Introduction to

Provence

The ancient Provençal version of Genesis maintains that prior to introducing Adam, the Creator realized he had several materials left over; large expanses of celestial blue, all kinds of rocks, arable soil filled with seeds for a sumptuous flora, and a variety of as yet unused tastes and smells from the most subtle to the most powerful. "Well," He thinks, "why don't I make a beautiful résumé of my world, my own special paradise?" And so Provence came into being.

This paradise encompasses the snow-peaked lower Alps and their foothills, which in the east descend to the sea's edge, and to the west extend almost to the Rhône. In central Provence the wild, high plateaux are cut by the deepest cleft in the surface of Europe – the Grand Canyon du Verdon. The coastal hinterland is made up of range after range of steep, forested hills in which the warm scent of pines, eucalyptus and wild herbs intoxicates the senses. The shore is an ever-changing series of geometric bays giving way to chaotic outcrops of glimmering rock and deep, narrow inlets, like miniature Norwegian fjords – the *calanques*. In the Camargue, the shoreline itself becomes an abstraction as land and sea merge in infinite horizons. Away from the Rhône delta there is nowhere that does not have its frame of hills, or mountains, or strange sudden eruptions of rock.

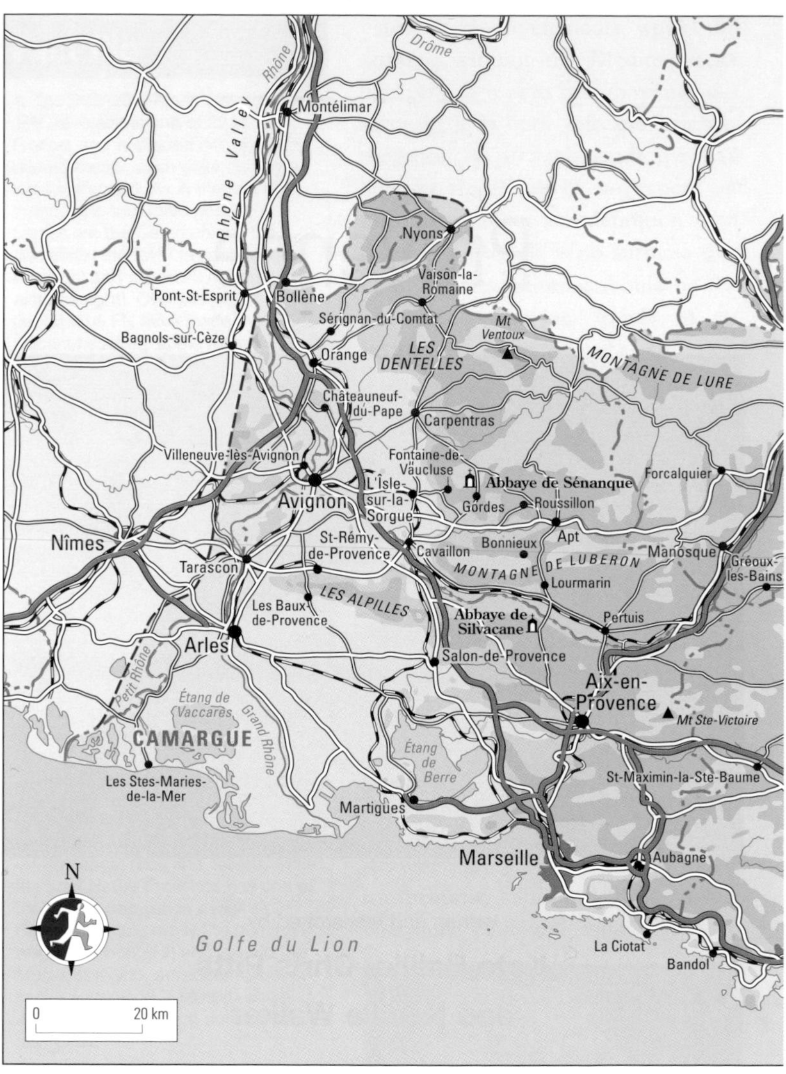
Drôme
Rhône
Montélimar
Rhone Valley
Nyons
Vaison-la-Romaine
Pont-St-Esprit
Bollène
Sérignan-du-Comtat
Mt Ventoux
Bagnols-sur-Cèze
Orange
LES DENTELLES
MONTAGNE DE LURE
Châteauneuf-du-Pape
Carpentras
Villeneuve-lès-Avignon
Fontaine-de-Vaucluse
Abbaye de Sénanque
Forcalquier
L'Isle-sur-la-Sorgue
Avignon
Gordes
Roussillon
Apt
Nîmes
St-Rémy-de-Provence
Cavaillon
Bonnieux
MONTAGNE DE LUBERON
Manosque
Gréoux-les-Bains
Tarascon
Lourmarin
LES ALPILLES
Les Baux-de-Provence
Abbaye de Silvacane
Pertuis
Arles
Salon-de-Provence
Petit Rhône
Étang de Vaccarès
Grand Rhône
Aix-en-Provence
Mt Ste-Victoire
CAMARGUE
Étang de Berre
St-Maximin-la-Ste-Baume
Les Stes-Maries-de-la-Mer
Martigues
Marseille
Aubagne
N
Golfe du Lion
La Ciotat
Bandol
0
20 km

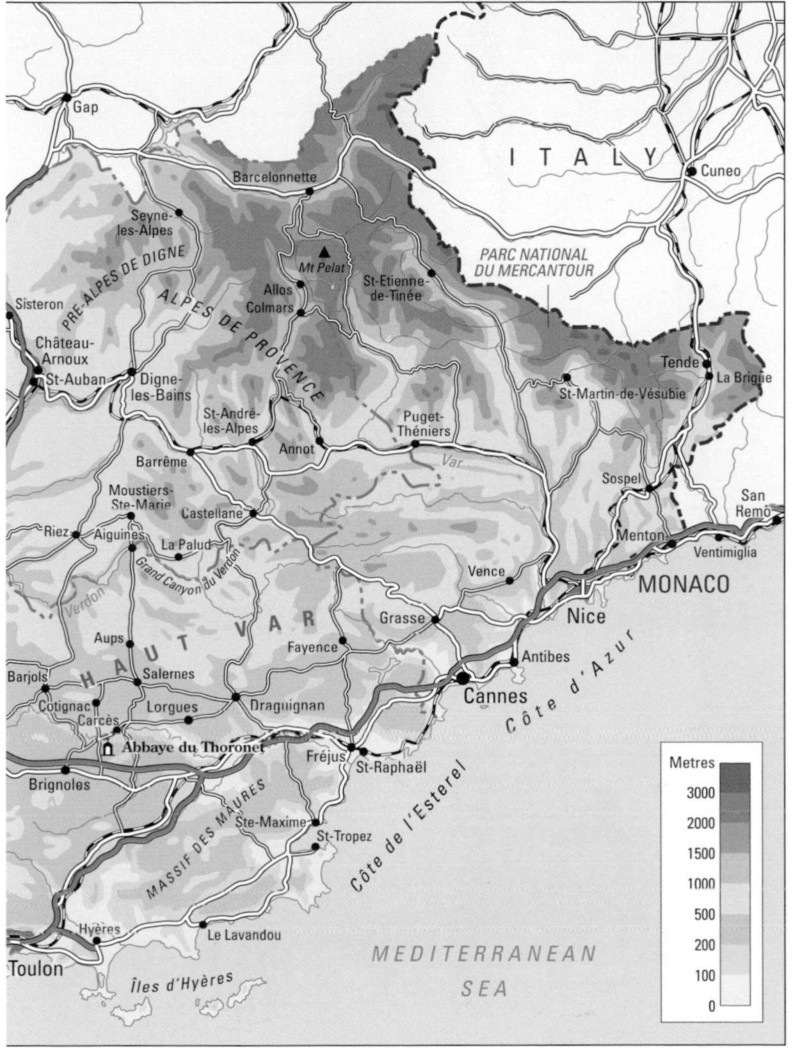
Gap
ITALY
Cuneo
Barcelonnette
Seyne-les-Alpes
PRE-ALPES DE DIGNE
ALPES DE PROVENCE
Mt Pelat
PARC NATIONAL DU MERCANTOUR
St-Etienne-de-Tinée
Allos
Colmars
Sisteron
Château-Arnoux
St-Auban
Digne-les-Bains
Tende
La Brigue
St-Martin-de-Vésubie
St-André-les-Alpes
Annot
Puget-Théniers
Var
Barrême
Moustiers-Ste-Marie
Castellane
Sospel
San Remo
Riez
Aiguines
La Palud
Menton
Ventimiglia
Grand Canyon du Verdon
Vence
MONACO
Verdon
HAUT VAR
Grasse
Nice
Aups
Fayence
Antibes
Barjols
Salernes
Côte d'Azur
Cannes
Cotignac
Lorgues
Draguignan
Carcès
Abbaye du Thoronet
Fréjus
St-Raphaël
Brignoles
MASSIF DES MAURES
Ste-Maxime
St-Tropez
Côte de l'Esterel
Hyères
Le Lavandou
MEDITERRANEAN SEA
Toulon
Îles d'Hyères
Metres
3000
2000
1500
1000
500
200
100
0

DROGUERIE
articles funéraires
droguerie conseil
Kodak

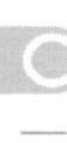

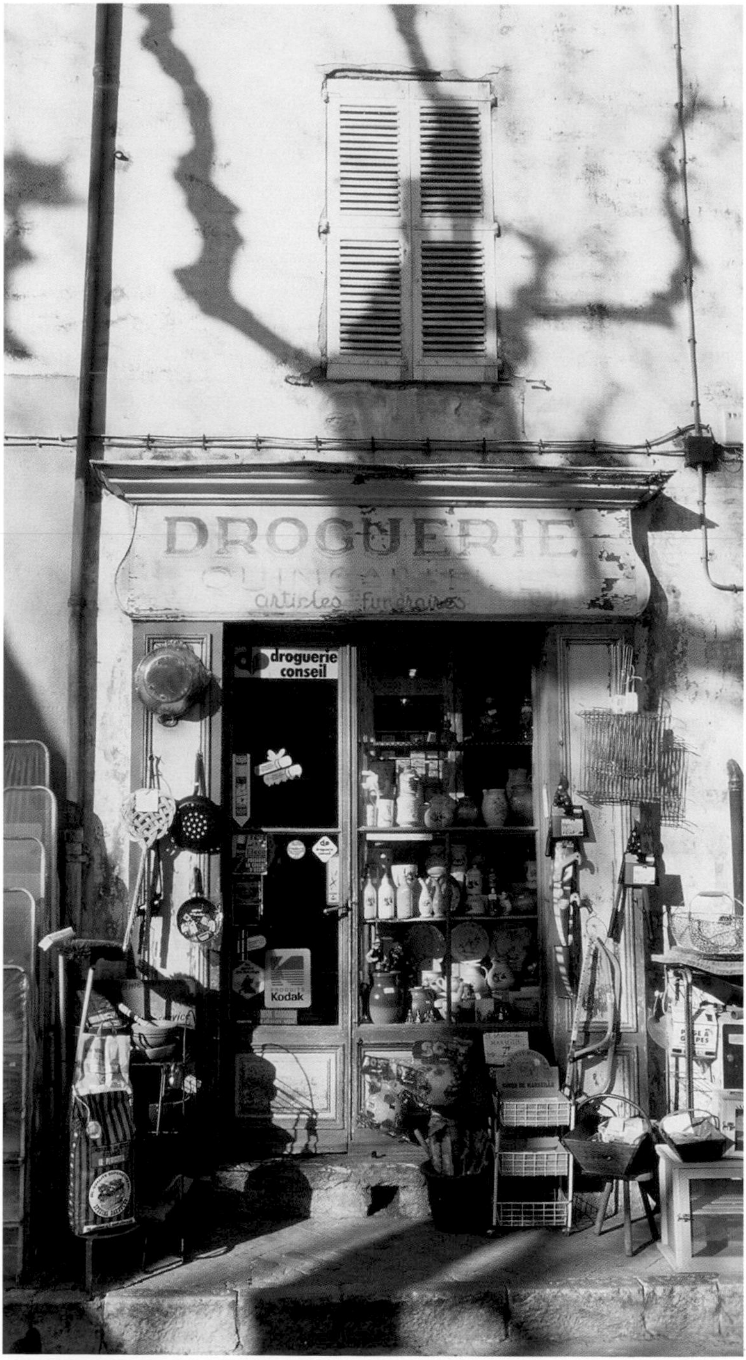

name but a few – forming an essential part of the hot, sensual environment. The wines, too, from the dry, light rosés of the Côtes de Provence to the deep and delicate reds of the Côtes du Rhône and Châteauneuf-du-Pape, both complement and owe their brilliance to the intensity of sunshine.

Such earthly pleasures, however, have been both a blessing and a curse. Successive waves of invaders and visitors have found the paradise they sought in Provence, and at the height of summer on the Riviera an unoccupied strip of beach can seem a far-fetched idea. Contemporary politics, too, fail to show the region in its best light, with support for the far-right *Front National* remaining disappointingly strong, despite the worldly sophistication of the Riviera and the rich ethnic mix of Marseille.

Where to go

This is a large region, and a diverse one, whose contrasting landscapes encompass the rural fields and villages of inland Provence, the remote mountainous regions of the Alpes-Maritime in the east and north, and the high-rise developments and *autoroutes* of the Riviera in the south. The Riviera's capital is **Nice**, an intriguing and vibrant blend of Italianate influence, faded *belle époque* splendour and first-class art. The town makes a perfect base from which to explore the region, with wonderful food, affordable accommodation and lively nightlife. To the north of

The cuisine of the south

The south of France is renowned for its simple, healthy cuisine, based on top-quality olive oil, herbs, garlic and vegetables, all grown or produced in the region. Fish is also essential to two of Provence's great dishes – *bourride* and *bouillabaisse.*

Not surprisingly, the region has been fertile territory for some great chefs. Auguste Escoffier, one of the best-known names of European cuisine, and creator of the peach Melba, was born in Villeneuve-Loubet in 1846 before going on to achieve international fame through his association with hotelier César Ritz. His style of cuisine, based very much on cream, butter and rich sauces, dominated the restaurant world for much of the twentieth century, though more recent Provençal chefs have turned to a healthier form of cooking. *Légion d'Honneur* winner Roger Vergé is one such chef, whose own creation the "cuisine of the sun" relies heavily on fresh herbs and local produce to give it its flavour. Vergé's cooking is taught at his cookery school *L'Amandier* in Mougins, and can be sampled at *Moulin de Mougins* near Cannes, one of the region's most renowned restaurants.

Current celebrity superchef Alain Ducasse is a Vergé protégé, and although not born in Provence, is very much associated with the region: his *Louis XV* restaurant at the *Hotel de Paris* in Monaco was the first hotel restaurant to win three Michelin stars. In addition to a culinary empire that stretches as far as Paris, London and New York, Ducasse still runs several restaurants in the south of France including the *Bar & Boeuf* in Monaco, *Spoon* at the *Byblos* hotel in St-Tropez and two country hotels, *La Bastide de Moustiers* at Moustiers Ste-Marie (see p.295) and *L'Hostellerie de l'Abbaye de la Celle* near Brignoles.

the city, densely wooded alpine foothills are home to a series of exquisite and unspoilt **perched villages**, while to the east, the lower Corniche links the picturesque coastal towns of **Villefranche**, **St-Jean-Cap-Ferrat** and **Beaulieu**: the higher roads offer some of Europe's most spectacular coastal driving en route to the perched village of **Èze** and the tiny principality of **Monaco**. Beyond here lie the resort and castle of **Roquebrune Cap Martin**, and the charming town of **Menton**, on the Italian border, with its lemon groves and atmospheric old quarter. The Riviera's western half claims its best beaches – at jazzy **Juan-les-Pins** and at **Cannes**, a glitzy centre of designer shopping and film. The Riviera also boasts some heavyweight cultural attractions, with the Picasso museum in **Antibes**, Renoir's house at **Cagnes-sur-Mer**, and the superb **Fondation Maeght** and **Fernand Léger** museums in the attractive perched villages of **St-Paul-de-Vence** and **Biot** respectively. The world's perfume capital, **Grasse**, and the ancient town of **Vence** both shelter in the hills behind the busy coastal resorts, while for a real escape from the bustle of the coast, the tranquil **Îles des Lérins** lie just a few kilometres offshore.

West of the ancient Massif of the **Esterel**, beyond the Roman towns of **Fréjus** and **St Raphaël**, lie the dark wooded hills of the **Massif des Maures**. Here, the coast is home to the infamous hot spots of **Ste-Maxime** and **St-Tropez**, still a byword for glamour and excess almost fifty years after Bardot put it firmly on the jetsetters' map. In dramatic contrast, the **Corniche des Maures** stretches to the west, with a series of low-key resorts interspersed by blissfully unspoilt stretches of Mediterranean coastline. Beyond lies the original Côte d'Azur resort of **Hyères** with its elegant villas, fascinating old town, and offshore **Îles d'Hyères**, a mecca for nature lovers, naturists and divers.

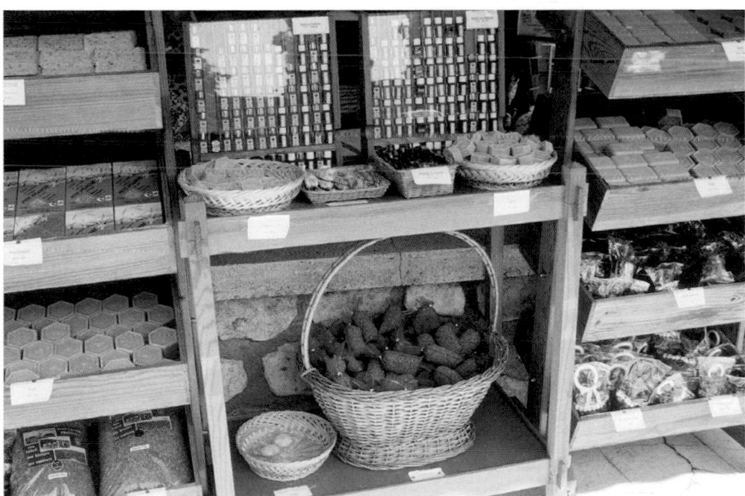

Further west, beyond the great natural harbour of **Toulon** and the superb wine country of the **Bandol** AC, lies the buzzing metropolis of **Marseille**. The region's largest city, this tough port has recently overcome its former sleazy reputation to become a lively, cosmopolitan, and often very likeable spot in which to spend a few days. On its eastern edge lie the **calanques**, a series of beautiful rocky coves accessible to walkers and boaters, with the picture-postcard village of **Cassis** and the working port of **La Ciotat** beyond, linked by the spectacular **Corniche des Crêtes**. North of Marseille is the elegant city of **Aix**, with its handsome stone houses, café-lined boulevards and some of Provence's best markets. It was here that Cézanne lived and painted, taking his inspiration from the countryside around the nearby **Mont Ste-Victoire**.

Beyond Aix lies the Lower Rhône Valley, home to some of Provence's most ancient cities: **Arles** and **Orange** both still boast some spectacular Roman structures, while **Avignon**, city of the popes and for centuries one of the great artistic centres of France, has an immaculately preserved medieval core and, of course, its famous bridge. The Rhône runs by the vineyards of **Châteauneuf-du-Pape** and the impressive fortifications of **Villeneuve-lès-Avignon**, before meeting the sea at the unique lagoon-studded marshlands of the **Camargue**, with its rich variety of wildlife including bulls, horses and flamingos.

Inland from Marseille is the **Luberon** region, a fertile rural hinterland whose attractive old villages are now dominated by second home owners. Nearby lie two of Provence's great medieval monasteries, at **Silvacane** and **Sénanque**. Beyond the **plateau de Vaucluse** rise the imposing **Mont Ventoux** and the jagged pinnacles of the **Dentelles de Montmirail**, with its brace of celebrated wine-producing towns including **Beaumes de**

Venise, known for its sweet dessert wines. East of the Luberon is the heartland of Provence, whose archetypal landscape of lavender fields dotted with old stone villages stretches northwards towards the dramatic **Grand Canyon du Verdon**. The countryside surrounding the canyon is rich in archeological evidence of man's long occupation of the region, with the area around the towns of **Riez**, **Valensole** and **Forcalquier** providing an exquisite taster of rural Provence.

Beyond the canyon but within easy reach of the Riviera, narrow **clues**, or

The art of Provence

Describing the south of France in a letter to Pissarro, Cézanne once wrote, "the silhouettes you see here are not only black and white, but also blue, red, brown and violet." His words go some way towards explaining the region's attraction for painters, and indeed over the last hundred years or so, Provence and the Côte d'Azur have been home and inspiration to some of the greatest names of modern art – Van Gogh, Renoir, Matisse and Picasso among them. The brilliant southern light was one of the most influential factors in their work here, with Matisse remarking that, had he gone on painting in the north, "there would have been cloudiness, greys, colours shading off into the distance…". Instead, during his time in Nice he produced some of his most famous, colourful works, such as *Interior with Egyptian Curtains* (*Le Rideau égyptien*) and *Icarus* (*Icare*). Van Gogh, too, was profoundly influenced by the region, and it was in Provence that he fully developed his distinct style of bright, contrasting colours. His landscapes of olive trees, cypresses and harvest scenes, such as *La Sieste* and *Champ de Blé et Cyprès* (*Wheat Field With Cypresses*), all pay tribute to the intensity of the Provençal sun.

Whilst the landscape and light of the south influenced the painters so strongly, they in turn had a major impact on the region. Hand-in-hand with the various writers and socialites who flocked to the Côte d'Azur during the interwar years, their artistic, and touristic, legacy helped to shape the region that exists today.

Movie mania

The Côte d'Azur may not be as synonymous with film-making as Hollywood, but its role in the evolution of cinema is just as important. It was in the seaside town of La Ciotat (see p.212) that the movie camera was invented by the Lumière brothers, who, in 1895, filmed the first ever moving picture – a less than glamorous shot of local workers leaving the family-owned car factory at closing time. As early as the 1920s, Nice was producing many of France's most innovative films in the Victorine Film Studios, and local writers Marcel Pagnol and Jean Cocteau were among the many who set their movies in the area. But it was Brigitte Bardot, and French New Wave cinema that really put the Riviera on the map, with Roger Vadim's *Et Dieu Créa la Femme* (1956) being the first in a long series of classic postwar films shot along the coast. Over the next few years, films such as Hitchcock's *To Catch a Thief* (1956), shot along the corniches, and *Masque de Fer* (1962) helped to confirm the south's reputation as a glamorous movie location. Today, although the production studios of Nice no longer make movies, the world's top stars are still drawn to the Riviera by the annual Cannes Film Festival, whose Palm d'Or awards remain among the film industry's most prestigious prizes.

gorges, open onto a secret landscape perfect for cycling and horse-riding, with the fortified towns of **Entrevaux** and **Colmars** marking the old frontier between France and Savoy. A third fortress town, **Sisteron**, on the Durance, marks the gateway to the mountains and the **Alps** proper, where the delightful town of **Barcelonette** provides skiing and snowboarding in winter and kayaking and hiking in the summer. Stretching south from here towards the **Roya valley** and the border with Italy is the **Parc National du Mercantour**, a genuine wilderness, whose only permanent inhabitants are its wildlife that includes such species as ibex, chamois, wolves and golden eagles.

When to go

Beware **the coast** at the height of summer. The heat and humidity can be overpowering and the crowds, the exhaust fumes and the costs overwhelming. For **swimming** the best months are from June to mid-October, with May a little on the cool side, but only by summer standards. As for sunbathing, that can be done from **February through to October**. February is one of the best months for the Côte d'Azur – museums, hotels and restaurants are mostly open, the mimosa is in blossom, and the contrast with northern Europe's climate at its most delicious. The worst month is **November** when almost everything is shut and the weather turns cold and wet.

Average daytime temperatures

	Jan	Feb	March	April	May	June	July	Aug	Sept	Oct	Nov	Dec
Central Provence												
	12.2	11.9	14.2	18.5	20.8	26.6	28.1	28.4	25.2	22.1	16.8	14.1
Rhône Valley												
	7.4	6.7	10.8	15.8	17.3	25.6	27.6	27.6	23.5	16.5	10.4	7.8
Riviera/Côte d'Azur												
	12.2	11.9	14.2	18.5	20.8	26.6	28.1	28.4	25.2	22.2	16.8	14.1

Average sea temperatures

	May	June	July	Aug	Sept	Oct
Montpellier to Toulon						
	15	19	19	20	20	17
Île du Levant to Menton						
	17	19	20	22	22	19

All temperatures are in **Centigrade**: to convert to **Fahrenheit** multiply by 9/5 and add 32. For a recorded **weather forecast** phone ⓣ32.50 (€0.34/min), or check ⓦwww.meteo.fr.

The same applies to inland Provence. Remember that the lower Alps are usually under snow from late November to early April (though recent winters have had snow in Nice followed by no falls on the lower ski resorts). October can erupt in storms that quickly clear, and in May, too, weather can be erratic. In summer, vegetation is at its most barren save for high up in the mountains. Wild bilberries and raspberries, purple gentians and leaves turning red to gold are the rewards of autumn walks. Springtime brings such a profusion of wild flowers you hardly dare to walk. In March a thousand almond orchards blossom.

The only drawback with the off seasons is the Mistral wind. This is a violent, cold, northern airstream that is sucked down the valley of the Rhône whenever there's a depression over the sea. It can last for days, wrecking every fantasy of carefree Mediterranean climes. Winter is its worst season but it rarely blows east of Toulon, so be prepared to move that way.

things not to miss

It's not possible to see everything that Provence has to offer in one trip – and we don't suggest you try. What follows is a selective taste of the country's highlights: outstanding beaches and ancient sites, natural wonders and colourful festivals. They're arranged in five colour-coded categories, which you can browse through to find the very best things to see and experience. All highlights have a page reference to take you straight into the guide, where you can find out more.

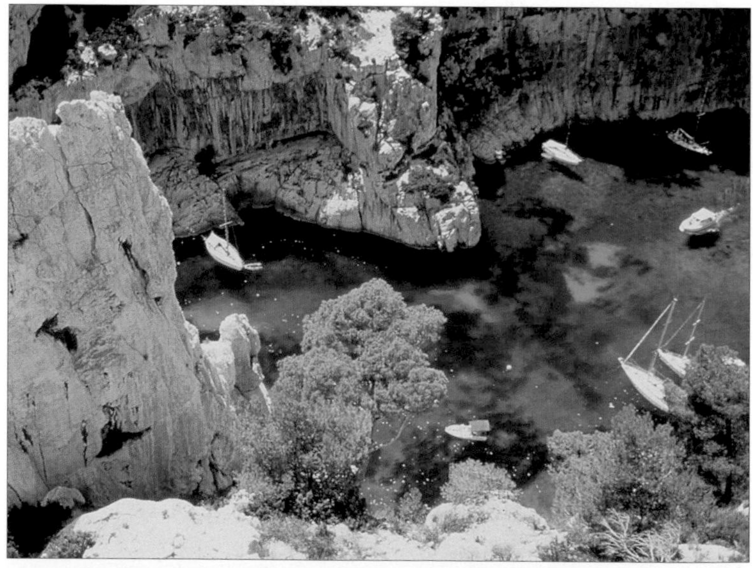

01 **Les Calanques** Page **211** • Take a boat trip to these hidden inlets east of Marseille, where the shimmering white rock shelters crystal-clear waters.

02 Dining al fresco in Vieux Nice Page **366** • Sit outside a Vieux Nice café watching the vibrant street life, and tuck into *salade niçoise*, *pissaladière* or a slice of *socca* straight from the pan.

03 Van Gogh's "Maison Jaune" in Arles Page **107** • Although the house itself no longer exists, you can stay in the hotel next door, and follow in the great artist's footsteps around the town where he lived and painted.

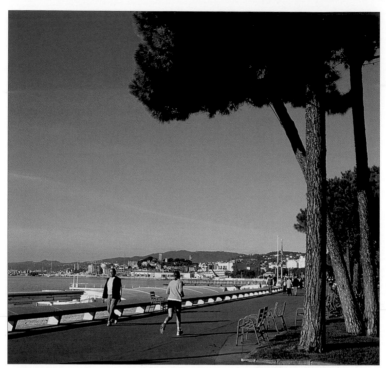

04 **Boulevard de la Croisette in Cannes** Page **322** • Walk, jog or rollerblade along the Riviera's best-known seafront promenade. In summer you'll share it with a jostling crowd and a few Hollywood starlets; in winter, you'll have the whole stretch to yourself.

05 **Mont Ste-Victoire by Paul Cézanne** Page **202** • Walk up to the top of the mountain that inspired so much of Cézanne's work.

06 **Abbaye de Sénanque** Page **149** • The twelfth-century Cistercian abbey of Sénanque is enhanced by its beautiful position, surrounded by lavender fields.

07 **Fondation Maeght** Page **352–353** • Don't miss this highly original art museum, whose building and setting are as impressive as the modern works of art inside.

08 **The vineyards of Châteauneuf du Pape** Page **67** • Sample a glass of Provence's world-famous wine at the *domaine* where it was made.

09 **Marseille** Pages **167–185** • Don't let its former reputation put you off visiting this earthy, multiethnic Mediterranean metropolis with good food, great bars, excellent football and bags of culture.

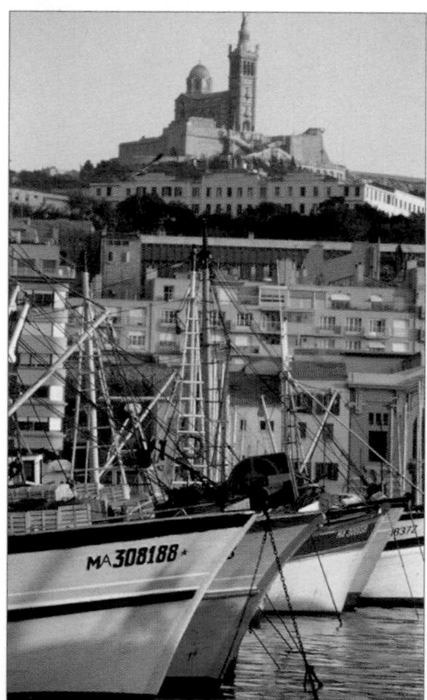

10 **Festival d'Avignon** Page **73** • July and early August is the time to visit Avignon, when its ancient monuments provide the backdrop to a riot of theatre, music and dance.

11 Bouillabaisse Page **182**
Marseille is the best place to sample this renowned fish stew.

12 Avignon's Palais des Papes Page **75–76** • The vast medieval building that was home to a succession of popes during Avignon's fourteenth-century heyday.

13 The perched village of Peille Page **370** • Built for defence, the region's *villages perchés* are much admired for their maze of streets, mellow stone houses and spectacular settings.

14 **The Camargue** Page **109** • Saddle up one of the white Camargue horses and explore this watery marshland on horseback.

15 **Breaking the bank at Monte Carlo** Page **383** • If you're going to lose your shirt, there's no finer place to do so than amid the *belle époque* elegance of Monaco's opulent casino.

16 The markets of Aix-en-Provence Page **202** • The cathedral city of Aix is home to Provence's best markets selling everything from live rabbits to hand-made clothes.

17 Cassis Page **211** • Cassis harbour is the place to sample spiky *oursins* (sea urchins), washed down with a bottle of crisp, white wine.

18 Grand Canyon du Verdon Page **291** • Cycle, walk or bungee-jump in Europe's largest canyon.

19 Parc National du Mercantour Page **417** • Ride, hike, canoe or ski in this alpine wilderness that is home to the Vallée des Merveilles and its four-thousand-year-old rock carvings

20 Relaxing on the Riviera Page **364** • Waiters will serve chilled wine and lobster mayonnaise on the swanky hotel beaches of Nice – if your wallet can stand the strain.

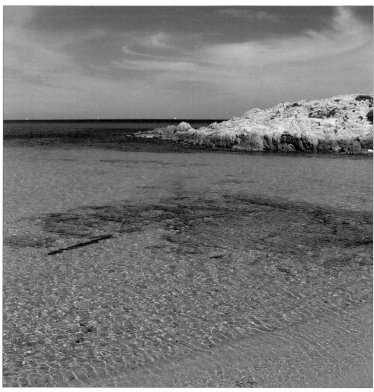

21 **Go topless in Saint Tropez** Page **252** • Despite the hype and commercialism, St-Tropez's beaches are still among the best on the Riviera.

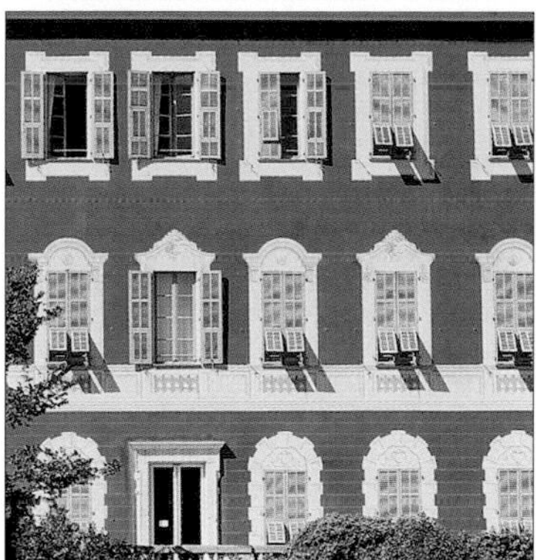

22 **Matisse Museum, Nice** Page **354** • Set amid Roman ruins and olive groves, Nice's Matisse Museum includes work from almost every period of the artist's life.

23 **Roman Amphitheatre, Orange** Page **65** • Beautifully preserved, Orange's fifth-century theatre is still used for performances in the summer.

24 **The gypsy pilgrimage, Ste Maries de la Mer** Page **115** • An annual spectacle of music, dancing and religious ritual dating from the sixteenth century.

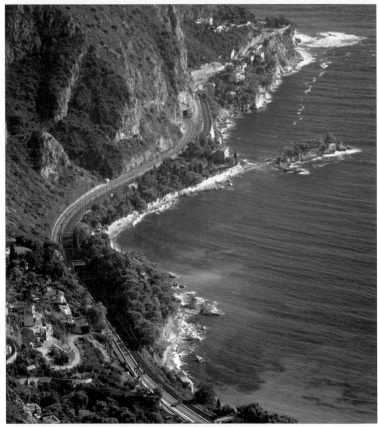

25 **Driving the Riviera's corniches** Page **372** • Check out the spectacular views on one of the world's most memorable drives.

Contents

Using this Rough Guide

We've tried to make this Rough Guide a good read and easy to use. The book is divided into six main sections, and you should be able to find whatever you want in one of them.

Colour section

The front colour section offers a quick tour of Provence. The **introduction** aims to give you a feel for the place, with suggestions on where to go. We also tell you what the weather is like and include a basic regional fact file. Next, our authors round up their favourite aspects of Provence in the **things not to miss** section – whether it's great food, amazing sights or a special hotel. Right after this comes a full **contents** list.

Basics

The Basics section covers all the **pre-departure** nitty-gritty to help you plan your trip. This is where to find out which airlines fly to your destination, what paperwork you'll need, what to do about money and insurance, about internet access, food, security, public transport, car rental – in fact just about every piece of **general practical information** you might need.

Guide

This is the heart of the Rough Guide, divided into user-friendly chapters, each of which covers a specific area. Every chapter starts with a list of **highlights** and an **introduction** that helps you to decide where to go, depending on your time and budget. Likewise, introductions to the various towns and smaller regions within each chapter should help you plan your itinerary. We start most town accounts with information on arrival and accommodation, followed by a tour of the sights, and finally reviews of places to eat and drink, and details of nightlife. Longer accounts also have a directory of practical listings. Each chapter concludes with **public transport** details for that area.

Contexts

Read Contexts to get a deeper understanding of what makes Provence tick. We include a brief history and a detailed further reading section that reviews dozens of **books** relating to the region.

Language

The **language** section gives useful guidance for speaking French and pulls together all the vocabulary you might need on your trip, including a comprehensive menu reader. Here you'll also find a glossary of words and terms peculiar to the country.

Index + small print

Apart from a **full index**, which includes maps as well as places, this section covers publishing information, credits and acknowledgements, and also has our contact details in case you want to send in updates and corrections to the book – or suggestions as to how we might improve it.

Chapter list and map

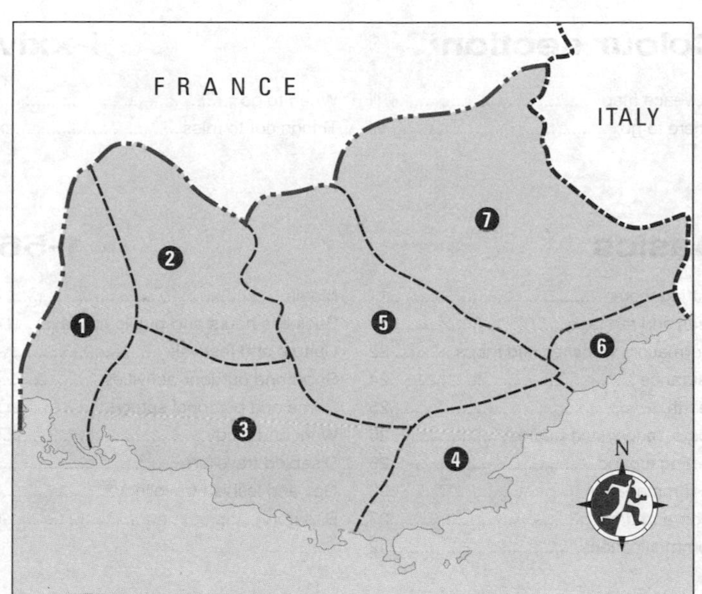

Contents

Colour section i–xxiv

Basics 1–56

The Guide 57–434

Contexts 435–461

Language 463–479

Index + small print 481–491

Map symbols

maps are listed in the full index using coloured text

- Motorway
- Road
- Minor road
- Steps
- Path
- Railway
- Ferry route
- National border
- Chapter division boundary
- River
- Airport
- Parking
- Bus stop
- Campsite
- Accommodation
- Restaurant
- Lodge
- Point of interest
- Viewpoint
- Cliffs
- Waterfall
- Mountain peak
- Tourist office
- Post office
- Métro station
- Wall
- Building
- Church
- Cemetery
- Park
- Beach

Basics

Basics

Getting there

Flying is the quickest and most straightforward way to get to Provence, with Nice and Marseille being the two main airports, though budget airlines from the UK now serve a variety of smaller regional airports too. If you're travelling long-haul – from Australia, Canada, the US or New Zealand, for example – you are most likely to come via Paris, from where the superfast TGV train now reaches Marseille in three hours. From the UK, driving (about a 24hr journey) or coming by train (now only about seven hours) are both options, though neither is likely to prove cheaper than taking one of the budget flights.

All airfares depend on the **season**, with the highest being around June to August, when the weather is best; fares drop during the "shoulder" seasons – September, April and May – and you'll get the best prices during the low season, October to March (excluding Christmas and New Year when prices are hiked up and seats are at a premium). Note also that flying on weekends ordinarily adds US$50–75/£30–50 to the round-trip fare; price ranges quoted below assume midweek travel.

You can often cut costs by going through a **specialist flight agent** – either a consolidator, who buys up blocks of tickets from the airlines and sells them at a discount, or a **discount agent**, who in addition to dealing with discounted flights may also offer special student and youth fares and a range of other travel-related services such as travel insurance, rail passes, car rentals, tours and the like. A further possibility is to see if you can arrange a **courier flight**, although you'll need a flexible schedule, and preferably be travelling alone with very little luggage. In return for shepherding a parcel through customs, you can expect to get a deeply discounted ticket. You'll probably also be restricted in the duration of your stay.

If Provence is only one stop on a longer journey, you might want to consider buying a **round-the-world** (RTW) ticket. Some travel agents can sell you an "off-the-shelf" RTW ticket that will have you touching down in about half a dozen cities (Paris is on many itineraries); others will have to assemble one for you, which can be tailored to your needs but is apt to be more expensive. Figure on US$1700/AUS$2400 for a RTW ticket including France.

Booking flights online

Many airline and discount travel **websites** offer you the opportunity to book your tickets online, cutting out the costs of agents and middlemen. Good deals can often be found through discount or auction sites, as well as through the airlines' own websites.

Useful websites

@www.cheapflights.com Flight deals, travel agents, plus links to other travel sites.
@www.cheaptickets.com Discount flight specialists.
@www.expedia.com Discount airfares, all-airline search engine and daily deals.
@www.gaytravel.com Gay online travel agent, concentrating mostly on accommodation.
@www.hotwire.com Bookings from the US only. Last-minute savings of up to 40 percent on regular published fares. Travellers must be at least 18 and there are no refunds, transfers or charges allowed. Log-in required.
@www.kelkoo.com European site with low prices for airfares and train tickets
@www.lastminute.com Offers good last-minute holiday package and flight-only deals.
@www.priceline.com Name-your-own-price website that has deals at around 40 percent off standard fares. You cannot specify flight times (although you do specify dates) and the tickets are non-refundable, non-transferable and non-changeable.
@www.sydneytravel.com.au Australian site with a decent range of packages and good-value flights.
@www.travelocity.com Destination guides, hot web fares and good deals on car rental, and

accommodation, as well as fares. Provides access to the travel-agent system SABRE, the most comprehensive central reservations system in the US.
@www.travelshop.com.au Australian website offering discounted flights, packages, insurance and online booking.
@travel.yahoo.com Incorporates a lot of Rough Guide material in its coverage of destinations, with information about places to eat and sleep.

Flights from Britain and Ireland

Flying to Provence and the Côte d'Azur is a real treat. For the last few hundred miles clear skies are virtually guaranteed, giving you breathtaking views of the Alps and the sea, and for most of the year there's the enveloping warmth when you get off the plane.

Nice and **Marseille** are the region's two main airports, though Marseille is not a particularly cheap destination. You're more likely to find cheap deals to Nice, which is better served by the budget airlines, while Marseille caters mainly for business travellers, with flights often booked up weeks in advance. Flight times are around two hours from London, and there are quick and frequent bus links to the city centres. Alternative points of arrival include **Montpellier, Nîmes, Toulon** and **Lyon**, and, slightly further afield, **Perpignan** and **Toulouse**, all of which have direct flights from London: Montpellier and Nîmes are especially convenient for exploring the west of Provence, such as Arles, Avignon or the Camargue.

Flying from Britain to any of these airports, you have a choice of **scheduled** flights, operated by both budget airlines and the big-name carriers, and **charter** flights, which are available through travel agents, with fixed dates for outward and return travel and a maximum stay of one month. Budget airlines often have good deals if you can juggle your travel dates, while the major airlines tend to be pricier (though reductions for children are bigger), but offer rather more flexibility.

Of the no-frills **budget airlines**, EasyJet has flights from Luton to Nice (6 daily in summer and 4 daily in winter) starting from £85, and a daily flight from Liverpool to Nice from £75; while Ryanair flies daily from Stansted to Nîmes, a forty-five-minute drive from Avignon, from £80, and from Stansted to Montpellier (1 daily; from £75). In addition, bmi/British Midland has direct flights to Nice from Heathrow (2 daily; from £80), and from East Midlands (1 daily; from £115). You have to book early to claim the cheapest deals, especially in July and August, though out of season it's also worth scanning the papers or looking online for last-minute bargains.

In response to the budget market, the **major airlines** have lowered their prices, and, if you're lucky, you can get some surprisingly good deals. British Airways flies from both Heathrow and Gatwick to Nice (6 daily) with fares staring from £100, and to Marseille (4 daily), starting from £80. It also has a daily flight from Gatwick to Montpellier from £110, while its franchise, GB Airways, flies from Gatwick to Toulon (1 daily; from £80). Air France flies daily from Heathrow direct to Nice (from £130), though its services to Marseille and Montpellier involve a change in Paris. Scheduled flights from other British regional airports tend to involve changing planes at Heathrow (or in Paris in the case of Air France). To get the best deals, most of the major airlines require you to stay at least a Saturday night, and are valid for a maximum of three months.

Most travel agents can advise on both charter and scheduled flights, though it's a good idea to contact some of the **specialist operators** detailed on p.15. It's also worth checking the **classified adverts** in the weekend papers. For charter flights, try the Charter Flight Centre (①0207/828 1090) or the holiday pages of Teletext, and you might strike it lucky and get a cheap last-minute deal. Full-time **students** and those **under 26** can get discounted flights from specialist agents such as STA (see p.13).

Aer Lingus operates the only direct flight **from Ireland** to the Côte d'Azur, flying from **Dublin** to Nice (1 daily), with fares starting at €195. Flights on all other airlines involve a change of planes: British Midland, for example, flies to Nice from both Dublin and **Belfast** via Heathrow; British Airways to Nice from Belfast via Manchester; and Air France from Dublin to Nice via Paris. Prices for all of these flights begin at around €300.

Airlines

Aer Lingus UK ①0845/084 4444, Ireland ①0818/365000, @www.aerlingus.com.
Air France UK ①0845/084 5111, Ireland ①01/605 0383, @www.airfrance.com.

British Airways UK ⓣ0845/773 3377, Ireland ⓣ0141/222 2345, ⓦwww.ba.com.
bmi/British Midland UK ⓣ0870/607 0555, Northern Ireland ⓣ0345/554554, Republic of Ireland ⓣ01/283 8833, ⓦwww.flybmi.com.
EasyJet ⓣ0870/600 0000, ⓦwww.easyjet.com.
GB Airways ⓣ0845/773 3377, ⓦwww.gbairways.com.
Ryanair UK ⓣ0871/246 0000, Ireland ⓣ0818/303 030, ⓦwww.ryanair.com.

Flight agents

Flightbookers ⓣ0870/010 7000, ⓦwww.ebookers.com. Low fares on a wide selection of scheduled flights.
French Holiday Centre Ireland ⓣ185/037 2623, ⓦwww.frenchholidaycentre.ie. Deals on flights to France.
Man Around Ltd ⓣ020/8902 7177, ⓦwww.manaround.com. Independent gay-run travel company.
North South Travel ⓣ01245/608291, ⓦwww.northsouthtravel.co.uk. Friendly, competitive travel agency, offering discounted fares to most destinations – profits are used to support projects in the developing world, especially the promotion of sustainable tourism.
STA Travel ⓣ0870/160 0599, ⓦwww.statravel.co.uk. Worldwide specialists in low-cost flights and tours for students and under-26s.
Trailfinders ⓣ020/7628 7628, ⓦwww.trailfinders.com. One of the best-informed and most efficient agents for independent travellers.
USIT Republic ⓣ01/602 1600, Northern Ireland ⓣ02890/327111, ⓦwww.usitnow.ie. Student and youth specialists for flights and trains.

Package deals, tour companies and specialist agents

There's no shortage of companies offering **package deals** to Provence, details of which can be found at any travel agent. As many include ferry crossings – or, occasionally, flights – in the deal, they can be very good value especially for a family or large group. In addition to the companies listed below, more complete lists are available from the **French Government Tourist Office** in the **French Travel Centre**, 178 Piccadilly, London W1V 0AL (Mon–Fri 10am–6pm, Sat 10am–5pm; information line ⓣ0906/8244 123 (60p/min) Mon–Fri 8.30am–8pm, Sat 9am–5pm; ⓦwww.franceguide.com).

The Alternative Travel Group ⓣ01865/315678, ⓦwww.atg-oxford.co.uk. "Walking through History" tours in Provence, with special-interest trips on the area's artistic legacy. Also fly-drive and cycling tours.
Belle France ⓣ01892/559595, ⓦwww.bellefrance.co.uk. Walking and cycling tours in Haute Provence and the Camargue, with the emphasis on food and family hotels.
Canvas Holidays ⓣ01383/629000, ⓦwww.canvasholidays.co.uk. Great camping packages and lots of sites.
Club Cantabrica Holidays ⓣ01727/866177, ⓦwww.cantabrica.co.uk. Specializing in the upper end of the mobile home, caravan and campsite market, with sites in Antibes and Port Grimaud. Also, air, bus or self-drive packages.
Dominique's Villas ⓣ0207/738 8772, ⓦwww.dominiquesvillas.co.uk. Upmarket agency with a diverse and tempting range of properties, mostly for large groups.
Eurocamp ⓣ0870/366 7558, ⓦwww.eurocamp.co.uk. Family-holiday specialist offering camping, self-drive and mobile-home packages with a selection of sites along the coast.
France Afloat ⓣ0870/011 0538, ⓦwww.franceafloat.com. Canal holidays throughout France, including the delta land of the Camargue. Cruisers from €568 per week in April to €905 in July & Aug.
Gîtes de France Ltd The UK operation of this French Government letting service is run by Brittany Ferries (ⓣ08705/360360), although you can still deal directly with Gîtes de France online (ⓦwww.gites-de-france.fr). It has a comprehensive list of houses, cottages and chalets all over France; ferry crossing extra.
Individual Travellers' Company ⓣ0179/886 9020, ⓦwww.indiv-travellers.com. Gîtes, cottages and farmhouses for rent along the Rhône Valley and in the Vaucluse.
Inntravel ⓣ01653/629 000, ⓦwww.inntravel.co.uk. Upmarket walking, cycling and horse-riding holidays with expert local guides in the Alpes Maritimes and around Manosque.
Keycamp Holidays ⓣ0870/700 0123, ⓦwww.keycamp.co.uk. Camping and mobile-home holidays. A two-week tent holiday on the Côte d'Azur costs £664 for two adults and two children in high season.
Lagrange ⓣ0207/371 6111, ⓦwww.lagrange-holidays.com. From camping to self-catering apartments and houses at coastal resorts and at the foot of Mont Ventoux. Specializes in the Côte d'Azur. From £163 a week for a studio in low season.

Martin Randall Travel ⊕0208/742 3355, ⊛www.martinrandall.com. Runs a programme of cultural tours led by specialists: "Art on the Côte d'Azur" (one week £990); "Gardens of the Two Rivieras" (one week £1220); plus the Aix Music Festival and other special-interest subjects. All prices include flights, half board at three- to five-star hotels and admission charges.

Martin Sturge ⊕01225/310623, ⊛www.holidayinfrance.co.uk. A range of upmarket, historic self-catering properties in the Var, Vaucluse and Avignon. High-season prices per week from £500 (sleeping 2) to £3200 (sleeping 10–11).

NSS Riviera Holidays ⊕01943/816949. Budget chalets, mobile homes and cottages in and around Fréjus. Mainly self-drive.

Susi Madron's Cycling for Softies ⊕0161/248 8282, ⊛www.cycling-for-softies.co.uk. Easy-going cycle holidays starting in St-Rémy-de-Provence. Seven-day tours with flight, half-board accommodation, bike and backup from around £860 per person.

Flights from North America

Delta/Air France offer the only direct service from the US **to Provence**, with three flights a week from New York (JFK) to Nice. However, there are also direct flights from over thirty major US cities **to Paris**, with connections from all over the continent. Some of the transatlantic airlines can book you through to Nice or Marseilles via Paris, though you may find it cheaper to pick up a bargain flight to Paris then continue your journey by TGV (see p.18). You can board direct trains to Provence from Charles de Gaulle airport.

Fares to France from the US are very reasonable thanks to intense competition, and there's no shortage of special deals, particularly if you're travelling from January to March. Tickets to Nice and Marseille from the east coast start at $400 in low season and $800 in high season, while from Chicago or San Francisco flights can be bought for as little as $600 in low season, and $900 in high season. Be aware, however, that the cheap seats go fast, and the price hikes for the remaining seats are particularly steep if you're travelling from the west coast.

The most comprehensive range of flights from the US is offered by **Delta/Air France**. As well as the direct JFK to Nice service, they also fly to Paris Charles de Gaulle with onward connections to Marseille, Nice, Toulon and Montpellier, from Atlanta, Boston, Chicago, Cincinnati, Houston, Los Angeles, Miami, New York, Philadelphia, San Francisco and Washington DC – in most cases, daily. Delta/Air France's fares are reasonable too, with its New York to Nice flight starting at just $425.

Other airlines flying daily nonstop into Charles de Gaulle airport include **American** from Chicago, Dallas Fort Worth, Miami and New York; **Continental** from its Houston and Newark hubs; and **United** from Chicago, Washington DC and San Francisco. Both Continental and United have a codeshare arrangement with SNCF (French railways), so that you can book your onward train trip to Provence through them, and earn frequent flyer mileage on the train journey too.

It can sometimes be cheaper to fly to Provence via a different **European hub**. Lufthansa, for example, flies daily from over 25 US cities to Nice and Marseille via either Frankfurt or Munich (NY from $400; Dallas from $475; LA from $600); and British Airways flies daily from nineteen US cities to London, from where you can pick up a connecting flight to Marseille or Nice (NY from $450; LA from $700).

Flights from Canada

The strong links between France and Québec's Francophone community ensure regular air services from Canada **to Paris**. Most departures are **from Toronto**, with Air Canada flying nonstop to Paris twice a day (from CN$1000), and Air France flying once daily (from CN$1100). Both companies also fly nonstop **from Montréal** (twice daily) for similar prices, while flights **from Vancouver** are routed either through Toronto or Montréal, starting at CN$1200 in low season and CN$1500 in high season.

There are no direct flights **to Provence** from Canada, but connecting flights to Nice or Marseille via Paris can be booked through either Air France or Air Canada, and generally only add on an extra CN$200 or so. Alternatively, you can continue the journey overland from Paris by TGV (see p.18).

Other options to consider are travelling via a different **European hub**: Lufthansa, for example, flies daily from Toronto to Nice via Frankfurt with fares starting at CN$1000 in low season. There are also **charter flights** from Toronto to Paris (from CN$700), and Montréal to Marseille (from CN$700) and Nice (from CN$1000) with **Air Transat**, though the flights vary according to demand, so you need to have a flexible schedule.

Airlines

Air Canada ⓣ1-888/247-2262, ⓦwww.aircanada.ca.
Air France US ⓣ1-800/237-2747, Canada ⓣ1-800/667-2747, ⓦwww.airfrance.com.
Air Transat ⓣ1-866-847-1112, ⓦwww.airtransat.com.
American Airlines ⓣ1-800/433-7300, ⓦwww.aa.com.
British Airways ⓣ1-800/247-9297, ⓦwww.ba.com.
Continental Airlines ⓣ1-800/525-0280, ⓦwww.continental.com.
Delta Airlines ⓣ1-800/221-1212, ⓦwww.delta.com.
Lufthansa US ⓣ1-800/645-3880, Canada ⓣ1-800/56-FLYLH, ⓦwww.lufthansa.com.
United Airlines ⓣ1-800/864-8331, ⓦwww.ual.com.

Discount flight agents and consolidators

Air Brokers International ⓣ1-800/883-3273, ⓦwww.airbrokers.com. Consolidator and specialist in RTW tickets.
Air Courier Association ⓣ1-800/282-1202, ⓦwww.aircourier.org. Courier flight broker.
Airhitch ⓣ212/736-0505, ⓦwww.airhitch.org. Standby-seat broker. For a set price, they guarantee to get you on a flight as close to your preferred destination as possible, within a week.
Council Travel ⓣ1-800/226-8624, ⓦwww.counciltravel.com. Student and youth travel organization offering discounted air fares, rail passes and travel gear.
Educational Travel Center ⓣ1-800/747-5551, ⓦwww.edtrav.com. Student, youth and consolidator fares.
Flight Centre ⓣ1-888/967-5331, ⓦwww.flightcentre.ca. Discount air fares from Canadian cities.
Nouvelles Frontières/New Frontiers ⓣ1-800/677-0720, ⓦwww.newfrontiers.com. French discount travel firm.
Now Voyager ⓣ212/431-1616, ⓦwww.nowvoyagertravel.com. Agent specializing in courier flights.
STA Travel ⓣ1-800/329-9537, ⓦwww.statravel.com. Worldwide discount travel firm specializing in student/youth fares; also student IDs, travel insurance, car rental, rail passes, etc.
TFI Tours International ⓣ1-800/745-8000, ⓦwww.lowestairprice.com. Consolidator.
Travel CUTS ⓣ1-866/246-9762, ⓦwww.travelcuts.com. Canadian specialist student and discount travel organization with branches all over the country.
Travel Avenue ⓣ1-800/333-3335, ⓦwww.travelavenue.com. Discount travel agent.
Worldtek Travel ⓣ1-800/243-1723, ⓦwww.worldtek.com. Discount travel agency.

Tour operators and specialist agents

Abercrombie & Kent ⓣ1-800/323-7308, ⓦwww.abercrombiekent.com. Deluxe trekking, biking, canal and rail packages.
Adventure Center ⓣ1-800/228-8747, ⓦwww.adventurecenter.com. Small-group hiking or cycling tours in France. Eight-day "Hiking in Provence" costs $620.
American Express ⓣ1-800/346-3607, ⓦwww.americanexpress.com. Seven-night package to Provence and the Riviera from $1150.
AESU Travel ⓣ1-800/638-7640, ⓦwww.aesu.com. Packages to the Riviera for the under 35s.
Back Door Travel ⓣ425/771-8303, ⓦwww.ricksteves.com. Small-group travel with Rick Steves and his guides. Fifteen-day "Best of Provence" tour costs $2550.
Backroads ⓣ1-800/462-2848, ⓦwww.backroads.com. Trendy bike tour company, offering a five-night "Taste of Provence" cycling trip from $2800.
Butterfield & Robinson ⓣ1-800/678-1147, ⓦwww.butterfield.com. Trekking tours including the "Provence Classic" seven-day walking tour ($3800); "Provence Getaway" six-day biking trip ($3300); and the "Provence Classic" seven-day biking trip ($3900).
Contiki Tours ⓣ1-888/CONTIKI, ⓦwww.contiki.com. Vacations in Provence for those aged between 18 and 35.
Cosmos Tourama/Globus ⓣ1-800/276-1241 or 1-888/755-8581, ⓦwww.globusandcosmos.com. Budget group tours by bus, including Provence on several of its programmes.
Euro-Bike Tours ⓣ1-800/321-6060, ⓦwww.eurobike.com. Luxury trekking tours including the "Taste of Provence" seven-day biking tour ($2465); "Walking in Provence" eight-day

walking tour ($2850); and the "Provence Complet" eleven-day biking tour ($3300).

The French Experience ⓣ1-800/283-7262, ⓦwww.frenchexperience.com. Offers self-drive and guided tours, including the four-day "Provence in your pocket" self-drive tour for $800.

International Gay & Lesbian Travel Association ⓣ1-800/448-8550, ⓦwww.iglta.com. Provides links to various tour operators and travel agents, with programmes in Provence.

Mountain Travel-Sobek ⓣ1-888/687-6235, ⓦwww.mtsobek.com. Trekking specialists with a "Hiking in Provence" nine-day tour starting at $2790.

Wilderness Travel ⓣ1-800/368-2794, ⓦwww.wildernesstravel.com. Trekking packages include the "Country Walks in Provence" nine-day walking tour in May, June, August and September ($3095).

Flights from Australia and New Zealand

There are no direct **flights to Provence** from Australia or New Zealand, and most people travel via Paris, either changing flights here onto Air France, or continuing to Provence by TGV (see p.18). All routes require either a transfer or stopover in the carrier's hub city, with many of the European airlines being able to add a Nice/Marseille leg onto an Australia/New Zealand–Europe ticket. Travelling time to Provence from east coast Australia is around 22 hours on flights via Asia and 30 hours via the US.

The lowest fares **to Paris from Australia's east-coast cities** start off at around A$1700, with Korean Airlines flying daily from Sydney via Seoul, and Malaysia Airlines flying daily from Sydney, Melbourne, Adelaide and Brisbane via Kuala Lumpur. More expensive flights include Qantas, which flies daily via Bangkok and London (from A$2150), Singapore Airlines, which flies daily via Singapore (from A$2200), and Thai Airways, with daily flights via Bangkok (also from A$2200). Flights **from Perth** with the same companies tend to cost A$100–200 less.

Connecting flights with Air France from Paris **to Nice, Marseille, Montpellier or Toulon** can be booked through Qantas, and will add on an extra A$200 or so.

Alternatively, you could fly via a different **European hub**. Lufthansa, for example, flies via Bangkok or Singapore and Frankfurt or Munich to Nice and Marseille (3 daily from Sydney, from A$2000; 1 daily from Perth, from A$1950); while **British Airways** flies daily from Sydney via Bangkok or Singapore and London to Nice and Marseille (from A$2250). **Emirates** flies to Nice three times a week from both Sydney and Perth, via Dubai and Florence (from Sydney, A$2250; from Perth, A$2000).

From New Zealand

From New Zealand, the best deals **to Nice/Marseille** from Auckland are with British Airways via Sydney and London, and Air New Zealand via Los Angeles and London. Both fly daily and offer similar fares of around NZ$2500 in low season and NZ$3300 in high season.

Alternatively, you can fly daily **to Paris** with Singapore Airlines, via Singapore (from NZ$2300), or with Malaysia Airlines via Kuala Lumpur (and sometimes Brisbane) for about the same price. From Paris, you can get an onward flight to Provence with Air France (see above for details), or continue overland on the TGV (see p.18).

Airlines

Air France Australia ⓣ02/9244 2100, New Zealand ⓣ09/308 3352, ⓦwww.airfrance.com.

Air New Zealand Australia ⓣ09/357 3000, New Zealand ⓣ0800/737 000, ⓦwww.airnz.co.nz.

British Airways Australia ⓣ13/0076 7177, New Zealand ⓣ0800/274 847, ⓦwww.ba.com.

Emirates Australia ⓣ02/9290 9700 or 1300/303 777, New Zealand ⓣ09/377 6004, ⓦwww.emirates.com.

Korean Air Australia ⓣ02/9262 6000, New Zealand ⓣ09/914 2000, ⓦwww.koreanair.com.au.

Lufthansa Australia ⓣ1300/655 727, ⓦwww.lufthansa-australia.com; New Zealand ⓣ09/303 1529, ⓦwww.lufthansa.com/index_en.html.

Malaysia Airlines Australia ⓣ13/2627, New Zealand ⓣ0800/777 747, ⓦwww.malaysiaairlines.com.

Qantas Australia ⓣ13/1313, New Zealand ⓣ09/357 8900, ⓦwww.qantas.com.

Singapore Airlines Australia ⓣ13/1011, New Zealand ⓣ09/303 2129, ⓦwww.singaporeair.com.

Travel agents

Accent on Travel Australia ⓣ07/3832 1777, ⓦwww.accentontravel.com.au. Discount airfares.

Budget Travel New Zealand ⓣ09/366 0061, ⓦwww.budgettravel.co.nz. Long established agent with budget airfares.
Destinations Unlimited New Zealand ⓣ09/373 4033, ⓦwww.travel-nz.com. Discount airfares as well as a good selection of tours and holiday packages to Provence.
Flight Centres Australia (for nearest branch call) ⓣ13/3133, New Zealand ⓣ0800/243 544, ⓦwww.flightcentre.com.au. Specialists in discounted airfares.
Passport Travel Australia ⓣ03/9867 3888. Discount airfares.
STA Travel Australia ⓣ13/0073 3035, New Zealand ⓣ05/0878 2872, ⓦwww.statravel.com.au. Airfare discounts for students and those under 26.
Student Uni Travel Australia ⓣ02/9232 8444, New Zealand ⓣ09/300 8266, ⓦwww.sut.com.au. Student/youth discounts and travel advice.
Trailfinders Australia ⓣ02/9247 7666, ⓦwww.trailfinders.com.au. One of the best-informed and most efficient agents for independent travellers.
Usit Beyond New Zealand ⓣ07/838 4242. Student and youth specialists for flights and trains.
Thomas Cook Australia ⓣ13/1771, New Zealand ⓣ03/434 9975. Bus and rail passes as well as reasonable rates on currency exchange.

Tour operators and specialist agents

Adventure Specialists Australia ⓣ02/9261 2927. Overland specialist and agent for numerous adventure-travel operators specializing in walking and camping trips throughout France.
Australians Studying Abroad (ASA) Australia ⓣ03/9509 1955, ⓦwww.asatravinfo.com.au. Lecture tours exploring the "Gardens and Chateaux of Provence" and the "Cultural Landscapes of France".
CIT World Travel Australia ⓣ02/9267 1255, ⓦwww.cittravel.com.au. Specializes in city tours and accommodation packages, plus bus and rail passes and car rental.
European Travel Office Australia ⓣ02/9267 7714. Offers a wide selection of tours and accommodation throughout France, from hotels to country inns, palaces and monasteries.
Explore Holidays Australia ⓣ02/9857 6200 or 1300/731 000, ⓦwww.exploreholidays.com.au Holidays including a good range of accommodation from B&B home-stays and hotels to chateaux and historic monuments.
France and Travel Australia ⓣ03/9670 7253. Holiday packages throughout France, with a good selection in Provence.
France Unlimited Australia ⓣ03/9531 8787. Can organize all French travel arrangements, as well as individually tailored trips, and guided walking and cycling holidays.
French Cottages and Travel Australia ⓣ03/9859 4944. International and domestic travel, independent tours and cottage rental.
French Travel Connection Australia ⓣ02/9966 1177. French travel arrangements, city accommodation and regional country cottages.
Peregrine Adventures Australia ⓣ03/9663 8611, ⓦwww.peregrine.net.au. Seven-day walking and cycling tours of Provence (A$1795).
Silke's Travel Australia ⓣ1800/807 860, ⓦwww.silkes.com.au. Specially tailored packages for gay and lesbian travellers.
Tempo Holidays Australia ⓣ1300/362 844, ⓦwww.yallatours.com.au. Wide range of accommodation, rail passes and car hire for custom-made holidays in Provence.
Walkabout Gourmet Adventures Australia ⓣ03/5159 6556, ⓦwww.walkaboutgourmet.com. All-inclusive fourteen-day food-and-wine walking trips, as well as cooking seminars in Provence.

By train from the UK

Most large travel agents sell train tickets from any station in Britain to any station in Provence. The routes will usually involve going through London and almost certainly Paris – where you may have to change from the Gare du Nord to the Gare de Lyon. For the London–Paris leg you can either take the **Eurostar** service through the Channel Tunnel, a journey of three hours, or catch a train to one of the southern ferry ports and then cross the Channel by **ferry** or **hovercraft**. From Paris you can take the world's fastest train, the **TGV**, as far as Marseille (three hours), continuing at slower speeds along the coast to Nice.

Eurostar runs services from London Waterloo to Paris Gare du Nord (up to 27 daily; journey time 3hr) and Lille (6 daily; journey time 2hr). A return ticket to Lille costs from around £69 for a second-class promotional advance fare, with fares for Paris starting at around £79. In addition, there's a direct Eurostar service from London to **Avignon** (Sat only; journey time 6hr 15min), from the end of May to mid-October, although seats are scarce and must be reserved well in advance. Bookings on all Eurostar services can be made online, through high-street travel agents, by calling Eurostar direct or through Rail Europe in

London (see p.19).

Combining a Eurostar deal with an onward journey on the **TGV** is a very easy and attractive option, though it does involve changing stations in Paris. By booking fourteen days in advance you can get to Marseille on Eurostar and the TGV for £124 in approximately seven hours, and to Nice for £132 in approximately ten hours.

Special fare options include thirty percent discounted BIJ tickets, available for anyone under 26 from Eurotrain or any student travel office. The over 60s who hold a British Rail Senior Card can extend the cover with a Rail Europe Senior Card – from major travel agents – which covers most of Western Europe and gives thirty to fifty percent reductions on train tickets. There are also discounts available with the various rail passes, detailed below.

Rail passes

If you plan to visit Provence as part of a wider tour of Europe, it may be worth considering a continent-wide pass like the **InterRail** (for those based in Britain and Ireland) or the **Eurail** (for North Americans and Antipodeans). Neither pass is valid on trains in Great Britain and Northern Ireland, but they will help you get across to France more cheaply, with substantial discounts on Eurostar and the Channel ferries. Once you get to France, you will still have to pay seat reservation supplements if you wish to use the TGV.

Most of the European-wide **rail passes** can be bought in advance through Rail Europe, the umbrella company for all national and international rail purchases. Its comprehensive website (Ⓦwww.raileurope.com) is the most useful source of information on which rail passes are available; it also gives all the current prices.

In addition to the Europe-wide passes, SNCF issues its own range of passes, which are valid only for travel within France (see p.28 for details).

Inter-rail passes

Inter-rail passes are only available to European residents, and you will be asked to provide proof of residency before being allowed to purchase one. They come in over-26 and (cheaper) under-26 versions, and cover 28 European countries (including Turkey and Morocco) grouped together in zones: France is in zone E, grouped together with Belgium, the Netherlands and Luxembourg. The passes are available for 22 days (one zone only), or one month, and you can purchase up to three zones or a global pass covering all zones.

Although Inter-Rail passes do not include travel between Britain and the continent, pass holders are eligible for discounts on rail travel in Britain and Northern Ireland and cross-Channel ferries, a discount on the London–Paris Eurostar, and free travel on the Brindisi–Patras ferry between Italy and Greece, plus discounts on other shipping services around the Mediterranean.

Eurail passes

A **Eurailpass** must be purchased before arrival in Europe (and cannot be purchased by European residents), allows unlimited free first-class train travel in France and 17 other European countries, and is available in increments of 15 days, 21 days, one month, two months and three months. If you're under 26, you can save money with a **Eurailpass Youth**, which is valid for second-class travel, or, if you're travelling with one to five other companions, a joint **Eurailpass Saver**, both of which are available in the same increments as the Eurailpass. You stand a better chance of getting your money's worth out of a **Eurail Flexipass**, which is good for ten or fifteen days' first-class travel within a two-month period. This, too, comes in under-26/second-class (**Eurailpass Youth Flexi**) and group (**Eurailpass Saver Flexi**) versions.

In addition, a scaled-down version of the Eurailpass Flexi, the **Eurail Selectpass**, is available which allows travel in your choice of three, four or five of the 17 countries Eurail covers (they must be adjoining, by either rail or ship) for any five, six, eight, ten or fifteen days (five-country option only) within a two-month period. With this pass, Belgium, the Netherlands and Luxembourg count as one "country" Like the Eurailpass, the Selectpass is also available in first-class, second-class youth, or first-class Saver options.

Details of prices for all these passes can be found on Ⓦwww.eurail.com, and the passes can be purchased from any of the agents listed below.

Eurodomino pass

Only available to European residents, the **Eurodomino pass** provides unlimited travel within France. It is available in increments of three, five and eight days' travel within a one-month period, though supplements apply on the TGV. It also offers reductions on Eurostar and Hoverspeed Channel crossings. The pass is available in adult and under-26 versions (children aged 4–11 pay half-price) and can be bought from Rail Europe and major travel agents.

France Railpass and France Rail 'n' Drive

Only available to North Americans and residents of Australia and New Zealand, the **France Railpass** provides four days of unlimited travel within France in a one-month period. It is available for first- and second-class travel, and in under-26 and group versions. Up to six additional days may be purchased.

Finally, the **France Rail 'n' Drive** pass, also only available to North Americans and residents of Australia and New Zealand, provides four days' of unlimited train travel and two days car rental. The price varies according to the size and class of car.

Both these passes must be purchased before departure; for details contact STA Travel (see p.13 and p.15) or one of the addresses below.

Rail contacts in the UK

Eurostar UK ⓣ0870/518 6186, France ⓣ08.92.35.35.39, ⓦwww.eurostar.com.
Rail Europe UK ⓣ0870/584 8848, ⓦwww.raileurope.co.uk.

Rail contacts in North America

BritRail Travel International ⓣ1-800/327-6097, ⓦwww.britishtravel.com.
CIT Rail ⓣ1-800/CIT-RAIL, ⓦwww.cit-tours.com.
Forsyth Travel Library ⓣ1-800/367-7984, ⓦwww.forsyth.com.
Rail Europe ⓣ1-877/257-2887, Canada ⓣ1-800/361-RAIL, ⓦwww.raileurope.com.

Rail contacts in Australia and New Zealand

CIT World Travel ⓣ02/9267 1255, ⓦwww.cittravel.com.au.
Rail Plus ⓣ03/9642 8644, ⓦwww.railplus.com.au.
Thomas Cook Australia ⓣ13/1771, New Zealand ⓣ03/434 9975.

By bus from the UK

Travelling to Provence **by bus** costs around fifteen to twenty percent less than by train. The journey, at around 22 hours, is tolerable, broken up by the ferry crossing, a couple of meal stops, one transfer, and additional short halts for coffee.

The route heads from London to Dover, ferry across to Calais, and continues on to Lyon. At Lyon you change buses, and then it's down to Nice via Sisteron, Grasse, Cannes, Juan-les-Pins and Antibes; or to St-Raphaël via Valence, Aix-en-Provence, Marseille, Toulon, Hyères and Fréjus.

All services are operated by **Eurolines** (UK ⓣ0207/730 8235 or 0990/143 219; Ireland ⓣ0183/66111; France ⓣ08.92.89.90.91, ⓦwww.eurolines.com) and leave London's Victoria Coach Station three times a week, with an extra express service in summer. Tickets are available from any National Express bus station in Britain, and add-on fares are sold from any British destination. Sample return fares from London are £109 to Nice and £97 to Marseille. Open-dated return tickets lasting up to six months give good long-stay flexibility, but the return journey must be booked four days in advance.

By car from the UK

Getting to the south of France **by car** isn't difficult, though it is a long trip, particularly if you're starting from Ireland. Using an overnight Channel ferry and the *autoroutes*, you'd be hard pressed to make the trip in much less than 24 hours, and using the Channel Tunnel will reduce the time by only a couple of hours. If you are going to drive, far better to break your journey and arrive at your destination in daylight.

The most convenient way of taking your car across to France is to drive down to the **Channel Tunnel**, load your car on the train shuttle, and be whisked under the Channel in 35 minutes, arriving at Coquelles on the French side, near Calais. The Channel Tunnel entrance is off the M20 at junction 11A, just outside Folkestone, and the sole operator, **Eurotunnel**, offers a frequent daily service (24hr; every 15min in peak periods). You can just turn up, but booking is advised, especially at weekends and in mid-summer, not least because it can be cheaper. Tickets are available through Eurotunnel (UK

Ferry details

Routes and prices

	OPERATOR	CROSSING TIME	FREQUENCY	ONE-WAY FARES Small car, 2 adults	Foot passenger
BRITTANY					
Portsmouth–St-Malo	Brittany Ferries	8hr	1–7 weekly	£200–230	£45–67
Plymouth–Roscoff	Brittany Ferries	6–8hr	1–12 weekly	£198–240	£46–88
Poole–St-Malo (via Jersey and Guernsey)	Condor Ferries	4–5hr	1 daily	£137–150	£38–50
Weymouth–St-Malo (via Jersey and Guernsey)	Condor Ferries	4–5hr	May–Oct 1 daily	£137–150	£38–50
NORMANDY					
Portsmouth–Cherbourg (Fastcraft)	P&O Portsmouth	2hr 45min	1–4 daily	£184	£57
Poole–Cherbourg	Brittany Ferries	2hr 15min–5hr 30min	1–2 daily	£132–161	£28–53
Portsmouth–Caen	Brittany Ferries	3hr 45min	2–3 daily	£139–212	£34–95
Portsmouth–Le Havre	P&O Portsmouth	5hr 30min	3 daily	£152–187	£49–84
Newhaven–Dieppe (Super SeaCat)	Hoverspeed	2hr	3–5 daily	£163–188	£29
PAS-DE-CALAIS					
Dover–Calais	P&O Stena Line	1hr 15min	30 daily	£116–124	£28
Dover–Calais	Sea France	1hr 30min	15 daily	£94	£17
Dover–Calais (SeaCat)	Hoverspeed	1hr	6–10 daily	£128–143	£26
FROM IRELAND					
Cork–Roscoff	Brittany Ferries	12–13hr	April to early Oct 1 weekly	€200–279	€55–134
Rosslare–Roscoff	Irish Ferries	17hr	mid-April to early Oct, 1–3 weekly	€240–307	€61–128
Rosslare–Cherbourg	Irish Ferries	17–19hr	3 weekly	€240–307	€61–128
Rosslare–Cherbourg	P&O Irish Sea	18hr	3 weekly	€257	Not allowed
Dublin–Cherbourg	P&O Irish Sea	18hr	1 weekly	€334	Not allowed

Ferry operators in England and Ireland

Brittany Ferries UK ⓣ0870/366 5333, Ireland ⓣ021/427 7801, ⓦwww.brittany-ferries.co.uk.
Condor ⓣ0845/345 2001, ⓦwww.condorferries.co.uk.
Hoverspeed ⓣ0870/240 8070, ⓦwww.hoverspeed.co.uk.
Irish Ferries ⓣ1890/313131, ⓦwww.irishferries.ie
P&O Irish Sea ⓣ1800/409049, ⓦwww.poirishsea.com.
P&O Portsmouth ⓣ0870/242 4999, ⓦwww.poportsmouth.com.
P&O Stena Line ⓣ0870/600 0600, ⓦwww.posl.com.
Sea France ⓣ0870/571 1711, ⓦwww.seafrance.com.

☎0870/535 3535; France ☎08.10.63.03.04; ®www.eurotunnel.com) or from local travel agents, and fares are calculated per car, regardless of the number of passengers. Rates depend on the time of year, time of day, length of stay, and whether or not you book in advance (the cheapest ticket is for a day-trip, followed by a five-day return); it's cheaper to travel between 10pm and 6am, while the highest fares are reserved for weekend departures and returns in July and August. As an example, a five-day fully flexible return costs £197 (passengers included) in low season, and £267 in high season. You should arrive at least thirty minutes before departure.

Though you can meander through Normandy, the Loire and the Massif Central to get to Provence, the most direct **driving routes** go south from Paris. If you're crossing from Britain by **ferry**, the best ports to head for are Calais, Boulogne and Dunkerque as they offer the most direct connections to Paris and the routes south into Provence. Dieppe is an hour closer to Paris, but crossings are considerably more expensive. Note that the minimum age for driving in France is 18. For more about driving in France, see p.29. From Ireland, the best port to head for is Le Havre, which has excellent road links with Paris. Cherbourg is a long way west with more than 100km before you hit the autoroute to the capital.

If you can't face the drive through France, you could always put your car on the train in Calais for Avignon or Nice, with **SNCF's Motorail** (contact Rail Europe on ☎08702/415415; ®www.motorrail.com). Prices, however, are prohibitive; for example, the return fare in summer from Calais to Nice costs a minimum of £940 for a car and a four-berth couchette.

Red tape and visas

EU citizens can travel freely in France and can stay for an unlimited amount of time. Citizens of Australia, Canada, New Zealand and the United States, among other countries, do not need a visa to enter France, but can only stay for up to ninety days.

Non-EU citizens who plan on staying longer than three months in France can cross the border to Switzerland and re-enter for another ninety days legitimately. However, if your intention is to **study** or do an internship in France, you should check the visa requirements with the French embassy or consulate in your home country well before departure. Be forewarned that it is extremely difficult to get **working papers** if you aren't an EU citizen; for further details on working and studying in Provence, see p.52.

Visa requirements for **Monaco** (an independent principality) are identical to those of France; there are no border controls between the two.

Customs

With the Single European Market you can carry most things between EU countries, as long as you have paid **tax** on them in an EU country and you intend them for personal consumption. Customs may be suspicious if they think you are going to resell goods. Limits still apply to drink and tobacco bought in **duty-free** shops: 200 cigarettes, 250g of tobacco or 50 cigars; 1l of spirits or 2l of fortified wine, or 2l of sparkling wine and 2l of table wine; 50ml of perfume and 250ml of toilet water. Americans, Australians, Canadians and New Zealanders who want details about customs limits in their home countries should look online at ®www.customs.gov (US); ®www.customs.gov.au (Australia); ®www.ccra-adrc.gc.ca (Canada); or ®www.customs.govt.nz (New Zealand).

French embassies abroad

Contact information for all French embassies

abroad can be found at ⓦwww.expatries.diplomatie.gouv.fr/annuaires/annuaires.htm.
Australia 6 Perth Ave, Yarralumla, Canberra, ACT 2600 ⓣ02/6216 0100, ⓦwww.ambafrance-au.org.
Canada 42 Sussex Drive, Ottawa, ON K1M 2C9 ⓣ613-789-1795, ⓦwww.ambafrance-ca.org.
Ireland 36 Ailesbury Rd, Ballsbridge, Dublin 4 ⓣ01/260 1666, ⓦwww.ambafrance-ie.org.
New Zealand 34–42 Manners St, PO Box 11–343, Wellington ⓣ04/384 2555, ⓦwww.ambafrance-nz.org.
UK 58 Knightsbridge, London SW1X 7JT ⓣ020/7073 1000, ⓦwww.ambafrance-uk.org.
USA 4101 Reservoir Rd NW, Washington, DC 20007 ⓣ202-944-6000, ⓦwww.ambafrance-us.org.

Information, websites and maps

The French Government Tourist Office has branches throughout the world, where you can pick up information on the Provence-Alpes-Côte d'Azur region and on the five départements: Alpes-de-Haute Provence, Alpes-Maritimes, Bouches-du-Rhône, Var and Vaucluse. The information available includes maps and brochures as well as lists of hotels and campsites, with the footpath maps, and lists of festivals being particularly useful.

Tourist offices abroad

We've detailed below some of the **French Government Tourist Offices** abroad – for a full list of all its branches worldwide, check www.towd.com. The official French Government Tourist Office website, **La Maison de la France**, is at ⓦwww.franceguide.com.
Australia 25 Bligh Street, Level 20, Sydney NSW 2000 ⓣ02/9231 5244.
Canada 1981 av McGill College, Suite 490, Montréal, QUE H3A 2W9 ⓣ514/876-9881.
Ireland 30 Merrion St, Dublin 2 ⓣ15/6023 5235.
UK 178 Piccadilly, London W1V 0AL ⓣ0906/8244 123 (60p/min) or 020/7493 6594.
USA 444 Madison av, New York, NY ⓣ410/286-8310; John Hancock Center Suite 3214, 875 N Michigan Ave, Chicago, IL 60611 ⓣ312/751-7800; 9454 Wilshire Blvd Suite 715, Beverly Hills, CA 90212-2967 ⓣ310/271-6665; 1 Biscayne Tower Suite 1750, 2 South Biscayne blvd, Miami, FL 33131 ⓣ305/373-8177.

Tourist offices in Provence

In Provence itself, virtually every town and many villages have their own **tourist office** – usually an Office du Tourisme (OT) but sometimes a Syndicat d'Initiative (SI) – addresses and opening hours are detailed in the Guide. For the practical purposes of visitors, there is little difference between them: SIs have wider responsibilities for encouraging business, while OTs deal exclusively with tourism.

From these offices you can get specific **local information**, including listings of hotels and restaurants, leisure activities, car and bike rental, walks, laundries and countless other things – particularly useful is the free town plan. In the Alps they display daily meteorological information and have contacts for walking and climbing guides and ski schools. In the big cities you can usually also pick up free listings guides. In small villages where there is no OT or SI, the *mairie*, or town hall, will often offer a similar service. The regional or departmental tourist offices listed below also offer useful practical information.
Alpes-de-Haute-Provence 19 rue du Dr-Honnorat, Digne ⓣ04.92.31.57.29, ⓦwww.alpes-haute-provence.com.
Alpes-Maritimes 55 Promenade des Anglais, Nice ⓣ04.93.37.78.78.
Bouches-du-Rhône 13 rue Roux de Brignoles, Marseille 6e, ⓣ04.91.13.84.13.

Hautes-Alpes 8bis rue Capit de Bresson, Gap ⓣ04.92.53.62.00, ⓦwww.hautes-alpes.net.
Var 1bd Marcel Foch, Draguignan ⓣ04.94.50.55.50, ⓦwww.tourismevar.com.
Vaucluse 12 rue Collège de la Croix, Avignon ⓣ04.90.80.47.00, ⓦwww.provenceguide.com.

Websites

A general search for "Provence" on the Internet will return a long list of hits, many of them sites selling holiday homes in the region. However, there's no shortage of useful sites too, and we've listed the best below. Each offers an insight into the region: its history and culture, its food and wine, plus up-to-date information on the villages and cities, local festivals and activities, and accommodation and restaurants.

ⓦwww.visitprovence.com A useful portal to the region, with practical information (weather, accommodation, sites and monuments) and current events.
ⓦwww.provencebeyond.com Tourist information geared towards Provence's back country. Topics include adventure sports, flora & fauna and gastronomy.
ⓦwww.provence.guideweb.com Good introduction to Provence, with traditional crafts, tourist routes and gastronomy.
ⓦwww.parcs-naturels-regionaux.tm.fr Official website for France's National Parks.
ⓦwww.luberon-news.com Tourism, entertainment and real estate for the Luberon.
ⓦwww.cityvox.com Online guide to bars, clubs and restaurants, covering Aix, Avignon, Marseille and Nice.
ⓦwww.marseille.webcity.fr What's on in Marseille (in French).
ⓦwww.riviera-reporter.com Articles, current events and classified ads for the expat community.
ⓦwww.angloinfo.com Detailed guide to the Riviera.
ⓦwww.sncf.com Official website for the French rail service, particularly good for checking train fares and booking tickets in advance.
ⓦwww.pagesjaunes.fr Comprehensive online phone directory, in French and English.
ⓦwww.mappy.com Road trip itinerary planner. Directions, toll prices and fuel and time estimates.

Maps

In addition to the various free leaflets you pick up from the tourist offices, you're likely to need a reasonable **road map**. For most purposes, certainly for driving, the best options are the IGN red series no. 115 (scale 1:250,000) which charts the entire area, and the larger Michelin 1:200,000 no. 245. In the same scale in Michelin's yellow series, you'll need no. 84 for the coast and Alpes-Maritimes, and no. 81 for inland Provence.

For exploring a particular area, and for **walking or cycling**, the larger IGN maps – their green (1:100,000 and 1:50,000) and blue (1:25,000) series – are invaluable. For even greater detail IGN also do a 1:10,000 series (10cm on the map for every 1km on the ground). These maps can be bought at almost all newsagents and bookshops, and from some tourist offices.

If you're driving to Provence, the Michelin map no. 989 is the best for the whole of France. A useful free map, obtainable from French filling stations and traffic information kiosks, is the Bison Futé, showing alternative back routes to the potentially congested main roads.

Map outlets

UK & Ireland

Blackwell's Map and Travel Shop 50 Broad St, Oxford OX1 3BQ ⓣ01865/793 550, ⓦmaps.blackwell.co.uk.
Easons Bookshop 40 O'Connel St, Dublin 1 ⓣ01/858 3881, ⓦwww.eason.ie.
The Map Shop 30a Belvoir St, Leicester LE1 6QH, ⓣ0116/247 1400, ⓦwww.mapshopleicester.co.uk.
National Map Centre 22–24 Caxton St, London SW1H 0QU ⓣ020/7222 2466, ⓦwww.mapsnmc.co.uk.
Newcastle Map Centre 55 Grey St, Newcastle-upon-Tyne, NE1 6EF ⓣ0191/261 5622.
Ordnance Survey of Northern Ireland Colby House, Stranmillis Ct, Belfast BT9 5BJ ⓣ028/9025 5755, ⓦwww.osni.gov.uk.
Stanfords 12–14 Long Acre, London WC2E 9LP ⓣ020/7836 1321, ⓦwww.stanfords.co.uk.
The Travel Bookshop 13–15 Blenheim Crescent, London W11 2EE ⓣ020/7229 5260, ⓦwww.thetravelbookshop.co.uk.
Note: Maps by mail order are available from Stanfords, London and at esales@stanfords.co.uk.

North America

Book Passage 51 Tamal Vista Blvd, Corte Madera, CA 94925 ⓣ1-800/999-7909, ⓦwww.bookpassage.com.
Distant Lands 56 S Raymond Ave, Pasadena, CA

91105 ⓣ1-800/310-3220, ⓦwww.distantlands.com.
Elliot Bay Book Company 101 S Main St, Seattle, WA 98104 ⓣ1-800/962-5311, ⓦwww.elliotbaybook.com.
Globe Corner Bookstore 28 Church St, Cambridge, MA 02138 ⓣ1-800/358-6013, ⓦwww.globecorner.com.
Map Link 30 S La Patera Lane, Unit 5, Santa Barbara, CA 93117 ⓣ1-800/962-1394, ⓦwww.maplink.com.
Rand McNally US ⓣ1-800/333-0136, ⓦwww.randmcnally.com. Around 30 stores across the US; dial ext 2111 or check the website for the nearest location.
The Travel Bug Bookstore 2667 W Broadway, Vancouver V6K 2G2 ⓣ604/737-1122, ⓦwww.swifty.com/tbug.
World of Maps 1235 Wellington St, Ottawa, Ontario K1Y 3A3 ⓣ1-800/214-8524, ⓦwww.worldofmaps.com.

Australia & New Zealand

The Map Shop 6–10 Peel St, Adelaide, SA 5000 ⓣ08/8231 2033, ⓦwww.mapshop.net.au.
Specialty Maps 46 Albert St, Auckland 1001 ⓣ09/307 2217, ⓦwww.specialtymaps.co.nz.
MapWorld 173 Gloucester St, Christchurch ⓣ0800/627 967 or 03/374 5399, ⓦwww.mapworld.co.nz.
Mapland 372 Little Bourke St, Melbourne, Victoria 3000 ⓣ03/9670 4383, ⓦwww.mapland.com.au.
Perth Map Centre 900 Hay St, Perth, WA 6000 ⓣ08/9322 5733, ⓦwww.perthmap.com.au.

Insurance

Citizens of all EU countries are entitled to take advantage of French health services under the same terms as residents, if they have the correct documentation. British citizens need form E111, available from post offices. North American and other non-EU citizens have to pay for most medical attention and are strongly advised to take out some form of travel insurance. Even EU citizens are advised to take out an insurance policy before travelling to cover against theft, loss and illness or medical emergencies.

Before paying for a new policy, however, it's worth checking whether you are already covered: some all-risks home insurance policies may cover your possessions when overseas, and many private medical schemes include cover when abroad. In addition, bank and credit cards often have certain levels of medical or other insurance included and you may automatically get travel insurance if you use a major credit card to pay for your trip. In Canada, provincial health plans usually provide partial cover for medical mishaps overseas, while holders of official student/teacher/youth cards in Canada and the US are entitled to meagre accident coverage and hospital in-patient benefits. Students will often find that their student health coverage extends during the vacations and for one term beyond the date of last enrolment.

After exhausting the possibilities above, you might want to contact a specialist travel insurance company, or consider the travel insurance deal we offer (see box). A typical travel insurance policy usually provides cover for the loss of baggage, tickets and – up to a certain limit – cash or cheques, as well as cancellation or curtailment of your journey. Most of them exclude so-called dangerous sports unless an extra premium is paid: in Provence this can mean scuba-diving, whitewater rafting, windsurfing and trekking, though probably not kayaking or jeep safaris. Many policies can be chopped and changed to exclude coverage you don't need – for example, sickness and accident benefits can often be excluded or included at will. If you do take medical coverage, ascertain whether benefits will be paid as treatment proceeds or only after return home, and whether there is a 24-hour medical emergency number. When securing baggage cover, make sure that the per-article limit – typically under £500 – will cover your most valuable possession. If you need to make a claim, you should keep receipts for medicines and medical treatment, and in the event you have anything stolen, you must obtain an official statement from the police (called a *déclaration de vol*).

Rough Guides travel insurance

Rough Guides offers its own travel insurance, customized for our readers by a leading UK broker and backed by a Lloyd's underwriter. It's available for anyone, of any nationality and any age, travelling anywhere in the world.

There are two main Rough Guide insurance plans: **Essential**, for basic, no-frills cover; and **Premier**, with more generous and extensive benefits. Alternatively, you can take out **annual multi-trip insurance**, which covers you for any number of trips throughout the year (with a maximum of 60 days for any one trip). Unlike many policies, the Rough Guides schemes are calculated by the day, so if you're travelling for 27 days rather than a month, that's all you pay for. If you intend to be away for the whole year, the **Adventurer** policy will cover you for 365 days. Each plan can be supplemented with a "Hazardous Activities Premium" if you plan to indulge in sports considered dangerous, such as skiing, scuba-diving or trekking.

For a policy quote, call the Rough Guide Insurance Line on UK freefone ⊕0800/015 0906; or, if you're calling from elsewhere ⊕ +44 1392 314 665. Alternatively, get an online quote or buy online at ⊛www.roughguidesinsurance.com.

Health

There are no compulsory vaccinations for visiting Provence, though tetanus may be a good idea if you are heading to the more remote rural parts. Tap water is safe to drink everywhere in France, although most French prefer the neutral taste of bottled water. Water from fountains is also drinkable, except where there is a sign reading *eau non potable*.

Most travellers to Provence will encounter little in the way of **health problems**: sunburn, heat exhaustion and insect bites are the most usual complaints. As ever, it is always worth taking precautions against sexually transmitted diseases: condoms are widely available from supermarkets, pharmacies and most bars, and there are no reasons not to use them.

Under the French **social security system**, all hospital visits, doctor's consultations and prescribed medicines are charged. Although all employed French people are entitled to a refund of 75–80 percent of their medical expenses, this can still leave a hefty shortfall, especially after a stay in hospital (accident victims even have to pay for the ambulance that takes them there).

To find a **doctor**, stop at any *pharmacie* and ask for an address, or look under *médecin généraliste* in the phone book. Consultation fees for a visit should be around €20, and you'll be given a *Feuille de Soins* (Statement of Treatment) for later documentation of insurance claims. Prescriptions should be taken to a **pharmacie**, which is also equipped – and obliged – to give first aid (for a fee). The medicines you buy will have little stickers (*vignettes*) attached to them, which you must remove and stick to your *Feuille de Soins* together with the prescription itself. In serious emergencies, you will always be taken to the **local hospital** (*Centre Hospitalier*), either under your own power or by ambulance. The emergency number throughout France is ⊕15.

As getting a refund entails a complicated bureaucratic procedure, and in any case does not cover the full cost of treatment, it's always a good idea to take out ordinary travel insurance, which generally allows full reimbursement, less the first few pounds or dollars of every claim, and also covers the cost of repatriation.

Medical resource websites

@health.yahoo.com Information on specific diseases and conditions, drugs and herbal remedies, as well as advice from health experts.
@www.fitfortravel.scot.nhs.uk UK NHS website carrying information about travel-related diseases and how to avoid them.
@www.istm.org The website of the International Society for Travel Medicine, with a full list of clinics specializing in international travel health.
@www.tripprep.com Travel Health Online provides an online-only comprehensive database of necessary vaccinations for most countries, as well as destination and medical service provider information.

Costs, money and banks

The Côte d'Azur has a reputation for being excessively expensive and it certainly will be if you indulge in the quayside-cocktail-sipping, haute cuisine and nightclub-larking lifestyle that this coast notoriously caters for. Many, but by no means all, of the hilltop villages in Provence are equally geared up to the indulgences of the very rich. The major cities, including those on the coast, have budget options for accommodation and eating out that, as in the rest of France, are relatively low cost by northern European standards. However, prices do go up considerably in July and August, and the Côte d'Azur and Riviera are more expensive than the rest of the region.

For a comfortable existence, with a hotel room for two, a light restaurant lunch and a proper restaurant dinner plus transport, café stops and museum visits, you need to allow about **€100 a day** per person.

However, if you are careful, staying in hostels (€13) or camping (€5–10 a head) and being strong-willed about not sitting down in cafés, you could manage on **€40–50**, including a cheap restaurant meal.

For two or more people **hotel accommodation** can be almost as cheap as hostels, though a sensible average estimate for a double room would be around €50. As for food, you can spend as much or as little as you like. There are large numbers of reasonable **restaurants** with three- or four-course menus for between €12 and €20, with midday meals almost always cheaper than in the evening. **Picnic food**, obviously, is much less costly, especially when you buy in the markets and cheap supermarket chains. **Wine** and **beer** are both very cheap in supermarkets; buying wine from the barrel at village coop cellars will give you the best value for money. The mark-up on wine in restaurants is high, though the house wine in cheaper establishments is still very good value. **Drinks** in cafés and bars are what really make a hole in your pocket – you have to accept that you're paying for somewhere to sit. Black coffee, draught lager and pastis are the cheapest drinks to order.

Transport need not be a large item of

expenditure, unless you're planning to drive a lot on the autoroutes in a gas-guzzling **car**. The French autoroutes still have **tolls**, and these are particularly high in Provence. Petrol prices are around €1.20 a litre for leaded, around €1.05 for unleaded, and around €0.90 a litre for diesel; note that there are 3.8 litres to the US gallon.

French **trains** are good value (a typical return-trip fare between Marseille and Nice costs around €52; and from Nice to Menton is around €8), with many discounts available. **Buses** are cheaper, though prices vary enormously from one operator to another. **Bicycles** cost between €10 and €15 per day to rent.

Museums and **monuments** can make considerable dents in budgets. **Reduced admission** is often available for those over sixty, under eighteen, and for students under 26. Several towns operate a global ticket for their museums and monuments. These are detailed in the Guide.

Currency and the exchange rate

On January 1, 2002, France, along with eleven other European Union nations, introduced a new currency, the **euro** (€). The euro is split into 100 cents. There are seven euro **notes** – in denominations of 500, 200, 100, 50, 20, 10, and 5 euros – and eight different **coin** denominations, including 2 and 1 euros, then 50, 20, 10, 5, 2, and 1 cents. Euro coins feature a common EU design on one face, but different country-specific designs on the other. No matter what the design, all euro coins and notes can be used in any of the twelve member states (Austria, Belgium, Finland, France, Germany, Greece, Ireland, Italy, Luxembourg, Portugal, Spain and the Netherlands).

Despite the overall success of the transition to the euro, many French continue to speak of prices in terms of the former currency, the franc, especially for large sums. Thus, it is useful to know that 1 euro is worth approximately 6.55957 francs (fixed rate). For the most up-to-date exchange rates, consult the currency converter website ⓦwww.oanda.com.

Changing money

Standard **banking hours** are 9.30am–noon and 2–4pm, although you may find some places that don't close for lunch. Banks are always closed on Sunday and either Saturday or, less often, Monday. **Rates of exchange** and **commissions** vary from place to place – a €5 charge for changing €40 is not uncommon; the Banque Nationale de Paris usually offers the best rates and takes the least commission. There are **money-exchange counters** at airports and the train stations of all big cities, and usually one or two in town centres as well; these often keep much longer hours than the high-street banks. You'll also find automatic money **exchange machines** which take dollars and £10 and £20 notes but give a very poor rate of exchange. For cash advances, see below.

Credit and debit cards

Credit/debit cards are widely accepted throughout Provence for goods and services. Those backed by Visa are the most universally recognized; American Express and Mastercard/Access (sometimes called Eurocard) less so. It's always worth checking, however, that restaurants and hotels will accept your card; smaller ones often don't, and even train stations in small towns may refuse them. Be aware that French cards have a smart chip and machines may reject the magnetic strip of British, American or Australasian cards, even if they are valid. If your card is refused because of this, you can explain to the assistant by saying: "Les cartes britanniques/américaines/canadiennes/australiennes/de Nouvelle-Zélande ne sont pas cartes à puce, mais à piste magnetique. Ma carte est valable et je vous serais très reconnaissant(e) de demander la confirmation auprès de votre banque ou de votre centre de traitement."

Credit/debit cards are also the most **convenient way to get cash**, and they can be used in any French ATM displaying the Visa or Cirrus symbol. The PIN number should be the same as you use at home, but make sure before you leave. Most French ATMs give instructions in English and do not charge service fees, though it's worth making sure your own bank doesn't charge a fee for using other banks' ATMs – a £1.50 charge each time you use your card could add up quickly.

Before leaving home, ask your bank or credit card company for the number to ring if your credit/debit card is **lost or stolen**.

Travellers' cheques

Obtaining **euro travellers' cheques** can be worthwhile: they can often be used as cash, and French banks are obliged by law to give you the face value of the cheques when you change them, so commission is only paid on purchase.

It is worth getting a selection of denominations of travellers' cheques. Make sure you keep the purchase agreement and a record of cheque serial numbers safe and separate from the cheques themselves. In the event that cheques are lost or stolen, the issuing company will expect you to report the loss straightaway to their office in France; most companies claim to replace lost or stolen cheques within 24 hours.

Getting around

If you want to visit Provence's main cities, travelling by train is the most reliable and economical means. You can then use the bus network to radiate out from the towns, though this is much easier in western Provence than the less populated east. By far the best way of getting around, however, is with your own transport, preferably motorized as much of the terrain is daunting for all but the most superfit cyclist. Approximate journey times and frequencies for public transport can be found in "Travel details" at the end of each chapter and local peculiarities are also pointed out in the text of the Guide.

Trains

The main **rail line** in Provence and the Côte d'Azur links all the major cities of the coast and the Rhône Valley, with Marseille as its hub. From here a second major line runs north along the Durance Valley to Manosque and Sisteron on its way to Gap. From Nice a line runs north through Tende to Turin. From Avignon trains head west into Languedoc and to Marseille via Cavaillon. Nice and Digne are linked by the **Chemin de Fer de Provence** (a narrow-gauge line), which is a brilliant ride in itself, and connects with the main rail network north of Digne by bus. **InterRail** passes give you only a fifty percent reduction on this line – the French rail passes are fully valid.

The French national rail company, the **SNCF** (☎08.92.35.35.35 €0.34/min; ⓦwww.sncf.com), deserves its reputation for efficiency. Trains are fast, frequent and reliable, and the system is more or less idiot-proof. All but the smallest stations have an information desk, and, many have coin-operated lockers big enough to take a rucksack (*consignes automatiques*). For security reasons, however, these lockers are not always available – check with an attendant for the current status.

SNCF's latest success is the new **TGV Méditerranée** line, which opened in June 2001 and has cut the travelling time between Paris (Gare de Lyon) and Marseille to a mere three hours. Twelve years in the making and with a budget of more than €3.5 billion, the project included 250km of new track laid between Valence and Marseille, and the construction of three ultra-modern stations on the outskirts of Valence, Avignon and Aix-en-Provence. All TGV travellers heading to these cities will alight at one of the new stations, from where there are shuttles into the centre of town. Likewise, those departing by TGV from Valence, Avignon or Aix will need to first take the shuttle out to the station in order to board their train. The new line also links Lyon, Valence, Avignon, Aix and Marseille directly with Charles de Gaulle airport, north-east of Paris.

Fares are generally reasonable, though TGVs require a supplement at peak times and compulsory seat reservations. TGV prices vary according to demand so you may find a later, or earlier, train cheaper. Also bear in mind that if a TGV is more than thirty minutes late, all passengers on board are entitled to a partial refund (via post), provided their tickets have been stamped by an attendant upon arrival.

Tickets can be bought from automatic machines or the ticket office, and must be validated in the orange machines at station platform entrances – it is an offence not to "*Compostez votre billet*". Train journeys may be broken at any point for up to 24 hours.

Regional **rail maps** and **timetables** are on sale at tobacconist shops. Leaflet timetables for a particular line are available free at stations. *Autocar* at the top of a column means it's an SNCF bus service, on which rail tickets and passes are valid.

Discounts and passes

Within France, the main discounts available for all trains, including the TGV, are for **advance bookings**: the **J8**, which gives a 25 percent discount for reservations made up to eight days in advance; and the **J30**, which gives a 50 percent discount for reservations made thirty to sixty days in advance. However, only a limited number of discounted seats are available for each train, and these are sold on a first-come, first-served basis, so you're less likely to get a discount if you are travelling during peak hours, on a weekend or on a holiday.

In addition to these discounts, people travelling in groups of two to nine are entitled to a **découverte à deux**, a 25 percent discount on return journeys on all trains. This same discount applies to anyone who books a return journey of at least 200km, including a Saturday night away (known as a **séjour**). Anyone **under 26** or **over 60** is also entitled to a 25 percent discount, though, as above, the availability of all these discounts is limited, and it helps if you travel during off-peak hours; a leaflet showing the different travel periods is available from stations. The discounts are not valid if you buy your ticket from a conductor on the train.

A final option is to buy a **discount pass**, which has the main advantage of guaranteeing at the very least a 25 percent reduction, even when the normally discounted seats are already sold out. Over 60s can purchase a **Carte Senior** (€46), valid for a year, which gives up to fifty percent off tickets on all trains, including TGVs. The same terms are available for 12- to 25-year-olds with a **Carte 12–25** pass, which costs €44, and for 4- to 12-year-olds with the **Carte Enfant Plus**, which costs €58. The last also entitles the cardholder to secure the same ticket reductions for up to three travelling companions, also aged between 4 and 12. These train passes can be bought through most travel agents in France or from SNCF's main stations and website. For details of Europe-wide train passes, see p.18.

Buses

Provence is quite well served by **buses**, with good networks radiating out from Aix and Nice, plus inland services between the two and along the coast between Toulon and St-Raphaël which do not duplicate train routes. In the least touristy areas timetables tend to be geared to **school and market needs** which usually means getting up at the crack of dawn to catch them. You may need to time your visit for a particular day of the week and fix up accommodation in advance.

SNCF buses are useful for getting to places on the rail network where trains no longer stop; they are included on rail timetables. The rest of the bus network is run by a plethora of **private companies** that rarely manage to coordinate their services. Although most towns have a **gare routière** (bus station) – usually near the Gare SNCF – it's not necessarily used by all the operators. Instead of wading through the reams of different timetables, get the ticket office to help you or ask at the local tourist office.

Driving

Provence is superb **driving** country, whether on the coastal corniches or the zig-zagging mountain routes. Driving allows you to explore the more remote villages and the most dramatic landscapes, which are otherwise inaccessible, while roads like the **Route Napoléon**, the **Corniche Sublime** and the **Grande Corniche** were built expressly to give breathtaking views.

With a full car the costs of driving need not be excessive and the added ease of camping with a car or motorbike to carry the gear can allow you to save on the price of accommodation. **Fuel** costs around €1.20 a litre for leaded, €1.05 for unleaded, and

€0.90 a litre for diesel; prices are lower at supermarket chains such as Intermarché.

All the **highways** (*autoroutes*) in Provence have tolls except for the urban stretches, the A51 between Marseille and Aix, and the A55 from Marseille to Martigues. Some sample charges are: Aix to Nice €13.70; Aix to Sisteron €7.20; Aix to Toulon €6.20; Nice to Monaco €2. For up-to-date information on traffic conditions on the autoroutes call ☎08.92.68.10.77.

Car rental costs upwards of €280 a week. It is usually cheaper to arrange from Britain or the US before you leave, with Budget offering particularly competitive deals on pre-paid car rental in France (see below for details of car rental companies). You'll find the big firms – Hertz, Avis, Europcar and Budget – at airports and in most big cities, with addresses detailed throughout the Guide. Local firms can be cheaper but you need to check the small print and be sure of where the car can be returned to. It's normal to pay an indemnity of around €200 against any damage to the car – they will take your credit card number rather than cash. You should return the car with a full tank. Extras are often pressed on you, such as medical cover, which you may already have from travel insurance. The cost of car rental includes the compulsory car insurance. North Americans and Australians, in particular, should be forewarned that it is very difficult to arrange the rental of a car with **automatic** transmission – not popular in France. If you can't drive a manual, you should reserve well in advance, and be prepared to pay a higher price.

All the major car manufacturers have service stations in France – you'll find them in the Yellow Pages (*Pages Jaunes*) of the phone book under *Garages d'automobiles*. For **breakdown services** look under *Dépannages*. If you have **an accident or break-in**, you should make a report to the local police (and keep a copy) in order to make an insurance claim.

In **mountainous areas** fuel stations are few and far between so it's wise to carry a can. Many of the high passes are closed from mid-October to May, June or even July. Notices give you good warning. In **July and August** the traffic jams on the coastal roads can be horrendous, in particular between Hyères and Cannes, and Nice and Menton. For recorded information on **road conditions** call Inter Service Route on ☎08.26.02.20.22.

Car **parking** is usually free in towns between midday and 2pm; otherwise charges vary from €0.30 to €2 an hour.

And finally, if you smoke, never throw your cigarette end out of the window. The undergrowth of Provence and the Côte d'Azur in summer is bone-dry kindling wood, and a single spark can start a raging **fire**.

Rules of the road

British, EU and US **driving licences** are valid in France, though an International Driver's Licence makes life easier if you get a police officer unwilling to peruse a document in English. The vehicle's registration document (*carte grise*) and the insurance papers must be carried. If your car is right-hand drive, you must have your headlight dip adjusted to the right before you go – it's a legal requirement.

The law of **priorité à droite** – giving way to traffic coming from your right, even when it is coming from a minor road – is a major cause of accidents. Even though it has been phased out in some places, it still applies in built-up areas, so you have to be vigilant in towns. Look out for the signs – a yellow diamond on a white background gives you right of way, whilst the same sign with an oblique black slash indicates that vehicles emerging from the right have right of way. "*STOP*" means stop completely; "*CÉDEZ LE PASSAGE*" means "Give way".

Fines for driving violations are exacted on the spot, and only cash is accepted. Exceeding the speed limit by 1–30kmph can cost as much as €400. Speed limits are: 130kmph (80mph) on the tolled *autoroutes*; 110kmph (68mph) on two-lane highways; 90kmph (56mph) on other roads; and 60kmph (37mph) in towns. Despite the fines, people in the south of France tend to drive fast and recklessly, and to top it off, drinking and driving laws are rarely enforced, so it pays to stay alert – especially on back roads.

Car rental agencies

UK

Avis ☎0870/606 0100, ⓦwww.avis.co.uk.
Budget ☎0870/156 5656, ⓦwww.budget.co.uk.
Europcar ☎0870/607 5000, ⓦwww.europcar.co.uk.

Hertz ⓣ0870/844 8844, ⓦwww.hertz.co.uk.
Holiday Autos ⓣ0870/400 0099, ⓦwww.holidayautos.co.uk.
National ⓣ0870/400 4552, ⓦwww.nationalcar.co.uk.
Thrifty ⓣ01494/751 600, ⓦwww.thrifty.co.uk.

Ireland

Avis Northern Ireland ⓣ028/9024 0404, Republic of Ireland ⓣ01/605 7500, ⓦwww.avisworld.ie.
Budget Republic of Ireland ⓣ0903/277 11, ⓦwww.budget.ie.
Europcar Northern Ireland ⓣ028/9442 3444, Republic of Ireland ⓣ01/614 2888, ⓦwww.europcar.ie.
Hertz Republic of Ireland ⓣ01/676 7476, ⓦwww.hertz.ie.
Thrifty Republic of Ireland ⓣ1800/515 800, ⓦwww.thrifty.ie.

North America

Alamo US ⓣ1-800/522-9696, ⓦwww.goalamo.com.
Avis US ⓣ1-800/331-1084, Canada ⓣ1-800/272-5871, ⓦwww.avis.com.
Budget US ⓣ1-800/527-0700, ⓦwww.budget.com.
Europe by Car US ⓣ1-800/223 1516, in NY ⓣ212/581-3040, ⓦwww.europebycar.com.
Hertz US ⓣ1-800/654-3001, Canada ⓣ1-800/263-0600, ⓦwww.hertz.com.
Thrifty US ⓣ1-800/367-2277, ⓦwww.thrifty.com.

Australia and New Zealand

Avis Australia ⓣ13 63 33, New Zealand ⓣ0800/93 95 97, ⓦwww.avis.com.
Budget Australia ⓣ1300/362 848, New Zealand ⓣ09/976 2222, ⓦwww.budget.com.
Hertz Australia ⓣ13 30 39; New Zealand ⓣ0800/654 321, ⓦwww.hertz.com.
National Australia ⓣ13 10 45, New Zealand ⓣ0800/800 115, ⓦwww.nationalcar.com.
Thrifty Australia ⓣ1300/367 227, New Zealand ⓣ09/309 0111, ⓦwww.thrifty.com.

Hitching

Provence is one of the few areas in France where **hitching** is still fairly common, particularly along the coast in summer. Inland Provence is less easy, though in the remote areas it's an accepted way for locals to get around.

In general, looking as clean, ordinary and respectable as possible makes a very big difference, and hitching the less frequented **D-roads** paradoxically gets you to your destination more quickly. In **mountain areas** a rucksack and trekking gear often ensure lifts from fellow aficionados.

Autoroutes are a special case; hitching on the highway itself is strictly illegal, but you can make excellent time going from one service station to another. If you get stuck at least there's food, drink and shelter. It helps to have Michelin's *Guide des Autoroutes*, showing all the rest stops, service stations, tollbooths (*péages*) and exits. All you need apart from that is a smattering of French and not too much luggage. Remember to get out at the service station before your driver leaves the *autoroute*. The tollbooths are a second best (hitching there is legal), but ordinary approach roads are very difficult.

Cycling

The French have a great respect for **cycling** – it's a national sport and passion. This shows in the warm reception given to cyclists and to the care and courtesy extended by French drivers (except in large cities where bikes are not normally used as a means of transport and on the corniche roads where everyone drives crazily fast). In Provence you'll see cyclists beetling up **mountains**, often overtaking heavy vehicles, but if you're not up to such strenuous pedalling the **Rhône Valley** is the only area that is consistently easy-going. The other things to bear in mind are the high summer **temperatures** and relentless frazzling sun. If you are willing to tackle inclines, however, cycling is a wonderful way to explore the region, and will get you fit very quickly.

Restaurants and hotels along the way are nearly always obliging about looking after your bike, even to the point of allowing it into your room. Most large towns have well-stocked retail and **repair shops**, where parts are normally cheaper than at home. However, if you're using a foreign-made bike, it's a good idea to carry spare tyres, as French sizes are different. Inner tubes are not a problem, as they adapt to either size, though make sure you get the right valves.

The **train network** runs various schemes for cyclists, all of them covered by the free leaflet *Train et Vélo*, available from most stations. You can travel with a bike as free accompanied luggage on *autorails*, when marked with a bicycle in the timetable. On TGVs and Corail coaches, folding bikes or bikes with the wheels removed and packed in covers no bigger than 120 x 90cm (which you can buy at cycle shops) can be carried. Otherwise, you have to send your bike as registered luggage (€30, or €45 for a door-to-door service), which SNCF guarantees to deliver within two working days, although it may well arrive immediately; equally, you do hear stories of bicycles disappearing altogether. British Airways and Air France both take bikes free. You may have to box them though, and you should check with the airlines first.

Bikes for rent – usually mountain bikes (*vélos tous terrains* commonly abbreviated to *VTTs*) – are often available from campsites, youth hostels and *gîtes d'étape*, as well as specialist cycle shops, some tourist offices and train stations. Costs are €10–15 per day, and around €65 a week. Deposits of between €150 and €250 are required – you can give them credit card details rather than cash but make sure you get a proper receipt.

Rented bikes are often not insured and you will be presented with the bill for its replacement if it's stolen or damaged, so check whether you are covered for this by your travel **insurance**. If not, the UK-based Cyclists Touring Club, Cotterell House, 69 Meadrow, Surrey GU7 3HS (☎0870/873 0064, ⓦwww.ctc.org.uk), runs a particularly good bike insurance scheme, and can also suggest routes and supply advice for a small fee.

The best **maps** for cycling are the contoured IGN 1:10,000 series. For further information on maps of the region, and details of stockists, see p.23–24.

Some useful cycling vocabulary

to adjust	*ajuster*
axle	*l'axe*
ball bearing	*le roulement à billes*
battery	*la pile*
bent	*tordu*
bicycle	*le vélo*
bottom bracket	*le logement du pédalier*
brake cable	*le cable*
brakes	*les freins*
broken	*cassé*
bulb	*l'ampoule*
chain	*la chaîne*
cotter pin	*la clavette*
to deflate	*gonfler*
dérailleur	*le dérailleur*
frame	*le cadre*
gears	*les vitesses*
grease	*la graisse*
handlebars	*le guidon*
to inflate	*gonfler*
inner tube	*la chambre à air*
loose	*dévissé*
to lower	*baisser*
mudguard	*le garde-boue*
pannier	*le pannier*
pedal	*le pédale*
pump	*la pompe*
punctured	*la crevaison*
rack	*le porte-bagages*
to raise	*relever*
to repair	*réparer*
saddle	*la selle*
to screw	*visser*
spanner	*la clef (mécanique)*
spoke	*le rayon*
to straighten	*rédresser*
stuck	*coincé*
tight	*serré*
toe clips	*les cale-pieds*
tyre	*le pneu*
wheel	*la roue*

Mopeds and scooters

Mopeds and **scooters** are relatively easy to find: everyone in France, from young kids to grandmas, rides one, and although they're not built for any kind of long-distance travel, they're ideal for shooting around town and nearby. Places that rent out bicycles will often also rent out mopeds; you can expect to pay €26 a day for a 50cc Honda, for example, or €47 for a 100cc motorbike. Crash helmets are compulsory only on machines over 125cc, but you'd be a fool not to wear one even on a moped.

Walking

Provence has an extensive network of **footpaths** and some of France's most rewarding **trekking country**, both in the mountains and in the coastal hinterland. There's the national network of long-distance footpaths, known as *sentiers de grande randonnée* – GR for short – marked by horizontal red and white striped signs, of which numbers 4, 5, 6 and 9 plus various offshoots run through the region. The national and regional parks – the Camargue, the Lubéron and the

Mercantour – have additional networks, and there are also the smaller paths and forest tracks, all usually well signed. Coastal paths exist but only in short stretches.

Each GR is described in a **Topo guide** (available from Stanfords in London, see p.23, and from bookshops and newsagents in Provence), which gives a detailed account of the route (in French), including maps, campsites, refuge huts, sources of provisions, etc. In addition, tourist offices can put you in touch with guides and organizations for **climbing and walking expeditions**.

Specialized walking maps are produced by Didier Richard on a 1:50,000 scale. These include *Alpes-de-Provence* (no. 1), *Mercantour* (no. 9), *Haute-Provence* (no. 19), *Au Pays d'Azur* (no. 26) and *Maures et Haut Pays Varois* (no. 25); they are available in most major bookshops in the region and from Stanfords in London (see p.23). The best publishers for **French guidebooks** on walking are Editions Edisud.

In July and August it's important to book a bed at the **mountain refuge huts** in advance. Phone numbers for many of the Alpine refuges are given in the Guide; you can also get lists from local tourist offices. Several are run by the Club Alpin Français which takes bookings from its office in Nice (Ⓣ04.93.62.59.99, Ⓦwww.clubalpin.com).

The warning to drivers about cigarette ends applies to walkers too. If you stub one out on the ground you must make sure that it is completely extinguished. Equally never light **fires**, however much you think a clearing is big enough for safety. You may find many paths and tracks have *défense d'entrée* signs in summer. These restrictions are to protect the forest from the risk of fire and should be respected – you can also be heavily fined if you're found on out-of-bounds paths.

On the water

You don't have to own a yacht to **sail** into the Côte d'Azur resorts. There are companies offering transport services from the gares maritimes (maritime ports) of many coastal towns, either out to islands or to neighbouring ports. Though not the cheapest way to get about, this can sometimes be the quickest when the summer traffic jams on the coastal roads are at their worst.

Trips down the Rhône are always slow and expensive. The boats tend to be of the Parisian *bateaux-mouches* variety – huge and ugly – and the deals often involve overpriced dinner-dance affairs. Inland, the **rivers of Provence** are harnessed to hydroelectric power stations and an extensive irrigation system. There are numerous barrages and water levels change at the flick of a switch (and with no warning). Therefore **canoeing and rafting**, though possible on many stretches, should not be undertaken without local guidance. Details about boat trips and centres for canoeing and rafting are listed in the Guide.

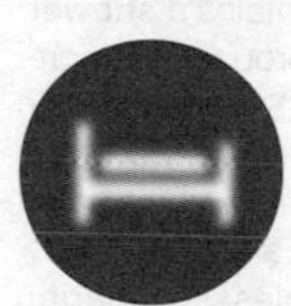

Accommodation

Finding accommodation on the spot in the main cities of Provence and the Côte d'Azur is not a major problem, other than in July and August. At any time of year, however, booking a couple of nights in advance can be reassuring, saving the effort of trudging round and ensuring that you know what you'll be paying.

The summer season in the **coastal resorts** lasts from around mid-May to mid-September, and hotels, youth hostels and campsites are all stretched beyond their limits. The worst time of all is between July 15 and August 15 when the French take their holidays en masse. Your chances of finding anything then without advance booking

Accommodation price categories

Throughout this guide, all hotels and guesthouses have been priced on a scale of ❶–❾, indicating the lowest price you could expect to pay for a double room in high season. What you get for your money varies enormously between establishments, but in the lower-priced hotels you should expect to pay considerably more for en-suite facilities. If you are staying anywhere for more than three days it's often possible to negotiate a discount, particularly out of season.

❶ Under €30	❹ €55–70	❼ €100–125
❷ €30–40	❺ €70–85	❽ €125–150
❸ €40–55	❻ €85–100	❾ Over €150

become very slim indeed, though most tourist offices will do their best to help.

The problems are rather different **inland**, where the villages are often dominated by *résidences secondaires* (second homes) rather than hotels; those **hotels** that there are, and **bed and breakfast** in private houses (chambres d'hôtes), can get booked up well in advance. **Campsites**, however, are plentiful and rarely full once you're north of the Autoroute La Provençale.

Aside from the summer, the one bad month is **November** when almost all hoteliers take their holidays and most campsites are closed.

Phone numbers as well as addresses have been given in the Guide and the "Language" section at the back should help you make a reservation, though many hoteliers and campsite managers, and almost all youth hostel managers, will speak some English.

Hotels

Hotel recommendations are given in the Guide for almost every town or village mentioned with a price range for each (see box above). Many hotels, particularly those in smaller resorts and the inland villages, **close for one day of the week** – this means that you can't check in or out on the day in question, but if you're already installed you'll be supplied with a key and expected to look after yourself. Where applicable, these days are also noted in the text.

If you're travelling in peak season it's worth having as many addresses as possible. Local **accommodation lists** are available from tourist offices, and lists for the Provence-Alpes-Côte-d'Azur region and each individual *département* can be obtained before you leave from any French Government Tourist Office (see p.22 for addresses).

A useful option, especially if it's late at night, is the **Formule 1 chain**, well signposted on the outskirts of larger towns. Characterless motels, they provide box-like rooms for up to three people for €30 in high season. With a Visa, Mastercard, Eurocard or American Express credit card, you can let yourself into a room at any hour of the day or night. Reservations can be made on ⓣ08.92.68.56.85 (€0.34/min) or at ⓦwww.hotelformule1.com. The hotels are not difficult to find as long as you're travelling by car, and a brochure with full details can be picked up at any one.

All French hotels are **graded** from **zero to four stars**. The price more or less corresponds to the number of stars, though the system is a little haphazard, often having more to do with ratios of bathrooms to guests than quality; ungraded and single-star hotels are often very good. At the cheapest level, what makes a difference in cost is whether a room contains a **shower**: if it does, the bill will be around €5 more. **Breakfast**, too, can add €5–10 per person to a bill – you will nearly always do better at a café, but some hotels will insist on providing it. **Single rooms** are only marginally cheaper than doubles so sharing always cuts costs considerably. Most hotels willingly provide rooms with extra beds, for three or more people, at good discounts.

In high season many hotels demand **demi-pension** (half board) which is not necessarily a bad deal, though it can get very boring eating in the same place all the time. Though it's illegal for hotels to insist on you taking meals when the cost is separate from the price of the room, many do and you may have little option but to agree. One plausible way out worth trying is to say you are *invité/e* (invited out).

Chambres d'hôtes

Chambres d'hôtes (bed and breakfasts in private houses) are fairly widespread, particularly in small villages. They vary in standard and are rarely an especially cheap option – usually costing the equivalent of a two-star hotel. However, if you're lucky, they may be good sources of traditional home-cooking. A selection is listed in the Guide; full lists are available from tourist offices and you can also find them detailed with Gîtes de France and gîtes d'étape (see below) by *département* in leaflets available from French Government Tourist Offices and the larger tourist offices.

Hostels, gîtes d'étape and refuges

At between €8 and €12.20 per night for a dormitory bed, **youth hostels** – *auberges de jeunesse* – are invaluable for single travellers on a budget. Some offer double rooms from €20, but it can be cheaper for couples, and certainly for groups of three or more people, to share a room in a hotel – particularly if you have to pay a bus fare out to the edge of town to reach the local hostel. However, many hostels are beautifully sited, and they allow you to cut costs by preparing your own food in their kitchens, or eating in their cheap canteens. To stay at many of the hostels you must be a member of **Hostelling International (HI)** (ⓦwww.iyhf.org), or its affiliate Youth Hostel Association (YHA), which currently costs £13/$25 for over 18s, £6.50/free for under 18s. Head offices are listed in the box below. However, if Provence is your first, or only, destination, you're much better off buying your **membership card** from a French hostel, where it will cost €15.25 for over 26s, and €10.70 for under 26s. Alternatively, you can buy a €2.90 "Welcome Stamp" which, once you've collected six, gives you international membership. If you don't have your own sleeping bag you'll have to pay €2.70 to rent bedding.

Youth Hostel Associations

Australia
Australian Youth Hostel Association, ⓣ02/9261 1111, ⓦwww.yha.org.au.

Canada
Hostelling International/Canadian Hostelling Association, ⓣ1-800/663 5777 or 613-237-7884, ⓦwww.hihostels.ca.

England and Wales
Youth Hostel Association (YHA), ⓣ0870/870 8808, ⓦwww.yha.org.uk.

France
Fédération Unie des Auberges de Jeunesse (FUAJ), ⓣ01.44.89.87.27, ⓦwww.fuaj.org.
Ligue Française pour les Auberges de Jeunesse (LFAJ), ⓣ01.44.16.78.78, ⓦwww.auberges-de-jeunesse.com.
Union des Centres de Rencontres Internationales de France (UCRIF), ⓣ01.40.26.57.64, ⓦwww.ucrif.asso.fr.

Ireland
An Oige, ⓣ01/830 4555, ⓦwww.irelandyha.org.
Youth Hostel Association of Northern Ireland, 22 Donegall Rd, Belfast BT12 5JN ⓣ028/9032 4733, ⓦwww.hini.org.uk.

New Zealand
Youth Hostel Association of New Zealand, PO Box 436, 193 Cashel St, Christchurch 1 ⓣ0800/278 299 or 03/379 9970, ⓦwww.yha.co.nz.

Scotland
Scottish Youth Hostel Association, ⓣ0870/155 3255, ⓦwww.syha.org.uk.

US
Hostelling International-American Youth Hostels (HI-AYH), ⓣ202-783-6161, ⓦwww.hiayh.org.

Slightly confusingly, there are three rival French hostelling associations, the main two being **Fédération Unie des Auberges de Jeunesse** (FUAJ; thirteen hostels in Provence), which has its hostels detailed in the *International Handbook*, and the **Ligue Française pour les Auberges de Jeunesse** (LFAJ; 5 hostels in Provence). HI membership covers both organizations, and you'll find all their hostels detailed in the text. The third organization is the **Union des Centres de Rencontres Internationales de France** (UCRIF) with hostels in Vaison-la-Romaine and Cannes; membership is not required.

In addition, you'll find other independent hostels that do not belong to the HI, and in the main cities there are **foyers** or *résidences* – residential hostels for young workers and students – which often have age limits or are women only, and university accommodation, usually available only in July and August. Prices are rarely more than €15 for a single or double room and all are detailed in the Guide.

A third hostel-type alternative is the **gîtes d'étape** found in rural Provence. These are less formal than other youth hostels, often run by the local village or municipality (whose mayor will probably be in charge of the key), and provide bunk beds and primitive kitchen and washing facilities for around €11. Designed primarily for people trekking or on bikes or horses, they are marked on the large-scale IGN walkers' maps and listed in the individual GR Topo guides, as well as in the *département* leaflets available from French Government Tourist Offices and local tourist offices.

In the mountains there are **refuge huts** on the main GR routes, normally open only in summer. They are extremely basic and not always very friendly places, and must be booked in advance in high summer (see "Walking" on p.32–33). Costs per night start at €10 depending on facilities. A list of refuge huts in the Alpes-Maritimes *département* is available from the Comité Régional de Tourisme, 55 promenade des Anglais, Nice (Ⓣ04.93.37.78.78), and for the Alpes-de-Haute-Provence *département* from the Comité Départemental de Tourisme, 19 rue du Dr-Honnorat, Digne-les-Bains (Ⓣ04.92.31.57.29).

Rented accommodation: Gîtes de France

If you are planning to stay a week or more in any one place it might be worth considering **renting a house**. You can do this by checking adverts placed by private and foreign owners in Sunday newspapers, or trying one of the many firms that market travel and accommodation packages (see p.13, p.15 & p.17).

The easiest and most reliable method, however, is to use the official French Government service, the **Gîtes de France**, run in Britain by Brittany Ferries (Ⓣ08705/360 360, Ⓦwww.gites-de-france.fr), and in Canada through Gîtes ruraux en France/Abracadabra (Ⓣ418/455-4331, Ⓦwww.abracadabra.qc.ca). The scheme includes properties all over France, varying in size and comfort, but all basically acceptable holiday homes. Costs vary, with sea-view houses on the Côte d'Azur and Riviera inevitably commanding very high prices. Inland you should be able to rent a comfortable house in the countryside with room for four or five people for around €500–600 a week in July and August. The properties are listed by *département*, with a short description of each one, and, through the online booking service, you can instantly reserve one for any number of weeks. For a more detailed description of the gîtes, there are seven *guides départementaux* (from €4.50) for Provence, available through the online bookshop and Gîtes de France regional offices.

Camping

Most towns and villages have at least one **campsite** (notable exceptions being Marseille which has none, and Nice which has only one a long way out). Camping is extremely popular with the French and, particularly for those from the north of the country, Provence is a favourite destination. The cheapest sites – at around €6 per person per night – are usually the **camping municipaux**, run by the local municipality. They are always clean and have plenty of hot water, and are often situated in prime positions. Some youth hostels also have space for tents.

On the **Côte d'Azur** campsites can cost three times regular prices for few (or no) extra facilities, and tend to be monstrously big. At full capacity in July and August they can be far too crowded for comfort. Most of the sites recommended in the Guide are the smaller ones. Inland, **camping à la ferme** – on somebody's farm – is another (generally facility-less) possibility. Lists of sites are detailed in the French Tourist Board's *Accueil à la*

Campagne booklet and are available from local tourist offices. You should make sure of what you'll be charged before you pitch up – it's easy to get stung the following morning.

Contact information for campsites is given in the text of the Guide so you can check ahead for space availability. We also give prices and the French grading from one to four stars which indicates the sophistication of the facilities.

Camping rough (*camping sauvage*, as the French call it) is possible, but you must ask **permission** from the owner of the land first. Farmers can be very nasty if you don't, and their weapons include guns as well as dogs. In the remote areas of northeastern Provence, where it may not be clear who owns the land, you'll probably be OK but don't camp within the protected area of the Parc de Mercantour. Nor should you ever camp in the forests in summer: however careful you think you might be, it takes only one stray spark to start a galloping inferno, and both local people and police are vigilant.

Camping **on the beach** is standard practice only on certain stretches in the Camargue; elsewhere you'll be vulnerable to theft and mugging. If the police find you, it's possible that you could be arrested.

If you're planning to do a lot of camping, an **international camping carnet** (£4.50/$10) is a good investment. The carnet serves as useful identification, covers you for third-party insurance when camping and is good for discounts at member sites. It's available from home motoring organizations, or from one of the following: in the UK, the Camping and Caravan Club (☎024/7669 4995, ⓦwww.campingandcaravanningclub.co.uk); in North America, the Family Campers and RVers (FCRV; ☎1-800/245-9755, ⓦwww.fcrv.org).

Food and drink

Food is as good a reason as any for going to Provence. The region has one of the great cuisines of France as well as some very fine wines in the Vaucluse, on the coast and at Châteauneuf-du-Pape.

For experiencing food and wine at their best, Provence boasts a considerable number of top gourmet **restaurants**, matched only in the rest of the country by Lyon and Paris. Many of these are cheap by British and American standards, their extravagance only relative to the prices of less elaborate but still gorgeously gluttonous meals you can have. Unfortunately, the chances of having a mediocre or even bad meal in the heavily touristed areas are on the increase, but if you take your time – treating the business of choosing a place as an interesting appetizer in itself – you should be able to eat consistently well without spending a fortune.

The **markets** of Provence (the best ones are detailed in the Guide) are a great sensual treat as well as lively social events. *Marchés paysans*, where *paysans* (smallholders, the backbone of French farming) sell directly to the public, are common.

Provence is also the homeland of **pastis**, the cooling aniseed-flavoured drink traditionally served with a bowl of olives before meals. For a full rundown of useful food and drink terms, see the food glossary on p.470–477.

Breakfast and snacks

A croissant, *pain au chocolat* (a choc-filled croissant) or a sandwich in a bar or café, with hot chocolate or coffee, is generally the best way to eat **breakfast** – at a fraction of the cost charged by most hotels. Croissants and sometimes hard-boiled eggs are displayed on bar counters until around 9.30 or 10am. If you stand – cheaper than sitting down – you just help yourself to these with your coffee, the waiter keeps an eye on how many you've eaten and bills you accordingly.

Provençal cuisine

Intense sunshine combined with all-important irrigation make Provence one of the great food regions of France. Just about everything flourishes here but pride of place must go to the olive tree, introduced to the region by the ancient Greeks two and a half thousand years ago, and perfectly suited to the warm, dry climate. Olives accompany the traditional Provençal aperitif of pastis; they appear in sauces and salads, on tarts and pizzas, and mixed with capers in *tapenade* paste spread on bread or biscuits. **Olive oil** is the starting point for almost all Provençal dishes. Spiced with chillies or **Provençal herbs** (wild thyme, basil, rosemary and tarragon), it is also poured over pizzas, sandwiches, and used to make vinaigrette and mayonnaise for all the varieties of salad, including the bitter leaves of the Niçois *mesclum*.

The ingredient most often mixed with olive oil is the other classic of Provençal cuisine, **garlic**. Whole markets are dedicated to strings of white and pale purple garlic. Two of the most famous concoctions of Provence are ***pistou***, a paste of olive oil, parmesan cheese, garlic and basil, and ***aïoli***, a garlic mayonnaise and the traditional Friday dish in which it's served with salt cod and vegetables.

Vegetables and fruit have double or triple seasons in Provence, often beginning while northern France is still in the depths of winter. **Ratatouille** ingredients – tomatoes, peppers, aubergines, courgettes and onions – are the favourites, along with purple-tipped asparagus and baby potatoes. Courgette flower fritters stuffed with *pistou* is one of the most exquisite Provençal delicacies. As for **fruit**, the melons, white peaches, apricots, figs, cherries and Muscat grapes are unbeatable. **Almond** trees grow on the plateaux of central Provence (with the nuts eaten when they are still green in summer), along with lavender, which gives Provençal **honey** its distinctive flavour.

Sheep, taken up to the mountains in the summer months, provide the staple meat, of which the best is *agneau de Sisteron*. But it is **fish** that features most on traditional menus. The fish soups of **bouillabaisse**, famous in Marseille, and *bourride*, served with a chilli-flavoured mayonnaise known as *rouille*, are served all along the coast, as are whole sea bream, monkfish, sea bass or John Dory, covered with Provençal herbs and grilled over an open flame. **Seafood**, from spider crabs to clams, sea urchins to crayfish, crabs, lobster, mussels and oysters, is piled onto huge *plateaux de fruits de mer*, not necessarily representing Mediterranean harvests, more the luxury associated with this coast. October to April is the prime seafood season.

The one source of food unsuited to the dry heat of Provence is cattle, which is why olive oil rather than butter and cream dominate Provençal cuisine, and why the **cheeses** are invariably made from goats' or ewes' milk. Famous *chèvres* (goats' cheeses) are Banon, wrapped in chestnut leaves and marinated in brandy, the aromatic Picadon from the foothills of the Alps, Poivre d'Ain, pressed with wild savory, and Lou Pevre with a pepper coating.

Provençal cuisine is extremely healthy. A traditional meal should leave you feeling perfectly able to dance the night away, or, more prosaically, to pig yourself without fear of heart attack. Except of course for the famous chocolates, candied fruit and chestnuts, almond sweets and nougat, plus all the extravagant ice-cream concoctions served with cocktails on the promenade cafés.

At **lunchtime**, and sometimes in the evening, you may find cafés offering a **plat du jour** (chef's daily special) at between €7 and €12 or *formules*, a limited or no-choice menu. The *croque-monsieur* or *croque-madame* (variations on the toasted-cheese sandwich) is on sale at cafés, brasseries and many street stands, along with *frites*, crêpes, *galettes* (buckwheat pancakes), *gaufres* (waffles), *glaces* (ice creams) and all kinds of fresh sandwiches. For variety, there are Tunisian snacks like *brik à l'œuf* (a fried pastry with an egg inside), *merguez* (spicy North African sausage) and Middle Eastern falafel (deep-fried balls of chickpea with salad). Local specialities include the Niçois *pan bagnat*, an oil-dripping bun stuffed with salad and fish, and *pissaladière*, an onion, black olive and anchovy flan.

Crêperies, serving filled pancakes from around €5 upwards, are very popular. But quality is variable, as it is with the ubiquitous **pizzerias** *au feu de bois* (wood-fire baked).

For **picnics**, the local outdoor market or supermarket will provide you with almost everything you need from tomatoes and avocados to cheese and pâté. Cooked meat, prepared snacks, ready-made dishes and assorted salads can be bought at *charcuteries* (delicatessens), which you'll find everywhere – even in small villages, though the same things are cheaper at supermarket counters. You purchase by weight, or you can ask for *une tranche* (a slice), *une barquette* (a carton), or *un part* (a portion). You'll also find hot, whole spit-roasted chicken on every high street and at most markets.

Salons de thé, which open from mid-morning to late evening, serve brunches, salads, quiches and the like, as well as gâteaux, ice cream and a wide selection of teas. They tend to be a good deal pricier than cafés or brasseries – you're paying for the posh surroundings. At **pâtisseries**, along with the usual cakes, breads and pastries, you'll find *fougasse* or *fougassette*, a five-finger-shaped bread containing olives, anchovies, sausage or cheese, or flavoured with orange, lemon or rose water. *Chichi* (a light, scented doughnut) are sold from street stalls; the region's other classic sweet nibble is nougat.

Full-scale meals

There's no difference between **restaurants** (*auberges* or *relais*) and **brasseries** in terms of quality or price range. The distinction is that brasseries, which resemble cafés, serve quicker meals at most hours of the day, while restaurants tend to stick to the traditional meal times of noon to 2pm and 7 to 9.30 or 10.30pm. After 9pm or so, restaurants often serve only à la carte meals – invariably more expensive than eating the set menu. In touristy areas in high season and for all the more upmarket places it's wise to make reservations – easily done on the same day. In small towns it may be impossible to get anything other than a bar sandwich after 10pm or even earlier; in major cities, town-centre brasseries will serve until 11pm or midnight and one or two may stay open all night.

Since restaurants change hands frequently and have their ups and downs, it's always worth asking local people for recommendations. This is the conversational equivalent of commenting on the weather in Britain and will usually elicit strong views and sound advice.

Prices and what you get for them are posted outside restaurants. Normally there is a choice between one or more **menus** where the number of courses has already been determined and the choice is limited. The *carte* (menu) has everything listed. *Service compris* or *s.c.* means the service charge is included. *Service non compris*, *s.n.c.* or *service en sus* means that it isn't and you need to calculate an additional fifteen percent. A glass of **wine** (*vin*) or an espresso may be included on midday menus. When ordering wine, ask for *un quart* (quarter-litre), *un demi-litre* (half-litre) or *une carafe* (a litre). You'll normally be given the house wine unless you specify otherwise; if you're worried about the cost ask for *vin ordinaire*. In the Guide the lowest-price menu or the range of menus is given; where average à la carte prices are given it assumes you'll have three courses and half a bottle of wine.

In the French sequence of **courses**, any salad (sometimes vegetables, too) comes separate from the main dish, and cheese precedes a dessert. You will be offered coffee, which is always extra (as much as €3) to finish off the meal. You can specify if you like it strong (*serré*) or weak (*léger*).

At the bottom of the price range, **menus** revolve around standard dishes such as steak and fries (*steack-frites*), chicken and fries (*poulet-frites*), stews (*daubes* or a whole variety of other terms) and various concoctions involving innards such as *pieds et paquets* (feet and tripe of sheep). If you're simply not that hungry, just go for the plat du jour.

Going **à la carte** offers much greater choice and, in the better restaurants, access to the chef's specialities. You pay for it, of course, though a simple and perfectly legitimate ploy is to have just one course instead of the expected three or four. You can share dishes or just have several starters – a useful strategy for vegetarians. There's no minimum charge.

The French are much better disposed towards **children** in restaurants than other nationalities, not simply by offering reduced-price children's menus, but in creating an atmosphere that positively welcomes kids, even in otherwise fairly snooty establishments; some even have in-house games and toys for them to occupy themselves with. It is regarded as self-evident that large family groups should be able to eat out together.

Less self-evident is the thinking behind allowing **dogs** in, too; it can be quite a shock to realize that some of your fellow diners are attempting to keep their pets under control beneath the tables.

Vegetarians

On the whole, **vegetarians** can expect a somewhat lean time in Provence and the Côte d'Azur. A few towns have specifically vegetarian restaurants (which are detailed in the text), but elsewhere you'll have to hope you find a sympathetic restaurant (crêperies can be good standbys). Sometimes restaurants are willing to replace a meat dish on the *menu fixe* with an omelette; other times you'll have to pick your way through the *carte*. Remember the phrase: *"je suis végétarien(ne); il y a des plats sans viande?"* (I'm a vegetarian; are there any non-meat dishes?).

Many vegetarians swallow a few principles and start eating fish and shellfish on holiday. **Vegans**, however, should probably forget about eating in restaurants and plan to cook for themselves.

Drinking

Wherever you can eat you can invariably drink and vice versa. **Drinking** is done at a leisurely pace whether it's as a prelude to food (*apéritif*), a sequel (*digestif*), or accompanying it, and **cafés** are the standard places to do it. Every bar or café displays the full **price list**, usually without the fifteen percent service charge added, for drinks at the bar (*au comptoir*), sitting down (*la salle*), or sitting on the terrace (*la terrasse*) – each progressively more expensive. You pay when you leave and you can sit for hours over just one cup of coffee.

Wine

Wine is drunk at just about every meal or social occasion. *Vin de table* or *vin ordinaire* – table wine – is generally drinkable and always cheap. A.O.C. (*Appellation d'Origine Contrôlée*) wines are better quality and considerably more expensive: even buying direct from the vineyard you won't get a bottle of Châteauneuf-du-Pape for less than €10, a Gigondas or Vacqueras for less than €8 or a Bandol for less than €7. But there are plenty of Côtes du Ventoux, Côtes du Luberon and Côtes de Provence wines that can be bought for €4 a bottle. Restaurant mark-ups on A.O.C. wines can be outrageous.

Wines of Provence

The best-known wine of the region, of course, is **Châteauneuf-du-Pape,** grown on the banks of the Rhône just north of Avignon. To the northwest, around the Dentelles, a clutch of villages have earned their own *appellations* within the Côtes du Rhône Villages region. They include the spicy and distinctive **Gigondas** and the sweet Muscat from **Beaumes-de-Venise**.

Further west, you'll find the light, drinkable but not particularly special wines of the Côtes du Ventoux and Côtes du Luberon.

Many of the vineyards in central Provence and along the coast were planted in World War I in order to supply, as speedily as possible, every French soldier with his ration of a litre a day. In the last 25 years, as the money to be made from property has soared, wine producers have had to up their quality in order for vineyards to compete with building as a profitable use of land. The Côtes de Provence *appellation* now has some excellent wines, in particular the rosés around the Massif des Maures.

The best of the coastal wines come from **Bandol**, with some gorgeous dusky reds; **Cassis** too has its own *appellation*; and around Nice the **Bellet** wines are worth discovering.

The basic **wine terms** are: *brut*, very dry; *sec*, dry; *demi-sec*, sweet; *doux*, very sweet; *mousseux*, sparkling; *méthode champenoise*, mature and sparkling. There are grape varieties as well but the complexities of the subject take up volumes. A glass of wine is simply *un rouge*, *un rosé* or *un blanc*. If it is an A.O.C. wine you may have the choice of *un ballon* (round glass) or a smaller glass (*un verre*). *Un pichet* (a pitcher) is normally a quarter-litre.

The best way to **buy bottles** of wine is directly from the producers (*vignerons*), either at vineyards, at *Maisons* or *Syndicats du Vin* (representing a group of wine-producers), or at *Coopératifs Vinicoles* (wine-producer coops). At all these places (for which you'll find details in the Guide) you can sample the wines first. It's best to make clear at the start how much you want to buy (if it's only one or two bottles) and you will not be popular if you drink several glasses and then leave without making a purchase. The most economical option is to buy *en vrac* – which you can also do at some wine shops (*caves*) – taking an easily obtainable plastic five- or ten-litre container (usually sold on the premises) and getting it filled straight from the barrel. In cities, supermarkets are the most economical places to buy your wine.

Spirits

Stronger alcohol is drunk from 5am as a pre-work fortifier, and then at any time through the day according to circumstance, though the national reputation for drunkenness has lost much of its truth. Cognac or Armagnac **brandies** and the dozens of ***eaux de vie*** (brandy distilled from fruit) and **liqueurs** are made with the same perfectionism as is applied to the cultivation of vines. Among less familiar names, try *Poire William* (pear brandy), *marc* (a spirit distilled from grape pulp), or just point to the bottle with the most attractive colour. Local specialities in Alpine areas include herb liqueurs that go by various names, and *gentiane*, distilled from the flower. Measures are generous, but they don't come cheap: the same applies for imported spirits like whisky, often called Scotch.

The aniseed drink **pastis**, served with ice (*glaçons*) and water, is a Provençal invention and one of the most popular **aperitifs** of the region. Pastis 51, Ricard and Pernod are all common brands whose names adorn every other glass and ashtray in Provence.

Cocktails are served at most late-night bars, discos and music places, as well as at upmarket hotel bars.

Beers and soft drinks

The familiar light Belgian and German brands, plus French brands from Alsace, account for most of the **beer** you'll find in Provence. Draught beer (*à la pression*, usually Kronenbourg) is the cheapest drink you can have next to coffee, wine and pastis – ask for *un demi* (1/3 litre). For a wider choice of draught and bottled beer you need to go to the special beer-drinking establishments or English-style pubs found in most coastal cities.

As for **soft drinks**, you can buy cartons of unsweetened fruit juice in supermarkets, although in the cafés the bottled (sweetened) nectars such as apricot (*jus d'abricot*) and blackcurrant (*cassis*) still hold sway. You can also get fresh orange and lemon juice (*orange/citron pressé*) – at a price. Otherwise there's the standard canned lemonade, cola (*coca*) and so forth.

Bottles of **spring water** (*eau minérale*) – either sparkling (*pétillante*) or still (*eau plate*) – are readily available, from the big brand names to the obscurest spa product. But there's not much wrong with the tap water (*l'eau du robinet*).

Coffee and tea

Coffee is invariably espresso and very strong. *Un café* or *un express* is black; *une crème* is with milk; *un grand café* or *une grand crème* is a large cup. In the morning you could also ask for *un café au lait* – espresso in a large cup or bowl filled up with hot milk. *Un déca* (decaf) is widely available.

Ordinary **tea** (*thé*) is usually Lipton's; to have milk with it, ask for *un peu de lait frais* (some fresh milk). **Herb teas** (*infusions* or *tisanes*), served in every café, can be soothing; the more common ones are *verveine* (verbena), *tilleul* (lime blossom), *menthe* (mint) and camomile. *Chocolat chaud* – **hot chocolate** – lives up to the high standards of French fare and can be had in any café.

Communications

As you would expect in a Western developed country, France's communication system is efficient and reasonably priced. In even the most rural outposts of Provence, international phone calls can be made relatively easily, and you'll find Internet access in all but the smallest of towns. The post is reasonably quick, with first-class letters taking around two days to the UK, five days to the US and seven days to Australia.

Mail

French **post offices** (*bureaux de poste*) are marked by bright yellow La Poste signs, and are generally open Mon–Fri 9am–noon and 2–5pm & Sat 9am–noon. Don't depend on these hours, though: in the larger towns you may well find the main office open throughout the day (usually 8am–7pm), while in the villages, lunch hours and closing times can vary enormously. French **postboxes**, too, are bright yellow.

As well as at the post office, **stamps** (*timbres*) can be bought from *tabacs*. In addition, inside many post offices you'll find a row of yellow *guichet automatiques* – automatic ticket machines, which will weigh your packages and sell you the appropriate stamps. You can also check the prices for sending **parcels** on the *guichet*, which is worth doing as small *postes*, in particular, don't often send foreign mail and may need reminding of the reductions for printed papers and books, for example.

You can **receive mail** at any post office; it should be addressed (preferably with the surname underlined and in capitals) **Poste Restante,** followed by the name of the town and its postcode, detailed in the Guide for all the main cities. To collect your mail you need a passport or other verifiable ID and there may be a charge of a few cent. You should ask for all your names to be checked, as filing systems are not brilliant. It's also worth noting that many post offices, particularly in rural areas, now have facilities for making photocopies, sending faxes, withdrawing cash and connecting to the Internet.

Phones

You can make domestic and international phone calls from any telephone box (or ***cabine***) and can receive calls where there's a blue logo of a ringing bell. Call boxes only take **phone cards** (*télécartes*), obtainable from post offices, FNAC shops, train stations and some *tabacs*; the cheapest card costs €7.50 for 50 units. Many call boxes also take credit cards. **Cheap rates** operate between 7pm and 8am on weekdays, after noon on Saturday and all day Sunday. A local six-minute call will cost around 15 cent.

For **calls** within France – local or long distance – simply dial all ten digits of the number. Numbers beginning with ☎08.00 or 08.04 or 08.05 are free numbers; other 08 numbers are premium rate calls (from €0.12/min). Those beginning with 06 are to mobiles and therefore also expensive to call. The major **international calling codes** are given in the box below; remember to omit the initial 0 of the local area code from the subscriber's number.

Calling cards bought in your home country are convenient, but tend to be an expensive option. The cheapest way to call home from France is to buy a **pre-paid calling card** once you're in France; there's a whole host of telecommunications companies offering cheap international phone calls, with cards starting at €7.50. The cards can be bought from *tabacs* and give you approximately 15 minutes to Australia, 30 minutes to North America and 45 minutes to the UK. First you dial a free number, then your account number and then the number you wish to call. The drawback is that the free number is often engaged and you have to dial a great many digits.

To avoid payment altogether, you can, of course, make a reverse-charge or **collect call** – known in French as "*téléphoner en PCV*". You can also do this through the operator in your home country by dialing the toll free numbers listed below; these numbers will also work if you have a calling card.

Mobile phones

If you want to use your **mobile phone** in France, you'll need to check with your phone provider whether it will work, and what the call charges are. Most French mobiles use GSM, so mobiles bought in Europe, Australia and New Zealand should work here. Unless you have a tri-band phone, a mobile bought in the US is unlikely to work in France, but it's worth checking first with your provider.

In the UK, for all but the very top-of-the-range packages, you'll have to inform your phone provider before going abroad to get **international access** switched on. You may get charged extra for this depending on your existing package and where you are travelling to. You are also likely to be charged extra for incoming calls when abroad, as the people calling you will be paying the usual rate. If you want to retrieve messages while you're away, you'll have to ask your provider for a new access code, as your home one is unlikely to work abroad. For further information about using your phone abroad, check out ⓦwww.telecomsadvice.org.uk/features/using_your_mobile_abroad.htm.

Minitel

Phone subscribers in most French cities have a **Minitel**, an online computer allowing access through the phone lines to all kinds of directories, databases, chat lines, etc. You may also find them in post offices. Most organizations, from sports federations to government institutions to gay groups, have a code consisting of numbers and letters to call up information, leave messages and make reservations. Dial the number on the phone, wait for a fax-type tone, then type the letters on the keyboard, and finally, press *Connexion Fin* (the same key ends the connection). If you're at all computer literate and can understand basic keyboard terms in French (*retour* – return, *envoi* – enter, etc), you shouldn't find them hard to use; but be warned that most services cost more than phone rates.

Useful phone numbers

IDD codes

From France: dial ⓣ00 + IDD code + area code minus first 0 + subscriber number
Britain ⓣ44
Ireland ⓣ353
US and Canada ⓣ1
Australia ⓣ61
New Zealand ⓣ64
From Britain to Provence: dial ⓣ00.33 + subscriber number minus the first 0 (this should then be a nine-digit number)
From the US and Canada to Provence: dial ⓣ011.33 + subscriber number minus the first 0 (a nine-digit number)
From Australia to Provence: dial ⓣ011.33 + subscriber number minus the first 0 (a nine-digit number)
From New Zealand to Provence: dial ⓣ044.33 + subscriber number minus the first 0 (a nine-digit number)

Useful numbers within France

Weather ⓣ32.50 (€0.34/min).
Telegrams by phone Internal ⓣ36.55; external ⓣ08.00.33.44.11 – all languages.
Time ⓣ36.99.
International operator ⓣ08.36.59.31.23 (€0.80/call).
International directory assistance ⓣ32.12 (€3/call).
French operator ⓣ13 to signal a fault.
French directory assistance ⓣ12 (€0.80/call).
Traffic and road conditions ⓣ08.92.68.10.77 (€0.34/min).

International access numbers within France (free)

AT&T ⓣ08.00.99.00.11.
Australia Optus ⓣ08.00.99.20.61.
Australia Telstra ⓣ08.00.99.00.61.
British Telecom ⓣ08.00.99.00.44.
Canada Direct ⓣ08.00.99.00.16.
MCI ⓣ08.00.99.00.19.
Sprint ⓣ08.00.99.00.87.

Time

France is **one hour ahead** of British time, except for a short period during October, when it's the same. It is **six hours ahead** of New York, and **nine hours behind** Sydney. This also applies during daylight saving seasons from the end of March to the end of September.

Email and the Internet

Email is the cheapest and most hassle-free way of staying in touch with home while in

France. Practically every reasonably sized town has a **cyber café** or Internet access of some sort, and in less populated areas many post offices now boast public Internet terminals. We have given details of cyber cafés and other Internet access points throughout the Guide.

One of the best ways to keep in touch while travelling is to sign up for a free email address that can be accessed from anywhere, for example **YahooMail** or **Hotmail** – accessible through ⓦwww.yahoo.com and ⓦwww.hotmail.com. Once you've set up an account, you can use these sites to pick up and send mail from any cyber café, or hotel with Internet access. If you're travelling with your own laptop, you may find ⓦwww.kropla.com a useful website – it gives details of how to plug your laptop in when abroad, phone country codes around the world, and information about electrical systems in different countries.

The existence of Minitel and the relatively low level of personal computer ownership in France contributed to the rather slow adoption of the **Internet** here, but in recent years the situation has changed and France as a nation has come fully online. Most tourist offices, hotels, restaurants and clubs have their own websites, although museums and festival organizations are less likely to be online in Provence than in the rest of France. Many of the most useful sites (SNCF, Yellow Pages) have **English-language** versions as well.

The media

English-language newspapers and magazines can be easily bought in the large cities and resorts, the easiest to find being the *International Herald Tribune*. Of the national French daily papers *Le Monde* is the most respected, although it can be a bit tedious. *Libération* is moderately left-wing, independent and more colloquial, with good, if choosy, coverage.

Regional newspapers enjoy much higher circulation than the Paris nationals and, though not brilliant for news, they are useful for listings. The right-wing *La Provence* and the very tabloid *Nice Matin* are the two big ones in Provence, followed by *Var-Matin* and *Le Dauphiné Vaucluse*. There's also *La Marseillaise* (available everywhere except the Alpes-Maritimes *département*) which originated as a Resistance paper during the war, and is firmly left-wing.

National weeklies include the wide-ranging and left-leaning *Nouvel Observateur* and its right-wing counterpart *L'Express*. The best and funniest investigative journalism is in the weekly satirical paper, *Le Canard Enchaîné*. *Charlie Hebdo* is a sort of *Private Eye* or *Spy Magazine* equivalent. For really in-depth analysis of national and international events and trends there's the **monthly** independent *Le Monde Diplomatique* or *Le Monde*'s own monthly *Le Monde Dossiers Documents*.

The Riviera Reporter is a free **English-language magazine** with a mix of culture and politics, which you can pick up at any of the English bookshops on the Riviera. A newish French cultural magazine for the Alpes-Maritimes is *Le Pitchoun*, available free from cultural venues and bookshops.

French TV broadcasts six channels, three of them public, along with many more cable and satellite channels, which include CNN and the BBC World Service. The main French TV **news** is at 8pm on TF1 and France 2; regional news is at 7 or 7.30pm on France 3. Arte, the fifth channel (after 7pm), shows undubbed movies. The best French documentaries are on the cable channel Planète.

If you've got a **radio**, you can tune into English-language news on the BBC World Service between 6.195 and 12.095MHz shortwave at intervals throughout the day and night. The Voice of America transmits on 90.5, 98.8 and 102.4FM. For **news** in French, there's the state-run France Inter (97.40 MHz) and Europe 1 (FM 94.9), or France Infos (FM 105.2) for round-the-clock news. **Local radio stations** include the English-language Riviera Radio (FM106.3 and 106.5) with news at 6–7am and 11am, and the BBC World Service overnight.

Business hours and public holidays

In Provence, almost everything closes for a couple of hours at midday, including shops, museums, tourist offices and most banks. The basic working hours are 8am to noon and 2 to 6pm, with shops usually staying open until 7pm. In summer the midday break often extends to 3pm.

There is of course some variation. **Food shops** often don't reopen till halfway through the afternoon, closing just before dinner time between 7.30 and 8pm. Sunday and Monday are the standard closing days; in villages you may not even find a single *boulangerie* (bakery) open. **Banks** close at 4pm and in small towns may be closed on Monday. Small hotels often close on Sunday or Monday, as do some restaurants.

Museums and monuments tend to open at around 10am and close between 5 and 6pm. Summer times may differ from winter times; if they do, both are indicated in the listings through the book. **Closing days** for museums and monuments are usually Monday or Tuesday, sometimes both.

Churches and cathedrals are almost always open all day, with charges only for the crypt, treasury or cloisters. Where churches are closed you can always take a look during Mass on Sunday morning or during other services, for which times are usually posted on the door. In small towns and villages, however, getting the key is not difficult – ask anyone nearby or hunt out the priest, whose house is known as the *presbytère*.

Public holidays

France celebrates thirteen national holidays (*jours fériés*), when most shops and businesses, though not all museums or restaurants, are closed. They are:

January 1
Easter Sunday
Easter Monday
Ascension Day (fourty days after Easter)
Pentecost or Whitsun (seventh Sunday after Easter, plus the Monday)
May 1 May Day/Labour Day
May 8 Victory in Europe Day
July 14 Bastille Day
August 15 Assumption of the Virgin Mary
November 1 All Saints' Day
November 11 1918 Armistice Day
Christmas Day

In addition to the above, **Monaco** has its own public holidays on January 27 (Fête de Ste-Dévote) and November 19 (Fête Nationale Monégasque).

Culture and festivals

Every town of any size in Provence or on the Côte d'Azur has its summer festival season, commonly called *Les Estivales*, which, more often than not, is pure tourist hype, bearing little or no relation to local customs or history. In the Camargue and the Crau, however, and throughout inland Provence, particularly in the remoter mountain areas, there are numerous small-scale fêtes which are genuine manifestations of traditional village life. The region continues to attract visual artists and their customers; the other arts, though not so dominant, are well catered for in the long-established festivals and in the theatres, opera houses and concert venues of the major cities.

The Arts

Marseille is the city for **all-round culture**, from classical theatre to experimental performance, major art retrospectives to contemporary photography, video and multimedia, opera and hip hop, plus football, political demonstrations and street happenings.

Avignon and Aix are the next most innovative cities on the arts front. Like Marseille, they have their own resident theatre companies and orchestras; the most renowned **drama and dance festival** in France takes place in **Avignon** with a large fringe component; and Aix has dance, contemporary music (including rock and jazz) festivals, and an excellent new cultural centre, the Cité du Livre. Monaco, like Nice, Avignon and Marseille, has its own opera house and attracts world-class musicians; it also hosts a circus festival. **Juan-les-Pins** has the best **jazz festival**, closely followed by Nice; **Châteauvallon** near Toulon is famous for **dance** and **Orange** for its **classical music festival** in the Roman theatre. Classical concerts are performed in many churches, often with free or very cheap admission; **Menton** has one of the most beautiful outdoor venues for its **festival of chamber music**.

Cinema is treated very seriously. The **Cannes film festival** has the highest status, both nationally and internationally; it is, though, very much a credentials-only event. Better to try the Festival of Cinema in **La Ciotat** where the techniques of film-making were originated by the Lumière brothers in 1895. On a day-to-day level, there are good cinemas throughout Provence and the Côte d'Azur where you can see undubbed **foreign films** (*version originale* or *v.o.*).

But of all the arts, it's **painting, sculpture** and **ceramics** that Provence is most famous for; as well as all the suberb art collections and exhibitions there are also numerous **art galleries** in the cities and coastal villages.

Santons

A speciality of Provence, particularly around Christmas time, **santons** are painted pottery nativity figures. They are unique in that they represent not just the holy family and shepherds but every nineteenth-century village character. So you'll have the olive-oil presser, the wine grower, the butcher, baker, soap maker and market gardener, women baking and carrying water, a gypsy band, plus the priest and mayor and even groups of *pétanque* players, all in immaculate detail. The figures are about 12cm high and their setting is a Provençal village with model houses, hillsides of pebbles and moss, twig vines and lime trees. In Aubagne, one of the main centres of *santon* art along with Aix and Marseille where they originated, scenes from Pagnol's novels are represented with *santons*. You can visit *santonnier* workshops, see displays in museums or special exhibitions, attend the great *santon* fair in Marseille, or buy them from every craft and souvenir shop.

All Provence's major cultural festivals are described in the Guide with details of where to get programme information and make bookings. For full details, try the local **listings magazines**, available free from the tourist offices: the best ones are *Ventilo* and *in situ*, which cover Marseille and the rest of the Bouches-du-Rhône; and *César*, covering Avignon to Arles. Otherwise the local papers, which have separate sections for the different areas, will be your best bet. The regional tourist office's magazine *Côte d'Azur en Fêtes* is good for an overall round-up of events and where to go. Annual brochures *Musées Galeries d'Art Côte d'Azur* and *Itinéraire Officiel de l'Art*, available from most of the Riviera tourist offices, list all the art museums, galleries and the big art exhibitions.

Traditional festivals

Throughout the region, special days are set aside to celebrate various aspects of Provençal life, such as **wine-making**, **transhumance** (the movement of sheep between their winter and summer pastures), **olive** and other **harvests** – chestnuts, lavender, jasmine, for example. In addition, there are one or two annual **village festivals**, for which local pipe bands, children in traditional costumes and the church with all its medieval superstitious trappings process to various shrines. These days they culminate with a beanfeast, much drinking and the sense of age-old community duly reaffirmed. Ever since the poet **Frédéric Mistral** and friends started the Provençal revival in the nineteenth century, these local traditions have been kept going, not as tourist attractions and not entirely as photo opportunities for the mayor. Their original meanings may have lost relevance, but they're still a real part of contemporary village life, and fun. As an outsider, the events may just look quaint, but watching people enjoy themselves can be a pleasure in itself and the festive spirit usually induces extra hospitality.

The Tarasque festival in **Tarascon** is a good one for kids. The gathering of the gypsies in **Les Stes-Maries-de-la-Mer** is one of the strangest and most exciting: it attracts vast crowds and, these days, a heavy police presence. The **folklore festivals** of Arles and Nice have rather more commercial origins, but can be very enjoyable nonetheless.

Bonfires are lit and fireworks set off for **Bastille Day** and for the **Fête de St Jean** on June 24, three days from the summer solstice. **May Day** is also commonly celebrated. **Mardi Gras** – the last blowout before Lent – is far less of an occasion than in other Roman Catholic countries, and where it is celebrated – in Nice and other Riviera towns – it's designed for commercial interests and municipal prestige.

Finally, at **Christmas**, Mass is celebrated in many Provençal churches, with real shepherds offering real sheep, and the crib scene enacted by parishioners in traditional garb. A thirteen-course non-meat supper is traditionally served on Christmas Eve.

You'll find details of the most popular events as well as many small, lower-key traditional festivities throughout the Guide.

Calendar of events

Dates may vary slightly from year to year, so it's always worth checking with local tourist offices.

January

Circus Festival (sometimes held in Dec or Feb) – Monaco
Monte Carlo Car Rally (end of month) – Monaco
Science Festival (last week) – Cavaillon

February

Classical Music Festival (end of Feb to March) – Cannes
Dance Festival (end of Feb to beginning of March) – Avignon
Lemon Festival (end of Feb to March) – Menton
Mardi Gras Carnival (week before Lent) – Nice
Mimosa Procession (third Sun) – Bormes
Olive Oil Festival (first Sun) – Nyons

March

Film Festival – Digne-les-Bains

April

Arts Festival – Monaco
Easter weekend bullfights (*Féria Pascale*) – Arles
Opening of the bull-fighting season (*Fête des Gardians*; last Sun in month to May 1) – Arles
Ski Grand Prix (early April) – Isola 2000
Tennis Open (mid-April) – Monaco

May

Arts Festival (end of May to mid-July) – Châteauvallon
Film Festival (second week) – Cannes

Formula 1 Grand Prix (Ascension weekend) – Monte Carlo
Gypsy Festival (24–25) – Les Stes-Maries-de-la-Mer
Processions (May 16–18 & June 15) – St Tropez
Processions (Ascension weekend) – Cavaillon
Rose Festival (second weekend) – Grasse

June

Bottle procession (1) – Boulbon
Cinema Festival (mid-June) – La Ciotat
Contemporary Music Festival (mid-June to first week July) – Aix
Dance, Music, Folklore and Theatre Festival (end of June and beginning of July) – Arles
Fête de la Musique (21) – throughout France
Fête de St-Jean (24) – throughout Provence
Jazz and Chamber Music Festival (last 2 weeks) – Aix
Music Festival (Whitsun) – Apt
Sacred Music Festival (last 3 weeks) – Nice
Sculpture Symposium (last 2 weeks) – Digne
Tarasque Festival (last full weekend) – Tarascon
Transhumance Festival (Whit Monday) – St-Rémy
Transhumance Festival (last weekend of month) – St-Étienne-de-Tinée
Triathlon (beginning of month) – Nice

July

Bastille Day (14)
Chorègies (operatic and choral music; mid-July to early Aug) – Orange
Dance Festival (mid-month) – Aix
Fête de St-Éloi (second Sun or penultimate Sun) – Graveson, Châteaurenard and Maillane
Firework Festival (July & Aug) – Cannes
Folklore Festival – Nice
Food Festival (around third weekend) – Carpentras
Gay Pride (July 6) – Marseille
Jazz Festival (last 2 weeks) – Juan-les-Pins
Jazz Festival (first 2 weeks) – Nice
Jazz Festival (third week) – Salon
Melon Festival (first weekend) – Cavaillon
Music Festival (*Suds*; third week) – Arles
Music Nights in the Citadel (end of July and beginning Aug) – Sisteron
Music, Theatre and Dance Festival (all month) – Carpentras
Olive Festival (weekend before July 14) – Nyons
Opera and Music Festival (mid-July to mid-Aug) – Aix
Painting Festival – Cagnes-sur-Mer
Photography Show (first week) – Arles
Provençal Festival (end July to early Aug) – Avignon and neighbouring towns
Regional *Boules* championship (first weekend) – Marseille
Sorgue Festival of music, theatre and dance (all month) – L'Isle-sur-la-Sorgue and neighbouring villages
Theatre, Dance and Music Festival plus Fringe Festival (mid-July to early Aug) – Avignon
Theatre, Dance and Music Festival (all month) – Marseille
Theatre, Jazz and Classical Music Festival (last 2 weeks) – Gordes
Theatre, Music and Art Festival (mid-July to end Aug) – Apt
Theatre, Music and Art Festival (mid-July to end Aug) – Vaison
Venetian Festival (first Sat) – Martigues
Wine Festival (14) – Vacqueyras
World Music Festival (*Nuits du Sud*) (mid-July to early Aug) – Vence

August

Chamber Music Festival – Menton
Garlic Festival (end of month) – Poilenc
Graphic Arts (last week) – Lurs
Harvest Festival (15) – St-Rémy
Haute-Provence Festival of Arts and Crafts (first 2 weeks) – Forcalquier and neighbouring villages
Jasmine Festival (first Sun) – Grasse
Lavender Festival (end of month) – Digne
Square *Boules* championship – Cagnes-sur-Mer
Wine Festival (first weekend) – Châteauneuf-du-Pape

September

Journées du Patrimoine (Architectural Heritage Weekend – open house for all historic and public buildings; third weekend) – throughout France
Rice Harvest (mid-month) – Arles
Sheep Fair – Guillaumes
Wine Festival (first weekend) – Cassis

October

Fiesta des Suds Music Festival (last 3 weeks) – Marseille
Sea procession and blessing (Sun nearest to 22) – Les Stes-Maries-de-la-Mer

November

Côtes du Rhône wine festival (mid-month) – Avignon
Dance Festival (Nov–Dec, every other year) – Cannes
Santons Fair (last Sun to end of Dec) – Marseille

December

Provençal Midnight Mass (24) – Aix, Les Baux, Fontveille, Lucéram, St-Michel-de-Frigolet, St-Rémy, Ste-Baume, Séguret, Tarascon
Wine and Traditions Festival (first Sun) – Séguret

Sports and outdoor activities

Football is the most popular spectator sport in Provence, with motor racing taking precedence in Monaco, while enthusiasm over cycle races is as great as in the rest of France. The most typically Provençal competitive pastime is *pétanque*. Outdoor activities in the region include hang-gliding, skiing, all types of water sports, climbing and mountain trekking.

Spectator sports

On every town or village square in Provence, in every park, or sometimes in a specially built arena, you'll see ***pétanque***, the Provençal version of *boules*, being played. The principle is the same as bowls but the terrain is always rough, never grass, and the area much smaller. The metal ball is usually thrown upwards from a distance of 10m or a little more, to land and skid towards the marker (*cochonnet*). In Provence, uniquely, the players are allowed to move as they "point" (the first throw) or "aim" (the adversary's throw). There are café or village teams, endless championships, and, on the whole, it's very male-dominated.

The spectator sport most passionately followed in Provence is *le foot* – **football**. The most popular team is Olympique de Marseille; after a few setbacks, including a conviction for cheating, the club was bought by Adidas and is back in the First Division. Marseille has spawned two famous football players: Eric Cantona, and the national hero after the French victory in the World Cup in 1998, Zinedine Zidane.

The **Tour de France** cycling race in July generally has a stage in Provence, as does the **Paris–Nice** race in March. Cycling combined with running and swimming brings in the crowds for Nice's and Antibes' **triathlons**.

In and around the **Camargue**, the number-one sport is **bullfighting** (for more details, see p.110). Though not to everyone's taste it is, at least, less gruesome than the variety practised by the Spanish.

The world-famous **Formula One Grand Prix** takes place in Monaco with some of Provence's remote inland routes being used for **rally-driving**. Monaco and Nice also host international **Tennis Open** championships.

Participatory sports

Water sports on the **Côte d'Azur** are practised on the whole for the glamour factor rather than for competition. The waters and winds of the Mediterranean are far too temperate to exercise high-powered sailing or windsurfing skills. But for learning and just playing about in the warm water, it's potentially ideal. The problem, though, is congestion, and no one following the rules of the water. So beware the madcap jet skiers and power-boat racers. The other great drawback is inevitably the cost of renting the equipment. Every resort has several outlets – for sailing, windsurfing, water-skiing, wet-biking, scuba-diving – so you can shop around for the best prices, but it will still take a major chunk out of your budget, and prices go up every year.

Airborne sports, particularly **hang-gliding**, are extremely popular in Provence. Fayence is the main centre for **gliding** and St-André-les-Alpes one of many places with an excellent hang-gliding centre. *Baptêmes* (initiations) are not too expensive.

More and more health-conscious holidaymakers are taking to **trekking** in the mountains, with most ski resorts now catering for summer activities – like pony-trekking and climbing – in a big way. The main areas for **climbing** are the Alps, the Dentelles and the Luberon; for more information, contact the Club Alpin Français (ⓦwww.clubalpin.com), 14 av Mirabeau, Nice (ⓣ04.93.62.59.99), or 5 rue St-Michel, Avignon (ⓣ04.90.82.66.17).

Horse-riding is catered for by numerous *Centres Equestres* throughout Provence, particularly in the Camargue. Normally what's offered is an accompanied ride in a group but there are some places where you can gallop off on your own; tourist offices will be able to supply more details.

The rivers and artificial lakes of Provence also provide opportunities for **canoeing**, **rafting**, and more gently paddling about in **boats**, windsurfing and yachting. Details of helpful organizations and centres catering for these pursuits are given in the Guide.

Skiing – whether downhill or cross-country – is enthusiastically pursued in Provence. There are over a dozen ski resorts within two hours' drive of the coast, the three biggest being **Auron**, **Valberg** and **Isola 2000**, though recent weather changes have affected snowfalls in the lower Alps. It can be an expensive sport to pursue on your own and the Provence resorts are rarely covered by the international package operators, though some, like La Foux d'Allos, are much cheaper in terms of ski-lift charges than the higher resorts north of Provence. Local deals are available; the Comités Départementals de Tourisme in Digne or Nice (see below) and the Club Alpin Français (see p.49) are the best sources of information.

Finally, two highly promoted activities on the Côte d'Azur, one with a long history and potentially ruinous, the other newly fashionable and environmentally suspect, are **gambling** and **golf**.

Information on sports and leisure activities

All the Comités Départementals de Tourisme, the departmental tourist boards or CDTs, produce helpful brochures on all leisure activities, with useful addresses of specialist organizations. The big city tourist offices are likely to have these, or you can go to the CDT office for more detailed information (see p.22 for addresses of the CDT offices).

Crime and personal safety

Petty theft is endemic along the Côte d'Azur and pretty bad in the more crowded part of the big cities. It makes sense to take the normal precautions: don't wave money or travellers' cheques around; carry your bag or wallet securely; and never let cameras and other valuables out of your sight. But the best security of all is to have a good insurance policy and keep a separate record of cheque numbers, credit card numbers and the phone numbers for cancelling them, as well as the relevant details of all your valuables.

Drivers face the greatest problems, most notoriously **break-ins** – though having your vehicle stolen, particularly in Nice or Marseille, is not uncommon. Also, Nice, in particular, is susceptible to car break-ins by thieves on foot or motorbike, while drivers are stopped at a red light – so, in congested or rough areas keep valuables out of sight, doors locked and windows rolled up.

It's always best to **park** overnight in guarded car parks; where that's not possible try to park in a busy street or in front of a police station. Never leave anything in the boot and remove your stereo system if you can. It's not just foreign number plates that attract thieves; rented cars are also favourite prey.

If you need to **report a theft**, go along to the local *commissariat de police* (addresses are given for all the main cities), and make sure you get the requisite piece of paper for a claim. The first thing they'll ask for is your passport, and vehicle documents if relevant.

If you have a **driving accident**, officially you have to fill in and sign a *constat à l'aimable* (jointly agreed statement); car insurers should give you this with a policy, though in practice few seem to have heard of it. For non-criminal **driving violations** such as speeding, the police can impose an on-the-spot fine. If you don't have the necessary cash you could find yourself passing several unpleasant hours at the police station.

Emergencies

Ambulance ☎15
Police ☎17
Fire Service ☎18
Note: It's common for the fire brigade, les sapeurs pompiers, *to be called for medical problems; they all have paramedical training and equipment.*

By law you are supposed to carry ID with you at all times and the police have the right to stop and ask to see it.

Committing crimes

Camping outside authorized sites can bring you into contact with the authorities, though it's more likely to be the landowner who tells you to move on. Police have been known to stalk the beaches, sweating in their uniforms, telling everyone to cover up their bottom halves, and in Cannes there are on-the-spot fines for toplessness on the street, but there's no equivalent of the British public decency laws. **Topless sunbathing** is universally acceptable; nudity is in principle limited to specifically naturist beaches.

More seriously, anyone caught smuggling or possessing **drugs**, even a few grammes of marijuana, is liable to find themselves in jail, and consulates will not be sympathetic. This is not to say that hard-drug consumption isn't a visible activity: there are scores of kids dealing in *poudre* (heroin) in Marseille and Nice and the authorities are unable to do much about it.

Should you be arrested on any charge, you have the right to contact your consulate (see "Listings" for Marseille, Nice or Monaco).

Racial and sexual harassment

The large industrial cities of Provence and the Côte d'Azur towns have the highest proportion of extreme right-wing voters in France. **Racist attitudes** in the populace and the police are rife. Being black, or particularly Arab, makes your chances of avoiding unpleasantness very low. Hotels claiming to be booked up, police demanding your papers, and abuse from ordinary people is horribly frequent. In addition, even entering the country can be difficult. Changes in passport regulations have put an end to outright refusal to let some British holidaymakers in, but customs and immigration officers can still be obstructive and malicious. In North-African-dominated areas of cities, identity checks by the police are very common and not pleasant. If you suffer a racial assault, you're likely to get a much more sympathetic hearing from your consulate than from the police. The national anti-racism organization, Ligue Internationale Contre le Racisme et Anti-Semitisme (LICRA), has an office in Marseille at 46 rue Ste-Victoire, ☎04.91.81.59.69.

Sexual harassment is generally no worse or more vicious than anywhere else, but it can be a problem making judgements about situations without the familiar linguistic and cultural signs. A "*Bonjour*" or "*Bonsoir*" on the street is usually a pick-up line. If you return the greeting, you've left yourself open to a persistent monologue and a difficult brush-off job. On the other hand, topless bathing doesn't usually invite bother and it's quite common, if you're on your own, to be offered a drink in a bar and not to be pestered even if you accept. Hitching is a risk, though some women do hitch alone in the more built-up areas of the Côte d'Azur.

If you need help, go to the police, although don't expect too much from them. The *mairie/hôtel de ville* (town hall) will have addresses of women's organizations (Femmes Battues, Femmes en Détresse or SOS Femmes), though this won't be much help outside business hours. The national **rape crisis** number, Viol Femme Information, is ☎08.00.05.95.95 (Mon–Fri 10am–6pm), but it may not have English speakers. Again your consulate may be the best source of sympathetic assistance.

Work and study

Temporary agricultural work in Provence and the Côte d'Azur is hard to come by and, in summer, catering work or work in the tourist industry is a better bet. For longer-term employment, au-pair positions and English teaching are distinct possibilities if you take time to plan and make contact in advance.

If you're looking for something secure, it's important to plan well in advance. The best general **sources for jobs** in France are the publications *Summer Jobs Abroad* (Vacation Work), *Work Your Way Around the World* by Susan Griffiths (Vacation Work) and *1000 Pistes de jobs étudiants* (L'Étudiant). *Living, Studying, and Working in France* by Saskia Reilly and Lorin Kalisky (Owl Books) and *Living and Working in France* by David Hampshire (Survival Press) are also useful references. The fortnightly, subscription-only *Overseas Jobs Express* (Ⓣ01273/699 611, Ⓦwww.overseasjobs.com), publishes a range of job vacancies around the world, while the travel magazine *Wanderlust* (every two months; £2.80) has a Job Shop section which often advertises vacancies with tour companies. The website Ⓦwww.studyabroad.com has useful links to study and work programmes worldwide. If you're already in Provence, check the job ads in the region's two main papers, *Nice Matin* and *La Provence*.

By law all **EU nationals** are entitled to exactly the same pay, conditions and trade-union rights as French nationals. **Non-EU** citizens will have a hard time finding jobs if they don't have working papers, which in most cases – unless you have a student visa authorizing part-time work – are near impossible to obtain. France has a **minimum wage** (the SMIC) of around €7 an hour. Employers, however, are likely to pay lower wages to temporary foreign workers who don't have easy access to legal resources.

Temporary work

Grape-picking during the wine harvest in September is possible, though many vineyards are automated and others too small to take on outsiders. Youth hostels in wine-growing areas sometimes recruit grape-pickers, or you could try asking at the local Agence Nationale de l'Emploi (ANPE), whose address you'll find in the phone book.

Getting a temporary job as a deckhand or skivvy **on a yacht** is also feasible, but you'll have to hang about the ports, and getting on board will be very much a matter of luck. Pay and conditions are likely to be abysmal – it's assumed that you're there for the glamorous ride and you'll certainly be made to work for it. Another casual option, if you speak some French, is **bar work** in the many clubs run by American, Dutch, English or Irish managers on the coast. Again it's a matter of being in the right place at the right time.

Temporary jobs in the **travel industry** revolve around courier work – supervising and working on bus tours or summer campsites. You'll need good French (and maybe even another language) and should write to as many tour operators as you can, preferably in early spring. Getting work as a courier on a campsite is slightly easier. It usually involves putting up tents at the beginning of the season, taking them down again at the end, and general maintenance and trouble-shooting work in the months between. Canvas Holidays (Ⓣ01383/629000, Ⓦwww.canvasholidays.co.uk) or Riviera Holidays (Ⓣ01943/816949) in Britain are worth approaching, as is the Union Française des Centres de Vacances (Ⓣ01.44.72.14.14, Ⓦwww.ufcv.asso.fr) in Paris.

Longer-term employment

Teaching English is one of the easier ways of getting a job in France. It's best to apply before leaving your home country; in the UK, check the ads in *The Guardian*'s "Education" section (every Tuesday), or in the weekly *Times Educational Supplement*. Late summer is usually the best time to apply. You don't need fluent French to get a post, but a degree and a TEFL (Teaching English as a Foreign Language) qualification are normally required. If you apply from home, most schools will fix you up with the necessary papers. A useful reference is Susan Griffith's *Teaching English Abroad* (Vacation Work; £12.95); while the British Council's website (ⓦwww.britishcouncil.org/work/jobs.htm) has a list of English-teaching vacancies. It's also quite feasible to find a teaching job when you're in France, but you may have to accept semi-official status and no job security. For the addresses of schools, look under *Écoles de Langues* in the Professions directory of the local phone book. Offering **private lessons** (via university noticeboards or classified ads), you'll have lots of competition, and it's hard to reach the people who can afford it, but it's always worth a try, particularly in Marseille where there are fewer native English-speakers around. In Aix, and particularly on the coast, there are already large numbers of established native English speakers to compete with.

Au-pair work is usually arranged through one of a dozen agencies, all of which are listed in *Working Holidays*. In Britain, the classified advert section of *The Lady* is the best place to look for such jobs. A couple of good places to try are Avalon Au Pairs in the UK (ⓣ01344/778 246, ⓦwww.aupairs-byavalon.com), or the American Institute for Foreign Study (ⓣ1-800/727-2437, ⓦwww.aifs.com) in the US. It's also worth contacting the Accueil Familial des Jeunes Étrangers (ⓣ01.42.22.50.34, ⓦwww.afje-paris.org) in Paris, who have positions for female au pairs only, and will fill you in on the standard terms and conditions (never very generous); as a general rule, you shouldn't get paid less than €300 a month (on top of board and lodging). It is wise to have an escape route (like a ticket home) in case you find the conditions intolerable.

Claiming benefit

If you're an EU citizen – and you do the paperwork in advance – you can sign on for **unemployment benefit**. To do so, you must collect form E303 before leaving home, available in Britain from any DSS office. The procedure is first to get registered at an ANPE office (Agence Nationale pour l'Emploi), then take the form to your local ASSEDIC (benefits office) and give them an address, which can be a hostel or a hotel, for the money to be sent to. You sign once a month at the ANPE and receive benefit a month in arrears, in theory. In practice payments can be delayed in small towns for up to three months. EU pensioners can arrange for their pensions to be paid in France, but not, unfortunately, to receive French state pensions.

Studying in France

It's relatively easy to be a **student** in France. All foreigners pay no more than French nationals (around €400 a year) to enrol for a course, and the only problem then is to support yourself. Your *carte de séjour* and – if you're an EU citizen – social security will be assured, and you'll be eligible for subsidized accommodation, meals and all the student reductions. In general, French universities are much less formal than British and American ones and many people perfect their fluency in the language while studying. There are strict entry requirements, including an exam in French for undergraduate degrees. For full details and prospectuses, contact the Cultural Service of any French embassy or consulate (see p.21–22).

Language schools all along the coast provide intensive French courses for foreigners; some are detailed in the Guide. A complete list is given in the leaflet *Cours de Français, Langue Etrangère. Repertoire des Centres de Formation en France*, also available from embassy or consular cultural sections. In addition, the **University of Aix and Marseille** has its science faculties in Marseille and arts faculties in Aix, both of which are very popular with American students. For US students, both the American Institute for Foreign Study (ⓣ1-800/727-2437, ⓦwww.aifs.org) and the Council on International Educational Exchange (CIEE; ⓣ1-800/40-STUDY, ⓦwww.ciee.org) run summer and academic-year programmes of language and culture in France.

Finally, it's worth noting that if you're a full-time student in France, you can get a part-time **work permit** for the following summer as long as your visa is still valid.

Travellers with disabilities

France has no special reputation for providing facilities for disabled travellers, and for people in wheelchairs the haphazard parking habits and stepped village streets are serious obstacles. In the major cities and coastal resorts, there are accessible hotels, and ramps or other forms of access are gradually being added to museums and other sites. Public toilets with disabled access are rare. APF, the French paraplegic organization, has an office in each *département* which will be the most reliable source of information on accommodation with disabled access.

Public transport is certainly not wheelchair-friendly, and although many train stations now have ramps to enable wheelchair users to board and descend from carriages, at others it is still up to the guards to carry the chair. The **TGVs** (including Eurostar) all have places for wheelchairs in the First Class saloon coach, which must be booked in advance, though no extra fee is charged; on other trains, a wheelchair symbol on the timetable denotes that the service offers special facilities, and you and your companion will be upgraded to first class at no extra charge.

There are **organized tours and holidays** specifically for people with disabilities – the contacts listed below will be able to put you in touch with any specialists for trips to Provence. If you would rather organize your trip independently, it's worth making sure that your airline or bus company is aware of your condition – they tend to be far more helpful if they are expecting you, with a wheelchair provided at airports and staff primed to help. A **medical certificate** of your fitness to travel, provided by your doctor, is also extremely useful; some airlines or insurance companies may insist on it. Make sure that you have extra supplies of drugs – carried with you in hand luggage if you fly – and a prescription including the generic name in case of emergency.

Contacts for travellers with disabilities

France

APF (Association des Paralysés de France) ☎3615 APF (€0.20/min), Ⓦwww.apf.asso.fr. National organization providing useful information and lists of accessible accommodation.

Avignon: 64 bd Jules Ferry, ☎04.90.16.47.40.
Manosque: rue Heures Claires, ☎04.92.71.74.50.
Marseille: 279 av de la Capelette, ☎04.91.79.99.99.
Nice: 3 av Antoine Véran, ☎04.92.07.98.00.

UK and Ireland

Access Travel UK ☎01942/888 844, Ⓦwww.access-travel.co.uk. Tour operator that can arrange flights, transfers and accommodation.
Holiday Care UK ☎0845/124 9973, Ⓦwww.holidaycare.org.uk. Information on all aspects of travel.
Irish Wheelchair Association Ireland ☎01/818 6400, Ⓦwww.iwa.ie. Offers information about travel and access for disabled travellers abroad.
RADAR UK ☎020/7250 3222, Ⓦwww.radar.org.uk. A good source of advice on holidays and travel abroad.
Tripscope UK ☎0845/758 5641, Ⓦwww.tripscope.org.uk. Travel information and advice service.

North America

Access-Able Travel Source US ☎303/232-2979, Ⓦwww.access-able.com. Offers information for disabled travellers.
Kéroul Canada ☎514/252-3104, Ⓦwww.keroul.qc.ca. Organization promoting and facilitating travel for mobility-impaired people. Annual membership CN$15.
Mobility International USA US ☎541/343-1284, Ⓦwww.miusa.org. Information and referral services, access guides, tours and exchange trips. Annual membership $35 (includes quarterly newsletter).
Society for Accessible Travel and Hospitality (SATH) US ☎212/447-7284, Ⓦwww.sath.org. Non-profit travel-industry referral service that passes queries on to its members as appropriate.

Wheels Up! US ⓣ1-888/389-4335, ⓦwww.wheelsup.com. Provides discounted airfares, tours and cruises for disabled travellers; also publishes a free monthly newsletter.

Australia and New Zealand

ACROD (Australian Council for Rehabilitation of the Disabled) Australia ⓣ02/6282 4333, ⓦwww.acrod.org.au. Provides lists of travel agencies and tour operators for people with disabilities.

Disabled Persons Assembly New Zealand ⓣ04/801 9100, ⓦwww.dpa.org.nz. Provides details of tour operators and travel agencies for people with disabilities.

Gay and lesbian travellers

France is more liberal on homosexuality than most other European countries. The legal age of consent is fifteen and, in general, the French consider sexuality to be a private matter.

The dominance of extreme-right sympathies in many parts of Provence, however, means that gay people tend to be discreet. Marseille is the only place where gay and lesbian pride is celebrated, though Nice has a thriving gay club scene. As in many Mediterranean cultures, physical contact between women or men is seen as "natural" but kissing in public may raise hackles. Addresses for clubs and bars are listed in the Guide – mainly in Marseille, Nice and Aix.

Gay contacts and information

ARCL (Les Archives, Recherches et Cultures Lesbiennes; ⓣ01.46.28.54.94, ⓦarcl.free.fr.), based at the Maison des Femmes (see below). ARCL runs a library (Tues 7–9.30pm) and organizes frequent meetings around campaigning, artistic and intellectual issues.

Centre Gai et Lesbien 3 rue Keller, Paris 11e, M° Ledru-Rollin ⓣ01.43.57.21.47, ⓦwww.cglparis.org. The main information centre for the gay, lesbian, bisexual and transsexual community in France.

Maison des Femmes 163 rue de Charenton, Paris 12e, M° Reuilly-Diderot ⓣ01.43.43.41.13, ⓦmaisondesfemmes.free.fr. Run by Paris Féministe, this is the home of the Groupe des Lesbiennes Féministes and the Mouvement d'Information et d'Expression des Lesbiennes, ARCL (Archives, Recherches et Cultures Lesbiennes). A cafeteria operates on Friday nights (8pm–midnight), and there are occasional events organized.

Minitel 3615 GPS is the Minitel number to dial for information on groups, contacts, messages, etc. There are also any number of chat lines.

Gay media

Radio FG (98.2 FM). 24hr gay and lesbian radio station with music, news, chat and information on groups and events.

Lesbia The most widely available lesbian publication, available from most newsagents. Each monthly issue features a wide range of articles, listings, reviews, lonely hearts and contacts.

Spartacus International Gay Guide Guidebook focusing mainly on gay travel in Europe; geared mostly towards males but with some info for lesbians. Available around the world at travel and gay bookshops.

Têtu Gay monthly magazine with intelligent, wide-ranging articles.

ⓦwww.gayguide.net Links to many online guides covering different areas in France. Usually written and updated by a local writer; including reviews of hotels, restaurants, shopping and clubs.

ⓦwww.gayvox.com French portal for gay men and lesbians. Comprehensive listings, articles, forums, chat rooms and links (in French).

Directory

ALARM OR WAKE UP CALLS dial ☎*55* then the time (for example 0715 for 7.15) followed by the # key; the cost is €0.56.

BEACHES are public property within 5m of the high-tide mark, so you can kick sand past private villas and hotel sunbeds. Camping, however, is illegal. Getting to many beaches and parking a car often requires entry through *terrain privé* (private land). In some instances, such "private beaches" charge a daily fee of €10 per car, but in return you may find facilities such as showers, beach bars and restaurants.

CAMERAS AND FILM Film is considerably cheaper in North America than in France or Britain, so stock up if you're coming from there. If you're bringing a video camcorder, make sure any tapes you purchase in France are VHS. The normal French format, PAL, will only give black and white when played on VHS machines. Again, American videotape prices are way below French prices.

CHILDREN AND BABIES pose few travel problems. They're generally welcome everywhere, including most bars and restaurants. **Hotels** charge by the room, with a small supplement for an additional bed or cot, and family-run places will usually babysit or offer a listening service while you eat or go out. Many **restaurants** have children's menus or will cook simpler food on request. You'll have no difficulty finding disposable nappies (*couches à jeter*), but nearly all baby foods have added sugar and salt, and French milk powders are very rich indeed. SNCF charge nothing on **trains and buses** for under-fours, and half-fare for four- to twelve-year-olds (see pp.18–19 for other reductions). Most local tourist offices have details of specific activities for children; along the coast there are a great number of funfairs, marinelands, zoos, go-karting tracks, etc, all designed to extract the maximum amount of money off you. But almost every town has a municipal **children's playground** with a good selection of activities. Something to beware of is the difficulty of negotiating a child's **buggy** over the cobbles and steps of many of the hilltop villages.

ELECTRICITY is 220V out of double, round-pin wall sockets.

FISHING You need to become a member of a fishing club to get rights – this is not difficult, and any tourist office will give you a local address.

FOREST FIRES Every summer, forest fires in Provence and the Côte d'Azur hit the international headlines. Vast tracts become blazing infernos long before the sprayers from Nice or Marseille can reach the area. Loss of life is common and people's homes are frequently destroyed. So always take the utmost care. The emergency number for the fire service is ☎18.

LAUNDRY Laundries are common in French towns, and some are listed in the Guide – elsewhere look in the phone book under *Laveries Automatiques*. The alternative *blanchisserie* or *pressing* services are likely to be expensive, and hotels in particular charge very high rates. If you're doing your own washing in hotels, keep quantities small as most forbid doing any laundry in your room.

LEFT LUGGAGE At the time of writing, left-luggage lockers at train stations are closed as a precaution against terrorist attacks.

SWIMMING POOLS Swimming pools (*piscines*) are well signposted in most French towns and reasonably priced. Tourist offices have their addresses.

TIME France is one hour ahead of British time for most of the year, except for a short period during October when it's the same. It is six hours ahead of Eastern Standard Time, nine hours ahead of Pacific Standard Time. This also applies during daylight-saving seasons, which are observed in France (as in most of Europe) from the end of March until the end of September.

TOILETS are usually to be found downstairs in bars, along with the phone, or there are the automatic self-cleaning ones outside on the street costing €0.25. Dirty, hole-in-the-ground, squatting loos are still common. The usual euphemism for toilet is "WC", pronounced "vé-sé".

WATER The fountains in the squares of towns and villages of Provence are there to provide water. Unless a notice says *Eau non potable* – a very rare occurrence – the water is drinkable and deliciously cool.

Guide

Guide

1

The Lower Rhône Valley

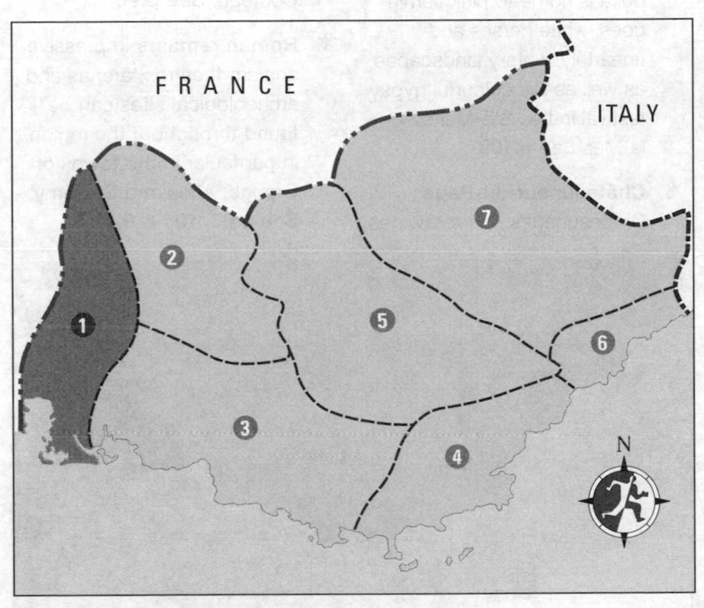

CHAPTER 1

Highlights

* **Avignon** The spectacular monuments and museums of the former City of Popes form an imposing backdrop for the Festival d'Avignon, held each July. **See p.69**
* **The Camargue** The expansive marshland of the Rhône delta is home to pink flamingoes, white horses and unearthly, watery landscapes, as well as the colourful gypsy festival in Les Ste-Maries-de-la-Mer. **See p.109**
* **Châteauneuf-du-Pape** Châteauneuf's rich red wines are some of the most famous in the world. **See p.67**
* **Cathédrale des Images** This former quarry in the Valley of Hell has been the inspiration for many artists, including Dante and Cocteau. **See p.96**
* **Roman remains** Impressive ancient theatres, arenas and archeological sites can be found throughout the region, in particular in the towns of Orange, Arles and St-Rémy. **See p.63, 105 & 92**

1

The Lower Rhône Valley

The lower stretch of the **Rhône Valley**, long a frontier between the rest of France and Provence, has seen centuries of fortification on its banks – at **Beaucaire** and **Villeneuve-lès-Avignon** on the French side, at **Tarascon**, **Boulbon** and **Barbentane** in Provence. It has been the north–south route of ancient armies, of medieval traders and of modern rail and road, and its river has been a vital trading route, bringing wealth and fame to the cities that line its banks.

Today, the prime settlement of the Provençal stretch is **Avignon**, the great city of the popes from medieval times until the Revolution and a major centre of art and architecture. To the north lies **Orange**, famous for its Roman amphitheatre, and the vineyards of the **Châteauneuf-du-Pape**, both drawing visitors into an otherwise heavily industrialized stretch of the valley.

The countryside attractions begin on the modest rural plains to the south of Avignon, **La Petite Crau** and **La Grande Crau** – the stretch of land enclosed by the River Durance and the Rhône and separated by the abrupt ridge of the **Alpilles**. Here the villages and small towns have retained a nineteenth-century charm, living out the old customs and traditions revived by the great Provençal poet **Frédéric Mistral**, a native of La Petite Crau. This is the countryside that **Van Gogh** painted when he spent a year at Arles and then sought refuge in St-Rémy. Both towns pay tribute to his tragic brilliance.

Arles lies to the south, at the mouth of the Rhône delta. It was the centre of Roman Provincia, which stretched from the Pyrenees to the Alps and became the capital of Gaul towards the end of the Roman era; the city's great amphitheatre, like that in the Roman city of **Orange**, still seats thousands for summer entertainments. Further evidence of Roman occupation is apparent at **Glanum**, outside **St-Rémy-de-Provence**, where you can see the overlaid remains of Greek and Roman towns, and between Arles and St-Rémy, where the Romans' brilliant use of water power is in evidence in the **Barbegal mill**.

Below Arles, where the Rhône divides, is the strange watery land of the **Camargue**, with a natural history and way of life quite distinct from surrounding regions. The wet expanses sustain flocks of flamingoes and a multitude of other birds, while black bulls and wild white horses graze on the edges of the marshes and lagoons. The Camargue also provides a sanctuary for unique social traditions – it is here, to the town of **Les Stes-Maries-de-la-Mer**, that

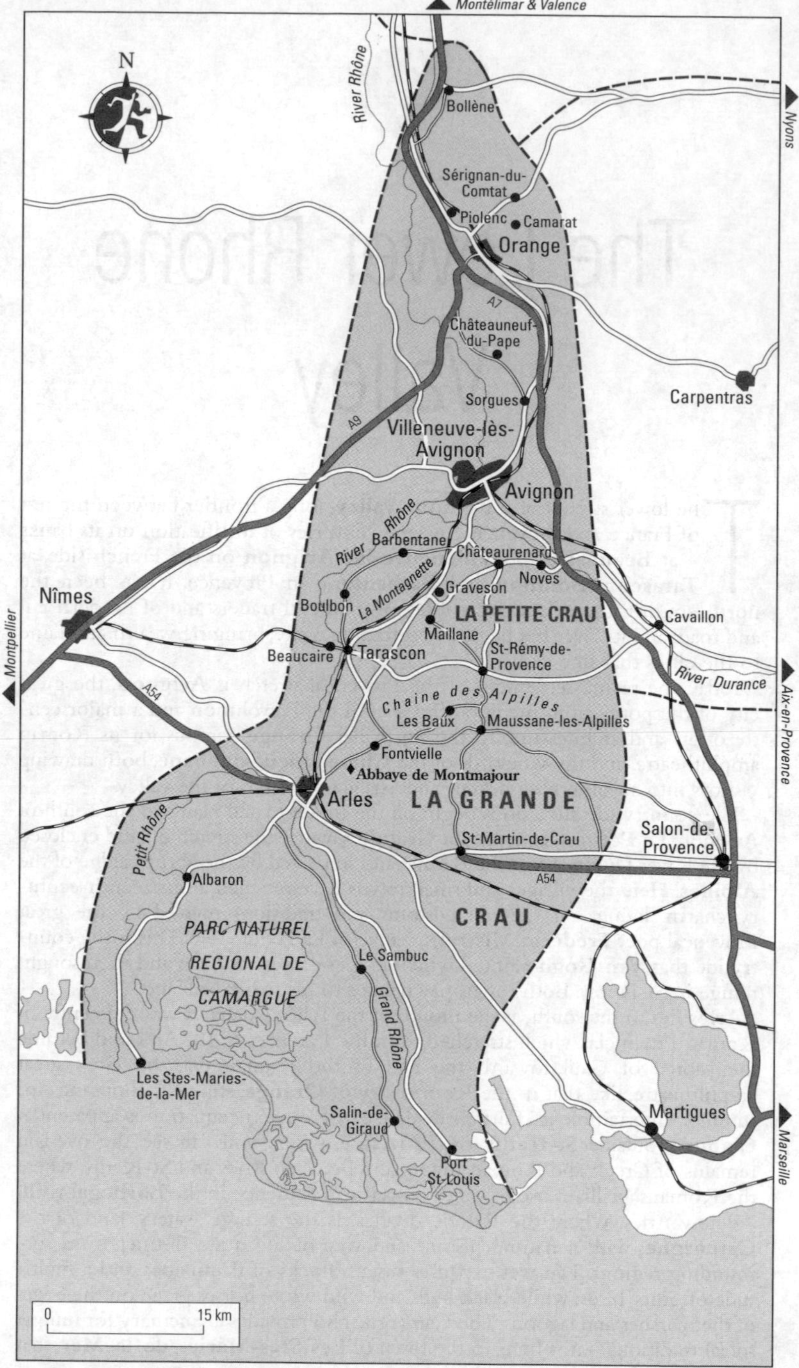
Montélimar & Valence
N
River Rhône
Bollène
Nyons
Sérignan-du-Comtat
Piolenc
Camarat
Orange
A7
Châteauneuf-du-Pape
Carpentras
Sorgues
A9
Villeneuve-lès-Avignon
Avignon
River Rhône
Barbentane
Châteaurenard
Noves
Nîmes
Boulbon
La Montagnette
Graveson
LA PETITE CRAU
Cavaillon
Maillane
Montpellier
Beaucaire
Tarascon
St-Rémy-de-Provence
River Durance
Aix-en-Provence
A54
Chaine des Alpilles
Les Baux
Maussane-les-Alpilles
Fontvielle
Abbaye de Montmajour
Arles
LA GRANDE
Petit Rhône
St-Martin-de-Crau
Salon-de-Provence
A54
Albaron
CRAU
PARC NATUREL REGIONAL DE CAMARGUE
Le Sambuc
Grand Rhône
Les Stes-Maries-de-la-Mer
Martigues
Marseille
Salin-de-Giraud
Port St-Louis
0
15 km

gypsies come every May from all over the Mediterranean to celebrate their patron saint's day.

Orange and around

The major routes south into the Rhône Valley all pass through **ORANGE**, best known for its spectacular **Roman theatre**. The city is the former seat of the counts of Orange, a title created by Emperor Charlemagne in the eighth century, and passed to the Dutch crown of Nassau in the sixteenth century. Its most memorable member was the Protestant Prince William, who ascended the English throne with his consort Queen Mary in 1689; the Protestant Orange Order in Ireland was founded to support William's military campaign against his Catholic predecessor, James II, which ended with the Battle of the Boyne.

Orange has never been the friendliest of towns, though its medieval street plan, Thursday market, fountained squares and houses with ancient porticoes and courtyards are attractive enough. Aside from the **Théâtre Antique**, the triumphal **Roman arch**, and **museum**, there's not much to detain you, and you may feel that, however distant, the parallels between Roman culture and today's neo-fascists are such that you can give the whole place a miss with a clear conscience. If you're happy to linger, however, there is a surprising treat in the old residence of the nineteenth-century scientist, the **Harmas** of **Jean-Henri Fabre**, in Sérignan-du-Comtat, just north of the city.

Today, the city hosts a major summer **music festival** (see box on p.65), held in the Roman theatre. However, the victory of Le Pen's *Front National* in the municipal elections of 1995, and again in 2001 (with a decisive sixty percent of the vote), has put the future of the festival in jeopardy. Opinions of French artists are split, with many of Arab or African origin arguing that it's now more important than ever for them to perform here, while others declare they will have nothing to do with events that increase the town hall's income and prestige. Between 1986 and 1996, the city also hosted an annual Festival BD (*Bandes-Dessinées* or cartoon strips), which used to bring in weird and wonderful characters, but this was pushed out of the city due to similar political differences.

Arrival, information and accommodation

The **gare SNCF** is about 1.5km east of the centre, at the end of av Frédéric-Mistral. The nearest bus stop is at the bottom of rue Jean-Reboul, the first left as you walk from the station towards the city centre. Bus #2 (direction Nogent) will take you to the Théâtre Antique, opposite which there's a seasonal **tourist office** (April–Sept Mon–Sat 10am–1pm & 2–7pm; July & Aug Sun 10am–6pm); the **main tourist office** is a stop beyond (Gasparin) on av Charles-de-Gaulle (April–Sept Mon–Sat 9am–7pm, Sun 10am–6pm; Oct–March Mon–Sat 10am–1pm & 2–5pm; ⓣ04.90.34.70.88, ⓦwww.provence-orange.com). The **gare routière** is close to the centre on place Pourtoules, just east of the Roman theatre. There's undergound **parking** here too.

You'll have no problem finding **accommodation** in Orange, except during the Chorégies festival in July.

Hotels

Arcotel 8 pl aux Herbes ⓣ04.90.34.09.23, ⓔjor8525@aol.com. Overlooking the pretty pl aux Herbes, this appealing hotel is a good budget option: it's simple, clean and quiet. ❷

L'Arène pl de Langes ⓣ04.90.11.40.40, ⓕ04.90.11.40.45. Spacious rooms with all mod

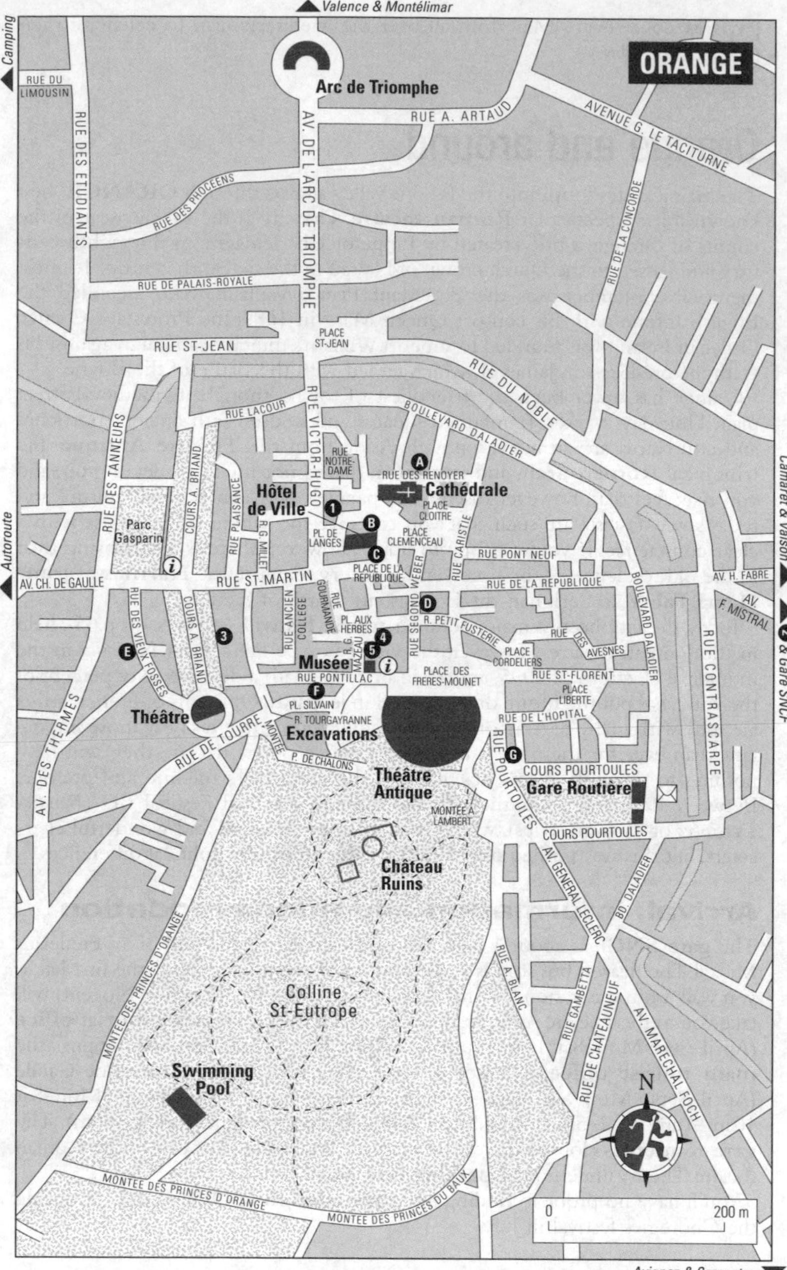

ACCOMMODATION				RESTAURANTS, BARS & CAFES					
Arcotel	4	Louvre et Terminus	2	Chez Daniel	D	Le Parvis	G	Café de l'Univers	C
L'Arène	1	St-Florent	5	Le Yaca	F	Les Négociants	B	Café des Thermes	E
Le Glacier	3			La Roselière	A				

cons, on a quiet pedestrianized square. ❺

Le Glacier 46 cours Aristide-Briand ☎04.90.34.02.01, www.le-glacier.com. A comfortable family-run hotel, offering the best value in Orange. ❸

Louvre et Terminus 89 av Frédéric-Mistral ☎04.90.34.10.08, www.louvre-terminus.com. A pleasant three-star hotel with a garden and pool, close to the train station. ❹

St-Florent 4 rue du Mazeau ☎04.90.34.18.53, membres.lycos.fr/stflorent. Rather kitsch decor, but central and cheap. ❸

Campsite

Le Jonquier 1321 rue Alexis-Carrel ☎04.90.34.49.48, Ⓕ04.90.51.16.97. Three-star site northwest of the centre, with tennis courts, pool and mini golf. €20 per tent; closed Nov to mid-March.

The Town

Orange is not a very big town and can be easily covered on foot. Its old streets lie north of the enormous Roman theatre which, with the hill of St-Eutrope behind, is the dominating feature.

Théâtre Antique

Days off in Orange circa 55 AD were spent at the **théâtre**, where an audience of ten thousand could watch farce, clownish improvisations, song and dance, and, occasionally, a bit of heavy Greek tragedy, usually in Latin. Today, although the action is mainly limited to summer music, the theatre (daily: April, May & Sept 9am–7pm; June–Aug 9am–8pm; Oct & March 9am–6pm; Nov–Feb 9am–5pm; combined ticket with the Musée Municipal €7) is still the focus of the town, an awesome shell at the heart of the old medieval centre, which survived periods as a fortification, slum and prison before its careful reconstruction in the nineteenth century. In 1879 the first performance in 350 years was staged, initiating the Orange **Chorégies**, a festival of musical and dramatic arts (see box below).

Said to be the world's best-preserved Roman theatre, Orange's theatre is the only one with the stage wall still standing – a massive 36m high and 103m across. The outer face, viewed from place des Frères-Mounets, resembles a monstrous prison wall, despite the ground-level archways leading into the backstage areas. Near the top you can see the blocks that held the poles of the awning which once hung over the stage and the front rows. Those at the back were protected from the sun by the hill of St-Eutrope into which the seats are built. Rows were allocated strictly by rank; an inscription "EQ Gradus III" (third row for knights) is visible near the orchestra pit. The enormous **stage** could accommodate vast numbers of performers, and the acoustics, thanks to the complex projections of the stage wall, allowed a full audience to hear every word. Though missing most of its original decoration, the inner side of the stage wall is an extremely impressive sight. Columned niches, now empty of their statues, run the length of the wall; below them a larger-than-life-size statue of Augustus, raising his arm in imperious fashion, looks down centre stage.

Orange festivals

In July Orange is packed with opera fanatics, here for the **Chorégies** or **choral festival**, performed in the Roman theatre. If you're interested in going, you'll need to make a reservation well in advance; details are available from the Bureau des Chorégies, 18 place Silvain, 84107 Orange (☎04.90.34.24.24), and from FNAC shops across the country. Ticket prices range from €4 to €160, depending on the performance.

The theatre is also used for jazz, film, folk and rock concerts. Prices range from €10 to €46, and some performances are free; details are available from the Service Culturel de la Ville, 14 place Silvain (☎04.90.51.57.57) as well as from FNAC shops.

If the spectators grew bored during the day-long performances they could slip out of the west door to a semicircle complex cut into the rock. According to some archeologists, this contained baths, a stage for combats and a gymnasium equipped with three 180-metre running tracks alongside the wall of rue Pontillac, parts of which still stand. Others say it was the forum, or even a circus. There are widely differing views on how the excavations should be interpreted, though all agree that the massive capital was part of a temple.

The best view of the theatre in its entirety, and one for which you don't have to pay, is from **St-Eutrope hill**. You can follow a path up the hill either from the top of cours Aristide-Briand, montée P. de Chalons, or from cours Pourtoules, montée Albert-Lambert, until you are looking directly down onto the stage. The **ruins** around your feet are those of the short-lived seventeenth-century **château** of the princes of Orange. Louis XIV had it destroyed and the principality annexed to France, a small setback for William of Orange who was to become William III of Britain and Ireland.

The Musée Municipal and Arc de Triomphe

Orange's **Musée Municipal** (municipal museum) stands across the road from the theatre entrance (same hours and price as the theatre). Its various documents concerning the Orange dynasty include a suitably austere portrait of the very first Orangeman, William (Guillaume) the Taciturn, grandfather to William III. The museum also has an interesting – for classical historians at least – property register and land survey of the city in 77 AD, and a display of various bits and pieces from the theatre. The rest of the collection is rotated on a yearly basis, but contains diverse items such as the contents of a seventeenth-century apothecary and a collection of pictures portraying British workers from early last century by Frank Brangwyn, a Welsh painter who learnt his craft with William Morris.

To the north of the centre, on the main road into Orange, stands the town's second major monument, the **Arc de Triomphe**, whose intricate friezes and reliefs celebrate imperial victories against the Gauls. Although highly regarded by classicists as one of the largest, best-preserved and oldest triple-bayed Roman arches in existence, the Arc's position in the middle of a major road detracts somewhat from its appeal.

Eating and drinking

Although **eating out** in Orange is unlikely to prove an exceptional experience, there's no shortage of choice. *Chez Daniel*, 12 rue Segond Weber (☎04.90.34.63.48; closed Tues evening & Wed), serves cheap pizzas and pasta (€7) as well as more expensive seafood platters (€25), while *Le Yaca*, in an old vaulted chamber at 24 place Silvain (☎04.90.34.70.03; closed Wed, plus Tues off-season & Nov), boasts a generous choice of Provençal dishes for under €21. Some of Orange's more inventive cooking can be found at *La Roselière*, 4 rue du Renoyer (closed Wed & Thurs midday; ☎04.90.34.50.42), a lovely little restaurant by the hôtel de ville, where you can dine à la carte for around €30. However, the best food you're likely to get in Orange is at *Le Parvis*, 3 cours des Pourtoules (☎04.90.34.82.00; closed Sun evening & Mon), which serves classic French *haute cuisine*, made with top-quality ingredients: weekday lunch menus start at €15.

For **drinking**, head for the central place de la République, where you'll find *Les Négociants* and the less expensive *Café de l'Univers*, both lively spots when the shops are open but much quieter at night. A better bet for evening entertainment is the *Café des Thermes* (8pm–1am) at 29 rue des Vieux-Fossés, to the west of cours Aristide-Briand, with a good selection of beers, a pool table and a youngish clientele.

Camarat and Sérignan-du-Comtat

For those with a car, it's an enjoyable drive from Orange to Sérignan, 8km northeast of the city; along the way are beautiful views of the smooth lower slopes of Mont Ventoux, and if you take the minor roads (D975, then D43) you'll pass the tiny wine-producing village of **CAMARAT**, guarded by a round-towered gateway topped with a campanile. Camarat's one claim to fame was its black Virgin Mary holding Jesus to her breast rather than on her lap, though this was burnt in 1736 on the orders of the bishop of Orange who considered the pose to be indecent.

Alternatively, there are three **buses** daily from Orange to **SÉRIGNAN-DU-COMTAT**, whose most celebrated resident, **Jean-Henri Fabre** (1823–1915), spent the last 36 years of his life here. A remarkable self-taught scientist, Fabre is famous primarily for his insect studies; he also composed poetry, wrote songs and painted his specimens with artistic brilliance as well as scientific accuracy. As a boy his family's poverty consistently interrupted his education, but with the help of scholarships and, later, with pure, stubborn self-discipline, he attained diplomas in mathematics and the sciences. In his forties, with seven children to support, he was forced to resign from his teaching post at Avignon because parents and priests considered his lectures on the fertilization of flowering plants licentious if not downright pornographic. His friend John Stuart Mill eventually bailed him out with a loan, allowing him to settle in Orange. Darwin was also a friend with whom he had lengthy correspondence, though Fabre was too religious to be an evolutionist.

A **statue of Fabre** stands beside the red-shuttered buildings of the *mairie*, while his actual house, which he named the **Harmas** (Latin for fallow land), is on the edge of the village on the N976 from Orange (Mon & Wed–Sat 9–11.30am & 2–5pm; €2.29). At the time of writing, the house is closed for renovation, so check first with the Orange tourist office. If it has re-opened, you'll be able to look round Fabre's study with its various specimens of insects and other invertebrates and his complete classification of the herbs of France and Corsica. The room gives a strong sense of a person in love with the world he researched, an impression echoed in the selection on the ground floor of Fabre's extraordinary **watercolours** of the fungi of the Vaucluse. The stunning colours and almost hallucinogenic detail make these pictures more like holograms. After visiting the house you're free to wander round the **garden** where over a thousand species grow in wild disorder, exactly as Fabre wanted it.

Sérignan is also home to a very smart **hotel-restaurant**, *L'Hostellerie du Vieux Château*, set in large grounds on rte de Ste-Cécile-les-Vignes (Ⓣ04.90.70.05.58, Ⓦwww.moulinetape.com/html/serignan.html; ❹).

Châteauneuf-du-Pape

Ten kilometres south of Orange, on the back road to Avignon, the large village of **CHÂTEAUNEUF-DU-PAPE** takes its name from the ruins of the fourteenth-century Avignon popes' summer château. However, neither this nor the medieval streets around **place du Portail**, the hub of the village, are why Châteauneuf is a household name. It is, of course, the local **vineyards** that produce the magic, with the grapes warmed at night by large pebbles that cover the ground and soak up the sun's heat by day. Their rich ruby red wine is one of the most renowned in France, though the lesser-known white, too, is exquisite.

If you can coincide your visit with the first weekend of August you'll find free *dégustation* stalls throughout the village, as well as parades, dances, equestrian contests, folklore floats and so forth, all to celebrate the ripening of the grapes in the **Fête de la Véraison**. As well as wine, a good deal of grape liqueur (*marc*) is imbibed.

At other times of the year, several places throughout the village offer free **tastings**: the Cave Père Anselme, on av Bienheureux-Pierre-de-Luxembourg, has its own **Musée du Vin** (daily 9am–noon & 2–6pm; free), and offers free tasting of its own and other Rhône wines, while the boutique **La Maison des Vins**, at 8 rue du Maréchal Foch (mid-June to mid-Sept daily 9am–7pm; mid-Sept to mid-June daily 10am–12.30pm & 2–6.30pm), will let you sample its excellent selection of different *domains*. If you'd rather buy direct from a producer, check the lists at the tourist office (see below) or the Fédération des Syndicats de Producteurs at 12 av Louis-Pasteur (ⓣ04.90.83.72.21). You could also ask for the details of the winner of the previous April 25 competition when the village celebrates the day of Saint Marc, patron saint of wine-growers, with a procession from the church and a tasting by professionals to determine the best wines from the last vintage. Otherwise, you can visit an *Association de Vignerons* such as Prestige et Tradition, 3 rue de la République (Aug & Sept daily 8am–noon & 2–6pm; Oct–July Mon–Sat 8am–noon & 2–6pm), Reflets, 2 chemin du Bois de la Ville (Mon–Fri 8am–noon & 2–6pm), or La Vinothèque, 9 rue de la République (daily 10am–6pm), who sell wines from several producers.

Practicalities

Buses from Orange (four daily) arrive at the bottom of av des Bousquets which leads up to place Jean-Moulin, rue de la République and place Portail, where you'll find the **tourist office** (July & Aug Mon–Sat 9.30am–7pm, Sun 10am–12.30pm & 2–6pm; Sept–June Mon–Sat 9.30am–12.30pm & 2–6pm; ⓣ04.90.83.71.08, ⓕ04.90.83.50.34).

Accommodation is confined to four very pleasant but small **hotels**: the cosy, five-roomed *La Garbure,* 3 rue Joseph-Ducos (ⓣ04.90.83.75.08, ⓦwww.la-garbure.com; ❹; closed mid-Oct to mid-Nov), whose rooms have all mod cons including cable tv; *La Mère Germaine*, av Cdt-Lemaître (ⓣ04.90.83.54.37, ⓦwww.lameregermaine.com; ❸), close to place du Portail, which is very welcoming with eight rooms and a tennis court; the four-star *Hostellerie du Château des Fines Roches*, a ten-minute walk out of town on the rte d'Avignon (ⓣ04.90.83.70.23, ⓦwww.chateaufinesroches.com; ❾), which has seven very plush rooms and is wonderfully situated with gorgeous views; and the charming *La Sommellerie* on route de Roquemaure (ⓣ04.90.83.50.00, ⓦwww.hotel-la-sommellerie.com; ❾, half-board obligatory), a renovated country house with a pool and superb restaurant. There are also two **chambres d'hôtes** – *chez Monsieur Melchor*, La Font du Pape (ⓣ04.90.83.73.97; ❸; closed Dec–Feb), and *chez Mme Dexheimer*, Clos Bimard, rte de Roquemaure (ⓣ04.90.83.73.16, ⓕ04.90.83.50.54; ❸; closed Dec–Feb) – and a two-star **campsite**, Islon St-Luc (ⓣ04.90.83.56.36; €15 per tent), about 2km down chemin de la Calade, south from place Portail.

You can eat well for around €15 at the brasserie *La Mule du Pape* at 2 rue de la République, which also has a gastronomic **restaurant** on the first floor (ⓣ04.90.83.79.22; restaurant closed Sun evening and Mon), where prices average around €35. Alternatively, *La Mère Germaine* (closed Sun evening out of season; €25–39) serves well-crafted Provençal dishes and has panoramic views. Top of the range, however, is *La Sommellerie* (closed Sun evening & Mon out of season; menus from €28–69), whose cook is one of France's master chefs: everything here is made on the premises, from the bread to the fine desserts, and the meat is cooked on an outdoor wood fire.

Avignon and around

AVIGNON, great city of the popes and for centuries one of the major artistic centres of France, can be very daunting. Its monuments and museums are huge, and the city is always crowded in summer and can be stiflingly hot. But it has an immaculately preserved medieval centre with a multitude of impressively decorated buildings, ancient churches, chapels and convents, and more places to eat and drink than you could cover in a month. The city is at its busiest during July and early August, when the **Festival d'Avignon** – a medley of theatre, dance, lectures, exhibitions and concerts – draws people from all over the country.

Old Avignon is only a small corner of a large modern industrial city whose suburbs reach out to the neighbouring towns along the Autoroute du Soleil 8km east. Among the main attractions are the cultivated open countryside on the Île de la Barthelasse, and the much less crowded town of **Villeneuve-lès-Avignon**, on the opposite bank and, as such, technically outside of Provence.

The papal city: some history

Avignon's monuments, and most of its history, are bound up almost entirely with the status it acquired in the fourteenth century as the residence of the popes. **Pope Clement V**, taking refuge from anarchic feuding in Rome and northern Italy, first moved the papal headquarters here in 1309, a temporary act that turned out to last over seventy years, and a few decades longer, if you count the city's last flurry in defence of its antipope pretenders.

Though the town, unlike nearby Châteauneuf-du-Pape, did not originally belong to the papacy, it had the advantage of excellent transport links and a good Catholic landlord. Clement was not entirely confident about his security, however, even in France, and shifted his base between here, Vienne and Carpentras. His successor, **Jean XXII**, had previously been bishop of Avignon, so he re-installed himself quite happily in the episcopal palace Clement V had established. The next Supreme Pontiff, **Benoît XII**, acceded in 1335; accepting the impossibility of returning to Rome, he demolished the bishop's palace to replace it with an austere fortress, now known as the **Vieux Palais**.

Number four of the nine Avignon popes, **Clement VI**, managed to buy Avignon from Queen Jeanne of Naples and Provence, apparently in return for absolution for any possible involvement she might have had in the assassination of her husband. He also built a **new palace** adjoining the old one, a much more luxurious affair showing distinctly worldly tastes. The fifth and sixth Avignon popes further embellished and fortified the papal palace, before the seventh, **Gregory XI**, after years of diplomacy, and an appeal from Catherine of Siena, moved the Holy See back to Rome in 1377. This did not please the French cardinals who promptly voted in the **Antipope Clement VII** to take up residence in Avignon, thus initiating the division in the Catholic Church known as the Great Schism. The courier business in excommunications and more worldly threats between Rome and Avignon flourished. **Antipope Benoît XIII**, who replaced Clement VII, became justifiably paranoid about

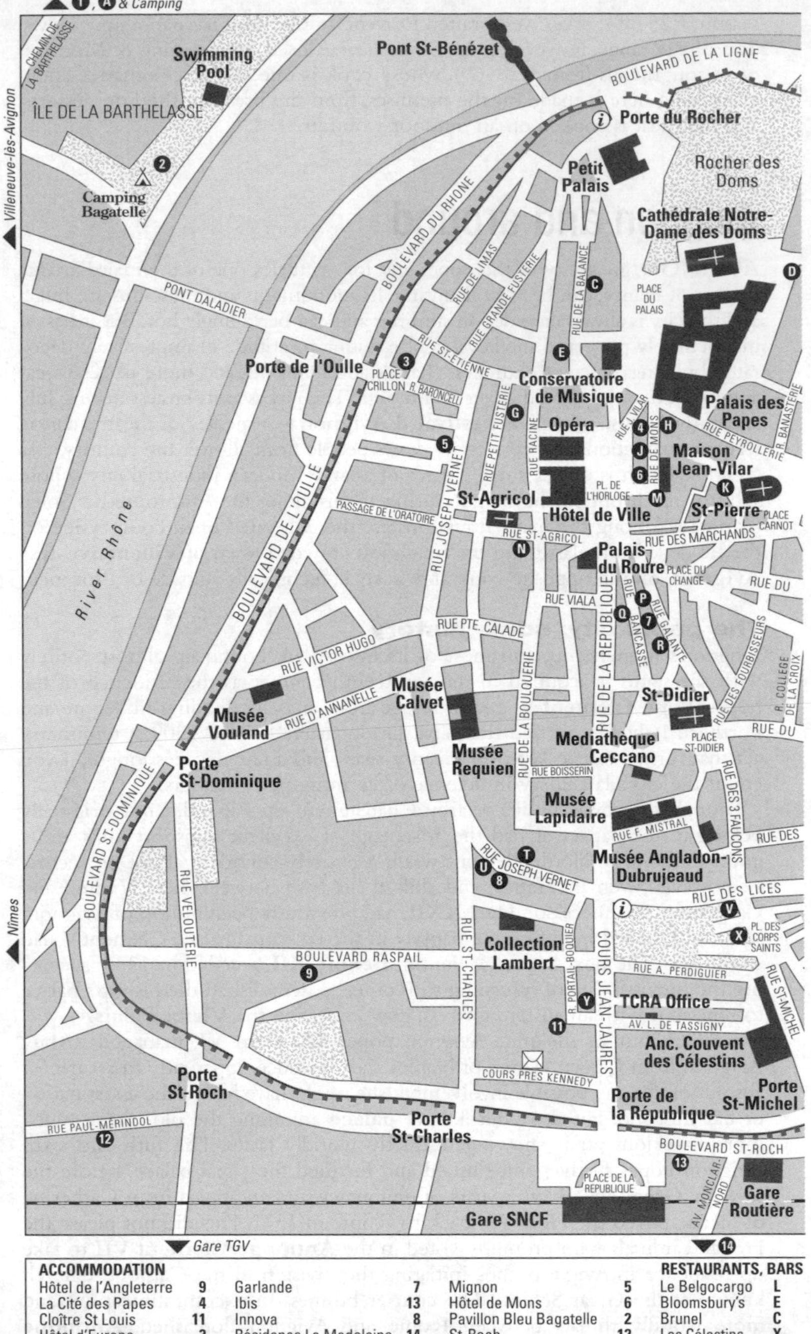

ACCOMMODATION						RESTAURANTS, BARS	
Hôtel de l'Angleterre	9	Garlande	7	Mignon	5	Le Belgocargo	L
La Cité des Papes	4	Ibis	13	Hôtel de Mons	6	Bloomsbury's	E
Cloître St Louis	11	Innova	8	Pavillon Bleu Bagatelle	2	Brunel	C
Hôtel d'Europe	3	Résidence La Madeleine	14	St-Roch	12	Les Célestins	X
La Ferme	1	Le Magnan	10			Chez Floriane	N

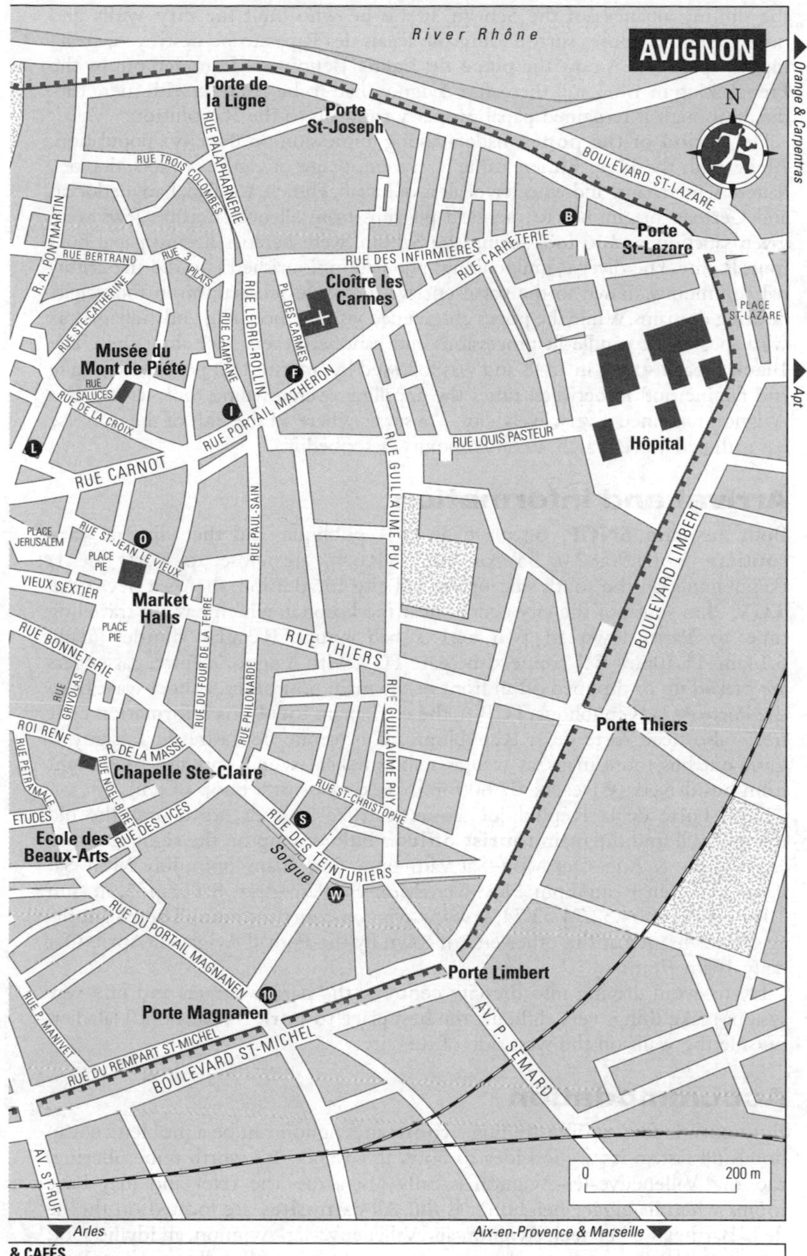

& CAFÉS

Christian Étienne	H	L'Empreinte	S	Hiély-Lucullus	Q	Shakespeare	B
La Cintra	Y	L'Entrée des Artistes	F	Koala Bar	V	Venaissin	J
La Compagnie des Comptoirs	T	L'Épicerie	K	Mon Bar	I	Tapalocas	R
Couscousserie de l'Horloge	M	La Ferme	A	Le Red Lion	O	Utopia Bar	D
D'ici et D'ailleurs	P	La Fourchette	G	Rose au Petit Bedon	U	Woolloo Mooloo	W

the shifting alliances of the Schism. It was he who built the **city walls** and ordered all the houses surrounding the Palais des Papes to be destroyed, creating the space that is now the **place du Palais**. Benoît was hounded out by the French king in 1403 and thereafter Avignon had to be content with mere cardinals, though it remained papal property right up to the Revolution.

The **period of the popes** made a lasting impression on the city's population. Along with the Holy Fathers came a vast entourage of clerks, lawyers, doctors, flatterers, merchants and wheeler-dealers of Italian, French, Catalan, Languedocian and German origin, not to mention pilgrims from all over Europe. Jews were given sanction, and so too, during the Schism, were heretics fleeing papal bulls from Rome. The diverse, multicultural population flourished – as did the criminal community, drawn to the papal enclave to escape prosecution in the neighbouring domains. While the popes entertained visiting monarchs and ambassadors with spectacular candle-lit processions and banquets, every vice flourished. The **Black Death** struck in 1348 and was followed by intermittent periods of plague and famine, and in between times the appalling overcrowding took its toll. But Avignon remained a very lively city – "a sewer where all the filth of the universe has gathered", as Petrarch, a contemporary, described it.

Arrival and information

Both the **gare SNCF**, on place de la République, and the adjacent **gare routière** (Ⓣ04.90.82.07.35) on bd St-Roch, are close to Porte de la République, on the south side of the old city. In addition, there's a new **gare TGV,** 2km south of the city centre, near the hospital, which has cut travelling time to Paris down to two and a half hours. Regular shuttles (daily 6.14am–11.10pm; €1) connect the gare TGV with Avignon centre; passengers are picked up or dropped off in front of the main post office, a short walk from the Porte de la République. TCRA, the city's main **local bus** information centre, is also near Porte de la République, at 1 avenue de Lattre de Tassigny. It gives out bus route maps, as well as selling tickets, which can also be bought from bus drivers (€1 each; €7.80 for a weekly pass or a book of ten).

From Porte de la République, cours Jean-Jaurès leads north into the old town; you'll find the main **tourist office** a little way up on the right at no. 41 (April–June & Aug–Oct Mon–Sat 9am–6pm, Sun 10am–5pm; July Mon–Sat 9am–7pm, Sun 10am–5pm; Nov–May Mon–Fri 9am–6pm, Sat 9am–5pm, Sun 10am–noon; Ⓣ04.32.74.32.74, Ⓦwww.avignon-tourisme.com). There's another smaller branch at the other end of town by the Pont d'Avignon (April–Oct daily 10am–7pm).

Try to avoid driving into the city centre as the narrow streets and one-way system make things very difficult: the best place **to park** is near Pont Daladier, outside the walls on the west side of the city.

Accommodation

Even outside festival time, finding a **room** in Avignon can be a problem: cheap hotels fill fast so it's a good idea to book in advance. It's worth remembering, too, that Villeneuve-lès-Avignon is only just across the river and may have rooms when its bigger neighbour is full. All **campsites** are located on the Île de la Barthelasse between Avignon and Villeneuve-lès-Avignon, an idyllic spot; take bus #10 from outside the post office to Porte de l'Oulle opposite Pont Daladier and then walk or take bus #20 onto the island. During the festival a temporary site is set up behind the Bagatelle with minimal facilities. Look out, also, for the odd **farmhouse** advertising rooms.

Hotels

Hôtel de l'Angleterre 29 bd Raspail ⓣ04.90.86.34.31, ⓦwww.hoteldangleterre.fr. Located in a quiet neighbourhood in the southwest corner of the old city, this is a traditional hotel with some very reasonably priced rooms. ❹

La Cité des Papes 1 rue J-Vilar ⓣ04.90.80.93.00, ⓕ04.90.80.93.01. Large chain hotel located between pl de l'Horloge and pl du Palais; good location and comfort assured in all rooms. ❼

Cloître St Louis 20 rue de Portail-Boquier ⓣ04.90.27.55.55, ⓦwww.cloitre-saint-louis.com. A large but friendly hotel in a renovated Jesuit cloister with all modern facilities, including TV, en-suite baths and a roof-top pool. ❽

Hôtel d'Europe 12 pl Crillon ⓣ04.90.14.76.76, ⓦwww.hotel-d-europe.fr. A sixteenth-century townhouse, very classy and set back in a shaded courtyard. Peaceful and luxurious. ❽

La Ferme chemin du Bois, Île de la Barthelasse ⓣ04.90.82.57.53, ⓦwww.hotel-laferme.com. A sixteenth-century farm on the island in the Rhône (signed right off Pont Daladier as you cross over from Avignon), with well-equipped and pleasant rooms. Closed Nov to mid-March. ❹

Garlande 20 rue Galante ⓣ04.90.85.08.85, ⓕ04.90.27.16.58. Delightful location on a narrow street right in the centre of the city. Well-known so booking ahead is essential. ❹

Ibis 42 bd St-Roch ⓣ04.90.85.38.38, ⓕ04.90.86.44.81. Chain hotel located in the train station complex. Noisy, but worth it for the front rooms which offer great views over the city. ❺

The festival d'Avignon

Unlike most provincial festivals of international renown, the **Festival d'Avignon** is dominated by theatre rather than classical music, though there's also plenty of that, as well as lectures, exhibitions and dance. The city's great buildings make a spectacular backdrop to the performances, which take place annually from the second week in July. During the three-week festival everything stays open late, and things get booked up very quickly; there can be up to 200,000 visitors, and getting around or attempting everyday activities becomes virtually impossible.

Founded in 1947 by actor-director **Jean Vilar**, the festival has included, over the years, theatrical interpretations as diverse as Euripides, Molière and Chekhov, performed by companies from across Europe. While big-name directors (Jacques Lasalle, Alain Françon) draw the largest crowds to the main venue, the Cour d'Honneur in the Palais des Papes, there is more than enough variety in the smaller productions, dance performances and lectures to keep everyone sufficiently entertained. In addition to the introduction of new works staged by lesser-known directors and theatre troupes, each year the festival spotlights a different culture, which in the past have ranged from showings of the Hindi epic *Ramayana* to the debut of THEOREM (Theatres from the East and from the West), a European cultural venture designed to bring together the two halves of Europe on stage. These days, however, it's the fringe contingent known as the **Festival Off** which gives the festival its true atmosphere of craziness and magic, with a programme of innovative, obscure and bizarre performances taking place in more than a hundred venues as well as in the streets.

The main festival programme, with details of how **to book**, is available from the second week in May from the Bureau du Festival d'Avignon, 20 rue du portail Boquier, 84000 Avignon (ⓣ04.90.27.66.50, ⓦwww.festival-avignon.com), or from the tourist office. Ticket prices are reasonable (between €16 and €33) and go on sale from the second week in June. As well as phone sales (Mon–Fri 9am–1pm & 2–5pm, daily during the festival; ⓣ04.90.14.14.14), tickets can be bought from FNAC shops in all major French cities. During the festival, tickets are available until 4pm for the same day's performances. The Festival Off programme is available from the end of June from Avignon Public Off BP5, 75521 Paris Cedex 11 (ⓣ01.48.05.01.19, ⓦwww.avignon-off.org). During the festival, the office is in the Conservatoire de Musique on place du Palais. Tickets prices range from €9 to €17 and a *Carte Public Adhérent* for €13 gives you thirty percent off all shows.

Innova 100 rue Joseph-Vernet ⓣ04.90.82.54.10, ⓔhotel.innova@wanadoo.fr. Small, friendly, and conveniently located: worth booking in advance. ❷
Le Magnan 63 rue Portail Magnanen ⓣ04.90.86.36.51, ⓦwww.avignon-et-provence.com/le-magnan. Just inside the walls by Porte Magnanen a short way east of the station. Quiet, and with a very pleasant shaded garden. ❹
Mignon 12 rue Joseph-Vernet ⓣ04.90.82.17.30, ⓦwww.hotel-mignon.com. Dated decor but good value and comfortable; reserve well in advance. ❹
Hôtel de Mons 5 rue de Mons ⓣ04.90.82.57.16, ⓦwww.hoteldemons.com. A central, imaginatively converted thirteenth-century chapel. All the rooms are odd shapes, and you breakfast beneath a vaulted ceiling. ❹
St-Roch 9 rue Paul-Mérindol ⓣ04.90.16.50.00, ⓕ04.90.82.78.30. Spacious, clean and quiet with a pleasant garden and cable TV in all the rooms. ❸

Hostels

Pavillon Bleu Bagatelle camping Bagatelle, Île de la Barthelasse ⓣ04.90.86.30.39, ⓕ04.90.27.16.23. Rather basic facilities, but set in a pleasant shady campsite with rooms for four to eight people for €10.50 (per person), or €13.50 including breakfast. Bus #10 from the post office to Porte de l'Oulle, then bus #20 to the Bagatelle stop.
Résidence La Madeleine 4 impasse des Abeilles, 25 av Monclar-Nord ⓣ04.90.85.20.63, ⓔla-madeline@web-office.fr. Studios with kitchenette for two people from €400 a week, €630 a week for three or four. Out of season it's possible to rent by the day at cheaper rates. Turn right out of the station and first right, away from the old town.

Campsites

Camping Bagatelle ⓣ04.90.86.30.39, ⓕ04.90.27.16.23. The closest site to the city centre. A three-star complex, visible as you cross the Daladier bridge from Avignon; bus #20 to Bagatelle stop. €11 per tent. Open all year.
Camping Municipal Pont St-Bénézet ⓣ04.90.82.63.50, ⓔinfo@camping-avignon.com. A four-star site about 3km from the centre overlooking Pont St-Bénézet; bus #20 (Bénézet stop). €20 per tent. Closed Nov–March.
Les Deux Rhônes chemin de Bellegarde, Île de la Barthelasse ⓣ04.90.85.49.70, ⓕ04.90.85.91.75. Around 4km from the city and smaller than the other three; bus #20 (Traille stop). €10.50 per tent. Open all year.
Parc des Libertés Île de la Barthelasse ⓣ04.90.85.17.73, ⓔparcdeslibertes@free.fr. The cheapest of the four campsites. €8.50 per tent. Open all year.

The City

Avignon's **walls** still form a complete loop around the city, though they now appear far too low to be a serious defence. In fact half their full height is buried beneath the city, as is its moat – though all the gates and towers were restored during the nineteenth century and there's still a strong sense of being in an enclosed space quite separate from the modern spread of the city.

Running north from the wall gate, cours Jean-Jaurès becomes **rue de la République**, the main axis of the old town, leading straight up to **place de l'Horloge**, the central square. Beyond that is **place du Palais**, the **Rocher des Doms** park and the **Porte du Rocher** overlooking the Rhône by the Pont d'Avignon, or Pont St-Bénézet as it's officially known. Avignon's major monuments occupy a compact quarter inside the northern loop of the walls. The **Palais des Papes**, northeast of the square and home of the medieval popes, is obviously the city's major sight, but there are other palaces dotted about

Discovery passports

The tourist offices in Avignon and Villeneuve-lès-Avignon distribute free **Discovery Passports.** After paying the full admission price for the first museum you visit, you and your family receive discounts of 20–50 percent on the entrance fees of all subsequent museums in Avignon. The pass also gives discounts on tourist transport (such as petits trains, riverboats and bus tours), and is valid for two weeks after its first use.

the centre and, as you'd expect, a fair smattering of churches (most with very limited opening hours). The best of the **city's museums** are the **Petit Palais** and the **Musée Calvet**, while, for a break from the monumental, have a wander around the pedestrian streets east of the papal palace towards place des Carmes, and to the southeast of the centre, the atmospheric **rue des Teinturiers**.

Palais des Papes

Serious sightseeing is bound to start off in the place du Palais, a huge cobbled square dominated by the **Palais des Papes** (daily: April–June & Oct–Nov 9am–7pm; July–Sept 9am–8pm; Nov–March 9.30am–5.45pm; last ticket 1hr before closing; €9.50, or €11 for palace and the Pont; ticket includes either an audioguide or a guided tour at 11.30am or 4.45pm in English). The palais is a monster of a building, best viewed from the rue Peyrolerie to its south; inside, so little remains of the original decoration and furnishings that you can be deceived into thinking that all the popes and their retinues were as pious and austere as the last official occupant, Benoît XII. The denuded interior certainly gives sparse indication of the corruption and decadence of fat, feuding cardinals and their mistresses, the thronging purveyors of jewels, velvet and furs, the musicians, chefs and painters competing for patronage, the riotous banquets and corridor schemings which took place here during the period of the popes.

Tours begin in the **Pope's Tower**, otherwise known as the Tower of Angels, entered via the **Treasury**, a vaulted room in the tower. Here the serious business of the church's deeds and finances went on and, beneath the flagging of the lower treasury, the papal gold and jewels were stored in four large safe holes. The same cunning storage device can be seen in the Chamberlain's quarters, in the **Chambre du Camérier**, just off the Jesus Hall. As the pope's right-hand man, the Chamberlain would originally have had lavishly decorated quarters, but successive occupants have left their mark and what is now visible is a confusion of layers. The other door in this room leads into the Papal Vestiary, where the pope would dress before sessions in the consistory. He also had a small library here and could look out onto the gardens below.

A door on the north side of the Jesus Hall leads to the **Consistoire** of the Vieux Palais, where sovereigns and ambassadors were received and the cardinals' council was held. The original flooring and the frescoes were destroyed by fire in 1413 and today it contains fragments of frescoes moved here from the cathedral plus a series of nineteenth-century paintings of the popes, all nine looking remarkably similar – unsurprisingly, given that the artist used the same model for each.

If it's medieval artistry you're after, however, go to the **Chapelle St-Jean**, off the Consistoire, and the **Chapelle St-Martial** on the floor above, reached via the cloisters. Both were richly decorated by the Sienese artist Matteo Giovanetti, and commissioned by Clement VI. The frescoes were damaged in the nineteenth century by soldiers using the building as barracks – they tried to chip off all the heads of the figures in order to sell them.

The **kitchen**, also on this floor, gives an idea of medieval times, and a hint of the scale of papal gluttony – its square walls becoming an octagonal chimney-piece for a vast central cooking fire. Major feasts were held in **Le Grand Tinel** which was also part of the conclave in which the cardinals were locked up in order to elect a new pope; clearly visible are the arches that led to additional rooms in the south and west in which the cardinals conspired and schemed in isolation from the world.

In the adjoining **Palais Neuf**, Clement VI's bedroom and study are further evidence of the pope's secular concerns, with wonderful food-oriented murals and painted ceilings. Beautifully restored, they illustrate in detail fishing, falconry, hunting and other courtly pursuits. However, austerity resumes in the cathedral-like proportions of the Grande Chapelle, or **Chapelle Clementine**, and in the Grande Audience on the floor below.

When you've completed the circuit, which includes a heady walk along the roof terraces, you can watch a glossy but informative film on the history of the palace (English headphones available). **Concerts** are also held here: programmes are available from the ticket office. During evening visits or concerts the illuminations give the palais a truly Gothic atmosphere.

North to Pont St-Bénézet

Opposite the entrance to the palais is the beautiful seventeenth-century **Hôtel des Monnaies**, the old mint, now the Conservatoire de Musique, with a facade of griffons, cherubs, eagles and swathes of fruit. To the north stands the **Cathédrale Notre-Dame-des-Doms** (daily 7.30am–7.30pm), which might once have been a luminous Romanesque structure, but the interior has had a bad attack of Baroque. In addition, nineteenth-century fanatics mounted an enormous gilded Virgin on the belfry, which would look silly enough anywhere, but, when dwarfed by the fifty-metre towers of the popes' palace, is absurd. To the west of the square is the redeveloped **Quartier de la Balance**, now teeming with souvenir shops, but once home to the gypsies in the nineteenth century.

Behind the cathedral is the **Rocher des Doms park**, a relaxing spot with lovely views over the river to Villeneuve and beyond. To the west is the **Petit Palais** (daily except Tues: July & Aug 10am–1pm & 2–6pm; Sept–June 9.30am–1pm & 2–5.30pm; €6), a former episcopal palace now housing a dauntingly huge gallery. There are almost a thousand paintings and sculptures here and it's easy to get stuck, with more than a dozen rooms still to go, on the mastery of colour and facial expressions of a Simone Martini or Fabriano, or to be fatigued by a surfeit of the Madonna and Child before you've reached Botticelli's masterpiece on the subject or the Niçois painter, Louis Bréa's *Assumption of the Virgin*. Anyone intrigued by labyrinths should look out for *Theseus and the Minotaur*, the labyrinth in the foreground is identical to the one on the floor of Chartres cathedral, and is thought by some to have mysterious powers of healing.

North of the Petit Palais, and well signposted, is the half-span of **Pont St-Bénézet**, or the Pont d'Avignon of the famous song (same hours as Palais des Papes; €3.50, €11 combined ticket with Palais des Papes). One theory has it that the lyrics say "*Sous le pont*" (under the bridge) rather than "*Sur le pont*" (on the bridge), and refer to the thief and trickster clientele of a tavern on the Île de la Barthelasse (which the bridge once crossed) dancing with glee at the arrival of more potential victims. Keeping the bridge repaired from the ravages of the Rhône was finally abandoned in 1660, three and a half centuries after it was built, and only four of the original twenty-two arches remain. Despite its limited use, the bridge remained a focus of river boatmen, who constructed a chapel to their patroness on the first of the bridge's bulwarks. Today, the bridge can be walked, danced or sat upon, but if you take small children, beware the precipitous, barely protected drops on either side.

The Festival Provençal

The Palais du Roure is the main Avignon venue for the **Festival Provençal**, which for over two decades has been celebrating the Provençal language and traditions in poetry, theatre, dance and song. It takes place during July and early August, with events in several Vaucluse cities. Details from the Palais du Roure on ⓣ04.90.80.80.88, or online in Provençal at ⓦwww.nouvello.com.

Around place de l'Horloge

South of the Palais des Papes is the busy, café-lined **place de l'Horloge**, site of the city's imposing nineteenth-century **Hôtel de Ville** with its Gothic **clock tower**, and of the **Opéra**. Around the square, on rues de Mons, Molière and Corneille, famous faces are painted on the windows of the buildings. Many of these figures from the past were visitors to Avignon, and of those who recorded their impressions of the city, it was the sound of over a hundred bells ringing that stirred them most. Though there's not quite so many today, on Sunday mornings, traffic lulls permitting, you can still hear myriad different peals from churches, convents and chapels in close proximity. Many ecclesiastical buildings were knocked down during the Revolution and in the years up to 1815, when a minority of Avignonnais were still fighting against union with France. It was a bloody time: in 1791 a supporter of the new order was murdered in church; in response sixty counter-revolutionaries were buried alive in the ice-house of the papal palace.

The restored fourteenth-century **Église St-Agricol**, just behind the hôtel de ville, is one of Avignon's best Gothic edifices, with a beautifully carved fifteenth-century facade; inside, there's a Renaissance altarpiece of Provençal origin, and paintings by Nicolas Mignard and Pierre Parrocel (Wed 10am–noon, Sat 4–6pm, Sun 8–10pm). Beyond here lie the most desirable addresses in Avignon. High, heavy facades dripping with cupids, eagles, dragons, fruit and foliage range along **rue Petite-Fusterie** and **rue Joseph-Vernet**, where you'll find the most expensive shops selling chocolate, haute couture and baubles, with restaurants and art galleries to match.

To the south of the square, just behind rue St-Agricol on rue Collège du Roure, is the elegant fifteenth-century **Palais du Roure**, a centre of Provençal culture, whose gateway and courtyard are worth a look. The Palais often hosts temporary art exhibitions, or you can take a rambling tour through its attics to see Provençal costumes, publications and presses, photographs of the Camargue in the 1900s and an old stage coach: the tour is on Tuesdays at 3pm (€4.60), or you can make an appointment (☎04.90.80.80.88).

On rue de Mons, to the east, the seventeenth-century Hôtel de Crochans is home to the **Maison Jean Vilar** (Tues–Fri 9am–noon & 1.30–5.30pm, Sat 10am–5pm; closed Aug; free; ☎04.90.86.59.64), named after the great theatre director who set up the "Week of Dramatic Art" in 1947, which was to become Avignon's annual festival (see p.73). The building houses festival memorabilia, an excellent library dedicated to the performing arts, and a collection of videos on everything from Stanislavski to last year's street theatre. These are sometimes shown in the foyer, or at special screenings, but you can also arrange your own viewing, with one day's notice – the catalogue is at the main desk. The Maison also puts on temporary exhibitions, workshops and public lectures hosted by renowned theatre people.

The Banasterie and Carmes quartiers

The **quartier de la Banasterie**, to the east of the Palais des Papes, is mostly seventeenth- and eighteenth-century. The heavy wooden doors with highly sculptured lintels bear the nameplates of lawyers, psychiatrists and dietary consultants. It's worth poking your nose into the courtyard of the Hôtel de Fonseca, built in 1600 at 17 rue Ste-Catherine, to admire its mullioned windows and old well. Between Banasterie and place des Carmes are a tangle of tiny streets guaranteed to get you lost. Pedestrians have priority over cars on many of them, and there are plenty of tempting cafés and restaurants along the way. At 6 rue Saluces you'll find the peculiar **Musée du Mont de Piété**

(Mon–Fri 8.30–11.30am & 1.30–5.00pm; free), an ex-pawnbroker's shop and now the town's archives, which has a small display of papal bulls and painted silk desiccators for determining the dry weight of what was the city's chief commodity.

Beyond, the **Cloitre les Carmes** (Carmelite convent) once spread over the whole of place des Carmes, right down to the bell tower on rue Carreterie, built in the 1370s with the bell cage added in the sixteenth century. Today, all that remains is the **Église St-Symphorien** (Mon–Fri 8–9am & 6.30–7.30pm, Sat 5–7pm, Sun 8.45am–noon), which contains a stunning painting of *St Éloi* by Nicolas Mignard. The cloisters have become a theatre for Avignon's oldest permanent company, the Théâtre des Carmes, run by André Benedetto.

Further up, at 155 rue Carreterie, you'll find Avignon's English bookshop which also serves as a tearoom, meeting place and venue for readings and performances (Tues–Sat 9.30am–12.30pm & 2–6.30pm; sometimes open Fri eve & Sun pm).

From St-Pierre to the rue des Teinturiers

To the south of rue Banasterie, on **place St-Pierre**, stands one of the most spectacular of Avignon's churches, the Renaissance **Église St-Pierre** (Fri 2.30–5.30pm, Sat 9–11am, Sun 8.30–11.30am). Its greatest artwork is the doors, which were carved in 1551, with the Annunciation depicted on the right, and St Jerome and St Michael on the left. Inside, sculpted angels form the base of the nave's ribbed vault, holding up the arches, while beneath the organ loft there's a painting by Nicolas Mignard, *Sainte Famille au Chardonnerot*.

To the south is the city's main pedestrian precinct, which centres on **place du Change**, and the old **Jewish quarter** around rue du Vieux-Sextier and place Jérusalem, where, during the time of the popes, Jews had to wear yellow caps and were locked in every night. To the east is **place Pie**, site of the ugly modern **market halls** and an open flower market. Just to the south, on rue du Roi-Réné is the **Chapelle St-Clare**, where, during the Good Friday service in 1327, the poet Petrarch first saw and fell in love with Laura, as recorded in a note on the pages of the poet's copy of Virgil.

From place Pie, rue Bonneterrie heads southeast, becoming **rue des Teinturiers**, the most atmospheric street in Avignon. Its name refers to the eighteenth- and nineteenth-century business of calico printing. The cloth was washed in the Sorgue canal, which still runs alongside the street, turning the wheels of long-gone mills. It's also an excellent street for restaurant-browsing, though the water tends to get a bit smelly as you reach the ramparts.

Place St-Didier and around

A short way south of place de l'Horloge and just east of the main drag, rue de la République, is **place St-Didier**. The square is dominated by the **Église St-Didier** (Mon–Sat 9am–noon & 2–7pm, Sun 10am–noon). Check out the altarpiece in the first chapel on the left which depicts Mary's pain with such realism that it has acquired the somewhat uncomfortable name of "Notre-Dame-du-Spasme". There are also some fourteenth-century frescoes in the left-hand chapel.

Between the noisy rue de la République and place St-Didier, on rue Labourer, is the impressive fourteenth-century former cardinal's residence, now the municipal library, the **Mediathèque Ceccano** (Mon 1–6pm, Tues–Sat 10am–6pm), where you could easily spend a tranquil afternoon reading in its quiet gardens; occasional exhibitions are also held in the beautifully decorated interior. Opposite, the **Musée Angladon-Dubrujeaud** (Wed–Sun 1–6pm, till

7pm in Aug; €5) displays the remains of the private collection of Jacques Doucet. It was once a mighty collection, containing such treasures as Picasso's *Demoiselles d'Avignon* and Douanier-Rousseau's *The Snake Charmer* (now in the Musée d'Orsay), but much of it was either given away or sold bit by bit. Testimony to grander days can be found in the first room, where photographs of Jacques Doucet's house, with rooms decorated according to the style of the paintings therein, reveal a man ahead of his time. The rest of the downstairs room shows what is left of his contemporary collection; *Portrait of Mme Foujita* and a self-portrait by Foujita, Modigliani's *The Pink Blouse*, various Picasso's, and Van Gogh's *Railway Wagons*, the only painting from Van Gogh's stay in Provence to be on display in Provence. The theme of decorating rooms around a style has been taken up in the rest of the museum with a room dedicated to the medieval and Renaissance periods, three dedicated to the eighteenth century (Doucet's first passion) and a Far East room.

Musée Calvet and around

West of rue de la République lies a cluster of museums, a couple of which are well worth checking out. Housed in an impressive eighteenth-century palace, the excellent **Musée Calvet**, on 65 rue Joseph-Vernet (daily except Tues 10am–1pm & 2–6pm; €6), has been undergoing gradual restoration and transformation for the past few years. Although several rooms on the ground floor remain closed to the public, the majority of the collection is now on display, beginning with the **Galerie des Sculptures**. A better introduction to a museum couldn't be wished for, with a handful of languorous nineteenth-century marble sculptures, including Bosio's *Young Indian*, perfectly suited to this elegant space. The end of the gallery houses the Puech collection with a large selection of silverware, Italian and Dutch paintings, but more unusually a Flemish curiosities cabinet, painted with scenes from the story of Daniel. Upstairs, the Provençal dynasties of the Mignards and the Vernets are well represented. Nicolas Mignard sets off with a fine set of Seasons in the Joseph Vernet room, whilst Joseph Vernet himself sticks to representing the different times of the day. Further down, Horace Vernet donated the subtle *The Death of Young Barra* by Jacques-Louis David as well as Géricault's *Battle of Nazareth*. On the way out don't miss the Victor Martin collection, including Vlaminck's *Sur le Zinc*, Bonnard's *Jour d'Hiver*, and the haunting portrait of *The Downfall* by Chaïm Soutine. The rest of the eclectic collection – from an Egyptian mummy of a five-year-old boy to intricate wrought-iron work, taking in Gallo-Roman pots and Gothic clocks along the way – is expected to be on show again by 2004.

The second museum worth visting is the **Musée Vouland**, which lies further west, at the end of rue Victor-Hugo, near Porte St-Dominique (Tues–Sat: May–Oct 10am–noon & 2–6pm; Nov–April 2–6pm; €4). Here you can feast your eyes on the fittings, fixtures and furnishings that French aristocrats once indulged in both before and after the Revolution. There's some brilliant Moustiers faïence, exquisite marquetry and Louis XV ink-pots with silver rats holding the lids.

Avignon's remaining museums are considerably less compelling: next door to the Musée Calvet, the **Musée Requien** (Tues–Sat 9am–noon & 2–6pm; free), is a rather uninspiring natural history museum; the **Musée Lapidaire**, housed in a Baroque chapel at 27 rue de la République (daily except Tues 10am–1pm & 2–6pm; April–Oct €2, Nov–March free), boasts a dull collection of Roman and Gallo-Roman stones; while Avignon's only contemporary art gallery, the **Collection Lambert**, just west of the tourist office, down rue Violette

(Tues–Sun 11am–7pm; €5.50; Ⓦ www.collectionlambert.com), houses a disappointing permanent collection, although the temporary exhibitions can sometimes be worthwhile.

Eating and drinking

Good-value midday **meals** are plentiful in Avignon and eating well in the evening needn't break the bank. The large terraced **café-brasseries** on place de l'Horloge, rue de la République, place du Change and place des Corps-Saints will all serve quick basic meals. Rue des Teinturiers and the streets of the Banasterie and Carmes are good places to try if you're on a tight **budget**, and the streets between place de Crillon and place du Palais are full of temptation if you're not.

Restaurants

Le Belgocargo 10 pl des Châtaignes Ⓣ04.90.85.72.99. Belgian restaurant specializing in mussels and beer. Midday menu with drink for €7.50. Closed Sun out of season.

Brunel 46 rue de la Balance Ⓣ04.90.85.24.83. Superb regional dishes, with menus from €21. Closed Sun & Mon, and mid-July to mid-Aug.

Chez Floriane 23 rue St-Agricol Ⓣ04.90.27.12.66. Tucked away at the end of a *cour*, romantic atmosphere and excellent Mediterranean cooking – even the mashed potatoes are astounding; €25 menu. Closed Sun & Mon.

Christian Étienne 10 rue de Mons Ⓣ04.90.86.16.50. One of Avignon's best restaurants, housed in a fourteenth-century mansion and offering exotic combinations such as fennel sorbet with a saffron sauce plus some great fish dishes. Menus from €30–85. Last orders 9.30pm. Closed Sun & Mon.

La Cintra 44 cours Jean-Jaurès. Dependable brasserie with a menu under €11.50. Daily till midnight.

La Compagnie des Comptoirs 83 rue Joseph Vernet Ⓣ04.90.85.99.04. Appearance reigns supreme in this redecorated Jesuit cloître, although the fusion cuisine – which varies from Mediterranean to southeast Asian, with vegetarian options as well – isn't far behind. A la carte around €40. Open daily noon–2pm & 7–10.30pm.

Couscousserie de l'Horloge 2 rue de Mons Ⓣ04.90.85.84.86. Popular Algerian-run restaurant with a jovial atmosphere and excellent North African food. Try the delicious *tajine aux prunes* at €12. Open daily noon–2pm & 7–10.30pm.

L'Entrée des Artistes 1 pl des Carmes Ⓣ04.90.82.46.90. Small, friendly bistro serving traditional French dishes, with a €16 weekday menu. Closed lunch Sat, Sun & first two weeks Sept.

L'Épicerie pl St Pierre Ⓣ04.90.82.74.22. A quiet spot in which to sample a selection of cheeses (€7) or starters (€10), or go for a relaxed meal (from €14). Closed Sun.

La Ferme chemin du Bois, Île de la Barthelasse Ⓣ04.90.82.57.53. A traditional farmhouse with well-prepared simple dishes from €20. Sept–June closes Mon & Wed.

La Fourchette 17 rue Racine Ⓣ04.90.85.20.93. The basic fixed menu (around €26) offers marinated sardines, vegetable terrine, stuffed tomatoes and excellent meat and fish stews. Last orders 9.30pm. Closed Sat, Sun & last two weeks in Aug.

Hiély-Lucullus 5 rue de la République Ⓣ04.90.86.17.07. Avignon's top gastronomic palace, serving beautiful Provençal cuisine – gratin of mussels and spinach, stuffed rabbit, sole in red pepper sauce, lamb grilled in rosemary, scallop salad, a huge selection of goats' cheese and wonderful puddings – all washed down with the best local wines. Menus from €30. Last orders 9.15pm. Closed Tues and Wed & last two weeks of June.

D'ici et D'ailleurs 4 rue Galante Ⓣ04.90.14.63.65. Provençal dishes from "here" mixed with international flavours from "there", and live music weekend nights. Good value; lunch for €11, dinner from €14. Closed Sun.

Rose au Petit Bedon 70 rue Joseph Vernet Ⓣ04.90.82.33.98. According to fellow chefs the "pot-belly" does the best meal for under €20 anywhere in the city. Last orders 10pm. Closed Mon eve, Sun & last two weeks in Aug.

Venaissin 16 pl de l'Horloge Ⓣ04.90.86.20.99. In the height of summer you'd be very lucky to get a table here. It's the only cheap brasserie on pl de l'Horloge serving more than just *steack-frites*. It offers two menus under €14.50. Open daily noon–2pm & 7–10.30pm.

Woolloo Mooloo 16 bis rue des Teinturiers Ⓣ04.90.85.28.44. An old printshop with all the presses still in place. Now serves dishes from around the world and a good selection of teas. Offers a lunch menu at €11, and €17 at dinner. Occasional theme nights. Closed Mon.

Cafés, bars and salons de thé

Bloomsbury's 11 rue de la Balance. As English a teahouse as you could find on this side of the Channel. Excellent cakes, and a good, quiet place to read the paper. Mon–Sat 1–6pm.

Les Célestins 38 pl des Corps-Saints. Café-bar with a young, fairly trendy clientele. Open Mon–Sat 7am–1am.

L'Empreinte 33 rue des Teinturiers. Inexpensive mint tea and Moroccan pastries. Closed Sun & Wed.

Koala Bar 2 pl des Corps-Saints. Loud and popular music emanates from this bar which attracts a young and mainly English-speaking crowd. Open daily till 2am.

Mon Bar 17 rue du Portail Matheron. Pleasant café with a laid-back atmosphere. Open Mon–Sat 8am–8pm.

Le Red Lion 21–23 rue St Jean le Vieux. Popular student bar on Place Pie. Open daily 7am–1.30am.

Shakespeare 155 rue Carreterie. English bookshop and *salon de thé*. Closed evenings and all Sun & Mon.

Tapalocas 10 rue Galante ⓣ04.90.82.56.84. Cheap drinks, tapas for €2.20 a dish and occasional live music. Daily 11.45am–1.30am.

Utopia Bar 4 rue Escaliers Ste-Anne. In the shadow of the Palais des Papes, this café has changing exhibitions adorning the walls, live jazz some nights, and is next door to a good cinema. Open daily noon to midnight.

Nightlife and entertainment

Though a lot of the city's energy is saved up for the festival, there's a fair amount of **nightlife and cultural events** in Avignon all year round, particularly café-theatre. For more information, get the free bi-monthly calendar *Rendez-Vous* from the tourist office, or the free, weekly arts, events and music magazine, *César*, also available from the tourist office and arts centres.

Live music and discos

Le 5/5 1 rempart St-Roch ⓣ04.90.82.61.32. Mainstream disco, popular with the locals. Thurs–Sat from 11pm.

AJMI Jazz Club c/o La Manutention, rue Escalier Ste-Anne ⓣ04.90.86.08.61, ⓦwww.jazzalajmi.com. Hosts major acts and some adventurous new groups.

The Cage 5 ave Monclar ⓣ04.90.27.00.84. A gay and lesbian club in the *gare routière* building. Thurs–Sun from 11pm.

L'Esclave Bar 12 rue du Limas. Gay bar and disco. Open daily 10.30pm–5am; shows Wed & Sun; drinks from €6.

Le Privé rte de Tavel, Les Angles ⓣ04.90.25.90.99. Club hosting international DJs and playing mainly house music. Free entry except for special shows. Fri & Sat from 11pm.

Pub Z corner of rue Bonneterie and rue Artaud. Rock bar, decorated in black and white in honour of the zebra, DJs at the weekend. Open till 1.30am; closed Sun & last two weeks Aug.

Le Red Zone 25 rue Carnot ⓣ04.90.27.02.44. Trendy bar with DJs and weekly concerts. Mon–Sat 7pm–3am.

Theatre and cinema

Théâtre du Balcon 38 rue Guillaume-Puy ⓣ04.90.85.00.80. A venue staging everything from African music and twentieth-century classics to contemporary theatre.

Théâtre des Carmes 6 pl Carmes ⓣ04.90.82.20.47. Run by one of the founders of Festival Off, this theatre specializes in avant garde performances.

Théâtre du Chêne Noir 8 bis rue Ste-Catherine ⓣ04.90.86.58.11. May have mime, a musical or Molière on offer.

Opéra pl de l'Horloge ⓣ04.90.82.81.40. Classical opera and ballet.

Péniche Dolphin Blues chemin de l'île Piot ⓣ04.90.82.46.96. One-person shows and café-theatre in a barge moored on the Île Piot.

Utopia 4 rue Escalier Ste-Anne ⓣ04.90.82.65.36. Cinema showing art-house, obscure or old-time favourites, always in the original language. The tourist office has programmes.

Listings

Airport Aéroport Avignon-Caumont ⓣ04.90.81.51.51. Internal flights only.

Bike rental Cycles Peugeot 84, 80 rue Guillaume-Puy ⓣ04.90.86.32.49; Provence Bike, 52 bd St-Roch ⓣ04.90.27.92.61 (also scooters and motorbikes).

Boat trips Grands Bateaux de Provence, allée de l'Oulle ☎04.90.85.62.25, Ⓦwww.avignon-et-provence.com/mireio/; runs year-round trips upstream towards Châteauneuf-du-Pape and downstream to Arles; two-week advance booking recommended; tickets from €33.50, meal included. Shorter hour-long cruises and the bateau bus (summer only) from €6.
Bookshops Shakespeare, 155 rue Carreterie ☎04.90.27.38.50 (closed Mon); Maison de la Presse, 36 cours Jean-Jaurès; FNAC, 19 rue de la République.
Bus Local buses: TCRA, 1 av Lattre de Tassigny ☎04.32.74.18.32, Ⓦwww.tcra.fr. Long-distance buses: 5 av Montclar ☎04.90.82.07.35.
Car parks Guarded parking (24hr) at 16 bd St-Roch, near the train station, and at 1 rue P-Mérindol; free guarded parking with regular shuttles on l'Île de Piot.
Car rental ADA, 23 bd St-Ruf ☎04.90.86.18.89; Hertz, 2a av Montclar ☎04.90.14.26.90; Rent a Car, 130 av Pierre Sémard ☎04.90.88.08.02; Sixt, 3 av St-Ruf ☎04.90.86.06.61.
Currency exchange Chaix Conseil, 43 cours Jean-Jaurès (Mon–Fri 10.10am–1pm & 3–7pm, Sat 9.40am–12.30pm & 1.30–7pm); 24hr automatic exchange at CIC, 13 rue de la République and at Caixa Bank, 64 rue Joseph-Vernet.
Emergencies For doctor/ambulance call: ☎15 or Médecins de Garde ☎04.90.87.75.00. Hospital: Centre Hospitalier H-Duffaut, 305 rue Raoul-Follereau ☎04.90.80.33.33.
Internet *Cyber Highway*, 30 rue des Infirmières; *Webzone* 3 rue St Jean le Vieux/Place Pie.
Laundry 113 av St-Ruf; 27 rue Portail Magnanen; 66 pl des Corps-Saints; and 9 rue Chapeau-Rouge.
Markets Antiques: pl Crillon (Sat morning). Flea market: pl des Carmes (Sun morning). Books and records: cours Jean-Jaurès (July 1 to Aug 5 every Sat; rest of year first Sat of the month). Flowers: pl des Carmes (Sat morning). Food: in the covered halls on pl Pie (Tues–Sun till 1pm) and on rue rempart St-Michel, between portes St-Michel and Magnanen (Sat & Sun till 1pm).
Pharmacy Call police at bd St-Roch on ☎04.90.16.81.00 for addresses of 24-hour pharmacies.
Police Municipale 13 ter quai St Lazare ☎08.00.00.84.00.
Post office cours Président-Kennedy (Mon–Fri 8am–7pm, Sat 8am–noon).
Swimming pool Piscine Olympique des Arènes, Île de la Barthelasse (May–Sept 10am–7pm; €4). Do not attempt to swjm in the Rhône.
Taxis pl Pie; ☎04.90.82.20.20.
Trains ☎08.92.35.35.35 (€.034/min).

Villeneuve-lès-Avignon

VILLENEUVE-LÈS-AVIGNON (also spelled Villeneuve-lez-Avignon) rises up a rocky escarpment above the west bank of the river, looking down upon its older neighbour from behind far more convincing fortifications. In the thirteenth and fourteenth centuries, when its citadel and bridge defences were built, the Rhône at Avignon was the French border, not just with the papal enclave but with the county of Provence, whose allegiances shifted between the many different rivals of the king of France. Despite that, and the French king's habit of claiming land, and therefore taxes, in areas of Avignon that the river flooded, Villeneuve operated largely as a suburb to Avignon, with palatial residences constructed by the cardinals and a great monastery founded by Pope Innocent VI.

To this day Villeneuve is, strictly speaking, part of Languedoc not Provence, and would score better in the hierarchy of towns to visit were it further from Avignon, whose monuments it can almost match for colossal scale and impressiveness. In summer, at least, it benefits, providing venues for the festival, as well as accommodation overspill; it's certainly worth a day, whatever time of year you visit.

Arrival, information and accommodation

From the Avignon post office, buses #10 and #11 (direction Les Angles) run every thirty minutes direct to place Charles-David (Bellevue stop) in Villeneuve; after 7.40pm you'll have to take a taxi or walk the 3km. Villeneuve's **tourist office** is on place Charles-David (July daily 10am–7pm; Aug daily 8.45am–12.30pm & 2–6pm; Sept–June Mon–Sat 8.45am–12.30pm & 2–6pm;

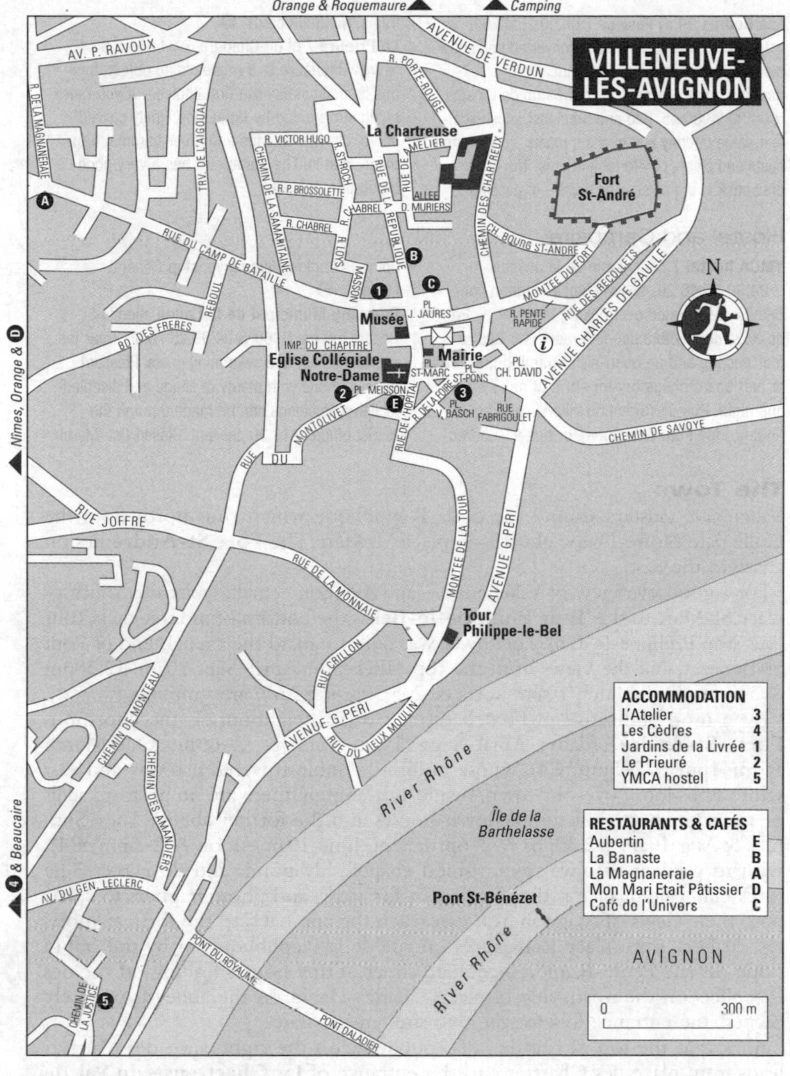

Ⓣ04.90.25.61.33, Ⓦwww.villeneuve-les-avignon.com), where there's also a food **market** on Thursday morning and a bric-a-brac market on Saturday morning. The tourist office can help with **accommodation**, as well as providing a list of furnished apartments available for short-term rental on their website. Outside the festival period you shouldn't have too many problems finding your own.

Hotels

L'Atelier 5 rue de la Foire Ⓣ04.90.25.01.84, Ⓔhotel-latelier@libertysurf.fr. A sixteenth-century house with huge open fireplaces and a walled garden. Excellent value. ❹

Les Cèdres 39 av Pasteur ⓣ04.90.25.43.92, ⓔlescedres.hotel@lemel.fr. A converted Louis XIV mansion with pool and restaurant. ❹
Jardins de la Livrée 4 bis rue Camp de Bataille ⓣ04.90.26.05.05. Bed and breakfast, plus excellent-value midday and evening meals; very friendly hosts and clean, comfortable rooms. The only drawback is the noise – all night – of passing trains. No credit cards. ❹
Le Prieuré 7 pl du Chapitre ⓣ04.90.15.90.15, ⓦwww.laprieure.fr. If money is no object, then this is indisputably the first choice – if you fancy being surrounded by tapestries, finely carved doors, old oak ceilings and other baronial trappings, that is. The restaurant has a very good reputation, too. ❽

Hostel and Campsite

YMCA hostel 7 bis chemin de la Justice ⓣ04.90.25.46.20, ⓦwww.ymca-avignon.com. Beautifully situated overlooking the river by Pont du Royaume, with balconied rooms for two to four people, and an open-air swimming pool. Full or half board obligatory for stays of more than one night. Bus #1 (direction Villeneuve–Les Angles, stop Pont d'Avignon), or bus #10 (direction Les Angles–Villeneuve, stop Général-Leclerc). ❸
Camping Municipal de la Laune chemin St-Honoré, off the D980 ⓣ04.90.25.76.06. Near the sports stadium and swimming pools. Pleasant three-star site with plenty of shade and disabled facilities. Bookings can be made through the tourist office. €11.30 per tent. Closed Oct–March.

The Town

Villeneuve clusters around rue de la République which runs north from the Collègiale Notre-Dame church on place St-Marc. The **Fort St-André** lies on a rise to the east.

For a good overview of Villeneuve – and Avignon – make your way south of place St-Marc to the **Tour Philippe-le-Bel** at the bottom of montée de la Tour (bus stop Philippe-le-Bel). The tower was built to guard the French end of Pont St-Bénézet, and the views from the top (Tues–Sun: April–Sept 10am–12.30pm & 3–7pm; Oct–March 10am–noon & 2–5.30pm; €1.60) are stunning.

Even more indicative of French distrust of its neighbours is the enormous **Fort St-André** (daily: April–Sept 10am–1pm & 2–6pm; Oct–March 10am–1pm & 2–5pm; €4), whose bulbous, double-towered gateway and vast white walls loom over the town. Inside, refreshingly, there are no postcard stalls or souvenir shops, just tumbledown houses and the former abbey (Tues–Sun: July & Aug 10am–12.30pm & 2–6pm; Sept–June 10am–noon & 2–5pm; €4), with its gardens of olive trees, ruined chapels, lily ponds and dovecotes. The fort's cliff-face terrace is the classic spot for artists and photographers to compose their views of Avignon. You can reach the approach to the fortress, montée du Fort, from place Jean-Jaurès on rue de la République, or by the "rapid slope" of rue Pente-Rapide, a cobbled street of tiny houses leading off rue des Recollets on the north side of place Charles-David. As the abbey is privately owned, the entrance fees for the two sites are separate.

Almost at the top of rue de la République, on the right, allée des Muriers leads from place des Chartreux to the entrance of **La Chartreuse du Val de Bénédiction** (daily: April–Sept 9am–6.30pm; Oct–March 9.30am–5.30pm; €5.50), one of the largest Charterhouses in France and founded by Innocent VI, the sixth of the Avignon popes, whose sharp profile is outlined on his tomb

Museums and monuments in Villeneuve

A **Passeport pour l'Art** (€6.86) gives you entry to the Fort St-André, Tour Philippe-le-Bel, La Chartreuse du Val de Bénédiction, the Collégiale Notre-Dame and its cloister and the Musée Pierre-de-Luxembourg. The ticket is available from each of the monuments and from the tourist office.

in the church. The buildings, which were sold off after the Revolution and gradually restored last century, are totally unembellished. With the exception of the Giovanetti frescoes in the chapel beside the refectory, all the paintings and treasures of the monastery have been dispersed, leaving a strong impression of the austerity of the strict practices of the Carthusian order. The only communication allowed was one hour of conversation a week plus the rather less congenial public confessions. Monks left the enclosure for one three-hour walk per week; within, their time was spent as much on manual labour as on prayer, and their diet was strictly vegetarian.

You are free to wander round unguided, through the three cloisters, the church, chapels, cells and communal spaces; there's little to see but plenty of atmosphere to be absorbed. It is one of the best venues in the Festival d'Avignon, along with the fourteenth-century **Église Collégiale Notre-Dame** and its cloister on place St-Marc (April to mid-June Tues–Sun 10am–12.30pm & 3–7pm; mid-June to Sept daily 10am–12.30pm & 3–7pm; Oct–Jan & March Tues–Sun 10am–noon & 2–5.30pm; free). The church is decorated with paintings by the Avignon School and with caring cupids tending Christ's hands and feet on the altar. However, Notre-Dame's most important treasure, a rare fourteenth-century smiling Madonna and Child made from a single tusk of ivory, supposedly carved by a convert from Islam, is now housed, along with many of the paintings from the Chartreuse, in the **Musée Pierre-de-Luxembourg** just to the north along rue de la République (same hours as Église Collégiale Notre-Dame; €3).

The museum's spacious layout includes a single room given over to the most stunning painting in the collection, *Le Couronnement de la Vierge*, painted in 1453 by Enguerrand Quarton as the altarpiece for the church in the Chartreuse. With fiercely contrasting colours of red, orange, gold, white and blue, the statuesque and symmetrical central figures of the coronation form a powerful and unambiguous subject. To either side of them, in true medieval style, the social hierarchy is defined, using a greater variety of form and colour. Along the bottom of the painting the scale of detail leaps several frames, with flames engulfing sinners, devils and their assistant beasts carrying away victims, walled towns with pin-size figures, and in the distance Mont St-Victoire and the cliffs of Estaque. No other painting in the collection matches Quarton's work and many are too obviously public relations pieces for their patrons, placing the pope, lord or bishop in question beside the Madonna or Christ.

Eating and drinking

Villeneuve's centre has a good choice of **eating** places for those who are ready to spend, but if it's affordable dining you're after, it's best to stick to Avignon. Cave St-Marc, just up to the right as you approach place St-Marc from place Charles-David (9.30am–12.15pm & 3.30–7.15pm; closed Wed & Sun), is a good place for **buying wine**.

Aubertin 1 rue de l'Hôpital ☎04.90.25.94.84. A sumptuous restaurant, serving a midday menu (€31; à la carte from €55) in the shade of the old arcades by the Collégiale Notre-Dame. Closed Sun & Mon out of season.

La Banaste 28 rue de la République ☎04.90.25.64.20. Good-value Provençal fare, but nicer indoors than on the noisy roadside. Menu at €21.50; closed Tues, Wed & Sat lunch out of season.

La Magnaneraie 37 rue Camp de Bataille ☎04.90.25.11.11. Excellent, upmarket restaurant, serving specialities such as courgette flowers stuffed with cream of mushrooms and a *gâteau d'agneau*. Menu for €40; à la carte over €70. Oct–April closed Sat lunch, Sun evening & Mon.

Mon Mari Etait Pâtissier 3 av Pasteur ☎04.90.25.52.79. A little way out from the town centre, and popular with the locals. Menus start at €17, and the desserts are particularly good. Closed Mon.

Café de l'Univers pl J-Jaurès. Ordinary café on a picturesque square, in the heart of Villeneuve. Open daily 6am–10pm.

La Petite Crau and La Montagnette

A short way downstream from Avignon, the Rhône reaches its confluence with the Durance. Between the two rivers and the Chaîne des Alpilles to the south is an area that was once a swampy wasteland. The rocky outcrop of **La Montagnette**, running parallel to the Rhône for 10km, and the hill at **Châteaurenard** were the only extensive bits of solid ground. However, the plain, known as **La Petite Crau**, has been steadily irrigated since Roman times, and today it is a richly cultivated area, with cherries and peaches as its main crops. It is crisscrossed with water channels, while row upon row of cypresses and poplars form windbreaks for the fruit trees. Villages in the area are few and far between, built on the scattered bases of rock, and many retain their medieval elements of fortified walls and churches and tangled narrow streets. It is this Provence that inspired **Frédéric Mistral** and Vincent Van Gogh.

If you have your own **transport**, La Petite Crau and La Montagnette can easily be reached as day-trips from Avignon, and from Tarascon or St-Rémy further south. By **bus**, it's more problematic, as services between the villages are sporadic. Buses from Avignon to Châteaurenard are most frequent, going on to Graveson and Maillane. Boulbon, Barbentane and Tarascon are served by buses to Nîmes. There are no trains.

Châteaurenard and Noves

CHÂTEAURENARD, just south of Avignon, is the main town in La Petite Crau and host to a massive wholesale fruit and vegetable market each Sunday; the produce is all locally grown and on market days the town is packed. Dominating the town's physical features are the two remaining towers of its Romanesque and Gothic medieval **castle** (July & Aug daily 10am–noon & 2.30–6.30pm; Sept–June Mon–Thurs & Sun 10am–noon & 3–5pm, Sat 3–5pm; €3.20), described by Frédéric Mistral as "twin horns on the forehead of a hill". Even if you're only passing through, it's worth taking the time to climb the castle's **Tour du Griffon** for the views across La Petite Crau to the Alpilles and La Montagnette. In a recess within the castle is engraved a 700-year-old troubadour poem, in Provençal, praising the beauty of the new building erected "by such a wise king".

Buses arrive on av Roger-Salengo, at the east end of which is the **tourist office** (July–Sept Mon–Sat 9am–noon & 3–7pm, Sun & public hols 10am–noon; Sept–June Mon–Sat 9am & 2–6pm; Ⓣ04.90.24.25.50, Ⓦwww.ville-chateaurenard.fr). For cheap and basic **accommodation** try *Le Central*, 27 cours Carnot (Ⓣ04.90.94.10.90, Ⓕ04.90.90.03.84; ❸); *Les Glycines*, 14 av Victor-Hugo (Ⓣ04.90.94.10.66, Ⓕ04.90.94.78.10; ❸); or, cheaper still, the somewhat dingy *Le Rustic*, place Victoire (Ⓣ04.90.94.13.36; ❶). *La Roquette* **campsite** on av J-Mermoz (Ⓣ & Ⓕ04.90.94.46.81; closed Nov–March;

Markets

If you're in La Petite Crau on a Friday, the **Marché Paysan in Graveson**, place du Marché (mid-May to Oct 4–8pm) is not to be missed, with *paysans* from La Grande and La Petite Crau, the Camargue and from across the Durance selling their goats' cheeses, honey and jams, rice, olives and olive oil, flowers and aromatic plants as well as fruit and vegetables picked the same morning.

The ordinary morning markets here are on Friday in **Graveson**, Thursday in **Maillane** and **Noves**, Sunday in **Châteaurenard**, Wednesday in **Barbentane**, and Tuesday in Rognonas, the village just across the Durance from Avignon.

€9.70 per tent) is small and inexpensive. For **food**, *La Buvette des Tours*, just below the castle, serves cheap salads, grills and pizzas on summer evenings (Thurs–Sun). Alternatively, the *Brasserie des Producteurs* at 4 rue R-Ginoux (Ⓣ04.90.94.04.61; closed Sun) serves menus from €11, while *Le Central* (see opposite) has a *plat du jour* for €8.50.

Five kilometres east of Châteaurenard, the little village of **NOVES** is typical of the area, with its fourteenth-century gateway. It is also where Laura, the subject of Petrarch's besotted sonnets, is reputed to have lived. If you fancy splashing out on a luxury stay, the *Auberge de Noves*, just outside Noves on the Châteaurenard road (Ⓣ04.90.24.28.28, Ⓦwww.aubergedenoves.com; ❾), is a seriously expensive hotel-restaurant in a beautiful farmhouse with exquisite furnishings and impeccable service. Its restaurant serves such delicacies as oysters cooked in Châteauneuf-du-Pape and duck en croûte with herbs and acacia honey (weekday menu €38.50; €47 menu with wine, otherwise over €66). For more basic comforts, Noves' **campsite** *Le Pilon d'Agel*, on the rte de Mollégès (Ⓣ04.90.95.16.23; closed Oct–March; €14), offers a pool, disabled facilities and horses to hire.

Maillane and La Montagnette

The poet Frédéric Mistral was born in **MAILLANE** in 1830 and buried there in 1914. Primarily responsible for the early twentieth-century revival of all things Provençal, he won the Nobel Prize for Literature, a feat no other writer of a minority language has ever achieved. The house that he built and lived in from 1876 till the end of his life has been preserved intact as the **Museon Mistral**, 11 rue Lamartine (daily except Mon: April–Sept 9.30–11.30am & 2.30–6.30pm; Oct–March 10–11.30am & 2–4.30pm; €3.50).

La Petite Crau was Mistral's "sacred triangle", and its customs and legends were very often his primary source of inspiration. Black Madonnas and various saints fêted in these villages were, and often still are, bestowed with the power to bring rain or cure diseases. In his memoirs Mistral describes the procession of St Anthime from **Graveson**, just north of Maillane, to **LA MONTAGNETTE**, where on reaching the abbey church of **St-Michel-de-Frigolet**, the people spread out a feast on the perfumed grass and knocked back bottles of local wine for the rest of the day. If it hadn't rained by the time they reached home, they punished the saint by dipping him three times in a ditch.

The name of the abbey derives from *ferigoulo*, Provençal for thyme, which grows profusely in these hills, hence the perfumed grass of the feast. The thyme is also used to make a liqueur, *Le Frigolet*, which can be bought at the end of a guided tour of the **abbey church** and **cloisters** (Sun & hols 4pm; €4). Mistral went to school in these buildings before they were returned to ecclesiastical use in the mid-nineteenth century. The highlight of the visit is the series of fourteen paintings on the *Mysteries of the Virgin Mary* by Mignard in the main church, though you may find the cloisters more spiritually inspiring.

The valleys that cut through the scrubbed white rock of La Montagnette are shaded by olive, almond and apricot trees, oaks and pines. The heights never extend above 200m, and the smell of thyme is omnipresent; easy and exhilarating walking country.

Boulbon and Barbentane

One footpath from St-Michel-de-Frigolet takes you over the ridge and, after 5km or so, down to **BOULBON**. A strategic site overlooking the Rhône, Boulbon was heavily fortified in the Middle Ages, and today the ruins of its

The Fête de Saint-Éloi

Boulbon celebrates the **Fête de Saint-Éloi** on the last Sunday of August. This involves chariots drawn by teams of horses in Saracen harness doing the rounds of the village, and much drinking by all the villagers. Elsewhere, notably in Graveson, Châteaurenard and Maillane, this saint, whose role is protector of beasts of burden, is celebrated on the penultimate Sunday of July.

enormous fortress, built half within and half above a rocky escarpment, look like some picture-book crusader castle. Here, on the first day of June, the men gather with a bottle of wine apiece and process to St-Marcellin chapel in the cemetery, one of Boulbon's six Romanesque places of worship. At the end of the service the wine is blessed, the bottles are lifted first in homage to the *Seigneur* and then to the lips. But some of the wine must remain undrunk, to be corked and preserved as an antidote to illness and misfortune.

Eight kilometres from Boulbon, at the northern edge of La Montagnette in **BARBENTANE**, the fourteenth-century **Tour Anglica** keeps watch on the confluence of the Rhône and Durance. The town has two medieval gateways and a beautifully arcaded Renaissance building, the **Maison des Chevaliers**, plus a much more recent **Château** (guided tours July–Sept daily 10am–noon & 2–6pm; April–June & Oct closed Wed; Nov & Feb–March Sun only; €6), designed for grandeur rather than defence. This is a seventeenth-century ducal residence with gorgeous grey and white Tuscan marble floors, and all the vases, painted ceilings, chandeliers and delicate antique furniture that you would expect of a house still owned by generations of the same family of aristocrats. The Italianate gardens are the highlight.

For **hotel** accommodation in Barbentane, you can choose from the rudimentary comforts of *Hôtel St-Jean*, 1 le Cours (Ⓣ & Ⓕ04.90.95.50.44; ❶), or the more comfortable *Castel Mouisson*, quartier Castel Mouisson (Ⓣ04.90.95.51.17, Ⓦwww.hotel-castelmouisson.com; ❸; closed mid-Oct to mid-March), with good facilities and a pleasant garden and pool. There are two **restaurants** worth going out of your way for: the hotel-restaurant *Auberge de Noves* (see p.87); and *L'Oustalet Maianen* in Maillane (Ⓣ04.90.95.76.17; closed Mon, Sun eve & mid-Oct to March), with an excellent-value midweek menu for €19.50, and a wonderful four-course menu for €28.50.

St-Rémy-de-Provence and around

The scenery of La Petite Crau changes abruptly with the eruption of the **Chaîne des Alpilles**, whose peaks look like the surf of a wave about to engulf the plain. At the northern base of the Alpilles nestles **ST-RÉMY-DE-PROVENCE**, a dreamy place where Van Gogh sought psychiatric help and painted some of his most lyrical works. St-Rémy is a beautiful spot, as unspoilt as the villages around, and its old town (the Vieille Ville) is contained within a circle of boulevards no more than half a kilometre in diameter. Outside this ring, the modern town is sparingly laid out, so you don't have to plough your way through dense developments before you reach the heart of the city. Outside the old town, all the attractions lie to the south: the **Roman arch**, the hospital of **St-Paul-de-Mausole** and the **Mas de la Pyramide** farmhouse in the old Roman quarries.

St-Rémy is ideally situated for exploration of the hills or, indeed, of La Petite Crau, and easy to get to by bus. A short way south are the remains of the ancient city of **Glanum**, and along the ridge of the Alpilles is the medieval stronghold of **Les Baux**, a place dedicated to luxury tourism; both are difficult to get to by public transport.

Arrival, information and accommodation

Arriving by **bus**, you'll be dropped at **place de la République**, the main square abutting the Vieille Ville to the west. The **tourist office** (June–Sept Mon–Sat 9am–noon & 2–7pm, Sun 9am–noon; Oct–May Mon–Sat 9am–noon & 2–6pm; ⓣ04.90.92.05.22, ⓦwww.saintremy-de-provence.com) is just south of the centre on place Jean-Jaurès, between av Pasteur and av Durand-Maillane and reached by following bd Marceau until it becomes av Durand-Maillane; it provides excellent free guides on **cycling** and **walking** routes in and around the Alpilles and has addresses for hiring **horses** and for **gliding** at a club that claims to hold the world record for the longest flight. If you want to rent a **bike**, try Telecycles (ⓣ04.90.92.83.15). It's difficult to get to Glanum or Les Baux except by foot or taxi (ⓣ06.07.02.25.64 or 06.09.31.50.38). The *Maison de la Presse* opposite *La Brasserie des Alpilles* stocks some **English-language newspapers** and paperbacks.

The town has a fairly wide choice of **accommodation**, though real bargains are quite hard to come by. You may prefer to use one of the three campsites close by.

Hotels

Hôtel des Antiques 15 av Pasteur ⓣ04.90.92.03.02, ⓕ04.90.92.50.40. A nineteenth-century mansion close to the tourist office with huge grounds, pools and wonderfully aristocratic furnishings in the dining room and salons. Closed mid-Oct–March. ❻

Les Arts–La Palette above the *Café des Arts* at 30 bd Victor-Hugo ⓣ04.90.92.08.50, ⓕ04.90.92.55.09. An excellent location and very friendly. A good budget choice. Closed Jan & Feb. ❷

Canto Cigalo chemin de Canto Cigalo ⓣ04.90.92.14.28, ⓔcantocigalo@wanadoo.fr. By the canal to the southeast of the old town, this quiet and comfortable hotel is in a secluded spot with a large garden. ❸

Le Castellet des Alpilles 6 pl Mireille ⓣ04.90.92.07.21, ⓦwww.castelet-alpilles.com. South of the old town, past the tourist office; small and friendly, and some rooms with great views. Closed mid-Jan to mid-Feb. ❹

Hostellerie le Chalet Fleuri 15 av Frédéric Mistral ⓣ04.90.92.03.62, ⓕ04.90.92.60.28. An old-fashioned boarding house with recently renovated rooms: breakfast is served in the garden. Closed Dec–Feb. ❸

Nostradamus 3 av Taillandier ⓣ04.90.92.13.23, ⓕ04.90.92.49.54. Studios for two to the north of the old town by the municipal pool. Not particularly atmospheric, but cheap. ❷

Villa Glanum 46 av Vincent-van-Gogh ⓣ04.90.92.03.59, ⓔvilla.glanum@wanadoo.fr. Next door to the archeological site; pleasant, not too overpriced and has a swimming pool. Most rooms with disabled facilities. Half board only. Closed mid-Nov to Easter. ❹

Ville Verte av Fauconnet/pl de la République ⓣ04.90.92.06.14, ⓦwww.hotel-villeverte.com. Central location with a garden and pool and seven rooms with disabled facilities. It also organizes walking, climbing and cycling trips. ❸

Campsites

Le Mas de Nicolas av Plaisance du Touch ⓣ04.90.92.27.05, ⓕ04.90.92.36.83. A four-star municipal site, with its own pool, 2km along the rte de Mollèges to the northeast. Closed Nov–Easter. €17 per tent.

Monplaisir chemin Monplaisir ⓣ04.90.92.22.70, ⓦwww.camping-monplaisir.fr. Slightly cheaper, two-star campsite, 1km to the north along the route de Maillane. Closed Nov–Feb. €13.50 per tent.

Pegomas rte de Noves ⓣ04.90.92.01.21, ⓕ04.90.92.56.17. Three-star, with a pool, 1km east on the road to Cavaillon. Closed Nov–Feb. €15 per tent.

The Town

St-Rémy's compact centre makes it a pleasant place for relaxed strolling round the picturesque streets and their stylish shops, galleries and restaurants. Rue Carnot cuts through the old town from bd Mirabeau to bd Marceau to place Favier, where the **Musée des Alpilles** and the **Musée Archéologique** can be found.

The impressive archeological sites of **Glanum** and **Les Antiques** along with St-Rémy's other attractions, including St-Paul-de-Mausole, the psychiatric hospital whose most famous former patient is **Van Gogh**, lie south of the old town along av Pasteur, which becomes av Vincent-van-Gogh after the canal.

The Vieille Ville

The **Vieille Ville** is encircled by boulevards Marceau, Gambetta, Mirabeau and Victor-Hugo. To explore the old town take any of the streets leading off these boulevards and start wandering up alleyways and through immaculate leafy squares. From place de la République, on av de la Résistance, you'll pass the town's main church, the **Collégiale St-Martin**, a Neoclassical lump of a building of interest only for its renowned organ, painted in a surreal lime-green (recitals every Sat from July to Sept at 5pm). The route from **rue du Parage** off bd Gambetta is particularly appealing with its central stream of clear water. Several ancient stately residences line its route as the street meanders up to the fountained **place Favier**, where you'll find St-Rémy's two main museums.

For an introduction to the region, a good first visit would be to the **Musée des Alpilles** on place Favier, housed in the Hôtel Mistral de Mondragon, a Renaissance mansion with a romantic interior courtyard (daily: July & Aug 10am–noon & 2–7pm; April–June & Sept–Oct 10am–noon & 2–6pm; Nov & Dec 10am–noon & 2–5pm; €2.75). Currently closed for renovation but scheduled to reopen in 2004, the museum features interesting displays on folklore, festivities and traditional crafts, plus intriguing local landscapes, some creepy portraits by Marshall Pétain's first wife and souvenirs of local boy Nostradamus.

The collection in the neighbouring **Musée Archéologique** housed in the fifteenth-century Hôtel de Sade on rue du Parage (daily: Feb, March & Oct–Dec 9am–noon & 2–5pm; April–Sept 9am–noon & 2–6pm; €2.50, €6 with entry to Glanum), comes from the archeological digs at the Greco-Roman town of Glanum (see p.92). Its primary function is for categorization of the finds, and the hour or so which it takes to wander around the museum may be a bit much for the casual visitor. Nevertheless, there are some stunning pieces, in particular the well-coiffeured heads of two women, possibly Livia and Octavia, wife and sister of Augustus.

St-Rémy's fêtes

The best time to visit St-Rémy is for the **Fête de Transhumance**, on Whit Monday, when a two-thousand-strong flock of sheep, accompanied by goats, rams and donkeys, does a tour of the town before being packed off to the Alps for the summer. There's also the **Carreto Ramado** on August 15, a harvest thanksgiving procession in which the religious or secular symbolism of the floats reveals the political colour of the various village councils. Other festivals include a pagan rather than workers' **Mayday** celebration, with donkey-drawn floral floats on which people play fifes and tambourines, while, on July 14, August 15 and the fourth Sunday in September, the intrepid local youth attempt to set loose six **bulls** that are herded round the town by their mounted chaperons.

Nostradamus

Born in St-Rémy in 1503, **Michel de Notredame** was educated as a physician and first received recognition for his innovative treatment of plague victims. It wasn't until the latter part of his life that his interest in astrology and the occult led to the publication of **The Prophecies of Michel Nostradamus**, a collection of 942 prophetic quatrains. Already well known, Nostradamus used a deliberately obscure and cryptic writing style for fear that he would be persecuted by the authorities were they to completely understand his predictions. The end result was some extremely ambiguous French verse, which has since been the subject of numerous forgeries, urban legends and some very liberal interpretations, to say the least. Today he is most often given credit for predicting the rise of Napoleon and Hitler, and major catastrophic events such as the Great Fire of London in 1666. While Nostradamus may or may not have been able to accurately foresee the future, his success as a writer remains undisputed: the collection of prophecies, now known as *Centuries*, has been in print continuously since its first publication in 1551.

To the east of place Favier, rue Millaud leads into **rue Hoche** where a fountain topped by a bust marks the house where **Nostradamus** was born on December 14, 1503. Only the facade of the house is contemporary with the futuristic savant, and it's not open to visitors. Heading south from here brings you to the eighteenth-century Hôtel d'Estrine, at 8 rue L'Estrine, now home of the **Centre d'Art Présence Van Gogh**. The centre hosts contemporary art exhibitions and has a permanent exhibition of Van Gogh reproductions and extracts from letters plus an audiovisual presentation on the painter (April–Dec Tues–Sun 10.30am–12.30pm & 2.30–6.30pm; €3.20). A wide selection of Van Gogh books, prints and postcards is available from the shop.

There are many **art galleries** and boutiques scattered throughout St-Rémy, of which Le Grand Magasin, 24 rue de la Commune (summer daily 10am–12.30pm & 2.30–7pm; winter closed Mon), is one of the most interesting: it combines contemporary works of art with jewellery, accessories and household objects of a stylish and original nature.

South of the Vieille Ville

Outside the old town enclosure, a short way south of the tourist office on rue Jean-de-Nostredame, is the beautiful Romanesque **chapel of Notre-Dame-de-Pitié** (daily: July & Aug 11am–1pm & 3–7pm; March–June & Sept–Dec 2–6pm; free), which exhibits the art of the twentieth-century Greek painter, Mario Prassinos, who settled in the village of Eygalières, near St-Rémy. Tree forms, a favourite motif of his work, become a powerful graphic language in the series of oil paintings created for the chapel, *Les Peintures du Supplice*, provoked by Prassinos' horror of torture.

If you keep heading south, following av Vincent-van-Gogh, you'll come to **Les Antiques**, a triumphal arch celebrating the Roman conquest of Marseille and a mausoleum thought to commemorate two grandsons of Augustus. Save for a certain amount of weather erosion, the mausoleum is perfectly intact. The arch is less so, but both display intricate patterning and a typically Roman sense of proportion. Les Antiques would have been a familiar sight to **Vincent van Gogh**, who, in 1889, requested that he be put away for several months. The hospital chosen by his friends was in the old monastery **St-Paul-de-Mausole**, a hundred yards or so east of Les Antiques, which remains a psychiatric clinic today. Although the regime was more prison than hospital, Van Gogh was allowed to wander out around the Alpilles and painted prolifically during his twelve-month stay. The *Champs d'Oliviers*, *Le Faucher*, *Le Champ Clôturé* and *La Promenade du Soir* are among the 150 canvases of this period. The church and cloisters can be visited (April–Oct daily 9.30am–7pm; €3); take av Edgar-Leroy or allée St-Paul from av Vincent-van-Gogh, go past the main entrance of the clinic and into the gateway on the left at the end of the wall.

Heading east along chemin des Carrières from the hospital you'll see signs to the right for the **Mas de la Pyramide** (daily: June–Aug 9am–noon & 2–7pm; Sept–May 9am–noon & 2–5pm; worth waiting if there's no immediate answer to the bell at the gate; €4), an old troglodyte farm in the Roman quarries of Glanum with a field of lavender and a cherry orchard surrounded by cavernous openings into the rock filled with ancient farm equipment and rusting bicycles. Standing in the centre of the lavender field is a twenty-metre slice of rock – the pyramid that gives the farm its name – revealing the depth of the ancient quarrying works. The farmhouse is part medieval, part Gallo-Roman and has some fascinating pictures of the owner's family who have lived here for generations.

Glanum

One of the most impressive ancient settlements in France, **GLANUM**, 500m south of Les Antiques, was dug out from the alluvial deposits at the foot of the Alpilles (daily: April–Sept 9am–7pm; Oct–March 9am–noon & 2–5pm; €5.50, or €6 with entry to the Musée Archéologique). The site was originally a Neolithic homestead until the Gallo-Greeks, probably from Massalia (Marseille), built a city here between the second and first centuries BC. The Gallo-Romans constructed yet another town here from the end of the first century BC to the third century AD.

Glanum can be very difficult to get to grips with. Not only were the later buildings moulded on to the earlier ones, but the fashion at the time of Christ was for a Hellenistic style. You can distinguish the Greek levels from the Roman most easily by the stones: the earlier civilization used massive hewn rocks while the Romans preferred smaller, more accurately shaped stones. The leaflet at the admission desk is helpful, as are the attendants if your French is good enough.

Where the site narrows in the ravine at the southern end you'll find a Grecian edifice around a **spring**, the feature that made this location so desirable. Steps lead down to a pool, with a slab above for the libations of those too sick to descend. An inscription records that Agrippa was responsible for restoring it in 27 BC and for dedicating it to Valetudo, the Roman goddess of health. But **altars** to Hercules are still in evidence, while up the hill to the west are traces of a prehistoric settlement which also depended on this spring. The Gallo-Romans directed the water through canals to heat houses and, of course, to the **baths** that lie near the entrance to the site. There are superb sculptures on the Roman **Temples Geminées** (twin temples), as well as fragments of mosaics, fountains of both periods, and first-storey walls and columns.

Eating and entertainment

Throughout the year, you'll find plenty of **brasseries** and **restaurants** open in and around old St-Rémy. There are a few good options on rue Carnot (leading from bd Victor-Hugo west through the old town to bd Marceau), including *Le Monocle* at no. 48 which, though not brilliant, maintains an eccentric atmosphere and has three menus for under €15; *La Gousse d'Ail* at no. 25

(☎04.90.92.16.87; closed for lunch Thurs & Sat; from €14.50), which hosts live jazz on Thursday nights; and *La Maison Jaune* at no. 15 (☎04.90.92.56.14; closed Mon & Sun evening in winter, Mon & Tues in summer), with polenta and pigeon roasted in Baux wines on the €52 menu, and an equally tasty €28 lunchtime menu. Alternatively, the trendy new *Xa*, 24 bd Mirabeau (☎04.90.92.41.23; closed Weds and Nov–March; €23 menu), serves excellent food, while *Lou Planet*, at 7 place Favier, is a scenic spot to dine on crêpes, and *Le Bistrot des Alpilles*, 15 bd Mirabeau (☎04.90.92.09.17; open till midnight; closed Sun), is a popular brasserie for *gigot d'agneau* and *tarte au citron* (€15 midday menu, evening €28). Lastly, try *Le Jardin de Frédéric*, 8 bd Gambetta (☎04.90.92.27.76; closed Wed & Thurs lunch), which has a €16 midday menu, and usually offers some interesting dishes.

For **café lounging** head for the *Café des Arts*, 30 bd Victor-Hugo (open till 12.30am; closed Tues & Feb), where the works of local painters are exhibited. Next door, the Librarie des Arts is a good bookshop selling lovely picture books on the region. If you're after **picnic fare**, do your shopping at the Wednesday morning **market** on the pedestrian streets of the old town or at the Saturday market in place de la Mairie. The *boulangerie* at 7 rue Carnot sells the special *épis de St-Rémy*, spiky baguettes. In season you'll see and smell great bunches of basil and marjoram which are grown in abundance around St-Rémy; aromatic oils are another speciality of the town, which are produced and sold at *Chez Florame*, at 34 bd Mirabeau (Easter–Sept daily 10am–12.30pm & 2.30–7pm; Oct–Easter closed Sun).

The Ciné Palace on av Fauconnet sometimes screens undubbed English-language films (programme from the tourist office), but if you fancy something a little more lively, try the two **discos**, *La Haute Galine*, quartier de la Galine (☎04.90.92.00.03), and *La Forge*, av de la Libération (☎04.90.92.31.52), or the *Cocktail Clun* **bar** on rue Roger-Salengro (running north from place de la République), which has a regular karaoke night.

Les Baux

At the top of the Alpilles ridge, 10km southwest of St-Rémy, lies the distinctly unreal fortified village of **LES BAUX**. Unreal partly because the ruins of the eleventh-century citadel are hard to distinguish from the edge of the plateau whose rock is both foundation and part of the structure. And unreal, too, because this Ville Morte (Dead City) and a vast area of the plateau around it are accessible only via a turnstile from the living village below, which remains a too-perfect collection of sixteenth- and seventeenth-century churches, chapels and mansions.

Les Baux once lived off the power and wealth of its medieval lords, who owed allegiance to none. When the dynasty died out at the end of the fourteenth century, the town, which had once numbered six thousand inhabitants, passed to the counts of Provence and then to the kings of France, who in 1632, razed the feudal citadel to the ground and fined the population into penury. From that date until the nineteenth century both citadel and village were inhabited almost exclusively by bats and crows, until the discovery of bauxite (the aluminium ore takes its name from Les Baux) in the neighbouring hills, which gradually brought back some life to the village. Today tourism is the most important industry, with around 1.5 million visitors a year descending on the population of four hundred.

△ Cathedrale des Images, Val d'Enfer

The village

The lived-in village has a great many beautiful buildings, among them those housing its half-a-dozen or so museums. One of the best museums is the **Musée Yves Brayer** in the Hôtel des Porcelets (mid-Feb to March & Oct–Dec daily except Tues 10am–12.30pm & 2–5.30pm; April–Sept daily 10am–12.30pm & 2–6.30pm; €4), showing the paintings of the twentieth-century figurative artist whose work also adorns the seventeenth-century **Chapelle des Pénitents Blancs** on place de l'Église. Changing exhibitions of the work of contemporary Provençal artists are displayed in the **Hôtel de Manville** (hours vary, so check with the tourist office; free). The museum of the **Fondation Louis Jou**, in the fifteenth-century Hôtel Jean de Brion (April–Oct Fri–Mon 2–5pm; Nov–March by reservation only, ⓣ04.90.54.34.17; €3), contains the presses, wood lettering blocks and hand-printed books of the master typographer whose workshop opposite is still used for manual printing (products on sale in the boutique). The **Musée des Santons** in the old hôtel de ville (daily 8am–7pm; free) displays traditional Provençal nativity figures.

Follow the signs to the château for the entrance to the **Citadelle de la Ville Morte**, the main reason for coming to Les Baux (daily: Jan & Feb 9am–5pm; March–June, Sept & Oct 9am–7.30pm; July & Aug 9am–9.30pm; Nov & Dec 9am–6pm; €6.50), where there are several more museums amid the ruins. The **Musée d'Histoire des Baux** in the vaulted space of Tour de Brau has a collection of archeological remains and models to illustrate the village's history from medieval splendour to bauxite works. The most impressive ruins are those of the feudal castle demolished on Richelieu's orders; there's also the partially restored **Chapelle Castrale** and the **Tour Sarrasine**, the cemetery, ruined houses half carved out of the rocky escarpment, and some spectacular views, the best of which is out across La Grande Crau from beside the statue of the Provençal poet Charloun Riev at the southern edge of the plateau.

Practicalities

The **tourist office** is at the beginning of La Grande Rue (daily: July & Aug 9am–7pm; Sept–June 9am–6pm; ⓣ04.90.54.34.39, ⓦwww.lesbauxdeprovence.com). You have to park – and pay – before entering the village and, as you'll soon discover, nothing in Les Baux comes cheap, least of all **accommodation**. There is just one moderately priced option, the *Hostellerie de la Reine Jeanne* (ⓣ04.90.54.32.06, ⓕ04.90.54.32.33; ❸; closed mid-Nov to mid-Feb), by the entrance to the village, which has very friendly staff and good **food** with menus starting from €20. If you feel like treating yourself, try the beautiful hotel-restaurant *Oustau de Baumanière* (ⓣ04.90.54.33.07, ⓦwww.oustaudebaumaniere.com; ❾), just west of Les Baux on the road to the Val d'Enfer, which is spectacularly situated and simply luxurious. For less sumptuous fare, there are a couple of places selling crêpes, pizzas and other **snacks** along rue du Château.

The Val d'Enfer

Within walking distance of Les Baux, along the D27 leading north, is the valley of quarried and eroded rocks that has been named the **Val d'Enfer** (Valley of Hell). Dante, it is thought, came here while staying at Arles, and took his inspiration for the nine circles of the *Inferno*. Jean Cocteau used the old bauxite quarries and the contorted rocks for his film *Le Testament d'Orphée*, some of which was filmed in Les Baux itself.

More recently, the very same quarries have been turned into an audiovisual experience under the title of the **Cathédrale des Images** (mid-Feb to Dec daily; €7), signposted to the right downhill from Les Baux's car park. The projection is continuous, so you don't have to wait to go in. You are surrounded by images projected all over the floor, the ceilings and the walls of the vast rectangular caverns, and by music that resonates strangely in the captured space. The content of the show, which changes yearly, doesn't really matter; it is just an extraordinary sensation, wandering on and through these changing shapes and colours. As an inventive use for an erstwhile worksite it can't be bettered.

Tarascon and Beaucaire

To the south of La Montagnette, the castles of **Beaucaire** and **Tarascon** face each other across the Rhône, the former in Languedoc on the west bank, the latter on the Provence side. Although the castles are regarded as classics, neither of the towns set below them is wildly alluring, but both are useful bases for excursions into Languedoc, with Nîmes and the Pont du Gard close at hand. Tarascon has one of the most famous Provençal carnivals, based on an amphibious monster known as the *Tarasque*, and is home to the **Souleïado** textile company. Near Beaucaire a reconstructed **Roman winery** has been put back to work.

Arrival, information and accommodation

Both towns are served by Tarascon's **train** station and have good **bus** links with Avignon, Arles, St-Rémy and Nîmes. The **gare SNCF** is south of Tarascon's centre on bd Gustave-Desplaces (ⓣ08.36.35.35.35). **Buses** arrive at the *Café des Fleurs* stop, in front of the station. Opposite the station, on the other side of bd Gustave-Desplaces, is a **car park**, beyond which cours Aristide-Briand leads north to the road bridge across the Rhône. Tarascon's **tourist office** is at 59 rue des Halles (July & Aug Mon–Fri 9am–noon & 2–7pm, Sat 9am–noon & 2–6pm, Sun 9.30am–12.30pm; Sept–June Mon–Fri 9am–noon & 2–6pm, Sat 9am–noon & 2–5pm, Sun 9.30am–12.30pm; ⓣ04.90.91.03.52, ⓦwww.tarascon.org), which leads off cours Aristide-Briand. You can **rent bikes** in Tarascon at *Cycles Christophe*, 66 boulevard Itam (ⓣ04.90.91.25.85), and **boats** in Beaucaire at very reasonable prices, from the Capitainerie du Port, on cours Sadi-Carnot on the south side of the canal, opposite the tourist office.

Beaucaire is bounded to the south by the Canal du Rhône which provides a pleasure port for the town before joining the river just below the bridge to Tarascon. Beaucaire's **tourist office** is at 24 cours Gambetta, overlooking the canal 300m from the bridge (April–June, Aug & Sept Mon–Fri 8.45am–12.30pm & 2–7pm, Sat 9.30am–12.30pm & 3–6pm: July Mon–Fri 8.45am–12.30pm & 2–7pm, Sat 9.30am–12.30pm & 3–6pm, Sun 9.30am–12.30pm; Oct–March Mon–Fri 8.45am–12.30pm & 2–7pm; ⓣ04.66.59.26.57, ⓦwww.ot-beaucaire.fr).

Tarascon has more **accommodation** to offer than Beaucaire, including a youth hostel, but it should be easy to find a room in either town, and as the centre of Beaucaire is just a kilometre's walk away from that of Tarascon, across the bridge, it doesn't really matter which of the two you choose.

Hotels

Le Castel 16 bd Victor-Hugo, Tarascon ⓣ04.90.43.55.90, ⓔle.castel.tarascon@wanadoo.fr. The cheapest hotel in town, with very friendly owners; all the basic rooms have TVs. ❶

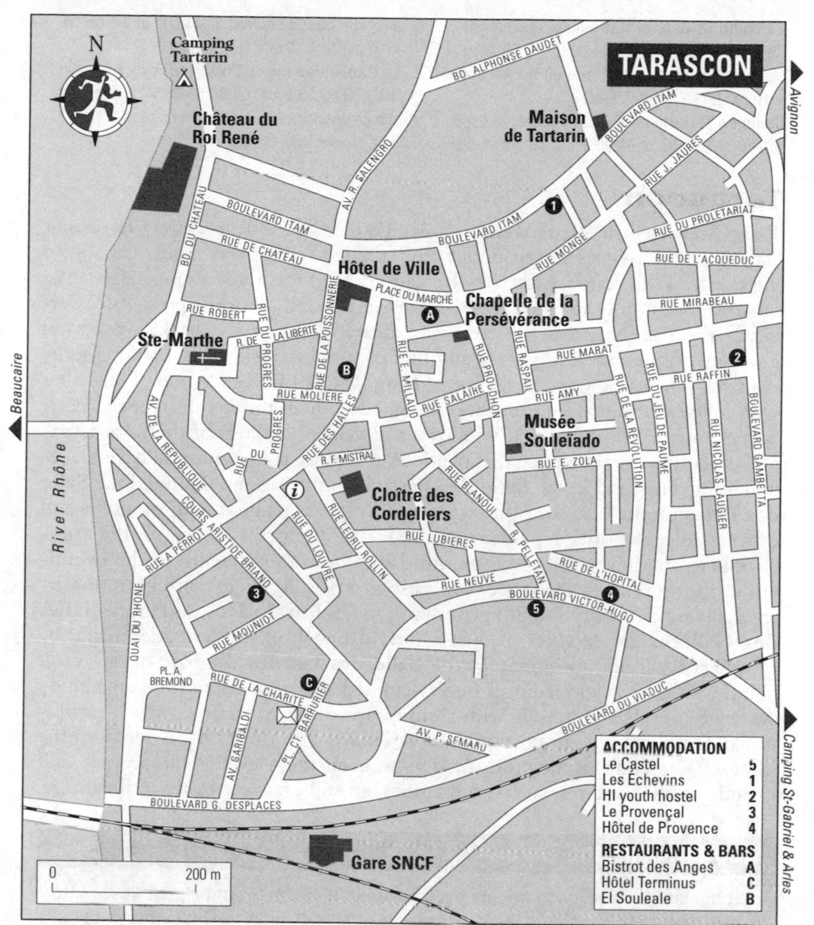

Les Échevins 26 bd Itam, Tarascon ☎04.90.91.01.70, ✉echevins@aol.com. Reasonable rooms in a handsome town house. Closed Nov–April. ❹

Napoléon 4 pl Frédéric-Mistral, Beaucaire ☎04.66.59.05.17. A good budget choice by the river with very cheap singles. Closed Mon. ❷

Le Provençal 12 cours A-Briand, Tarascon ☎04.90.91.11.41, ✉leprovencalmbc@wanadoo.fr. Family-run hotel with paper-thin walls, but each room has en-suite facilities. Good location. ❷

Hôtel de Provence 7 bd Victor-Hugo, Tarascon ☎04.90.91.06.43, ✉hoteldeprovence@wanadoo.fr. The best choice in Tarascon, with spacious air-conditioned rooms and balconies for breakfasting. Closed Fri out of season. ❹

Robinson rte de Remoulins, Beaucaire ☎04.66.59.21.32, ⓦwww.hotel-robinson.com. Two kilometres north of Beaucaire on the D986, with a pool and tennis court, and a warm welcome. ❹

Hostels and campsites

HI youth hostel 31 bd Gambetta, Tarascon ☎04.90.91.04.08, ✉tarascon@fuaj.org. About 850m northeast of the gare SNCF. Well-maintained town house with 65 dormitory beds; 11pm curfew. €11.30 per person, breakfast (€3.20) is compulsory on the first night. Closed mid-Dec to Feb.

Camping St-Gabriel Mas Ginoux, quartier St-Gabriel, Tarascon ⓣ & ⓕ04.90.91.19.83. A two-star site 5km southeast of town off the Arles road. €10 per tent. Closed Oct–May.

Camping Tartarin rte de Vallabrègues, Tarascon ⓣ04.90.91.01.46, ⓕ04.90.91.10.70. A two-star site right beside the river, just north of the castle. €10 per tent. Closed Nov to April.

Le Rhodanien rue du Champ de Foire, Beaucaire ⓣ04.66.59.25.50, ⓕ04.66.59.68.51. A three-star site centrally located on the riverbank. €13 per tent. Closed Nov–March.

Tarascon

The **Château du Roi René** (daily: Easter–Sept 10am–7pm; Oct–Easter 9am–noon & 2–5pm; closed public hols; guided tours every hour; €5.50), to the north of the centre, is the obvious site to head for, a vast impregnable mass of stone, beautifully restored to its defensive fifteenth-century pose. Its towers facing the enemy across the river are square, those at the back round, and nowhere on the exterior is there any hint of softness. Inside, however, is another matter. The castle was a residence of King René of Provence, and of his father who initiated the building, and was designed with all the luxury that the period permitted. The mullioned windows and vaulted ceilings of the royal apartments and the spiral staircase that overlook the **cour d'honneur** all have graceful Gothic lines, and in the **Salle des Festins** on the ground floor and the **Salle des Fêtes** on the first floor the wooden ceilings are painted with monsters and other medieval motifs. Tapestries of a later date (François I) hang in the king's chambers, and in several rooms graffiti dating from the fifteenth to the twentieth century testify to the castle's long use as a prison. There's an inscription by an eighteenth-century English prisoner in the **Salon du Roi**, and in the **Salles des Gallères** are carvings of boats, some dating from the crusades, made by prisoners awaiting judgement. In the **Salle des Gardes** the base of one vault column shows a man reading a book, sculpted at a time when such an activity was truly novel. A visit ends with a climb up to the **roof**, from which revolutionaries and counter-revolutionaries were thrown in the 1790s. Aside from the sight of Tarascon's paper mill just downstream, the views are impressive and include, to the west, the far less substantial but still dramatic castle of Beaucaire.

The Tarasque and Tartarin

On the last full weekend of June, the **Tarasque**, a mythical 6m-long creature with glaring eyes and shark-size teeth, storms the streets of Tarascon in the fashion of a Chinese dragon, its tail swishing back and forth to the screaming delight of all the children. It is said to have been tamed by Saint Martha after a long history of clambering out of the Rhône, gobbling people and destroying the ditches and dams of the Camargue with its long crocodile-like tail. The monster serves as a reminder of natural catastrophe, in particular floods, kept at bay in this region by the never totally reliable drainage ditches and walls.

Also celebrated at the same time is another local legend, that of **Tartarin**, a mid-nineteenth-century literary character, created by Alphonse Daudet who came from this part of Provence. For a long time the writer dared not set foot in the city, thanks to the garrulous, bragging caricature of a Provençal petty bourgeois he had invented. Tartarin makes out he is a great adventurer, scaling Mont Blanc, hunting leopards in Algeria, bringing back exotic trees for his garden at 55 bis bd Itam. The address is real, and is dedicated to the fictional character: **Maison de Tartarin** (mid-April to mid-Sept 10am–noon & 2–7pm; mid-Sept to mid-Dec & mid-March to mid-April 10am–noon & 1.30–5pm; €2), where a waxwork figure waits, gun in hand, in the hall. During the Tarasque procession, a local man, chosen for his fat-bellied figure, strolls through the town as Tartarin.

The **Collégiale Royale Sainte-Marthe** (daily: 8am–noon & 2–6pm; free), which stands across the street from the castle, contains the tomb of Martha, the saint who saved the town from the Tarasque monster in its crypt; St Martha also appears in the paintings by Nicolas Mignard and Vien that decorate the Gothic interior along with works by Pierre Parrocel and Van Loo.

It's apparent from a wander round **the town** that the castle creams off most of the budget for old-building restoration, but it can be quite a pleasant change not to be surrounded by immaculate historic heritage. The streets of Renaissance town houses interspersed with older houses with Gothic decoration, the classical town hall and medieval arcades along rue des Halles are all very subdued, with just the shutters adding a soft diversity of colour. The town really only comes to life during the Tuesday morning **market**.

In the centre of the town, on place Frédéric-Mistral off rue Ledru-Rollin, the sixteenth-century **Cloître des Cordeliers** (mid-Feb to Sept daily 10am–noon & 2–6pm; free) has had its three aisles of light cream stone beautifully restored. It's used for exhibitions, sometimes of contemporary paintings, often by young artists. Other exhibitions take place alongside a permanent collection of crib figures in the **Chapelle de la Persévérance** at 8 rue Proudhon (hours and price depend upon the exhibition; check at the tourist office), part of an erstwhile "refuge" for securing women and girls suspected of living "bad lives". Further down rue Proudhon, at no. 39, is the **Musée Souleïado** (May–Sept daily 10am–6pm; Oct–April Tues–Sat 10am–5pm; ☎04.90.91.50.51; €6.10), a tribute to the family business that revived the 200-year-old Tarascon tradition of making brightly coloured, patterned, printed fabrics, now sold in shops all over Provence. The museum houses the eighteenth-century wood blocks from which many of the patterns are still made, and tastefully displays products including a table setting dedicated to the bulls of the Camargue.

Beaucaire

A statue of a bull standing at the head of the Canal du Rhône greets you as you arrive in **BEAUCAIRE** from Tarascon. To the north, between the castle and the river, is a bullring and a theatre on the site of the old **champs de foire**. The fair, founded in 1217, was one of the largest in medieval Europe, attracting traders from both sides and both ends of the Mediterranean as well as merchants from the north along the Rhône. The fairs reached their heyday in the eighteenth century but died out in the nineteenth with the onset of rail freight.

The faded facades of the classical mansions and arcades around **place de la République**, **rue de la République** and **place Clemenceau** speak of former fortunes but are gradually being restored. The Mansart-designed **Hôtel de Ville** and the much more modern market halls on place Clemenceau are very attractive, as is the seventeenth-century house at 23 rue de la République. Between the two is the eighteenth-century church of **Notre-Dame-des-Pommiers**, with a frieze from its Romanesque predecessor embedded in the eastern wall, visible from rue Charlier.

To reach the **Château Royale de Beaucaire**, follow the ramparts north of the bridge and then cut into town on rue Victor-Hugo, cross place de la République and follow rue de la République until you reach place du Château. Every afternoon an hourly **falconry display** with medieval costumes and music is staged here (daily except Wed: April–June 2–4.30pm; July & Aug 3–6pm; March & Sept–Nov 2.30–4.30pm; €7.50). It's great for kids, and the birds perform very well, but it's a shame you can no longer ramble freely around the ruins, nor climb to the top of the tower to appreciate the great advantage it had over Tarascon, whose castle lies far below. The **gardens**, however, are open for independent exploration (daily except Tues: April–Oct 10am–noon & 2.15–6.45pm; Nov–March 10.15am–noon & 2–5.15pm; closed public hols; free), and contain the **Musée Auguste-Jacquet** (same hours; €2.20) with its small but interesting collection of Roman remains, mostly from a mausoleum, and documents relating to the medieval fair.

The castle was destroyed in 1632 on Richelieu's orders when the town gave support to one of the cardinal's rivals, the duc de Montmorency. However, one irregular-sided tower still stands intact with the battlements and machicolations typical of thirteenth-century military strategy and, despite Richelieu's efforts, most of the walls overlooking the river have survived, as has the monumental staircase linking the upper and lower sections of the castle and a Romanesque chapel.

A much more enlivening Roman find is the winery with its original oak trunk press and amphorae containers at **La Mas des Tourelles** (July & Aug 10am–noon & 2–7pm; March–June, Sept & Oct daily 2–6pm; Nov–Feb Sat only 2–6pm; €4.60, includes a tasting and guided tour in English), 4km along the road to Bellegarde. The wine-maker and archeologist proprietor has put the Roman cellars to work again, using precise classical methods and recipes. Some of these are rather strange; apparently the Romans liked fortifying their wine with honey or seasoning it with fenugreek, dried iris bulbs, quince and pigs' blood.

Eating, drinking, markets and festivals

Eating cheaply in Tarascon and Beaucaire is not a problem, but eating well is another matter. The best bet is the *Bistrot des Anges*, on pl du Marché in Tarascon, which usually has an interesting plat du jour (☎04.90.91.05.11; €10–16). The *Hôtel Terminus* by Tarascon's station on place Col-Berrurier (☎04.90.91.18.95; closed Wed & Sat midday) offers a wide but unexciting selection of starters and main dishes on a €13 menu, while *Napoléon* in Beaucaire has pizzas and the like starting at €10. Otherwise Beaucaire's quai Gén-de-Gaulle, on the north side of the canal, is where you'll find the best concentration of restaurants and cafés. Both towns are very quiet most evenings – *El Souleale* **bar** on rue des Halles in Tarascon is one of the few bars to stay open after 10pm.

Market day in Tarascon is on Tuesday and takes place along rue des Halles; in Beaucaire there's a market on Thursday and Sunday in the covered halls on place Clemenceau and cours Gambetta. On the first Friday of the month Beaucaire also has a **bric-a-brac** market on cours Gambetta.

Tarascon's end-of-June **Tarasque festival** (see box on p.98) involves public balls, bull and equestrian events and a firework and music finale. Beaucaire has its summer **Estivales**, a week of bullfighting, medieval processions, music, fireworks and so forth around July 21, plus its own Rhône monster legend, the **Drac**, fêted on the first weekend in June and followed by a jazz concert.

La Grande Crau

La Grande Crau (or just plain La Crau) stretches south from the Alpilles and east from the Rhône delta to Salon, and was once, a very long time ago, the bed of the Rhône and the Durance. The name Crau derives from a Greek word for "stony", certainly a dominant feature of this landscape. Legend has it that Hercules, having trouble taking on local Ligurians and the Mistral wind both at once, called on Zeus for aid, which arrived in the form of a pebble-stone storm, water off a duck's back to the classical hero.

Much of the area, like La Petite Crau, is irrigated and planted with fruit trees protected by windbreaks of cypresses and poplars. But other parts are still a stony desert in summer when the grass between the pebbles shrivels up. As winter approaches sections of the old Roman Via Aurelia are used as drove roads for sheep leaving their summer pastures in the mountains. In winter there are only the winds to contend with; in summer it is unbearably hot and shadeless.

There are some interesting stopoffs in the more amenable countryside between the western end of the Alpilles and Arles. The first is the extremely old **Chapelle St-Gabriel**, just 5km from Tarascon on the D33 to Les Baux, immediately after the junction with the main Avignon–Arles road. It's built on the site of a Gallo-Roman settlement, with a very appealing facade, possibly sculpted by the same artists responsible for St-Tromphime's tympanum in Arles; Tarascon's tourist office has the keys, but there's not that much to see inside. Between the chapel and a ruined medieval tower the GR6 footpath heads up towards the Alpilles ridge and Les Baux (see p.93). For a ten-kilometre round walk you could follow the GR6 until you hit a small road, turn left down to **St-Étienne-du-Grés** and left again along the D32.

South of St-Gabriel is **FONTVIEILLE**, a popular pilgrimage for the French as the place where the writer Alphonse Daudet used to stay. The road past the small literary museum, **Moulin de Daudet** (daily: April–Sept 9am–7pm; Oct–March 10am–noon & 2–5pm; €2), leads south to the crossroads with the D82 where the remains of two Roman aqueducts are visible. A little further south a left turning, signposted *Meunerie Romain*, brings you to the dramatic excavation of the **Barbegal mill**, a sixteen-wheel system powered by water from one of the aqueducts and constructed in 3 or 4 BC; it is estimated that the mill produced up to three tonnes of flour a day.

The road from Fontvieille to Arles takes you past the Romanesque ruins of the **Abbaye de Montmajour** (April–Sept daily 9am–7pm; Oct–March Mon & Wed–Sun 10am–1pm & 2–5pm; €5.50), a five-minute bus ride from Arles itself. Take heed when you climb the 124 steps of the fortified watchtower, as your arrival will undoubtedly startle dozens of pigeons; the view from the top of La Grande Crau, the Rhône and the Alpilles is stunning. Below, in the **cloisters**, an excellent stone menagerie of beasts and devils enlivens the bases of the vaulting. Just 200m from the abbey, back in the direction of Fontvieille, the eleventh-century funerary chapel of **Ste-Croix** with its perfect proportions and frieze of palm fronds stands amid tombs cut out of the rock in a farmyard.

Arles

ARLES, on the east bank of the Rhône, is a major town on the tourist circuit, its fame sealed by the extraordinarily well-preserved Roman arena, **Les Arènes**, at the city's heart, and backed by an impressive variety of other stones and monuments, both Roman and medieval. Roman Arles provided grain for most of the western empire and was one of the major ports for trade and ship-building; under Constantine, it became the capital of Gaul, Britain and Spain. After the Roman Empire crumbled, the city, along with Aix, regained its fortunes as a base for the counts of Provence before unification with France. For centuries it was Marseille's only rival, profiting from the inland trade route up

ARLES

ACCOMMODATION				RESTAURANTS, CAFÉS & BARS			
Hôtel de l'Amphithéâtre	8	Grand Hôtel Nord Pinus	9	Andalucia	M	L'Entrevue	C
D'Arlatan	5	HI youth hostel	13	L'Affenage	L	Le Grillon	K
Calendal	10	Mireille	3	Bistrot Arlésian	G	La Gueule de Loup	I
Le Cloître	11	Musée	4	Boitel	F	Le Jardin du Manon	O
Constantin	12	Terminus et Van Gogh	1	Le Café La Nuit	J	L'Olivier	A
Du Forum	7			Cargo de Nuit	P	La Paillote	D
Galoubet	6			La Charcuterie	H	Soleileïs	E
Gauguin	2			Le Cloître & Lou Marquès	N	Toast Vin & Cie	B

the Rhône whenever France's enemies were blockading the port of Marseille. Arles began to decline when the arrival of train routes put an end to this advantage, and it was an inward-looking, depressed town that **Van Gogh** came to in the late nineteenth century. It was a prolific though lonely and unhappy period for the artist, ending with his self-mutilation and asylum in St-Rémy-de-Provence (see p.88). The **Fondation Vincent Van Gogh** pays tribute to him through the works of modern artists.

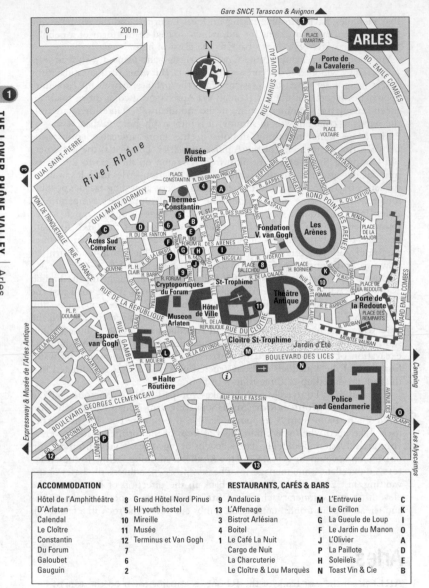

Today, Arles is a staid and conservative place, whatever the politics of its mayors, but it comes to life for the **Saturday market** that brings everyone from the Camargue and La Crau into town. It also fills the year with a crowded calendar of festivals, of which the best are the **Rencontres Internationales de la Photographie**, based around the National School of Photography, in July; the dance, music, folklore and theatre **Fêtes d'Arles** at the end of June and beginning of July; and the **Mosaïque Gitanes** with gypsy and flamenco dance and song in mid-July. For the locals, who say the photographic festival is only for Parisians, the key events are the annual opening of the bullfighting season with the **Fête des Gardians** on May 1, the crowning of the **Reine d'Arles**, once every three years – the last one took place in May 2002 – and the **rice harvest** festivities in mid-September.

Arrival and information

The **gare SNCF** is conveniently located a few blocks to the north of Les Arènes, with the adjacent **gare routière** (Ⓣ04.90.49.38.01) being the terminus for most **buses**, though some, including all local buses, use the *halte-routière* on the north side of bd Georges-Clemenceau, just east of rue Gambetta.

From the station, av Talabot leads south to **place Lamartine**, right by one of the old gateways of the city, **Porte de la Cavalerie**. From here rue de la Cavalerie takes you to Les Arènes and the centre. **Rue Jean-Jaurès**, with its continuation **rue Hôtel-de-Ville**, is the main axis of old Arles. At the southern end it meets bd G-Clemenceau and **bd des Lices**, the promenading and market thoroughfare, with the main **tourist office** directly opposite the junction (April–Sept daily 9am–6.45pm; Oct–Nov Mon–Sat 9am–5.45pm, Sun 10.30am–2.30pm; Dec–March Mon–Sat 9am–4.45pm, Sun 10.30am–2.30pm; Ⓣ04.90.18.41.20, Ⓦwww.tourisme.ville-arles.fr): there's also an annexe in the gare SNCF (Mon–Sat 9am–1pm). You can rent **bikes** from Peugeot at 15 rue du Pont or Europbike at the newspaper kiosk on esplanade Charles-de-Gaulle. To connect to the **Internet**, head for *Hexaworld*, on rue 4 Septembre, near place Voltaire.

Accommodation

Arles is well used to visitors and there are plenty of **hotel rooms** to suit all budgets. The best place to look for cheap rooms is in the area around Porte de la Cavalerie near the station. If you get stuck, the tourist office will find you accommodation for a €1 fee.

Hotels

Hôtel de l'Amphithéâtre 5 rue Diderot Ⓣ04.90.96.10.30, Ⓦwww.hotelamphitheatre.fr. Situated close to Les Arènes, this comfortable hotel has tasteful modern decor and great deals on four-person rooms. Closed Dec–March. ❸

D'Arlatan 26 rue du Sauvage Ⓣ04.90.93.56.55, Ⓦwww.hotel-arlatan.fr. This may not be Arles' most expensive hotel, but it is probably the most luxurious, set in a beautiful old fifteenth-century mansion and decorated with antiques. ❻

Calendal 22 place Pomme Ⓣ04.90.96.11.89, Ⓦwww.lecalendal.com. Welcoming hotel with generous, air-conditioned rooms overlooking a garden. ❹

Le Cloître 16 rue du Cloître Ⓣ04.90.96.29.50, Ⓕ04.90.96.02.88. A cosy hotel with some rooms having views of St-Trophime. Closed Dec–March. ❹

Constantin 59 bd de Craponne, off bd Clemenceau Ⓣ04.90.96.04.05, Ⓔhotelconstantin@wanadoo.fr. Pleasant, well maintained and comfortable, with prices kept down by its close proximity to the busy Nîmes highway (some traffic noise) and its location some distance from the centre. Closed Jan to mid-March. ❸

Du Forum 10 pl du Forum Ⓣ04.90.93.48.95, Ⓦwww.hotelduforum.com. Spacious rooms in an old house at the ancient heart of the city, with a swimming pool in the garden. A bit noisy and hot but very welcoming. Closed Nov–March. ❺

Galoubet 18 rue du Dr-Fanton ⓣ04.90.93.18.11, ⓔgaloubet.hotel@wanadoo.fr. Lovingly restored building in the old part of town. Simply furnished and decorated rooms in rustic Provençal style. ❹

Gauguin 5 pl Voltaire ⓣ04.90.96.14.35, ⓕ04.90.18.98.87. Comfortable, inexpensive and well run. Booking advisable. ❷

Grand Hôtel Nord Pinus 14 pl du Forum ⓣ04.90.93.44.44, ⓦwww.nord-pinus.com. Favoured by the *vedettes* of the bullring and decorated with their trophies, including a selection of stuffed bulls' heads. Despite all this, it's still one of the most luxurious and elegant options. ❾

Mireille 2 pl St-Pierre ⓣ04.90.93.70.74, ⓦwww.hotel-mireille.com. On the other side of the river with the more expensive and very luxurious rooms overlooking a swimming pool. Closed mid-Nov to Feb. ❻

Musée 11 rue du Grand-Prieuré ⓣ04.90.93.88.88, ⓦwww.hoteldumusee.com.fr. In a quiet location opposite the Musée Réattu, with small rooms and lots of charm. Closed Jan. 

Terminus et Van Gogh 5 place Lamartine ⓣ & ⓕ04.90.96.12.32. A cheap but basic option just outside the city gates, close to the train and bus stations. Next door to the former site of Van Gogh's "Yellow House". Closed Dec & Jan. ❷

Hostel and campsites

HI youth hostel 20 av Maréchal-Foch ⓣ04.90.96.18.25, ⓕ04.90.96.31.26. Take the "Starlett" from the gare routière, and then bus #4 to the auberge. A rather dismal option, with rock-hard beds (€8) in large dorms and spartan facilities. Reception 7.30–10am and 5–11pm; 11pm curfew. Closed late-Dec to Feb.

La Bienheureuse on the N453 at Raphèle-lès-Arles, ⓣ04.90.98.48.06, ⓕ04.90.98.35.64. Two-star site 7km out, but with regular buses from Arles (direction Aix, stop Raphèle). This is the best of the local campsites. Its restaurant is furnished with pieces similar to those on display in the Museon Arlaten, and is full of pictures of popular Arles traditions. €9 per tent. Closed Nov–March.

Camping City 67 rte de Crau ⓣ04.90.93.08.86, ⓦwww.camping-city.com. Two-star site close to town on the Crau bus route (direction Aix, stop Crau). €16 per tent. Closed Oct–March..

The City

The centre of Arles fits into a neat triangle between bd Émile Combes to the east, bds Clemenceau and des Lices to the south, and the Rhône to the west. The main square, with the cathedral and town hall, is **place de la République**, while the hub of popular life is **place du Forum**. Apart from the **Musée de l'Arles Antique**, south of the expressway, and **Les Alyscamps**, across the train lines to the south, the city's **Roman and medieval monuments** are all within easy walking distance of the centre.

Les Arènes and around

The amphitheatre, known as **Les Arènes** (see box below for opening hours; €4), in the centre of the city, is the most impressive of the Roman monuments. It dates from the end of the first century AD and, to give an idea of its size, it used to shelter over two hundred dwellings and three churches, built into the two tiers of arches that form its oval surround. This medieval *quartier* was cleared in

Museums and monuments

If you're planning on visiting several of the city's sights, it's worth buying a **Pass Monument** (€12), which gives free admission to all Arles' museums and monuments except the Fondation Vincent Van Gogh. It's available from the tourist office and at the sights themselves. Opening hours for all Arles' monuments are the same – daily: March & April 9am–noon & 2–6pm; May–Sept 9am–7pm; Oct 9am–noon & 2–6pm; Nov–Feb 10am–noon & 2–5pm. Note that in winter the Amphithéâtre and the Cloître do not close for lunch.

1830 and Les Arènes was once more used for entertainment. Today, though not the largest Roman amphitheatre in existence and missing its third storey and most of the internal stairways and galleries, it is a very dramatic structure and a stunning venue for performances, seating 20,000 spectators. Although restoration work is scheduled to continue until 2006, the amphitheatre remains open to the public.

Facing Les Arènes from the west, at 26 Rond-Point des Arènes, the Palais de Luppé houses the **Fondation Vincent Van Gogh** (June–Sept daily 10am–7pm; Oct–May Tues–Sun 9.30am–noon & 2–5.30pm; €7), which exhibits works by contemporary artists inspired by Van Gogh. Francis Bacon was the first to contribute with a painting based on Van Gogh's *The Painter on the Road to Tarascon* that had been destroyed during World War II. Roy Lichtenstein repaints *The Sower*; Hockney, Christo, César and Jasper Johns also pay homage, as do musicians, poets, photographers and the fashion designer Christian Lacroix who grew up in Arles. The collection sometimes goes on tour, at which times it is replaced by an exhibition on one of the contributors.

The **Théâtre Antique** (see box opposite for opening hours; €3), just south of Les Arènes, comes to life in July during the dance and theatre festival and for the *Fête du Costume*, in which local folk groups parade in traditional dress. A resurrected Roman, however, would be appalled at the state of this entertainment venue, with only one pair of columns standing, all the statuary removed and the sides of the stage littered with broken bits of stone. It was built a hundred years earlier than Les Arènes and quarried for stones to build churches not long after the Roman Empire collapsed; it then became part of the city's fortifications, with one of the theatre wings being turned into the **Tour Roland** whose height gives you an idea of where the top seats would have been. A convent and houses were later built over the area and it was only excavated at the turn of the twentieth century. Below the theatre the pleasant **Jardin d'Été** leads down to bd des Lices.

The quiet and attractive southeast corner of the city between bd Émile-Combes, Les Arènes and the theatre has vestiges of the ramparts built over the Roman walls down montée Vauban and in the gardens running alongside the boulevard past the old Roman gateway, the **Porte de la Redoute**. Just by the gate you can see where the aqueduct from Barbegal brought water into the city.

Place de la République and around

West of Les Arènes stands the **place de la République**, dominated by the **Cathédrale St-Trophime**, whose doorway boasts one of the most famous bits of twelfth-century Provençal stone carving in existence. It depicts the Last Judgement, trumpeted by angels playing with the enthusiasm of jazz musicians, while the damned are led naked and in chains down to hell; the blessed, all female and draped in long robes, processing upwards.

The cathedral itself was started in the Dark Ages on the spot where, in 597 AD, Saint Augustine was consecrated as the first bishop of the English. It was largely completed by the twelfth century. A font in the north aisle and an altar in the north transept illustrating the parting of the Red Sea were both originally Gallo-Roman sarcophagi. The high nave is decorated with d'Aubusson tapestries; you'll find more Romanesque and Gothic stone carving, this time with New Testament scenes enlivened with other myths such as Saint Martha leading away the tamed Tarasque, in the extraordinarily beautiful **cloisters**, accessible from place de la République to the right of the cathedral (see box opposite for opening hours; €3.50).

An obelisk of Egyptian granite, that may once have stood in the middle of the Cirque Romaine (see opposite), stands in front of the cathedral, placed there by Louis XIV who fancied himself as a latter-day Augustus. Across place de la République from the cathedral stands the palatial seventeenth-century **Hôtel de Ville**, inspired by the Palace of Versailles. You can walk through its vast entrance hall with its flattened vaulted roof, designed to avoid putting extra stress on the **Cryptoportiques** below (see box on p.104 for opening hours; €3.50). This is a huge, dark, dank and wonderfully spooky horseshoe-shaped underground gallery, built by the Romans, possibly as a food store, possibly as a barracks for public slaves, but certainly to provide sturdy foundations for the forum above. It's less extraordinary than the cloisters, but still worth a visit. Access is from the Jesuits' church on rue Balze.

On nearby rue de la République is the **Museon Arlaten** (daily: April–May & Sept 9.30am–12.30pm & 2–6pm; June–Aug 9.30am–1pm & 2–6.30pm; Oct–March 9.30am–12.30pm & 2–5pm; €4), set up in 1896 by Frédéric Mistral with his Nobel Prize money. In the room dedicated to the poet, a cringing notice piously instructs you to salute the great man's cradle. That apart, the collections of costumes, documents, tools, pictures and paraphernalia of Provençal life are extensive and intriguing. The evolution of Arlesian dress is charted in great detail for all social classes from the eighteenth century to World War I and includes a scene of a dressmaking shop. Two other life-size scenes portray a visit to a mother and newborn child, and a bourgeois Christmas dinner, not to be looked at if you're hungry. The room devoted to Provençal mythology, including a Tarasque from the Tarascon procession, is entertaining if not very enlightening.

Heading down rue du Président-Wilson from the Museon Arlaten and right into rue P.F-Rey brings you to the **Espace Van Gogh**, the former Hôtel-Dieu where Van Gogh was treated. It now houses a *mediathèque* and university departments, with a bookshop and a *salon de thé* in the arcades. The flowerbeds in the courtyard are a recreation of the hospital garden based on Van Gogh's painting and the descriptions he wrote of the plants in letters to his sister.

Place du Forum to the river and Van Gogh

North of place de la République, **place du Forum** is still the centre of life in Arles today. In the square, you can see the pillars of an ancient archway and the first two steps of a monumental stairway that gave access to the Roman forum, now embedded in the corner of the *Nord-Pinus* hotel. The statue in the middle of the square is of Frédéric Mistral.

Heading north towards the river you reach the **Thermes de Constantin** (see box on p.104 for opening hours; €3), the considerable ruins of what may well have been the biggest Roman baths in Provence. You can see the heating system below a thick Roman concrete floor and the divisions between the different areas, but there's nothing to help you imagine the original. The most striking feature, an apse in alternating brick and stonework, which sheltered one of the baths, is best viewed from outside on place Constantin.

To the right, along rue du Grand Prieuré, is the entrance to the must-see **Musée Réattu** (daily: March–April & Oct 10am–12.30pm & 2–5.30pm; May–Sept 10am–12.30pm & 2–7pm; Nov–Feb 1–5.30pm; €4) where, beside the rigid eighteenth-century classicism of works by the museum's founder and his contemporaries, there are some stunning twentieth-century pieces. Of the modern works, Picasso is the best represented with the sculpture *Woman with Violin* and 57 ink and crayon sketches from between December 1970 and February 1971 which he donated to the museum. Amongst the split faces, clowns and hilarious Tarasque, is a beautifully simple portrait of Picasso's mother. Zadkine's study in bronze for the two Van Gogh brothers, Mario Prassinos' black and white studies of the Alpilles, César's *Compression 1973* and works by contemporary artists are dotted about the landings, corridors and courtyard niches of this very beautiful fifteenth-century priory; there are also some very good temporary exhibitions.

If you walk to the back of the building, you'll see its gargoyles jutting over the river. There are lanterns along the river wall (and some wonderful sunsets), though much of the river front and its bars and bistros, where weary workers once drank and danced away their woes, was destroyed during World War II.

Another casualty of the bombing was the "Yellow House", on place Lamartine to the north of the centre, where **Van Gogh** lived before entering the hospital at St-Rémy. However, the café painted in *Café de Nuit* is still open for business in place du Forum. Van Gogh had arrived by train in February 1888 to be greeted by snow and a bitter Mistral wind. But he started painting straightaway, and in this period produced such celebrated canvases as *The Sunflowers*, *Van Gogh's Chair*, *The Red Vines* and *The Sower*. He used to wander along the riverbank wearing candles on his hat, watching the light of night-time; *The Starry Night* is the Rhône at Arles.

Van Gogh was desperate for Gauguin to join him, though at the same time worried about his friend's dominating influence. From the daily letters he wrote to his brother Théo, it was clear that the artist found few kindred souls in Arles. Gauguin did eventually come and moved in with Van Gogh. The events of the night of December 23, when Vincent cut off his ear after rushing after Gauguin brandishing a razor blade, were recorded by the older artist fifteen years later. No one knows the exact provocation. Van Gogh was packed off to the Hôtel-Dieu hospital where he had the good fortune to be treated by a young and sympathetic doctor, Félix Rey. Van Gogh painted Rey's portrait while in the hospital as well as the hospital itself, in which the inmates are clearly suffering, not from violent frenzy, but from inexpressible unhappiness.

Musée de l'Arles Antique and the Cirque Romaine

The **Musée de l'Arles Antique** (daily: March–Oct 9am–7pm; Nov–Feb 10am–5pm; €5.35) stands on the spit of land between the Rhône and the Canal du Rhône just west of the city centre. The triangular building, designed by Peruvian architect Henri Ciriani, is positioned on the axis of the **Cirque Romaine**, an enormous chariot racetrack that stretched for 450m from the museum to the town side of the expressway. Built in the middle of the second century AD, the track was 101m wide and allowed an audience of 20,000 to watch the chariot races. Although excavation of the track has been temporarily halted due to lack of funding, you can still look down into the existing digs crossed by av de la 1er Division Française Libre, the road in front of the museum. The models inside the museum, however, will give you a much better idea of Roman Arles' third major entertainment venue.

Inside, the museum is a treat: open-plan, flooded with natural light and immensely spacious. It covers the prehistory of the area and then takes you through the centuries of Roman rule from Julius Caesar's legionnaire base and the development during the reign of Augustus through to the Christian era from the fourth century when Arles was Emperor Constantine's capital of Gaul, to the fifth century, the height of the city's importance as a trading centre when Emperor Honorius could say "the town's position, its communications and its crowd of visitors is such that there is no place in the world better suited to spreading, in every sense, the products of the earth". The exhibits are arranged chronologically as well as thematically, so, for example, there are sections on medicine, on the use of water power (with more details on the Barbegal mill; see p.101), on industry and agriculture. Fabulous mosaics are laid out with walkways above; and there are numerous sarcophagi with intricate sculpting depicting everything from music and lovers, to gladiators and Christian miracles.

Les Alyscamps

The Romans had their burial ground, **Les Alyscamps** (see box on p.104 for opening hours; €3.50), southeast of the centre and it was used by the well-to-do Arlesians well into the Middle Ages. Now only one alleyway, foreshortened by a rail line, is preserved; to reach it follow av des Alyscamps from bd des Lices. Sarcophagi still line the shaded walk, whose tree trunks are azure blue in Van Gogh's rendering. Some of the tombs have an axe engraved on them which is thought to have been the contemporary equivalent of a notice warning "Burglar alarm fitted". There are numerous tragedy masks, too, though any with special decoration have long since been removed to serve as municipal gifts, as happened often in the seventeenth century, or to reside in the museums. But there is still magic to this walk which ends at the church of **St-Honorat** where more sarcophagi are stored.

Eating, drinking and entertainment

Arles has a good number of excellent-value **restaurants**. If you're looking for quick meals, or just want to watch the world go by, there's a wide choice of **brasseries** on the main boulevards, of which the most appealing is *Andalucia*, 14 bd des Lices, which serves tapas, and plays up the bullfighting theme.

Saturday is the big day of the week in Arles for the **market** that extends the length of bd Georges-Clemenceau, bd des Lices and bd Émile-Combes and many of the adjoining streets. The atmosphere is festive with all the brasseries full of friends having their weekly get-together, and stunning displays of local produce, in particular the cheeses and olives. A smaller food market takes place every Wednesday on bd Émile-Combes and bric-a-brac stalls spread down bd des Lices the first Wednesday of the month.

For all-round **entertainment**, the *Actes Sud* complex, at 23 quai Marx-Dormoy (☎04.90.93.33.56), offers **classical concerts** and **films**, along with meals and a bookshop.

Restaurants

L'Affenage 4 rue Molière ☎04.90.96.07.67. In the stables of an eighteenth-century coach house, this restaurant serves generous portions of Provençal specialities. Menus at €17 and €25. Closed Sun.

La Charcuterie 51 rue des Arènes ☎04.90.96.56.96. A lyonnaise-style deli; cramped, lively, with a variety of *assiettes de charcuterie* starting at €12. Closed Sun & Mon.

Le Cloître & Lou Marquès *Hôtel Jules César*, bd des Lices ☎04.90.52.52.52. *Le Cloître* is the hotel's cheaper restaurant, with something to suit most budgets including a midday menu at €18. The real gourmet delight, however, is the far more expensive *Lou Marquès*, where the specialities include *baudroie* (monkfish), langoustine salad and Camargue rice cake, all served with the utmost pomposity; menus from €35 to €53, à la carte over €50. Both closed Nov & Dec.

L'Entrevue 23 quai Marx Dormoy ☎04.90.93.37.28. Hip Moroccan café with an attached hammam. Tajines for around €13; for the adventurous, a hammam/tajine combo at €17. Closed Sun evening.

Le Galoubet 18 rue du Dr-Fanton ☎04.90.93.18.11. Pleasant, vine-covered terrace on which to sample modern Provençal cuisine; the €20 menu is particularly good value. Closed Sun and Mon lunch.

Le Grillon corner of rond-point des Arènes & rue Girard-le-Bleu ☎04.90.96.70.97. Pleasant place overlooking Les Arènes with menus from €9.50. Closed Sun & Wed.

La Gueule de Loup 39 rue des Arènes ☎04.90.96.96.69. Cosy restaurant serving traditional dishes with menus from €25, reservations recommended. Closed Sun & Mon lunch.

Le Jardin du Manon 14 av des Alyscamps ☎04.90.93.38.68. Hospitable Provençal restaurant serving elaborate regional dishes and delicious desserts, which you can enjoy in a small patio garden. Menus from €17. Closed Wed.

L'Olivier 1 bis rue Réattu ☎04.90.49.64.88. Small, elegant and very agreeable restaurant serving wine by the glass and with a delicious €28 menu.

La Paillote 28 rue Dr-Fanton ☎04.90.96.33.15. Very friendly place with a good €15 menu. Closed Thurs.

Cafés, bars and ice cream

Cargo de Nuit 7 av Sadi-Carnot ☎04.90.49.55.99. A café-bar with an excellent line-up of live jazz, electronic and world music concerts. Open Thurs–Sat evenings, food served till 2am, drinks till 5am.

Boitel 4 rue de la Liberté. A *salon de thé* with a whole pâtisserie full of goodies to go with the Earl Grey. Closed Sun.

Le Café La Nuit pl du Forum. If you sit on the terrace of this café you'll find yourself in quite a few holiday snaps, as this is the famous café in Van Gogh's *Café La Nuit*.

Bistrot Arlésian pl du Forum. Young and noisy, its waiters are greeted by each new arrival with kisses on both cheeks. The best of the pl du Forum bars.

Soleileïs 9 rue du Dr-Fanton ☎04.90.93.30.76. Delicious home-made ice cream.

Toast Vin & Cie 2 rue Dr-Fanton ☎04.90.96.22.26. Hearty open sandwiches served with tasty salads (€12); free but limited Internet access for customers. Closed Tues & Wed lunch.

Listings

Car parks Parking des Lices, off bd des Lices; free parking off bd E-Combes.

Car rental Avis at the gare SNCF (☎04.90.96.82.42); Europcar, bd Victor-Hugo (☎04.90.93.23.24); Eurorent, bd Victor-Hugo (☎04.90.93.50.14); Hertz, bd Victor-Hugo (☎04.90.96.75.23).

Currency exchange Rond-point des Arènes; several banks on pl de la République.

Emergencies ☎15; Centre Hospitalier J-Imbert, quartier Fourchon (☎04.90.49.29.29).

Pharmacy For a list of late-night pharmacies, call the gendarmerie on ☎04.90.18.45.00.

Police On bd des Lices opposite the Jardin d'Été (☎04.90.18.45.00).

Post office 5 bd des Lices, 13200 Arles (Mon–Fri 8.30am–7pm, Sat 8.30am–noon).

Swimming pool Stade Municipal off av Maréchal-Foch (June to mid-Sept Tues–Sun).

Taxis ☎04.90.96.90.03, ☎04.90.49.69.59 or ☎04.90.93.31.16.

Trains Local ☎08.91.67.68.69; national ☎08.36.35.35.35 (€.034/min).

The Camargue

The Camargue is one of those geographically enclosed areas that are separate and unique in every sense. Its ever-shifting boundaries, the **Petit Rhône**, the **Grand Rhône** and **the sea**, are invisible until you stumble upon them; its horizons infinite because land, lagoon and sea share the same horizontal plain. And both animal and human life have traits peculiar to this drained, ditched and now protected delta land.

The region is home to the **bulls** and the **white horses** that the Camargue *gardians* or herdsmen ride. Neither animal is truly wild though both run in semi-liberty. In recent times new strains of bull have been introduced because numbers were getting perilously low. The Camargue horse remains a distinct breed, of origin unknown, that is born dark brown or black, and turns white around its fourth year. It is never stabled, surviving the humid heat of summer and the wind-racked winter cold outdoors. The **gardians** likewise are a hardy

Bullfighting in Arles and the Camargue

Bullfighting, or more properly *tauromachie* (roughly, "the art of the bull"), in Arles and the Camargue is generally not the Spanish-style *mise-à-mort*, and it's usually the bullfighters, or *razeteurs*, who get hurt, not the animal. The sport remains a passion with the locals, who treat the champion *razeteurs* like football stars, while the bulls are fêted and adored – before retirement they are given a final tour around the arena while people weep and throw flowers.

The **shows** involve various feats of daring and, being much closer to the scene, you will feel more involved than with other dangerous sports. The most common show is where the bull has a cockade at the base of its horns and ribbons tied between them. Using blunt razor-combs, the *razeteurs* have to cut the ribbons and get the cockades. The drama and grace of the spectacle is the stylish way the men leap over the barrier away from the bull. For some shows involving horsemen arrows are shot at the bull, though these don't go in deep enough to make the animal bleed.

All this may leave you feeling cold, or sick, but it is your best way of experiencing **Les Arènes in Arles**. It may help to know that no betting goes on; people just add to the prize money as the game progresses. The tourist office, local papers and publicity around the arena will give you the details (€5–15 per seat); be sure to check shows are not *mise-à-mort*.

community. Their traditional homes, or *cabanes*, are thatched and windowless one-storey structures, with bulls' horns over the doors to ward off evil spirits. They still conform, to some extent, to the popular cowboy myth, and play a major role in guarding Camarguais traditions. Throughout the summer, with spectacles involving bulls and horses in every village arena, they're kept busy and the work carries local glamour. Winter is a good deal harder, and fewer and fewer Camarguais property owners can afford the extravagant use of land that bull-rearing requires.

The two towns of the Camargue are as distant and as different as they could possibly be. **Les Stes-Maries-de-la-Mer** is the area's overcrowded resort, famous for its gypsy gathering, while **Salin-de-Giraud** is linked to the industrial complex around the Golfe de Fos. Such villages as are found are little more than hamlets. The rest of the habitations are farmhouses, or *mas*, set well back from the handful of roads, and not within easy walking distance of their neighbours.

There's really no **ideal time** for visiting the Camargue. If you have the sort of skin that attracts **mosquitoes**, then the months from March to November could be unbearable. Staying right beside the sea will be okay, but otherwise you'll need serious chemical weaponry. Biting flies are also prevalent and can take away much of the pleasure of cycling around this hill-less land. The other problem is the winds, which in autumn and winter can be strong enough to knock you off your bike. Conversely, in summer the weather can be so hot and humid that the slightest movement is an effort. For this reason, it may be better to make Arles your base and visit the Camargue on day-trips.

Transport

There are fairly frequent **bus services** between Arles and Stes-Maries, but fewer between Arles and Salin, and there's no direct service between Stes-

Maries and Salin. Timetables are available in Arles at Les Cars de Camargue on rue J-M-Artaud, and at the gare routière. For **drivers and cyclists** the main thing to be wary of is taking your car or bike along the dykes. Maps and road signs show which routes are closed to vehicles and which are accessible only at low tide, but they don't warn you about the surface you'll be driving along. The other problem is **theft** from cars. There are well-organized gangs of thieves with a particular penchant for foreign licence plates. You can **rent bikes** at Stes-Maries from Le Vélociste, on rte d'Arles (☎04.90.97.83.26), and at Le Vélo Saintois at 19 av de la République (☎04.90.97.74.56). **Canoes** can also be rented from Kayak Vert in Sylvéréal, on RD 38 direction Aigues-Mortes (☎04.66.73.57.17). The other means of transport to consider is **horse-riding**. There are around thirty farms that hire out horses, by the hour, half day or whole day.

For transport as an end in itself, the **paddle steamer** *Le Tiki III* leaves from the mouth of the Petit Rhône, off the route d'Aigues-Mortes 2.5km west of Stes-Maries (mid-March to mid-Nov; ☎04.90.97.81.68), and runs upriver. Alternatively, the *Soleil*, a much less pretty vessel but designed for very shallow water, leaves from the port in Stes-Maries and follows the shoreline to the Petit Rhône (April–Sept; 1hr 30min trips; ☎04.90.97.85.89). Other boats offer **fishing expeditions**: the tourist office in Stes-Maries (see p.115) can provide details.

Wildlife, agriculture and industry

The bulls and horses are just one element in the Camargue's exceptionally rich **wildlife**, which includes flamingoes, marsh- and seabirds, waterfowl and birds of prey; wild boars, beavers and badgers; tree frogs, water snakes and pond turtles; and a rich **flora** of reeds, wild irises, tamarisk, wild rosemary and famous juniper trees, which grow to a height of 6m, and form the Bois des Rièges on the islands between the Étang du Vaccarès and the sea, part of the central **National Reserve** to which access is restricted to those with professional research credentials. The whole of the Camargue is a Parc Naturel Régional, with great efforts made to keep an equilibrium between tourism, agriculture, industry and hunting on the one hand, and the indigenous ecosystems on the other.

After World War II the northern marshes were drained and re-irrigated with fresh water. The main crop planted was rice, established so successfully that by the 1960s the Camargue was providing three-quarters of all French consumption of the grain – although these days the industry is struggling to hold its own against cheaper imports. Vines were also reintroduced, and in the nineteenth century they survived the infestation of phylloxera that devastated every other wine-producing region because their stems were under water. There are other crops – wheat, fruit orchards and the ubiquitous rapeseed – as well as trees in isolated clumps. To the east, along the last stretch of the Grand Rhône, the chief business is the production of salt, first organized in the Camargue by the Romans in the first century AD, and now one of the biggest saltworks in the world. The saltpans and pyramids cannot help but add an extraterrestrial aspect to the Camargue landscape.

Though the Étang du Vaccarès, the Réserve des Impériaux and the central islands are out of bounds, there are paths and sea dykes from which their inhabitants can be watched, and special nature trails (detailed on p.114). The ideal months for bird-watching are the mating period of April to June, with the greatest number of flamingoes present between April and September.

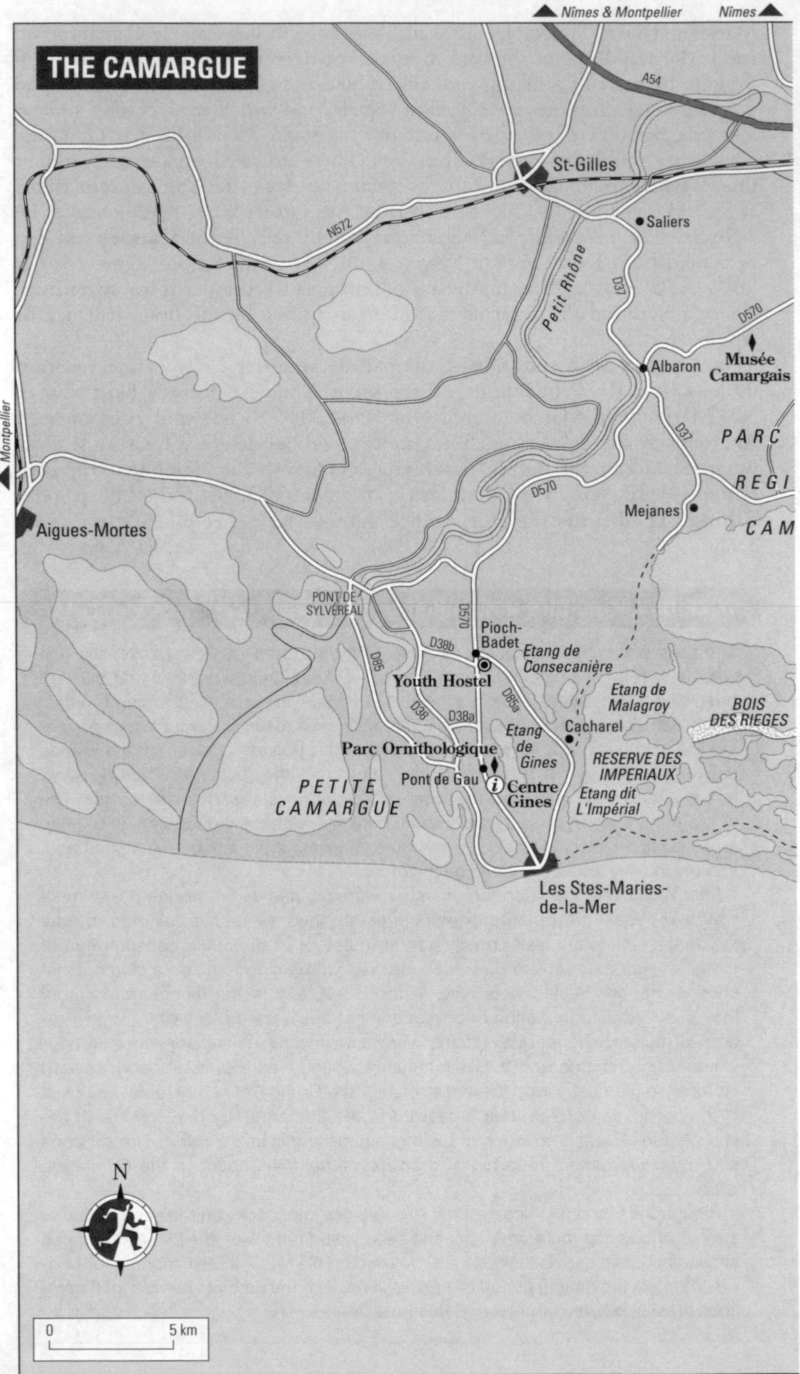
THE CAMARGUE
Nîmes & Montpellier
Nîmes
A54
St-Gilles
N572
Saliers
Petit Rhône
D37
D570
Albaron
Musée Camargais
PARC
REGI
CAM
Mejanes
Montpellier
Aigues-Mortes
D570
PONT DE SYLVÉREAL
D570
Pioch-Badet
Etang de Consecanière
D38b
D85
Youth Hostel
Etang de Malagroy
D85a
BOIS DES RIEGES
D38
D38a
Cacharel
Etang de Gines
Parc Ornithologique
RESERVE DES IMPERIAUX
Pont de Gau
Centre Gines
PETITE CAMARGUE
Etang dit L'Impérial
Les Stes-Maries-de-la-Mer
N
0
5 km

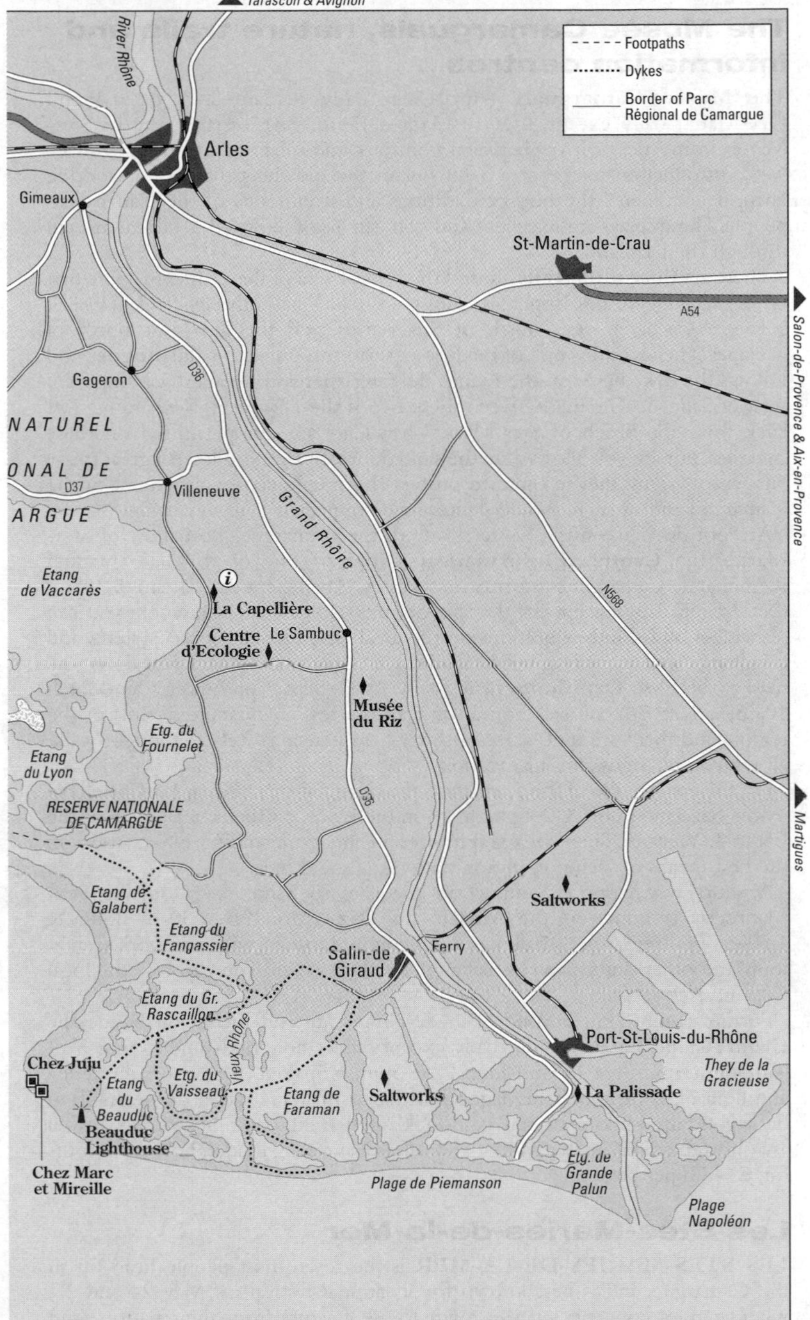
Tarascon & Avignon
River Rhône
Footpaths
Dykes
Border of Parc Régional de Camargue
Arles
Gimeaux
St-Martin-de-Crau
A54
Salon-de-Provence & Aix-en-Provence
Gageron
D36
NATUREL
ONAL DE
ARGUE
D37
Villeneuve
Grand Rhône
Etang de Vaccarès
La Capellière
Centre d'Ecologie
Le Sambuc
N568
Musée du Riz
Etg. du Fournelet
Etang du Lyon
RESERVE NATIONALE DE CAMARGUE
D36
Martigues
Etang de Galabert
Etang du Fangassier
Saltworks
Salin-de Giraud
Ferry
Etang du Gr. Rascaillon
Vieux Rhône
Port-St-Louis-du-Rhône
Chez Juju
Etang du Beauduc
Etg. du Vaisseau
Etang de Faraman
Saltworks
La Palissade
They de la Gracieuse
Beauduc Lighthouse
Chez Marc et Mireille
Plage de Piemanson
Etg. de Grande Palun
Plage Napoléon

The Musée Camarguais, nature trails and information centres

The **Musée Camarguais** (April–Sept daily 9.15am–5.45 or 6.45pm; Oct–March daily except Tues 10.15am–4.45pm; €4), on the way to Stes-Maries from Arles, halfway between Gimeaux and Albaron, gives a straightforward introduction to the area. Laid out in the old sheep barn of a working farm, it documents the history, traditions and livelihoods of the Camarguais people. The displays are excellent and you can also follow a 3.5-kilometre trail through the farmland.

There are three main **trails** around the central area of the Camargue. The first skirts the Réserve des Impériaux along a drover's path, the *draille de Méjanes*, between Cacharel, 4km north of Ste-Maries, and the D37 just north of Méjanes. The second is one of the best observation points for **flamingoes** and follows the dyke between the Étangs du Fangassier and Galabert, starting 5km west of Salin-de-Giraud. Between these two is the *Digue à la Mer* running just back from the beach of Stes-Maries' bay. Cars are not permitted on these stretches, nor are you allowed on the sand dunes. In fact, you'll see a great many "no entry" signs; they're there to protect the fragile eco-environment of the Camargue and, as such, should definitely be respected.

At Pont de Gau, on the western side of the Camargue, 4km short of Stes-Maries, the **Centre d'Information Ginès** is one of the Parc Naturel Régional de Camargue's information centres (April–Sept daily 10am–5.30pm; Oct–March daily except Fri 9.30am–5pm; ⓣ04.90.97.86.32), where you can see videos, slides and exhibitions on the local environment, its ecosystems and fragility, as well as picking up detailed maps of paths and dykes. Just down the road at the **Parc Ornithologique** (daily: April–Sept 9am–sunset; Oct–March 10am–sunset; €6), aviaries house some of the less easily spotted birds of the region, and there are trails across a thirty-acre marsh as well as a longer walk, all with ample signs and information.

On the eastern side of the Camargue, the main nature trail is at **La Capelière** (Mon–Sat 9am–noon & 2–5pm; free) on the D36b on the eastern edge of the Étang du Vaccarès. There are exhibitions on Camargue wildlife, information on the best means of seeing it, plus initiation trails and hides.

A short way past Le Sambuc on the way to Salin, the Domaine Petit Manusclat is home to the **Musée du Riz** (Mon–Fri 8.30am–noon & 1.30–5.30pm; €3.80), a small museum dedicated to rice, with waxwork scenes, tools and other dusty paraphernalia, plus a shop where you can buy the local rice and rice cakes.

Further south, 7km beyond Salin-de-Giraud just off the D36d beside the Grand Rhône, **La Palissade** (daily except public hols: mid-June to mid-Sept 9am–6pm; mid-Sept to mid-June 9am–5pm; €3) concentrates on the fauna and flora of its neighbouring lagoons. It has a small and rather dull exhibition but a good nine-kilometre trail past duck and flamingo nesting grounds, as well as a shorter 1.5-kilometre path. It also offers hour-long guided horseback tours for €14.70 per person.

Les Stes-Maries-de-la-Mer

LES STES-MARIES-DE-LA-MER is the town most people head for in the Camargue, and is best known for its annual festival on May 24 and 25, when gypsies converge on the town to ask favours from their patron saint Sarah. It is swamped by people throughout the summer and, as the Camargue's

The legend of Sarah and the gypsy festivals

Sarah was the servant of Mary Jacobé, Jesus's aunt, and Mary Salomé, mother of two of the apostles, who, along with Mary Magdalene and various other New Testament characters, were driven out of Palestine by the Jews and put on a boat without sails and oars – or so the story goes.

The boat subsequently drifted effortlessly to an island in the mouth of the Rhône where the Egyptian god Ra was worshipped. Here Mary Jacobé, Mary Salomé and Sarah, who was herself Egyptian, settled to carry out conversion work while the others headed off for other parts of Provence. In 1448 their relics were "discovered" in the fortress **church** of Stes-Maries on the erstwhile island, around the time that the Romanies were migrating into western Europe from the Balkans and from Spain. It's thought the two strands may have been reunited in Provence.

Whatever the explanation, the gypsies have been making their **pilgrimage** to Stes-Maries since the sixteenth century. It's a time for weddings and baptisms as well as music, dancing and fervent religious activities. On May 24, after Mass, the shrines of the saints are lowered from the high chapel to an altar where the faithful stretch out their arms to touch them. Then the statue of Black Sarah is carried by the gypsies to the sea. On the following day the statues of Mary Jacobé and Mary Salomé, sitting in a wooden boat, follow the same route, accompanied by the mounted *gardians* in full Camargue dress, Arlesians in traditional costume, and all and sundry present. The sea, the Camargue, the pilgrims and the gypsies are blessed by the bishop from a fishing boat, before the procession returns to the church with much bell-ringing, guitar playing, tambourines and singing. Another ceremony in the afternoon sees the shrines lifted back up to their chapel.

In recent years the authorities have considered the event to be getting out of hand and there's now a heavy police presence and the all-night candle-lit vigil in the church has been banned. There is a certain amount of hostility between some townspeople and the *gitans*, though the municipality has actively countered the racism. It's a wonderful event to be part of, but inevitably makes finding accommodation in the town impossible. Another pilgrimage takes place on the Sunday closest to October 22, dedicated solely to Mary Jacobé and Mary Salomé and without the participation of the gypsies.

only real resort, is becoming grossly overdeveloped, catering for every leisure activity. Apart from peace and quiet you're not going to want for anything here. There are miles of beaches; a new pleasure port with boat trips to the lagoons; horses to ride; water sports; and the arenas for bullfights, cavalcades and other entertainment (events are posted on a board outside).

Arrival and accommodation

Buses from Arles arrive at the end of av d'Arles. The **tourist office** is on the seafront at 5 av van-Gogh (daily: Jan, Feb, Nov & Dec 9am–5pm; March & Oct 9am–6pm; April–June & Sept 9am–7pm; July & Aug 9am–8pm; Ⓣ04.90.97.82.55, Ⓦwww.saintesmariesdelamer.com), five minutes' walk from the bus stop.

From April to October **rooms** in Stes-Maries need to be booked in advance, and for the Romany festival, several months before. Prices go up considerably during the summer and at any time of the year are more expensive than at Arles. Outlying *mas* (farmhouses) renting out rooms tend to be quite expensive. **Camping** on the beach is not officially tolerated, but even at Stes-Maries people sleeping beneath the stars rarely get told to move on. The fifteen-kilometre plage de Piemanson, also known as the plage d'Arles, south of Salin-de-Giraud, 10km east of Stes-Maries, is a favoured venue for *camping sauvage* in summer.

Hotels

La Brise de Mer 31 av G-Leroy ⓣ04.90.97.80.21, ⓔdauphin.bleu@wanadoo.fr. Overlooking the sea, with a moderately priced restaurant. Halfboard obligatory (€60 per person) in July & Aug. ❺

Camille 13 av de la Plage ⓣ04.90.97.80.26, ⓕ04.90.97.98.01. Characterless interior, but with a sea view. Closed Nov–Feb. ❷

Le Fangassier Rte de Cacharel ⓣ04.90.97.85.02, ⓦwww.fangassier.camargue.fr. Pleasant hotel in the centre of town, with friendly staff. Closed mid-Nov to mid-Dec & Jan to Feb. ❸

Le Flamant Rose in Albaron between Arles and Stes-Maries ⓣ04.90.97.10.18, ⓔfrederic.lacave@worldonline.fr. Acceptable hotel-restaurant with some bargain rooms. ❸

Mangio Fango rte d'Arles ⓣ04.90.97.80.56, ⓔmangio.fango@wanadoo.fr. About 600m from Stes-Maries, overlooking the Étang des Launes with pool and patios. Closed mid-Nov to mid-Dec & Jan. ❺

Hostellerie du Mas de Cacharel rte de Cacharel, 4km north on D85a ⓣ04.90.97.95.44, ⓦwww.hotel-cacharel.com. Expensive rooms in one of the Camargue's oldest farms, with horses to ride. ❼

Mas des Rièges rte de Cacharel, Stes-Maries ⓣ04.90.97.85.07, ⓔhoteldesrieges@wanadoo.fr. Down a track signed off the D85a close to Stes-Maries. An upmarket hotel in an old farmhouse, with swimming pool and garden. Closed mid-Nov to mid-Dec & Jan. ❹

Le Mediterranée 4 rue Frédéric-Mistral ⓣ04.90.97.82.09, ⓦwww.hotel-mediterranee.camargue.fr. A very verdant and charming hotel in a good, central location. The inexpensive rooms have been recently renovated. Closed Jan. ❸

Hôtel de la Plage 2 rue Victor-Hugo ⓣ04.90.97.85.09, ⓦwww.chez-boisset.camargue.fr. Modern hotel 100 metres from the sea, all rooms with air con, en-suite bathrooms and satellite TV. Closed Jan & Feb. ❸

Hostellerie du Pont du Gau rte d'Arles, Pont de Gau, 4km north of Stes-Maries ⓣ04.90.97.81.53, ⓕ04.90.97.98.54. Old-fashioned Camarguais decor, pleasant rooms and a good restaurant. Closed Jan & Feb. ❸

Les Vagues 12 av T-Aubunal ⓣ & ⓕ04.90.97.84.40. A friendly option overlooking the sea on the rte d'Aigues-Mortes. Closed Feb. ❷

Hostel, campsites and chambre d'hôtes

HI hostel in Pioch-Badet hamlet, 10km north of Stes-Maries on the Arles–Stes-Maries bus route ⓣ04.90.97.51.72, ⓕ04.90.97.54.88. Set in an old school, with rooms holding three to ten beds (€15 per person; €20 half board). Horse rides organized and bikes for rent.

Mas de Pioch Pioch-Badet, 10km north of Stes-Maries ⓣ04.90.97.50.06, ⓦwww.manadecavallini.com. Chambre d'hôtes run by Mme Cavallini, with a pool and large rooms. It's excellent value but needs booking well in advance. ❸

Camping La Brise rue Marcel-Carrière on the east side of the village ⓣ04.90.47.84.67, ⓕ04.90.97.72.01. On the Arles to Stes-Maries bus route (stop La Brise). Three-star site with a pool and laundry facilities, and tents and caravans for rent. €9.70 per tent. Open all year.

Camping Le Clos du Rhône at the mouth of the Petit Rhône, 2km west of the village on the rte d'Aigues-Mortes ⓣ04.90.97.85.99, ⓕ04.90.97.78.85. Only two of the Arles to Stes-Maries buses continue to here (stop Clos du Rhône). Busy four-star site with a pool, laundry and shop. €12 per tent. Closed Oct–March.

The Town

Though grossly commercialized, Stes-Maries is still an extremely pretty town with its streets of white houses and the grey-gold Romanesque **church**, fortified in the fourteenth century in response to frequent attacks by pirates. Inside, at the back of the crypt, is the tinselled and sequined statue of Sarah (see box on p.115), always surrounded by candles and abandoned crutches and calipers. The church itself has beautifully pure lines and fabulous acoustics, and during the time of the Saracen raids it provided shelter for all the villagers and even has its own freshwater well. Between March and Oct the church tower is open (10am–12.30pm & 2pm–sunset; €2), affording panoramic views over the Camargue.

The local **Musée Baroncelli** (opening hours vary, so check with tourist office; €1.50), on rue Victor-Hugo, is named after the man who, in 1935, was responsible, along with various *gardians*, for initiating the gypsies' procession down to the sea with Sarah. This was motivated by a desire to give a special place in the pilgrimage to the Romanies. The museum covers this event, other Camarguais traditions and the region's fauna and flora.

Eating and drinking

On summer evenings every other bar and restaurant has flamenco guitarists playing on the *terrasses* while the streets are full of buskers with a crazy variety of instruments. The atmosphere can be carnival or tackily artificial, depending on your mood.

Although there are plenty of **restaurants** to choose from in Stes-Maries, few are inexpensive: out of season, however, the quality improves, and the prices come down. The specialities of the Camargue include *tellines*, tiny shiny shell-fish served with garlic mayonnaise; *bœuf gardian*, bull's meat; eels from the Vaccarès; rice, asparagus and wild duck from the district; and *poutargue des Stes-Maries*, a mullet roe dish. The town **market** takes place on place des Gitans every Monday and Friday.

Le Delta 1 pl Mireille ⓣ04.90.97.81.12. Serves local specialities such as *bourride* and *aïoli de morue*, menus from €9.10 to €23. Closed Wed & Jan.

L'Impérial 1 pl des Impériaux ⓣ04.90.97.81.84. Good fish dishes with interesting sauces. Menus from €19.50. April–June, Sept & Oct closed Tues; July & Aug open daily; closed Nov–March.

Le Kahlua 1 rue Jean-Roche ⓣ04.90.97.98.41. Tapas, pizzas, grills and cheap wine on the *terrasse* overlooking pl des Gitans, from about €15. Open till 1am. Closed Jan & Feb and Wed out of season.

Les Montilles 2 rue Paul Peyron ⓣ04.90.97.73.83. Inexpensive menus (from €12.50), often including a delicious duck mousse. Closed Jan.

Salin-de-Giraud and around

In total contrast to Stes-Maries, **SALIN-DE-GIRAUD** is an industrial village, based on the saltworks company and its related chemical factory, with workers' houses built on a strict grid pattern during the Second Empire.

If you want to take a look at the lunar landscape of the **salt piles**, there's a viewing point with information panels just south of Salin off the D36d. The saltworks here are the world's highest-capacity salt-harvesting site, covering an area of 110 square kilometres and producing 800,000 tonnes a year for domestic use and export. Across the Grand Rhône (there's a daily ferry at Salin; every 20min; €4) and downstream you can see **Port-St-Louis**, where the rice and salt of the Camargue are loaded onto ships, and where, surprisingly, a small fishing fleet still operates.

There are two inexpensive **hotels** in the village: *Les Saladelles*, 4 rue des Arènes (ⓣ04.42.86.83.87, ⓕ04.42.48.81.89; ❶), a traditional, family-run hotel with a popular restaurant; and *La Camargue*, 58 bd de la Camargue (ⓣ04.42.86.88.52, ⓕ04.42.86.83.95; ❶), with a little less character, but more mod cons. The centre of social life is the *Bar des Sports*, next to the *Saladelles* hotel, where *belote* (a card game) championships are held and where the local fan club for Marseille's football team is based. Original paintings by local artists are on the walls, there's a model ship crystallized in salt, pinball, bar football, arcade games, and a normally gregarious clientele. On Friday evenings in July and August, entertainment shifts to the *arènes* between the main road and the river.

In summer three of the Arles–Salin buses continue on to the long, sandy **Plage d'Arles** which stretches westwards from the mouth of the Grand Rhône. Due west of Salin a tortuous route of dyke-top tracks takes you to the **Pointe de Beauduc**, a wide spit of sand facing Stes-Maries across the bay. Amidst the shacks and caravans you'll find *Chez Juju* (closed Thurs; Oct–March weekends only) and *Chez Marc et Mireille* (closed Wed), two fish **restaurants** where you can try freshly scooped *tellines*. It's a bit like barbecuing on the beach, and not cheap, but it's the best Camarguais dining experience.

Travel details

Trains

Ordinary trains

Arles to: Avignon (9–13 daily; 20min); Avignon TGV (5 daily; 45 min); Marseille (every 40 min; 45min–1hr); Narbonne (3 daily; 2hr); Nîmes (hourly; 30min); Tarascon (4 daily; 10min).

Avignon to: Arles (9–13 daily; 20min); Cavaillon (14 daily; 25 min); Marseille (7 daily; 1hr 20min); Montpellier (8 daily; 1hr); Orange (9 daily; 15min); Tarascon (10 daily; 10min); Toulouse (2 daily; 4hr 10min).

Orange to: Avignon (9 daily; 15min).

TGV

Avignon to: Aix-en-Provence TGV (11 daily; 20min); Lyon (14 daily; 1hr 10min); Marseille (hourly; 35min); Paris (12 daily; 2hr 40min); Paris CDG Airport (6 daily; 3hr 30min).

Buses

Arles to: Aix (5 daily; 2hr); Albaron (5 daily; 30min); Avignon TGV (9 daily; 45min); Les Baux (4 daily; 30min); Le Sambuc (Mon–Sat 6 daily, Sun 2 daily; 35min); Raphèle (10 daily; 15min); Salin (Mon–Sat 6 daily, Sun 2 daily; 1hr); Salon (8 daily; 1hr–1hr 25min); Stes-Maries (5 daily; 1hr); St-Rémy (1 daily; 35min); Tarascon (3 daily; 20min).

Avignon to: Aix (4 daily; 1hr–1hr 15min); Apt (5 daily; 1hr 10min); Arles (5 daily; 50min); Barbentane (4 daily; 20min); Beaucaire (4 daily; 45min); Boulbon (4 daily; 30min); Carpentras (hourly; 40min); Cavaillon (8 daily; 45min); Châteauneuf-du-Pape (4 daily; 20min); Châteaurenard (hourly; 20min); Digne (1 daily; 3hr 30min); Fontaine de Vaucluse (9 daily; 1hr); Gordes (1 daily; 2hr); Graveson (2 daily; 50min); Les Baux (2 daily; 1hr); L'Isle-sur-la-Sorgue (hourly; 40 min); Lourmarin (4 daily; 1hr 30min); Maillane (2 daily; 1hr); Marseille (4 daily; 2hr 30min); Montélimar (1 daily; 2hr 40min); Nîmes (4 daily; 1hr 15min); Orange (4–6 daily; 45min); Pertuis (4 daily; 2hr); St-Rémy (8 daily; 40min); Tarascon (4 daily; 40min); Vaison (2 daily; 1hr).

Avignon TGV to: Apt (4 daily; 1hr 30min); Arles (5 daily; 45min); Carpentras (3 daily; 45min); Cavillon (1 daily; 50min).

Orange to: Avignon (hourly; 45min–1hr 10min); Carpentras (5 daily; 45min); Châteauneuf-du-Pape (4 daily; 25min); Nyons (1 daily; 1hr 15min); Sérignan (3 daily; 20min); Vaison (5 daily; 45min).

St-Rémy to: Arles (1 daily; 35min); Les Baux (2 daily; 15min); St-Rémy (3 daily; 20min).

Tarascon to: Arles (3 daily; 20min); St-Rémy (3 daily; 20min).

The eastern Vaucluse

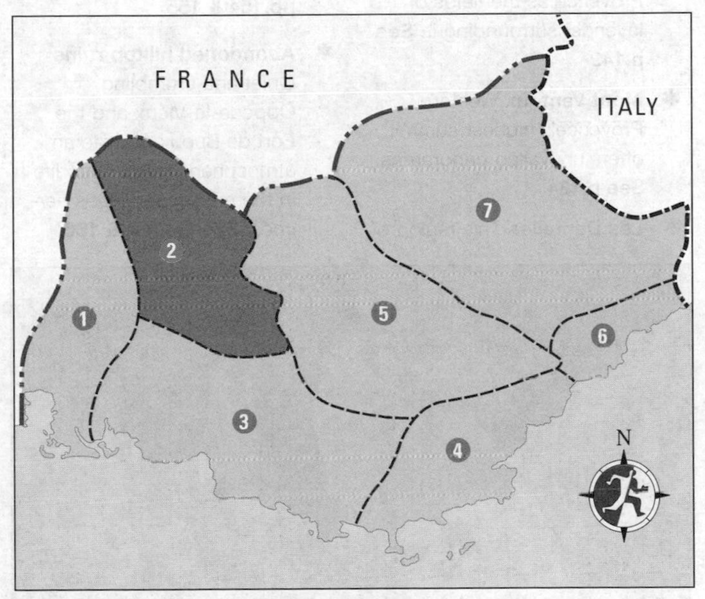

CHAPTER 2

Highlights

* **Medieval hilltop villages** Though Gordes is the best known, Bonnieux, Saignon and Le Crestet are equally picturesque, and much less busy. **See pp.130, 151 & 155**
* **Abbaye de Sénanque** The ancient Cistercian monastery is as much a symbol of Provence as the fields of lavender surrounding it. **See p.149**
* **Mont Ventoux** Western Provence's highest summit offers unrivalled panoramas. **See p.134**
* **Les Dentelles** This region of jagged limestone pinnacles is home to some exceptional and varied wines, as well as plenty of good hiking trails. **See p.130**
* **Colorado Provençal** Eroding ochre-coloured landscapes enfold the friendly villages of Rustrel and Roussillon. **See pp.154 & 155**
* **Abandoned hilltop ruins** Quiet and crumbling, Oppède-le-Vieux and the Fort de Buoux provide an atmospheric insight into life in the medieval *villages perchés*. **See pp.150 & 156**

2

The eastern Vaucluse

As an area with a distinct identity the **Vaucluse département** dates only from the Revolution. It was created to tidy up all the bits and pieces: the papal territory of the Comtat Venaisson that became part of France in 1791, the principality of Orange won by Louis XIV in 1713, plus parts of Provence that didn't fit happily into the initial three *départements* drawn up in 1791. It's still a bit untidy, with the **Papal Enclave** surrounded by the Drôme *département*, but that apart, it has the natural boundaries of the Rhône, **Mont Ventoux**, the limit of the **Vaucluse plateau** and the **River Durance**. The Rhône Valley is covered in Chapter 1; this chapter deals with everything Vauclusian to the east.

The main urban centres of **Vaison-la-Romaine**, **Cavaillon**, **Carpentras** and **Apt** were once part of the imperial Roman belt, while the outlying villages remained tribal strongholds. During the Wars of Religion Carpentras was strongly papal, whereas the settlements of the southern Luberon supported the new religion. To this day there is very little unifying character to the area, save that its people have always been Provençal, whether ruled by Rome, Holland or France.

Today, Cavaillon, Carpentras and Apt are basically market towns, with life centred on the seasons of the best fruit and vegetables in Provence. Of far greater appeal are the villages and countryside. The jagged rocky teeth of the **Dentelles**, the panorama from the windswept heights of Mont Ventoux and the great green surge of the **Luberon** give three complete landscape contrasts. Then there are the multi-hued ochre mines of **Rustrel** and **Roussillon**, and the **River Sorgue** with its many channels and mysterious source at **Fontaine-de-Vaucluse**.

The villages are just as diverse: the dedicated wine-producing communities of the Dentelles, the chic medieval hilltop habitats surrounding Apt, the abandoned villages at **Buoux** and **Oppède-le-Vieux**, romantic **Fontaine**, and **Cucuron**, which is strongly Provençal in character; while you'll find great examples of twelfth-century Cistercian monasteries at **Sénanque** and **Silvacane**.

The Enclave des Papes and Nyons

The **Enclave des Papes**, centred on the town of **Valréas**, is not part of the Drôme *département* that surrounds it, but part of Vaucluse, an anomaly dating back to 1317 when the land was bought by Pope Jean XXII as part of his pol-

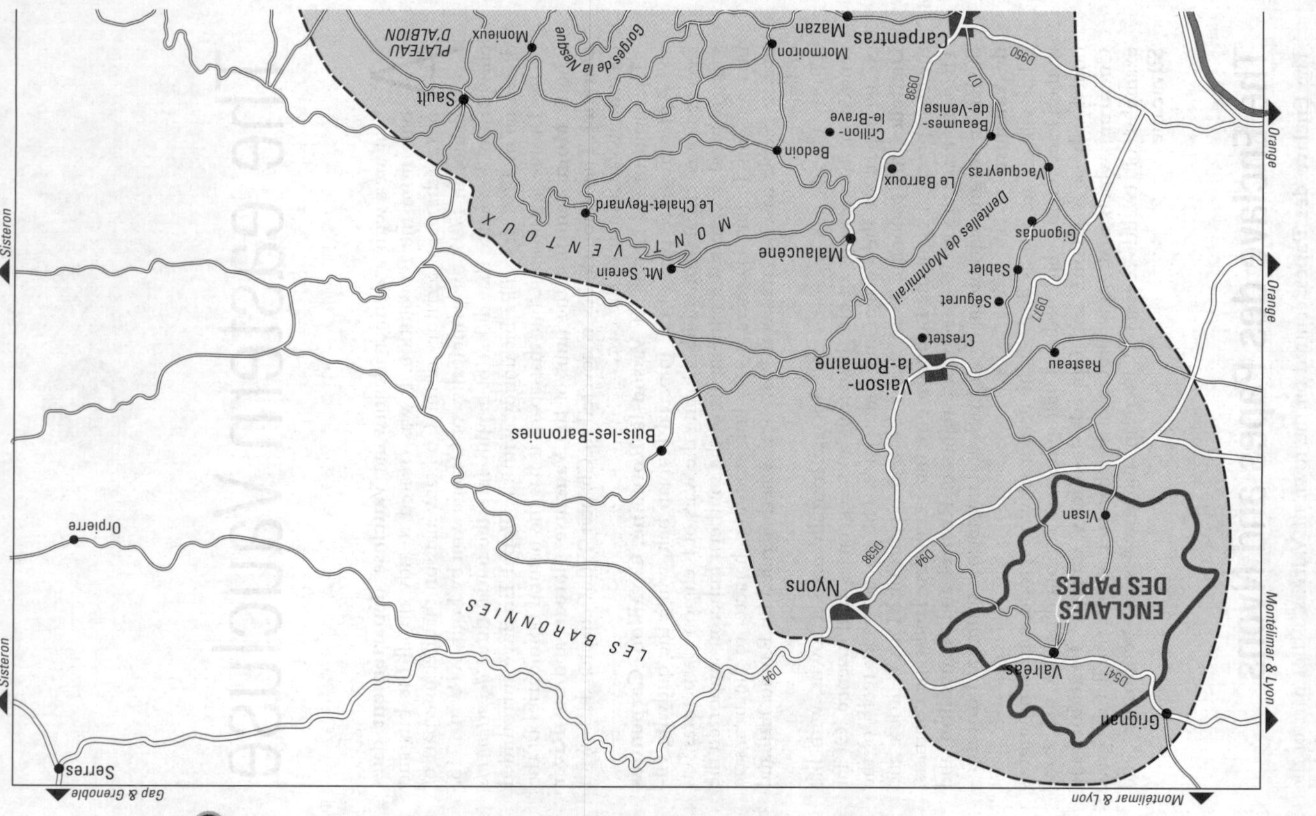

Sisteron
Sisteron
Gap & Grenoble
Serres
Orpierre
Montélimar & Lyon
Montélimar & Lyon
Orange
Orange
LES BARONNIES
Buis-les-Baronnies
MONT VENTOUX
Mt. Serein
Le Chalet-Reynard
Sault
Monieux
PLATEAU D'ALBION
Gorges de la Nesque
Nyons
D94
D538
Vaison-la-Romaine
Malaucène
Bedoin
Mormoiron
Mazan
Crillon-le-Brave
Le Barroux
Crestet
Séguret
Sablet
Dentelles de Montmirail
Beaumes-de-Venise
Carpentras
D938
D7
D950
Vacqueyras
Gigondas
Rasteau
D977
Valréas
Visan
Grignan
D541
ENCLAVES DES PAPES

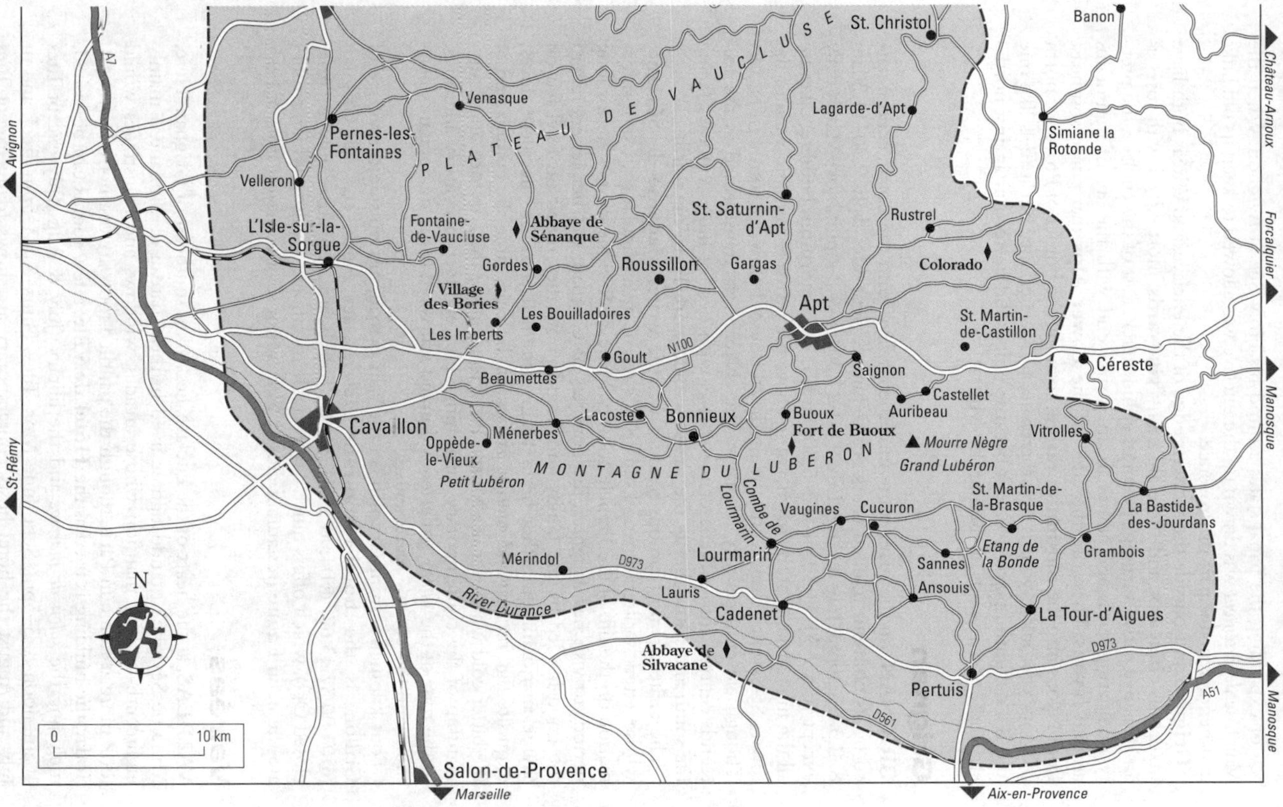

Château-Arnoux
Forcalquier
Manosque
Manosque
Aix-en-Provence
Marseille
St-Rémy
Avignon
Banon
Simiane la Rotonde
Céreste
La Bastide-des-Jourdans
Grambois
Vitrolles
La Tour-d'Aigues
St. Martin-de-Castillon
St. Martin-de-la-Brasque
Etang de la Bonde
Mourre Nègre
Grand Lubéron
Castellet
Auribeau
Sannes
Ansouis
Pertuis
St. Christol
Lagarde-d'Apt
Rustrel
Colorado
Saignon
Fort de Buoux
Buoux
Cucuron
Vaugines
Apt
L U B E R O N
St. Saturnin-d'Apt
Gargas
Combe de Lourmarin
Lourmarin
Cadenet
Abbaye de Silvacane
Lauris
Roussillon
N100
Bonnieux
M O N T A G N E D U
Goult
Lacoste
Les Bouilladoires
Abbaye de Sénanque
Beaumettes
Ménerbes
Mérindol
D973
D561
A51
Gordes
Village des Bories
Les Imberts
Oppède-le-Vieux
Petit Lubéron
River Durance
Venasque
P L A T E A U D E V A U C L U S E
Fontaine-de-Vaucluse
Cavaillon
Salon-de-Provence
Pernes-les-Fontaines
L'Isle-sur-la-Sorgue
Velleron
A7
N
0
10 km

icy of expanding the papal states around his Holy See at Avignon. When the Vaucluse *département* was drawn up the enclave was allowed to keep its old links and hence remains part of Provence.

Grignan, just outside the western edge of the enclave, and Valréas both have luxurious **châteaux**, and there are many **vineyards**, most edged with roses as an attractive early-warning system of aphid attack. East of the enclave, the pretty, undulating landscape comes to an abrupt end with the arc of mountains around **Nyons**. These are the edge of the **Lower Alps** that curve southeast from Nyons into the **Baronnies range**, forming the border of Provence north of Mont Ventoux. Nyons is not, therefore, a Provençal city but it feels like one and is a delightful place, not least because of its solid protection against northern and eastern winds, including the Mistral.

Grignan

GRIGNAN, on the main route into the enclave from the north, is dominated by its **château** (guided tours: April–June & Sept–Oct daily 9.30–11.30am & 2.30–5.30pm; July & Aug daily 9.30–11.30am & 2–6pm; Nov–March daily except Tues 9.30–11.30am & 2–5.30pm; €5). The enormous building takes up all the high ground of the town, rising above the heavy towers and walls of the town's St-Saveur's church and the medieval houses below the southern facade. Though eleventh-century in origin, the château was transformed in the sixteenth century into a Renaissance palace, with tiers of huge windows facing the south and statues lining the roof; the older parts lie to the north.

The château's most famous resident was the writer **Madame de Sévigné**, whose letters, written during Louis XIV's reign, are a popular source of information on the life of the French nobility. Mme de Sévigné came here for long periods to visit her daughter, the countess of Grignan, and her letters record the good life led by the family and friends: how they dined on fowl fed on thyme, marjoram and other herbs to give them flavour, on succulent doves, exquisite figs, melons and muscat grapes. At the same time she complained of the bitter cold whenever the Mistral blew. You can see the comforts and craftsmanship of the contemporary furnishings, plus eighteenth-century additions, in the tour of the *salons*, galleries and grand stairways, Mme de Sévigné's bedroom and the count's apartments.

Four kilometres from Grignan on the Valréas road, just outside the village of Grillon, is the **hotel-restaurant** *Auberge des Papes,* rte de Grignan (Ⓣ04.90.37.43.67, Ⓕ04.90.35.51.28; ❺; half board obligatory July & Aug; closed Oct), which offers quiet, comfortable rooms and meals in which truffles are the main feature (restaurant closed Wed out of season; menus from €19).

Valréas

VALRÉAS, at the heart of the enclave, lies 10km southeast of Grignan. Here, Mme de Sévigné's granddaughter lived in the Château de Simiane, a mainly eighteenth-century mansion whose arcades, windows and balustrades would look more at home in Paris, though the pantiled roofs are distinctly Provençal. Today, the building is used as the **Hôtel de Ville**; a few rooms can be visited, including the *salon de mariage* and the library (July & Aug daily except Tues 10am–noon & 3–5pm; Sept–June Mon, Tues, Thurs–Sat 3–5pm; free), and in July and August the hôtel hosts contemporary art shows (daily except Tues 10am–noon & 2–8pm; free). The town's other example of *ancien régime* ornamentation is the painted wooden ceiling of the **Chapelle des Pénitents**

Blancs on place Pie (July & Aug guided tours twice weekly; ask at the tourist office for details), which stands to the west of the much more subdued eleventh-century **Église Notre-Dame-de-Nazareth**.

Valréas is an important centre of cardboard production and, just outside the town in a warehouse on the road west to Orange, there's a museum dedicated to the use of the product: the **Musée du Cartonnage et de l'Imprimerie** (April–Oct Mon & Wed–Sat 10am–noon & 3–6pm, Sun 3–6pm; €3.50), a surprisingly intriguing museum of packaging.

Valréas is at its busiest on June 23 and 24, for the night-time procession and show of the **Nuit de Petit St-Jean**, and on the first Sunday in August, when the **Fête des Vins de l'Enclave** takes place. At other times, it's a pleasant, if quiet, place to spend some time. The most interesting diversions lie in buying local **wines**. As well as the Côtes du Rhône appellation there's also Valréas Villages and Visan Villages, distinctive enclave wines, with flavours of violet, red fruits and pepper; it's said that these distinctive wines were what persuaded Pope Jean XXII to buy this area in the first place. The **Cave Coopérative** is at the Caveau St-Jean, av de l'Enclave des Papes; you can also visit the private cellars (full list from the tourist office).

The **tourist office** is to the north of town on avenue Maréchal Leclerc (July & Aug Mon–Sat 9.15am–12.15pm & 2–7pm, Sun 9.15am–12.15pm; Sept, Oct & March–June Mon–Sat 9.15am–12.15pm & 2–6pm; Nov–Feb 9.15am–12.15pm & 2–5pm; ⓣ04.90.35.04.71, ⓦwww.ot-valreas.info). The best places **to stay** are the *Grand Hôtel,* 28 av Gén-de-Gaulle (ⓣ04.90.35.00.26, ⓕ04.90.35.60.93; ❸), on the outskirts of town, and the more moderate *Camargue*, 49 cours Jean-Jaurès (ⓣ04.90.35.01.51; ❷), both of which have reasonable restaurants. There's also a two-star **campsite**, *Camping de la Couronne*, by the river on the rte du Pègue (ⓣ04.90.35.03.78; closed Nov–Feb; €10 per tent).

A good place **to eat** is *La Ferme Champ-Rond*, chemin des Anthelmes (ⓣ04.90.37.31.68), off rte de St-Pierre to the southeast of town; it uses local produce with menus from €18. In town, *L'Oustau,* 2 cours Tivoli (ⓣ04.90.35.05.94; closed Sun eve & Mon), has menus starting from €18 and specializes in seafood à la carte. You can sample the **local wines** at the beautiful *Café de la Paix* on rue de l'Hôtel-de-Ville. The **market** is held on Wednesday on place Cardinal-Maury and cours du Berteuil on the eastern side of town, with local truffles figuring prominently between November and March.

Nyons

After Grignan and Valréas, **NYONS**, on the River Aigues, seems like a metropolis, though its population is well under ten thousand. It is an extremely attractive place, perfect for lazing about in cafés or strolling through, with its medieval centre and aromatic riverside gardens. If Nyons is on your route into Provence you can begin to appreciate the essentials of the region's cooking here: olives and olive oil, garlic, wild mushrooms, and countless varieties of fruit and vegetables, with seasons quite different to the north. If Nyons is on your way out, then this is the place to do the final shop.

Arrival and accommodation

Nyons has no train links but is served by a regular bus from Montélimar and Avignon. **Buses** arrive at place Buffaven on the edge of the old town, just northeast of the large central square, place de la Libération, where you'll find the **tourist office** (April–June & Sept Mon–Sat 9.30am–noon & 2.30–6pm, Sun 10am–1pm & 2–5pm; July & Aug Mon–Sat 9am–12.30pm & 2.30–7pm, Sun 10am–1pm & 2–5pm; Oct–May Mon–Sat 9.30am–noon & 2.30–6pm; ⓣ04.75.26.10.35, ⓦwww.nyonstourisme.com). Accommodation is easy to find: as well as the two excellent **campsites** – the four-star *Camping des Clos*, 1km along the road to Gap (ⓣ04.75.26.29.90; €19.50 per tent), which has its own pool, and the two-star *Camping l'Or Vert*, 2km along the road to Gap (ⓣ04.75.26.24.85; €11 per tent; closed Oct–March) – there are plenty of **hotel** rooms. Inexpensive options include *Le Petit Nice*, 4 av Paul-Laurens (ⓣ04.75.26.09.46; ❷), just to the west of pl de la Libération; and *Les Oliviers*, 2 rue A-Escoffier (ⓣ04.75.26.11.44, ⓕ04.75.26.05.03; ❸), a small, pleasant hotel with a garden bordering the old town to the north. For a bit more luxury, try *La Caravelle*, 8 rue des Antignans (ⓣ04.75.26.07.44, ⓕ04.75.26.23.79; ❺; closed mid-Nov to mid-Dec), a small hotel, looking out over gardens to the river, close to the town centre; or *La Picholine,* promenade de la Perrière (ⓣ04.75.26.06.21, ⓕ04.75.26.40.72; ❹), a quiet, secluded and comfortable place in the hills north of the town, with its own swimming pool and a good restaurant. Finally, *Une Autre Maison*, on place de la République, is small but lavish, with six south-facing rooms, a pool and garden (ⓣ04.75.26.43.09; ⓦwww.uneautremaison.com; ❼).

The Town

The pavement terraces of **place de la Libération**'s cafés and brasseries are a pleasant place to while away an afternoon, people-watching against a background of fountains, plane trees, palms and curly wrought-iron lampposts, and taking in the views beyond of steep wooded slopes. On Thursdays the square and its neighbour to the northeast, place Buffaven, are taken over by a huge and wonderful **market**. A smaller one takes place on Monday – and in July and August there's a Sunday-morning market in the old town.

East of place de la Libération, the arcaded **place du Dr-Bourdongle** leads into a web of streets, covered passages and stairways running up to the **quartier des Forts**, so named for the now ruined feudal castle; the fourteenth-century **Château Delpinal**, of which three towers remain; and the extraordinary **Tour Randonne**, which houses a nineteenth-century chapel, with a neo-Gothic pyramid supporting a statue of the Madonna, sitting delicately on the heavy crenellated base of a thirteenth-century keep.

Olive produce

Nyons is famous for its **olives**. Black eating olives are a speciality, as is *tapenade* (a paste of olives, capers and herbs), but the biggest business is making olive oil, a process you can watch between December and February. Among firms that welcome visitors are **J Ramade**, av P-Laurens (just before place Oliver-de-Serres on the left), who show a video explaining all the subtleties, and **Moulin à Huile Autrand-Dozol**, on av de la Digue by the Pont Romain. The tourist office can provide more addresses, and there's also a small **museum** on the subject on rue des Tilleuls (June–Oct Mon–Sat 10am–11am & 2.45–6pm; Nov–May Tues–Sat 2.45–6pm, Sun 2.30–6pm; €2).

The **Coopérative Agricole du Nyonsais** on place Oliver-de-Serres (Mon–Sat 8.45am–12.30pm & 2–7pm, Sun 10am–12.30pm & 2.30–6.30pm) sells a full range of the olive products under the trademark "Nyonsolive", as well as nut and chilli oils, wines and honey.

Towards the river, which is crossed by a single-spanned Romanesque bridge, the Pont Romain, there are pleasantly untouristy streets, scattered with bars, restaurants and some highly unusual **shops**, such as the Galerie du Pontias at 20 rue des Bas Bourgs, selling the sort of traditional crafts and antiques normally seen only in folklore museums. Just beside the bridge, at 4 av de la Digue, is **Les Vieux Moulins** (July & Aug daily 10am–noon & 2.30–6pm; Sept–June closed Sun & Mon; €4), an old artisanal complex of two eighteenth- and nineteenth-century oil presses, an eighteenth-century soap works, and a traditional Provençal kitchen.

About 500m west of the bridge, along the river, is the small but sensual **Jardin des Arômes**, a garden of aromatic plants from which essential oils are made.

Eating and drinking

In addition to the many **brasseries** on place de la Libération there's *Le Petit Caveau*, 9 rue Victor-Hugo (☎04.75.26.20.21; set menu from €26-39; closed Sun eve & Mon out of season), which serves very good, classic Provençal food and wines. The best place for *steack-frites* is the *Bar du Pont*, at 10 place Jules Laurent, with great views over the old Pont Romain. At the restaurant *Les Alpes*, 9 rue des Déportés (☎04.75.26.04.99), you can get paella and couscous from €9.15, while, on the same street, there's a choice of Tex-Mex at *Le Tex* (from €10), pizzas at *L'Alicoque* (from €7), or large open **sandwiches** and salads for around €8 at *La Tartinière*.

Vaison-la-Romaine and around

VAISON-LA-ROMAINE lies between Nyons and Orange to the southeast of the Enclave des Papes. The most dramatic approach, however, is from the southeast along the Malaucène road, from where the first glimpse of the town is of a ruined twelfth-century castle outlined against the sky. As you get closer you see the storeys of old pale stone houses and towers beneath it, and the eighteenth-century town laid around its Roman predecessor. The two are linked by a Roman bridge, spanning the River Ouvèze in a single arch. The population of Vaison began to settle on both sides of the river only late this century. The original Celtic Voconces, like the late medieval Vaisonnais, chose the high ground, for defensive reasons. Their eighteenth-century descendants moved back to the right bank, abandoning the citadel to wait for twentieth-century romantics to bring it back into fashion.

The older generation in Vaison recalls the days when shops were little more than front rooms and you would interrupt the cooking or other household chores when you went in to be served. They talk of a barber who played the violin and would always finish the final bars before getting out the soap and towels. These days the population of the town and its tourist visitors can keep several dozen bars, hotels and restaurants busy, as well as numerous souvenir and sports shops.

Vaison hit the headlines in 1992 when the River Ouvèze burst its banks, killing thirty people, and destroying riverside houses, the modern road bridge, and an entire industrial quarter. Though the town has recovered remarkably, its character has changed. It seems much more commercialized, and less friendly, perhaps because of the mass of ghoulish "tourists" who flocked to the town to see the damage.

Today, its main attractions are the medieval **Haute Ville** with a ruined clifftop castle, the **Pont Romain** that held out against the floods, a cloistered former cathedral and the exceptional excavated remains of two **Roman districts**. Just south of Vaison, the **Crestet Centre d'Art** is home to an array of sculptures displayed in natural settings.

Arrival, information and accommodation

Buses to and from Avignon, Orange and Carpentras stop at the **gare routière** on av des Choralies, near the junction with av Victor-Hugo east of the town centre on the north side of the river. Heading down av Victor-Hugo you'll come to the main square, **place de Montfort**, from where it's a short walk further to **Grande Rue** which leads left to the **Pont Romain** and right, becoming av Général-de-Gaulle, to **place du Chanoine-Sautel**. The **tourist office** is to the north of the modern town, on pl du Chanoine-Sautel (July & Aug daily 9am–1pm & 2–6.45pm; Sept–June Mon–Sat 9am–noon & 2–5.45pm, Sun 9am–noon; ⓣ04.90.36.02.11, ⓦwww.vaison-la-romaine.com), between the two Roman archeological sites.

Accommodation is thin on the ground and consequently somewhat expensive.

Hotels

Le Beffroi rue de l'Evêché in the Haute Ville ⓣ04.90.36.04.71, ⓦwww.le-beffroi.com. Stylish lodgings in a sixteenth-century residence; the rooms are furnished in keeping with the building and are not outrageously expensive. Closed Feb to mid-March. ❻

Le Burrhus 2 pl Montfort ⓣ04.90.36.00.11, ⓦwww.burrhus.com. The cheapest rooms in town and noisy at weekends as it's above several cafés with terraces. ❸

La Fête en Provence pl du Vieux Marché in the Haute Ville ⓣ04.90.36.36.43, ⓦwww.la-fete-en-provence.com. Studios and duplexes in the Haute Ville, let on a day-to-day basis. ❸

Hôtel des Lis 20 cours Henri-Fabre ⓣ04.90.36.00.11, ⓕ04.90.36.39.05. Right in the centre, with some very large rooms. ❹

Le Logis du Château Les Hauts de Vaison ⓣ04.90.36.09.98, ⓦwww.logis-du-chateau.com. Along montée du Château south of the river, and to the west of the Haute Ville; spacious rooms with lovely views. ❸

Hostel and campsite

Centre Culturel à Coeur Joie Le Moulin de César, rte de St-Marcellin ⓣ04.90.36.00.78, ⓔcentracj.france@wanadoo.fr. Just 1km east of town down av Geoffroy from the Pont Romain, with basic but adequate rooms for two to four people at €28.50 per person.

Camping du Théâtre Romain chemin du Brusquet, off av des Choralies, quartier des Arts ⓣ04.90.28.78.66. Small three-star campsite with good facilities. €16.80 per tent. Closed Nov to mid-March.

The Town

Of all the distinctive periods in Vaison's history, it is the style and luxuries of the **Roman** population that are the most intriguing. The two excavated Roman residential districts in Vaison lie to either side of av Général-de-Gaulle: the **Fouilles Puymin** to the east and the **Fouilles de la Villasse** to the west (Feb & Oct daily 10–12.30pm & 2–5.30pm; March–May daily 10am–12.30pm & 2–6pm; June–Sept daily 9.30am–6.15pm; Nov–Jan Wed–Sun 10am–noon & 2–4.30pm; €7 includes both sites, plus Puymin museum and cathedral cloisters).

The Puymin excavations (*fouilles*) contain the theatre, several mansions and houses thought to be for rent, a colonnade known as the *portique de Pompée* and the museum for all the items discovered. The Villasse site reveals a street with pavements and gutters with the layout of a row of arcaded shops running parallel, more patrician houses (some with mosaics still intact), a basilica and the baths. The houses require a certain amount of imagination, but the street plan of La Villasse, the colonnade with its statues in every niche, and the theatre, which still seats seven thousand people during the July festival, make it easy to visualize a comfortable, well-serviced town of the Roman ruling class.

Most of the detail and decoration of the buildings is displayed in the **museum** (closes 15 minutes before the main sites; admission included in site ticket) in the Puymin district. Tiny fragments of painted plaster have been jigsawed together with convincing reconstructions of how whole painted walls would have looked. There are mirrors of silvered bronze, lead water pipes, taps shaped as griffins' feet, dolphin door knobs, weights and measures, plus household and building implements. The busts and statues are particularly impressive: among them a silver head of one of the Villasse villas' owners; the emperor Domitian, under whose reign the conquest of Britain was completed, wearing a breastplate of Minerva and the Gorgon's head; and a statue of another famous emperor, Hadrian.

The former **Cathédrale Notre-Dame** lies west down chemin Couradou which runs along the south side of La Villasse. The apse of the cathedral, which was badly flooded, is a confusing overlay of sixth-, tenth- and thirteenth-century construction, some of it using pieces quarried from the Roman ruins. The **cloisters** (closes 15 minutes before the main sites; admission included in site ticket) are fairly typical of early medieval workmanship, pretty enough but not wildly exciting. The only surprising feature is the large inscription visible on the north wall of the cathedral, a convoluted instruction to the monks to bring peace upon the house by loving the monastic rule and following God's grace.

Just south of the Roman districts, the **Pont Romain** leads across the river to the Haute Ville. The bridge has undergone extensive repair works since its battering in the 1992 flood, but it says a lot for Roman engineering that it fared better than the modern road bridge to the west. Its new casings need weathering to return it to its former beauty, but the grace of the high-arched structure remains.

From the bridge, rue du Pont climbs upwards towards place des Poids and the fourteenth-century gateway to the medieval **Haute Ville**. More steep zigzags take you past the Gothic gate and overhanging portcullis of the belfry and into the heart of this sedately quiet, uncommercialized and rich *quartier*. There are fountains and flowers in all the squares, and right at the top, from the twelfth- to fifteenth-century **Castle**, you'll have a great view of Mont Ventoux. In summer the Haute Ville livens up every Tuesday when Vaison's **market** spreads up here.

Eating and drinking

The **restaurant** to head for in Vaison is *Le Bateleur* at 1 place Théodore-Aubanel, downstream from the Pont Romain on the north bank (☎04.90.36.28.04; closed Mon, Tues, Fri lunch & mid-Nov to mid-Dec; weekday lunch menu €16, à la carte around €35): the lamb stuffed with almonds and the *rascasse* soufflé are highly recommended. Alternatively, *L'Auberge de la Bartavelle*, 12 place Sus-Auze (☎04.90.36.02.16; closed Mon & Tues lunch), serves specialities from southwest France for €19–45, while *Charlie's Pub*, 12 av Général-de-Gaulle (open 8am–3am), is good for salads and pizzas as well as traditional *plats* at around €10.

In the Haute Ville, the restaurant at *Le Beffroi* hotel has a surprisingly inexpensive menu (€25.50), and the food is good though served with stiff formality. At the far end of rue de l'Evêché on place du Vieux-Marché, *La Fête en*

Provence includes grilled dishes using organic produce on its excellent €25 menu. Alternatively, there's the *Crêperie la Pomme*, at 3 rue du Pont, which also serves pizza.

Standard **brasserie fare** is available on place de Montfort, which is also the best place to head for **drinks**. If you want to be in a more "local" ambience try *Vasio Bar* on cours Taulignan. For buying **wine** to take home, the Maison des Vins (Tues–Sat 9–noon & 2–5.45pm), in the same building as the tourist office, has all the wines from the vineyards of the Dentelles and Ventoux.

Le Crestet

South of Vaison, 3.5km down the Malaucène road, a turning to the right leads up to **LE CRESTET**, a tiny hilltop village with a private château at the top and a little snack bar *Le Panorama* (summer daily till 9pm; winter Sat & Sun only), from where you can admire the fantastic view, taking in the ruined château of Entrechaux, the Barronnies range and Mont Ventoux. From the village, signs direct you to the nearby **Crestet Centre d'Art** (always open; July & Aug €3; Sept–June free), where you can explore the sculptures placed within the surrounding forest of oak, pine and honeysuckle. None of the sculptures is titled or signed and most are off the main path, but there's a map on the wall at the entrance to the building: from behind here, head right and then turn sharp left within 20m; the path then makes a clockwise loop – if you reach a dirt road you've gone too far. Some of the sculptures are formed from the trees themselves, others are startling metal structures like a mobile and a Meccano cage. One of the first ones you're likely to come across is Parvine Curie's *La Grande Tête*, concrete cubes positioned so that Vaison's ruined château is framed directly behind.

South of Le Crestet, signed off the D76 to the Vaison–Malaucène road, is a lovely **hotel** in the middle of nowhere, *Le Mas de Magali* (Ⓣ04.90.36.39.91, Ⓦwww.masdemagali.com; ❽, half board obligatory; closed mid-Oct to mid-March), run by a Dutch couple, with its own pool and a *terrasse* looking eastwards to the mountains.

The Dentelles

The jagged hilly backdrop of the **DENTELLES DE MONTMIRAIL** is best appreciated from the contrasting landscape of level fields, orchards and vineyards lying to their south and west. The range is named after lace (*dentelles*), its pinnacles slanting, converging, standing parallel or veering away from each other, like the contorted pins on a lace-making board – though the alternative connection with "teeth" (*dents*) is equally appropriate. For geologists, the Dentelles are Jurassic limestone folds, forced upright and then eroded by the wind and rain.

The Dentelles run northeast to southwest between Vaison and Carpentras. On the western and southern slopes lie the **wine-producing villages** of **Gigondas**, **Beaumes-de-Venise**, **Sablet**, **Séguret**, **Vacqueyras** and, across the River Ouzère, **Rasteau**. Several carry the distinction of having their own individual *appellation contrôlée*, within the Côtes du Rhône or Côtes du Rhône Villages areas, meaning their wines are exceptional. If you're in the region over the July 14 holiday, head straight to Vacqueyras for the bacchanalian **Fêtes des Vins**, while at any other time of the year a more sober introduction to the subject is on offer at Rasteau's museum.

△ Gargoyle in Le Crestet

Besides wine-tasting and bottle-buying, the Dentelles are good for long **walks**, happening upon mysterious ruins or photogenic panoramas of Mont Ventoux and the Rhône Valley. The jagged hills are also favourite destinations for apprentice **rock-climbers**: the Col de Cayron is one of the favourite pinnacles for serious climbing; the Dent du Turc needs only decent shoes and a head for heights to give a thrill. To the east of the range lies the *village perché* of **Le Barroux**, with a fine twelfth-century château.

Although it's possible to get to the villages by public transport from Vaison or Carpentras, having your own vehicle is definitely an advantage. You can **rent bikes** at the *Café du Cours* in the centre of Vacqueyras; for **walking and climbing information** go to the *Gîte d'Etape des Dentelles* in Gigondas (see opposite), or pick up a local footpath map (€2.50) from the tourist office in Gigondas (see opposite). Alternatively, Edisud publishes a more detailed guide, *Randonnées au Ventoux et dans les Dentelles* by I. & H. Agresti, which is available from most of the region's tourist offices.

Rasteau

For a good introduction into the art and science of wine-making and the whole business of wine-tasting, head for **RASTEAU** and the **Musée du Vigneron** (Mon & Wed–Sat: July & Aug 11am–6pm; April–June & Sept 2pm–6pm; €2.50). The museum is on the D975 between Rasteau and Roaix and belongs to the Domaine de Beaurenard which also has vineyards in Châteauneuf-du-Pape. Along with a fairly predictable collection of bottles and nineteenth-century implements, there's a half-hour video on the whole Côtes du Rhône area. The charts and panels are rather harder work, but instructive on geology, soil, vine types, fossils, parasites and wine-growing throughout the world. There's also a free wine-tasting with no obligation to buy.

If you want **to stay** in Rasteau, the *Belle Rive* on route Violes (ⓣ04.90.46.10.20; ❾, half board obligatory; closed mid-Nov to March) is a quiet hotel with a fine view from its terrace, and serves good food, including a rosemary-flavoured *crème brûlée*. For walkers, the *Centre Départemental d'Animation et d'Accueil*, rte du Stade (ⓣ04.90.46.15.48), offers dormitory accommodation for €24.72 per night (half board), and €29.70 (full board). It also has three two-bed rooms for the same price, but the place is often reserved for large groups, so always call in advance.

Séguret and Sablet

The star Dentelles village, **SÉGURET**, whose name means "safe place" in Provençal, is an alluring spot blending into the rocky cliff rising above. With its steep cobbled streets, vine-covered houses and medieval structures, including an old stone laundry and a belfry with a one-handed clock, the village embodies many of Provence's charms. On Christmas Eve, in place of the standard Provençal crib, it hosts a living re-enactment of the Nativity in which people play the parts their grandparents and great-grandparents played before them. The **Fête des Vins et Festival Provençal Bravade** in the last two weeks of August is a relatively recent festival, incorporating processions for the Virgin Mary and the patron saint of wine-growers.

Séguret has two very smart **hotels**, *Domaine de Cabasse*, rte de Sablet (ⓣ04.90.46.91.12, ⓦwww.domaine-de-cabasse.fr; ❼, half board obligatory in July & Aug; closed Nov–March), and *La Table du Comtat* in the village (ⓣ04.90.46.91.49; ❻), both with a few rooms and good restaurants. A slightly cheaper and a more rustic option is the *Bastide Bleue*, rte de Sablet (ⓣ & ⓕ04.90.46.83.43; ❹; closed Wed), 500m from the village on the Vaison road.

For **food**, try *Le Mesclun*, rue des Poternes (Ⓣ04.90.46.93.43; closed Mon & Nov–Easter), which is renowned for using fresh local ingredients in its dishes; menus start at €25.

Just south of Séguret lies **SABLET**, the largest of the villages, and the least obviously chic. One road spirals up the dome on which the oldest houses are built; near the summit stands the *Café des Sports* and a cheap pizzeria. There's also a **campsite**, *Le Panoramic* (Ⓣ04.90.46.96.27; closed at the time of writing, so call ahead), 2km from the village on the rte d'Orange.

Gigondas and Vacqueyras

Known as "Jocunditas" (light-hearted joy) in Roman times, the village of **GIGONDAS** sits at the base of a hill, spreading upwards to the église Ste-Catherine. From the church, you get one of the region's best views of limestone pinnacles emerging from the vineyards below. Also in the upper reaches of the village are the vestiges of the old fortifications and château, which have now been transformed into a *Cheminement de Sculptures*, a collection of contemporary sculptures and installations.

Gigondas' wine has the best reputation of all the Dentelles *appellations*. It is almost always red, quite strong, has a back taste of spice or nuts and is best aged at least four or five years. Sampling the varieties could not be easier since the **Syndicat des Vins** runs a *caveau des vignerons* (daily 10am–noon & 2–5.30pm) in place de la Mairie where you can taste and ask advice about the produce from forty different *domaines*. It's also a good place to buy as the bottles cost exactly the same as at the vineyards.

Gigondas' **tourist office** is on place du Portail (daily: July & Aug 10am–noon & 2–7pm; Sept–Oct 10am–noon & 2–6pm; Ⓣ04.90.65.85.46, Ⓔot-gigondas@axit.fr), and can provide lists of particular *domaines* or *caves* grouping several *vignerons* for the other villages. If you want **to stay**, the *Gîte d'Etape des Dentelles* at the entrance to Gigondas (Ⓣ04.90.65.80.85; Ⓦwww.provence-trekking.com; closed Jan & Feb), has double rooms (❶), and dormitory accommodation (€11 per person). There's also a charming hotel, *Les Florets*, 2km from the village towards the Dentelles (Ⓣ04.90.65.85.01, Ⓕ04.90.65.83.80; ❻, half board obligatory in season), with an excellent Provençal **restaurant** (menus from €22; closed Wed, also Tues out of season). Alternative food options include *L'Oustalet*, on place du Portail in the village (Ⓣ04.90.65.85.30; closed Sun eve & Mon), with a pleasant shaded terrace and menus from €29.

Three kilometres to the south, the village of **VACQUEYRAS** is best known as the birthplace of a troubadour poet **Raimbaud**, who wrote love poems to Beatrice in Provençal and died in the Crusades in 1207. It is also home to an annual **wine festival** (on July 14) and a wine-tasting competition on the first weekend of June. You'll see plenty of signs for wine producers to visit around the village.

For **accommodation**, there's the upmarket *Hôtellerie de Montmirail*, just south of the centre on the road to Vacqueyras (Ⓣ04.90.65.84.01, Ⓦwww.hotel-montmirail.com; ❺), with an excellent Provençal restaurant (menus from €18).

Beaumes-de-Venise

The most distinctive wine of the region, and elixir for those who like it sweet, is Beaumes-de-Venise muscat. Pale amber in colour and with a hint of roses and lemon following the muscat flavour, it can usually convince the driest palates of its virtue. The place to buy it is at **BEAUMES-DE-VENISE**, in the Cave des Vignerons (Mon–Sat 8.30am–noon & 2–6pm, Sun 9am–12.30pm &

2–6pm), a huge low building on the D7 overlooked by the Romanesque bell tower of Notre-Dame-d'Aubune. The *cave* also sells red, rosé and white Côtes du Rhône Villages, and the light Côtes du Ventoux. The **church** in Beaumes reflects the key concern of the area in the trailing vines and classical wine containers sculpted over the door. The **tourist office** (June–Sept daily 9am–noon & 2–7pm; Oct–May Mon–Sat 9am–noon & 2–5pm; ⓣ04.90.62.94.39), near the church, can also provide lists of *domaines* or *caves* for the area.

The village has two quiet, old-fashioned **hotels,** both with good restaurants: the *Auberge St-Roch*, av Jules-Ferry (ⓣ04.90.65.08.21; ❷), and, across the street, *Le Relais des Dentelles* (ⓣ04.90.62.95.27; ❷). Both are located on the other side of the river from the old village, but only a short distance away. There's also a **campsite** on the edge of the village, the *Municipal les Queyrades* (ⓣ04.90.62.95.07; closed Sept–March; €6 per tent), 2km towards Malaucène.

Le Barroux

To the east of the Dentelles, on the Vaison–Malaucène road, the largely untouristy **LE BARROUX** is a perfect *village perché* with narrow, twisting streets leading up to its château at the top. Dating from the twelfth to eighteenth century, the **château** (Easter–Nov daily 10am–7pm; €3) was restored just before World War II, burnt by the Nazis then restored again from 1960 to 1990, and is now open to the public.

In the heart of the village, on place de la Croix, *Les Géraniums* (ⓣ04.90.62.41.08, ⓕ04.90.62.56.48; ❸; closed Jan & Feb) is a very peaceful, comfortable and unpretentious **hotel** with views of the Dentelles; its *terrasse* restaurant serves decent food with menus from €21.

Mont Ventoux and around

From the Rhône, Luberon and Durance, the summit of **MONT VENTOUX** repeatedly appears on the horizon. White with snow, black with storm-cloud shadow or reflecting myriad shades of blue, the barren pebbles of the final 300m are like a coloured weather vane for all of western Provence. From a distance the mountain looks distinctly alluring, a suitable site for what was the first recorded notion of landscape in European thought. The fourteenth-century Italian poet Petrarch climbed the heights simply for the experience; the local guides he chartered for the two-and-a-half-day hike considered him completely crazy.

Meteorological information is gathered, along with TV transmissions and Mirage fighter jet movements, from masts and dishes at the top. The tower directing the conglomeration of receptors is in consequence no beauty, its essential design characteristic being to withstand winds from every direction, including the northern Mistral that can accelerate to 250km per hour across Ventoux. Wind, rain, snow and fearsome sub-zero temperatures are the dominant natural accompaniments to this tarmacked mountain top.

The deforestation of Mont Ventoux dates from Roman times, and by the nineteenth century it had got so bad that the entire mountain appeared shaved. Oaks, pines, boxwood, fir and beech have since been replanted and the owls and eagles have returned, but the greenery is unlikely ever to reach the summit again. The road that zigzags up the 1900m and down again with such consummate, if convoluted, ease was built for the purposes of testing prototype cars, an activity that continued up till the mid-1970s. Mont Ventoux is also a sporadic highlight of the Tour de France, hence its appeal in summer for passionately committed cyclists. Around the tree line is a memorial to the great British cyclist Tommy Simpson, who died here from heart failure in 1967, on one of the hottest days ever recorded in the race; legend has it that his last words were – "Put me back on the bloody bike."

Despite the unpromising environment, rest assured that from the summit you have one of the most wonderful **panoramas**, not just in France, but in the whole of Europe. Between **November and May** all the road graffiti is covered by snow, with only the tops of the black and yellow poles beside the road still visible; then, people ascending Mont Ventoux will be on **skis**, leaving base either at Mont Serein on the north face or from the smaller southern station of Le Chalet-Reynard.

If you want to make the **ascent on foot** the best path to take is from Les Colombets or Les Fébriers, hamlets off the D974 east of **BEDOIN** whose **tourist office**, on Espace M.L-Gravier (July–Aug Mon–Fri 9am–12.30pm & 2–7pm, Sat 9.30am–12.30pm & 2.30–6.30pm, Sun 9.30am–12.30pm; Sept–June Mon–Fri 9am–12.30pm & 2–6pm, Sat 9am–noon; ⓣ04.90.65.63.95), can provide details. They also organize a weekly **night-time ascent**, in July and August, leaving around 10pm to camp near the summit and await the sunrise; check with the tourist office for the day. Bedoin location, on chemin de la Feraille (ⓣ04.90.65.94.53), rents out **bikes** if you want to join the superfit cyclists in braving the gusts and horribly long steep inclines. If you're not that fit, you could take one of the tourist office's monthly mountain biking trips, in which you are transported to the summit, and can cycle back down. In **Mont Serein** the Chalet d'Accueil Mt-Serein (ⓣ04.90.63.42.02) can provide info on **ski-rental**, runs and lifts.

Bedoin has several **campsites**, including the two-star *Camping Pastory* on the Malaucène road (ⓣ04.90.12.85.83; closed mid-Oct to mid-March), and more than a dozen **gîtes ruraux** for anyone considering spending a week or more in the area.

Le Chalet-Reynard, on the south face, has a small **restaurant** (ⓣ04.90.61.84.55; menus from €14.20) that fills with walkers in the summer and skiers in the winter. There's a very good gîte d'étape, *Les Écuries de Ventoux* (ⓣ04.90.65.29.20; ❶), 2km outside Malaucène, down a track off the road to Beaumont-de-Ventoux. At the other end of the scale, the *Hostellerie de Crillon le Brave*, place de l'Église (ⓣ04.90.65.61.61, ⓦwww.crillonlebrave.com; ❾), in **Crillon-le-Brave** just west of Bedoin, offers exquisitely tasteful luxury.

Gorges de la Nesque

The **GORGES DE LA NESQUE** lies to the south of Ventoux, on the D942 from Carpentras to Sault. The River Nesque is dry most of the year and invisible from most of the road which clings to the rocks above it – a feat of engineering even more impressive than the geological fault itself. It's a barren area with just one landmark, located on the southern side before the gorge turns northeast again towards the village of Monieux. The 200-metre-high **Rocher du Cire** is coated in wax from numerous hives that wild bees have made, and supposedly provided the men of the nearby village with the reputation-enhancing exploit of abseiling down it to gather honey. This may well be a macho myth; certainly no one does it now. In **MONIEUX**, there's a cheap **gîte d'étape** for walkers, the *Ferme St-Hubert* (ⓣ04.90.64.04.51; ❶; closed Mon–Thurs), and a little **restaurant**, *Les Lavandes* (ⓣ04.90.64.05.08; around €22; closed Mon out of season).

Sault and the Plateau d'Albion

At **SAULT**, 6km northeast of Monieux, the steep forested rocks give way to fields of lavender, cereals and grazing sheep. Wild products of the woods – lactaire and grisel mushrooms, truffles and game, as well as honey and other lavender products – are bought and sold at its Wednesday **market**; autumn is the best time for these local specialities. If you miss the market, La Maison des Producteurs on rue de la République can sell you all the goodies. Sault also has **fairs** on the Wednesday before Palm Sunday, St John's feast day (June 23) and on August 16.

At the **PLATEAU D'ALBION**, south of Sault, Mount Ventoux recedes from view. A ring of hills guards this treeless, undulating plain in which the chalky ground is riven by fissures, subterranean caverns and tunnels. Habitation is almost nonexistent and it's a shock when the narrow, badly surfaced and traffic-less D30 suddenly becomes a three-lane, superbly smooth highway which continues through St-Christol and down to Lagarde d'Apt. Part of the reason for this change is the enormous **airforce base** with its massive hangars and tall, rectangular, khaki-coloured blocks just north of St-Christol. Until recently, it was the base for France's eighteen land-based nuclear missiles, all of which have now been disarmed.

Carpentras and south

CARPENTRAS, with a population approaching thirty thousand, is one of the larger towns of the Vaucluse with a history dating back to around 5 BC, when it was the capital of a Celtic tribe. The Greeks, who founded Marseille, came here to buy honey, wheat, goats and skins, but it wasn't until the fourteenth century that the town really flourished – during the period of the popes, it briefly became the papal headquarters and gave protection to Jews expelled from France. Today, however, despite so many ancient remains, the town has a ghost-like and desolate atmosphere, especially in the evenings – only during the Friday **market** (see below), and the **festival** in the last two weeks of July (see p.138), does it really come to life.

Arrival, information and accommodation

Only freight trains stop at Carpentras, while **buses** arrive either on avenue Victor-Hugo or on place Terradou. From the latter it's a short walk to avenue Georges-Clemenceau and then right to place Aristide-Briand, where the **tourist office** is housed in the Hôtel-Dieu (July & Aug Mon–Sat 9am–7pm, Sun 9.30am–1pm; Sept–June Mon–Fri 9am–12.30pm & 2–6.30pm, Sat 9am–noon & 2–6pm; ⓣ04.90.63.00.78, ⓦwww.tourisme.fr/carpentras). The town proper is small enough to cover easily on foot, but if you fancy renting a **bike**, try Egobike on rue Vigne (ⓣ04.90.67.05.58).

Carpentras market

Friday is the major **market** day in Carpentras. The local **fruit and vegetables** that appear so early in the lowlands of Vaucluse are available all round the town; **flowers and plants** are sold on av Jean-Jaurès; **antiques and bric-a-brac** on rue Porte-de-Monteux and place Colonel-Mouret; while, from the annual St-Siffrein fair (November 27) to the beginning of March, place Aristide-Briand and place du 25 Août 1944 are given over to the selling of **truffles**, the rooted not the chocolate kind.

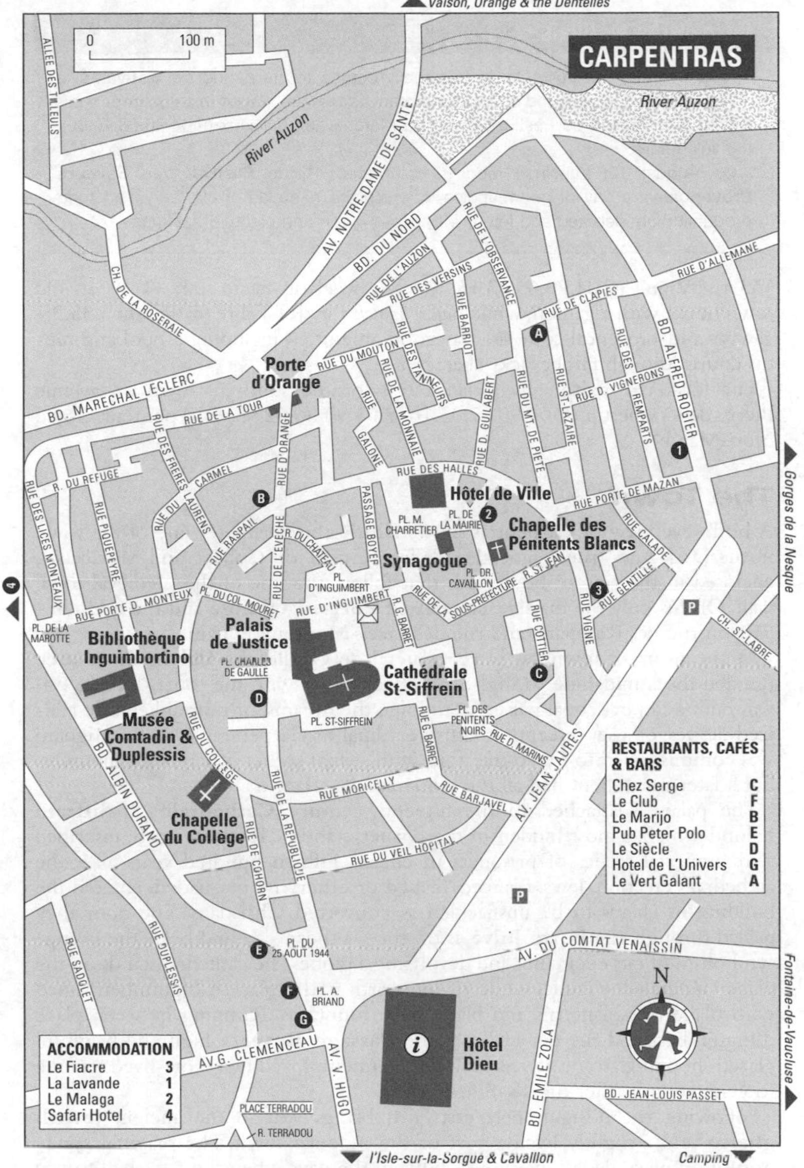

Most of Carpentras' **hotels** are on the boulevards which circle the old town; there are plenty of bargains to be had, but don't expect to find anywhere particularly atmospheric. *La Lavande*, 282 bd A-Rogier (Ⓣ04.90.63.13.49, Ⓕ04.90.63.55.12; ❷), is a basic but clean budget option with just twelve beds: it fills up quickly, so booking is recommended. Alternatively, there's the rather kitsch but central *Le Malaga*, on place Maurice-Charretier (Ⓣ04.90.60.57.96; ❷), where all the rooms have en-suite facilities. For a bit more luxury, *Le Fiacre*,

Carpentras festivals

The last fortnight in July, Carpentras really comes to life during the **Estivales**, a series of music, theatre and dance performances that are staged in an outdoor auditorium. The Bureau du Festival, place du Marché aux Oiseaux (Ⓣ04.90.60.46.00), has full details.

On August 15, Vaucluse food is celebrated in the **Festival des Saveurs Provençales**, a day of gourmandise in which the minutiae of old-fashioned food production are debated and fêted, with prizes given and plenty of tastings.

153 rue Vigne (Ⓣ04.90.63.03.15, Ⓦwww.hotel-du-fiacre.com; ❸), is an old town house with a garden, while *Safari Hotel*, 1 av JH-Fabre (Ⓣ04.90.63.35.35, Ⓦwww.nid-provencal.com; ❺), has good amenities, including a pool and tennis courts, though rather lacks character.

The local **campsite**, *Lou Comtadou*, is located south of town on avenue Pierre de Coubertin (Ⓣ04.90.67.03.16, Ⓕ04.90.86.62.95; €10 per tent; closed Nov–March).

The Town

A bird's-eye view of Carpentras shows clearly the perimeter line of the town in the Dark Ages (rues Vigne, des Halles, Raspail, du Collège and Moricelly), enclosed in the ring of boulevards that follow the line of the medieval town wall. Of this only the massive, crenellated **Porte d'Orange** and the odd rampart on rue des Ramparts and rue des Lices-Monteux remain.

At the heart of town on place Général-de-Gaulle, the **Palais de Justice** (guided tours mid-June to mid-Sept; check times with the tourist office; €4) was built as an episcopal palace to indulge the dreams, or more likely the realized desires, of a seventeenth-century cardinal of Carpentras. Nicolas Mignard was commissioned to fresco the walls with sexual scenes of satyrs and nymphs, but a later incumbent had all the erotic details effaced.

The palais is attached to the fifteenth-century **Cathédrale St-Siffrein** behind which, almost hidden in the corner, stands a **Roman arch**, inscribed with imperial scenes of prisoners in chains. Fifteen hundred years after the cathedral's erection, Jews, coerced, bribed or otherwise persuaded, entered the building in chains to be unshackled as converted Christians. The door they passed through, the **Porte Juive**, is on the southern side and bears the strange symbolism of rats encircling and devouring a globe. The cathedral stands on the place Général-de-Gaulle, while to the north is the place d'Inguimbert, lined with plane trees, lanterns and black swan fountains. Running between place d'Inguimbert and rue des Halles is the **Passage Boyer**, a high and beautiful glazed shopping arcade. It was built by the unemployed in a short-lived scheme to generate jobs after the 1848 revolution.

Following rue d'Inguimbert eastwards brings you to the ancient **Jewish ghetto** and a slightly livelier part of the modern town. The original **synagogue** on place de la Juiverie was built in the days when the Jews had to pay movement taxes every time they left or entered the ghetto, and when their rights to be in Carpentras at all depended on papal whim. In 1741, when the present synagogue was constructed on the old foundations, Bishop d'Inguimbert would not allow it to be as high as the **Chapelle des Pénitents Blancs** on rue Bidault. The rabbi's response was to paint the ceiling blue with stars, "for then I'll have all the skies". This, along with its low hanging chandeliers, the purification baths (for women after menstruation and for brides) and the bread ovens, can all be visited (Mon–Thurs 10am–noon & 3–5pm, Fri closes 4pm; closed Jewish feast days).

To the west of the centre on bd Albert-Durand, the **Musée Comtadin** (daily except Tues. April–Sept 10am–noon & 2–6pm; Oct–March 10am–noon & 2–4pm; €1 combined ticket with Musée Duplessis) contains an unimaginative collection of keys, guns, *santons*, seals, ex-votos, papal bulls, bells and bonnets. The dimly lit pictures are of more interest, among them the portraits of famous Carpentrassiens including François-Vincent Raspail, after whom so many French streets are named. Born just after the Revolution and condemned to death during the White Terror, Raspail was a committed republican all his life, criticising every brand of nineteenth-century conservatism and dedicating much of his work as a doctor to making medicine available to the poor. The work of one of his fellow radical Vaucluse *députés* in the 1876 parliament, Alfred Nacquet, who proposed divorce rights for women, also hangs in these musty rooms. A painting by Denis Bonnet of medieval Carpentras features a nonexistent hill to show the separate Jewish area within the city walls.

On the floor above is the **Musée Duplessis** (same hours and ticket as Musée Comtadin), named after a mediocre eighteenth-century painter from Carpentras whose wealth and influence had much to do with the people he painted. Roman artefacts, an Egyptian tablet with a pharaonic scene captioned in Aramaic, and some very wonderful Renaissance miniatures are also on display. Also in the complex, on the left as you enter the courtyard, is the **Bibliothèque Inguimbertine**, which used to contain several hundred thousand volumes on the history of Provence, Books of Hours, musical scores and early manuscripts: the collection is currently being transferred to the Hôtel-Dieu, so ask at the tourist office for details. Contemporary art is displayed in changing exhibitions at the nearby **Chapelle du Collège** on rue du Collège (Mon–Sat 9.30am–12.30pm & 2–6pm; free).

To the south of the centre, just beyond place Aristide-Briand, is the huge eighteenth-century **Hôtel-Dieu** building, which still functions as a hospital though you can visit its original opulent **pharmacy** (Mon, Tues & Fri 9am–noon, Wed & Sat 9am–noon & 3–6pm; free). As well as gorgeously decorated vials and boxes containing cat's foot extract, Saturn salt, deer antler shavings and dragon blood, the painted lower cupboards tell a very "Age of Reason" moral tale of wild and happy monkeys ending up as tame and dutiful labourers.

Eating, drinking and entertainment

One of the best places to **eat** in Carpentras is *Le Marijo*, at 73 rue Raspail (☎04.90.60.42.65; closed Sun), which has excellent Provençal menus from €16 – local truffles, melon and wines feature, according to the season. Alternatively, *Chez Serge*, at 90 rue Cottier (☎04.90.63.21.24; closed Sun) has a tree-shaded terrace and serves pizzas as well as reasonably priced local dishes (€12.80), while *Le Vert Galant*, 12 rue de Clapies (☎04.90.67.15.50; closed Sat midday & Sun), serves more sophisticated fare, with menus from €25.50.

For **drinking** the *Pub Peter Polo* on the corner of place Aristide-Briand attracts a trendy crowd. There are several more café-brasseries on the square and, during the truffle season, the buyers, middlemen and *truffiers* do great business in the bar of the *Univers* hotel. There are some good cafés on place Charles-de-Gaulle, including *Le Siècle*, but all of them close by 7.30pm. Once the sun goes down in Carpentras, the only place with any semblance of life is *Le Club*, a pizzeria/bar at 106 place Aristide-Briand.

Pernes-les-Fontaines

South of Carpentras, on the road to L'Isle-sur-la-Sorgue, lies the exquisite small town of **PERNES-LES-FONTAINES**. The fountains for which it's named (36 in all), the ramparts, gateways, castle, towers, covered market hall, Renaissance streets and half a dozen chapels all blend into a single complex structure, and the passages between its squares feel more like corridors between rooms.

Approaching from Carpentras, you cross the River Nesque before reaching place Gabriel-Moutte on the left, the site of Pernes' Saturday market and tourist office; from here av Jean-Jaurès follows the line of the fourteenth-century ramparts, of which only three gates now remain. Second on the left is the Park Villeneuve, dating from 1550, which leads to rue Gambetta and the old town. At the end of rue Gambetta is the **Tour Ferrande** (guided tours arranged by the tourist office) which contains the town's great medieval artwork – **frescoes** dating from the era of the Bayeux tapestry and similar in style; they portray religious scenes of the Virgin and Child as well as scenes from the legend of William of Orange and the life of Charles of Anjou.

Heading down rue Victor-Hugo and along rue de la Halle brings you to the sixteenth-century Porte Notre-Dame and the **cormorant fountain** with the seventeenth-century market hall. From this gateway, rue Raspail heads south past the fifteenth-century **reboul fountain**, the oldest of Pernes' fountains, and onto the other remaining gate, the Porte St-Gilles.

Practicalities

The **tourist office** is on place Gabriel-Moutte (May–Sept Mon–Fri 9am–12.30pm & 2.30–7pm, Sat 9am–12.30pm & 2.30–6pm, Sun 9am–noon; Oct–April Mon–Fri 9am–noon & 2–5pm, Sat 9am–noon; ⓣ04.90.61.31.04). An afternoon's wander may well be enough to sample Pernes-les-Fontaines' charms, but if you find yourself seduced, some **hotel** possibilities include *La Margelle*, place Aristide-Briand, on the boulevard ring to the south of the village (ⓣ04.90.61.25.83; ❹, half board obligatory in season), with a rambling back garden and inexpensive menus; or *Prato-Plage* (ⓣ04.90.61.37.75, ⓦwww.pratoplage.com; ❹), just outside the town on the Carpentras road overlooking an artificial lake. The municipal **campsite** is in the quartier Coucourelles (ⓣ04.90.66.45.55; closed mid-Sept to mid-April; €9.50 per tent); campervans can park overnight on quai de Verdon (not Fri).

There's a delightful **restaurant** on place L-Giraud, *Au Fil de Temps* (ⓣ04.90.66.48.61; closed Wed; lunch menu €26; evening menu from €37), which serves exquisite food, or try *Lou Cigalou*, on place Aristide-Briand (closed Wed eve, Sat & Sun lunch), for its reasonably priced woodfire **pizzas**.

Venasque

VENASQUE, 9km east of Pernes just before the road starts to wind over the Plateau de Vaucluse towards Apt, is a perfectly contained village on a spur of rock. At its highest end are three round towers and a curtain wall, at its lowest end a sixth-century baptistry, built on the site of a Roman temple which is thought to have been dedicated to Venus. Like most Provençal villages it swings between a sleepy winter state and a tourist honey pot in summer. The best time to visit is in May and June, before the main tourist season begins, and when the daily **market** concentrates exclusively on the sale of local cherries.

Besides its location, Venasque's attractions lie in its food. **Haute cuisine**, with all the ingredients fresh from the market, can be sampled at the *Auberge de la*

Fontaine, on place de la Fontaine (Ⓣ04.90.66.02.96; from €38; closed Wed eve); you'll need to book for the main restaurant, but on the ground floor *Le Bistro* (closed Sun eve & Mon) serves less expensive (€18) and less sophisticated dishes of the same high quality. The hotel-restaurant, *Les Remparts*, at the top of the main street, rue Haute (Ⓣ04.90.66.02.79; around €17; closed mid-Nov to early March), also has an excellent restaurant – the *dorade des agrumes* (sea bream with citrus fruits) is particularly good.

The **tourist office**, on Grande Rue (April, May, Sept & Oct Mon–Thurs, Sat & Sun 10am–noon & 2–6pm, Fri 2–6pm; June–Aug Mon–Thurs & Sat 10am–noon & 2.30–6pm, Fri & Sun 2.30–6pm; Ⓣ04.90.66.11.66), can help with **accommodation**, which is fairly thin on the ground: aside from rooms at the *Auberge* (Ⓣ04.90.66.02.96, Ⓕ04.90.66.13.14; ❸) and *Les Remparts* (Ⓣ04.90.66.02.79, Ⓕ04.90.66.61.67; ❸), the only other **hotel** in town is *La Garrigue*, rte de l'Appiè (Ⓣ04.90.66.03.40, Ⓕ04.90.66.61.43; ❸; closed mid-Oct to Easter).

L'Isle-sur-la-Sorgue

L'ISLE-SUR-LA-SORGUE, not to be confused with Sorgues on the Rhône, lies 23km east of Avignon, halfway between Carpentras and Cavaillon. The town straddles five branches of the River Sorgue, its waters once full of otters and beavers, eels, trout and crayfish, and its currents turning the power wheels of a **medieval cloth industry**. Tanneries, dyeing works, and, in the eighteenth century, silk production, all ensured considerable prosperity for "the Island".

Those times are largely past. An epidemic killed off all the crayfish a hundred years ago and the eels and aquatic animals have long since gone, while the huge blackened wheels of the cloth industry turn now only as mementoes, the mills and tanneries standing empty, plants growing through the crumbling brickwork. But in summer fishing punts continue to crowd the streams and L'Isle is a cheerful place, particularly on Sundays, when people arrive for its well-known **antiques market**. L'Isle is also a useful, less expensive base for visiting nearby **Fontaine-de-Vaucluse**.

Arrival, information and accommodation

Trains from Avignon and Cavaillon arrive at the **gare SNCF**, southwest of the town centre, and **buses** arrive by place Gambetta. The **tourist office** is in the former granary on place de l'Eglise (July & Aug Mon–Sat 9am–1pm & 2.30–6.30pm, Sun 9am–1pm; Sept–June Mon–Sat 9am–12.30pm & 2–6pm, Sun 9am–12.30pm; Ⓣ04.90.38.04.78, Ⓦwww.ot-islesurlasorgue.fr). **Bikes** can be rented from Loca'Bike, at 1081 chemin de la Muscadelle (Ⓣ04.90.38.65.99), and Web@nna at 10 rue Autheman has **Internet** access.

L'Isle-sur-la-Sorgue is not a major tourist destination, so **rooms** tend to be fairly cheap – but watch out for water-loving midges. *Au Vieux Isle*, 15 rue Danton (Ⓣ04.90.38.00.46; ❶), in one of the narrow alleyways of the old town, is pretty basic but has a pool table, bar football and occasional concerts. Other inexpensive rooms can be found above the restaurant *La Saladelle*, at 33 rue Carnot (Ⓣ04.90.20.68.59; ❶; closed Fri eve & Sat), but it's best to call first as it's more of a boarding house than a hotel. Fifteen hundred metres upstream of the town, *Le Pescador* in Partages-des-Eaux 1 (Ⓣ04.90.38.09.69, Ⓕ04.90.38.27.80; ❸; closed Mon, Jan & Feb), is in an idyllic spot at the point where the waters divide – follow signs to Carpentras and turn right immediately after crossing the main branch of the river. Or try the eighteenth-century coach house out in the countryside, *Le Mas de Cure Bourse*, chemin de la Serre (Ⓣ04.90.38.16.58, Ⓕ04.90.38.52.31; ❻), a few kilometres southwest of town signed left off the D25 to Caumont, the continuation of av de l'Égalité. The rooms are decorated in traditional Provençal style and the restaurant is very good.

The municipal three-star **campsite**, *La Sorguette*, 41 Les Grandes Sorgues (Ⓣ04.90.38.05.71, Ⓔsorguette@wanadoo.fr; €15 per tent; closed Nov to mid-March), is by the river on the Apt road.

The Town

Though L'Isle-sur-la-Sorgue's claim to be the Venice of Provence stretches a point, it is a pleasant waterside location in which to spend an afternoon. The central **place de l'Église** and **place de la Liberté** provide reminders of past prosperity, most obviously in the Baroque seventeenth-century **church** (Tues–Sat 10am–noon & 3–6pm), by far the richest religious edifice for miles around. Each column in the nave supports a sculpted Virtue: whips and turtle-doves are Chastity's props, a unicorn accompanies Virginity, and medallions and inscriptions carry the adornment down to the floor. Above the west door, angels, Christ, the Supreme Being and Mary veer heavenwards in gilded relief like flying ducks. Only the ceiling is bare. Heading north of the place de l'Église, you'll come to the eighteenth-century **Hôtel Donadeï de Campredon** at 20 rue du Docteur-Tallet (April–Sept Tues–Sun 10am–1pm & 3–6pm; Oct–March Tues–Sun 9.30am–noon & 2–5.30pm), which is currently closed for renovation, but usually hosts temporary exhibitions of modern sculpture and painting. The **Hôpital** on quai des Lices at the western edge of the old town is in a much more restrained eighteenth-century style, with a monumental staircase bearing de Sade's arms. Its chapel and fountained gardens are open to the public (daily 10am–6pm; free).

Every year the Isle fishermen retain their medieval guild tradition of crowning a king of the Sorgue, whose job is to oversee the rights of catch and sale. The **Festival de la Sorgue** at the end of July sees them out in traditional gear, with two teams battling from boats in an ancient jousting tournament. On the **spring equinox** the people of Velleron, 5km downstream, process down to the river and launch a fleet of tiny luminous rafts to celebrate the start of spring. If you want to get on the river yourself Canoë Evasion (Ⓣ06.86.67.65.74), signed right off the D25 towards Fontaine-de-Vaucluse, organizes **canoe trips**.

The Sunday market of **antiques** and secondhand goods centres on the Village des Antiquaires on av de l'Égalité spilling out onto the boulevards. Interesting **bric-a-brac** is also for sale at La Petite Curieuse, 23 impasse de la République, off the main shopping street of rue de la République.

Eating and drinking

Traditional **local specialities** include *écrevisse* (crayfish) *en coquille* and an omelette flavoured with a Sorgue weed, but today grilled trout is the staple – a good place to try it is on the terrace overlooking the river at *Lou Soloy*, 2 avenue Charles de Gaulle (Ⓣ04.90.38.03.16; from €18). For something more special, *La Prévoté*, behind the church at 4 rue J.J.-Rousseau (Ⓣ04.90.38.57.29; closed Sun eve & Mon), has weekday lunchtime menus for around €24, and a gastronomic evening menu for €41. *Le Pescador* hotel in Partages-des-Eaux (see "Arrival"; closed Mon, Jan & Feb; menu from €19.50) serves good fish dishes, and the *Mas de Cure Bourse* hotel (see "Arrival"; closed Mon & Tues lunch; menu around €26) also has a reputable restaurant. For a lighter meal,

Bistro de l'Industrie, on quai de la Charité by place E-Char, serves excellent coffee and plats du jour for €8, or there's the busy brasserie, *Café de la Sorgue*, on quai Jean-Jaurès. Good ice cream can be found at *Gelateria Isabella* on 2 esplanade Robert Vasse. The best place to head for a **drink** is place de l'Église, where you'll find the *Bar Le César* with its faded mirrors, and the swish fin-de-siècle *Café de France*.

Thursday is **market** day but the best place to buy food is at nearby Velleron where producers sell their goods direct at a busy *marché paysan* (summer Mon–Sat 6–8pm; winter Tues, Fri & Sat 4.30–6pm). For inexpensive **wine**, Le Caveau de la Tour de l'Isle at 12 rue de la République is the place to go (closed Sun & Mon).

Fontaine-de-Vaucluse

The diverging streams of L'Isle-sur-la-Sorgue have their source only 6km to the east in a mysterious tapering fissure deep below the sheer 230-metre cliffs at the top of a gorge above **FONTAINE-DE-VAUCLUSE**. Fascination with the **source**, one of the most powerful natural springs in the world, coupled with the beauty of the ancient riverside village where the fourteenth-century poet Petrarch pined for his Laura, makes this a very popular tourist spot – well over a million visitors a year converge here. But despite the crowds, Fontaine is still a fairly romantic place.

The source and the village

In spring, the waters of the Sorgue often appear in spectacular fashion, bursting down the gorge, at other times they seep stealthily through subterranean channels to meet the riverbed further down. The best time to admire them is in the early morning before the crowds arrive.

If you're intrigued by the source, and understand French, visit the **L'Ecomusée du Gouffre** (Feb–June & Sept–Nov daily except Tues 10am–noon & 2–6pm; July & Aug daily 9.30am–7.30pm; closed Dec & Jan: hourly 45-minute tours in French; €5) in the underground commercial centre alongside chemin de la Fontaine. It's run by volunteers eager to communicate their passion for crawling about in the bowels of the earth, who lead the tour through a series of mock-up caves and passages. The museum winds up with a collection of underworld concretions gathered by Casteret, one of France's most renowned cavers, ranging from huge, jewellery-like crystals to pieces resembling fibre optics. Displays also document the intriguing history of the exploration of the spring, from the first 23-metre descent in 1878 to the robotic camera that reached the bottom a few years ago, its blurry pictures apparently showing a horizontal passage disappearing into the rock. It's thought that water seeping through a vast plateau of chalk (stretching as far north as Banon) hits an impermeable base that slopes down to Fontaine.

However the water arrives, it has long been put to use in turning the wheels of manufacturing. The first paper mill was built at Fontaine in 1522, and the last, built in 1862, ceased operations in 1968. The medieval method of pulping rags to paper has been re-created in the **Moulin à papier Vallis Clausa** (daily 9am–12.20pm & 2–6.20pm; Sun opens 10.30am; free), 500m beyond the Ecomusée du Gouffre alongside the river. Here, flowers are added to the pulp and the resulting paper is printed with all manner of drawings, poems and prose, from Churchill's "Blood, Sweat and Tears" speech to the legend of how

God created Provence, on sale in the vast Vallis Clausa shop. There are other quality craft shops in the complex, including one selling household objects carved in olive wood, and an exhibition of *santons*.

Further along chemin de la Fontaine is the impressive and intense **Musée d'Histoire 1939–1945** (March & Nov–Dec Sat & Sun 10am–noon & 2–6pm; April–June & Sept–Oct daily except Tues 10am–noon & 2–6pm; July & Aug daily except Tues 10am–7pm; €5). The overriding purpose of the museum is not to judge or apologize, but to remind people of the humanity of resistance. In so doing it acknowledges the extent to which the war period still perturbs the collective memory of the French. The museum looks at Marshall Pétain's anti-Semitic laws, which were not instructions from Berlin, and stresses how many French people must have opposed them since three-quarters of the French Jewish population escaped deportation. The re-created classroom and other displays of daily life bring home the authoritarian, anti-intellectual and patriarchal nature of France's fascist regime, its insistence on work, family and *patrie*, and the military cult of Pétain. A section is dedicated to the artists who refused to collaborate, another to the German Resistance.

In total, and grotesque, contrast, the **Musée de la Justice et des Châtiments**, a few doors down (daily 10am–6pm; free), displays torture equipment and the methods of carrying out the death penalty based around the collection of the official French executioner in occupied Algeria from 1949 to 1953. There are appropriate statements by sociologists, but no mention that the horrors it evokes continued after the 1950s.

Across the river, through an alleyway just past the bridge, the **Musée de Pétrarque**, on quai du Château Vieux (mid-April to mid-Oct Wed–Sun 9.30am–noon & 2–6pm; mid-Oct to Nov Sat & Sun only; €3.50), is home to a collection of beautiful old books dating back to the fifteenth century, and some pictures of Petrarch, his beloved Laura and of Fontaine where he passed sixteen years of his unrequited passion. The museum also hosts temporary art exhibitions.

Practicalities

Buses from L'Isle-sur-la-Sorgue drop you by the car park just before the church. The **tourist office** is on chemin de la Fontaine (Mon–Sat: July & Aug 9am–7pm; Sept–June 10am–7pm; Ⓣ04.90.20.32.22; Ⓔofficetourisme.vaucluse@wanadoo.fr), off to the left towards the source.

Rooms in Fontaine are likely to be full in summer, so booking ahead is advisable: alternatively, you could base yourself in L'Isle-sur-la-Sorgue and visit on a day-trip. Fontaine's **place de la Colonne** is a particularly pleasant spot to stay, with hotel balconies, terraced restaurants and cafés overhanging the river. The cheapest and most characterful **hotel** here is the *Grand Hôtel des Sources* (Ⓣ04.90.20.31.84, Ⓦwww.hoteldessources.com; ❺), with a whole variety of *vieille France* rooms. About 3km out of the village on the road back to L'Isle, on the right, are two decent options: the excellent-value *L'Ermitage* (Ⓣ04.90.20.32.20, Ⓕ04.90.20.28.95; ❸) and, just beyond, down a track, the smaller, more basic *Font de Lauro* (Ⓣ & Ⓕ04.90.20.31.49; ❷; closed Oct–March). About 1km from the village, on chemin de la Vignasse, there's a very pleasant HI **youth hostel** (reception 8–10am & 5–11pm; Ⓣ04.90.20.31.65; Ⓔfontaine@fuaj.org; closed mid-Nov to Feb; €8 per bed), while the year-round *Les Prés* **campsite**, 500m downstream from the village (Ⓣ04.90.20.32.38), has tennis courts and a swimming pool.

Fontaine has a choice of several reasonably priced **restaurants**, including *Château* on quai du Château Vieux (Ⓣ04.90.20.13.54; closed Sun & Mon evenings out of season), and *Lou Fanau* on place Colonne (Ⓣ04.90.20.31.90;

closed Wed), both of which have menus of solid regional food for about €16. If you arrive early, the *boulangerie Le Moulin de la Fontaine* near the church does breakfasts, and a few doors down there's a crêperie. **Market** day is on Tuesday.

On the north side of the river, above the aqueduct, you can rent **fishing** rods and lines from the little hut called *Pêche de la Truite*, while *Kayak Vert*, just upstream (☎04.90.20.35.44), rents **canoes** for a half-hour or hour's paddling, or for a fairly effortless eight-kilometre trip down to L'Isle-sur-la-Sorgue (where the canoes can be left).

Cavaillon

Approaches to **CAVAILLON** pass through fields of fruit and vegetables, watered by the Durance and Coulon rivers. Market gardening is the major business of the city and to the French, Cavaillon, its Roman origins notwithstanding, is known simply as a melon town. The **melon** in question is the Charentais, a small pale green ball with dark green stripes and brilliant orange flesh, in season from May to September. Together with asparagus and early spring vegetables, they are sold every weekday morning at one of the largest **wholesale markets** in Europe.

In the last week of January, Cavaillon is home to a **science festival**, bringing together serious boffins, journalists, artists and celebrities with free events open to all. It also hosts a couple of low-key, traditional festivals – the *Fête de St-Gilles* in the first week of September, and the *Foire St-Véran* in the second

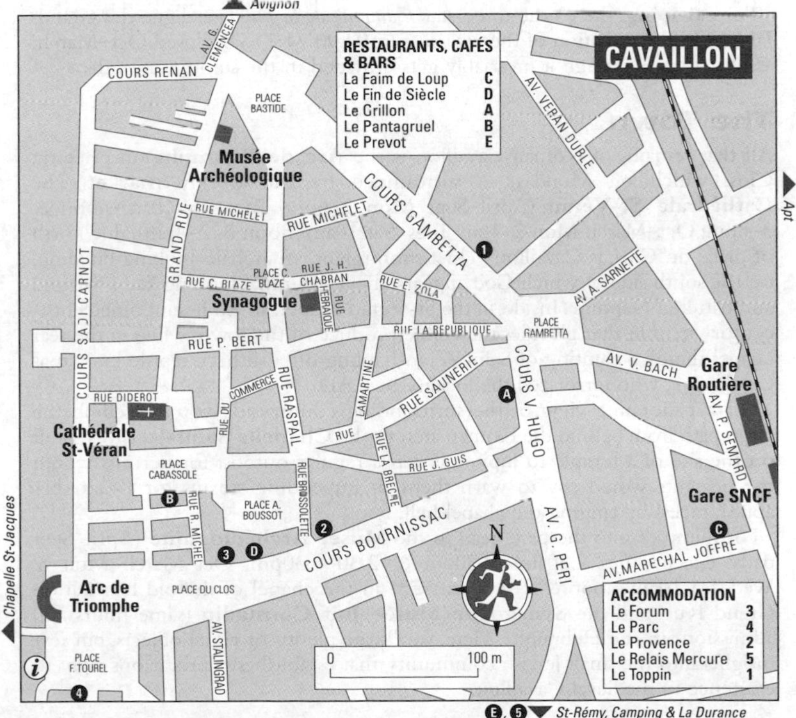

week in November. It must be said, however, that this doesn't make Cavaillon very interesting for much of the year, although it's certainly a useful stopover, with train and bus connections to Avignon, Salon, Aix and Carpentras, as well as to the Luberon to the east.

Arrival, information and accommodation

The **gare SNCF** and the **gare routière** are on av P-Semard on the east side of town, while the **tourist office** is on the opposite side of town, on pl François-Tourel (Mon–Sat 9am–12.30pm & 2–6.30pm, Sun 10am–noon; ⓣ04.90.71.32.01, ⓦwww.cavaillon-luberon.com): it can be reached by taking av du Malechal Joffre, opposite the train station, turning right at the end, then turning first left onto cours Bournissac and following it to the end. **Bikes** can be rented from Cycles Rieu, 25 av Mal-Joffre (ⓣ04.90.71.45.55).

In the centre of town, the most attractive budget **hotel** is *Le Toppin*, 70 cours Gambetta (ⓣ04.90.71.30.42, ⓔhotel.toppin.gesnot@wanadoo.fr; ❷), with rustic-style, comfortable rooms, while *Le Parc*, a former *maison bourgeoise* at 183 place F-Tourel (ⓣ04.90.71.57.78, ⓔhotelduparc.cavaillon@wanadoo.fr; ❸), is also very agreeable: its flamboyant decor suits the building and all the rooms have air conditioning. If these are full, there a couple of basic but cheap options near the tourist office – the clean, quiet *Le Forum*, 68 place du Clos (ⓣ04.90.78.37.55, ⓦwww.hotelforum.fr.st; ❷), and *Le Provence*, at 9 cours Bournissac (ⓣ04.90.78.03.38, ⓕ04.90.78.22.25; ❶), with simple rooms above a bar. At the top end of the scale, *Le Relais Mercure*, digue des Grands Jardins, quartier Boscodomini (ⓣ04.90.71.07.79, ⓕ04.90.78.27.94; ❻), is a modern, luxurious hotel overlooking the Durance, with pool and tennis courts.

For **camping**, there's the three-star *Camping de la Durance*, digue des Grands Jardins, in the direction of the *autoroute* (ⓣ04.90.71.11.78; closed Oct–March; €12 per tent), though it invariably gets crowded in the summer months.

The Town

All that remains of Roman Cavaillon is the **Arc de Triomphe** on place du Clos, which on Mondays is surrounded by the weekly **market**. The **Cathédrale St-Véran** (April–Sept Mon 3–6pm, Tues–Sat 10am–noon & 3–6pm; Oct–March Mon 2–4pm, Tues–Sat 10am–noon & 2–4pm), due north of place du Clos, is Cavaillon's chief monument, an archaic-looking building, on the south side of which God appears above a sundial looking like a winged and battered Neptune. Inside, in the St-Véran chapel, an exuberant nineteenth-century marble altar glorifies the edible produce of the town, while in the rear chapel there's a painting of Saint Véran hauling off a slithery reptile known as Couloubre, who terrorized the locality in 6 AD.

For a panoramic view of the surrounding countryside you can climb the steep path from behind the Roman arch to the **Chapelle Saint-Jacques**. Built on the site of a temple to Jupiter, it was a regular outpost for hermits whom the peasants would pay to warn them of impending storms (or Couloubre appearances) by ringing the chapel bell.

For glimpses into the past, head to the **Musée Archéologique** (April–Sept daily except Tues 9.30am–12.30pm & 2.30–6.30pm; Oct–March Mon & Wed–Fri 10am–noon & 2–4.30pm; €3) in the chapel of the old hospital on Grand Rue, and the **Synagogue/Musée Juif Comtadin** (same hours and admission) in rue Hebraïque. Here, you'll see plenty of ritual objects, but few insights into the small Jewish community that established a precarious right to existence in medieval Cavaillon.

Eating and drinking

For all its fresh produce, **eating** in Cavaillon isn't all that spectacular. To sample the local speciality, head to *Le Prevot*, at 353 av de Verdon on the road out to St-Rémy (☎04.90.71.32.43; closed Mon & Sun eve), and order its "melon menu" (June to September; €70), which includes lobster with petals of melon, fillet of beef on dried melon and iced melon with nougat and Beaumes-de-Venise muscat. Alternatively, *Le Pantagruel*, 5 place de Cabassole (☎04.90.76.11.98; closed Sun & Mon lunch), serves a good range of organic produce and charcoal grills on its menus starting at €21.50. For a lighter meal, *La Faim de Loup*, 129 av Marechal Joffre (☎04.90.78.31.68; around €11.50), serves seafood and salads, while *Le Grillon*, 50 cours Victor-Hugo (☎04.90.71.33.87; from €7.50; closed Tues), is good for tagines, couscous and pastillas, plus Provençal specialities and excellent Algerian wines.

The most stylish place for a **drink** is *Le Fin de Siècle*, 46 place du Clos, with heavy gold cornices and fantasy pictures; it also has a glitzy restaurant upstairs (☎04.90.71.12.27; menus from €19.50; closed Tues, Wed & Aug lunch).

Gordes and around

GORDES, 6km north of the main Avignon–Apt road, and the same distance east of Fontaine-de-Vaucluse (but only as the crow flies) is a picturesque hilltop village, popular with film directors, media personalities, musicians and painters, many of whom have added a Gordes address to their main Paris residence. As a result, the place is full of expensive restaurants, cafés and art and artisanal shops.

There are good reasons for its popularity with the rich and famous. The approach at sunset is picture perfect, with the ancient stone turning gold as you climb the winding roads towards the centre. In addition, in the vicinity, you can see a superb array of dry-stone architecture in **Village des Bories**, as well as the **Abbaye de Sénanque**, and a couple of museums dedicated to glass and olive oil. There's also a **festival** in the last two weeks of July when the village is awash with theatrical performances, jazz and classical music concerts.

The village

In the past, near-vertical staircases hewn into the rock gave the only access to the summit of the village, where the church and houses surround a twelfth- to sixteenth-century **castle** with few aesthetic concessions to the business of fortification. At the turn of the century most of Gordes' villagers had abandoned the old defensive site and the place was in ruins. A centre of resistance during World War II, Gordes was rediscovered by various artists, including Chagall and the Hungarian scientist of art and design, Victor Vasarely.

Vasarely undertook the restoration of Gordes castle and, in 1970, opened his Didactic Museum within its Renaissance interior. However, on his death in 1995, the collection was reclaimed by his family (although the Aix-en-Provence collection remains in situ) and the space devoted to the very different and less accessible **Musée Pol Mara** (daily 10am–noon & 2–6pm; €4). The career of the Belgian artist, also seduced by the beauty of Gordes, moves from Post-Expressionism to Pop Art with one dominant theme – the female body.

Practicalities

Infrequent **buses** cover the 16km from Cavaillon to Gordes, stopping at place du Château. **Bikes** can be rented at the Elf station at Les Imberts on the D2 halfway between Gordes and the Avignon–Apt road.

Gordes' helpful **tourist office**, in the Salle des Gardes of the castle (daily 10am–noon & 2–6.30pm; ⓣ04.90.72.02.75, ⓦwww.gordes-village.com), has lists of accommodation and details of local events, as well as displaying an extraordinary model of the village made out of matchsticks. One of the best value **hotels** in the village is the reasonably priced *Le Provençal*, on place du Château (ⓣ04.90.72.10.01, ⓕ04.90.72.04.20; ❹), with just seven rooms. Overlooking the village, the old country house *Les Romarins*, on the rte de Sénanque (ⓣ & ⓕ04.90.72.12.13; ❻), has traditionally styled comfortable rooms, as does the similar *La Gacholle*, rte des Murs (ⓣ04.90.72.01.36, ⓦwww.lagacholle.com; ❼; closed mid-Jan to mid-Feb), with unbeatable views over the Luberon. The most luxurious option is *Domaine de l'Enclos*, on the rte de Sénanque (ⓣ04.90.72.71.00, ⓕ04.90.72.03.03; ❼), set in a terraced garden with spacious rooms. Halfway between Gordes and Murs on the D15 is a very pleasant two-star **campsite**, *Camping des Sources* (ⓣ04.90.72.12.48, ⓕ04.90.72.09.43; closed Nov–March); early booking is advisable.

There are two excellent **restaurants** within easy reach of Gordes: *Le Bistrot à Michel* on Grande Rue in Cabrières d'Avignon, 7km along on the winding road to Fontaine (ⓣ04.90.76.82.08; last orders 9.15pm; closed Tues, also Mon lunch out of season), is a favourite with the second-home-owning Parisians and serves up exquisitely simple food in a dining room decorated with Pagnol film posters, or in the garden (*plats* from €10). Five kilometres south of Gordes in Les Imberts, at *Le Mas Tourteron*, chemin de St-Blaise (ⓣ04.90.72.00.16; closed Mon & Tues; weekday lunchtime menu €28.50, otherwise €45.50), you can eat gorgeous Provençal specialities in a shaded garden, or much cheaper quick lunches at *Le Petit Comptoir* bistro in the same establishment. In Gordes itself, the most popular place to eat is the *Comptoir des Arts*, place du Château (ⓣ04.90.72.01.31; closed Tues eve & Wed out of season; from €30.50), which is always full of Parisians in summer. The restaurant at *La Gacholle* hotel is pleasant but pricey (€50 à la carte), while *Le Teston*, on place du Château (ⓣ04.90.72.02.54; closed Sun eve & Wed out of season; ❹), is a bit less expensive (*plats* from €16), and also has *chambres d'hôtes*.

Village des Bories

About 4km east of Gordes, signed off the D2 to Cavaillon, is an unusual rural agglomeration, the **Village des Bories** (daily 9am–sunset; €5.50). This walled enclosure contains dry-stone houses, barns, bread ovens, wine stores and workshops constructed in a mix of unusual shapes: curving pyramids and cones, some rounded at the top, some truncated and the base almost rectangular or square. They are cleverly designed so that rain runs off their exteriors and the temperature inside remains constant whatever the season. To look at them, you might think they were prehistoric, and Neolithic rings and a hatchet have been found on the site, but most of these buildings in fact date from the eighteenth century and were lived in until about one hundred years ago. Some may well have been adapted from or rebuilt over earlier constructions, and there are extraordinary likenesses with a seventh- or eighth-century oratory in Ireland, and with huts and dwellings as far apart as the Orkneys and South Africa.

Abbaye de Sénanque

About 4km north of Gordes, **Abbaye de Sénanque** (March–Oct Mon–Sat 10am–noon & 2–6pm, Sun 2–6pm; Nov–Feb Mon–Fri 2–5pm, Sat & Sun 2–6pm; €5) is one of a trio of twelfth-century monasteries established by the Cistercian order in Provence, and predates both the *bories* and the castle. It stands alone, amid fields of lavender in a hollow of the hills, its weathered stone sighing with age and immutability. It's still in use as a monastery and you can visit the church, cloisters and all the main rooms of this huge and austere building, although the monks ask that all visitors respect the silence to which the abbey is consecrated. The shop at the end of the visit sells the monks' produce, including liqueur, as well as honey and lavender essence.

From the abbey, the loop back to Gordes via the D177 and D15 reveals the northern Luberon in all its glory.

Les Bouilladoires

The area around Gordes was famous for its olive oil before severe frosts killed off many of the trees. A still-functioning Gallo-Roman press made from a single slice of oak two metres in diameter, as well as ancient oil lamps, jars and soap-making equipment, can be seen at the **Moulin des Bouillons** (April–Oct daily except Tues 10am–noon & 2–6pm; €4) in **LES BOUILLADOIRES**, on the D148 just west of St-Pantaléon, 3.5km south of Gordes, and well signed from every junction. The Gordes bus from Coustellet, on the main Avignon–Apt road, stops just outside.

The ticket for the Moulin also gives you access to the **Musée du Vitrail Frédérique Duran** (April–Oct daily except Tues 10am–noon & 2–5pm), signalled by a huge and rather gross sculpture by Duran and housed in a semi-submerged bunker next to the Moulin. Duran's contemporary stained-glass creations are extremely garish, but if you want to learn about the long history of stained glass, you can, though perhaps the most attractive items are the gorgeous, strutting fowl and hedges of rosemary in the gardens around the two museums.

The Petit Luberon

The great fold of rock of the Luberon runs for fifty-odd kilometres between the Coulon and the Durance valleys from **Manosque** to Cavaillon. It is divided by the **Combe de Lourmarin**, the only way to cross the mountain for 20km on either side, into the Grand Luberon to the east and the **Petit Luberon** to the west. Though many forestry tracks cross the ridge, they are in fact barred to cars (and too rough for bikes), and where the ridge isn't forested it opens into table-top pastures where sheep graze in summer. The northern slopes have Alpine rather than Mediterranean leanings: the trees are oak, beech and maple; and cowslips and buttercups announce the summer. But it is still very hot and there are plenty of **vines** on the lower slopes.

The Luberon has long been popular as a country escape for Parisians, Germans, the Dutch and the British – it was the setting for Peter Mayle's *A Year in Provence* – and *résidences secondaires* are everywhere. Ruins, like **de Sade**'s **château** in **Lacoste** and the **Abbaye de St-Hilaire** near Bonnieux, are also being restored by their private owners.

There are few **hotels** in these parts, and, as a consequence, those that there are, are fairly expensive. Basing yourself at Cavaillon or Apt may be the most sensible option.

Oppède-le-Vieux

OPPÈDE-LE-VIEUX, above the vines on the steeper slopes of the Petit Luberon, remains relatively free of the yuppie invasion. There are a couple of cafés, the *Petit Café* being the most pleasant, and a quirky shop on the road alongside selling stones and fossils, oddments made from lavender, *santons*, post-cards and good books on the locality. With its Renaissance gateway, the square in front of the ramparts suggests a monumental town within, but behind the line of restored sixteenth-century houses there are only ruins which stretch up to the remains of the medieval **castle**. Take care when exploring the ruins, as there are no fences or warning signs, steps break off above gaping holes, paths lead straight to precipitous edges and at the highest point of the castle you can sit on a foot-wide ledge with a drop of ten or more metres below you.

For **accommodation** in the village try *M et Mme Bal* (ⓣ04.90.76.93.52, ⓕ04.90.76.89.08; ❸), though it's so popular that you really need to book months in advance. There are no **restaurants** in the village, but the *Petit Café* serves light snacks.

Ménerbes

Heading east from Oppède-le-Vieux, **MÉNERBES** is the next hilltop village you come to. Shaped like a ship, its best site, on the prow as it were, is given over to the dead. From this cemetery you look down onto an odd jigsaw of fortified buildings and mansions, old and new. In the other direction houses with exquisitely tended terraces and gardens, all shuttered up outside holiday time, ascend to the mammoth wall of the citadel, now another *résidence secondaire*.

Outside Ménerbes, left off the D103 towards Beaumettes, is the wine-producing Domaine de la Citadelle's **museum of corkscrews** (April–Oct daily 10am–noon & 2–7pm; Nov–March Mon–Fri 10am–noon & 2–6pm, Sat 9am–noon; €4), housed in a château dating back to the seventeenth century. The intriguing collection includes a Cézar compression, a corkscrew combined with pistol and dagger, others with erotic themes and many with beautifully sculpted and engraved handles. You can also visit the wine cellars for a free tasting. Between Ménerbes and Lacoste, on the D109, is the **Abbaye de St-Hilaire** (daily: April–Sept 10am–7pm; Oct–March 10am–5pm), with its fine seventeeth-century cloisters, exquisite Renaissance stairway and ancient dovecotes.

The wars of religion in the Luberon

During five days in April 1545 a great swathe of the Petit Luberon, between **Lourmarin** and **Mérindol**, was burnt and put to the sword. Three thousand people were massacred and six hundred sent to the galleys. Their crime was having Protestant tendencies in the years leading up to the devastating Wars of Religion. Despite the complicity of King Henri II, the ensuing scandal forced him to order an enquiry which then absolved those responsible – the Catholic aristocrats from Aix.

Lourmarin (see p.157) itself suffered minor damage but the castle in Mérindol was violently dismantled, along with every single house. Mérindol's remains, on the hill above the current village on the south side of the Petit Luberon, are a visible monument to those events, and to this day the south face of the Petit Luberon remains sparsely populated.

If you're looking **to stay** in Ménerbes itself, your best option is the welcoming *Le Galoubet* in the centre of the village, at 104 rue Marcellin-Poncet (Ⓣ & Ⓕ04.90.72.36.08; ❹; closed Jan). It has charming but small rooms and a very pleasant **restaurant** serving classic Provençal cuisine on the terrace (menus at €9–25; closed Tues night and Wed). Alternatively, there's the quiet and very agreeable *Hostellerie Le Roy Soleil* (Ⓣ04.90.72.25.61, Ⓦwww.roy-soleil.com; ❽), just outside Ménerbes, on rte des Baumettes.

Lacoste

LACOSTE and its **château** are visible from all the neighbouring villages, and are particularly enticing in moonlight while a wind rocks the hanging lanterns on the narrow cobbled approaches to the château. Its most famous owner was the Marquis de Sade, who retreated here when the reaction to his writings got too hot, but in 1778, after seven years here, he was locked up in the Bastille and the castle destroyed soon after. Semi-derelict, the château now belongs to *couturier* Pierre Cardin, and is closed to the public.

For **accommodation** in the village, there are eight rooms above the excellent *Café de France* (Ⓣ04.90.75.82.25; ❷), which itself provides sandwiches, quiches and pizzas, for under €10. **Market** day is on Tuesday.

Bonnieux and around

From the *terrasse* by the old church on the heights of the steep village of **BONNIEUX** you can see Gordes, Roussillon and neighbouring Lacoste, 5km away. Halfway down the village, on rue de la République, there's a museum of traditional bread-making, the **Musée de la Boulangerie** (July & Aug daily except Tues 10am–1pm & 3–6.30pm; Oct Sat, Sun & hols same hours; €3.50), and on av des Tilleuls the **Église Neuve** exhibits four fifteenth-century wood paintings (summer 9am–noon & 2.30–5.30pm; free).

From Bonnieux the D149 joins the Apt Avignon road just after the triple-arched **Pont Julien** over the Coulon which dates back to the time when Apt was the Roman base of Apta Julia. Before you reach the bridge you'll see signs for the **Château La Canorgue**, a good place to sample the light and very palatable Côtes de Luberon wines (Mon–Sat 9.30am–noon & 2.30–5.30pm).

The best **accommodation** option in Bonnieux is *La Bouquière*, quartier St-Pierre (Ⓣ04.90.75.87.17, Ⓦwww.labouquiere.com; ❺), though it's very popular, so you'll need to book months in advance. Failing that, there's a couple of unexceptional options – the *César*, on place de la Liberté at the top of the village (Ⓣ04.90.75.96.35, Ⓔinfo@hotel-cesar.com; ❸), and the central but rather snooty *Hostellerie du Prieuré* on rue Jean Baptiste Aurard (Ⓣ04.90.75.80.78, Ⓔhotelprieur@hotmail.com; ❻). For **eating**, try *Le Fournil*, overlooking the fountain in place Carnot (Ⓣ04.90.75.83.62; lunch menu €24; dinner from €34; closed Mon & Tues, summer also Sat lunch), which serves lovely Provençal dishes laced with olive oil and garlic. Friday is **market** day.

Apt and around

APT, the main settlement in the Luberon, lies to the east of the Combe de Lourmarin in the Grand Luberon, and is best known for its crystallized fruit and preserves. The town itself is not much of a place for sightseeing; its large confectionery factory spews mucky froth into a concrete-channelled River

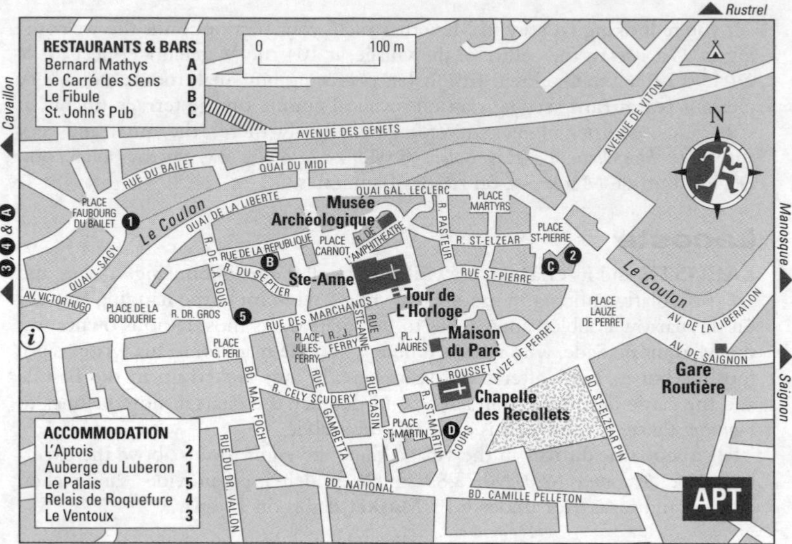

Coulon, and in early spring, when mimosa is blossoming down on the coast, the temperature around Apt can drop to well below freezing. If you have your own transport, however, it makes a useful base for visiting the surrounding villages: **Rustrel** and **Roussillon** to the north, with their **ochre mines**, and to the south, the hilltop villages of **Saignon** and **Buoux**, with its fascinating **abandoned village**, are all within a ten-kilometre radius of the town. Apt itself has excellent shops and a very lively Saturday **market**, and from mid-July through August *Les Tréteaux de Nuit* **festival** provides a choice of shows with concerts, plays, café-theatre and exhibitions.

Arrival, information and accommodation

Buses drop you off either at the main **place de la Bouquerie** or at the **gare routière** (☎04.90.74.20.21) on av de la Libération at the eastern end of the town; the train station is for freight only. The **tourist office** is at 20 av Philippe-de-Girard (July & Aug Mon–Sat 9am–7pm, Sun 9.30am–12.30pm; Sept–June Mon–Sat 9am–noon & 2–6pm; ☎04.90.74.03.18, Ⓔ omt.apt@free.fr), just up to your left as you face the river from place de la Bouquerie. Arriving by **car**, you may have to park along the quays, but place de la Bouquerie is still the focal point to head for. You can **rent bikes** from Guy Agnel, 86 quai Général-Leclerc (☎04.90.74.17.16), or Cycles Ricaud, 44 quai de la Liberté (☎04.90.74.16.43). Infotelec, at 88 rue de la Sous-Préfecture, has **Internet** access.

There's a reasonable choice of **accommodation** in and around Apt; hotels in the town are less likely to be booked up here than in the more scenic hilltop villages.

Hotels

L'Aptois 289 cours Lauze-de-Perret ☎04.90.74.02.02, Ⓦ www.aptois.fr.st. Overlooking place Lauze-de-Perret and the Saturday market, this clean, basic hotel is reasonably priced, and most rooms have TVs. ❷

Auberge du Luberon 8 place Faubourg du Ballet ☎04.90.74.12.50, Ⓦ www.auberge-luberon-peuzin.com. Directly across the river, with pleasant rooms and a quiet setting, this is probably the most desirable hotel in town. ❸

Le Palais 24 pl Gabriel-Péri ⓣ04.90.04.89.32, ⓕ04.90.04.71.61. Cheap option bang in the centre of town, above a rather uninspired pizzeria. Closed mid-Nov to April. ❷

Relais de Roquefure Le Chêne, 6km from Apt on the N100 towards Avignon ⓣ04.90.04.88.88, ⓦwww.relaisderoquefure.com. A large renovated country house with a pool, and ochre-tinted rooms with en-suite bathrooms. Also runs a separate gîte d'étape (€13 per bed). Both closed Dec & Jan. ❹

Le Ventoux 785 av Victor-Hugo ⓣ04.90.04.74.60. On the outskirts of town opposite the old train station, this inexpensive, unassuming hotel is pleasant enough if you get a room looking out on the courtyard. ❷

Campsites

Camping les Cèdres av de Viton ⓣ04.90.74.14.61, ⓔcamping.lescedres@free.fr. A two-star site within easy walking distance of the town, across the bridge from pl St-Pierre. €7.30 per tent. Closed Nov–Feb.

Camping le Luberon rte de Saignon ⓣ04.90.04.85.40, ⓦwww.campingleluberon.com. Three-star site, less than 2km from town, with swimming pool, restaurant and disabled facilities. €17 per tent. Closed Oct–Easter.

The Town

Saturday is the best day to visit Apt, when cars are barred from the town centre to allow artisans and cultivators from the surrounding countryside to set up stalls. As well as featuring every imaginable Provençal edible, including 200-year-old species of vegetables grown by one trader (see "Saignon", p.155), the **market** is accompanied by barrel organs, jazz musicians, stand-up comics, aged hippies and notorious local characters. Everyone, from successful Parisian artists with summer studios here, to military types from the St-Christol base, serious ecologists, rich foreigners and local Aptois, can be found milling around the central **rue des Marchands** for this weekly social commerce.

The great local speciality of fruits – crystallized, pickled, preserved in alcohol or turned into jam – features at the market, but during the rest of the week you can go to La Bonbonnière on the corner of rue de la Sous-Préfecture and rue de la République for every sort of sweet and chocolate and the Provençal speciality *tourron*, an almond paste flavoured with coffee, pistachio, pine kernels or cherries. If you're really keen on sticky sweets you can ring Aptunion, the

Parc Naturel Régional du Luberon

The **Parc Naturel Régional du Luberon** is administered by the Maison du Parc in Apt at 60 place Jean-Jaurès (April–Sept Mon–Sat 8.30am–noon & 1.30–7pm; Oct–March Mon–Sat 8.30am–noon & 1.30–6/7pm, Sat 8.30am–noon; ⓣ04.90.04.42.00, ⓦwww.parcs naturels-regionaux.tm.fr/lesparcs/lubea.html). It's a centre of activity with laudable aims – nature conservation and the provision of environmentally friendly tourist facilities – though many people have misgivings about the practicalities of the project.

Any glance at a map will show the area covered by the park to be shot through with holes, *communes* where the local mayor has chosen to opt out. This makes a bit of a mockery of the park's key purpose of protecting the environment. In fact, the park has very few powers and even less money and mostly has to be content with giving technical and architectural advice that doesn't have to be followed. Certain attempts to assist small local producers have, according to the park's critics, backfired badly.

Be that as it may, the Maison du Parc is the place to go for information about the fauna and flora of the Luberon, footpaths, cycle routes, pony-trekking, gîtes and campsites. The centre also houses a small **Musée de la Paléontologie** (€1.50), designed for children. A submarine-type "time capsule" door leads down to push-button displays that include magnified views of insect fossils and their modern descendants.

confectionery factory, in quartier Salignan, 2km from Apt on the Avignon road (Mon–Fri 10.30am–2pm; ⓣ04.90.76.31.43) for a tour or just to visit the shop which sells all the possible fruit concoctions.

Other **shops** worth looking at are Tamisier, on rue du Docteur-Gros, selling kitchenware and the traditional fly-proof open boxes for storing cheese and sausage; Station Peintre, on place de la Bouquerie, with artists' materials at very good prices; Jean Faucon's ceramics on av de la Libération; and the Librarie Dumas, on the corner of rue des Marchands and place G-Péri, with some English books for sale.

While window-shopping along rue des Marchands, you'll see the **Tour de L'Horlage** (bell tower) spanning the street, and the former **Cathédrale de Ste-Anne**, which houses a selection of relics and ancient objects (Tues–Sat 10am–noon & 3–6pm, Sun 10am–noon; guided tour July to mid-Sept Tues–Sat 11am & 5pm; mid-Sept to June Sat 11am; free). The highlight is a fragment of Egyptian cloth, known as "Saint Anne's veil", which was used to transport some of the other artefacts in the collection back from Palestine in the twelfth century The **Musée Archéologique** at 4 rue de l'Amphithéatre (June–Sept Mon & Wed–Sat 10am–noon & 2.30–5pm; Oct–May Mon & Wed–Fri 2.30–4.30pm, Sat 10am–noon & 2.30–5.30pm; €2) is not wildly exciting, with a few remains of a Roman theatre in the basement. Temporary exhibitions of contemporary art are sometimes held in the **Chapelle de Recollets** at 26 rue Louis-Rousset, organized by Artifices, 47 rue de la République (ⓣ04.90.74.50.62), which represents some of the best artists based in the Luberon and arranges visits to their studios.

Eating and drinking

One of the best **restaurants** in Apt is *Le Carré des Sens*, on Place St-Martin at the top of cours Lauze-de-Perrez (ⓣ04.90.74.74.00; closed Mon lunch; €24 menu, à la carte €44), where you can sample such exquisite dishes as bluefin tuna in a Sichuan peppercorn sauce; the cheaper, affiliated *bar à vins* round the back on rue St-Martin offers the same plat du jour for €11 (closed Sun & Mon lunch). For more traditional cuisine, and a superb choice of desserts, try the *Auberge du Luberon*, (see p.152; closed Mon & Sun eve out of season; from €26). Alternatively, the ever-popular *Le Fibule*, at 128 rue de la République (ⓣ04.90.4.05.29; closed Sun & Mon lunch), serves good tajines and couscous (€13). Five kilometres out of town at Le Chêne (off the Avignon road), *Bernard Mathys* on chemin des Platanes (ⓣ04.90.04.84.64; menus from €25; closed Tues & Wed) offers more good food and a chance to try a wide selection of local goats' cheeses, plus a delicious lavender *crème brûlée*. The best place for a **drink** is any of the brasseries on place de la Bouquerie, or *St. John's Pub*, at 16 rue St-Pierre.

Roussillon

Perching precariously above soft-rock cliffs 10km northwest of Apt, the buildings of **ROUSSILLON** radiate all the different shades of the seventeen ochre tints once quarried here. A spiralling road leads past potteries, antique shops and restaurants up to the summit of the village, which is worth the effort for the views over the Luberon and Ventoux. If you want to see the **ochre quarries** themselves, a well-signed footpath leads from the car park on place de la Poste, where you'll also find the **tourist office** (Easter–Nov Tues–Fri 9am–noon & 1.30–6.30pm, Sat & Mon 10am–noon & 2–5.30pm; Dec–Easter daily 2–6pm; ⓣ04.90.05.60.25, ⓦwww.roussillon-provence.com) and a Centre Social et Culturel with occasional art exhibitions. Just outside Roussillon, on the Apt road,

Ochre quarrying

Ochre quarrying has been practised in the Vaucluse since prehistoric times, producing the natural dye that gives a range of colours, which don't fade in sunlight, from pale yellow to a blood red. By the nineteenth century the business had really taken off, with overloaded donkeys, then, by the 1880s, trains, carrying truckloads of the dust to Marseille to be shipped round the world. At its peak, in 1929, forty thousand tonnes of ochre were exported from the region. Twenty years later it was down to 11,500 tonnes, and in 1958 production was finally stopped, in part because of reduced demand with competition from synthetic dyes, but also because the foundations of Roussillon were being undermined.

an old **ochre factory**, the Usine Mathieu, has been renovated and you can look round the various washing, draining, settling and drying areas (tours daily: July & Aug 10am–noon & 2–6pm; March–June & Sept–Nov 11am & 2–5pm; €5). It also hosts excellent exhibitions on themes related to the use and production of ochre, with accompanying workshops for both adults and children.

If you need somewhere to stay, the *Rêves d'Ocres* **hotel**, on rte de Gordes (Ⓣ04.90.05.60.50, Ⓕ04.90.05.79.74; ❺), is warm, welcoming and has some rooms with good views of the Luberon. There's also a very pleasant two-star **campsite**, *Camping L'Arc en Ciel*, in pine woods, 2km along the D104 to Goult (Ⓣ04.90.05.73.96; €10 per tent; closed Oct to mid-March). For **meals**, try Roussillon's *La Treille*, 1 rue du Four (Ⓣ04.90.05.64.47), which serves a mixture of North African, Turkish and Scandinavian specialities with menus from €20, or you can get a crêpe at *La Gourmandine* on place l'Abbé-Avon.

Rustrel and around

RUSTREL, 10km northeast of Apt, is a very sweet little village with a small and welcoming **hotel**, the *Auberge de Rustréou*, 3 pl de la Fête (Ⓣ04.90.04.90.90; ❸), and a convivial **bar**, *Les Platanes* (Ⓣ04.90.04.93.99), which serves good beers and has live music most Saturday nights.

It, too, is home to a series of dramatic ochre quarries, known as the **Colorado Provençal**, signed off the D22 towards Gignac, just before you reach Rustrel from Apt. The track round the quarries begins at the car park entrance. Having passed the remains of old settling tanks that look like unearthed foundations and a small ruined building, take the track on the right marked with white. The full, circular, route takes about 1hr 30min to walk and the **map** (€2.50), available from the snack bar in the car park, will prove useful, as the route can be quite hard to follow – particularly when the stream meanders onto the creamy ochre sand of the path. Persevere and you will end up in an amphitheatre of coffee, vanilla and strawberry ice-cream-coloured rock, whipped into pinnacles and curving walls. If you continue up above a little waterfall, you can turn left, then left again onto a wider path, which soon brings you to the gods' seats over the quarry. Continue and you'll end up on the same route leading back to the settling tanks.

Saignon

SAIGNON is only 4km from Apt but already high enough up the Luberon to have an eagle's-eye view of the town. From below, the village rises like an immense fort with natural turrets of rock; on closer inspection it turns out to be a mix of crumbling farmhouses and perfectly restored summer residences. The gardener, Monsieur Danneyrolles, whose ancient species of organic vegetables are on sale in Apt's markets, lives here at La Molière; if you phone him (Ⓣ04.90.74.44.68), he may show you round his fabulous **garden**.

There's a pleasant **hotel** in the centre of the village, the *Auberge du Presbytère*, pl de la Fontaine (Ⓣ04.90.74.11.50, Ⓕ04.90.04.68.51; ❹), offering some wonderful views. Alternatively, 2.5km north of Saignon, just before Auribeau, is the *Auberge de Jeunesse Le Regain* (Ⓣ04.90.74.39.34, Ⓕ04.90.74.50.90; €23 per person half board, €4 per tent; closed mid-Jan to mid-Feb), which also has plenty of information on local **walks**.

Buoux

The fortified, abandoned hilltop village known as the **Fort de Buoux**, 10km south of Apt, stands on the southern edge of a canyon, forged by the once powerful River Aiguebrun at the start of its passage through the Luberon. To reach the fort follow the road signed off the D113 to the gateway at the end, beyond which it's a ten- to fifteen-minute walk to the entrance (daily sunrise till sunset; €3).

Numerous relics of prehistoric life have been found in the Buoux Valley, and in the earliest Christian days anchorite monks survived against all odds in tiny caves and niches in the vertical cliff face. In the 1660s, Fort de Buoux was demolished by command of Richelieu for being a centre of Protestantism, but the remains of old Buoux – including water cisterns, storage cellars with thick stone lids, arrow-slitted ramparts, the lower half of a Romanesque chapel and a pretty much intact keep – still give a good impression of life here over the centuries. Today, the spot is popular with **climbers**, many of whom can be seen clinging to the cliff face as you approach the fort. Most of them will be denizens of the corporate or municipal holiday homes that cluster round the road into the valley.

Back at the junction with the D113, a left turn takes you past the slender Romanesque tower of the former Prieuré de St-Symphorien and onto the Lourmarin road, while a right turn brings you to the present-day village of **BUOUX** (the "x", by the way, is pronounced). Just outside the village, the *Auberge de la Loube* **restaurant** (Ⓣ04.90.74.19.58; closed Thurs & Wed eve out of season) has a considerable local reputation: some say it's pretentious and overpriced, others that it's *génial* and delicious. You can judge for yourself with the midday €21 menu. For **accommodation** try the *Auberge des Seguins*, quartier de la Combe (Ⓣ04.90.74.16.37, Ⓕ04.90.74.03.26; ❸; closed mid-Nov to March), tucked away in the spectacular canyon not far from the Fort de Buoux.

From Buoux, and indeed from Apt, there are fabulous views west from the road to the Combe de Luberon; in the gorge itself you can stop off by the river, at its most spectacular in spring.

From the Luberon to the Durance

The **southern slopes of the Luberon** come into the climatic sphere of the Mediterranean. They are filled with the smell of pines and wild thyme, the yellow and gold of honeysuckle and immortelle, and the quick movements and stillnesses of sun-basking reptiles. Unlike the humid northern face, here it is hot and dry. The lower slopes are taken up by cherry orchards and vines, grown both for wine and grapes. Where the land levels out, 12km or so back from the Durance, the ground is highly fertile and all the classic crops of Provence are grown. The smaller holdings, divided aesthetically and environmentally by organic windbreaks, specialize in one or other of the ingredients for ratatouille. Because of the importance of agriculture, the villages here are still very Provençal in character, with far fewer Parisians and other foreigners than in the northern Luberon.

The beautiful villages of **Lourmarin**, **Vaugines** and **Cucuron** sit amidst vineyards and the unspoilt countryside of the Grand Luberon foothills, while **La Tour d'Aigues** and **Ansouis** boast elegant châteaux. **Pertuis** has the best transport links and accommodation possibilities in the area, though **Cadenet** has a certain charm, across the Durance from the ancient **Abbaye de Silvacane**.

Lourmarin

LOURMARIN stands at the bottom of a *combe*, its Renaissance **château** guarding with nonchalant ease a small rise to the west. A fortress once defended this strategic vantage point but the current edifice dates from the sixteenth century when comfort was beginning to outplay defence; hence the generous windows.

Since 1929 the château has belonged to the University of Aix, who use it to give summer sabbaticals to artists and intellectuals of various scientific and philosophical persuasions. Many have left behind works of art, which you can see on a 45-minute **guided tour** (daily: Jan Sat & Sun 2.30–4.30pm; Feb–April & Oct–Dec 11am & 2.30–4.30pm; May, June & Sept 10–11am & 2.30–5.30pm; July & Aug 10–11.30am & 3–6pm; €5) through vast rooms with intricate wooden ceilings, massive fireplaces and beautifully tiled floors where the favoured cultural workers socialize. **Concerts** are held in the château every Saturday evening during July and August, and throughout the summer **exhibitions** of all sorts are staged (contact the tourist office for more information).

The most famous literary figure associated with Lourmarin town is the writer Albert Camus, who spent the last years of his life here and is buried in the cemetery.

Practicalities

Lourmarin's **tourist office** is at 9 av Philippe-de-Girard (Feb–Dec Mon–Sat 9.30am–1pm & 3–7pm, Sun 9.30–noon; ⓣ04.90.68.10.77, ⓦwww.lourmarin.com). The best place **to stay** is the wonderfully situated *Hostellerie Le Paradou* on the D943 at the start of the *combe* (ⓣ04.90.68.04.05, ⓕ04.90.08.54.94; ❹). Alternatively, back towards Lourmarin, the gîte *Le Four à Chaux* (ⓣ04.90.68.24.28, ⓕ04.90.68.11.10) has dormitory beds (€11.50) and a few rooms (❶). There's a three-star **campsite**, *Les Hautes Prairies*, on rte de Vaugines (ⓣ04.90.68.02.89, ⓕ04.90.68.23.83; closed Dec–March), with a pool, bar and restaurant.

There are several **restaurants** around the fountained squares of the village, including *La Récréation*, 15 rue Philippe-de-Girard (ⓣ04.90.68.23.73; closed Wed), which serves good and reasonably priced organic dishes, with menus from €20. Further out of town, the expensive but excellent *La Fenière* on rte de Cadenet (ⓣ04.90.68.11.79; menus from €42; closed Mon, Tues lunch, and mid-Nov to Jan) uses absolutely fresh ingredients to create seriously gourmet concoctions.

East to Pertuis

East from Lourmarin, the first place along the minor D56 road is **VAUGINES**, a gorgeous little village with a nice old-fashioned café, *Café de la Fontaine*, opposite the *mairie*, and a **hotel** with great views, the *Hostellerie du Luberon* (ⓣ04.90.77.27.19, ⓦwww.hostellerieduluberon.com; ❻). Vaugines is the meeting point of the GR97 from the Petit Luberon and the GR9 which crosses the Grand Luberon to Buoux in one direction and in the other loops above Cucuron and skirts the Mourre-Nègre summit before running along the eastern end of the ridge.

The neighbouring village of **CUCURON** is a bit larger and almost as fetching, with some of its ancient ramparts and gateways still standing and a bell tower with a delicate campanile on the central place de l'Horloge. Cucuron had a glimpse of fame when it was taken over by the film industry for the shooting of Rappeneau's *The Horseman on the Roof*, based on a Giono novel, and, at the time, the most expensive French film made. The village's main business, however, is olive oil and it has a sixteenth-century mill in a hollow of the rock face on rue Moulin à l'Huile that is still used to press olives. At the top of the rock a **park** surrounds the site of the former citadel. At the other end of the village is the **Église Notre-Dame-de-Beaulieu**, which contains a sixteenth-century painting on wood amongst its art treasures. From the end of May to the middle of August a huge felled poplar leans against the church, a tradition dating back to 1720 when Cucuron was spared the plague. On rue de l'Église, a short way from the church, is a small **museum** (10am–noon & 3–7pm; closed Tues morning; free) on local traditions and early history, with a collection of daguerreotypes.

On the north side of the village, by the reservoir bordered by plane trees, the **hotel-restaurant** *L'Étang* (ⓣ04.90.77.21.25, ⓕ04.90.77.10.98; ❹) serves very pleasant food (menus from €18.30). There are two **campsites**: *Lou Badareu* at La Rasparine, southeast of the village towards La Tour d'Aigues (ⓣ04.90.77.21.46; €8 per tent; closed Dec to mid-March) next to a rather expensive gîte d'étape; and *Le Moulin à Vent* on chemin de Gastoule off the D182 to Villelaure (ⓣ04.90.77.25.77; €9 per tent; closed Oct–March). A Tuesday **market** is held on place de l'Étang.

Halfway between Cucuron and Pertuis, the hilltop village of **ANSOUIS** has a **château** (guided tours only: May–Oct daily 2.30–6pm; Nov–April closed Tues; €6), lived in since the twelfth century by the same family; the mother of the current ducal resident wrote a bestseller called *Bon Sang Ne Peut Mentir* (Good Blood Cannot Lie). The real attraction of this superb castle, however, is its remarkably rich furnishings, from Flemish tapestries and silver chandeliers to kitchen pots and pans. In the village below, the **Musée Extraordinaire** (daily: June–Sept 2–7pm; Oct–May 2–6pm; €3.50) is dedicated to underwater life and has some extremely kitsch touches. The village **market** is held on Thursday.

Just south of the D27, before the Etang de la Bonde, the seventeenth-century **Château de Sannes** produces Côtes de Luberon wines *au naturel* – in other words with no fertilizers, pesticides or additives – as it would have been done when the eighteenth-century château was first inhabited; the wines are on sale in the château's shop (daily 8am–noon & 2–7pm). The setup is somewhat snooty, and if you don't fancy this you could try the Vins Coopératives in La Motte d'Aigues or in Grambois. For picnic food, **ST-MARTIN-DE-LA-BRASQUE** has a smallholders' **market** every Sunday between May and October as well as a rather surprising trompe l'oeil mural of Roman ruins.

Pertuis and La Tour d'Aigues

The one sizeable place this side of the Durance is **PERTUIS**, which hasn't a great deal to offer other than places to stay. Like so many Vaucluse towns, it only really comes to life on **market** day, Friday in this case. At the beginning of May the **festival** of street theatre and strip cartoons can be fun, too.

Pertuis is served by the TER (regional train network) on the Marseille to Aix line. However, the **train station** is a kilometre to the south of town, whereas buses stop at the **gare routière**, on place Garcin, within easy walking distance of the centre: leave the square on the opposite side from the bus station and turn left up rue Henri-Silvy. The town centres around place Parmentier, where you'll find flowers for sale on Friday, rue Colbert, the main clothes shopping street leading up to place Jean-Jaurès, and place du 4 Septembre and place Mirabeau just to the north. The **tourist office** is on place Mirabeau (Mon–Fri 9am–noon & 2–6pm, Sat 9.30am–noon & 2.30–6pm; ⓣ04.90.79.15.56, ⓦwww.vivreleluberon.com) in the old keep, all that remains of Pertuis' castle. The narrow streets of the Vieille Ville to the north are, for the most part, low lit and lifeless.

Of the **places to stay**, the best central options are the *Hôtel du Cours*, place Jean-Jaurès (ⓣ04.90.79.00.68, ⓕ04.90.79.14.22; ❷), which is small and friendly, and *L'Aubarestiero* on place Garcin (ⓣ04.90.79.14.74, ⓕ04.90.79.00.57; ❷), a very quiet hotel where the only disturbances are on Wednesday and Saturday mornings when vegetable stalls are set up in the square. The *Sévan*, on av de Verdon on the way out towards Manosque (ⓣ04.90.79.19.30, ⓦwww.le-sevan.com; ❼), is the most expensive option; it belongs to a chain and is unappealing from the outside, though the rooms and the swimming pools are pleasant enough. The three-star municipal **campsite** *Les Pinèdes*, av Pierre-Augier (ⓣ04.90.79.10.98; €10 per tent; closed mid-Oct to mid-March), has excellent facilities.

You'll find plenty of **brasseries** and **restaurants** on the main squares and streets, but nothing wildly special: your best bet is *Lou Pistou*, on 145 rue de Croze (ⓣ04.90.79.04.34; closed Mon night), where baked swordfish with capers and grilled salmon in a Roquefort sauce can both be sampled on the €23 menu. **Bikes** can be rented at Cycles Genin (ⓣ04.90.79.49.43), on bd des Jardins across from the Super U, and there's also a smoke-filled **Internet** café, *La Cave aux Loups*, at 31 rue Murette.

Heading northeast from Pertuis towards Grambois brings you to **LA TOUR D'AIGUES** where a vast shell of a **château** dominates the village centre. The castle was half destroyed during the Revolution but the most finely detailed Renaissance decoration, based on classical designs including Grecian helmets, angels, bows and arrows and Olympic torches, has survived on the gateway arch. You can admire most of the ruins' glories from the outside but there's also a **Musée de Faïence**, and a **Salle de l'Habitat Rural du Pays d'Aigues** inside (July & Aug daily 10am–1pm & 2.30–6.30pm; April–June, Sept & Oct Mon & Wed–Fri 9.30am–noon & 2–6pm, Tues 9.30am–noon, Sat & Sun 2–6pm; Nov–March Mon & Wed–Fri 9.30am–noon & 2–5pm, Tues 9.30am–noon, Sat & Sun 2–5pm; €4.50), covering local archeological finds, the development of traditional rural homes (*mas*) in the area, plus temporary exhibitions. The château is also a popular venue for year-round music and dance concerts (ⓣ04.90.07.50.33, ⓦwww.chateau-latourdaigues.com). There's a shaded **café** on the far side of the main road from the castle and one **hotel**, *Les Fenouillets*, not far from the centre on the Pertuis road (ⓣ04.90.07.48.22, ⓦwww.lesfenouillets.com; ❹).

Cadenet and around

The main road heading south from Lourmarin detours round **CADENET**. There's little reason to stop here save to see the statue, in the central place du Tambour d'Arcole, of a manic drummer-boy, hair and coat-tails flying as he runs. The monument commemorates André Étienne for his inspired one-man diversion that confused the Austrians and allowed Napoleon's army to cross the River Durance in 1796. Also on place du Tambour d'Arcole is Cadenet's **tourist office** (Mon–Sat 9.30am–12.30pm & 2.15–6.15/7pm; ☎04.90.68.38.21), which rents out **bikes**. There's an excellent lakeside **campsite** southwest of the village off chemin de Pile, the four-star *Val de Durance* (☎04.90.68.37.75; €24.50 per tent; closed Oct–March), and a **restaurant**, *Stéfani*, 35 rue Gambetta (☎04.90.68.07.14; closed Tues & Wed eve), with menus from €16. **Market** day is Monday.

Abbaye de Silvacane

Eight kilometres south of Cadenet, on the other side of the Durance, stands the **Abbaye de Silvacane**, built by the same order and in the same period as the abbeys of Sénanque and Le Thoronet, although the "wood of rushes", from which the name Silvacane derives, had already been cleared by Benedictine monks before the Cistercians arrived in 1144. As at the other two great monasteries, the architecture of Silvacane reflects precisely the no-nonsense, no-frills rule of Saint Benedict (Benoît) in which manual work, intellectual work and worship comprised the three equal elements of the day.

The buildings that remain look pretty much as they did seven hundred years ago, with the exception of the refectory, rebuilt in 1423 and given Gothic ornamentation that the earlier monks would never have tolerated. The windows in the church would not have had stained glass either; and the only heated room was the *salle des monies* where the work of copying manuscripts was carried out. The daily reading of "the Rule" and public confession by the monks took place in the *salle capitulaire* and the *parloir* was the only area where conversation was allowed. You can still visit the stark, pale-stoned splendour of the church and its compact surrounding buildings and cloisters (April–Sept daily 10am–6pm; Oct–March daily except Tues 10am–1pm & 2–5pm; closed public hols; €5.50).

Travel details

Trains

Cavaillon to: Avignon (14 daily; 25min); L'Isle-sur-la-Sorgue (12 daily; 10min); Marseille (3 daily; 1hr 10min).
L'Isle-sur-la-Sorgue to: Avignon (12 daily; 15–30min); Cavaillon (12 daily; 10min); Marseille (change at Miramas; 6 daily; 1hr 10min–2hr 10min).

Buses

Apt to: Aix (2 daily; 2hr); Avignon (5 daily; 1hr 25min); Avignon TGV (4 daily; 1hr 40min); Bonnieux (2 daily; 25min); Cadenet (2 daily; 1hr); Carpentras (3 weekly in school term; 1hr); Digne (2 daily; 3hr 10min); Lourmarin (2 daily; 40min); Pertuis (2 daily; 1hr); Roussillon (1 daily; 20min); Rustrel (2 daily; 15min); Sault (1 weekly; 1hr).
Carpentras to: Aix (2 daily; 1hr 40min); Apt (3 weekly in school term; 1hr); Avignon (hourly; 45min); Avignon TGV (3 daily; 1hr); Beaumes-de-Venise (2 daily; 20min); Bedoin (2–3 daily; 40min); Cavaillon (6 daily; 45min); Gigondas (2 daily; 35min); L'Isle-sur-la-Sorgue (6 daily; 25min); Malaucène (2 daily; 30min); Marseille (3 daily; 2hr 15min); Orange (5 daily; 45min); Pernes-les-Fontaines (6 daily; 5min); Sablet (2 daily; 45min); Sault (1 daily; 1hr 30min); Vacqueyras (2 daily; 25min); Vaison (3 daily; 45min); Venasque (2 daily; 30min).

Cavaillon to: Aix (3 daily; 1hr 10min); Apt (2 daily; 45min); Avignon (8 daily; 45min); Avignon TGV (2 daily; 45min); Bonnieux (3 weekly; 1hr); Carpentras (6 daily; 45min); Gordes (2 daily; 45min); Lacoste (3 weekly, must be booked in advance; 40min); L'Isle-sur-la-Sorgue (6 daily; 20min); Lourmarin (4 daily; 45min); Oppède-le-Vieux (3 weekly, must be booked in advance; 20min); Pernes-les-Fontaines (6 daily; 35min); Pertuis (4 daily; 1hr).
L'Isle-sur-la-Sorgue to: Avignon (hourly; 40min); Carpentras (6 daily; 25min); Cavaillon (6 daily; 20min); Fontaine-de-Vaucluse (4 daily; 15min).
Nyons to: Avignon (2 daily; 1hr 40min–2hr); Grignan (4 daily; 40min); Orange (1 daily; 1hr 15min); Vaison (6 daily; 30min); Valréas (3 daily; 20min).
Pertuis to: Aix (6 daily; 30min); Ansouis (1 daily; 10min); Apt (2 daily; 1hr); Avignon (4 daily; 2hr); Cadenet (4 daily; 15min); Cavaillon (4 daily; 1hr); Cucuron (1 daily; 20min); Lourmarin (4 daily; 20 min); Meyrargues (3 daily; 15min); La Tour d'Aigues (3 daily; 10min).
Vaison to: Avignon (3 daily; 1hr); Camaret (3–4 daily; 40min); Carpentras (2 daily; 45min); Nyons (4 daily; 30min); Orange (5 daily; 45min); Rasteau (1 daily; 15min); Séguret (4 daily; 15min); Sablet (3–4 daily; 20min).
Valréas to: Avignon (3 daily; 1hr 30min); Grignan (4 daily; 20min); Nyons (3 daily; 20min); Orange (3 daily; 45min).

Marseille and Metropolitan Provence

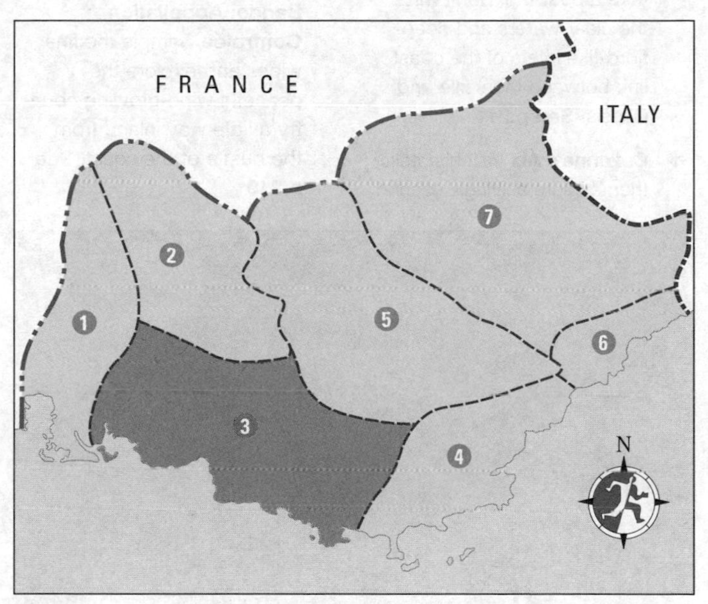

CHAPTER 3

Highlights

* ✱ **Marseille** Experience the history, the food and the cosmopolitan brio of France's great Mediterranean metropolis. **See p.165–185**
* ✱ **The Calanques** Whether you walk, swim or simply take a boat trip, don't miss the clear waters and deep fjord-like inlets of the coastline between Marseille and Cassis. **See p.211**
* ✱ **Cézanne's Aix** Visit his atelier then explore a living Cézanne landscape in the country around the Mont Ste-Victoire. **See pp.199 & 204**
* ✱ **Corniche des Crêtes** Don't get blown away by the coast's most spectacular drive, from Cassis to La Ciotat. **See p.212**
* ✱ **Bandol Appellation Controlée** Sample the fine wines and explore the peaceful wine-growing country a little way inland from the bustle of the coast. **See p.216**

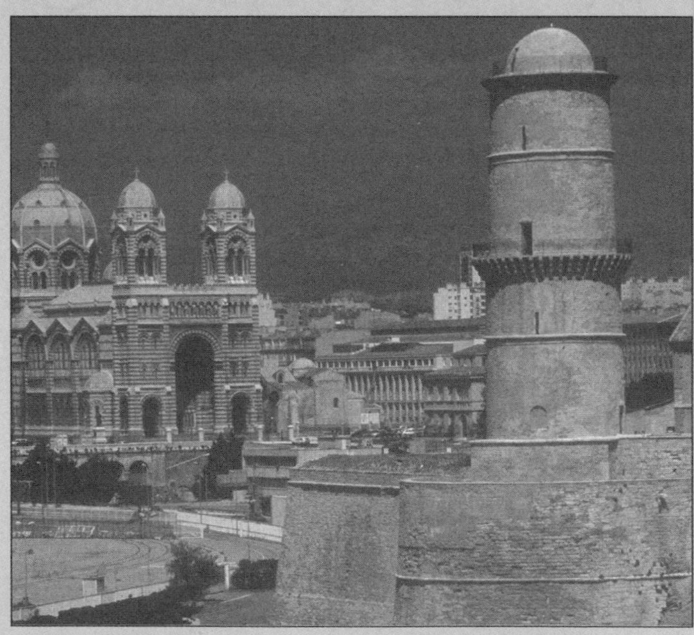

3

Marseille and Metropolitan Provence

Encompassing Marseille, Aix and Toulon, 'Metropolitan Provence' is by far the most populated and industrial part of the region, and indeed of southern France. It's cosmopolitan, culturally dynamic and wields considerable political and economic influence, not least for the way it dramatizes the severe consequences of dated industries and recession. But the area also has vast tracts of deserted mountainous countryside and a shoreline of high cliffs, deep jagged inlets and sand beaches with stretches still untouched by the holiday industry.

The two great poles of attraction are the contrasting cities of **Marseille** and **Aix-en-Provence**. Marseille, a vital commercial port for more than two millennia and France's second largest city, is, for all its notorious reputation, a wonderful place with a distinctive, unconventional character that never ceases to surprise. The charms of Aix, with a historic core as perfect as any in France, are much more commonly sung. It glories in the medieval period of independent Provence and the riches of its seventeenth- and eighteenth-century growth.

The first foreigners to settle in Provence, the ancient **Greeks** from Phocaea and their less amiable successors from **Rome**, left evidence of their sophistication around the **Étang de Berre**, at **Les Lecques**, and most of all at Marseille. Museums in Marseille and Aix guard reminders of the indigenous peoples of Provence whose civilization the Romans destroyed.

Military connections are strong in this region. **Salon-de-Provence** trains French air-force pilots and **Toulon** is home to the French navy's Mediterranean fleet. Until very recently the planes for the one and the ships for the other, plus the freighters for Marseille, were all built at **Istres**, **La Seyne** and **La Ciotat**.

But between the battleships of Toulon and the petrochemical industries and tanker terminals around the Étang de Berre there are still great **seaside attractions**: the pine-covered rocks of the **Estaque**; the *calanques* (rocky inlets) between Marseille and **Cassis**; the sand beaches of La Ciotat bay and the coastal path to **Bandol**; and the heights from which to view the coast, close-up on the **route de Crêtes** or **Cap Sicié**, and at a distance from **Le Gros Cerveau** and **Mont Caume**.

For countryside, you can escape **inland** from the conurbations, following in Cézanne's steps from Aix to **Mont-Victoire**; in those of Pagnol's characters around **Aubagne**; or explore the legends of Mary Magdalene in the **Chaîne**

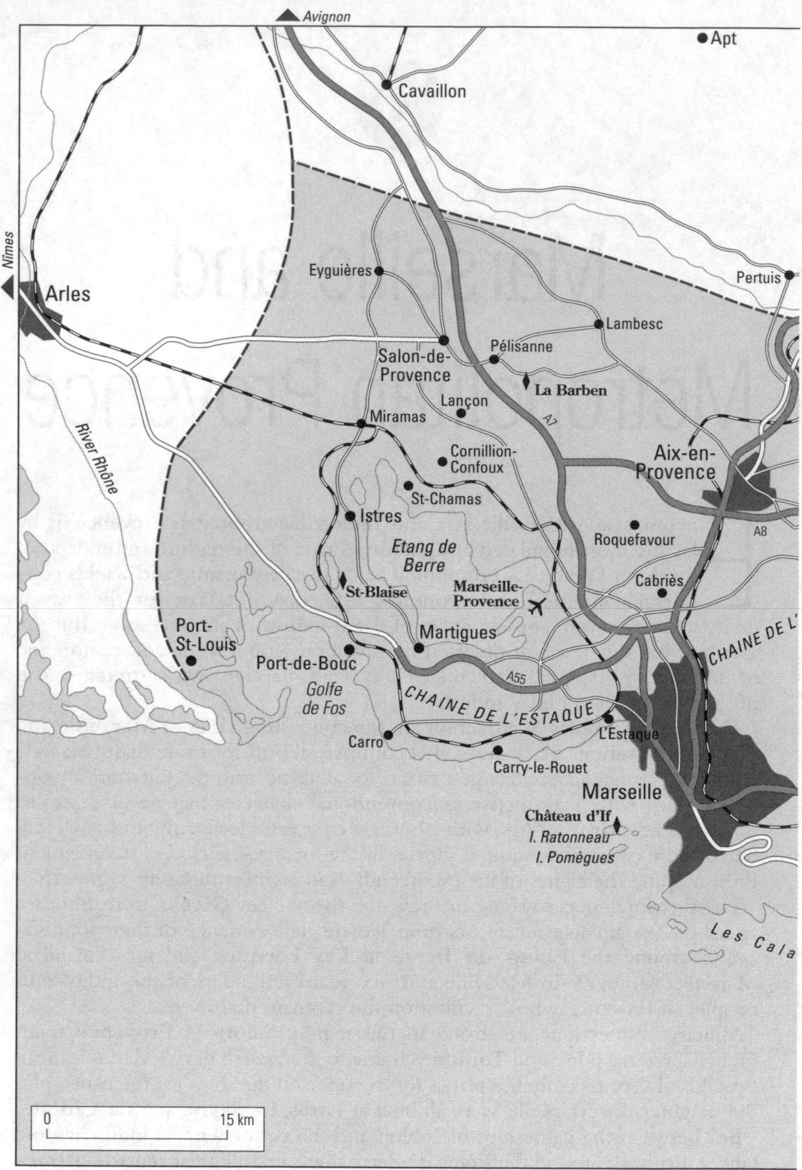

de la Ste-Baume. In the last you'll find great expanses of hillside and forest, with only birds and squirrels for company, and little villages like **Signes**, where time seems to stand still.

The area also has great **wines** at Bandol and Cassis, and great **seafood** gourmandize, particularly in Marseille, home of the famous sea-fish dish, bouillabaisse.

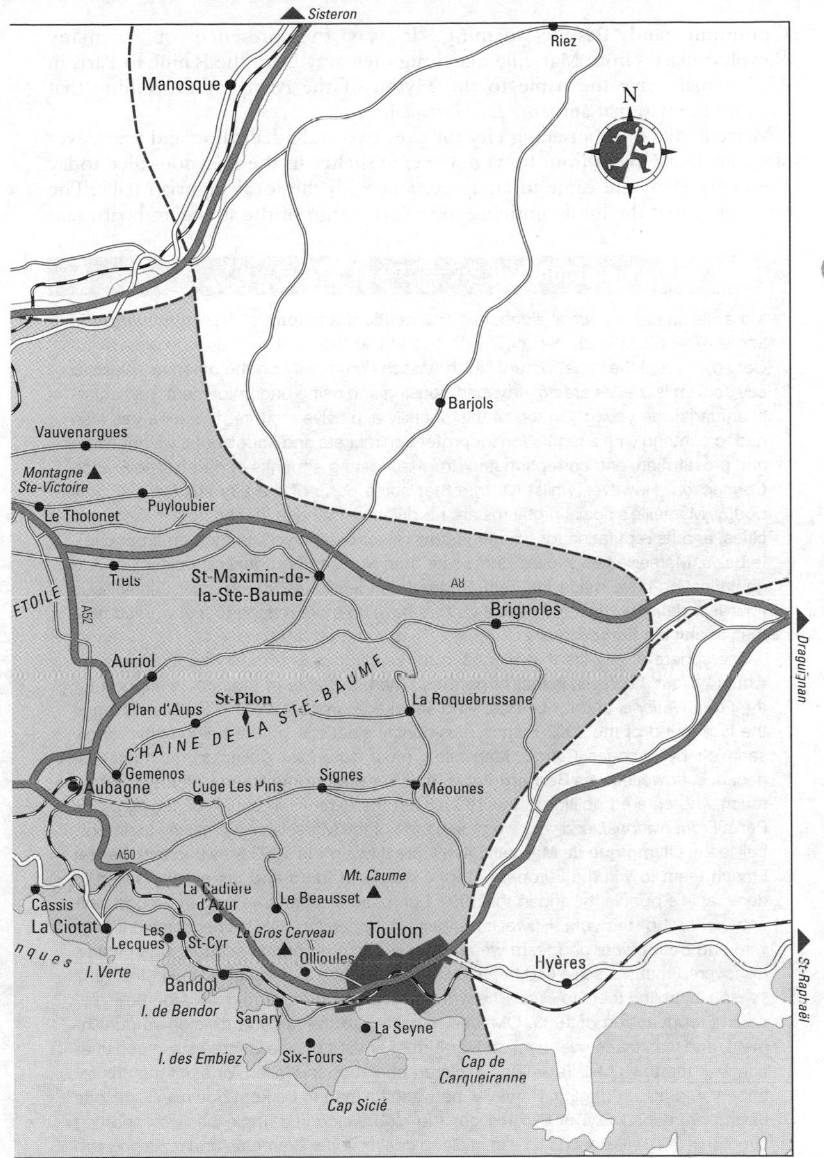

Marseille

The most renowned French city after Paris, **MARSEILLE** has, like the French capital, prospered and been ransacked over the centuries. It has lost its privileges to sundry French kings and foreign armies, refound its fortunes, suffered plagues, religious bigotry, republican and royalist terror and had its own

Commune and Bastille-storming. It was the presence of so many Revolutionaries from Marseille marching their way from the Rhine to Paris in 1792 which gave the name to the Hymn of the Army of the Rhine that became the national anthem, '*La Marseillaise*'.

Marseille has been a trading city for over two and a half thousand years, ever since ancient Greeks from Ionia discovered shelter in the Lacydon inlet, today the Vieux Port, and came to an agreement with the local Ligurian tribe. The story goes that the locals, noticing the exotic cargo of the strangers' boats, sent

Race, politics and football

Marseille has all the social, economic and **political tensions** of France writ large. To some extent it is a divided city, with the ethnic French living on one side of La Canebière, and the large, vibrant North African community on the other: needless to say, racism is rife, as are poverty, bad housing and rising unemployment, particularly amongst the young. On top of this socially explosive mixture, Marseille has also had to contend with a reputation for protection rackets and shoot-outs, violent crime and prostitution, and corruption and drug-laundering – thanks in part to *The French Connection*. However, whilst it's true that some parts of the city still feel palpably dodgy, Marseille's social problems are no different to those in many other European cities, and its reputation for danger is now rather overplayed. In fact, on a per capita basis, Marseille has a lower crime rate than Nice, and gradual refurbishment and gentrification have made the central streets, at least, feel much safer. Marseille is now very definitely 'in', and casual visitors have no more reason to feel worried here than in any big European city.

One sphere of city life that has been as tumultuous and murky as its reputation would have it, however, is that of **politics**. There is plenty of grassroots support for the *Front National* and for Le Pen, who shocked Europe with his strong showing in the first round of the 2002 French presidential elections before being convincingly seen off by Jacques Chirac. Marseille's most notorious politician during recent decades, however, was **Bernard Tapie**, a millionaire businessman with the common touch who entered politics in the 1980s with the express intention of seeing off Le Pen's *Front National*, and who won the hearts of the Marseillais by making their football team, **Olympique de Marseille** (OM), great again – in 1993 they became the first French team to win the European Cup. Charges of fraud and tax evasion failed to dent Tapie's popularity, and in the 1994 European elections he gained around seventy percent of the vote. However, under his ownership, OM's finances went haywire and both owner and team were embroiled in a notorious scandal when it was discovered that Marseille had been guilty of chicanery and match-fixing in the 1992 season, enabling them to clinch the national Championship and qualify for their 'glorious' European run of 1993. OM was relegated to the second division as punishment, and was taken over by a consortium of private business interests in conjunction with the town hall. Tapie was declared bankrupt and jailed for eight months for bribery and match-rigging. However, he wasn't a man to be kept down and, despite having defrauded OM of $15 million, the club welcomed Tapie back as sporting director in 2001. He lost no time in sacking coach Javier Clemente and replacing him with OM stalwart Tomislav Ivic, and by the end of 2002 OM were once again at the top of *Le Championnat*.

A more universally admired – and multicultural – symbol of Marseille's footballing prowess is French national idol **Zinedine Zidane**, the Marseille-born son of Algerian parents and one of the leading members of the so-called 'rainbow team' which won the 1998 World Cup. Zidane made use of his hero status during the 2002 election to speak out against Le Pen and in favour of Chirac. A giant portrait of the city's favourite son covers one side of a building on the Corniche.

them off to the king's castle where the princess's wedding preparations were in full swing. The Ligurian royal custom at the time was that the king's daughter could choose her husband from among her father's guests. As the leader of the Greek party walked through the castle gate, he was handed a drink by a woman and discovered that she was the princess and that he was the bridegroom. The king gave the couple the hill on the north side of the Lacydon and Massalia came into being. And there ends, more or less, Marseille's association with romance.

Which is not to say Marseille cannot be romantic. It has a powerful magnetism as a true Mediterranean city, surrounded by mountains and graced with hidden corners that have the unexpected air of fishing villages. Built (for the most part handsomely) of warm stone, it has its triumphal architecture; it has, too, the cosmopolitan atmosphere of a major port. Perhaps the most appealing quality is the down-to-earth nature of its inhabitants, who are gregarious, generous, endlessly talkative and unconcerned if their style seems provocatively vulgar to the snobs of Aix or the Côte d'Azur. Their animation makes this one of the most delightful European cities in which to spend a few days, and one which – thanks in part to the new TGV link with Paris – is fast becoming popular with visitors.

Arrival and information

Arriving by **car**, you'll descend into Marseille from the surrounding heights of one of three mountain ranges. From any direction the views encompass the barricade of high-rise concrete on the lower slopes, the vast roadstead with docks stretching miles north from the central **Vieux Port** and Marseille's classic landmark, the **Basilique de Notre-Dame-de-la-Garde**, perched on a high rock south of the Vieux Port. Follow signs for the Vieux Port to reach the city centre.

The city's **airport**, the Aéroport de Marseille-Provence, is 20km northwest of the city centre; a shuttle bus runs to the **gare SNCF St-Charles** (6am–10pm; every 20min; later buses meet flights; €8), on the northern edge of 1er arrondissement on esplanade St Charles. The **gare routière** stands to the right of the station entrance, on place Victor-Hugo. From esplanade St-Charles, a monumental staircase leads down to bd d'Athènes, which becomes bd Dugommier before reaching **La Canebière**, Marseille's main street. La Canebière runs to the head of the **Vieux Port**, a fifteen-minute walk to the right of the intersection. Marseille's main **tourist office** is at 4 La Canebière (June Aug Mon–Sat 9am–7.30pm, Sun 10am–6pm; Sept–May Mon–Sat 9am–7pm, Sun 10am–5pm; ⓣ04.91.13.89.00, ⓦwww.mairie-marseille.fr).

City transport

Marseille has an efficient **bus**, **tram** and **métro** network. You can get a plan of the **transport system** from RTM at 6 rue des Fabres, one street north of La Canebière near the Bourse, the city's stock exchange. **Tickets** are flat rate for buses, trams and the métro and can be used for journeys combining all three as long as they take less than one hour. You can buy individual **tickets** (€1.40) from bus and tram drivers, and from métro ticket offices, or **multi-journey** *Cartes Libertés* (in increments of €6.50 and €13), which are valid for any number of journeys up to the value of the card; these can be bought from métro stations, RTM kiosks and shops displaying the RTM sign. If you're 25 or under, and going to be in Marseille for a while, you can buy a **Carte Personelle travelcard**, which gives seven days' unlimited travel for €10, and 30 days for €37. You have to buy the card itself (€6.40) from the RTM office and you'll need a photo, but you can then recharge it as often as you like at métro stations. Tickets need to be punched in the machines on the bus, on tramway platforms or at métro gates. The métro runs Monday to Thursday 5am to 9pm, and until 12.30am at weekends or when the football team is playing. **Night buses** run out from the centre from 9.30pm to 12.45am, from rue des Fabres: pick up a timetable from the RTM office or métro sales points.

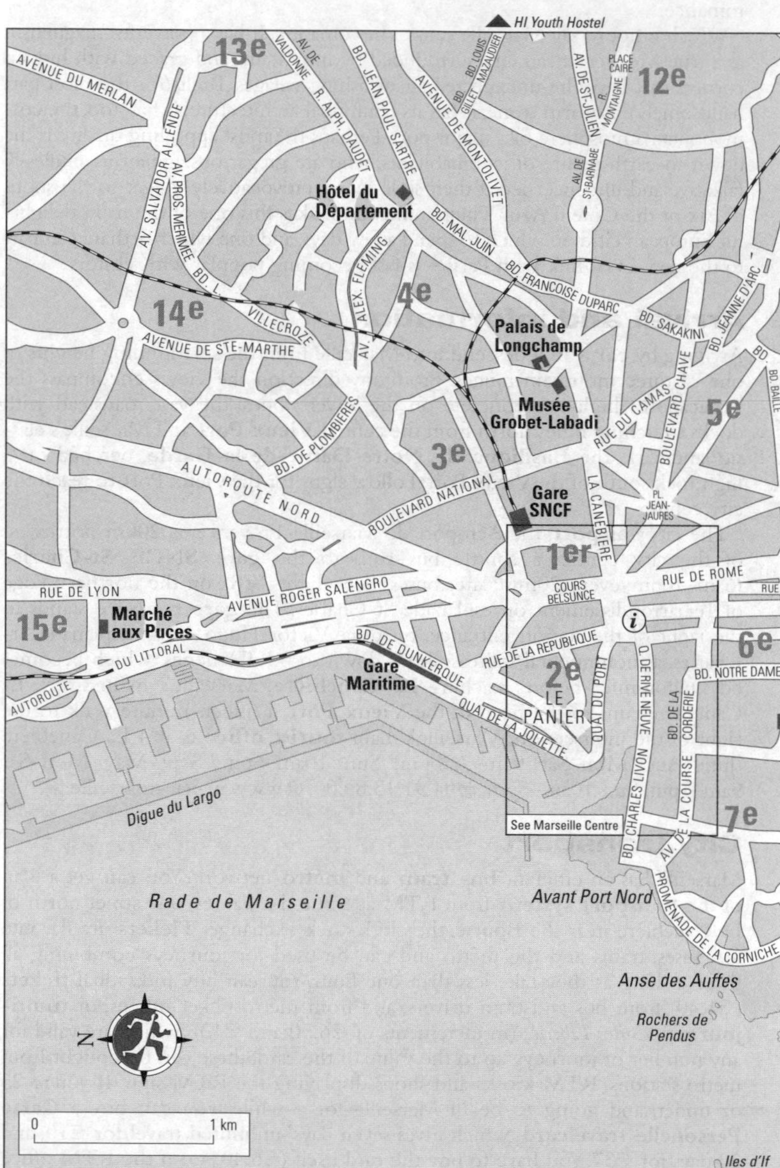

Accommodation

Demand for accommodation in Marseille isn't as tied to the **tourist season** as in the coastal resorts, and finding a room in August is no more difficult than in November. **Hotels** are plentiful with lots of reasonable options around the Vieux Port and on the streets running south from La Canebière. If you get stuck for a room, the main tourist office offers a free accommodation service.

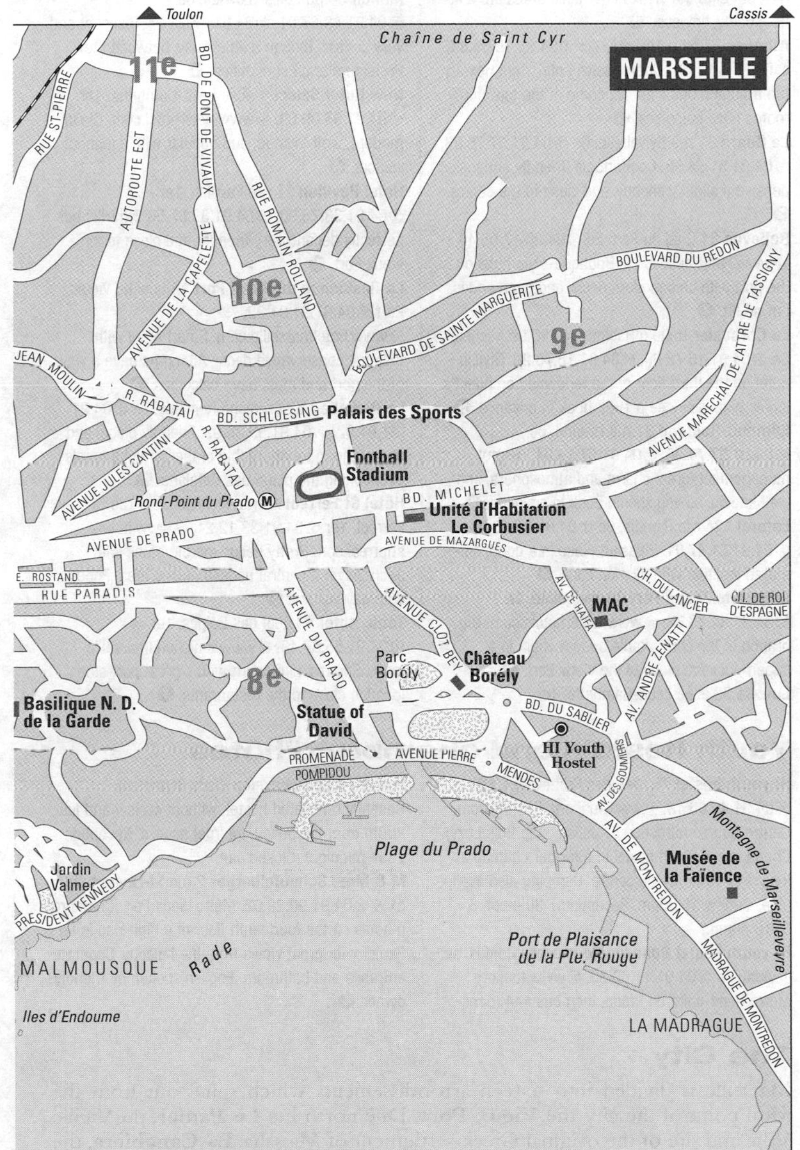

The cheapest options are the city's **youth hostels**, both quite a way from the centre.

Hotels

Alizé 35 quai des Belges, 1er ⓣ04.91.33.66.97, ⓦwww.alize-hotel.com. Comfortable, bright, soundproofed rooms; the more expensive ones look out onto the Vieux Port. Public areas are a little gloomy, however. ❹

Athènes 37 bd d'Athènes, 1er ⓣ04.91.90.03.83, ⓕ04.91.90.72.03. Inexpensive hotel, right next to the train and bus stations; some of the top-storey rooms have balconies. ❸

Le Béarn 63 rue Sylvabelle, 6e ⓣ04.91.37.75.83, ⓕ04.91.81.54.98. Comfortable, friendly and inexpensive if slightly shabby, and close to the centre. ❷

Bellevue 34 Quai du Port, 2e ⓣ04.96.17.05.40, ⓦwww.hotel-bellevue.fr. Boutique-style hotel on the port with chic modern decor and good prices, but no lift. ❹

Le Corbusier Unité d'Habitation, 280 bd Michelet, 8e ⓣ04.91.16.78.00, ⓕ04.91.16.78.28. Stylish hotel on the third floor of the renowned architect's iconic high-rise (see p.180); book in advance. ❸

Edmond-Rostand 31 rue Dragon, 6e ⓣ04.91.37.74.95, ⓕ04.91.57.19.04. Helpful management, great charm and atmosphere, and well known, so you should book in advance. ❸

Esterel 124 rue Paradis, 6e ⓣ04.91.37.13.90, ⓕ04.91.81.47.01. Pleasant place in a good, animated location with all mod cons. ❸

Etap Hotel Vieux Port 46 rue Sainte, 1e ⓣ04.91.54.73.73, ⓦwww.accorhotels.com. Big branch of the comfortable budget chain in a superb location close to the Vieux Port. ❸

Lutétia 38 allée Léon-Gambetta, 1er ⓣ04.91.50.81.78, ⓕ04.91.50.23.52. Right in the thick of things with pleasant, soundproofed and air-conditioned rooms. ❸

Manon 36 bd Louis-Salvator, 6e ⓣ04.91.48.67.01, ⓕ04.91.47.23.04. Pleasant and very central, though a little noisy, between the Préfecture and cours Julien. ❷

New Hotel Select 4 allée Léon-Gambetta, 1er ⓣ04.91.95.09.09, ⓦwww.new-hotel.com. Clean, modern, well-located, and popular with Japanese visitors. ❹

Hotel Pavillon 27 rue Pavillon, 1er ⓣ04.91.33.76.90, ⓕ04.91.33.87.56. No frills but perfectly decent, very friendly, and close to the Vieux Port. ❶

La Residence du Vieux Port 18 quai du Vieux Port ⓣ04.91.91.91.22, ⓦwww.hotelmarseille.com. Smart hotel with tasteful, conservative decor. All rooms have a view of the port and most have balconies. ❼

Le Richelieu 52 Corniche Kennedy, 7e ⓣ04.91.31.01.92, ⓕ04.91.59.38.09. Friendly place, and one of the more affordable of the corniche hotels, overlooking the plage des Catalans. ❷

Hôtel St Ferréol 19 rue Pisançon, cnr rue St-Ferréol, 1er ⓣ04.91.33.12.21, ⓦwww.hotel-stferreol.com Pretty decor, marble baths with Jacuzzis, in a central pedestrianized area. Popular with gay visitors. ❺

Tonic Hotel 43 quai des Belges, 1er ⓣ04.91.55.67.46, ⓦwww.tonichotelmarseille.com. Smart and modern with a great port-side location close to the restaurants. ❼

Youth hostels and chambre d'hôtes

HI youth hostel 76 allée des Primevères, 12e ⓣ04.91.49.06.18, ⓦwww.fuaj.org. Bus #8 from Centre Bourse (direction St-Julien, stop Bois Luzy). Cheap, clean youth hostel in a former château a long way out from the centre. Camping also available. Curfew 10.30pm. Reception 7.30–noon & 5–10.30pm.

HI youth hostel Bonneveine impasse Bonfils, av J-Vidal, 8e ⓣ04.91.17.63.30, ⓦwww.fuaj.org. Métro Rond-point du Prado, then bus #44 (direction Roy d'Espagne, stop Place Bonnefon). Recently renovated hostel, without curfew and just 200m from the beach. Internet access. Reception 7am–midnight. Closed Jan.

M & Mme Schaufelberger 2 rue St-Laurent, 2e ⓣ & ⓕ04.91.90.29.02. Métro Vieux Port. Chambre d'hôtes on the fourteenth floor of a high-rise in Le Panier with great views from the balcony. Separate entrance and bathroom. English spoken by friendly owner. ❹

The City

Marseille is divided into sixteen arrondissements which spiral out from the focal point of the city, the **Vieux Port**. Due north lies **Le Panier**, the Vieille Ville and site of the original Greek settlement of Massalia. **La Canebière**, the wide boulevard starting at quai des Belges at the head of the Vieux Port, is the central east-west axis of the town, with the **Centre Bourse** and the little streets of **quartier Belsunce** bordering it to the north and the main shopping streets to the south. The main north-south axis is **rue d'Aix**, becoming **cours Belsunce** then **cours St Louis**, **rue de Rome**, **av du Prado** and **bd Michelet**. The lively, youngish quarter around **place Jean-Jaurès** and the trendy **cours Julien** lie to the east of rue de Rome. On the headland west of the Vieux Port are the villagey *quartiers* of **Les Catalans** and **Malmousque** from where the **Corniche** heads south past the city's most favoured residential districts towards the main beaches and expensive promenade bars and restaurants of the **Plage du Prado**.

The Vieux Port

The **Vieux Port** is, more or less, the ancient harbour basin, and the original inlet that the ancient Greeks sailed into. Historic resonances, however, are not exactly deafening on first encounter, drowned as they are by the stalling or speeding lanes of traffic. But the sunny **cafés** on the north and east side of the port indulge the sedentary pleasures of observing street life; the morning **fish market** on the quai des Belges provides some natural Marseillais theatre; and the mass of seafood restaurants on the **pedestrianized streets** between the southern quay and cours Estienne d'Orves ensure that the Vieux Port remains the life centre of the city.

Two fortresses guard the harbour entrance. **St-Jean**, on the northern side, dates from the Middle Ages when Marseille was an independent republic, and is now only open when hosting exhibitions. Its enlargement of 1660, and the construction of **St-Nicolas** fort, on the south side of the port, represent the city's final defeat as a separate entity. Louis XIV ordered the new fort to keep an eye on the city after he had sent in an army, suppressed the city's council, fined it, arrested all opposition and, in an early example of rate-capping, set ludicrously low limits on Marseille's subsequent expenditure and borrowing. The Fort St-Nicolas is still a military installation today.

The best view of the Vieux Port is from the **Palais du Pharo**, built on the headland beyond Fort St-Nicolas by Emperor Napoleon III for his wife and now used as a conference centre. Its surrounding park (summer 7am–10pm; winter 7am–9pm) hides an underground *mediathèque* and exhibition space. For a wider-angle view, head up to the city's highest point, **Notre-Dame-de-la-Garde**, on bd André Aune (daily: summer 8–10am & 11.30–5pm; winter 8–10am & 11.30am–4.30pm; bus #60), which tops the hill south of the harbour. Crowned by a monumental gold Madonna and Child, the Second Empire landmark is a monstrous riot of neo-Byzantine design, crammed with bizarre offerings – some touching, others creepy – from those rescued from shipwrecks, plane crashes, house fires and the like.

There are two small museums on the south side of the port which are worth checking out. The **Musée du Santon**, 47 rue Neuve Ste-Catherine (Tues–Sun 10am–12.30pm & 2–6.30pm; free), is part of the Carbonel workshop, one of the most renowned producers of the crib figures for which

Carte Privilèges

If you're planning on visiting several of Marseille's museums it may be worth investing €15.25 in the **Carte Privilèges**, which gives a day's free access to fourteen of the city's museums, mini-cruises, city tours, tourist trains and the public transport network. Two- (€22.87) and three-day (€30.49) versions are also available.

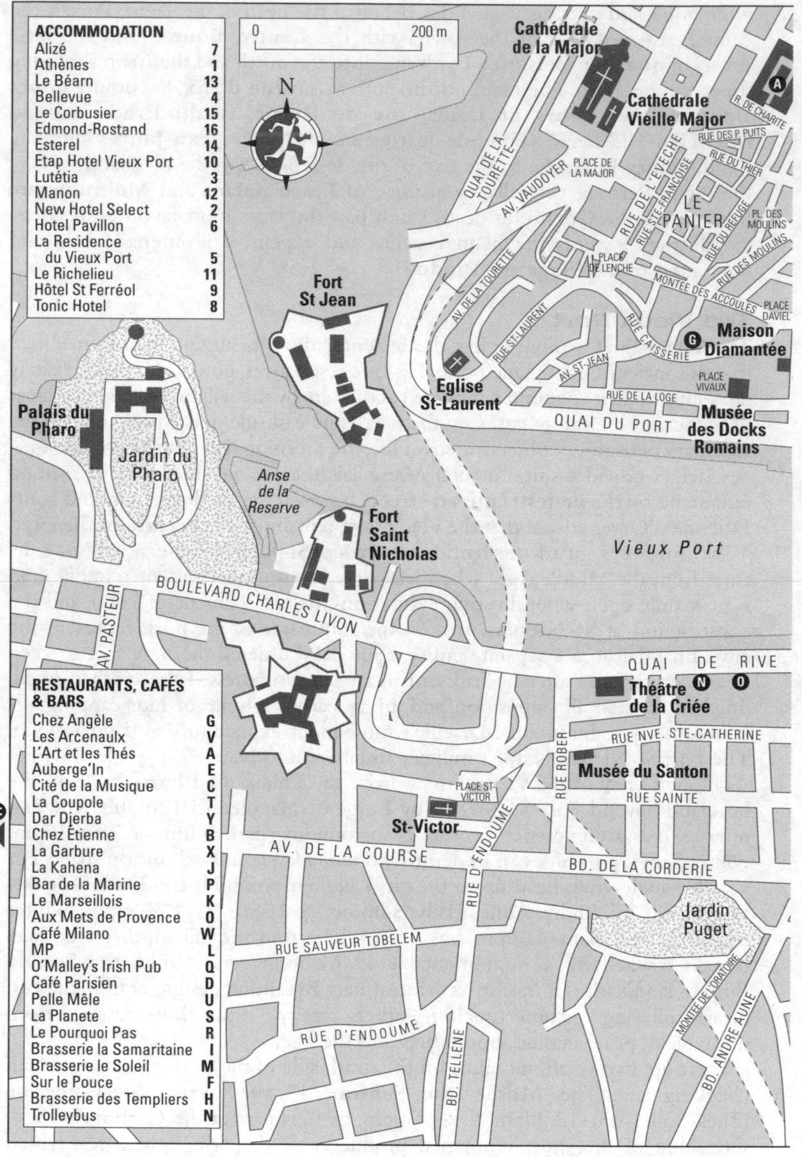

Provence is famous. The **Maison de l'Artisanat et des Métiers d'Art**, 21 cours Estienne d'Orves (Tues–Sat 1–6pm; free), hosts excellent temporary exhibitions on Marseillais themes. Two doors away is the intellectual haunt of *Les Arcenaulx*: a restaurant, *salon de thé* and bookshop.

A short way inland from the Fort St-Nicolas, above the Bassin de Carénage and the slip road for the Vieux Port's tunnel, is Marseille's oldest church, the

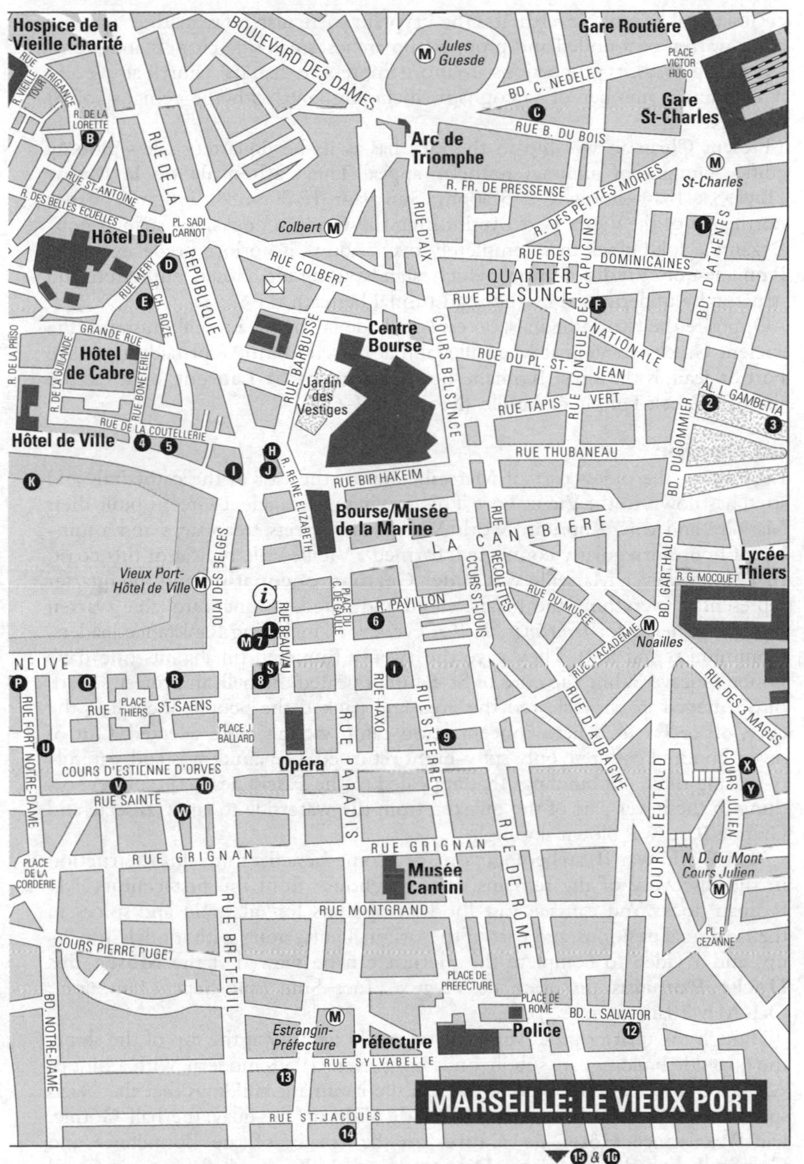

Abbaye St-Victor (daily 8.30am–6.30pm; €2 entry to crypt). Originally part of a monastery founded in the fifth century on the burial site of various martyrs, the church was built, enlarged and fortified – a vital requirement given its position outside the city walls – over a period of two hundred years from the middle of the tenth century. It certainly looks and feels more like a fortress with the walls of the choir almost three metres thick, and it's no conventional ecclesiastical beauty. Nevertheless the crypt, in particular, is fascinating: a crumbling warren of rounded and propped-up arches, small side chapels and secretive passageways, its proportions are more impressive than the church above and it contains a number of sarcophagi, including one with the remains of St Maurice.

Present Christian worship in the city has as its headquarters a less gloomy edifice but one of minimal aesthetic appeal. The **Cathédrale de la Major** (Tues–Sat 10am–noon & 2–5.30pm; Sun 9am–12.30pm & 2–6pm), on the north side of the Vieux Port overlooking the modern docks, is a striped neo-Byzantine solid block that completely overshadows its forlorn predecessor, the Romanesque **Vieille Major**, which stands alongside, closed, shuttered and structurally undermined by the road tunnel beneath it.

Opposite the two cathedrals, on esplanade de la Touret, a mural illustrates the ancient Greeks arriving at Marseille, and at the end of the esplanade, opposite Fort St-Jean, is the small Romanesque **Church of St-Laurent**, built on the site of a Greek Temple of Apollo (Mon–Fri 2–6pm).

Le Panier

Le Panier, the oldest part of Marseille, lies to the east of the cathedrals and stretches down to the Vieux Port. This is where the ancient Greeks built their Massalia, and where, up until World War II, tiny streets, steep steps and a jumble of houses irregularly connected, formed a Vieille Ville typical of this coast. In 1943, however, Marseille was under **German occupation** and the quarter represented everything the Nazis feared and hated, an uncontrollable warren providing shelter for *Untermenschen* of every sort, including Resistance leaders, Communists and Jews. They gave the twenty thousand inhabitants one day's notice to leave. While the curé of St-Laurent pealed the bells in protest, squads of SS moved in; they cleared the area and packed the people, including the curé, off to Fréjus, where concentration camp victims were selected. Out of seven hundred children, only sixty-eight returned. Dynamite was laid, carefully sparing three old buildings that appealed to the Fascist aesthetic, and everything in the lower part of the quarter, from the waterside to rue Caisserie and Grande Rue, was blown sky high.

After World War II, archeologists reaped some benefits from this destruction in the discovery of the remains of a warehouse from the first-century AD Roman docks. You can see vast food-storage jars for oil, grain and spices in their original positions, and part of the original jetty, along with models, mock-ups and a video to complete the picture, can be viewed at the **Musée des Docks Romains** on place de Vivaux (Tues–Sun: June–Sept 11am–6pm; Oct–May 10am–5pm; €2).

Though the quarter preserves some of its old identity at the top of the slope, the quayside buildings are solidly built but austere 1950s modern, with a hint of Art Deco in places. Amongst all this are the landmark buildings that the Nazis spared: the seventeenth-century **Hôtel de Ville** on the quay; the half-Gothic, half-Renaissance **Hôtel de Cabre** on the corner of rue Bonneterie and Grande Rue; and the **Maison Diamantée** of 1620, so called for the pointed shape of its facade stonework, on rue de la Prison. This exceptionally beautiful building normally houses the Musée de Vieux Marseille, but is currently closed for repairs: its exhibits can sometimes be seen in other venues around the city, including the Charité (check with tourist office for latest information).

Overlooking the small **place Daviel** nearby is an impressive eighteenth-century bell tower, all that remains of the Église des Accoules, destroyed in 1794 as it had served as a meeting place for counter-revolutionaries after the French

Revolution. To the north of here, above the place Daviel, is the vast nineteenth-century **Hôtel Dieu**, now a nursing college. At the junction of rue de la Prison and rue Caisserie, the steps of montée des Accoules lead up and across to **place de Lenche**, site of the Greek agora, a few blocks south of the cathedrals and a good café stop.

What's left of old Le Panier is above here, though the fifteen windmills of place des Moulins disappeared in the nineteenth century. If you climb rue du Réfuge you'll find yourself in a modern piazza, with new buildings in traditional styles, and an uninterrupted view of the refined **Hospice de la Vieille Charité** at the far end. This seventeenth-century workhouse, with a gorgeous Baroque chapel surrounded by handsome columned arcades in pink stone, is now a cultural centre, hosting some excellent temporary exhibitions and popular evening concerts. It is also home to two museums, a café and a bookshop. The **Musée d'Archéologie Méditerranéenne** (Tues–Sun: June–Sept 11am–6pm; Oct–May 10am–5pm; €2; combined ticket for entire complex €4.57) contains some very beautiful fourth- and fifth-century BC pottery and glass, an Egyptian collection with mummies and their accompanying boxes for internal organs plus a mummified crocodile. It also displays fascinating finds from a Celto-Légurian settlement at Roquepertuse, between Marseille and Aix, including a double-headed statue. The other permanent collection is the **Musée des Arts Africains, Océaniens et Amérindiens** (same hours and prices as Musée d'Archéologie), which in addition to its sculptures and masks has a collection of dried heads.

La Canebière and around

La Canebière, the grandiose, if dilapidated, boulevard that runs for about a kilometre east from Marseille's port, is the undisputed hub of the town. Named after the hemp (*canabé*) that once grew here and provided the raw materials for the town's thriving rope-making trade, it was originally modelled on the Champs Elysées, though today it's too scruffy for pavement café idling and its shops are fairly lacklustre. It is also home, at the port end, to two museums. The **Musée de la Marine et de l'Economie** (Mon & Wed–Sun 10am–6pm; €2) is housed on the ground floor of the Neoclassical stock exchange and contains a superb collection of model ships, including the legendary 1930s transatlantic liner *Normandie* and Marseille's very own prewar queen of the seas, the *Providence*. A bit further up at no. 11, the **Musée de la Mode** (Mon–Sat noon–7pm; €2) displays fashion and swimwear from 1945 to the present day, as well as hosting regular exhibitions; it also has a chi-chi restaurant.

Marseille's Commune

Within the space of four years from its completion in 1867, the Marseille **Préfecture** had flown the imperial flag, the red flag and the tricolour. The red flag was flying in 1871, during Marseille's Commune. The counter-revolutionary forces advanced from Aubagne, encountering little resistance, and took the heights of Notre Dame de la Garde from where they directed their cannons down onto the Préfecture. The defeat was swifter but no less bloody than the fate of the Parisian Communards. One of the Marseillaise leaders, Gaston Crémieux, a young idealistic bourgeois with great charisma, escaped the initial carnage but was subsequently caught. Despite clemency pleas from all quarters of the city, Thiers, president of the newly formed Third Republic and a native of Marseille, would not relent and Crémieux was shot by a firing squad near the Pharo Palace in November 1871.

Behind the stock exchange is the ugly **Centre Bourse** shopping centre and the **Jardin des Vestiges**, where the ancient port extended, curving northwards from the present quai des Belges. Excavations have revealed a stretch of the Greek port and bits of the city wall with the base of three square towers and a gateway, dated to the second or third century BC. The beautifully lit and spaced **Musée d'Histoire de Marseille**, inside the Centre Bourse (Mon–Sat noon–7pm; €2), shows the main finds of Marseillaise excavations, of which the most dramatic is a third-century AD wreck of a Roman trading vessel. There are models of the city, reconstructed boats, everyday items such as shoes and baskets, and a beautiful Roman mosaic of a dolphin, plus a great deal of information on text panels and a video about the Roman, Greek and pre-Greek settlements. Laws that were posted up in Greek Massalia are cited, forbidding women to drink wine and allowing would-be suicides to take hemlock if the 600-strong parliament agreed.

The vast new **central library** on cours Belsunce is the latest in a series of regeneration projects gradually supplanting the dilapidated tenements north of La Canebière, though for the time being the area's knife shops remain. The continuation of cours Belsunce, rue d'Aix, stretches to **Porte d'Aix**, Marseille's Arc de Triomphe, modelled on the ancient Roman arch at Orange. This was part of the city's grandiose mid-nineteenth-century expansion which included the Cathédrale de la Major and the new Joliette docks, paid for with the profits of military enterprise, most significantly the conquest of Algeria in 1830. Today it's a popular meeting place for the North African male community, as is the **quartier Belsunce** to the east. Bordered by cours Belsunce/rue d'Aix, bd d'Athènes and St-Charles, this dynamic district is home to hundreds of tiny shops selling North African food, music, household goods and clothes.

At the top end of bd d'Athènes, a monumental stairway leads up to **Gare St-Charles**. It was laid out in the 1920s with Art Deco railings, lamps and mammoth statues and has steps wide enough for people to sit and chat, play cards or, for some, simply to lie drunk without constituting an obstruction. The building of a road tunnel link to the A7 autoroute beneath the steps, however, is unlikely to add to its appeal.

More Arab trading, on a smaller scale, takes place just south of La Canebière around the lively **Marché des Capucins** (Mon–Sat 8am–7pm) by the former Gare de l'Est. The streets around here are pretty seedy, with plenty of insalubrious hotels and, come nightfall, prostitutes on every corner, particularly along the handsome rue Sénac de Meilhan.

The prime shopping quarter of Marseille centres around three streets running south from La Canebière: rue de Rome, rue Paradis and rue St-Ferréol, which terminates at the pseudo-Renaissance **Préfecture**, where demonstrations in the city traditionally converge. The streets are full of chic, designer boutiques, whose shop fronts have been renovated to their original architectural condition. Tempting cafés and pâtisseries are dotted throughout the *quartier*, making it a good place to stop for a midday meal.

Between rue St-Ferréol and rue Paradis, on rue Grignan, is the city's most important art museum, the **Musée Cantini** (Tues–Sun: June–Sept 11am–6pm; Oct–May 10am–5pm; €2), housing paintings and sculptures dating from the end of the nineteenth century up to the 1950s. The Fauvists and Surrealists are well represented along with works by Matisse, Léger, Picasso, Ernst, Le Corbusier, Miró and Giacometti. Only a proportion of the permanent collection is displayed at any one time, and even less during the many excellent temporary exhibitions.

A few blocks east of rue de Rome, the streets around **cours Julien** are full of bars and music shops, and the *cours* itself, with pools, fountains, and restaurant tables, is one of the most pleasant places to idle in the city. Madame Zaza of Marseille, an original and affordable Marseillaise couturier, has her shop at no. 73; there are bookshops and art galleries to browse in, plus a stamp and secondhand book market, with antiques and junk every second Sunday in summer months. The **daily market**, known as **La Plaine**, on place Jean-Jaurès is at its best on Saturday when there's a good mix of food and clothing, including bargain Italian shoes.

Palais de Longchamp and around

The **Palais de Longchamp**, 2km inland from the port (buses #8, #80, #81 or #41 from La Canebière, or métro Longchamp-Cinq-Avenues), was completed in 1869, the year the Suez Canal opened, bringing a new boom for Marseillaise trade. It was built as the grandiose conclusion of an aqueduct at Roquefavour (no longer in use) bringing water from the Durance to the city. Water is still pumped into the centre of the colonnade connecting the two palatial wings of the building. Below, an enormous statue looks as if it's honouring some great feminist victory: three well-muscled women stand above four bulls wallowing passively in a pool from which a cascade drops the four or five storeys to ground level.

The palace's north wing houses the **Musée des Beaux-Arts** (Tues–Sun: June–Sept 11am–6pm; Oct–May 10am–5pm; €2), a slightly stuffy place but with its fair share of delights. Italian, French and Flemish old masters, including works by Rubens and Jordaens, occupy the lower level, while upstairs is dedicated to nineteenth-century French art, with works by Corot and Signac. Most unusual are the three paintings by Françoise Duparc (1726–76), while the nineteenth-century Marseille satirist Honoré Daumier, imprisoned for his vicious caricatures of Louis Philippe's government, has an entire room dedicated to his cartoons. The other wing of the palace is taken up with the **Musée d'Histoire Naturelle** (same hours and prices), and its collection of mouldy stuffed animals and lots of fossils. Opposite the palace, at 140 bd Longchamp, is the **Musée Grobet-Labadi** (same hours and prices as the Musée des Beaux-Arts), a typically elegant late-nineteenth-century bourgeois town house filled with exquisite tapestries, paintings and objets d'art.

About 1km northeast of the palace, at the end of bd Mal-Juin, stands the futuristic **Hôtel du Département** (métro St-Just). Deliberately sited in the run-down St-Just-Chartreux *quartier*, the new seat of government for the Bouches-du-Rhône *département* was the biggest public building to be built in the French provinces in the twentieth century. Designed by English architect Will Alsop in characteristically expressive style, the building is, unfortunately, closed to the public for security reasons. In front of the Hôtel stands the **Dôme**, a venue for shows and exhibitions.

Parc Chanot, Unité d'Habitation and beyond

Av du Prado, the continuation of rue de Rome, is an eight-lane highway, with impressive fountains and one of the city's biggest **daily markets** between métros Castellane and Périer. At the rond-point du Prado, the avenue turns west to meet the corniche road.

The north-south axis continues as Bd Michelet past **Parc Chanot**, home to Olympique de Marseille's ground. OM's reputation for occasional brilliance means that home matches are almost always sold out, but tickets may be available from the *OM Café* on the quai des Belges on the Vieux Port, with prices starting around €25. At the far side of the stadium on rue Raymond Teisseire, the vast modern **Palais des Sports** hosts boxing matches, ice-skating, circuses and other spectacles.

Beyond Parc Chanot, set back from the west side of the boulevard, is a mould-breaking piece of architecture, **Le Corbusier's Unité d'Habitation**, designed in 1946 and completed in 1952. A seventeen-storey housing complex on stilts, the Unité was the prototype for thousands of apartment buildings the world over, though the difference in quality between this – the *couture* original – and the industrially-produced imitations becomes immediately apparent after a visit to the Unité. Confounding expectations, this concrete modernist structure is extremely complex, with 23 different apartment layouts, to suit single people and varying sized families: the larger appartments are split across two floors with balconies on both sides of the building, giving unhindered views of mountains and sea. Many of the original tenants are still in residence. At ground level the building is decorated with Corbusier's famous human figure, the Modulor, while on the third floor is a small café-bar with its terrace and superlative Mediterranean views, and a hotel (see p.172). Sadly, the iconic, sculptural rooftop recreational area is off limits to visitors, though you can ride the lift to the top and peer out at it. To reach the Unité take the métro to Rd-Pt du Prado, then bus #21 (direction Vaufrèges or Luminy).

Further south, at 69 av d'Haïfa (bus #23 or #45 from métro Rd-Pt du Prado; stop Haïfa or Marie-Louise), is the contemporary art museum, **MAC** (Tues–Sun: June–Sept 11am–6pm; Oct–May 10am–5pm; €2). The permanent collection, displayed in perfect, pure-white surroundings, is the continuation of the Cantini collection, with works from the 1960s to the present. The artists include the Marseillais César and Ben, along with Buren, Christo, Klein, Niki de St-Phalle, Tinguely and Warhol. There's also the CinéMAC (☎04.91.25.01.07), a cinema showing feature films, shorts and videos on different themes each month.

Between av d'Haïfa and the sea, just off av Prado, is **Parc Borély**, with ponds, palm trees, a rose garden, botanical gardens (daily 6am–9pm; free) and no restrictions about walking or picnicking on the grass. It was originally the grounds of the **Château Borély** (daily 10am–6pm; €2), an eighteenth-century mansion hosting temporary art exhibitions. Next to the park is the racecourse with its old, elegant stands on the promenade by the Plage du Prado.

The corniche and south to Les Goudes

The most popular stretch of sand close to the city centre is the small plage des Catalans, a few blocks south of the Palais du Pharo. This marks the beginning of Marseille's **Corniche Président-Kennedy**, initiated and partly built after the 1848 revolution, and currently being doubled in width by extending it out over the sea. Despite its inland bypass of the Malmousque peninsula, it's a corniche as good as any on the Riviera, with *belle époque* villas on the slopes above, the Îles d'Endoume and the Château d'If in the distance, cliffs below and high bridge piers for the road to cross the inlets of La Fausse-Monnaie and Les Auffes. Here, the Monument aux Morts de l'Armée d'Orient frames its statue against the setting sun, while further along the corniche, a modernist memorial commemorates the *pieds noirs* who returned from North Africa.

Prior to 1948, Malmousque and the **Vallon des Auffes** were inaccessible from the town unless you followed the 'customs men's path' over the rocks or took a boat. There was nothing on Malmousque, but the Vallon des Auffes had a freshwater source and a small community of fishermen and rope-makers. Amazingly, it is not much different today, with fishing boats pulled up around the rocks, tiny jumbled houses and restaurants serving the catch. Only one road, rue du Vallon-des-Auffes, leads out; otherwise it's the long flights of steps up to the corniche.

Malmousque is now a very desirable residential district, favoured by the champagne-socialist set, and home to Marseille's most expensive hotel-restaurant, *Le Petit Nice*. Behind La Fausse-Monnaie inlet, a path leads to the Théâtre Silvain, an open-air theatre set in a wilderness of trees and flowers. There's more greenery, of a formal nature, a short way further along the corniche in the **Jardin Valmer** (bus #83; stop Corniche J-Martin), and you can explore the tiny streets that lead up into this prime district of mansions with high-walled gardens.

The Corniche J-F Kennedy ends at the Plage du Prado, the city's main sand beach backed by a wide strip of lawns and the ugly Espace Borély complex of shops and restaurants. The promenade continues, however, all the way to Montredon, with a glittering array of restaurants, clubs and cafés, best seen at night. Marseille's newest museum, the **Musée de la Faïence** (Tues–Sun: June–Sept 11am–6pm; Oct–May 10am–5pm; €2), is at 157 av de Montredon, in the elegant nineteenth-century Château Pastré, set in a huge park that extends to the foot of the Montagne de Marseilleveyre (bus #19 from métro Rd-Pt du Prado; stop Montredon-Chancel). The eighteenth- and nineteenth-century ceramics, many of them produced in Marseille, are of an exceptionally high standard, such as the vibrant productions of Théodore Deck, but there is also a small collection of novel modern pieces.

From Montredon to Les Goudes, where the gleaming white, beautifully desolate hills finally meet the sea and the coast road ends, there are easily accessible *calanques* (rocky inlets) that face the setting sun, ideal for evening swims and supper picnics. If you prefer to walk, the GR98 to Cassis starts from the top of av de la Grotte-Roland, off av de Montredon a short way beyond the Pastré park. It splits into the 98a which follows the ridge inland and 98b which descends to the sea at Callelongue, the last outpost of Les Goudes. *La Grotte* bar here is where walkers gather.

The islands

Blacker than the sea, blacker than the sky, rose like a phantom the giant of granite, whose projecting crags seemed like arms extended to seize their prey.

So the **Château d'If** (April–Sept daily 9.30am–6.30pm; May–Oct Tues–Sun 9.30am–5.30pm; €4.60) appears to Edmond Dantès, hero of Alexandre Dumas' *The Count of Monte Cristo*, having made his watery escape after five years of incarceration as the innocent victim of treachery. In reality most prisoners of this island fortress died before they reached the end of their sentences – unless they were nobles living in the less fetid upper-storey cells, like one de Niozelles who was given six years for failing to take his hat off in the presence of Louis XIV, and Mirabeau who had run up massive debts with shops in Aix. More often, the crimes were political. After the revocation of the Edict of Nantes in 1685, thousands of Marseillais Protestants who refused to accept the new law were sent to the galleys and their leaders entombed in the Château d'If. Revolutionaries of 1848 drew their last breath here.

Apart from the castle, there's not much else to the Île d'If; it's little more than a rock that you can swim off, with a small café-restaurant. Dumas fans will love it, others may raise an eyebrow at the cell marked 'Dantès' in the same fashion as non-fictional inmates' names. But it's a horribly well-preserved sixteenth-century edifice and the views back towards Marseille are wonderful.

Boats leave from the quai des Belges from 9am onwards (hourly in summer; at least 5 daily in winter; €8), with the last boat back timed to coincide with the château's closing time; the journey takes twenty minutes. Alternatively, you can do a round trip taking in the other two islands of the Frioul archipelago, **Pomègues** and **Ratonneau** (€13), which are joined by a causeway enclosing a yachting harbour. In days gone by these islands were used as a quarantine station, most ineffectually in the early 1720s when a ship carrying the plague was given the go-ahead to dock in the city, resulting in the decimation of half the population.

Eating and drinking

Fish and seafood are the main ingredients of the Marseillais diet, and the superstar of dishes is the city's own expensive invention, **bouillabaisse**, a saffron- and garlic-flavoured fish soup with croûtons and *rouille* to throw in. There are conflicting theories about which fish should be included and where and how they must be caught, though it's generally agreed that *rascasse* is essential. The other city speciality is *pieds et paquets*, mutton or lamb belly and trotters.

The best, and most expensive, **restaurants** are close to the corniche, though for international choice the trendy cours Julien is the best place to head. The pedestrian precinct behind the south quay of the Vieux Port is more upmarket and fishy, with plenty more restaurants between the Opéra and La Canebière. Le Panier has a few tiny, inexpensive **bistros**, while cheap **snacks** can be found from the stands along cours Belsunce where you can buy fries and sandwiches stuffed with meat for under €3.

As Marseille is a Mediterranean city, people tend to stay up late in summer. Around the Vieux Port, from place Jean-Jaurès to cours Julien, and the Plage du Prado are the areas where there are always lots of people around and the **cafés** and **restaurants** open well into the night. Be warned that many restaurants take very long summer breaks.

Restaurants and cafés

L'Abri Côtier bd des Baigneurs, 8e ☎04.91.72.27.29. Lovely fish restaurant overlooking the sea in Montredon. It's a block or so down from the boulevard and a little tricky to find, despite the many signs. Menus from around €22. Closed Oct–April.

Chez Angèle 50 rue Caisserie, 2e ☎04.91.90.63.35. Packed Le Panier local, dishing up fresh pasta and pizza. Closed Sat lunch & Sun.

Les Arcenaulx 25 cours d'Estienne-d'Orves, 1er ☎04.91.59.80.30. Superb lunchtime plats for €11 in this intellectual haunt, which is also a bookshop; otherwise there's a €24.50 menu and a *ménu dégustation* at around €45. Last orders 11pm. Closed Sun.

L'Art et les Thés Centre de la Vieille Charité, 2e. The cultural centre's tearoom; it's a little gloomy inside, but one of few decent lunchtime options in this part of town. Closed Mon.

Auberge'In 25 rue du Chevalier-Roze, 2e ☎04.91.90.51.59. In a health-food shop on the edge of Le Panier. Has a vegetarian *menu fixe* for €10 at lunch and in the early evening. Closed Sun.

Pizzaria des Catalans 3 rue des Catalans, 7e ☎04.91.52.37.82. Excellent pizzas served just above the beach. Closed Mon, and open midday only out of season.

La Coupole 5 rue Haxo, 1er ☎04.91.54.88.57. Elegant brasserie serving a midday plat du jour with a glass of wine for €12. The seafood salads are a temptation. Open lunchtimes only; closed Sun.

Dar Djerba 15 cours Julien, 6e ☎04.91.48.55.36. Excellent Tunisian restaurant with beautiful tiling and friendly service. Tackle one of their gargantuan couscouses from €15. There is a second branch in the Aquaforum shopping complex opposite the plage du Prado. Open daily.

L'Épuisette Vallon des Auffes, 7e ☎04.91.52.17.82. This is the place to eat the Auffes catch at the water's edge. Expect to pay upwards of €60. Closed Sat lunch, Sun eve & Mon.

Chez Étienne 43 rue Lorette, 2e. An old-fashioned Le Panier pizzeria; hectic, cramped and crowded.

La Garbure 9 cours Julien, 6e ☎04.91.47.18.01. Rich specialities from southwest France, including Bresse chicken. Menus around €22. Closed Sat midday & Sun.

La Kahena 2 rue de la République, 2e ☎04.91.90.61.93. Popular Moroccan restaurant near the Vieux Port, with grills and couscous from €7.50. Open daily.

Le Marseillois quai du Port, 2e ⓣ04.91.90.72.52. Restaurant on the deck of an old sailing vessel in the Vieux Port. Lunchtime menus from €19, otherwise from €23. Closed Sun.

Aux Mets de Provence 18 quai Rive-Neuve, 7e ⓣ04.91.33.35.38. A Marseille institution with authentic Provençal cooking. Lunch menu at €35, otherwise €49. Closed Sat midday, Sun & Mon.

Chez Michel 6 rue des Catalans, 7e ⓣ04.91.52.30.63. There's no debate about the bouillabaisse ingredients here. A basket of five fishes, including the elusive and most expensive one, the *rascasse*, is presented to the customer before the soup is made. Quite simply the place to eat this dish. Expect to pay €47 per person for the bouillabaisse alone.

Café Milano 43 rue Sainte, 1er ⓣ04.91.33.14.33. Sleek, rather *BCBG* and hugely popular Italian. À la carte around €30. Closed Sun.

Café Parisien 1 pl Sadi-Carnot, 2e. Very stylish mix of old elegance and modern chic, where people play cards and chess. Hosts occasional painting exhibitions. Closed all day Sun, plus Mon–Wed evenings.

La Planete 45 Quai des Belges, 1er ⓣ04.91.33.14.82. About the cheapest bouillabaisse with *rascasse* you'll find, at around €15, and they show you the fish first. Open daily.

Brasserie la Samaritaine 2 quai du Port, 2e. The sunniest port-side bar with comfy terrace chairs. Plats du jour around €8–9; salads from €6. Open daily.

Brasserie le Soleil 3 Quai des Belges 1er. The main daytime gathering place for the city's gay community. Slick and modern, with huge salads for €10–12. Open daily.

Sur le Pouce 2 rue des Convalescents, 1er. Very cheap, studenty Tunisian restaurant in the quartier Belsunce. Couscous €5.

Bars

O'Malley's Irish Pub 9 Quai du Rive Neuve, 1er. Wildly popular Vieux Port boozer with the usual 'Oirish' trimmings plus, of course, Beamish and Guinness, and occasional live music.

Bar de la Marine 15 quai Rive-Neuve, 1er. A favourite bar for Vieux Port lounging, and inspiration for Pagnol's celebrated Marseille trilogy. Closed Sun.

MP 10 rue Beauvau, 1er. Smart bar close to the opera, attracting a very mixed gay/hetero, male and female crowd. Open daily 6pm–3am.

Bar Le Petit Nice 26 pl Jean-Jaurès, 1er. The place to head for on Saturday morning during the market, with an interesting selection of beers.

Brasserie des Templiers 21 rue Reine-Elizabeth, 1er. Next to the Centre Bourse, with good beers, including Belgian varieties and Guinness, and quick *croques*.

Markets and food shops

The city's copious **street markets** provide a feast of fruit and veg, olives, cheeses, sausages and spit-roast chickens – everything you'd need for a picnic except for wine, which is most economically bought at supermarkets. The markets are also good for cheap clothes, particularly shoes. La Plaine and av du Prado are the biggest; the Capucins the oldest.

Marseille's Sunday flea market, **Marché aux Puces**, is a brilliant spectacle, and good for serious haggling. There's a relaxed atmosphere, plenty of cafés, and everything and anything for sale, including very cheap fruit and veg.

The markets

Quai des Belges Vieux Port, 1er; métro Vieux Port. Fish sold straight off the boats. Daily 8am–1pm.

Capucins pl des Capucins, 1er; métro Noailles. Fish, fruit and veg sold here and in the Halles Delacroix on nearby rue Halles-Delacroix, towards rue de Rome. Mon–Sat 8am–7pm.

Place Carli 1er; métro Noailles. Antiquarian books and records. Daily.

Cours Julien 6e; métro N.-D.-du-Mont-Cours Julien. Food Mon–Sat 8am–1pm; stamps Sun 8am–1pm; antiquarian books second Sat of month 8am–1pm; bric-a-brac third Sun of month 8am–7pm; organic produce Fri 8am–1pm; flowers Wed & Sat 8am–1pm.

Allées de Meilhan La Canebière, 1e; métro Réformés. Flowers Tues & Sat 8am–1pm; santons daily in Dec 10am–7pm.

Cours Pierre Puget 1er, métro Préfecture Estrangin. Fruit, veg and fish, Mon & Fri 8am–1pm; flowers Mon 8am–1pm.

La Plaine pl Jean-Jaurès, 5e; métro N.-D.-du-Mont Cours Julien. Food daily 8am–1pm; shoes on

Sat 8am–1pm; flowers Wed 8am–1pm.
Prado av du Prado, 6e; métro Castellane and Périer. Fruit, veg, fish and general food products daily 8am–1pm; flowers Fri 8am–1pm.
Marché aux Puces av du Cap-Pinède, 15e; bus #35 from the Vieux Port (stop Cap-Pinède) or buses #25, #26, #36, #70 from métro Bougainville (stop Lyon). Food Tues–Sun 8am–7pm; antiques Fri–Sun 10am–7pm; bric-a-brac Sat; flea market Sun 9am–7pm.
Joseph Thierry 1er, métro Réformés. Fruit, herbs and fish Mon–Sat 8am–1pm.

Shops

Le Carthage 8 rue d'Aubagne, 1er. Best Tunisian pâtisseries and Turkish delight.
Pâtisserie d'Aix 1 rue Nationale, 1er. More excellent Tunisian sweetmeats.
Plauchut 168 La Canebière, 1er. Excellent *pâtissier-chocolatier-glacier* and *salon de thé*, established in 1820.

Nightlife and entertainment

Marseille's **nightlife** has something for everyone, with plenty of live rock and jazz, nightclubs and discos, as well as theatre, opera and classical concerts. Theatre is particularly innovative and lively in Marseille. The Virgin Megastore at 75 rue St-Ferréol and the tourist office's ticket bureau are the best places to go for **tickets and information** on gigs, concerts, theatre, free films and cultural events. Virgin also stocks a wide selection of English books and runs a café on the top floor, open, like the rest of the store, seven days a week until midnight. Other places to head for information are the book and record shop FNAC on the top floor of the Centre Bourse; the travel agency and comic shop La Passerelle on rue des Trois-Mages; and the New Age music shop Tripsichord next door. There's also a free weekly **listings** mag *Ventilo*, with articles at the front, which you can pick up from FNAC, Virgin, tourist offices, museums and cultural centres.

Live music and nightclubs

L'Affranchi 212 bd de St Marcel, 11e ⓣ04.91.35.09.19. Venue in the eastern suburbs with a varied programme of clubs and live gigs, including rai, hip-hop and reggae.
New Cancan 20 rue Sénac, 1er ⓣ04.91.94.08.43. Marseille's best known and longest running gay disco.
Le Dôme 48 av de St Just, 4e ⓣ04.91.12.21.21. Marseille's large-capacity live venue, hosting big-name and tame middle-of-the-road acts.
Cité de la Musique 4 rue Bernard du Bois, 1er ⓣ04.91.39.28.28. Jazz cellar and auditorium.
La Maison Hantée 10 rue Vian, 6e ⓣ04.91.92.09.40. Country music, R&B and rock. Closed Mon.
Le Moulin 47 bd Perrin, 13e; métro St-Just; ⓣ04.91.06.33.94. An obscure venue in the northwest of the city, specializing in weird and wonderful European bands.
Pelle Mêle 45 cours d'Estienne d'Orves, 1er ⓣ04.91.54.85.26. Intimate, smart and lively jazz bistro and piano bar. Open from 6pm; closed Sun.
Le Pourquoi Pas 1 rue Fortia, 1er. Offers Caribbean music and punch to get drunk on, just off the Vieux Port.
Stairway to Heaven 9 rue Horace Berlin, 5e ⓣ04.91.42.68.73. Blues and rock bar with live acts at weekends.
Trolleybus 24 quai de Rive-Neuve, 7e ⓣ04.91.54.30.45. Disco in a series of vaulted rooms; mainly popular rock and techno. Closed Sun–Wed.

Film, opera, theatre and concerts

Alhambra 2 rue du Cinéma, 16e ⓣ04.91.03.84.66. Cinema showing undubbed English-language films (*v.o*).
Ballet National de Marseille 20 bd Gabès, 8e ⓣ04.91.32.72.72. The home venue of the famous dance company, founded in 1972 by Roland Petit.
Bastide de la Magalone 245 bis, bd Michelet, 9e ⓣ04.91.39.28.28. Classical music concerts in the south of the city.
Chocolat Théâtre 59 cours Julien, 6e ⓣ04.91.42.19.29. Theatre, restaurant and exhibition space with shows ranging from male striptease to avant-garde improvisations.
Cinémathèque 31 bis bd d'Athènes, 1e

☎04.91.50.64.48. Cinema showing undubbed English-language films (*v.o*).

Théâtre de la Criée 30 quai de Rive-Neuve, 7e ☎04.96.17.80.00. Home of the Théâtre National de Marseille and Marseille's best theatre.

Creuset des Arts 21 rue Pagliano, 4e ☎04.91.06.57.02. Drama, comedy, live music and dance venue.

Espace Julien 33 cours Julien, 6e ☎04.91.24.34.10. A mixed-bag arts centre, showing theatre, jazz, dance and exhibitions.

Opéra 2 rue Molière, 1er ☎04.91.55.11.10. Symphony concerts and operas in a magnificent setting, part Neoclassical, part Art Deco.

Théâtre de Lenche 4 pl de Lenche, 2e ☎04.91.91.52.22. Everything from Cervantes to Beckett is showcased at this Le Panier theatre.

Théâtre Massalia 23 rue Guibal, 3e ☎04.95.04.95.70. Lively puppet theatre with changing programme of adult (evening) and children's (matinee) shows.

Variétés 37 rue Vincent Scotto, 1e ☎04.96.11.61.61. Cinema showing the odd undubbed English-language film (*v.o*).

Listings

Airlines Air France 14 La Canebière, 1er, ☎0820.820.820; Delta 41 La Canebière, 1er, ☎04.91.90.07.90.

Airport information ☎04.42.14.14.14, ⓦwww.Marseille-aeroport.fr.

Bike rental Holiday Bikes, 129 Cours Lieutaud; ☎04.91.92.76.04, ⓦwww.holiday-bikes.com.

Bookshops Fuéri-Lamy, 21 rue Paradis, 1er (Mon–Sat), sells a few English books; and Maupetit, 140 La Canebière, 1er, is a good general French bookshop.

Bus information ☎04.91.91.92.10.

Car parks cours Estienne-d'Orves, 1er; cours Julien, 6e; allées Léon-Gambetta, 1er; pl Monthyon, 6e; Centre Bourse, 1er; Gare St-Charles, 1er; pl Félix-Baret, 6e; and pl Gal-de-Gaulle, 1er.

Car rental Avis, Gare St-Charles ☎04.91.64.71.00; Budget, 40 bd de Plombières ☎04.91.64.40.03; National Citer, 96 bd Rabatau, 8e ☎04.91.83.05.05; Europcar, 7 bd Maurice-Bourdet, 1er ☎04.91.99.40.90; Hertz, 21 bd Maurice-Bourdet, 1er ☎04.91.90.14.03. All also have head offices at the airport.

Consulates Britain, 24 av du Prado, 6e ☎04.91.15.72.10; USA, pl Varian Fry/12 bd Paul-Peytral, 6e ☎04.91.54.92.00.

Currency exchange Comptoir Marseillais de Bourse, 22 La Canebière; American Express, 35 La Canebière.

Disabled information Office Municipal pour Handicappés, 128 av du Prado, 8e ☎04.91.81.58.80.

Emergencies Ambulance ☎15; SOS Médecins ☎04.91.52.91.52; 24hr casualty departments at La Conception, 144 rue St-Pierre, 5e ☎04.91.38.36.52; and SOS Voyageurs, Gare St-Charles, 3e ☎04.91.62.12.80.

Ferries SNCM, 61 bd des Dames ☎08.91.70.18.01, ⓦwww.sncm.fr, runs ferries to Corsica, Tunisia and Algeria.

Internet *Web Café* 1 quai du Rive Neuve, 1er ☎04.91.33.53.05.

Lost property 18 rue de la Cathédrale, 2e ☎04.91.90.99.37.

Pharmacy Gare St-Charles (Mon–Fri 7am–10pm, Sat 7am–8pm).

Police Commissariat Centrale, 2 rue Antoine-Becker, 2e (24 hr; ☎04.91.39.80.00).

Post office 1 pl de l'Hôtel-des-Postes, 1er.

Taxis ☎04.91.02.20.20; Eurotaxi (mulitilingual drivers) ☎04.91.05.31.98; disabled facilities Monsieur P. Dahan ☎06.11.54.99.99.

Train information ☎08.36.35.35.35.

L'Estaque and westwards

Marseille's docks and its northern coastal sprawl finally end at **L'ESTAQUE**, an erstwhile fishing village much loved by painters in the nineteenth century, and easy to get to by train (10min on Miramas train). It was no rural paradise even in 1867, as a gouache by Cézanne of the factory chimneys of L'Estaque shows (originally given to Madame Zola and now exhibited in his studio in Aix). Yet it still has fishing boats moored alongside yachts, and the new artificial beaches to the west ensure that L'Estaque remains a popular escape from the city. The simple terrace restaurant *L'Hippocampe* on the coast road a little west of the village (☎04.91.03.83.78; closed Sun) is the place to go for a fish

dinner, or if you simply want a **snack**, the local *chichis* (hot, doughnut-like confections) from the Chichis Fruguis kiosk on the promenade are delicious.

Between L'Estaque and Carry-le-Rouet, the hills of the **Chaîne de l'Estaque** come right down to the coast, a gorgeous wilderness of white rock, pines and brilliant yellow scented broom. The shore is studded with *calanques* where the water is exceptionally clean and you can look across the roadstead of Marseille to the islands and the entrance of the Vieux Port. The train tunnels its way above the shore while the main road, the N568, then D5, takes an inland route through **La Rove** and **Ensues-la-Redonne**, with smaller roads looping down to the fishing villages and summer holiday homes of **Niolon**, **Méjean** and **La Redonne**. At Méjean simple meals of grilled fish and *petites fritures* are served overlooking the tiny port at *Le Mange Tout* (☎04.42.45.91.68; closed Dec–Feb).

The peace and intimate scale of this coast end at the small but bustling resort of **CARRY-LE-ROUET**, its harbour encircled by popular restaurants. Carry was the home of the jazz singer Nina Simone towards the end of her life, and it was here that she died in 2003. The **tourist office** in the Espace Fernandel (July & Aug Mon–Sat 9am–noon & 2–6pm; Sept–June Tues–Sat 10am–noon & 2–5pm; ☎04.42.13.20.36) has a list of hotels and private rooms, but there's no real reason to stop other than to visit the wonderful **restaurant**, *L'Escale*, on a terrace above the right-hand side of Carry's port, where the *gâteau de poissons* is divine (☎04.42.45.00.47; menus from €32; closed Sun eve & Mon, plus Oct–Feb). If you're **camping**, head further west to the tiny, relatively peaceful village of Tamaris, where there are several campsites including *Lou Cigalon*, Corniche des Tamaris (☎04.42.49.61.71; €17 per tent; closed Oct–March), and *Les Tamaris*, Calanque des Tamaris (☎04.42.80.72.11; €18 per tent; closed Oct–March).

Carry merges into its western neighbour Sausset-les-Pins, where the beaches are stony and artificial, without any break in the seaside houses and apartment buildings. For **beaches** it's best to head beyond Tamaris where there are long, sandy beaches around the pleasantly downmarket family resorts of **CARRO** and **LA COURONNE**, though you may be put off by the proximity of the petrochemical plants at the mouth of the Étang de Berre.

Around the Étang de Berre

The shores of the 22-kilometre-long and 15-kilometre-wide **Étang de Berre**, northwest of L'Estaque, are not the most obvious holiday destination. The lagoon is heavily polluted, especially around the southern edges near Marseille's airport, and the sources are only too visible: oil refineries, petrochemical plants and tankers heading in and out of the Caronte Canal linking the lagoon with the vast industrial complex and port on the Golfe de Fos.

There are, however, some unexpected pockets worth exploring: the ancient remains at **St-Blaise**, the perched villages of **Miramas-le-Vieux** and **Cornillon-Confoux**, and, despite its close proximity to Europe's largest oil refinery, the town of **Martigues**.

Martigues

MARTIGUES straddles both sides of the Caronte Canal and the island in the middle, at the southwest corner of the Étang de Berre. In the sixteenth century when the union of three separate villages, Jonquières to the south, Ferrières to the north and the island, known simply as l'Île, created Martigues, there were many more canals than the three that remain today. But Martigues has joined the long list of places with waterways to be dubbed the 'Venice' of the region, and it deserves the compliment, however fatuous the comparison.

In the centre of l'Île, in front of the sumptuous facade of the airy Église de la Madeleine, a low bridge spans the Canal St-Sébastien where fishing boats moor and houses in ochre, pink and blue look straight down onto the water. This appealing spot is known as the **Miroir aux Oiseaux** and was painted by Corot, Ziem and others at the turn of the twentieth century. Some of these artists' works, including Ziem's *Vieux Port de Marseille*, can be seen in the wonderful **Musée Ziem** on bd du Juillet in Ferrières (Wed–Sun 2.30–6.30pm; free). The collection includes works by the likes of Dérain, Dufy and Signac, while François Picabia's 1905 *Étang de Berre* shows the lagoon to be every bit as choppy as it is today. Upstairs is a well-presented local history display, as well as some more contemporary art exhibits.

Behind the idle strolling quaysides of l'Île's canal, new housing has been designed on a pre-modern, acute-angled layout. From **quai Toulmond** the white and green geometric shapes of the ridiculously expensive municipal offices across the water and the towering highway bridge above the Caronte Canal contrast with the masts and bright hulls of the pleasure boats tied up along the quay.

A nineteenth-century swing bridge alongside a more dilapidated modern metal road bridge joins l'Île to **Ferrières**, whose tiny streets of shops and bars spread back from the relaxed focal point of place Jean-Jaurès. To the south, the tanker passage of the Canal Galiffet is spanned by a drawbridge taking you into **Jonquières**, the third and most lively of Martigues' centres, with the best concentration of bars and restaurants lining the main axis of cours du 4 Septembre and esplanade des Belges.

Practicalities

Buses from Marseille stop on the quayside opposite the *Bar du Port* in Ferrières, a little west of the bridge. From the **gare SNCF** take bus #3 (direction Ferrières), to the centre. The plush modern **tourist office** (Mon–Sat 9am–6.30pm, Sun 9am–1pm; ⓣ04.42.42.31.10; ⓦwww.mairie-martigues.fr) is in Ferrières, on the Rond Point, close to the police station and the *mairie*.

The best of the **hotels** is the *St-Roch*, allée P-Signac, off av Georges-Braque, Ferrières (ⓣ04.42.42.36.36; ⓦwww.hotelsaintroch.com; ❺), while *Le Cigalon*, 37 bd du 14 Juillet, Ferrières (ⓣ04.42.80.49.16; ❷), is in a noisy spot but a lot cheaper.

A good time to visit is between late June and the end of August to see the spectacle of the *Sardinades*, when thousands of plates of grilled sardines are sold cheaply each evening along the quays near the *mediathèque* in the Quartier de L'Île (except during the folklore festival towards the end of July). Aside from these, the **food** to look out for is *poutargue*, a paste made from salted mullet, and *melets*, seasoned fish fry fermented in olive oil. Three **restaurants** to try, all on l'Île, are *Bouchon à la Mer*, 19 quai Toulmond (ⓣ04.42.49.41.41; menus from €20); the scenically situated *Le Miroir*, quai Brescon (ⓣ04.42.80.50.45; menus from €19.50); and *Chez Marraine*, 6 rue des Cordonniers (ⓣ04.42.49.37.48; menus from €20), where the fish soup is especially good.

St-Mître-les-Remparts, St-Blaise and Istres

About 6km beyond Martigues, on the road to Istres, lies the walled village of **ST-MÎTRE-LES-REMPARTS**, with two original gateways allowing entrance to its minuscule, cramped heart. From the unusual church at the culmination of the corkscrew nest of streets you can see westwards over the Étang du Pourra and Étang d'Engenier towards the Fos complex.

From the main road the D51 leads away from St-Mître village up to a hill between two more lagoons, the Étang de Citis and Étang de Lavalduc. On the hill stands the twelfth-century Chapelle St-Blaise beside a thirteenth-century wall and the **Oppidum St-Blaise** archeological site (April–Sept Wed–Sun 9.30am–12.30pm & 1.30–5.30pm; Oct–March closes at 4.30pm; free). The ancient inhabitants of this well-defended site left their mark throughout eight distinct periods, from 7 BC to the fourteenth century. If the site is closed you can still walk around it, see the extraordinary surviving Greek ramparts through the fence, and generally enjoy the woods and water, which can sometimes appear pink because of the algae encouraged by a high salt content.

Back on the main road north, 6km beyond St-Mitre, is **ISTRES**. The town, whose main business has been the construction of military jets, has a delightful, residential Vieille Ville, with fine views from the upper terrace of the fortified **Notre-Dame-de-Beauvoir church** at the top of the hill, and numerous winding medieval streets to explore. Istres' **Musée Archéologique** lies to the west of the church on place du Puits Neuf (daily 2–6pm; €2.30), and houses an impressive collection of Greek amphorae gathered from wrecks in the Golfe de Fos, many with their hand-painted destinations still visible. The museum also contains a unique bronze ship's figurehead of a boar. Abutting the bd Paul-Painlevé, part of the ring road around the old town, the **Centre d'Art Contemporain** (Mon, Wed, Thurs & Fri 9am–6pm, Tues, Sat & Sun 2–6pm; €2.29) mounts prestigious exhibitions of contemporary art.

The modern **tourist office** is at 30 allées Jean-Jaurès (Mon–Fri 9am–noon & 2–6pm; Sat 10am–noon; Ⓣ04.42.55.51.15), by the eighteenth-century Portail d'Arles archway at the northwest corner of the Vieille Ville, and there's a pleasantly situated **hotel**, *Le Castellan*, rue Léon Blum (Ⓣ04.42.55.13.09, Ⓕ04.42.56.91.36; ❸), north of the Vieille Ville by the park overlooking the Étang de l'Olivier. There's also a three-star **campsite** *Camping Vitou* on rte de St-Charmas (Ⓣ04.42.56.51.57) for those with tents. Near the Centre d'Art Contemporain, place Hôtel-de-Ville has several pleasant **cafés**, while the best **restaurant**, *Le Saint-Martin*, 2 chemin Source Saint Martin (Ⓣ04.42.56.07.12; menus around €27; closed Tues eve & Wed), is over to the east by the *Des Heures Claires* pleasure port on the Étang de Berre.

Miramas-le-Vieux, St-Chamas and Cornillon-Confoux

The town of Miramas, to the north of the Étang de Berre, is a bland nineteenth-century creation, which exists solely because of its rail connections to the heavy industries of the coast. You're really only likely to find yourself here if you're travelling by train between Arles or Avignon and Marseille, or using it as a stopoff for exploring the villages of **Miramas-le-Vieux**, **St-Chamas** and **Cornillon-Confoux** to the south.

In contrast, the honey-coloured, crumbly **MIRAMAS-LE-VIEUX**, perched on a hill 3km south of Miramas train station, is a typical Provençal medieval village – and refreshingly free of tourists. Narrow cobbled streets lead up past the pretty public gardens below place de la Marie to the immaculately restored **St-Vincent church** and its tiny predecessor. Beyond is place du Château and its **castle** ruins. There are pottery shops and a couple of excellent ice-cream parlours, including *Le Quillé*, whose mouthwatering choice of flavours and fine terrace view attract a small evening crowd from the towns in the area.

Just to the south, on the Étang de Berre, is **ST-CHAMAS**, where portside workers' houses are separated from the rest of the town by an aqueduct between two high rocks, one of which is colonized by a scenic grid of tightly terraced houses. Here, on the Monté des Pénitents, is a helpful little **tourist office** (Mon–Sat: mid-June to mid-Sept 9am–noon & 3–7pm; mid-Sept to mid-June 9am–noon & 1.30–5.30pm; ⓣ04.90.50.90.54). A few metres further on up the hill is the path that accesses the top of the nineteenth-century **Pont de l'Horloge aqueduct**, an astonishing creation that affords the best (if slightly vertigo-inducing) views of the town from alongside its hallmark clock. This unpretentious town has several other interesting monuments, including a grandiose Hispanic-looking, seventeenth-century church, with a severely cracked, leaning bell tower, and **La Poudrerie gunpowder factory** that Louis XIV initiated in 1690, and which was the economic mainstay of the town until shortly before its closure in 1974. A twenty-minute walk south of the centre brings you to the elegant **Pont Flavien**, a first-century BC Roman triumphal bridge spanning the River Touloubre – an unexpected sight in the wasteland to the left of the main road to Aix.

Though not on the lagoon itself, the neighbouring rock-perched village of **CORNILLON-CONFOUX**, 4km east of St-Chamas, gives even better views of the Étang de Berre, taking in the Alpilles, the Luberon and sometimes even Mont Ventoux as well.

Salon-de-Provence and around

The northern exit from the Autoroute du Soleil to **SALON-DE-PROVENCE** takes you past a memorial to **Jean Moulin**, the Resistance leader who was parachuted into the nearby Alpilles range in order to coordinate the different *maquis* groupings in Vichy France. He was caught on June 21, 1943, tortured, deported and murdered by the Nazis. The bronze sculpture, by Marcel Courbier, is of a lithe figure landing from the sky like some latterday Greek god, very beautiful though somewhat perplexing if you're not aware of the invisible parachute.

Today, one of Salon's principal activities is teaching pilots to fly Mirage jets – indeed, legendary 1930s singer Charles Trenet was just one of thousands to undertake their military service here – and at times the planes scream overhead day and night. The clientele of the town's bars and restaurants usually includes blue-uniformed cadets from the École de l'Air at the **airforce base** to the south of the town. Salon is very proud of its role in the nation's strategic forces, not least because the base has given a welcome boost to the local economy for the last fifty years.

Nostradamus and the Canal de Craponne

Salon lies at the eastern edge of Provence's most arid region, La Crau, and suffered perennial droughts until the mid-sixteenth century, when the town's most famous resident, Michel de Nostradamus, financed the building of a canal. Engineered by Adam de Craponne, the waterway ran from the River Durance through a gap in the hills at Lamanon and across La Crau to the Étang de Berre, and today the area west of Salon is criss-crossed with similar canals. A contemporary account describes the people of Salon greeting the arrival of the waters with 'applause, astonishment and joyful incredulity'.

In medieval times, Salon's economy was dependent on its tanneries, a saffron crop and flocks of sheep reputed for the quality of their mutton. However, true prosperity arrived in the shape of the small black **olives** that produced an oil, *olivo selourenco*, of great gastronomic renown. By the end of the nineteenth century the Salonais were making soap from their oil, a highly profitable commodity manufactured in the most appalling conditions in subterranean mills. Those to whom the dividends accrued built spacious *belle époque* residences outside the old town walls, the grandest of which lie between the town centre and the gare SNCF to the west.

The famous predictions of **Nostradamus** were composed in Salon, though the museum dedicated to him is less appealing than the mementoes of **Napoleon** in Salon's castle, the Château de l'Empéri. A good time to visit the town is mid-July when, on odd-numbered years, the **jazz festival** takes place, or in August for the annual **chamber music festival** in the château.

Arrival, information and accommodation

From the **gare SNCF** on av Émile-Zola, the long straight bd de la République leads you on to cours Pelletan, at the edge of the Vieille Ville. Local buses depart from the north end of the cours, while the **gare routière** is on place Jules Morgan, at its southern end. The **tourist office** (mid-June to mid-Sept Mon–Sat 9am–12.30pm & 2.30–7pm, Sun 10am–2pm; mid-Sept to mid-June Mon–Sat 9am–noon & 2–6pm; ⓣ04.90.56.27.60, ⓦwww.salon-de-provence.org) is on the other side of the ring road around the Vieille Ville, at 56 cours Gimon.

Finding **accommodation** should not be too difficult, whatever time of year you visit. The *Regina*, 245 av Kennedy (ⓣ04.90.56.28.92, ⓕ04.90.56.77.43; ❶), is the best of the budget options; the *Grand Hôtel de la Poste*, 1 av Kennedy (ⓣ04.90.56.01.94, ⓕ04.90.56.20.77; ❸), and the *Hôtel d'Angleterre*, cours Carnot (ⓣ04.90.56.01.10, ⓕ04.90.56.71.75; ❸), are comfortable and central; and the *Vendôme*, 34 rue Maréchal-Joffre (ⓣ04.90.56.01.96, ⓦwww.hotelvendome.com; ❸), has a pleasant courtyard setting. If you prefer to be in the country, the *Domaine de Roquerousse* (ⓣ04.90.59.50.11, ⓦwww.domaine-deroquerousse.com; ❹), in the opposite direction to Salon from the northern *autoroute* exit, has sixteen rooms and ten self-contained units set in an extensive park. Otherwise, there's the seriously expensive *Hostellerie de L'Abbaye de Sainte-Croix*, 3km from Salon on the D16, route du Val-de-Cuech (ⓣ04.90.56.24.55, ⓦwww.relaischateaux.com/saintecroix; ❾), an ancient abbey in beautiful surroundings.

The canal-bank three-star **campsite**, *Camping Nostradamus* (ⓣ04.90.56.08.36, ⓦperso.wanadoo.fr/camping.nostradamus; closed Nov–Feb), on the D17 towards Eyguières and the Arles bus route (rte d'Eyguières), also has some **mobile homes**.

The Town

In the mid-1960s the town council initiated a programme of demolition and rebuilding in the **Vieille Ville**, which was completed in the late 1980s. Despite the swathes of redevelopment, however, Salon's commercial life has firmly established itself in the boulevards ringing the Vielle Ville, and the old town today has an artificial and rather forlorn feel to it.

Given the lack of life in this part of town, you might as well concentrate on the **Château de l'Empéri**, the centrepiece of the Vieille Ville. This massive structure is a proper medieval fortress, built to suit the worldliness of its former proprietors, the archbishops of Arles. It now houses the **National Military Art and History Museum** (July & August daily 10am–6pm; Sept–June Mon & Wed–Sun 10am–noon & 2–6pm; €3.05), covering the period from Louis XIV to World War I; the sections devoted to the Revolution and Napoleon are particularly fascinating.

Flights of gleaming steps run down the castle rock to place des Centuries, a wide-open space with little obvious purpose. It's overlooked by the Centre Commerciale St-Michel which houses the **Musée Grévin de la Provence** (July & Aug Mon–Fri 10am–6pm, Sat & Sun noon–6pm; Sept–June Mon–Fri 9am–noon & 2–6pm; €3.05, or €5.35 including the Maison de Nostradamus), a series of waxwork scenes illustrating episodes from the legends and history of Provence, with taped commentaries available in several different languages. Opposite the Centre Commerciale, the thirteenth-century **Église St-Michel**, with two belfries, adds a touch of old-world charm to this rather dull windswept area, as does **rue Moulin-d'Isnard**, leading off the place de L'ancienne Halle, to the north of the square.

Just east of the place de L'ancienne Halle stands the **Maison de Nostradamus** (same hours as Musée Grévin; €3.05), on the street now named after the soothsayer. Nostradamus arrived in Salon in 1547, already famous for his aromatic plague cure, administered in Aix and Lyon, and married a rich widow. After some fairly long Italian travels, he returned to Salon and settled down to study the stars, the weather, cosmetics and the future of the world. Translations in numerous languages of his *Centuries*, the famous predictions, are displayed in the house along with pictures of events supposedly confirming them. There are waxwork tableaux and visuals meant to fill you with wonder, but nothing particularly earth-shattering – the most interesting exhibit is the 1979 sculpture by François Bouché in the courtyard. Nostradamus died in Salon in 1566 and his tomb is in the Gothic Collégiale St-Laurent, at the top of rue du Maréchal-Joffre, north of the Vieille Ville.

To reach Collégiale St-Laurent from the museum, you'll pass through **Porte de l'Horloge**, the principal gateway to the Vieille Ville. This is a serious bit of seventeenth-century construction, with its Grecian columns, coats of arms, gargoyles and wrought-iron campanile. Through the arch is place Crousillat, which centres on a vast mushroom of moss concealing a three-statued fountain; a wonderful spot for a café break.

To the west of the Vielle Ville and located within a working savonnerie, the **Musée du Savon de Marseille**, 148 av Paul-Bourret (Mon–Thurs 9.30–11.30am & 2–5pm, Fri 9.30–11.30am & 2–4pm; €3.85), tells the story of soap-making in Provence from the Middle Ages onwards. Tours of the factory take place on Monday and Thursday at 10.30am and there is an on-site shop.

Eating and drinking

The best of Salon's **restaurants** is *La Salle a Manger*, 6 rue Maréchal-Joffre (☎04.90.56.28.01; closed Sun eve & Mon), with wonderful Italianate decor and lovely Provençal food at very reasonable prices (weekday lunch menu at €15, otherwise €23; closed Sun & Mon) – it's very popular so book ahead. The *Hostellerie de L'Abbaye de Ste-Croix* (see p.191) and *Le Mas du Soleil*, 38 chemin de St-Côme (☎04.90.56.06.53), are both top-notch gourmet restaurants, the latter being slightly more affordable with two menus under €40. A more economical alternative is *La Brocherie des Cordeliers*, 20 rue d'Hozier (☎04.90.56.53.42; closed Sun eve & Mon), in a former thirteenth-century chapel, which has menus at around €20 and €30, and for cheap, filling couscous there's the *Restaurant Bleu*, 32 rue Palamard (☎04.90.56.51.93, menu at €11).

The place for **café lounging** is around the fountain on place Crousillat, where you'll find *Bar de la Fontaine, Nostradamus* and the *Café des Arts*. On rue A-Moutin, opposite the hôtel de ville, there's a piano bar, *Le Grenier d'Abondance*.

Salon's famous olive oil and other produce can be bought at the busy Wednesday **market** on place Morgan or the Sunday market on place de-Gaulle.

Around Salon

Ten kilometres north of Salon, the main road and highway pass through a narrow gap in the hills by **LAMANON**, a village which was never much more than a stopover on the transhumance routes (used for the moving of flocks, and still followed by the Crau shepherds every June), though it does have a château. Above the village, hidden amongst rocks and trees, is a strange troglodyte village, the **GROTTES DE CALES**, which was inhabited from Neolithic times until the nineteenth century. Stairs lead down into grottoes, part natural, part constructed, with hooks and gutters carved into the rock; at the centre is a sacrificial temple. Access is free: follow the road going up to the right of the church which turns into a path, from which the Grottes are signed to the right.

EYGUIÈRES, just west of Lamanon, is a town of five thousand inhabitants with a fairly uninspiring eighteenth-century church, several old fountains and wash houses, a ruined medieval castle, the remains of a Roman aqueduct, an eighteenth-century oil press and a Gallo-Grecian necropolis on the hill above. The countryside here is typical of the dry Crau region, but less predictably you may also see llamas grazing along with goats and horses. Llamas are excellent at keeping trim forest firebreaks – so, too, are goats, but goats are forbidden from running loose in the forests, thanks to an unrevoked Napoleonic law.

Bears, elephants, big cats, hippos and a host of other non-native mammals and birds are kept for more conventional purposes at the **Château de la Barben** (Château: guided tours daily 10am–noon & 2–6pm; €7; Zoo: daily 10am–6pm; €10), 12km east of Salon, just beyond Pélissanne. This is a place to take young children, with plenty of entertainment such as miniature train rides, as well as the standard zoo delights. The château was lived in for a while by Napoleon's sister, Pauline Borghese, and her apartments are still decorated in imperial style, while the rest retains a seventeenth-century luxury.

Aix-en-Provence and around

AIX-EN-PROVENCE lies just 25km north of Marseille, but historically, culturally and socially it is moons apart from its neighbour. Aix is complacently conservative, and a stunningly beautiful town, its riches based on land owning and the liberal professions. Marseille's successful financiers, company directors and gangsters live in Aix; people dress immaculately; hundreds of foreign students, particularly Americans, come to study here; and there's a certain snobbishness, almost of Parisian proportions, in the air.

Aix began life as Aquae Sextiae, a Roman settlement based around its **hot springs** of sodium-free water – still used for cures in a thermal establishment on the site of the Roman baths in the northwest corner of the Vieille Ville. From the twelfth century until the Revolution Aix was the capital of Provence. In its days as an independent fiefdom, its most mythically beloved ruler, King René of Anjou (1409–80), held a brilliant court renowned for its popular festivities and patronage of the arts. René introduced the muscat grape to the region, and today he stands in stone in picture-book medieval fashion, a bunch of grapes in his left hand, looking down the majestic seventeenth-century replacement to the old southern fortifications, the cours Mirabeau.

The humanities and arts faculties of the university Aix shares with Marseille are based here, where the original university was founded in 1409. In the nineteenth century Aix was home to two of France's greatest contributors to painting and literature, Paul Cézanne and his close friend Émile Zola.

Arrival, information and accommodation

Aix's **gare TGV** lies 8km from the town, connected every thirty minutes by minibus (€3.60) to the **gare routière** (☎04.42.91.26.80), which is on ave de l'Europe, southwest of the multi-fountained place Général-de-Gaulle and the city's main drag, **Cours Mirabeau.** Local trains, including those from Marseille, arrive about 500 metres from here at the old **gare SNCF** on rue Gustavo-Desplace. The **tourist office** (Mon–Sat 8.30am–7pm, Sun

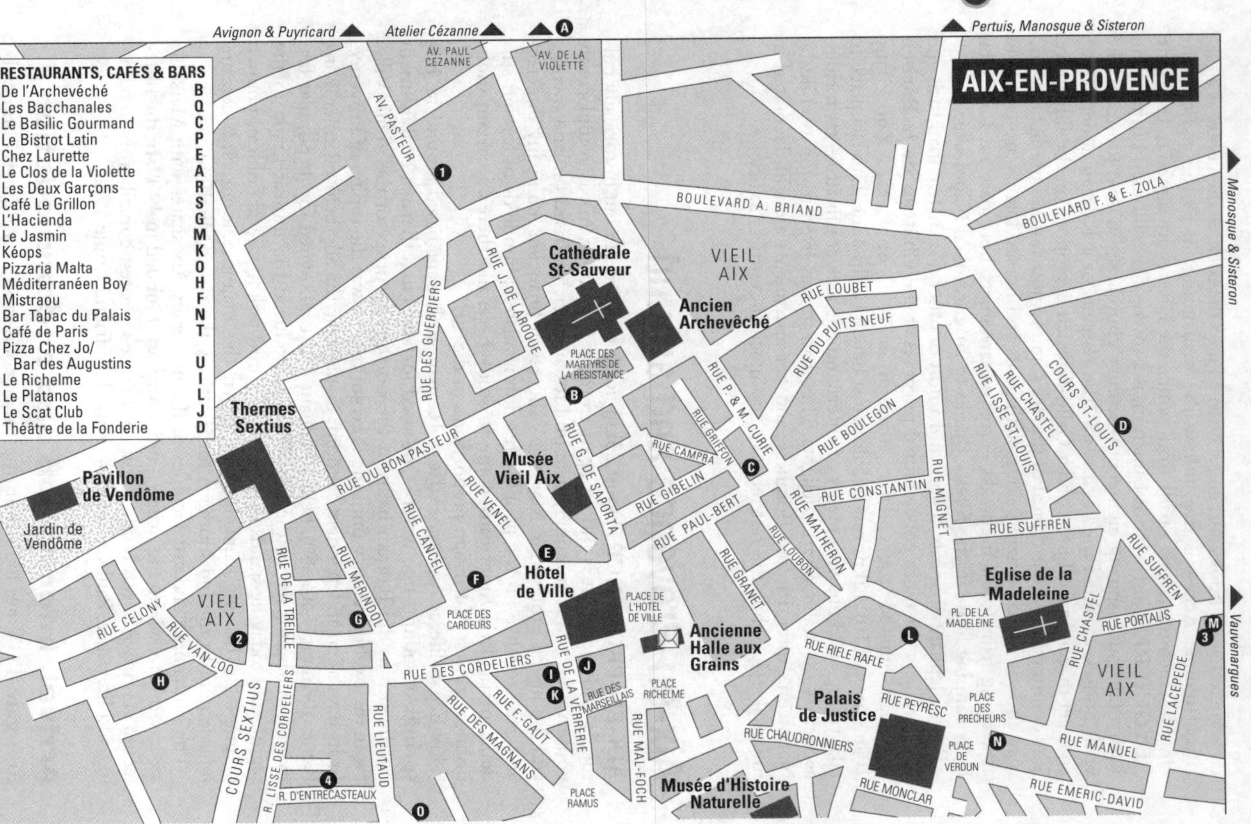
AIX-EN-PROVENCE
RESTAURANTS, CAFÉS & BARS
De l'Archevéché B
Les Bacchanales Q
Le Basilic Gourmand C
Le Bistrot Latin P
Chez Laurette E
Le Clos de la Violette A
Les Deux Garçons R
Café Le Grillon S
L'Hacienda G
Le Jasmin M
Kéops K
Pizzaria Malta O
Méditerranéen Boy H
Mistraou F
Bar Tabac du Palais N
Café de Paris T
Pizza Chez Jo/ Bar des Augustins U
Le Richelme I
Le Platanos L
Le Scat Club J
Théâtre de la Fonderie D
Avignon & Puyricard
Atelier Cézanne
Pertuis, Manosque & Sisteron
Manosque & Sisteron
Vauvenargues
Avignon
AV. PAUL CEZANNE
AV. DE LA VIOLETTE
AV. PASTEUR
BOULEVARD A. BRIAND
BOULEVARD F. & E. ZOLA
VIEIL AIX
Cathédrale St-Sauveur
Ancien Archevêché
RUE LOUBET
RUE DU PUITS NEUF
RUE J. DE LAROQUE
PLACE DES MARTYRS DE LA RESISTANCE
RUE DES GUERRIERS
Thermes Sextius
RUE P. & M. CURIE
RUE GRIFFON
RUE CAMPRA
RUE BOULEGON
RUE LISSE ST-LOUIS
RUE CHASTEL
COURS ST-LOUIS
RUE DU BON PASTEUR
Musée Vieil Aix
RUE G. DE SAPORTA
RUE GIBELIN
RUE CONSTANTIN
RUE MIGNET
Pavillon de Vendôme
Jardin de Vendôme
RUE VENEL
RUE CANCEL
RUE PAUL-BERT
RUE MATHERON
RUE LOUBON
RUE SUFFREN
Hôtel de Ville
RUE GRANET
Eglise de la Madeleine
PL. DE LA MADELEINE
RUE CHASTEL
RUE PORTALIS
RUE CELONY
RUE MERINDOL
PLACE DES CARDEURS
PLACE DE L'HOTEL DE VILLE
Ancienne Halle aux Grains
RUE RIFLE RAFLE
RUE VAN LOO
RUE DE LA TREILLE
RUE DES CORDELIERS
RUE DE LA VERRERIE
RUE DES MARSEILLAIS
PLACE RICHELME
Palais de Justice
RUE PEYRESC
PLACE DES PRECHEURS
RUE LACEPEDE
RUE F.-GAUT
RUE CHAUDRONNIERS
RUE MANUEL
COURS SEXTIUS
R. LISSE DES CORDELIERS
RUE LIEUTAUD
RUE DES MAGNANS
RUE MAL-FOCH
PLACE DE VERDUN
R. D'ENTRECASTEAUX
PLACE RAMUS
Musée d'Histoire Naturelle
RUE MONCLAR
RUE EMERIC-DAVID

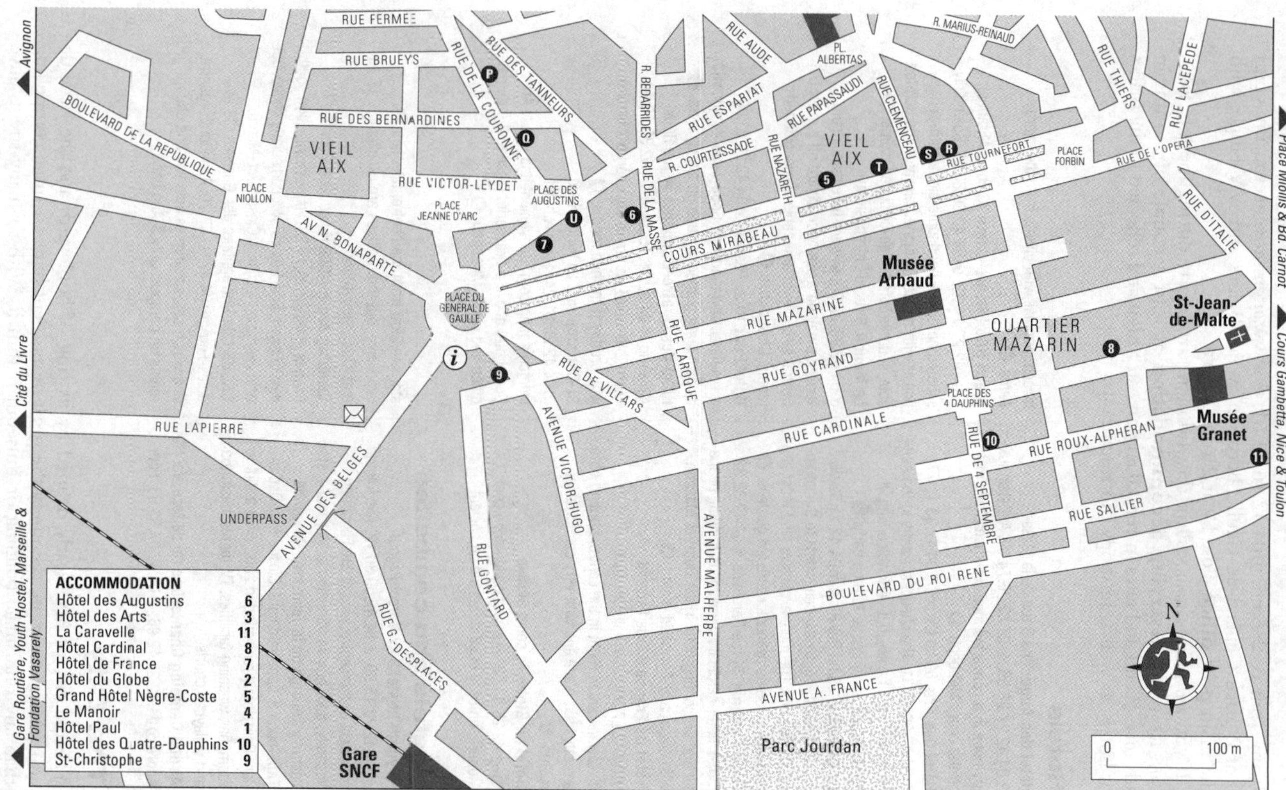
Avignon
Cité du Livre
Gare Routière, Youth Hostel, Marseille & Fondation Vasarely
Place Miollis & Bd. Carnot
Cours Gambetta, Nice & Toulon
RUE FERMEE
RUE BRUEYS
RUE DES BERNARDINES
BOULEVARD DE LA REPUBLIQUE
VIEIL AIX
RUE DE LA COURONNE
RUE DES TANNEURS
RUE VICTOR-LEYDET
PLACE NIOLLON
PLACE JEANNE D'ARC
PLACE DES AUGUSTINS
AV N. BONAPARTE
PLACE DU GENERAL DE GAULLE
RUE LAPIERRE
AVENUE DES BELGES
UNDERPASS
RUE G. DESPLACES
Gare SNCF
RUE GONTARD
AVENUE VICTOR-HUGO
RUE DE VILLARS
R. BEDARRIDES
RUE DE LA MASSE
RUE AUDE
RUE ESPARIAT
R. COURTESSADE
RUE NAZARETH
COURS MIRABEAU
RUE LAROQUE
AVENUE MALHERBE
PL. ALBERTAS
RUE PAPASSAUDI
VIEIL AIX
RUE CLEMENCEAU
R. MARIUS-REINAUD
RUE TOURNEFORT
PLACE FORBIN
RUE THIERS
RUE LACEPEDE
RUE DE L'OPERA
RUE D'ITALIE
Musée Arbaud
RUE MAZARINE
RUE GOYRAND
RUE CARDINALE
QUARTIER MAZARIN
PLACE DES 4 DAUPHINS
RUE DE 4 SEPTEMBRE
RUE ROUX-ALPHERAN
RUE SALLIER
St-Jean-de-Malte
Musée Granet
BOULEVARD DU ROI RENE
AVENUE A. FRANCE
Parc Jourdan
N
0 100 m
ACCOMMODATION
Hôtel des Augustins 6
Hôtel des Arts 3
La Caravelle 11
Hôtel Cardinal 8
Hôtel de France 7
Hôtel du Globe 2
Grand Hôtel Nègre-Coste 5
Le Manoir 4
Hôtel Paul 1
Hôtel des Quatre-Dauphins 10
St-Christophe 9

10am–1pm & 2–6pm; ⓣ04.42.16.11.61; ⓦwww.aixenprovencetourism.com) is at 2 place Général-de-Gaulle, between av des Belges and av V-Hugo, with the main **post office** close by at 2 rue Lapierre.

If you are planning to visit in the summer, particularly during the July festivals, it's worth **reserving accommodation** at least a couple of months in advance. Rents and rates in central Aix are very high and reflected in the prices of hotels, as well as in shops and restaurants.

Hotels

Hôtel des Augustins 3 rue de la Masse ⓣ04.42.27.28.59, ⓕ04.42.26.74.87. A stylish luxury hotel in a converted medieval monastery, just off the cours Mirabeau. ❻

Hôtel des Arts 69 bd Carnot ⓣ04.42.33.11.77, ⓕ04.42.26.77.31. The cheapest rooms in the centre of Aix – a bit noisy, but very welcoming. It doesn't take bookings, so turn up early. ❷

La Caravelle 29 bd Roi-René ⓣ04.42.21.53.05, ⓕ04.42.96.55.46. By the boulevards to the south-east of the city. The more expensive (and most likely quietest) rooms overlook courtyard gardens. ❹

Hôtel Cardinal 24 rue Cardinale ⓣ04.42.38.32.30, ⓔhotel-cardinal@wanadoo.fr. A clean, peaceful and welcoming hotel in the Quartier Mazarin, with classically-furnished rooms. ❹

Hôtel de France 63 rue Espariat ⓣ04.42.27.90.15, ⓔhoteldefrance-aix@wanadoo.fr. Right in the centre, fronting onto a pretty little *place* and with very comfortable rooms. ❸

Hôtel du Globe 74 cours Sextius ⓣ04.42.26.03.58, ⓦwww.hotelduglobe.com. Modern, unfussy comfort behind an ancient facade, popular with clients from the nearby *baths.* ❸

Grand Hôtel Nègre-Coste 33 cours Mirabeau ⓣ04.42.27.74.22, ⓕ04.42.26.80.93. Splendidly-situated hotel in a handsome eighteenth-century house with an old-fashioned elevator and comfortable, soundproofed, high-ceilinged rooms. ❹

Le Manoir 8 rue d'Entrecasteaux ⓣ04.42.26.27.20, ⓦwww.hotelmanoir.com. Tucked away on a pretty courtyard off a quiet but central street, with agreeable air-conditioned rooms. Closed Jan. ❸

Hôtel Paul 10 av Pasteur ⓣ04.42.23.23.89, ⓔhotel.paul@wanadoo.fr. Good value for Aix, with its own leafy garden, though on a busy road. ❷

Hôtel des Quatre-Dauphins 54 rue Roux-Alphéran ⓣ04.42.38.16.39, ⓕ04.42.38.60.19. Warm, old-world charm in the quartier Mazarin, with prettily furnished rooms. ❹

St-Christophe 2 av Victor-Hugo ⓣ04.42.26.01.24, ⓦwww.hotel-saintcristophe.com. Convenient and classy Art Deco hotel above a brasserie. Close to the tourist office and cours Mirabeau. ❺

Hostels and campsites

HI youth hostel 3 av Marcel-Pagnol ⓣ04.42.20.15.99, ⓕ04.42.59.36.12. Two kilometres west of the centre, next to the Fondation Vasarely; take bus #4 (direction la Mayanalle, stop Vasarely Auberge de la Jeunesse). Reception 7am–noon & 5pm–midnight. Closed mid-Dec to Jan. Completely renovated in 2002, with a dining room, bar, washing facilities, TV, tennis, basketball and volleyball courts.

Airotel Camping Chanteclerc rte de Nice, Val St-André ⓣ04.42.26.12.98, ⓕ04.42.27.33.53. Four-star site 3km from the centre; take bus #3. Expensive, but the facilities are excellent. €17 per tent. Open year-round.

Camping Arc-en-Ciel rte de Nice, Pont des Trois Sautets ⓣ04.42.26.14.28. Four-star site 3km south-east of town; take bus #3. Not particularly cheap, but with very good facilities. Closed Oct–March.

CROUS Cité Universitaire des Gazelles, 38 av Jules-Ferry ⓣ04.42.93.47.70. A student organization which can sometimes help you find cheap rooms on campus. July & Aug only.

The City

The old city of Aix, clearly defined by its ring of boulevards and the majestic cours Mirabeau, is in its entirety the great monument here, far more compelling than any one single building or museum within it. With so many streets alive with people, so many tempting restaurants, cafés and shops, plus the best markets in Provence, it's easy to pass several days wandering around without needing any itinerary or destination. Beyond **Vieil Aix**, there are a few museums in the

Aix for less

Aix's excellent-value **Visa** card (€2) gives discounted admission to the principal museums, plus half-price guided tours and reduced-rate travel on Aix's buses.

Mazarin quartier south of **cours Mirabeau**, and, further out, the **Vaserely foundation** and **Cézanne's studio**. The Cité du Livre cultural complex is part of a major regeneration across the entire west side of Vieil Aix.

Cours Mirabeau

As a preliminary introduction to life in Aix, take a stroll beneath the gigantic plane trees of **cours Mirabeau**, stopping off along the way at one of the many cafés along its north side; the south side is lined with banks and offices, all lodging in seventeenth- to eighteenth-century mansions. These have a uniform hue of weathered stone, with ornate wrought-iron balconies and Baroque decorations, at their heaviest in the tired old musclemen holding up the porch of the Hôtel d'Espargnet at no. 38.

Opposite the hotel is Aix's most famous café, *Les Deux Garçons*, with a reputation dating back to World War II of serving intellectuals, artists and their entourage. The interior is all mirrors with darkening gilt panels and reading lights that might have come off the old *Orient Express*. The other cafés have a shifting hierarchy of kudos. All are pricey, though very tempting with cocktails, ice creams, and wicker armchairs from which to watch the milling street.

Vieil Aix

To explore the heart of Aix, wander north from cours Mirabeau and then anywhere within the ring of cours and boulevards. The layout of **Vieil Aix** is not designed to assist your sense of direction but it hardly matters when there's a fountained square to rest at every fifty metres and a continuous architectural backdrop of treats from the sixteenth and seventeenth centuries.

Starting from the eastern end of cours Mirabeau, heading north into place de Verdun, brings you to the **Palais de Justice**, a Neoclassical construction on the site of the old counts of Provence's palace. Count Mirabeau, the aristocrat turned champion of the Third Estate, who accused the États de Provence, meeting in Aix for the last time in 1789, of having no right to represent the people, is honoured here by a statue and allegorical monument. Just to the north, on place des Prêcheurs, is the **Église de la Madeleine** (closed Sun afternoon). The church's crumbling interior is decorated with paintings by Jean-Baptiste Van Loo, born in Aix in 1684, and by Rubens, as well as a three-panel medieval Annunciation in which Gabriel's wings are owl feathers and a monkey sits with its head just below the deity's ray of light.

Further west, in place de l'Hôtel-de-Ville at the heart ofVieil Aix, a delicate though fairly massive foot hangs over the architrave of the old corn exchange, now the **post office**. It belongs to the goddess Cybele dallying with the masculine River Rhône. On the west side of the place, the **Hôtel de Ville** itself displays perfect classical proportions and embroidery in wrought iron above the door. Alongside stands a **clock tower** which tells the season as well as the hour of day.

Rue Gaston-de-Saporta takes you up from place de l'Hôtel-de-Ville to the **Cathédrale St-Sauveur** (daily: 7.30am–noon & 2–6pm), a conglomerate of fifth- to sixteenth-century buildings, full of medieval art treasures. Its most notable painting, *The Burning Bush,* commissioned by King René in 1475, is currently undergoing restoration and consequently not on show, though the beautiful Romanesque **cloisters** have recently emerged from restoration work and their carved pillars are perhaps the best sculptures in the cathedral. The four corner pillars depict the four beasts of the Revelation: man-Matthew-Adam-incarnation; lion-Mark-Resurrection; eagle-John-Ascension; and calf-Luke-expectation. Also remarkable are the cathedral's west doors, carved by Toulon carpenter Jean Guiramand in the early sixteenth century to depict four Old Testament prophets and twelve sybils, the wise women of antiquity who supposedly prophesied Christ's birth, death and resurrection.

Close by, across place des Martyrs-de-la-Résistance at the side of the cathedral, is the former bishop's palace, the **Ancien Archevêché**, the setting, each July, for part of Aix's grandiose music festival. It also houses the **Musée des Tapisseries** (Mon & Wed–Sun 10–11.45am & 2–5.45pm; €2), a collection of wonderful tapestries. Highlights include the musicians, dancers and animals in a 1689 series of *Grotesques*; nine scenes from the life of Don Quixote, woven in the 1730s, including one with a club-footed cat being divested of its armour by various *demoiselles*; and four *Jeux Russiens* (Russian Games) from a few decades later with superb miscellaneous detail to them. There's also a contemporary section which hosts temporary exhibitions, and a section given over to the costumes, stage designs and history of the music festival.

The **Musée du Vieil Aix**, at 17 rue Gaston-de-Saporta (Tues–Sun 10am–noon & 2–5pm; €4), is worth a glance while you're in this part of town. It has a set of marionettes that were a vital part of the old Fête-Dieu religious procession, and a huge collection of *santons*. Among the other odds and ends are paintings on velvet and a portrait of an Englishman receiving honorary citizenship for charitable works.

South of place de l'Hôtel-de-Ville is the elegant, cobbled eighteenth-century **place d'Albertas**, where, on summer evenings, concerts are held. The square is just off rue Espariat, which runs west to place du General-de-Gaulle and has a distinctly Parisian style. Many of Aix's classiest couturier shops cluster in this area: Escada and Yves Saint Laurent are on rue Marius-Reinaud, and Yohiji Yamamoto on rue Fabrot.

At 6 rue Espariat, a seventeenth-century mansion houses the **Musée de l'Histoire Naturelle** (daily 10am–noon & 1–5pm; €2). The cherubs and garlands decorating the ceilings are slightly at odds with the stuffed birds and beetles, ammonites and dinosaur eggs below; this is a rainy day – or sunstroke – refuge.

Quartier Mazarin

Taking rue Clemenceau south over cours Mirabeau brings you into the heart of the **Quartier Mazarin**, built in five years in the mid-seventeenth century by the archbishop brother of the cardinal who ran France when Louis XIV was a baby. It's a very dignified district, and very quiet.

Before you reach the beautiful place des Quatre Dauphins with its four-dolphin fountain, you'll pass **Musée Paul Arbaud**, at 2 rue du 4-Septembre, a dark, musty old house, to which you are reluctantly granted admission after ringing the bell (Mon–Sat 2–5pm; €2.50). The museum's main collection is of Marseillais and Moustiers ceramics, but there are more interesting items tucked away in the claustrophobic rooms of leather-bound books, silk wallpaper and painted and panelled ceilings. The best is a portrait by Pierre Puget of his mother. There are also portraits of Mirabeau and family and royalist trinkets such as nobles' rings that were offered as bail for Louis XVI while he was imprisoned in Paris.

A couple of blocks east of the dolphin fountain, on place St-Jean-de-Malte in the former priory of the Knights of Malta, is the most substantial of Aix's museums, the **Musée Granet** (Mon & Wed–Sun 10am–noon & 2–6pm; €2). Covering art and archeology, it exhibits the ever-growing finds from the Oppidum d'Entremont (see p.203), a Celto-Légurian township 3km north of Aix, which flourished for about a hundred years, along with the remains of the Romans who routed them in 124 BC. The museum's paintings are a mixed bag: Italian, Dutch, French, mostly seventeenth- to nineteenth-century, not very well hung or lit. François Granet (1775-1849), whose collection initiated the museum, was an Aixois painter; his portrait by Ingres hangs here but his own works are better represented in the Musée Paul Arbaud. The portraits of Diane de Poiters by Jean Capassin and Marie Mancini by Nicolas Mignard are an interesting contrast and there is also a self-portrait by Rembrandt. One wall is dedicated to the most famous Aixois painter, **Paul Cézanne**, who studied on the ground floor of the building, which at that date was the art school. Two of his student drawings are here as well as a handful of canvases, including *Bathsheba*, *The Bathers* and *Portrait of a Woman*.

The Atelier Paul Cézanne, Vasarely Foundation and the Cité du Livre

Cézanne used many studios in and around Aix, but at the turn of the twentieth century, four years before his death, he had a house built for the purpose at what is now 9 av Paul-Cézanne, overlooking Aix from the north. It was here that he painted the *Grandes Baigneuses*, the *Jardinier Vallier* and some of his greatest still-lifes. The **Atelier Paul Cézanne** (daily: April to mid-June 10am–noon & 2.30–6pm; mid-June to Sept 10am–6.30pm; Oct–March 10am–noon & 2–5pm; €5.50) has been left exactly as it was at the time of his death in 1906: coat, hat, wine glass and easel, the objects he liked to paint, his pipe, a few letters and drawings – everything save the man himself, who would probably have been horrified at the thought of it being public. The guides are true enthusiasts, and provided the atelier isn't too busy a visit is a real joy. To get to the house, take bus #1 (stop terminus Beisson); otherwise it's a ten-minute walk or so uphill from the north end of the Vieille Ville.

Cézanne was born in Vieil Aix at 28 rue de l'Opéra, but grew up in a house to the southwest of the city on the slopes of the hill known as Jas de Bouffon. The hill is now dominated by the **Vasarely Foundation**, 1 av Marcel-Pagnol (April–Oct Mon–Fri 10am–1pm & 2–7pm, Sat & Sun 10am–7pm; Nov–March Mon–Fri 10am–1pm & 2–6pm, Sat & Sun 10am–6pm; ☎04.42.20.01.09), a building in black and white geometric shapes created by the Hungarian-born artist in 1976. To get there take bus #4 (stop Fondation Vasarely). The seven hexagonal spaces of the ground floor are each hung with dramatic tapestries and paintings, while upstairs sliding showcases reveal hundreds of drawings, designs, collages and paintings related to all Vasarely's favourite themes; most importantly, the collective and social nature of art. The Foundation has only recently reopened after a long period of closure when its then director was imprisoned for selling off works privately and pocketing the cash.

Collective cultural life is the basis of the **Cité du Livre** in the old matchmaking factory at 8–10 rue des Allumettes (Tues, Thurs & Fri noon–6pm, Wed & Sat 10am–6pm; free), a short way south of the gare routière. It includes libraries, a cinema, theatre space, a *videothèque d'art lyrique* (where you can watch just about any French opera performance), and any number of exhibitions, as well as being home to the internationally renowned Ballet Preljocaj, one of the jewels in Aix's cultural crown. The most stunning features, however, are the two entrances at the ends of the conglomerate of buildings: giant books leaning together as if on a shelf, a wonderful example of French imaginative design flair. The whole complex testifies to a continuing determination to keep culture safe from the free play of market forces by creating beauty in public places. It would have made Vasarely very happy.

Eating and drinking

Aix is stuffed full of **restaurants** of every price and ethnic origin. Place des Cardeurs, just northwest of the Hôtel de Ville, is filled with restaurant, brasserie and café tables, while rue de la Verrerie running south from rue des Cordeliers is good for ethnic choices – Thai, Egyptian and Tunisian, in particular. Rue des Tanneurs is also good for those who don't want to pay gourmet prices, with a mix of ethnic and Provençal options. The **café-brasseries** on cours Mirabeau are also tempting, with cheaper snacks and pedlars of delicious fresh fruit juice, dotted in between.

Cafés, bars and restaurants

De l'Archevéché pl des Martyrs-de-la-Résistance ☎04.42.21.43.57. Smart place with good midday pasta, tapas, tagines and salads from €10, plus a €13 menu. Closed Sun in winter.

Les Bacchanales 10 rue Couronne ☎04.42.27.21.06. Inventive cooking, featuring dishes such as salmon with *cèpes*, and rabbit with marjoram; lunch menus at €17; otherwise €26 upwards. Closed all day Tues & Wed eves.

Le Basilic Gourmand 6 rue du Griffon ☎04.42.96.08.58. Classic Provençal food on an €11.50 lunch menu, in an appealing dining room with old advertisements and paraphernalia as decor. Occasional live music too. Closed Sun & Mon.

Le Bistrot Latin 18 rue Couronne ☎04.42.38.22.88. *Escargot* and black olive sauce, profiteroles and honey, and garlic rabbit are three of the top dishes here. Menus at €21 and €26. Closed Sun, Mon, Tues, last week of August & first week of September.

Chez Laurette 6 pl des Cardeurs ☎04.42.96.95.40. Pleasantly situated restaurant, a little more upmarket than its neighbours, with fairly traditional dishes on its €13 and €29 menus. Open daily.

Le Clos de la Violette 10 av de la Violette ☎04.42.23.30.71. Aix's most renowned restaurant with dishes that might not sound too seductive – stuffed lamb's feet and *pieds et paquets* – but are in fact gastronomic delights. More obviously alluring are the puddings: a clafoutis of greengages and pistachios with peach sauce, and a tart of melting dark chocolate. Lunch menu at €54, otherwise €117. Closed Sun, plus Mon & Wed lunchtimes.

Les Deux Garçons 53 cours Mirabeau ☎04.42.26.00.51. The erstwhile haunt of Camus is done up in faded 1900s style and still attracts a motley assortment of literati. Good brasserie food, but not cheap, with plats at around €23. Open daily.

Café Le Grillon 49 cours Mirabeau ☎04.42.27.58.81. One of the biggest and best brasseries on the cours with an €11.50 menu. Open daily.

L'Hacienda cnr rue Mérindol/pl des Cardeurs ☎04.42.27.00.35. Tapas place with €10.50 lunch menu including wine – try the delicious hacienda beef à la carte served al fresco. Closed all day Sun, plus Mon & Tues evening.

Le Jasmin 6 rue de la Fonderie ☎04.42.38.05.89. Iranian food on €15.50 and €20.50 menus. Closed Sun.

Kéops 28 rue de la Verrerie ☎04.42.96.59.05. Egyptian cuisine featuring falafel, stuffed pigeon and gorgeous milk-based desserts. Menus from €8.

Pizzeria Malta 28 pl des Tanneurs ☎04.42.26.15.43. Nice atmosphere and cheap plonk to accompany the pizzas or pasta. Menu €18.

Mistraou 38 place des Cardeurs ☎04.42.96.98.69. Provençal restaurant in an atmospheric cellar with a veggie menu at €20; other menus from €20.

Bar Tabac du Palais cnr rue Manuel/pl des Prêcheurs. Small, pleasant bar from which to view the market.

Café de Paris 41 cours Mirabeau ☎04.42.26.04.51. A classic, expensive café on the cours. Open daily.

Pizza Chez Jo/Bar des Augustins 59 rue Espariat ☎04.42.26.12.47. Cheap pizzas and traditional plats du jour from €11 upwards; usually packed, but you won't have to wait long for a table. Closed Sun.

Le Platanos 13 rue Rifle-Rafle ☎04.42.21.33.19. Very cheap and popular Greek restaurant with a €10 menu.

Nightlife and entertainment

Surprisingly, Aix does not have the variety of theatre that you can find in Marseille, though it is home to the renowned contemporary **dance** company, Ballet Preljocaj, which is based at the Cité du Livre. There are also some good **pubs** with **live music**, excellent **jazz** venues, and **classical concerts** given in the city's churches. If you fancy a trip to the **cinema**, try La Mazarin, 6 rue Laroque (☎04.42.26.36.50), an independent cinema where most foreign films are shown in their original language.

A selection of concerts and other mainstream cultural events is listed in *Le Mois à Aix*, available free from the tourist office; the best place for bookings and for more information is the FNAC book and record shop on place Forbin. The best time for Aix nightlife is during the summer **festivals** when much of the entertainment happens in the street.

Book in Bar 1 bis, rue Cabassol ☎04.42.26.60.07. English café and bookshop with regular book signings, lectures and theme nights.

Cité du Livre 8–10 rue des Allumettes ☎04.42.91.98.88. Concerts, plays, cutting-edge contemporary dance, poetry readings and films.

La Fontaine d'Argent 5 rue de La Fontaine-d'Argent ☎04.42.38.43.80. Café-theatre with a diverse programme including dance.

Hot Brass chemin de la Plaine-des-Verguetiers, rte d'Eguilles-Célony ☎04.42.21.05.57. The best jazz club in Aix, filling up around midnight and going on until 4 or 5 in the morning. Entrance €15–20 depending on the night and act.

Méditerranéen Boy 6 rue Paix ☎04.42.27.21.47. Aix's only gay bar is small but packed and very friendly.

Le Richelme 24 rue de la Verrerie ☎04.42.96.25.31. Mainstream disco. Daily from 11.30pm.

Le Scat Club 11 rue de la Verrerie ☎04.42.23.00.23. All kinds of jazz, rock, funk – the best live music venue in Vieil Aix; reasonable prices. Daily from 11pm.

Théâtre de la Fonderie 14 cours St-Louis ☎04.42.63.10.11. New plays and dance.

The festivals

For much of June and July, Vieil Aix is taken over by its music festivals and the accompanying street entertainers of the alternative scene; street theatre, rock concerts and impromptu gatherings turn the whole area into one long party. The main events are the **Aix en Musique**, a rock, jazz, experimental and classical music event in June; the **Danse à Aix**, covering everything from classical to contemporary dance in the last two weeks of July and the first week of August; and the **Festival International d'Art Lyrique**, dedicated to opera and classical concerts in the last two weeks of July.

Tickets for the festivals' mainstream events average €15–30: for the Aix en Musique festival, they are available from Espace Forbin, on place John-Rewald (☎04.42.21.69.69); for the Festival International d'Art Lyrique from the festival shop at 11 rue Gaston de Saporta (☎04.42.17.34.34); tickets for Danse à Aix are also available from the Espace Forbin, on place John-Rewald (☎04.42.96.05.01), though you can watch several public rehearsals and performances for free.

Shopping and markets

Aix's **markets** provide the greatest retail pleasures, but there are also some very good **specialist shops**. For English-language **books** there's Paradox Bookstore, 15 rue du 4-Septembre, and Book in Bar at 1 bis, rue Cabassol, while the best place for French-language books is Vents du Sud, on rue du Maréchal Foch. **Santons**, the Provençal crib figures, are made and sold at Fouque, 65 cours Gambetta.

Some of the best shops around, however, are those specializing in food. If you like your **bread** fresh and warm, the Boulangerie-Pâtisserie on rue Tournefort is open around the clock, even on Christmas day, and sells pizzas, pastries and other snacks as well as bread. Claude Poulain, at 42 rue Espariat, also sells wonderful bread and cakes, and there is a fantastic selection of **cheeses** at Paul Gérard on rue Marseillais. Should you want to try the local **Coteaux d'Aix wines**, contact the Maison des Agricultures, 22 av Henri-Pontier (☎04.42.23.01.92), who can also advise you on where to buy **olive oil**. On the last weekend in July, the Coteaux d'Aix **wines** are celebrated with a fair on cours Mirabeau.

The finest **chocolates and sweets** are sold at Puyricard, 7 rue Rifle-Rafle, though they cost around €62 a kilo. If you're really keen, you can visit the famous chocolatier's factory at Puyricard, on the D14 north of Aix. For Aix's speciality **almond biscuits**, *calissons*, head to Du Roi René, 10 rue Clémenceau.

Markets

On **Saturdays** the whole of Vieil Aix is taken up with **markets**. Fruit and veg are sold on **place Richelme**, as they are every morning: purple, white and copper onions; huge sprigs of herbs; the orange flowers from young courgettes; and, according to season, different forest mushrooms or red fruits in mouth-watering displays. Fish stalls spread down rue des Marseillais and, behind the post office, **place de l'Hôtel-de-Ville** is filled with lilies, roses and carnations. Across rue Méjanes to the east you can buy clothes – new, mass-produced, hand-made or second-hand – from stalls in rues Peyresc, Rifle-Rafle, Bouteilles, Chaudronniers and Monclar. Beyond the Palais de Justice, **place de Verdun** hosts its flea market with bric-a-brac and anything from real rabbit hats to plastic earrings, while the neighbouring **place des Prêcheurs** and **place de la Madeleine** display regional specialities. The same thing happens on a smaller scale on Tuesdays and Thursdays.

Listings

Bike rental Cycles Zammit, 27 rue Mignet ☎04.42.23.19.53; closed Sun & Mon.

Car rental ADA, 1 av Henri-Mouret ☎04.42.52.36.36; Avis, 11 bd Gambetta ☎04.42.21.64.16; Budget, 16 av des Belges ☎04.42.38.37.36; Europcar, 55 bd de la République ☎04.42.27.83.00; National Citer, 42 av Victor Hugo ☎04.42.93.07.85.

Currency exchange L'Agence, 15 cours Mirabeau ☎04.42.26.84.77; Change Or, 22 rue Thiers ☎04.42.38.23.01; La Poste, 2 rue Lapierre. There are cash machines at most banks, but since the introduction of the euro fewer ordinary commercial banks exchange foreign currency.

Emergencies SAMU ☎15; Centre Hospitalier, chemin de Tamaris (emergencies reception ☎04.42.33.90.28); SOS Médecins (☎04.42.26.24.00).

Laundry 60 rue Boulégon; 36 cours Sextius; 11 rue des Bernardines; and 4 rue de la Treille.

Pharmacy For the name and address of a late-night pharmacy, ring the police on ☎04.42.26.31.96, check the notice on any pharmacy's door, or ask at the tourist office.

Police Av de l'Europe ☎04.42.93.97.00; emergency ☎17.

Post office 2 rue Lapierre, 13100 Aix.

Taxis Allo Taxi ☎06.09.32.24.62; Taxi Radio Aixois 24hr service ☎04.42.27.71.11; and Aix Taxi ☎06.09.88.68.68.

Around Aix

If city life begins to pall, there is gorgeous countryside to be explored around Aix, particularly to the east, where you'll find **Cézanne**'s favourite local subject, the **Mont Ste-Victoire**, which he painted over fifty times, and west where he also often painted, along the **Arc River**. In addition, there are the ancient sites at **Oppidum d'Entremont** and a strange artist's château in **Vauvenargues**.

Roquefavour and Cabriès

The Arc River, which runs south of Aix, and inspired Cézanne's *Grande Baigneuse*, can be followed westwards along the D65 to the **AQUADUC DE ROQUEFAVOUR**. Alternatively, take the D64 from Jas de Bouffan, which is good cycling terrain and offers several wine *dégustation* stops, to reach Roquefavour. The valley steepens as you approach the three-tiered aqueduct, built to take Durance water to Marseille. Further downstream, by the junction of the D10 and D65, is the site of the **Oppidum de Roquepertuse** whose finds are displayed in Marseille's history museum.

CABRIÈS, 11km south of Aix off the road to Marseille, is a totally untouristy *village perché*, topped by a wonderfully spooky **château** (Mon & Wed–Sat 10am–noon & 2–5pm, Sun 2–5pm €4.60), built in the Dark Ages for the counts of Provence. In 1934, the château was bought by the artist **Edgar Mélik** who used to play the role of a fiendish count, filling the château with wolf-like dogs, playing his blood-red piano all night long, and painting demonic figures on the walls. Today, the château contains works by Mélik as well as temporary exhibitions of other artists.

Oppidum d'Entremont

Three kilometres north of Aix is the archeological site of the **Oppidum d'Entremont** (Mon & Wed–Sun 9am–noon & 2–6pm; free), once the chief settlement of one of the strongest confederations of indigenous people in Provence. Built in the second century BC, it was divided into two parts: the upper town, where the leading fighters were thought to have lived; and the lower town, for artisans and traders. The site lay on an important trade crossroads from Marseille to the Durance Valley and from Fréjus to the Rhône and was protected by curtain walls and towers, within which the streets were laid out on a grid pattern. It was the Marseille merchants who finally persuaded the Romans to dispose of this irritant to their expanding business (see Musée Granet on p.199).

The plateau on which this Celtic-Ligurian stronghold was built is as interesting for its views over Aix and across to the dramatic Mont Ste-Victoire, as for the ancient layout marked by truncated walls but denuded of all other objects. Take av Pasteur out of Aix centre, then turn right after 2.5km just before you cross the N296. A special tourist bus runs here from Aix: for times and details, call ☎04.42.26.37.28.

Vauvenargues

Leaving Aix via bd des Poilus, the D10 road to Vauvenargues passes the lake and barrage of Bimont from where you can walk south past Mont Ste-Victoire to Le Tholonet (see p.204). If you want to drive, the sixty-kilometre circuit round the mountain offers wonderful views. At peaceful **VAUVENARGUES**, a perfect, weather-beaten, red-shuttered fourteenth-century **Château**, bought by Picasso in 1958, stands just outside the village with nothing between it and the slopes of the mountain. **Picasso** lived there till his death in 1973, and is buried in the gardens, his grave adorned with his sculpture *Woman with a Vase*. The château, still owned by his stepdaughter, is strictly private, and the otherwise friendly locals are taciturn when it comes to discussing the connection. If the village appeals, you can stay at the pleasant, small **hotel**, *Le Moulin de Provence*, 33 av des Maquisards (☎04.42.66.02.22, ⓔmoulin.de.provence@wanadoo.fr; ❷), with views over Mont Ste-Victoire and Picasso's château, a terrace restaurant, and friendly owners.

Mont Ste-Victoire

If you're interested in **climbing Mont Ste-Victoire**, 8km east of Aix, the northern approach is a little easier than that of the southern face, which has a sheer 500-metre drop, though it'll still require some determination. Don't underestimate the fierce sun either: avoid attempting the walk between about 11am and 3pm, especially in the summer months when you should always wear a hat, and bring suncream and a minimum of two litres of water per person. The path leaves the D10 just before Vauvenargues, after a parking bay called Les Cabassols. The round trip to the monumental **Cross of Provence** and back takes around three to four hours, depending on fitness, and the path is steep and poorly marked towards the top. Once at the top of the ridge, at 945m – marked by a chapel and a cross that doesn't figure in any of Cézanne's pictures – serious hikers can follow the path east to the summit of the Ste-Victoire massif at **Pic des Mouches** (1011m), along some breathtakingly vertiginous cliff faces. Just beneath the Pic des Mouches on the north side is the **Gouffre du Garagaï** chasm, that was once rumoured, among other things, to be the bottomless pit into hell. The path branches to the north about 200m past the summit, and after about fifty minutes rejoins the road at the **Col des Portes** pass (a good alternative starting point for climbing the massif). Otherwise stay on the ridge and descend southwards to **Puyloubier** (about 15km from the cross).

Le Tholonet and Puyloubier

The D17 south of Ste-Victoire skirts the edge of woods leading up to the defensive face of the mountain. There are two parking places with confusing maps of paths. Heading upwards you soon get views of Ste-Victoire, from this angle looking like a wave with surf about to break. Modern aqueducts pass overhead, the responsibility of the Société du Canal de Provence which has its headquarters in the Italianate seventeenth-century château in **LE THOLONET**. The grounds are used for open-air concerts during the Aix music festival, but the château is otherwise closed to the public. On the east side of the village, an old windmill, the **Moulin de Cézanne**, has been converted into an exhibition space for art and sculpture, with a bronze relief of Cézanne on a stele outside.

At the main crossroads there's a popular **restaurant**, *Chez Thome* (ⓣ04.42.66.90.43), with outdoor tables under the trees and menus starting at €22. For those with lots of cash to blow, there's the modern, swish **hotel-restaurant** *Relais Sainte-Victoire* in Beaurecueil, roughly 4km east of Le Tholonet (ⓣ04.42.66.94.98, ⓦwww.relais-sainte-victoire.com; restaurant closed Mon, Fri lunch & Sun eve; menus from €33; ❺). Also in Beaurecueil is the two-star *Ste-Victoire* **campsite** (ⓣ04.42.66.91.31, ⓕ04.42.66.96.43; €14.75 per tent), which can be reached by bus from Aix.

East of Le Tholonet, the D17 takes you beneath the mighty face of the massif, past the **Maison de Ste-Victoire** (Mon–Fri 10am–6pm, Sat & Sun 10am–7pm), a tourist centre with information and hiking maps as well as a boutique and a restaurant, and on to **Puyloubier**, where military enthusiasts can visit the French Foreign Legion's Pensioners' Château. Its small **museum** (Tues–Sun 10am–noon & 2–5pm; free) is really only for devotees of the Legion with its collection of uniforms and ceramics, metalworking and bookbinding workshops. From here, the road continues through vineyards towards **Pourrières**, before twisting up a marvellous wooded road, and looping back round to Col des Portes and Vauvenargues.

St-Maximin-de-la-Ste-Baume

Forty kilometres east of Aix, the attractive old town of **ST-MAXIMIN-DE-LA-STE-BAUME** is where, in 1279, the count of Provence claimed to have found the crypt with the relics of Mary Magdalene and Saint Maximin hidden by local people during a Saracen raid. The count started the construction of a **basilica** and **monastery** on place de l'Hôtel-de-Ville, which finally took their present shape in the fifteenth century, and have since seen lavish decoration of stone, wood, gold, silk and oil paint added, particularly during the reign of Louis XIV, one of many French kings to make the pilgrimage to the nearby Ste-Baume *grotte* (see p.208) and the crypt.

There is, therefore, plenty to look at in the **basilica** (daily 8am–6pm), with its beautifully detailed wood panelling in the choir and the paintings on the nave walls, as well as Ronzen's lovely *Retable de la Passion* (1520), with its eighteen scenes from the Passion. Also look out for the wonderfully sculptured fourth-century sarcophagi and the grotesque skull once venerated as that of Mary Magdalene, encased in a glass helmet framed by a gold neck and hair, in the **crypt**. The building itself is a substantial Gothic affair, unusual for Provence, but the thirteenth-century **cloisters** and chapterhouse of the monastery (access through the *Couvent Royal* on av de la Libération; free) are much more delicate. Look down the well to see the escape route that the Dominican friars used on several occasions in the sixteenth century when the monastery was placed under siege. Today, the monastery is the setting for classical concerts (call ⓣ04.94.59.84.59 for details).

To the south of the church a covered passageway leads into the beautiful arcaded rue Colbert, a **former Jewish ghetto**. All the medieval streets of St-Maximin with their uniform tiled roofs at anything but uniform heights have considerable charm, and there's a reasonable choice of restaurants, and shops selling the work of local artisans.

Practicalities

The **tourist office** is in the hôtel de ville next to the basilica (daily 9am–12.30pm & 2–6pm; ⓣ04.94.59.84.59; ⓦwww.stmaximin.com). If you walk west from the basilica along rue Général-de-Gaulle, the well-run, friendly **hotel**, *Plaisance*, at 20 place Malherbe (ⓣ04.94.78.16.74, ⓕ04.94.78.18.39; ❸), is a grand town house with spacious rooms, while the newly expanded *Couvent Royal* on place Jean-Salusse (ⓣ04.94.86.55.66, ⓔhotelfp-stmaximin.com; ❹) is a particularly atmospheric option, with clean, excellent-value rooms, some looking out over the cloister itself. The local three-star **campsite**, *Provençal* (ⓣ04.94.78.16.97; €13 per tent), is 3km out along the chemin de Mazaugues, the road to Marseille. **Cafés** and **brasseries** congregate on place Malherbe, the present-day hub of St-Maximin, but for a more formal meal, the restaurant in the former chapterhouse at the *Couvent Royal* has an elegant ambience, with menus from €42 (closed Sun eve, Mon & Tues). There's also a *Maison des Vins de Pays du Var* within the *Couvent* complex, if you'd like to taste the local **wines**.

Brignoles

BRIGNOLES, 18km east of St-Maximin, is a good base for a night or two's stay. For years the town made a living from mining bauxite for the aluminium works in Marseille and Gardanne. The mine closed in 1969, and today

Brignoles is ringed with modern commercial zones much like those of any other sizeable French town and, to the north of the Vieille Ville, suffers thundering lorries passing through on the N7. But there's plenty of life in its centre, with piped music in the main shopping streets adding a surreal touch, and a substantial, warren-like medieval quarter full of quiet, shaded squares and old facades with faded painted adverts and flowering window boxes.

At the southern end of the old quarter is a thirteenth-century summer residence of the counts of Provence, now adapted as the **Musée du Pays Brignolais** (April–Sept Wed–Sat 9am–noon & 2.30–6pm, Sun 9am–noon & 3–6pm; Oct–March Wed–Sat 10am–noon & 2.30–5pm, Sun 10am–noon & 3–5pm; €4). This fascinating, old-style museum dips into every aspect of local life that the town is proud of: from one of the oldest palaeo-Christian sarcophagi ever found to a reinforced concrete boat made by the inventor of concrete in 1840. There's a statue of a saint whose navel has been visibly deepened by the hopeful hands of infertile women, a reconstruction of a bauxite mine, a crèche of *santons*, a fine collection of *ex voto* paintings, some Impressionist Provençal landscapes by Frédéric Montenard and the chapel of the palace, cluttered with ancient religious statuary from around the area. Climb the tower for the best view of the town and its surroundings. Next door to the main museum is the **Office de la Culture**, an elegantly converted space hosting contemporary art shows (Mon–Fri 10am–noon & 3–6pm, Sun 3–6pm; free).

Rue des Lanciers, with fine old houses where the rich Brignolais used to live, leads up from place des Comtes-de-Provence to **St-Sauveur**, a tweflth-century church in which, on the left-hand side, you can see the remains of an older church. Behind St-Sauveur the stepped street of rue Saint-Esprit runs down to rue Cavaillon and place Carami, the café-lined central square of the modern town.

Practicalities

Buses stop at place St-Louis. The excellent modern **tourist office** (Mon–Fri 9.30am–noon & 2–5.30pm; ⓣ04.94.72.04.21, ⓦwww.la-provence-verte.org) is on the north side of the River Carami by the carrefour de l'Europe roundabout; there's also a smaller, helpful tourist office in the Vieille Ville, in the Hôtel de Clavier, rue du Palais (daily 10am–noon; ⓣ04.94.69.27.51, ⓦwww.ville-brignoles.fr). The only **hotel** in the centre of Brignoles is *Le Provence*, on place du Palais de Justice (ⓣ04.94.69.01.18; ❷), but to the west of town, there's the small *Hostellerie St Louis* (ⓣ04.94.69.09.20, ⓕ04.94.59.01.13; ❶) on the N7, and a *Formule I* in the Ratan industrial quarter signed off the N7 (ⓣ04.94.69.45.05; ❶). There's also an *Ibis* on chemin du Val, north of the town centre (ⓣ04.94.69.19.29; ❹). The two-star municipal **campsite** is 1km down the rte de Nice (ⓣ & ⓕ04.94.69.20.10; €9 per tent; closed mid-Oct to mid-March).

There's also a profusion of places to **eat** and **drink**, none of them very expensive. On place Carami, you can get meals or snacks at *Le Central* bar-brasserie (plats du jour from €7.60) and the *Café de l'Univers*. *Le Pourquoi Pas* on rue Cavaillon (ⓣ04.94.69.00.76; closed lunchtimes & Mon) serves couscous, steaks and *moules frites* from around €10, while *La Gousse d'Ail*, at 7 rue Louis-Maître (ⓣ04.94.59.28.92; lunch menu at €10, otherwise from €13), offers good-value Provençal dishes. In the heart of the Vieille Ville, *Les Romarins*, at 5 rue St-Esprit (ⓣ04.94.59.20.99; closed lunchtimes & Wed), serves pizzas from €8 and grills, while *Lou Crespeu*, across the bridge from the tourist office at 56 rue Barbaroux (ⓣ04.94.69.33.43; closed Sun & Mon lunch), makes delicious, inexpensive crêpes from €2–8 – try the buckwheat *galettes de sarrasin* with any of the fillings.

For summer evening entertainment, check out the **open-air theatre** in an olive grove 3km south of town on the rte de Camps-la-Source, which puts on classical concerts, jazz, theatre and variety acts from late June through to the end of July.

The Chaîne de la Ste-Baume

Marseille's suburbs extend relentlessly east along the highway and N8 corridor north of the Chine de St-Cyr. You reach **Aubagne** almost before you realize you've left Marseille, even though the landscape is now dominated by mountains on all sides. The range to the east is the **Chaîne de la Ste-Baume**, a sparsely populated region of rich forests and one of the least spoilt areas in the region. Once you're up on the plateau to the north, it's wonderful territory for walks and for bicycling, the woods, flowers and wildlife of the northern face showing a profusion rare in these hot latitudes. All of the area north to St-Maximin, south to **Signes**, west to **Gémenos** and east to **La Roquebrussanne** is protected. You are not allowed to camp in the woods or light fires, and a still extant royal edict forbids the picking of orchids.

For details of the numerous **footpaths**, including the GR9, GR98 and GR99, the best guide is Josianne Alor-Treboutte and Alexis Lucchesi's *Rando-Sainte Baume à pied et à VTT*, one of Edisud's series of French-only walking and cycling guides (Ⓦwww.edisud.com).

Aubagne

With a triangle of *autoroutes* around it and a series of dismal postwar developments which encroach on its historic core, **AUBAGNE** is easy to pass by. Yet the town is not without cultural interest, as the headquarters of the French Foreign Legion and a major centre for the production of *santons*, the traditional Provençal Christmas figures. Its main claim to fame, however, is as the birthplace of writer and film-maker Marcel Pagnol (1895–1974) and the now much-altered setting for his tales. The international success in the 1980s of Claude Berri's films of Pagnol's *Jean de Florette* and *Manon des Sources*, starring Gérard Depardieu and Emmanuelle Béart, has widened Pagnol's appeal. In *Jean de Florette* an outsider inherits a property on the arid slopes of the Garlaban mountain, whose rocky crest rears like a stegasaurus's back, north of Aubagne. The local peasants who have blocked its spring watch him die from the struggle of fetching water, delighted that his new scientific methods won't upset their market share.

The soil around Aubagne is very fertile, and on Tuesday, Thursday, Saturday and Sunday mornings and Friday afternoons, you can take your pick of the flowers, fruit and vegetables from the excellent **market** stalls on cours Voltaire, cours Foch and the Esplanade de Gaulle. The soil also makes excellent pottery; hence the town's renown for *santons* and ceramics, and the only School of Ceramics in Provence, founded in 1989. From mid-July to the end of August and in December, a huge daily **market of ceramics** and **santons** takes place on the central street of cours Maréchal Foch, and in December a giant crèche is set up with 120 figures. At any time of the year you can visit the potters' workshops in the Vieille Ville to the east of cours Maréchal Foch: rue F-Mistral beyond the hôtel de ville is a good street to try. Other interesting displays of the art can be found at the top of the Vieille Ville in the **Ateliers Thérèse Neveu** (Tues–Sun 10am–noon & 2–6.30pm; free), in the cour de Clastre behind St-Saveur church.

The most impressive display of *santons* is to be found at **Le Petit Monde de Marcel Pagnol** (daily 9am–12.30pm & 2.30–6pm; free) in a diorama on Esplanade de Gaulle opposite the helpful **tourist office** on av Antide Boyer (Mon–Sat 9am–noon & 2–6pm; ⓣ04.42.03.49.98, ⓦwww.aubagne.com). The finely detailed figures of Pagnol characters play out their parts on a model of the local district, complete with windmills, farms and villages. For real Pagnol fans, the tourist office supplies a map of all the places in his stories, and offers a range of guided tours in *Pays de Pagnol*.

Gémenos to Plan-d'Aups

GÉMENOS, 3km east of Aubagne, has a beautiful seventeenth-century château as its **Hôtel de Ville** and is a tempting place to stop. The area around the château has several **cafés**, **bars** and good **pâtisseries**, in particular the Pain Doré on place Georges-Clémenceau, and the **restaurant** *Le Fer à Cheval* on place de la Mairie (ⓣ04.42.32.20.97), with menus from around €12. For **accommodation**, there's a fantastic luxury hotel, the *Relais de la Magdeleine* (ⓣ04.42.32.20.16, ⓦwww.relais-magdeleine.com; meals from €56; ❼; closed Dec to mid-March), set in a lovely, vine-covered eighteenth-century manor house in a park designed by Le Nôtre; it lies just off the Rond Point de la Fontaine on the N396 rte d'Aix on the way out of town. Two minutes' walk further along the N396 is a less expensive option, the friendly *Le Provence* (ⓣ04.42.32.20.55, ⓕ04.42.32.23.48; ❶), which also has family rooms for up to four people.

From Gémenos the D2 follows the narrow valley of St-Pons, past an open-air municipal theatre cut into the rock and the **Parc Naturel de St-Pons** with beech, hornbean, ash and maple trees around the ruins of a thirteenth-century Cistercian abbey, before beginning the zigzagging ascent to the Espigoulier pass. A footpath beyond the park soon links to the GR98 which climbs directly up the Ste-Baume and then follows the ridge with breathtaking views.

At **PLAN-D'AUPS** the dramatic climb levels out to a forested plateau running parallel to the ridge of Ste-Baume, which cuts across the sky like a massively fortified wall. A comfortable small **hotel**, *Lou Pèbre d'Aï*, in the quartier Ste-Madeleine (ⓣ04.42.04.50.42, ⓕ04.42.62.55.52; ❸; menus from €18), offers one of the very few **restaurants** in this scattered settlement. There's a tiny Romanesque church and a **tourist office** next to the *mairie* (Mon, Tues, Thur & Fri 9.15–11.45am & 4–5.30pm; Wed & Sat 9.15–11.45am; ⓣ04.42.62.57.57).

Four kilometres on from Plan-d'Aups is the starting point for a **pilgrimage** based on Provençal mythology, or simply a walk up to the peaks. The myth takes over from the sea-voyage arrival in Stes-Maries-de-la-Mer of Mary Magdalene, Mary Salomé, Mary Jacobé and St-Maximin (see p.205). **Mary Magdalene**, for some unexplained reason completely at odds with the mission of spreading the gospel, gets transported by angels to a cave just below the summit of Ste-Baume. There she spends 33 years, with occasional angel-powered outings up to the summit, before being flown to St-Maximin-de-la-Ste-Baume (see p.205) to die.

The difficult **paths** up from the *Hôtellerie*, a roadside pilgrimage centre run by Dominican friars and open for prayers, information, food and accommodation (ⓣ04.42.04.54.84; ❶), are dotted with oratories, calvaries and crosses, before reaching the fabled *grotte*, where mass is held daily at 10.30am. The *grotte* is suitably sombre, while the path beyond to the **St-Pilon summit** makes you wish for some of Mary's winged pilots. For further information enquire at the *Hôtellerie* or at the **Écomusée de la Sainte Baume** opposite (daily mid-April to Oct 9am–noon & 2–6pm; Nov to mid-April 2–5pm; €3), which has exhibitions on the cultural and natural heritage of the Ste-Baume and organizes seasonal events.

East to La Roquebrussane

The road east from Plan-d'Aups crosses the range through miles of unspoiled forest. The groves of spindly, stunted oaks and beeches have exerted a mystical pull since ancient times, and it is believed they were once a sacred Druidical forest. Around the village of **MAZAUGUES**, just before you reach La Roquebrussane, you pass huge, nineteenth-century covered stone wells, built to hold ice which could then be transported on early summer nights down to Marseille or Toulon; an industry which once gave livelihoods to many an inhabitant of the Ste-Baume. There's a small **Musée de la Glace** here (phone ⓣ04.94.86.39.24 for opening hours), which traces the history of ice-making in Provence and worldwide. From Mazaugues the GR99 takes you, after an initial steep climb, on a gentle three- to four-hour walk down to Signes (it also links halfway with the GR98 from Ste-Baume); while continuing east by road will bring you to **LA ROQUEBRUSSANE**, and its **gliding-school**, Fly Azur, in quartier Le Riolet (ⓣ04.94.86.97.52). The village itself is attractive, with a large Saturday food **market** and a pleasant **hotel**, *La Loube* (ⓣ04.94.86.81.36, ⓕ04.94.86.86.79; ❹; menus from €21.50).

Méounes-les-Montrieux and Signes

Continuing south on the D5 you pass through **MÉOUNES-LES-MONTRIEUX**, with a couple of **hotels**, including the small, welcoming *Hôtel de France* on place de L'Église (ⓣ04.94.33.95.92; ❸; closed mid-Oct to Feb), and two **campsites** of which the best equipped is *Camping Blue Garden* (ⓣ04.94.48.95.34; €20 per tent), 1.5km from the village at the Château de Gavauden.

From Méounes you can follow the lovely Gapeau stream west, which has its source just before **SIGNES**. This is yet another appealing little village, a place where palm trees and white roses grow around the war memorial, where the clock tower is more than 400 years old, and where the people make their living from wine, olives, cereals and market gardening, or, in the case of two small enterprises, biscuits and nougat. At Lou Goustetto on the main road as you leave the village westwards, you can sample biscuits in a multitude of completely natural flavours that include Provençal herbs and nuts, lemon, cinnamon, cocoa and honey. They are hard and unsweetened and excellent to munch as you climb the Ste-Baume. The other delicious edible comes from Nougat Fouque, 2 rue Louis-Lumière, whose seasonal black or white nougat provides a honey overdose that manages not to stick to your teeth (Oct–Dec only).

The village has a Thursday **market** on place Marcel Pagnol, and a **tourist office** at 29 rue Pasteur (Wed–Sat 10am–noon & 2–6.30pm; ⓣ04.94.98.87.80; ⓦwww.signes.com), which has details of local gîtes d'étape. Alternatively, there's one small **hotel**, the *Auberge des Espéréguins* (ⓣ04.94.90.87.35; ❸ out of season, otherwise €320 per week only), on the rte de Méones, and a three-star **campsite**, *des Promenades*, on the edge of the village on the road from Méounes (ⓣ04.94.90.88.12; €17 per tent). Rue Bourgade has a couple of places to **eat**, *La Marmite de Mathilde* (ⓣ04.94.9083.21) and *Pizzeria Chez Flo* (ⓣ04.94.90.82.11).

Cassis

It's hard to imagine the little fishing port of **CASSIS**, on the main coast road south from Marseille, as a busy industrial harbour in the mid-nineteenth century, trading with Spain, Italy and Algeria. Its fortunes had declined by the time Dérain, Dufy and other Fauvist artists started visiting at the turn of the twentieth century. In the 1920s Virginia Woolf stayed while working on *To the Lighthouse*, and later Winston Churchill used to come to paint. These days it's scarcely an undiscovered secret, as one glance at the local property prices or the crowds in the port-side restaurants will tell you. The place bustles with activity: stalls sell artisans' handicrafts, guitarists busk round the port, and day-trippers endlessly circle the one-way system trying to find a parking space. But many people still rate Cassis the best resort this side of St-Tropez, its residents most of all.

Arrival, information and accommodation

Vehicle access to the central port area of Cassis is restricted, so **buses** drop their passengers at the *Gendarmerie* a little above the town, from where it's a short walk downhill to the port. The **gare SNCF** is 3km out of town, and connected to the *Gendarmerie* by buses which stop at the pont de la Gare, a few hundred metres from the gare itself. The modern **tourist office** is on the port at quai des Moulins (March–May & Oct Mon–Fri 9.30am–6pm, Sat 10am–noon & 2–5pm, Sun 10am–noon; June–Sept Mon–Fri 9am–7pm, Sat & Sun 9am–1pm & 3–7pm; Nov–Feb Mon–Fri 9.30am–12.30pm & 2–5pm, Sat 10am–noon & 2–5pm, Sun 10am–noon).

Hotels

Le Clos de Arômes 10 rue Abbé Paul-Mouton ⓣ04.42.01.71.84, ⓕ04.42.01.31.76. Charming, quiet hotel a short way inland from the bustle of the port, with a lovely garden restaurant that is well regarded by locals. Closed Jan & Feb. ❹

Le Golfe 3 place du Grand Carnot ⓣ04.42.01.00.21, ⓕ04.42.01.92.08. In the middle of all the action, overlooking the port, and with a lunchtime brasserie. Closed Nov–March. ❹

Le Grand Jardin 2 rue Pierre-Eydin ⓣ04.42.01.70.10, ⓕ04.42.01.33.75. A pleasant hotel on a side street next to the Jardin Public and close to the centre of town. Has parking and is open all year. ❸

Joli Bois rte de la Gineste ⓣ04.42.01.02.68, ⓕ04.42.0118.24. Just off the main road to Marseille, 3km from Cassis. A bargain but it has only ten rooms, so it's best to book ahead. It's in a pretty remote spot, but there's plenty of parking. Half board or full board only. ❷ including half board.

Laurence 8 rue de l'Arène ⓣ04.42.01.88.78, ⓕ04.42.01.81.04. A short way inland from the port and market. Closed Nov and Dec. ❷

Les Roches Blanches av des Calanques ⓣ04.42.01.09.30, ⓦwww.roches-blanches-cassis.com. Handsome old hotel in a perfect position overlooking the bay, with smart rooms, terraces and a pine wood leading down to the water. ❺

Le Commerce 1 rue de Ste-Clair ⓣ04.42.01.09.10, ⓕ04.42.01.14.17. One block back from the port. Closed mid-Nov to mid-Jan. ❷

Hostel and campsite

HI youth hostel *La Fontasse* ⓣ04.42.01.02.72. In the hills above the *calanques* west of Cassis. By car from Cassis, take the D559 for 4km then turn left. The Cassis–Marseilles bus stops on the D559 (bus stop Les Calanques). On foot it's 2.5km from the centre of Cassis, towards the Col de la Gardiole; take av des Calanques from the port. The hostel's facilities are basic (there are no showers, and power and water are rationed), but if you want to explore this wild, uninhabited stretch of limestone heights, the people running it will advise you enthusiastically. Reception 8–10am & 5–10pm.

Les Cigales ⓣ04.42.01.07.34, ⓕ04.42.01.34.18. Campsite on the corner of the route de Marseille and av de la Marne, 1km from the port. €15 per tent. Closed mid-Nov to mid-March.

The Town

The white cliffs hemming it in and the value of its vineyards on the slopes above have prevented Cassis becoming a relentless sprawl, and the little modern development there is, is small scale. Port-side posing, eating *oursins* (sea urchins) and

The Cosquer Cave

In 1991, **Henri Cosquer**, a diver from Cassis, discovered paintings and engravings of animals, painted handprints and finger tracings in a cave between Marseille and Cassis, whose sole entrance is a long, sloping tunnel which starts 37m under the sea. The cave would have been accessible from dry land no later than the end of the last ice age and carbon dating has shown that the oldest work of art here was created around 27,000 years ago. Over a hundred animals have been identified, including seals, auks, horses, ibex, bisons, chamois, red deer and a giant deer known only from fossils. Fish are also featured along with sea creatures that might be jellyfish. Most of the finger tracings are done in charcoal and have fingertips missing, possibly to convey a sign language by bending fingers. For safety reasons it's not possible to visit the cave, though Marseille's tourist office (see p.169) sometimes runs an exhibition on it.

drinking aside, there's not much to do except sunbathe and look up at the ruins of the town's medieval **Castle**. It was built in 1381 by the counts of Les Baux and refurbished last century by Monsieur Michelin, the authoritarian boss of the family tyres and guides firm, and it remains a private home.

Cassis has a small **museum** (summer Wed–Sat 10.30am–12.30pm & 3.30–6.30pm; winter Wed–Sat 10.30am–12.30pm & 2.30–5.30pm; free) in the seventeenth-century presbytery on rue Xavier d'Authier just behind the tourist office. It has a bit of everything: nineteenth-century paintings and photographs of Cassis and Marseille, old furniture, costumes and Roman amphorae.

One of the most popular tourist activities is to take a **boat trip to the calanques** (€10–15), the long, narrow, deep, fjord-like inlets that cut into the limestone cliffs. Several companies operate from the port, but check if they let you off or just tour in and out, and be prepared for rough seas. If you're feeling energetic, you can **walk** along the GR98 footpath from the av des Calanques behind the western beach; it's about a ninety-minute walk to the furthest and best inlet, **En Vau**, where you can climb down rocks to the shore. Intrepid pine trees find root-holds, and sunbathers find ledges on the chaotic white cliffs. The water is deep blue and swimming between the vertical cliffs is an experience not to be missed.

Eating and drinking

Sea urchins accompanied by the delicious, crisp Cassis white wine are the speciality here. **Restaurant** tables are abundant along the port side on quai des Baux, quai Calandal and quai Barthélemy; prices vary but the best bet is to follow your nose, and seek out the most enticing fish smells. The authentic Provençal ratatouille and freshly caught fish at *Chez Gilbert*, 19 quai Baux (☎04.42.01.71.36; €20 menu; closed Tues eve & Wed), are hard to beat; it also serves great bouillabaisse. *Nino*, at 1 quai Barthélemy (☎04.42.01.74.32; menus from €30; closed Sun eve & Mon), is an attractive blue-and-white restaurant, serving pasta, bouillabaisse and wonderful grilled fish, while *Romano*, 15 quai Barthélemy (☎04.42.01.08.16; lunch menu at €15.60, otherwise menus from €21), dishes up elaborate creations such as a *mille feuilles* of smoked salmon with spinach. The most beautiful gourmet restaurant in town is *La Presqu'Île*, on rte des Calanques in the quartier de Port-Miou, overlooking both the *calanques* and the bay of Cassis and offering exquisite fish dishes and traditional Provençal fare (☎04.42.01.03.77; menus from €43; booking essential; closed Sun eve & Mon). For **drinking**, the *Bar Canaille*, on the corner of quai Calandal and quai des Baux, has the best *terrasse*, under the shade of a plane tree.

Cassis **wines**, from grapes grown on the slopes above the D559, are very special. Mistral described the white as 'shining like a limpid diamond, tasting of the rosemary, heather and myrtle that covers our hills'. If you arrive by train you can stop off at two **vineyards** on your way down the D1: the Domaine des Quatres Vents (Ⓣ04.42.01.88.10, Ⓕ04.42.01.01.12) and Clos d'Albizzi (Ⓣ & Ⓕ04.42.01.11.43). There are more along the D41 which loops east from the station, and along the D559 towards La Ciotat, and the tourist office's small English-language guide lists all the others. For **picnic food** to go with the wine, head for the **market**, held around rue de l'Arène south of the port on Wednesday and Friday mornings, and for the numerous *boulangeries* in av Victor Hugo.

The Corniche des Crêtes

If you have a car or motorbike, the spectacular **Corniche des Crêtes** road south from Cassis to La Ciotat (the D141) is definitely a ride not to be missed. From Cassis the chemin St-Joseph turns off av de Provence, climbs at a maximum gradient to the Pas de la Colle, then follows the inland slopes of the Montagnes de la Canaille. Much of the landscape is often blackened by fire but every so often the road loops round a break in the chain to give you dramatic views over the sea. You can walk it as well in about three and a half hours: the path, beginning from *Pas de la Colle*, takes a precipitous straighter line passing the road at each outer loop.

La Ciotat and around

Cranes still loom incongruously over the old ship-building town of **LA CIOTAT**, where 300,000-tonne oil and gas tankers were built as recently as 1989. Today, the town's economy relies on property development, tourism, and providing facilities for yachts, yet it remains a pleasantly unpretentious place, with a golden Vieille Ville above the bustling quayside, affordable hotels and restaurants, and an attractive beach stretching northeast from the port.

In 1895 **Auguste and Louis Lumière** filmed the first ever moving pictures in La Ciotat and in 1904 went on to develop the first colour photographs. The town celebrates its relatively unknown status as the cradle of cinema with an annual **film festival** in June and a script writers' festival in April.

Arrival, information and accommodation

The **gare SNCF** is 5km from the town centre but a bus meets every train and gets you to the Vieux Port in around thirty minutes. The Vieille Ville and port look out across the Baie de la Ciotat, whose inner curve provides the beaches and resort-style life of La Ciotat's beach-side extension, **La Ciotat Plage**. The **gare routière** is next to the **tourist office** (June–Sept Mon–Sat 9am–8pm, Sun 10am–1pm; Oct–May Mon–Sat 9am–noon & 2–6pm; Ⓣ04.42.08.61.32, Ⓦwww.laciotatourisme.com), at the end of bd Anatole-France by the Vieux Port. **Bikes** can be rented from Cycle Lleba at 3b av F-Mistral (Ⓣ04.42.83.60.30).

Hotels

Beaurivage 1 bd Beaurivage Ⓣ04.42.98.04.34, Ⓕ04.42.71.88.80. Two-star hotel with parking, restaurant and a terrace. The more expensive rooms have sea views. Closed Nov–March. ❷

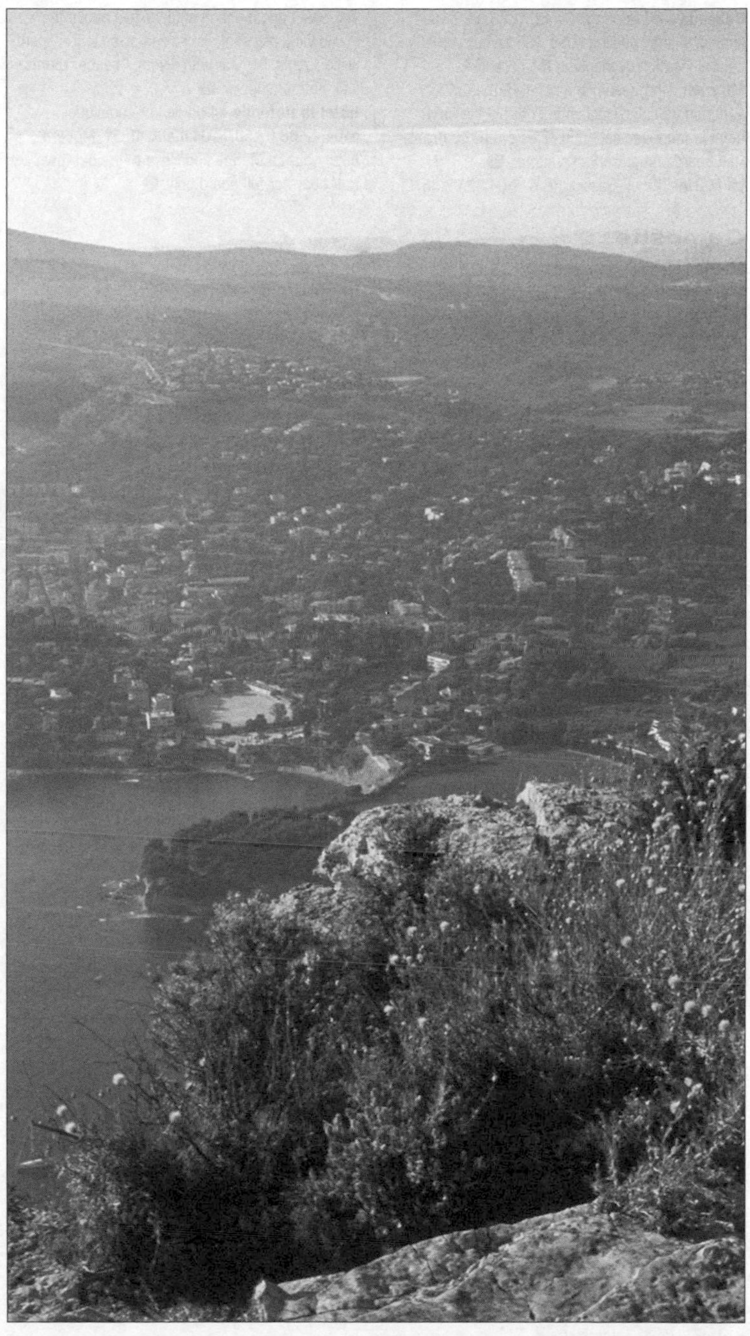
△ Cassis-route-des-Cretes

Bellevue 3 bd Guérin ⓣ04.42.71.86.01. Small, simple, slightly peeling hotel with an incredibly central location overlooking the port. ❷
Miramar 3 bd Beaurivage ⓣ04.42.83.33.79, ⓔmiramarlaciotat@aol.com. Possibly the best hotel in the town, set amid pines on the seafront. Half board compulsory in summer. ❾
La Marine 1 av F-Gassion ⓣ & ⓕ04.42.08.35.11. The best budget option in town, just above the Vieille Ville; pleasant, very clean place with decent-sized rooms. Popular with divers. Cheaper rooms lack bath or shower. ❶
Hôtel la Rotonde 44 bd de la République ⓣ04.42.08.67.50, ⓕ04.42.08.45.21. Modern hotel near La Marine and close to the old town. Half board or full board only. ❺

Campsite

St-Jean 30 av St-Jean ⓣ04.42.83.13.01, ⓦwww.asther.com/stjean. Take bus #40 (direction gare SNCF; stop St-Jean Village). Three-star site by the sea, the closest one to the centre. €16 per tent. Closed Oct–March.

The Town

The resplendently ornate nineteenth-century former *mairie* at the end of quai Ganteaume now houses the **Musée Ciotaden** (June–Sept Wed–Mon 4–7pm; Oct–May 3–6pm; €3.20), charting the history of the town back to its foundation by the ancient Greeks of Marseille when local shipbuilding began. Further down the quay is the seventeenth-century church, **Notre-Dame-du-Port**, with its Baroque facade and a striking early-seventeenth-century painting by André Gaudion of the *Descent of the Cross* alongside modern works of art. The streets of the Vieille Ville behind the church are uneventful and a bit run-down.

To the east along the seafront, on the corner of bd A-France and bd Jean-Jaurès, is the crumbly **Eden Cinema**, the world's oldest movie house, sadly no longer open to the public. Further on, at plage Lumière, is a solid 1950s monument to Auguste and Louis Lumière who shot the world's first films in the garden of the family **château** at the top of allée Lumière. The house survives, but is private property and not open to the public. The brothers appear again in a mural on the covered market halls which house the modern **cinema** on pl Evariste Gras, visible as you walk up rue Régnier from bd Guérin north of the port. If you want to learn more about the brothers, the **Espace Simon Lumière** at 20 rue Maréchal Foch (Tues–Sat 10am–noon & 3–6.30pm; free) has a small exhibition.

Boat trips depart from the Vieux Port for the ten-minute trip to the tiny offshore **Île Verte**, topped by a fort and with a small restaurant, *Chez Louisette*, which serves pizzas, grills and baked fish. Both Vedette Voltigeur (ⓣ04.42.83.11.44) and Vedette Monte Cristo (ⓣ04.42.71.53.32) make the crossing to Île Verte daily, while Catameran Le Citharista (ⓣ06.09.35.25.68) runs trips to the *calanques* of Cassis and Marseille (€14–17) from quai Ganteaume.

Alternatively, you could explore the remarkable contorted cliff beyond the shipyards that the city's founders named 'the eagle's beak' and which is now protected as the **Parc du Mugel** (daily: June–Sept 8am–7pm; Oct–May 9am–6pm). A path leads up from the entrance through overgrown vegetation and past scooped vertical hollows to a narrow terrace overlooking the sea. The cliff face looks like the habitat of some gravity-defying, burrowing beast rather than the result of erosion by wind and sea. To get there, take bus #30 (direction La Garde; stop Mugel).

If you continue on bus #30 to Figuerolles you can reach the **Anse de Figuerolles** *calanque* down the avenue of the same name, and its neighbour, the **Gameau**. Both have pebbly beaches and a completely different dominant colour from the *calanques* of Cassis.

Film in La Ciotat

La Ciotat's train station has a commemorative plaque to the film *L'Arrivée d'un train en gare de La Ciotat*, which was one of a dozen or so films, including *Le déjeuner de bébé* and the comedy *L'Arroseur arrosé*, shown in the Château Lumière in September 1895. The audience jumped out of their seats as the image of the steam train hurtled towards them. Three months later the reels were taken to Paris for the capital's citizens to witness cinema for the first time.

The town's film festival, the **Cinestival**, is a public and affordable event which takes place in early June, usually revolving around a particular theme or genre. The venues include the Lumière and Eden cinemas and the Chapelle des Pénitents Bleus. A full programme for the festival, and films, theatre and music throughout the summer, is available from the tourist office. An associated film conference, **Berceau du Cinema** takes place a week or two later at the Cinéma Lumière, and there's also an annual scriptwriters' conference in April.

Eating, drinking and entertainment

La Ciotat's **restaurants** are not gastronomically renowned, though *Coquillages Franquin*, at 13 bd Anatole-France (Ⓣ04.42.83.59.50), serves perfectly respectable fish dishes for around €32, and *La Marmite Provençal*, 8 quai Ganteaume (Ⓣ04.42.08.15.07), does the Provençal basics proficiently for around €20. Also on the port, pizzeria *La Mamma* (Ⓣ04.42.08.30.08) is much the busiest place in town, with decent pizzas for €10. There are plenty of **cafés** and **brasseries** on the quays; *L'Escalet* has a fixed lunchtime menu at €10; and there's an ample selection of **beers** at the *Le Palais de la Bière*, where everyone seems to end up. The *Bar à Tine* overlooking the Cinema Lumière and the Tuesday market on place E-Gras is another pleasant place to drink. Also on place E-Gras, the *Atelier Convergences* gives **jazz concerts** every Friday and Saturday evening. La Ciotat has a surprisingly animated cultural scene, including several gallery/exhibition spaces and the smart new *Theatre du Golfe* on the seafront at bd Anatole France (Ⓣ04.42.08.92.87).

There's a Sunday **market** on the quays, though the main shopping street is rue des Poilus, a little inland from the church of Notre Dame du Port. For a takeaway lunch, *Lou Pecadou*, a fishmonger's at no. 20, sells paella and other fish dishes from huge iron pans.

Les Lecques and St-Cyr

Across La Ciotat bay are the fine sand and shingle beaches and unremarkable family resort of **LES LECQUES**, which is gradually merging with the inland village of **ST-CYR-SUR-MER**. The one reminder of the past here dates back to Caesar and Pompey's contest for the control of Marseille. The decisive naval battle, which Caesar won, took place near a town called Taureontum, whose precise location is unknown. On the rte de la Madrague at the east end of the bay are the remains of a **Roman villa**, dated first century AD. With three extant mosaics, patches of frescoes, a couple of interesting sarcophagi, numerous beautiful Greek and Roman vases and other household paraphernalia, the villa forms the **Musée de Taureontum** (June–Sept Mon & Wed–Sun 3–7pm; Oct–May Sat & Sun 2–5pm; €3).

St-Cyr has a few sites to detain you briefly: the small **Centre d'Art Sébastien** on bd Jean-Jaurès (Mon & Wed–Sun 9am–noon & 2–6pm; €1) displays the paintings and tender terracotta statues of this Parisian-born artist and friend of

Picasso in a beautifully restored former caper storehouse, while the **Espace Provence**, next door (Tues–Sat 9am–noon & 3–6pm), exhibits local crafts and produce. On place de Portalis is a miniature, golden **Statue of Liberty**, sculpted by Bartholdi, the artist who created its better-known sister. Beyond these, St-Cyr's main attraction is its **vineyards**, which belong to the excellent Bandol *appellation*. One of the best reds comes from the Château des Baumelles, a seventeenth-century manor house just out of St-Cyr to the right off the Bandol road, which can be visited by appointment only (ⓣ04.94.32.63.20), while the Domaine du Cagueloup on the D66 towards La Cadière d'Azur (Mon–Fri 9am–noon & 2.30–6pm; ⓣ04.94.26.15.70) has open *dégustations*. St-Cyr also has a food **market** on Sunday in the G Péri car park in the Vieille Ville.

The **gare SNCF** lies midway between St-Cyr-sur-Mer and Les Lecques; from the station it is a twenty-minute walk down to Les Lecques. The **tourist office**, which caters for both towns, is on place de l'Appel du 18 Juin, off av du Port in Les Lecques (June & Sept Mon–Sat 9am–6pm; July & Aug Mon–Sat 9am–7pm, Sun 10am–1pm & 4–7pm; Oct–May Mon–Fri 9am–6pm, Sat 9am–noon & 2–6pm; ⓣ04.94.26.73.73, ⓦwww.saintcyrsurmer.com).

Of the Les Lecques **hotels**, the very small *Beau Séjour*, 34 av de la Mer (ⓣ04.94.26.54.06, ⓕ04.94.26.63.78; ❷; closed Jan), is a reasonably priced option close to the sea, or there's the comfortable *Grand Hôtel*, 24 av du Port (ⓣ04.94.26.23.01, ⓕ04.94.26.10.22; July & Aug halfboard only, €117 per person, otherwise ❸; closed mid-Nov to March), set in a large garden. Simple, less expensive places can be found up the hill in St-Cyr, including the *Auberge Le Clos Fleurie*, at 27 av du Général-de-Gaulle near the train station (ⓣ04.94.26.27.46; ❶), and the *Hôtel-Bar Café de France* on place Portalis, in the centre of town (ⓣ04.94.26.22.55; ❶). Les Lecques also has a large three-star **campsite**, *Les Baumelles* (ⓣ04.94.26.21.27; €14 per tent; closed Nov–Feb), on the beach right in the centre of the resort.

The widest choice of **restaurants** in Les Lecques is along av du Port on the seafront. Alternatively, head along the coastal path, which runs from La Madrague at the east end of Les Lecques' beach down to the Pointe du Déffend – east of here, on the calanque de Port-d'Alon, there's a gorgeous fish restaurant, *La Calanque* (ⓣ04.94.26.20.08; menu €20; closed Sun eve, Mon and Oct–Jan). If you'd rather **picnic**, the coastal path offers plenty of secluded spots, and continues on to Bandol (3hr 30min).

Bandol and around

Continuing southeast on the coastal road to Toulon, the next stop is **BANDOL**, an unpretentious coastal resort fringed by unappealing apartment complexes. It bustles with day-trippers attracted by the cheap clothes shops, and with yachties milling around the vast marina, which obliterates most of the town's sea view. The town is rightly proud of its wines which have their own, distinct Bandol *Appellation Controlée*. As well as all the usual casinos, discos, cocktail bars and water sports, Bandol has some cheap accommodation so makes a good coastal base from which to explore Toulon. Along the coast, the wines and the hinterland are the main attractions, along with the **Île de Bendor**, which aptly houses France's largest exposition of wines, spirits and alcohols.

Arrival, information and accommodation

From Bandol's **train station**, head straight downhill and you'll reach the town centre above the port. The **tourist office** is on allées Vivien by the quayside (last two weeks of June and first two weeks of Sept daily 9am–noon & 2–6pm; July & Aug daily 9am–7pm; mid-Sept to mid-June Mon–Fri 9am–noon & 2–6pm, Sat 9am–noon; Ⓣ04.94.29.41.35, Ⓦwww.bandol.fr). You can rent **bikes**, motorized or not, at Holiday Bikes, 127 rte de Marseille (Ⓣ04.94.32.21.89), west down av Loste on the other side of the rail lines from the station.

A couple of the cheaper **hotels** worth considering are the basic *Le Provence* on a little impasse up from av du 11 Novembre (Ⓣ04.94.32.32.25; ❷), with a friendly restaurant and parking space, just down the steps from the station, where *pétanque* players gather to play and drink pastis, and *La Brise*, 12 bd Victor-Hugo (Ⓣ04.94.29.41.70; ❷), located on a small rise just back from the port and with its own restaurant. Slightly more upmarket is *Roses Mousses*, 22 rue des Écoles (Ⓣ04.94.29.45.14; ❹; closed mid-Oct to mid-April), in a residential area between the town centre and Rènecros, and the very pleasant good-value *Golf Hôtel*, right on Rènecros beach (Ⓣ04.94.29.45.83, Ⓦwww.golhotel.fr; ❹). Bandol's top hotel, *Île Rousse*, 17 bd Louis-Lumière (Ⓣ04.94.29.33.00, Ⓦwww.ile-rousse.com; ❾), has a terrace leading down to the beach from the west of the port, vast light rooms and a choice of restaurants. If you're **camping**, try the three-star *Vallongue* (Ⓣ04.94.29.49.55; €15.50 per tent; closed Oct–March), 2.5km out of town on the rte de Marseille.

There are also a couple of hotels on **Île de Bendor**, both aimed at the company expense account market: the *Soukana* (Ⓣ04.94.25.06.06, Ⓕ04.94.25.04.89; ❺; closed Oct–March) at the far end of the island is the best bet, but you'd still have to book months in advance.

The town

Bandol's charms are based principally on wine, in particular the town's own *appellation* produced in the area encompassing St-Cyr (see p.216). The reds have the best reputation, maturing for over ten years on a good harvest, with bouquets sliding between pepper, cinnamon, vanilla and black cherries; the rosé is equally wonderful. Back from the port on allées Vivien, the **Maison des Vins du Bandol** (Ⓣ04.94.29.45.03) sells its own selection of wines and will give you lists of local *propriétaires* to visit. For cheese, sausages and the like to accompany your wine, there's a Tuesday morning **market** on the quayside, supplemented in summer by a regular evening crafts market at the same place. Bandol's most scenic sandy **beach** is around the **Anse de Rènecros**, an almost circular inlet just over the hill west of the port, reached via bd Louis-Lumière. Better still are the coves and beaches along the coastal path to Les Lecques which you reach from av du Maréchal-Foch on the western side of the Anse de Rènecros (signed in yellow).

The Île de Bendor

Île de Bendor was an uninhabited rocky island when it was bought by the rags-to-riches pastis man **Paul Ricard** in the 1950s, and today the atmosphere is somewhat surreal, with unlikely statues, an uneasy discrepancy between the people and the place, and a 1950s architectural style severely stamped on most of its buildings. Ricard himself died in 1997, but his family still owns the place, and there's an exhibition on the island covering his life and works (Mon & Wed–Sun 10am–noon & 2–6pm). Boats leave for the seven-minute crossing to Bendor from Bandol's quai de l'Hôtel-de-Ville on the port (April to mid-June & mid-Sept to Oct daily 7am–11pm; mid-June to mid-Sept daily 7am–2am; Nov–Mar 7am–5pm; €6 return).

For most of the year, activities on the island revolve around the **Club International de Plongée** (Ⓣ04.94.29.55.12, Ⓔcipbendor@hotmail.com), which offers diving training from beginner to instructor level, and has a sea school for 8- to 12-year-olds, and the **Club Nautique** (☎04.94.29.52.91), which runs a sailing school and rents catamarans, dinghies and windsurf boards. Inland, there's also the cavernous **Exposition Universelle des Vins et Spiritueux** (April–Sept Mon & Wed–Sat 10am–noon & 2–6pm; free) to the west of the port. Decorated with murals by art-school students, the hall has a comprehensive display of French wines and liquors and a slowly expanding selection of liquid intoxicants from around the world. The exposition's claim that no culture has ever failed to produce alcohol has yet to be refuted, and there are some weird and wonderful items, including an evil bottle of Chinese spirit in which a large gecko floats.

Eating and drinking

In the centre of Bandol, you'll find plenty of **restaurants** along rue de la République and allée Jean-Moulin, running parallel to the port side promenade. The *Auberge du Port*, 7 allée Jean-Moulin (☎04.94.29.42.63), has classic fish dishes, with menus at €29 and €40; while *La Marmite*, at 1 rue F-Fabre (☎04.94.25.05.60), serves good-value dishes including *gambas à la plancha*, with menus from €14. The elegant restaurant *Les Oliviers* at the hotel *Île Rousse* (see p.217) is the place for braised knuckle of veal with truffles and confit of shallots, plus elaborate desserts including a peppermint chocolate *gratinée*; menus start at €37. Arguably as good is *Le Clocher*, 1 rue de la Paroisse (☎04.94.32.47.65; menus from €20; à la carte from €29; closed Nov), with specialities including home-made *foie gras* and pesto.

Bandol's **bars** tend towards the sophisticated: *Le Bistro* at 6 av Jean Moulin is chic and modern, with a long cocktail list and light meals from €12, while *Le 38 Caffe*, *Poupoune* and *L'Escale*, all along quai Charles-de-Gaulle above the beach, are similarly fashionable cocktail-sipping spots.

Around Bandol

Despite the creeping suburbanization, the countryside north of Bandol makes good **cycling** country: you could head for the perched medieval village of **La Cadière d'Azur** (take the road above the station, left on the D559, then right), and then across the valley to the more touristy fortified hamlet of **Le Castellet** with its vast car parks, gloomy, crypt-like bastion of a twelfth-century church, perfumed boutiques and wonderful panorama of the vineyards below.

Approximately 6km southeast of Le Castellet, south of Le Beausset, is **Le Vieux Beausset**, whose Romanesque **Chapelle Notre-Dame** (Mon, Tues, Thur, Fri 2–5.30pm, Sat 9am–5.30pm, Wed & Sun 9.30am–5.30pm) rewards the long and winding approach with a suberb panoramic view.

The Cap Sicié peninsula and Ollioules

The coastal approach to Toulon from Marseille takes you via the congested neck of the **Cap Sicié peninsula**. On the western side, Six-Fours-les-Plage sprawls between Bandol's neighbour **Sanary-sur-Mer** and **Le Brusc** on the western tip where you can get boats to another Ricard-owned island, **Île des Embiez**. The eastern side of the peninsula merges with Toulon's former shipbuilding suburb of **La Seyne-sur-Mer**, while at the southern end a semi-wilderness of high cliffs and forest reigns.

Approaching Toulon on the Aubagne road, you'll pass through the twisting **gorge d'Ollioules**, where the heights of **Le Gros Cerveau** and **Mont Caume** above it are well worth visiting.

Sanary-sur-Mer and around

The little fishing harbour of **SANARY-SUR-MER** is approximately 5km east of Bandol on the Cap Sicié peninsula. With its palm trees, nineteenth-century church spire, pastel pink and yellow facades along the seafront, and fountains with statues representing agriculture and fishery, the harbour retains its charm despite the urban conglomoration it's now immersed in. It hasn't sold its soul to the yachting crowd as much as Bandol, either. Housed in the thirteenth-century **Tour Romane** by the port is a small **diving museum** (July & Aug daily 9am–noon & 4–8pm; Sept–June Sat & Sun 9am–12.30pm & 3–6.30pm; free), based around the collection of one of the pioneers of the modern sport, Frédéric Dumas, who worked with Jacques Cousteau. Also by the port in the Jardin de la Ville is a plaque commemorating the German-speaking artistic community that made Sanary its base in the 1930s, having fled from the strictures of Hitler's NSDAP party: the exiles included Thomas, Golo and Heinrich Mann, Erwin Piscator and Arthur Koestler.

Practicalities

Buses run frequently from Bandol's quai de l'Hôtel-de-Ville to Sanary. The town's **train station**, which it shares with Ollioules (see p.220), is 2.5km north of the centre, but the buses into town don't always link up with train arrivals. The **tourist office** is by the port in the Jardin de la Ville (July & August Mon–Sat 9am–12.30pm & 2–7pm, Sun 9.30am–12.30pm; May, June, Sept & Oct Mon–Fri 9am–noon & 2–6pm, Sat 9am–noon & 2–5pm; Nov–April Mon–Fri 9am–noon & 2–5.30pm, Sat 9am–noon & 2–5pm; ⓣ04.94.74.01.04, ⓦwww.sanarysurmer.com).

If you want **to stay**, the *Centre Azur* hostel, 149 av du Nid (ⓣ04.94.74.18.87, ⓔcentre-azur@wanadoo.fr; ❶), is between Portissol and La Cride, a little west of the centre, or there's the attractive *Hôtel de la Tour*, 24 quai Général-de-Gaulle (ⓣ04.94.74.10.10, ⓕ04.94.74.69.49; ❹), with a perfect location right on the port. There's also a good three-star **campsite**, *Les Girelles*, on the chemin de Beaucours, by the sea on the Bandol road (ⓣ04.94.74.13.18, ⓕ 04.94.74.60.04; €22 per tent; closed Oct–Easter).

The **restaurant** *Relais de la Poste*, on place Chanoine Arnaldi (ⓣ04.94.74.22.20; closed Sun eve & Mon; menus from €22), serves interesting dishes, such as veal andouilettes stuffed with prawns, while *Le Cabanon*, on the pretty Plage de Portissol (ⓣ04.94.74.13.89), offers delicious low-priced fish dishes – to get there, head 1km west from the port along av Gallieni and av de Portissol.

Around Sanary

From Sanary the D559 and D63 head towards Toulon through **SIX-FOURS-LES-PLAGES**, which seems nothing but sprawling, suburbs littered with hoardings, though its shingly beaches are well-kept. A small road off the D63, to the north, however, takes you up to **Notre-Dame-de-la-Pépiole** (open Mon & Wed–Sat 3–6pm; mass Sundays at 9.30am; free), a stunning sixth-century chapel in the midst of pines, cypresses and olive trees.

The southeast reaches of the peninsula are not exactly wilderness, but the sturdy sentinel of **Notre-Dame-de-Mai** (Oct–April every first Sat of the month;

throughout May for pilgrimages, plus 15 August and 14 Sept), once a primitive lighthouse, provides a reason to **hike** for an hour or two up the pretty backroads towards Cap Sicié. The local tourist map marks several routes, some starting in the midst of Six-Fours' traffic-choked suburban sprawl, but the best one is *sentier du littoral*, starting from chemin des Cargadoux, which runs east from the quay in **LE BRUSC** and follows the coast. It's a walk of several kilometres, worth it for the heady views in every direction; it can get pretty windy up here, and even on a calm day exploring the cliffs should be done with a certain amount of caution. Back in Le Brusc, you can reward yourself with a generous fish dinner at *Le St-Pierre*, 47 rue de la Citadelle (Ⓣ04.94.34.02.52; menus at €17, €23 and €31; closed Tues eve & Wed out of season).

Île des Embiez

Paul Ricard's second island, the **Île des Embiez** (Ⓦwww.ile-des-embiez.com), greets visitors with mock classical goddesses on pillars around its large **pleasure port** and scattered Greco-Roman picnic tables. The **Fondation Océanographique Ricard** (April–June, Sept & Oct Mon–Fri & Sun 10am–12.30pm & 1.30–5.30pm, Sat 2–5.30pm; July & Aug daily 10am–12.30pm & 1.30–5.30pm; Nov–March Mon, Tues, Thur & Fri 10am–12.30pm & 1.30–5.30pm, Wed, Sat & Sun 2–5.30pm; €3.81) has aquariums and exhibitions on underwater matter. There are pony and go-kart rides for the under-twelves and in summer a miniature road-train does a circuit of the island (adult €4; child over 6 €2.40), all great fun for pre-teens. Away from the paying attractions, much of the island has been laid waste by various 'works'. In spring the more or less untrammelled south-facing cliffs are a riot of yellow flowers but the rest of the year they're covered in dull scrub and, with the exception of a few pocket-handkerchief-sized beaches of fine gravel and crystal water, there's not much to induce a lengthy stay.

There are frequent **ferry crossings** from Le Brusc (daily: mid-June to mid-Sept 7am–12.45am; mid-March to mid-June & mid-Sept to mid-Nov 7am–10.45pm; mid-Nov to mid-March 7am–8.20pm; journey time 10min; €7.50). If you want to stay, there's a small **hostel** (no membership needed but book well in advance; Ⓣ04.94.88.08.30), and a couple of **hotels** – the de luxe *Hélios* (Ⓣ04.94.10.66.10, Ⓦwww.helios-embiez.com; ❾), and the more modest *Le Canoubié* (Ⓣ04.94.74.94.94, Ⓦwww.lecanoubie.com; ❻) – plus a few rented apartments.

Ollioules

OLLIOULES, north of the peninsula, derives its name from 'olive', and it's one of those small Provençal towns that, despite a ruined medieval castle, arcaded streets, fountains and a Romanesque church, still manages to have an economy not totally dependent on tourism. Much of this rests on its floral wholesale and export market, the biggest in France, though open to the public only during the *Foire aux Plantes* at the end of April on the central place Jean-Jaurès. Small-scale artisans are also much in evidence, earning their keep making barrels, pots, nougat or reeds for musical instruments, as well as wine and olive oil. On the cultural front, the *commune* contains the **Centre National de Création et de Diffusion Culturelles** in the château of Châteauvallon (off the D92 towards Toulon), with an impressive calendar of arts events including music, theatre, circus and film. It also hosts an **international dance festival** every July (details from the centre Ⓣ0800.089.090, or from Ollioules or Toulon tourist offices).

Practicalities

Ollioules shares its **gare SNCF** with Sanary; it lies between the two, about 3.5km south of Ollioules. There's a regular bus (#120) between the town and the station, and you can also catch a bus (#12) from place de la Liberté in the centre of Toulon. Ollioules' **tourist office** is in the Espace Culturel at 116 rue Ph De Hautecloque (Mon–Fri 9am–noon & 2–6pm, Sat 9am–noon; ⓣ04.94.63.11.74). **Bikes** can be rented at Oki Bike, 18 av Georges Clémenceau, across the bridge from the tourist office (ⓣ04.94.63.46.37). A **market** takes place on place Jean-Jaurès on Thursday and Saturday mornings.

Very cheap **rooms** can be had at *L'Escale* hotel-bar-restaurant, 1 rue Hoche (ⓣ04.94.63.21.07; ❶), and *Au Bon Coin* hotel-crêperie, 11 rue Marceau (ⓣ04.94.63.22.26, ⓕ04.94.63.30.45; ❶), both run by friendly couples and both just off place Jean-Jaurès. For **meals**, *Au Bon Coin's* crêpes and salads are reasonably priced, while *Restaurant les Temps des Copains* on pl Henri Duprat is popular and jolly, with a brochette-dominated menu at €22. For some very special Bandol AOC **wine**, head for the Domaine de Terrebrune, 724 chemin de la Tourelle, signed off the rte du Gros Cerveau (Mon–Sat 9am–12.30pm & 2–6.30pm), which produces a wonderful deep and dusky red wine and has an expensive but very good Provençal restaurant, *Le Table du Vigneron*, with menus at €39 and €42 (Tues–Sun, closed Sun eve & Mon; ⓣ04.94.88.36.19).

Mont Caume and Le Gros Cerveau

Though less dramatic in their inclines than the Cap Sicié cliffs, the mountain ranges to the north of the peninsula give the best panorama of this complex coast. **Mont Caume** to the east is, at 804m, by far the highest point in the locality. Access at the top is restricted by the military, but you can get a view northwards across acres of forest to the Chaîne de la Ste-Baume and the distinctively sharp drop of the Montagne de la Loube by La Roquebrussanne.

The road between Mont Caume and the gorges takes in the villages of **Le Broussan** and **Evenos**, the latter perched up in the winds around a ruined castle.

West of the gorges, the **Gros Cerveau** ridge reveals the islands of Embiez and Bendor, the Toulon roadstead, Cap Sicié and La Ciotat's shipbuilding yards. From an abandoned military barracks you can look down northwards onto the strange rock forms. This is good walking country, though watch out in the hunting season for *chasse gardée* signs.

Toulon

Viewed from the distant heights of Mont Caume or Notre-Dame-du-Mai, it's clear why **TOULON** had to be a major port. The heart-shaped bay of the Petite Rade gives over 15km of shoreline around Toulon and its suburb **La Seyne-sur-Mer** to the west. Facing the city, about 3km out to sea, is **St-Mandrier**, a virtual island, connected to the Cap Sicié peninsula by the isthmus of Les Sablettes and protecting the Grande Rade both northwards and eastwards. All in all it's a magnificent natural harbour, deserving of a Rio or Hong Kong to grace its shores. But that, the cynics might say, is the trouble: instead of Rio, they built Toulon.

The city was half-destroyed in World War II and its rebuilt whole is dominated by the military and associated industries. The arsenal that Louis XIV created is one of the major employers of southeast France and the port is home

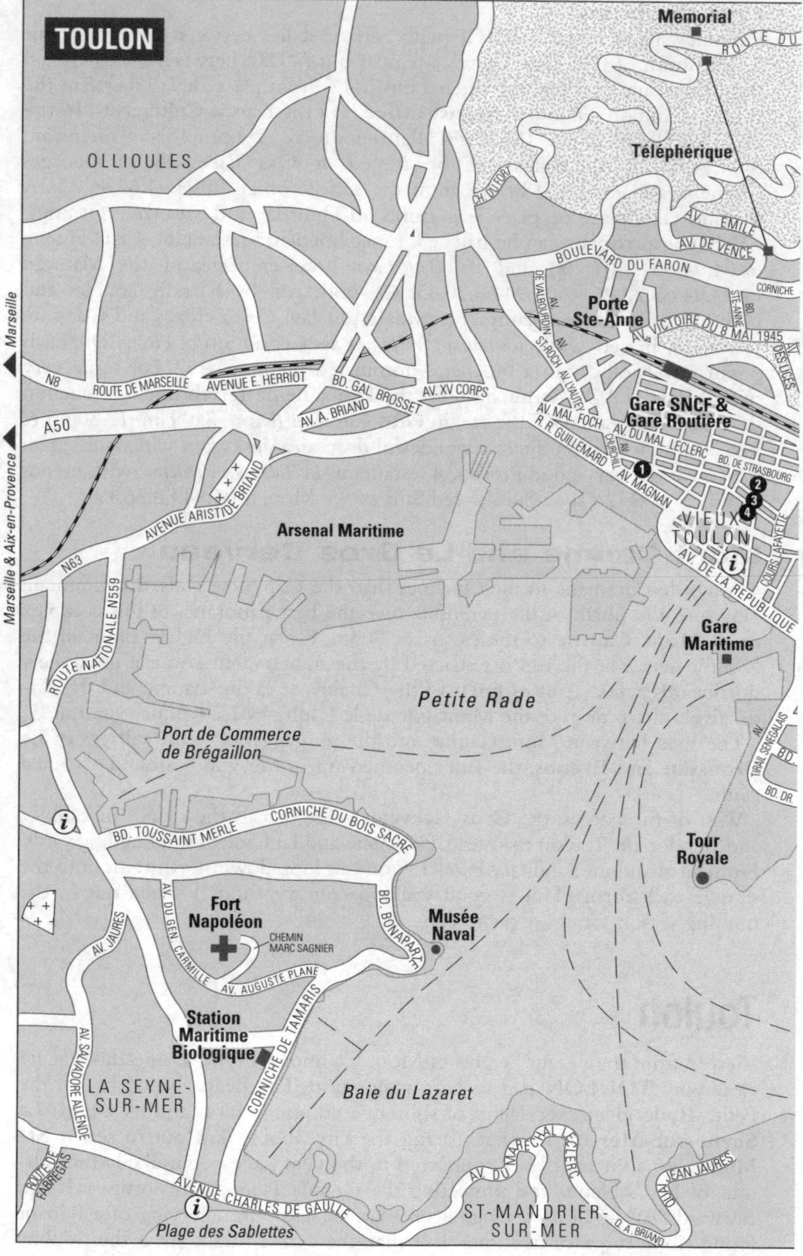
TOULON
Memorial
ROUTE DU
Téléphérique
OLLIOULES
CH. DU FORT
AV. EMILE
AV. DE VENCE
BOULEVARD DU FARON
CORNICHE
AV. DE VALBOURDIN
Porte Ste-Anne
BD. STE-ANNE
AV. VICTOIRE DU 8 MAI 1945
AV. DES LICES
AV. ST-ROCH
AV. LYAUTEY
N8
ROUTE DE MARSEILLE
AVENUE E. HERRIOT
BD. GAL. BROSSET
AV. XV CORPS
AV. A. BRIAND
AV. MAL. FOCH
R. R. GUILLEMARD
Gare SNCF & Gare Routière
AV. DU MAL. LECLERC
AV. CHURCHILL
BD. DE STRASBOURG
AV. MAGNAN
A50
AVENUE ARISTIDE BRIAND
Arsenal Maritime
VIEUX TOULON
COURS LAFAYETTE
AV. DE LA REPUBLIQUE
N63
ROUTE NATIONALE N559
Gare Maritime
Petite Rade
Port de Commerce de Brégaillon
AV. TIRAIL SENEGALAIS
BD.
BD. DR.
CORNICHE DU BOIS SACRE
BD. TOUSSAINT MERLE
Tour Royale
Fort Napoléon
AV. DU GEN. CARMILLE
BD. BONAPARTE
CHEMIN MARC SAGNIER
Musée Naval
AV. JAURES
AV. AUGUSTE PLANE
Station Maritime Biologique
CORNICHE DE TAMARIS
AV. SALVADORE ALLENDE
LA SEYNE-SUR-MER
Baie du Lazaret
AV. DU MARECHAL LECLERC
QUAI JEAN JAURES
ROUTE DE FABREGAS
AVENUE CHARLES DE GAULLE
Plage des Sablettes
ST-MANDRIER-SUR-MER
Q. A. BRIAND
Marseille
Marseille & Aix-en-Provence

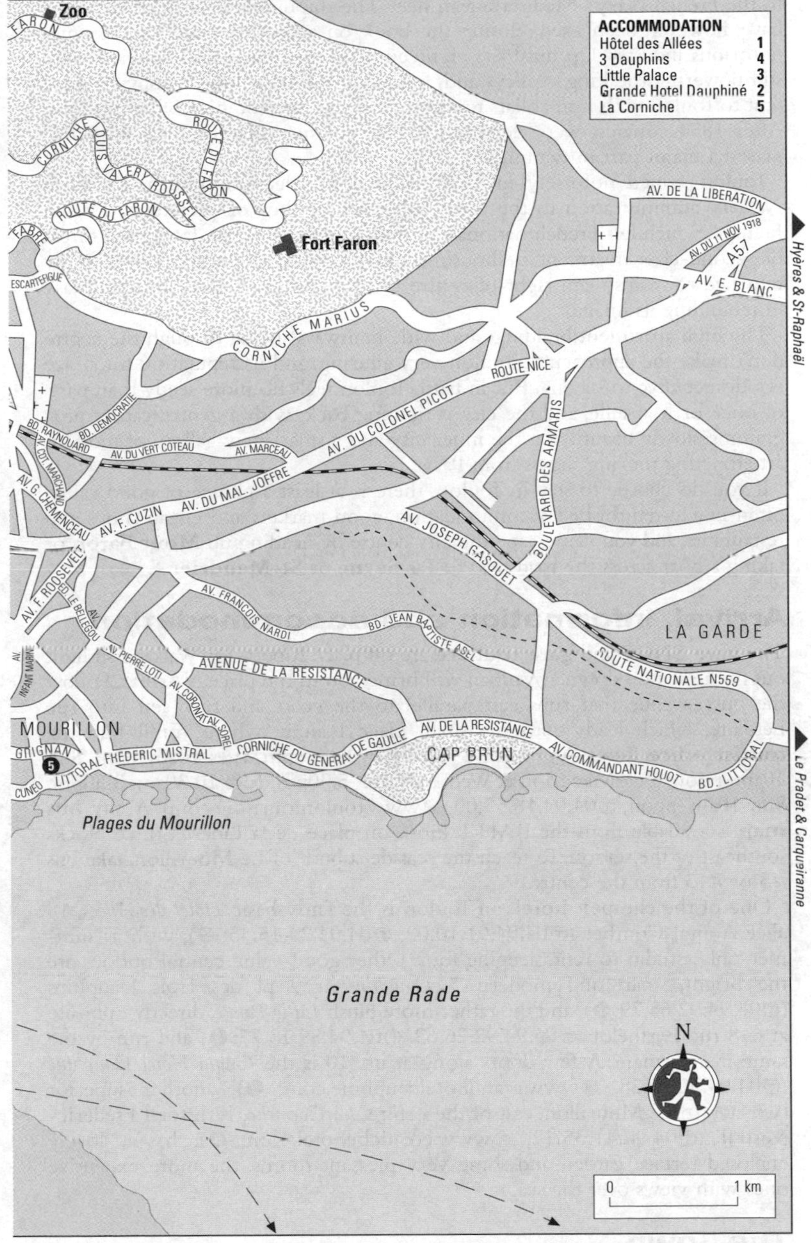
ACCOMMODATION
Hôtel des Allées 1
3 Dauphins 4
Little Palace 3
Grande Hotel Dauphiné 2
La Corniche 5
Zoo
Fort Faron
ROUTE DU FARON
CORNICHE LOUIS VALERY ROUSSEL
AV. DE LA LIBERATION
AV. DU 11 NOV 1918
A57
AV. E. BLANC
CORNICHE MARIUS
ROUTE NICE
AV. DU COLONEL PICOT
BD. DEMOCRATIE
BD. RAYNOUARD
AV. DU VERT COTEAU
AV. MARCEAU
AV. COT. MARCHAND
AV. G. CHEMENCEAU
AV. F. CUZIN
AV. DU MAL. JOFFRE
AV. JOSEPH GASQUET
BOULEVARD DES ARMARIS
AV. F. ROOSEVELT
BD. LE BELLEGOU
AV. FRANCOIS NARDI
BD. JEAN BAPTISTE ASEL
LA GARDE
ROUTE NATIONALE N559
AV. PIERRE LOTI
AVENUE DE LA RESISTANCE
AV. CORONAT
AV. SOREL
INFANT MARIE
MOURILLON
AV. DE LA RESISTANCE
CAP BRUN
LITTORAL FREDERIC MISTRAL
CORNICHE DU GENERAL DE GAULLE
AV. COMMANDANT HOUOT
BD. LITTORAL
CUNEO
Plages du Mourillon
Hyères & St-Raphaël
Le Pradet & Carqueiranne
Grande Rade
N
0
1 km

to the French Navy's Mediterranean fleet. The shipbuilding yards of La Seyne have, however, been axed, closing the book on a centuries-old and at times notorious industry. Up until the eighteenth century, slaves and convicts were still powering the king's galleys and, following the Revolution, convicts were sent to Toulon with iron collars round their necks for sentences of hard labour. After 1854 convicts were deported to the colonies that Toulon's ships had played a major part in winning.

Toulon gained notoriety in 1995 when local elections returned a *Front National* administration to the town hall with a policy of 'preference for the French', which left French nationals of non-European origin facing the threat of second-class treatment in housing and provision of local services. Now returned to mainstream right-of-centre (RPR) control, it faces an uphill task in rebuilding its image.

The high apartment buildings and wide highways slicing through the centre don't make the approach to Toulon very alluring, and its reputation for sleaze is a disincentive to staying. But in truth Toulon feels no more seedy than parts of Nice or Marseille, and the city is fighting back, with a gentrification programme slowly beautifying the inner city and a smart new gallery of modern art attracting touring shows from Paris.

If you do choose to stay in Toulon, there is at least a choice of good value, often newly-refurbished accommodation, good markets and cheap shops and restaurants, and you can escape the city centre by heading up **Mont Faron** or taking a boat across the roadstead to **La Seyne** or **St-Mandrier**.

Arrival, information and accommodation

The **gare SNCF** and **gare routière** are on place Albert-1er. Walking straight out of the station down av Vauban will bring you to the place d'Armes. Follow the busy avenue that runs east parallel to the coast and turn left into rue Letuaire, which leads onto the small place Raimu, where you'll find the **tourist office** (June–Sept Mon & Wed–Sat 9am–6pm, Tues 10am–6pm, Sun 10am–noon; Oct–May Mon & Wed–Sat 9am–5.30pm, Tues 10.30am–5.30pm, Sun 10am–noon; ⓣ04.94.18.53.00, ⓦwww.toulontourisme.com). A city **bus map** is available from the RMTT kiosk on place de la Liberté, three blocks southeast of the station. To reach the seaside suburb of Le Mourillon, take bus #3 or #13 from the centre.

One of the cheapest **hotels** in Toulon is the fairly basic *Hôtel des Allées*, 18 allée Amiral-Courbet (ⓣ04.94.91.10.02, ⓕ04.94.24.15.45; ❶), with a (summer-only) studio to rent, sleeping four. Other good-value central options are the bright, smart and modern *3 Dauphins* at 9 pl des Trois Dauphins (ⓣ04.94.92.65.79; ❶), and the rather more plush *Little Palace*, directly opposite at 6–8 rue Berthelot (ⓣ04.94.92.26.62, ⓕ04.94.89.13.77; ❸) and run by the same management. A few doors along at no. 10 is the *Grand Hotel Dauphiné* (ⓣ04.94.92.20.28, ⓦwww.grandhoteldauphine.com; ❷), another superior two-star. In Le Mourillon, east of the centre, *La Corniche*, 17 littoral Frédéric-Mistral (ⓣ04.94.41.35.12, ⓦwww.cornichehotel.com; ❺), has a lovely enclosed terrace garden and some very pleasant rooms, the more expensive ones with views over the sea.

The Town

Vieux Toulon, crammed in between bd de Strasbourg and av de la République on the old port, is pleasant enough during the day. It has a fine scattering of fountains, more often than not of dolphins, a decent selection of shops, particularly for clothes, and an excellent **market** (Tues–Sun) around rue Landrin and cours Lafayette. Big chunks of the Vieille Ville have disappeared with the construction of a gleaming new lycée and shopping centre, and place Victor-Hugo around the opera is all cleaned up and full of café tables, as is the quai Cronstadt fronting the port. However, one block behind the port, along av de la République, the streets are still a little seedy by night; here, Toulon's only gay bar, *Texas*, offers a pleasant haven to heterosexual and gay alike. Alternatively, you may want to head east to the **Mourillon quartier** where trendy nightlife glitters down the littoral Frédéric-Mistral and the beaches face the open sea.

The vast expanse of the **Arsenal**, on place Monsenergue, marks the western end of the Vieille Ville, with its grandiose eighteenth-century gateway leading to the **Musée de la Marine** (Mon & Wed–Sun 10am–noon & 2–7pm; €4.60), where French and English visitors alike are greeted by Pierre-Louis Ganne's depiction of the battle of Trafalgar. The museum displays figureheads, statues of admirals, an extensive collection of model ships and an enormous fresco showing the old arsenal before it was burnt by the British (see below), as well as stark black-and-white photos showing the aftereffects of the scuttling of the French fleet in Toulon harbour during World War II. To the north, beyond the rather scruffy formal gardens of **place d'Armes** and up the main boulevard, the grandiose **Musée d'Art**, 113 bd Maréchal-Leclerc (currently closed for refurbishment; check opening times with tourist office), has a collection spanning seventeenth- and eighteenth-century Provençal artists, the Provençal Fauves and more modern works including some from the Support-Surfaces movement. It shares a building with the **Muséum d'Histoire Naturelle** (Mon–Fri 9.30am–noon & 2–6pm, Sat & Sun 1–6pm; free), whose musty collection of mineral and dinosaur displays outshine the stuffed animals and mounted butterflies.

Further east, at 236 bd Maréchal Leclerc, is the handsome **Hôtel des Arts** (daily 11am–6pm; free), housed in the beaux arts, former Conseil General building and intended as a home for touring exhibitions of modern art. The building itself is architecturally conservative, but the gallery pulls in shows from the major Parisian galleries, and it's always worth a look to see what's on. The most impressive public artwork in the city, however, is Pierre Puget's sculptures of **Atlantes**, holding up all that is left of the old town hall on av de la République. It's thought that Puget, working in 1657, modelled these immensely strong, tragic figures on galley slaves as allegories of might and fatigue.

Around the Petite Rade

Several companies offer **boat tours** with commentary around both the Grande and Petite Rade, but a much cheaper option is to take one of the public transport **boats** from quai Stalingrad, along the av de la République, across the Petite Rade to **La Seyne** (#8M; 20 min); **St-Mandrier** (#28M; 20min); or **Les Sablettes**, the isthmus between them, which stops at Tamaris on the way (#18M; 20 min).

Although it now has the merchant shipping port, the loss of **LA SEYNE**'s naval shipyards at the end of the 1980s took a heavy toll on this industrial working-class community. However, it reverted to its old red colours by electing a communist mayor when Toulon voted for the *Front National*. The **Musée Naval du Fort Balaguier** on bd Bonaparte (mid-June to mid-Sept Tues–Sun 10am–noon & 3–7pm; mid-Sept to mid-June Tues–Sun 10am–noon & 2–6pm; €2) explores La Seyne's long association with naval history. In 1793, after Royalists had handed Toulon over to the British and Spanish fleet, the

British set up a line of immensely secure fortifications between this fort and the fort now known as **Fort Napoleon**, a kilometre or so inland from the museum on chemin Marc Sangnier. Despite its ability to rain down artillery on any attacker, Fort Balaguier was taken by a Captain Bonaparte with a bunch of volunteers, who sent the enemies of revolutionary France packing, though not before they burnt the arsenal, the remaining French ships and part of the town. Fort Napoleon now houses a cultural centre and gallery, which occasionally hosts excellent contemporary art exhibitions; for details, check with La Seyne's **tourist office**, on corniche Georges Pompidou in Les Sablettes (summer Mon–Sat 9am–7pm, Sun 10am–12.30pm & 3.30–7pm; winter Mon–Sat 9am–12.30pm & 2–6pm; ⓣ04.98.00.25.70, ⓦwww.ot-la-seyne-sur-mer.fr).

Between Fort Balaguier and the sand spit of Les Sablettes is the shoreline of the peaceful former resort of **Tamaris**, with its rickety wooden jetties and fishing huts on stilts overlooking the mussel beds of the Baie du Lazaret. The beautiful oriental building on the front, now the Institut Michel Pacha Marine Physiology Institute, was constructed in the nineteenth century by a local who had made his fortune in Turkey.

At **Les Sablettes** you can lounge on the south-facing beach; beyond the neck of sand is the little port of **SAINT-MANDRIER-SUR-MER**, sandwiched between the high walls of *terrain militaire*, where you can look across the harbour, past all the battleships, to the grim metropolis.

Mont Faron

Aside from the harbour boat trips, the best way to pass an afternoon in Toulon is to leave the town 542m below you and ascend to the summit of **Mont Faron**. By road, av Emile Fabre to the northwest of the centre becomes rte du Faron, snaking up to the top and descending again from the northeast, a journey of 18km in all. The road is a one-way, narrow slip of tarmac with no barriers on the cliff-edge hairpin bends, looping up and down through luscious vegetation. To reach the summit as the crow flies, take bus #40 (direction Super Toulon or Mas du Faron; stop Téléphérique) to bd Amiral-Vence where a **cable car** operates (daily 9.30am–noon & 2–5.30pm; ⓣ04.94.92.68.25; €5.80 return; closed mid-Nov to early Feb and in poor weather); it's a bit pricey but a treat.

At the top of Mont Faron there's a **memorial museum** to the Allied landings in Provence of August 1944 (May & June Tues–Sun 9.45am–12.45pm & 2–6pm; July–Sept daily 9.45am–12.45pm & 1.45–6.30pm; Oct–April Tues–Sun 9.45am–12.45pm & 2–5.45pm; €3.80), with screenings of original newsreel footage. In the surrounding park are two restaurants, and a little further up to the right, a **zoo** (daily 2–4.30pm; ⓣ04.94.88.07.89; €7) specializing in big cats. Beyond the zoo you can walk up the hillside to an abandoned fort and revel in the cleanliness of the air, the smell of the flowers and the views beyond the city way below.

Eating and drinking

Toulon's best rewards are mainly in **eating**. There are plenty of brasseries, cafés and restaurants along the quayside, some selling just sandwiches, others offering seafood-based fixed menus for under €10. Toulon's oldest restaurant, *Au Sourd*, 10 rue Molière, in the Vieille Ville (ⓣ04.94.92.28.52; closed Mon, Sun eve & most of July), specializes in fish dishes including bouillabaisse, and has a good menu at €23, with main courses à la carte from €12–40. Good couscous can be enjoyed at *Chez Mimi*, 83 av de la République (ⓣ04.94.92.79.60; closed Wed), for around €12. North of bd Strasbourg, close to the opera and in an area with several pizza restaurants, the *Pizzeria Stromboli*, 40 rue Picot (☎04.94.62.44.02; closed Sun), stands out, serving pizzas and pasta until midnight with a €10 lunch menu. The littoral Frédéric-Mistral in Le Mourillon is chock-a-block with restaurants; try *Brasserie La Corniche* in the *Hotel La Corniche* at no. 17 (☎04.94.41.10.04; closed Sat, Sun eve & Mon), which serves good-value *plateaux de fruits de mer* and Bandol wines, with menus from €12. The hotel also has a more upmarket restaurant, with menus from €32.

East towards Hyères

Beyond Le Mourillon to the east, Toulon merges with **LE PRADET** where old houses with lovely gardens are shaded by pines above the cliffs leading to the **Pointe de Carqueiranne**. A path follows the coast all the way round the headland to Carqueiranne and steep steps lead down to beaches which are crowded during the day but lovely in the evening as they catch the sun setting over Toulon's harbour. At Plage de la Garonne, 10km east of Toulon (bus #23 or #39 to Flamencq, then #91 to La Garonne), the terrace **restaurant** *L'Adventure* (☎04.94.21.72.27) serves up Provençal specialities accompanied by panoramic sea views.

Past Pointe de Carquieranne, between Pointe du Bau Rouge and the D559, the chemin du Bau Rouge crosses the side of a hill guarded by two old forts with views of the Presqu'Ile de Giens and the Île de Porquerolles (see p.239). Along this road you'll also find the **Musée de la Mine de Cap Garonne** (July & Aug daily 2–5.30pm; Sept–June Wed, Sat & Sun 2–5pm; €6.20), with its treasure trove of semi-precious minerals, including malachite, azurite and cyanotrichite. There's also an exhibition on the history of the miners themselves.

If you're **cycling** from Toulon to Hyères there's a proper track running beside the D559.

Travel details

Trains

Aix TGV to: Paris (7 daily; 3hr).

Aix to: Briançon (3 daily; 3hr 30min); Château-Arnoux-St Auban (4–5 daily; 1hr–1hr 15min); Marseille (hourly; 40min); Manosque/Gréoux Bains (5–6 daily; 40–50min); Meyrargues (13–16 daily; 15–20min); Sisteron (4–5 daily; 1hr 15min–1hr 20min).

Aubagne to: Bandol (15–23 daily; 30 min); Cassis (15–23 daily; 8 min); La Ciotat (15–23 daily; 15 min); Marseille (18–30 daily; 15–20min); Toulon (15–23 daily; 40–45 min).

Marseille to: Aix (approx every 30min; 35–40min); Arles (21–33 daily; 45min); Aubagne (approx every 30min at peak times; 15–20min); Avignon (approx 15 daily; 1hr 10min); Bandol (26 daily; 35–50 min); Cannes (frequent; 2hr–2hr 15min); Carry-le-Rouet (11 daily; 25min); Cassis (16–24 daily; 21min); Cavaillon (1–3 daily; 1hr 15min); Hyères (2–4 daily; 1hr 20–1hr 30min); Istres (7–11 daily; 1hr); L'Estaque (10–16 daily; 10–15min); La Ciotat (17–26 daily; 30min); La Couronne (7–11 daily; 32min); La Redonne-Ensués (7–11 daily; 20min); La Seyne-Six Fours (16–24 daily; 50 min); Les Arcs-Draguignan (14–18 daily; 1hr 15min–2hr); Lyon (8–18 daily; 3hr 30min); Martigues (7–11 daily; 40min); Menton (3 daily; 3hr–3hr 20min); Miramas (approx every 15min at peak times; 30min–1hr 20min); Nice (20–22 daily; 2hr 40min); Niolon (4–6 daily; 15–20min); Ollioules-Sanary (16–24 daily; 50min); Paris (TGV: 18 daily; 3hr 15min); St-Chamas (3–5 daily; 40min); St Cyr/Les-Lecques (16–24 daily; 30–35min); St-Raphaël (20–22 daily; 1hr 45min); Salon (2–3 daily; 50–55min); Sausset-les-Pins (7–11 daily; 25–30min); Tarascon (2–3 daily; 1hr); Toulon (every 20min at peak times; 45min–1hr 5min).

Miramas to: Arles (15–18 daily; 20min); Avignon (13–15 daily; 35min); Marseille (approx every 15min at peak times; 40min–1hr 20min).

Salon to: Avignon (5–7 daily; 40–55min); Marseille (2–3 daily; 45–55min); Miramas (8–13 daily; 10–30min).

Toulon to: Marseille (every 15 min at peak times; 45min–1hr 5min).

Buses (Sundays and holidays reduced services)

Aix TGV to: Aix (every 30min; 15min); Digne-les-Bains (3 daily; 1 hr 45min).
Aix to: Apt (2 daily; 1hr 50min); Arles (4 daily; 1hr 30min); Avignon (6–7 daily; 1hr 15min); Bandol (2 daily in summer; 1hr); Beaureceuil (5 daily; 25 min); Brignoles (2 daily; 55min–1hr 5min); Cabriès (7 daily; 30min); Carpentras (2–3 daily; 1hr 25min–1hr 40min); Cavaillon (2 daily; 1hr); La Ciotat (9 daily; 1hr 5min–1hr 30min); Martigue (7 daily; 1hr 10min–1hr 30min); Marseille (every 5 min at peak times; 30–50min); Nice (5 daily; 2hr 15min–3hr 30min); St-Cyr (2 daily in summer; 1hr); St-Maximin (2 daily; 30–40min); Salon (23 daily; 35–45min); Sanary (2 daily in summer; 1hr 15min); Sisteron (4 daily; 1hr 55min); Six-Fours (2 daily in summer; 1hr 30min); Toulon (6 daily; 1hr 15min).
Aubagne to: Aix (8 daily; 40min); Bandol (8 daily; 1hr); Brignoles (9 daily; 1hr 10min–1hr 20min); Cassis (9 daily; 30min); Gémenos (hourly Mon-Sat; 20min); La Ciotat (8 daily; 50min) Marseille (9 daily; 30–40min); St-Maximin (9 daily; 50 min–1hr).
Marseille to: Aix (every 5min at peak times; 30–50min); Arles (5 daily; 2hr 10min–2hr 20min); Aubagne (7 daily; 30min); Bandol (6 daily; 1hr 30min); Barcelonnette (3 daily; 3hr 30min–4hr 45min); Brignoles (7 daily; 1hr 45min); Carpentras (2–3 daily; 2hr 5min–2hr 20min); Carry le Rouet (3 daily; 40min); Cassis (7 daily; 50min); Digne (4 daily; 2hr 10min–2hr 50min); Draguignan (3 daily; 3 hr 20min); Forcalquier (2 daily; 1hr 50min–2hr); Gémenos (4 daily; 45min); Grenoble (1 daily; 4hr); La Ciotat (8 daily; 1hr); Les Lecques (4 daily; 1hr 15min–1hr 30min); Manosque (9 daily; 1hr 5min–1hr 25min); Martigues (hourly; 45–50 min); St-Chamas (3 daily; 1hr 20min); St-Maximin (7 daily; 1hr 20min–1 hr 30min); Salon (5 daily; 1hr 5min–1hr 30min); Sisteron (4 daily; 1hr 40min–2hr 25min).
Martigues to: Aix (6 daily; 1hr 25min); Istres (5 daily; 35min–1hr 5min); Marseille (13 daily; 45 min–1hr); Salon (5 daily; 1hr 30min).
Salon to: Aix (20 daily; 35–55min); Arles (11 daily; 50min–1hr 10min); Eyguières (7 daily; 15min); Istres (6 daily; 35min); La Barben (2 daily; 20min); Les Baux (4 daily; 30–40min); Marseille (8 daily; 1hr 10min–1hr 20min); Martigues (6 daily; 1hr 35min); Miramas (6 daily; 20min).
Toulon to: Aix (4 daily; 1hr 15min); Bandol (every 30min; 1hr); Brignoles (6 daily; 1hr 30min); Draguignan (5 daily; 2hr 10min); Hyères (every 45min; 30–40min); Le Brusc (6–7 daily; 25min); Le Pradet (every 30min; 20min); Méounes (2 daily; 50min); Nice (2 daily; 2hr 30min); St-Maximin (1 daily; 1hr 40min); St-Raphaël (4 daily; 2hr); St Tropez (8 daily; 2hr–2hr 10min); Sanary (every 30min; 35–45min); Signes (2 daily; 1hr 15min); Six-Fours (frequent; 25min)

Ferries

Marseille to: Corsica (4–6 daily in summer; 12hr).
Toulon to: Corsica (1 weekly; 8hr).

Flights

Marseille to: Paris (18 daily; 1hr 20min).

The Côte d'Azur: Hyères to the Esterel

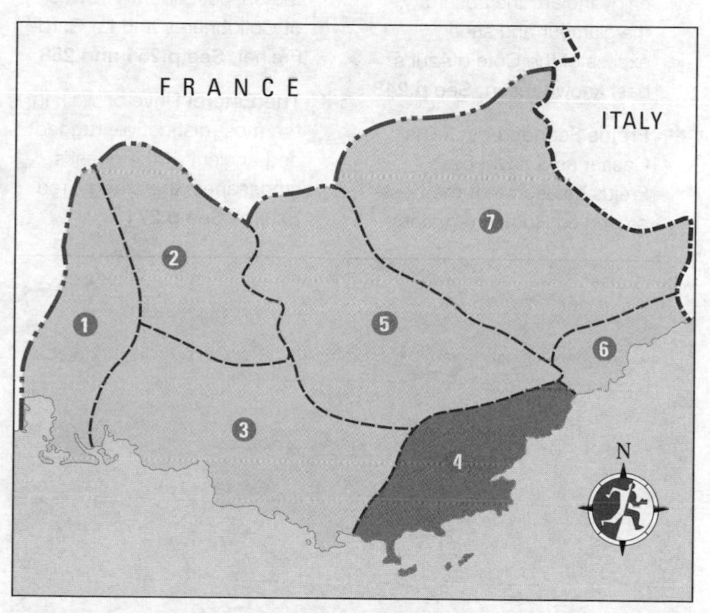

CHAPTER 4

Highlights

* **The island of Port-Cros** Take a glass-bottomed boat to explore the fascinating marine life off France's smallest national park. **See p.241**

* **St-Tropez** Suspend your cynicism for one day and enjoy the art, the absurdity, the glamour and sheer excess of the Côte d'Azur's best known resort. **See p.248**

* **Fréjus** Founded by Julius Caesar as a naval base, Fréjus has some of the best-preserved Roman remains along this coast, including a theatre, an amphitheatre and the ruins of a Roman aqueduct. **See p.264**

* **Massif des Maures** Escape the glitz and development of the coast to explore the sombre wooded hills, and the unspoilt country towns of Collobrières and La Garde Freinet. **See p.254 and 258**

* **The Esterel** Drive or walk in the most distinctive, rugged and ancient of the coast's landscapes, the craggy, red Esterel. **See p.271**

The Côte d'Azur: Hyères to the Esterel

The **Côte d'Azur** is the most desirable and, at times, the most detestable stretch of Mediterranean coast. The glimmering rocks along its shore and the translucent sea, the February mimosa blossom, the springtime scents of pine and eucalyptus or the golden autumn chestnut crop and reddening vines all combine with the Mediterranean light to create a sensual magic landscape. It can still cast the spell that attracted the Impressionist and Post-Impressionist painters over a hundred years ago – whose work can be seen at St-Tropez – as well as their bohemian successors, and the 1950s film world. But in summer it also has the worst traffic jams and public transport, the most crowded quaysides, campsites and hitching queues, the most short-tempered locals – and outrageous prices.

Unlike the Riviera further east, or the Toulon-Marseille stretch to the west, the Côte d'Azur proper is off the main routes and has no major cities. Between the largest town, Hyères, and the conurbation of St-Raphaël-Fréjus, lies a string of fishing villages turned resorts. Pre-eminent among them is **St-Tropez**, or 'St-Trop' as its aficionados like to call it, a brand name for sea, sun, celebrity and sex.

There's such a tangle of small resorts that it's sometimes hard to distinguish one from another; but in **Cavalière**, **Pramousquier**, **Le Rayol** with its fabulous **garden**, and **Le Trayas** you can get glimpses of how this coast all once looked. There are even stretches which have held out against the construction mania altogether, including the section west of **Cap Bregançon**, the southern end of **St-Tropez**'s **peninsula**, little snatches of the **Corniches des Maures**, and along the **Corniche d'Esterel** west of Le Trayas, below the dramatic red volcanic crags of the **Massif d'Esterel**. For real coastal wilderness though, you need to head out to sea to the gorgeous **Îles d'Hyères**.

Hyères, which attracted foreign visitors in the eighteenth century, while Cannes was still a fishing village, thrives on its horticulture as much as on its tourism and is an affordable place to stay. **Fréjus** is the most historical of the major towns, dating back to Roman times; its neighbour **St-Raphaël** ignores its ancient origins, and dedicates itself to holiday-makers, with rooms and food for every budget.

Inland, the dark wooded hills of the **Massif des Maures** form a backdrop east to St-Raphaël. Hidden amid the sweet-chestnut trees and cork oaks are

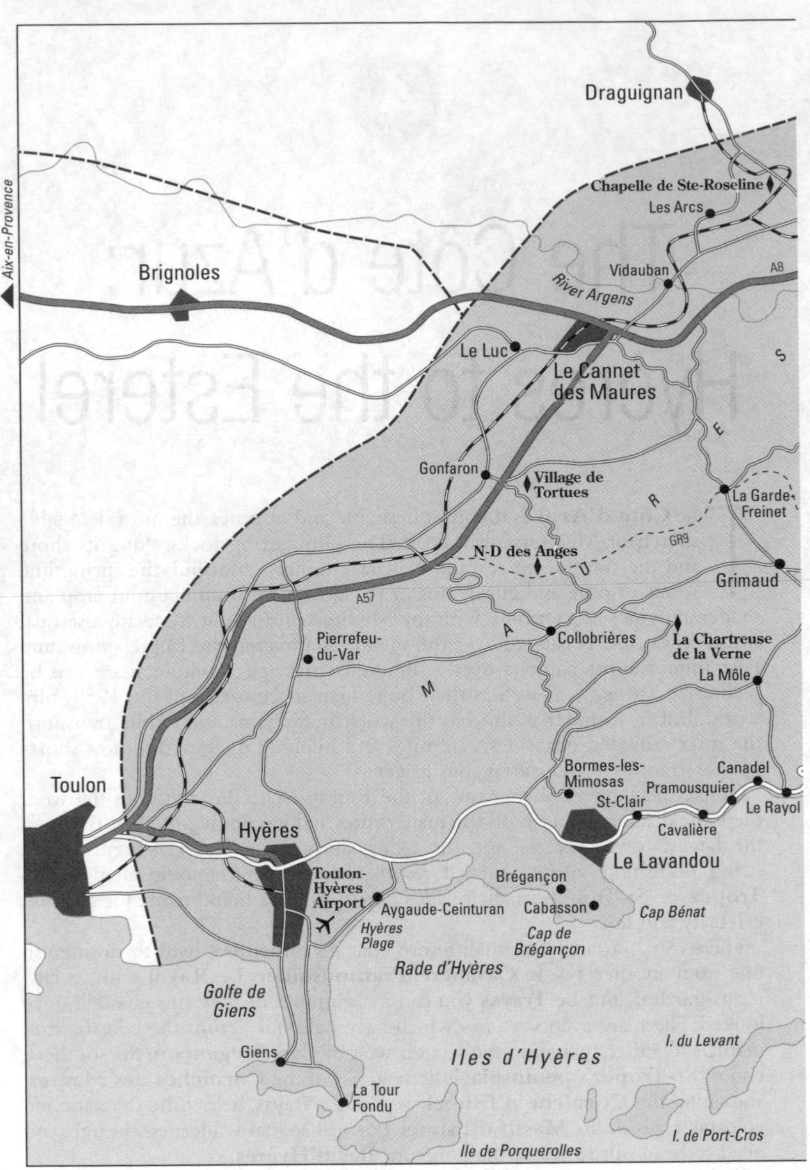

ancient monasteries and medieval villages. **Collobrières** and **La Garde-Freinet** have not forsaken traditional livelihoods and carry on their wine, cork and chestnut businesses beyond the tourist season, while on the Massif's eastern edge **Grimaud** and **Rocquebrune** provide exclusive second homes for the more discerning Côte clientele.

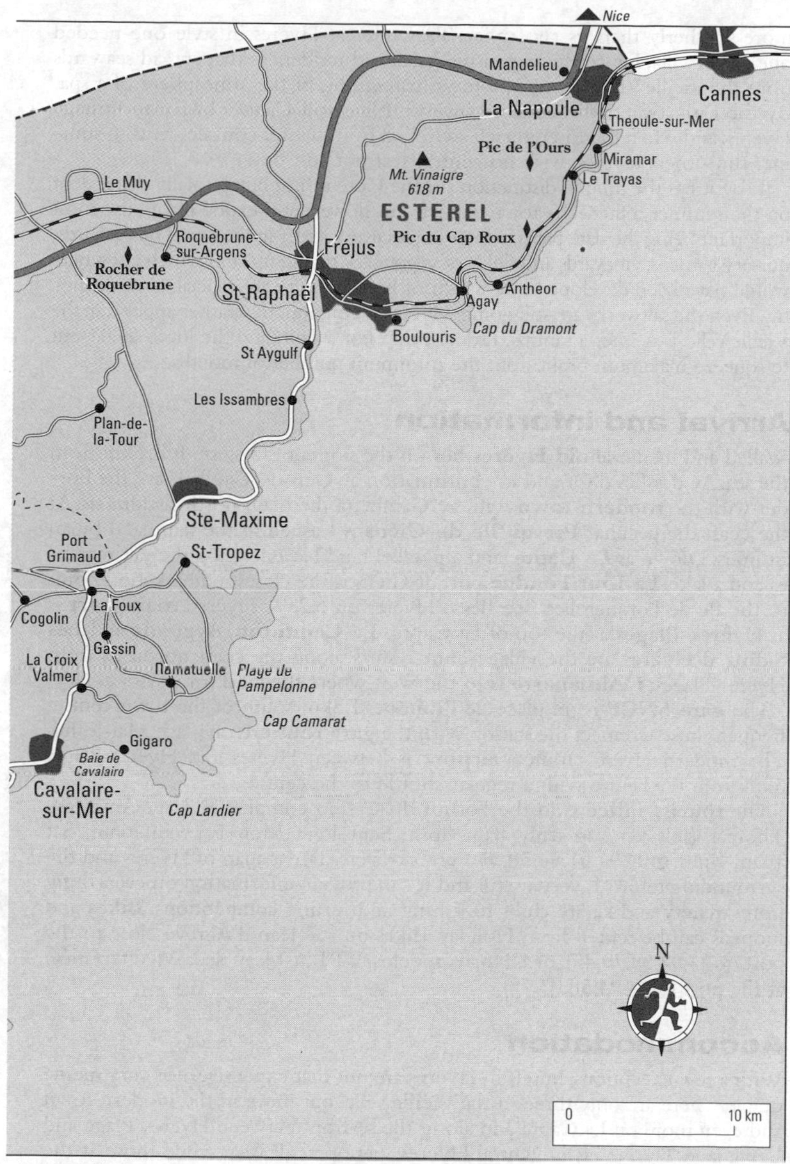

Hyères

HYÈRES is the oldest resort of the Côte d'Azur, listing among its pre-twentieth-century admirers Empress Joséphine, Queen Victoria, Tolstoy and Robert Louis Stevenson. It was particularly popular with the British, being closer, and more southerly, than its rival Nice. To winter at Hyères in style one needed one's own villa, hence the expansive gardened residences that spread seawards from the Vieille Ville, giving the town something of the atmosphere of a spa. By the early twentieth century, however, Nice and Cannes began to upstage Hyères, and when the foreign rich switched from winter convalescents to summer sunbathers Hyères, with no central seafront, lost out.

Today it has the unique distinction on the Côte of not being totally dependent on the summer influx. The town exports cut flowers and exotic plants, the most important being the date palm, which graces every street in the city. The orchards, nursery gardens, vineyards and fields of vegetables, taking up land which elsewhere would have been developed into a rash of holiday units, are crucial to its economy. Even the saltworks are still going. Hyères is consequently rather appealing: the Vieille Ville is neither a sanitized tourist trap nor a slum and the locals aren't out to squeeze maximum profit from the minimum number of months.

Arrival and information

Walled and medieval **old Hyères** lies on the slopes of Casteou hill, 5km from the sea. Av des Îles d'Or and its continuation av Gén-de-Gaulle mark the border with the **modern town** with av Gambetta the main north-south axis. At the coast the peculiar **Presqu'Île de Giens** is leashed to the mainland by an isthmus, known as **La Capte**, and a parallel sand bar enclosing the salt marshes and a lake. **La Tour Fondue** port at Giens is the closest embarkation point to the Île de Porquerolles (see Îles d'Hyères on p.239); Hyères' **main port** is at **Hyères-Plages** at the top of La Capte. **Le Ceinturon**, **Ayguade** and **Les Salins d'Hyères** are the village-cum-resorts along the coast northeast from Hyères-Plages; **L'Almanarre** is to the west where the sand bar starts.

The **gare SNCF** is on place de l'Europe, 1.5km south of the town centre; frequent buses connect the station with the **gare routière** on place Mal-Joffre. The modern Hyères-Toulon **airport** is between Hyères and Hyères-Plage, 3km from the centre with a regular shuttle to the centre.

The **tourist office** is in the Forum du Casino complex at 3 ave Ambroise Thomas (July & Aug daily 8am–8pm; Sept–June Mon–Fri 9am–6pm, Sat 10am–4pm; ⓣ04.94.01.84.50, ⓦwww.ot-hyeres.fr). Its map of Hyères and the surrounding resorts is very useful and it can provide information on everything from archery and karate clubs to fishing and surfing competitions. **Bikes** and mopeds can be rented from Holiday Bikes on rue Jean d'Agrève close to the port (ⓣ04.94.38.79.45), or L'Horizon Vélos-VTT at 14, av. de la Méditerranée, at the port (ⓣ04.94.58.03.78).

Accommodation

With a few exceptions, hotels in Hyères are not that expensive, nor very memorable. There are only three in the Vieille Ville, but more in the modern town and even more on La Capte and along the seafront between Hyères-Plage and L'Ayguade. The hotels in central Hyères stay open all year, while those at the coast tend to close for the winter.

Hotels

Le Calypso 36 av de la Méditerranée, Hyères-Plage ⓣ 04.94.58.02.09; ⓔOlivier.tillie@wanadoo.fr; closed Dec & Jan. A small hotel in a quiet, suburban location near the sea. ❷

Casino des Palmiers 1 av Ambroise Thomas ⓣ04.94.12.80.80, ⓕ04.94.12.80.94. Staying at the casino itself may be fun and it *is* the swishest hotel in town, though it's a modern building and rather lacking in atmosphere. ❼

Les Orangers 64 av des Îles d'Or

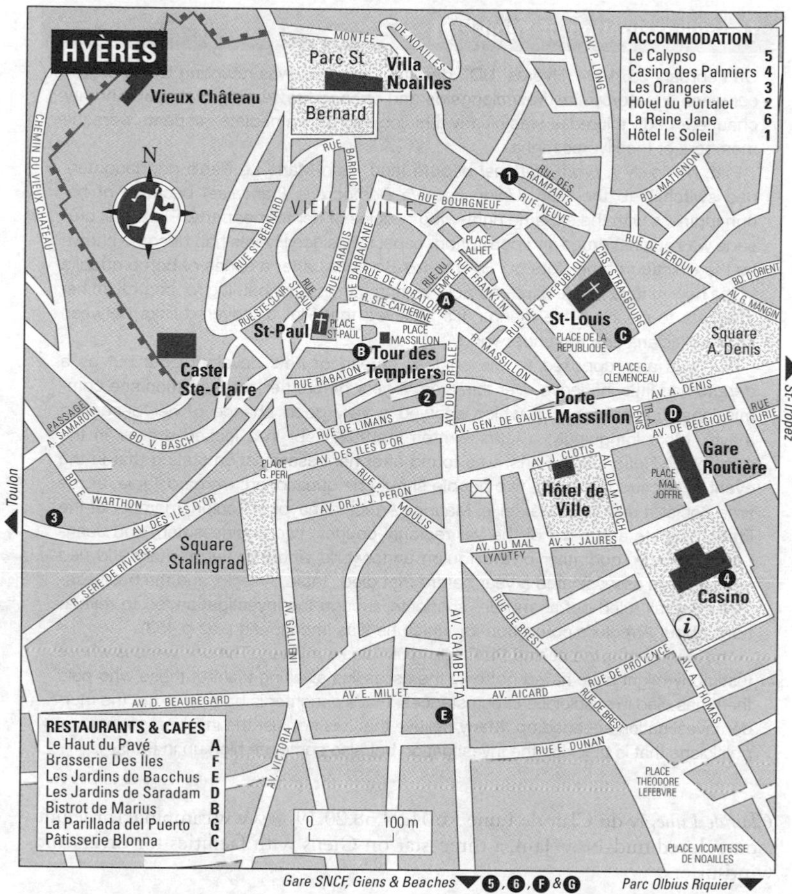

☎04.94.00.55.11, ©orangers@infonie.fr. This pleasant small hotel is situated in an attractive villa district, west of the modern centre. It has an attractive garden and terrace. ❸

Hôtel du Portalet 4 rue de Limans ☎04.94.65.39.40, ©chbenit@oreka.com. In the lower, and busier, part of the old town, this hotel has TVs in all the rooms and accepts pets. ❷

La Reine Jane le port de l'Ayguade ☎04.94.66.32.64, ©reine.jane@wanadoo.fr; closed Jan. Overlooking the port at Ayguade, this is a friendly place with a restaurant, bar and terrace to make up for its out-of-town location. ❻

Hôtel le Soleil rue du Rempart ☎04.94.65.16.26, ⓦwww.hoteldusoleil.com. Well positioned in the Vieille Ville, high up at the foot of parc St-Bernard, this popular hotel is not particularly cheap in summer, but offers better value outside high season. ❶

Campsites

There are plenty of **campsites** on Presqu'Île de Giens, La Capte and all along the coast, some of them housing over a thousand pitches. Some of the smaller, more pleasant ones include the two-star *Camping-Bernard*, close to the beach in Le Ceinturon (☎04.94.66.30.54, ⓕ04.94.66.48.30; closed Oct–Easter); *Le Capricorne* on rte des Vieux Salins, 1.5km from the beach at Les Salins (☎04.94 .66.40.94, ⓦsite.voila.fr/capricorne; closed Oct–March), also a two-star; and

The assassination of Yann Piat

On February 25, 1994, Hyères' UDF député, Yann Piat, was returning to the city by car when a motorcyclist drew alongside and opened fire, leaving Piat dead and her chauffeur badly injured. It was clearly a hit job and the immediate suspects were the members of the Hyères mafia.

Piat, originally a *Front National député* (and Jean-Marie Le Pen's goddaughter), had switched to the UDF (*Union pour la Démocratie Française*) because of her unhappiness with the extreme right-wing policies of her former party. Piat's real crusade was against drugs and corruption, especially since Hyères had become known as the Chicago of the Côte or "Hyères-les-Bombes" after a series of bomb attacks in the new marina where different racketeering gangs were battling for control. In her attempts to clean up the marina, it's believed that Piat discovered links between local politicians and the underworld.

Piat was also opposed to the endless spread of new developments but as a *député* had little influence over this area. A year before her assassination she commissioned an opinion poll which showed a very good chance of her becoming mayor. More intriguingly, a letter written in 1992, kept in a locked drawer in the Assemblée Nationale in Paris, was found after her assassination stating that in the event of her sudden death, five people should be questioned: Bernard Tapie, at the time Socialist *député* in Marseille; Maurice Arreckx, mayor of Toulon, member of the French senate and head of the Var regional council; two businessmen; and Jean-Louis Fargette, godfather of the Toulon underworld who had fled to Italy and had himself been assassinated a year before Piat died. Tapie, Arreckx and the businessmen were all ruled out as murder suspects, though the investigation led to revelations about Arreckx's corruption for which he was imprisoned (see p.453).

The identity of those behind Piat's killing remains a mystery. The one witness whose testimony might have nailed not only the assassins awaiting trial but those who paid them has died in suspicious circumstances. Piat's daughter is battling to get the murder investigation speeded up. Many believe that it is not just the involvement of local politicians that is blocking the investigation but also someone high up in Paris.

Clair de Lune, av du Clair de Lune (ⓣ04.94.58.20.19, ⓦwww.campingclairdelune.com; closed mid-Nov–Jan), a three-star on Giens with facilities for divers and windsurfers.

The Vieille Ville

To the west of place Clemenceau a medieval gatehouse, **Porte Massillon**, opens onto rue Massillon and the Vieille Ville. At **place Massillon**, you encounter a perfect Provençal square, with terraced cafés looking onto the twelfth-century **Tour des Templiers** (April–Oct Wed–Sun 10am–noon & 3–7pm; Nov–March 10am–noon & 2–5.30pm; free), the remnant of a Knights Templar lodge. The tower now houses contemporary art exhibitions, though these are frequently less impressive than their dramatic setting: don't miss the narrow staircase that leads up onto the roof for a bird's-eye view of the medieval centre. Behind the tower, rue Ste-Catherine leads uphill to place St-Paul, from where you have another panoramic view over a section of medieval town wall to Costabelle hill and the Golfe de Giens. It is round here, where the crumbly lanes are festooned with bougainvillea, wisteria and yuccas, that the real charm of the Vieille Ville begins to be apparent.

Dominating the square is the former collegiate church of **St-Paul** (April–Sept Tues–Sun 10am–noon & 4–7pm; Oct–March Wed–Sun 10am–noon & 2–5.30pm), whose wide steps fan out from a Renaissance door.

Its distinctive belfry is pure Romanesque, as is the choir, though the simplicity of the design is masked by the collection of votive offerings hung inside. The decoration also includes some splendid wrought-iron candelabras and a Christmas crib with over-life-size *santons*. Today, the church is used only for special services – the main place of worship is the mid-thirteenth-century former monastery church of **St-Louis** on place de la République.

To the right of St-Paul's, a Renaissance house bridges rue St-Paul, its turret supported by a pillar rising beside the steps. Through this arch you can reach rue St-Claire which leads past the neo-Gothic Porte des Princes to the entrance of **parc Ste-Claire** (daily 8am–dusk; free), the exotic gardens around **Castel Ste-Clair**. Now housing the offices of the Parc National de Port Cros, the castle was originally owned by the French archeologist Olivier Voutier (who discovered the Venus de Milo), before becoming home to the American writer Edith Wharton.

Back at St-Paul's church, if you follow rue Paradis north, you'll pass an exquisite Romanesque house at no. 6, before reaching the **Porte Barruc**. At the side of the *porte* you can ascend to **parc St-Bernard** (8am–dusk; free), an enjoyable warren full of almost every Mediterranean flower known. At the top of the park, along montée des Noailles – which can be reached by car from cours de Strasbourg and rue Long – is the **Villa Noailles**, an angular Cubist mansion designed by Mallet-Stevens in the 1920s, with gardens enclosed by part of the old citadel walls. All the luminarics of Dada and Surrealism stayed here and left their mark, including Man Ray who used it as the setting for one of his most inarticulate films, *Le Mystère du Château de Dé*. The villa is currently being restored, and is only open to the public during the various exhibitions that it hosts throughout the year (Mon & Wed–Sun 10am–noon & 2–5.30pm during exhibitions; free).

To the west of the park and further up the hill you come to the remains of Hyères' **Vieux Château** (daily 9am–noon & 2–5pm, but currently restricted due to restoration work), whose keep and ivy-clad towers outreach the oak and lotus trees and give stunning views out to the Îles d'Hyères and east to the Massif des Maures.

The modern town

The switch from medieval to eighteenth- and nineteenth-century Hyères is particularly abrupt, with wide boulevards and open spaces, opulent villas, waving palm fronds and stuccoed walls marking the modern town. Most of the former aristocratic residences and grand hotels now have more prosaic functions, though the **casino** (daily 10am–4pm), south of the gare routière, is still in use. Unfortunately its elegant beaux arts exterior and interior have lost much of their original character due to some crude modernization, and the current gloomy interior will disappoint all but the most hardened gamblers.

South of the casino, at the bottom of av Olbius Riquier, is Hyères' botanic garden, the **Parc Olbius Riquier** (Jan–March 7.30am–6pm; April, May & Sept 7.30am–7pm; June–Aug 7.30am–8pm; Nov & Dec 7.30am–5pm; free), which opened in 1868. Pride of place is given to the palms, of which there are 28 varieties, plus yuccas, agaves and bamboos. There's a hothouse full of exotics including banana, strelitzia, hibiscus and orchids, and a small zoo and miniature train to keep children amused.

Down to the coast

There are plenty of beaches around Hyères' coastal suburbs, though mosquitoes can be a problem, so bring insect repellent just in case. The eastern side of

La Capte, the built-up isthmus of the **Presqu'Île de Giens**, is one long sand beach, with very warm and shallow water, and gets packed out in summer. To the northeast, traffic fumes and proximity to the airport detract from the charms of the seaside between Hyères-Plage and Le Ceinturon, despite the pines and ubiquitous palms. It's far more pleasant further up by the little fishing port of **Les Salins d'Hyères**. East of Les Salins, where the coastal road finally turns inland, you can follow a path between abandoned salt flats and the sea to a naturist beach.

Alternatively, there's the less sheltered **L'Almanarre** beach to the west of the Presqu'Île de Giens, where you can swim from a narrow crescent of sand: the French sailing championships are sometimes held here, and it's a popular surfers' hangout, too. L'Almanarre is also the site of the ancient Greek town of **Olbia**, whose ruins you can wander round today (April–June 9.30am–12.30pm & 2.30–7pm; July–Sept 9.30am–12.30pm & 3–7pm; €4). Founded in the fourth century BC on a small knoll by the sea, Olbia was a maritime trading post, and excavations here have revealed Greek and Roman remains, including baths, temples and homes, plus parts of the medieval abbey of St-Pierre de L'Almanarre.

South of L'Almanarre, the route du Sel (closed to cars mid-Nov to mid-April) leads down the sand bar on the western side of the Presqu'Île, giving you glimpses of the saltworks and the lake with its flamingoes, that lies between the sand bar and the built-up La Capte. At the far end of the sand bar sits the placid suburban seaside resort of Giens, with its **Tour Fondue**, a Richelieu construction on the eastern side, overlooking the small port that serves the Îles d'Hyères.

Regular **buses** from Hyères' gare routière run to Giens, L'Almanarre, Hyères-Plage and Le Ceinturon.

Eating, drinking and markets

The best places to eat and drink in Hyères are the terraced **café-brasseries** in and around place Massillon, where you'll also find a good choice of crêperies, pizzerias and little bistros that serve plats du jour for €10–15. **Restaurants** worth trying include *Le Haut du Pavé*, 2 rue du Temple (☎04.94.35.20.98; menus €15 & €21; closed Mon), with live jazz in the basement; the more upmarket *Bistrot de Marius*, 1 pl Massillon (☎04.94.35.88.38; closed Mon and Tues, menus at €15, €23 & €30), which serves excellent *soupe de poisson*; and *Les Jardins de Bacchus*, on the edge of the new town at 32 av Gambetta (☎04.94.65.77.63; menus from €31), where you can try novel concoctions such as caramelized pears on salmon with prawns and bacon. Alternatively, *Les Jardins de Saradam*, opposite the gare routière at 35 av de Belgique (☎04.94.65.97.53; around €20), is a pretty North African restaurant serving reasonable *brik*, *tagines* and *couscous*. Down at the port, *La Parillada del Puerto* (☎04.94.57.44.82; menus from €19; closed Nov to mid-March) specializes in Spanish dishes based on fresh fish, while the swish *Brasserie Des Îles* (☎04.94.57.49.75) has menus from €23 and a big *plateau de fruits de mer* for €34. For the best **cakes and ice creams**, try *Pâtisserie Blonna* at 1 place Clemenceau (closed Mon).

A food **market** takes place on place de la République on Tuesday and Thursday mornings and along av Gambetta on Saturday morning, while organic produce is sold on place Vicomtesse de Noailles on Tuesday, Thursday and Saturday mornings. There's also a food market at Giens on Tuesdays, at Ayguade on Wednesday mornings, at Les Salins on Thursdays, and in La Capte on Friday mornings. Back in Hyères, there's a flea market along av des Îles d'Or on Saturday mornings.

The Îles d'Hyères

Originally a haven from tempests in ancient times, then the peaceful habitat of monks and farmers, in the Middle Ages the **Îles d'Hyères** (also known as the Îles d'Or) became a base for piracy and coastal attacks by a relentless succession of aggressors, against whom the few islanders were powerless. In 1550, Henri II tried to solve the problem by turning the islands into penal colonies, but unfortunately the convicts themselves turned to piracy, even attempting to capture a ship of the royal fleet from Toulon. Forts were built all over the islands from the sixteenth century onwards, when François I started a trend of underfunded fort building, to the twentieth century, when the German gun positions on Port-Cros and Levant were knocked out by the Americans. Some of the forts exist to this day, with a few having been rebuilt, others left half-destroyed or abandoned.

The military presence remains, too, thanks to the habit of the French armed forces of acquiring prime beauty sites for their bases. This has at least prevented the otherwise inevitable development, and in the non-military areas the Parc National de Port-Cros and the Conservatoire Botanique de **Porquerolles** have been protecting and documenting the islands' rare species of wild flowers. **Port-Cros** and its small neighbour Bagaud are just about uninhabited, so the main problem there is controlling the flower-picking and litter-dropping habits of visitors. On **Levant**, the military rule all but a tiny morsel of the island.

Overall, the Îles d'Hyères are a very fragile environment, with their wild, scented greenery and fine sand beaches contrasting with the overpopulated, overdeveloped coastline nearby. A host of measures protect the islands, and in hot, dry weather some of the forest areas may well be out of bounds due to the fire risk. If you want to **stay**, the only reasonably priced options are on Levant, and then you need to book months in advance. Accommodation on Porquerolles is limited to pricey hotels and rented apartments; on Port-Cros it is almost nonexistent.

Getting to the islands

There are ferries to the Îles d'Hyères, from seven ports along the Côte d'Azur, though some services only operate in summer. Departures are from **Cavalaire** (summer only; ☎04.94.71.01.02) to Port-Cros (45min) and Porquerolles (1hr 5min); **La Croix Valmer** (summer only; ☎04.94.71.01.02) to Port-Cros (1hr) and Porquerolles (45min); **La Londe** Port de Miramar (summer only; ☎04.94.05.21.14) to Port-Cros (45min) and Porquerolles (30min); **Le Lavandou** Gare Maritime (☎04.94.71.01.02) to Île de Levant (35min–1hr), Port-Cros (35min–1hr) and Porquerolles (50min); **Port d'Hyères** (☎04.94.57.44.07) to Île de Levant (1hr 30min), Port-Cros (30min) and Porquerolles (summer only; 1hr 15min); **Toulon** quai Stalingrad (summer only; ☎04.94.92.96.82) to Porquerolles (1hr 15min); and **La Tour Fondue** Presqu'Île de Giens (☎04.94.58.21.81; bus #67 from the Port d'Hyères) to Porquerolles (20min), plus summer-only cruises in a glass-bottomed catamaran to Île de Levant and Port-Cros (4 daily; €16.50). Parking at the ferry in La Tour Fondue costs €10 daily; cheaper car parking is available further back from the port.

Porquerolles

PORQUEROLLES is the most easily accessible of the islands and has a permanent village around the port, with a few hotels and restaurants, and plenty of cafés. In summer, the island's population expands dramatically, but there is some activity year-round. This is the only cultivated island and it has its own wine, with three Côte de Provence *domaines* which can be visited.

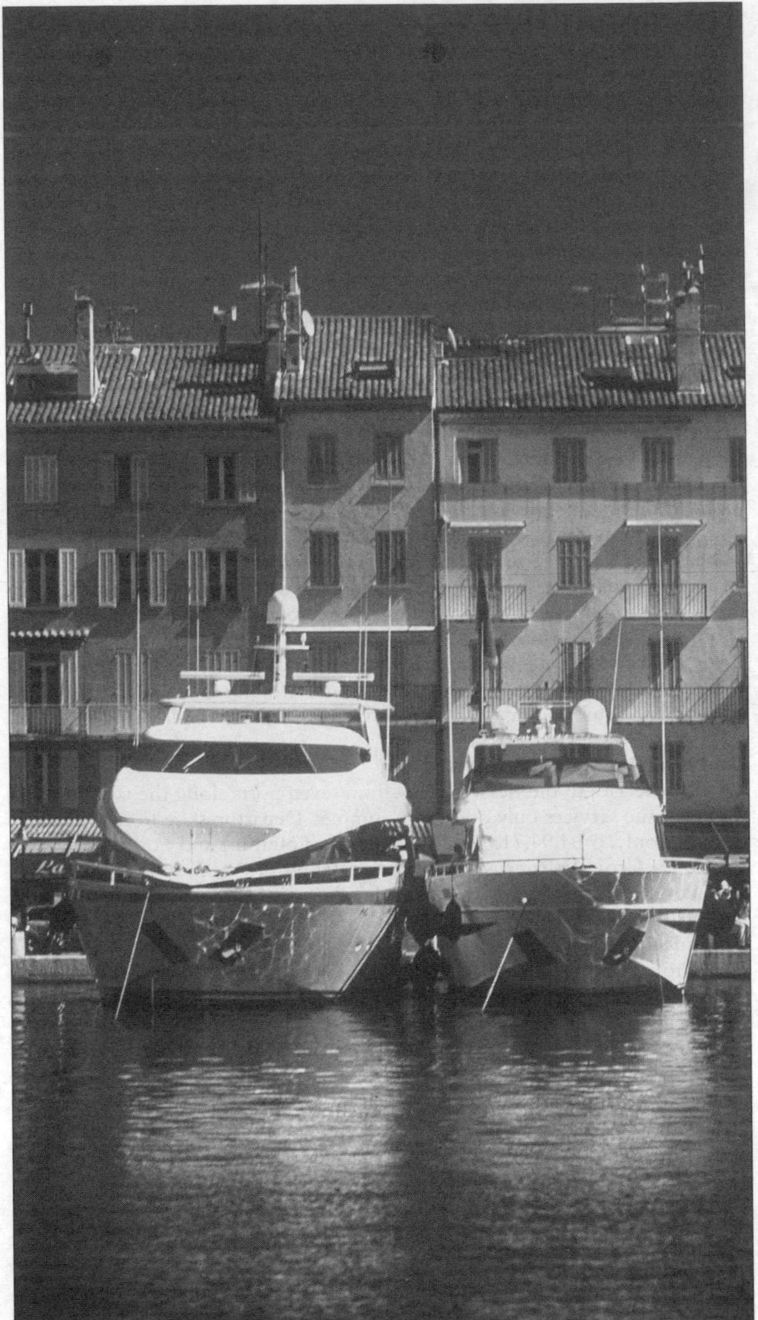

△ St-Tropez, Vieux Port

The **village of Porquerolles** began life as a nineteenth-century military settlement, with its central square, the place d'Armes, being the old parade ground. It achieved notoriety of the non-military kind in the 1960s, when Jean-Luc Godard filmed the bewildering finale of his film *Pierrot le Fou* here, as well as at the calanque de la Treille, at the far end of the plage de Notre-Dame. Overlooking the village is the ancient **Fort Sainte-Agathe**, whose origins are unknown, though evidence suggests it was already in existence by 1200, and was refortified in the sixteenth century by François I, who built a tower with five-metre-thick walls to resist cannon fire. The fort has a small **museum** (May–Sept daily 10am–noon & 2–5.30pm; €4), which traces the history of the island and the work of the national park.

Five minutes south of the village, in Le Hameau, the **Conservatoire Botanique National Méditerranéen de Porquerolles** (May to Sept 9.30am–12.30pm & 1.30–5pm; free) opens its gardens and orchards to the public to wander around. The orchards are particularly interesting, as the Conservatoire is concerned with preserving biodiversity through protecting traditional and local varieties of fruit trees. If you prefer a wilder environment, however, you're better off heading south to the **lighthouse** (July & Aug 10am–noon & 4–5pm; Sept to June by appointment with the information centre; see below) and the **calanques** to its east, both of which make good destinations for an hour's walk. Be aware, though, that it's not safe to swim on this side of the island, as the southern shoreline is all cliffs with scary paths meandering close to the edge through exuberant Provençal vegetation. The best swimming is to be found at the sandy **beaches** on either side of the village: the closest is the **plage d'Argent**, a 500-metre strip of white sand around a curving bay, backed by pine forests and a single restaurant; the longest beach is the **plage de Notre-Dame**, 3km northeast of the village.

Practicalities

There's a small **information centre** by the harbour (April–Sept daily 9am–5.30pm; Oct–March daily 9am–12.30pm; ⓣ04.94.58.33.76, ⓦwww.porquerolles.com), where you can pick up basic maps of the island. **Hotels** in Porquerolles cost upwards of €100 a night and need to be booked months in advance. The most luxurious is *Le Mas du Langoustier* (ⓣ04.94.58.30.09, ⓦwww.langoustier.com; ❾; closed Oct–April) at the western end of the island, which insists on either full or half board. More reasonable are *Les Medes* (ⓣ04.94.12.41.24, ⓦwww.hotel-les-medes.fr; ❽) on the edge of the village, and *Auberge l'Arché de Noé* (ⓣ04.94.58.33.71, ⓔauberge-arche-denoe@wanadoo.fr; ❼) on place d'Armes. There is no **campsite** and *camping sauvage* is strictly forbidden.

Most of the **cafés** and **restaurants** in the village cater for wealthier tourists, who can snack on lobster at *Le Mas du Langoustier* (lunch menus from €32). Slightly more affordable is the grilled fish at the *Auberge des Glycines* on place d'Armes (ⓣ04.94.58.30.36; menus from €16), while *La Plage d'Argent* (ⓣ04.94.58.32.48; closed Oct–March), overlooking the beach, serves decent fish lunches for €13–17.

If you fancy cycling around the island, you can rent **bikes** from one of nine outlets in the village: La Becane (ⓣ04.94.58.37.94) and L'Indien (ⓣ04.94.58.30.39) are both on the central place d'Armes.

Port-Cros

The dense vegetation and mini mountains of **PORT-CROS** make exploring this island considerably harder going than Porquerolles, even though it is less than half the size. Aside from ruined forts and a handful of buildings around the port, the only intervention on the island's wildlife is the classification labels on some of the plants and the extensive network of paths. You are not supposed to stray from these and it would be difficult to, given the thickness of the undergrowth.

With just 35 permanent residents, the island is France's smallest national park and a protected zone – smoking is forbidden outside the port area, as is picking any flowers. It's the only one of the islands with natural springs, and boasts the richest **fauna and flora**: kestrels, eagles and sparrowhawks nest here; there are shrubs that flower and bear fruit at the same time, while more common species such as broom, lavender, rosemary and heather flourish in abundance. If you come armed with a botanical dictionary, and the leaflet provided by the **Maison du Parc** (Ⓣ04.94.01.40.72) at the port, you'll have no problem spotting all the different species.

One kilometre northeast of the port is the nearest beach, the **plage de la Palud**, backed by dense vegetation. On the way to the beach, you'll find the **Fort de L'Estissac** (July–Sept 10am–6pm; free), housing an exhibition on the national park and the island's protected marine life. The best way to see some of the marine life for yourself is to take a glass-bottomed boat-trip from La Tour Fondue (see p.239 for details), though more serious divers will want to head for the island's southern shore to explore the waters round the **Ilot de la Gabinière**.

Walkers will enjoy the paths that cross the island from the port via the **Vallon de la Solitude** and **Vallon de la Fausse-Monnaie** to the cliff-bound south coast; alternatively, there's a signed ten-kilometre **circuit of the island**.

Staying on Port-Cros is, sadly, not much of an option: the only hotel, *Le Manoir d'Hélène* (Ⓣ04.94.05.90.52, Ⓕ04.94.05.90.89; closed mid-Oct to mid-April; ❾), is prohibitively expensive, as are the five rooms at the *Hostellerie Provencale* (Ⓣ04.94.05.90.43, Ⓦwww.hostellerie.provencale.com; closed Nov–Easter; ❾). The island's **restaurants** are not cheap either, though there are a few places where you can pick up a sandwich or a slice of pizza. Camping is forbidden.

Île de Levant

Ninety percent military reserve, the **ÎLE DE LEVANT** is almost always humid and sunny. Cultivated plant life goes wild with the result that giant geraniums and nasturtiums climb three-metre hedges, overhung by gigantic eucalyptus trees and yucca plants.

The tiny bit of the island spared by the military is dominated by the **nudist colony** of **Héliopolis,** founded in the early 1930s, and nudity is compulsory on the beaches of Bain de Diane and Les Grottes. About sixty people live here year-round, joined by thousands of summer visitors and many more day-trippers. The residents' preferred street dress is '*les plus petits costumes en Europe*', on sale as you get off the boat.

Visitors who come just for a few hours tend to be treated as voyeurs. If you stay, even for one night, you'll generally receive a much friendlier reception, but in summer without advance booking you'd be lucky to find a room or camping pitch. **Hotel** rooms need to be reserved well in advance. The cheapest places are the nine-roomed *La Source* (Ⓣ04.94.05.91.36, Ⓕ04.94.05.93.47; ❸; closed Nov–March), and *Les Arbousiers* (Ⓣ04.94.05.90.73; ❸), with just eight rooms. Slightly more upmarket is the small and very charming *La Brise Marine*, in the centre of the village (Ⓣ04.94.05.91.15, Ⓦwww.labrisemarine.fr; ❻). For total luxury, try the cliff-top *Le Ponant* (Ⓣ04.94.05.90.41, Ⓦwww.ponant.fr; ❾; closed Oct–May), with stunning views from its terrace, or the very smart

Héliotel (☎04.94.00.44.88, ⓦwww.heliotel.info; ❸; closed Nov–Easter), near the centre of the village, with luxuriant gardens. In addition, there are two naturist **campsites**: *Le Colombero* (☎04.94.05.90.29; €14 per tent; closed Oct–March) and *La Pinède* (☎04.94.05.92.81; €17 per tent).

Levant has a better choice of **places to eat** than the other islands, with the hotel restaurants being the best bet: *La Source* offers decent plats du jour from €9, while *La Brise Marine* has a menu at €21, served on an attractive Andalucian-style patio complete with fountain.

The Corniche des Maures

The Côte d'Azur really gets going to the east of Hyères, with the resorts of the **Corniche des Maures**, a twenty-kilometre stretch of coast from Le Lavandou to the Baie de Cavalaire; multi-million-dollar residences lurk in the hills, pricey yachts in the bays, and seafront prices start edging up. This is where the rich and famous go to seed: Douglas Fairbanks Jr (a house in Bormes) and the late grand duke of Luxembourg to name but two, plus a whole host of titled names familiar to readers of *Tatler*. And though aristos and celebrities are not always known for their good taste, when it comes to living in the best locations, they can usually be relied upon.

The Corniche des Maures has beaches that shine silver from the mica crystals in the sand, shaded by tall dark pines, oaks and eucalyptus; glittering rocks of purple, green and reddish hue; and chestnut-forested hills keeping winds away. There are even unspoilt stretches where it's possible to imagine what all this coast looked like in bygone years, notably around **Cap de Brégançon**, at the **Domaine de Rayol gardens**, and between **Le Rayol** and the resort of **Cavalaire**.

Transport around the Corniche is the biggest problem. The coast road is narrow and littered with hairpin bends: it's served by regular buses year-round, though they are very slow, as are the cars that follow. Cycling is strenuous and hair-raising until you get east of Le Lavandou, when a decent bridleway follows much of the coast. There are no trains.

Bormes-les-Mimosas

You can almost smell the money as you spiral uphill from the D559 into immaculate **BORMES-LES-MIMOSAS**, 20km east of Hyères. It's indisputably medieval, with a restored castle at the top, protected by spiralling lines of pantiled houses backing onto short-cut flights of steps. The castle is private, but there is a public terrace alongside it, which offers attractive views. The winding alleys of the village are oddly named, with addresses such as 'alleyway of lovers', 'street of brigands', 'gossipers' way', and 'arse-breaker street'. They're stuffed full of arts and crafts ateliers, and there's a small **Musée d'Art et d'Histoire**, at 103 rue Carnot (Mon & Wed–Sat 10am–noon & 2.30–5pm; Sun 10am–noon; free), displaying early twentieth-century regional painting.

Although it only dates from 1968, Bormes-les-Mimosas' name is apt, particularly in February when you'll see a spectacular display of the tiny yellow pom-poms. Despite their popularity along the whole of the Côte d'Azur, mimosa are no more indigenous to the region than Porsches, having been introduced from Mexico in the 1860s.

Bormes' ugly pleasure port at **La Favière** is flanked by spot-the-spare-foot-of-sand beaches. To the south the tip of **Cap Bénat** can be reached on foot along a coastal path from La Favière's beach. From Cap Bénat westwards to the bland modern seaside extension of **La Londe**, vineyards and private woods will block your way, as well as the security arrangements around the château at **Cap de Brégançon**, which is the holiday home of the president of the Republic. In summer you will have to pay for parking if you want to use the public tracks down to the shore from the La Londe-Cabasson road (cars around €7). However, once you've reached the water you can wander along the gorgeous beaches as far as you like, with no apartment buildings amongst the pine trees, not even villas, just the odd mansion in the distance surrounded by its vineyards.

Practicalities

In July and August Bormes-les-Mimosas is served by a **minibus** from Le Lavandou (6 daily; 30min); otherwise, it's a two-kilometre walk uphill from Le-Pin-de-Bormes on the main Hyères-Le Lavandou road. Minibuses arrive at the top of the village, near place Gambetta, where you'll also find the **tourist office** (June & Sept daily 9am–12.30pm & 2.30–7pm; July & Aug daily 9am–12.30pm & 3–8pm; Sept–March Mon–Sat 9am–12.30pm & 3–6.30pm; ⓣ04.94.01.38.39, ⓦwww.bormeslesmimosas.com). If you want **to stay** overnight, there are a couple of basic, but clean and pleasant, options on place Gambetta in old Bormes: *La Terrasse*, at no. 19 (ⓣ04.94.71.15.22; ❷; closed Nov & Dec), and the *Bellevue* (ⓣ04.94.71.15.15; ⓦwww.bellevuebormes.fr.st; ❷). In nearby Cabasson there's a very attractive and peaceful hotel, *Les Palmiers*, at 240 chemin du Petit Fort (ⓣ04.94.64.81.94, ⓔles.palmiers@wanadoo.fr; closed mid-Nov to Feb; ❻), with its own path to the beach. There are several **campsites** in the vicinity, all of which need to be booked in advance in high season. These include the four-star *Camp du Domaine* right by the sea on the rte de Bénat in La Favière (ⓣ04.94.71.03.12, ⓦwww.campdudomaine.com; €21 per tent; closed Nov–March); a much smaller four-star site, *Clos-Mar-Jo*, 895 chemin de Bénat, between the D559 and the port (ⓣ04.94.71.53.39; closed Oct–March); the two-star *La Célinette*, 30 impasse du Houx, just off the main rte de Benat south of the port (ⓣ04.94.71.07.98; closed Oct–March); and the two-star *Les Cyprès* on av de la Mer, close to the port in La Favière (ⓣ04.94.64.86.50, ⓕ04.94.15.21.01; €15 per tent; closed Oct–March).

This being the Côte proper, there's no shortage of interesting, if costly, **restaurants**. A couple of reasonably priced and excellent quality options are *La Tonnelle*, on place Gambetta (ⓣ04.94.71.34.84; closed Wed & Sun eve), with menus from €30, and *L'Escoundudo*, 2 ruelle du Moulin (ⓣ04.94.71.15.53; closed Tues & Wed plus mid-Feb to mid-March), which serves delicious Provençal specialities, with menus at €33 and €48. *Pâtes...et Pâtes*, on place du Bazar, serves the best pasta in town from around €10, while more run-of-the-mill meals including pizzas can be had at *La Pastourelle*, 41 rue Carnot (ⓣ04.94.71.57.78), with menus from €14.

Le Lavandou

Five kilometres from Bormes, **LE LAVANDOU** is an out-and-out seaside resort, with sandy beaches, a scattering of high-rise hotels and an unpretentious holiday atmosphere. Its origins as a Mediterranean fishing village are betrayed by the dozen or so remaining fishing vessels, which are kept in business by the region's upmarket seafood restaurants. Merging with Bormes to the west and St Clair to the east, Le Lavandou concentrates its charm in the tiny area between av du Gal-de-Gaulle and quai Gabriel-Péri where café tables overlook the *boules* pitch and the traffic of the seafront road. Three narrow stairways lead back from here to rue Patron Ravello, place Argaud and rue Abbé-Helin, each lined with specialist shops and cafés.

However, it's the coast that is the real attraction, and there's no shortage of water sports and boat trips on offer: the École de Plongée offers initiation **dives** (ⓣ04.94.71.83.65; €25 from St Clair beach, or €38 from the club's boat), while Cap Sud on quai Gabriel-Péri (ⓣ04.94.71.59.33) rents out **motor boats**. **Ferries** to the Îles d'Hyères (daily), to St-Tropez (April–Sept; every Tues), and to Brégançon (April–June & Sept; every Mon), leave from the Gare Maritime in front of the tourist office (see below). For escaping into the hills or hunting out secluded beaches, you can rent **bikes** from Starbike, Quai Baptistin Pins (ⓣ04.94.01.03.82), or Holiday Bike, av Vincent-Auriol (ⓣ04.94.15.19.99). For **beaches**, St Clair, just to the east of town, is pleasant enough, but if you're after the fabled silver stretches of sand you need to carry on east to any of the string of villages between here and Cavalaire-sur-Mer.

Practicalities

Buses stop on the av de Provence, close to the Shopi supermarket and a short walk west of the **tourist office** on quai Gabriel-Péri (June–Sept daily 9am–12.30pm & 3–7pm; Oct–May Mon–Sat 9am–noon & 3–6pm; ⓣ04.94.00.40.50, ⓦwww.lelavandou.com).

In summer your chances of finding a **hotel** room are pretty slim. Prices are similar to Bormes, but with rather less charm at the bottom end of the range. A few central options worth trying are *L'Îlot Fleurie*, bd Front de Mer, right next to the beach but also to a rather loud disco (ⓣ04.94.71.14.82, ⓔlilot-fleuri@9online.fr; ❸); *Hôtel l'Oustaou*, 20 av Gal-de-Gaulle (ⓣ04.94.71.12.18, ⓕ04.94.15.08.75; ❸); and *L'Auberge Provençale*, 11 rue Patron Ravello (ⓣ04.94.71.00.44, ⓔaubprovencal@aol.com; ❷). Far nicer, however, are the more upmarket *Auberge de la Calanque*, 62 av du Gal-de-Gaulle (ⓣ04.94.71.05.96, ⓔlacalanque@wanadoo.fr; ❼; closed Nov–March), and the *Belle-Vue*, chemin du Four des Maures in St Clair (ⓣ04.94.00.45.00, ⓕ04.94.00.45.25; ❾; closed Nov–March), which has charming rooms overlooking the sea. If you really want to push the boat out, *Les Roches*, on av des trios Dauphins in Aiguebelle (ⓣ04.94.71.05.07, ⓦwww.hotelprestige-provence.com; ❾), is the place to go for – it stands right on the water's edge, has stunning views from its restaurant (menus from €50) and a list of illustrious former guests that includes Churchill and Bogart; sea-view rooms start at €250. For **campsites**, there's *Caravaning St-Clair*, av André-Gide in St Clair (ⓣ04.94.01.30.20; closed Nov to mid-March), though it only takes campervans and caravans.

For gastronomy with a sea view, *L'Algue Bleue* in the *Auberge de la Calanque* (ⓣ04.94.71.05.96; closed mid-Oct to March) is a good, if pricey, choice, while the busy **restaurant** at *L'Auberge Provençale* (menus from €29; closed all day Mon, Tues plus Wed lunch) may not have sea views, but the food is excellent if a touch expensive à la carte. For fresh fish caught by the restaurant's owner, *Le Pêcheur*, on quai des Pêcheurs (ⓣ04.94.71.58.01; menus €17.50 and €26.50; closed Sun), is a good bet. As for **café** lounging, you can take your pick along quai Gabriel-Péri: *Le Rhumerie La Rade* has live music at weekends and the most comfy terrace chairs, while *Chez Mimi* has good beers and perhaps the edge on the ice cream front. For cocktails in a stylish setting, try the *Brasserie du Centre* on place Ernest-Reyer.

Along the corniche

The D559 east from Le Lavandou is lined with pink oleander interspersed with purple bougainvillea, a classic feature of the Côte d'Azur corniche as it curves its way through the steep wooded hills that reach down to the sea. This, along with the St-Tropez peninsula it leads to, is the most beautiful part of the Côte d'Azur, boasting silvery beaches and sections of unspoiled tree-backed coastline.

The first **beaches** you come to, between Aiguebelle and Cavalière, are the tiny, secluded *calanques*, either side of **Pointe du Layet**, at Plage du Rossignol and the naturist Plage du Layet. **CAVALIÈRE** itself has a long, wide beach and hill horizons that easily outreach the highest houses, while a couple of kilometres further on at **PRAMOUSQUIER**, you can look up from the turquoise water to woods undisturbed by roads and buildings. A further 4km east, the villages of **LE CANADEL** and **LE RAYOL** have gradually merged and colonized the hills behind them. At Le Canadel, the sinuous D27 to La Môle (see p.256) leaves the coast road and quickly spirals up past cork-oak woodland to the **Col du Canadel**, giving unbeatable views en route.

Le Rayol, however, is best known as home to the huge and stunning **Domaine du Rayol gardens** (daily: Feb–June & Sept to mid-Nov 9.30am–12.30pm & 2.30–6.30pm; July & Aug 9.30am–12.30pm & 3–8pm; €6.50), which extend down to the Figuier bay and headland. The land originally belonged to a banker who, before going bust at Monte Carlo in the 1930s, built the Art Nouveau mansion through which you enter the gardens, the Art Deco villa, farmhouse and classical pergola to which a later owner added the dramatic long flight of steps lined with cypresses. Areas of the garden are dedicated to plants from different parts of the world that share the climate of the Mediterranean: Chile, South Africa, China, California, Central America, Australia and New Zealand. Apart from the extraordinary diversity of the vegetation, some of which is left alone to spread and colonize at will, there's sheer brilliance in the landscaping that entices you to explore, to retrace your steps and get to know every path and every vista. In July and August, you can take a snorkelling tour of the 'Jardin Marine' (book at least a week in advance; ⓣ04.98.04.44.00; €13). There are also highly informative and engaging guided tours of the garden (French only: July & Aug 10.15am, 4.30pm & 5pm; Sept–June 3pm), given by professional gardeners.

East from Le Rayol, the corniche climbs away from the coast through 3km of open countryside, sadly scarred most years by fire, before ending with the sprawl of **CAVALAIRE-SUR-MER**. Here the tiny *calanques* give way to a long stretch of sand and flat land that has been exploited for the maximum rentable space. In its favour, Cavalaire is very much a family resort and not too stuck on glamour.

Practicalities

In Le Rayol, the helpful **tourist office**, on place Michel Goy (Mon, Wed & Fri 9.30am–12.30pm & 2.30–4.30pm; Tues, Thurs & Sat 9.30am–2.30pm; closed mid-Nov to early Dec; ⓣ04.94.05.65.69), has details of possible walks including the *Ex-Voie Férée*, a former railway track. Cavalaire-sur-Mer's **tourist office**, in the Maison de la Mer (mid-June to mid-Sept daily 9am–7pm; mid-Sept to mid-June Mon–Fri 9am–12.30pm & 2–6pm; Sat 9am–12.30pm; ⓣ04.94.01.92.10), is prominently sited where av des Alliés meets promenade de la Mer, and has lists of hotels and campsites. **Bikes** can be rented nearby at Holiday Bikes, les Régates, rue du Port (ⓣ04.94.64.18.17).

Finding **rooms** in this area outside July and August should not present a problem; if you get stuck there are a number of hotels in Cavalaire-sur-Mer, with first choice being the small, upmarket *La Calanque*, rue de la Calanque (☎04.94.00.49.00, ⓦwww.hotel-la-calanque.com: ❾); it's beautifully perched on a low cliff overlooking the sea, a little way out of town. In Pramousquier, *Le Mas*, 9 av Capitaine Ducourneau, above the main road (☎ & ⓕ04.94.05.80.43; ❹), is a good option with a pool and great views. In Le Rayol, you can rent apartments sleeping four at *Les Îles de la Mer*, close to the beach on av des Américains (☎04.94.05.63.76, ⓕ04.94.05.63.23; closed Nov–Feb), or there are simple low-priced rooms at the *Auberge des Silaques*, on the main road (☎04.94.05.60.13; ❸; closed mid-Nov to mid-Dec).

The place to **eat and drink** is *Le Maurin des Maures* on the main road at Le Rayol (☎04.94.05.60.11; Mon–Sat lunchtime menu €11, otherwise €19), serving fresh grilled fish, bourride and aioli. In Cavalaire, *Le Quai des Moules* on the Nouveau Port (☎04.94.15.44.63; closed Dec–Jan) serves moules-frites in all its variety, for around €9, while *La Crêperie Bretonne* on rue du Port (☎04.94.64.16.98; April–Oct only; menu at €9.20) serves decent crêpes. For **nightlife**, *Le Tropicana* **disco** on Le Canadel's beach (July & Aug Thurs, Fri & Sat; ☎04.94.05.61.50) stays open until the early hours.

La Croix-Valmer

At the eastern end of Cavalaire-sur-Mer's bay lies another exceptional stretch of wooded coastline, the **Domaine de Cap Lardier**. This pristine coastal conservation area snakes around the southern tip of the St-Tropez peninsula, and is best accessed from **LA CROIX-VALMER**, even though the village centre is some 2.5km from the sea. Being slightly inland, however, adds charm, since some of the land between is taken up by vineyards that produce a decent wine. Local legend maintains that Emperor Constantine stopped here with his troops on his way to Rome and had his famous vision of the sun's rays forming a cross over the sea which converted him, and therefore ultimately all of Europe, to the new religion; hence the 'cross' in the name of the village which only came into existence in 1934.

To reach the best **beach** in the vicinity, Plage du Gigaro, and the start of the paths to Cap Lardier, you need to take bd Georges Selliez from place des Palmiers (the D93), turn right into bd de Sylvabelle, then left along bd de la Mer. It's a four-kilometre walk, so you may prefer to catch the *navette* or **shuttle bus** (15 June–15 Sept; 9 daily) from outside the tourist office (see below) to the beach.

Practicalities

La Croix-Valmer's **tourist office** (mid-June to mid-Sept Mon–Sat 9.15am–12.30pm & 2.30–7pm, Sun 9am–1pm; mid-Sept to mid-June Mon–Fri 9.15am–noon & 2–6pm, Sat & Sun 9am–noon; ☎04.94.55.12.12) is in Les Jardins de la Gare, just up from the central junction place des Palmiers, and has a list of walks in the area. **Bikes** and scooters can be rented from Holiday Bikes on bd Georges Selliez, east of the village centre; ☎4.94.79.75.12).

One of the cheapest places **to stay** in La Croix-Valmer is *La Bienvenue* on rue L-Martin (☎04.94.79.60.23, ⓕ04.94.79.70.08; ❷; closed Nov–Easter), right in the centre of the village, while the small, family-run *Hostellerie La Ricarde*, quartier de la Plage du Débarquement (☎04.94.79.64.07, ⓕ04.94.54.30.14; ❸; closed Oct–March), is a good option near the beach. At the other end of the scale, *Le Château de Valmer* on rte de Gigaro (☎04.94.79.60.10, ⓦwww.chateau-valmer.com; ❾; closed Nov–March) is a seriously luxurious old Provençal manor house within walking distance of the sea. There's one **campsite**, the pricey four-star *Sélection* on bd de la Mer, just 400m from the sea and with excellent facilities (ⓣ04.94.55.10.30, ⓕ04.94.55.10.39; €30 per tent; closed mid-Oct to mid-March; booking essential in summer); it's 2.5km southwest of the village on the main road towards Cavalaire.

There are some tempting **restaurants** along the beach, though none is particularly cheap; the best is *Soule'as* (ⓣ04.94.55.10.55; closed mid-Oct to March), with menus from €30–69, while good, inexpensive pizzas are guaranteed at *Le Coin de l'Italien* (ⓣ04.94.79.67.16), the last restaurant before the conservation area.

The St-Tropez peninsula

The origins of **ST-TROPEZ** are not unusual for this stretch of coast: a fishing village that grew up around a port founded by the Greeks of Marseille, it was destroyed by the Saracens in 739 and finally fortified in the late Middle Ages. Its sole distinction was its inaccessibility. Stuck out on a peninsula that never warranted real roads, St-Tropez could only really be easily reached by boat. This was the case as late as the 1880s, when the novelist **Maupassant** sailed his yacht into the port during his final high-living binge before the onset of syphilitic insanity. The Tropeziens were a little shocked but it was the beginning of their induction to bizarre strangers seeking paradise in their home.

Soon after Maupassant's visit, the painter and leader of the Neo-Impressionists, **Paul Signac**, sailed down the coast in his boat named after Manet's notorious painting *L'Olympia*. Bad weather forced him to moor in St-Tropez and, being rich and impulsive, he decided to have a house built there –

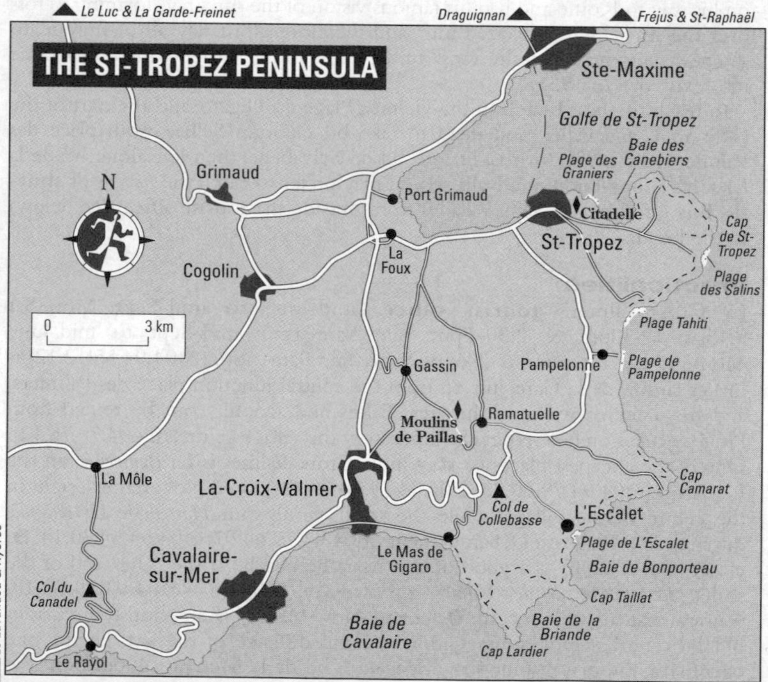

La Hune, on what is now rue Paul-Signac, was designed by fellow painter Henri van de Velde. Signac opened his doors to impoverished friends who could benefit from the light, the beauty and the distance from the respectable convalescent world of Cannes and Nice. **Matisse** was one of the first to take up his offer; the locals were shocked again, this time by Madame Matisse modelling in a kimono. **Bonnard**, **Marquet**, **Dufy**, **Derain**, **Vlaminck**, **Seurat**, **Van Dongen** and others followed, and by the eve of World War I, St-Tropez was fairly well established as a hang-out for bohemians.

The 1930s saw a further artistic influx, this time of writers as much as painters: **Jean Cocteau** came here; **Colette** lived for fourteen years in a villa outside the village, describing her main concerns as "whether to go walking or swimming, whether to have rosé or white, whether to have a long day or a long night"; while **Anaïs Nin**'s journal records "girls riding bare-breasted on the back of open cars; an intensity of pleasure" and undressing between bamboo bushes that rustled with concealed lovers.

But it wasn't until after World War II that St-Tropez achieved international celebrity. In 1955, Roger Vadim arrived to film **Brigitte Bardot** in *Et Dieu Créa La Femme*, and the cult of Tropezian sun, sex and celebrities took off, creating a tourist boom which continues to this day. Recent celebrity visitors include Puff Daddy, Robbie Williams and David and Victoria Beckham, while the elite list of St-Tropez property owners numbers George Michael and Jean-Paul Belmondo, as well as Harrods owner Mohamed Al Fayed. Bardot, for decades the very icon of the place, finally left in the late 1990s, some years after famously denouncing the "black tide of human filth" that was physically and morally polluting her beloved village. When questioned about Bardot's criticisms, the mayor agreed: "It's true that St-Tropez is a dying village, but who brought all this vice and indecency here in the first place?"

In 1991 the village was dealt a further blow, with the discovery that the hundred-year-old **plane trees** on place des Lices were rotting. Several had to be cut down; the remainder underwent intensive surgery and their hollow trunks are now propped up with metal crutches. They are perhaps a fitting metaphor for St-Tropez itself: a recent report suggests the village's permanent population is shrinking, with many locals fleeing to neighbouring communes where essential shops are still plentiful and prices are more reasonable.

Arrival, information and accommodation

On entering St-Tropez, the road from La Foux divides into av Général-Leclerc and av Gén-de-Gaulle, which itself quickly becomes av 8 du Mai 1945 at the **gare routière**, and runs parallel to a vast port-side car park before becoming av du 11 Novembre 1918. The harbour here is the **Nouveau Port** for yacht overspill. Follow av du 11 Novembre 1918 past the **post office** and you'll hit the **Vieux Port**, with the Vieille Ville rising above the eastern quay. The **tourist office** is opposite you on the Vieux Port at the start of quai Jean-Jaurès (April–June, Sept & Oct 9.30am–12.30pm & 2–7pm; July & Aug daily 9.30am–8.30pm; Nov–March 9.30am–12.30pm & 2–6pm; ⓣ04.94.97.45.21, ⓦwww.saint-tropez.st). You can rent **bikes** from MAS, 3 rue Joseph-Quaranta (ⓣ04.94.97.00.60; closed mid-Sept to March), or Holiday Bikes, 14 av Général-Leclerc (ⓣ04.94.97.09.39).

The tourist office can help with **hotel** reservations, although with ever more people wanting to pay homage to St-Tropez, accommodation is a problem. Between April and September you won't find a room unless you've booked months in advance and are prepared to pay exorbitant prices. If you have your own transport, you may be better off staying in La Croix-Valmer or even

Cavalaire-sur-Mer (see p.246). Out of season you may be luckier, though in winter few hotels stay open.

Camping near St-Tropez can be just as difficult as finding a room. The nearest two sites are on the plage du Pampelonne, though both charge extortionate rates and are massively crowded in high summer. In summer it's worth checking out the signs for **camping à la ferme** that you'll see along the D93. Pitching on a farm can be more pleasant that the overcrowded official sites, but make sure you know the charges first.

Hotels

Le Baron 23 rue de l'Aïoli ⓣ04.94.97.06.57, ⓦwww.hotel-le-baron.com. A comfortable hotel overlooking the citadel, and a bit quieter than those in the centre. It's small and cosy with just ten rooms and a restaurant. ❹

L'Ermitage av Paul-Signac ⓣ04.94.97.52.33, ⓕ04.94.97.10.43. Above pl des Lices, charming and very comfortable, and away from the bustle of the village centre. Closed mid-Nov to mid-March. ❻

Les Lauriers rue du Temple ⓣ04.94.97.04.88, ⓕ04.94.97.21.87. Small and very good value, with its own garden. Close to pl des Lices. Closed Jan. ❹

Lou Cagnard 18 av Paul-Roussel ⓣ04.94.97.04.24, ⓕ04.94.97.09.44. Dreary-looking from the outside, but with a decent garden and quiet at night time. Closed Nov & Dec. ❸

La Ponche 3 rue des Remparts ⓣ04.94.97.02.53, ⓦwww.laponche.com An old block of fishermen's houses, luxuriously furnished and with a host of famous names in its guest book. Closed Nov to mid-Feb. ❾

Le Sube 15 quai Suffren ⓣ04.94.97.30.04, ⓦwww.nova.fr/sube. Unique views over the port, and decor to make you think you're in a yacht with mirrors everywhere. ❻

Maison Blanche pl des Lices ⓣ04.94.97.52.66, ⓦwww.hotellamaisonblanche.com. Gorgeous white designer hotel in a fine bourgeois villa, with an elegant garden and lots of quirky touches. Rooms start at €267 in high season. ❾

Campsites

La Croix du Sud rte des Plages ⓣ04.94.55.51.23, ⓕ04.94.79.89.21. A four-star site 3km from Ramatuelle towards the Plage de Pampelonne (see p.252). €24 per tent. Closed Oct–March.

Parc St James Montana off the road to Bourrian near Gassin ⓣ04.94.55.20.20, ⓕ04.94.56.34.77. A pricey four-star site. €32 per tent. Closed Dec.

Les Tournels on rte de Camarat ⓣ04.94.55.90.90, ⓕ04.94.55.90.99. Vast site but well situated, 1km from the sea. €24 per tent.

The Town

Beware of coming to St-Tropez in high summer, unless by yacht and with limitless funds. The 5km of road from La Foux is an unpleasant introduction, lined with out-of-town superstores, fast-food restaurants and interminable traffic jams in summer. The pedestrian jams in the port are not much better, while the hotels and restaurants are full and expensive, and the beaches are not that clean, having lost their Blue Flag award for water quality in 2000, due to oil pollution and smelly drains. That said, if you can time your trip for a spring or autumn day, you'll understand why this place has charmed so many for so long.

The **Vieux Port** is where you get the classic St-Tropez experience: the quayside café clientele eyeing the yacht-deck Martini-sippers, with the latest fashions parading in between, defining the French word *frimer* (derived from sham) which means exactly this – to stroll ostentatiously in places like St-Tropez. You may well be surprised at just how entertaining this spectacle can be, especially when accompanied by the jugglers, fire-eaters and mimics who ply their trade in the streets. The oversized yachts pretty much obliterate the views across the port, though the owners are as likely to be banks as aristocrats or celebrities. They tend to be registered in Britain, the US, the Caribbean or France, with Union Jacks predominating.

The other pole of St-Trop's life is **place des Lices**, southeast of the Vieux Port, with its sad but surviving plane trees and the benches and *boules* games underneath. The café-brasseries have become a bit too Champs-Elysées in style, and a new commercial block has been added near the northern corner, but you can still sit down for free and ponder the unchanged dusty surface that is so essential for the momentum of Provence's favourite pastime. In the streets between place des Lices and the port – rue Sibilli and rue Clemenceau – and the smaller lanes in the heart of the old village you can window-shop or buy haute couture, antiques, *objets d'art* and classy trinkets to your heart's content.

Heading east from the port, from the top end of quai Jean-Jaurès, you pass the **Tour Suffren**, originally built in 980 by Count Guillaume 1er of Provence, and enter place de l'Hôtel-de-Ville where the *mairie* with its attractive earthy pink facade and dark green shutters is one of few reminders that this is a real town. A street to the left takes you down to the tiny, rocky **Baie de la Glaye**; straight ahead, rue de la Ponche passes through an ancient gateway to place du Revelin above the lovely **fishing port** with its tiny beach. Turning inland and upwards, struggling past shop fronts, stalls and café tables, you can finally reach the open space around the sixteenth-century **citadel** (April–Sept Mon & Wed–Sun 10am–12.30pm & 1.30–6.30pm; Oct & Dec–March closes at 5.30pm; closed Nov; €4), which houses a small museum of local history. Far more interesting, however, is to take a walk round the ramparts, whose excellent views of the gulf and the back of the town have not changed since their translation into oil on canvas in the early twentieth century.

These paintings can be seen at the **Musée de l'Annonciade** (June–Sept Mon & Wed–Sun 10am–noon & 3–7pm; Oct & Dec–May Mon & Wed–Sun 10am–noon & 2–6pm; €4.60), reason in itself for a visit to St-Tropez. It was originally Signac's idea to have a permanent exhibition space for the Neo-Impressionists and Fauves who painted here, though it was not until 1955 that collections owned by various individuals were put together in the deconsecrated sixteenth-century chapel on place Georges-Grammont just west of the port. The museum features representative works by Signac, Matisse and most of the other artists who worked in St-Tropez: grey, grim, northern scenes of Paris, Boulogne and Westminster, and then local, brilliantly sun-lit scenes by the same brush. Two winter scenes of the village by Dufy contrast with Camille Camoin's springtime *Place des Lices* and Bonnard's boilingly hot summer view. The museum is a real delight for its contents, unrivalled outside Paris for the 1890 to 1940 period, for the way it displays them, and for the fact that it can sometimes be the least crowded place in town.

Eating and drinking

There are **restaurants** for every budget in St-Tropez, as well as plenty of **snack bars** and takeaway joints, particularly on rue Georges-Clemenceau and place des Lices. Almost all are open daily from June to September; many close altogether in the winter months. Place aux Herbes has a daily (except Mondays in winter) fish **market** with some fruit and veg also on sale, though the main food market takes place on place des Lices on Tuesday and Saturday mornings.

Cafés and snack bars

Bar du Port Vieux Port. With its stylish retro sixties decor, this bar is the epitome of St-Tropez idling.

Café des Arts pl des Lices. The number-one café-brasserie on the square, with old-timers still gathering in the bar at the back; expect to pay around €30.

Le Cohiba Café 23 rue du Portail Neuf. Trendy cigar bar, with a tapas menu from €8.

Le Gorille quai Suffren. Straightforward quayside

fare,where you can get a brasserie-style meal for under €12. July & Aug open 24hr.

La Patate rue Clemenceau. Snack bar serving omelettes, pasta, *pan bagnat* and so forth.

Café Sénéquier on the port. The top quayside café: it's horribly expensive, but sells sensational nougat (also available from the shop at the back).

Rotisserie Tropezienne bd Vasserot and rue F-Sibille. One of a series of snack stalls in a complex on the edge of place des Lices; this one sells the ubiquitous roast chicken on a spit, the others include an Asian fast food stall, a crêperie and a kebab stall.

La Tarte Tropezienne pl des Lices and 36 rue G-Clemenceau. A celebrated pâtisserie which claims to have invented this eponymous sponge and cream custard cake.

Restaurants

Auberge des Maures 4 rue du Dr-Boutin, off rue Aillard ☎04.94.97.01.50. Specializes in chargrilled fish and meat from around €20, with a menu at €39. Evenings only; closed mid-Nov to mid-Dec & Jan.

Bistrot des Lices 3 pl des Lices ☎04.94.55.82.82. *Fin-de-siècle* decor for traditional preening and spectacular food, from *salade de langoustines* to *croustillant du loup*, with particularly chocolatey puds to follow. The midday menu is €18, otherwise from €28.

Café de Paris Quai de Suffren ☎04.97.00.56. Pizzas, salads, sashimi and light meals at round €15, all served in elegant port-side surroundings.

L'Echalote 35 rue du Gal-Allard ☎04.94.54.83.26. Rich, meaty dishes and a great scallop salad, which you can enjoy in the tranquillity of the garden. There's a menu at €18, otherwise expect to pay around €31 à la carte. Closed Thurs.

Joseph 1 pl de l'Hôtel-de-Ville ☎04.94.97.01.66. Good bouillabaisse, *bourride* and desserts. Menus from €18, à la carte around €50.

Le Petit Charron 6 rue des Charrons ☎04.94.97 .73.78. Tiny terrace and dining room serving beautifully cooked Provençal specialities, for around €50. Closed mid-Nov to mid-Feb.

Regis 19 rue de la Citadelle ☎04.94.97.15.53. Small, friendly bistro and snack bar; around €20 à la carte.

La Table du Marché 38 rue Clemenceau ☎04.94.97.85.20. Hard to get a table here but worth the wait for true bistro-style gourmandise; menus at €18 and €25.

Nightlife

In season St-Tropez stays up late, as you'd expect. The **boules games** on place des Lices continue till well after dusk; the port-side spectacle doesn't falter till the early hours; and even the shops stay open well after dinner. If you have pots of cash and want to sample the infamous St-Tropez **nightlife**, head for *La Bodega du Papagayo* in the Résidence du Nouveau Port, with world music and theme nights; the glitzy *VIP Room* at the same location; or *Les Caves du Roy* in the flashy *Hôtel Byblos* on rue Paul-Signac, which is the most expensive and probably the tackiest. Alternatively, there's the **gay** disco *L'Esquinade*, 2 rue du Four, a long-standing St-Tropez institution, popular with gays and straights alike. All the clubs open every night in summer, and usually Saturday only in winter, though your chances of getting in will depend on who's on the door, and whether they think you look the part.

The beaches

The nearest beach to St-Tropez, within easy walking distance, is **Les Graniers** below the citadel just beyond the Port des Pêcheurs along rue Cavaillon. From here a path follows the coast around the **Baie des Canebiers**, which has a small beach, to Cap St-Pierre, Cap St-Tropez, the very crowded **Salins** beach and right round to **Plage Tahiti**, 12.5km from St-Tropez. This eastern area of the peninsula is where the rich and famous have their vast villas with helipads and artificial lakes in acres of heavily guarded grounds.

Tahiti-Plage is at the top end of the almost straight five-kilometre north-south **Plage de Pampelonne**, famous bronzing belt of St-Tropez and initiator of the topless bathing cult. The water is shallow for 50m or so and exposed to the wind, and it's sometimes scourged by dried sea vegetation, not to mention slicks of industrial pollutants. But spotless glitter comes from the rash of beach bars and restaurants built out over the coarse sand, all with patios and sofas, all serving cocktails and ice creams (as well as full-blown meals), and all renting out beach mattresses and matching parasols. Though you'll see people naked on all stretches of the beach, only some of the bars welcome visitors carrying wallets and nothing else. *Club 55*, named after the year when Vadim's film crew scrounged food from what was then a family beach hut, is supposed to be a favourite with the celebrities (à la carte from €46; closes at sundown).

The beach ends with the headland of **Cap Camarat**, beyond which the private residential settlement of **Villa Bergès** grudgingly allows public access to the **Plage de l'Escalet**. Another coastal path leads to the next bay, the **Baie de la Briande**, where you'll find the least populated beach of the whole peninsula. Beyond here the villas end and you can continue to **Cap Lardier** with a choice of paths upwards and downwards and along the gorgeous shore all the way round to La Croix-Valmer.

To **get to the beaches** from St-Tropez, there's a frequent minibus service from place des Lices to Salins, and an infrequent **bus** from the gare routière to Ramatuelle, the nearest you'll get to any of the beaches by bus. Alternatively, you could rent **bikes** in St-Tropez (see p.249) and cycle out to the beaches. For **drivers**, if you want to avoid the high parking fees that all the beaches charge, you'll need to leave your car some distance from the sea and risk being prey to thieves.

The interior of the peninsula

Though the coast of the St-Tropez peninsula continues to sprout holiday homes and even golf courses, the **interior** is almost uninhabited, thanks to government intervention, complex ownerships and the value of some local wines. The best view of this richly green, wooded and flowering countryside is from the hilltop village of **Gassin**, its lower neighbour **Ramatuelle**, or the tiny road between them, the beautiful route des Moulins de Paillas where three ruined windmills could once catch every wind.

Gassin

The highly chic village of **GASSIN** gives the impression of a small ship perched on a summit. Once a Moorish stronghold, it is now best known as the birthplace of French soccer idol David Ginola and the place where Mick and Bianca Jagger married. It's a perfect place for a blow-out dinner, sitting outside by the village wall with a spectacular panorama east over the peninsula. Of the handful of restaurants, *Bello Visto*, 9 place dei Barri (Ⓣ04.94.56.17.30, Ⓕ04.94.43.45.36; restaurant closed Tues & Nov–Easter), serves decent Provençal specialities, with menus from €23 to €31, and also has nine good-value rooms (❸). The nearby *Au Vieux Gassin* (Ⓣ04.94.56.14.26; closed mid-Oct to late March) also serves good Provençal dishes, as well as lobster, and has menus from €20–38.

Ramatuelle

RAMATUELLE is bigger than its neighbour, though just as old, and is surrounded by some of the best Côte de Provence vineyards (the top selection of wines can be tasted at Les Maîtres Vignerons de la Presqu'île de St-Tropez by the La Foux junction on the N98). The twisting and arcaded streets are inevitably full of arts and crafts shops selling works of dubious talent, but the village itself is very pleasant nonetheless. The central Romanesque **Église Notre-Dame** that formed part of the old defences has heavy gilded furnishings from the Chartreuse de la Verne (see p.255) and an impressive early-seventeenth-century door carved out of serpentine.

Opposite the church, on place de l'Ormeau, the small **tourist office** (April–June, Sept & Oct Mon–Sat 9am–1pm & 3–7pm; July & Aug daily 9am–1pm & 3–7.30pm; Nov–March Mon–Fri 9am–12.30pm & 2–6pm; ⓣ04.98.12.64.00) has a good list of *campings à la ferme*. Of the few **hotels** in the village, try the fairly basic *Le Giulia*, 31 rue Clemenceau (ⓣ04.94.79.20.46; ❷), or *Lou Castellas* (ⓣ & ⓕ04.94.79.20.67; ❹), just outside the village on the road to Gassin, with panoramic views and its own restaurant. At the foot of the old village, there's the luxurious *Hostellerie Le Baou* (ⓣ04.98.12.94.20; ⓦwww.chateauxhotels.com/baou; ❾; closed late Oct to late March), with a pool, and where every room has its own terrace or balcony. The best place in the village to **eat** is *Au Fil à la Pâte*, 7 rue Victor-Léon (ⓣ04.94.79.16.40; à la carte from €13–30; closed Nov–Feb), which serves great dishes of fresh pasta as well as a meat or fish special.

The Massif des Maures

The secret of the Côte d'Azur is that despite the gross conglomeration of the coast, Provence is still just behind – old, sparsely populated, village-oriented and dependent on the land for its produce as much as for its value as real estate. Between Marseille and Menton, the most bewitching hinterland is the sombre **Massif des Maures** that stretches from Hyères to Fréjus.

The highest point of these hills stops short of 800m but the quick succession of ridges, the sudden drops and views, and the curling, looping roads are pervasively mountainous. Where the lie of the land gives a wide bowl of sunlit slopes, vines are grown. Elsewhere the hills are thickly forested, with Aleppo and umbrella pines, holly, sweet-chestnut trees, and tremendous gnarled cork oaks, their trunks scarred in great bands where their precious bark has been stripped. On a windy autumn day chestnuts the size of grenades explode upon your head, while water from a thousand springs cascades down each face of rock. In the heat of summer there is always the darkest shade alternating with one-way light – the rocks that compose this massif absorb rather than reflect – and it's hardly surprising that its name derives from the Provençal and Latin words for dark, *mauram* and *mauro*.

Much of the massif is inaccessible even to **walkers**. However, the GR9 follows the most northern and highest ridge from Pignans on the N97 past Notre-Dame-des-Anges, La Sauvette, **La Garde-Freinet** and down to the head of the Golfe de St-Tropez. There are other paths and tracks, such as the one following the Vallon de Tamary from north of La Londe-des-Maures to join one of the roads snaking down from the Col de Babaou to Collobrières. Some of the smaller backroads don't go very far and many are closed to the public in summer for fear of forest fires, but when they are open, this makes exceptional countryside for exploring by mountain bike or on foot. Bear in mind, however, that at certain times of the year the entire Massif is thick with hunters.

For **cyclists**, the D14 that runs through the middle, parallel to the coast, from Pierrefeu-du-Var north of Hyères to **Cogolin** near St-Tropez, is manageable and stunning.

Collobrières and around

At the heart of the massif is the ancient village of **COLLOBRIÈRES**, reputed to have been the first place in France to adopt cork-growing from the Spanish. From the Middle Ages until recent times, **cork** production has been the major business of the village, and it is still the best place in the region to buy items roughly fashioned from raw cork bark such as fruit platters and plant pots, sold from a couple of roadside stalls in the centre of the village by the old men who own the cork-collecting concessions. However, the main industry now is *marrons glacés* and every other confection derived from sweet chestnuts.

From the terrace of the main *bar-tabac* that overlooks the River Collobrier, the forests that surround the village appear to go on for hundreds of miles, while in the village itself, the church, the *mairie* and the houses look like they come straight out of the nineteenth century. Yet on the other side of the river, at the eastern end of the village, a streamlined, no-nonsense, gleaming bright-blue building, the **Confiserie Azurienne**, exudes efficiency and modern business skills. Workers clock in and out, production schedules are met, profits are made, all from the conker's sister fruit. The factory itself can't be visited but there's a shop that sells chestnut ice cream, chestnut jam, chestnut nougat, chestnut purée, *chestnut glacées* and chestnut bonbons. For the fanatic, there's always the annual *Fête de la Châtaigne*, the **chestnut fair**, at the height of the harvest on the last three Sundays of October, with special dishes served in restaurants and roast chestnuts sold in the streets.

Practicalities

Collobrières' welcoming **tourist office** on bd Charles-Caminat (Tues–Sat 2–6pm; ⓣ04.94.48.08.00, ⓦwww.collotour.com) can supply details of various **walks** through the massif (€2) and some excellent local gîtes d'étape in the surrounding hills. There are two **hotels** in the village, both of them small, so it is advisable to book in advance in summer: *Notre-Dame*, 15 av de la Libération (ⓣ04.94.48.07.13, ⓕ04.94.48.05.95; ❷), and the excellent-value *Auberge des Maures*, 19 bd Lazare-Carnot (ⓣ04.94.48.07.10, ⓕ04.94.48.02.73; ❶). There are also two great **chambres d'hôtes**: *L'Atelier du Rempart*, Colette Brésis's ceramic studio at Le Vallon des Fées, 2km west of the village along the D14 (ⓣ04.94.48.05.92; ❸; Nov–March closed weekdays outside school holidays); and Andrée Cécile de Saleneuve's *La Bastide de La Cabrière*, 6km towards Gonfaron on the D39 (ⓣ04.94.48.04.31, ⓦwww.provenceweb.fr/83/cabriere; ❻). The small, one-star municipal **campsite**, the *St-Roch*, is open mid-June to mid-September (ⓣ04.94.13.83.83). *Camping sauvage* is forbidden: you might just get away with pitching up in the woods in late autumn or early spring, but when it's hot and dry don't even consider it – one stray spark and you could be responsible for a thousand acres of burnt forest.

For food, other than chestnuts and the fare at *L'Auberge des Maures*, the **restaurant** *La Petite Fontaine*, 1 place de la République (ⓣ04.94.48.00.12; closed Sun eve & Mon), is congenial and affordable with a menu at around €25, though it books up fast. South of the village, signed off the D41 to Bormes at the Col de Babaou, the *Ferme de Peïgros* (ⓣ04.94.48.03.83; daily lunch only) is an isolated farmhouse in wonderful surroundings serving its own produce on a €20 menu. If you want to buy some local **wines**, head for the *Cave Cooperative* on av de la Libération; the **market** in place de la Libération is on Thursdays (summer only) and Sundays.

Around Collobrières

Writing at the end of the nineteenth century, Maupassant declared that there was nowhere else in the world where his heart had felt such a pressing weight of melancholy as at the ruins of **La Chartreuse de la Verne** (Mon & Wed–Sun: June–Sept 11am–6pm; Oct–Dec & Feb–May 11am–5pm; €5). Since then a great deal of restoration work has been carried out on this

Carthusian monastery, abandoned during the Revolution and hidden away in total isolation, 12km east of Collobrières on a winding, partially tarmacked track off the D14 towards Grimaud. It remains a desolate spot; the buildings of this once vast twelfth-century complex, in the dark reddish-brown schist of the Maures, combined for decorative effect with local greenish serpentine, appear gaunt and inhospitable, but the atmosphere is indisputable. However, if the nutty, chocolate-brown olive bread on sale in the shop is anything to go by, life here for the monks couldn't have been that deprived.

Another religious settlement concealed in these hills is **Notre-Dame-des-Anges**, 11km north of Collobrières on the Gonfaron road, almost at the highest point of the Maures (daily: June–Aug 10am–7pm; April & May 10am–5pm; Sept–May Sat & Sun 10am–5pm). As a place of worship it goes back to pagan times, but in its nineteenth-century remodelled form it lacks the atmosphere of La Verne. The main point of a visit for most people is to take in the expansive views stretching from the Alps to the sea.

About 20km north of Collobrières and 2km east of Gonfaron on the D75 to Les Mayons, **Le Village des Tortues** (March–Nov daily 9am–7pm; €8) is not just a tourist attraction but a serious conservation project to repopulate the native Hermann tortoise. A million years ago the tortoises populated a third of France, but now, due to the ever-increasing threat of urbanization, forest fires, theft of eggs and sale as pets, this rare creature only just survives in the Massif des Maures. The tortoises are cared for and protected here, and you can look round their large enclosures where you'll see the tiny babies, "juveniles" and those soon to be released back into the wild. The visit is both relaxed and educational.

La Môle

Southeast of Collobrières, **LA MÔLE** sits on the fast N98 between Bormes and Cogolin in a fabulous bowl of meadows and vineyards, with old farmhouses dotted along the lanes leading into the hills. There are three reasons to stop here: the *Auberge de la Môle* **café** (closed Mon & mid-Nov to mid-March) serving good strong coffee and decked out with wooden fittings, ancient framed posters and a wonderfully old-fashioned petrol pump; the *Relais d'Alsace* **restaurant** (☎04.94.49.57.02; out of season closed Mon, Sat & Sun; menus from €10) with hearty specialities from northeast France; and, best of all, the *Boulangerie de la Môle* (Tues–Sun 8am–1pm & 3.30–7pm) that bakes amazing olive and raisin breads, *pain de campagne* and *pain rustique*, as well as selling their own jam. As you leave La Môle for Cogolin, you'll pass the tiny airport used by St-Tropez-bound celebrities and, more down-to-earth, a one-star **campsite**, *Les Caramagnols* (☎04.94.54.40.06; €14 per tent; closed mid-Sept to mid-June), with caravans to rent in July and August.

Cogolin

Eight kilometres east of La Môle, and a mere 8.5km from St-Tropez, **COGOLIN** is renowned for its craft industries, including reed-making for wind instruments, pipes for smoking, wrought-iron furniture, silk yarn and knotted wool carpets, all offering one-off, made-to-order, high-quality and high-cost goods for the Côte d'Azur market.

It's possible to visit some of the **craft factories**; the helpful tourist office (see opposite) can provide a *guide pratique*, and help with making appointments. Alternatively, you can just wander down av Georges-Clemenceau and pop into the retail outlets. For **carpets**, the Manufacture de Tapis just off av Clemenceau on bd Louis-Blanc (exhibition room Mon–Thurs 8am–noon & 2–6pm; closed 4–17 Aug) is known for its recreations of designs by famous artists such as Léger and Mondrian. Each carpet is hand-made, taking up to a year to finish, and the order book includes presidential residences, embassies and local palaces. The production of **pipes** from briarwood is on show at Courrieu, 58 av Clemenceau (Mon–Sat 9am–noon & 2–7pm), while world-famous musicians drop in on Rigotti, on rue F. Arago, to replace the reeds of their oboes, bassoons and clarinets; unfortunately, they open their doors only to professionals.

On the way out of town before joining the N98 heading west, the **Cave des Vignerons**, on rue Marceau (summer Mon–Sat 8.30am–12.30pm & 2.30–7.30pm, Sun 9am–12.30pm; winter Mon–Sat 8.30am–12.30pm & 2–6pm), is worth a visit to sample some of the local wines, which are said to have particularly impressed Julius Caesar.

Practicalities

From the **gare routière** on av Georges-Clemenceau head upwards to the central place de la République, where you'll find the **tourist office** (July & Aug Mon–Fri 9am–1pm & 2–7pm, Sat 9am–1pm & 3–7pm, Sun 9.30am–12.30pm; Sept–June Mon–Fri 9am–12.30pm & 2–6.30pm, Sat 9am–12.30pm; Ⓣ04.94.55.01.10, Ⓦwww.cogolin-provence.com).

Hotels in Cogolin are reasonable and are a viable alternative to staying in congested St-Tropez: the best option is the comfortable and amiable *Le Coq* on place de la Mairie (Ⓣ04.94.54.13.71, Ⓕ04.94.54.03.06; ❸), while *Le Clemenceau*, 1 rue Carnot (Ⓣ04.94.54.15.17, Ⓕ04.94.54.42.78; ❸), is good value but on a noisy junction. For **food**, try *La Grange*, 7 rue du 11 Novembre (Ⓣ04.94.54.60.97; closed Mon), with menus at €13 and €24, or *Taverne du Siffleur*, 9 rue Nationale (Ⓣ04.94.54.67.02; menus from €18; closed Oct–March), which overlooks a fountain on a very quiet street.

Grimaud and around

Four kilometres north of Cogolin, **GRIMAUD** is a film set of a *village perché*, where the cone of houses enclosing the twelfth-century church and culminating in the spectacular ruins of a medieval castle appears as a single, perfectly unified entity, decorated by its trees and flowers. The most vaunted street in this ensemble is the narrow **rue des Templiers**, which leads up past the arcaded Gothic house of the Knights Templars to the pure Romanesque **Église St-Michel**. The views from the château ruins (currently undergoing restoration) are superb, and the monumental, sharply cut serpentine window frames of the shattered edifice stand in mute testimony to its former glory.

These days Grimaud is an exclusive little village whose "corner shop" sells antiques and contemporary art. There's a small **tourist office** at 1 bd des Aliziers, just off the main road passing the village (Mon–Sat: July & Aug 9am–12.30pm & 3–7pm; April–June & Sept 9am–noon & 2.30–6.15pm; Oct–March 9am–12.30pm & 2.15–5.30pm; Ⓣ04.94.43.26.98, Ⓦwww.grimaud-provence.com). If you're on a budget and need a place to stay it's worth carrying on to La Garde-Freinet (see p.258), although *Le Coteau Fleuri* (Ⓣ04.94.43.20.17, Ⓔcoteaufleuri@wanadoo.fr; menu from €30; ❺), on place des Pénitents at the western edge of the village, offers a few reasonable **rooms** above its good restaurant. **Campers** should head for the *Camping Charlemagne* (Ⓣ04.94.43.22.90), at le Pont de Bois, 2km outside the village on the road to Collobrières. For food, you can get crêpes and omelettes at *Le Boubou* on the fountained place du Cros (closed Oct–March), or decent plats du jour at *L'Écurie de la Marquise*, 3 rue du Gacharel (Ⓣ04.94.43.27.26; menu from €18).

For more serious fare, settle down on the vine-covered terrace of the *Café de France* on place Neuve (☎04.94.43.20.05; €20 menu; closed Nov–Feb). On the lower side of place Neuve, the *Pâtisserie du Château* tearoom sells wonderful cakes and fresh nutty breads. The village **market** is held on Thursdays.

Port Grimaud

Avoiding the St-Tropez traffic chaos is tricky if you're visiting **PORT GRIMAUD**, the ultimate Côte d'Azur property development, half standing, half floating at the head of the Golfe de St-Tropez just north of La Foux.

It was created in the 1960s by developer François Spoerry – whose tomb is in the village church – as a private pleasure lagoon with waterways for roads and yachts parked at every door. The houses are in exquisitely tasteful old Provençal style and their owners, amongst them Joan Collins, are more than a little well heeled. The development is not wired off, and anyone can wander in for a gawp: the main visitors' entrance is 800m up the well-signed road off the N98, surrounded by vast (and distinctly unpicturesque) parking areas. You don't pay to get in, but you can't explore all the islands without hiring a boat (€18) or taking a boat tour with Les Coches d'Eau (€3.50). Even access to the church tower costs €1. There are plenty of places to **eat** and **drink**, though they are clearly aimed at visitors rather than the residents, and are not particularly good value, though affordable enough.

La Garde-Freinet

The attractive village of **LA GARDE-FREINET**, 10km north of Grimaud, was founded in the late twelfth century by people from the nearby villages of Saint Clément and Miremer. The original fortified settlement sat further up the hillside, and the foundations of its **fort** are visible above the present-day village beside the ruins of a fifteenth-century castle. To explore the ancient fort, it's a steep one-kilometre clamber along a path signposted "Aire de la Planète", leading from the tourist office car park. The fort can also be reached from La Croix des Maures car park.

During the insurrectionary days of Louis Napoleon's coup d'état, La Garde-Freinet played a radical role. Not only did its cork workers form a successful cooperative in 1851, but in their struggle with the landowners women played as strong a role as men. So much so that the prosecuting magistrate of Aix wrote to the minister of justice warning him that La Garde-Freinet, with its new form of socialism in which women took part, would encourage other villagers to abandon public morals and descend into debauchery.

Although today La Garde-Freinet's residents include Oxbridge professors and other Anglos with time on their hands, the village still feels like it belongs to the locals, thanks to the regeneration of the cork and chestnut forestry business, and the number of young local children around. It also has top-notch medieval charm; easy walks to stunning panoramas; markets each Wednesday and Sunday; a sweet-chestnut cooperative on the main road as you leave the village heading north; and tempting food shops such as *La Voute*, 38 rue St-Jacques, selling organic produce and good local wines. For hikers, the 21-kilometre GR9 **route des Crêtes** to the west of the village passes along a tremendously scenic forested ridge. The going is good as it used to be open to vehicles, and half the route is surfaced, though traffic has now been banned due to fire risk.

Practicalities

The helpful **tourist office** operates from 1 place Neuve (Easter–Oct Mon–Sat 10am–12.30pm & 3–6pm, Sun 10am–12.30pm; Nov–Easter Mon–Sat 10am–12.30pm & 3–6pm; ☎04.94.43.67.41, Ⓦwww.lagardefreinet

-tourisme.com), and provides information on all the Maures region, including suggested walks. Above it, a small **museum** (same hours as tourist office) displays archeological finds from the fortifications.

Accommodation prospects are reasonable: *La Sarrazine*, on the D588 after it turns west at the top of the village (ⓣ04.94.55.59.60, ⓕ04.94.55.58.18; ❺; closed Nov–Easter), has pleasant rooms to rent, while *La Claire Fontaine* on place Vieille (ⓣ04.94.43.60.36, ⓕ04.94.43.63.76; ❷) and *Le Fraxinois* on rue François-Pelletier (reception at the *Tabac-Presse*; ⓣ04.94.43.62.84, ⓕ04.94.43.69.65; ❸) are incredibly good value for this part of the world. There are two three-star **campsites** close at hand: the municipal *Saint-Éloi* (ⓣ04.94.43.62.40; €11 per tent; closed Oct–April) opposite the municipal pool, and *La Ferme de Bérard* (ⓣ04.94.43.21.23; €11 per tent; closed Nov–Feb) 5km along the D558 towards Grimaud, with its own pool and restaurant. **Walkers** can stay at a **gîte d'étape**, the *Hameau de La Cour Basse*, on the GR51 towards the coast (ⓣ04.94.43.64.63).

In the evenings, *Le Lézard* **restaurant** and **bar** on the exquisite place du Marché is the place to be (ⓣ04.94.43.62.73; menus at €20 and €34), with regular jazz and blues concerts. More elaborate food is served up in the rampant garden of *La Faucado* on the main road to the south (ⓣ04.94.43.60.41; around €25; booking essential; closed Jan & Feb & Tues out of season). Pigeon fanciers, in the culinary sense, should try *La Colombe Joyeuse* on the place Vieille (ⓣ04.94.43.65.24; €15–20; closed Mon & Nov–Jan) for its game and pigeon in honey and red wine.

Ste-Maxime and around

STE-MAXIME, which faces St-Tropez across the gulf, is an archetypal Côte resort: palmed corniche and enormous pleasure boat harbour, beaches crowded with confident bronzed windsurfers and waterskiers, a local history museum in a defensive tower that no one goes to, and a proliferation of estate agents. It sprawls a little too far – like many of the towns along this coast – but the magnetic appeal of the water's edge is hard to deny. Compared to its more famous neighbour, though, it's all rather lacking in atmosphere.

Its **beaches**, however, have the Blue Flags for cleanliness that St-Tropez's lack, and **Cherry Beach** or its neighbours on the east-facing Plage de la Nartelle, 2km from the centre round the Pointe des Sardinaux towards Les Issambres, is the strip of sand to head for. As well as paying for shaded, cushioned comfort, you can enter the water on a variety of different vehicles, eat grilled fish, have drinks brought to your mattress, and listen to a piano player as dusk falls. Four kilometres further on, with much the same facilities, is **Plage des Eléphants**, named after the cartoons of Jean de Brunhoff, creator of Babar the elephant, who had a holiday home in Ste-Maxime.

In addition to the beaches, Ste-Maxime's Vieille Ville has several good **markets**: there's a covered flower and food market on rue Fernand-Bessy (July & Aug Mon–Sat 7am–1pm & 4–8pm, Sun 7am–1pm; Sept–June Tues–Sun 7am–1pm); a Thursday morning food market on and around place du Marché; a bric-a-brac market every Friday morning (9am–noon) on place Jean-Mermoz; and arts and crafts in the pedestrian streets daily (mid-June to mid-Sept 10am–11pm).

Ten kilometres north of town on the road to Le Muy, the **Musée du Phonographe et de la Musique Mécanique** at parc St-Donat (Easter–Oct Wed–Sun 10am–noon & 3–6pm; €3) is the result of one woman's forty-year obsession with collecting audio equipment. This marvellous museum's facade resembles Hansel and Gretel's fantastical biscuit house but is actually modelled on an eighteenth-century Limonaire mechanical music machine. Inside, the owner has on display one of Thomas Edison's "talking machines" of 1878, the first recording machines of the 1890s and an amplified lyre (1903). One of the first saucer-shaped amplifiers, made of paper, is still in remarkably good condition, along with a 1913 audiovisual language-teaching aid and the wonderfully neat portable record players of the 1920s. In addition, there's an extraordinarily wide selection of automata, musical boxes and pianolas. Almost half the exhibits still work, and you may find yourself listening to the magical, crackling sounds of an original wax cylinder recording from the 1880s played on the equipment it was made for.

Practicalities

Buses arrive in town along the seafront and stop in front of the **tourist office** on the promenade Simon-Lorière (June & Sept daily 9am–8pm; July & Aug Mon–Sat 9am–8pm; Oct–May Mon–Sat 9am–noon & 2–6pm; Ⓣ04.94.55.75.55, Ⓦwww.ste-maxime.com). If you're heading for St-Tropez it's a good idea to do the journey by **boat**; the service from Ste-Maxime's **gare maritime** on the quai L-Condroyer runs daily all year round, with crossings every thirty minutes in July and August (Ⓣ04.94.49.29.39; €10.20). **Bikes** and **mopeds** can be rented at Rent Bike, 13 rue Magali (Ⓣ04.94.43.98.07), or Holiday Bikes, 10 rte du Plan de la Tour (Ⓣ04.94.43.90.19).

The tourist office can advise on **hotel** vacancies, which are very rare in summer. Among the less expensive options are the welcoming *Auberge Provençale*, 49 rue Aristide-Briand (Ⓣ04.94.55.76.90, Ⓕ04.94.55.76.91; ❹), which has a decent restaurant attached, or the small *Castellamar*, 21 av G-Pompidou (Ⓣ04.94.96.19.97; ❸; closed Oct–March), on the west side of the river but still close to the centre and the sea. Slightly further out, the *Marie-Louise*, 2km west in the Hameau de Guerre-Vieille (Ⓣ04.94.96.06.05, Ⓔmarielouise1@club-internet.fr; ❹), is tucked away in greenery but within sight of the sea. Pricier alternatives include the smart *Hôtellerie de la Poste*, 11 bd Frédéric-Mistral (Ⓣ04.94.96.18.33, Ⓕ04.94.96.41.68; ❻), which has very nice rooms and is right in the centre, and the pleasant *Les Palmiers*, on rue Gabriel-Péri by the church and Tour Carrée (Ⓣ04.94.96.00.41, Ⓕ04.94.96.74.30; ❻). For **campers**, there's *Les Cigalons*, in quartier de la Nartelle, a two-star seaside site (Ⓣ04.94.96.05.51, Ⓕ04.94.96.79.62; €17 per tent; closed Nov–March), or *La Baumette*, rte du Plan de la Tour (Ⓣ04.94.96.14.35, Ⓕ04.94.96.35.38; €18 per tent; closed Oct–March), 2km out of town, up in the hills off the D74.

There's plenty of choice for places **to eat**, with the pedestrian streets jam-packed with restaurants – one way of choosing from those on rue Hoche is to check them from the kitchen side along rue Fernand-Bessy. The *Hostellerie de la Belle Aurore*, 4 bd Jean-Moulin (Ⓣ04.94.96.02.45; menu at €35; closed Wed lunch & mid-Oct to mid-March), serves gourmet dishes on a sea-view terrace, while *L'Hermitage*, 118 av Gal-de-Gaulle (Ⓣ04.94.96.04.05; around €15), specializes in fish dishes at around half the price.

Along the coast to St-Aygulf

Beyond Ste-Maxime, its suburb **Val d'Esquières** merges with **Les Issambres**, the seaside extension of Roquebrune, and **St-Aygulf**, belonging to the *commune* of Fréjus, along the fast and rather dangerous coast road. For all that, this stretch has its attractions, revealing traditional colour-washed, pantiled Provençal architecture amid the filing-cabinet condominiums, and a shoreline of rocky coves and *calanques* alternating with golden crescents of sand. In Les Issambres there's even a narrow band of pines that almost lets you pretend that the corniche apartments and villas don't exist. If the seaside development gets too much, you can always head up and away into the empty eastern extremity of the Massif des Maures.

Practicalities

Hotels worth trying in Les Issambres include *La Quiétude*, set back from the corniche (ⓣ04.94.96.94.34, ⓔlaquietude@hotmail.com; ❹; closed mid-Oct to late Feb), and *La Bonne Auberge*, on the N98 at Calanque des Issambres (ⓣ04.94.96.90.74; ❷; closed Nov–Feb), overlooking the sea. In St-Aygulf, *Le Catalogne*, av de la Corniche d'Azur (ⓣ04.94.81.01.44, ⓕ04.94.81.32.42; ❽; closed mid-Oct to Easter), has a pleasant, shaded garden, while *Athéna Motel* at 69 impasse Corot (ⓣ04.94.81.21.15; ❻; closed Nov–Feb), sits at the start of the long, straight beach that stretches from St-Aygulf to St-Raphaël. There's no shortage of **campsites** along this stretch, all well signed off the corniche. **Bikes** can be rented from Holiday Bikes, at 595 av Corniche d'Azur, the main road through St-Aygulf (ⓣ04.94.81.35.94).

The *Villa St-Elme* is the fancy **restaurant** on the corniche des Issambres, where elaborate and delicate fish dishes can be consumed overlooking the Golfe de St-Tropez: it also has a few rooms for well-heeled guests (ⓣ04.94.49.52.52; menus from €43.50; ❾). At the other end of the scale, *Le Pointu*, on place de la Galiote in St-Aygulf, dishes up a brilliant *moules marinières* for €8.50. St-Aygulf has a good daily **market**, too, and great *poulets rôtis* from a permanent stall overlooking the main square on bd Honoré-de-Balzac.

Inland: the Argens Valley

The **River Argens** meets the Mediterranean in unspectacular style between St-Aygulf and St-Raphaël. It is an important source of irrigation for orchards and vines, but as a waterway it has little appeal, being sluggish, full of breeding mosquitoes and on the whole inaccessible. The geographical feature that dominates the lower Argens Valley, and acts as an almost mystical pole of attraction, is the **Rocher de Roquebrune** between the village of **Roquebrune-sur-Argens** and the town of **Le Muy**.

Roquebrune-sur-Argens and the Rocher de Roquebrune

The village of **ROQUEBRUNE-SUR-ARGENS** lies on the edge of the Massif des Maures, 12km from the sea, facing the flat valley of the Argens opening to the northeast. Some of its sixteenth-century defensive towers and ramparts remain, and almost every house within them is four hundred years old or more, joined together by vaulted passageways and tiny cobbled streets. The central square is a satisfying slice of small-town France, with graceful ironwork balconies and shady arcades.

To sample some of the delicious local red and rosé **wines** (phone first), visit the Domaine de Marchandise, rte des Marchandises (ⓣ04.94.45.42.91), or the Domaine des Planes on the D7 to St-Aygulf (ⓣ04.98.11.49.00). Alternatively, you can fill up with quality plonk at the Coopérative Vinicole, at rond point St Pierre, on the D7 just east of the village centre. Delicious nougat and chocolate can be bought from Courreau, 2 montée St-Michel, and there's a **market** on Tuesday on pl Germain Ollier, and Friday morning on pl Alfred Perrin.

The **tourist office**, on rue Jean-Aicard (Feb to mid-June & mid-Sept to Oct Mon–Sat 9am–noon & 2–6pm; mid-June to mid-Sept daily 9am–1pm & 3–7pm; Nov–Jan Mon–Fri 9am–noon & 2–5pm; ⓣ04.94.45.72.70; ⓦwww.ville-roquebrune-argens.fr), can provide addresses for accommodation, as well as information on walks and sports. **Accommodation** in the village is limited to a *Formule I* hotel on rond point des 4 Chemins (ⓣ04.94.81.61.61, ⓦwww.accor.com; ❶), between Roquebrune and Le Muy, or the nearby *Villages Hôtel*, at La Garillans on the D7 (ⓣ04.94.45.45.00, ⓕ04.94.81.63.53; ❷), a similarly modern and impersonal establishment, that has several rooms with facilities for the disabled. Between the village and St-Aygulf the road is lined with mega **campsites**, but more pleasant pitches can be found on local farms; ask at the tourist office. Of the **restaurants**, *Le Gaspacho*, 21 av Gal de Gaulle (ⓣ04.94.45.49.59; closed Nov), serves Provençal specialities; or you can get a filling meal at *Le Mas des Oliviers* (ⓣ04.94.81.25.81), 6km from the village along the D7 in the direction of St-Aygulf.

Rocher de Roquebrune

Three kilometres west of Roquebrune, the rust-red mass of the **Roquebrune rock** erupts unexpectedly out of nothing, as if to some purpose. Even the Autoroute du Soleil thundering past its foot fails to bring it into line with the rest of the coastal scenery glimpsed from the fast lane. To reach it, coming from Roquebrune, take the left fork just after the village, signed to La Roquette; at the next fork you can go left or right depending on which side of the mountain you want to skirt. The right-hand route runs alongside the highway towards **Notre-Dame-de-la-Roquette**, an erstwhile place of pilgrimage (now closed to the public), while the left-hand fork takes you round the quieter, steeper southern side.

The rock itself is private property and casual visitors are far from welcome. However, the tourist office in Le Muy (in whose *commune* the rock actually stands) can organize guided visits, usually on a Tuesday.

Le Muy and around

Although not a wildly exciting place, **LE MUY** is interesting politically, having had one of the sole surviving communist mayors of the Côte d'Azur in the 1980s, switching to a coalition of right-wing and *Front National* in 1989, and shifting in the late 1990s to a centrist administration.

The town's political history and ideological leanings are often mirrored in the names of its streets, its buildings and architecture. One street is named after Maurice Lachâtre, a revolutionary writer, publisher and printer who escaped from the 1871 Paris Commune and was sheltered in Le Muy. The *Provençal* **bar** that surrounds and hides the apse of the town's church was built during the 1930s period of militantly atheist socialism.

The **tour Charles-Quint** takes its name from the attempted assassination of the Emperor Charles V in 1536 by the people of Le Muy. Unfortunately for the Le Muy natives, the king was aware of his unpopularity and had paid a Spanish poet, Garcilaso de la Vega, to masquerade as him. Consequently the Muyoise killed the Spaniard, retreated to the tower, were told by the invader that they would be spared if they surrendered, came out with their hands up and were promptly massacred; the tower was renamed after their arch enemy. Today, the tower houses a **Musée de la Libération** (April–June Sun

10am–noon; July & Aug Thurs & Sun 10am–noon; Sept–April by appointment at the tourist office), commemorating 1944's Operation Dragoon, which opened a second front in the south of France against the Germans.

If you want to **stay** in the village, try the *Hôtel les Allées*, 2 allée Victor-Hugo (Ⓣ04.94.45.08.30, Ⓕ04.94.45.95.25; ❷), a fairly basic place in the centre of the village. For **food**, *Le Vieux Piano*, 7 bis av Cavalier (Ⓣ04.94.45.83.86), has a €15.50 menu, and theatrical portraits on the walls. Le Muy's Sunday morning **market** is one of the largest in the region.

Chapelle de Ste-Roseline

A short way up the road to Draguignan (see p.280–281) from Le Muy, the D91 leads left to the **Chapelle de Ste-Roseline** (Tues–Sun: March–May 2–6pm; June–Sept 3–7pm; Oct–Feb 2–5pm; free). The old abbey buildings of which the chapel is part are a private residence belonging to a wine grower, and you can also visit the cellars and taste the *cru classé* named after the chapel (Mon–Fri 9am–noon & 2–6.30pm, Sat & Sun 10am–noon & 2–6pm).

The chapel's interior is really rather ghoulish. Saint Roseline was born in 1263 and spent her adolescence disobeying her father by giving food to the poor. On one occasion he caught her and demanded to see the contents of her basket; the food miraculously turned into rose petals. She became the prioress of the abbey and when she died her body refused to decay. It was paraded around Provence until it got lost. A blind man found it and it now, supposedly, lies in a glass case in the chapel, shrivelled and brown but not quite a skeleton. What's worse are her eyes – one lifeless, the other staring at you – displayed in a gaudy frame on a wall. Louis XIV is said to be responsible for the dead eye. On a pilgrimage here he reckoned the eyes smacked of sorcery so had his surgeon pierce one. Life immediately left it. Horror objects apart, the chapel has a fabulous mosaic by **Chagall** showing angels laying a table for the saint; some beautifully carved seventeenth-century choir stalls; and an impressive Renaissance rood-loft in which peculiar things happen to the legs of the decorative figures.

Les Arcs-sur-Argens and beyond

Eight kilometres west of Le Muy, the picturesque medieval village of **LES ARCS** has been carefully restored, with its skyline dominated by a Saracen lookout tower, the sole remnant of a thirteenth-century castle. Les Arcs is one of the centres for the Var wine industry, and at the **Maison des Vins** (daily 10am–1pm & 1.30–7pm; July–Aug until 8pm) you can taste and buy wine and cheeses and pick up details of local *vignerons* to visit and *routes du vin* to follow: it's on the main road from Le Muy, past the turning to the village and the bridge across the Argens.

The **tourist office** on place Gén-de-Gaulle (Mon–Fri 10.30am–12.30pm & 2–5pm; Ⓣ04.94.73.37.30) has plenty of information on the surrounding area. The nicest place to **stay**, if your budget will stretch, is the exclusive hotel *Le Logis du Guetteur* on place du Château (Ⓣ04.94.99.51.10, Ⓕ04.94.99.51.29; ❼), with panoramic views of the Saracen tower. Less expensive rooms are available at *L'Avenir*, av de la Gare (Ⓣ04.94.73.30.58; ❶), by the gare SNCF, halfway between the village and the N7. The **restaurant** in *Le Logis* is good (menus from €27), as is *Le Bacchus Gourmand* (Ⓣ04.94.47.48.47; menus from €29; closed Sun eve out of season, and Mon), the Maison des Vins' very beautiful restaurant, which serves Provençal specialities. The best day to visit Les Arcs is Thursday when a busy **market** is held on the central square.

Vidauban

Following the road west from Les Arcs, after 8km you'll come to the village of **VIDAUBAN**, as attractive as its neighbour, particularly at night when its old-fashioned lamps are lit. The village has a charming **restaurant**, *Le Concorde*, 9 place Clemenceau (☎04.94.73.01.19; menus from €26–55; closed Wed), and some interesting wine *domaines*, including the Vieux Château d'Astros (to arrange an appointment, call ☎04.94.73.00.25) and the Château St-Julien d'Aille (to arrange an appointment, call ☎04.94.73.02.89).

St-Raphaël and Fréjus

The major conurbation of **St-Raphaël** on the coast and **Fréjus**, centred 3km inland, has a history dating back to the Romans. Fréjus was established as a naval base under Julius Caesar and Augustus, St-Raphaël as a resort for its veterans. The ancient port at Fréjus, or Forum Julii, had 2km of quays and was connected by a walled canal to the sea, which was considerably closer back then. After the battle of Actium in 31 AD, the ships of Antony and Cleopatra's defeated fleet were brought here.

The area between Fréjus and the sea is now the suburb of **Fréjus-Plage** with a glitzy 1980s marina, **Port-Fréjus**. St-Raphaël merges with Fréjus and Fréjus-Plage, which in turn merge with **Boulouris** to the east. West of Fréjus a vast modern out-of-town shopping strip – amongst the largest in the South of France – spreads west as far as the A8 autoroute.

Despite the obsession with facilities for the seaborne rich – there were already two pleasure ports at St-Raphaël before Port-Fréjus was built – this is no bad place for a stopover. There's a wide range of hotels and restaurants, some interesting sightseeing in Fréjus, and good transport links with inland Provence and the coast eastwards along the Corniche d'Esterel.

Fréjus

The population of **FRÉJUS**, remarkably, was greater in the first century BC than it is today if you count only the residents of the town centre, which lies well within the Roman perimeter. But very little remains of the original **Roman walls** that once circled the city, and the **harbour** that made Fréjus an important Mediterranean port silted up early on and was finally filled in after the Revolution. It is instead the **medieval centre**, with its lively shopping and cafés and intimate, small-town side streets full of tiny houses, that evokes a feel for this ancient town.

Arrival and information

Around a dozen trains a day from St-Raphaël stop at **Fréjus gare SNCF**, a journey of between three and six minutes. Buses between the two towns are much more frequent and take fifteen minutes, arriving at the Fréjus **halte routière** on place Paul-Vernet on the east side of the town centre, opposite the small **tourist office**, 325 rue Jean-Jaurès (July & Aug Mon–Sat 9am–7pm, Sept–June Mon–Sat 9am–noon & 2–6pm, Sun 10am–noon & 3–6pm; ☎04.94.51.83.83, ⓦwww.ville-frejus.fr). Here, you can pick up a helpful street map of the entire Fréjus-St Raphaël conurbation. **Bikes** can be rented from Holiday Bikes, Rond Point des Moulins (☎04.94.52.30.65).

Accommodation

Hotels are not as plentiful in Fréjus as in St-Raphaël, but it's generally a quieter place to stay. There's a **youth hostel** a couple of kilometres from the cen-

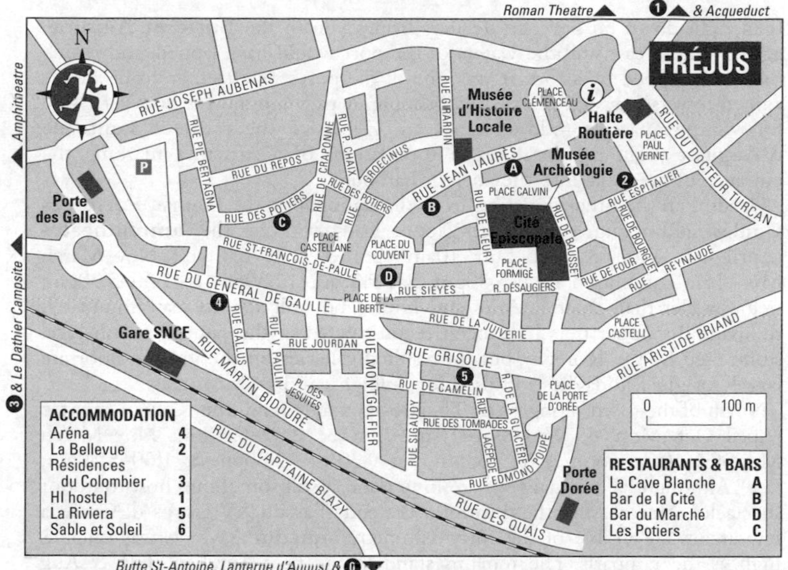

tre, and plenty of **campsites** along the rte des Combattants d'Afrique du Nord west of the town. These are mostly on a vast scale, however – the largest has almost 800 pitches – and only a few are especially close to the sea.

Hotels

Aréna 145 av Général-de-Gaulle ⓣ04.94.17.09.40, ⓦwww.arena-hotel.com. Rather elegant, with pretty rooms, if a bit small, in a converted bank in Fréjus centre. Pleasant swimming pool. 6

La Bellevue pl Paul-Vernet ⓣ04.94.17.27.05, ⓕ04.94.51.32.25. Right in town so not the quietest location, but convenient and inexpensive. 4

Résidences du Colombier 1239 rte des Combattants d'Afrique du Nord ⓣ04.94.51.45.92, ⓕ04.94.53.82.85. A series of modern bungalows in a pine wood north of town; all rooms have their own garden and terrace. Closed Nov–Jan. 5

La Riviera 90 rue Grisolle ⓣ04.94.51.31.46, ⓕ04.94.17.18.34. Very small hotel in the centre of Fréjus. Not very modern, but clean and perfectly acceptable. 1

Sable et Soleil 158 rue Paul-Arène, Fréjus-Plage ⓣ04.94.51.08.70, ⓕ04.94.53.49.12. A pleasant, small, modern hotel, 300m from the sea. 4

Hostels and campsites

HI hostel Auberge de Jeunesse de Fréjus, chemin du Counillier ⓣ04.94.53.18.75, ⓕ04.94.53.25.86. Located in a small pine grove, 2km from Fréjus centre; take bus #4, #8 or #9 from St-Raphaël or Fréjus (direction L'Hôpital, stop Les Chênes) and walk up av du Gal-d'Armée Jean-Calliès – the chemin du Counillier is the first left. In the mornings a minibus departs from the hostel for the station and the beach. Reception closed 10am–6pm; 11pm curfew (10pm in winter).

Le Dattier rte des Combattants d'Afrique du Nord ⓣ04.94.40.88.93, ⓕ04.94.40.89.01. A four-star site 3.5km north of Fréjus. Closed Oct–Easter.

Site de Gorge Vent quartier de Bellevue ⓣ04.94.52.90.37, ⓕ04.94.44.41.24. A two-star site off the N7 towards Cannes, 3km from the town centre. €20 per tent.

The Roman town

Taking a tour of the **Roman remains** gives you a good idea of the extent of Forum Julii, but they are scattered throughout and beyond the town centre and to see them all would take a full day. Turning right out of the gare SNCF and then right down bd Séverin-Decuers brings you to the **Butte St-Antoine**, against whose east wall the waters of the port would have lapped, and which once was capped by a fort. It was one of the port's defences, and one of the ruined towers may have been a lighthouse. A path around the southern wall follows the quayside (odd stretches are visible) to the medieval **Lanterne d'Auguste**, built on the Roman foundations of a structure marking the entrance of the canal into the ancient harbour.

Heading in the other direction from the station, past the Roman **Porte des Gaules** and along rue Henri-Vadon, leads you to the **amphitheatre** (April–Oct Mon & Wed–Sun 10am–1pm & 2.30–6.30pm; Nov–March Mon–Fri 10am–noon & 1–5.30pm, Sat 9.30am–12.30pm & 1.30–5.30pm; free), smaller than those at Arles and Nîmes, but still able to seat around ten thousand. Its upper tiers have been reconstructed in the same greenish local stone used by the Romans, but the vaulted galleries on the ground floor are largely original. Today, it's still used for bullfights and rock concerts.

North of the town, along av du Théâtre-Romain, stands the Roman **theatre** (April–Oct Mon & Wed–Sun 10am–1pm & 2.30–6.30pm; Nov–March Mon–Fri 10am–noon & 1–5.30pm, Sat 9.30am–12.30pm & 1.30–5.30pm; free). Although its original seats are long gone, it still sometimes hosts outdoor spectacles. Northeast of the theatre, at the end of av du XV Corps-d'Armée, a few arches are visible of the forty-kilometre **aqueduct**, which was once as high as the ramparts. The remains stand in the parc Aurelien (July & Aug Mon–Fri 9am–7pm, Sat & Sun 9am–6pm; Sept–June daily 9am–5pm; free), also home to the large beaux arts Villa Aurélienne, which hosts cultural events and exhibitions. Closer to the centre, where bd Aristide-Briand meets rue des Quais, are the arcades of the **Porte d'Orée**, positioned on the former harbour's edge alongside what was probably a bath complex.

The medieval town

The **Cité Episcopale**, or cathedral close, takes up two sides of **place Formigé**, the marketplace and heart of both contemporary and medieval Fréjus. It comprises the cathedral, flanked by the fourteenth-century bishop's palace, now the hôtel de ville, the baptistry, chapterhouse, cloisters and archeological museum. Visits to the cloisters and baptistry are guided and leave approximately every hour (April–Sept Mon & Wed–Sun 9am–7pm; Oct–March Mon & Wed–Sun 9am–noon & 2–5pm; €4); access to the cathedral is free (daily 9am–noon & 2.30–6.30pm), but you'll have to peer through a glass partition to see the baptistry and will miss the fascinating seventeenth-century carved wooden portals with their depictions of a Saracen massacre unless you take the tour.

The oldest part of the complex is the **baptistry**, one of France's most ancient buildings, built in the fourth or fifth century and, as such, contemporary with the decline and fall of the city's Roman founders. Its two doorways are of different heights, signifying the enlarged spiritual stature of the baptized, and it was used in the days of early Christianity when adult baptism was still the norm. Parts of the early Gothic **cathedral** may belong to a tenth-century church, but its best features, apart from the coloured diamond-shaped tiles on the spire, are Renaissance: the choir stalls, a wooden crucifix on the left of the entrance, and the intricately carved doors with scenes of a Saracen massacre. By far the most beautiful and engaging component of the whole ensemble, however, is the **cloisters**. Slender marble columns, carved in the twelfth century, support a fourteenth-century ceiling of wooden panels painted with apocalyptic creatures. Out of the original 1200 pictures, 400 remain, each about the size of this page. The subjects include multiheaded monsters, mermaids, satyrs and scenes of bacchanalian debauchery. The **Musée Archéologique** (April–Oct Mon & Wed–Sat 10am–1pm & 2–6.30pm; Nov–March Mon–Fri 10am–noon & 1.30–5.30pm, Sat 9.30am–12.30pm, Sun 1.30–5.30pm; free) on the upper storey of the cloisters has as its star pieces a complete Roman mosaic of a leopard and a copy of a renowned double-headed bust of Hermes. You can wander through the modern courtyard of the hôtel de ville, but you get a better view of the orange Esterel stone walls of the episcopal palace from rue de Beausset.

Close by, in an old bourgeois town house at 153 av Jean Jaurès, is the small **Musée d'Histoire Locale** (mid-June to mid-Sept Tues–Sat 9am–noon & 3–7pm; mid-Sept to mid-June Tues–Sat 9am–noon & 2–6pm), with reconstructions of past life including an old school classroom, plus displays on traditional local trades.

Around Fréjus

The environs of Fréjus hold several reminders of France's colonial past. About 2km north of town, there's a Vietnamese pagoda and a Sudanese mosque, both built by French colonial troops. The **Pagode Hong Hien** (daily 9am–noon & 2–7pm), at the crossroads of the N7 to Cannes and rue Henri-Giraud (bus #L13), is still maintained as a Buddhist temple. There's also a **memorial** to the Indochina wars close by. About four kilometres north of Fréjus, the **Mosquée Missiri de Djenné** is on rue des Combattants d'Afrique du Nord, off the D4 to Bagnols 2km from the RN7 junction. It's a strange, guava-coloured, fort-like building in typical West African style, and decorated inside with fading murals of desert journeys gracefully sketched in white on the dark pink walls.

There are plenty of activities for children around Fréjus, including a **zoo** at Le Capitou, 5km north of the town (June–Sept daily 9.30am–6pm; Oct–May daily 10am–5.30pm; €10), and the **Aquatica water park**, off the RN98 to St-Aygulf (July & Aug daily 10am–7pm; June & Sept daily 10am–6pm; €22, children €18; bus #L9), complete with Europe's biggest wave pool, paddle boats, galleons and other water-based attractions, plus an 18-hole miniature-golf course. Next to Aquatica, Fréjus' **Base Nature** (☎04.94.51.91.10) offers a vast range of sporting activities including sand-yachting, skateboarding and rollerblading, while more gentle pursuits, such as walking and bird-spotting, can be indulged at the **Étangs de Villepey** wetland nature reserve (dawn–dusk; free), off the RN98 between Fréjus and St-Aygulf.

Eating, drinking and nightlife

Fréjus is not a bad place for menu-browsing and café-lounging, with the cheaper **eateries** found on place Agricola, place de la Liberté and the main shopping streets. At Fréjus-Plage there's a string of eating houses to choose from, with more upmarket seafood outlets at Port-Fréjus. For **nightlife**, the port and beach are the places to aim for, with Fréjus' two discos, *L'Odysée* and *La Playa*, both on the seafront bd de la Libération.

Aréna 145 av Général-de-Gaulle ☎04.94.17.09.40. Attached to the hotel of the same name (see p.265), this decent restaurant serves excellent fish dishes; menus start at €23. Closed Mon & Sat lunch.

La Cave Blanche on pl Calvini above the Cité Episcopale ☎04.94.51.25.40. Offers *rascasse* on a menu of €18.50. Closed Sun eve and all day Mon.

Bar de la Cité 152 rue Jean-Jaurès. A pleasant, ordinary bar.

Bar du Marché pl de la Liberté. A classic café for snacks and sipping beers under the shade of plane trees.

Les Potiers 135 rue des Potiers ☎04.94.51.33.74. Charmingly located in a tiny backstreet, this is one of the best restaurants in Fréjus; it serves dishes of fresh seasonal ingredients, with menus from €21.50. Closed Tues lunch & Wed.

St-Raphaël

A large resort and now one of the richest towns on the Côte, **ST-RAPHAËL** became fashionable at the turn of the twentieth century. It lost many of its *belle époque* mansions and hotels in the bombardments of World War II; some, like the *Continental*, have been rebuilt virtually from scratch in a modern style, others have undergone more gradual restoration. Meanwhile, the tiny **old quar-**

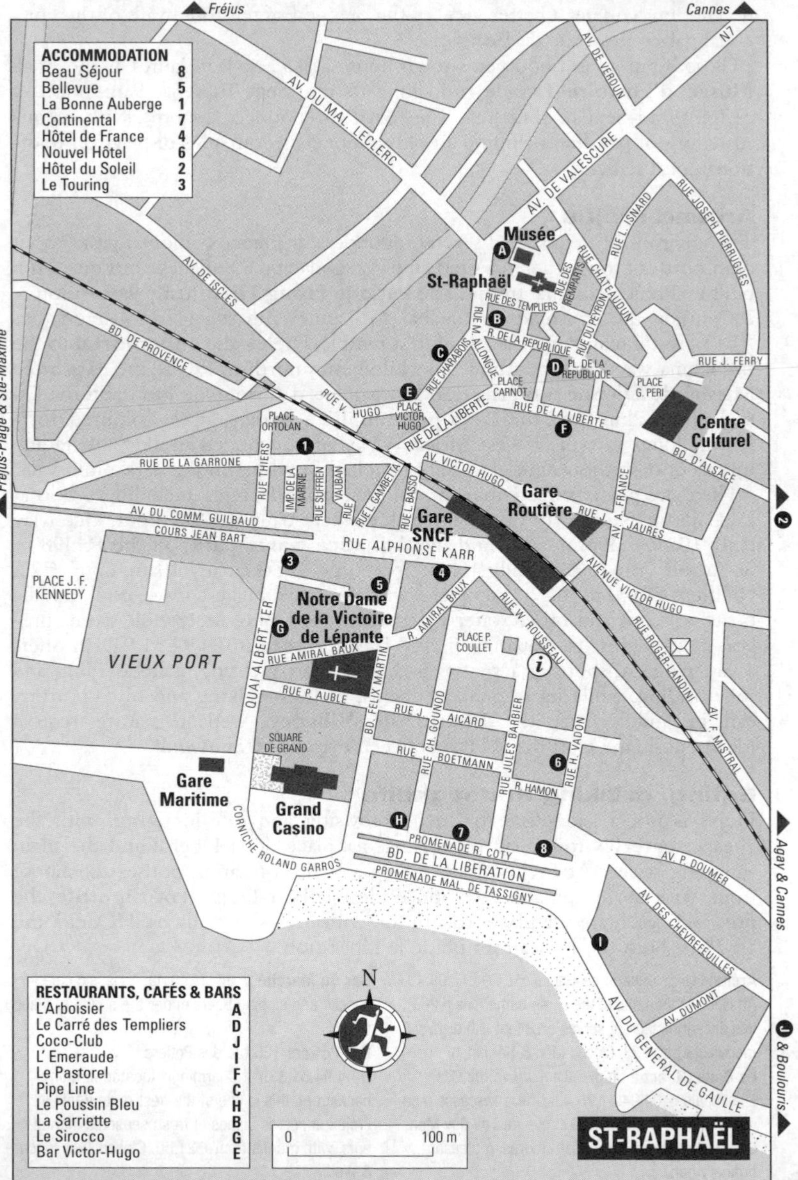

ter (*vieux quartier*) beyond place Carnot on the other side of the rail line is pleasantly low-key, no longer the town's major commercial focus but one of the better places to stroll and browse.

Arrival and information

St-Raphaël's gare SNCF, on rue Waldeck-Rousseau in the centre of the town, is the main station on the Marseille-Ventigmilia line; the **gare routière** is just across the rail line from the gare SNCF, on place du Dr Régis. The **tourist office** is also on rue Waldeck-Rousseau (July & Aug daily 9am–7pm; Sept–June Mon–Sat 9am–12.30pm & 2–6.30pm, Sun hours vary; ⓣ04.94.19.52.52, ⓦwww.ville-saintraphael.fr).

Accommodation

There are plenty of **hotels** in St-Raphaël, from seafront palaces to backstreet budget options. They can all get extremely busy in summer, however, so it's worth booking in advance. If you prefer **camping**, head for the area east of St-Raphaël along the Esterel coast – the large three-star *International de L'Ile d'Or*, above the N98 at Boulouris (ⓣ04.94.95.52.13), is a good bet with sea views.

Beau Séjour promenade René-Coty ⓣ04.94.95.03.75, ⓕ04.94.83.89.99. One of the less expensive seafront hotels with a pleasant terrace. Closed Nov–March. ❸

Bellevue 22 bd Félix-Martin ⓣ04.94.19.90.10, ⓔhotel.bellevue3@wanadoo.fr. Excellent value for its central location, but book well in advance. ❸

La Bonne Auberge 54 rue de la Garonne ⓣ04.94.95.69.72. Close to the old port, half board only in summer (€39 per person). Closed mid-Nov to Feb. ❺

Continental promenade René-Coty ⓣ04.94.83.87.87, ⓦwww.hotelcontinental.fr. A modern, air-conditioned seafront hotel with private parking and light, spacious rooms, rebuilt on the site of its illustrious predecessor in 1993. ❻

Hôtel de France 25 pl Galliéni ⓣ04.94.95.19.20, ⓕ04.94.95.61.84. A plain and simple option, but not seedy, in a potentially noisy location, opposite the station. ❸

Nouvel Hôtel 6 av Henri-Vadon ⓣ04.94.95.23.30, ⓕ04.94.95.75.41. A cheerful and reasonably smart tourist hotel, near the station. ❹

Hôtel du Soleil 47 bd du Domaine de Soleil, off bd Christian-Lafon ⓣ04.94.83.10.00, ⓦwww.perso.wanadoo.fr/hotel-du-soleil. A small, pretty villa with its own garden to the east of the centre. The hotel also has studios to rent. ❹

Le Touring 1 quai Albert 1er ⓣ04.94.95.01.72, ⓔletouring@wanadoo.fr. Port-side location, so not that quiet, but you can't get more central than this. Closed mid-Nov to mid-Dec. ❹

The Town

On rue des Templiers, to the north of the stations, in the courtyard of a crumbling fortified Romanesque church, you'll find fragments of the Roman aqueduct that brought water from Fréjus. Further along rue des Templiers, there's a local history and underwater archeology **museum** (June–Sept Tues–Sat 10am–noon & 3–6.30pm; Oct–May Tues–Sat 10am–noon & 2–5.30pm; €1.50), which contains Neolithic, Paleolithic and Bronze Age artefacts and a large collection of amphorae. The streets in this *vieux quartier* are home to some of St-Raphaël's more interesting and sophisticated restaurants and bars, while just to the east, on pl Gabriel Péri, stands the town's spanking new **Centre Culturel** (Tues–Sat 8.30am–7pm). Primarily a library, it also hosts interesting temporary art exhibitions.

Heading back towards the port, you'll pass St Raphaël's principal landmark, the towering, florid late-nineteenth-century church of **Notre Dame de la Victoire de Lépante**, on bd Félix Martin. Its interior houses a representation of St Raphaël, the symbol of the city. From here, it's a brief stroll to the broad promenade René-Coty lined with grand hotels – look out for the Art Deco stucco flowers adorning La Rocquerousse apartment buildings, next to the *Hôtel Beau Séjour*. The promenade culminates with the grandiose Résidence La

Méditerranée, built in 1914, at 1 av Paul-Doumer: continue along here, and you'll find a pretty English church and a *fin-de-siècle* villa.

The sandy **beaches** stretch between the Vieux Port in the centre and the newer Port Santa Lucia, with opportunities for every kind of water sport. **Boats** leave from the gare maritime on the south side of the Vieux Port to St-Tropez, Port Grimaud, the Îles d'Hyères and the islands off Cannes as well as the much closer *calanques* of the Esterel coast. If you're tired of sea and sand and want to lose whatever money you have left on slot machines or blackjack, the **Grand Casino** on Square de Gand overlooking the Vieux Port (daily 10am–4am; open until 5am in July & August) will be only too happy to oblige.

Eating and drinking

You'll find reasonable **brasseries**, pizzerias, crêperies and **restaurants** of varying quality around the port and along the promenades, with smaller and more individual (but not necessarily more expensive) places inland in the *vieux quartier*. Many of St-Raphaël's restaurants are family-friendly with specific children's menus. **Cafés** such as *Bar Victor-Hugo*, overlooking the market on pl Victor-Hugo, are also a good, cheap option. For **snacks**, cakes, ice creams, beers and cocktails try *L'Emeraude*, 3 bd du Gal-de-Gaulle. **Food markets** are held daily on place Victor-Hugo and place de la République, with fish sold in the mornings at the Vieux Port.

L'Arboisier 6 ave de Valescure ⓣ04.94.95.25.00. Inventive cuisine from chef Philippe Troncy includes tagine of lobster with fresh coconut. €26 lunch menu. Closed Sun eve, Wed eve and Mon out of season.

Le Carré des Templiers 2 pl de la République ⓣ04.94.19.19.19. Smart new *vieux quartier* restaurant that turns into a cigar bar and nightclub on Fri and Sat, after 11pm. Lunch menu at €17, dinner from €33. Closed Sun eve.

Le Pastorel 54 rue de la Liberté ⓣ04.94.95.02.36. This place has been serving traditional Provençal dishes since 1922. Menus start around €28. Closed Sun eve, Mon & Tues.

Le Poussin Bleu cnr of promenade René-Coty and rue Charles-Gounod ⓣ04.94.95.25.14. Moderately priced seafront brasserie.

La Sarriette 45 rue de la République ⓣ04.94.19.28.13. Likeable family restaurant on a small place in the *vieux quartier*, serves wonderful lavender scented *crème brûlée*. Menus at €15 and €20 accompanied by a soundtrack from the Hot Club de France. Closed Sun eve & all day Mon.

Le Sirocco 35 quai Albert 1er ⓣ04.94 95 39.99. Smart, but staid, sea-view restaurant specializing in fish. The menus range from €16–44, but the wine is expensive.

Nightlife and entertainment

For **drinking**, *Blue Bar* on rue Jules Barbier above Plage du Veillat has a decent selection of beers, or, for something more upmarket, there's cocktails and piano music at *Coco-Club* at Port Santa Lucia (till dawn), and *Le Seven*, at 171 Quai Albert 1er. *Pipe Line*, at 16 rue Charabois, is St Raphaël's only gay bar, with regular cabaret (weekends only out of season). *La Réserve*, on promenade René-Coty, is the stereotypical Côte d'Azur **disco** (open from 11pm), with ladies' nights and popular hits. *Le Kilt*, at 130 rue Jules-Barbier, is a little more exciting, billing itself as the disco for the over-30s, while *Le C Hype*, on rue de la Liberté, is slicker, with a cigar bar.

If you're in St-Raphaël in early July, try to catch some of the bands playing in the international competition of New Orleans **jazz** bands: ask at the tourist office for details of venues.

Listings

Bike rental Atout Cycles, 330 bd Jean Moulin ⓣ04.94.95.56.91.

Boat rental Club Nautique, at the western end of Port Santa Lucia ⓣ04.94.95.11.66.

Car rental Most are in or near the gare SNCF: Avis is on pl de la Gare ⓣ04.94.95.60.42; Budget

is on rue Waldeck-Rousseau ☎04.94.82.24.44; and Europcar on pl-Coulet ☎04.94.95.56.87.
Currency exchange Most banks have cashpoint machines, or try the Crédit Agricole Change Service, 26 av du Commandant-Guilbaud, on the Vieux Port.
Diving Club Sous l'Eau, at Port Santa Lucia to the east of the town centre (☎04.94.95.90.33), takes divers out to the numerous wartime wrecks and underwater archeological sites off the coast; Club de Plongée Aventure Sous-Marine, 56 rue de la Garonne (☎04.94.19.33.70, ⓦwww.plongee83.com), specializes in night-diving.
Emergency ☎15; Hôpital Intercommunal Bonnet, av André-Léotard, Fréjus ☎04.94.40.21.21; SOS Médecins ☎04.94.95.15.25.
Laundry Top Pressing, 34 av Général Leclerc; Lav'Matic, Port Santa Lucia.
Pharmacy For the name of an emergency pharmacy, call the Police Municipale in St-Raphaël by day ☎04.94.95.00.17; or in Fréjus by night ☎04.94.51.90.00.
Police Commissariat, av Amiral-Baux, St-Raphaël ☎04.94.95.00.17
Post office Poste Principale, av Victor-Hugo.
Taxi ☎04.94.95.04.25 or 04.94.83.24.24.

The Esterel

The 32-kilometre **Corniche de l'Esterel**, the sole stretch of wild coast between St-Raphaël and the Italian border, remains untouched by property development – at least between **Anthéor** and **Le Trayas** – its backdrop a 250-million-year-old arc of brilliant red volcanic rock tumbling down to the sea from the harsh crags of the **Massif de l'Esterel**. From the two major routes between Fréjus and **La Napoule**, the coastal N98 and rail line, and the inland N7, minor roads lead into this steeply contoured and once deeply wooded wild terrain. The **shoreline**, meanwhile, is a mass of little beaches, some sand, some shingle, cut by rocky promontories.

The inland route

The high, hairpin **inland route** is a dramatic but sometimes heart-rending drive; for every 2km of undisturbed ancient olive trees and gravity-defying rock formations, you have to suffer 1km of new motels and "residential parks" with real-estate hoardings. The Esterel is – or was – one of the most beautiful areas on the planet, with an interior uninhabited for centuries, save for reclusive saints, escaped convicts from Toulon, and Resistance fighters. It has no water and the topsoil is too shallow for cultivation. Prior to the twentieth-century creation of the corniche, the coastal communities were linked only by sea. The inland route (N7), however, is ancient, following in parts the Roman Via Aurelia.

Because of the fire risk many of the minor roads are barred to vehicles and even bicycles during the summer months, and some are closed throughout the year between 9am and 6pm: call the information line on ☎04.98.10.55.41 for details. All fires, and even cigarettes, are banned all year round. This makes **walking** even more enjoyable, though camping is strictly forbidden. The tourist office in St-Raphaël (see p.264) can provide details of paths and of the peaks that are the most obvious destinations. The highest point is **Mont Vinaigre**, which you can almost reach by road on the N7; a short, signposted footpath leads up to the summit. At 618m it's hardly a mountain, but the view from the top is spectacular.

The corniche

With half a dozen train stations and ten buses a day between St-Raphaël and Le Trayas, this is a very accessible coastal stretch for non-drivers. Boats also run along the coast from St-Raphaël's gare maritime. Along the stretch between

Anthéor and Le Trayas each easily reached beach has its summer snack-van, but by clambering over rocks you can usually find a near-deserted cove.

Le Dramont, Agay and Anthéor

The merest snatch of clear hillside and brasserie-less beach distinguishes Boulouris from **LE DRAMONT**, 7km east of St-Raphaël, where the landing of the 36th American division in August 1944 is commemorated. A cliff-top path around the **Cap du Dramont** headland gives fine views out to sea, though looking inland the most severe and recent encroachment on the Esterel is revealed – the tasteful but utterly unreal "designer village" of **Cap Esterel**, squatting smugly on the ridge between Le Dramont and Agay.

In contrast, Le Dramont's close neighbour **AGAY** is one of the least pretentious resorts of the Côte d'Azur, and beautifully situated around a deep horseshoe bay edged by sand beaches, red porphyry cliffs and pines. Both Agay and its eastern neighbour **ANTHÉOR** suffer a little from the creeping contagion of housing estates with rural names like Mas and Hameaux edging ever higher up their hills, but once you get above the concrete line, at the **Sommet du Rastel**, for example (signed up Agay's av du Bourg or bd du Rastel), you can begin to appreciate this wonderful terrain.

There are at least ten **campsites** in this area: along the Valescure road near the River Agay you'll find the four-star *Les Rives de L'Agay* (Ⓣ04.94.82.02.74; closed Nov–Feb), and the three-star *Agay-Soleil*, by the beach at 1152 bd de la Plage (Ⓣ04.94.82.00.79, Ⓔcampaing-agay-soleil@wanadoo.fr; closed mid-Nov to mid-March); or there's the three-star *Azur Rivage*, around the headland in Anthéor-Plage (Ⓣ04.94.44.83.12, Ⓕ04.94.44.84.39; €23 per tent; March–Oct). There's also no shortage of **hotels**: both Agay's *France Soleil* on bd de la Plage (Ⓣ04.94.82.01.93, Ⓕ04.94.82.73.95; ❹; closed Nov-Easter) and *Sol e Mar*, on the N98 in Le Dramont (Ⓣ04.94.95.25.60, Ⓕ04.94.83.83.61; ❻), have sea views. Less expensive options include *Hôtel l'Esterella* on the bd de la Plage in Agay (Ⓣ04.94.82.00.58, Ⓕ04.94.82.02.05; ❸), and *Les Flots Bleus* on bd Eugène Brieux in Anthéor (Ⓣ04.94.44.80.21, Ⓕ04.94.44.83.71; ❷; closed mid-Nov to late March).

Le Trayas

LE TRAYAS is on the highest point of the corniche and its shoreline is the most ragged, with wonderful inlets to explore. You can also trek to the Pic de l'Ours from here (about 3hr; the path is signed from the gare SNCF).

The **hotel** *Relais des Calanques*, rte des Escalles (Ⓣ04.94.44.14.06, Ⓕ04.94.44.10.93; ❻), nestles above a cove, the water almost lapping at its terrace where good sea-fish is served (around €25). Less expensive rooms can be found at *L'Auberge Blanche*, 1061 rte des Calanques/RN98 (Ⓣ04.94.44.14.04, Ⓕ04.94.44.17.27; ❸), where the bus stops. Le Trayas also has an **HI youth hostel**, the *Villa Solange*, 9 av de la Véronèse (Ⓣ04.93.75.40.23, Ⓕ04.93.75.43.45; closed Nov–Feb), a two-kilometre slog uphill from the stop outside the *Auberge Blanche* on the Cannes–St-Raphaël bus route.

Miramar and Théoule-sur-Mer

At **MIRAMAR** and neighbouring **THÉOULE**, the proximity of Cannes begins to show: you can see the city's outskirts, and the local architecture is infected with its style. From the Pointe de l'Esquillon you get an unhindered view of the private residential estate designed by Jacques Couelle at Porte-La-Galère on the neighbouring headland.

If you want **to stay**, *La Tour de l'Esquillon*, on the N98 coast road in Miramar

(ⓣ04.93.75.41.51, ⓦwww.esquillon.com; ❼), is worth splashing out on, with spectacular views from high up on the corniche, its own beach, a pool and a good restaurant. The coastline becomes less rugged at Théoule, where the most precipitous cliff scenery finishes and the beaches begin again. Théoule's **tourist office**, at 1 corniche d'Or (daily 9am–7pm; ⓣ04.93.49.28.28), provides the usual local information and rents out cars.

La Napoule

A fantasy castle, built onto the three towers and gateway of a fourteenth-century fort, announces **LA NAPOULE** and heralds the Riviera. The **castle** ranks high amongst the classic pre-World War I follies built by foreigners on the Côte; the creators, in this instance, being the American sculptor Henry Clews and his wife. The castle and its lovely gardens can be visited (Feb–Oct daily 10am–6pm; tours at 11.30am, 2.30pm, 3.30pm & 4.30pm; Nov–Jan daily 2–6pm; €4), with their collection of Clews' odd and gloomy works, represented on the outside by the grotesques on the gateway.

The **tourist offices** at the autoroute exit in Termes and on av Henri-Clews opposite La Napoule's port (July & Aug daily 10am–12.30pm & 1.30–7pm; Sept–June Mon–Fri 10am–2.30pm & 1.30–7pm; ⓣ04.93.49.95.31, ⓦwww.ot-mandelieu.fr) can help with **accommodation**. There are two hotels worth trying: *La Calanque* on bd Henri-Clews (ⓣ04.93.49.95.11, ⓕ04.93.49. 67.44; ❹) has a good restaurant and rooms with views of the castle and the sea; or the better-value and more peaceful *Villa Parisiana*, on rue de l'Argentière (ⓣ04.93.49.93.02, ⓦwww.villaparisiana.com; ❸). If you get stuck, the characterless inland golfing resort of Mandelieu-La Napoule has plenty of hotels, though little appeal to non-golfers.

If you have the money to splash out on a special meal, head for the gourmet **restaurant** *L'Oasis*, on rue Jean-Honoré-Carle (book in advance; ⓣ04.93.49.95.52; closed Sun eve & Mon); evening menus range from €58–145, but there is also a good lunch menu at €45. For something more down-to-earth, the restaurant at *La Calanque* (see above) serves some fine Provençal fish dishes, with menus from €16.50.

Travel details

Trains

Les Arcs to: Fréjus (25 daily; 15–20min); Gonfaron (4 daily; 20min); St-Raphaël (25 daily; 20–25min); Toulon (20 daily; 35–40min); Vidauban (4 daily; 5min).
Hyères to: Toulon (9 daily; 20min).
St-Raphaël to: Agay (9 daily; 10–12min); Anthéor (9 daily; 15min); Boulouris (13 daily; 4min); Cannes (approx. every 20min; 25–35min); Les Arcs-Draguignan (21 daily; 15–20min); Le Dramont (9 daily; 10min); Le Trayas (9 daily; 20–25min); Mandelieu-La Napoule (13 daily; 20–30min); Marseille (22 daily; 1hr 35min–2hrs); Nice (approx. every 20min; 50min–1hr 20min); Théoule-sur-Mer (9 daily; 25min); Toulon (25 daily; 55min–1hr 15min).

Buses

Fréjus to: Nice Airport (2 daily: 55min–1hr 20min).
Hyères to: Bormes (frequent; 25min); La Croix-Valmer (8 daily; 1hr 15min); Le Lavandou (16 daily; 30min); Le Rayol (9 daily; 50min); St-Tropez (7 daily; 1hr 30min); Toulon (13 daily; 35–50min).
Le Lavandou to: Bormes (14 daily; 5min); Cavalaire-sur-Mer (9 daily; 30min); Cavalière (9 daily; 10min); Hyères (13 daily; 35min); La Croix-Valmer (8 daily; 40min); Le Rayol (9 daily; 20min); St-Tropez (8 daily; 1hr); Toulon (14 daily; 45min–1hr 10min).
Ste-Maxime to: Cogolin (8 daily; 30min); La Foux (8 daily; 35min); Les Arcs (2 daily; 30–35min); Grimaud (8 daily; 20min); St-Tropez (9 daily; 45min)

St-Raphaël to: Cogolin (7 daily; 55min–1hr 5min); Grimaud (7 daily; 55min–1hr); La Foux (8 daily; 1hr–1hr 15min); Les Issambres (8 daily; 20–30min); Nice Airport (1 daily; 2hr); Ste-Maxime (8 daily; 30–40min); St-Tropez (8 daily; 1hr 10min–1hr 25min).

St-Tropez to: Bormes (8 daily; 1hr–1hr 15min); Cavalaire-sur-Mer (8 daily; 25–35min); Cavalière (8 daily; 45–55min); Cogolin (10 daily; 15min); Gassin (2 weekly; 25min); Grimaud (10 daily; 20–25min); Hyères (8 daily; 1hr 20min–1hr 35min); La Croix-Valmer (8 daily; 15–20min); Le Lavandou (8 daily; 55min–1hr 5min); Le Rayol (8 daily; 35–45min); Les Issambres (8 daily; 50min–1hr); Ramatuelle (2 weekly; 25min); Ste-Maxime (8 daily; 45min); St-Raphaël (8 daily; 1hr 20min–1hr 30min); Toulon (8 daily; 2hr–2hr 15min).

Flights

Hyères to: Clermont-Ferrand (2 daily; 1hr 40min); and Paris (Orly) (6 daily; 1hr 25min).

5

The Heartland of Provence

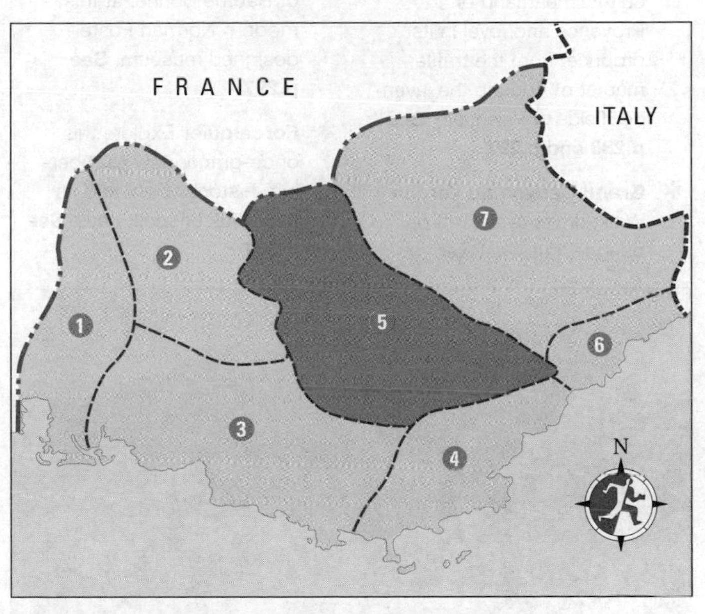

CHAPTER 5

Highlights

* **Abbaye du Thoronet** An exquisite rose-coloured monastic complex, and the oldest of Provence's three great Cistercian monasteries. **See p.284**

* **Provençal produce** Discover the peaceful, agricultural heartland of Provence and revel in its produce, from the truffle market of Aups to the lavender fields of Valensole. **See p.288 and p.297**

* **Grand Canyon du Verdon** Walk, drive, cycle, raft or bungee, but whatever you do, don't miss Europe's largest and most spectacular gorge. **See p.291**

* **Musée de Préhistoire des Gorges du Verdon** Gain an insight into 400,000 years of human habitation in Provence, and visit the cave of Baume Bonne, at this modern Norman Foster-designed museum. **See p.297**

* **Forcalquier** Explore this once-grand, now slumbering, historic town, and its beautiful, unspoilt *pays*. **See p.301**

5

The Heartland of Provence

This chapter takes in the Upper Var – the northern half of the Var *département* – and the western section of the Alpes-de-Haute-Provence. It is one of the least populated of France's non-mountainous areas and is the **heartland of Provence** not because it is geographically central, but because it is here that you can escape the region's over-commercialized resorts and begin to discover the individuality and true beauty of Provence.

Small towns and villages such as **Aups**, **Riez**, **Cotignac**, **Forcalquier** and **Simiane-la-Rotonde** still thrive on their traditional industries of cultivating lavender, making honey, tending sheep, digging for truffles and pressing olive oil; and in isolated places like **Banon** and the hamlets around Sisteron, it's hard to believe this is the same country, never mind province, as the Côte d'Azur.

True, foreigners have bought second homes in the idyllic **Haut Var villages**, but the tidal wave of new-house building does not yet extend north of the Autoroute Provençale (A8). Nor has the Marseille-Gap highway, which follows the **River Durance**, encouraged major industrialization, aside from an industrial park north of Sisteron. Prices here remain much lower than on the coast or in western Provence.

Landscapes are exceptional, from the gentle countryside of the Haut Var or Pays de Forcalquier to the rolling plains and wide horizons of the **Plateau de Valensole** and the high harshness of the **Montagne de Lure**; the wild emptiness of the **Plateau de Canjuers**, the untrammelled forests east of Draguignan and, most spectacularly of all, Europe's largest ravine, the **Grand Canyon du Verdon**, matched only in grandeur by the snowcapped mountains on the northern horizons.

Food is fundamentally Provençal: lamb from the high summer pastures, goats' cheese, honey, almonds, olives and wild herbs. The soil is poor and water scarce, but the Côtes de Provence **wine** *appellation* extends to the Upper Var.

The towns, busy but workaday **Draguignan**, quiet **Manosque** and strategically-sited **Sisteron**, the mountain gateway to Provence, are not the prime appeal. First and foremost, this is an area for **walking** and **climbing**, or **canoeing** and **windsurfing** on the countless dammed lakes that provide power and irrigation. The Grand Canyon du Verdon is a must, even if only seen from a car or bus. But the best way of discovering the area is just to stay in a village that takes your fancy, eating, dawdling and letting yourself drift into the rhythms of local life.

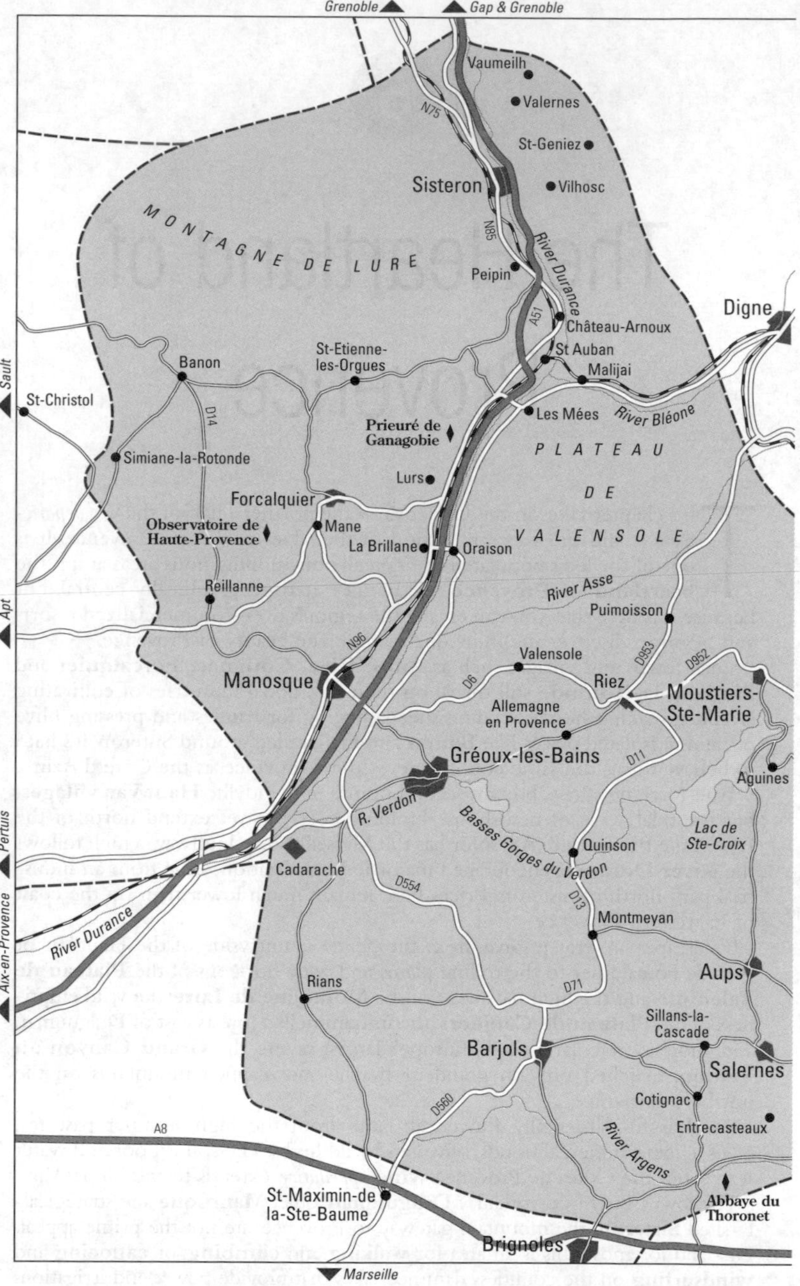

5

THE HEARTLAND OF PROVENCE

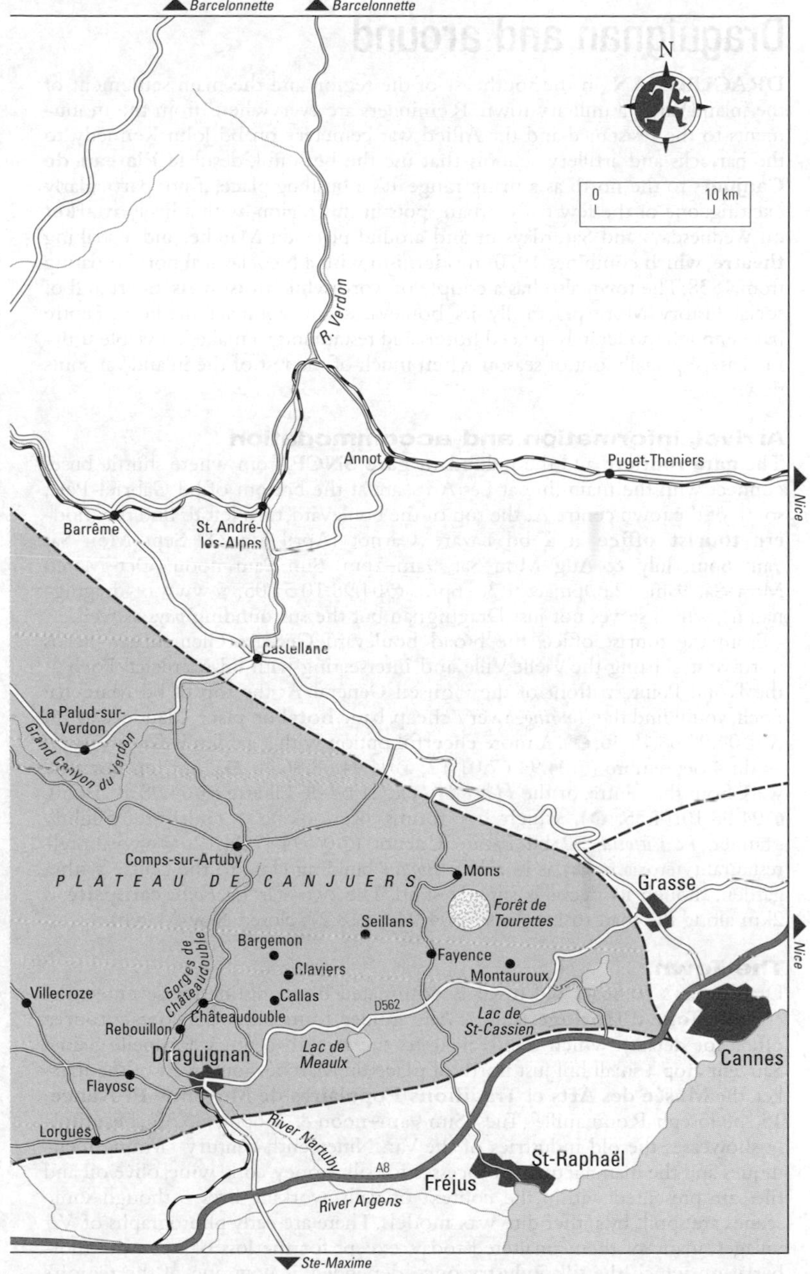
Barcelonnette
Barcelonnette
N
0
10 km
R. Verdon
Annot
Puget-Theniers
Nice
Barrême
St. André-
les-Alpes
Castellane
La Palud-sur-
Verdon
Grand Canyon du Verdon
Comps-sur-Artuby
PLATEAU DE CANJUERS
Mons
Grasse
Forêt de
Tourettes
Seillans
Bargemon
Fayence
Nice
Claviers
Montauroux
Gorges de
Châteaudouble
Villecroze
Callas
Châteaudouble
D562
Lac de
St-Cassien
Rebouillon
Draguignan
Lac de
Meaulx
Cannes
Flayosc
River Nartuby
Lorgues
St-Raphaël
A8
Fréjus
River Argens
Ste-Maxime

Draguignan and around

DRAGUIGNAN, in the southeast of the region and the main settlement of the inland Var, is a military town. Reminders are everywhere, from the monuments to the resistance and the Allied war cemetery on bd John Kennedy, to the barracks and artillery schools that use the beautiful, desolate **Plateau de Canjuers** to the north as a firing range. It's a bustling place, if not particularly exciting; one of the few truly urban spots in this region, with a lively **market** on Wednesdays and Saturdays in and around place du Marché, and a striking **theatre**, which combines 1970s modernism with a Neoclassical portico dating from 1838. The town also has a couple of worthwhile **museums**, of art and of social history. More practically, its boulevards and compact medieval centre have enough moderately-priced hotels and restaurants to make it a viable touring base, especially out of season when much of the rest of the inland Var shuts down.

Arrival, information and accommodation

The **gare routière** and the redundant **gare SNCF**, from where shuttle buses connect with the main line at Les Arcs, are at the bottom of bd Gabriel-Péri, south of the town centre. At the top of the boulevard, turn left to find the modern **tourist office** at 2 bd Lazare Carnot (April–June & Sept Mon–Sat 9am–6pm; July & Aug Mon–Sat 9am–7pm, Sun 9am–noon; Oct–March Mon–Sat 9am–12.30pm & 1.30–6pm; ⓣ04.98.10.51.05, ⓦwww.ot-draguignan.fr), which serves not just Draguignan but the surrounding *pays* as well.

From the tourist office, the broad boulevard Georges Clemenceau heads northwest, skirting the Vielle Ville and intersecting with bd Maréchal Foch at the Rond Point, in front of the Conseil Général. At the top of bd Maréchal Foch, you'll find the *Touring*, a very cheap, basic **hotel** on place Claude-Gay (ⓣ & ⓕ04.94.68.15.46; ❶). A more cheerful option with a garden is *La Pergola* on av du 4 Septembre (ⓣ04.94.67.01.12, ⓕ04.94.68.86.46; ❸), just ten minutes' walk from the centre, or the *Hôtel du Parc*, 21 bd de Liberté (ⓣ04.98.10.14.50, ⓕ04.98.10.14.55; ❸), which has rooms overlooking a courtyard. Slightly grander, *Le Victoria*, 52 bd Lazare Carnot (ⓣ04.94.47.24.12, ⓦwww.hotel-restaurantvictoria.fr; ❹), is in a *belle époque* building close to the centre with a garden, though its decor is slightly staid. The two-star *La Foux* **campsite** is 2km along the road to Les Arcs (ⓣ04.94.68.18.27; closed Nov-March).

The Town

Draguignan's compact old town is dominated by its distinctive seventeenth-century **Tour d'Horloge** (July & Aug guided tours only; €3; contact tourist office for details), which stands next to the twelfth-century Chapelle Saint-Sauveur atop a small hill just north of place du Marché. Southwest of the market, the **Musée des Arts et Traditions Populaires de Moyenne Provence**, 15 rue Joseph-Roumanille (Tues–Sun 9am–noon & 2–6pm, €3.50), beautifully showcases the old industries of the Var. Nineteenth-century farming techniques and the manufacturing processes for silk, honey, cork, wine, olive oil and tiles are presented within the context of daily working lives – though some scenes are spoilt by rather dire wax models. There are early photographs of Var villages, many of them unaltered today, except for the loss of trees: the mulberry, on which the silk industry once depended, is now one of the region's rarest species.

On rue de la République, the **Musée Municipale** (Mon–Sat 9am–noon & 2–6pm; free) is housed in a former bishop's palace. Its highlights include *Child*

Blowing Bubbles by Rembrandt; a delicate marble sculpture by Camille Claudel; Greuze's *Portrait of a Young Girl*; two paintings of Venice by Ziem; a Renoir; and upstairs in the library, a copy of the *Romance of the Rose* and early Bibles and maps.

Eating and drinking

There's a generous choice of inexpensive **places to eat** in the Vieille Ville and surrounding boulevards, though nothing very special. If you've come from the coast, however, you'll be relieved to be in **cafés** charging well under €2 for a sit-down terrace coffee. A couple of good choices for a meal are the *Bar de Négociants* amidst the flower stalls on place du Marché, and *Les Mille Colonnes*, on place aux Herbes, with a decent menu at €16. If sugary things are your passion, seek out the De Neuville *confiserie* at 191 rue du Combat.

Châteaudouble and Comps-sur-Artuby

About 5km northwest of Draguignan along av de Montferrat is **Rebouillon**, an exquisitely peaceful village built around an oval field on the banks of the River Nartuby. Beyond here, the scenery changes dramatically with the start of the **Gorges du Châteaudouble**. Though a mere scratch compared to the great Verdon gorge, it has some impressive sites, not least the village of **CHÂTEAUDOUBLE** hanging high above the cliffs. Nostradamus predicted that the river would grind away at the base until the village fell; he is yet to be proved right. Almost deserted except during the summer holidays, Châteaudouble consists of little more than a couple of churches; a handful of houses; a potter's workshop; a beekeeper and his hives; *La Tour* restaurant (Ⓣ04.94.70.93.08; menus at €16 and €25.20) with a terrace overlooking the gorge; and a ruined tower and ramparts, which you can reach from a path beside the *Bar du Château* (Ⓣ04.94.70.90.05; menu at €42).

North of Châteaudouble, the D955 crosses the increasingly bleak military camp of Canjuers before reaching the isolated settlement of **COMPS-SUR-ARTUBY**, after 20km. There are few specific sights here, other than the fortified chapel of **St André**, and the magnificent scenery surrounding the village, but there's a pleasant **hotel-restaurant**, the *Grand Hotel Bain*, on av de Fayet (Ⓣ04.94.76.90.06, Ⓕ04.94.76.92.24; ❸), with menus from €13 and a sunny garden.

Towards Lac de St-Cassien

If you're heading east towards Grasse from Draguignan a number of medieval villages north of the main Draguignan–Grasse road (the D562) may detain you. Sheltering below the inhospitable wilderness of the plateau of Canjuers to the north, the settlements of **Callas**, **Claviers**, **Bargemon**, **Seillans**, **Mons**, **Fayence**, **Tourettes** and **Montauroux** were all virtually inaccessible less than a hundred years ago. Not so now, though they retain their charm, despite a nasty rash of commercial development along the main D562. South of it is a wonderful, almost uninhabited expanse of forest where, between January and June, you may see untended cattle with bells round their necks and sheep chewing away at the undergrowth. After a long period of campaigning, farmers have managed to persuade the authorities to allow the animals to roam some of the old pasturing grounds of the transhumance routes, which has great ecological benefits in maintaining the diversity of the forest fauna.

Callas and Bargemon

Twelve kilometres northeast of Draguignan, **CALLAS** is a pleasant place to stop, with a lovely square by the church at the top of the village and a very reasonable **hotel-restaurant**, the *Hôtel de France*, further down on the shaded place Georges-Clemenceau (Ⓣ04.94.76.61.02, Ⓕ04.94.39.11.63; ❷, menu at €16). For somewhere much grander, the *Hostellerie des Gorges de Pennafort* overlooks Pennafort waterfalls, with its own pool, lake and olive grove (Ⓣ04.94.76.66.51, Ⓦwww.hostellerie-pennafort.com; ❽): it's still in the *commune* of Callas, but 7km south of the village, below the Draguignan-Grasse road on the D25.

Continuing north from the village of Callas, the steep narrow D25 leads through luscious valleys for 6km, to **BARGEMON**, tucked behind fortified gates. With its fountained squares shaded by towering plane trees, the village is particularly picturesque in spring, when its streets are filled with orange petals and mimosa blossom. The little **Chapelle St-Étienne**, which forms part of the defences, is now home to the **musée-galerie Honoré Camos** and hosts exhibitions of local painters (daily: May–Sept 3–6pm; Oct–April 2.30–5.30pm; free). The two angel heads on the high altar are attributed to the great Marseillais sculptor Pierre Puget.

For **food** and **accommodation**, there's the excellent *L'Oustaloun*, 12 av Pasteur (Ⓣ04.94.76.60.36, Ⓕ04.94.76.68.33; menus from €27; restaurant closed Wed eve & Thurs out of season; ❹).

Seillans

Heading east from Bargemon to **SEILLANS**, 13km away, the long-distance view suddenly opens out to the mountains. As you approach the village you'll see the effects of Côte-style property development in an ugly rash of white villas, while the Vieux Village, where the painter Max Ernst spent his last years, hides behind medieval walls. A small **collection** of lesser-known lithographs by Ernst, as well as some by his companion Dorothea Tanning, is on display a few doors down from the tourist office on rue de l'Église (Tues–Sat: summer 3–6pm; winter 2–6pm; €2). Seillans' most spectacular piece of artistry, however, lies 1km beyond the village on the road to Fayence. A Renaissance retable, attributed to an inspired Italian monk, is housed in the Romanesque **Chapelle de Notre-Dame-de-l'Ormeau** (Thurs 11am–noon; guided tours July & Aug Tues at 5.30pm). To book guided tours of the chapel, contact Seillans' **tourist office**, at 1 rue du Valat (April–Sept Mon–Sat 9.30am–12.30pm & 2.30–6.30pm; Oct–March closes at 6pm; Ⓣ04.94.76.85.91, Ⓦwww.seillans-var.com).

The best place to **stay** or **eat** in Seillans is the *Hôtel de France Clariond* on place de Thouron (Ⓣ04.94.76.96.10, Ⓕ04.94.76.89.20; menus from €30; ❺; closed Wed out of season), with its own pool and panoramic views. A few cheaper rooms are available at the equally pleasant *Les Deux Rocs* on the fountained place Font-d'Amont by the old wash house (Ⓣ04.94.76.87.32, Ⓕ04.94.76.88.68; ❸; closed Tues & Nov–March).

Fayence and around

FAYENCE, called Favienta Loca (favourable place) by the Romans, is today better known as one of the main centres for **gliding** in France. Larger and livelier than most of its neighbours, it makes a good base for exploring the surrounding countryside. Fayence's charm lies in the contrast between its small-town bustle and the peaceful traffic-free side streets spilling over with flowers. Its Vieille Ville curls tightly around the steep slopes of a hill, with the imposing porchway of the *mairie* guarding the entrance to it; within the Vieille Ville, stands a fourteenth-century gateway, the **Porte Sarrazine**. There's a market on place de l'Église on Tuesdays, Thursdays and Saturdays, as well as the inevitable ateliers and souvenir shops, and great views over the countryside.

For information, there's the **tourist office** on place Léon-Roux (June–Sept daily 9am–12.10pm & 2.30–6pm Sun 9am–noon; Oct–May Mon–Sat 9am–12.10pm & 2–6pm; ⓣ04.94.76.20.08, ⓦwww.mairiedefayence.com), and the Castle bookshop, at 1 rue St-Pierre (Mon 2.30–7pm; Tues–Sat 9am–12.30pm & 2.30–7pm), near the car park, which sells a reasonable selection of local guides and maps in English. The **gliding school**, the Association Aéronautique Provence Côte d'Azur, is based at Fayence-Tourettes aerodrome, just south of the village (ⓣ04.94.76.00.68, ⓦwww.aapca.net; temporary membership €70 or €35 for under-25s).

Fayance's **accommodation** options include *La Sousto* on rue du Paty (ⓣ04.94.76.02.16, ⓔhotel.sousto@wanadoo.fr; ❸), in the peaceful old heart of the village, with five well-equipped studio rooms for two to four people; and *Les Oliviers*, just below the village on the D19 (ⓣ04.94.76.13.12, ⓦhotel.olivers.fayen.free.fr; ❺), with a pool. Alternatively, try the *Auberge de la Fontaine*, 3km away on the road to Fréjus, beyond the junction with the main Draguignan–Grasse road (ⓣ04.94.76.07.59, ⓔbernard.MARTIN80@wanadoo.fr; ❸); here, Provençal cooking, with a menu at €13, adds to the attraction of its isolation. For really special surroundings, however, book in at *Le Moulin de la Camandoule*, a converted mill 1km from town on the road out to Notre-Dame-des-Cyprès (ⓣ04.94.76.00.84, ⓕ04.94.70.10.40; ❺); it's run by an English couple, but the meals (menus from €18.50) are prepared by a skilled and inventive French chef. Options for **camping** include the three-star *Lou Cantaire*, 7km out on the road to Draguignan (ⓣ04.94.76.23.77; €15 per tent; closed Oct–March), and the four-star *Le Parc*, in the Quartier Trestaure (ⓣ04.94.76.15.35; €14 per tent; closed Oct–March).

In addition to the hotel **restaurants**, there's *Le France* on Grand Rue du Chateau (ⓣ04.94.76.00.14; closed Sat lunch, Sun eve & all day Mon in winter), which has dependable chefs and menus at €18 for lunch and €28 in the evenings. A few paces away on place Léon-Roux, the *Entracte* is open for light lunches, and snacks all day. For a quieter, more substantial meal, try *La Farigoulette*, at the top of the village (ⓣ04.94.84.10.49), or the *Patin Couffin*, placette de l'Olivier (ⓣ04.94.76.29.96; menu at €22; closed Mon), which is known for its large portions of good food. For a gourmet treat, try *Le Castellaras*, signed off the Seillans road (ⓣ04.94.76.13.80; menus from €28; closed Mon & Tues out of season), where you can eat lobster, wild mushrooms, pigeon and courgette flowers, by a rose garden.

Tourettes and Mons

The distinctly un-medieval **château** in **TOURETTES**, Fayence's neighbour 1km to the east, is a copy of an early nineteenth-century cadet school set up in St Petersburg for Tsar Nicholas I by a French colonel. He built this replica for his retirement and it's still a private residence and not open to the public.

For an energetic ten-kilometre walk from Fayence, take the GR49 (off the D563 just north of town) through the Fôret de Tourettes, across the valley of La Siagnole River and up to the truly perched village of **MONS**. Once there, you can reward yourself with a drink at one of the cafés on place St-Sébastien and the tremendous views, which sometimes extend as far as Corsica and Italy.

Callian, Montauroux and the Lac de St-Cassien

CALLIAN, 9km east of Fayence, and **MONTAUROUX**, its larger neighbour, have merged together, with just a short stretch of forest to the east separating them from the suburbs of Grasse. Callian is more obviously picturesque but Montauroux is livelier, and its large open place du Clos makes a change from narrow, twisting medievalism, as does the grassy summit of the village with its fig tree, church and little chapel of St-Barthélemy whose ceiling and walls are covered in painted panels.

The **Lac de St-Cassien** reservoir lies 4km to the south of here. You can use the reservoir for swimming (best access from the D37 after you've crossed the lake), sailing or rowing, and eat pizzas, grills and ice creams at the various lakeside establishments. No motor boats are allowed and the water is very clean.

The Haut Var

The **Haut Var**, stretching west from Draguignan from the Argens Valley to the Verdon Gorge, is the true heart of Provence, with soft enveloping countryside of woods, vines, lakes and waterfalls, streaked with rocky ridges before the high plateaux and mountains further north. To the outsider, its picturesque medieval villages – amongst them, **Flayosc** and **Lorgues**, **Cotignac** and **Entrecasteaux** – merge together; to know them properly you'd have to live here for winter after winter, limiting your world to just a few square miles. For, despite the proliferation of *résidences secondaires*, these villages hold on to their identity, however guarded it is from the casual eyes of visitors. The region is also home to the **Abbaye du Thoronet**, the oldest of Provence's three surviving Cistercian monasteries.

Flayosc and Lorgues

From Draguignan you can head west for 5km to **FLAYOSC**, or 11km south-west to **LORGUES**, both of which make excellent **eating** stops. *L'Oustaou* on place Brémond, the main square of Flayosc (☎04.94.70.42.69; menus from €20; closed all day Mon, plus Thurs & Sun eves), serves delicious local specialities accompanied by a rare genuine Provençal atmosphere. *Chez Bruno*, on rte de Vidauban in Lorgues (☎04.94.85.93.93; menus at €52 and €100; closed all day Mon plus Sun eve out of season), is considerably more expensive, but if you're prepared to pay serious sums, you can try wonderful wild local ingredients in a chestnut and *chanterelle* soup and in the truffle and game dishes, followed by *crème brûlée* with figs in wine. The restaurant also has a few rooms attached (❺), but it's worth pointing out that the chef, M Bruno, is one of France's celebrity chefs and may well be away cooking dinners for presidents or royalty.

The Abbaye du Thoronet

Fifteen kilometres west of Lorgues, across the River Argens, deep in the forest of La Daboussière, is one of Provence's three great Cistercian monasteries, the austere, rose-coloured **Abbaye du Thoronet** (April–Sept Mon–Sat

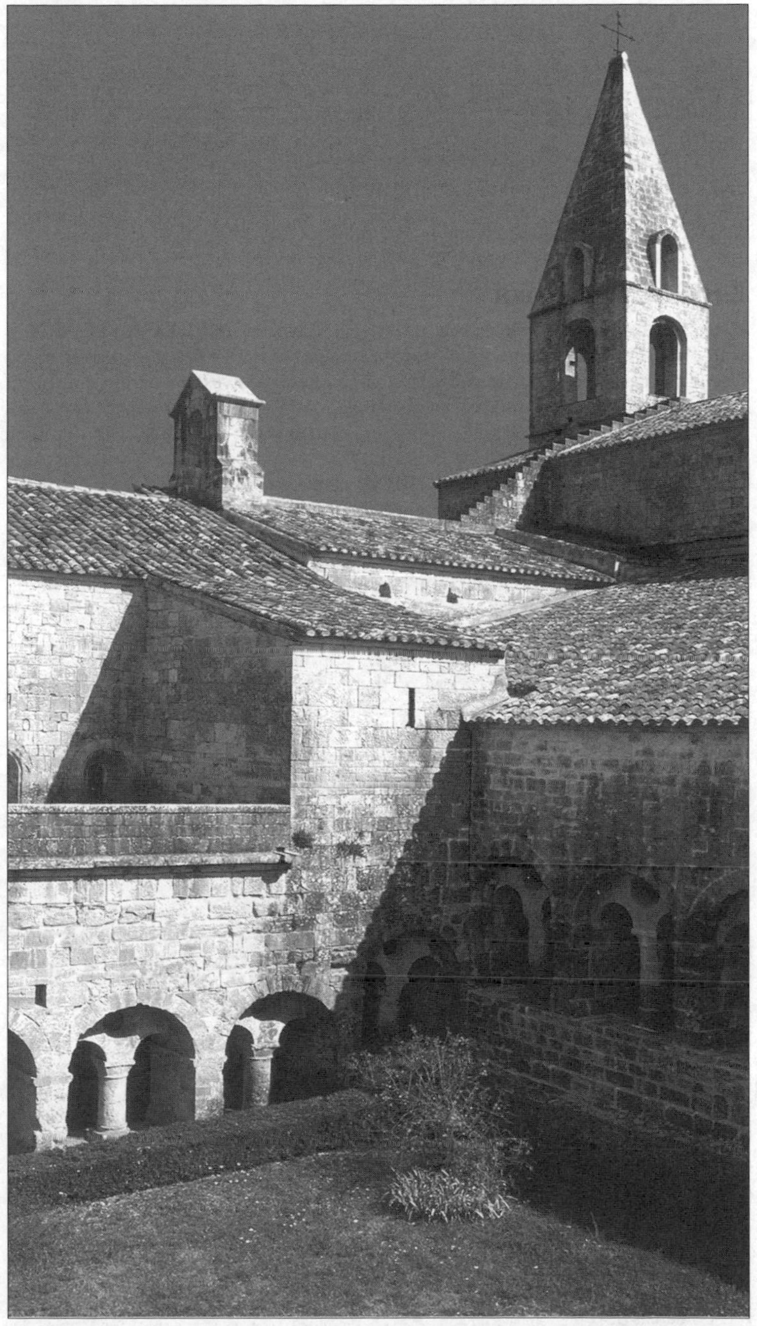

△ Abbaye-du-Thoronet

10am–6.30pm, Sun 10am–noon & 2–6.30pm; Oct–March 10am–1pm & 2–5pm, Sun 10am–noon & 2–5pm; €5). Like Silvacane and Sénanque (see pp.160 & 149), it was founded in the first half of the twelfth century, but Thoronet is the oldest of the three and the one that was completed in the shortest time, giving it an aesthetic coherence that transcends its relatively modest size. Finally abandoned in 1791, it was kept intact during the Revolutionary era as a historic monument. Restoration started in the 1850s, and a more recent campaign has brought it to graceful, melancholy perfection. The *abbaye* is off the D79, between the hamlet of Le Thoronet and Cabasse; there are no buses, so you'll need your own transport to get there.

Entrecasteaux

A circuitous 16km north of the *abbaye*, via Carcés, **ENTRECASTEAUX** is scarcely more than a stone frame for its château, which rises from box-hedged formal gardens to dominate the village. The château owes its current condition to a Scottish painter, Ian McGarvie-Munn (1919–81), who trained as a naval architect after World War II and later became the head of the National Workshops for Applied Arts in Colombia. Soon after his wife's father became president of Guatemala, McGarvie-Munn took over as head of the Guatemalan navy, following that with a stint as the country's ambassador to London. In 1974, by now retired, he bought the ruined shell of Entrecasteaux's seventeenth-century château, and spent the rest of his life and wealth on the massive restoration job. His family continued the work after his death, but sold up in 1995. The château is still privately owned.

You can visit the **château** (Easter–Nov daily except Sat, guided visits at 11am, 3pm & 4pm; Dec–Easter, groups only by appointment; ☎04.94.04.43.95; €6), and the publicly owned **Le Nôtre** gardens (dawn–dusk; free), which separate it from the village. Its interior is spacious, light and charmingly rustic, typified by

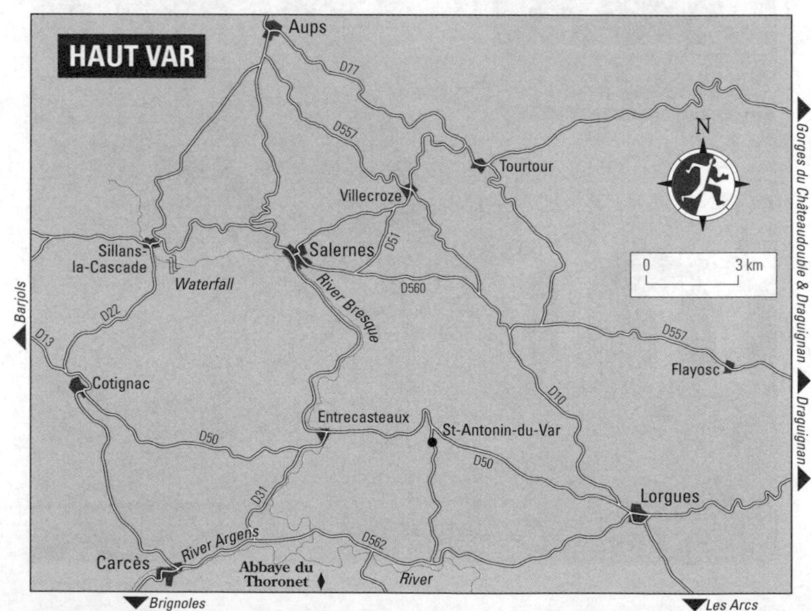

the terracotta tiles, a style that was all the rage when the Count and Countess of Grignan used the château as their summer residence; the opulence of the countess's bedroom, however, gives some idea of the status of the one-time inhabitants. Exhibitions on the first floor relate to later occupants, including Raymond Bruny, who charted part of the coast of western Australia and Tasmania, and photos of the sorry state in which McGarvie-Munn first found the château.

Practicalities

Places to stay are thin on the ground here, but the very welcoming hotel-restaurant *Lou Cigaloun* in St-Antonin-du-Var, Entrecasteaux's even smaller neighbour to the east (Ⓣ04.94.04.42.67, Ⓕ04.94.04.48.19; closed Nov–Feb; ❹), is a good bet; its restaurant (closed Wed; menu around €21–24) offers simple but fine cooking.

Decent **meals** can also be had in Entrecasteaux at *La Forchette*, up beyond the château entrance (Ⓣ04.94.04.42.78; around €13; closed all day Mon & Sun eve), and at *Lou Picateou*, below the château (Ⓣ04.94.04.47.97; menus from €15).

Cotignac

Of all the Haut Var villages, **COTIGNAC**, 9km west of Entrecasteaux, is the most beautiful, and one of the most upmarket. From its utterly photogenic place de la Mairie, rue de l'Horloge leads under the clock tower and up to the church; from here, a path takes you to the foot of the eighty-metre cliff that forms the village's back wall, a troglodyte mass of passages and odd little structures. At the summit stand two ruined towers of a long-abandoned castle, between which the rock is riddled with caves and subterranean passages of white rock and stalactite formations. You can ascend the nerve-racking cliff pathway from Easter to mid-October (€2).

Centre stage in the history of Cotignac are the now defunct tanning works, once a major industry of the Haut Var, and the miraculous Virgin in the **Chapelle de Notre-Dame-des-Grâces**, on the summit across the valley to the south. Long venerated as a saviour from the plague, this Virgin finally hit the big time in 1638 when Louis XIII and Anne of Austria – married for 22 childless years – made their supplications to her. Nine months after the royal visit, the future Sun King let out his first demanding squall.

If you want to sample some of Cotignac's local produce, head for Les Ruchers du Bessillon, at 2 rue des Naïfs, which sells an exceptional variety of **honey**, and the Vignerons de Cotignac, 100m out of town on the Salernes road (D13), for **wine**.

Practicalities

Cotignac's **tourist office** is just off the cours Gambetta at 2 rue Bonaventure (Tues–Fri 9am–1pm & 2–6pm, Sat 9am–1pm; Ⓣ04.94.04.61.87). **Accommodation** options are limited to a couple of chambres d'hôtes: the *Domaine de Nestuby*, amid vineyards about 4km south of the village on the D22 (Ⓣ04.94.04.60.02, Ⓔnestuby@wanadoo.fr; ❹), and the atmospheric *Maison Gonzagues*, in a former tannery in the village at 9 rue Lúon Gúrard (Ⓣ04.94.72.85.40, Ⓦwww.maison-gonzagues-cotignac.com; ❻). The municipal **campsite** *Les Pouverels* is on the Aups road on your right about 3km outside Cotignac (Ⓣ04.94.04.71.91; €7.50 per tent).

The cours Gambetta is the heart of the village's social life: here, you'll find a good pizzeria, *Les Trois Marches*, and a posher restaurant, *du Cours* (menus at €15, €20 & €28), as well as the *Bar de l'Union*, where the community's various clans

– beekeepers, *vignerons* and immigrants working as fig-packers or labourers – gather for a **drink**. Cotignac's **market** is on cours Gambetta on a Tuesday.

Salernes and Sillans

Compared with Cotignac, **SALERNES**, 13km northeast, is quite a metropolis, with a thriving tile-making industry and enough near-level irrigated land for productive agriculture. Sunday and Wednesday are the best days to visit the **market** beneath the ubiquitous plane trees on the *cours*. There are also twenty or so **pottery and tile workshops**, selling a mix of designs you'd find in any home improvement shop as well as items with more local flair. In the nineteenth century the workshops churned out the hexagonal terracotta floor tiles that have been reproduced in various synthetic materials ever since. You'll find shops in the centre of the town and larger *ateliers-magasins* on the outskirts: Maurice Emphoux, Jacques Polidori and Pierre Boutal on the road to Draguignan; Alain Vagh on the road to Entrecasteaux; and Ateliers de la Baume 4km east on the D560. Remember, if you want to take home some originals, these are artisans' artefacts and priced accordingly.

Salernes' tourist office is on pl Gabriel Péri (July–Aug Mon–Sat 9am–7pm; Sept–June Tues–Sat 9.30am–12.30pm & 2–6pm ⓣ04.94.70.69.02, ⓦwww.ville-salernes.fr). For somewhere **to stay**, there's a fourteenth-century farmhouse, *La Bastide Rose*, across the River Bresque towards La Colle Riforan (ⓣ04.94.70.63.30, ⓕ04.94.70.77.34; ❹), and a four-star campsite, *Les Arnauds*, just outside the town on the Sillans road (ⓣ04.94.67.51.95; €18 per tent; closed Oct–April). **Places to eat** in Salernes include *Le Temps des Mets*, place du 8 mai 1945 (ⓣ04.94.70.64.51), with menus at €22 and €26, and *La Cuillère*, on rue Pierre Blanc (closed Mon), with decent pizzas from €9. There's a range of cafés on the *cours* serving light meals and snacks, and a **bar** with a good selection of beers opposite the tourist office.

Six kilometres west of Salernes, tiny **SILLANS** is not in itself overtly picturesque, but its **waterfall** is stunning, gushing down into a turquoise pool that makes for a brilliant swim. It's signed down a delightful path from the main road (a 20-minute walk from the car park). If you want to **stay** in Sillans, there's *Les Pins* hotel-restaurant (ⓣ04.94.04.63.26, ⓕ04.94.04.72.71; menus from €13; ❷), or the three-star **campsite**, *Le Relais de la Bresque* (ⓣ04.94.04.64.89), 1km out along the road to Aups.

Villecroze

Five kilometres northeast of Salernes, **VILLECROZE**, like Cotignac, sits beneath a water-burrowed cliff, whose intriguing grottoes can be visited in summer (daily 10am–noon & 2.30–7pm; €2). The gardens around the base are delightfully un-Gallic and the same lack of formality extends throughout the town. It's an appealing place, with lovely vaulted arcades down rue des Arcades and rue de France, and a Romanesque church with a wall of bells.

Aside from its attractiveness, Villecroze is of interest as home to the early radical ecologist, Jean Pain, who in the 1970s ran his heating, lighting and 2CV on compost made from the undergrowth of the surrounding woods, material otherwise destroyed to avoid the risk of fire. Pain's compost gave back nutrients to the forest soil and agricultural land of this harsh terrain, and his methods of generating power from compost have been taken up as far afield as Canada, California and Senegal.

If Villecroze tempts you to **stay**, one of the best deals in the region can be found at the seven-roomed *Auberge des Lavandes* on place du Général-de-Gaulle

(Ⓣ04.94.70.76.00, Ⓕ04.94.67.56.45; closed Jan & Feb; ❸). Failing that, the secluded and very comfortable *Au Bien Être*, in quartier Les Cadenières, 3.5km south along the D557 (Ⓣ04.94.70.67.57; ❹), is also a good bet. There are two three-star **campsites**, *Les Cadenières* (Ⓣ04.94.67.59.66; €19 per tent; closed Nov–March) and *Le Ruou* (Ⓣ04.94.70.67.70; €21 per tent; closed Nov–March), both on the D560 towards Flayosc. For food, the **restaurant** at the *Au Bien Être* has menus at €24, €29 and €34 (out of season closed all day Mon & Tues plus Wed lunchtimes), while the well-reputed *Le Colombier* on rte de Draguignan (Ⓣ04.94.70.63.23; menus from €25; closed Mon plus Sun eve out of season), has a truffle menu from December to March, and a few rooms (❼).

Tourtour

TOURTOUR sits 300m higher than Villecroze, atop a ridge from where the view extends to the massifs of Maures, Ste-Baume and Ste-Victoire. The village has a seemingly organic unity, soft-coloured stone growing into stairways and curving streets, branching to form arches, fountains and towers. The ruin of an old mill looks as if it has always been like this; the elephant-leg towers of the sixteenth-century bastion stand around the *mairie* and the post office as if of their own volition, while the twelfth-century **Tour du Grimaldi** might have erupted spontaneously from the ground. The two elms on the main square, planted when Anne of Austria and Louis XIII visited Cotignac, are almost as enormous as the bastion towers, but are beginning to show signs of decrepitude.

Having said this, Tourtour is all a bit unreal, full of *résidences secondaires* and *salons de thé* selling expensive fruit-juice cocktails. It also has the region's most upmarket **hotel-restaurant**, the *Bastide de Tourtour* (Ⓣ04.98.10.54.20, Ⓦwww.chateauxhotels.com/tourtour; menus from €24.50; ❾), specializing in classic local cuisine, and with Jacuzzis, tennis courts and a gym to accompany the lavish rooms.

Aups

For those with their own transport, the village of **AUPS**, 10km north of Salernes, makes an ideal base for visiting the villages of the Haut Var or the Grand Canyon du Verdon. Though only 500m or so above sea level, it was considered by the ancients to be the beginning of the Alps; the Romans called it Alpibus which became Alps then Aups. The chief town of one of the Ligurian tribes and the location for a Roman army hospital, it then thrived in the Middle Ages, and by the eighteenth century its prosperity was inducing delusions of grandeur in the local abbot. Having mathematically proved Aups to be at the centre of Europe, he drew a map of the continent on the tiles of his house to illustrate the fact. He also erected a column in his garden inscribed with the scientific knowledge of his day and was responsible for one of the seven sundials that decorate the village.

Arrival, information and accommodation

Coming from Sillans, Salernes or Villecroze, you enter **Aups** along av Georges-Clemenceau ending up at place Frédéric-Mistral and place Martin-Bidouré. The very helpful **tourist office** is to your left in the former town hall (April–June & Sept Mon–Sat 9am–noon & 2.30–6.30pm; July–Aug 9am–1pm & 3.30–7.30pm; Oct–May Mon–Sat 9.30–noon & 2–5.30pm; Ⓣ04.94.84.00.69, Ⓦmembres.lycos.fr/otsiaups/), and has details of local walks. The Vieille Ville is in front of you with the church to the right.

The **hotels** in Aups itself are good value: the recently refurbished *Provençal* on place Martin-Bidouré (Ⓣ04.94.70.00.24, Ⓕ04.94.84.06.25; ❸) is the most expensive; and the *Grand Hôtel* on place Duchâtel (Ⓣ04.94.70.10.82; ❷; closed Feb–March) is the cheapest. Outside town, about 3km along the road to Moustiers-Ste-Marie, *Bastide de l'Estré* (Ⓣ04.94.84.00.45, Ⓦwww.estre.com; ❹) provides bed and breakfast accommodation, a gîte to rent, and a camping barn for walkers and cyclists, in an attractive rural location. For more luxury, try *La Bastide du Calalou* in the village of Moissac-Bellevue, 5km from Aups on the D9 (Ⓣ04.94.70.17.91, Ⓕ04.94.70.50.11; closed mid-Nov to March; ❻). There are two **campsites** close to town: the two-star *Camping Les Prés*, to the right off allée Charles-Boyer towards Tourtour (Ⓣ04.94.70.00.93; €11 per tent); and the three-star *Saint Lazare*, 2km along the Moissac road (Ⓣ04.94.70.12.86; €11 per tent; closed Oct–March), which has a pool. The big three-star *International Camping* (Ⓣ04.94.70.0680; €20 per tent; closed Oct–March) is 500m out of town, on the road to Fox-Amphoux.

The Town

On place Martin-Bidouré a monument commemorates a period of republican resistance all too rarely honoured in France. Its inscription reads: "To the memory of citizens who died in 1851 defending the Republic and its laws", the year being that of Louis Napoleon's coup d'état. Peasant and artisan defiance was strongest in Provence, and the defeat of the insurgents, who flew the red flag because the tricolour had been appropriated by the usurper, was followed by a massacre of men and women alike. At Aups, the badly wounded Martin Bidouré escaped, but was found soon afterwards being succoured by a peasant, and shot dead on the spot.

This event might explain the strident "République Française, Liberté, Egalité, Fraternité" sign on the **Église St-Pancrace**, proclaiming the supremity of state before religion – a common feature of French churches, though it's usually more discreet. The church was designed by an English architect five hundred years ago and has had its doors restored in the last ten years by two resident British carpenters. The Renaissance portal is in good shape, there are some altarpieces inside and the attractive nineteenth-century stained-glass windows have been cleaned and repaired.

Another plus for Aups is its **museum of modern art** – the Musée Simon Segal, in the former convent chapel on av Albert-1er (mid-June to mid-Sept 10am–noon & 4–7pm; €2.30). The best works are by the Russian-born painter Simon Segal, but there are interesting local scenes in the other paintings, such as the Roman bridge at Aiguines, now drowned beneath the artificial lake of Ste-Croix.

Unfortunately La Fabrique, the former abbot's house, is a private residence and can't be visited. But the old streets, the sixteenth-century clock tower with its campanile, and the Wednesday and Saturday morning **market** which fills place Martin-Bidouré, all make this a very appealing place to be. Aups has become more geared to tourism in recent years but its living still comes from agriculture and there's prime local produce on sale in the shops. Along with honey, the Aups speciality is truffles, and if you're here on a Thursday between November and the end of February you'll witness the **truffle market**. The local lamb has a gourmet reputation: marinaded and roasted with thyme is the traditional preparation. Other delicacies include small birds cooked with juniper berries; the gun shop in the main street explains the ready supply. For food shopping, Bernard Georges sells **honey** from his farm, Mas du Vieux Moulin, on rue de la Piscine east of place Martin-Bidouré; the Pâtisserie

Brunet à la Claire Fontaine sells **nougat** and other local sweets; and, at 7 rue Maréchal-Foch, L'Herbier sells soaps, **liqueurs** and dried flowers. The best place for **bread** and cakes (olive oil *fougasses*, in particular) is the Boulangerie-Pâtisserie Canut on place du Marché, while the Domaine Valmoisine, on the ave Albert-1er, is the place to go for **wine** *en vrac*.

Eating, drinking and entertainment

For **meals**, your first choice should be the hotel-restaurant *St-Marc* (☎04.94.70.06.08; ❸; closed Tues, Wed & middle two weeks of June), a nineteenth-century mill on rue Aloisi. Serving local dishes, truffles and boar in season, it offers menus from €10.50 to €30. For standard, reliable food, try *Yucca* at 3 rue Mal-Foch (☎04.94.70.12.11; closed Mon & Tues), and for snacks, the *boulangerie-pâtisserie* at no. 12 av Albert-1er (closed Dec–April). The **bar** opposite the church is the place to sip pastis. The tourist office has details of the theatre, film and other **entertainment** that takes place in the Centre Culturel, on chemin des Prés.

Barjols

Springs, streams and above all mossy fountains are the chief attraction of **BARJOLS**, 16km west of Cotignac. There are 28 fountains dotted around the village, but particularly in its older, eastern half, the *Quartier du Réal*: the **tourist office** on bd Grisolle, one block east of the broad place Rouguière (Mon–Sat 10am–noon & 2–6pm; ☎04.94.77.20.01, Ⓦwww.ville-barjols.fr), can provide a map to follow the circuit of fountains. The glum, rickety buildings of the town's now-defunct local tanning industry have been taken over by artists and craft workers; you can visit their studios (follow signs to *Art-Artisanal*) down the old road to Brignoles, east of the Vieille Ville. Looking back upwards from here at the industrial ruins is a good spooky night-time experience.

In January a strange **festival** takes place which commemorates the miraculous arrival of an ox during a famine, but is in honour of the town's patron saint, St-Marcel: the cow gets killed and roasted to the accompaniment of flutes and tambourines and the refrain "Saint Marcel, Saint Marcel, the little tripe, the little tripe".

The **hotel-restaurant** *Le Pont d'Or* on rte de St-Maximin (☎04.94.77.05.23; closed mid-Nov to mid-Jan; ❸) serves the best **food** in town with menus from €18. Nightlife, such as it is, centres around the bars and cafés in place Capitaine Vincens and along av Eugène Payan.

The Grand Canyon du Verdon

North of Aups, the D957 skirts the military Camp de Canjuers and crosses the River Verdon at the bottom of the gorge, just before it enters the vast Lac de Ste-Croix. This is the quickest approach from the south to Europe's widest and deepest gorge, the **Grand Canyon du Verdon**, though not the most dramatic. For that you must approach from Draguignan via the Gorges de Châteaudouble and Comps-sur-Artuby, following one of the few public roads through the Camp de Canjuers. After Comps the road turns westwards through 16km of end-of-the-earth heath and hills, with each successive horizon higher than the last. When you reach the canyon, it is as if a silent earthquake had taken place while you journeyed.

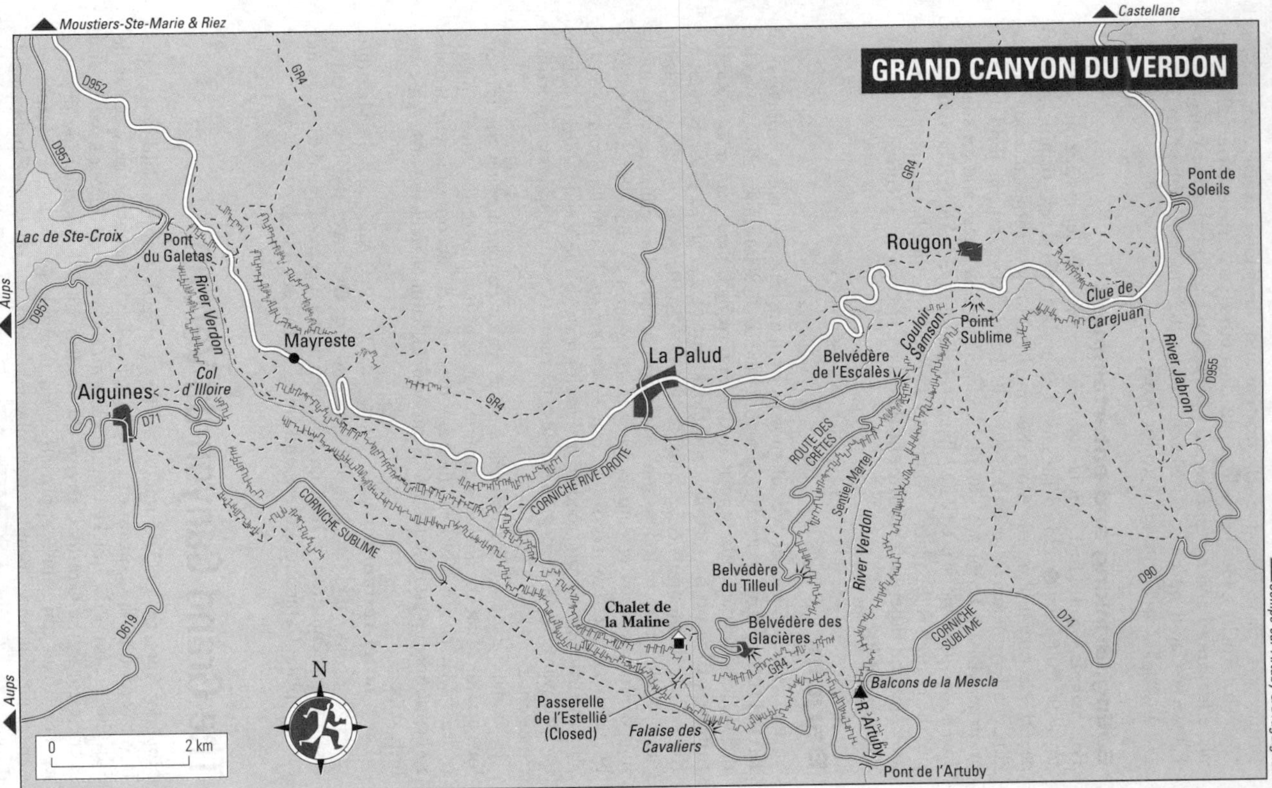
GRAND CANYON DU VERDON
Moustiers-Ste-Marie & Riez
Castellane
Comps-sur-Artuby & Draguignan
Aups
Aups
D952
D957
D957
GR4
GR4
GR4
GR4
Lac de Ste-Croix
Pont du Galetas
River Verdon
Mayreste
Col d'Illoire
Aiguines
D71
D619
La Palud
Rougon
Pont de Soleils
Clue de Carejuan
River Jabron
D955
Point Sublime
Couloir Samson
Belvédère de l'Escalès
ROUTE DES CRÊTES
Sentier Martel
River Verdon
CORNICHE RIVE DROITE
CORNICHE SUBLIME
Belvédère du Tilleul
Chalet de la Maline
Belvédère des Glacières
Balcons de la Mescla
CORNICHE SUBLIME
D71
D90
R. Artuby
Pont de l'Artuby
Passerelle de l'Estellié (Closed)
Falaise des Cavaliers
N
0
2 km

Information and guides: a checklist

There are plenty of organizations and individual guides with whom you can arrange expeditions on foot, horseback, raft, canoe or by air, especially in La Palud, Castellane, Moustiers and Aiguines. The Bureau des Guides and Le Perroquet Vert in La Palud will also give advice if you don't want to be part of a group. Prices vary with the season and the number of people taking part, but they are generally reasonable.

Aboard Rafting Castellane, ⓣ04.92.83.76.11, ⓦwww.aboard-rafting.com. Masses of water-based activities including rafting, canoeing, canyoning, hydrospeed, water rambling, and mountain biking.

Bureau des Guides La Palud, ⓣ04.92.77.30.50, ⓦescalade-verdon.com. Association of professional guides for walks, canyoning and rock-climbing.

Bruno Potié Moustiers, ⓣ04.92.77.37.04. Professional walking guide and rock-climber.

Parc Naturel Région du Verdon Domaine de Valx, Moustiers, ⓣ04.92.74.68.00, ⓦwww.parcduverdon.fr. National park authority.

Le Perroquet Vert La Palud, ⓣ04.92.77.33.39. Climbing shop.

Ranch Les Pioneers La Palud, ⓣ04.92.77.38.30. Horse-rides with your own guide.

UCPA La Palud, ⓣ04.92.77.31.66. Climbing, walking, canoeing and nautical trekking with a trained guide.

Verdon Passion Moustiers, ⓣ04.92.74.69.77, ⓦwww.verdon-passion.com. Canyoning, climbing and paragliding.

Latitude Challenge Marseille, ⓣ04.91.09.04.10, ⓦwww.latitude-challenge.fr. Bungee jumps from the Pont de l'Artuby.

Approached from Comps, the first vantage point, the **Balcons de la Mescla**, is a memorable *coup de théâtre*, with the view withheld until you are almost upon it. Nothing prepares you for the 250-metre drop to the base of the V-shaped, 21km-long gorge incised by the Verdon through piled strata of limestone. Ever-changing in its volume and energy, the river falls from **Rougon** to the east of the gorge, decelerating for shallow languid moments and finally exiting in full steady flow at the **Pont de Galetas** to fill the huge reservoir of the **Lac de Ste-Croix**.

Running west from the Balcons is the **corniche sublime**, built expressly to give the most breathtaking and hair-raising views. On the north side, the **Route des Crêtes** serves the same function, at some points looking down a sheer 800-metre drop to the sliver of water below, though the views are not as consistently good. The entire circuit is 130km long and it's cycling country solely for the preternaturally fit. Even for drivers it's hard work, as the hidden bends and hairpins in the road are perilous and, in July and August, so is the traffic.

Public transport around the canyon is poor. There's one **bus** between Marseille, Aix, Moustiers, La Palud, Rougon and Castellane (July to mid-Sept on Mon, Wed & Sat; mid-Sept to June on Sat only); and one other bus twice daily between La Palud, Rougon and Castellane (July & Aug Mon–Sat; Easter–June & Sept Sat & Sun only, plus public hols). **Drivers** should note that petrol stations are few and far between, so fill up whenever you see one.

By far the best way to explore the canyon, if your legs are strong enough, is to descend to the river and follow it by foot; to **walk** from La Maline to the Point Sublime on the **Sentier Martel** takes seven hours, and is best undertaken as part of a guided group (see box above). You can do it independently, but beware of the sudden changes in water levels, caused by the Verdon's hydroelectric activity – drownings can and do occur. Unaccompanied shorter excursions into the canyon include the **Sentier du Lézard**, a relatively easy marked walk from the **Point Sublime**, with various routes from 30 minutes to four hours, passing though the **Couloir Samson**, a 670-metre tunnel with occasional "windows" and a stairway down to the chaotic sculpture of the river banks.

Canoeing or **rafting** the entire length of the gorge should not be attempted unless you are very experienced and strong, as you will have to carry your craft for long stretches. However, you can pay (quite a lot) to join a group and tackle certain stretches of the river. Because of the electricity board's operations these trips aren't always possible, so be prepared for disappointment. A cheaper, though less exciting option, is to paddle about on the last stretch of the gorge: you can rent canoes and pedalos at the Pont du Galetas. **Rock-climbing** is also possible, as is **horse-riding** on the less precipitous slopes around the gorge. For the ultimate buzz, you can **paraglide**, or **bungee jump** from the **Pont de l'Artuby**, at 182 metres the highest bridge in Europe.

La Palud-sur-Verdon

LA PALUD-SUR-VERDON is the closest village to the gorge and makes a good base for exploring the area. There's not much to the village itself, which all but closes down out of season, though it does have a certain bleak appeal.

Housed in La Palud's château, the **Maison des Gorges du Verdon** is a centre for environmental tourism that includes the **tourist office** and an exhibition on the gorge (mid-June to mid-Sept Mon & Wed–Sun 10am–1pm & 4–7pm; mid-March to mid-June & mid-Sept to mid-Nov Mon & Wed–Sun 10am–noon & 4–6pm; Ⓣ04.92.77.32.02, Ⓦwww.lapaludsurverdon.com; entrance to exhibition €4). The tourist office can help with accommodation and information on **walking tours** of the area. Before setting out on any walk in the gorge, always get details of the route and advice on **weather conditions** (recorded information Ⓣ08.36.68.02.04, Ⓦwww.meteoconsult.fr). You'll also need drinking water, a torch/flashlight (for the tunnels), and a jumper for the cold shadows of the narrow corridors of rock. Always stick to the path and don't cross the river except at the *passerelles* as the EDF (electricity board; Ⓣ04.92.83.62.68 for recorded information) may be opening dams upstream.

There is plenty of **accommodation** in and around the village. Of the hotels *Le Provence*, rte de la Maline (Ⓣ04.92.77.38.88, Ⓔhotelleprovence@aol.com; ❸; closed Nov to late March), has the most stunning position, just below the village, while *Les Gorges du Verdon*, 500m from the start of the route des Crêtes and a few minutes' walk from the trails down into the gorge (Ⓣ04.92.77.38.26, Ⓦwww.hotel-des-gorges-du-verdon.fr; ❻; closed Oct–April), has all mod cons and is beautifully isolated. In La Palud itself, *Le Panoramic*, rte de Moustiers, (Ⓣ04.92.77.35.07, Ⓦwww.hrpanoramic.com; ❹; closed Nov–March), may not have such good views, but it's an agreeable enough place, and there's also the small *Auberge des Crêtes*, 1km east of La Palud (Ⓣ04.92.77.38.47, Ⓔaubergedescretes@wanadoo.fr ❸; closed Oct–March), with just twelve rooms. The youth **hostel**, *L'Immense Botte de Paille*, is on the D23 route des Crêtes (Ⓣ04.92.77.38.72), and there's a two-star **campsite** on the route de Castellane (Ⓣ04.92.77.38.13).

The centre of La Palud's social life is *Lou Cafetie* **bar-café** where conversation is inevitably thick with stories of near-falls, near-drownings and near-death from exposure. Most people eat at the hotel **restaurants**, but there's also a pizzeria, *Pépino*, and a crêperie, *Les Tilleuls*. The **market** is on Sunday.

Aiguines

AIGUINES, at the western end of the Corniche Sublime, is perched high above the Lac de Ste-Croix, with an enticing château (closed to the public) of pepperpot towers that dazzle with their coloured tiles. The town was formerly a wood-turning centre, with its speciality being the crafting of *boules* for *pétanque* from ancient boxwood roots; in the 1940s the industry sustained a population of six hundred people. Women would bang the little nails into the *boules* to give them their metal finish, inventing intricate and personalized designs. There's a tiny **Musée des Tourneurs sur Bois** (mid-June to mid-Sept Tues–Sun 9am–noon & 2–6pm; €2), devoted to the intricate art of wood-turning, while the **Galerie d'Art**, opposite the tourist office, sells some very expensive and beautiful woodwork, as well as pottery and faïence.

Every conceivable water sport is practised on the nearby **Lac de Ste-Croix**, and you should find gear available for rent at Les Salles-sur-Verdon or Ste-Croix-du-Verdon and at other outlets around this enormous reservoir. Swimming is good, with easy access from the D957 between Aups and Moustiers, though sometimes when the water levels are low it's a bit muddy round the edges.

There are plenty of places to stay around Aiguines. For central **hotels**, try *Le Vieux Château*, on the main road (Ⓣ04.94.70.22.95; closed mid-Oct to March; €51 per person half board only), or *Altitudes 823*, just below the main road (Ⓣ04.98.10.22.17 Ⓕ04.98.10.22.16; ❸; closed Nov–March). Alternatively, there's chambre d'hôtes accommodation in the *Château de Chanteraine*, signposted off the D19 1km out of Aiguines on the Lac de Ste-Croix road (Ⓣ04.94.70.21.01, Ⓔchanteraine@free.fr; ❸). For a bit more style and comfort, *Le Grand Canyon* on the Corniche Sublime, halfway between Aiguines and Comps (Ⓣ04.94.76.91.31, Ⓕ04.94.76.92.29; ❹; closed mid-Oct to mid-April), has comfortable rooms, balconies and a dining terrace teetering on the edge of a 300-metre drop. There's also a two-star **campsite**, *Le Galetas*, on the D957 (Ⓣ04.94.70.20.48; closed Nov–March), almost within diving distance of the lake, a long way down from the village.

Moustiers-Ste-Marie

The 800 or so car-parking spaces tell you all you need to know about the summer popularity of **MOUSTIERS-STE-MARIE**, 17km north of Aiguines. Glutted with *ateliers* making and selling glazed pottery – Moustiers' traditional speciality – the village amounts to little more than a picturesque location for a shopping spree. But it is *very* picturesque, almost absurdly so; the backdrop of sheer cliffs with a star slung between them will be familiar from a thousand calendars. There's rather more appeal out of season, and if you want to escape the commercialism you can at least puff your way uphill to the aptly-named chapel of **Notre Dame de Beavoir**, high above the village proper. If, however, plates and jugs are your thing, this is the place to buy them: the pottery, like the village, is pastel and pretty. There's also a small **musée de la Faience** (April–Oct Mon & Wed–Sun 9am–noon & 2–6pm; July–Aug closes at 7pm; €1) in the hôtel de ville.

The **tourist office** is on rue de la Bourgade at the top of the village (daily: May, June & Sept 10.30am–12.30pm & 2–5.30pm; July & Aug 9.45am–12.30pm & 2–7.30pm; Oct–April 2–5pm; Ⓣ04.92.74.67.84). If you want to **stay**, the *Hotel-Café du Relais* is right in the heart of the village (Ⓣ04.92.74.66.10, ⒺLe.Relais@wanadoo.fr; ❸), with menus from €22.70, though you may want to splash out on the rather more luxurious *La Bastide de Moustiers*, on the main road just below the village (Ⓣ04.92.70.47.47,

Ⓦ www.bastide-moustiers.com; ❾), run by celebrity chef Alain Ducasse. Each of the rooms has its own theme, there's a herb garden and a helicopter pad and the **restaurant** offers weekday set menus at a (relatively) modest €40. If that's too much, the *Bar-Resto le Bellevue*, next to the lower of the two bridges in the heart of the village, lives up to its name with a plum riverside site.

Riez and around

Fourteen kilometres south west of Moustiers, and in total contrast to its commercialism, **RIEZ** is one of the least spoilt small towns of inland Provence. Its main business comes from the lavender fields that cover this part of the region. Just over the river, about a kilometre away on the road south, is a **lavender distillery**, a building strangely reminiscent of 1950s Soviet architecture, which produces essence for the perfume industry.

Information and accommodation

The **tourist office** is at 4 cours allées Louis-Gardiol (July–Aug daily 9am–7pm & 2.30–6.30pm; Sept–June Mon–Sat 8.30am–noon & 1.30–5.30pm; Ⓣ 04.92.77.99.09). **Accommodation** options are limited to the modern, executive-style *Carina*, across the river in the quartier St-Jean (Ⓣ 04.92.77.85.43, Ⓕ 04.92.77.74.93; ❸; closed mid-Nov to March), with views back across to the town, or the out-of-town *Hôtel Cigalou* (Ⓣ 04.92.77.75.60; ❸) on the rte de Roumoules, and the *Château de Pontfrac* (Ⓣ 04.92.77.78.77, Ⓦ www.chateaudepontfrac.com; ❹) on the rte de Valensole. There's a two-star **campsite** on rue Edouard-Dauphin, across the river (Ⓣ 04.92.77.75.45; €10 per tent; closed mid-Oct to March).

The Town

Although today Riez is more village than town, a brief stroll around will soon uncover its grander past. Some of the houses on Grande Rue and rue du Marché – the two streets above the main allées Louis-Gardiol – have rich Renaissance facades, and the former hôtel de ville on place Quinconces was once an episcopal palace. The cathedral, which was abandoned four hundred years ago, has been excavated just across the river from allées Louis-Gardiol. Beside it is a **baptistry** (mid-June to Sept Tues, Fri & Sat 3–7pm; Oct to mid-June by arrangement with the tourist office; €2), originally constructed, like the cathedral, around 600 AD and restored in the nineteenth century. If you recross the river and follow it downstream you'll find the even older and more startling relics of four **Roman columns** standing in a field.

A rather more strenuous **walk** – head first for the clock tower above Grande Rue, then take the path up past the cemetery (on the left) – brings you to a cedar-shaded platform at the summit of the hill. This is the site of the Roman town, though the only building remaining is the eighteenth-century **Chapelle St-Maxime**, with a patterned interior that is gaudy or gorgeous, depending on your taste.

The **Maison de l'Abeille**, 1km out of the village along the road to Digne (daily 10am–12.30pm & 2.30–7pm; closed Jan & Feb; free), is a fascinating research and visitors' centre where you can buy various **honeys** as well as hydromel, or mead – the honey alcohol of antiquity. The enthusiastic staff are very keen to share their knowledge of all aspects of a bee's life, from anthropology, to sexuality and physiology, and may even show you the bees themselves.

Eating and drinking

Rue du Marché and the open squares along allées Louis-Gardiol are where you'll find most of Riez's **eating** and **drinking** options. *L'Arts des Mets* in allée Louis-Gardiol (☎04.92.77.82.60) has menus at €15 and €19, while the restaurant *Le Rempart* on rue du Marché (☎04.92.77.89.54) serves Italian and Provençal dishes, with menus from €15. The pleasant *Bar Central* is on the corner of allées Louis-Gardiol and pl Maxime Javelly.

The Plateau de Valensole

Riez lies to the south of the **Plateau de Valensole**, bordered by the Bléone and Durance rivers and cut in two by the wide, stony course of the River Asse. Roads and villages north of the river are sparse. It's a beautiful landscape: a wide, uninterrupted tableland whose horizons are the sharp, high edges of mountains.

The most distinctive sight of the plateau is row upon row of **lavender** bushes, green in early summer, turning purple in July. Every farm advertises *lavandin* (a hybrid of lavender used for perfume essence) and *miel de lavande* (lavender honey). There are fields of golden grain, of almond trees blossoming white in early spring, and the gnarled and silvery trunks of olive trees. Even for Provence, the warm quality of the light is exceptional: the ancient town of Valensole, midway between Riez and Manosque, the village of Puimoisson on the road to Dignes, and the tiny hamlets along the Asse exude warmth from it even on wintry days.

This region is well off the beaten track, and there are few hotels. For campers, there's a two-star municipal **campsite**, *Les Lavandes* (☎04.92/74.86.14), on the road to Puimoisson, and most farmers hereabouts won't mind you camping on their land, provided you ask first.

Fourteen kilometres west of Riez, the village of **VALENSOLE** itself is a photogenic huddle of stone houses piling up to an eleventh-century hilltop church. It has its own **Maison de l'Abeille**, on the edge of the village on the Manosque road (Tues–Sat 8–11.30am & 1.30–5pm; free), where they will be happy to sell you as much of the sweet stuff as you can stomach.

The Lower Verdon

Southwest of Riez, along the Colostre and the last stretch of the Verdon, the land is richer and more populated. People commute to the Cadarache nuclear research centre at the confluence of the Durance and the Verdon, or to the new high-tech industries that are very gradually following the wake of the Marseille-Grenoble *autoroute*. The main reason to head this way is to visit the well-preseved **château** at Allemagne en Provence (tours July to mid-Sept Wed–Sun at 4 and 5pm; April–June & mid-Sept to Oct Sat & Sun at 4 & 5pm; €5), halfway between Riez and the long-established but rather dull spa town of Gréoux-Les-Bains. Built in the twelfth century and converted into a Renaissance residence during the sixteenth century, the château now boasts an impressive mix of warlike battlements and delicate stone pinnacles.

Quinson and the Musée de Préhistoire des Gorges du Verdon

On the far more attractive route south from Riez towards Barjols, **QUINSON** sits at the head of the **Basses Gorges du Verdon**. If you have not yet explored the Grand Canyon du Verdon, these 500-metre depths will strike you as quite dramatic, although, unfortunately, they are not as accessible. The GR99 makes a short detour to the south side of the gorge a couple of kilometres downstream from Quinson, and there are paths from the road between Quinson and Esparron that lead to the gorge's edge.

The chief attraction hereabouts, however, is Quinson's **Musée de Préhistoire des Gorges de Verdon**, rte de Montmeyan (April–June & Sept Mon & Wed–Sun 10am–7pm; July & Aug daily 10am–8pm; Oct to mid-Dec, Feb & March Mon & Wed–Sun 10am–6pm; €7), designed by the British architect Norman Foster in a clean and sympathetic modern style. Opened in 2001, it's the largest museum of human prehistory in Europe, and uses the latest audiovisual techniques to chart one million years of human habitation in Provence. There is a multimedia presentation of the cave of Baume Bonne and a fifteen-metre long reconstruction of the caves of the canyon of Baudinard, with their six-thousand-year-old red sun paintings. A themed path leads from the museum past reconstructed prehistoric homes and through a Neolithic garden to the most important of the sixty or so archeological sites in and around Quinson, the cave of **Baume Bonne** itself, where excavations over the last fifty years or so have traced human occupation back 400,000 years.

There's a pleasant, old-fashioned **hotel**, the *Relais Notre-Dame* (ⓣ04.92.74.40.01, ⓕ 04.92.74.02.10; ❷; menus from €14.50; closed mid-Dec to Jan), on the main road just south of Quinson, close to the river before it enters the gorge.

Manosque

MANOSQUE, 33km west of Riez, is an ancient town, strategically positioned just above the right bank of the River Durance. Its small old quarter is surrounded by ugly tower blocks and beyond them by ever-spreading industrial units and superstores. It is a major population centre in the *département* of Alpes-de-Haute-Provence and busy profiting from the new corridor of affluence that follows the river. Many of its residents work at the Cadarache atomic centre, or in Aix, or even in Marseille now that the highway gives speedy access.

For the French, Manosque is most famous as the home town of the author **Jean Giono** who was born here in 1895. As well as mementoes of the writer, the town also contains an extraordinary work of art on the theme of the Apocalypse by the Armenian-born painter **Jean Carzou**.

Arrival, information and accommodation

The **gare SNCF** is 1.5km south of the centre and served by regular **buses** up av Jean-Giono, the main route into town which ends at Porte Saunerie. From the **gare routière** on bd Charles-de-Gaulle (ⓣ04.92.87.55.99), turn left and then right onto av Jean-Giono. The **tourist office** (July & Aug Mon–Sat 9am–7pm, Sun 10am–noon; Sept–June Mon–Sat 9am–12.15pm & 1.20–6pm/6.30pm; ⓣ04.92.72.16.00) is to the left on place du Dr-Joubert just before you reach Porte Saunerie.

Staying in Manosque presents few problems. For low-priced rooms in the centre, try *François 1er*, 18 rue Guilhempierre (ⓣ04.92.72.07.99, ⓕ04.92.87.54.85; ❷), or the *Grand Hôtel de Versailles*, 17 av Jean-Giono (ⓣ04.92.72.12.10, ⓦwww.hotel-versailles.com; ❸), just outside the Vieille Ville's ring of boulevards. Further out still, the charming *Le Prést Michel* on rte

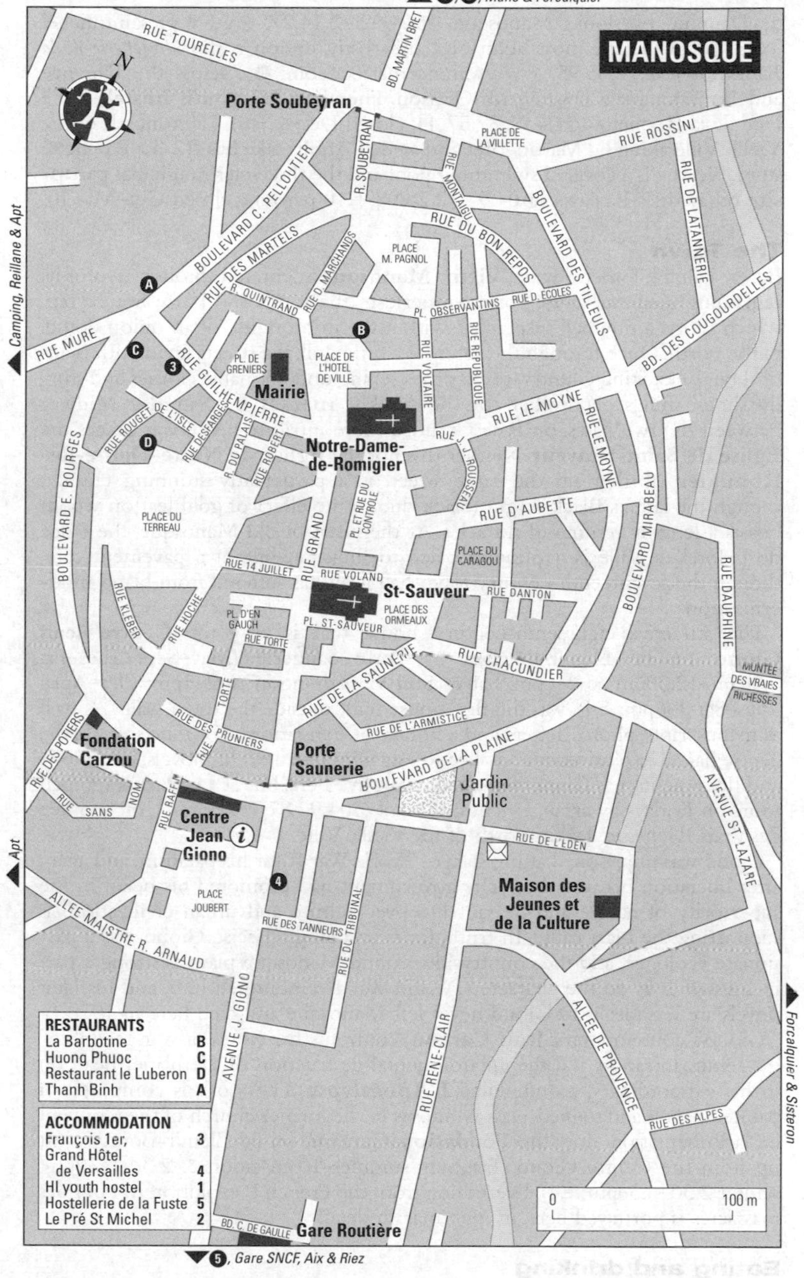
MANOSQUE
1, 2, Mane & Forcalquier
Camping, Reillane & Apt
Apt
Forcalquier & Sisteron
5, Gare SNCF, Aix & Riez
Porte Soubeyran
Mairie
Notre-Dame-de-Romigier
St-Sauveur
Fondation Carzou
Porte Saunerie
Jardin Public
Centre Jean Giono
Maison des Jeunes et de la Culture
Gare Routière
RESTAURANTS
La Barbotine B
Huong Phuoc C
Restaurant le Luberon D
Thanh Binh A
ACCOMMODATION
François 1er, 3
Grand Hôtel de Versailles 4
HI youth hostel 1
Hostellerie de la Fuste 5
Le Pré St Michel 2
0 100 m

de Dauphin overlooks Manosque (ⓣ04.92.72.14.27, ⓦwww.presaintmichel.com; ❹), while the most luxurious, and costly, option is the *Hostellerie de la Fuste* (ⓣ04.92.72.05.95, ⓦwww.francemaricet.com; ❽), across the Durance and 1km along the D4 towards Oraison. There's an **HI youth hostel** in the Parc de la Rochette (ⓣ04.92.87.57.44; closed Dec & Jan), 750m north of the Vieille Ville along bd Martin-Bret and av de l'Argile; take bus #2 (La Rochette stop). Nearby is a covered swimming pool and the three-star municipal **campsite** on av de la Repasse (ⓣ04.92.72.28.08; €10 per tent; closed Oct–March).

The Town

Barely half a kilometre wide, **Vieux Manosque** is entered through two of its remaining medieval gates: Porte Saunerie in the south and Porte Soubeyran, which sports a tiny bell suspended within the iron outline of an onion dome, in the north. Once through the gates it's a little dull, the streets lined with practical but unexciting country-town shops selling unfashionable clothes and sturdy shoes; things get livelier for the weekly **market** on Saturday. Midway between the two gates, on Rue Grand, a more intricate bell tower graces the **Église de Saint-Sauveur**. Neither this nor the **Église de Notre-Dame-de-Romigier**, further up the same street, is a particularly stunning church, though the latter's Black Virgin (black due to the effect of gold leaf on wood) boasts a lengthy resumé of miracles. At the heart of old Manosque, the Place de l'Hôtel de Ville is a pleasant place to linger awhile at a pavement café, though the seventeenth-century town hall itself has suffered from bland modernization.

The attractive eighteenth-century house that is now the **Centre Jean Giono**, on bd Elémir-Bourges by Porte Saunerie (May–Sept Tues–Fri 9.30am–12.30pm & 2–6pm; Sat & Sun 9.30am–noon & 2–6pm; Oct–April Tues–Sat 2–6pm; €4), was the first house built outside the town walls. As well as manuscripts, photos, letters and a library of translations of Giono's work, the centre has an extensive video collection of films based on his novels, interviews and documentaries. Giono himself did not live here, but at **Le Paraïs** (guided tours on Fridays by arrangement only: call ⓣ04.92.87.73.03; free), off montée des Vrais Richesses 1.5km north of the Vieille Ville.

Giono was imprisoned at the start of World War II for his pacifism, and again after liberation because the Vichy government had promoted his belief in the superiority of nature and peasant life over culture and urban civilization, as supporting the Nazi cause. In truth, far from being a fascist, Giono was a passionate ecologist, and the countryside around Manosque plays as strong a part in his novels as do the characters. World War II embittered him, and his later novels are less idealistic. Giono never left Manosque and died here in 1970.

Giono's contemporary, **Jean Carzou**, confronts the issues of war, technology, dehumanization and the environmental destruction of the planet head on in his extraordinary, monumental **L'Apocalypse**. The work is composed of painted panels and stained-glass windows in the former church of the Couvent de la Présentation, now the **Fondation Carzou**, on bd Elémir-Bourges just up from the Centre Giono (Fri–Sun: summer 10am–noon & 2.30–6.30pm; winter 2.30–6.30pm; €4). Everything from the French Revolution to Pol Pot's massacres is portrayed here, in nightmarish detail.

Eating and drinking

The **restaurants** in the Vieille Ville are generally great value: simple but satisfying meals can be had from around €11 at *La Barbotine* on place de l'Hôtel-de-Ville (ⓣ04.92.72.57.15; closed Sun), while the *Restaurant le Luberon*, at 21 bis place du Terreau (Ⓣ04.92.72.03.09; closed Mon & Sun eve out of season), has menus from €20. If you want a change from Provençal cuisine, try one of the town's excellent Vietnamese/Chinese restaurants, such as *Thanh Binh*, 7 bd Casimir-Pelloutier (Ⓣ04.92.87.36.83), or *Huong-Phuoc*, 38 bd Elémir-Bourges (Ⓣ04.92.72.84.96; menus from €10). For something a bit more upmarket, *La Source* at the hotel *Le Pré St Michel*, on rte de Dauphin (Ⓣ04.92.72.14.27; menus at €22, €28 & €35; closed Mon & Sat lunchtimes), has a broad terrace, and serves a wonderful chocolate pudding.

Forcalquier and around

In contrast with bustling Manosque, mellow **FORCALQUIER**, 17km to the north, is a very low-key town, despite the modern industrial development at its foot. It's not on any rail line, the main square is often deserted, the bars empty, and the masonry of the ancient houses is fraying at the edges. It is not surprising, therefore, that Forcalquier's past glories, and the surrounding soft, hilly countryside, are the real attraction. That said, things are a good deal livelier on Monday, when it's **market day**.

Arrival, information and accommodation

Buses drop you off at place Martial Sicard, one block back from the main place du Bourguet, where you'll find the **tourist office** at no. 13 (mid-June to mid-Sept Mon–Sat 9am–12.30pm & 2–7pm, Sun 10am–1pm; mid-Sept to mid-June Mon–Sat 9am–noon & 2–6pm; Ⓣ04.92.75.10.02, Ⓦwww.forcalquier.com). You can **rent bikes** from Moto Culture on bd de la République (Ⓣ04.92.75.12.47), from Forcalquier Auto, on av Saint Promesse (Ⓣ04.92.75.01.38), or from the campsite (see below).

The best place **to stay** is the attractive *Auberge Charembeau* (Ⓣ04.92.70.91.70, Ⓦwww.charembeau.com; ❸; closed mid-Nov to mid-Feb), 2km out of town, at the end of a long drive signed off the road to Niozelles. *Le Colombier* (Ⓣ04.92.75.03.71, Ⓕ04.92.75.14.30; July & Aug demi-pension compulsory from €59 per person, otherwise ❸) is another pleasant countryside retreat, 3km south of Forcalquier off the D16. In town, the *Hostellerie des Deux Lions*, next door to the tourist office at 11 place du Bourguet (Ⓣ04.92.75.25.30, Ⓕ04.92.75.06.41; ❹; closed Tues eve & Wed out of season), is a seventeenth-century coach house, with comfortable rooms and an excellent restaurant serving game and fowl dishes flavoured with all the herbs of Provence. The three-star municipal **campsite** (Ⓣ04.92.75.27.94; €10 per tent; closed Nov–March) is 500m out of town on the road to Sigonce, past the cemetery; it also rents out caravans.

The Town

Despite its slumbering air, Forcalquier was once a place of some significance, as its **public buildings** betray. In the **twelfth century** the counts of Forcalquier rivalled those of Provence, with dominions spreading south and east to the Durance and north to the Drôme. Gap, Embrun, Sisteron, Manosque and Apt were all ruled from the **citadel** of Forcalquier, which even minted its own currency. When this separate power base came to an end, Forcalquier was still renowned as the *Cité des Quatre Reines*, since the four daughters of Raimond Béranger V, who united Forcalquier and Provence, all married kings. One of them, Eleanor, became the wife of Henry III of

England, a fact commemorated by a modern plaque on the Gothic fountain of place Bourguet.

Not much remains of the ancient citadel at the summit of the rounded, wooded hill that dominates the town. Beside the ruins of a tower, sole vestige of the counts of Forcalquier's castle, and the half-buried walls of the original cathedral, stands a nineteenth-century chapel, **Notre-Dame-de-Provence**.

Looming over the central place du Bourguet, the former **Cathédrale Notre-Dame** has an asymmetric and defensive exterior, a finely wrought Gothic porch and a Romanesque nave which has recently been restored. Behind the cathedral you enter the **Vieille Ville** where the houses date from the thirteenth to the eighteenth century. From place Vieille or rue Mercière you can bear right for place St-Michel and the ancient street fronts of Grande Rue, rue Béranger, place du Palais and rue du Collège. Place St-Michel has another fountain, whose decorative figures are embroiled in activities currently banned under biblical sanction in half the states of the USA.

At the top and to the left of rue Passère, running south off place Vieille, and with more crumbling historic facades, you reach the start of montée St-Mari, which leads up to the citadel. East of place Vieille on rue des Cordeliers stands the old **synagogue**, which marks the site of the former Jewish quarter; just beyond it is the one remaining gateway to the Vieille Ville, the Porte des Cordeliers. The superior power of the Roman Catholic Church is represented by the **Couvent des Cordeliers** at the end of bd des Martyrs. Built between the twelfth and fourteenth centuries, it bears the scars of wars and revolutions but preserves a beautifully vaulted scriptorium and a library with its original wooden ceiling. It's used for concerts and exhibitions (programme from the tourist office) and is open for **guided tours** (mid-June to mid-Sept daily at 11am, 2.30 & 4.30pm; Feb to mid-June & mid-Sept to Nov enquire at tourist office; €3.80).

On the northeastern edge of town, on the road to Sigonce, the town's **cemetery** is in a much better state of repair than the houses of the living. Many of the oddly conical vaults were lived in until this century, like the Neolithic *bories* they resemble. The elegant staircase leading down to the geometric paths, the clipped yews and high box hedges, and the detailed inscriptions on many of the tombs make this an especially appealing place.

Eating and drinking

Place du Bourguet has a couple of decent places to eat: the *Deux Lions* (☎04.92.75.25.30; menus from €13), offering traditional fare, and *L'Estable*, at no. 4 (☎04.92.75.39.82), serving Provençal cuisine with menus starting at €16. *Oliviers & Co*, on rue des Cordeliers (☎04.92.75.00.75; closed evenings out of season), specializes in more modern creations, with a tempting array of olive oils and other local produce on sale. *La Crêperie*, at 4 rue des Cordeliers, does great salads, grills, ice creams and crêpes, with menus from €12.50, while *Le Commerce* on place du Bourguet (☎04.92.75.00.08; plats at €8) is a good place to try the wonderful local lamb.

Another product of the town, based on fruits and nuts from further south, is **exotic alcohol**. The Distillerie et Domaines de Haute-Provence has its shop on av St-Promasse just down from the tourist office, where you can buy cherries, pears and mixes of different fruits and nuts pickled in liqueur. Of its fruit wines, the *de brut de pêche*, a sparkling peach aperitif, needs to be tasted to be believed. For ordinary **café drinking**, the *Brasserie La Fontaine* on place St-Michel is a friendly locals' watering hole, and the *Café L'Hôtel de Ville*, on place Bourguet, is perfectly positioned for *pétanque*-watching.

Mane

The village of **MANE**, 4km south of Forcalquier at the junction of the roads from Apt and Manosque, still has its feudal citadel – now a private residence and closed to the public – and Renaissance churches, chapels and mansions remarkably intact. The most impressive building is a former Benedictine priory, **Notre-Dame-de-Salagon**, half a kilometre out of Mane off the Apt road. It comprises fifteenth-century monks' quarters, seventeenth-century stables and farm buildings, and an enormous fortified twelfth-century Romanesque church with traces of fourteenth-century frescoes and sculpted scenes of rural life. Archeological digs in the choir have revealed the remnants of an earlier, sixth-century church. Three **gardens**, one of aromatic plants, another of medicinal plants, and one cultivated as the medieval monks would have used it, have been recreated to illustrate the way in which the monks used the land; there are also modern and ecological gardens. A number of exhibitions and activities are organized each year by the Conservatoire du Patrimoine Ethnologique of the Alpes-de-Haute-Provence *département* which runs the site (May–Sept daily 10am–noon & 2–7pm; Oct–April daily 2–6pm; €5).

Further along the Apt road, past a medieval bridge over the River Laye, you come to a palatial residence that has been called the Trianon of Provence. The pure eighteenth-century ease and luxury of the **Château de Sauvan** (guided tours July & Aug Mon–Fri & Sun at 3.30pm; Sept–June Thurs, Sun & hols at 3.30pm; €5.60) come as a surprise in this harsh territory, leagues from any courtly city. Though there are hundreds of mansions like it around Paris and along the Loire, the residences of the rich and powerful in Haute-Provence tend towards the moat and dungeon, not to French windows giving onto lawns and lake. The furnishings are predictably grand and the hall and stairway would take some beating for light and spaciousness, but what's best is the setting: the swans and geese on the square lake, the peacocks strutting by the drive, the views around and the delicate solidity of the aristocratic house.

The Centre d'Astronomie de Saint-Michel l'Observatoire

The tourist literature promoting the pure air of Haute-Provence is not just hype. Proof of the fact is the National Centre for Scientific Research **observatory** on the wooded slopes west of Mane, sited here because it has the fewest clouds, the least fog and the lowest industrial pollution in all France. Visible from miles around, it presents a peculiar picture of domes of gleaming white mega-mushrooms pushing up between the oaks. It's open for **guided tours** (April–Sept Wed 2–4pm; Oct–March Wed at 3pm; €2.30), so you get to see some telescopes and blank monitors, and the mechanism that opens up the domes and aims the lens. More exciting, however, are the night-time sky watching vigils (July and Aug only) and the festival of astronomy.

Simiane-la-Rotonde, Banon and the Montagne de Lure

The gentle countryside of the Pays de Forcalquier gives way to the north to the great barrage of the **Montagne de Lure** and to the west, past **Simiane-**

la-Rotonde and **Banon**, to the desolate Plateau d'Albion (see p.136). The more northern villages, including Banon, are where you're likely to hear Provençal being spoken and see aspects of rural life that have hardly changed over centuries. It was in a tiny place on the Lure foothills due north of Banon called Le Contadour where Jean Giono (see p.300) set up his summer commune in the 1930s to expostulate the themes of peace, ecology and the return to nature.

Simiane-La-Rotonde

The spiralling cone of **SIMIANE-LA-ROTONDE** marks the horizon with an emphasis greater than its size would warrant. However many *villages de caractère* (Simiane's official classification) you may have seen, this is one to re-seduce you. Neither over-spruce nor on the verge of ruin, it gives the feeling of a place that people love and are prepared to work for.

The modern town – post office, banks, *boulangerie* and bars – all lies in the plain by the D51, cleanly separated from the old village's winding streets of honey-coloured stone in which each house is part of the medieval defensive system. The zigzags end at the **Rotonde** (April to mid-June & Sept Mon & Wed–Sun 3–5.30pm; last two weeks of June daily 10am–12.30pm & 3–5.30pm; mid-July & Aug Mon–Sat 10am–7pm, Sun 3–7pm; €2), a large domed building that was once the chapel of the castle but looks more like a keep. Nineteenth-century restoration work added smooth limestone to its rough-hewn fortress stones, but the peculiar feature is the asymmetry between its interior and exterior, being hexagonal on the outside and irregularly dodecagonal on the inside. The set of the stones on the domes is wonderfully wonky and no one knows what once hung from or covered the hole at the top. In July and August the Rotonde is used for various cultural functions.

Beyond the Rotonde there's a path to the chapel of **Notre-Dame-de-Pieté**, which stands amongst old windmills. As you head back down through the village you pass all sorts of architectural details which catch the eye: heavy carved doors with stone lintels in exact proportion, wrought-iron street lamps, the scrolling on the dark wooden shutters of the building opposite the **covered hall of the old market**, Simiane's most stunning building. With its columns framing open sky, the hall almost overhangs the hillside on the steepest section of the village; no longer used as a marketplace, it's where people stop on their daily rounds to pass the time of day or stare into the middle distance, where cats stretch out in the sun, and where, each July 14, the **village dance** is held.

Tourism is not Simiane's main preoccupation, but it does have a **tourist office**, housed in the Rotonde (same hours as the Rotonde; ⓣ04.92.75.90.14, ⓦwww.simiane-la-rotonde.com); when the office is closed, go to the *mairie* in the upper village for information. There's only one **hotel**, the *Auberge du Faubourg* (ⓣ04.92.75.92.43; ❷; closed Nov–Feb), which has just eight rooms. There are, however, several **gîtes** and **chambres d'hôtes** in and around Simiane, including *Le Chaloux*, run by M Rider (ⓣ04.92.75.99.13, ⓦwww.chaloux.free.fr; ❸; closed Jan to mid-March): it's off the D51 about 3km south of the village, and right on the GR4 footpath. There's also a two-star **campsite**, *Camping de Valsaintes*, on the main road (ⓣ04.92.75.91.46, ⓦwww.valsaintes.com; closed late Oct to March). Simiane isn't richly endowed with places to **eat** or **drink**: there's a bar-tabac, *Le Chapeau Rouge*, and a salon de thé, *Aux Plaisir des Yeux*, where you can also buy honey, liqueurs and *crème de marrons*.

Banon

Like Simiane, the houses of the Haute Ville of **BANON** form a guarding wall. Within the fortified gate, the protective huddling of the buildings is even closer, forcing one street to tunnel underneath the others.

Banon is famous for its **cheese**. The *plateau des fromages* of any half-decent Provence restaurant will include a round goats' cheese marinaded in brandy and wrapped in sweet chestnut leaves, but there's nothing like tasting different ages of the untravelled cheese, sliced off for you by the *fromager* at a market stall on place de la République. As well as ensuring that you taste the very young and the well-matured varieties, they may give you an accompaniment in the form of a sprig of savory, an aromatic local plant of the mint family. The *boulangerie* on the square sells the local variety of *fougasse* bread, stuffed with Banon cheese.

Accommodation options are limited to the **hotel-bar-restaurant** *Les Voyageurs* on the main square (ⓣ04.92.73.21.02; ❷), or the **campsite** *L'Épi Bleu* at the foot of the village (ⓣ04.92.73.30.30, ⓦperso.wanadoo.fr/epibleu; €15 per tent; closed Oct–March), with a pool and organized children's activities. For snacks, there's the *Café de France* on the main street, or *La Braserade* pizzeria.

The Montagne de Lure

Roads north of Banon peter out at the lower slopes of the **Montagne de Lure**. To reach the summit of the Lure, by road or the GR6, you have to head east to St-Étienne-les-Orgues, 12km north of Forcalquier. The footpath avoids the snaking road for most of the way, but you're walking through relentless pine plantation and it's a long way without a change of scenery (about 15km). Just below the summit you'll see the **ski lifts**.

When the trees stop you find yourself on sharp and rubbly stones without a single softening blade of grass. The summit itself is a mass of telecommunications aerials and dishes; a grimmer high-perched desert would be hard to find. That said, the point of the climb is that the Lure has no close neighbours, giving you 360 degrees of mountainscape, as if you were airborne. The view of the distant snowy peaks to the north is the best; those with excessive stamina can keep walking towards them along the GR6 to Sisteron.

Up the River Durance

The Marseille-Grenoble *autoroute* now speeds along the River Durance, bypassing the industrial town of **St-Auban** and its older neighbour **Château-Arnoux**, renowned for its superb restaurant, *La Bonne Étape*. The views from the fashionable little village of **Lurs** and the ancient **Prieuré de Ganagobie** have not been affected, nor has their isolation. La Brillane is the nearest gare SNCF to Lurs; Ganagobie is between La Brillane and Peyruis with no public transport links.

Lurs

Perched on a narrow ridge above the west bank of the Durance, **LURS** is another *village de caractère*, but much more keen on its picturesque status than Simiane-la-Rotonde. Immaculately restored houses stand amid immaculately maintained ruins; there's a tiny, Roman-style theatre, but little commerce beyond a shop selling prints, the café *Chez Justine*, and a pâtisserie. From the top of the village, you can see across the wide, multi-branching river to the abrupt step up to the Plateau de Valensole, with the snowy peaks beyond; to the south the land drops before rising again in another high ridge along the river; while to the west and north the views are just as extensive, from the rolling hills around Forcalquier to the Montagne de Lure.

The best way to appreciate this geography is to follow the paths to the small chapel of **Notre-Dame-de-Vie** along the narrowing escarpment. The right-hand path goes through the woods and is less clearly defined than the eastern path, the **Promenade des Evêques**, which is marked by fifteen small oratories.

By the late 1940s Lurs was deserted save for the odd passing bandit, but it gained international notoriety in 1952 when the British scientist Sir Jack Drummond and his family were murdered while camping alongside the Durance below the village. The case was never satisfactorily solved: the man convicted of the murder was spared execution and ultimately released from custody, and in recent years it has been suggested that Sir Jack was a victim of the Cold War, assassinated because he was a British spy.

In recent years, the village has become a centre for **graphic artists and printers**, including the author of the universal nomenclature for typefaces, and it is they who have brought life back to Lurs. They even hold an annual conference here, the Rencontres Internationales de Lurs, which brings in practitioners of the graphic arts from calligraphers to computer-aided-design consultants for the last week in August.

For somewhere **to stay**, there's the hotel-restaurant, *Le Séminaire*, near the car park on place de la Fontaine (ⓣ04.92.79.94.19, ⓦwww.hotel-leseminaire.com; ❼; menus from €15.50 to €58), housed in the old summer residence of the bishops of Sisteron. Alternative eating options include the nearby *La Bello Visto* **restaurant**, on pl du Château (ⓣ04.92.79.95.09; menus from €14; closed Tues & Wed), and *Chez Justine*, on the way into the village from the car park.

The Prieuré de Ganagobie

About 7km north of Lurs, in the twelfth-century **Prieuré de Ganagobie** (Tues–Sun 3–5pm), you'll find some fine examples of complex design skills that far predate the invention of printing. The floor of the priory church is covered with mosaics composed of red, black and white tiles: they depict fabulous beasts whose tails loop through their bodies, and the four elements represented by an elephant (Earth), a fish (Water), a griffon (Air) and a lion (Fire). Interlocking and repeating patterns show a strong Byzantine influence, and there's a dragon slain by a St George in Crusader armour. The porch of the church is also an unusual sight, its arches carved to a bubbly pattern that's thought to be an imitation of medieval bunting.

If you're not in a hurry, you can pass the time walking through the oaks and broom, pines and lavender eastwards along the allée des Moines to the edge of the Plateau de Ganagobie on which the priory stands, 350m above the Durance, or westwards following the allée de Forcalquier for views to the Montagne de Lure and beyond Forcalquier to the Luberon.

Château-Arnoux

North of the priory, the impending confluence of the Durance and Bléone is announced by the **Pénitents des Mées**, a long line of pointed rocks on the east bank, said to be the remains of cowled monks, literally petrified for desiring the women slaves a local lord brought back from the Crusades. Beyond here, the landscape is not very promising, with industry covering the right bank of the Durance at **St-Auban**, a dull suburb laid out in 1916.

Once you reach **CHÂTEAU-ARNOUX** itself, however, the hills once more close in, blocking St-Auban's plain from view, and the river takes on a smoother and more majestic prospect, as a seven-kilometre-long artificial lake ending at the barrage just south of the town. Dominating the centre of Château-Arnoux is an imposing Renaissance **castle**, now the *mairie*, with two round towers at the back, two square ones at the front and a hexagonal tower in the middle. All 84 steps of the tower staircase are carved from one block of stone. The roofs are covered in tiles of different colours, with gargoyles glaring from below the eaves. You can't visit the castle, but you can wander in its **park**, which has the best and most diverse collection of trees in Haute-Provence: Chinese mulberries, bananas, Judas trees and ebony, as well as native species.

Château-Arnoux practicalities

The **tourist office** is at Ferme Font Robert (mid-June to Aug Mon–Sat 10am–7pm; Sept to mid-June Mon–Fri 9am–noon & 2–6pm; ⓣ04.92.64.02.64, ⓦwww.district-moyenne-durance.com), signed off the N85 heading north out of the Vieille Ville.

Hotels here range from the de luxe *La Bonne Étape*, on chemin du Lac (ⓣ04.92.64.00.09, ⓦwww.bonneetape.com; ❾), to *La Taverne Jarlandine* on pl Jean-Jaurès (ⓣ04.92.64.04.49; ❶), an old-fashioned cheapie in the centre of the village. *La Bonne Étape* (ⓣ04.92.64.00.09; menus from €40–90; closed Mon out of season & Sun eve), has one of the best **restaurants** in Provence, where the cooking celebrates the produce of the region without trendy foreign influences. If your budget won't stretch to this, the excellent *Casa Mia* pizzeria on av Général-de-Gaulle (ⓣ04.92.62.63.96) has menus from €12.50, and the *Tchin-Tchin* **bar**, on the central place Camille-Reymond, serves snacks and ice creams to a young clientele accompanied by loud music. The Centre Culturel des Lauzières on av Jean-Moulin, the main road coming in from the south, has its own restaurant *Le Stendhal* (ⓣ04.92.64.45.56; menus from €11), as well as a **cinema** and **exhibition space**.

Sisteron and around

The last Provençal stretch of the Route Napoleon (see p.343) runs from Château-Arnoux to **SISTERON**. The most picturesque approach is to follow Napoleon's footsteps via the D4 on the left bank of the Durance. The first sight of Sisteron reveals its strategic significance as the major mountain gateway of Provence. The site, fortified since ancient times, was half-destroyed by the Anglo-American bombardment of 1944, but its **citadel** still stands as a fearsome sentinel over the city and the solitary bridge across the river. After heavy rains the Durance, the colour of *café au lait*, becomes a raging torrent pushing through the narrow Sisteron gap.

Sisteron gave Napoleon something of a headache. Its mayor and the majority of its population were royalist, and given the fortifications and geography of the town, it was impossible for him to pass undetected. However, luck was still with the Corsican in those days, as the military commander of the *département* was a sympathizer and removed all ammunition from Sisteron's arsenal. Contemporary accounts say Napoleon sat nonchalantly on the bridge, con-

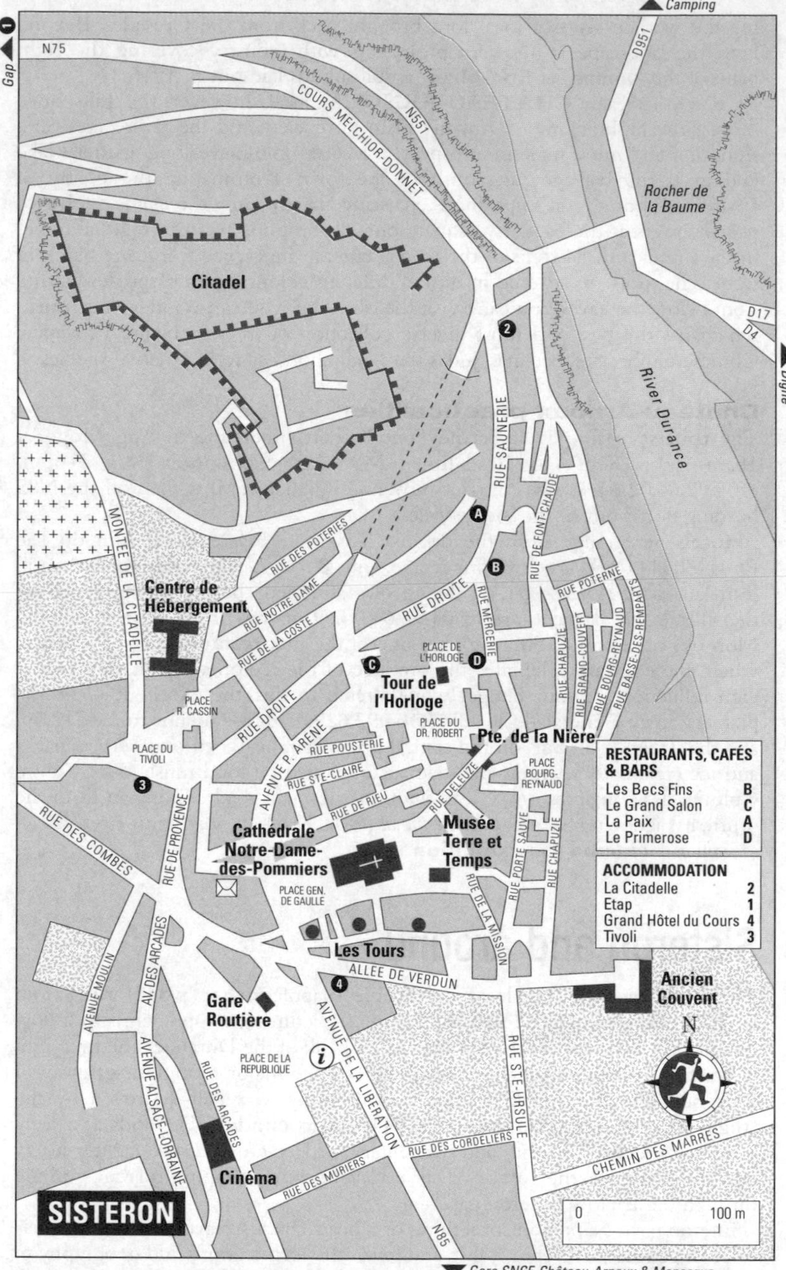
SISTERON
Camping
Gap
Digne
Gare SNCF, Château-Arnoux & Manosque
N75
D951
N551
D17
D4
N85
COURS MELCHIOR-DONNET
Rocher de la Baume
River Durance
Citadel
Centre de Hébergement
MONTEE DE LA CITADELLE
RUE DES POTERIES
RUE NOTRE DAME
RUE DE LA COSTE
RUE DROITE
RUE SAUNERIE
RUE DE FONT-CHAUDE
RUE MERCERIE
RUE POTERNE
RUE CHAPUZIE
RUE GRAND-COUVERT
RUE BOURG-REYNAUD
RUE BASSE-DES-REMPARTS
PLACE DE L'HORLOGE
Tour de l'Horloge
PLACE R. CASSIN
PLACE DU TIVOLI
AVENUE P. ARENE
RUE POUSTERIE
RUE STE-CLAIRE
RUE DE RIEU
RUE DELEUZE
PLACE DU DR. ROBERT
Pte. de la Nière
PLACE BOURG-REYNAUD
RUE PORTE SAUVE
RUE DES COMBES
RUE DE PROVENCE
Cathédrale Notre-Dame-des-Pommiers
Musée Terre et Temps
PLACE GEN. DE GAULLE
RUE DE LA MISSION
Les Tours
ALLEE DE VERDUN
Ancien Couvent
AVENUE MOULIN
AV. DES ARCADES
Gare Routière
AVENUE DE LA LIBERATION
PLACE DE LA REPUBLIQUE
RUE STE-URSULE
AVENUE ALSACE-LORRAINE
RUE DES ARCADES
RUE DES CORDELIERS
RUE DES MURIERS
CHEMIN DES MARRES
Cinéma
N
0
100 m
RESTAURANTS, CAFÉS & BARS
Les Becs Fins B
Le Grand Salon C
La Paix A
Le Primerose D
ACCOMMODATION
La Citadelle 2
Etap 1
Grand Hôtel du Cours 4
Tivoli 3

templating the citadel above and the tumultuous waters below, while his men reassembled and the town's notables, ordered to keep their pistols under wraps, looked on impotently. Eventually Napoleon entered the city, took some refreshment at a tavern and received a tricolour from a courageous peasant woman before rejoining his band and taking leave of Provence.

Sisteron's prosperity today is based as much on the extensive industrial zone that has grown up to the north along the N75 as it is on tourism. The truth of the town's claim to be a gateway to the mountains, however, is effectively demonstrated if you try to use a mobile phone: reception is terrible.

Arrival, information and accommodation

From Sisteron's **gare SNCF** turn right and head along av de la Libération until you reach place de la République. Here you'll find the **gare routière**, post office and **tourist office** (Sept–June Mon–Sat 9am–noon & 2–5pm; July & Aug Mon–Sat 9am–7pm, Sun 10am–noon & 2–5pm; ⓣ04.92.61.12.03 or 04.92.61.36.50, ⓦwww.sisteron.com), which can provide details of good walks and advise on **bike rental**.

For pleasant, comfortable and exceptionally good-value **rooms**, try *La Citadelle*, overlooking the river at the end of rue Saunerie (ⓣ04.92.61.13.52; ❷); the *Tivoli*, 21 place René Cassin (ⓣ04.92.61.15.16, ⓕ04.92.61.21.72; ❷), or the genteel and old-fashioned three-star *Grand Hôtel du Cours*, allée de Verdon (ⓣ04.92.61.04.51, ⓔhotelducours@wanadoo.fr; ❸). Further out, there's a modern, well-equipped *Etap* hotel (ⓣ04.92.61.28.22, ⓦwww.accor.com; ❷) at the *autoroute* exit, 4km north of town on the N75, and the four-star **campsite**, *Les Prés-Hauts*, with a pool (ⓣ04.92.61.19.69; €11 per tent; closed Nov–Feb); it's over the river, and 3km along the D951 to the left.

The Town

To do the **citadel** justice (April–June & Sept to mid-Nov 9am–6pm; July & Aug daily 9am–8pm; €4) can easily take up half a day. There are no guides, just tape recordings in French attempting to recreate historic moments, such as Napoleon's march and the imprisonment in 1639 of Jan Kazimierz, the future king of Poland. Most of the extant defences were constructed after the Wars of Religion, and added to a century later by Vauban when Sisteron was a frontline fort against neighbouring Savoy. No traces remain of the first Ligurian fortification nor of its Roman successor, and the eleventh-century castle was destroyed in the mid-thirteenth century during a pogrom against the local Jewish population.

As you climb up to the fortress, there seems no end to the gateways, courtyards and other defences. The outcrop on which the fortress sits abruptly stops at the lookout post, **Guérite du Diable**, 500m above the narrow passage of the Durance, and affording the best views. On the other side of the ravine, the vertical folds of the **Rocher de la Baume** provide a favourite training ground for local mountaineers.

In the fortress grounds, a **festival** known as *Nuits de la Citadelle* takes place in late July and early August, with open-air concerts and performances of opera, drama and dance. There is also a **museum** on the history of the citadel with a room dedicated to Napoleon, and temporary art exhibitions in the vertiginous late medieval chapel, **Notre-Dame-du-Château**, restored to its Gothic glory and given very beautiful subdued stained-glass windows in the 1970s.

Outside the citadel, perhaps the most striking features of Sisteron are the three huge **towers** which belonged to the ramparts built around the expanding town in 1370. Though one still has its spiralling staircase, only ravens use them now. Beside them is the much older former **Cathédrale Notre-Dame-des-Pommiers**, whose strictly rectangular interior contrasts with its riot of stepped roofs and an octagonal gallery adjoining a square belfry topped by a pyramidal spire. The altarpiece incorporates a Mignard painting; other seventeenth-century works adorn the chapels.

At the rear of the cathedral, a former convent of the Visitandine order houses the **Musée Terre et Temps** (April & Oct Wed–Sun 9.30am–12.30pm & 2–6pm; May, June & Sept daily 9.30am–12.30pm & 2–6pm; July & Aug daily 10am–1pm & 3–7pm; €2), which charts the measurement of time from ancient sundials through calendars to the latest atomic clocks, in parallel with the measurement of geological time. From the museum, you can follow a signposted route through the lower town, past tall houses enclosing narrow passages with steep steps and ramps that interconnect through vaulted archways, known here as **andrônes**. Houses on the downslope side of rue Saunerie, overlooking the river, often descend at the back a further three or four storeys to the lanes far below. In the troubled days of 1568 (during the Wars of Religion) sixty lanterns were put in place to light the alleyways and deter conspiracies and plots; there's no such luxury today, and Old Sisteron can take on a sinister aspect at night. In the upper town, on the other side of rue Saunerie and rue Droite, the houses, like the citadel above them, follow the curves of the rock.

Place de l'Horloge, at the other end of rue Deleuze from the church, is the site for the Wednesday and Saturday **market**, where stalls congregate to sell sweet and savoury *fougasse*, lavender honey, nougat and almond-paste *calissons* that rival those from Aix. On the second Saturday of every month the market becomes a **fair**, and there are likely to be flocks of sheep and lambs, and cages of pigeons as well as stalls selling clothes and bric-a-brac.

Eating and drinking

Sisteron has no outstanding **restaurants**, though you can certainly have a filling meal at a reasonable price. Of the hotel-restaurants, *La Citadelle* has plats at €5.50, menus from €13, plenty of salads, and a terrace above the river where you can eat; while the *Grand Hôtel du Cour* serves copious meals including the renowned *gigot d'agneau de Sisteron* (menus at €14–24). *Les Becs Fins*, in rue Saunerie (☎04.92.61.12.04), specializes in delicious ingredients like *trompettes de mort*, with menus from €14. Alternatively, there's no shortage of crêperies, brasseries, Tex-Mex and pizzerias along rue Saunerie and on the squares around the Tour de l'Horloge – the pizzeria *La Paix*, at 41 rue Saunerie (☎04.92.62.62.29), does particularly good pizzas at €9 as well as more elaborate dishes. The best nougat and *calissons* come from Canteperdrix on place Paul-Arène, which also runs *Le Grand Salon*, a *salon de thé* serving salads, cakes and ice creams. For anchovy *fougasse* head to Boulangerie Bernaudon, 37 rue Droite, and for *charcuterie* to Traiteur des Gourmets, 136 rue de Provence. *Le Primerose* **bar** on place de l'Horloge stays open late.

Vilhosc and Vaumeilh

If you're staying in Sisteron for several days there are some worthwhile expeditions into the wilds. To the east along the D17 you come to **VILHOSC** whose priory has an eleventh-century crypt hidden in its walls; a few kilometres further on is the graceful fourteenth-century **Pont de la Reine Jeanne**, which crosses the River Vançon. The roads end here, but the long-distance walkers' route, the GR6, leads onwards and upwards, past villages that are almost all abandoned and in ruins.

If you're keen on **flying**, the Aérodrome de Sisteron (☎04.92.62.17.45) can arrange for you to go up in a glider or microlight. It's 10km to the north of Sisteron, through Valernes off the D951 in the village of **VAUMEILH**.

Travel details

Trains

Manosque to: Aix (5 daily; 45min); Château-Arnoux (6 daily; 25min); La Brillane (4 daily; 12min); Marseille (5 daily; 1hr 15min); Sisteron (6 daily; 40min).

Buses

Aups to: Aiguines (5 weekly; 25min); Brignoles (1–2 daily; 1hr 15min); Cotignac (1–2 daily; 50min); Draguignan (3–4 daily; 1hr 15min); Salernes (1 weekly; 10min); Scillans (1–2 daily; 10min); Tourtour (3–4 daily; 15min).
Banon to: Aix (1 daily; 2hr 5min); Marseille (1 daily; 2hr 35min); Simiane (2 daily; 10min).
Draguignan to: Aix (3 daily; 2hr 30min); Aups (1 daily; 1hr–1hr 20min); Bargemon (5 daily; 45min); Barjols (1 daily; 1hr 10min); Brignoles (3 daily; 1hr); Callas (3 daily; 40min); Entrecasteaux (2 weekly; 45min); Fayence (4 daily: 1hr 40min); Grasse (2 daily; 2hr 45min); Les Arcs (frequent; 20min); Lorgues (4 daily; 20min); St-Raphaël (12 daily; 1hr 15min–1hr 30min); Salernes (3 daily; 1 hr 15min–1hr 45min); Seillans (3 daily; 1hr 20min); Toulon (4 daily; 2hr 15min); Tourtour (1 daily; 50 min); Villecroze (2 weekly; 1hr).
Fayence to: Draguignan (Mon–Sat 3 daily; 1hr 30min); Grasse (Mon–Sat 3 daily; 1hr); St Raphaël (Mon–Sat 4 daily; 1hr 20min).
Forcalquier to: Apt (1–2 daily; 55min); Avignon (1–2 daily; 2hr 10min); Château-Arnoux (2 daily; 45min); Digne (2 daily; 1hr 10min); La Brillane (1–2 daily; 10min); Lurs (1–2 daily; 15min); Mane (1–2 daily; 5min); Marseille (5 daily; 1hr 35min–1hr 50min); Peyruis (1–2 daily; 25min); St-Auban (1–2 daily; 35min); St Michel l'Observatoire (1–2 daily; 10min); Sisteron (1 daily; 1hr 5min).
Manosque to: Aix (14 daily; 40min–1hr); Château-Arnoux (1–2 daily; 35min); Digne (1–2 daily; 1hr 5min); Marseille (14 daily; 1hr–1hr 30min); Riez (3 daily; 1hr); St-Auban (3 daily; 35min); Sisteron (4 daily; 35min–1hr).
Riez to: Barjols (1 daily; 45min); Digne (1 daily; 1hr 15min); Manosque (1 daily; 1hr); Marseille (1–2 daily; 2hr) Moustiers-Ste-Marie (1–4 daily; 15min).
Sisteron to: Aix (7 daily; 1hr 25min–2hr); Château-Arnoux (6 daily; 20min); Digne (2 daily; 1hr); Forcalquier (1 daily; 1hr) Lurs (3 daily; 45min); Manosque (4 daily; 45min–1hr); Marseille (4 daily; 1hr 55min–2hr 25min); Nice (1 daily; 3hr 55min); Peipin (3 daily; 10min).

6

The Riviera: Cannes to Menton

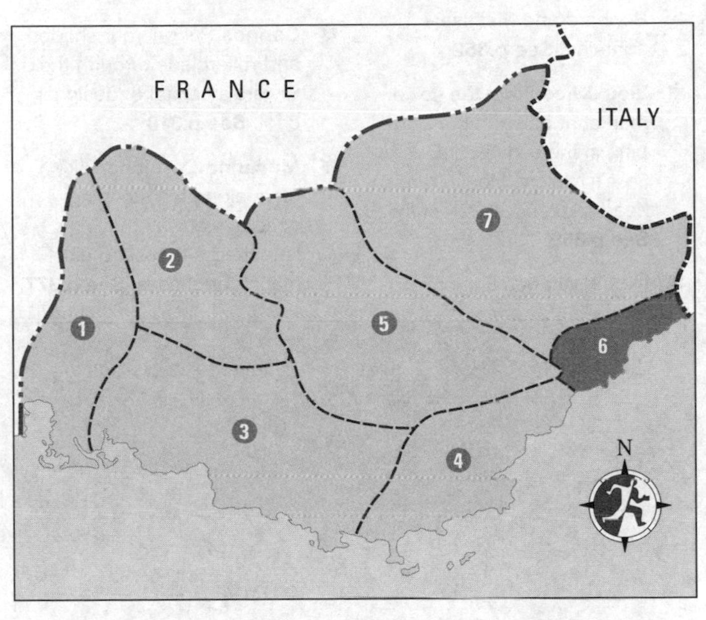

CHAPTER 6

Highlights

* **Fondation Maeght** Art and architecture fuse with landscape and the dazzling Provençal light to create this astonishing museum, whose building is as stunning as the works of art – by the likes of Miró, Chagall, Kandinsky, Bonnard and Matisse – it contains. **See p.352**

* **Vieux Nice** From the flower market at dawn to bar hopping in the early hours, Nice's mellow, Mediterranean heart buzzes with street life. **See p.359**

* **Niçois villages** Explore craggy Peillon and unspoilt Luceram, the *villages perchés* of Nice's wild and underpopulated hinterland, where villagers still live off the land, producing olives, goats' cheese, herbs and vegetables. **See p.369 and p.371**

* **Cannes** Put on your shades and rollerblade through the Riviera's capital of designer cool. **See p.318**

* **Moyenne Corniche** Take a drive along the stunning coastal highway that launched a thousand cinematic car chases. **See p.377**

6

The Riviera: Cannes to Menton

The seventy-kilometre stretch of the coast between Cannes and the Italian border known as the Riviera was once an inhospitable shore with few natural harbours, its tiny local communities preferring to cluster around feudal castles high above the sea. It is now an almost uninterrupted promenade, lined by palm trees and megabuck hotels, with speeding sports cars on the corniche roads and yachts like minor ocean liners moored at each resort. The sea is speckled with boats, boards, bikes and skis; the beaches – many of them shingle or made from imported sand – with a vivid pattern of parasols and beds. The occasional breaks in the garish, intermittently gorgeous facades overlooking the Mediterranean are filled by formal parks or gardens, and, where vertical contours limit construction, roads and rail lines have been cut on the water's edge.

The Riviera's largest city, **Nice**, became fashionable as a winter resort in the eighteenth century. The fishing village of **Cannes** was discovered in the 1830s by a retired British chancellor who couldn't get to Nice because of a cholera epidemic. Up until World War I, aristocrats and royals from all ends of Europe came here to build their Riviera mansions, and artists like **Renoir** sought warm retreats here while the local population continued to farm and fish. The interwar years saw the advent of more artists – **Picasso, Matisse, Dufy, Bonnard, Miró** – and the beginnings of a switch from winter to summer as the favoured season.

Tourist passes

There are a couple of passes worth considering if you want to cut costs along the Riviera. The **Carte Isabelle** offers a day's unlimited first- or second-class train travel along the whole coast between Fréjus and Ventigmilia. It costs €10, is valid between July and September, and can be bought from train stations, newsagents and *tabacs*.

The **Museum Pass** allows unlimited access to sixty of the most important art and history museums, monuments and gardens in the Riviera region. A one-day pass costs €10, a three-day pass costs €17 and a seven-day pass €27. Available at participating museums, principal tourist offices, FNAC stores or Thomas Cook foreign exchange offices.

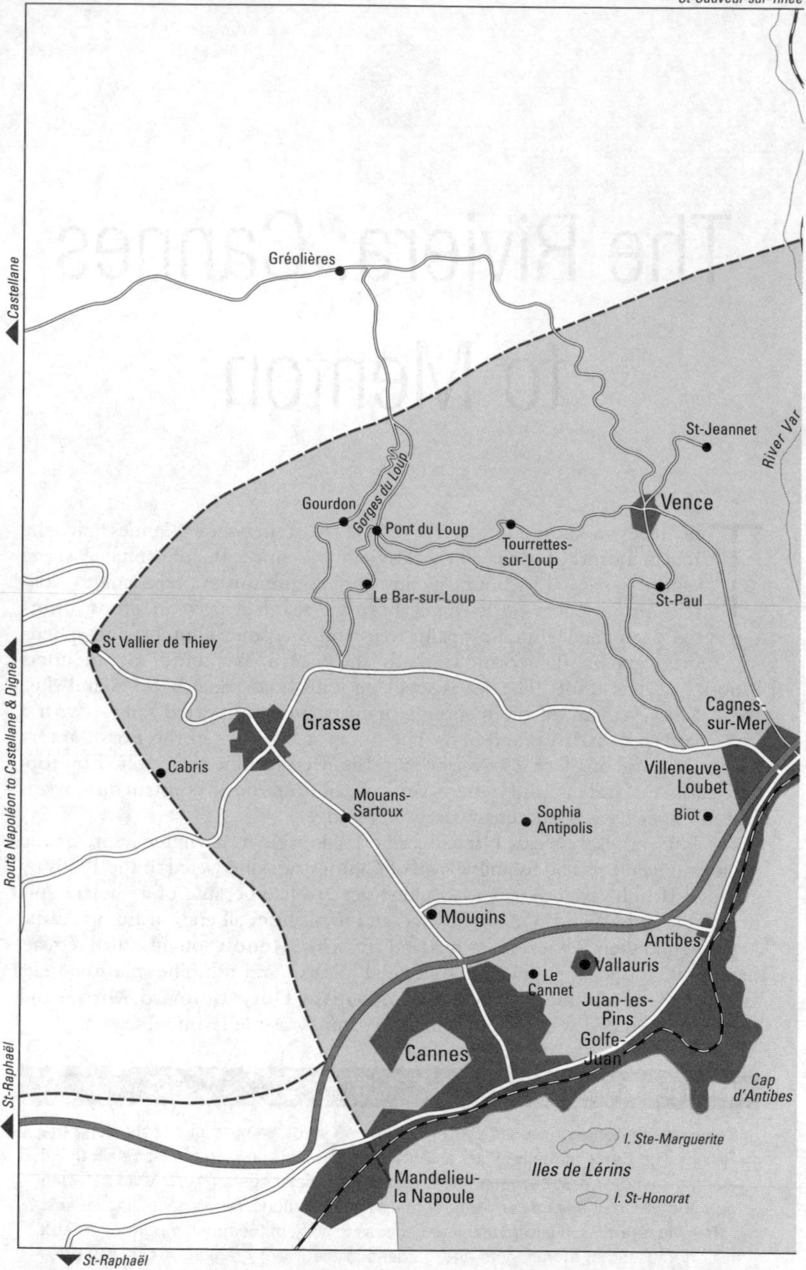
St-Sauveur-sur-Tinée
Castellane
Gréolières
St-Jeannet
River Var
Vence
Gourdon
Gorges du Loup
Pont du Loup
Tourrettes-
sur-Loup
Le Bar-sur-Loup
St-Paul
St Vallier de Thiey
Route Napoléon to Castellane & Digne
Grasse
Cagnes-
sur-Mer
Cabris
Villeneuve-
Loubet
Mouans-
Sartoux
Sophia
Antipolis
Biot
Mougins
Antibes
Vallauris
Le
Cannet
Juan-les-
Pins
Golfe-
Juan
Cannes
St-Raphaël
Cap
d'Antibes
I. Ste-Marguerite
Iles de Lérins
Mandelieu-
la Napoule
I. St-Honorat
St-Raphaël

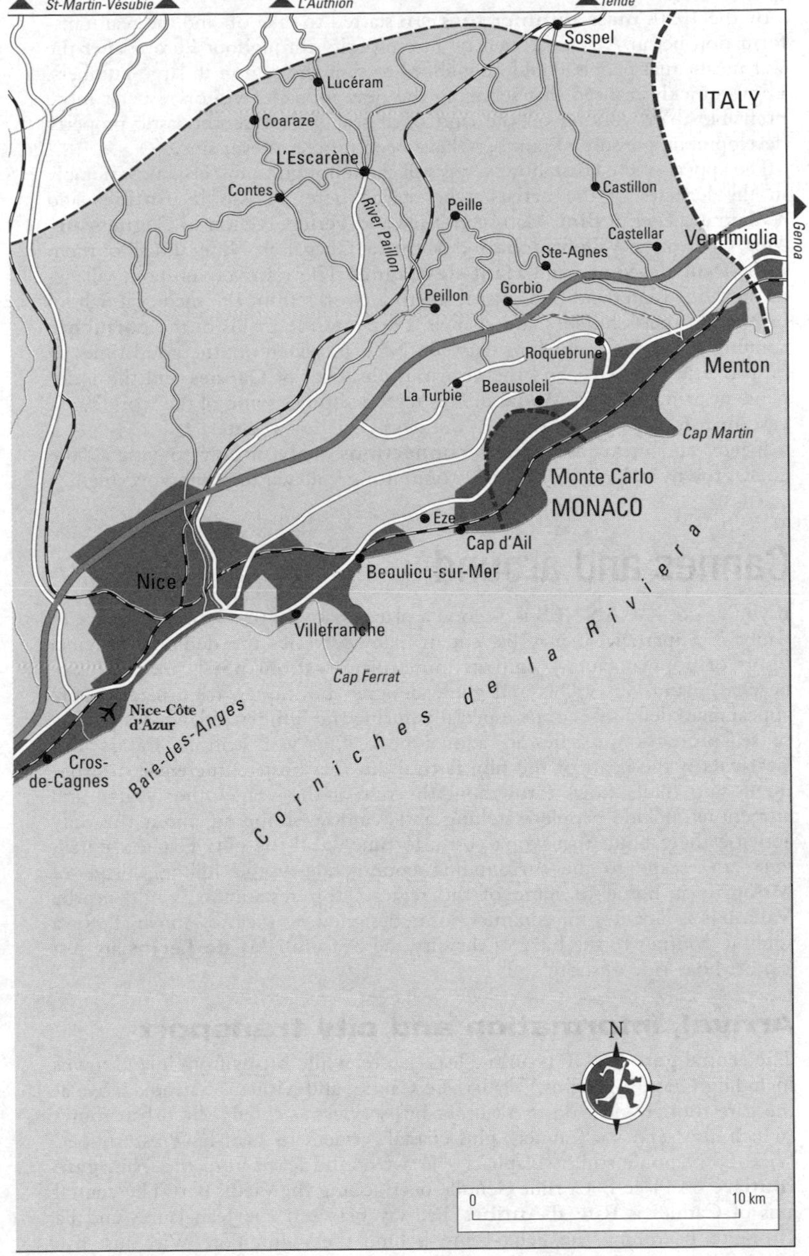
St-Martin-Vésubie
L'Authion
Tende
Sospel
Lucéram
ITALY
Coaraze
L'Escarène
Contes
Castillon
Peille
River Paillon
Genoa
Castellar
Ventimiglia
Ste-Agnes
Gorbio
Peillon
Roquebrune
Menton
La Turbie
Beausoleil
Cap Martin
Monte Carlo
MONACO
Eze
Cap d'Ail
Beaulieu-sur-Mer
Nice
Villefranche
Cap Ferrat
Corniches de la Riviera
Nice-Côte d'Azur
Baie-des-Anges
Cros-de-Cagnes
N
0
10 km

By the 1950s **mass summer tourism** started to take off and the real transformation began. A general increase in prosperity throughout Europe after the war meant that people could now afford to visit the region in large numbers. Locals quickly realized that servicing the new influx of visitors was far more profitable than working on the land or at sea, and overenthusiastic property development, pressure of numbers, have been problems ever since.

The appeal of the coast, however, is still easy enough to discern, most notably in the legacies of the **artists** who stayed here: Picasso in **Antibes** and **Vallauris**; Léger in **Biot**; Matisse in **Nice** and **Vence**; Renoir in **Cagnes-sur-Mer**; Cocteau in **Villefranche** and **Menton**; Chagall in **Nice**; and all of them in **St-Paul-de-Vence** and **Haut-de-Cagnes**. The relatively unspoilt villages in the Nice hinterland, too, guard superb artworks from the medieval School of Nice in their churches and chapels. There are the thrills of the **corniches** running across the mountains between Nice and Menton; the good times to be had in Vieux Nice; and the vicarious pleasures of **Cannes** and the independent principality of **Monaco**. This region also has some of the world's best **restaurants**, catering for some of the world's richest clientele.

Speedy and inexpensive **train connections** make it easy to visit all the coastal towns and villages without committing yourself to staying overnight.

Cannes and around

If you've got it, **CANNES** is as good a place as any in the South of France to flaunt it. Superficial it may be, but in many ways it's the definitive Riviera resort of popular fantasy, with its immaculate seafront hotels and exclusive beaches, glamorous yachts and glitzy designer boutiques. It's a place where appearances definitely count, especially during the film festival, when the orgy of self-promotion reaches its annual peak. The vast seafront **Palais des Festivals** is the heart of the film festival but also hosts conferences, tournaments and trade shows throughout the rest of the year. Other year-round attractions include people-watching and window-shopping, about the only activities hereabouts that won't cost a fortune. If all the glitz gets too much, you can escape to the surrounding countryside – the hilltop village of **Mougins** is home to some of the region's top restaurants, while nearby **Vallauris** is a centre for ceramics, some designed by Picasso. Above all, for a sublime contrast to the buzz of the city, the peaceful **Îles de Lérins** are just a short boat-ride offshore.

Arrival, information and city transport

The central **gare SNCF** is on rue Jean-Jaurès, while **buses** from inland towns including Grasse, Mougins, Vallauris, Le Cannet and Mouans-Sartoux arrive at the gare routière next door. All other bus services – chiefly the urban routes (which also serve Le Cannet), plus coastal services to Juan-les-Pins, Antibes, Nice, La Napoule and St-Raphaël – arrive at and leave from the main **gare routière** on Place B-Cornut Gentille overlooking the Vieux Port. The central axis of Cannes is **Rue d'Antibes**, halfway between rue Jean-Jaurès and La Croisette, becoming rue Félix-Faure behind the Vieux Port. With just five blocks between rue Jean-Jaurès and the seafront, central Cannes is not particularly big, though it manages to look daunting. **Le Suquet**, the hill overlooking the modern town from the west, is the heart of Old Cannes. **Urban buses** run from outside the hôtel de ville; you can buy individual **tickets** for €1.25, a *carnet* of ten for €8.30 and a weekly pass, the *Carte Palm'Hebdo*, for €9.20. A useful service is the #8 bus along the seafront from the hôtel de ville to Palm Beach Casino on Pointe Croisette, at the other end of the bay. If you prefer to cycle, **bikes** can be rented from Alliance Location, 19 rue des Frères Pradignac (ⓣ04.93.39.93.03); or Holiday Bikes, 32 av du Maréchal Juin (ⓣ04.93.94.34.48, ⓦwww.holiday-bikes.com/maps/cannes.htm).

There are **tourist offices** at the gare SNCF (Mon–Fri 9am–noon & 2–6pm; ⓣ04.93.99.19.77); at 1 rue Sémard in La Bocca (Tues–Sat 8.30am–12.20pm & 3–6.30pm; ⓣ04.93.47.04.12); and at the Palais des Festivals (Mon–Sat 9am–6.30pm; ⓣ04.93.39.24.53, ⓦwww.cannes.fr).

Accommodation

There's a wide choice of **hotels** in central Cannes, and you shouldn't have much trouble finding somewhere to stay, whatever your budget; for the cheaper options it's important to book in advance. The tourist offices have a free **reservation service** (ⓣ04.93.99.99.00, ⓦwww.cannes-reservation.com), but can't guarantee rooms for late arrivals or at the price you specify. **Camping** opportunities are not good: the sites are well over capacity and far from central; pitching in Mandelieu, 7km west, is likely to be easier and cheaper. As sleeping on the beach is out of the question, it is not a good idea for anyone on a tight budget to get stuck in Cannes late at night, especially after public transport services have stopped.

Hotels

Alnea 20 rue Jean-de-Riouffe ⓣ04.93.68.77.77, ⓔalnea@free.fr. Moderately priced with just fourteen rooms, the *Alnea* is air-conditioned and has the service and style that you'd expect from a pricier place. ❹

Beau Séjour 5 rue des Fauvettes ⓣ04.93.39.63.00, ⓦwww.cannes-beausejour.com. Just to the northwest of Le Suquet, with good facilities and a quiet location. The hotel is modern with an extensive garden, pool and attractive terrace, and all the rooms have balconies. ❽

Best Western Hotel Univers 2 rue Maréchal Foch ⓣ04.93.06.30.00, ⓦbw-hotelunivers.com. Comfortable if rather conventional hotel in a central location, but well-soundproofed. There's a rooftop terrace with views over the town. ❻

Bleu Rivage 61 La Croisette ⓣ04.93.94.24.25, ⓕ04.93.43.74.92. A seafront hotel in a nineteenth-century building with its own stretch of beach, neighbouring all the de luxe establishments but rather more affordable. ❾

Bourgogne 120 rue du 24 Août ⓣ04.93.38.36.73, ⓕ04.92.99.28.41. No-frills place, but well-kept and very central. Closed Dec. ❹

Canberra 11 rue d'Antibes ⓣ04.97.06.95.00, ⓔhotelcanberra@wanadoo.fr. Newly-refurbished and central, with classy modern decor. ❽

Carlton Intercontinental 58 La Croisette ⓣ04.93.06.40.06, ⓦhttp://cannes-interconti.com. Legendary *belle époque* palace hotel that starred in Hitchcock's *To Catch a Thief*, along with Cary Grant and Grace Kelly. The rooms are surprisingly modern, but will set you back €450 for a double in August. ❾

Chanteclair 12 rue Forville ⓣ & ⓕ04.93.39.68.88. Budget place in a side street close to Le Suquet, with quiet rooms and no TVs. ❺

Cristal 13 rond-point Duboys-d'Angers ⓣ04.93.39.45.45, ⓦwww.hotel-cristal.com. Just off La Croisette and with palatial decor. There's a panoramic restaurant, bar and pool on the sixth floor. ❾

Cybelle 14 rue du 24 Août ⓣ04.93.38.31.33, ⓕ04.93.38.43.47. A small, good value place, with just ten rooms. It's well known for its excellent restaurant. Closed mid-Nov to mid-Dec. ❸

Eden 133 rue d'Antibes ⓣ04.93.68.78.00, ⓦwww.eden-hotel-cannes.com. As swanky Cannes places go, this stylish, airy, contemporary boutique hotel, close to the designer shopping action, has relatively sane prices: doubles in high season from €165. ❾

Hôtel le Florian 8 rue du Commandant-André ⓣ04.93.39.24.82, ⓦwww.hotel-florian-cannes.com. A pleasant two-star hotel with friendly owners, in a central location. Closed mid-Nov to mid-Jan. ❹

Little Palace 18 rue du 24 Août

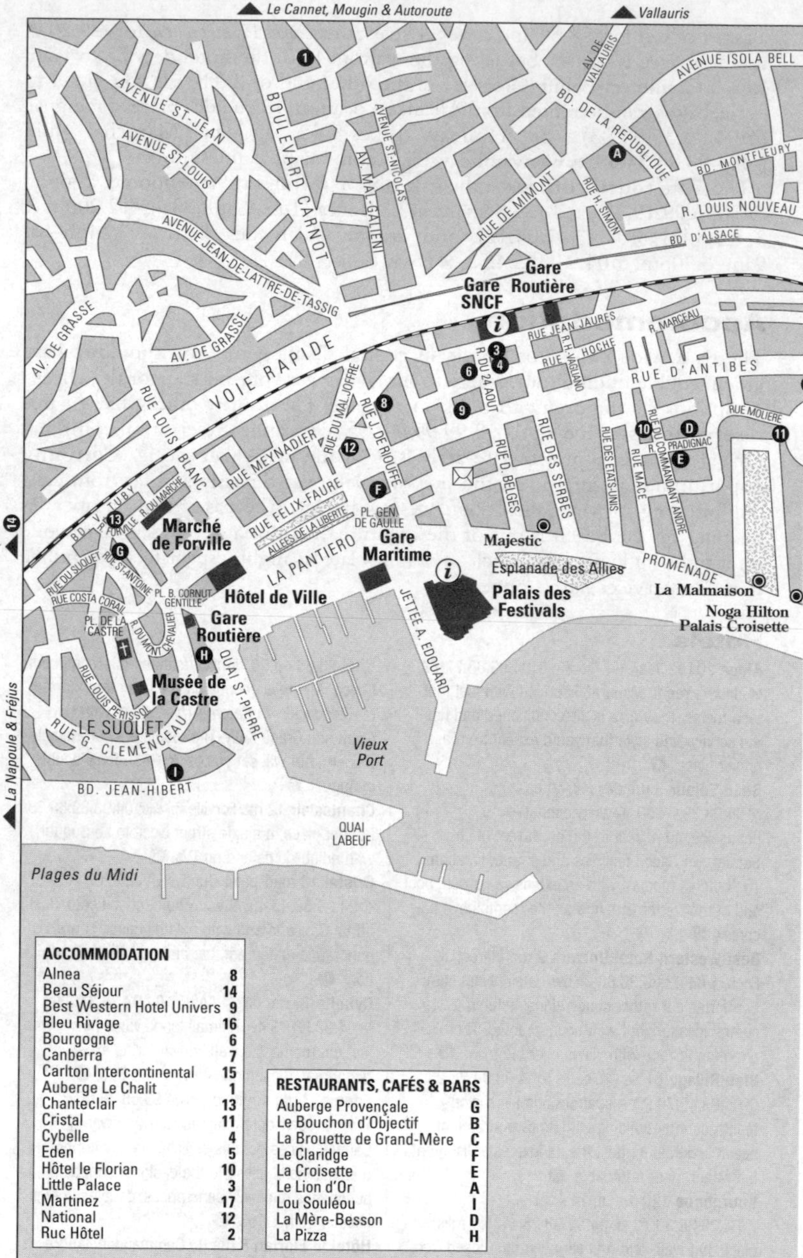
Le Cannet, Mougin & Autoroute
Vallauris
AVENUE ISOLA BELL
AV. DE VALLAURIS
BD. DE LA REPUBLIQUE
BD. MONTFLEURY
R. LOUIS NOUVEAU
BD. D'ALSACE
RUE H. SIMON
RUE DE MIMONT
AVENUE ST-JEAN
AVENUE ST-LOUIS
BOULEVARD CARNOT
AVENUE ST-NICOLAS
AV. MAL-GALIENI
AVENUE JEAN-DE-LATTRE-DE-TASSIG
AV. DE GRASSE
AV. DE GRASSE
VOIE RAPIDE
Gare Routière
Gare SNCF
RUE JEAN JAURES
R. MARCEAU
R.H. VAGLIANO
RUE HOCHE
RUE D'ANTIBES
R. DU 24 AOUT
RUE MOLIERE
RUE LOUIS BLANC
RUE DU MAL JOFFRE
RUE J. DE RIOUFFE
RUE MEYNADIER
RUE FELIX-FAURE
ALLEES DE LA LIBERTE
PL. GEN DE GAULLE
RUE D. BELGES
RUE DES SERBES
RUE DES ETATS-UNIS
RUE MACE
RUE DU COMMANDANT ANDRE
R. PRADIGNAC
BD. V. TUBY
R. DU MARCHE
R. FORVILLE
Marché de Forville
RUE DU SUQUET
RUE ST-ANTOINE
RUE COSTA CORAIL
PL. B. CORNUT GENTILLE
PL. DE LA CASTRE
R. DU MONT CHEVALIER
Hôtel de Ville
LA PANTIERO
Gare Maritime
Gare Routière
Majestic
Esplanade des Allies
PROMENADE
Palais des Festivals
JETTEE A. EDOUARD
QUAI ST-PIERRE
Musée de la Castre
RUE LOUIS PERISSOL
LE SUQUET
RUE G. CLEMENCEAU
BD. JEAN-HIBERT
La Napoule & Fréjus
Vieux Port
QUAI LABEUF
Plages du Midi
La Malmaison
Noga Hilton Palais Croisette
ACCOMMODATION
Alnea 8
Beau Séjour 14
Best Western Hotel Univers 9
Bleu Rivage 16
Bourgogne 6
Canberra 7
Carlton Intercontinental 15
Auberge Le Chalit 1
Chanteclair 13
Cristal 11
Cybelle 4
Eden 5
Hôtel le Florian 10
Little Palace 3
Martinez 17
National 12
Ruc Hôtel 2
RESTAURANTS, CAFÉS & BARS
Auberge Provençale G
Le Bouchon d'Objectif B
La Brouette de Grand-Mère C
Le Claridge F
La Croisette E
Le Lion d'Or A
Lou Souléou I
La Mère-Besson D
La Pizza H

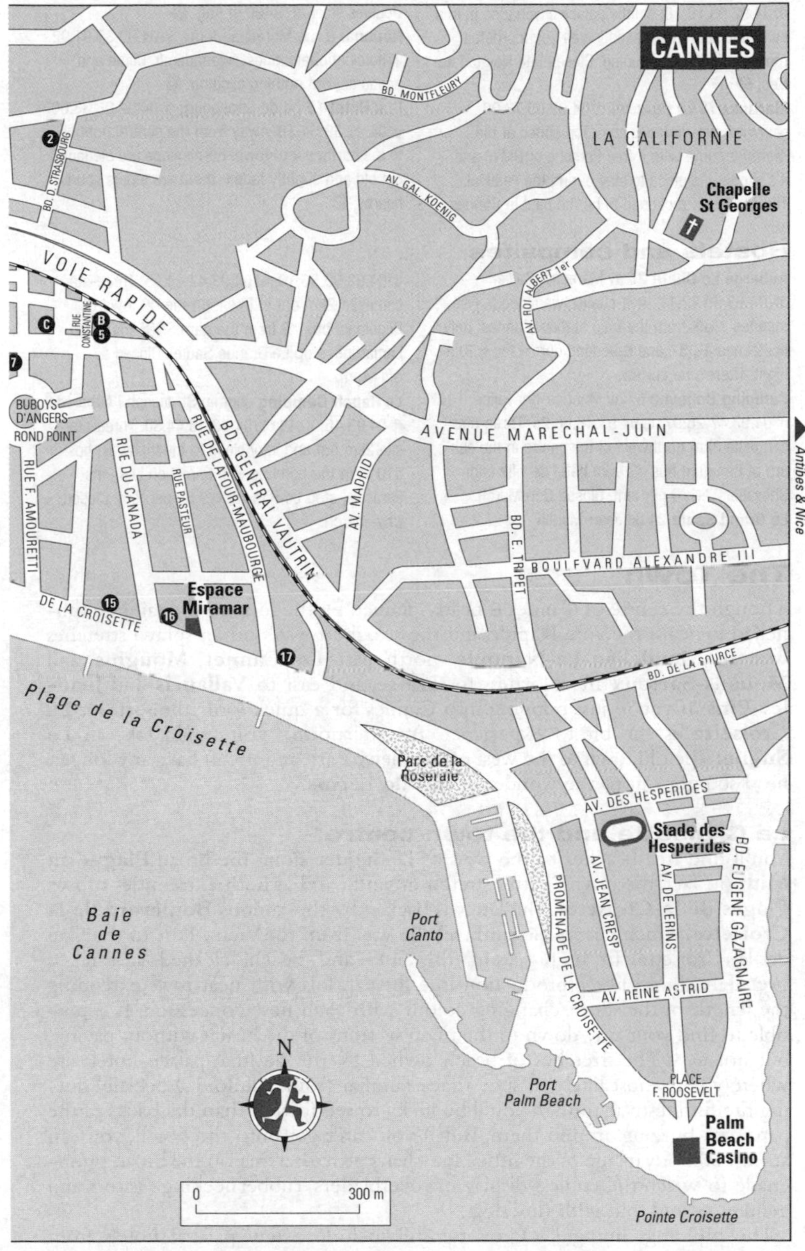
CANNES
BD. MONTFLEURY
LA CALIFORNIE
BD. D. STRASBOURG
AV. GAL. KOENIG
Chapelle
St Georges
VOIE RAPIDE
AV. ROI ALBERT 1er
RUE CONSTANTINE
BUBOYS
D'ANGERS
ROND POINT
RUE F. AMOURETTI
RUE DU CANADA
RUE PASTEUR
RUE DE LATOUR-MAUBOURGE
BD. GENERAL VAUTRIN
AV. MADRID
AVENUE MARECHAL-JUIN
Antibes & Nice
BD. E. TRIPET
BOULEVARD ALEXANDRE III
DE LA CROISETTE
Espace
Miramar
BD. DE LA SOURCE
Plage de la Croisette
Parc de la
Roseraie
AV. DES HESPERIDES
Stade des
Hesperides
AV. JEAN CRESP
AV. DE LERINS
BD. EUGENE GAZAGNAIRE
PROMENADE DE LA CROISETTE
Baie
de
Cannes
Port
Canto
AV. REINE ASTRID
N
Port
Palm Beach
PLACE
F. ROOSEVELT
Palm
Beach
Casino
0
300 m
Pointe Croisette

Ⓣ04.92.98.18.18, Ⓔlittle.palace@wanadoo.fr. In a central location with twenty well-soundproofed rooms and air conditioning. Closed late Nov to late Dec. ❺

Martinez 73 La Croisette Ⓣ04.92.98.73.00, Ⓦwww.hotel-martinez.com. Top suites at the *Martinez* come with a free Porsche or BMW, and it's simply *the* place to stay during the Festival. The service is reckoned to be the best in Cannes. Doubles start at €400 in Aug. ❾

National 8 rue Maréchal-Joffre Ⓣ04.93.39.91.92, Ⓔhotelnationalcannes@wanadoo.fr. Clean and adequate, but nothing exciting. ❸

Ruc Hôtel 15 bd de Strasbourg Ⓣ04.92.98.33.60, Ⓕ04.92.39.54.18. Away from the central hubbub to the northeast of town. Furnishings are elegant but old and slightly faded; there are tennis courts nearby. ❺

Hostels and campsites

Auberge Le Chalit 27 av Maréchal Galliéni Ⓣ 04.93.99.22.11, Ⓔle-chalit@wanadoo.fr. Five minutes' walk from the train station, Cannes' only hostel has 4-, 5-, and 6-bedded dorms for €20 a night. There's no curfew.

Camping Bellevue 67 av Maurice-Chevalier Ⓣ04.93.47.28.97, Ⓕ04.93.48.66.25. Three-star campsite 3km northwest of the centre in the suburb of Ranguin; bus #2 from hôtel de ville (stop Chevaliers). €20 per tent. Closed Oct–March.

Le Grand Saule 24 bd Jean-Moulin Ⓣ04.93.90.55.10, Ⓕ04.93.47.24.55. Three-star campsite 2km out of town, off the D9 towards Pégomas; bus #9 from the gare SNCF (direction Lamartine, stop Le Grande Saule). Closed Oct–April.

Le Ranch Camping chemin St-Joseph l'Aubarède Ⓣ04.93.46.00.11, Ⓕ04.93.46.44.30. Three-star site 2km out and very close to the highway; bus #10 from the hôtel de ville (direction Les Pins Parasols, stop Le Ranch). €9.50 per tent. Closed Nov–March.

The Town

Though the centre of Cannes is neatly defined by the loop of the rail line tunnelled beneath the Voie Rapide and the sea, the town's urban sprawl stretches west to **Mandelieu-La-Napoule**, north past **Le Cannet**, **Mougins** and **Mouans-Sartoux** more or less to **Grasse**, and east to **Vallauris** and **Juan-les-Pins**. If you're just popping into Cannes for a quick look, the seafront **La Croisette** is the bit to experience. An afternoon's visit could take in **Le Suquet**, the old town to the west of the Vieux Port, and if you have any longer, head straight out to the wonderful **Îles de Lérins**.

La Croisette and the town centre

You'll find free beaches to the west of Le Suquet along the broad **Plages du Midi** (in fact, the town's better stretch of sand), and at both extremities of **Les Plages de la Croisette**. The latter is backed by the famous **Boulevard de la Croisette**, which curves elegantly all the way from the Vieux Port to the Cap de la Croisette. In high season, the fine sand beach, cleaned and raked overnight, looks like a production line for parasols with neat rows extending the length of the shore, changing colour with each new concession. It is possible to find your way down to the main sections of the beach without paying, but not easy. The stretches of beach owned by the de luxe palace-hotels are where you're most likely to spot a face familiar from celluloid, especially during the film festival, though you'll be lucky to see further than the backs of the paparazzi buzzing around them. But if you can't get onto the beach, you can at least take advantage of the little blue chairs provided free on the broad promenade to watch the endless display of rollerbladers, rubbernecking visitors and genteel retired folk with tiny dogs.

The buildings lining La Croisette still include a few palatial hotels from Cannes' golden age, notably the **Carlton Intercontinental**, whose cupolas were inspired by the breasts of a famous courtesan, and the Art Deco *Martinez*. But there are also some modern monstrosities, such as the *Noga Hilton* and the *Hôtel de la Reine* next door to and overshadowing the beautiful **La Malmaison**

△ Côte d'Azur, Cannes, Hotel Carlton

The Cannes Film Festival

Each May Cannes hosts the most famous of all movie media events, the **Festival International du Film** (www.festival-cannes.com). It was first conceived as a rival to the Venice film festival, then under Mussolini's influence. Since only pro-fascist films had any chance of winning prizes, an alternative competition was planned for 1939 in Cannes. World War II dictated otherwise and it was not until 1946 that the first Cannes festival took place.

Winning the top prize, the **Palm d'Or**, can't compete with Oscars for box-office effect, but within the movie world it is unrivalled. Some years it seems as if the big names are all too busy talking finance in LA to come to Cannes; the next they are all begging for the accolades. Even if the Hollywood moguls keep their new blockbusters under wraps, they still send minions to wheel and deal.

There are over thirty thousand film professionals, journalists and hangers-on who get accreditation for the festival. Though most tickets are pre-allocated for the media, ten percent of the **tickets** to the official selections are reserved for local people – they elect the *Prix Populaire*. The **Palais des Festivals** sells tickets for some screenings one week in advance, and hands out a select number of **passes** to those considered to be true cineastes (a student card for an internationally recognized film school is helpful), plus free **programmes** to anyone who asks for them.

Cultivating contacts reaches fever pitch as the festival progresses and casual visitors are left excluded. However, not all the new films being shown are official entries to the festival, nor are all screened within the heavily guarded Palais des Festivals. Every cinema and conference hall in town is a venue and at some of these you can buy tickets, but don't expect to do so on the day.

at no. 47, which has an excellent palm tree mural on its side wall. This is the home of the city's cultural affairs department, where temporary exhibitions of modern and contemporary art are often staged (Tues–Sun 10am–1.30pm & 2.30–6.30pm; €3). Further east, the **Espace Mirarar** (Tues–Sun 1–6pm; free) also hosts temporary exhibitions.

Though walking around town in swimsuits or bikini bottoms used to be the norm in Cannes, there's now a fine for "indecent" dress anywhere other than the beaches themselves, and in town the style is to dress up, rather than down. The western end of La Croisette, **Rue d'Antibes** and the streets between them form the South of France's most extensive luxury shopping district, stuffed with designer names, such as Bulgari, Cartier, Chanel, Lacroix and Vuitton. This part of town looks its best in the weeks leading up to Christmas, when the streets glitter with tasteful white lights and the crowds of summer are long forgotten. A small Christmas market takes place on the **Vieux Port**, while in summer you can watch the millionaires eating meals served by white-frocked crew on enormous yacht decks. Between here and La Croisette stands the **Palais des Festivals**, where you can compare hand sizes with the imprints of those film stars that have, Hollywood-style, been set in tiles on the pavement in front of the main entrance. Opposite stands a phone booth in the shape of a reel of film, paying tribute to the importance of the film industry to Cannes' economy.

Le Suquet

The old town is known as **Le Suquet** after the hill on which it stands. Back in the eleventh century it became the property of the Îles de Lérins monks, and a castle built by the *abbé* in 1088 still stands. Alongside it is the white stone twelfth-century Romanesque **Chapelle de Ste-Anne**. After several centuries in which a small town took root around the religious settlement, a dispute arose between the monks and the townsfolk who wanted their own parish and priest. Two hundred years after their initial demand in 1648, **Notre-Dame de l'Espérance** was finally built beside the Chapelle de Ste-Anne, in Gothic style as if to emphasize just how overdue it was.

Inside the castle and the chapel is the **Musée de la Castre** (Tues–Sun; April, May & Sept 10am–1pm & 2–6pm; June–Aug 10am–1pm & 3–7pm; Oct–March 10am–1pm & 2–5pm; €3), which has some interesting pictures and prints of old Cannes and strong ethnology and archeology displays. Its highlight, however, is the brilliant collection of musical instruments from all over the world, including Congolese bell bracelets, an Ethiopian ten-string lyre, an Asian 'lute' with a snakeskin box and an extraordinary selection of drums. Climb the medieval tower in the museum courtyard for the best view of Le Suquet and the town below.

Although Le Suquet started out as home to the city's poorer residents, its streets leading to the summit are now gentrified, and the various places to **eat** and **drink** increasingly chic and expensive. From the top, the panorama across La Croisette is superb.

Eating and drinking

Cannes' **restaurants** tend to stay open very late; getting a meal after midnight is no great problem. There are hundreds of places to eat, covering the whole range from €11 fixed menus to €70 blowouts, though quality across the board can be patchy. The vigour of the Forville **market**, two blocks north of the Vieux Port, however, means that every chef in town has access to the finest and freshest ingredients. The best areas for less expensive dining are **rue Meynardier**, **Le Suquet** and **quai St-Pierre** on the Vieux Port, lined with **brasseries** and **cafés**. Reserving a table is advisable at almost all the restaurants listed below.

Restaurants

Au Bec Fin *Hôtel Cybelle*, 12 rue du 24 Août ☎04.93.38.35.86. Traditional cooking with an excellent choice of plats du jour and large portions. Menus at €18 and €22. Closed Sat & Sun evening & mid-Nov to mid-Dec.

Auberge Provençale 10 rue Saint-Antoine ☎04.92.99.27.17. Generous portions of Provençal cooking in a rustic setting at Cannes' oldest restaurant. Menus from €23. Open daily all year.

Le Bouchon d'Objectif 10 rue de Constantine ☎04.93.99.21.76. An excellent local bistro serving aïoli, duck à l'orange and other staple dishes with admirable simplicity. Menus at €15 and €25. Closed Sun & mid-Nov to mid-Dec.

La Brouette de Grand-Mère 9 bis rue d'Oran ☎04.93.39.12.10. A single menu (around €30) that includes an aperitif and as much wine as you can drink, with filling dishes such as a five-meat stew, quails in grapes, or Bresse chicken steamed in tarragon for the main course. Fun and good value. Closed at lunchtime, Sun & Nov to mid-Dec.

Le Claridge 2 place du Gal de Gaulle ☎04.93.39.05.86. Fashionable bar/ice cream parlour with a broad terrace, in a grandstand location opposite the Palais des Festivals – wear your shades. It serves generous panini from €4.50, and lunchtime plats at around €10. Open daily all year.

La Croisette 15 rue du Commandant-André ☎04.92.98.62.82. Grilled fish is the speciality here, cooked to perfection. If the supplements on some of the fish dishes astound you, take a look at the Forville market to see just how few fish are caught. Closed Sun out of season.

Le Lion d'Or 45 bd de la République ☎04.93.38.56.57. On the north side of the Voie Rapide with no pretensions to gastronomy, but edible and filling home-made food all the same. Menus from €12. Closed Sat.

Lou Souléou 16 bd Jean-Hibert ☎04.93.39.85.55. A fish specialist serving a good range of seafood on very reasonably priced menus in view of the sea west of Le Suquet. Menus from €24. Closed Mon, Wed evenings & Nov.

La Mère-Besson 13 rue des Frères-Pradignac ☎04.93.39.59.24. Each day has a different speciality: *estouffade*, aïoli and *lottes niçoises* (tiny fried monkfish) among them. Menus at €26 and €30. Evenings only.

La Palme d'Or *Hôtel Martinez*, 73 La Croisette ☎04.92.98.74.14. A renowned temple of taste, where the stars celebrate their film festival prizes with some of the most exquisite and original food this coast has to offer. Menus at €65, €82 and €130 without drinks, à la carte €120. Closed Mon, Tues & mid-Nov to mid-Dec.

La Pizza 3 quai St-Pierre ☎04.93.39.22.56. Kitschy Vieux Port pizzeria serving reliable Italian food with large peppermills and no surprises. The fresh ravioli are good, helpings are generous, and they write your tab on the paper tablecloths. Plats around €11. Open til late year-round.

Nightlife

As you'd expect, Cannes abounds with exclusive **clubs**. The clientele that step off their yachts or out of a festival prize-giving disappear behind closed doors: the more private and unmarked a club is, the more expensive it will be. After a night out at even the cheapest **bars** and **clubs** you're unlikely to have much change from €50, so you may prefer to stick to the late-night restaurants, which can be the most congenial after-dark venues. If you are determined to lose money in Cannes, choose from **casinos** at the Palais des Festivals, the *Carlton Intercontinental* or the *Noga Hilton* hotels. There's also a fairly lively year-round **theatre**, **dance** and **music** scene, centred on the Palais des Festivals, the Théâtre Palais Croisette in the *Noga Hilton*, and the Theatre La Licorne in La Bocca. The **Stade des Hespérides** in the district of La Croisette is the venue for occasional visits by big-name bands.

Cat Corner 22 rue Macé. Fashionable, central disco just off La Croisette.

Chinks 88 rue Meynadier. Tiny but trendy cocktail bar close to the Vieux Port and Le Suquet.

Le Havana Room 42 La Croisette. Champagne and cocktail bar with garden terrace in a prime seafront location.

The Quays 17 Quai St Pierre. The inevitable Irish pub opposite the swanky yachts of the Vieux Port. Internet access. Open until 2.30am.

Le Whisky à Go-Go 115 av des Lérins. The disco where everyone beneath the jet set goes to be seen.

Le Zanzibar 85 rue Félix-Faure. Wildly nostalgic seventies disco meets matelot chic at this long-established gay bar. Open 6pm–6am.

Listings

Airport Cannes-Mandelieu, 6km from the centre of town ☎04.93.90.40.40.

Banks Most banks on rue d'Antibes have cash dispensers.

Boat terminal Gare maritime, jetée Albert-Edouard ☎04.93.39.11.82.

Bookshop Librairie Anglaise, 11 rue Bivouac-Napoleon ☎04.93.99.40.08; sells new and some second-hand English-language books.

Car rental Avis, 69 La Croisette ☎04.93.94.15.86 and at the gare SNCF ☎04.93.39.26.38; Budget, 160 rue d'Antibes ☎04.93.99.44.04; Citer National, 160 rue d'Antibes ☎04.93.94.64.41; Europcar, 3 rue du Commandant-Vidal ☎04.93.06.26.30.

Currency exchange American Express, 1 bis rue Notre Dame ☎04.93.99.05.45.

Emergencies ☎18 or ☎15; SOS médecins ☎0.825.005.004; Hôpital des Broussailles, 13 av des Broussailles ☎04.93.69.71.50.

Lost property 1 av St Louis ☎04.93.68.91.92.

Parking Cheap overnight parking between 8pm and 8am beneath the Palais des Festivals and gare SNCF.

Pharmacy Call ☎04.93.06.22.22 for address of emergency pharmacy after 7.30pm.

Police Commissariat Central de Police, 1 av de Grasse ☎04.93.06.22.22.

Post office 22 rue Bivouac-Napoleon, Cannes 06400.

Taxis Cannes Allo Taxi ☎04.92.99.27.27; gare SNCF ☎04.93.38.30.79.

Îles de Lérins

The **Îles de Lérins** would be lovely anywhere, but at only a fifteen-minute ferry ride from Cannes, they're a haven away from the madness of the modern city. Known as Lerina or Lero in ancient times, the two islands have a long historical pedigree, and today seem a long way from the modern world.

Getting to the islands

Boats for both islands leave from the Vieux Port. There are regular services to **Ste-Marguerite** (summer 15 daily; winter 14 daily), run by two companies, Compagnie Esterel Chanteclair (ⓣ04.93.39.11.82, ⓦwww.ilesdelerins.com; €9), and Compagnie Maritime Cannoise (ⓣ04.93.38.66.33, ⓔcmcrgm@aol.com; €8): the last boats back to Cannes leave Ste-Marguerite at 6pm, 6.30pm or 7pm, depending on the season. **St-Honorat** is served by Société Planaria, run by the Abbaye de Lérins (ⓣ04.92.98.71.38, ⓦwww.abbayedelerins.com; summer 10 daily; winter 8 daily; €9): the last boat back to Cannes leaves at 5pm in winter and 6pm in summer. Taking a **picnic** is a good idea, as eating places on the islands tend to be expensive.

Ste-Marguerite

Of the two islands, **STE-MARGUERITE** is the more touristy, though it still has beautiful parts, and is large enough for visitors to find seclusion if they're prepared to leave the crowded port and follow paths through the thick woods of Aleppo pines and evergreen oaks. The **Chemin de la Chasse** from the harbour crosses to the southern shore where rocky inlets provide good bathing points. The **Chemin de la Ceinture** follows the island's edge for about 3km to the battery on the eastern headland. Returning via the northern shore provides you with views back to Cannes.

The dominating structure and crowd puller of the island is the **Fort Ste-Marguerite** (April–Sept Tues–Sun 10.30am–1.15pm & 2.15–5.45pm; Oct–March Tues–Sun 10.30am–1.15pm & 2.15–4.45pm; €3), a Richelieu commission which failed to prevent the Spanish occupying both Lérins islands between 1635 and 1637. Later, Vauban rounded it off, presumably for Louis XIV's glory, since the strategic value of greatly enlarging a fort facing the mainland without upgrading the one facing the sea is pretty minimal. The main interest in the Fort Ste-Marguerite today is the identification of one cell as having held the **Man in the Iron Mask**, a mythical character given credence by Alexandre Dumas – author of *The Three Musketeers* and *The Count of Monte Cristo* – and by Hollywood. Other cells undoubtedly held the prisoners attributed to them, mostly Huguenots imprisoned for refusing to submit to Louis XIV's vicious suppression of Protestantism. Also housed in the fort is the **Musée de la Mer**, containing mostly Roman local finds, as well as the remnants of a tenth-century Arab ship.

St-Honorat

ST-HONORAT, the smaller southern island, has been owned by monks almost continuously since its namesake and patron founded a monastery here in 410 AD. Honoratus, a Roman noble turned good, is said to have chosen the isle of Lerina because of its reputation for being haunted, full of snakes and scorpions, and lacking any fresh water. Quickly divining a spring and gradually exterminating all the vipers, the saint and his two companions found themselves with precisely the peace and isolation they sought. In time, visitors started to increase in frequency and numbers; the monastic order was established to structure a growing community. By the end of Honoratus's life the Lérins monks had monasteries all over France, held bishoprics in cities such as Arles and Lyon, and were renowned throughout the Catholic world for their contributions to theology. St Patrick was one of the products of the seminary, training here for seven years before setting out for Ireland.

The present **abbey** buildings are mostly nineteenth-century, though vestiges of medieval and earlier construction survive in the church and cloisters. Visiting the austere church is free, but there is a small entrance charge for the monastery between June and September (no beach clothes; tours daily 10am–12.30pm & 2.30–4.45pm; Oct–May free access daily 10.30am–4pm; ☎04.92.98.71.38). Today, 28 Cistercian monks live and work here, tending an apiary and a vineyard that produces a sought-after white wine, as well as making liqueurs, all of which are on sale in the abbey's shop. Behind this complex, on the sea's edge, stands an eleventh-century **fortress**, a monastic bolthole that was connected to the original abbey by a tunnel, and used to guard against the threat of invaders, especially the Saracens. Of all the protective forts built along this coast, this is the only one that looks as if it could still serve its original function.

The other buildings on St-Honorat are the churches and chapels that served as retreats. **St-Pierre**, beside the modern monastery, **La Trinité**, in the east of the island, and **St-Sauveur**, west of the harbour, remain more or less unchanged. By **St-Cabrais**, on the eastern shore, is a furnace with a chute for making cannonballs, evidence that the monks were not without worldly defensive skills.

Today, the main attraction of the island is its tranquillity. There is just one small restaurant by the landing stage, and no cars or hotels: just the cultivated vines, lavender, herbs and olive trees mingled with wild poppies and daisies; and pine and eucalyptus trees shading the paths beside the white rock shore and mixing with the scent of rosemary, thyme and wild honeysuckle.

The suburbs: Le Cannet and La Californie

To the north of Cannes, the city's outskirts merge imperceptibly with **LE CANNET** along the busy bd Sadi-Carnot. Although the town's built-up area is indistinguishable from Cannes' sprawl, Le Cannet's old part, along rue St-Sauveur, preserves some villagey charm. The original town was built on land belonging to the Îles de Lérins monks to house 140 families summoned from Liguria to cultivate the orange trees. These original 'Le Cannois' are commemorated by the mural and orange trees on **place Bellevue**. If you approach the *place* from the south you'll pass the tiny fifteenth-century **Chapelle de St-Sauveur** on rue St Sauveur (guided visits Fri–Mon & Wed 2–6pm; free), exuberantly decorated by the contemporary artist Tobiasse and, further up at no. 190, a mural by Peynet of a bride, bridegroom and cherubs floating away to wedded bliss.

It's an easy journey to Le Cannet: **buses** #4 or #5 from the hôtel de ville in Cannes stop at place Leclerc at the foot of the old village. There's a **tourist office** just above the start of rue St-Sauveur (Mon–Fri 9am–noon & 2–6pm; ☎04.93.46.74.00). Le Cannet has a good Provençal **restaurant**, *Le Pezou*, 346 rue St-Sauveur (☎04.93.69.32.50; menus at €20 and €27.50), and the popular family-run *Le Clos Fleuri*, 347 rue St-Sauveur (☎04.93.46.69.05; closed Thurs), with menus from €12. For a simple lunch, *Le Tivoli* at 25 bd Carnot serves *couscous*, *choucroute* or *bourride*.

Two kilometres east of Cannes, the suburb of **LA CALIFORNIE** was a favourite hang-out of the Russian and British aristocracy. It preserves something of its former patrician atmosphere, though there are few specific attractions. On av du Roi Albert the **Chapelle St Georges**, formerly the town's Anglican church, is one of the best examples of English Victorian church architecture on the Riviera. It was built as a memorial to King Edward VIII's brother, the Duke of Albany, who died young in Cannes as a result of an accident in 1884. The church was consecrated on 12 February 1887, with the future king in attendance. A fountain, erected by the people of Cannes in the Duke's memory, stands close to where he lived on **Boulevard des Pins**.

Vallauris

Pottery and Picasso are the attractions of **VALLAURIS**, an otherwise unremarkable town in the hills above Golfe-Juan, 6km east of Cannes. Vallauris' association with ceramics dates from Roman times, but it was in the early sixteenth century, after the Plague had decimated the population, that **pottery** became the major industry. The bishop of Grasse rebuilt the village from its infested ruins and settled Genoese potters to exploit the clay soil and the fuel from the surrounding forests, and the industry flourished. By the end of World War II, however, aluminium had become a much cheaper and easier material to use for pots and plates, and the pottery began rapidly to lose its popularity.

It took the intervention of Picasso to reverse this decline. In 1946, while installed in the castle at Antibes, the artist met some of the town's few remaining potters, and was invited to Vallauris by the owner of a ceramics studio, Georges Ramié. Picasso got hooked on clay and spent the next two years working at Ramié's **Madoura workshop**. The result, apart from adding pages to the catalogue of the Picasso *oeuvre*, was a rekindling of the local industry. Today the main street, av Georges-Clemenceau, sells nothing but pottery, much of it garish and indifferent. The Madoura pottery is on av Georges et Suzanne Ramié, to the right as you come down av Georges-Clemenceau, and still has sole rights on reproducing Picasso's designs, which are on sale, at a price, in its shop (April–Sept Mon–Fri 10am–12.30pm & 2.30–6pm; Oct–March Mon–Fri 10am–12.30pm & 2.30–7pm).

A bronze **Man with a Sheep**, Picasso's gift to the town, stands in the main square, place de la Libération, beside the church and castle. The municipality had some misgivings about the sculpture but decided that the possible affront to their conservative tastes was outweighed by the benefits to tourism of Picasso's international reputation. They needn't have worried; the statue looks quite simply like a shepherd boy and sheep.

The local authorities then offered Picasso the task of decorating the early medieval deconsecrated **chapel** in the castle courtyard (Mon & Wed–Sun: mid-June to mid-Sept 10am–12.15pm & 2–6pm; mid-Sept to mid-June 10am–12.15pm & 2–5pm; €3), which he finally did in 1952. The space is tiny and, with the painted panels covering the vault, has the architectural simplicity of an air-raid shelter. Picasso's subject is *War and Peace*. At first glance it's easy to be unimpressed (as many critics still are) – it looks mucky and slapdash with paint runs on the unyielding plywood surfaces. Stay a while, however, and the passion of this violently drawn pacifism slowly emerges. On the War panel a music score is trampled by hooves and about to be engulfed in flames; a fighter's lance tenuously holds the scales of justice and a shield bears the outline of a dove, while from a deathly chariot skeletons escape. Peace is represented by Pegasus; people dancing and suckling babies; trees bearing fruit; owls; books – and the freedom of the spirit to mix up images and concepts with innocent mischief.

The **ticket** for the chapel also gives admission to the **Musée de Céramique/Musée Magnelli** (same hours) in the castle, which for some years has exhibited many of the ceramics Picasso made at the Madoura, in addition to several Pre-Columbian pieces and a collection of paintings by Alberto Magnelli.

Buses from Cannes and Golfe-Juan gare SNCF arrive at the rear of the castle, on bd Maurice Rouvier. The **tourist office** is at the bottom of av Georges-Clemenceau on square du 8 mai 1945 (daily: July & Aug 9am–7pm; Sept–June 9am–noon & 2–6pm; ⓣ04.93.63.82.58). You can **eat** cheaply at *La Grupi*, 47 av

Georges-Clemenceau, and very well at *La Gousse d'Ail*, 11 av de Grasse (☎04.93.64.10.71; menus from €21; closed Sun evening, Mon & Tues evening).

Mougins and around

The hilltop village of **MOUGINS**, 8km north of Cannes, is a welcome oasis in a desert of sprawling suburbia. It's a pretty rarified place, immaculately maintained by its wealthy residents and thick with refined *ateliers* and chic restaurants. Its understated elegance was rudely disturbed a few years ago by the antics of exiled Haitian dictator 'Baby Doc' Duvalier, who finally fled his home here and creditors after running up vast bills. More distinguished former residents include Pablo Picasso and the photographer Man Ray.

Just beyond the Porte Sarrazine, there's an excellent **photography museum** (July–Sept daily 10am–8pm; Oct & late Dec to June Wed–Sat 10am–noon & 2–5pm; €2), which hosts changing exhibitions every two months. It also has its own small collection, which includes some pictures of Jacques Lartigue (who lived in the neighbouring village of Opio) and rather too many portraits of Picasso. At the top end of the village, the old wash house, **Le Lavoir**, on av JC Mallet (March–Oct daily 11am–8pm), forms another exhibition space for the visual arts, its wide basin of water playing reflecting games with the images and the light, while the **Musée Municipal**, on place du Commandant Lamy (late Dec to Oct Mon–Fri 9am–5pm; free), holds classy exhibitions of art and design.

Three kilometres southeast of Mougins, just off the D3 slip road and alongside the A8 *autoroute* to Nice, is a museum that will delight even those who don't share the passion of its subject, the **Musée de l'Automobiliste** (Dec–Oct daily 10am–6pm/7pm; €7). No expense has been spared on this indulgent dedication to the motorcar and its two-wheeled relations. Sculptures made of shiny, tangled exhaust pipes line the pathway to the hangar-like exhibition space. Inside, the exhibits include glamorous cars, such as a 1933 Hispano-Suiza; toy cars; German army vehicles; record-breaking racing cars; a simulation of the traffic control room for the Nice–Menton *autoroute*; bizarre prototypes; and films of classic races.

Practicalities

The frequent #600 **bus** service from Cannes to Grasse stops at Mougins. If price is no object you should **stay** at *Le Mas Candille* bd Clément Rebuffel (☎04.92.28.43.43, ⓦwww.lemascandille.com; ❾), a de luxe spa amid olive groves and cypresses, or at *Les Muscadins*, 18 bd Courteline (☎04.92.28.28.28, ⓦwww.lesmuscadins.com; ❾), the last word in relaxed luxury. For smaller budgets, there's *Les Liserons de Mougins*, 608 av St-Martin (☎04.93.75.50.31, ⓦwww.hotel-liserons-mougins.com; ❺), a pleasant two-star place with its own pool.

Mougins has some very fine **restaurants**, none of them cheap. The most famous is *Le Moulin de Mougins*, on av Notre Dame de Vie (☎04.93.75.78.24; menus at €100 and €132; closed Dec to mid-Jan), run by celebrity-chef Roger Vergé, whose modern reinterpretation of Provençal cooking is internationally renowned. If your budget doesn't stretch this far, you can sample Vergé's style of cuisine more cheaply at his cooking school, *L'Amandier*, pl des Patriotes (☎04.93.90.00.91; menus from €28). The restaurant at *Le Mas Candille* (☎04.92.28.43.43; around €75) also serves inventive modern Mediterranean cuisine; the desserts, in particular, are highly original. Place du Commandant Lamy is home to a trio of less grand but still pleasant and dependable options: the congenial *Bistrot de Mougins* (☎04.93.75.78.34; menus from €20; closed Wed), serving Provençal specialities; the *Brasserie de la*

Méditeranée (Ⓣ04.93.90.03.47; menus from €29); and *Le Feu Follet* (Ⓣ04.93.90.15.78; menus from €23; closed Mon).

Mouans-Sartoux

Three kilometres northwest of Mougins, the village of **MOUANS-SARTOUX** lies to the north of the Cannes-Grasse highway (N85), laid out on a grid system and protected from the Mistral winds beneath a high wall. The #600 **bus** between Cannes, Mougins and Grasse stops here.

The main focus for a visit to the village is the **château**, just north of the old village centre between chemin des Bastions and av de Grasse. Rebuilt to its medieval design in the nineteenth century, and chosen by the Socialist former minister for culture, Jack Lang, to be one of twenty provincial venues for modern and contemporary art, it houses the beautiful white **L'Espace de l'Art Concret** (daily: June–Sept 11am–7pm; Oct–May 11am–6pm; €2.30). The gallery stages three exhibitions a year, concentrating on the rationalist form of art defined by Théo Van Doesburg as "concrete rather than abstract because nothing is more real than a line, a colour or a surface". The gallery staff are keen to welcome visitors and to help them appreciate the art on show: you can get a personal guided tour just by asking. Mouans-Sartoux also has a **Centre Culturel**, 77 allé des Cèdres (Mon–Fri 10am–noon & 2–7pm), boasting one of the biggest collections of literature in the Provençal language.

Grasse

With its medieval heart, uninterrupted sea views, and hilly location amongst scented flowers, **GRASSE** has been capital of the **perfume industry** for over two hundred years. Making perfume is usually presented as a mysterious process, an alchemy, turning the soul of the flower into a liquid of luxury and desire. The reality, including traditional methods of *macération* – mixing the blossoms with heated animal fat – and *enfleuration* – placing the flowers on cold fat, then washing the result with alcohol and finally distilling it into the ultimately refined essence – are far more vividly described in Patrick Süskind's novel *Perfume*, set in the city, than in the perfume factories in Grasse. Since the 1920s synthetic ingredients have been added to the perfumeries' repertoire, but locally grown jasmine and roses are still used, with the industry preferring to keep quiet about modern innovations and techniques.

Arrival, information and accommodation

Grasse's **gare routière** is to the north of the Vieille Ville at the Notre-Dames-des-Fleurs car park. Turning left out of the compound and heading downhill on av Thiers, you'll pass an annexe of the tourist office immediately on your right, where av Thiers becomes bd du Jeu de Ballon. Five minutes' walk further down, on cours Honoré-Cresp, is the old casino, now converted into a Palais des Congrès and housing the main **tourist office** (July to mid-Sept Mon–Sat 9am–7pm, Sun 9am–12.30pm & 1.30–6pm; mid-Sept to June Mon–Sat 9am–1pm & 2–6pm; Ⓣ04.93.36.66.66).

Of the **hotels**, the best budget options are the rather spartan *Napoléon*, 6 av Thiers (Ⓣ04.93.36.05.87, Ⓕ04.93.36.41.09; ❷), 50m from the gare routière, and *Les Palmiers*, 17 av Y-Baudoin (Ⓣ & Ⓕ04.93.36.07.24; closed Jan; ❷), which has a pleasant garden with good views of the surrounding countryside and

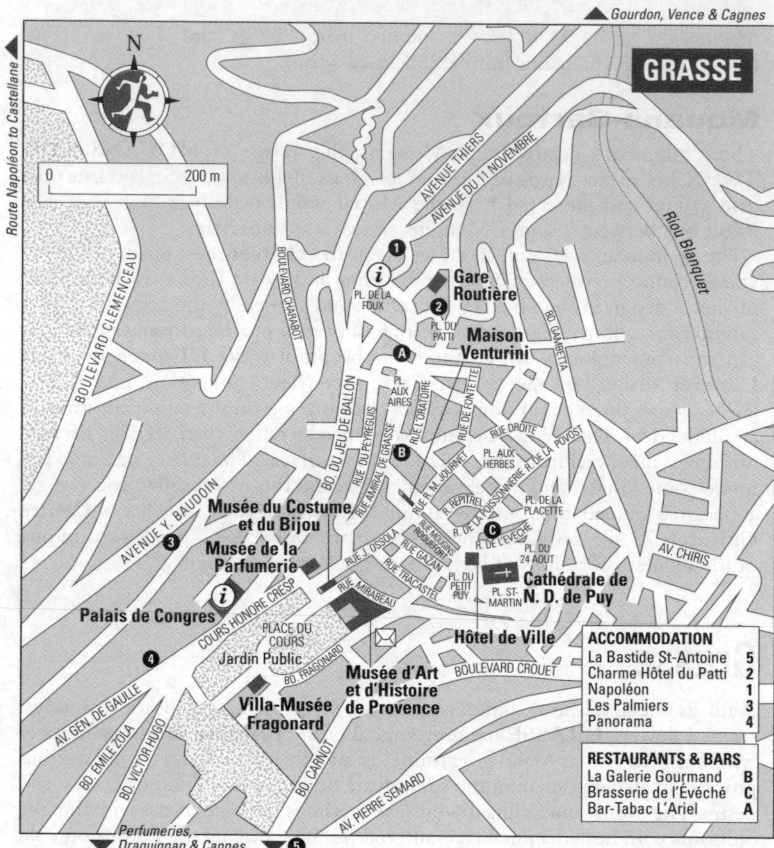

down to the coast. Slightly more expensive is the *Panorama* on place du Cours (☎04.93.36.80.80, Ⓦwww.hotelpanorama-grasse.com; closed Jan; ❹), which offers rooms with a view and all mod cons. Even more comfortable, if less well located, is the *Charme Hôtel du Patti*, place du Patti (☎04.93.36.01.00, Ⓔcharme-hotel-du-patti@wanadoo.fr; ❺), with two rooms designed for wheelchair users. If it's luxury in country-house surroundings you want, *La Bastide St-Antoine*, 48 av Henri Dunant (☎04.93.70.94.94, Ⓦwww.Jacques-chibois.com; ❾), is the finest place in Grasse.

The Town

Vieux Grasse is surprisingly run-down: despite subsidies to encourage refurbishment, life and economic activity are visibly draining away, leaving whole streets seedy and desolate behind rusting shutters and 'for sale' boards. Even when Grasse was part of the aristocratic tourist boom of the late nineteenth century, the desirable addresses, Queen Victoria's among them, were all east of the Vieille Ville. Today, the Vielle Ville's houses – the former homes of sixteenth-century tanning merchants, seventeenth-century perfumed-glove manufacturers and eighteenth-century *parfumiers* – have all been turned into museums and municipal offices, or divided into apartments.

The perfume factories

There are thirty major **parfumeries** in and around Grasse, most of them producing the different essences-plus-formulas which are then sold to Dior, Lancôme, Estée Lauder and the like, who make up their own brand-name perfumes. To extract 1kg of essence of lavender takes 200kg of lavender; for 1kg of cabbage rose essence, over 3000kg of roses are needed. Perfume contains twenty percent essence (eau de toilette contains ten percent; eau de Cologne five or six percent) and the bottles are extremely small. The major cost to this multi-billion-pound business is marketing, with millions spent on advertising alone. The grand Parisian couturiers, whose clothes, on strictly cost-accounting grounds, serve simply to promote the perfume, go to inordinate lengths to sell their latest fragrance. As you might imagine, however, the rates paid to those who pick the raw materials, mostly in the Third World, are notoriously low.

A good place to get an overview, and a fairly close-up look at the production, is the **Parfumerie Fragonard** (Feb–Oct daily 9am–6.30pm; Nov–Jan Mon–Sat 9am–12.30pm & 2–6.30pm; free), which is spread over two venues, one in the centre of town at 20 bd Fragonard and the other 3km towards Cannes at Les Quatre Chemins. The first shows traditional methods of extracting essence and has a collection of antique cosmetics bottles and bejewelled flagons. The one outside town is more informative and at least admits to modernization of the processes. A map of the world shows the origins of all the various and strange ingredients: resins, roots, moss, beans, bark join civet (extract of a wild cat's genitals), ambergris (whale intestines), bits of beaver, and musk from Tibetan goats all help to produce the array of scents the 'nose' – as the creator of the perfume's formula is known – has to play with. A professional 'nose' (of whom there are less than fifty in the world) can recognize up to five or six thousand different scents.

Other parfumeries to tour include Galimard, 73 rte de Cannes (guided visits daily: summer 8.30am–6.30pm, winter 9am–noon & 2–6pm; free), and Molinard at 60 bd Victor-Hugo (April–June & Sept Mon–Fri 9am–6pm, Sat & Sun 9am–noon & 2–6pm; July & Aug daily 9am–7pm; Sept–March Mon–Fri 9am–12.30pm & 2–6pm; Sat 9am–noon & 2–6pm; free). All have shops and give frequent tours in French and English, as well as offering you the chance to create your own personal fragrance.

Place aux Aires, at the top of the Vieille Ville, however, retains its vitality and is the venue for the daily **flower and vegetable market** (mornings only). It is ringed by arcades of different heights with an elegant wrought-iron balcony on the Hôtel Isnard at no. 33, and at one time was the exclusive preserve of the tanning industry.

Spiritual power was concentrated at the opposite end of Vieux Grasse, around place du Petit-Puy and place du 24 Août, one of the darkest, most deserted quarters at night. The **cathedral** (Mon–Sat 8.30–11.30am & 3–6.30pm) and **Bishop's Palace**, between the two squares, were built in the twelfth century, replacing a 200-year-old fortress of which part of a tower remains, incorporated in the palace that now serves as the hôtel de ville. The cathedral, despite endless additions and alterations, still has its high gaunt nave in which the starkly unadorned ribbed vaulting is supported from the side walls. Its astonishing, weighty columns and the walls surrounding the altar were fractured in a fierce fire that blazed through the church after the Revolution, giving the masonry an incredible, organic, cave-like feel that is most arresting. In the south aisle hang various paintings, a Fragonard, three early Rubens and, best by far, a poorly lit triptych by the sixteenth-century Niçois painter Louis Bréa.

You can see more works by Fragonard in the **Villa-Musée Fragonard** at 23 bd Fragonard (June–Sept daily 10am–7pm; Oct & Dec–May Weds–Mon

10am–12.30pm & 2–5.30pm; €3). The painter was the son of an early and not very successful Grassois perfumed-glove maker and returned to live in this villa after the Revolution, when his work fell out of favour.

Another museum worth a quick visit is the **Musée d'Art et d'Histoire de Provence**, 2 rue Mirabeau (same opening times and entrance fee as the Villa-Musée Fragonard), set in a luxurious town house commissioned by Mirabeau's sister for her social entertainment duties. As well as all the gorgeous fittings and the original eighteenth-century kitchen, the historical collection adds an eclectic touch. It includes wonderful eighteenth- to nineteenth-century faïence from Apt and Le Castellet, Mirabeau's death mask, a tin bidet, six prehistoric bronze leg bracelets; costumes, *santons* and oil presses. There is an opulent eighteenth-century Turkish bed, a collection of brutal, leaden-faced portraits of the seventeenth-century Provençal nobility, and a tremendous sunset painted by René Seyssaud a century ago, whose cracked surface augments the movement of a hazy evening sky near the Étang de Berre.

Just around the corner are another couple of museums: the small **Musée Provençal du Costume et du Bijou**, 2 rue Jean Ossola (June–Oct 10am–1pm & 2–6pm; free), with displays of the region's traditional dress and jewellery, and the **Musée International de la Parfumerie**, 8 place du Cours (same opening times and entrance fee as the Villa-Musée Fragonard), whose exhibits are fascinating and fun, even if you're not an enthusiast of the perfume industry. There are lots of perfume bottles dating from the ancient Greeks to the present, via Marie-Antoinette. There's also a greenhouse full of roses, jasmine, vanilla and other prized plants, and you can take a test on recognizing perfumes.

A more relaxed flower-smelling takes place at the **Jardin de la Villa de Noailles**, 59 av Guy-de-Maupassant (tours for fifteen people or more can be arranged through Grasse tourist office from Mon–Fri; €10), to the west of the town centre: take rue Jeanne-Jugan off av Gén-de-Gaulle, then left down Chemin Noailles, and left again. Camelias, magnolias and peonies are the star attractions here.

Eating and drinking

Grasse's best **restaurant** is *La Bastide St-Antoine*, at the hotel of the same name on the south side of the town (☎04.93.70.94.94; menus at €45, €107 & €135): its owner Jacques Chibois is a former Gault Millau chef of the year. Cheaper eating options include *La Galerie Gourmand* on rue Fabreries (☎04.93.36.80.69; menus from €14), and the rather basic *Brasserie de l'Évéché*, on the place de l'Évéché (☎04.93.36.40.12), which serves decent midday menus from about €10. If you want to make your own picnic, the *Maison Venturini*, 1 rue Marcel-Journet (closed Sun & Mon), sells fabulous sweet *fougassettes*, flavoured with the Grasse speciality of orange blossom. The **bars** on place aux Aires offer the best opportunity for encounters with the locals; the *Bar-Tabac L'Ariel* is a good place to start.

Around Grasse

The countryside around Grasse is pleasant for a day or two's stay, especially if you have a car. To the north is the **Plateau de Calern**, almost deserted save for the British archeologists who arrive every September to map the changing patterns of land use and ownership by the commune of **Cipières**. Running northwest is the **Route Napoléon**, and to the northeast the gorges of the **Loup River** pass the cliff-hanging stronghold of **Gourdon** and **Le-Bar-sur-**

Loup's reminders of mortality. To the west, towards the Upper Var, there are good dinners to be had at **Cabris** and musical caves to witness at **St-Cézaire**.

Cabris

CABRIS, just 6km southwest of Grasse, has all the trappings of a picture-postcard village: a ruined château providing panoramas from the Lac de St-Cassien to the Îles de Lérins, sometimes even Corsica, and arty residents who decamped here from Grasse. If you want to **stay**, the *Auberge du Vieux Chateau* on place Mirabeau (ⓣ04.93.60.50.12; ❹) is the best bet, with wonderful views. The warm and welcoming *Le Petit Prince* **restaurant** at 15 rue Frédéric-Mistral (ⓣ04.93.60.63.14; closed Dec and Tues & Wed out of season), overlooking the park lined with chestnut trees, is a treat, with a weekday menu at €17. The puddings are gorgeous, as is the smoked salmon *mille feuilles* and the wild-mushroom dishes.

The Grottes des Audides and Grottes de St-Cézaire

Three kilometres northwest of Cabris, on the road to St-Vallier, are the **Grottes des Audides** (mid-Feb to June, Sept, Oct & Wed–Sun 2–5pm; July & Aug daily 10am–noon & 12.30–6pm; Nov to mid-Feb phone for information; ⓣ04.93.42.64.15; €5 for caves), formerly neolithic dwellings. You descend 60m into the caves, to see scenes of prehistoric life that have been recreated using stone tools and implements found in the caves.

A further set of **caves**, the **Grottes de St-Cézaire** (tours: mid-Feb to May & Oct daily 2.30–5pm; June & Sept daily 10.30am–noon & 2–6pm; July & Aug daily 10.30am–6.30pm; Nov to mid-Feb Sun 2.30–5pm; €5), can be found just outside St-Cézaire-sur-Siagne (signed off the road from Cabris). The visit to the caves doesn't involve a deep descent, and visually it is no great treat. What *is* special is the aural experience of the stalagmites and stalactites with the most iron in them; the guide plays them like a xylophone, with an eerie resonance in this most irregular of acoustic chambers.

Heading west from Grasse towards Draguignan along the D562, there's a great **lunch** stop, *Le Pont de la Siagne* (ⓣ04.93.66.10.36; closed Tues), about ten kilometres out of town, where the €23 menu is an enormous feast in the best French tradition, served with a minimum of pomp but with considerable respect and designed to be eaten leisurely over a couple of hours.

The Route Napoléon: St-Vallier-de-Thiey

The road north from Grasse is the **Route Napoléon**, the path taken by the emperor in March 1815 after his escape from Elba, in pursuit of the most audacious recapture of power in French history. In typically French fashion the road was built in the 1930s specifically to commemorate their greatest leader's journey.

The route doesn't follow the imperial boot tracks precisely, going miles off course in some places, but it serves a useful purpose. After several kilometres of zigzagging bends you get fantastic views back to Grasse, its basin and the coast. The first village you come to is **ST-VALLIER-DE-THIEY**, 12km from Grasse, with some prehistoric dolmens and tumuli: the **tourist office** on place du Tour (March–Oct Mon–Sat 9am–noon & 3–6pm; Nov–Feb 9am–noon & 3–5pm; ⓣ04.93.42.78.00, ⓦwww.saintvallierdethiey.com) can provide a walking map of how to get to the prehistoric sites. The place to **eat** and **stay** is *Le Préjoly* at place Rougière (ⓣ04.93.42.60.86, ⓕ04.93.42.67.80; menus at €17 and €33; ❸; closed Dec & Jan & Mon in winter). There are three **campsites** in the vicinity, including the three-star *Parc des Arboins* on the rte Napoléon, (ⓣ04.93.42.63.89, ⓕ04.93.09.61.54; €16 per tent).

Beyond St-Vallier, the Route Napoléon heads, almost uninterrupted by settlements, towards Castellane (see p.408–410). Wayside stalls sell honey and perfume; each little hamlet has a petrol station and hotel-restaurant, and every so often you see a commemorative plaque carved with Napoleon's winged eagle.

Along the Gorges de Loup

The main southern approach to the Gorges de Loup is via **LE-BAR-SUR-LOUP**, 10km from Grasse. The little **Église de St-Jacques** contains an altarpiece attributed to the Niçois painter, Louis Bréa, and a fifteenth-century *Danse Macabre* painted on a wooden panel at the west end of the nave. The latter is a tiny but detailed illustration of courtly dancers being picked off by Death's arrows, their souls gathered up by devils, failing Saint Michael's test of blessedness and being thrown into the teethed and tongued mouth of hell. Alongside is a poem, in Provençal, warning of mortality and of the heavy risk involved in committing sins as grievous as dancing.

From here, you can follow the **gorges road**, through dark, narrow twists of rock beneath cliffs that look as if they might tumble at any minute, through the sounds of furiously churning water, to corners that appear to have no way out. Alternatively, you could miss out Le-Bar-sur-Loup and take the D3 from **Châteauneuf-Grasse** up along the northern balcony of the gorges to Gourdon.

Gourdon

Tiny **GOURDON** teeters on the edge of the Gorges de Loup, and the view from place Victoria at the top is as extraordinary as any in the Pays de Grasse. Unfortunately, you have to run the gauntlet of this *village perché*'s many souvenir shops to get there.

The village's **château**, to the right of the main street as you walk up from the car park (June–Sept daily 11am–1pm & 2–7pm; Oct–May Mon & Wed–Sun 2–6pm; €4), is an immaculately restored private residence containing a historical museum and a **museum of decorative arts and modernity** (guided tours only: €10). The first houses a self-portrait by Rembrandt (not always on show), a glowing *Descent from the Cross* by Rubens and other religious paintings of the early sixteenth century, as well as Saracen helmets made in Damascus, a writing desk used by Marie-Antoinette and letters signed by Henri IV. Highlights of the latter include a complete Art Deco ensemble by Eileen Gray. The best place **to eat** in Gourdon is *Le Nid d'Aigle*, place Victoria (☎04.93.77.52.02; closed Mon and Tues), at the top of the village with great views. It has a reasonable brasserie menu (€15–20), as well as pasta dishes from €8.

Antibes, Cap d'Antibes and Juan-les-Pins

Graham Greene, who lived in **Antibes** for more than twenty years, considered it the only place on this stretch of coast to have preserved its soul. And it is true that whilst Antibes and its twin, **Juan-les-Pins**, have not completely escaped the overdevelopment that blights much of this region, they have avoided the worst excesses suffered by some of their immediate neighbours. Antibes itself is a pleasing old town, with animated streets full of bars and restaurants, and one of the finest **markets** along the coast. Its castle has a superb **Picasso collection**, and the views from the town's ramparts towards the Alps are wonderful. **Cap d'Antibes** is dominated by the world's super-rich, many of whom live, or at least maintain homes, here, though the southern cap still retains its pinewoods to hide the exclusive mansions. On Sundays, it's one of the rare spots on the Riviera where the supremacy of the car is challenged, with walkers, cyclists and rollerbladers taking over the coast road. There's intermittent access to the wonderful rocky shore here, as well as a couple of beautiful gardens to visit, the **Jardin Thuret** and the **Villa Eilenroc**. Though perhaps not as swish as it was, Juan-les-Pins is one of the region's more appealing beach resorts, with plenty of nightlife and a renowned **jazz festival**.

Antibes

Very little remains of the medieval centre of **ANTIBES**, thanks to border squabbles from the fifteenth century until the Revolution, when Antibes belonged to France and Nice to Savoy. Today, luxury yachts and humble fishing boats shelter in the harbour, beneath the splendidly situated **Fort Carré** (May–Aug Tues–Sun 10am–6pm; Sept–April 10am–4.30pm; €3), transformed in the seventeenth century by Vauban into an impregnable fortress. Solid

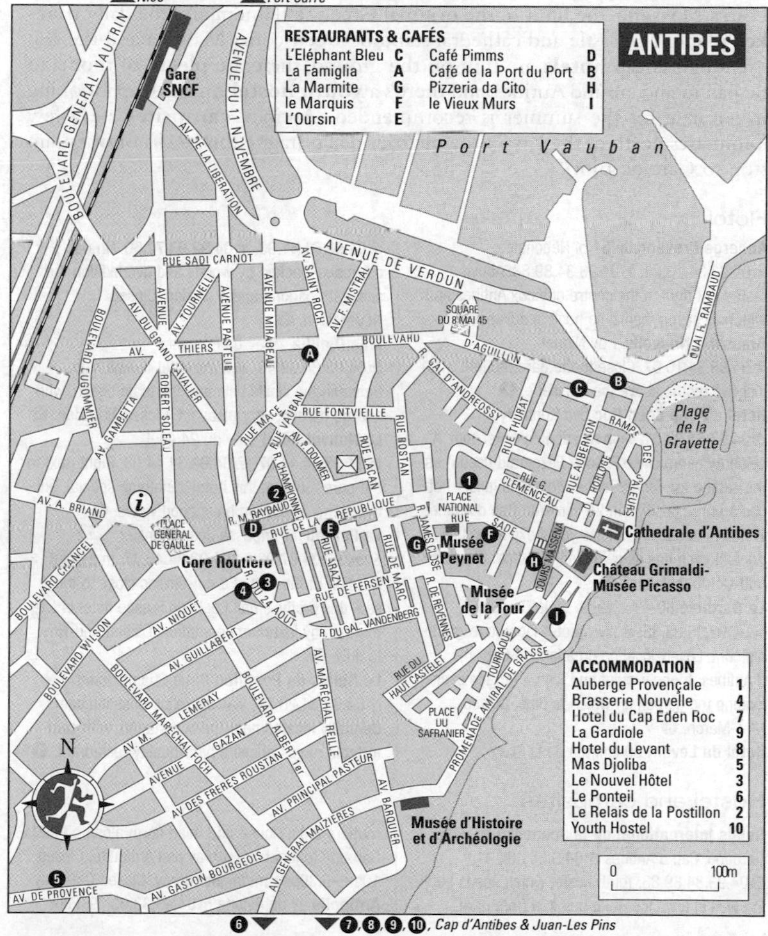

ramparts separate the port from the Vieille Ville, whose twin points of focus are the medieval **Château Grimaldi** and the belfry of the former **cathedral** rising above the sea wall.

Arrival, information and accommodation

The Vieille Ville fits into a triangle formed by the coast, the port and the main railway line, with Antibes' **gare SNCF** at the apex. From the station, turn right and it's a short walk along av R-Soleau to place du Général-de-Gaulle and the **tourist office**, at no. 11 (July & Aug daily 9am–7pm; Sept–June Mon–Fri 9am–12.30pm & 1.30–6pm, Sat 9am–noon & 2–6pm; ⓣ04.92.90.53.00; ⓦwww.antibesjuanlespins.com). The **gare routière** is east of here on place Guynemer with frequent buses to and from the gare SNCF. Bus #2A goes to Cap d'Antibes; bus #1A and #3A to Juan-les-Pins, and #10A to Biot. **Bikes** can be rented from Midi Location Service, Galerie du Port, rue Lacan (ⓣ04.93.34.48.00), and Holiday Bikes, 122 bd Wilson (ⓣ04.93.61.51.51).

From the gare routière, rue de la République leads into the heart of Vieux Antibes around **place Nationale**, which in turn is linked by rue Sade to the **cours Masséna**, the limit of the original Greek settlement and the daily **market place**. The castle and cathedral stand between cours Masséna and the sea.

Though cheap **hotels** are thin on the ground, there are plenty of rooms to be had in and around Antibes, and there's a **youth hostel** on the Cap. Booking in advance for the summer is recommended. Antibes' **campsites** are a few kilometres north of the city in the quartier de la Bragué (bus #10a or one train stop to Gare de Biot).

Hotels

Auberge Provençale 61 pl Nationale ⓣ04.93.34.13.24, ⓕ04.93.34.89.88. Above a restaurant right in the centre of Vieux Antibes and with only seven rooms, so book in advance. ❹

Brasserie Nouvelle 1 av Niquet ⓣ04.93.34.10.07. Close to the gare routière, with just five rooms above the brasserie. ❷

Hotel du Cap Eden Roc bvd Kennedy ⓣ04.93.61.39.01, ⓦwww.edenroc-hotel.com. A celebrity haunt since F. Scott Fitzgerald used it as the setting for *Tender is the Night*, this luxury hotel has a prime position in 25 acres on Cap d'Antibes. With all the usual comforts you'd expect at this price, it even has its own landing stage. Closed mid-Oct to mid-April. ❾

La Gardiole 60–74 chemin de la Garoupe ⓣ04.92.93.33.33, ⓦwww.hotel-lagaroupe-gardiole.com. Lovely location on a lane in Cap d'Antibes; friendly, quiet and with a terrace overlooking the garden on which to dine. Closed Nov–March. ❻

Hotel du Levant 50 chemin de la Plage ⓣ04.93.61.41.33, ⓕ04.92.93.72.60. On Cap d'Antibes, backed by woods and overlooking the sea, with parking and a garden. Closed Nov–March. ❺

Mas Djoliba 29 av de Provence ⓣ04.93.34.02.48, ⓦwww.hotel-djoliba.com. Between the Vieille Ville and the main beach, with a large garden; very pleasant. Closed Nov–Jan. ❺

Le Nouvel Hôtel 1 av du 24 Août ⓣ04.93.34.44.07, ⓕ04.93.34.44.08. Right next to the gare routière, this hotel is nothing special, but the rooms at the top have good views. ❸

Le Ponteil 11 impasse Jean-Mensier ⓣ04.93.34.67.92, ⓕ04.93.34.49.47. In a quiet location at the end of a cul-de-sac close to the sea, this pretty, small Logis de France hotel is surrounded by luxuriant vegetation. Closed mid-Nov to July. ❺

Le Relais du Postillon 8 rue Championnet ⓣ04.93.34.20.77, ⓦwww.relais-postillon.com. Centrally located near the bus station, with comfortable rooms above a high-quality restaurant. ❹

Hostel and campsites

Relais International de la Jeunesse bd de la Garoupe, Cap d'Antibes ⓣ04.93.61.34.41, ⓕ04.93.34.89.88. Youth hostel which needs booking well in advance. Take bus #2a from gare routière to La Bouée and head north along bd de la Garoupe to junction with av de l'Antiquité. Closed 10am–5.30pm; midnight curfew. Closed Oct–May.

Antipolis av du Pylone ⓣ04.93.33.93.39. Four-star campsite, 800 m from the sea. Closed Oct–March.

Les Embruns 63 rte de Biot ☎04.93.33.33.35. Three-star site just north of Biot's station; and close to the sea. €20 per tent. Closed Oct to late May.

The Town

The most atmospheric approach to the castle and cathedral is from the south through the **quartier du Safranier**. Place du Safranier and the little residential streets hereabouts, including rue de Lavoir with its old public **wash house**, have an appealing villagey atmosphere. By turning right on rue de l'Orme – rather than continuing straight into cours Masséna, then left into rue du Bateau, you'll find yourself on place Marie-Jol, in front of the **Château Grimaldi**.

Rebuilt in the sixteenth century but still with its twelfth-century Romanesque tower, the château served briefly as Picasso's studio in 1946, and is now home to the **Musée Picasso** (June–Sept Tues, Thurs, Sat & Sun 10am–6pm; Wed & Fri 10am–8pm; Oct–May Tues–Sun 10am–noon & 2–6pm; €4.60). Picasso spent several extremely prolific months in the château before moving to Vallauris, and leaving all his Antibes output to the museum. Although he donated other works later on, the bulk of the collection belongs to this one period. At this time, he was involved in one of his better relationships; his friend Matisse was just up the road in Vence; the war was over; and the 1950s had not yet arrived to change the Côte d'Azur for ever. There's an uncomplicated exuberance in the numerous still lifes of sea urchins, the goats and fauns in Cubist non-disguise, and the wonderful *Ulysses and the Sirens*, a great round head against a mast around which the ship, sea and sirens swirl. The materials reveal postwar shortages – odd bits of wood and board instead of canvas, and boat paint rather than oils. Picasso is also the subject here of other painters and photographers, including André Villers, Brassai, Man Ray and Bill Brandt. The photo of him holding a sunshade for Françoise Gilot catches the happiness of this period in the artist's life.

By contrast, on the second floor, in Picasso's old studio, are displayed the anguished works of Nicolas de Staël, who eventually killed himself. He stayed in Antibes for a few months from 1954 to 1955, painting the sea, gulls and boats with great washes of grey. A disturbing red dominates *The Grand Concert* and purple the *Still Life with Candlestick*. Works by other great twentieth-century artists are included in the museum's **modern art** collection, including several by German artist Hans Hartung. The wonderful terrace overlooking the sea is adorned by Germaine Richier sculptures along with works by Miró, César and others, and a violin homage to Picasso by Arman.

Alongside the castle is the **cathedral**, built on the site of an ancient temple. The choir and apse survive from the Romanesque building that served the city in the Middle Ages, while the nave and stunning ochre facade are Baroque. Inside, in the south transept, is a sumptuous altarpiece by Louis Bréa surrounded by immaculate panels of tiny detailed scenes.

One block inland, on cours Masséna, the **covered market** (June–Aug daily 6am–1pm; Sept–May Tues–Sun 6am–1pm) overflows with Provençal goodies including delicious olives, and a profusion of cut **flowers**, the traditional and still flourishing Antibes business. In the afternoons, a **craft market** (Easter–Sept Thurs–Sun; Oct–Easter Thurs–Sat) takes over from about 3pm (4.30pm on Sat), and when the stalls pack up, café tables take their place.

As well as the Picasso museum, there's a trio of further museums that may take your fancy. The museum of local history, the **Musée de la Tour** (Wed, Thurs & Sat 3–5pm; €3.50) in a medieval tower at the southern end of cours Masséna, is not wildly interesting, but it does house the world's first ever water-skis, invented locally in the 1930s. Further south, on the ramparts along pde Amiral de Grasse, the Bastion St-André houses the **Musée d'Histoire et d'Archéologie** (Tues–Sun 10am–noon & 2–6pm; €3), which gathers together the Greek, Roman, medieval and later finds of the region. The **Musée Peynet** on place Nationale (Tues–Sun: mid-June to mid-Sept 10am–6pm; mid-Sept to mid-June 10am–noon & 2–6pm; €3.50) pays homage to the Antibes cartoonist whose most famous creation was the 1940s series of 'the lovers', a truly old-fashioned conception of romance which, if you're not careful, may even induce nostalgia.

Eating and drinking

Place Nationale and cours Masséna are lined with **cafés**; rue James-Close has nothing but **restaurants**, and rue Thuret and its side streets also offer numerous menus to browse through. In addition to the market, there are some excellent **food shops** on rue du Sade, including the Charcuterie Lorraine at no. 15.

Auberge Provençale 61 pl Nationale ☎04.93.34.13.24. Fish grills and seafood are served in the covered garden of this welcoming hotel; menus from €17.50.

Restaurant de Bacon bd de Bacon, Cap d'Antibes ☎04.93.61.50.02. One of the coast's best fish restaurants, overlooking Vieux Antibes and serving fabulous fish soups and stews, including a superb bouillabaisse. Lunch menu €45; dinner €75. Closed Mon, Tues lunch & Nov–Jan.

L'Eléphant Bleu 28 bd de l'Aguillon ☎04.93.34.28.80. Thai and Vietnamese specialities with good vegetarian dishes. Midday menu €13, dinner menus at €20 and €39.

La Famiglia 34 av Thiers ☎04.93.34.60.82. A cheap, family-run outfit serving good pizzas and pasta, from around €12. Closed all day Wed, Sat & Sun lunch.

La Marmite 20 rue James-Close ☎04.93.34.56.79. One of the best restaurants along this street, with a menu at €23.50. Closed mid-Nov to mid-Dec & Mon out of season.

Le Marquis 4 rue Sade ☎04.93.34.23.00. Traditional Provençal food in a charming setting. Closed Mon & Tues lunch.

Chez Olive 2 bd Maréchal-Leclerc ☎04.93.34.42.32. Provençal specialities. Closed Mon.

L'Oursin 16 rue de la République ☎04.93.34.13.46. Superb fish and traditional seafood, with menus starting at €16.50. Closed Sun, Mon & Tues eve.

Café Pimms cnr of rue de la République and pl Guynemer. Brasserie with carousel decor and friendly atmosphere. Closed Sun.

Café de la Porte du Port bd de l'Aiguillon by the archway through the ramparts. One of many lively cafés in the rampart arcades.

Le Romantic 5 rue Rostan ☎04.93.34.59.39. Charming, small restaurant with menus at €23 and €37. The grilled sardines are good. Closed Sun, Mon lunch.

Pizzeria da Cito in the covered market, at 23 cours Masséna. Café with a wide selection of beers; *moules* for around €12. Close all day Mon and Tues lunchtime.

Les Vieux Murs near the castle at av Amiral-de-Grasse ☎04.93.34.06.73. In a perfect setting on the ramparts, this restaurant serves very classy food, such as oysters cooked in champagne. Menus at €28, €38 or €60. Closed Mon & Oct–March.

Nightlife

Many **cafés** and **bars** stay open late, with bvd Aguillon next to the port being the liveliest spot for a drink. Antibes' most popular **nightclub** is the refurbished *La Siesta*, on the route du Bord-de-la-Mer, between Antibes and La Brague, with gaming rooms, a disco, restaurant and bar. Serious dancers, however, will have more choice in nieghbouring Juan-les-Pins (see below). Antibes has a couple of decent **jazz** clubs – *La Tour International*, 6 Cours Massena, Vieil Antibes, and *Bar en Biais*, 600 1iere av, Nova Antipolis – and one **gay club**, the *Golden Gate* at 4 rue Honoré Ferrare.

Cap d'Antibes

The sandy **Plage de la Salis**, Antibes' longest beach, runs along the eastern neck of **Cap d'Antibes** and is a rarity along the Riviera – access to it is free, with no big hotels blocking the way. The success of Juan-les-Pins spared this side of the Cap from unchecked development in the days before planning laws were tightened. Above the southern end of the beach, at the top of chemin du Calvaire, stands the **Chapelle de la Garoupe** (daily 9am–noon & 3–6.30pm), full of ex-votos for deliverances from accidents, ranging from battles with the Saracens to collisions with speeding Citroëns. It also contains a medieval Russian icon and a painting on silk, both spoils from the Crimean War. Next to the church is a viewing platform and a powerful lighthouse whose beam is visible 70km out to sea.

A second public beach, **Plage de la Garoupe**, stretches along bd de la Garoupe before the promontory of Cap Gros. From here a footpath follows the shore to join the chemin des Douaniers. At the southern end of the Cap d'Antibes, on av Mrs LD Beaumont, stands the grandiose **Villa Eilenroc** (gardens Tues & Wed 9am–5pm; free: villa Wed 9am–noon & 1.30–5pm; free), designed by Charles Garnier, architect of the casino at Monte Carlo, and surrounded by 28 acres of lush gardens.

To reach the southernmost tip of the Cap d'Antibes, the Pointe de l'Îlette, you have to take chemin de la Mosquée from av J-F-Kennedy, past the superstars' favourite hang-out, the *Hôtel du Cap Eden Roc*. Staying on av J-F-Kennedy to the end will bring you to the **Musée Naval et Napoléonien** (Nov–Sept Mon–Fri 9.30am–noon & 2.15–6pm, Sat 9.30am–noon; €3), which documents the general's return from Elba (see p.335) with the usual paraphernalia of hats, cockades, model ships and signed commands. It also offers views over the woods of the southern Cap, all parcelled up into large private domains. From here walking or cycling up the western side of the Cap is very pleasant; you pass the tiny **Port de l'Olivette** full of small, unflashy boats, as well as rocks, jetties, tiny sandy beaches, and grand villas hiding behind high walls.

Dominating the middle of the Cap, on bd du Cap between chemins du Tamisier and G-Raymond, is the **Jardin Thuret** (summer Mon–Fri 8am–6pm; winter Mon–Fri 8.30am–5.30pm; free), established in the mid-nineteenth century by a botanist, Gustav Thuret. It now belongs to INRA, a national research institute which tests out and acclimatizes subtropical trees and shrubs in order to diversify the Mediterranean plants of France. You can wander freely around the gardens, and are sure to be surprised by some of the species of trees and shrubs that grow here.

Juan-les-Pins

JUAN-LES-PINS, just 1.5km west of Antibes, is another of those infamous Côte d'Azur names. It's the legendary summer night-time playground for the most expensively outfitted and consistently photographed celebrities who retreat at dawn, like supernatural creatures, to their well-screened cages on Cap d'Antibes.

Arrival, information and accommodation

Walking from the **gare SNCF** on av de l'Esterel down av Dr-Fabre and rue des Postes you reach the carrefour de Nouvelle Orléans, beyond which is La Pinède; by bus from Antibes the most central stops are Pin Doré and Rond Point Joffre. The **tourist office** is at 51 bd Guillaumont on the seafront at the western end of the town (July & Aug daily 9am–7pm; Sept–June Mon–Fri 9am–12.00pm & 2–6.00pm, Sat 9am–noon; ⓣ04.92.90.53.05).

Most of the town's **hotels** are clustered around av Gallet, between av de l'Esterel and the seafront, and av Alexandre III which crosses it. *Hôtel de la*

Pinède, 7 av Georges-Gallice (ⓣ04.93.61.03.95; ❸; closed Dec–Feb), has some cheap rooms and is right in the centre, while the *Parisiana*, 16 av de l'Esterel (ⓣ04.93.61.27.03, ⓕ04.93.67.97.21; ❸), is close to the station. For something more luxurious, try the peaceful *Pré-Catelan* in attractive gardens on the corner of av des Palmiers and av des Lauriers (ⓣ04.93.61.05.11, ⓦwww.precatalan.com; ❻; closed mid-Nov to Jan), or the upmarket and central *Hôtel du Parc*, set back from the seafront between av Maupassant and av Gallet (ⓣ04.93.61.61.00, ⓦwww.hotel-duparc.net; ❾; closed Nov–March).

The Town

Beyond the image, Juan-les-Pins has very little in the way of history. Unlike St-Tropez it was not a fishing village, just a pine grove by the sea, and although its casino was built in 1908, it wasn't until the late 1920s that it really took off as the original summer resort of the Côte d'Azur. In the 1930s, revealing swimsuits were reputedly first worn here and water-skiing was invented, and Juan-les-Pins' trailblazing style continued to attract aristocrats, royals, writers, dancers and screen stars throughout the 1950s and 1960s. Today, some of the glamour has undoubtedly gone: the modern *Meridien* hotel and casino is an oversized blot on the seafront, while one of the grandest 1920s hotels stands empty, awaiting its transformation into apartments. However, as a resort it has more appeal than many, with 2km of sheltered sandy **beach**, and a dizzying array of architectural styles along its streets. In addition, its ancient, beautiful pine grove, **Jardin de La Pinède** (known simply as La Pinède), plays host to the region's best **jazz festival**.

Eating and drinking

La Terrasse overlooking La Pinède on av Gallice (ⓣ04.93.61.20.37) is one of the star **restaurants** on this coast, and needs booking several weeks in advance. The set menu starts at €49 for lunch, and €84 at other times, but the expense is worthwhile for the exquisite fish and seafood dishes. That apart, Juan-les-Pins is not blessed with dependable restaurants, so take pot luck from the countless menus on offer on the boulevards around La Pinède. *Le Café de la Plage*, at 1 bd Edouard Baudouin (ⓣ04.93.61.37.61; lunchtime plats €15), is a good bet, serving seafood, cocktails and ice cream in a pleasant seafront spot, while *Cyber Pizza*, at 59 bd Wilson, dishes up light meals including pizzas and crêpes from around €6. You can also get brasserie food, crêpes, pizzas and similar snacks from street stalls till the early hours, and many shops and bars also keep going in summer till 3 or 4am.

Nightlife

The fads and reputations of the different **discos** in Juan-les-Pins change by the month (and all the starry *boîtes* are members-only). In general, however, opening hours are 11pm to dawn, and you can count on paying at least €20 for entrance plus your first drink. Some of the current hotspots include *Whisky a Gogo*, on Rue Jacques Leonetti, and *Le Village Voom Voom* and *Les Colonies Britanniques*, both at 1 bd de La Pinède. The town's only **gay club** is *Le Keops*, 12 av Guy de Maupassant. The most popular **live music** venue is currently *Le Pam-Pam*, 137 bd Wilson, which often has Brazilian bands, but you'll need to go early to get a seat.

The Côte d'Azur Festival International de Jazz

The best jazz event on the Côte d'Azur, the **Festival International de Jazz** (known simply as Jazz à Juan), takes place during the **last two weeks of July** in the open air. The main venues are La Pinède and Square Gould, above the beach by the casino, separated from each other by bd Edouard Baudouin.

The festival attracts performers of the calibre of Joe Cocker, Keith Jarrett, Wynton Marsalis, and Didier Lockwood. The music is always chosen with serious concern for every kind of jazz, both contemporary and traditional, rather than commercial popularity. Programme details and **tickets** are available from the tourist offices in Antibes and Juan-les-Pins, and tickets can also be bought from FNAC and Virgin shops.

Biot and Sophia-Antipolis

Twenty years ago, the area inland from Antibes above the *autoroute* was still the more or less untouched Forêt de la Brague, stretching from Mougins in the west to Biot in the east. Now transnational companies have offices and laboratories linked by wide roads cut through the forest, notably at **Sophia-Antipolis**, a futuristic science park. Nearby **Biot**, meanwhile, has become one of the most visited places on the Côte for its glassworks and the Fernand Léger museum.

Biot

Although the *village perché* of **BIOT**, above the coast 8km north of Antibes, is pretty enough, the real draw is its rich arts and crafts tradition. Formerly a centre of pottery production and now home to several glassworks, the village has long been a magnet for artists and craftspeople. Inevitably, Biot is packed out in high season, but it's not a place to miss if you can help it.

Arrival, information and accommodation

Biot's **gare SNCF** is actually 4km from the village, by the sea at La Brague. It's not a very pleasant walk along a dangerous road to the village, so you're better off catching one of the Antibes buses (12 daily to Biot). From the bus stop in the village head up Chemin Neuf, and rue St-Sébastien, the main street, runs

The Route Napoléon

The pines and silver sand between Juan-les-Pins and Cannes, now **Golfe-Juan**, witnessed Napoleon's famous return from exile in 1815. The emperor knew the bay well, having been in command of the Mediterranean defences as a general in 1794 with Antibes' Fort Carré as his base. This time, however, his emissaries to Cannes and Antibes were taken prisoner upon landing, though the local men in charge decided not to capture him. The lack of enthusiasm for his return was enough to persuade the ever-brilliant tactician to head north, bypassing Grasse, and take the most isolated snowbound mule paths up to Sisteron and onwards – the path commemorated by the modern **Route Napoléon**. By March 6 he was in Dauphiné. On March 19 he was back in the Tuileries Palace in the capital. One hundred days later he lost the battle of Waterloo and was finally and absolutely incarcerated on St Helena.

An anecdote relates that on the day of landing at Golfe Juan, Napoleon's men accidentally held up the prince of Monaco's coach travelling east along the coast. The Revolution incorporated Monaco into France but the restored Louis XVIII had just granted back the principality. When the prince told the former emperor that he was off to reclaim his throne, Napoleon replied that they were in the same business and waved him on his way.

For **other sections of the Route Napoléon**, see 'Grasse' on p.335, 'Sisteron' on p.307, and 'Castellane' on p.409.

off to your right. The **tourist office** (July–Aug Mon–Fri 10am–7pm, Sat & Sun 2.30–7pm; Sept–June Mon–Fri 9am–noon & 2–6pm, Sat & Sun 2–6pm; ⓣ04.93.65.78.00; ⓦwww.biot-coteazur.com) is at no. 46, and can provide copious lists of art galleries, should you need them.

There's not a lot of **accommodation** in Biot. If you book well in advance you could stay at the very reasonable *Hôtel des Arcades*, 16 place des Arcades (ⓣ04.93.65.01.04, ⓕ04.93.65.01.05; ❸), in the medieval centre of the village. There are plenty of **campsites** in the vicinity – the best are the one-star *Le Mistral* on rte de la Mer (ⓣ04.93.65.61.48), and the three-star *L'Eden*, chemin du Val-de-Pôme (ⓣ04.93.65.63.70; closed Oct–March), a couple of hundred metres from the Léger Museum.

The village

The highlight of a visit to Biot is its stunning collection of paintings by Fernand Léger, who lived in the village for a few years at the end of his life. His life-affirming works of art are on display at the **Musée Fernand Léger**, southeast of the village on the chemin du Val-de-Pôme, a thirty-minute walk from the gare SNCF (Mon & Wed–Sun: July–Sept 10.30am–6pm; April–June 10am–12.30pm & 2–6pm; Oct–March 10am–12.30pm & 2–5.30pm; €3.81). Even the museum building itself is a pleasure: with its giant murals, it transcends the mundane suburban setting.

Léger was turned off from the abstraction of Parisian painters by his experiences of fighting alongside ordinary working people in World War I. Not that he favoured realism, but he wanted his paintings to have popular appeal: he understood that in the modern world art competed with images generated by advertising, cinema and public spectacle. Léger set himself the task of producing paintings that could rival the visual power of such images. He was vocal on the politics of culture, too, arguing for museums to be open after working hours; for making all the arts more accessible to working people; and for public spaces to be adorned with art in the way of "incidental background", on which he often collaborated with Le Corbusier.

Without any realism in the form or facial expressions, the people in such paintings as *Four Bicycle Riders* or the various *Construction Workers* are forcefully present as they engage in their work or leisure, and are visually on an equal footing with the objects. Léger's art has the capacity for instant pleasure – the pattern of the shapes, the vibrant colour, particularly in his ceramic works – though he can also draw it back to stark horror as with *Stalingrad*. It's instructive to compare Léger's life and work with that of Picasso, his fellow **Cubist** pioneer and long-time comrade in the Communist Party. While Léger's commitment to working-class life never wavered, Picasso waved at it only when he needed it.

It was the **potteries** that first attracted Léger to Biot, where one of his old pupils had set up shop to produce ceramics of his master's designs. A year after Léger's death, in 1956, the Biot **glassworks** were also established, confirming the village's position as a centre for arts and crafts. Today, there are several glassmakers in the area, all keen for you to visit and buy their products. The **Verrerie de Biot** on chemin des Combes, the third turning off the D4 after the Léger museum (summer Mon–Sat 9.30am–8pm, Sun 10am–1pm & 2.30–7.30pm; winter Mon–Sat 9.30am–6pm, Sun 10.30am–1pm & 2.30–6.30pm; free), is a good choice, where you can watch the glass-blowers at work, visit an Eco-musée du Verre (guided tours only), and admire the famous and beautiful hand-blown bubble glass (*verre bullé*).

There's no shortage of attractions for **children**, all back on the main sea road. They include the performing dolphins of **Marineland** on the N7 (daily from

10am; adult €24, child €16), which is also home to the water toboggans, chutes and slides of **Aquasplash** (adult €16, child €13). Opposite Marineland, there's a funfair, **Antibesland** (June Mon–Fri 8.30pm–2am, Sat 4pm–2am, Sun 2pm–2am; July & Aug daily 4pm–2am, Sun 2pm–2am; Sept daily 4pm–2am; €2).

Eating and drinking

Among the **restaurants**, *L'Auberge du Jarrier*, 30 passage de la Bourgade (☎04.93.65.11.68; menus at €36 & €40; closed Mon, Tues, Wed & Thurs lunchtimes, out of season closed Mon & Tues), serves up Biot's best dinners, while the *Hôtel des Arcades* (closed Sun evening & Mon; lunchtime menu €26) has an appealing combination of café, art gallery and restaurant with traditional Provençal dishes.

Sophia-Antipolis

If Cap d'Antibes symbolizes old money, **SOPHIA-ANTIPOLIS** represents the power of the multinational. When capital and plant can be shifted anywhere, why not have your research facility or information technology centre in the planet's most desirable corner, the hills above Antibes? Bayer, Intel, Motorola and Siemens are among the companies to have set up in this vast **science park**, cut out of the forest 6km west of Biot. Although things have slowed down since the end of the dotcom boom, the city of Nice is still hatching plans for a rival science park of its own.

You can explore Sophia-Antipolis with your own transport (it's signed off the D4 from Biot, and from the A8 Antibes exit), but despite some daring architecture, the low-density design and extensive shrubbery makes it all rather elusive. Bus #2VB will bring you up from Antibes.

Villeneuve-Loubet and Cagnes

Villeneuve-Loubet and **Cagnes** flash past on the speedy train and road connections between Cannes, Antibes and Nice. Glimpses in transit suggest these places are the direst consequence of modern commercial development, but the messy seaside extensions have little to do with Cagnes and Villeneuve-Loubet proper. Both are worth a look: Villeneuve for its castle and place in culinary history; Cagnes for its wonderfully preserved medieval quarter and its artistic connections, with Renoir in particular.

Villeneuve-Loubet

Villeneuve-Loubet-Plage is dominated by the giant marina, **Baie des Anges**, built in the 1970s to a design by André Minangoy, with petrified sails visible from Cap d'Antibes to Cap Ferrat. By the time the French government began to be concerned at the despoliation of the Côte d'Azur, apartments in this marina were worth far too much for it to be demolished. So there it stays, a clever but conspicuous piece of modernism. The commercial squalor immediately surrounding it, however, is harder to stomach.

On the other side of the *autoroute*, the tiny, quiet village of **VILLENEUVE-LOUBET**, on the river Loup, clusters around an undamaged twelfth-century castle (closed to the public), which was once home to François I. Villeneuve's riverside park and pastures are a stopover point for migrating birds, but its main claim to fame is the **Musée de l'Art Culinaire**, 3 rue Escoffier (Tues–Sun 2–6pm; closed Nov; €4.50), in the house where a king of culinary arts was born in 1846. The son of a blacksmith, **Auguste Escoffier** began his career in restaurants at thirteen, skivvying for his uncle in Nice. By the end of the century he had reached the top in a business the French value as much as design or art. In London he was the *Savoy*'s first head chef, then the *Carlton*'s, and he fed almost every European head of state. *Pêche melba* was his most famous creation, but his significance for the history of *haute cuisine* was in breaking the tradition of health-hazard richness and quantity. He also showed concern for those who would never be his clients, publishing a pamphlet in 1910 proposing a system of social security to eliminate starvation and poverty.

The museum itself is of limited appeal to all but the most dedicated gastronomes, and unfortunately there's nowhere there to eat.

Cagnes

The various parts of **CAGNES** are rather confusing: the nondescript coastal strip is known as **Cros-de-Cagnes**; **Cagnes-sur-Mer**, which constitutes the town centre, is actually inland above the *autoroute*; while **Haut-de-Cagnes**, the original medieval village, overlooks the town and coast from the northwest heights. Cros-de-Cagnes has plenty of pebbly beach, and a Hippodrome wedged between the seafront and the A8 *autoroute*, with horse-racing from December to March and trotting in July and August. Cagnes-sur-Mer is a busy and rather characterless town, notable only for Renoir's house. Haut-de-Cagnes, however, has a stunning **castle** containing the fabulous **Donation Suzy Solidor** (see opposite) and a changing array of contemporary art.

Arrival and information

The **gare SNCF Cagnes-sur-Mer**, one stop from the station SNCF Cros-de-Cagnes, is southwest of the centre beside the *autoroute*. Turn right on the northern side of the *autoroute* along av de la Gare to reach the town centre. If you want to rent a **bike**, take the second right, rue Pasqualini, where you'll find Cycle Marcel at no. 5 (Ⓣ04.93.20.64.07). The sixth turning on your right, rue des Palmiers, leads to the **tourist office** at 6 bd Maréchal-Juin (July & Aug Mon–Sat 9am–7pm, Sun 9am–noon; June & Sept Mon–Sat 9am–noon & 3–7pm; Oct–May Mon–Sat 8.30am–12.15pm & 2–6pm; Ⓣ04.93.20.61.64; Ⓦwww.cagnes-tourisme.com).

Bd Maréchal-Juin, which becomes av de l'Hôtel-des-Postes and then av Mistral, is the main street. It runs parallel to av de la Gare, which becomes av Renoir then veers eastwards into place M. Bourdet. This is where you'll be dropped if you arrive from Cannes or Nice by **bus**. From here, local bus #2 runs to the gare SNCF; bus #1 to Cros-de-Cagnes and the seafront; bus #4 to the Renoir museum; and the free *Navette* to Haut-de-Cagnes. On foot it's a steep ascent along rue Général-Bérenger, which forks left at the end of av de la Gare and turns into montée de la Bourgade.

Accommodation

Cros-de-Cagnes has the largest choice of **hotels**, but also plenty of traffic: *Beaurivage*, 39 bd de la Plage (Ⓣ04.93.20.16.90, Ⓦwww.beaurivage.org; closed Dec & Jan; ❸), is a good choice, but ask for one of the quieter rooms at the back; or try *Chez Nous*, 96 bd de la Plage (Ⓣ04.93.07.02.56 Ⓕ04.92.27.06.63; ❸), which is set back slightly from the road. Top choice in Haut-de-Cagnes, if your budget will stretch, is the luxurious *Le Cagnard*, rue Sous Barri

(Ⓣ04.93.20.73.21, Ⓦwww.le-cagnard.com; ❾), the ancient guard room for the castle. A far cheaper option, opposite the castle, is one of the six rooms at *Le Grimaldi*, 6 place du Château (Ⓣ04.93.20.60.24, Ⓕ04.92.02.19.47; ❷). Also in Haut-de-Cagnes, on place Notre Dame de la Protection, *Les Terrasses du Soleil* (Ⓣ04.93.73.26.56, Ⓦwww.terrassesdusoleiel.com; ❻) is an attractive chambre d'hôtes in the former home of songwriter Georges Ulmer.

Campsites are plentiful, and mostly in wooded locations inland. Try the three-star *Le Todos*, 4km north of Cros-de-Cagnes at 159 chemin Vallon des Vaux (Ⓣ04.93.31.20.05, Ⓕ04.92.12.81.66; €17 per tent; closed mid-Oct to Feb), with a pool, bar and restaurant, or the well-equipped two-star *le Val de Fleuri*, adjacent to *Le Todos*, at 139 chemin Vallon des Vaux, also with a pool, tennis and children's activities (Ⓣ04.93.31.21.74, Ⓦwww.campingvalfleuri.fr; €15 per tent; closed Nov & Dec). There is also a two-star site, *La Rivière*, at 168 chemin des Salles, 4km north of Cros-de-Cagnes (Ⓣ04.93.20.62.27, Ⓕ04.93.31.02.61).

Renoir's house

Les Collettes, the house that **Renoir** had built in 1907 and where he spent the last twelve years of his life, is now a museum, the **Musée Renoir**, chemin des Collettes (Mon & Wed–Sun: May–Sept 10am–noon & 2–6pm; Oct & last week in Nov to April 10am–noon & 2–5pm; €3), surrounded by olive and rare orange groves. Renoir was captivated by the olive trees and by the difficulties of rendering "a tree full of colours": remarking on how a gust of wind would change the tree's tonality, he said, "The colour isn't on the leaves, but in the spaces between them." One of the two studios in the house, north-facing to catch the late afternoon light, is arranged as if Renoir had just popped out. Despite the rheumatoid arthritis that had forced him to seek out a warmer climate than Paris, he painted every day at Les Collettes, strapping the brush to his hand when moving his fingers became too painful. There are portraits of him here by his closest friends: a painting by Albert André, *À Renoir Peignant*, showing the ageing artist hunching over his canvas; a bust by Aristide Maillol; and a crayon sketch by Richard Guido. Bonnard and Dufy were also visitors and there are works of theirs here, including Dufy's *Homage to Renoir*, transposing a detail of *Moulin de la Galette*. Renoir himself is represented by several sculptures including two bronzes – *La Maternité* and a medallion of his son Coco – some beautiful, tiny watercolours in the studio, and ten paintings from his Cagnes period (the greatest, the final version of *Les Grandes Baigneuses*, hangs in the Louvre).

To **get to Les Collettes**, take bus #4 from place Bourdet or, on foot, follow av Renoir eastwards and turn left up passage Renoir.

Haut-de-Cagnes

For many years the haunt of successful artists, **HAUT-DE-CAGNES** is as perfect a hilltop village as you'll find on the Riviera: there are no architectural excrescences to spoil the tiers of tiny streets, and even the flowers spilling over terracotta pots or climbing soft stone walls appear perfect.

The ancient village backs up to the crenellated **château**, which once belonged to the Grimaldis of Monaco and now houses the **Musée Méditerranéan d'Arte Moderne**, the **Musée de l'Olivier** and the **Donation Solidor** (May–Sept daily 10am–noon & 2–6pm; Oct–April daily 10am–noon & 2–5pm; €5). The castle's Renaissance interior is itself a masterpiece, with tiers of arcaded galleries, vast frescoed ceilings, stuccoed reliefs of historical scenes and gorgeously ornamented chambers and chapels. The

Donation Solidor consists of wonderfully diverse portraits of the cabaret star, Suzy Solidor, whose career spanned the 1920s to the 1970s, and who spent the last 25 years of her life in Cagnes. She was painted by many of the great painters of the period, including Dufy, Cocteau, Laurençin, Lempicka, Van Dongen and Kisling, all of whom have works on display here. Solidor was quite a character: extremely talented, totally independent and immensely sexy. She declared herself a lesbian years before the word, let alone the preference, was remotely acceptable, and, incidentally, was the inspiration for the music-hall song "*If you knew Suzy, like I know Suzy*". The qualities that most endeared her to each artist, or the fantasies she provoked, are clearly revealed in every one of the canvases, giving a fascinating insight into the art of portraiture as well as a multifaceted image of the woman.

Downstairs is a reconstruction of an olive mill and exhibitions concerning the importance of the olive to the region, whilst upstairs plays hosts to temporary exhibitions of modern art and, from July to September, the *Festival International de la Peinture*. The latter is the big event of the year, with the paintings chosen by an august body similar to Britain's Royal Academy.

On place du château, the former cabaret where Solidor performed now houses the **Espace Solidor**, a venue for regular displays of contemporary jewellery. There's also a small **tourist office** here (April–June & Sept Wed–Sun 2–6pm; July & Aug daily 10am–1.30pm & 4–7pm; Oct–March Wed–Sun 2–5pm), and in July concerts are held on the square.

Eating and drinking

Haut-de-Cagnes and Cros-de-Cagnes have the town's best eating places, and for café lounging, place du Château or place Grimaldi, to either side of the castle in Haut-de-Cagnes, are the obvious spots.

In Haut-de-Cagnes, the area around montée de la Bourgade is thick with **restaurants**: a good choice is *Le Clap*, just off here at 4 rue Hippolyte-Guis (☎04.92.02.06.28; menu at €14; closed Wed), which serves very reasonably priced specialities from southwest France. *Le Cagnard* hotel has a predictably smart restaurant (☎04.93.20.73.21; menus from €53; closed Nov to mid-Dec), or there's *Josy-Jo*, 8 place Planastel (☎04.93.20.68.76; around €25; closed Sat lunch, Sun & first two weeks of Aug), with Provençal delicacies dished up in the space that served as Soutine's workshop in the interwar years.

In Cros-de-Cagnes, *Le Neptune* on rte du Bord de Mer (☎04.93.20.10.59; menus from €17) and *La Villa du Cros* on the port (☎04.93.07.57.83; menus from €25) both serve good seafood.

Vence and around

Set up in the hills 10km from the sea, and with abundant water and the sheltering Pre-Alpes behind, **VENCE** has always been a city of significance. Its Ligurian inhabitants, the Nerusii, put up stiff opposition to Augustus Caesar, but to no avail; Roman funeral inscriptions and votive offerings from the period remain embedded in the fabric of the old cathedral. In the Dark Ages of Visigoth and Ostrogoth invasions, the bishop of Vence, **Saint Véran** from the St-Honorat seminary, was as effective in organizing the defence of the city as in rebuilding its moral fabric. When he died in 481 he was canonized by popular request – in those days the democratic principle of *vox populi vox Dei* (the voice of the people is the voice of God) operated. But the people of Vence had no spiritual or temporal power to call on to save them from the Saracens who razed both the town and St-Véran's cathedral to the ground.

In the twelfth century the second patron saint of Vence, St-Lambert, took up residence at the same time as the baron **Romée de Villeneuve**, chief minister of Raymond Béranger IV, count of Provence. It was Villeneuve who arranged the powerful marriages of Béranger's four daughters, as part of his strategic scheming (see p.301). From then on, until the Revolution, Vence was plagued by rivalry between its barons and its bishops.

In the 1920s Vence became yet another haven for **painters and writers**, including André Gide, Paul Valéry, Soutine, Dufy and D.H. Lawrence (who died here, in 1930). Near the end of World War II **Matisse** moved to Vence to escape the Allied bombing of the coast and his legacy is the town's most famous building, the **Chapelle du Rosaire**, built under his design and direction. **Vieux Vence** too has its charms, with its ancient houses, gateways, fountains and chapels as well as the **St-Véran Cathedral**.

In late July or early August the open-air Latin and World music festival, **Les Nuits du Sud**, takes place. The festival attracts a high calibre of bands and its reputation is growing fast.

Arrival and information

From Cagnes-sur-Mer there are two **roads into Vence**. One enters the town as av Général-Leclerc, leading straight up to the eastern end of the old walled city. The other, along with the roads from Grasse, St-Paul and the north, arrives at carrefour Maréchal-Juin and the two main avenues of the modern town, av de la Résistance and av des Poilus/Henri Isnard. Coming by bus you'll be dropped at the **gare routière** on place du Grand-Jardin, next door to place du Frêne and the western gateway of Vieux Vence. On place du Grand-Jardin you'll find the **tourist office** (Mon–Sat 9am–5pm, summer until 7pm; Sun 9am–1pm; ⓣ04.93.58.06.38). You can hire **bikes** from Vence Motos at 7 av des Poilus.

Accommodation

Although Vence has a good choice of **places to stay**, catering for all budgets, it's as well to book ahead in the summer.

Hotels

Hôtel des Alpes 2 av Général-Leclerc ⓣ04.93.58.13.30. On the eastern edge of Vieux Vence and nothing fancy, but friendly and the most economical option. Closed Nov; restaurant closed Sat & Sun. ❷

La Closerie des Genêts 4 impasse Maurel, off av M-Maurel on southern edge of Vieux Vence ⓣ04.93.58.33.25, ⓕ04.93.58.97.01. Pleasant, peaceful hotel and very welcoming, with an attractive garden and sea views from some rooms. ❷

Diana av des Poilus ⓣ04.93.58.28.56, ⓦwww.hotel-diana-vence.com. Modern building in a quiet and convenient location. ❻

Le Provence 9 av Marcellin-Maurel ⓣ04.93.58.04.21, ⓕ04.93.58.35.62. Decent value for the price, with a lovely garden. Closed mid-Jan to mid-Feb. ❸

La Roseraie 14 av H-Giraud ⓣ04.93.58.02.20, ⓕ04.93.58.99.31. Classic, rich Provençal homestead with ancient cedars and magnolias overhanging the terrace on the road to the Col de Vence northwest of town. Charming reception and lovely pool in the garden. ❺

Auberge des Seigneurs pl du Frêne ⓣ04.93.58.04.24, ⓕ04.93.24.08.01. Just within Vieux Vence, with rooms named after the painters who lodged there; the food is excellent. Closed mid-Nov to mid-Dec. ❹

La Victoire pl du Grand-Jardin ⓣ04.93.58.61.30, ⓕ04.93.58.74.68. Noisy but very central and reasonable for the money. ❷

Campsite

La Bergerie rte de la Sine ⓣ04.93.58.09.36, ⓕ04.93.59.80.44. Three-star site 3km west off the road to Tourrettes-sur-Loup. Closed mid-Oct to mid-March.

The Town

Vieux Vence has its fair share of chic boutiques and arty restaurants, but it also has an everyday feel about it with ordinary people going about their business, seeking out the best market deals, stopping for a chat and a *petit verre* at run-of-the-mill cafés. The **castle** and the **cathedral** are the two dominant buildings in this part of town; while **Matisse's chapel** (with its limited opening hours) is the main diversion in the modern town.

Vieux Vence

The 450-year-old ash tree that gives its name to **place du Frêne** stands in front of Vence's castle, the **Château de Villeneuve** (June to mid-Oct daily 10am–6pm; mid-Oct to May Tues–Sun 10am–12.30pm & 2–6pm; €5), built just outside the city walls in a calm period of fifteenth-century expansion. It was rebuilt in the seventeenth century and renovated in 1992 to become a beautiful temporary exhibition space for the works of artists like Matisse, Dufy, Dubuffet and Chagall – all associated with the town – along with other modern and contemporary art.

The **Porte du Peyra** and its sheltering tower that adjoins the castle have remained more or less untouched from the twelfth century and provide the best entry into Vieux Vence. **Place du Peyra**, within the medieval walls, has the town's oldest fountain. The narrow, cobbled **rue du Marché** off to the right is a wonderfully busy street of tiny and delectable food shops, all with stalls; it is said to be one of the most expensive streets in France for food. Behind rue du Marché you'll find **place Clemenceau**, which centres on the cathedral and hosts the main Tuesday and Friday **market**, spilling into place Surian.

The **St-Véran Cathedral** is a tenth- and eleventh-century replacement for the church St-Véran presided over in the fifth century, which in turn was built on the ruins of a Roman temple to Mars and Cybele. Like so many of the oldest Provençal churches, it is basically square in shape, with an austere exterior which gives the appearance of monastic exclusion. Over the centuries bits have been demolished and other bits added, leaving none of the clear lines of Romanesque architecture. But with each project, including the initial construction, fragments of the Merovingian and Carolingian predecessor and Roman Vence were incorporated. In the chapel beneath the belfry two reliefs from the old church show birds, grapes and an eagle. More stone birds, flowers, swirls of leaves and interlocking lines are embedded in the walls and pillars throughout the church. Roman inscriptions from an aqueduct adorn the porch and more have found their way into the walls of the southwestern tower. The purported **tomb of St-Véran**, in the southern chapel nearest the altar, is a pre-Christian sarcophagus. St-Véran and his fellow patron saint of Vence, St-Lambert, survive in reliquary form in the neighbouring chapel. Of later adornments there are some superb, irreverent Gothic carved **choir stalls** that are housed alongside some powerfully human, if crude, polychrome wooden statues of the calvary, up above the western end of the nave (summer only Mon–Fri 9am–6pm). In the baptistry, a **Chagall mosaic** depicts the infant Moses being saved from the Nile by the Pharaoh's daughter. Church-as-museum devotees can have a field day examining all the treasures, but those who go for a sense of awesome space will probably be disappointed.

On the east side of the cathedral is **place Godeau**, almost totally medieval save for the column in the fountain that was given to the city, along with its twin on place du Grand-Jardin, by the Republic of Marseille some time in the third century. Rue St-Lambert and rue de l'Hôtel-de-Ville lead from place Godeau down to the original eastern gate, the **Porte du Signadour**, with another fifteenth-century fountain just outside on place Antony-Mars celebrating the town's expansion. In the thirteenth century the only other gate was the Portail Levis on the opposite corner of the city to Porte du Signadour.

The fountain on **place Vieille**, between the Portail Levis and the cathedral, was redesigned in 1572, this time to celebrate the town getting the better of both its feudal and spiritual lords. The town's bishop had been condemned as a heretic for his dabblings with Protestantism. The people of Vence kicked him out not because of the new religion but because he'd sold his seigneurial rights to Baron Villeneuve, who now had exclusive jurisdiction over them. Using the courts both of Rome and of Provence, the town acquired the illegally transferred rights itself. What is more, when the baron laid siege to Vence with Protestant troops in 1592, the town held out. The townspeople didn't like it when Rome sent a new envoy the same year, accepting him only after he had won the approval of the new king in 1594.

Matisse's Chapelle du Rosaire

Henri Matisse was never a Christian believer, though some have tried to explain the **Chapelle du Rosaire** at 466 av Henri-Matisse, the road to St-Jeannet from the Carrefour Jean-Moulin at the top of av des Poilus (Dec–Oct Mon & Wed–Sat 2–5.30pm; Tues & Thurs 10–11.30am & 2–5.30pm; Sunday Mass 10am; additional openings during school holidays, check with tourist office; €2.50), as proof of a late-life conversion. "My only religion is the love of the work to be created, the love of creation, and great sincerity," he said in 1952, when the five-year project was completed.

A serious illness in 1941 had left Matisse an invalid. In August 1943, during his convalescence in Vence, where he was nursed by the Dominican sisters who were to involve him in the design of the chapel, he wrote to Louis Aragon: "I am an elephant, feeling, in my present frame of mind, that I am master of my fate, and capable of thinking that nothing matters for me except the conclusion of all these years of work, for which I feel myself so well equipped."

The artist moved back to his huge rooms in Nice in 1949 in order to work on the designs using the same scale as the chapel. There is a photograph of him in bed drawing studies for the figure of St-Dominic on the wall with a paintbrush tied to a long bamboo stick. It's not clear how much this bamboo technique was a practical solution to his frailty, and how much a solution to an artistic problem. According to some critics, Matisse wanted to pare down his art to the basic essentials of human communication, and to do this he needed to remove his own stylistic signature from the lines.

The drawings on the chapel walls – black outline figures on white tiles – succeed in this to the extent that many people are bitterly disappointed, not finding the 'Matisse' they expect. The east wall is the most shocking; it shows the Stations of the Cross, each one numbered and scrawled as if it were an angry doodle on a pad. Matisse described the ceramic murals as "the visual equivalent of an open book where the white pages carry the signs explaining the musical part composed by the stained-glass windows." The full-length windows in the west and south walls are the aspect of the chapel most likely to live up to expectations. They are the only source of colour in the chapel, changing with the day's light through opaque yellow, transparent green and watery blue, and playing across the black and white murals, floor and ceiling.

Every part of the chapel is to Matisse's design (with some architectural input from Auguste Pérret): the high cross with oriental leanings on the roof; the brightly coloured silk vestments (still worn by the priest at Mass), chasubles, crucifix and candelabra; the layout of the chapel; the decoration on the floors, steps and roof. It is a total work and one with which Matisse was content. It was his "ultimate goal, the culmination of an intense, sincere and difficult endeavour".

The Galerie Beaubourg

More art can be seen at the **Galerie Beaubourg** in the Château Notre-Dame des Fleurs, halfway along the road from Vence to Tourrettes-sur-Loup (July & Aug Tues–Sat 11am–7pm; Sept–June 12.30–5.30pm; €4.60). Temporary exhibitions take place here throughout the year, featuring works by the likes of César, Klein, Arman, Ben, Tinguely and Warhol.

Eating and drinking

There are plenty of **cafés** in the squares of Vieux Vence: *Le Clemenceau* on place Clemenceau is the best location, though *Henry's* on place de Peyra is more congenial. *La Régence* on place du Grand-Jardin serves excellent coffee to sip beneath its stylish parasols. Rue du Marché is the place for **picnic** food: *Au Poivre d'Âne* at no. 12 specializes in **cheeses** and serves cheese dishes at the back.

Restaurants

Château Saint-Martin rte de Coursegoules ☎04.93.58.02.02. Housed in a Templars' castle perching on a rock and complete with stunning views, this is the most extravagant and beautiful place to eat. Classic French food served with due pomp and ceremony. The weekday midday menu is €53, otherwise from €73. Closed Wed out of season & Nov–March.

La Farigoule 15 av Henri-Isnard ☎04.93.58.01.27. Not always brilliant food but a great atmosphere. Menus from €22. Closed Tues & Wed.

Maximin Restaurant 689 chemin de la Gaude ☎04.93.58.90.75. Gourmet cuisine from one of France's fabled chefs, Jacques Maximin, with menus starting from €40, and rising steeply in price and indulgence.

Le Pêcheur du Soleil 1 pl Godeau ☎04.93.58.32.56. An astounding choice of pizzas, costing from €7–13. Closed Fri lunchtime.

La Vieille Douve 10 av Henri-Isnard ☎04.93.58.10.02. Lovely *terrasse* with a view of the zigzagging blue roof of the Chapelle du Rosaire. Menu at €12. Closed Wed evening & Thurs.

St-Paul-de-Vence and the Fondation Maeght

Three kilometres south of Vences, on the road down to Cagnes, is the fortified village of **ST-PAUL-DE-VENCE**, where visitors flock to see the grave of **Marc Chagall** in the little cemetery at the southern end of the village or to browse through the seventy or so contemporary art galleries and *ateliers*. Its chief draw, however, is the remarkable **Fondation Maeght** (daily: July–Sept 10am–7pm; Oct–June 10am–12.30pm & 2.30–6pm; €10), the artistic centre that most fully represents the link between the Côte d'Azur and modern European art. The foundation was created in the 1950s by Aimé and Marguerite Maeght, art collectors and dealers who knew all the great artists who worked in Provence. They commissioned the Spanish architect José Luis Sert to design the building, and a number of the painters, sculptors, potters and designers who were on their books to decorate it. Both structure and ornamentation were conceived as a single project with the aim of creating a museum in which the concepts of entrance, exit and *sense de la visite* would not apply. It worked.

Once through the gates, any idea of dutifully checking off a catalogue of priceless museum pieces crumbles. Giacometti's *Cat* is sometimes stalking along the edge of the grass; Miró's *Egg* smiles above a pond and his totemed *Fork* is outlined against the sky. It's hard not be bewitched by the Calder mobile swinging over watery tiles, by Léger's flowers, birds and a bench on a sunlit rough stone wall, by Zadkine's and Arp's metallic forms hovering between the pine trunks, or by the clanking tubular fountain by Pol Bury. And all this is just a portion of the garden.

The building itself is a superb piece of architecture: multilevelled and flooded with daylight, with galleries opening on to terraces and courtyards, blurring the boundaries between inside and outside. The collection it houses – sculpture, ceramics, paintings and graphic art by Braque, Miró, Chagall, Léger, Kandinsky, Dubuffet, Bonnard, Dérain and Matisse, along with more recent artists and the young up-and-comings – is impressive. Not all the works are exhibited at any one time, however, and during the summer, when the main annual exhibition is mounted, the only ones on show are those that make up the decoration of the building.

There are several major **exhibitions** every year, from retrospectives to shows on contemporary themes, along with workshops by musicians or writers with strong links to the visual arts, concerts, theatre and dance, and films screened daily throughout the summer until mid-October.

Bus #400 from Nice to Vence serves St-Paul via Cagnes, but at certain times of the day it speeds through without stopping, so check before boarding. The Fondation Maeght is approximately ten minutes' walk from the bus stop in the village. By **car or bike**, follow the signs just before you reach the village, off the D7 from La-Colle-sur-Loup or the D2 from Villeneuve.

Tourrettes-sur-Loup

Six kilometres west of Vence, **TOURRETTES-SUR-LOUP** is an artisans' paradise, preserving just the right balance between crumbly attractiveness and modern comforts. The three towers from which the village derives its name plus the rose-stone houses which cling to the high escarpment, almost all date from the fifteenth century; the best views can be had from the curious rock shelf known as Les Loves, just above the town. The Grande-Rue is lined with expensive *ateliers* selling clothes, sculpture, jewellery, leather, fine art and many other desirable designer items.

The town is famous for its **violet festival**, held on the first or second Sunday of March, when floats are decorated with thousands of these blooms. Violets, which thrive in the mild microclimate, are grown here in vast quantities for the perfume trade as well as for subsidiary cottage industries such as old-fashioned candied violets.

Tourrettes' **tourist office** is at 2 place de la Libération (Mon–Sat 9.30am–12.30pm & 2.30–6.30pm; Ⓣ04.93.24.18.93, Ⓦwww.tourrettessur-loup.com). If you want **to stay**, first choice is pleasant *L'Auberge de Tourrettes*, 11 rte de Grasse (Ⓣ04.93.59.30.05, Ⓦwww.aubergedetourrettes.fr; ❻), on the edge of the village, with good views. Local **campsites** include the three-star *La Camassade*, 523 rte de Pie Lombard (Ⓣ04.93.59.31.54, Ⓕ04.93.59.31.81; €18 per tent), about 3km along the road to Pont du Loup, and, further on, the three-star *Les Rives du Loup*, rte de la Colle (Ⓣ & Ⓕ 04.93.24.15.65; closed Oct to March). For somewhere to **eat** that won't break the bank, try *Le Médiéval* at 6 Grand' Rue (Ⓣ04.93.59.31.63; menus at €16, €25 and €32; closed Wed eve & Thurs), or *Le Petit Manoir* at 21 Grand' Rue (Ⓣ04.93.24.19.19; menus at €21, €30 or €40; closed Mon, Tues & Wed lunch).

Nice

The capital of the Riviera and fifth-largest town in France, **NICE** lives off a glittering reputation, its former glamour now gently faded. First popularized by English aristocrats in the eighteenth century, Nice reached its zenith in the *belle époque* of the late nineteenth century, an era that left the city with several extraordinary architectural flights of fancy. Today, many of Nice's permanent residents are retired, their pensions and investments contributing to the high ratio of per capita income to economic activity. Among visitors Italians dominate, especially on summer weekends.

Far too large to be considered simply a beach resort, Nice nevertheless manages to be a delightful, vibrant Mediterranean metropolis with all the advantages and disadvantages its city status brings: superb cultural facilities, wonderful street life and excellent shopping, eating and drinking, but also a high crime rate, graffiti and – in summer – a truly horrendous traffic problem. Yet somehow things never seem as bad as they might be: the sun shines, the sea sparkles and a thousand sprinklers keep the lawns and flowerbeds lush even as temperatures soar into the thirties. Along the famous seafront the frayed but sturdy palms survive, and on summer nights the old town buzzes with contented crowds. It's hard not to be utterly seduced by the place.

Nice's easy-going charm, however, is at odds with its reactionary **politics**. For decades municipal power was the monopoly of a dynasty whose corruption was finally exposed in 1990, when Mayor Jacques Médecin fled to Uruguay, only to be extradited and jailed. From his prison cell, Médecin backed Jacques Peyrat, the former *Front National* member and close friend of Jean-Marie Le Pen, in the 1995 local elections. Peyrat won with ease and has been mayor ever since, while the *Front National* retains significant support in the city.

Nice has retained its historical styles almost intact: the medieval rabbit warren of **Vieux Nice**, the Italianate facades of **modern Nice** and the rich exuberance of **fin-de-siècle residences** dating from when the city was Europe's most fashionable winter retreat. It has also retained mementoes from its ancient past, when the Romans ruled the region from here, and earlier still, when the Greeks founded the city. Nice's many **museums** are a treat for art lovers: within France the city is second only to Paris for the sheer range on offer. The **Musée Matisse**, the **Musée d'Art Moderne**, the **Musée des Beaux-Arts**, **Musée International d'Art Naif**, Chagall's **Message Biblique** and the **Musée Départmental des Arts Asiatiques** all vie for the visitor's attention. Many of the artists represented by these collections have a direct connection to the city.

Arrival, information and city transport

From terminal 1 at the **airport**, two bus services connect with the gare SNCF – the fast shuttle #99 (15min; €3.50) and the regular bus #23 (30min; €1.30). **Taxis** are plentiful at the airport and will cost about €19 into the town centre. The ugly **gare routière** is close to the Vieille Ville beneath the promenade du Paillon on bd Jean-Jaurès; the **gare SNCF** is a little further out, just west

Chemin de Fer de Provence

The **Chemin de Fer de Provence** runs one of France's most scenic and fun railway routes from the Gare de Provence on Nice's rue Alfred-Binet (4 daily; 3hr 15min). The line runs up the Var valley into the hinterland of Nice, and climbs through some spectacular scenery, past places such as the tremendous fortified town of **Entrevaux** (see p.405–406), before terminating at **Digne-les-Bains** (see p.410–415).

of the top end of av Jean-Médecin on av Thiers. The **Gare de Provence** is ten minutes' walk north of the gare SNCF on rue A-Binet, west of av Malaussena: buses #4 and #5 from bd Joseph Garnier, a block away, run down av Jean-Médecin.

The main **tourist office** is beside the gare SNCF on av Thiers (June–Sept daily 8am–8pm; Oct–May 8am–7pm; ⓣ0892.707.407, ⓦwww.nicetourisme.com). It's one of the most useful, helpful and generous of the Côte tourist offices, and has annexes at 5 promenade des Anglais (June–Sept Mon–Sat 8am–8pm, Sun 9am–6pm; Oct–May Mon–Sat 9am–6pm; ⓣ0892.707.407), at Nice-Ferber further along the promenade des Anglais near the airport (June–Sept daily 8am–8pm; ⓣ0892.707.407), and at terminal 1 of the airport (daily 8am–10pm; ⓣ0892.707.407).

Buses are frequent and run until about 9pm, after which four buses serve most areas from place Masséna until 1.10am. Fares are flat rate and you can buy a single ticket (€1.30), a Sunmaxi *carnet* of fourteen tickets (€16), or a day pass (€4) on the bus; five-day passes (€12.96) and seven-day passes (€16.77) are available from *tabacs*, kiosks, newsagents and from Sunbus, the transport office, at 10 av Félix-Faure, where you can also pick up a free route map. From the gare SNCF, bus #15 will take you to place Masséna and along rue Gioffrédo, from where it's a short walk to the Sunbus office (stop Alberti-Gioffrédo). For some years there has been detailed discussion of a new **tramway** system for the city. The route of the first line was approved in 2001, and the first trams are scheduled to begin operation in 2006.

Taxis around town are hard to come by, and cost €1.14 per kilometre by day; night rates operate from 7pm to 7am, and are €1.71 per kilometre. **Bicycles, mopeds** and **motorbikes** can be rented from Holiday Bikes at 34 av Aubers, just by the gare SNCF (ⓣ04.93.16.01.62).

Accommodation

Before you start doing the rounds, it's well worth taking advantage of the NiceRes **reservation service** offered by the tourist office. The area around the train station teems with cheap, seedy hotels, but it's perfectly possible to find reasonably priced rooms in **Vieux Nice**, even in summer. Options for **camping** are poor: the nearest site is *Camping Terry*, 768 rte de Grenoble St-Isodore (ⓣ04.93.08.11.58), 6.5km north of the airport on the N202 – take bus #700, #740 or #750 from the gare routière to La Manda stop, or the Chemin de Fer de Provence railway to Bellet-Tennis des Combes.

Hotels

La Belle Meunière 21 av Durante ⓣ04.93.88.66.15. Efficiently-run backpacker hotel in fabulously wasted old bourgeois house. The top-floor rooms are rather sweaty. ❷

Canada 8 rue Halévy ⓣ04.93.87.98.94, ⓔhotel-canada@caramail.com. Plain but clean and reasonable with a good, central location close to the sea. ❸

Le Capitole 4 rue de la Tour ⓣ04.93.80.08.15, ⓕ04.93.85.10.58. A good, if potentially noisy,

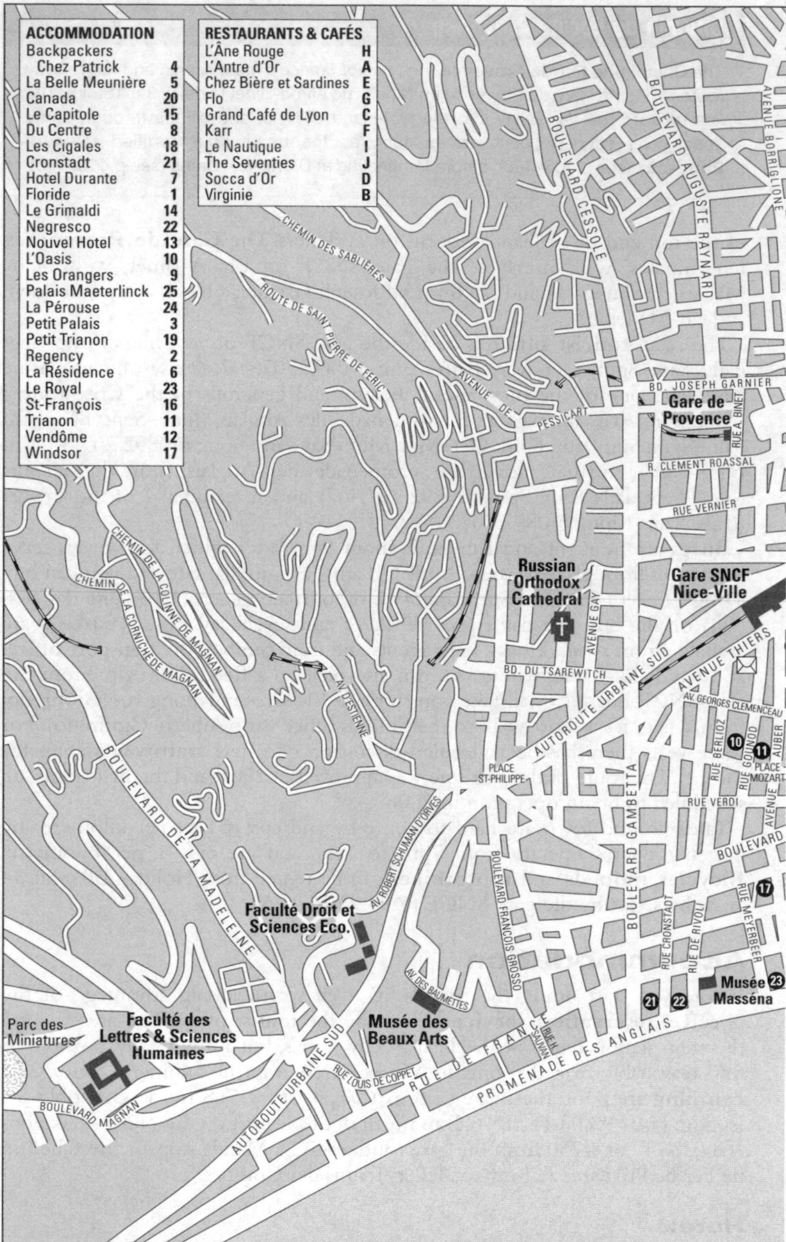
ACCOMMODATION
Backpackers Chez Patrick 4
La Belle Meunière 5
Canada 20
Le Capitole 15
Du Centre 8
Les Cigales 18
Cronstadt 21
Hotel Durante 7
Floride 1
Le Grimaldi 14
Negresco 22
Nouvel Hotel 13
L'Oasis 10
Les Orangers 9
Palais Maeterlinck 25
La Pérouse 24
Petit Palais 3
Petit Trianon 19
Regency 2
La Résidence 6
Le Royal 23
St-François 16
Trianon 11
Vendôme 12
Windsor 17
RESTAURANTS & CAFÉS
L'Âne Rouge H
L'Antre d'Or A
Chez Bière et Sardines E
Flo G
Grand Café de Lyon C
Karr F
Le Nautique I
The Seventies J
Socca d'Or D
Virginie B
Gare de Provence
Russian Orthodox Cathedral
Gare SNCF Nice-Ville
Faculté Droit et Sciences Eco.
Faculté des Lettres & Sciences Humaines
Parc des Miniatures
Musée des Beaux Arts
Musée Masséna
Musée d'Art Naït & Nice-Côte d'Azur Airport
BOULEVARD CESSOLE
BOULEVARD AUGUSTE RAYNARD
AVENUE BORRIGLIONE
CHEMIN DES SABLIÈRES
ROUTE DE SAINT PIERRE DE FERIC
AVENUE DE PESSICART
BD. JOSEPH GARNIER
RUE A. BINET
R. CLEMENT ROASSAL
RUE VERNIER
AVENUE GAY
BD. DU TSAREWITCH
AUTOROUTE URBAINE SUD
AVENUE THIERS
AV. GEORGES CLEMENCEAU
RUE BERLIOZ
RUE GOUNOD
AUBER
PLACE MOZART
RUE VERDI
AVENUE
BOULEVARD
PLACE ST-PHILIPPE
BOULEVARD GAMBETTA
BOULEVARD FRANÇOIS GROSSO
RUE CRONSTADT
RUE DE RIVOLI
RUE MEYERBEER
CHEMIN DE LA COLINNE DE MAGNAN
CHEMIN DE LA CORNICHE DE MAGNAN
AV. D'ESTIENNE
AV. ROBERT SCHUMAN D'ORVES
BOULEVARD DE LA MADELEINE
AV. DES BAUMETTES
RUE DE FRANCE
RUE H. SAUVAN
RUE LOUIS DE COPPET
PROMENADE DES ANGLAIS
BOULEVARD MAGNAN

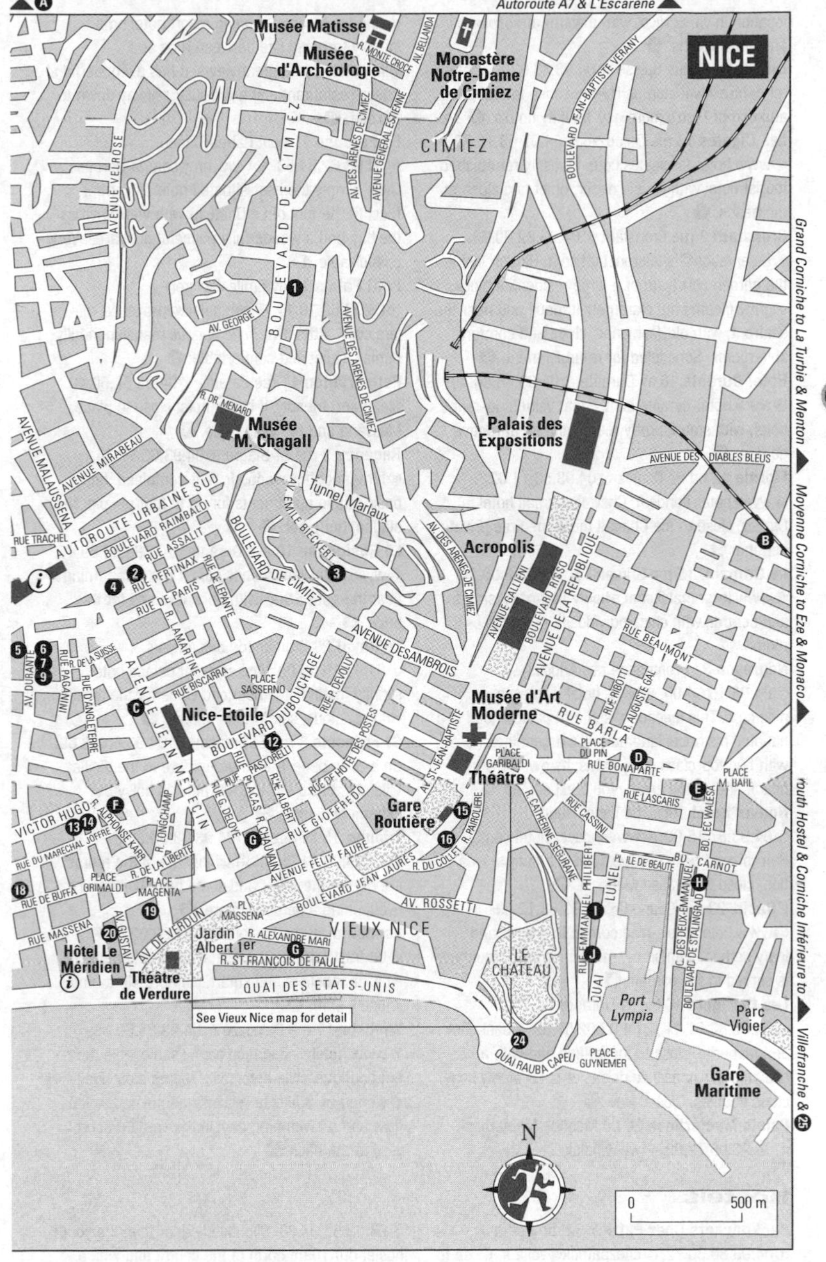
NICE
Autoroute A7 & L'Escarène
Grand Corniche to La Turbie & Menton
Moyenne Corniche to Eze & Monaco
Youth Hostel & Corniche Inférieure to Villefranche & 25
Musée Matisse
Musée d'Archéologie
Monastère Notre-Dame de Cimiez
CIMIEZ
Musée M. Chagall
Palais des Expositions
Acropolis
Musée d'Art Moderne
Nice-Etoile
Théâtre
Gare Routière
VIEUX NICE
Jardin Albert 1er
LE CHATEAU
Port Lympia
Parc Vigier
Gare Maritime
Hôtel Le Méridien
Théâtre de Verdure
See Vieux Nice map for detail
BOULEVARD DE CIMIEZ
AVENUE DES ARENES DE CIMIEZ
AVENUE GENERAL ESTIENNE
AV. BELLANDA
R. MONTE CROCE
BOULEVARD JEAN-BAPTISTE VERANY
AVENUE VELROSE
AV. GEORGE V
R. DR. MENARD
AVENUE MALAUSSENA
AVENUE MIRABEAU
AUTOROUTE URBAINE SUD
BOULEVARD RAIMBALDI
RUE ASSALIT
RUE PERTINAX
RUE DE PARIS
RUE DE LEPANTE
R. LAMARTINE
RUE TRACHEL
Tunnel Marlaux
AV. EMILE BIECKERT
AVENUE DESAMBROIS
AVENUE DES DIABLES BLEUS
AVENUE GALLIENI
BOULEVARD RISSO
AVENUE DE LA REPUBLIQUE
RUE BEAUMONT
RUE RIBOTTI
R. AUGUSTE GAL
RUE BARLA
PLACE DU PIN
RUE BONAPARTE
PLACE M. BAIL
RUE LASCARIS
RUE CASSINI
PLACE GARIBALDI
R. CATHERINE SEGURANE
R. PAIROLIERE
R. DU COLLET
AV. ST JEAN-BAPTISTE
PLACE SASSERNO
R. P. DEVOLUY
BOULEVARD DUBOUCHAGE
RUE BISCARRA
AVENUE JEAN MEDECIN
R. DE LA SUISSE
RUE PAGANINI
RUE D'ANGLETERRE
AV. DURANTE
RUE PASTORELLI
RUE PLACAS
RUE G. DELOYE
R. ALBERT
RUE DE HOTEL DES POSTES
RUE GIOFFREDO
R. CHAUVAIN
AVENUE FELIX FAURE
BOULEVARD JEAN JAURES
AV. ROSSETTI
VICTOR HUGO
R. ALPHONSE KARR
RUE DU MARECHAL JOFFRE
R. LONGCHAMP
R. DE LA LIBERTE
PLACE GRIMALDI
PLACE MAGENTA
RUE DE BUFFA
RUE MASSENA
AV. GUSTAV V
AV. DE VERDUN
PL. MASSENA
R. ALEXANDRE MARI
R. ST FRANCOIS DE PAULE
QUAI DES ETATS-UNIS
QUAI RAUBA CAPEU
PLACE GUYNEMER
RUE EMMANUEL PHILIBERT
QUAI LUNEL
PL. ILE DE BEAUTE
BD. CARNOT
BD. LEC WALESA
C. DES DEUX-EMMANUEL
BOULEVARD DE STALINGRAD
N
0
500 m

location in Vieux Nice, with a warm atmosphere and small rooms. ❸

Du Centre 2 Rue Suisse ⓣ04.93.88.83.85; ⓔhotel-centre@webstore.fr. No-nonsense tourist place, and one of Nice's more gay-friendly hotels. ❸

Les Cigales 16 rue Dalpozzo ⓣ04.97.03.10.70, ⓦwww.hotel-lescigales.com. Stylishly refurbished tourist hotel with simple decor; quiet and close to the beach. ❼

Cronstadt 3 rue Cronstadt ⓣ04.93.82.00.30, ⓔreservation@hotelcronstadt.com. Hidden inside the garden courtyard of a large residential block, slightly gloomy but extremely tranquil and near the seafront, with old-fashioned, clean and comfortable rooms. Scheduled for refurbishment. ❹

Hotel Durante 16 av Durante ⓣ04.93.88.84.40, ⓦwww.hotel-durante.com. Great value mid-range hotel, with smart, pretty rooms and an attractive garden. ❹

Floride 42 bd de Cimiez ⓣ04.93.53.11.02, ⓦwww.hotel-floride.fr. Charming small hotel in Cimiez, close to the Chagall museum. Free private parking. ❸

Le Grimaldi 15 rue Grimaldi ⓣ04.93.16.00.24, ⓦwww.le-grimaldi.com. Highly-regarded, smart and central, with chic, individually-designed rooms. ❻

Negresco 37 Promenade des Anglais ⓣ04.93.16.64.00, ⓦwww.hotel-negresco-nice.com. This legendary seafront palace hotel is a national historical landmark. It's a genuine one-off, with two top-class restaurants, its own private beach and all the luxury you'd expect. ❾

Nouvel Hotel 19bis, bd Victor Hugo ⓣ04.93.87.15.00, ⓦwww.nouvel-hotel.com. Refurbished *belle époque* hotel in a central location, close to av Jean Médecin. ❻

L'Oasis, 23 rue Gounod ⓣ04.93.88.12.29, ⓦwww.hotel-oasis-nice.com.fr. In a quiet and leafy setting, with small, modern rooms: breakfast is served in the garden. ❺

Les Orangers 10 bis av Durante ⓣ04.93.87.51.41, ⓕ04.93.82.57.82. A backpackers' favourite, close to the station and with a choice of no-nonsense dorms or surprisingly spacious doubles. Closed Nov. ❷

Palais Maeterlinck 30 bd Maurice Maeterlinck ⓣ04.92.00.72.00, ⓦwww.palais-maeterlinck.com. Stunning resort hotel on a steeply terraced site between Nice and Villefranche, with great views. It has a wonderful al fresco restaurant and a funicular railway down to the sea. ❾

La Pérouse 11 quai Rauba-Capeu ⓣ04.93.62.34.63, ⓦwww.hroy.com/la-perouse. Quite simply the best-situated hotel in central Nice, at the foot of Le Château with views across the bay and a wonderfully peaceful pool area. Very comfortable. ❽

Petit Palais 10 av Émile-Bieckert ⓣ04.93.62.19.11, ⓔpetitpalais@provence-riviera.com). Attractive *belle époque* mansion in hilly Cimiez. Quiet and comfortable. ❺

Petit Trianon 11 rue Paradis ⓣ04.93.87.50.46. Clean and friendly, if basic, hotel close to place Masséna and the Vieille Ville. ❷

Regency 2 rue St-Siagre ⓣ04.93.62.17.44, ⓔh.regency@wanadoo.fr. Self-contained, fairly basic studio apartments for up to four people. Near station, but quiet. ❷

La Résidence 18 ave Durante ⓣ04.93.88.89.45, ⓦwww.hotel-laresidence.com. On a side turning near the gare SNCF, with decent rooms for the price. ❹

Le Royal 23 Promenade des Anglais ⓣ04.93.16.43.00. Vast seafront palace hotel, slightly institutional but good value for the location, with spacious, comfortable rooms. ❺

St-François 3 rue St-François ⓣ04.93.85.88.69. On a busy pedestrian thoroughfare in the Vieille Ville, this basic backpacker hotel is noisy but extremely central. ❷

Trianon 15 av Auber ⓣ04.93.88.30.69, ⓕ04.93.88.11.35. Old-fashioned, but the rooms are big for the price, and some have balconies overlooking a garden square. ❸

Vendôme 26 rue Pastorelli ⓣ04.93.62.00.77, ⓕ04.93.13.40.78. Traditional hotel with high ceilings, chandeliers and smart, comfortable rooms. Friendly staff. ❼

Windsor 11 rue Dalpozzo ⓣ04.93.88.59.35, ⓦwww.hotelwindsornice.com. Fashionable modern boutique-style hotel, with rooms individually designed by artists, a relaxation suite on the top floor and a swimming pool in the verdant courtyard at the back. ❼

Hostels

Backpackers Chez Patrick 32 rue Pertinax ⓣ04.93.80.30.72, ⓔchezpatrick@voila.fr. Close to the station, with kitchen facilities and no curfew. €20 per dorm bed.

Clairvallon Relais International de la Jeunesse 26 av Scudéri ⓣ04.93.81.27.63, ⓕ04.93.53.35.88. Slightly cheaper than the youth hostel but 10km north of the centre and with a 10.30pm curfew. Location apart, it's pleasantly informal and has a pool; take bus #15 (stop Scudéri). Reception closes 6pm. €16 per dorm bed.

HI youth hostel rte Forestière du Mont-Alban ⓣ04.93.89.23.64, ⓕ04.92.04.03.10. Four kilometres out of town and not a lot cheaper than sharing a hotel room. Take bus #14 from pl Masséna (direction pl du Mont-Boron, stop L'Auberge); the last bus from the centre leaves at 7.30pm. Curfew 11.30pm. €14 per dorm bed. Reception 7am–noon & 5–11pm. Open Jan–Oct.

The City

It doesn't take long to get a feel for the layout of **Nice**. Shadowed by mountains that curve down to the Mediterranean east of its port, it still breaks up more or less into old and new. Vieux Nice groups beneath the hill of **Le Château**, its limits signalled by boulevard Jean-Jaurès, built along the course of the **River Paillon**. Along the seafront, the celebrated **promenade des Anglais** runs for 5km until forced to curve inland by the runways of the airport. The central square, **place Masséna**, is at the bottom of the modern city's main street, **avenue Jean-Médecin**, while off to the north is the exclusive hillside suburb of **Cimiez**.

Le Château

For initial orientation, with brilliant sea and city views, fresh air, a cooling waterfall and the scent of Mediterranean vegetation, the best place to head for is the park of **Le Château** (daily: April, May & Sept 9am–7pm; June–Aug 9am–8pm; Oct–March 10am–5.30pm). In fact, there's no château here; the city's fortress was destroyed by the French in the early eighteenth century when Nice belonged to Savoy. But this is where Nice began as the ancient Greek city of Nikea: hence the mosaics and stone vases in mock Grecian style. Excavations have revealed Greek and Roman levels beneath the foundations of the city's first, eleventh-century cathedral on the eastern side of the summit. Rather than ruin-spotting, however, the real pleasure here lies in looking down on the scrambled rooftops and gleaming mosaic tiles of Vieux Nice, on the yachts and fishing boats in the port on the eastern side, along the sweep of the promenade des Anglais, and of course at the sea itself in the smooth arc of the Baie des Anges between Antibes and the rock on which you stand. At the top of the hill a viewing platform points out the direction of St Petersburg among other places. In the **cemetery** to the north of the park are buried the two great Niçois revolutionaries, Giuseppe Garibaldi and Léon Gambetta, though casual visitors aren't particularly welcome. A moving Jewish war memorial includes an urn of ashes from the crematoria of Auschwitz.

To reach the park, you can either take the lift (€0.60) by the **Tour Bellanda**, at the eastern end of quai des États-Unis, or climb the steps from rue de la Providence or rue du Château in Vieux Nice.

Vieux Nice

Only a handful of years ago, any expat or police officer would tell you that picturesque **Vieux Nice** was a dangerous place, brimming with drug-pushers,

Museum charges

Most of Nice's museums used to be free, but since the city's financial troubles resulting from Médecin's embezzling reign, **free admission** is now limited to the first and third Sunday of each month. At all other times, the entrance charge is approximately €4 per museum, but it makes much more sense to buy the €6 **seven-day pass**, which is valid for all the city's museums, with the exception of the Musée Chagall and the Musée Départmental des Arts Asiatiques.

The galleries of Vieux Nice

Vieux Nice has more than its fair share of commercial art galleries. **Galerie des Ponchettes**, 77 quai des États-Unis (Tues–Sun 10am–6pm; free), and the neighbouring **Galerie de la Marine**, 59 quai des États-Unis (Tues–Sun 10am–6pm; free), both host temporary exhibitions displaying the work of promising young artists. **Espace Sainte Réparate**, 4 rue St-Réparate (Tues–Sun 10am–6pm; free), is a municipal gallery that loans out works to schools and institutions. Also worth tracking down are **Galerie Renoir**, 8 rue de la Loge on the corner of rue Droite (Tues–Sun 10am–6pm; free), and, diagonally opposite at 14 rue Droite, the **Galerie du Château/Espace Photographique Quinto Albicocco** (Tues–Sun 10am–6pm; free).

muggers and car thieves. That was always a gross exaggeration, but it still reveals how much the teeming *quartier* has changed. Over the last twenty years or so most of the former residents – ethnic minorities and native Niçois alike – have moved out and a host of restaurants, souvenir shops and classy commercial art galleries have moved in. Yet Vieux Nice certainly doesn't feel sanitized: its dark and mysterious side alleys are resistant to over-prettification and alongside the galleries and elegant home-furnishing boutiques ordinary life goes on. Clothes lines are strewn high across the streets and in summer there's an almost Neapolitan vibrancy and chaos to the place. What is undeniable, however, is the extent to which Vieux Nice today is dominated by tourism: throbbing with life day and night during August, much of it seems eerie and deserted in winter.

The streets of Vieux Nice are too narrow for buses and much of it is effectively car- (though not necessarily scooter-) free. It's an area made for walking. The central square is **place Rossetti** where the soft-coloured Baroque **Cathédrale de St-Réparate** just manages to be visible from the eight narrow streets which meet here. There are cafés to relax in, with the choice of sun or shade, and a magical ice-cream parlour, *Fenocchio*, with an extraordinary choice of flavours.

The real magnet of Vieux Nice, however, is the **cours Saleya**, with its splendidly Baroque **Chapelle de la Miséricorde** (currently closed for renovation, but normally open for Sunday Mass at 10.30am and by guided tour; €3, book through the Palais Lascaris; see opposite), and its adjacent places Pierre-Gautier and Charles-Félix. These wide-open, sunlit spaces, lined with grandiloquent municipal buildings and Italianate chapels, are the site of the city's main **market** (Tues–Sun 6am–1pm), where there are gorgeous displays of fruit, vegetables, cheeses and sausages – along with cut flowers and potted roses, mimosa and other scented plants till 5.30pm. On Monday the stalls sell bric-a-brac and second-hand clothes. On summer nights café and restaurant tables fill the *cours*. Leading west off the *cours*, rue St-François-de-Paule is home to the suitably grand *belle époque* **Opéra**, opened in 1885, with its plush red and gold interior.

Heading north past the **place du Palais de Justice** with its Saturday market of old paintings, books and postcards, the narrow **rue du Marché** and its continuations – rue de la Boucherie, rue du Collet, rue St-François-de-Paule and rue Pairolière – have the atmosphere of a covered market, lined with food stores and invitingly laid out clothes, with special offers and sales year-round. The diminutive **fish market** is in place St-François (Tues–Sun 6am–1pm), its odours persisting till late at night when all the old streets are hosed down with enough water to go paddling. A short detour north from here will bring you to the Baroque **L'Église St-Martin-St-Augustin** on place St-Augustine (open for Mass Sat 4pm & Sun 9am), which contains a fine *Pietá* by Louis Bréa.

Heading back south along Rue Droite, you'll pass the **Palais Lascaris** at no. 15 (daily except Tues; 10am–6pm; closed Nov; free), an extravagantly decorated, seventeenth-century palace built by a family whose arms, engraved on the ceiling of the entrance hall, bear the motto "Not even lightning strikes us". It's all very noble, with frescoes, tapestries and chandeliers, along with a collection of porcelain vases from an eighteenth-century pharmacy. Further down the road, more Baroque splendours can be seen at the seventeenth-century **Église du Gésu**.

Place Masséna and the course of the Paillon

The stately, red-ochre **place Masséna** is the hub of the new town, built in 1835 across the path of the River Paillon, with good views north past fountains and palm trees to the mountains. A balustraded terrace and steps on the south of the square lead to Vieux Nice; the new town lies to the north. To the west, the **Jardins Albert-1er** lead down to the promenade des Anglais; to the east, the **Espace Masséna** provides cooling fountains, and a focus for al fresco music concerts and the city's Christmas decorations. Further east, along the

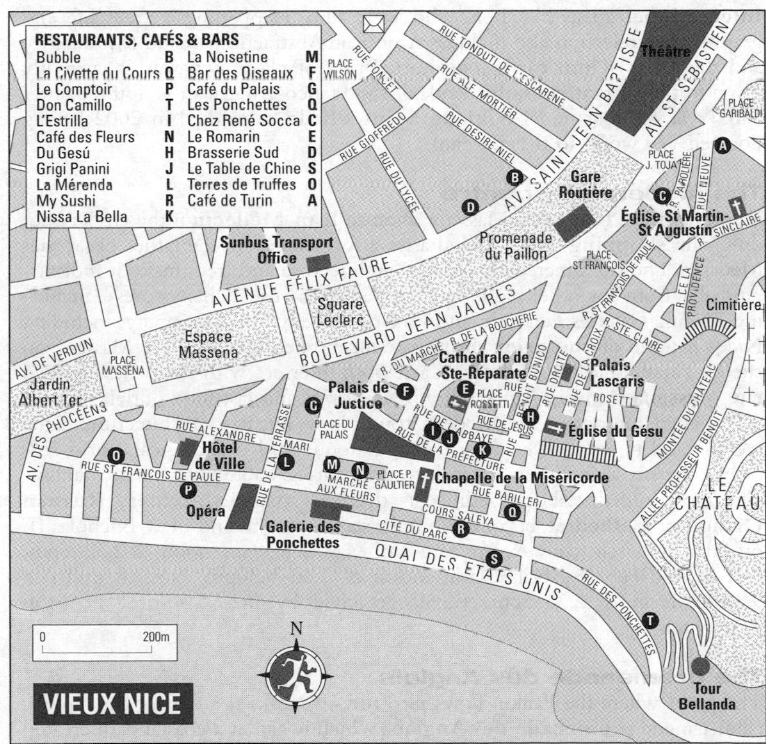

covered course of the Paillon, the **Jardins Suspendus** are an unsuccessful attempt to camouflage car parking with a latter-day hanging garden of Babylon.

The course of the Paillon is the site of the city's more recent municipal prestige projects, which create an unfortunate physical barrier between Vieux Nice and the modern city. The giant, unsubtle concrete **Acropolis** conference centre, up beyond traverse Barla, is the most banal of the buildings, though far more impressive is the vast, futuristic **Musée d'Art Moderne et d'Art Contemporain** (MAMAC; Tues–Sun 10am–6pm; €4), composed of four marble-clad towers linked by steel and glass bridges. It's undeniably a bold and confident work of architecture, though the building's fabric is ageing badly, with cladding panels crumbling, the roof terrace decaying and the beautiful terraced garden permanently closed to visitors. Nevertheless, MAMAC is one of the cultural highlights of Nice and not to be missed. It has a rotating exhibition of its collection of the avant-garde French and American movements of the 1960s to the present. **Pop Art** highlights include Lichtenstein cartoons and Warhol's Campbell's soup tin, while the **French New Realists** are represented in Arman's *The Birds II* – a flock of flying wrenches – and Nice artist Yves Klein's two massive sculptures, *Wall of Fire* and *Garden of Eden*, along with works by other members of the school, including César, Spoerri, Christo and Jean Tinguely. The **Supports-Surfaces** group, led by Alocco, Bioulès and Viallat, take paintings themselves as objects, concentrating on the frame, the texture of the canvas, and so on, and there are also sections on the **Fluxus International** artists like Ben, who were into 'Happenings', street life and graffiti. The collection also includes American Abstractionists and Minimalists, and the 1980s return to figurative art. Pride of place, however, is currently given to the vibrant, colourful work of the Franco-American sculptor, painter and *Vogue* fashion model **Niki de Saint Phalle**, who died in 2002 having donated 170 works to the museum.

The modern city centre

Running north from place Masséna, **avenue Jean-Médecin** is the city's rather dull main **shopping** street, named after a former mayor, the father of Jacques Médecin. The late nineteenth-century architecture and trees make it indistinguishable from any other big French city, as do the usual chain stores – including FNAC, Galeries Lafayette and Virgin. More inviting shopping, including Nice's handful of **couturier shops**, is concentrated west of place Masséna on rue du Paradis and rue Alphonse Karr. Both intersect with the pedestrianized **rue Masséna**, a tourist haunt full of bars, *glaciers* and fast food outlets.

The chief interest of the modern town, however, is its architecture: eighteenth- and nineteenth-century Italian Baroque and Neoclassical, florid *belle époque*, the occasional slice of art deco, and unclassifiable exotic aristo-fantasy. The most gilded, elaborate edifice is the early twentieth-century **Russian Orthodox Cathedral**, beyond the train station, at the end of av Nicholas II, off bd Tsaréwitch (daily except Sun am: May–Sept 9am–noon & 2.30–6pm; Oct & mid-Feb to April 9.15am–noon & 2.30–5.30pm; Nov to mid-Feb 9.30am–noon & 2.30–5pm; €2.50), reached by bus #14 or #17 (stop Tsaréwitch).

The promenade des Anglais

The point where the Paillon flows into the sea marks the start of the famous palm-fringed **promenade des Anglais**, which began as a coastal path created by nineteenth-century English residents for their afternoon stroll. Today it's the city's main traffic artery, bordered by some of the most fanciful architecture on the Côte d'Azur.

Past the first building, the glittery Casino Ruhl, is the 1930s Art Deco facade of the **Palais de la Méditerranée**, all that remains of the original municipal casino, closed due to intrigue and corruption, and finally demolished. A commercial centre is being built behind the old facade. Nearby, at 2 rue du Congrès, **Galerie Ferrero** is something of an institution in the art world, with a collection including works by Yves Klein.

Further along, with its entrance at 65 rue de France, is the **Musée Masséna**, which houses gothic art, primitive paintings, armour and porcelain. It is currently closed for renovation, and is likely to reopen in 2005.

The most celebrated of all the promenade buildings is the opulent **Negresco Hotel** at no. 37, filling up the block between rues de Rivoli and Cronstadt. Built in 1912, it's one of the great surviving European palace-hotels, still independently owned and run. If you are dressed smartly enough you can wander past the liveried doormen to take a look at some of the public rooms. The Salon Louis XIV, on the left of the foyer, has a seventeenth-century painted oak ceiling and mammoth fireplace plus royal portraits that have all come from various French châteaux. The Salon Royale in the centre of the hotel is a vast oval room with a dome built by Gustav Eiffel's workshops. The stucco and cornices are decorated with 24-carat gold leaf, the carpet is the largest ever made by the Savonnerie factory and the bill for it accounted for a tenth of the cost of the hotel. The chandelier is one of a pair commissioned from Baccarrat by Tsar Nicholas II – the other hangs in the Kremlin.

A kilometre or so west and a couple of blocks inland at 33 av des Baumettes, is the **Musée des Beaux-Arts** (Tues–Sun 10am–6pm; €4), housed in a mansion built by a Ukrainian princess in 1878. The museum's highlights include 28 works by Raoul Dufy, the result of a bequest to the city from Mme Dufy. There are also whimsical canvases by Jules Chéret, who died in Nice in 1932, a great many *belle époque* paintings, a room dedicated to Vanloo, plus a bust of Victor Hugo by Rodin and some very amusing Van Dongens, including the *Archangel's Tango*. In addition, works by Monet, Sisley and Degas grace the walls. The museum is reached by bus #38 (stop Chéret).

Further west still, the **Musée International d'Art Naïf Anatole Jakovsky** is behind the promenade and the expressway at av Val-Marie (Mon & Wed–Sun 10am–6pm; €4), and reached by bus #9, #10 or #12 (stop Fabron), then bus #34 (stop Art Naïf). Housed in the Château Ste-Hélène, former home of the parfumier Coty, the museum displays six hundred examples of art naïf from the eighteenth century to the present day, including works by Vivin, Rimbert, Bauchant and the Yugoslavian masters of the art, Yvan, Generaliå and Laakoviå.

Right out by the airport, the **Phoenix Parc Floral de Nice**, 405 promenade des Anglais (Tues–Sun: April–Sept 9am–7pm; Oct–Dec, Feb & March 9am–5pm; €6; exit St-Augustin from the highway or bus #9, #10 or #23 from Nice), is a cross between botanical gardens, bird and insect zoo, and theme park: a curious jumble of automated dinosaurs and mock Mayan temples, alpine streams, ginkgo trees, butterflies and cockatoos. The greenhouse full of fluttering butterflies is the star attraction. The park is also home to the **Musée Départmental des Arts Asiatiques**, beside the lake (Mon & Wed–Sun: May to mid-Oct 10am–6pm; mid-Oct to April 10am–5pm; €5.35). Housed in a beautiful building designed by Japanese architect Kenzo Tange, the museum displays artworks from India, China, Japan and Cambodia, as well as hosting touring exhibitions: there are also regular afternoon tea ceremonies.

The beaches and the port

Although the water is reasonably clean, Nice's beach is pebbly, and the stretch west of Le Château is broken up by fifteen private beaches that, from April to October, charge steep fees to enter. South of Le Château, below the sea wall of the port, the **Plage de Païolle** is a more secluded option, while east of the port a string of rocky coves includes the **Plage de la Réserve** opposite Parc Vigier (bus #32 or #30), and Coco Beach, popular with the local gay community.

The **port**, flanked by gorgeous red-ochre eighteenth-century buildings and headed by the Neoclassical Notre-Dame du Port, is full of bulbous yachts but has little quayside life despite the restaurants along quai Lunel. There is a **flea market** at place Robilante (Tues–Sat 10am–6pm).

Cimiez

Nice's northern suburb, **Cimiez**, has always been posh. The approach up bd de Cimiez is punctuated by vast *belle époque* piles; at the foot of the hill stands the gargantuan *Majestic*, while the summit is dominated by the equally vast *Hotel Régina*, built for a visit by Queen Victoria. The heights of Cimiez were the social centre of the town's elite some 1700 years ago, when the city was capital of the Roman province of Alpes-Maritimes. Part of a small amphitheatre still stands, and excavations of the Roman baths have revealed enough detail to distinguish the sumptuous facilities for the top tax official and his cronies from the plainer public and women's baths. The **archeological site** is overlooked by the impressive, modern **Musée d'Archéologie**, 160 av des Arènes (Mon & Wed–Sun 10am–6pm; €4), which displays all the finds and illustrates the city's history up to the Middle Ages; take bus #15, #17, #20 or #22 to the Les Arènes stop.

Close by is the **Musée Matisse**, 164 av des Arènes (Mon & Wed–Sun 10am–6pm; €4), housed in a seventeenth-century villa painted with *trompe l'oeil*. Matisse wintered in Nice from 1916 onwards, staying in hotels on the promenade – from where he painted *Storm over Nice* – and then from 1921 to 1938 renting an apartment overlooking place Charles-Félix. It was in Nice that he painted his most sensual, colour-flooded canvases featuring models as oriental odalisques posed against exotic draperies. In 1942, when he was installed in the *Régina*, he said that if he had gone on painting in the north "there would have been cloudiness, greys, colours shading off into the distance". As well as the Mediterranean light, Matisse loved the cosmopolitan life of Nice and the presence of fellow artists Renoir, Bonnard and Picasso in neighbouring towns. He returned to the *Régina* from Vence in 1949, having developed his solution to the problem of "drawing in colour" by cutting out shapes and putting them together as collages or stencils. Most of his last works in Nice were these cut-out compositions, with an artistry of line showing how he could wield a pair of scissors as deftly as a paintbrush. He died in Cimiez in November 1954, aged 85.

The museum's collection has work from every period, including an almost complete set of his bronze sculptures. There are sketches for one of the *Dance* murals; models for the Vence chapel plus the priests' robes he designed; book illustrations including those for a 1935 edition of Joyce's *Ulysses*; and excellent examples of his cut-out technique, of which the most delightful are *The Bees* and *The Creole Dancer*. Among the paintings are the 1905 portrait of Madame Matisse; *Storm over Nice* (1919–20), which seems to get wetter and darker the further you step back from it; *Odalisque Casquette Rouge* from the place Charles-Félix years; the 1947 *Still Life with Pomegranates*; and one of his two earliest attempts at oil painting, *Still Life with Books*, painted in 1890.

The Roman remains and the Musée Matisse back onto an old **olive grove**, one of the best open spaces in Nice and venue for the July **jazz festival** (see p.368). At its eastern end on place du Monastère is the **Monastère Notre-Dame de Cimiez** (daily 9am–6pm), with a pink flamboyant Gothic facade of nineteenth-century origin topping a much older and plainer porch. Inside there's more gaudiness, reflecting the rich benefactors the Franciscan order had access to, but also three masterpieces of medieval art: a *Pietá* and *Crucifixion* by Louis Bréa and a *Deposition* by Antoine Bréa. Adjoining the monastery is the **Musée Franciscain** (Mon–Sat 10am–noon & 3–6pm; free), which paints a picture of the mendicant friars and relates the gruesome fate that befell some early martyrs. You can also look into the first cloister of the sixteenth-century **monastic buildings**, and visit the peaceful **gardens**. To the north of the monastery is the **cemetery** where Matisse and Raoul Dufy are buried.

At the foot of Cimiez hill, just off bd Cimiez on av du Docteur-Menard, **Chagall's Biblical Message** is housed in a perfect custom-built museum (Mon & Wed–Sun: July–Sept 10am–6pm; Oct–June 10am–5pm; €5.49, €6.71 during temporary exhibitions), opened by the artist in 1972. The rooms are light, white and cool, with windows allowing you to see the greenery of the garden beyond the pinky red shades of the *Song of Songs* canvases. The seventeen paintings are all based on the Old Testament and are complemented by etchings and engravings. To the building itself, Chagall contributed a mosaic, the painted harpsichord and the *Creation of the World* stained-glass windows in the auditorium. To get there, take bus #15 (stop Musée Chagall).

The Villa Arson

The **Villa Arson**, 20 av Stephen-Liégeard (July–Sept daily 1–7pm; Oct–June Tues–Sun 1–6pm; free; bus #36 stop Villa Arson), lies in the district of St-Barthélemy, also in the north of the city but much further west than Cimiez. It is an unlikely mix of seventeenth-century mansion surrounded by 1960s concrete construction and houses a national school for the plastic arts and an international centre for the teaching of contemporary art. Along with several exhibitions a year and displays of work by pupils, the school has fantastic views over the city to the sea, a pleasant garden to lounge about in, a cafeteria, bookshop and a very friendly, unelitist atmosphere.

Just to the south, at 59 av St-Barthélemy, the **Prieuré du Vieux Logis** (Wed, Thurs, Sat & first Sun of the month 3–5pm; free; bus #5, stop Gorbella) contains a collection of fourteenth- to sixteenth-century furniture, household objects and works of art in a sixteenth-century farm, turned into a priory by a Dominican father in the 1930s.

Eating and drinking

Nice is a great place for **food**, whether you're picnicking on market fare, snacking on **Niçois specialities** like *pan bagnat* (a bun stuffed with tuna, salad and olive oil), *salade niçoise*, *pissaladière* (onion tart with anchovies) or *socca* (a chickpea flour pancake), or dining in the palace hotels. The **Italian** influence is strong, with pasta on every menu; **seafood** and **fish** are also staples, with good *bourride* (fish soup), *estocaficada* (stockfish and tomato stew), and all manner of sea fish grilled with fennel or Provençal herbs. The local Bellet wines from the hills behind the city provide the perfect light accompaniment. For **snacks**, many of the cafés sell sandwiches with typically Provençal fillings such as fresh basil, olive oil, goats' cheese and *mesclum*, the unique green-salad mix of the region.

Despite the usual fast-food chains and tourist traps dotted around, most areas of Nice have plenty of reasonable **restaurants**. Vieux Nice has a dozen on every street catering for a wide variety of budgets, while the port quaysides have excellent, though pricey, fish restaurants. From June till September it's wise to **reserve** tables, or turn up before 8pm, especially in Vieux Nice.

Vieux Nice restaurants

The restaurants below are all marked on the Vieux Nice map on p.361

Café des Fleurs 13 cours Saleya ☎04.93.62.31.33. Huge salads and *bruschetta*, plus a grandstand view of the flower market. Menu at €13.75. Open daily.

Café de Turin 5 pl Garibaldi ☎04.93.62.29.52. Queues around the block for the spectacular seafood at this restaurant on the edge of Vieux Nice. Plateaux de fruits de mer from €15.50. There are seafood stalls in the street outside if you get tired of waiting. Open daily.

Chez René Socca 2 rue Miralhéti, off rue Pairolière ☎04.93.92.05.73. The cheapest meal in town: you can buy helpings of *socca, pissaladière*, stuffed peppers, pasta or calamares at the counter and eat with your fingers on stools ranged haphazardly across the street; the bar opposite serves the drinks. Closed Mon & Nov.

Le Comptoir 20 rue St-François-de-Paule ☎04.93.92.08.80. Very chic 1930s-style brasserie by the Opéra. Serves superb sea bass in salt crust, though the waiting staff can be a little superior and unhelpful. Menu from €30. Evenings only until 1am, closed Sun.

Don Camillo 5 rue des Ponchettes ☎04.93.85.67.95. A strong Italian influence, and ingredients straight from the cours Saleya market. Menus from €29. Closed Sun.

L'Estrilla 13 rue de l'Abbaye ☎04.93.62.62.00. Reservations essential in summer for this popular restaurant that serves superb *petites fritures* and paella in huge earthenware pots. Around €15 to €20. Closed Mon midday & Sun.

Du Gesú 1 place du Jésus ☎04.93.62.26.46. Extremely popular restaurant with a great atmosphere, serving no-nonsense Niçois/Provençal food, including good *daube* and pizzas. In an attractive church square in the heart of Vieux Nice. Pizzas from €6.50, main courses from €9.50. Closed Sun.

Grigi Panini 5 rue St-Réparate. Hot *panini* from the counter, plus plats du jour.

La Mérenda 4 rue de la Terrasse. The menu scribbled up on a blackboard usually includes courgette fritters, fresh pasta with pistou, *trulle* (a Niçois black pudding) and gorgeous chocolate mousse. À la carte only, from €11. Closed Mon, Sat, Sun, Feb & Aug.

My Sushi 18 cours Saleya ☎04.93.62.13.32. Chic and reasonably priced sushi bar, with menus at €13, €19 and €24. Open daily until 11pm.

Nissa La Bella 6 rue Ste-Réparate ☎04.93.62.10.20. Good pizzas, *daube de bouef* and other Provençal specialities washed down with good-value *pichets* of house wine. Menu €18.50. Closed all day Tues; Wed & Thurs lunchtime.

La Noisetine cours Saleya, near rue Gassin. One of the cheapest places to eat on the cours Saleya, with generous and tasty crêpes, huge salads from €7, nice desserts and fresh fruit juices. Occasionally brusque service. Open till midnight.

Le Romarin 2/4 pl de la Halle aux Herbes ☎04.93.85.65.20. A plum Vieux Nice position on a small square, and generous portions of Niçois specialities. Mixed crowd of tourists and locals. Menus from €14. Closed out of season all day Mon & Tues lunch; summer closed Mon, Tues & Wed lunchtimes.

Le Table de Chine 57 quai des États-Unis ☎04.93.80.94.70. Chinese cuisine amid stunning decor including aquariums in the floor, plus views of the sea. From €15. Closed Wed.

Terres de Truffes 11 rue St-François-de-Paule ☎04.93.62.07.68. Fashionable, but intimate and tasteful restaurant with dishes based on a wide variety of fresh truffles. Highly recommended. From €7 to €35.

Greater Nice restaurants

The restaurants below are all marked on the Nice map on pp.356–357

L'Âne Rouge 7 quai des Deux-Emmanuel ☎04.93.89.49.63. Lobster is the speciality of this port-side gourmet's palace: grilled, baked or stuffed into little cabbages. Sea bass on a bed of fresh asparagus, turbot with salmon eggs, and the creamiest *bourride* are some of the other delights. Classic and very expensive. Menus from €24. Closed all day Wed, Thurs lunch & most of Jan.

L'Antre d'Or 19 av Audiffret. Good, affordable Chinese and Vietnamese food in the northern suburbs; around €7 to €10. Closed Sat.

Chantecler and La Rotonde Hôtel Negresco, 37 promenade des Anglais ⓣ04.93.16.64.00. The *Chantecler* is the best restaurant in Nice, with seriously expensive à la carte, but chef Dominique Le Stanc provides a lunchtime menu, including wine and coffee, for €50, which will give you a good idea of how sublime Niçois food is at its best. At *La Rotonde* you can taste less fancy but still mouthwatering dishes on the €22.50 or €29 menus. Open daily.

Chez Bière et Sardines 20 Rue Arson ⓣ04.93.26.63.46. Gay/lesbian restaurant north of the port, with varied tapas menu and eccentric decor. Around €13. Closed Mon.

Chez Flo 4 rue Sacha-Guitry ⓣ04.93.13.38.38. Wonderful big brasserie in the grand, Parisian manner, serving *choucroute, confit de canard*, seafood and great *crème brûlée* in the Art Deco surroundings of a theatre where Mistinguett and Piaf performed. Lunch menu €19.50, evening €29. Last orders midnight. Open daily.

Karr 10 rue Alphonse Karr ⓣ04.93.82.18.31. Elegantly modern restaurant with an international menu of grilled fish, chicken and steak. Popular pit stop for the designer shopping crowd. Two courses €12.95; three courses €15.95.

Le Nautique 20 Quai Lunel ⓣ04.93.26.77.79. Good, simply prepared seafood and a relaxed atmosphere. Swordfish €13; menus at €13 and €20. Open daily.

Socca d'Or 45 rue Bonaparte ⓣ04.93.56.52.93. Extremely cheap socca and pizza a few blocks back from the port. Closed Tues & Wed.

Virginie 2 pl A-Blanqui ⓣ04.93.55.10.07. Pizza and excellent *plateau des fruits de mer*, close to the Acropolis. Open daily.

Cafés and bars

The bars and cafés below are all marked on the Vieux Nice map on p.361, except Grand Café de Lyon *and* The Seventies, *which are marked on the Nice map on pp.356–357.*

Bar des Oiseaux 9 rue St-Vincent. Named for the birds that fly down from their nests in the loft and the pet parrot and screeching myna bird that perch by the door. Serves delicious baguette sandwiches. Erratic opening hours, closed Tues from mid-Aug to mid-Sept; live jazz some evenings.

Brasserie Sud 10 Félix Faure. Grungy, laid-back café bar with good value *panini*. Open until 2.30am at weekends.

Bubble 10 Félix Faure. Self-consciously trendy bar attracting a cute crowd. Cocktails €7.50 before 9pm, € 8.50 after. Daily until 2.30am.

Le Café du Palais Place du Palais. Prime al fresco lounging spot on the handsome square by the Palais de Justice.

Grand Café de Lyon 33 av Jean Médecin. One of the more attractive big *terrasse* cafés on the main street.

Les Ponchettes and La Civette du Cours cours Saleya. At Le Château end of the marketplace, neighbouring cafés with cane seats fanning out a good 50m from the doors. Open late in summer.

The Seventies 24 quai Lunel. Groovy port-side bar-restaurant with food, cocktails and gaudy, Bond villain 1970s decor.

Nightlife

Pubs have long been a very popular element of Nice nightlife, particularly with the young. For the older, more affluent generation, the luxury **hotel bars** with their jazzy singers and piano accompaniment have justly held sway for decades, as an essential ingredient of Riviera nightlife. There are plenty of **discos**, too, and, particularly in Vieux Nice, a wide choice of venues for drinking and dancing, though the music tends not to be very original. As for the **clubs**, bouncers judging your wallet or exclusive membership lists are the rule.

Bodéguita del Havana 14 rue Chauvain. Wildly popular salsa bar; open daily until 2am.

De Klomp 6 rue Mascoïnat. Dutch-style brown café with 18 beers on draught, plus regular live music. Open daily 7.30pm–2.30am.

Dizzy Club 26 quai Lunel. Bar and mainstream disco; entrance fee including first drink €15, cocktails from €10. Wed–Sun from 11.30pm.

Blue Whales 1 rue Mascoïnat. Intimate venue with friendly atmosphere, and live music after 10pm ranging from Latin to rock. Open daily till 4.30am.

L'Iguane 5 quai des Deux-Emmanuel. Very stylish (and expensive) bar with dance floor. Open Thurs–Sun 8pm–5am.

Pub Oxford 4 rue Mascoïnat. English-style pub, with an excellent range of beers; live music every evening from 9.30pm; closes at 4am.

Le 6 6 rue de la Terrasse. Smart, trendy gay bar, with regular live entertainment including drag, rai

(Algerian funk/rap music) and karaoke. Daily from 9.30pm.

Le Klub 6 rue Halevy. Nice's largest and best gay club attracts a young, stylish crowd including women and some heteros. Open Wed–Sun from midnight.

La Suite 2 rue Bréa. A fashionable late-night disco bar in Vieux Nice. You won't get in unless they like the look of you. Open daily until 2.30am.

O'Hara's Tavern 22 rue Droite. Tiny, long-established Irish folk bar on the corner of rue Rosetti, serving up food and satellite TV sports. Open daily until 2.30am.

Ruby's 2 8 Descente Crotti. Afro-Latin salsa club.

Subway 19 rue Droite. Reasonably priced disco, specializing in reggae, soul and rock. Closed Sun & Mon.

Wayne's 15 rue de la Préfecture. Big, popular bar on the edge of Vieux Nice run by an expat who shares the French penchant for good old rock'n'roll. Fri & Sat nights see live bands performing, of greatly varying quality. Satellite TV sports. Open daily.

Le Zoom 6 cours Saleya. Tapas bar with live soul and acid jazz on Thurs, Fri & Sat nights; reasonable prices. Open daily 6pm–2am.

Entertainment, sport and festivals

Of Nice's many **festivals** – which begin with the Mardi Gras **Carnival** in February – probably the most interesting is the **Festival de Jazz**, staged in the fourth week of July in the amphitheatre and gardens of Cimiez (for details, check ⓦwww.nicejazzfest.com). The city's biggest sporting event is the **Triathlon de Nice** in late September when competitors from all round the world swim 4km in the Baie des Anges, cycle 120km in the hills behind the city and run 30km ending up along the promenade des Anglais.

Nice's **opera**, Opéra de Nice, 4–6 rue St-François-de-Paule (ⓣ04.92.17.40.00), and **theatre**, Théâtre de Nice, promenade des Arts (ⓣ04.93.13.90.90), put on the usual run-of-the-mill stuff, with some of the smaller independent theatres, such as Théâtre de la Cité, 3 rue Paganini (ⓣ04.93.16.82.69), staging the most exciting shows. The best **cinema** is Cinéma Mercury, 16 place Garibaldi (ⓣ08.36.68.81.06), which shows subtitled films in the original language, as do the Cinémathèque de Nice, 3 Esplanade Kennedy (ⓣ04.92.04.06.66), and the Rialto, 4 rue de Rivoli (ⓣ08.36.68.00.41). The major touring **rock concerts** are usually held at the Palais Nikaïa, 163 rte de Grenoble (ⓣ04.92.29.31.29).

The best place for up-to-date **listings** for concerts, plays, films and sporting events is FNAC in the Nice-Étoile shopping complex on av Jean-Médecin, where you can also buy **tickets** for most events.

Listings

Airlines Air France ⓣ0820.820.820; Delta ⓣ0800.35.40.80; Easyjet ⓣ0825.08.25.08.

Airport information ⓣ0820.423.333.

Boat trips Trans Côte d'Azur, quai Lunel (ⓣ04.92.00.42.30, ⓦwww.trans-cote-azur.com) runs summer trips to Îles de Lérins, Cannes, Monaco, St-Tropez and the Esterel.

Bookshop English-language books are available from The Cat's Whiskers, 26 rue Lamartine ⓣ04.93.80.02.66.

Car breakdown Dépannage Côte d'Azur Transport 24hr service ⓣ04.93.29.87.87.

Car parks Acropolis; promenade du Paillon; promenade des Arts; gare SNCF; pl Masséna; and cours Saleya.

Car rental Most firms have offices at the airport and at the gare SNCF, on av Thiers. Try also: Avis, 2 av Phocéens ⓣ04.93.80.63.52; Europcar, 3 av Gustave V ⓣ04.92.14.44.50; or Hertz, 12 av de Suède ⓣ04.93.87.11.87.

Consulate Canada, 10 rue Lamartine ⓣ04.93.92.93.22; UK, 26 av Notre Dame ⓣ04.93.62.13.56; USA, 7 av Gustave V, 3rd floor ⓣ04.93.88.89.55.

Currency exchange American Express, 11 promenade des Anglais; Change Or, 7 av Thiers; Thomas Cook, 13 av. Thiers.

Disabled access Transport for people with reduced mobility ⓣ04.93.96.09.99.

Emergencies SAMU ⓣ15; SOS Médecins ⓣ04.93.85.01.01; Nice Médecins ⓣ04.93.52.42.42; Hôpital St-Roch, 5 rue Pierre-Dévoluy ⓣ04.92.03.33.75; SOS Dentaire ⓣ04.93.76.53.53.

Ferries to Corsica SNCM gare maritime, quai du Commerce ☎04.93.13.66.66, ⓦwww.sncm.fr; Corsica Ferries, quai Amiral Infernet ☎08.25.09.50.95.
Internet Alexso Info, 1 rue de Belgique; Communications Sans Frontières, 25 rue Paganini.
Laundry Assalit, 29 rue Assalit; Best One, 16 rue Pertinax; Lavomatique, 11 rue du Pont-Vieux; and Taxi-Lav, corner of rue Lamartine & Pertinax.
Lost property Police Municipale, 1 rue de la Terrasse ☎04.97.13.44.00; SOS Voyageurs gare SNCF Mon–Fri only ☎04.93.16.02.61.
Pharmacy 7 rue Masséna ☎04.93.87.78.94; open daily 7.30pm–8am.
Police Commissariat Central de Police, 1 av Maréchal-Foch ☎04.92.17.22.22.
Post office PTT, pl Wilson, 06000 Nice; and at 23 av Thiers.
Taxis ☎04.93.13.78.78.
Trains General information and reservations ☎08.36.35.35.35; information on the Chemin de Fer de Provence, 4 bis rue Alfred-Binet ☎08.91.67.68.69.
Youth information Centre Information Jeunesse, 19 rue Gioffredo ☎04.93.80.93.93.

Niçois villages

The **foothills of the Alps** come down to the northern outskirts of Nice, and right down to the sea on the eastern side of the city: a majestic barrier, snow-capped for much of the year, beyond which crest after crest edges higher while the valleys get steeper and livelihoods more precarious. From the sea, the wide course of the Var to the west appears to be the only passage northwards. But the hidden river of Nice, the **Paillon**, also cuts its way to the sea through the mountains past small, fortified medieval settlements. The **Nice–Turin railway line** follows the Paillon for part of its way – one of the many spectacular train journeys of this region. If you have your own transport this is serious, hairpin-bend country where the views are a major distraction. **Buses** from Nice to its villages are infrequent.

With their proximity to the metropolis, the *villages perchés* of **Peillon**, **Peille**, **Lucéram**, **L'Escarène**, **Coaraze** and **Contes** are no longer entirely peasant communities, though the social make-up remains a mix. You may well hear Provençal spoken here and the **traditional festivals** are still communal affairs, even when the participants include the well-off Niçois escaping from the coastal heat. The links between the city and its hinterland are strong: the villagers still live off the land and sell their olives and olive oil, goats' cheese or vegetables and herbs in the city's markets; many city dwellers' parents or grandparents still have homes within the mountains, and for every Niçois this wild and underpopulated countryside is the natural remedy for city stress.

Peillon

For the first 10km or so along the River Paillon, after you leave the last of Nice, the valley is marred by quarries, supplying the city's constant demand for building materials. However, once you reach Peillon's nearest gare SNCF at Ste-Thècle, the road begins to climb, looping for 5km through olive groves, pine forest and brilliant pink and yellow broom before you reach the gates of **PEILLON**'s medieval enclave. By bus from Nice, the closest you can get is the Les Moulins stop, from where it is a 3.5-kilometre uphill walk.

Peillon is beautifully maintained, right up to the lovely place de l'Église at the top. There is very little commerce, save for the gallery of Gabriel Mariani's bronze and wood sculptures in Le Vieux Logis and the craft shop La Maiouneta, and very little life during the week – most of the residents commute to their jobs in Nice. Just outside the village stands the **Chapelle des Pénitents Blancs**, decorated with violent fifteenth-century frescoes similar to those by

Jean Canavesio at La Brigue (see pp.431–432). You can peer through the grille across the chapel door, but you'll have to contact the *mairie* (ⓣ04.93.79.91.04; €1.50) to arrange a closer look inside. From the chapel a path heads off across the hills northwards to Peille. It's a two-hour walk along what was once a Roman road, and a more direct route than going via the valley.

Peillon has an extremely attractive **hotel-restaurant**, *Auberge de la Madone* (ⓣ04.93.79.91.17, ⓕ04.93.79.99.36; booking essential; closed late Oct to mid-Dec & middle two weeks of Jan; ❻), with balconies overlooking the valley. If you're on a tighter budget, try *Le Pourtail*, under the same management, across the street (❷), or the two-star **campsite**, *La Laune*, at the *Moulins de Peillon*, chemin des Prés (ⓣ04.93.79.91.61; closed Nov–April). The **restaurant** at the *Auberge de la Madone* (closed Wed) is excellent, offering a *menu gastronomique* at €50, with à la carte costing €75–80.

Peille

PEILLE lies 6.5km of hairpin bends above its gare SNCF in the valley below. The atmosphere here is very different to that in Peillon. It was excommunicated several times for refusing to pay its bishop's tithes, and the republicanism of the small town was later manifested by the domed thirteenth-century Chapelle de St-Sébastien being turned into the **Hôtel de Ville**, and the Chapelle des Pénitents Noirs into a communal **oil press**. Peille claims to be the birthplace of the Roman emperor Pertinax who was assassinated within thirteen weeks of his election on account of his egalitarian and democratic tendencies.

The main square, **place de la Colle**, is graced with a Gothic fountain and two half-arches supporting a Romanesque pillar. It's also home to the medieval **court house** bearing a plaque recalling Peille's transfer of its rights over Monaco to Genoa. On nearby rue St-Sébastien the former salt tax office, the **Hôtel de la Gabelle**, still stands. Peille's small **Musée du Terroir** on pl de l'Armée (Sat & Sun only) is fascinating, not so much for the exhibits but because the captions are written in the village's own dialect, Peillasque. The only thing detracting from the beauty of the village is the view to the southwest, marred by the cement-quarrying around La Grave, its suburb down in the valley by the rail line. You can, however, take labyrinthine winding routes to La Turbie, Ste-Agnes or L'Escarène from the village, on which precipitous panoramas – and slow progress – are assured.

Regular weekday **buses** make the connection between Peille's **gare SNCF** and the village. If you want to **stay** you'll need to have booked in advance at Peille's one **hotel-restaurant**, *Le Belvédère* (ⓣ04.93.79.90.45; ❸; closed Dec), at the western entrance to the village. *Restaurant Cauvin/Chez Nana* on place Carnot (ⓣ04.93.79.90.41; closed Tues & Wed; menu at €17) does a great Sunday lunch with real Provençal cooking and a generous choice of hors d'oeuvres; or you can snack at the *Havana K'fe* and *L'Absinthe* (closed Tues) **bars** at the end of rue Centrale, where *panini* cost €4.

L'Escarène

At **L'ESCARÈNE** the rail line leaves the Paillon and heads northeast to **Sospel**. In the days before rail travel, this was an important staging post on the road from Nice to Turin, when drivers would rig up new horses to take on the thousand-metre Braus pass, which the rail line now tunnels under. The village's single-arched bridge (rebuilt after its destruction in World War II) was the crucial river crossing, yet the people who first lived beside it obviously mistrusted all travellers; their houses had no windows overlooking the river, nor any doors, and access was by retractable ladders.

If you want to stop off for the day – there's nowhere to stay – head for the beautiful **place de l'Église** surrounded by pale yellow, green and ochre houses; opposite the great Baroque church is the *Café de l'Union* bar.

Lucéram

Following the Paillon upstream for 6km from L'Escarène, you pass the fifteenth-century **Chapelle de St-Grat** with frescoes by Jean Beleison, a colleague of Louis Bréa. Just 1km further on, clinging to the side of the valley, the village of **LUCÉRAM** has the friendliness of a still-peasant community, full of thin cats and mangy dogs. Its communal oil press remains in service and at the start of the olive season in October the villagers dip their traditional *brissaudo* – toasted garlic bread – in the virgin oil. At Christmas the shepherds bring their flocks into church and after Mass make their offerings of dried figs and bread.

Above the village houses, the belfry of **Ste-Marguerite** rises in defiance, its Baroque cupola glittering with polychrome Niçois tiles (Wed–Sun 10am–noon & 2–6pm). Inside, you can see some of the best late-medieval artworks in the Comté de Nice, though several have been removed and taken to Nice's Musée Masséna (see p.363). All these works belong to the School of Nice, and both the Retable de Ste-Marguerite, framed by a tasteless Baroque baldaquin, and the painting of Saints Peter and Paul, with its cliff-hanging castle in the distance, are attributed to Louis Bréa. There are more local landscapes in the Retable de St-Antoine, painted on flamboyant Gothic panelling, with generous additions of gold, and said to be by Jean Canavesio. Popular art is present in a thirteenth-century plaster *Pietà*, probably by a local craftsman, to the left of the choir, and the black and red processional lanterns kept in the choir.

You can see more examples of work by Jean Beleison, who painted the walls and ceilings of the **Chapelle de Notre-Dame de Bon Coeur**, 2km north-west of the village off the road to the St-Roch pass. Although you can't go inside the chapel, you can view the paintings from outside.

Lucéram has a small **tourist office** on place Adrien Barralis (daily 9am–noon & 2–6pm; ⓣ04.93.79.46.50), and one **hotel**, the *Hotel Restaurant de la Méditerranée*, 1 pl Adrien Barralis (ⓣ04.93.91.35.65; menus from €23; closed Mon; ❸). There's a small cluster of eating places around the *Mairie*, including pizzeria *Bocca Fina*, with menus at €14.

Coaraze

COARAZE overlooks the valley of the Paillon de Contes, a tributary running west of the main Paillon. From Lucéram and the pass of St-Roch the road hangs over near-vertical descents, turning corners onto great open views of these beautiful but inhospitable mountains.

The population of Coaraze is less than five hundred, though this is one of the more chic Niçois villages, with many an artist and designer in residence. The facades of the post office and *mairie*, and place Félix-Giordan near the top of the village, are decorated with **sundials** signed by various artists including Cocteau and Ponce de Léon. The latter decorated the **Chapelle Notre-Dame du Gressier** just north of the village in 1962, known now as the Chapelle Bleu from the single colour he used in the frescoes. Place Félix-Giordan also has a **lizard mosaic** and a Provençal poem engraved in stone. The church, destroyed and rebuilt three times, is famous for the number of angels in its interior decoration, 118 in all.

Coaraze has a volunteer-run **tourist office** on place A-Mari below the village (Tues–Sat 10am–noon & 2.30–5pm; Mon 10am–noon; Sun 9–11.30am; ⓣ04.93.79.37.47), which has the key to the church and chapel. There's also an excellent **hotel-restaurant**, the *Auberge du Soleil*, 5 chemin de la Bégude (ⓣ04.93.79.08.11, ⓕ04.93.79.37.79; ❹), with wonderful views from the rooms and the dining terrace. Access is on foot only, but you won't be expected to drag your cases up yourself.

Contes

The story always told about **CONTES**, 9km downstream from Coaraze, is of its **caterpillar plague** in 1508, which was so bad the bishop of Nice had to be called in to exorcise the leaf-eating army. With the full weight of ecclesiastical law the caterpillars were sentenced to exile on the slopes of Mont Macaron on the other side of the valley. A procession to the mountain was organized with all the villagers plus saintly relics, holy oil and so forth, and lo and behold, every last caterpillar joined the ranks and never bothered Contes again.

Contes has spread down the valley from its old village, and is quite a major town for these parts with a population of over four thousand, though there's nowhere to stay and no real reason to either. The **tourist office** is on place A-Olivier in the modern town (Mon–Sat 2–5pm; ⓣ04.93.79.13.99, ⓦwww.ville-contes.fr); buses #300 and #302 leave from the square for Haute Contes.

Châteauneuf-de-Contes

Across the river from Contes a road winds up the mountainside to **CHÂTEAUNEUF-DE-CONTES**, a hilltop gathering of houses around an eleventh-century Romanesque church. About 2km further on a path to the left leads to a more recent but **ruined village**, also called Châteauneuf-de-Contes, which was last inhabited before World War I. That this village was abandoned gradually is evident from the varying degrees of building decay and vegetation growth. Ivy-clad towers and crumbling walls rise up among once-cultivated fig trees and rose bushes, and insects buzz in the silence and butterflies flit about the wild flowers that have replaced the gardens. The crescent of walled terraces where the people grew their vegetables is still clearly defined. The passing of time rather than some cataclysm saw its decline – there are no ghosts, nor even a whiff of eerieness; just immense, unthreatening horizons on either side.

Apart from the odd railings around the most insecure bits of masonry, there are no gates or fences and you can wander around at any time of the day or night. On the Monday of Pentecost the inhabitants of the surviving village make a pilgrimage to the ruins which finishes with a communal meal.

The corniches

Three **corniche roads** run east from Nice to the independent principality of Monaco and on to Menton, the last town of the French Riviera. Napoleon built the **Grande Corniche** on the route of the Romans' Via Julia Augusta. The **Moyenne Corniche** dates from the first quarter of the twentieth century, when aristocratic tourism on the Riviera was already causing congestion on the coastal road, the **Corniche Inférieure**. The upper two are popular for shooting car commercials, and action films. They're dangerous roads: Grace

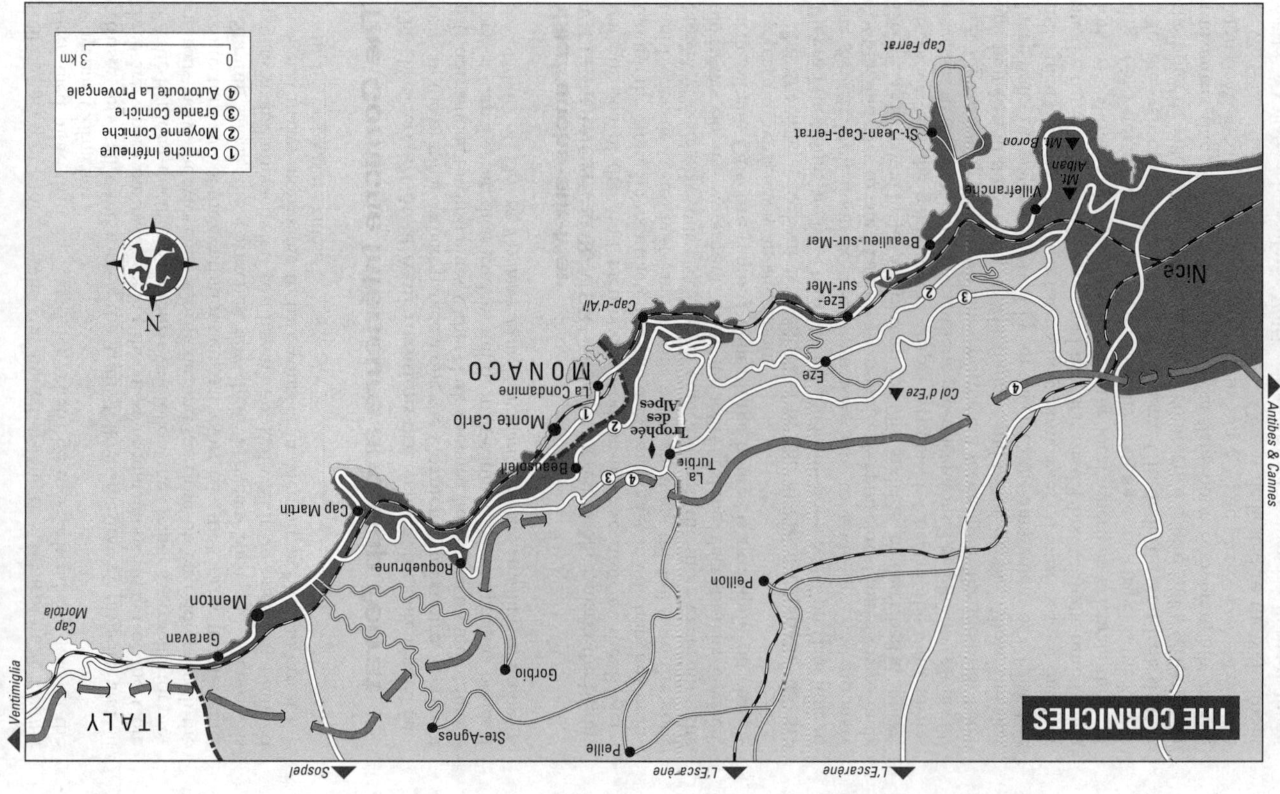
THE CORNICHES
Ventimiglia
ITALY
Cap Mortola
Garavan
Menton
Sospel
Cap Martin
Ste-Agnes
Gorbio
Roquebrune
Monte Carlo
Beausoleil
La Condamine
MONACO
Peille
L'Escarène
Trophée des Alpes
La Turbie
Cap-d'Ail
Peillon
L'Escarène
Eze
Eze-sur-Mer
Beaulieu-sur-Mer
Col d'Eze
St-Jean-Cap-Ferrat
Cap Ferrat
Villefranche
Mt. Boron
Mt. Alban
Nice
Antibes & Cannes
N
① Corniche Inférieure
② Moyenne Corniche
③ Grande Corniche
④ Autoroute La Provençale
0
3 km

Kelly, princess of Monaco, who was filmed driving the cornices in *To Catch a Thief*, died more than 25 years later when she took a bend too fast on the Moyenne Corniche.

Buses serve all three routes; the **train** follows the lower corniche; and all three are superb means of seeing the most mountainous stretch of the Côte d'Azur. For long-distance panoramas you follow the Grande Corniche; for precipitous views the Moyenne Corniche; and for close-up encounters with the architectural riot of the continuous coastal resort, take the Corniche Inférieure.

Staying along the corniches, anywhere between Nice and Menton, is expensive and impractical if you haven't booked well in advance. On a limited budget it makes more sense to base yourself in Menton or Nice and treat the corniches as pleasure rides.

The Corniche Inférieure and Cap Ferrat

The characteristic **Côte d'Azur mansions** that represent the unrestrained fantasies of the original owners parade along the **Corniche Inférieure**, a series of pale dots among the lush pines. Others lurk screened from view on the promontory of **Cap Ferrat**, their gardens full of man-eating cacti and piranha ponds if the plethora of *'Défense d'entrer – Danger de Mort'* signs are anything to go by.

Villefranche-sur-Mer

VILLEFRANCHE-SUR-MER, the resort closest to Nice, marks the beginning of one of the most picturesque and unspoilt sections of the Riviera, though the cruise liners attracted by the deep anchorage in Villefranche's beautiful bay ensure a steady stream of tour buses climbing the hill from the port. However, as long as your visit doesn't coincide with the shore excursions, the old town on the waterfront, with its active fishing fleet and its covered, medieval **rue Obscure** running beneath the houses, is a tranquil and charming place to while away an afternoon.

The tiny fishing harbour is overlooked by the medieval **Chapelle de St-Pierre** (Tues–Sun: late March to late June 9.30am–noon & 3–7pm; late June to late Sept 9.30am–noon & 4–8.30pm; late Sept to mid-Nov 9.30–noon & 2–6pm; mid-Dec to late March 9.30–noon & 2–5pm; closed mid-Nov to mid-Dec; €2), decorated by **Jean Cocteau** in 1957 in shades he described as "ghosts of colours". In the guide to the chapel written by Cocteau, the artist invites travellers to enter without any aesthetic preconceptions. The ghostly colours fill drawings in strong and simple lines, portraying scenes from the life of St Peter and homages to the women of Villefranche and to the gypsies. Above the altar Peter walks on water supported by an angel, to the amusement of Christ. The fishermen's eyes are drawn as fishes; the ceramic eyes on either side of the door are the flames of the apocalypse and the altar candelabras of night-time fishing forks rise above single eyes. On June 29, the local fishermen celebrate the feast day of St Peter and St Paul with a Mass, the only time the chapel is used.

To the west of the fishing port, the massive **Citadelle de St-Elme** shelters the hôtel de ville, an open-air cinema, a conference centre and a series of **art museums** (June & Sept Mon & Wed–Sat 9am–noon & 3–6pm; July & Aug Mon & Wed–Sat 10am–noon & 3–7pm, Sun 3–7pm; Oct & Dec–May Mon & Wed–Sat 10am–noon & 2–5pm; free). One is dedicated to the voluptuous works of Villefranche sculptor **Volti**, whose bronze woman lies in the fountain outside the citadel gates; another, dedicated to the couple **Henri Goetz** and **Christine Boumeester**, contains two works by Picasso and one by Miró. A third collection, the **Roux**, is devoted to ceramic figurines.

Villefranche's **tourist office** is in the Jardins François-Binon (July & Aug daily; Sept–June Mon–Sat 8.30am–noon & 2–8pm; ⓣ04.93.01.73.68), just below the corniche as it changes from bd Princesse-Grace-de-Monaco to av Albert-1er. Of the local **hotels**, *Pension Patricia*, on chemin des Pépinières, Pont St-Jean (ⓣ04.93.01.06.70, ⓦwww.hotel-patricia.Riviera.fr; ❷; closed mid-Nov to Dec), is a good-value, low-budget option, while the highly recommended *Hôtel Welcome*, 1 quai Amiral-Courbet (ⓣ04.93.76.27.62, ⓕ04.93.76.27.66, ⓦwww.welcomehotel.com; closed mid-Nov to mid-Dec; ❽), is the former convent where Cocteau used to stay, in a prime position overlooking the port. Of the fish **restaurants** on quai Amiral-Courbet, *L'oursin Bleu* (ⓣ04.93.01.90.12; menus from €28) and *La Fille du Pecheur* (€25) are the ones to try, while inland, the welcoming *La Grignotière*, 3 rue du Poilu (ⓣ04.93.76.79.83; closed Wed), is a delightful small restaurant whose excellent €25 menu includes delicious *amuse-bouches*.

Cap Ferrat

Closing off Villefranche's bay to the east is **Cap Ferrat**, justifiably the Côte d'Azur's most desirable address, due to the lack of through traffic and its pretty, indented coast. The one town, **ST-JEAN-CAP-FERRAT**, is a typical Riviera hideout for the wealthy: old houses overlooking modern yachts in a fishing port turned millionaires' resort. The not-too-frequent #111 **bus** service does a circuit of the promontory.

The St-Jean **tourist office** is at 59 av Dénis-Séméria (July & Aug Mon–Sun 8.30am–6pm; Sept–June 8.30am–noon & 1–5pm, ⓣ04.93.76.08.90). Cheaper **hotel** options are thin on the ground, with *La Frégate*, 11 av Denis Séméria (ⓣ04.93.76.04.51, ⓕ04.93.76.14.93; ❸) being the best bet. For deeper pockets, *Brise Marine*, 58 av J-Mermoz (ⓣ04.93.76.04.36, ⓕ04.93.76.11.49; ❼; closed Nov–Jan) has spacious rooms 100m from the sea, while the pleasant *Clair Logis*, 12 av Centrale (ⓣ04.93.76.04.57, ⓦwww.hotel-clair-logis.fr; ❼), boasts a lovely garden and balconies in every room. If you really want to blow your savings, *La Voile d'Or*, av Jean Mermoz (ⓣ04.93.01.13.13, ⓦwww.lavoiledor.fr; ❾), has airy, palatial interiors and a stunning setting overlooking the port.

The best **restaurants** in the area are both on the pleasure port and both have exceptional service: *Le Sloop* (ⓣ04.93.01.48.63; menu at €25; closed Wed out of season) serves prime fish cooked in delicate and original ways; and *La Voile d'Or* (ⓣ04.93.01.13.13; menu at €64; closed Nov to mid-March) provides very sophisticated and imaginative Mediterranean cuisine. There are also cheaper options on the port: *Le Pirate* (ⓣ04.93.76.12.97) serves good-value plats du jour, salads and pasta, while *La Goélette* (ⓣ04.93.76.14.38) dishes up zarzuela and paella for around €20.

East of St-Jean's pleasure port you can follow av Jean-Mermoz then a **coastal path** out along the little peninsula, past the Plage Paloma to **Pointe Hospice**, where a nineteenth-century chapel cowers behind a twelve-metre-high turn-of-the-twentieth-century metal *Virgin and Child*. Back in St-Jean, another coastal path runs from av Claude-Vignon right round to chemin du Roy on the opposite side of the peninsula. At the southernmost point of the Cap you can climb a **lighthouse** for an overview of what you cannot reach – most of Cap Ferrat. Two exceptions to the formidable restrictions of passage are the **zoo** at the northern end of bd Général-de-Gaulle (July & Aug 9.30am–7pm; Sept–June 9.30am–5.30pm; €9.50), in the park of King Léopold of Belgium's old residence, and the Villa Ephrussi on the road from the mainland.

The **Villa Ephrussi** (Feb–Oct daily 10am–6pm/7pm; Nov–Jan Mon–Fri 2–6pm, Sat & Sun 10am–6pm; last entry 30min before closing; €8) was built in 1912 for Baroness Ephrussi née Rothschild, a woman of unlimited wealth and highly eclectic tastes. The result is a wonderful profusion of decorative art, paintings, sculpture and artefacts ranging from the fourteenth to the nineteenth century and from European to Far Eastern origin. Among the highlights are a fifteenth-century d'Enghien tapestry of fabled hunting scenes; paintings by Carpaccio and other works of the Venetian Renaissance; Dresden porcelain; Ming vases; Mandarin robes; and canvases by Monet, Sisley and Renoir. Visits to the villa are unguided, allowing you to wander round at your own pace. In order to make the **gardens**, the baroness had a hill removed to level out the space in front, and then had tons of earth brought back in order that her formal French design could grow above the rock. She named the house after an ocean liner and had her 35 gardeners wear sailors' costumes. They tended Spanish, English, Japanese and Florentine gardens, all on a grand scale with attendant statuary and pools. One part of the park, the eastern slope, remained wild, because funds eventually ran out. In 1915 the baroness divorced and moved to Monaco, after just three years in her extraordinary creation.

Beaulieu

To the eastern side of the Cap Ferrat peninsula, overlooking the pretty Baie des Fourmis and accessible by foot from St-Jean along the promenade Maurice-Rouvier, is **BEAULIEU**, sheltered by a ring of craggy hills that ensures its temperatures are amongst the highest on the Côte, and that the town itself is one of its less developed spots. Beaulieu still has a working harbour, where you can buy freshly caught fish from the quayside, and retains a couple of fine examples of *belle époque* architecture – most notably La Rotonde on av Fernand Dunan, an opulent former hotel. Undoubtedly its most interesting attraction, however, is the **Villa Kérylos** (July & Aug daily 10am–7pm; Feb–June & Sept–Oct daily 10am–6pm; Nov–Jan Mon–Fri 2–6pm, Sat & Sun 10am–6pm; €7.50), a near perfect reproduction of an ancient Greek villa, just east of the casino on av Gustave-Eiffel. The only concessions made by Théodore Reinach, the archeologist who had it built, were glass in the windows, a concealed piano, and a minimum of early twentieth-century conveniences. He lived here for twenty years, eating, dressing and behaving as an Athenian citizen, taking baths with his male friends and assigning separate suites to women. However perverse the concept, it's visually stunning, with faithfully reproduced frescoes, ivory and bronze copies of mosaics and vases, authentic antiquities and lavish use of marble and alabaster.

The **tourist office** on av Georges Clémenceau (July & Aug Mon–Sat 9am–12.30pm & 2–7pm, Sun 9am–12.30pm; Sept–June Mon–Fri 9am–12.15pm & 2–6pm, Sat 9am–12.15pm; ⓣ04.93.01.02.21) is next to the **gare SNCF**, five minutes' walk from Villa Kérylos. A couple of economical **accommodation** options include the family-run *Hôtel Riviera*, at 6 rue Paul-Doumer, right in the centre near the sea (ⓣ04.93.01.04.92, ⓕ04.93.01.19.31; ❸) and *Select*, 1 place Gén-de-Gaulle (ⓣ04.93.01.05.42, ⓕ04.93.01.34.30; ❹), which is basic but clean and comfortable, and excellent value for this part of the coast. For those on a bigger budget, *La Résidence Carlton*, 9 bis av Albert-1er (ⓣ04.93.01.06.02, ⓕ04.93.01.29.62; ❼), has pretty rooms with balconies, 200m from the sea.

The best **restaurant** in town is *La Réserve* at 5 bd du Gal-Leclerc (ⓣ04.93.01.00.01; closed mid-Nov to mid-Dec; menus from €55), which features the grand old dishes of French cuisine in suitably opulent surroundings. If you prefer something a little more low-key, *Dar Marrakech*, 18 bd Gal-Leclerc (ⓣ04.93.01.48.59), is an atmospheric Moroccan restaurant with a €25 menu, and *La Pignatelle*, 10 rue Quincenet (☎04.93.01.03.37; closed Wed), has inexpensive seafood menus from €12. *Le Beaulieu*, 45 bd Marinoni, is a good bet for **drinks** and coffee in smart surroundings.

Èze-sur-Mer and Cap d'Ail

The next stop on the train is **ÈZE-SUR-MER**, the little seaside extension of **Èze** village on the Moyenne Corniche (see below), with a narrow shingle beach and less pretensions than its western neighbours.

There's a small **tourist office** (July & Aug Mon–Sat 10am–1pm & 3–6.30pm) by the train station and a shuttle bus up to Èze village every hour. Reasonable **accommodation** is available at *Auberge Le Soleil*, av de la Liberté (☎04.93.01.5146, Ⓦwww.auberge-lesoleil.com; ❸; closed Nov), right on the seafront.

CAP D'AIL feels equally informal though it suffers from the noise and congestion of the lower and middle corniches running closely parallel. Having said that, its tiny eastern promontory has for years maintained one of the few open public spaces left on the Riviera, around the little **bar-restaurant** *Le Cabanon* on Point des Douaniers, which serves its faithful customers who come down here to fish, play *boules* or just look out to sea. A short coastal path leads east from here to **Monaco** and west to Cap Mala and the pretty little *Plage Mala*.

The Moyenne Corniche

The first views from the **Moyenne Corniche** are back over Nice as you grind up Mont Alban, which, with its seaward extension, Mont Boron, separates Nice from Villefranche. Two forts command these heights: **Fort Boron** which is still in naval service, and **Fort Alban**, as endearing a piece of military architecture as is possible to imagine – though now overgrown, it still remains in one piece, with its four tiny turrets glimmering in glazed Niçois tiles. The fort was continually taken by the enemies of Villefranche, who could then make St-Elme (see p.374) surrender in seconds. You can wander freely around the fort and see why Villefranche's citadel, so unassailable from the sea, was so vulnerable from above. To reach it you turn sharp right off the corniche along rte Forestière before you reach the Villefranche pass. The #14 bus from Nice stops at Chemin du Fort from which the fort is signed.

Once through the pass, the cliff-hanging car-chase stretch of the Moyenne Corniche begins, with great views, sudden tunnels and little habitation.

Èze

ÈZE is unmistakable long before you arrive, its streets wound around a cone of rock below the corniche, whose summit is 470m above the sea. From a distance the village has the monumental medieval unity of Mont St-Michel and is a dramatic sight to behold, but seen up close, its secular nature exerts itself. Of the *villages perchés* in Provence, only St-Paul-de-Vence can compete with Èze for catering so single-mindedly to tourists. It takes a mental feat to recall that the labyrinth of tiny vaulted passages and stairways was designed not for charm but from fear of attack.

The ultimate defence, the castle, no longer exists, but the cacti **Jardin Exotique** (July & Aug daily 9am–8pm; Sept–June 9am–noon & 2–6/7pm; €2.50) which replaces it offers fantastic views from the ruins and a respite from the commerce below. Also worth visiting for atmosphere alone is the **Chapelle des Pénitents Blancs** on place du Planet, where the crucifix, of thirteenth-century Catalan origin, has Christ smiling down from the cross.

From place du Centenaire, just outside the old village, you can reach the shore through open countryside, via the **sentier Frédéric-Nietzsche**. The philosopher Nietzsche is said to have conceived part of *Thus Spoke Zarathustra* on this path. You arrive at the Corniche Inférieure at the eastern limit of **Èze-sur-Mer**.

Èze's **tourist office**, on place du Gal-de-Gaulle to the right of the post office (April–Oct daily 9am–7pm; Nov–March Mon–Sat 9am–6.30pm, Sun 9.30am–1pm & 2–6.30pm; ⓣ04.93.41.26.00, ⓦwww.eze-riviera.com), can supply a map of the many footpaths through the hills linking the three corniches.

If you want to stay, *Hôtel le Belèze*, place de la Colette on the Moyenne Corniche (ⓣ04.93.41.19.09, ⓕ04.93.41.13.62; ❸), is the most reasonable option, if a bit noisy. Alternatively, if you want to really splash out, there are two four-star luxury **hotels**, both with top-quality **restaurants**: *Château Eza* (ⓣ04.93.41.12.24, ⓦwww.chateza.com; menus from €45; ❾; closed Nov–March), where a fortune can be spent on ravioli stuffed with white truffle or *langoustine*, and rooms start at €350; and the *Château de la Chèvre d'Or*, on rue de Barri (ⓣ04.92.10.66.66, ⓦwww.chevredor.com; ❾; closed Dec–Feb), where rooms start at €260, and the cheapest menu is a cool €54. Far more affordable meals can be found at *La Taverne* (also known as *Le Grill du Château*), rue du Barri ⓣ04.93.41.00.17; menu €28), which serves grills and pizzas; *Le Nid d'Aigle*, at the very top of the village (ⓣ04.93.41.19.08; menus from €22; closed Tues & Wed eve); and the *Crêperie Le Cactus*, as you enter the village (ⓣ04.93.41.19.02; menus from €18).

The Grande Corniche

At every other turn on the **Grande Corniche** you're tempted to park your car and enjoy the distant views, which uniquely extend both seaward and inland, but there are frustratingly few truly safe places to stop. At certain points, such as **Col d'Èze**, you can turn off upwards for even higher views.

Col d'Èze

The upper part of Èze is backed by the **Parc Forestier de la Grande Corniche**, a wonderful oak forest covering the high slopes and plateaux of this coastal range. Paths are well signed, and there are picnic and games areas and orientation tables – in fact it's rather over-managed, but at least it isn't built on. If you take a left (coming from Nice) to cross the col and keep following rte de la Revère, you come, after 1.5km or so, to an observatory, **Astrorama** (Sept–June Fri & Sat 6–10pm; July & Aug Mon–Sat 6–11pm; €9), where you can admire the evening and night sky through telescopes.

If you want **to stay**, the *Hôtel L'Hermitage*, on the corniche (ⓣ04.93.41.00.68, ⓕ04.93.41.21.11; ❸; closed Dec–Jan), has magnificent views, and a **restaurant** serving passable meals (closed Thurs, Fri, Dec & Jan; menus from €16).

La Turbie

After eighteen stunning kilometres from Nice, you reach **LA TURBIE** and the **Trophée des Alpes**, a sixth-century monument to the power of Rome and the total subjugation of the local peoples. Originally a statue of Augustus Caesar stood on the 45-metre plinth which was inscribed with the names of 45 vanquished tribes and an equally long list of the emperor's virtues. In the fifth century the descendants of the suppressed were worshipping the monument, to the horror of St Honorat who did his best to have the graven image destroyed. However, it took several centuries of barbarian invasions, quarrying, and incorporation into military structures before the trophy was finally reduced to rubble in the early eighteenth century by Louis XIV's engineers, who blew the fortress up to prevent it being used by the king's enemies. Its painstaking reconstruction was undertaken in the 1930s, and it now stands, statueless, at 35m.

Viewed from a distance along the Grande Corniche, however, the *Trophée* can still hold its own as an imperial monument. If you want to take a closer look and see a model of the original, you'll have to buy a ticket for the fenced-off plinth and its little **museum** (April–June daily 9am–6pm; July–Sept daily 9am–7pm; Oct–March 9.30am–5pm; €4). You can climb up to the viewing platform and enjoy the spectacular view, extending to the Esterel in the west and Italy in the east.

In the town, just west of the *Trophée*, the eighteenth-century **Église de St-Michel-Archange** is a Baroque concoction of marble, onyx, agate and oil paint, with pink the overriding colour, and, among the paintings, a superb *St Mark writing the Gospel* attributed to Veronese. The rest of the town is less colourful, with rough-hewn stone houses, most of them medieval, lining rue Comte-de-Cessole, the main street which was part of the Via Julia leading to the *Trophée*.

If you're thinking of **staying**, try *Hôtel Le Napoléon*, 7 av de la Victoire (Ⓣ04.93.41.00.54, Ⓕ04.93.41.28.93; ❸; closed Tues out of season), on the main road, with views over the *Trophée* and a good **restaurant**, or the more atmospheric *Hostellerie Jérôme*, 20 Comte de Cessole (Ⓣ04.92.41.51.51, Ⓕ04.92.41.51.50; ❻), on the via Julia in the heart of the old village and with a beautiful restaurant.

Roquebrune Cap Martin

As the corniche descends towards Cap Martin, it passes the eleventh-century castle of **ROQUEBRUNE** and its fifteenth-century village nestling round the base of the rock. The **castle** (daily: Feb, March & Oct 10am–12.30pm & 2–6pm; April–June & Sept 10am–12.30pm & 2–6.30pm; July & Aug 10am–12.30pm & 2–7pm; Nov–Jan 10am–12.30pm & 2–5pm; €3.50) might well have become yet another Côte-side architectural aberration, thanks to its English owner in the 1920s. He was prevented from continuing his 'restorations' after a press campaign brought public attention to the mock-medieval tower by the gateway, now known as the *tour anglaise*. The local authority has since made great efforts to kit the castle out in an authentic medieval fashion, and one of the best, if perhaps not most authentic, ideas has been to create an **open-air theatre** for the concerts and dance performances held here in July and August, with a spectacular natural backdrop down the precipitous slopes to Monaco and the coast.

The village itself is a real maze of passages and stairways that eventually lead either to one of the six castle gates or to dead ends. If you find yourself on rue de la Fontaine you can leave the village by the Porte de Menton and see, on the hillside about 200m beyond the gate, an incredible spreading **olive tree** that was perhaps one hundred years old when the count of Ventimiglia first built a fortress on Roquebrune's spur in 870 AD.

Southeast of the old village, just below the joined middle and lower corniches and the station, is the peninsula of **Cap Martin**, with a **coastal path** giving you access to a wonderful shoreline of white rocks and wind-bent pines. The path is named after **Le Corbusier**, who spent several summers in Roquebrune and drowned tragically off Cap Martin in 1965. His grave – a work of art designed by himself – is in the cemetery (square J near the flagpole), high above the old village on promenade 1er DFL, and his beach house (visits arranged through the tourist office; Tues & Wed at 10am; €8) is on the shore just east of Plage du Buse, the beach just below the station.

Roquebrune Cap Martin's main **beach** is the Plage de Carnolès, a long stretch of shingle running northeast from Cap Martin. At the junction of the Via Aurelian and Via Julia is a remnant from the Roman station. Known as the **Tombeau de Lumone**, it comprises three arches of a first-century BC mausoleum, with traces of frescoes still visible under the vaulting.

Practicalities

To get to Roquebrune's Vieux Village from the **gare SNCF**, it's a forty-minute walk uphill: turn east and then right up av de la Côte d'Azur, then first left up escalier Corinthille, across the Grande Corniche and up escalier Chanoine JB Grana. Between the station and the beach, on av Aristide Briand, you'll find the **tourist office** at no. 218 (July & Aug Mon–Sat 9am–1pm, 3–7pm, Sun 10am–12.30pm & 3–7pm; ⓣ04.93.35.62.87).

Hotels to try on the coast in Roquebrune are *Westminster*, 14 av Louis-Laurens (ⓣ04.93.35.00.68, ⓦwww.westminster06.com; ❹), close to the sea, west of the station, and *Reine d'Azur*, 29 promenade du Cap (ⓣ04.93.35.76.84, ⓕ04.93.28.02.91; closed Nov to mid-Dec; ❹), overlooking the Plage de Carnolès. In the old village, try *Les Deux Frères*, place des Deux-Frères (ⓣ04.93.28.99.00, ⓦwww.lesdeuxfreres.com; ❹-❻), where rooms #1 and #2 have awesome views, so it's worth booking these well in advance.

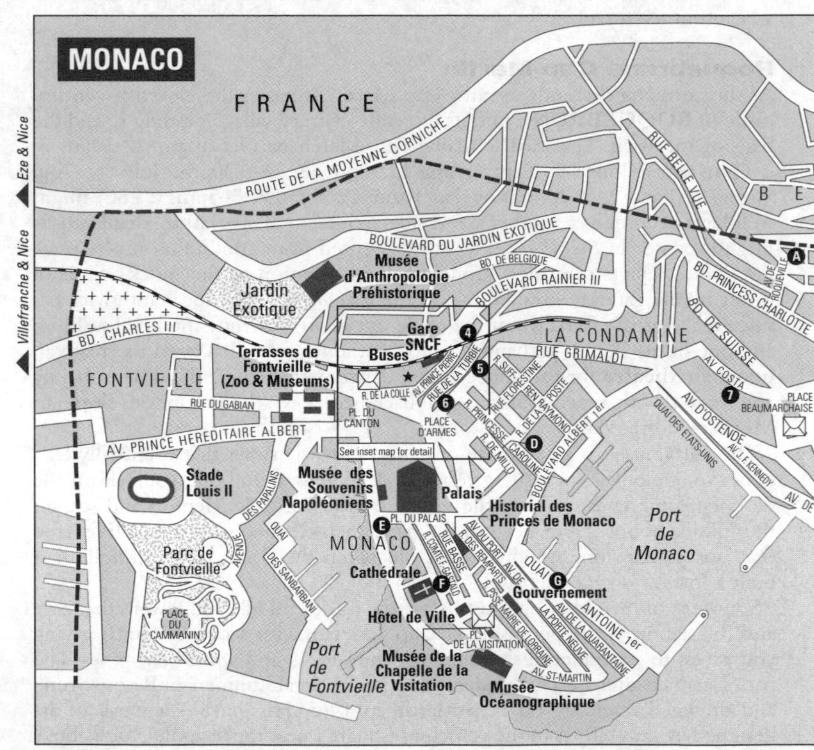

Several of the smarter **restaurants** in Roquebrune are rather overpriced: stick with *La Dame Jeanne*, 5 chemin Ste-Lucie (☎04.93.35.10.20; menu at €40; closed Sun), or *Au Grand Inquisiteur*, 18 rue du Château (☎04.93.35.05.37; menus at €24 & €35; closed Mon & Tues lunchtime and Nov to mid-Dec). Alternatively, the **bar** *La Grotte*, on place des Deux-Frères (closed Wed), serves generous plats du jour for around €9. For a real gourmet treat, try the panoramic **restaurant** *Le Vistaero* in the *Vista Palace Hotel* on the Grande Corniche (☎04.92.10.40.00; closed Feb), with menus at €53 and €91.

Monaco

Viewed from a distance, there's no mistaking the thick cluster of towers that is **MONACO**. Rampant property development over the last forty years or so has elbowed aside much of the principality's former Italianate prettiness, leaving it looking like nowhere else on the Riviera. This tiny independent state, no bigger than London's Hyde Park, has been in the Grimaldi family's hands since the fourteenth century – save for the two decades following the French Revolution – and, legally, Monaco would again become part of France were the royal line to die out. For the last hundred years the principality has lived off gambling and catering for the desires of the idle international rich. The latest mega-project is the construction of a new semi-floating breakwater, which

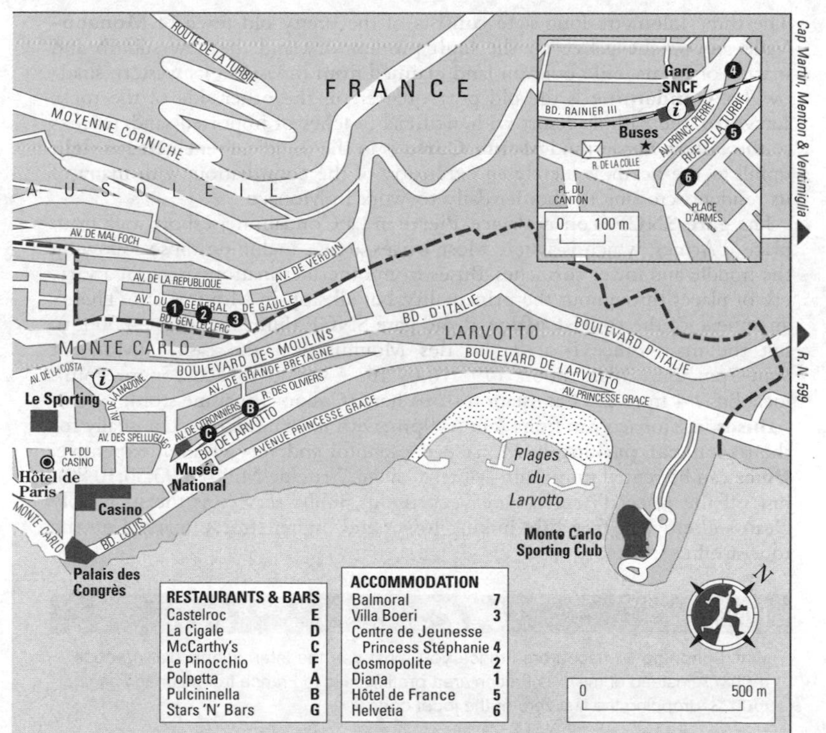

will virtually double the size of the harbour, provide yet more commercial space, and enable the principality to attract profitable cruise-ship visits.

Prince Rainier is the one constitutionally autocratic ruler left in Europe. There is a parliament, but it is of limited function and elected only by Monégasque nationals, about sixteen percent of the population. A copy of every French law is automatically sent to it, reworded and put to the prince. If he likes the law it is passed; if not, it isn't. The only other power is the Société des Bains de Mer (SBM), which owns the casino, the opera house, four of the grandest hotels, a handful of the most expensive cafés, restaurants, nightclubs and sports clubs, and large chunks of land including the Monte Carlo beach.

What the citizens and residents like so much is that they pay no income tax and their riches are protected by rigorous security forces. There are more police per square metre than in any other country in the world, and probably more closed-circuit television cameras, too. Despite all this, the principality's reputation as a safe haven took a knock in 1999 with the bizarre murder of billionaire banker Edmond Safra in a fire at his penthouse apartment, and by the subsequent trial and conviction of his male nurse, who later escaped from prison in Monaco only to be re-arrested in Nice.

One time to avoid Monaco – unless you're a motor-racing fan – is the end of May, when racing cars burn around the port and casino for the **Formula 1 Monaco Grand Prix**. Every space in sight of the circuit is inaccessible without a ticket, making casual sightseeing out of the question.

Arrival and information

The three-kilometre-long state consists of the pretty old town of **Monaco-Ville** around the palace on the high promontory, and the new suburb and marina of **Fontvieille** built on land claimed from the sea in its western shadow. **La Condamine** is the old port quarter on the other side of the rock; **Larvotto**, the bathing resort with artificial beaches of imported sand, reaches to the eastern border; and **Monte Carlo** is in the middle. French **Beausoleil**, uphill to the north, is merely an extension of the conurbation, with many of its residents crossing the border daily to work in Monaco.

The **gare SNCF** is on av Prince-Pierre in La Condamine, a short walk from place d'Armes, which is where most **buses** arrive, including those following the middle and lower corniches. Buses from other destinations arrive at a variety of places throughout the principality, but all stop in Monte Carlo. There's an annexe of the **tourist office** at the gare SNCF (June–Sept 9am–4.30pm), but the main office is at 2a bd des Moulins near the casino (Mon–Sat 9am–7pm, Sun 10am–noon; ⓣ92.16.61.16, ⓦwww.Monaco-congres.com); local bus #4 from the train station stops here (Casino-Tourisme stop).

Buses in Monaco run from 7am to 9pm, with flat-rate tickets. Unusually for the region, **car parking** in Monaco is plentiful and very clean, if expensive. **Bikes** can be rented from Auto-Moto-Garage, 7 rue de Millo (ⓣ93.50.10.80), just off the place d'Armes. One very useful public service is the incredibly clean and efficient **free lifts** linking lower and higher streets (marked on the tourist office's map).

Phones

When **phoning** Monaco from France you must use the international dialling code ⓣ00377 (instead of the ⓣ04 French area prefix); calls to France from Monaco begin ⓣ0033, dropping the first zero of the local code.

As for the practicalities of statehood, there are no **border formalities** and the euro is valid **currency**.

Accommodation

La Condamine is the best area for cheaper **hotels** within the principality, though don't expect bargains. For something a little more affordable, you can cross the invisible border and look for a room in Beausoleil. The prestige hotels cluster around the casino in **Monte Carlo**.

If you're under 31 and arrive early in the day, you may be able to get a **dormitory bed** at the *Centre de Jeunesse Princess Stéphanie*, near the station at 24 av Prince-Pierre on the junction with bd Rainier III (ⓣ93.50.83.20, ⓕ93.25.29.82; reception 7am–1am; ❶). Be prepared to hang about all morning before you know whether one of the forty beds (seventy in summer) is yours.

Monaco has no **campsite**, and **caravans** are illegal in the state (as are bathing costumes, bare feet and chests once you step off the beach). Camping vehicles must be parked at the Parking des Écoles in Fontvieille which is open around the clock.

Hotels

Balmoral 12 av Costa ⓣ93.50.62.37, ⓦwww.hotel-balmoral.mc. An elegant old building in Monte Carlo, with good views over the port. ❻

Villa Boeri 29 bd du Général-Leclerc, Beausoleil, France ⓣ04.93.78.38.10, ⓕ04.93.41.90.95. A cheapish option with reasonably sized rooms, some with sea views, and only a couple of minutes' walk from Monte Carlo centre. Don't be put off by the scruffy exterior – it's rather better inside. ❷

Cosmopolite 19 bd du Général-Leclerc ⓣ04.93.78.36.00, ⓔhotel.cosmopolitesoleil@wanadoo.fr. A reasonable, Italian-run two-star hotel. ❹

Diana 17 bd du Général-Leclerc, Beausoleil, France ⓣ04.93.78.47.58, ⓕ04.93.41.88.94. Cheap, fairly cheerful, and very close to Monte Carlo centre. ❷

Hôtel de France 6 rue de la Turbie ⓣ93.30.24.64, ⓕ 92.16.13.34. Bright rooms, good value for the principality and plenty of cheaper eating options nearby. ❹

Helvetia entrances at 1bis rue Grimaldi and rue de la Turbie ⓣ93.30.21.71, ⓕ92.16.70.51. A fairly basic option, but clean and comfortable. ❸

Monte Carlo

The heart of **MONTE CARLO** is its **casino**, the one place not to be missed on a trip to Monaco. Entrance is restricted to those over 21 and you may have to show your passport; dress code is strict, with shorts and T-shirts frowned upon, and skirts, jackets, ties and so forth more or less obligatory. Any coats or large bags must be left in the cloakroom, which charges a hefty fee.

In the first gambling hall, the Salons Européens (open from noon; €10), slot machines surround the American roulette and blackjack tables, the managers are Vegas-trained, the lights low and the air oppressively smoky. Above this slice of Nevada, however, the decor is turn-of-the-twentieth-century Rococo extravagance, while in the adjoining Pink Salon Bar, female nudes smoking cigarettes adorn the ceiling.

The heart of the place is the Salons Privés (June–Oct Mon–Fri from 4pm, Sat & Sun from 3pm; Nov–May daily from 3pm), through the Salles Touzet. You must look like a gambler, not a tourist (no cameras), to get in, and hand over €20 at the door. More richly decorated than the Salons Européens and much bigger, the atmosphere in here in the early afternoon or out of season is that of a cathedral: no clinking coins, just quiet-voiced croupiers and sliding chips.

Charles Garnier, the nineteenth-century architect of the Paris Opera, designed both the casino and the adjacent **Opera House** which is open to ticket holders only during the January to March season. Its typically Baroque interior is an excess of gold and marble with statues of pretty Grecian boys, frescoed classical scenes and figures waving palm leaves.

Around **place du Casino** are more casinos and the city's hôtels-palais and grands cafés, all owned by the SBM monopoly. The *American Bar* of the *Hôtel de Paris* is *the* place for the elite to meet, while the turn-of-the-twentieth-century *Hermitage* has a beautiful Gustave Eiffel iron-and-glass dome. Around the casino and along **bd des Moulins** is where most of the principality's luxurious shops are to be found, with another cluster on av Princesse Grace by Larvetto beach. People here really do live up to their stereotypes: you may not catch sight of Caroline and Stéphanie, but you can be sure of a brilliant fashion parade of clothes and jewels, cars and luggage.

For an alternative to people-watching, head for the **Musée National** at 17 av Princesse-Grace (Easter–Sept daily 10am–6.30pm; Oct–Easter daily 10am–12.15pm & 2.30–6.30pm; €5). Dedicated to the history of **dolls and automata** from eighteenth-century models to the latest Barbie dolls, it's better than you might think. Some of the doll's-house scenes and the creepy automata are quite surreal and fun.

Monaco-Ville

Though rather over-restored and lifeless, **MONACO-VILLE** is the one part of the principality where the developers have been reined in, and it retains a certain toy-town charm despite the surfeit of shops selling Prince Rainier mugs and assorted junk. It is also home to the **Palais Princier**, whose state apartments and throne room can be visited on a guided tour (June–Sept daily 9.30am–6.20pm; Oct daily 10am–5pm; €6). If you're outside the palace at 11.55am, you'll catch the daily changing of the guard.

There are also a number of small museums and attractions in Monaco-Ville more or less connected to the Grimaldis: you can look at waxwork princes in **L'Historial des Princes de Monaco**, 27 rue Basse (daily: Feb–Sept 9.30am–6pm; Oct–Jan 11am–4pm; €3.50); see the tombs of the former princes and Princess Grace in the nineteenth century **cathedral** (daily 10am–7pm) on rue Colonel; study old uniforms and bits of Monaco's history at the **Musée des Souvenirs Napoléoniens** on place du Palace (June–Sept daily 9.30am–6.30pm; Oct 10am–5pm; Dec–May Tues–Sun 10.30am–12.30pm & 2–5pm; €4); and even watch Monaco the movie, at the **Monte Carlo Story**, parking des Pecheurs (July & Aug 2–6pm; Sept–June 2–5pm; €6.50).

If you've had your fill of Grimaldis, check out the **Musée de la Chapelle de la Visitation**, place de la Visitation (Tues–Sun 10am–4pm; €3), which displays part of the religious art collection of Barbara Piasecka Johnson (an heir to the Johnson & Johnson fortune). This small but exquisite collection includes works by Zurbarán, Rivera, Rubens, and a rare, early religious work by Vermeer, *St Praxedis*.

One of Monaco's best, though pricey, sites is the **aquarium** in the basement of the **Musée Océanographique**, av St-Martin (April–Sept 9am–7pm; Oct–March 10am–6pm; €11), where delicate leafy sea dragons, living nautiluses and hideous angler fish are just some of the bizarre and colourful creatures you will witness. This is also an institute for serious scientific research, and claims to be the only place in the world that has succeeded in keeping living corals in its aquariums. Films by the famous underwater explorer Jacques Cousteau, who for many years was the director of the institute, are screened in the museum's conference hall.

Bus #1 or #2 will take you from place d'Armes to Monaco-Ville; **by car** head for the Parking du Chemin des Pêcheurs from where there's a lift up to av St-Martin by the Musée Océanographique. Only Monégasque- and Alpes Maritimes-registered cars are allowed in Monaco-Ville itself.

Fontvieille, the Jardin Exotique and La Condamine

Below the rock of Monaco-Ville by the Port de Fontvieille a new complex, the **Terrasses de Fontvieille** (bus #5), houses yet more museums. These include the prince's collection of private cars, everything from Cadillacs and Rollers to Trabants, Morris Minors and US jeeps (daily 10am–6pm; €6); a **Musée Naval** (daily 10am–6pm; €4) containing His Serene Highness's toy ships; a **zoo** (June–Sept 9am–noon & 2–7pm; Oct–Feb 10am–noon & 2–5pm; March–May 10am–noon & 2–7pm; €4); and a museum of stamps and coins, the **Musée des Timbres et des Monnaies** (July–Sept daily 10am–6pm; Oct–June 10am–5pm; €3).

Surrounded by car parks, the **Parc de Fontvieille** and Princess Grace's **rose garden** on the west side of the port are rather more rewarding than the museums. The prime garden in Monaco, however, is the **Jardin Exotique**, full of bizarre cacti emerging from the hillside high above Fontvieille on bd du Jardin Exotique (mid-May to mid-Sept 9am–7pm; mid-Sept to mid-May 9am–6pm; €6.40; bus #2). Admission also includes entry to the **Musée d'Anthropologie Préhistorique**, tracing the history of the human race from Neanderthal man to Grimaldi prince, and the **Grotte de l'Observatoire**, prehistoric caves with illuminated stalagmites and stalactites.

The yachts in the **Port de Monaco** in **La Condamine** are, as you might expect, gigantic. If the idea of getting on one and sailing out of the harbour gives you a buzz, try a mini **cruise** on the *Monte-Carlo* catamaran, quai des Etats-Unis, which has a glass hull for underwater viewing (☎92.16.15.15; €11). Also down by the port is a fabulous public Olympic-size, saltwater **swimming pool** with high-dive boards (May–Oct 9am–6pm except during the Grand Prix; €4.20).

Eating and drinking

La Condamine and Monaco-Ville are replete with **restaurants, brasseries** and **cafés,** but good food and reasonable prices rarely coincide: the best-value cuisine is usually Italian. It's really not worth going upmarket in Monaco unless you're prepared to pay €90 a head, in which case you should lunch in the *belle époque* glory of the *Louis XV* in the *Hôtel de Paris*, one of two Monte Carlo restaurants overseen by superstar chef Alain Ducasse (the other is *Bar & Boeuf* at the Sporting Club). As for **food shopping**, you can buy caviar, champagne and smoked salmon without any problem on and around av St-Charles, but finding *boulangeries* can be difficult. The best daily food **market** is in rue du Marché in Beausoleil.

Restaurants

Castelroc pl du Palais ☎93.30.36.68. A crowded but convenient place if you've been doing the palace tours. It serves fish dishes and Monégasque specialities, with a menu at €20; only open at lunchtimes. Closed Sat, Dec & Jan.

La Cigale 18 rue de Millo ☎93.30.16.14.

Between the station and the Port de Monaco, with a terrace. Serves seafood and Italian dishes on a €15 menu. Closed Sat eve.

Le Pinocchio 30 rue Comte F-Gastaldi ☎93.30.96.20. Dependable Italian in Monaco-Ville; plats from €10. Open till midnight in summer. Closed mid-Dec to mid-Jan.

Polpetta 2 rue Paradis ☎93.50.67.84. A pleasant restaurant with attractive terrace and vaulted dining hall in Monte Carlo, serving Italian food; menu at €23. Closed Tues & Sat lunch.

Pulcinella 17 rue du Portier ☎93.30.73.61. Traditional Italian cooking in Monte Carlo; menu at €25, plats from €12.

Nightlife, entertainment and festivals

There are better places to throw away money on **nightlife** than Monaco, and the top discotheques like *Jimmy'z*, by the Monte-Carlo Sporting Club, are not going to let you in unless you're dripping with real jewels. American- or British-style **bars** and pubs abound and your best bet is the large, informal bar on the quai Antoine-1er, *Stars 'N' Bars*, which is packed out on Fridays and Saturdays, with a lively club upstairs. Otherwise, there's *McCarthy's*, 7 rue du Portier, for Guinness and occasional live music.

By contrast, the **opera season** (Nov–March) is pretty exceptional, the SBM being able to book up star companies and performers before Milan, Paris or New York gets hold of them. The programme of **theatre**, **ballet** and **concerts** throughout the year is also impressive, with the **Printemps des Arts** festival (April–Sept) seeing performances by famous classical and contemporary dance troupes from all over the world. The main booking office for ballet, opera and concerts is the casino foyer, place du Casino, Monte Carlo (Tues–Sun 10am–5.30pm; ☎92.16.22.99); for theatre, book at the Théâtre Princesse Grace, 12 av de l'Ostende, Monte Carlo (☎93.25.32.27).

Monaco's **festivals** are spectacular, particularly the **International Fireworks Festival** in July and August, which can be seen from as far away as Cap d'Ail or Cap Martin. Mid- to late-January sees vast trailers entering Monaco for the **International Circus Festival** at the Espace Fontvieille, a rare chance to witness the world's best in this underrated performance art (details on ☎92.05.23.45). **Holidays** in Monaco are the same as in France, with the addition of January 27 (*Fête de Ste-Dévote*) and November 19 (*Fête Nationale Monégasque*).

The **Monte-Carlo Automobile Rally** takes place at the end of January and the **Formula 1 Grand Prix** at the end of May. Every space in sight of the circuit, which runs round the port and the casino, is inaccessible without a ticket (☎93.15.26.00). Monaco also has a first-division **football team**, AS Monaco, whose home ground is the enormous Stade Louis II in Fontvieille, 2 av du Prince-Héréditaire-Albert (☎92.05.40.00).

Listings

Banks Most banks have a branch in Monaco, centred around bd des Moulins, av de Monte-Carlo and av de la Costa; opening hours are Mon–Fri 9am–noon & 2–4.30pm.

Bookshop Scruples, 9 rue Princesse-Caroline ☎93.50.43.52, sells English-language books.

Consulates Britain, 33 bd Princesse-Charlotte ☎93.50.99.66; Ireland, 1 pl Ste-Dévote ☎93.15.70.00.

Currency exchange American Express, 35 bd Princesse Charlotte, Cie; Monégasque de Change, parking du Chemin des Pêcheurs.

Emergencies ☎18 or 93.30.19.45; Centre Hospitalier Princesse Grace, av Pasteur ☎97.98.97.69.

Pharmacy Call ☎141 or 93.25.33.25 from public phones.

Police and lost property 3 rue Louis Notari ☎93.15.30.15.

Post office PTT Palais de la Scala, Place Beaumarchais (Mon–Fri 8am–7pm & Sat 8am–noon).

Taxis ☎93.15.01.01.

Menton and around

Of all the Riviera resorts, **MENTON**, the warmest and the most Italianate, is the one that most retains an atmosphere of aristocratic tourism. Today it is even more of a rich retirement haven than Nice, and it's precisely that genteel, slow promenading pace of the town that makes it easy to imagine the presence of arch duchesses, grand dukes, tsars and other autocrats, as well as sick artists such as Guy de Maupassant and Katherine Mansfield. Menton does not go in for the ostentatious wealth of Monaco nor the creative cachet of Cannes or some of the hilltop towns. What it chiefly glories in is its climate and its all-year-round lemon crops. Ringed by protective mountains, hardly a whisper of wind disturbs the suntrap of the city. Winter is when you notice the difference most, with Menton several vital degrees warmer than St-Tropez or St-Raphaël.

Perched in the hills around Menton are some stunning little unspoilt villages, with spectacular views: **Ste-Agnes** and **Castillon** are both known for their arts and crafts studios, while **Castellar** and **Gorbio** are great for walkers.

Arrival and information

Roquebrune and Cap Martin merge into Menton along the three-kilometre shore of the **Baie du Soleil**. The modern town is arranged around three main streets parallel to the promenade du Soleil. The **gare SNCF** is on the top one, rue Albert-1er, from where it's a short walk northeast to the **gare routière** on av de Sospel. The **tourist office** is at 8 av Boyer (July & Aug Mon–Sat 9am–7pm, Sun 9am–1pm; Sept–June Mon–Fri 8.30am–12.30pm & 1.30–6pm, Sat 9am–noon & 2–6pm; ⓣ04.92.41.76.76, ⓦwww.villedementon.com), inside the Palais de l'Europe, a former casino which now hosts various cultural activities, annual contemporary art exhibitions and an international art *biennale*. The Vieille Ville lies further east, above the old port and the start of the Baie de Garavan. The district of Garavan, further east again, is the most exclusive residential area and overlooks the modern marina.

Accommodation

Accommodation, though good value, is difficult to find. Menton is as popular as the other major resorts, so in summer you should definitely book ahead. The tourist office won't make reservations for you, though they will tell you where rooms are still available.

Hotels

L'Aiglon 7 av de la Madone ⓣ04.93.57.55.55, ⓦperso.wanadoo.fr/aiglon. Spacious rooms in a nineteenth-century residence surrounded by a large garden, with a heated pool. ❺

Auberge Provençale 11 rue Trenca ⓣ04.93.35.77.29, ⓦwww.hotelmenton.com/l'auberge-provencale. Centrally located above a restaurant, with sound-proofed rooms and a garden. ❷

Beauregard 10 rue Albert-1er ⓣ04.93.28.63.63, ⓔbeauregard.menton@wanadoo.fr. Traditionally furnished rooms and a relaxed atmosphere. Closed Oct–Dec. ❷

Belgique 1 av de la Gare ⓣ04.93.35.72.66, ⓦperso.wanadoo.fr/hotel.de.belgique. A bit mundane but clean, friendly and conveniently close to the station. Closed Dec. ❷

Chambord 6 av Boyer ⓣ04.93.35.94.19, ⓦwww.hotelmenton.com/hotel-chambord. Large modern rooms, many with balconies. Well located. ❼

Hotel des Ambassadeurs 3 rue Partouneaux, ⓣ04.93.28.75.75, ⓦwww.ambassadeurs-menton.com. A traditional grand hotel that retains the character and atmosphere of the *belle époque*. ❼

Moderne 1 cours George V ⓣ04.93.57.20.02, ⓦwww.hotelmenton.com/hotel-moderne. Good-value modern, central hotel: many rooms have balconies. ❺

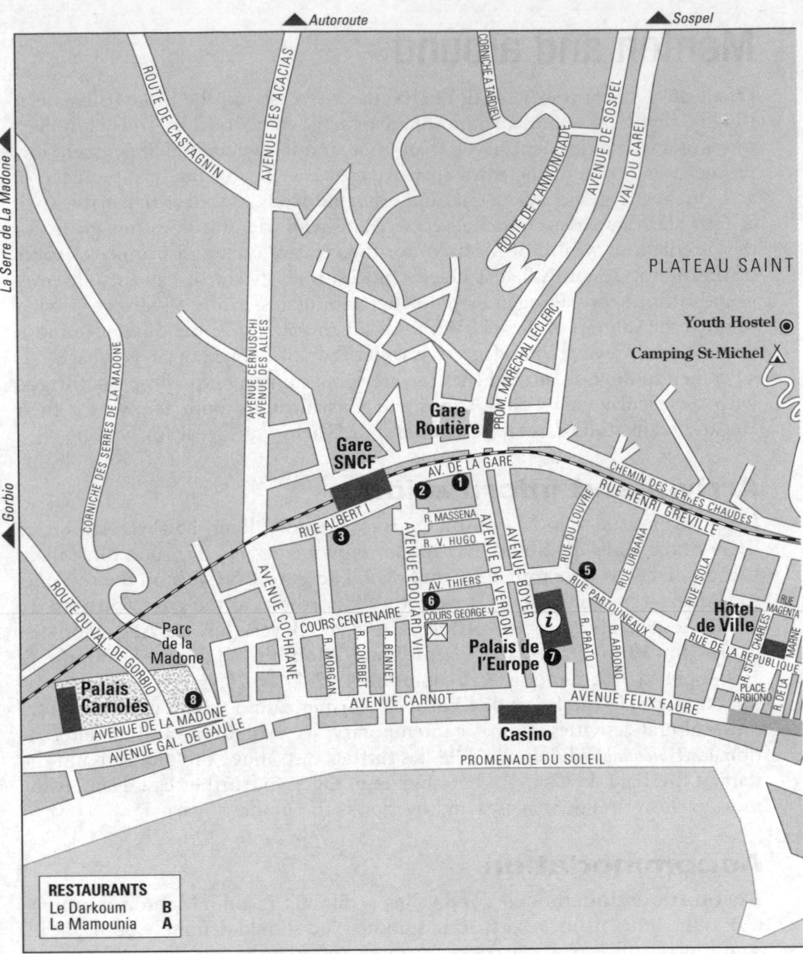

Napoléon, 29 porte de France, Garavan ⓣ04.93.35.89.50, ⓦwww.napoleon-menton.com. Traditionally furnished modern hotel. Mountain or sea views from the rooms. ❻

Le Terminus pl de la Gare ⓣ04.92.10.49.80, ⓦwww.hotelmenton.com/hotel-le-terminus. Basic and inexpensive, right by the station and with a cheap restaurant. ❶

Hostel, chambre d'hôtes and campsite

HI youth hostel plateau St-Michel ⓣ04.93.35.93.14, ⓕ04.93.35.93.07. This well-run hostel is up a gruelling flight of steps (sign-posted Camping St-Michel) from the northern side of the railway to the east of the station, or take bus #6 from the gare routière (direction Ciappes de Castellar; stop Camping St-Michel). Good food and views; 11pm curfew. €12 per dorm bed. April–Sept reception 7am–noon & 5pm–midnight; Oct–March 7–10am & 5–11pm.

Chambre d'hôtes M. Paul Gazzano, 151 rte de Castellar ⓣ04.93.57.39.73. Two kilometres from Menton, a delightful house with a terrace and pool looking down over the wooded slopes to the sea. Open all year. ❹

Camping St-Michel plateau St-Michel ⓣ04.93.35.81.23, ⓕ04.93.57.12.35. Reasonably priced campsite in the hills above the town, with plenty of shade and good views out to sea; follow directions for HI youth hostel. €14 per tent. Closed Dec–Feb.

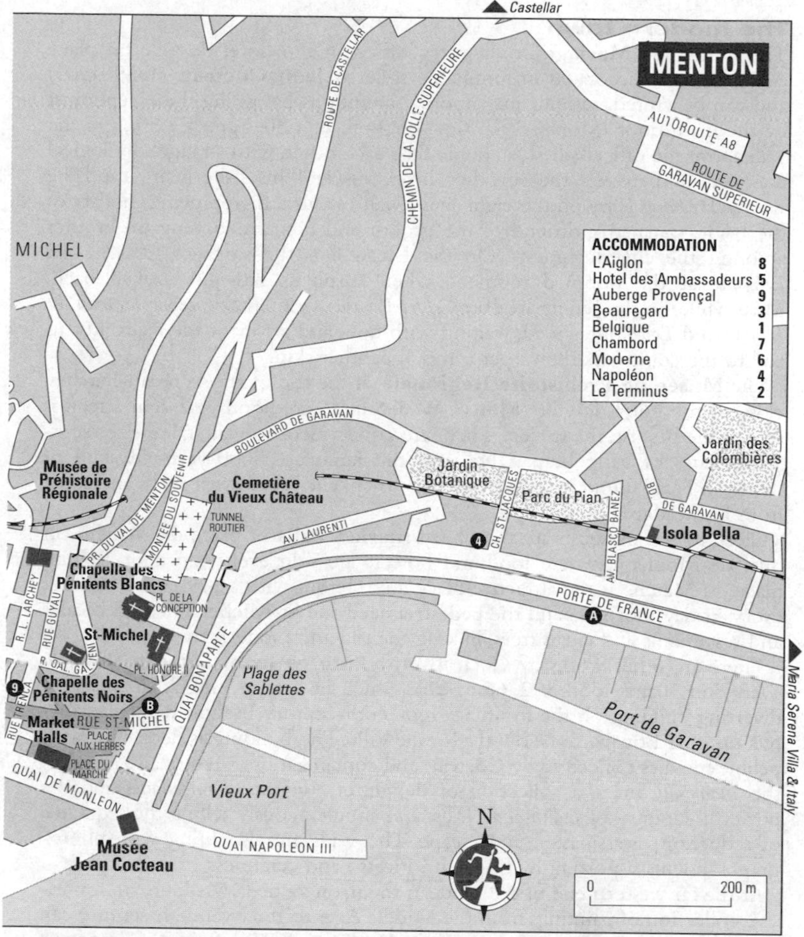

The Town

Menton's history, like that of Monaco, almost took an independent path. In the revolutionary days of 1848, Menton and Roquebrune, both at the time under Monaco's jurisdiction, declared themselves an independent republic under the protection of Sardinia. When the prince of Monaco came to Menton in the hope that his regal figure would sway the people, he had to be rescued by the police from a furious crowd and locked up overnight for his own protection. Eventually, following an 1860 vote by Roquebrune and Menton to remain in France, Grimaldi agreed to the sale of the towns to the French state for four million francs.

Today, the town's greatest attraction is not its seafront or pebble beach, but the fabulous facade of the **Vieille Ville** around the parvis St-Michel. Other highlights include the works of **Jean Cocteau** – in particular his decoration of the registry office – and the **gardens** in Garavan.

The modern town

The **Salle des Mariages**, or registry office, in the hôtel de ville on place Ardoiono, was decorated in inimitable style by **Jean Cocteau** (1889–1963) and can be visited without matrimonial intentions by asking the receptionist by the main door (Mon–Fri 8.30am–12.30pm & 1.30–5pm; €1.50). On the wall above the official's desk a couple face each other, with strange topological connections between the sun, her headdress and his fisherman's cap. The *Saracen Wedding Party* on the right-hand wall reveals a disapproving mother of the bride, spurned girlfriend of the groom and her armed vengeful brother amongst the cheerful guests. On the left wall is the story of *Orpheus and Eurydice* at the doomed moment when Orpheus has just looked back. Meanwhile, on the ceiling are *Poetry rides Pegasus*, tattered *Science juggles with the Planets* and *Love*, open-eyed, waiting with bow and arrow at the ready. Just to add to the confusion, the carpet is mock panther skin.

The **Musée de Préhistoire Régionale**, at the top of rue Lorédan-Larchey close to the hôtel de ville (Mon & Wed–Sun 10am–noon & 2–6pm; free), is one of the best on the subject. There are good videos to watch, life-size recreated scenes of early human life, and the famous 27,000-year-old skull of 'Menton Man' found in a cave near the town, encrusted with shells and teeth from his headgear.

Close to the museum are the pretty **market halls** of place du Marché off quai de Monléon, where food and flowers are sold every morning. Behind place du Marché is the attractive place aux Herbes with a bric-a-brac market every Friday morning, and the pedestrianized rue St-Michel, lined with cafés and restaurants and citrus trees, linking the old and modern towns.

There are other works by Cocteau in the **Musée Jean Cocteau** (Mon & Wed–Sun 10am–noon & 2–6pm; €3), which he set up himself in the most diverting building on the front, a seventeenth-century bastion with tiled turrets on quai Bonaparte below the Vieille Ville. The building is decorated with pebble mosaics conceived by Cocteau and contains more Mentonaise lovers in the *Inamorati* series, a collection of delightful *Animaux Fantastiques* and the powerful tapestry of *Judith and Holopherne* simultaneously telling the sequence of seduction, assassination and escape. The walls are also hung with photographs, poems, a portrait by his friend Picasso and ceramics.

At the far western end of the modern town, on av de la Madone, an impressive collection of paintings from the Middle Ages to the twentieth century can be seen in the sumptuous **Palais Carnolès** (Mon & Wed–Sun 10am–noon & 2–6pm; free; bus #3 or #7 from the gare routière to Madone Parc), the old summer residence of the princes of Monaco. Of the early works, the *Madonna and Child with St Francis* by Louis Bréa is exceptional; there are excellent Dutch and Venetian portraits; and an anonymous sixteenth-century École Français canvas of a woman holding a scale. The small modern and contemporary collection includes a wonderful Suzanne Valadon and works by Graham Sutherland, who spent some of his last years in Menton. The downstairs of the building is given over to temporary exhibitions and there's a **jardin des sculptures** in the adjoining lime, lemon and orange grove. Due north of here, at 74 route du Val de Gorbio, is **La Serre de la Madone** (Feb–Sept; guided tours only during restoration work; ⓣ04.93.57.73.90; €8), a botanical garden of great tranquillity created by an Englishman in the interwar years.

The Vieille Ville

Where the *quai* bends round the western end of the Baie de Garavan from the Cocteau museum, a long flight of black and white pebbled steps leads to the

parvis St-Michel and the perfect pink and yellow proportions of the **Église St-Michel** (Mon–Fri 10am–noon & 3–5.15pm; Sat 3–5.15pm). The interior of the church is a stupendous Italian Baroque riot of decoration, with an impressive vast organ casing, a sixteenth-century altarpiece in the choir by Antonio Manchello and a host of paintings, sculptures, gilded columns, stucco and frescoes.

From the church, take a few more steps up to another square and the apricot-and-white marbled **Chapelle des Pénitents Blancs** (Mon–Sat 3–5pm), home to a collection of processional lanterns and with a fine trompe-l'oeil over the altar. All this, as well as the pastel campaniles and disappearing stairways between long-lived-in houses, are a sure sign that you've arrived at the most Italianate and beautiful of the Riviera's Vieilles Villes.

From here, head north, or uphill. At the top you'll reach the **Cimetière du Vieux Château** which is low on gloom and high on views, with cream-coloured mid-nineteenth-century sculpted stone and diverse foreign names ranging from Russian princes to William Webb-Ellis, credited, in public schools throughout the land, with the invention of rugby.

Garavan

If it's cool enough to be walking outside, the public **parks** up in the hills and the **gardens** of **Garavan**'s once elegant villas make a change from shingle beaches. From the Vieux Cimetière you can walk or take bus #8 along bd de Garavan past houses hidden in their large, exuberant gardens.

The first public garden you come to is the **Jardin Botanique** (daily: April–Sept 10am–12.30pm & 3–6pm; Oct–May 10am–12.30pm & 2–5pm; €4), which surrounds the Villa Val Rahmeh. Though there's a good variety of plants, it's not brilliantly maintained and you can get the same views for free from the **Parc du Pian**, an olive grove reached from the boulevard just past the Jardin Botanique. Further on, down av Blasco-Ibañez and north up rue Webb-Ellis and chemin Wallaya, is the villa Isola Bella, the former Menton home of author Katherine Mansfield, though sadly it is not open to the public. Back on the seafront, the very last house before the Italian border is the **Maria Serena Villa** (guided tours on Tues, arranged by the Heritage Centre, rue Ciapetta, ☎04.92.10.33.66), designed by Charles Garnier for the family of Ferdinand de Lesseps.

Eating, drinking and entertainment

Menton has few exceptional **restaurants** so most people usually cross into Italy for a blowout meal. If you're not that bothered what you eat as long as it's cheap, the pedestrianized rue St-Michel is promising ground. There are plenty of snack bars among the burger houses, as well as outlets for omelettes or steak and chips and occasionally interesting plats du jour. There are two excellent Moroccan restaurants, both offering plats from around €12: *Le Darkoum*, 23 rue St-Michel (☎04.93.35.44.88), and *La Mamounia*, 51 porte de France, Garavan (☎04.93.57.95.39). Many of Menton's **bars** are on the seafront and port, including *Gran Caffe*, at 25 quai de Monléon, and *Mini Pub*, 51 quai Bonaparte.

In August the pebbled mosaic of the Grimaldi arms on the parvis St-Michel is covered by chairs, music stands, pianos and harps for the **Festival de Musique de Chambre**. The nightly concerts are superb and can be listened to from the quaysides without buying a ticket. If you want a proper seat, make a reservation at the tourist office.

More bizarrely, the town's **lemons** are celebrated in a citrus fruit festival every February. Sadly, despite the profusion of local produce, a *citron pressé* served in a Menton bar still costs twice as much as an imported Belgian beer.

Around Menton

In the hills above Menton and Roquebrune are the tiny villages of **Gorbio** and **Ste-Agnes**, and on the road to Sospel, **Castellar** and **Castillon**. All give stupendous views over steep, forested slopes to the sea.

Ste-Agnes

Ten kilometres northwest of Menton and 800m above sea level is **STE-AGNES**, the place which claims to be the highest coastal village in Europe, milling with crystal engravers, painters, herbalists, jewellers and leather workers. Perched at the foot of a cliff, it commands breathtaking views, especially from the ancient Saracen fortress currently being restored, at the top of the crag above. The Saracens had an impeccable eye for choosing defensive positions: such is the site's commanding vantage point that another important **fort** was built into the mountain top a millennium later, this time as part of the Maginot defences of the 1930s (guided tours daily 3pm & 4.30pm; €3.05).

The village is also an excellent starting point for **walks**, and the syndicat d'initiative, in the Espace de Culture at the entrance to the village, will provide you with a free list (in French only) of suggested hikes. One popular route, offering the best chance of glimpsing Corsica, is up the **Pic/Cime de Baudon** (1hr 45min to the summit at 1264m), with possibilities of continuing on to Gorbio or Peille.

A hospitable place to stay in the village is the **hotel-restaurant** *Saint Yves* (Ⓣ04.93.35.91.45, Ⓕ04.93.35.65.85; ❶), some of whose rooms have good views. The best-quality **food** is served in *Le Logis Sarrasin* (Ⓣ04.93.35.86.89; closed Mon; menus at €17 & €13), where they prepare a fine *tarte Agnésoise*, made with courgette flowers; while *Le Righi*, around the Maginot fort (Ⓣ04.92.10.90.88; menus from €12), has the best views. **Bus** #902 runs from Menton to Ste-Agnes (3 daily; 30min).

Gorbio

GORBIO, to the southwest of Ste-Agnes, is an exquisite hilltop village with very few arts and crafts boutiques or other tourist fodder, lending it a tranquil atmosphere that's rare for so scenic a place. Though the two villages are only 2km apart as the crow flies, the roads between them meet approximately 8km away, below the *autoroute*. Walkers can take a more direct route (a 45-minute walk): the road from Ste-Agnes drops downhill, and then crosses the path to Gorbio at L'Auribel bus stop, on a sharp hairpin bend after about 2km. You can also get to the village directly from Menton; bus #901 makes the climb five times daily from the gare routière in thirty minutes.

On the Thursday after Corpus Christi in June, the annual rite of the **Procession des Limaces** takes place, when the streets are illuminated by tiny lamps of snail shells filled with olive oil – a custom dating back to medieval times and occurring in villages throughout this area (check with the tourist office in Menton for exact dates).

Castillon and Castellar

A railway used to run along the Carei valley from Menton up to Sospel. Though the tracks and tunnels are still there, it's been closed for over forty years and there are currently no plans to revive it, which is a great pity as this valley offers one of the best roller-coasting descents to the sea. The villages are few and far between and much of the valley is thickly forested. The Sospel bus (#910) from Menton passes through **Castillon** (3 daily; 25min); for **Castellar** there's a local bus (#903; 5 daily; 25min).

To the east of the Carei valley, and closer to Menton, **CASTELLAR** marks the point where the pines start to take over from the lemon groves. It is another old *village perché*, but not overrun by tourist commerce. It's also good for **walks**, with several paths radiating out into the hills around it as well as the GR52 from Gorbio and Ste-Agnes, which turns north along the Italian border to Sospel. Details of the paths, plus **rooms** and **food**, can be found at the *Hôtel des Alpes*, place Georges-Clemenceau (Ⓣ04.93.35.82.83, Ⓕ04.93.28.24.25; ❺), whose terrace has lovely views. To the north of the village, there is a tiny **campsite** at *La Ferme St-Bernard* (Ⓣ04.93.28.28.31; €8 per tent; open April–Sept), with just six pitches but fantastic views from high up a mountain slope.

CASTILLON, a few kilometres south of Sospel, has twice been destroyed and rebuilt, by an earthquake in 1887 and by bombing in 1944. The current village, a short way down from Vieux Castillon, dates from the 1950s, with **Les Arcades des Serres**, a terrace of artists' and crafts workers' studios, added in the 1980s. Its status as an artists' village – the turning from the main road is marked by a dazzling ceramic – is not based on the normal Riviera riches market; the studios and galleries are provided at low rents in a genuine attempt to help local practitioners; and the works you see are very original and of a high standard. The **hotel-restaurant** *La Bergerie* (Ⓣ04.93.04.00.39; ❹; closed Oct–Dec), on the southern edge of the village, has great views and pleasant rooms.

Travel details

Trains

Cannes to: Antibes (every 20min peak time; 10–15min); Biot (every 40–50min; 15min); Cagnes-sur-Mer (every 40–50min; 25min); Cros-de-Cagnes (every 40–50min; 30min); Golfe Juan-Vallauris (every 40–50min; 7min); Juan-les-Pins (every 40–50min; 12min); Marseille (22 daily; 2hr;); Nice (every 20min peak time; 40min); St-Raphaël (every 30min; 25–35min); Villeneuve-Loubet-Plage (every 40–50min; 20min).

Nice to: Annot (4 daily; 1hr 45min); Beaulieu (every 20–30min; 10min); Breil-sur-Roya (6 daily; 55min); Cap d'Ail (25 daily; 15min); Cap Martin-Roquebrune (25 daily; 30min); Digne (4 daily; 3hr 10min); Entrevaux (4 daily; 1hr 30min); L'Escarène (3 daily; 40min); Èze-sur-Mer (25 daily; 15min); Marseille (2hr 45min–3hr 15min); Menton (every 15–40min; 25–35min); Monaco (every 15–40min; 25min); Peille (3 daily; 30min); Peillon (2 daily; 20min); Puget-Théniers (4 daily; 1hr 20min); St-Raphaël (1hr–1hr 20min); Sospel (6 daily; 45min); Tende (2 daily; 1hr 50 min); Touét-sur-Var (4 daily; 1hr 10min); Villars-sur-Var (4 daily; 1hr); Villefranche (25 daily; 10min).

Buses

Cannes to: Aéroport Nice-Côte-d'Azur (every 20min; 55min); Golfe-Juan (frequent; 12min); Grasse (every 30min; 45min); Mouans-Sartoux (every 30min; 20min); Mougins (every 30min; 20min);); Nice (every 20min; 1hr 25min); St-Raphaël (3–7 daily; 1hr 10min); Vallauris (frequent; 15min).

Grasse to: Le-Bar-sur-Loup (10 daily; 15–20min); Cabris (5 daily; 10min); Cannes (frequent; 35min); Digne (1 daily; 2hr 20min); Grenoble (1 daily; 6hr 25min); Mouans-Sartoux (frequent; 15min); Mougins (frequent; 25min); Nice (frequent; 1hr); St-Cézaire (5 daily; 30min); St-Vallier (6 daily; 15min); Vence (3 daily; 50min).

Menton to: Nice (every 15min; 1hr 20min); Sospel (5 daily; 30–55min).

Monaco to: Èze gare SNCF (every 15min; 13min); Menton (every 20min; 30min); Nice (every 15min; 40min); La Turbie (6 daily; 30min).

Nice to: Aix (5 daily; 2hr 15min–5hr 10min); Beaulieu (every 20min; 20min); Cagnes-sur-Mer (frequent; 30–50min); Cap d'Ail (every 20min; 20–30min); Coaraze (3 daily; 1hr); La Colle-sur-

Loup (every 30min at peak times; 1 hr); Contes (every 45min; 30min); Cros-de-Cagnes (every 20min; 25min); Digne (2 daily; 3hr–3hr 30min); L'Escarène (9 daily; 45min–1hr); Èze-sur-Mer (14 daily; 20min); Èze-Village (7 daily; 40min); Geneva (1 daily; 10hr 15min); Grasse (10 daily; 1hr–1hr 15min); Grenoble (1 daily; 7hr 30min); Lucéram (6 daily; 1hr); Marseille (5 daily; 2hr 45min–4hr 5min); Menton (every 20min; 1hr 20min); Monaco (every 20min; 25–40min); Peille (3 daily; 1hr); Roquebrune (every 20min; 40min–1hr); St-Paul (hourly; 1hr); Sisteron (1 daily; 3hr 45min–4hr 10min); Toulon (2 daily; 2hr 30min); La Turbie (5 daily; 40min); Vence (hourly; 1hr 5min); Villefranche (every 20min; 10min).

Ferries

Nice to: Corsica (summer 8 daily; winter 1 weekly; 2hr 30min–12hr).

Flights

Nice to: Amsterdam (10 daily; 2hr); Birmingham (6 weekly; 2hr); Dublin (9 weekly; 2hr 30min); East Midlands (2 weekly; 2hr); London (15 daily; 2hr); Manchester (1 daily; 2hr 10min); New York (2 daily; 9hr); Paris (23 daily; 1hr 20min); Rome (4 daily; 2hr).

7

Haute Provence

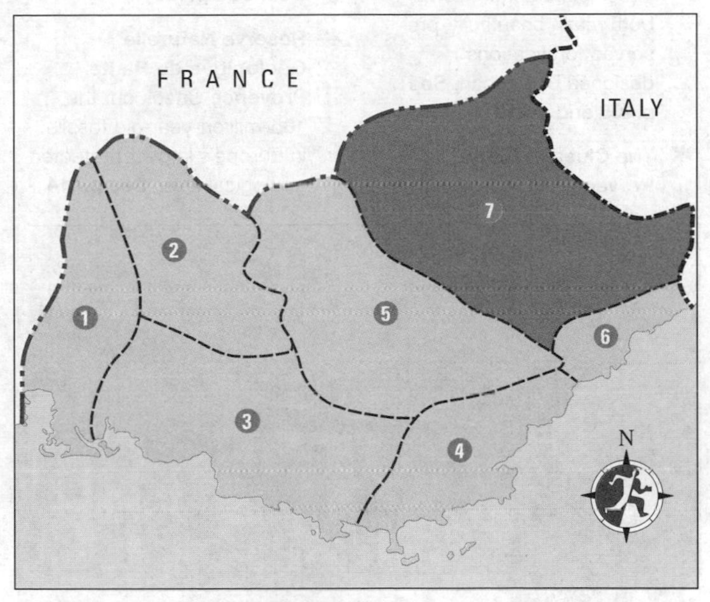

CHAPTER 7

Highlights

* **Parc National du Mercantour** An unspoilt alpine wilderness that is home to the Vallée des Merveilles and its mysterious four-thousand-year-old rock carvings. **See p.422**

* **Entrevaux and Colmars** These picturesque towns both retain beautifully-preserved fortifications designed by Vauban. **See p.405 and p.419**

* **The Clues of Haute Provence** A hidden landscape of rocky gorges, tiny villages and rural tranquillity, a mere 40km from the Riviera. **See p.399**

* **Sospel** An attractive Italianate Baroque town at odds with its surrounding rugged Provençal countryside. **See p.429**

* **Réserve Naturelle Géologique de Haute Provence** Check out the 185-million-year-old fossils in Europe's largest protected geological area. **See p.414**

7

Haute Provence

The mountainous northeastern corner of Provence, **Haute Provence**, is a different world from season to season. In **spring** the fruit trees in the narrow valleys blossom, and melting waters swell the Verdon, the Vésubie, the Var, the Tinée and the Roya, sometimes flooding villages and carrying whole streets away. In the foothills, the groves of chestnut and olive trees bear fruit in **summer** and **autumn**, while higher up the pine forests are edged with wild raspberries and bilberries, and the moors and grassy slopes with white and gold alpine flowers. Above the line where vegetation ceases there are rocks with eagles' nests and snowcaps that never melt.

In **winter** the sheep and shepherds retreat to warmer pastures, leaving the snowy heights to antlered mouflons and chamois, and the perfectly camouflaged ermine. The villages where the shepherds came to summer markets are battened down for the long cold haul, while modern conglomerations of Swiss-style chalet houses, sports shops and discotheques come to life around the ski lifts. From November to April many of the mountain passes are closed, cutting off the dreamy northern town of **Barcelonnette** from its lower neighbours.

This is not an easy place to live. Abandoned farms and overgrown terraced slopes bear witness to the declining viability of mountain agriculture. But the **ski resorts** bring in money and summer brings the dedicated **trekkers**, naturalists and **climbers**. One area, covering 75km from east to west, protected as the **Parc National du Mercantour**, has no permanent inhabitants at all. It's crossed by numerous paths, with refuge huts providing basic food and bedding for trekkers.

For centuries the border between Provence and Savoy ran through this part of France, a political divide embodied by the impressive fortifications of Entrevaux and **Colmars**, the principal town of the Haut Verdon. To this day most of the region is not considered to be part of Provence. The French refer to it by the geographical term, the **Alpes-Maritimes**, which is also the name of the *département* that stretches from between the Haut Var and Verdon valleys and just above the source of the Tinée Valley to the Italian border, and includes the Riviera. Where Provence ends and the Alps begin is debatable, with the Tinée Valley usually cited as definitely belonging to the latter – the mountains here are pretty serious and the Italian influence becomes noticeable.

Running along the southern limit of the Alps is the **Nice–Digne rail line**, known as the Chemin de Fer de Provence, the only remaining segment of the region's turn-of-the-twentieth-century narrow-gauge network. One of

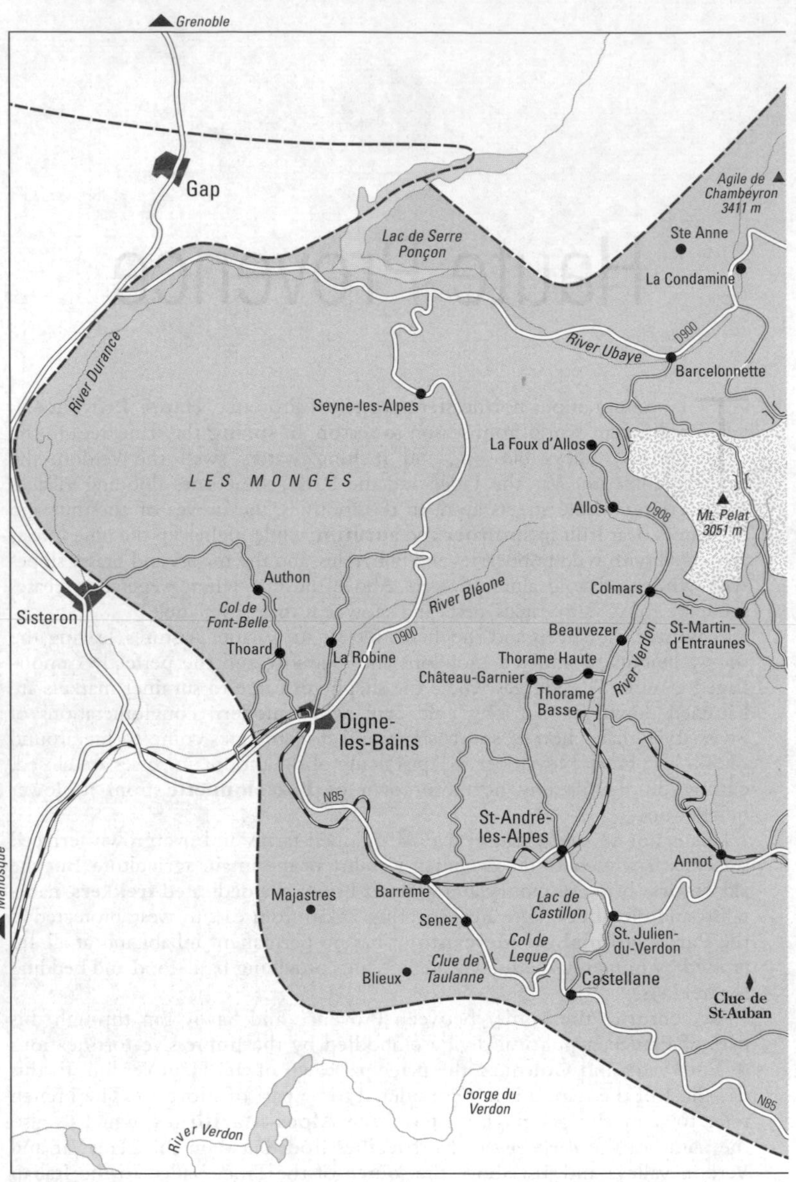

the great train rides of the country, it takes in the isolated Var towns of **Puget-Théniers** and **Entrevaux**, and ends at **Digne**, a low-key but intriguing regional capital that serves as the centre of the lavender industry. Away from the Nice–Digne line, transport is a problem save in the **Roya Valley**, over in the east, where the **Nice–Turin rail line** links the Italianate towns

of **Tende** and **Sospel**. **Buses** are infrequent and many of the best starting points for walks or the far-flung pilgrimage chapels are off the main roads. If you have your own transport, you'll face tough climbs and long stretches with no fuel supplies, but you'll be free to explore the most exhilaratingly beautiful corner of Provence.

Clues de Haute Provence

To the west of the River Var, north of Vence and the Route Napoléon in the Pre-Alpes de Grasse, lies the area known as the **Clues de Haute Provence**, *clues* being the word for the gorges cut through the limestone mountain ranges by their torrential rivers. This is an arid, sparsely populated region, its seclusion disturbed only by the winter influx of skiers from the coastal cities to the 1777-metre summit of the **Montagne du Cheiron**, and the car rallies along the route des Crêtes, which follows the contours of the Montagne de Charamel and the Montagne St-Martin between the Cols de Bleine and Roquestéron.

Each claustrophobic and seemingly collapsible *clue* opens onto a wide and empty landscape of white and grey rocks with a tattered carpet of thick oak and pine forest. The horizons are always closed off by mountains, some erupting in a space of their own, others looking like coastal cliffs trailing the **Cheiron**, the **Charamel** or the 1664-metre-high **Montagne de Thorenc**. It's the sort of scenery that fantasy adventure games take place in, with wizards throwing laser bolts from the mountains.

To appreciate it, though, you really need your own **transport**. Not all the passes are open in winter – notices on the roads forewarn you of closures – and you should keep an eye on your fuel gauge, as garages are scarce. Routes that go through the *clues* rather than over passes are manageable for cyclists: this is gorgeous, clean-air, long-freewheeling and panoramic terrain. There are plenty of footpaths, with the **GR4** as the main through-route for walkers from Gréolières to Aiglun across the Cheiron. The Conseil Général des Alpes

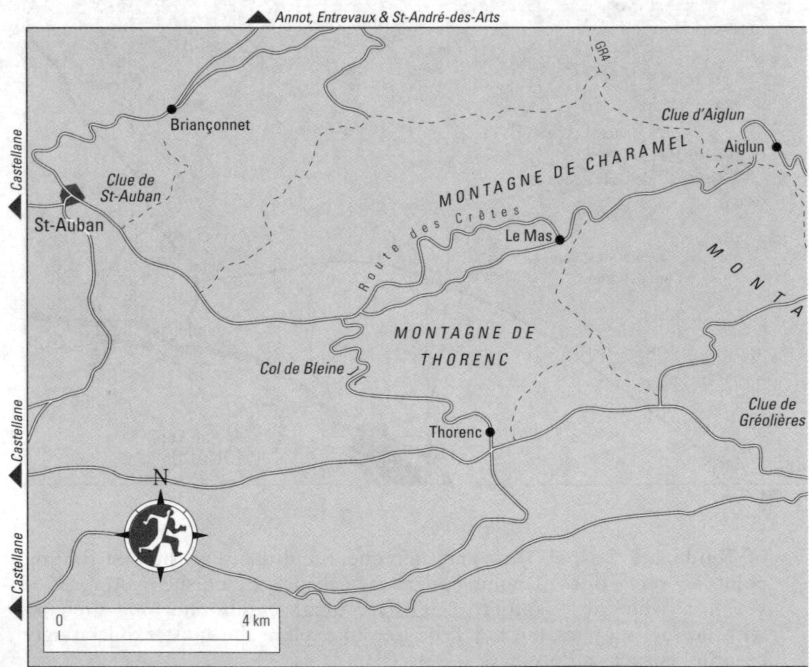

Maritimes produces an excellent series of walking guides for the region, available online (Ⓦwww.cg06.fr), and the *Guide Rand Oxygène Moyen Pays* covers the Esteron.

Accommodation isn't plentiful. What hotels there are tend to be very small, with a faithful clientele booking them up each year. Campsites are also thin on the ground, though is are a variety of gîtes scattered about. Even winter accommodation at **Gréolières** and **Gréolières-les-Neiges** is fairly minimal, as people tend to come up for a day's skiing or have their own weekend places. Most of the villages offer tourist information at the *mairie*. If you get stuck, the towns of Vence, Grasse, Puget-Théniers, Castellane or Nice are not far away.

Coursegoules and Gréolières

Coming from Vence you approach the *clues* via the Col de Vence, which brings you down to **Coursegoules**. Approaching from Grasse and the Loup Valley, the road north leads to **Gréolières**, 11km west of Coursegoules.

Coursegoules

The bare white rocks that surround **COURSEGOULES** are not the most hospitable of sites for a working village, so it's no surprise that many of the smartly restored houses here are now second homes. The population has steadily declined to around three hundred or so people who don't need to eke out a living from the soil-scoured terrain. **Accommodation** possibilities here, all

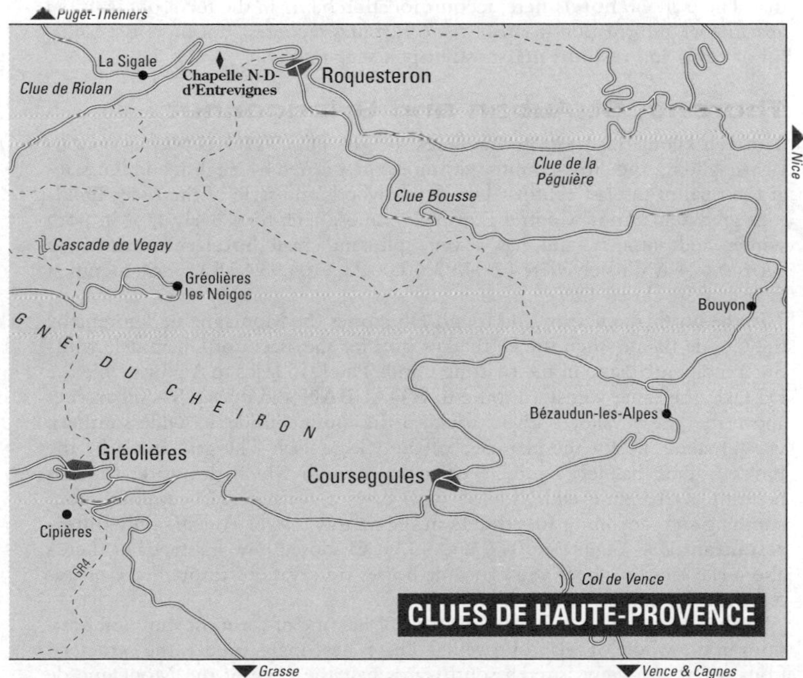

of which have superb views, include a chambre d'hôtes, 400m from the village (M et Mme Durand, L'Hébergerie; ⓣ04.93.59.10.53; ❸), and the hotel *L'Auberge de l'Escaou* on the lovely place des Tilleuls in the old village (ⓣ04.93.59.11.28, ⓦwww.hotel-escaou.com; ❹). The hotel has a perfectly good **restaurant** and there's also a crêperie and small bistro in the village.

Gréolières and around

GRÉOLIÈRES, 10km west, seems an equally unpromising site for habitation. Originally a stopping point on the Roman road from Vence to Castellane, it's now surrounded by ruins, of Haut-Gréolières to the north and a fortress to the south. The church, opposite the fortress, has a Romanesque facade and a fifteenth-century retable of St Stephen. The village is liveliest during the winter, but passes as a summer resort as well; it's a popular site for paragliding.

The **tourist office**, at 21 Grande-Rue (Mon–Fri 9am–noon & 2–6pm; ⓣ04.93.59.97.94, ⓦwww.pays-accueil-provence06.net), has plenty of information on sports and activities in Gréolières and its neighbouring villages. For **hotel-restaurants** the only choice is the very reasonable *La Vieille Auberge*, on place Pierre-Merle (ⓣ04.93.59.95.07; ❷), in the centre of the village. A good and inexpensive place to **eat** in the village is *La Barricade* pizzeria (menus at €11–18; closed Mon & Tues).

Heading west around the mountains from Gréolières brings you through the Clue de Gréolières, carved by a tributary of the Loup, to the ski station **GRÉOLIÈRES-LES-NEIGES**, 18km by road from Gréolières. This is the closest ski resort to the Mediterranean and a centre for **cross-country skiing** (information on ⓣ04.93.59.70.57). Fourteen lifts ascend Mount Cheiron in winter, and in July and August a single chairlift operates for summer panoramas. There are no **hotels** here, accommodation being in the form of furnished apartments (information from tourist office in Gréolières), but there is a handful of **cafés** and **restaurants**, mostly open year-round.

Thorenc, St-Auban and Briançonnet

Thirteen kilometres west of Gréolières, off the D2, **THORENC** is a popular paragliding and cross-country-skiing resort, created by English and Russians at the turn of the last century. The dense woods and style of the older buildings give it an almost Central European atmosphere. It's a lively spot in both winter and summer, and has a very pleasant small **hotel-restaurant** *Les Merisiers*, 24 av du Belvédère (ⓣ04.93.60.00.23, ⓕ04.93.60.02.17; ❷; menus at €22 & €28; closed Tues).

To the north, the narrow and rough D5 crosses the Montagne de Thorenc by the Col de Bleine, then the D10 takes over for the ascent of Charamel, without a moment's pause in the twisting climb. The D10 leads to Aiglun while the D5 takes the easier westward route to **ST-AUBAN** and its *clue*. St-Auban rises above the grassy valley with its back to the mountainside, its wide southern views making up for the plainness of the village itself. The gash made by the River Esteron has left a jumble of rocks through which the water tumbles beneath overhanging cliffs riddled with caves and fissures. In summer, rock-climbing and canyoning are possible in the narrow *clue*. St-Auban's only **hotel-restaurant** is *Le Tracastel* (ⓣ04.93.60.43.06; ❸; closed Nov–Easter), but there's also a *gîte equestre* where you can rent horses (reservations through the *mairie*; ⓣ04.93.60.41.23 or 04.93.60.43.20; ❷).

Further downstream, **BRIANÇONNET** has one of the most stunning positions in the whole of inland Provence. This is best appreciated at the cemetery, from where the views stretch southwards past the edge of the Montagne de

Charamel across miles of uninhabited space. The Romans had a settlement here and the present houses are built with stones from the ancient ruins, with odd bits of Latin still decipherable in the walls. There's just one street with a *boulangerie*, a *tabac*, a small museum of local history, the church – which contains a retable of *The Madonna of the Rosary* by Louis Bréa, showing Mary protecting the ecclesiastical and secular potentates in her cloak – and one tiny **hotel-restaurant**, *Le Chanan* (☎04.93.60.46.75; ❶).

From here you can head north across the **Col de Buis** (usually closed Nov to mid-April) to Entrevaux or Annot (see p.405 and p.406), or east towards the Clue d'Aiglun and the Clue de Riolan.

The Route des Crêtes

Clinging to the steep southern slope of the Montagne de Charamel, the switchback **Route des Crêtes** (D10) requires concentration and nerve. For long stretches there are no distracting views, only thick forest matted with mistletoe. After Le Mas, which hangs on the edge of a precipitous spur below the road, trees can no longer get a root-hold in the near-vertical golden and silver cliffs; the narrowing road crosses high-arched bridges over cascading streams which fall to smoothly moulded pools of aquamarine.

Just before Aiglun you cross the Esteron as it shoots out from the high-pressure passage (too narrow for a road) that splits the Charamel and the Montagne St-Martin. This is the most formidable of all the *clues* and is impossible to explore. You can, however, walk along the GR4 southwards from the D10, 1.5km west of the *clue*, to the **Vegay waterfall**, halfway between Aiglun and Gréolières-les-Neiges (a distance of about 3km), where water destined for the Esteron plummets down a vertical cliff face.

In the village of **AIGLUN** you can **stay**, if you're lucky, in one of the six rooms at the *Auberge de Calendal* (☎04.93.05.82.32; ❷; closed Feb & first week of March), which also manages a dormitory-style *gîte communale* on the GR4 (enquiries to the tourist office at Gréolières; ☎04.93.59.97.94). East from Aiglun, the campanile and silvery olive groves of the ancient fortified village of La Sigale flicker into view.

Beyond La Sigale, midway to Roquesteron, the **Chapelle Notre-Dame d'Entrevignes** has preserved fragments of fifteenth-century frescoes including the unusual scene of Mary, ready to give birth, with Joseph expressing deep suspicion. To visit, apply to La Sigale's *mairie* (Mon–Fri 8.30am–noon & 2.30–5pm; ☎04.93.05.83.52) for keys: you will have to leave a passport behind as security.

ROQUESTERON, about 10km east of St-Aiglun, was divided for a hundred years by the France–Savoy border, which followed the course of the Esteron. There's one **hotel** here, the *Passeron* at 25 bd Salvago (☎04.93.05.91.01; ❷). From Roquesteron you have the choice of following the D17 above the Esteron to the river's confluence with the Var, or taking the tangled D1, through passages of rock seamed in thin vertical bands to **BOUYON**, from where the D8 takes you back to Coursegoules. Both routes take you through a succession of eagle's-nest villages. At Bouyon you'll find an excellent **hotel-restaurant**, the *Catounière* in place de la Mairie (☎ & ⓕ04.93.59.07.15; ❷; closed Oct–Easter).

The Lower Var Valley

From Nice both the Chemin de Fer de Provence and the road stick to the left bank of the Var, which is wide, turbulent and not greatly scenic downstream of its confluence with the Esteron. Past the confluence with the Vésubie, a short way further north, you enter the **Défilé de Chaudan**, a long gorge between vertical cliffs through which the rail line and road have to tunnel. At the northern extremity of the gorge, the River Tinée comes rushing out of the **Gorges de la Mescla** to join the Var in a twisted, semi-subterranean junction of rock and water. From here the course of the Var runs almost due west for 40km, passing tiny medieval villages and the towns of **Puget-Théniers** and **Entrevaux**. The main road and the rail line then continue west along the River Vaïre to **Annot**.

Villars-sur-Var

VILLARS-SUR-VAR, 11km west of the Gorges de la Mescla, may have the northernmost vineyards of the Côtes de Provence *appellation*, but the quantity of wine produced is only just sufficient for local consumption, so you'll be lucky to get a glass of it in one of the two cafés.

The reason for stopping here – apart from the charm of a *village perché* with stepped streets – is to see the **Église de St-Jean-Baptiste**. The carefully restored Baroque church is decorated with trompe-l'oeil frescoes and an eighteenth-century ex-votive painting to "Saint Patron de la Bonne Mort", thanking him for killing off only 66 residents in the previous year's plague. The main altar has a striking retable, with another on the left wall from the Nice School.

Touët-sur-Var and the Gorges du Cians

Crammed against a cliff 10km west of Villars-sur-Var, **TOUËT-SUR-VAR** also has a church that's rather special, though for a very different reason: it's built over a small torrent, visible through a grille in the floor of the nave. The village's highest houses look as if they are falling apart, but in fact the gaps between the beams are open galleries where the midday sun can reach the rows of drying figs.

There's nowhere to stay in Touët, but it has a good **restaurant**, the *Auberge des Chasseurs*, on the main road (☎04.93.05.71.11; menus at €23 & €32; closed Tues), serving local fare which in autumn involves game and wild mushrooms. The specialities of the area are squash ravioli with nut sauce and *tartes des blettes* (Swiss chard tarts).

The River Cians joins the Var just west of Touët. The road along this tributary, the D28, leads to the ski resort of Beuil, passing first through the Gorges Inférieures du Cians, close to the confluence, and then the **Gorges du Cians** proper, an ominous chaos of water tumbling between looming red schist cliffs. Much of the route is tunnelled. This and the Gorges de Daluis to the west (see p.430) are well-signed tourist routes, so be prepared for traffic.

Puget-Théniers

Arriving by train at **PUGET-THÉNIERS**, the first monument you see, on the *cours* below the old town, is a statue of a woman with bound hands. Sculpted by Maillol and titled *L'Action Enchaînée*, it commemorates **Auguste Blanqui**, born here in 1805. Blanqui was one of the leaders of the Paris Commune of 1871, and spent forty years in prison for – as the inscription states – "fidelity to the sacred cause of workers' emancipation". There are few French revolutionaries for whom the description "heroic defender of the proletariat" is so true, and none who came from a more isolated, unindustrialized region.

To some extent, dilapidated Puget-Théniers is the ugly duckling of the *pays*, though its **Vieille Ville**, on the right bank of the River Roudoule, is full of thirteenth-century houses, some with symbols of their original owners' trades on the lintels. The left bank is dominated by the great semicircular apse of the Romanesque **church**, outreaching even the ancient cedar alongside, and suggesting a fort or prison more than a place of worship. It's not a pretty structure, but it does contain a brilliantly realistic Flemish *Entombment*, painted in the 1500s, and an expressive calvary sculpted in wood.

Practicalities

The **tourist office** (June–Aug daily 9am–12.30pm & 3–7pm; Sept–May daily 9am–noon and 2–5.30pm; ⓣ04.93.05.05.05, ⓦwww.provence-val-dazur.com) is on the main road by the gare Chemin de Fer de Provence and has information on walks, canoeing and the steam trains that run between Puget-Théniers and Annot.

The *Laugier*, at 1 place A-Conil (ⓣ04.93.05.01.00; ❷), is the best place to **stay**; alternatively, try the modern *Alizé* (ⓣ04.93.05.06.20, ⓦhotel.alize@wanadoo.fr; ❸), which is by the busy N202, but has its own swimming pool. Puget's two-star municipal **campsite** is by the river (ⓣ04.93.05.10.53; €11 per tent; closed Oct–Feb).

On summer evenings the **cafés** and **restaurants** on place A-Cornil in the Vieille Ville and down along the Roudoule towards the Var are livelier than you'd expect from a small *haut-pays* town. The restaurant in the *Laugier* hotel is a good bet in the centre of town, but first choice for food is *Les Acacias* (ⓣ04.93.05.05.25; closed Wed), 1km east of Puget-Théniers on the main road, where *cuisine de terroir* using the local produce can be enjoyed on a €12 lunch menu, or for €18 in the evenings. Excellent old-fashioned *boulangeries*, *charcuteries* and *fromageries* can be found in the old quarter and, if you happen to be here at Pentecost, nearby La Croix-Sur-Redoule has a communal feast of bean soup cooked in a vast cauldron.

Entrevaux

Upstream from Puget-Théniers the valley widens, allowing space for pear, apple and cherry orchards. After 13km you reach the absurdly photogenic **ENTREVAUX**, whose most striking feature is its fortified old town on the north bank of the river. Built on the site of a Roman settlement, this was once a key border town between France and Savoy.

The single-arched drawbridge across the rushing Var – the only access – was fortified by Vauban, and it is Vauban's linking of the town with the ruined **Château** (access at any time; €3) that gives the site its menacing character. Perched 135m above the river at the top of a steep spur, the château originally could be reached only by scrambling up the rock. By the seventeenth century this had become unacceptable, perhaps because soldiers leaving the garrison on their hands and knees did not do much for the army's image. Consequently, Vauban built the double-walled ramp, plus attendant bastions, that zigzags up the rock in ferocious determination.

The former **cathedral** (summer 9am–7pm; winter 9am–5pm), in the lower part of the old town, is well integrated into the military defences, with one wall forming part of the ramparts and its belfry a fortified tower. The interior, however, is all twirling Louis Quinze, with misericords, side altars and organ as overdecorated as they could possibly be. Just beyond the church, through the **Porte d'Italie**, you can escape from Baroque opulence and military might alike.

Practicalities

The **gare Chemin de Fer de Provence** is just downstream from the bridge on the south bank, and the **tourist office** (June–Aug daily 9am–7pm;

March–May & Sept daily 9am–noon & 2–5pm; Oct–Feb Tues–Sat 9am–noon & 2–5pm; ⓣ04.93.05.46.73) is in the left-hand tower of the drawbridge; it organizes guided tours of the town (May–Sept; €3.80) in medieval costume.

For places to stay, there's the rudimentary **hotel** *Hostellerie Vauban*, 4 place Moreau (ⓣ04.93.05.42.40; ❷), south of the river, and two **gîtes d'étapes**: the *Gîte des Moulins* (❶) and the *Gîte de Plan* (❶), both bookable through the tourist office.

For **food and drink** try the *Bar au Pont-Levis* opposite Vauban's bridge, where English-speaking tourists congregate, or head up to place Charles-Panier where you'll find *L'Échauguette* (ⓣ04.93.05.46.89; menus from €16), a restaurant specializing in trout, pasta and the local dry beef sausage (*secca de boeuf*), and *Le Planet* snack bar, serving omelettes, *pan bagnat* and pizzas. The Lovera *charcuterie* (closed Mon), two doors from *Le Planet*, sells *secca de boeuf* to take away, though it's best seasoned with lemon and olive oil.

Annot

Surrounded by hills, **ANNOT** is primarily a holiday centre for its climate, pure health-giving waters and clean air. The Vieille Ville, if not outstanding, does have some pretty arcades and a Renaissance clock tower on its church; the modern town is grouped around its *cours*, a large open space lined by plane trees to the south of the medieval quarter. It is an excellent base for walks, up past strange sandstone formations to rocky outcrops with names like *Chambre du Roi* (the King's Chamber) and *Dent du Diable* (the Devil's Tooth).

The **gare Chemin de Fer de Provence** is to the southeast of the town, at the end of av de la Gare, which leads to the main *cours*. The helpful tourist office on bd St Pierre (Mon 3–6pm; Tues, Wed, Fri 9am–noon & 3–6pm, Sat 3–5pm; ⓣ04.92.83.23.03, ⓦwww.annot.fr) has plenty of details on walks, rides, sports facilities, the steam train to Puget-Théniers, exhibitions and local festivities. It also organizes guided tours of the Vieille Ville on Tuesdays in season.

Accommodation is easy to come by and reasonably priced. Of the **hotels**, budget options include the recently renovated *La Cigale* to the north on bd St-Pierre (ⓣ & ⓕ04.92.83.33.37; ❷); the *Beau Séjour*, by the entrance to the Vieille Ville on place du Revelly (ⓣ04.92.83.21.08, ⓕ04.92.83.39.67; ❶); and *Hôtel Le Parc* (ⓣ04.92.83.20.03, ⓕ04.92.83.29.84; ❷; closed Oct–April) in an old house on the eastern side of the *cours*. The hotel on av de la Gare, *L'Avenue* (ⓣ04.92.83.22.07; ⓕ04.92.83.33.13; ❸; closed Nov–March), has small cosy rooms and the best **restaurant** in town (menus from €15). For **campers** there's a very pleasant two-star site, *La Ribière*, on the road to Fugeret (ⓣ04.92.83.21.44; €8 per tent; mid-Feb to mid-Nov) just north of the town.

St-André-les-Alpes, Castellane and the Route Napoléon

From Annot, the Chemin de Fer de Provence heads due north before tunnelling through to the Verdon Valley and **Thorame-Haute**'s station, where you can take buses further north up the Verdon. Here, the rail line turns south again, with the next major stop at **St-André-les-Alpes**. St-André stands at the head of the **Lac de Castillon**, one of the Verdon's many artificial lakes, stretching a good 10km southwards to the Barrage de Castillon and the smaller Lac de Chaudanne from where the Verdon descends dramatically into **Castellane**, the second most significant town on the **Route Napoléon** after Grasse.

The main road along the Var Valley, the N202 from Entrevaux, skirts Annot and heads west through the Clue de Rouaine to the Lac de Castillon at **St-Julien-du-Verdon**, then takes over from the D955 as the lakeside corniche up to St-André. The road and rail line run parallel again west from St-André along a beautiful stretch of rock, river and forest to meet the Route Napoléon at **Barrême**.

With good train and road access, plenty of accommodation and well-organized facilities for outdoor activities, particularly water and airborne sports, this is an easy corner of Haute Provence to explore. Castellane and St-Julien can feel a bit too subservient to entrepreneurial tourism, but traditional Provence is never far away, as the sight of sheep taking over the roads on their way to or from their summer pastures may well remind you.

St-André-les-Alpes

Unlike so many tightly huddled Provençal villages, **ST-ANDRÉ-LES-ALPES** has a straggly feel, with its streets and squares open to the magnificent views of the surrounding mountains and the lake. Accommodation and food are cheap; the only difficulty is choosing which of the beautiful routes out from St-André to explore.

The **gare Chemin de Fer de Provence** is a few minutes' walk north west of the village centre, across the N202. The **tourist office** lies between the two on place Marcel-Pastorelli (mid-June to mid-Sept Mon–Sat 9am–noon & 2–7pm, Sun 10am–1pm; mid-April to mid June & mid-Sept to mid-Oct Mon–Fri 9am–noon & 2–5.30pm, Sat 10am–12.30pm & 4–6pm; mid-Oct to mid-April Mon–Fri 9am–noon & 2–5pm; ⓣ04.92.89.02.39, ⓦwww.ot-st-andre-les-alpes.fr), and is very helpful, offering information on the surrounding area, including St-Julien, Thorame and Moriez.

Of the seven **hotels** in and around St-André, the *Lac et Forêt* on the road to St-Julien (ⓣ04.92.89.07.38, ⓕ04.92.89.13.88, ⓔlacforet@club-internet.fr; ❸; closed Nov–Feb) has the best views over the lake, while the *France*, on place de l'Église (ⓣ04.92.89.02.09; ❶), is the cheapest, with budget rooms right in the centre of the village. The two-star municipal **campsite**, *Les Iscles*, by the confluence of the Verdon and the Issole on the road to St-Julien (ⓣ04.92.89.02.29, ⓕ04.92.89.02.56; €9 per tent; closed Oct–April), has good facilities. If you prefer a **gîte d'étape**, try the one in Moriez, the next stop on the Chemin de Fer de Provence or a five-minute drive west of St-André (ⓣ04.92.89.13.20, ⓦwww.verdon-provence.com/gitemoriez; closed mid-Nov to Feb). Several of the hotels have their own **restaurants**, or try *La Table de Marie*, pl Charles Bron (ⓣ04.92.89.16.10). There's a good choice of beers available at *Le Commerce* **bar** on place de l'Église.

Paragliding and **hang-gliding** are popular here, around Mont Chalvet to the west of the village. It's very well organized and regulated by the École de Vol Libre 'Aerogliss' at the Base de Loisirs des Iscles to the south of the village (ⓣ04.92.89.11.30; ⓦwww.aerogliss.com). Short flights for the less experienced take place in the morning, and a five-day beginners' course starts at €390. **Bikes** can be rented at Pro-Verdon Activités Nature on Grande Rue (ⓣ04.92.89.04.19), who also organize **walks**, and **rafting**, **canyoning** and **canoeing** on the Lac de Castillon and Gorges de Verdon.

North to Château-Garnier and Thorame

From St-André, following the River Issole along the D2 brings you to Château-Garnier, 15km north. The narrow road stays close to the banks most of the time, and well-signed footpaths lead off into the wooded hills, which are prone to landslides, as the frequent boulder-strewn scars on the slopes show. After 8km you can turn left towards **TARTONNE** where there's a pleasant gîte d'étape with a good restaurant, *Les Robines* (c/o Mme Pascale Reybaud; ⓣ04.92.34.26.07; ❷; menus from €13), or keep going to La Bâtie where the valley opens out into meadows ringed by hills. Between La Bâtie and Château-Garnier, along the footpath to Tartonne, is the twelfth-century **Chapelle St-Thomas**, decorated with medieval frescoes (the key is available from the *miellerie* in Château-Garnier).

The main reason to stop in **CHÂTEAU-GARNIER**, however, is to visit the serious and dedicated **honey** business Miellerie Chailan at the far end of the village on the left (Mon–Fri 8am–noon & 1.30–6.30pm, Sat 9am–noon & 2–5pm). Though only groups are given tours of the hives, you may see the gleaming machinery in action, and you can certainly buy superb honey with such flavours as rosemary, acacia, "thousand flowers", sunflower, pine and lavender, plus nougat, sweets, candles and medicinal derivatives.

From Château-Garnier the road veers east through **THORAME BASSE**, where the church has an unlikely clock on the spire and the *Café du Vallée* serves inexpensive plats du jour. The road then continues through wide open meadows to **THORAME HAUTE** where the landscape is scarred by gravel extraction. There's a **hotel-restaurant** here, *Au Bon Accueil* (ⓣ04.92.83.90.79; ❷), a *charcuterie* and a one-star municipal **campsite** *Fontchaude* (ⓣ04.92.83.47.37; €7 per tent), down by the river.

South along the Lac de Castillon

Slightly milky and an unearthly shade of aquamarine, the hundred-metre-deep **Lac de Castillon** is a popular bathing spot in high summer, with closely-supervised **beaches** and **boats** for rent, south of St-André along the N202. The landscape gets more dramatic after the road crosses over the lake and the hills start to close in.

ST-JULIEN-DU-VERDON was a casualty of the creation of the lake. Today it's a tiny place with a two-star **campsite**, *Camping du Lac* (ⓣ04.92.89.07.93; €10 per tent; open mid-June to mid-Sept), and a **hotel**, *Lou Pidanoux* (ⓣ04.92.89.05.87, ⓦwww.verdon-provence.com/pidanoux.htm; ❶), but nothing to suggest that this was once Sanctus Julienetus, on the Roman road from Nice to Digne. Still, it's a pleasant, quiet spot if you just want to laze about by calm water with a gorgeous backdrop of mountains.

The main road east to Annot from St-Julien leads through the dramatic *clues* of Vergons and Rouaine, and past the exquisite Romanesque chapel of Notre-Dame de Valvert. The road south to Castellane follows the lake, with plenty of opportunities for water-skiing. The gleam of gold up in the hills on the opposite bank is the Buddhist centre of Mandaron. At the southern tip of the lake, the road crosses the awe-inspiring **Barrage de Castillon**, where there's a small parking area if you want to stop for a closer look, though bathing is forbidden.

Castellane

Few towns can have as dramatic a site as **CASTELLANE**, dominated by a 180m cliff that looms over the Vieille Ville and is topped by the chapel of **Notre Dame du Roc**. Billed as the "gateway" to the Gorges du Verdon, some 17km away (see p.291), Castellane has long been a major tourist camp, and your reason for stopping is likely to be for the range of restaurants, hotels and cafés which in summer gives the town an animation rare in these parts. The place where Napoleon stopped to dine on March 3, 1815 is now the **Musée des Arts et Traditions**

Populaires de Castellane et Moyen Verdon, 34 rue Nationale (late May, June & Oct Tues–Sat 9am–noon & 2–6pm; July–Sept daily 10am–1pm & 2.30–6.30pm; €2), which has temporary exhibitions of variable interest.

Houses in Castellane's old quarter are packed close together, as if huddling for protection from the sheer violence of the surrounding landscape; some of the lanes are barely shoulder wide. The path up to the chapel of Notre Dame du Roc starts behind the parish church at the head of place de l'Église, winding its way up past the Vieille Ville and the machicolated **Tour Pentagonal**, standing uselessly on the lower slopes. Twenty to thirty minutes should see you at the top, from where you can't actually see the gorge, but you do get a pretty good view of the river disappearing into it and the mountains circling the town.

Practicalities

There are two **buses** a day in July and August into the Gorges du Verdon (1hr 20min to La Maline). The **tourist office** is at the top of rue Nationale (July & Aug Mon–Sat 9am–12.30pm & 1.30–7pm, Sun 10am–1pm; Sept–June Mon–Fri 9am–noon & 2–6pm; ⓣ04.92.83.61.14, ⓦwww.castellane.org) and can provide a full list of hotels and campsites.

The best **hotel** deals in Castellane are the *Hostellerie du Roc*, place de l'Église (ⓣ04.92.83.62.65, ⓕ04.92.83.73.76; ❸; closed Mon, Nov & Dec), *Le Verdon*, bd de la République (ⓣ04.92.83.62.02, ⓕ04.92.83.73.80; ❷), and the *Auberge Bon Accueil*, place Marcel-Sauvaire (ⓣ04.92.83.62.01, ⓕ04.92.83.62.01; ❷; closed Oct to mid-April). The *Hôtel du Commerce* in place de l'Église (ⓣ04.92.83.61.00, ⓦwww.hotel-fradet.com; ❹; menus from €20; closed Nov–Feb) is the most upmarket, with questionable decor but wonderful **food** served in the garden. You can get pasta dishes for €7.50 at *La Main à la Pâte* on rue de la Fontaine and there's a pleasant ice-cream bar at the end of the same street. Wednesday and Saturday are **market** days and there's a good wine shop on rue Nationale.

There are eleven **campsites** within 3km of the town. The closest is *Le Frédéric-Mistral* (ⓣ04.92.83.62.27; €12 per tent), by the river on the rte des Gorges du Verdon. Further on down the same road you'll see the caravans and bungalows of the *Camping Notre-Dame* (ⓣ04.92.83.63.02; closed mid-Sept to April), and 1.5km out of town the four-star *Camp du Verdon* (ⓣ04.92.83.61.29; ⓦwww.camp-du-verdon.com; €24 per tent; closed mid-Sept to mid-May). In summer all the sites along this road are likely to be full. A good one to try that's further afield and away from the gorge is *La Colle* on the GR4 off the rte des Gorges (ⓣ & ⓕ04.92.83.61.57; €14.50 per tent; closed Nov–March).

For **canoeing** and **rafting** on Lac de Castillon and the Gorges du Verdon, Aqua-Verdon at 9 rue Nationale (ⓣ04.92.83.72.75), and Activité Montagne Rivières, at 20 rue Nationale (ⓣ04.92.83.73.57), are the places to get information. It's easy enough to rent a mountain **bike** in Castellane: try Aboard Rafting, 8 pl de l'Église (ⓣ04.92.83.76.11), or Aqua Viva Est, 12 bd de la République (ⓣ04.92.83.75.74).

Along the Route Napoléon

North of Castellane the barren scrubby rocks lining the Route Napoléon need the evening light to turn them a more becoming pinkish hue. The town's landmark remains visible all the way up the zigzags to the **Col de Leque**, from where the Route Napoléon traverses the **Clue de Taulanne**, then opens out onto a marvellous northward view of a circle of crests. To either side of the road lie some of the most obscure and empty quarters of Provence. The populations of villages such as **Blieux** and **Majastres**, on the slopes of the Mourre ridge to the west, have dwindled close to the point of desertion. Life here is a picture of rural poverty at its starkest, for all the seeming promise of the springtime or early summer land to the amateur's eye.

Back on the only significant road, the village of **SENEZ** speaks of the same decline, with its barn-like Romanesque former cathedral that could easily accommodate ten times the present number of residents. The episcopal see established here in the fourth century, one of the earliest in France, was throughout the centuries one of the poorest bishoprics in the country. The church is only open on Sunday, but at other times the key is available from Mme Mestre on pl de la Fontaine behind the cathedral. There's a **gîte** on place du Coulet (ⓣ04.92.34.29.21, ⓔcarpediemsenez@aol.com; ❶), should you wish to stay.

Digne-les-Bains and around

The traffic-choked spa town of **DIGNE-LES-BAINS** is the capital of the Alpes-de-Haute-Provence *département*, and by far the largest town in northeastern Provence, with about 17,000 inhabitants. Yet despite the almost metropolitan swank of the main street, boulevard Gassendi, and its superb position between the Durance Valley and the start of the real mountains, it can be a dull place to explore. Aside from the crumbling Vieille Ville with its tasteful modern infill, the town is principally a centre for administration and functional shopping, particularly in the vast retail park southwest of the town along the N85.

Digne does, however, have a busy calendar of festivals, including a "lavender month" in summer (see p.414), a couple of interesting museums, and a Tibetan foundation that has been visited by the Dalai Lama. It also has a good range of affordable places to stay, and, if you have your own transport, makes a decent base for trips into the surrounding mountains. This is serious walking country, much of which is protected by the **Réserve Naturelle Géologique de Haute Provence**, which encompasses a huge area surrounding the town.

Arrival, information and accommodation

From the Durance Valley the Route Napoléon enters Digne along the west bank of the Bléone, arriving at the rond-point du 4 Septembre, with the **gares SNCF** (bus connection to St-Auban and Aix TGV; ⓣ04.92.31.50.00) and **Chemin de Fer de Provence** (ⓣ04.92.31.01.58) just to the west, along av Paul-Sémard. Avenue de Verdon continues to Grand Pont, the main bridge, over which is the rond-point du 11 Novembre 1918, where you'll find the **tourist office** (April–June & Sept Mon–Sat 8.45am–noon & 2–6pm, Sun 10am–noon; July & Aug Mon–Sat 8.45am–12.30pm & 1–6.30pm, Sun 10am–12.30pm & 3–6pm; Sept–May Mon–Sat 8.45am–noon & 2–6pm; ⓣ04.92.36.62.62, ⓦwww.ot-dignelesbains.fr), the **gîtes de France** office and the **gare routière**. From the south the Route Napoléon comes in along the east bank of the river to the rond-point du 11 Novembre 1918. From the rond-point, the main street, bd Gassendi, leads northeast up to place du Gal-de-Gaulle, while bd Thiers, which becomes av du 8 mai 1945, leads east towards the Établissement Thermal, 3km from the centre. The **old town** lies between these two. **Bikes** can be rented from Gallardo, 8 cours des Arès (ⓣ04.92.31.05.29).

The best-value **hotels** in Dignes are the simple but pleasant *Le Petit Saint-Jean*, 14 cours des Arès (ⓣ04.92.31.30.04, ⓕ04.92.31.30.04; closed mid-Dec to mid-Jan; ❶), with a restaurant serving Spanish specialities (plats from €9); the

Origan, 6 rue Pied-de-la-Ville (Ⓣ04.92.31.62.13, Ⓕ04.92.31.68.31; ❶), which also serves good food (menus from €19; closed Sun); and the very comfortable *Central*, 26 bd Gassendi (Ⓣ04.92.31.31.91, Ⓦwww.hotel-central.fr.st; ❶). For those on a larger budget, *Le Grand Paris*, 19 bd Thiers (Ⓣ04.92.31.11.15, Ⓔgrandparis@wanadoo.fr; closed Dec–Feb; ❺), provides considerably more luxury in a seventeenth-century former convent with tastefully decorated large rooms and Digne's top gourmet restaurant (menus from €23–68; closed Dec–Feb).

The two-star municipal **campsite** *du Bourg* is 2km out from the centre along the D900 to Seynes-les-Alpes (Ⓣ04.92.31.04.87; €10.50 per tent; closed Nov–March); take av Ste-Douceline left from the top of bd Gassendi and then turn right into av du Camping. Alternatively, the three-star *Camping des Eaux Chaudes*, av des Thermes (Ⓣ04.92.32.31.04; €12.50 per tent; closed Nov–March), is more pleasantly situated, 1.5km out of town towards the Établissement Thermal.

The City

Late medieval Digne had **two centres**: the area to the north around Notre-Dame du Bourg, where pre-Roman Digne developed; and the existing Haute Ville where the Cathédrale St-Jérôme was built as a small church at the end of the fifteenth century, to be successively enlarged as it took over the functions of Notre-Dame.

Standing in splendid isolation on placette du Prévat, **Notre-Dame du Bourg** (June–Oct daily 3–6pm) is typical of Provençal Romanesque architecture, save for its relative bulk and the lightness of its yellowy stone. Built between 1200 and 1330, it contains fragments of early medallions and late medieval murals, the least faded illustrating the Last Judgement. Archeological digs have revealed a first-century construction and a fifth-century church from which a Merovingian altar and a mosaic floor remain.

In contrast, the fifteenth-century **Cathédrale St-Jérôme** in the Haute Ville (June–Oct Tues, Wed, Thurs & Sat 3–6pm) stands weed-encrusted and dilapidated. Its Gothic facade is still impressive and the features inside, in particular the Gothic stained-glass windows, clearly indicate that this was once an awesome place of worship. Sadly, some of the surrounding streets remain as run-down as the cathedral itself, with commercial life draining from the Vieille Ville, and a quarter of the shops in rue de l'Hubac, its principal street, standing empty.

The Wednesday and Saturday **markets** bring animation to the otherwise lifeless and windswept **place Général-de-Gaulle**, to the north of the cathedral, with lots of lavender products, including honey, on sale. To the east, a statue of **Pierre Gassendi**, a seventeenth-century mathematician and astronomer, stands within the balustrades that separate the boulevard named after him from place Général-de-Gaulle. Gassendi used to dispute the precise location of the immortal soul with Descartes, but showed more materialism on his deathbed when he remarked that he would not now be dying had he not been so compliant with his doctors.

The **Musée Municipal**, at 64 bd Gassendi (currently closed for restoration; check with the tourist office for the latest details), has a good art collection that ranges from the sixteenth century to the present, plus a collection of nineteenth-century scientific instruments and Gassendi mementoes.

Southeast of the old town, on place Paradis, is the **Musée de la Seconde Guerre Mondiale** (May, June & Sept to mid-Oct Wed 2–5pm; July & Aug Mon–Fri 2–6pm; Oct–April by appointment with Jacques Teyssier on

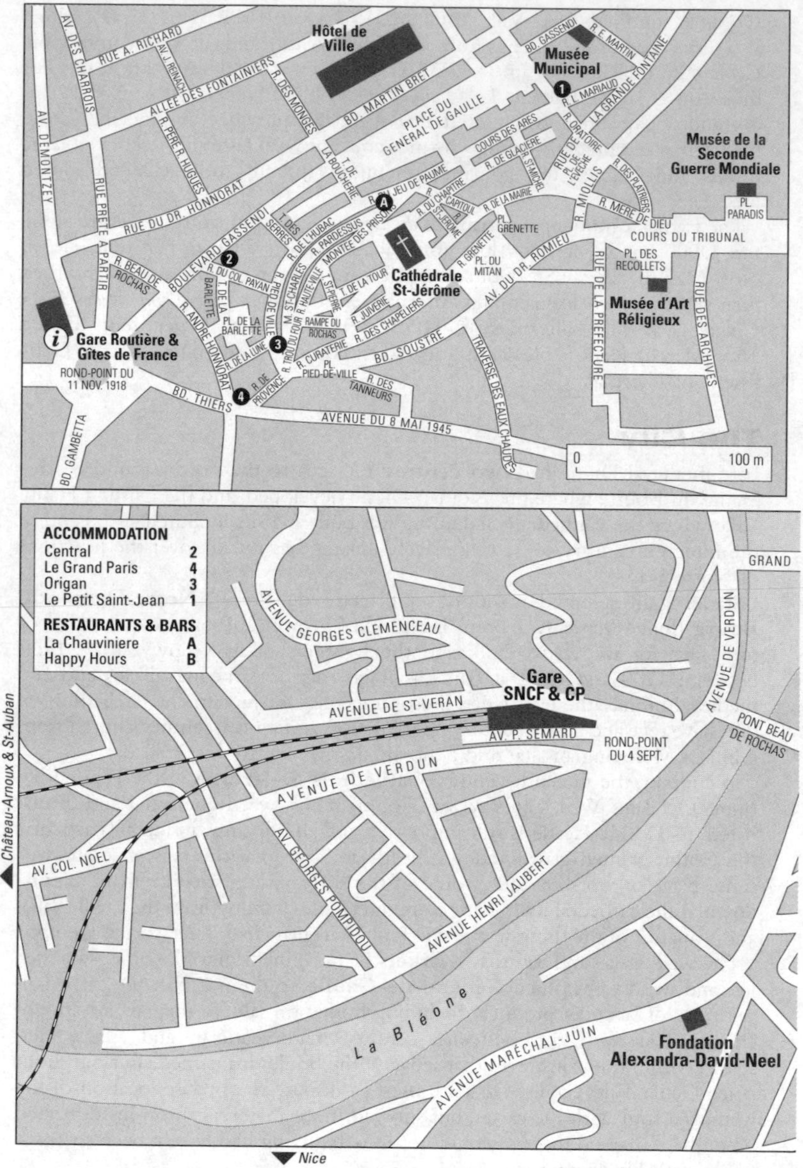

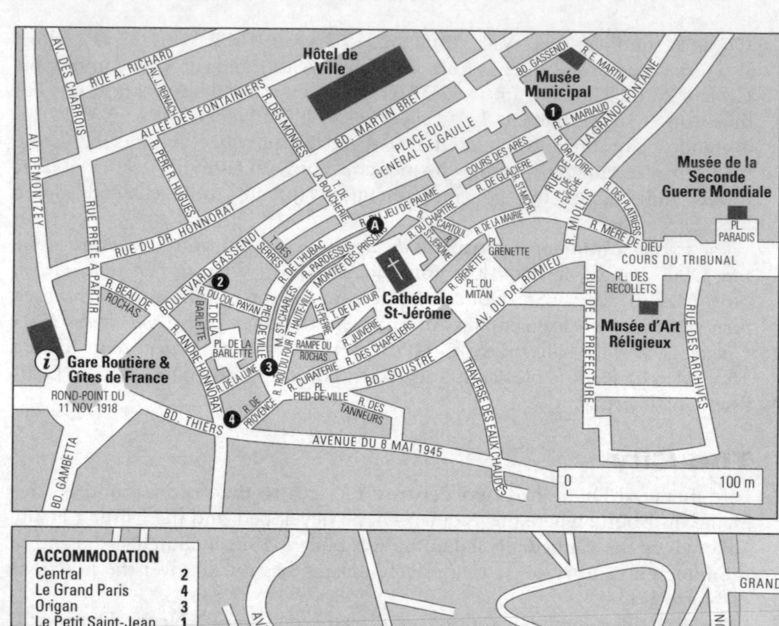

Ⓣ04.92.31.28.95; free). Digne was under Italian occupation from the end of 1942 to September 1943, when the Germans took over. The names of people in the photographs have had to be covered up in an effort to avoid the rows that still erupt here over who resisted and who did not. For a foreign visitor, however, this is a fascinating exposé of one town's experience of the war that left the people here, as throughout France, scarred by bitter divisions, even within the ranks of the Resistance.

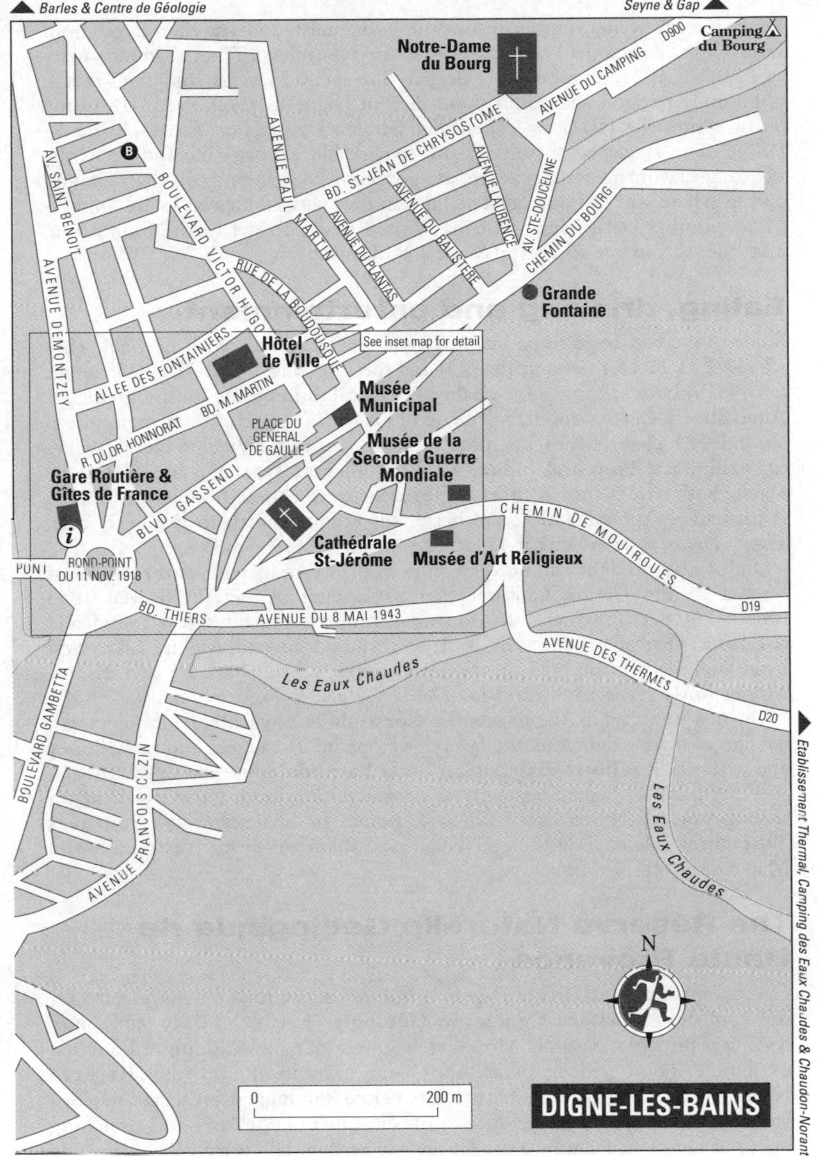

The collection of reliquaries, chalices, robes and crucifixes on show at the **Musée d'Art Religieux** on nearby place des Récollets (June–Sept daily 10am–6pm; free) is less inspiring. The museum does, however, have fairly interesting videos on Romanesque architecture, Baroque altarpieces, and the Cathédrale St-Jérôme.

A very different world is conjured up in the **Fondation Alexandra-David-Neel** at 27 av Maréchal-Juin, the Nice road, south of the centre (guided tours daily: June–Sept 10.30am, 2pm, 3.30pm & 5pm; Oct–May 10.30am, 2pm &

4pm; free). A writer, musician, one-time anarchist, and traveller throughout Indo-China, Alexandra David Neel spent two months in Tibet's forbidden city of Lhasa in 1924, disguised as a beggar. She spent 25 years studying Tibetan philosophy, religion and culture, and died in Digne in 1969, aged 101, in the house – now the *Fondation* – she called Samten Dzong, her "fortress of meditation". The *Fondation* documents this remarkable woman's life and pays tribute to her favourite country; there are gorgeous silk hangings on the walls and a shop where you can buy current Tibetan products, all blessed by the Nobel-Prize-winning Dalai Lama, who has visited twice. To get to the foundation, take bus #2 and get off at stop Stade J. Rolland.

Eating, drinking and entertainment

Some of the best **food** to be had in Digne is at the hotels, with *Le Grand Paris* (☎04.92.31.11.15; menus from €23) and the *Origan* (☎04.92.31.62.13; menus from €19) both serving good-quality Provençal dishes using local ingredients. Alternatively, *La Chauvinière*, 54 rue de l'Hubac (☎04.92.31.40.03; menus from around €21; closed Mon), is a more intimate spot in the Vieille Ville, also serving traditional Provençal dishes. Whilst Boulevard Gassendi and pl Gal de Gaulle both have plenty of **cafés** and **brasseries** to choose from, none of them is particularly special, and you're better off heading north to the lively café, *Happy Hours*, at 43 bd Victor-Hugo (☎04.92.31.23.37; closed Sun).

Out of season Digne can be very quiet in the evening, with **entertainment** limited to the Centre Culturel Pierre Gassendi, 45 av du 8 Mai 1945 (☎04.92.30.87.10), which puts on shows, concerts and films year-round, and also has a cybercafé. If you want to dance, head out towards Aiglun, 12km west from Digne along the N85 on rte de Marseille, where there are two **discos**, *Meteore* (☎04.92.34.75.89) and *Les Douze Chênes* (☎04.92.34.65.10).

The first weekend in August sees the **Corso de la Lavande**, a jamboree with parades of floats celebrating the lavender crop and its two key products, honey and perfume. The **Foire-Exposition de la Lavande** at the end of August and the beginning of September is more commercially minded but excellent for buying pots of goodies to take back home. In September the **Journées Tibétaines** celebrate all things Tibetan; and there are special **film** seasons in March, July and November.

The Réserve Naturelle Géologique de Haute Provence

On the northern outskirts of Digne, at the end of the road off to the left after the Pont des Arches, the **Centre de Géologie** (April–Oct daily 9am–noon & 2–5.30pm; Nov–March Mon–Fri 9am–noon & 2–5.30pm; €4.60) has extremely good videos, workshops and exhibitions on the **Réserve Naturelle Géologique de Haute Provence**, the biggest protected geological area in Europe, covering an area of 150 square kilometres and stretching north of Digne and south to the Gorges du Verdon. The reserve's sites include imprints and fossils of various Miocene creatures – crabs, oysters, ammonites, an ichthyosaurus – which record the time before the Alps had forced the sea southwards. In spring the Centre runs guided walks to various sites in the Réserve (for information call ☎04.92.34.91.20). To get to the Centre, take bus #2 from Dignes' gare routière, and get off at stop Champourcin. If you're driving, note that it's a fifteen-minute walk from the car park to the Centre.

Close to the Centre, on the road to Barles, you can see on the left of the road a wall of ammonites, the fossils of shells whose creatures lived off these rocks

185 million years ago. Beyond here, the road forks left to **LA ROBINE**, starting point for a one-hour walk to the extraordinarily well-preserved fossilized skeleton of an ichthyosaurus, a 4.5-metre-long reptile that was swimming around these parts while dinosaurs lumbered about on land. The walk starts from the car park near La Robine's school at the far end of the village, and the path is well signed with the logo of an ichthyosaurus.

Along the Eaux Chaudes

The sulphurous water (29–49°C), whose health-giving properties have been known since antiquity, spouts out of the Falaise St-Pancrace just east of the town above av des Thermes; the stream called Eaux Chaudes, which runs alongside the avenue, however, is actually no warmer than any mountain stream. If you want to take a cure, the **Établissement Thermal** (Ⓣ04.92.32.32.92) will be only too happy to oblige, and if you're not sure what it entails there's a guided tour (March–Aug & Nov Thurs 2pm; bus #1, stop Thermes).

If you're more interested in stunning landscapes, the D20 along the Eaux Chaudes which meets the Route Napoléon at Chaudon-Norante is a great route to follow. Meadows contrast with the great wall of mountain to the north; acacia trees give way to larch forests as you climb to the Col du Corobin where the views open up to a vast expanse southwards. Near Digne you may notice women wearing floral scarves and long skirts of a distinctly un-Provençal style. They are likely to be Albanians, one of several foreign communities who have settled in this harsh and marginalized environment.

Massif les Monges and Seyne

North of Digne the mountains that reach their highest peak at Les Monges (2115m) form an impassable barrier, as far as roads go, between the valleys running down to Sisteron and the Durance and those of the Bléone's tributaries. There are footpaths for serious walkers (which begin at Digne on the west bank of the Bléone north of the Grand Pont), and just one road loops south of Les Monges linking Digne and Sisteron via **Thoard** and **Authon** across the **Col de Font-Belle**. Fantastic forested paths lead off past vertical rocks from the pass.

The D900a, which follows first the course of the Bléone, and then the Bès torrent, before joining the main D900 and continuing north to **Seyne-les-Alpes**, passes many of the protected sites of the Réserve Naturelle Géologique de Haute Provence, where shrubs, flowers and butterflies are now the sole visible wildlife. After heavy rain the waters tear through the **Clues de Barles and Verdaches** like a boiling soup of mud in which it's hard to imagine fish finding sustenance.

Making any decent livelihood from the land here is difficult. A lot of "*marginaux*" (hippies or anyone into alternative lifestyles) manage to survive, making goats' cheese and doing seasonal work; the indigenous *paysans* are more likely to be opening gîtes and servicing the increasing numbers of city dwellers who come for trekking or skiing trips. But it's still very wild and deserted, with little accommodation other than gîtes and chambres d'hôtes; petrol stations are also few and far between.

Seyne-les-Alpes

SEYNE-LES-ALPES lies in a distinctly alpine landscape some 40km north of Digne, its highest point topped by a Vauban fort. The town's main influx is in winter, when its three skiing stations, **St-Jean**, **Chabanon** and **Le Grand Puy**, are in operation. The rest of the year Seyne is quieter, but still has plenty of accommodation on offer and scope for walking and riding into the mountains. It also has the only surviving horse fair in southeast France – held on the second Saturday of October – and a mule breeder's competition at the beginning of August.

The **tourist office** is on Grande-Rue, the road past the church (Mon–Fri 9am–noon & 2–5pm, ⓣ04.92.35.11.00, ⓔvallee.de.la.blanche@wanadoo.fr), and provides information about skiing, walking and horse-riding. For **accommodation**, there's *La Chaumière* hotel-restaurant, also on Grande-Rue (ⓣ04.92.35.00.48; ❶), and *Au Vieux Tilleil* (ⓣ04.92.35.00.04, ⓦwww.vieux-tilleul.fr; ❷), 1km from the town centre at Les Auches, with its own pool/skating rink. Below the town, on either side of the river, are two **campsites**, the three-star *Les Prairies* (ⓣ04.92.35.10.21, ⓦwww.campinglesprairies.com; €18 per tent; closed Oct–March) and the two-star *Camping la Blanche* (ⓣ04.92.35.02.55, ⓦwww.campinglablanche.com). There are a couple of **bars** on Grande Rue and one pizzeria, *La Bugade* (from €6).

Along the Ubaye to Barçelonnette

From the northern border of Provence at the Lac de Serre-Ponçon, the D900 follows the River Ubaye to **Barçelonnette**. It passes through a dramatic landscape of tiny, irregular fields backed by the jagged silhouettes of the mountains at the head of the valley, looking like something out of a vampire movie. There are **campsites** on the river bank in each village, and **canoeing**, **rafting**, **canyoning** and **hydrospeed** bases at Le Lauzet-sur-Ubaye and Meolans-Revel. The Aérodrome de Barçelonnette-St-Pons is announced by a grounded aeroplane transformed into a restaurant.

Barçelonnette

Snow falls on **BARÇELONNETTE** around Christmas and stays till Easter, yet, despite the proximity of several ski resorts, summer is the main tourist season. The town is immaculate, with sunny squares where old men wearing berets play *pétanque*, backed by views of snowcapped mountains. The houses all have tall gables and deep eaves, and a more ideal spot for doing nothing would be hard to find. The central square, **place Manuel**, has a white clock tower commemorating the centenary of the 1848 revolution. The Spanish association of the town's name, "Little Barcelona", is due to its foundation in the thirteenth century by Raimond Béranger IV, count of Provence, whose family came from the Catalan city.

Some of the larger houses on av de la Libération are particularly opulent, having been built by Barçelonette's sheep farmers and wool merchants who emigrated to Latin America in the nineteenth century to make their fortunes, before returning home to build their dream houses. One of these grand

Skiing

The tourist office in Barçelonnette has brochures for all the local **ski resorts**, which can also be contacted direct: Pra-Loup (ⓣ04.92.84.10.04, ⓦwww.praloup.com); Ste-Anne/La Condamine (ⓣ04.92.84.30.30, ⓦwww.sainte-anne.com); Jausiers (ⓣ04.92.81.21.45, ⓦwww.jausiers.com); Le Sauze/Super-Sauze (ⓣ04.92.81.05.61, ⓦwww.sauze.com). During the skiing season a **free bus** does the rounds of the resorts from Barçelonnette. Pra-Loup's pistes link up with La Foux d'Allos (see p.418).

villas, *La Sapinière*, at 10 av de la Libération, houses the **Musée de la Vallée** (June & Sept Tues–Sat 3–7pm; July & Aug daily 10am–noon & 2.30–7pm; €3.10), which details the life and times of the people of the Ubaye Valley, the emigration to Mexico and the travels of a nineteenth-century explorer from the town. In summer, the ground floor becomes an information centre for the **Parc National du Mercantour** (mid-June to mid-Sept daily 10am–noon & 3–7pm; ⓣ04.92.81.21.31), a national reserve stretching from the mountain passes south of Barçelonnette almost to **Sospel** (see map on pp.429–430). They can provide maps, advise on walks and mountain refuges, and tell you about the fauna and flora of the area.

Practicalities

Barçelonnette is very small. **Buses** from Marseille or Gap arrive on place Aimé-Gassier, three blocks south of the main street, rue Manuel, which leads to place F-Mistral. In a small courtyard just off place F-Mistral you'll find the **tourist office** (July & Aug daily 9am–8pm; Sept–June Mon–Sat 9am–noon & 2–6pm; ⓣ04.92.81.04.71, ⓦwww.barcelonnette.net). **Bikes** can be rented from Rando Passion, 31 rue Jules Béraud (ⓣ04.92.81.43.34), and **canoeing** and **rafting** trips can be organized through Alligator, Pont Long (ⓣ04.92.81.06.06).

The best budget **places to stay** in the centre of town are the cosy *Touring*, 4 rue Jules Béraud (ⓣ04.92.81.07.57; ❶), or the old-fashioned and comfortable *Grand Hôtel*, 6 place Manuel (June to mid-Oct & Jan to mid-May; ⓣ04.92.81.03.14, ⓔgrandhotelbarcelonnette@hotmail.com; ❷; closed mid-Oct to Jan and first two weeks of May). Slightly more upmarket are the excellent-value *Grande Épervière* at 18 rue des Trois-Freres-Arnaud (ⓣ04.92.81.00.70, ⓔvillamex@9online.fr; ❸), surrounded by its own park, and *L'Azteca*, 3 rue François-Arnaud (ⓣ04.92.81.46.36, ⓔhotel-azteca@wanadoo.fr; ❸), an extremely pleasant hotel in a Mexican-style house, with superb views of the mountains. There are two **campsites** on av Émile-Aubert, the D902 leading to the Col de la Cayolle: the closer, three-star *Camping du Plan* (ⓣ & ⓕ04.92.81.08.11; closed Oct to mid-May) is 500m out of town; the two-star *Le Tampico* (ⓣ04.92.81.02.55; €11 per tent) is 1km further out.

Beautifully prepared and delicious **food** can be had at *La Mangeoire Gourmande*, place des Quatre-Vents (ⓣ04.92.81.01.61; menus from €15; closed Mon, Tues, last two weeks of May & Nov), in the rustic setting of an old sheep barn. For a more alpine feel, there's raclette and fondue on the menu at *La Bergerie*, on rue Grenette (ⓣ04.92.81.29.90, around €18), and pizza is available at *Le Coco-Loco*, pl Manuel (ⓣ04.92.81.50.72; closed in winter). Most of Barçelonnette's **cafés** cluster around pl Manuel; *Saint Tropez* is the most elegant, with salads from €7 and pasta from €6.

Wednesday and Saturday are **market** days on place Aimé-Gassier and place St-Pierre, where you'll find all manner of sweets, jams and alcohol made from locally picked bilberries, pâtés made from local birds – thrush, partridge, pheasant – and the favourite liqueurs of this part of the world, distilled from alpine plants and nuts. There are also farmers' markets in summer on place de la Mairie, and in November, December, February, April and May on place Manuel.

Moving on from Barçelonnette: the mountain valleys

From Barçelonnette there are four routes across the watershed of Mont Pelat, La Bonette, Chambeyron and their high gneiss and granite extensions. The Col d'Allos leads into the **Haut-Verdon** Valley; the Col de la Cayolle into the **Haut-**

Var Valley; the road across the summit of La Bonette to the **Tinée** Valley; and the Col de Larche into Italy. All but the last are snowed up between November and April, and can sometimes be closed as late as June. Further east the **Vésubie** rises just below the Italian border; like the Tinée and the Verdon it runs into the Var.

The Haut-Verdon Valley

The most westerly route from Barçelonnette crosses the **Col d'Allos** (closed Nov–May) at 2250m to join the River Verdon just a few kilometres from its source. A mountain refuge, *Col d'Allos* (☎04.92.83.85.14; closed Sept–July), on the pass, marks the junction with the GR56, which leads west to the Ubaye Valley and Seyne-les-Alpes, and east to the Col de Larche and the Tinée Valley. In late June pale wild pansies and deep blue gentians flower between patches of ice. The panorama is magnificent, though once you start backstitching your way down the side of the pass to the Verdon, the hideous vast hotels of **La Foux d'Allos** come into view.

La Foux d'Allos

If you're going to ski or snowboard, scruffy **LA FOUX D'ALLOS** is probably the cheapest Provençal resort in which to do it. The lifts and *pistes* join up with Pra-Loup to the north, and the resort is quite high (1800–2600m), so melting snow shouldn't be a problem.

La Foux d'Allos and its neighbours are also keen to promote themselves as summer resorts, with all kinds of activities on offer at the Parc de Loisirs in Allos, from trampolining to horse-riding, archery, courses in wildlife photography, and water sports. The **tourist office** in the Maison de la Foux (July, Aug & 20 Dec to April daily 9am–noon & 2–6.30pm; ☎04.92.83.80.70) can provide details.

The best-value place to stay is the **youth hostel**, *HI La Foux d'Allos* (☎04.92.83.81.08, Ⓦwww.fuaj.org; closed mid-Sept to Nov & mid-May to mid-June), which must be booked well in advance. Other options include the **hotels** *Le Sestrière* (☎04.92.83.81.70, Ⓦwww.lesestriere.com; ❸; closed May, Oct & Nov) and *Le Toukal* (☎04.92.83.82.76; ❸; closed May to late June & mid-Sept to Nov), or the *Hameau de la Foux* **chalets** (☎04.92.83.82.26; from €381 a week). For details of the ski school, phone the École de Ski du Val d'Allos (☎04.92.83.81.64).

Allos and its lake

The medieval village of **ALLOS**, 9km south of La Foux d'Allos, was all but destroyed by fire in the eighteenth century; one tower of the ramparts half survived and was turned into the current clock tower. The old livelihoods of tending sheep and weaving woollen sheets only just made it past the turn of the twentieth century when tourism began with the discovery of the **Lac d'Allos**, 13km east and 800m above Allos. Once skiing became an established pastime the agricultural days of Allos were numbered. But for all its *résidences secondaires*, it's not a bad place to spend a day or two.

The road to the lake stops 6km from Allos, leaving you with a long walk to reach what was once the head of a glacier. If you want to walk the whole way from Allos, follow the path which starts by the church. Round and blue, reflecting the high amphitheatre half-circling it, the lake nourishes trout and char in its pure cold waters. Looking in the direction of the one-time glacier flow, you can just see the peak of **Mont Pelat**, the highest mountain in the Parc du Mercantour.

Practicalities

For information on paths, weather conditions and so forth, the Parc du Mercantour has an office (Ⓣ04.92.83.04.18) in the same building as the **tourist office** (July, Aug & mid-Dec to mid-April Mon–Sat 8.30am–noon & 2–6.30pm, Sun 9am–noon & 3–6.30pm; Sept to mid-Dec and mid-April to June Mon–Sat 9am–noon and 2–5pm, Sun 9am–noon; Ⓣ04.92.83.02.81, Ⓦwww.valdallos.com), at the northern end of the old village. Note that the only **bank** in this stretch of the valley is the Crédit Agricole opposite (Tues–Sat).

Hotels include the *Pascal* (Ⓣ04.92.83.00.04; ❷) in the old village, and the more upmarket but characterless *Plein Soleil* (Ⓣ04.92.83.02.16, Ⓔfyerou@aol.com; ❸) in Super-Allos, the modern extension northeast of the village. There's a very comfortable **chambre d'hôtes**, *La Ferme*, on rte de la Foux (Ⓣ04.92.83.04.76, Ⓔlafermegp@aol.com; ❷), and a **gîte d'étape**, the *Chalet Auberge L'Autapie* (Ⓣ04.92.83.06.31; ❶). Walkers can also stay at the *Refuge du Lac d'Allos* on the lake itself (Ⓣ04.92.83.00.24; ❶; closed Oct–June), but will have to book well in advance.

The choice of places to **eat** in Allos is limited. You can get pasta and fondue at *Le Bercail*, 1 Grand rue (Ⓣ04.92.83.07.53; menus from €14), while upmarket picnic food can be bought from *La Ferme Gourmande* opposite the tourist office. A useful place to shop, for food and anything else you might need, is the Shopi supermarket on the main road (Mon–Sat 8.45am–12.15pm & 3.30–7pm; closed Wed pm).

Colmars-les-Alpes

The next town downstream from Allos is **COLMARS-LES-ALPES**, an extraordinarily well-preserved stronghold, whose name comes from a temple to Mars built by the Romans on the hill above the town. The sixteenth-century ramparts with their arrow slits and small square towers are complete; and though the two main entrances, the Porte de France and Porte de Savoie, have been reduced to just gateways, the impression is still that this is a perfect historical model. The ramparts were constructed on the orders of François I of France to reinforce the defences that had existed since 1381 when Colmars became a border town between Provence and Savoy. When Savoy declared war on France in 1690, Vauban was called in to make the town even more secure. He designed the **Fort de Savoie** and the **Fort de France** at either end of the town.

Having passed through the Porte de France, the Porte de Savoie or the smaller Porte de Lance halfway between them – all adorned with climbing roses – you find yourself in an exquisite old and quiet Provençal town with cobbled streets and fountained squares. The Fort de Savoie is open for guided tours in July and August (daily 10am; €4; tickets from the tourist office), when exhibitions of art or local traditions are set up beneath the magnificent larch-timbered ceilings. All in all, there's not a lot to do in Colmars except wander around and soak up the atmosphere, or you could take a twenty-minute walk east of the town to the Lance waterfall.

The **tourist office** is by Porte de la Lance (July & Aug daily 8am–7pm; Sept–June Mon–Sat 9am–12.15pm & 2–5.45pm; Sun 9am–12.15pm; Ⓣ04.92.83.41.92). There is one **hotel**, *Le Chamois*, just off the D908 opposite the walled town (Ⓣ04.92.83.43.29; ❷; closed mid-Nov to Dec); a **gîte d'étape**, the *Gassendi*, rue St Joseph, housed in a twelfth-century Templar hospice

(☎04.92.83.42.25; ❶); and a very scenic **campsite**, *Le Bois Joly*, by the river (☎04.92.83.40.40; closed Oct–April). For **food** there's *Le Lézard* restaurant and *salon de thé*, on the corner of Grande-Rue and place Neuve, which serves *raclette*, and the *Café Rétro* on place J-Girieud by the *mairie*. For picnic supplies, there's a *boulangerie*, *charcuterie* and wine shop, all on Grande-Rue.

Colmars lies at the junction of the Verdon Valley road with the D78 which climbs up between the Frema and Encombrette mountains and descends to the Var Valley at St-Martin-d'Entraunes. Six kilometres along the road, signed left, is the **Ratery ski-station** (☎04.92.83.40.92), which rents out **bikes** in summer. You can trek from here over the Encombrette to the Lac d'Allos or east across the Col des Champs (closed mid-Nov to mid-May) to the Var at Entraunes.

Beauvezer

If you're heading south towards Thorame, Annot or St-André (see pp.406–408), you can follow the D908 for 5km to **BEAUVEZER** – experienced cross-country skiers can take a looping route there through the Forêt de Monier and across the summit of the Laupon. The road sticks to the Verdon, a wide dramatic torrent in winter or spring, a wide messy track of scattered boulders and branches in summer. Beauvezer perches high above its right bank, a wonderful ancient village smelling of old timbers whose business used to be making linen. Beside the beautiful ochre church is one of the prettiest **hotel-restaurants** in Haute Provence, *Le Bellevue*, place de l'Église (☎04.92.83.51.60, ⓦwww.hotellebellevue.org; ❸).

The Haut-Var Valley

The route to the Haut-Var Valley from Barçelonnette first follows the River Bachelard through its gorge then east following its course between Mont Pelat to the south and the ridge of peaks to the north whose shapes have given them the names Pain de Sucre (Sugarloaf), Chapeau de Gendarme (Gendarme's Hat) and Chevalier (Horseman). At the *Bayasse* refuge (☎04.92.81.07.31, ❶), the main road turns south towards the **Col de la Cayolle**, while a track and the GR56 continue east towards La Bonette and the Tinée Valley.

The Var makes its appearance below the Col de la Cayolle and pours southwards through Entraunes and St-Martin-d'Entraunes to Guillaumes and on down through the **Gorges de Daluis** to Entrevaux. Its banks are punctuated with chapels built before and after disasters of avalanches, floods, landslides and devastating storms. Many are superbly decorated, like the Renaissance Chapelle de St-Sébastien, just north of Entraunes and the church at St-Martin-d'Entraunes, with its Bréa retable.

Tucked beneath the ruined Chateau de la Reine Jeanne, **GUILLAUMES**, the valley's minor metropolis and a favourite with cyclists in summer, is a traditional resting place for sheep on their way between the Haut-Var summer pastures and Nice. Though most flocks now travel by lorry, the old **sheep fairs** on September 16 and the second Saturday of October are still held. Winter sees a migration in the opposite direction, as the residents of the Côte d'Azur flock to the ski resorts of Valberg and Beuil, to the east of Guillaumes, on the fabulous road that climbs over to the Tinée Valley.

The biggest **tourist office** in the area is in Valberg (daily 9am–noon & 2–6pm; ☎04.93.23.24.25, ⓦwww.valberg.com), although Guillaume has a

△ Alpine view near Valberg

"chalet du tourisme" on the main road operating sporadic hours in season (☎04.93.05.57.76; Tues, Wed, Fri & Sat 9am–noon & 2–6pm, Thurs 9am–noon). For **accommodation** in Guillaumes, there's the *Les Chaudrons* hotel on the main road (☎04.93.05.50.01; ❷), and *La Renaissance*, an old-fashioned establishment 100m up on the right just past the bridge (☎04.93.05.59.89; ❷), whose restaurant has menus at €12 and €16.

About 5km south of Guillaumes, the Var enters the dramatic red-rocked **Gorges de Daluis**. The Pont de la Mariée across the gorge is a popular spot for bungee-jumpers. It's worth noting that the road upstream has the better view while the downstream carriageway is in tunnels much of the way. Walkers can get a closer look at the gorge by following the two-kilmetre *Sentier du Point Sublime* from Pont de Berthèou on the D2202 to the Point Sublime itself.

The Tinée Valley

The longest of the Var's tributaries, the Tinée rises just below the 2800-metre summit of **La Bonette**. The mountains on its left bank – under whose shadow **St-Étienne** and **Auron** nestle – rise up to the Italian border, while the river heads south to cut a steep, narrow valley before joining the Var 30km from the sea.

Across La Bonette

Claiming to be the highest stretch of tarmac in Europe, the road across **La Bonette** gives a feast of high-altitude views. The summit of the mountain, a ten-minute scrabble up scree from the road, is not particularly exciting, and is made more ugly by its military training camp. But the green and silent spaces of the approach, circled by barren peaks, are magical.

Before the hairpins begin for the southern descent, at Camp des Fourches, you can abandon your wheels and take the **GR5/56** north and parallel with the Italian border to the Col de Larche, then northwest towards Larche, where there's a gîte (☎04.92.84.30.80; ❷). It's not exactly a stroll, but once you've climbed to the Col de la Cavale (after 5km or so) it's more or less downhill all the way, with the Ubayette torrent as your guide, and the **Lac de Lauzanier**, 5km on from the Col de la Cavale, a spot you may never want to leave.

A short way down from the Camp des Fourches is the *Gîte de Bousiéyas* (☎04.93.02.42.20; closed mid-Sept to mid-June). About 5km on, a track on the left to the tiny hamlet of **Vens** leads to a footpath that follows the Vens torrent to the Lacs de Vens and a refuge at 2380m (☎04.93.02.44.87; closed mid-Sept to mid-June).

St-Étienne-de-Tinée and Auron

Continuing on the road, with the Tinée alongside, you descend to the small, isolated town of **ST-ÉTIENNE-DE-TINÉE** that comes to life only during its sheep fairs, held twice every summer, and the Fête de la Transhumance at the end of June. The **tourist office** at 1 rue des Communes-de-France (daily 9am–noon & 2–5pm; ☎04.93.02.41.96, ⓦwww.auron.fr.st), organizes tours (€3.10) of the town's chapels, the museums of milk-making and traditional crafts and of the old school. Just up from the Pont St-Antoine at the northern end of the village is the **Maison du Parc National du Mercantour** (daily 2–5.30pm; ☎04.93.02.42.27), with displays and information about the park.

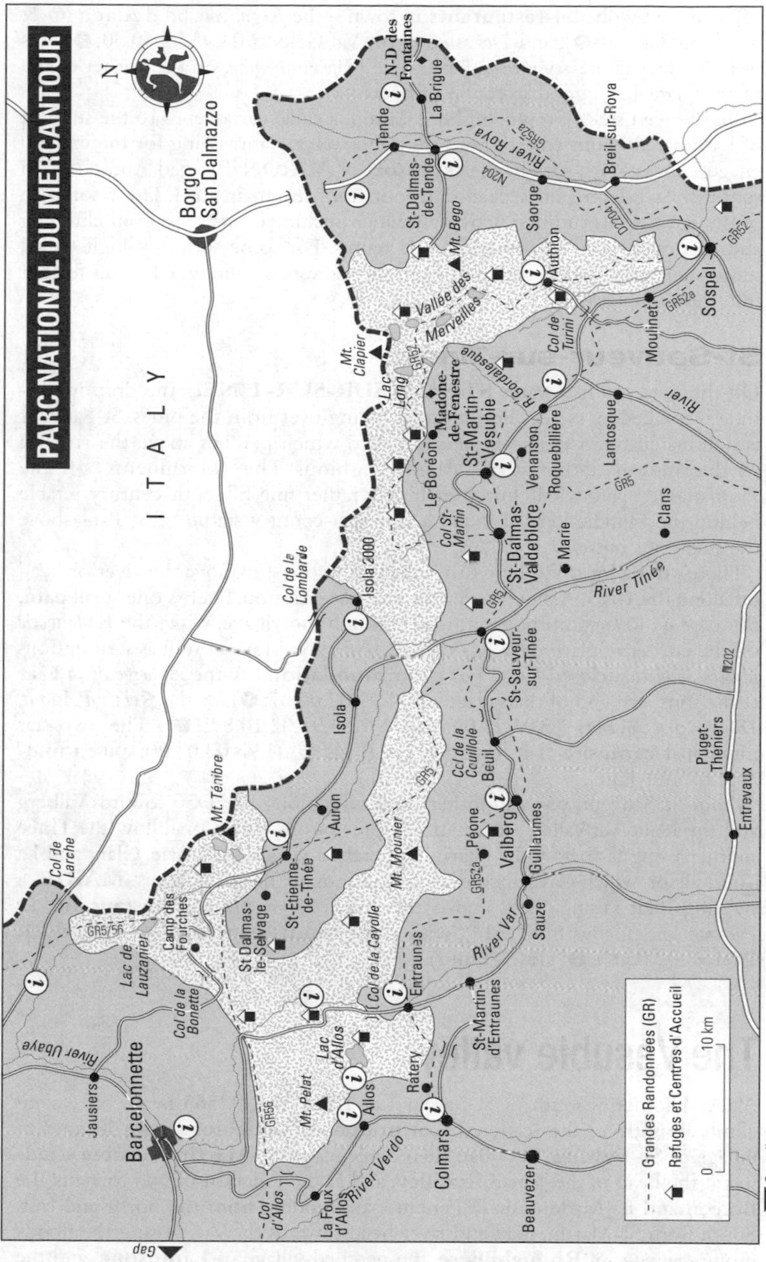

PARC NATIONAL DU MERCANTOUR

ITALY
Borgo San Dalmazzo
N
Col de Larche
Jausiers
River Ubaye
Barcelonnette
Gap
Lac de Lauzanier
Camp des Fourches
Col de la Bonette
Mt. Ténibre
GR5/56
St Dalmas-le-Selvage
St-Etienne-de-Tinée
Auron
Isola
Isola 2000
Col de la Lombarde
Col d'Allos
GR56
Mt. Pelat
Lac d'Allos
La Foux d'Allos
Allos
River Verdo
Col de la Cayolle
Entraunes
Mt. Mounier
GR5
Ratery
Colmars
St-Martin-d'Entraunes
River Var
GR52a
Péone
Valberg
Col de la Couillole
Beuil
St-Sauveur-sur-Tinée
Sauze
Guillaumes
Beauvezer
Mt. Clapier
Lac Long
GR52
Le Boréon
Madone-de-Fenestre
Col St-Martin
St-Martin-Vésubie
St-Dalmas-Valdeblore
Venanson
Roquebillière
R. Gordalesque
Vallée des Merveilles
Mt. Bego
Authion
Col de Turini
Marie
Lantosque
River Tinée
Clans
River
Moulinet
Sospel
Tende
St-Dalmas-de-Tende
La Brigue
N-D des Fontaines
N204
River Roya
Saorge
D2204
Breil-sur-Roya
Puget-Théniers
N202
Entrevaux
Castellane
Nice
Nice

Grandes Randonnées (GR)
Refuges et Centres d'Accueil
0 10 km

There are two **hotel-restaurants** in town – the *Regalivou*, bd d'Auron (Ⓣ & Ⓕ04.93.02.49.00; ❸), and *Des Amis*, 1 rue Val Gélé (Ⓣ04.93.02.40.30; ❷) – as well as a few alpine-style restaurants. The *Café Autheman*, on the corner of the main square, has a good selection of beers.

On the west side of town, off bd d'Auron, a cable car ascends to the summit of La Pinatelle from where there are good walks – and skiing for the experienced – including a path to the **ski resort** of **AURON**. By road, Auron is 7km south of St-Étienne, on a dead-end spur from the main road. The resort also prides itself on its summer activities, which include everything from climbing and mountain golf to pony rides and tennis. For some seriously high **treks**, more cable cars, which operate in summer as well as winter, take you further into the mountains.

St-Sauveur-sur-Tinée

On the road south towards **ST-SAUVEUR-SUR-TINÉE**, the drop in altitude is marked by sweet chestnut trees taking over from the pines. St-Sauveur is dominated by its medieval needle belfry, which perches above the river in Mediterranean rather than Alpine fashion. The adornments of the Romanesque gargoyled church include a rather fine fifteenth-century retable behind the bloodied crucifix and a fifteenth-century statue of St Paul above the side door outside.

There's not a lot to do here other than sit in the sun above the river or head off along the GR52A, but it's an attractive place to stop. There's one small **café**, the *Café du Village*, on the main road through the village, while the *boulangerie* on the corner of place de la Mairie sells basic provisions as well as scrumptious *tourtes de blettes* (closed Tues). For **accommodation**, try the *Auberge de la Gare* at the southern end of the village (Ⓣ04.93.02.00.67; ❶), or the *Relais d'Auron*, 18 av des Blavets (Ⓣ04.93.02.00.03, Ⓕ04.93.02.10.89; ❷). The two-star municipal **campsite** is in quartier Les Plans (Ⓣ04.93.02.03.20; closed mid-Sept to mid-June).

From St-Sauveur, you can either head west along the D30 towards Valberg and the Haut-Var Valley, a dramatically precipitous climb, or follow the Tinée south, passing far below the charming perched villages of Marie, Clans and La Tour, all of which have medieval decorations in their churches. **MARIE**, a twisting, hair-raising 3km above the road, has a pleasant **restaurant**, *Le Panoramique* (menus from €14), with a few **rooms** as well (Ⓣ04.93.02.03.01, Ⓕ04.93.02.03.85; ❷; closed Thurs).

The Vésubie valley

A few kilometres south of St-Saveur-sur-Tinée, the D2565 heads off east to climb abruptly to the scattered **Commune of Valdeblore**, with its ancient village of **St-Dalmas**. The road then descends to **St-Martin-Vésubie** standing at the head of the **Vésubie valley**, and at the junction of two torrents, Le Boréon and La Madone de la Fenestre, descending from the north and east. South from St-Martin, road and river head towards the Var, passing the flood-prone *commune* of **Roquebillière**, the perched village of **Lantosque**, and the approach to the pilgrimage chapel of **Madonne d'Utelle**. An alternative southern route from the valley crosses east to the **Col de Turini** and down the **River Bévéra** towards Sospel.

The Commune de Valdeblore and St-Dalmas

Straddling the Col St-Martin between the Tinée and Vésubie valleys, the **COMMUNE DE VALDEBLORE** consists of a series of settlements strung along the D2565, starting with La Bolline and La Roche, then the ancient village of St-Dalmas, finishing, on the eastern side of the Col, with the ski resort of **La Colmiane**, where you can take a chairlift for stunning views from the **Pic de Colmiane** (Christmas–March daily 10am–4.50pm; July & Aug daily 10am–6pm; €3.50). The **tourist office** is in La Roche (daily 9am–noon & 2–6pm; ⓣ04.93.23.25.90, ⓦwww.colmiane.com).

The most interesting of Valdeblore's villages is **ST-DALMAS**, which was built on the remains of a Roman outpost, and lies at the strategic crossroads between the most accessible southern route across the lower Alps, linking Piedmont with Provence, and a north–south route linking Savoy with the sea. The former importance of this region is clear from the dimensions of the **Église Prieurale Bénédictine** (mid-June to mid-Sept afternoons only; mornings and mid-Sept to mid-June by request; call Jean Alcoy on ⓣ04.93.02.82.29), parts of which are thought to date from the tenth century. A gruesome glazed tomb reveals a 900-year-old skeleton; more appealing are the fragments of fourteenth-century frescoes in the north chapel. The present structure is Romanesque, plain and fierce with its typically Alpine bell tower and rounded apsidal chapels on which eleventh-century Lombardian decoration is still visible. If your French is good it's worth getting a guided tour from Jean Alcoy, who can be found at the **Musée du Terroir** just up from the church (same hours as the church; €3), which displays traditional agricultural tools, household items, and a large model train set.

St-Martin-Vésubie and around

Eleven kilometres east of St-Dalmas, **ST-MARTIN-VÉSUBIE** is at its busiest in July and August, though even at the height of the season, it's not jam-packed. In late spring and early autumn it's a perfect base for exploring the surrounding mountains, and in winter you can go for wonderful walks in snowshoes, or tackle some of the cross-country skiing routes that pass through the town.

The main artery of the old quarter, the **rue du Docteur-Cagnoli**, is a single-file cobbled street of Gothic houses with overhanging roofs and balconies, through which flows a channelled stream designed in the fifteenth century for sewage and now charged with rainwater or melting snow. Halfway down on the left is the **Chapelle des Pénitents Blancs**, decorated with eighteenth-century paintings. At the end of the street is St-Martin's **church**, with works attributed to Louis Bréa, a mirror on the high altar reflecting the stained-glass window above the door, and a venerated polychrome wooden statue of the Madonna that is taken up to the Chapelle de Madone de Fenestre (see p.426) at the beginning of July and brought back towards the end of September. Southeast of the church you can look down at the Madone de Fenestre torrent from place de la Frairie. In the opposite direction a narrow lane leads to the junction of rue Kellerman and the main road, beyond which is the old wash house and **Le Vieux Moulin**, the town's one museum (June & Sept Thurs, Sat & Sun 2.30–6.30pm; July & Aug daily 2.30–6.30pm; Oct–May Sat & Sun 2.30–6.30pm; €3), which illustrates the traditional way of life of the Vésubiens.

Heading back towards the main **place Félix-Fauré** along rue Kellerman, you'll pass the **Maison du Parc** with occasional wildlife exhibitions as well as information about the Parc du Mercantour (currently closed for renovation; ⓣ04.93.03.23.15 for information). The **fountain** on allées de Verdun, the *cours* in front of place Félix-Fauré, has a placard detailing its mineral contents and citing the ministerial declaration of 1913 that claims the water has negative pathogenic germs.

Practicalities

St-Martin's **gare routière** is on place de la Gare, where av de la Gare loops south into av de Caqueray, while the **tourist office** is on place Félix-Fauré (June–Aug daily 9am–12.30pm & 3–7pm; Sept–May Mon–Sat 9am–noon & 2.30–5.30pm, Sun 10am–noon; ⓣ04.93.03.21.28, ⓦwww.saintmartinvesubie.fr) along with the *mairie*, post office and a bank.

The tourist office has lists of gîtes and mountain refuges for St-Martin and the surrounding area posted up outside, plus lists of walking guides and weather information. On rue du Dr-Cagnoli, just below place du Marché, the Bureau des Guides et Accompagnateurs de la Haute Vésubie (ⓣ04.93.03.26.60) can organize **walks**, including winter expeditions with snowshoe rental, and give advice for your own expeditions. The Guides du Mercantour, on pl de Marché (ⓣ04.93.03.31.32), can arrange **canoeing**, **climbing**, **horse rides**, **walks** and **skiing**. Maps, compasses and the like can be purchased from Aux Milles Articles, 50 rue du Dr-Cagnoli.

Accommodation is plentiful. The least expensive of the town's five **hotels** is the *Hotel des Alpes* on place Félix-Fauré (ⓣ04.93.03.21.06; ❷), while *La Bonne Auberge*, a short way up the allées de Verdun (ⓣ04.93.03.20.49, ⓕ04.93.03.20.69; ❷; closed mid-Nov to Jan), and the *La Châtaigneraie*, also on the allées de Verdun (ⓣ04.93.03.21.22, ⓕ04.93.03.33.99; demi-pension only, €50 per person; closed Oct–May), offer slightly more comfort. The closest **campsite** is the two-star *Ferme St-Joseph* on the rte de Nice by the lower bridge over La Madone (ⓣ04.93.03.20.14; €10 per tent). In the opposite direction 1.5km out of town, on the rte de la Colmiane, there's *La Mério* (ⓣ04.93.03.30.38; €15 per tent; open June to mid-Sept) and, to the southwest, on the rte de Venanson, the two-star *Le Champouns* (ⓣ & ⓕ04.93.03.23.72; €8 per tent), which also has apartments to let and dormitory accommodation.

The nicest **restaurant** in town is *La Trappa* on place du Marché (closed Mon in term time), which offers a four-course meal for €14, and the restaurant in *La Bonne Auberge* is also worth trying (menus at €16). For snacks, *La Mavorine café-boulangerie* on place Félix-Fauré serves *bruschettas* for around €6, plus ice creams, crêpes and cakes.

Finally, there's an après-ski **disco**, *Le Piolet*, off rue du Dr-Cagnoli on the east slope of the old town.

Around St-Martin: Le Boréon and Madone de Fenestre

The main reason for heading to **LE BORÉON**, some 10km north of St-Martin and just inside the Parc du Mercantour, is to eat trout, either caught yourself or by those who supply the clutch of **restaurants** and **hotels** at this small, scenic mountain retreat. During the fishing season, from mid-March to early September, you can get a licence from the hotels here or from most of the bars in St-Martin. The two **hotel-restaurants** are *Le Boréon*, Quartier du Cascade (ⓣ04.93.03.20.35, ⓕ04.93.03.34.53; menus from €15; ❸ closed mid-Nov to Dec), and *Le Cavalet*, Lac du Boréon (ⓣ04.93.03.21.46, ⓕ04.93.03.34.34; demi-pension only, €60 per person). There's also a **gîte** at 248 rte de Salése (ⓣ04.93.03.27.27; ❶).

Returning to St-Martin then heading east for 11.5km along the D94 will bring you to the **Chapelle de Madone de Fenestre** standing above the tree-line in a setting of barren rocks, also just within the borders of the Parc du

Wildlife of the Mercantour

The least shy of the mammal inhabitants of these mountains is the **marmot**, a cream-coloured, badger-sized creature often to be seen sitting on its haunches in the sun. Chamois, mouflon and ibex are almost equally unwary of humans, even though it was not so long ago that they were hunted here. The male **ibex** is a wonderful, big, solid beast with curving, ribbed horns that grow to a metre long; the species very nearly became extinct, and it is one of the successes of the park that the population is now stable. Another species of goat, the **chamois**, is also on the increase. The male is recognizable by the shorter, grappling-hook horns and white beard. The **mouflon**, introduced to the Mercantour in the 1950s, is the ancestor of domestic sheep. Other animals that you might see include **stoats**, rare species of **hare**, and **foxes**, the most numerous predators since bears and lynxes became extinct in the region. The most problematic predator, however, is the **wolf**, once extinct, but stalking the region again since 1992, having crossed the border from Italy. With eight hundred sheep killed by wolves in a single year, sheep farmers are not happy, and the predators have been found killed despite their protected status.

The Mercantour is a perfect habitat for **eagles**, who have any number of crags on which to build their nests, and plenty to eat – including marmots. Pairs of **golden eagles** are now breeding, and a rare vulture, the **lammergeier**, has been successfully reintroduced to the region. Other birds of prey, **kestrels**, **falcons** and **buzzards**, wing their way down from the scree to the Alpine lawn and its torrents to swoop on lizards, mice and snakes. The **great spotted woodpecker** and the black and orange **hoopoe** are the most colourful inhabitants of the park. **Ptarmigan**, which turn snowy-white in winter, can sometimes be seen in June parading to their would-be mates on the higher slopes in the north. **Blackcocks**, known in French as *tétras-lyre* for their lyre-shaped white tails, burrow into the snow at night and fly out in a flurry of snowflakes when the sun rises.

The **flowers** of the Mercantour are an unmissable glory, with over two thousand species represented, about forty of which are unique to the region. The moment the snow melts, the lawn between the rocky crags and the tree line begins to dot with golds, pinks and blue. Rare species of **lily** and **orchid** grow here, as do the elusive **edelweiss** and the wild ancestors of various cultivated flowers – pansies, geraniums, tulips and gentian violets. Rarest of all is the **multi-flowering saxifrage** (*saxifraga florulenta*), a big spiky flower that looks as if it must be cultivated, though it would hardly be popular in suburban gardens since it flowers just once every ten years. Wild strawberries, raspberries and bilberries tempt you into the woods.

Camping, lighting fires, picking flowers, playing ghetto blasters or doing anything that might disturb the delicate environment is strictly outlawed.

Mercantour. Half a dozen gloomy, rough-hewn stone buildings, one of them housing a refuge and restaurant, surround the chapel, named after the hole in the rock above it through which you can see the sky. The main purpose for coming up here is to **trek** along the GR52, which passes by the sanctuary and leads eastwards to the Vallée des Merveilles (see p.432). This is not the shortest route but it's a very dramatic path that rarely descends below 2000m.

In summer there is a weekly **bus** on Thursdays from St-Martin to Le Boréon, and one, on Sunday, to Madone de Fenestre.

Downstream to Madone d'Utelle

South from St-Martin on the other side of the valley, but approached by a circuitous route that heads north out of the town, is the little village of **VENANSON**, which dubs itself, appropriately, a "zone of silence". It has just one

hotel-restaurant, the *Bella-Vista* on place St Jean (Ⓣ04.93.03.25.11, Ⓕ04.93.64 .45.60; ❷), a dark **chapel** with Baleison frescoes, and an excellent view over St-Martin.

Back on the left bank you come to the village of **ROQUEBILLIÈRE**, which has been rebuilt six times since the Dark Ages after catastrophic landslides and floods. The last major disaster was in 1926, with a less lethal upheaval in the 1980s. Apart from the archeological interest of the various superseded settlements and the beauty of the frequently rebuilt church, the new village on the right bank has a wonderful *boulangerie*, Chez Somiani (closed Sun pm) on the main street, av C-Moulinie.

The road along the **Gordolesque Valley** above old Roquebillière heads north for 16km with paths leading off eastwards towards the Vallée des Merveilles. Where the road ends you can continue upstream past waterfalls and high crags to Lac de la Fous where you meet the GR52 running west to Madone de la Fenestre and east to the northern end of the Vallée des Merveilles (see p.432). This triangle between the Mont Clapier on the Italian border (3045m), Mont Bego (2873m) to the east and Mont Neiglier (2785m) to the west is a fabulous area for walking, but not to be taken lightly. All the **mountain refuges** here belong to the Club Alpin Français (Ⓣ04.93.62.59.99) and may well be unsympathetic if you turn up unannounced.

South of Roquebillière, the D70 leaves the Vésubie Valley to head east through the chic resort of La-Bollène-Vésubie to the Col de Turini (see below). Staying with the Vésubie, you reach **LANTOSQUE**, which, like Roquebillière, has had its share of earth tremors and was badly flooded in 1993. Yet it survives in picturesque form, a pyramid of winding, stepped streets full of nervous cats, with a wonderful café-brasserie, the *Bar des Tilleuls*, on the lower *place*, serving copious and delicious plats du jour for around €8. The village has one swish **hotel** on the other side of the river, the *Hostellerie de L'Ancienne Gendarmerie*, in Quartier Rivet (Ⓣ04.93.03.00.65; Ⓕ04.93.03 .06.31; ❺; closed mid-Nov to Feb), with an excellent restaurant (lunch menu from €10).

Just before the river starts to pick up speed through the gorge leading to its confluence with the Var, you can detour upwards to yet another far-flung **chapel**, dedicated to **La Madone d'Utelle**. It stands on a plateau above the village of Utelle, high enough to be visible from the sea at Nice. According to legend, two Portuguese sailors lost in a storm in the year 850 navigated safely into port by a light they saw gleaming from Utelle. They erected a chapel here to give thanks, though the current one dates from 1806. Pilgrimages still take place on Easter Monday, the Monday of Pentecost, August 15 and September 8, and are concluded with a communal feast on the grassy summit. You'll find reasonable fare in the village at *La Bellevue* **hotel-restaurant** on rte de la Madone (Ⓣ04.93.03.17.19; menus from €12; ❷; restaurant closed Jan).

The Col de Turini

At the **Col de Turini**, 15km east of Roquebillière, you know you're in a popular spot from the litter and snack bars. Four roads and two tracks meet at the pass, all giving access to the **Forêt de Turini**, which covers the area between the Vésubie and Bévéra valleys. Larches grow in the highest reaches of the forest, giving way further down to firs, spruce, beech, maples and sweet chestnuts.

The road north from the col through the small ski resort of **Camp d'Argent** to L'Authion gives a strong impression of limitless space, following the curved ridge between the two valleys and overlooking a hollow of pastures. There are plenty of walks hereabouts, but the sun, the flowers and the wild strawberries and raspberries are so pleasant you might just want to stop in a field and listen to the cowbells. The nicest place **to stay** is *Le Relais du Camp d'Argent*, Camp d'Argent, Turini (☎04.93.91.57.58; demi-pension only, at €42 per person), which serves decent **meals** from €16.

Sospel and the Roya Valley

From the Col de Turini the D2566 follows the valley of the River Bévéra southeast to **Sospel**, which straddles the main road and rail links from the French coast to the **Roya Valley**. Though it's the most easterly valley of Provence, the Roya is also the most accessible, being served by train lines from Nice, via Sospel, and from Ventimiglia in Italy: the lines converge just south of **Breil-sur-Roya**. When Nice became part of France in 1860, the upper Roya Valley was kept by the newly appointed King Victor Emmanuel II of Italy to indulge his passion for hunting, despite a plebiscite in which only one person in Tende and La Brigue voted for the Italian option. It was not until 1947 that the valley was finally incorporated into France. As you would expect from the result of the vote, everyone speaks French, though they do so with a distinctly Italian intonation.

Sospel

The ruggedness of the surrounding terrain only serves to emphasize the placid idyll of **SOSPEL**, a dreamy Italianate town spanning the gentle River Bévéra. Its main street, av Jean-Médecin, follows the river on its southern bank before crossing the most easterly of the three bridges to become bd de Verdun heading for the Roya Valley. The central bridge, the **Vieux Pont** with its tower between the two spans for collecting tolls, was built in the early eleventh century to link the town centre on the south bank with its suburb across the river. Impossibly picturesque, it's the architectural lynchpin of Sospel's townscape. The scene is made yet more alluring by the balconied houses along the north bank which back on to the grimy rue de la République. The banks are lush with flowering shrubs and trees, and one house even has a trompe-l'oeil street facade. Viewed from the eastern end of av Jean-Médecin, with the hills to the west and the bridge tower reflected in the water, this scene would be hard to improve.

Yet there's another vista in the town that rivals the river scene. For maximum effect it's best approached down rue St-Pierre from the eastern place St-Pierre. The street, which is deeply shadowed and gloomy with equally uninviting alleyways running off it, suddenly opens onto **place St-Michel** and you have before you one of the most beautiful series of peaches-and-cream Baroque facades in all Provence. In front of you is the **Église St-Michel** with its separate austere Romanesque clock tower. To the left are the **Chapelle des Pénitents Gris** and the **Chapelle des Pénitents Rouges**, and to the right are the medieval arcades and trompe-l'oeil decoration of the **Palais Ricci**. St-Michel contains an altarpiece by François Bréa in which the background to the red and gold robes of the Madonna is a bewitching river landscape of mountains, monasteries and dark citadels. On the right-hand panel Saint Martha has the snarling *Tarasque* well under control on a lead.

The road behind the church, rue de l'Abbaye, which you can reach via the steps between the two chapels, leads up to an ivy-covered **castle ruin**, from where you get a good view of the town. Further up, along chemin de St-Roch, an even better view can be had from the **Fort St-Roch**, part of the ignominious interwar Maginot line, which houses the **Musée de la Résistance** (April–June Sat & Sun 2–6pm; July–Sept Tues–Sun 2–6pm; €5), illustrating the courageous local resistance movement during World War II. Although under Italian occupation after June 1940, the town hall continued to fly the French flag; when the Germans took over in 1943, however, life became much harsher, and only a few of the Jews who had taken refuge here managed to escape south to Monaco. After Menton was liberated in September 1944 the Allied force advanced north, carrying out airborne attacks on Sospel, but stopping 5km short of the town. Sospel, therefore, was left to the mercy of the Germans, but with Allied artillery attacks adding to the casualties. At the end of October the Germans were forced to retreat, but not far enough, and the battle for Sospel continued until April 1945.

Practicalities

The **gare SNCF** is southeast of the town on av A-Borriglione, which becomes av des Martyrs-de-la-Résistance, before leading down to the riverside place des Platanes. Sospel's **tourist office** is housed in the Vieux Pont (Easter–Sept Mon 2.30–6pm, Tues–Sun 9.30am–12.30pm & 2.30–6pm; Oct–Easter Mon 2.30–4.30pm, Tues–Sat 9.30am–12.30pm & 2.30–4.30pm, Sun 9.30am–12.30pm; ⓣ04.93.04.15.80, ⓦwww.royabevera.com).

The *Auberge du Pont-Vieux*, 3 av J-Médecin (ⓣ04.93.04.00.73; ❷), is Sospel's cheapest **hotel**. The *Hôtel des Étrangers* at 7 bd de Verdun (ⓣ04.93.04.00.09, ⓕ04.93.04.12.31; ❹; closed Nov–Feb) has good service, the use of a pool and can arrange **bike** rental, while the *Hôtel de France* next door (ⓣ04.93.04.00.01, ⓔhotel-france@wanadoo.fr; ❸; closed mid-Nov to mid-Dec) is pleasant and welcoming. For more comfort, the *Auberge Provençale*, on rte du Col de Castillon 1.5km uphill from the town (ⓣ04.93.04.00.31, ⓕ04.93.04.24.54; ❹), has a pleasant garden and terrace from which to admire the town. There are four **campsites** around the town, the closest of which is one-star *Le Mas Fleuri* in quartier La Vasta (ⓣ04.93.04.14.94; €16 per tent; closed Oct–Feb), with its own pool, 2km along the D2566 to Moulinet following the river upstream.

There are various **eating places** along av J-Médecin including the *Bistrot Sospellois* which serves plats du jour for around €7. At *L'Escargot d'Or*, 3 rue de Verdun (ⓣ04.93.04.00.43; closed Tues), just across the eastern bridge, you can eat for between €11.50 and €28 on a terrace above the river, while the restaurant of the *Hôtel des Étrangers* next door has menus from €22. A Thursday **market** is held on place des Platanes, and on Sunday local produce is sold on place du Marché. There's a wonderful boulangerie/pâtisserie/chocolatier, *Papasergio*, at 13 bis av J-Médecin.

Breil-sur-Roya

Twenty-three kilometres north of Sospel, the town of **BREIL-SUR-ROYA** sits in a deep, narrow valley, 8km from the Italian border. Here, the river Roya has picked up enough volume to justify a barrage, behind which a placid and aquamarine lake makes a perfect location for canoeing. A town of modest industries – leather, olives and dairy products – Breil spreads back from both banks, with the old town on the eastern edge. A Renaissance chapel with a golden angel blowing a trumpet from its rooftop cross faces pl Bianquieri, while the vast eighteenth-century **Église Santa-Maria-in-Albis**, by the pont Charabot, is topped by a belfry with shiny multicoloured tiles, and has an impressive organ loft.

Several good **walks** are signed from the village; if you just want a short stroll, follow the river downstream past the barrage and the wash houses, then fork upwards through an olive grove to a tiny chapel and an old Italian gatehouse. The path eventually leads up to the summit of the Arpette, which stands between Breil and the Italian border. Alternatively, if you want to do some white-water **canoeing** or **rafting** up through the Gorges de Saorge, or simply paddle more gently through the village, Roya Evasion, at 1 rue Pasteur (Ⓣ04.93.04.91.46), rents out all the equipment, and organizes guided trips.

Of the three **hotels** in town, the *Castel du Roy*, chemin de l'Aigara, off the rte de Tende (Ⓣ04.93.04.43.66; ❹; closed Nov–Mar), is the most luxurious and has a very good **restaurant** (menus from €20), though the other two – *La Bonne Auberge* on rue Pasteur (Ⓣ04.93.04.41.50, Ⓕ04.93.04.92.70; ❷), with a restaurant serving local dishes on menus starting at €8, and *Le Roya* on place Biancheri (Ⓣ04.93.04.48.10; ❸) – are more central. The municipal two-star **campsite** (Ⓣ04.93.04.46.66) is by the river, just upstream from the village.

Saorge and Fontan

Seven kilometres north of Breil, the pretty village of **SAORGE** consists of a clutter of houses in grey and mismatched shades of red tumbling across a hillside, brightened by its church and chapel towers shimmering with gold Niçois tiles. Almost nothing in the village is level: vertical stairways turn into paths lined with bramble, and there's just one near-horizontal main street, and even that goes up and down flights of steps and through arches formed by the houses. At the end of the street a path leads across the cultivated terraces to **La Madone del Poggio**, an eleventh-century chapel guarded by an impossibly high bell tower topped by an octagonal spire; the chapel is private property and can't be visited. Back in the village, there's a seventeenth-century **Franciscan convent** (daily: April & May 10am–noon & 2–6pm; June–Oct 10am–6pm; Nov–March 10am–5pm; €4) with rustic murals around its cloisters, and the **Église St-Sauveur** (daily 9am–5pm), with its rich examples of ecclesiastical art.

The **gare SNCF**, which it shares with Fontan, is 1.5km below the village in the valley, while **chambre d'hôtes** accommodation is available from M & Mme Chimène, quartier Bergiron (Ⓣ04.93.04.55.49, Ⓔbergiron@free.fr; ❶). For **food**, there's a pizzeria, *Lou Pountin*, rue Revelli (closed Mon & Tues lunch & Wed eve), and one *bar-tabac, Chez Gilou*.

FONTAN, 2km upstream and with another shining Niçois-tiled belfry, has one **hotel** to fall back on; the *Terminus* (Ⓣ04.93.04.34.00, Ⓕ04.93.04.34.04; ❷), overlooking the Roya at the north end of the village: its restaurant has some decent menus starting at €9, and a beautifully painted ceiling. Here and at the **restaurant** *Les Platanes*, at the other end of the village, the speciality is fresh trout from the river.

La Brigue and Notre-Dame-des-Fontaines

The very appealing village of **LA BRIGUE**, 8km northeast of Fontan, lies on an eastern tributary of the Roya, just south of Tende, surrounded by pastures and with the perennial snowcap of Mont Bego visible to the west. Its Romanesque church, the **Église St-Martin**, is full of medieval paintings, including several by Louis Bréa, most of them depicting hideous scenes of torture and death. But the church, and the octagonal seventeenth-century **Chapelle St-Michel** alongside it, pale into insignificance compared with the sanctuary of **Notre-Dame-des-Fontaines**, 4km east of the village.

From the exterior this seems to be a plain, graceful place of retreat, but inside it's something more akin to an arcade of video nasties. Painted in the fifteenth century by Jean Baleison (the ones above the altar) and Jean Canavesio (all the rest), the sequence of restored **frescoes** contains 38 episodes. Each one, from Christ's flagellation, through the torment on the Cross to devils claiming their victims, and, ultimate gore, Judas's disembowelment, is full of violent movement and colour. The chapel is open daily in summer (9.30am–7pm; €1.50; guided tours organized by the tourist office; €3.20; ⓣ04.93.04.36.07), and in the winter you can let yourself in with a key obtained from the *mairie* or the *Auberge St-Martin* in La Brigue. There's no bus, but it's a very pleasant walk up the D43 for 2km, then turning right over the Pont du Coq, built, like the chapel, in the fifteenth century.

If you want **to stay** in La Brigue, place St-Martin by the church has a couple of options – the *Auberge St-Martin* (ⓣ04.93.04.62.17, ⓕ04.93.04.89.66; ❷; closed mid-Nov to Feb) and the *Fleurs des Alpes* (ⓣ04.93.04.61.05, ⓕ04.93.04.69.58; ❷; closed Dec–Feb) – both with **restaurants** serving very satisfying meals for less than €15. The more upmarket *Le Mirval* (ⓣ04.93.04.63.71, ⓕ04.93.04.79.81; ❸; closed Nov–March), downstream from place St-Martin on rue Vincent-Ferrier, has rooms overlooking the Levenza stream.

The Vallée des Merveilles

The **Vallée des Merveilles** lies between two lakes over 2000m up on the western flank of Mount Bego. The first person to record his experience of this high valley of lakes and bare rock was a fifteenth-century traveller who had lost his way. He described it as "an infernal place with figures of the devil and thousands of demons scratched on the rocks". What his contemporary readers must have imagined to be delusions brought on by the terror of the place were no imaginings. The rocks of the valley are carved with thousands of images, of animals, tools, people working and mysterious symbols, dating from some time in the second millennium BC. More are to be found in the **Vallée de Fontanable** on the northern flank of Mont Bego, and west from the Vallée des Merveilles across the southern slopes of Mont des Merveilles. Very little is known about them and the instruments that fashioned them have never been found.

Over the centuries other travellers, shepherds and eventually tourists have added their own engravings to the collection. As a result explorations of the Vallée de Fontanable, and the Mont des Merveilles area, are restricted to one path unless accompanied by an official Mercantour guide.

The easiest route to the Vallée des Merveilles is the ten-kilometre trek (6–8hr) that starts at *Les Mesces* refuge, about 8km west of St-Dalmas-de-Tende on the D91. The first part of the climb is through woods full of wild raspberries, mushrooms and bilberries, not all of it steeply uphill. Eventually you rise above the treeline and **Lac Long** comes into view. A few pines still manage to grow around the lake, and in spring the grass is full of flowers, but encircling you is a mountain wilderness. From the *Refuge des Merveilles* by the lake, you continue up through a fearsome valley where the rocks turn from black to green according to the light. From here to just beyond the **Lac des Merveilles** you can start searching for the engravings. For the Vallée de Fontanable the path starts 4.5km further up the D91 from the *Mesces* refuge, just before the Casterino information point.

Several companies organize **guided walks** in the area: the Association Merveilles Gravures et Découverte, 18 rue A. Operto in Tende (June Sat &

Sun; July & Aug daily; Sept Fri–Mon; €8, ⓣ06.86.03.90.13), the Bureau des Guides in St-Martin-Vésubie (see p.425; ⓣ04.93.03.44.30), and Destination Merveilles in Villeneuve-Loubet (ⓣ04.93.73.09.07) are all recommended. Going alone, it's perfectly possible to miss the engravings altogether, and blue skies and sun can quickly turn into violent hailstorms and lightning.

Tende

TENDE, the highest town on the Roya, guards the access to the Col de Tende, which connects Provence with Piedmont but is now bypassed by a road tunnel. Though not especially attractive, Tende is fairly busy, with plenty of cheap accommodation, places to eat, bars to lounge around in and shops to browse round.

The town's old and gloomy houses are built with green and purple schist, but blackened by fumes from the heavy trucks that cross to and from Italy. Above the houses rise the cherry-coloured belfry of the **collegiate church**, the peachy-orange towers and belfries of various **chapels**, and a twenty-metre needle of wall which is all that remains of a château destroyed by the French in the seventeenth century. Tende's main attraction is the **Musée des Merveilles** at the northern end of town on av du 16 Septembre 1947 (March to mid-Oct daily 10am–6pm; mid-Oct to Feb Mon & Wed–Sun 10am–5pm; €4.55), which details the geology, archeology and traditions of the areas where engravings have been found. Scenes from the daily lives of Copper- and Bronze-Age man have been set up, and reproductions of the rock designs are on display along with attempts to decipher the beliefs and myths that inspired them. Whether you've been to the Vallée des Merveilles or not, the museum is an invaluable insight into an intriguing subject.

The **Vieille Ville** is fun to wander through, looking at the symbols of old trades on the door lintels, the overhanging roofs and the balconies on every floor. On place de l'Église, the **Collégiale Notre-Dame de l'Assumption** is more a repository of the town's wealth than a place of contemplation, with Baroque excess throughout, though the Apostles wearing their halos like lids on the Renaissance porch and the lions supporting the two Doric columns are a nice touch. At the other end of town near the station, the seventeenth-century **Église St-Michel**, on place du Grande Marché, was entirely remodelled in the 1960s, when its chevet was replaced by a wall of glass looking onto the trees and shrubs of the former convent gardens. It was decorated by a local artist, some of whose dream-inspired paintings of a semi-symbolist, semi-surrealist nature, are dreadful, while others strike an eerily appropriate note.

Practicalities

The **gare SNCF** is set back from the top of the main street, av du 16 Septembre (becoming av Aimable-Gastaud and av Georges-Bidault as it runs southwards), at the end of av Vassalo. Turning right out of the station you'll see the **tourist office** at the back of the *mairie* on your left before you reach the avenue (Mon–Sat plus Sun am: May–Sept 9am–1pm & 2.30–6pm; Oct–April 9am–12.30pm & 2–5.30pm; ⓣ04.93.04.73.71, ⓦwww.tendemerveilles.com). This central axis leads down left towards place de la République; the Vieille Ville is further down on your right to either side of the Roya's tributary.

Hotels in Tende are inexpensive: there's the *Miramonti* at 5–7 av Vassalo (ⓣ04.93.04.61.82, ⓕ04.93.04.61.82; ❷; closed Nov), just by the station, or the *Hôtel du Centre*, 12 place de la République (ⓣ04.93.04.62.19; ❷; closed Nov–March). If you follow chemin Ste-Catherine, off rue St-Jean past the cathedral, you'll come to the edge of the town and the **gîte d'étape** *Les Carlines* (☎04.93.04.62.74; ❶; closed Oct to mid-April), which has gorgeous views down the valley. The one-star municipal **campsite** *Saint Jacques* is 500m down a path to the left of the gare SNCF (☎04.93.04.76.08; June–Aug only).

There's no shortage of **restaurants** to be found on av du 16 Septembre and rue de France: nothing very special but plenty of Italian dishes. *La Margueria* pizzeria, on av du 16 Septembre, with beams strung with dried herbs and garlic, and stuffed foxes on the walls, is the most popular.

Travel details

Trains

Chemin de Fer de Provence (Nice–Digne)

Nice to: Annot (4–5 daily; 2hr); Barrême (4–5 daily; 1hr 45min); Digne (4–5 daily; 3hr 15min); Entrevaux (4–5 daily; 1hr 30min); Puget-Théniers (4–5 daily; 1hr 30min); St-André-des-Alpes (4–5 daily; 2hr 25min); Thorame-Gare (4–5 daily; 2hr 15min); Touët-sur-Var (4–5 daily; 1hr 10min); Villars-sur-Var (4–5 daily; 1hr).

From **Digne** a regular SNCF bus links the Chemin de Fer de Provence with the SNCF Marseille–Sisteron line at St-Auban–Château-Arnoux (30min).

From **Thorame-Gare** a bus meets 3 trains daily (during the ski season, July and August) for connections to: Beauvezer (20min); Colmars-les-Alpes (30min); Allos (45min); La Foux d'Allos (1hr 10min).

SNCF line

Nice to: Breil-sur-Roya direct (6 daily; 55min); Breil-sur-Roya, via Ventimiglia (8 daily; 1hr 15min–1hr 25min); La Brigue, via Ventimiglia (4–5 daily; 1hr 45min); St-Dalmas-de-Tende, via Ventimiglia (4–5 daily; 1hr 40min); Saorge-Fontan (8 daily; 1hr 15min–1hr 40min); Sospel (6 daily; 45min); Tende via Ventimiglia (8 daily; 1hr 45min–2hr 30min).

Buses

Barçelonette to: Digne (1 daily; 1hr 30min); Gap (3 daily; 1hr 20min); Marseille (2–3 daily; 4hr).

Digne to: Avignon (3 daily; 3hr 30min); Barçelonnette (1 daily; 1hr 30min); Castellane (2 daily; 1hr 15min); Grenoble (1 daily; 3hr 55min); Manosque (4 daily; 1hr 15min); Marseille (5 daily; 2hr–2hr 25min); Nice (1 daily; 3hr 15min); Puget-Théniers (1 daily; 2hr); Pra-Loup (1 daily; 1hr 50min); St-André-les-Alpes (2–3 daily; 1 hr); Seyne-les-Alpes (1 daily; 40min); Sisteron (2–3 daily; 1hr).

Gréolières to: Grasse (1–2 daily; 35–50min).

Puget-Théniers to: Annot (1 daily; 20min); Barrême (1 daily; 1hr 10min); Digne (1 daily; 2hr); Entraunes (1 daily; 1hr 30min); Entrevaux (1 daily; 10min); St-André-les-Alpes (1 daily; 1hr); St-Martin-d'Entraunes (1 daily; 1hr 20min).

St-André-les-Alpes to: Allos (1–3 daily in high season; 1hr); Barrême (1 daily; 10min); Digne (1 daily; 1hr); La Foux d'Allos (1–3 daily; 1hr 15min); Nice (1 daily; 2hr).

St-Étienne-de-Tinée to: Auron (1–5 daily; 15min); Isola (1–4 daily; 15min); La Tour (1–4 daily; 1hr 5min); Nice (1–4 daily; 2hr 30min); St-Sauveur-de-Tinée (1–4 daily; 45min).

St-Martin-Vésubie to: Lantosque (3 daily; 30min); Nice (3 daily; 1hr 45min); Roquebillière (3 daily; 15min); St-Dalmas (1 weekly; 20min).

Sospel to: Menton (5 daily; 35min–1hr); Moulinet (2 daily; 40min).

Thorame-Gare to: Allos (3 daily; 45min); Beauvezer (3 daily; 20min); Colmars-les-Alpes (3 daily; 30min); La Foux d'Allos (3 daily; 1hr 10min).

Contexts

Contexts

The historical framework

From the Stone Age to the Celto-Ligurians

Almost all the great discoveries of **Stone Age** life in France have been made in the southwest of the country. In Provence a few Paleolithic traces have been found at Nice and in Menton (the skull of "Grimaldi man", for example), but nothing to compare with the cave drawings of Lascaux. It's assumed, however, that the area, including large tracts now submerged under the sea, was equally populated.

The development of farming, characterizing the **Neolithic Era**, is thought to have been started in Provence around 6500 BC with the domestication of the indigenous wild sheep. Around 3000 BC the **Ligurians** came from the east, settling throughout southern France and cultivating the land for the first time. It is to these people that the carvings in the Vallée des Merveilles, the few megalithic standing stones, and the earliest *bories* belonged. It's also thought that certain Provençal word endings in place names and names of rivers and mountains, such as *-osc*, *-asc*, *-auni* and *-inc*, derive from the Ligurian dialects passed down through Greek and Latin.

At some later point the **Celts** from the north moved into western Provence, bringing with them bronze technology. The first known fortified hilltop retreats, the *oppidi* (of which traces remain in the Maures, the Luberon, the upper Durance and the hills in the Rhône Valley), are attributed to this new ethnic mix, the **Celto-Ligurians**.

The Ancient Greeks discover Provence

As the Celto-Ligurian civilization developed, so did its trading links with the other Mediterranean peoples. The name of the River Rhône may have been given by traders from the Greek island of Rhodes (in French the name can be made into an adjective, *Rhodien*). Etruscans, Phoenicians, Corinthians and Ionians all had links with Provence. The eventual **Greek colonies** set up along the coast, starting with **Massalia** (Marseille) around 600 BC, were not the result of military conquest but of gradual economic integration. And while Massalia was a republic with great influence over its hinterland, it was not a base for wiping out the indigenous peoples. Prestige and wealth came from its port, and the city prided itself on its independence, which was to last well into the Middle Ages.

The Greeks introduced olives, figs, cherries, walnuts, cultivated vines and money. During the two hundred years following the foundation of Massalia, **colonies** were set up in La Ciotat, Almanarre (near Hyères), Brégançon,

Cavalaire, St-Tropez (known as Athenopolis), Antibes, Nice and Monaco. Mastrabala at St-Blaize and Glanum by St-Rémy-de-Provence developed within Massalia's sphere of influence. The **Rhône** was the corridor for commercial expeditions, including journeys as far north as Cornwall to acquire tin. Away from the coast and the Rhône Valley, however, the Celto-Ligurian lifestyle was barely affected by the advantages of Hellenic life, continuing its harsher and more basic battle for survival.

Roman conquest

Unlike the Greeks, the **Romans** were true imperialists, imposing their organization, language and laws by military subjugation on every corner of their empire. During the third century BC Roman expansion was concentrated on Spain, the power base of the Carthaginians – from where Hannibal had set off with his elephants to cross the Rhône somewhere above Orange and the Alps in order to attack the Romans in upper Italy. During this time Massalia nurtured good diplomatic relations with Rome which stood the city in good stead when Spain was conquered and the Romans decided to secure the land routes to Iberia.

This they achieved in a remarkably short time. From 125 to 118 BC, **Provincia** (the origin of the name Provence) became part of the Roman Empire. It encompassed the whole of the south of France from the Alps to the Pyrenees, stretching as far north as Vienna and Geneva, and with Narbonne as its capital.

While Massalia and other areas remained neutral or collaborated with the invaders, many Ligurian tribes fought to the death, most notably the Salyens, whose Oppidum d'Entremont was demolished and a victorious new city, Aquae Sextiae (Aix), built at its foot in 122 BC. Pax Romana was still a long way off, however. **Germanic Celts** moving down from the Baltic came into conflict with the ruling power, managing to decimate several Roman legions at Orange in 105 BC. A major campaign was undertaken to prevent the Barbarians from closing in on Italy. The northern invaders were defeated, as were local uprisings. Massalia exploited every situation to gain more territories and privileges; the rest of Provence knuckled under, suffering the various battles and the requisitions and taxes to pay for them. Finally, from 58 to 51 BC all of Gaul was conquered by **Julius Caesar**.

It was then that Massalia finally blew its hitherto successful diplomatic strategy by supporting Pompey against Caesar, who then laid siege, defeated the city and confiscated all its territories which had stretched from the Rhône to Monaco. Unlike earlier emperors, Julius Caesar started to implant his own people in Provence (St-Raphaël was founded for his veterans). His successor Octavian followed the same policy. While the coastal areas duly Latinized themselves, the **Ligurians** in the mountains, from Sisteron to the Roya Valley, refused to give up their identity without a fight. Fight they did, keeping Roman troops busy for ten years until their eventual defeat in 14 BC, which the Trophie des Alpes at La Turbie gloats over to this day.

This monument to Augustus Caesar was erected on the newly built **Via Aurelia**, which linked Rome with Arles, by way of Cimiez, Antibes, Fréjus and Aix, more or less along the route of the present-day N7. The **Via Agrippa** went north from Arles, through Avignon and Orange. Only the rebellious mountainous area was heavily garrisoned. Western Provence, with Arles as its main town (Narbonne was still the capital of Provincia), dutifully served the imperial interests, providing oil, grain and, most importantly, ships for the superpower that ruled western Europe and the borders of the Mediterranean for five centuries.

Christianity appeared in Provence during the third century and spread fair ly rapidly in the fourth when it became the official religion of the Roman Empire. The **Lérins Monastery** was founded around 410 AD and the **Abbey of St-Victor** in Marseille about six years later.

Rome falls: more invasions

For a while in the early fifth century, when the Roman Empire was beginning to split apart, the invasions by the Germanic tribes bypassed Provence. But by the time the Western Roman Empire was finally done for in 476 AD, Provence was under the domination of both the **Visigoths**, who had captured Arles and were terrorizing the lower Rhône valley, and the **Burgundians**, another Germanic tribe, who had moved in from the east. The new rulers confiscated land, took slaves and generally made life for the locals even more miserable than usual.

Over the next two hundred years **Goths** and **Franks** fought over and partitioned Provence; famine, disease and bloodshed diminished the population; lands that had been drained returned to swamp; intellectual life declined. Under the **Merovingian dynasty** in the eighth century Provence was, in theory, part of the **Frankish empire**. But a new world power had emerged – **Islam** – which had spread from the Middle East into North Africa and most of Spain. In 732 a Muslim army had reached as far as Tours before being defeated by the Franks at Poitiers. At this point the local ruler of Provence rebelled against the central authority, and called on the **Saracens** (Muslims) to assist. Armies of Franks, Saracens, Lombards (allies of the Franks) and locals rampaged through Provence, putting the Franks back in control.

Though the ports had trouble carrying on their lucrative trade while the Mediterranean was controlled by Saracens, agriculture developed under the Frankish **Carolingian dynasty**, particularly during the relatively peaceful years of **Charlemagne's rule**. But when, during the ninth century, Charlemagne's sons and then grandsons started squabbling over the inheritance, Provence once again became easy prey.

Normans took over the lower Rhône, and the **Saracens** returned, pillaging Marseille and destroying its abbey in 838, doing over Arles in 842, and attacking Marseille again in 848. For a century they maintained a base at Fraxinetum (La Garde-Freinet), from where they controlled the whole Massif des Maures.

The **hilltop villages** along the coast are commonly explained as the frightened response to the Saracens, though few date back this far. Well inland, people were just as prone to retreat to whatever defensive positions were available. In the cities this would be the strongest building (the Roman theatre at Orange, for example). The Rhône Valley villagers took refuge in the Luberon and the Massif de la Ste-Baume.

For all the terrors and bloodshed, the period was not without its evolution. The Saracens introduced basic medicine, the use of cork bark, resin extraction from pines, flat roof tiles, and the most traditional Provençal musical instrument, the tambourine.

The counts of Provence

The Saracens were expelled for good at the end of the tenth century by **Guillaume Le Libérateur**, count of Arles, who claimed Provence as his own feudal estate. After several centuries of anarchy a period of relative stability ensued. Forestry, fishing, irrigation, land reclamation, vine cultivation, beekeeping, salt-panning, river transport and renewed learning (under the auspices of the Benedictine monasteries) began pulling Provence out of the Dark Ages.

Politically, Guillaume and his successors retained considerable independence from their overlords (first the kingdom of Burgundy then the Holy Roman Empire). In turn they tended to confine their influence to the area around Arles and Avignon, while local lords held sway throughout the rest of the countryside and the cities developed their own autonomy. The Rhône formed the border between France and the Holy Roman Empire but for much of the time this political division failed to cut the old economic, cultural and linguistic links between the two sides of the river.

In the **twelfth century**, Provence passed to the counts of Toulouse and was then divided with the counts of Barcelona, while various fiefdoms – amongst them Forcalquier, Les Baux and Beuil on the eastern side of the Var – refused integration. Power was a bewildering, shifting pattern, but, sporadic armed conflicts apart (confined mainly to the lower Rhône Valley), the titleholder to Provence hardly affected the ordinary people who were bound in serfdom to their immediate seigneur.

As a consequence of the Crusades, **maritime commerce** flourished once again, as did trade along the Rhône, giving prominence to Avignon, Orange, Arles and, most of all, Marseille. In Nice, then under the control of the Genoese Republic, a new commercial town started to develop below the castle rock. The cities took on the organizational form of the Italian consulates, increasingly separating themselves from feudal power.

Troubadour poetry made its appearance in the langue d'oc language that was spoken from the Alps to the Pyrenees (and from which the **Provençal dialect** developed). Church construction looked back to the Romans for inspiration, producing the great Romanesque edifices of Montmajour, Sénanque, Silvacane, Thoronet and St-Trophime in Arles.

Raymond Béranger V, Catalan count of Provence in the early thirteenth century, took the unprecedented step of spending time in his domains. While fighting off the count of Toulouse and the Holy Roman Emperor, he made Aix his capital, founded Barcelonnette and travelled throughout the Alps and the coastal regions. Provence became, for the first time since the Romans, an organized mini-state with a more or less **unified feudal system** of law and administration.

The Angevins

After Béranger's death, Provence turned towards France, with the **house of Anjou** gaining control and holding it until the end of the fifteenth century. The borders changed: Nice, Barçelonnette and Puget-Théniers passed to Savoy in 1388 and remained separate from Provence until 1860. New extraneous powers claimed or bought territories within the country – the **popes at Avignon** (see p.69) and in the **Comtat Venaissin**; the Prince of Nassau in Orange. Though armed conflicts, revolts and even civil war in 1388 chequered its medieval history, Provence was at least spared the devastations of the Hundred Years' War with England, which never touched the region.

By the end of this period the established trading routes from the Orient to Genoa and Marseille, and from Marseille to Flanders and London, were forming the basis of **early capitalism**, and spreading new techniques and learning. Though Marseille was not a great financial centre like Antwerp or Florence, its expanding population became ever more cosmopolitan. Away from the coast and the Rhône, however, feudal villages continued to live in isolation, unable to survive if a harvest failed. For a shepherd or forester in the mountains, life in Marseille or in the extravagant papal city of Avignon would have appeared to belong to another planet.

Provençal Jews exercised equal rights with Christians, owning land and practising a wide variety of professions in addition to finance and commerce. Though concentrated in the western towns, they were not always ghettoized. But the moment any kind of disaster struck, such as the Black Death in the mid-fourteenth century, latent hostility would violently manifest itself. **The Plague**, however, made no distinctions between Jew or Christian, rich or poor: around half the population died from the recurring epidemics.

In **cultural and intellectual life** the dominant centres were the **papal court at Avignon**, and later **King René of Anjou's court at Aix**. However, despite the area's key position between Italy and northern Europe, and the cosmopolitan influence of the popes, Angevin rulers and foreign trade, art and architecture remained surprisingly unmarked by the major movements of the time. The popes tended to employ foreign artists and it was not until the mid-fifteenth century that native art developed around the **Avignon School** – represented by such works as Nicolas Froment's *Le Buisson Ardent* and *La Couronnement de la Vierge* by Enguerrand Quarton. At the same time the **School of Nice** developed, more directly under Italian influence, represented by the frescoes of Canavesio and Baleison and the paintings of Louis and François Bréa. Avignon was the chief city of great **Gothic architecture** – the Palais des Papes and many of the churches – but outside this city the only major examples of the new style were Tarascon's castle and the basilica of St-Maximin-de-la-Ste-Baume.

The **legends of the saints** fleeing Palestine and seeking refuge in Provence began to take root around this time, too, with pilgrimages to the various shrines bringing glimpses of the outside world to small towns and villages. It was at this time that the popes founded a **university in Avignon** (1303) which became famous for jurisprudence; Aix university was established a century later and in the mid-fourteenth century the first paper mills were in use. By King René's time, French was the official language of the court.

Union with France

The short-lived Charles III of Provence, René's heir, bequeathed all his lands to **Louis XI of France**, a transfer of power that the *parlement* of Aix glossed over and approved in 1482. Within twelve months every top Provençal official had been sacked and replaced by a Frenchman; the castles at Toulon and Les Baux were razed to the ground; garrisons were placed in five major towns.

The *parlement* protested in vain, but after Louis XI's death a more careful approach was taken to this crucial border province. The **Act of Union**, ratified by *parlement* in 1486, declared Provence to be a separate entity within the kingdom of France, enshrining the rights to its own law courts, customs and privileges. In reality, the ever-centralizing power of the French state was systematically to erode these rights as it did with Brittany and the other once-autonomous provinces.

The **Jewish population** provided a convenient diversion for Provençal frustrations. Encouraged, if not instigated, by the Crown, there were massacres, expulsions and assaults in Marseille, Arles and Manosque in the last two decades of the fifteenth century. The royal directive was convert or leave – some, such as the parents of **Nostradamus**, converted, many fled to the Comtat. During the sixteenth century more expulsion threats and special taxes were the rule. In 1570 the Jews lost their papal protection in the Comtat.

Meanwhile Charles VIII, Louis XII and François I involved Provence in their **Italian Wars**. **Marseille** became a **military port** in 1488, and in 1496 **Toulon** was fortified and its first **shipyards** opened. While the rest of the province suffered troop movements and requisitions, Marseille and Toulon benefited from extra funds and unchecked piracy against the enemies of France. Genoese, Venetian and Spanish vessels were regularly towed into Marseille's port.

The war took a more serious turn in the 1520s after the French conquest of Milan. **Charles V**, the new Holy Roman Emperor, retaliated by sending a large army across the Var and into Aix. The French concern was to protect Marseille at all costs – the rest of the province was left to fend for itself. After the imperial forces had failed to take Marseille and retreated, the city was rewarded with the pomp and carnival of a royal wedding between François' second son, the future Henri II, and **Catherine de Medici**. The Château d'If was built to protect the roadstead.

Another round in the war soon commenced. Charles V took back Milan, the French invaded Savoy and occupied Nice. In 1536 an even bigger **imperial army invaded**, and again the French abandoned inland Provence to protect Marseille and the Rhône Valley. The people of **Le Muy** stopped the emperor for one day with fifty local heroes, who were subsequently hanged for their pains. Elsewhere people fled to the forests, their towns and villages pillaged by the invaders. **Marseille** and **Arles** held out; French troops finally moved south down the Durance; dysentery and lack of sure supply lines weakened the imperial army. Twenty thousand Savoyards were dead or imprisoned by the time the imperial troops were safely back across the Var.

One effect of the Italian Wars was that Provence finally now identified itself with France, making it easier for the Crown to diminish the power of the États, impose greater numbers of French administrators, and, in 1539, decree that all administrative laws were to be translated from Latin into French, not Provençal.

Life in the early sixteenth century

Sixteenth-century Provence was ruled by two royal appointees – a governor and grand *sénéchal* (the chief administrator) – but the **feudal hierarchy** failed to achieve the same command over the structure of society as it did elsewhere in France. Few nobles lived on their estates and those that did were often poorer than the merchants and financiers of the major cities. In remoter areas people cultivated their absent seigneur's land as if it were their own; in other areas towns bought land off the feudal owners. It is estimated that nearly half the population had their own holdings. Advances in irrigation, such as **Craponne's canal through the Crau**, were carried out independently from the aristocracy.

While not self-sufficient in grain, Provence had surpluses of wine, fish and vermilion from the Camargue to export; as well as **growing industries** in textiles, tanneries, soap and paper; and new foods, such as oranges, pepper, palm dates and sugar cane, introduced along the coast from across the Mediterranean. Olives provided the basic oil for food, orchards began to be cultivated on a commercial scale, and most families kept pigs and sheep: only vegetables were rare luxuries. People lived on their land, with the **old fortified villages** populated only in times of insecurity. Most small towns had weekly **markets**, and **festivals** celebrated the advance from survival being a non-stop struggle. Epidemics of the plague continued, however, and sanitation left a lot to be desired – a contemporary noted that even in Aix it "rained shit as often as it did in Arles or Marseille".

Free schools were set up by some of the larger towns, and secondary colleges established in Aix, Marseille, Arles and Avignon. **Nostradamus** (1503–1566) achieved renown throughout France – from the royal court down to his Salon and St-Rémy neighbours. His books had to be printed in Lyon, though, as there was as yet no market for printers in Provence.

Châteaux such as La Tour d'Aigue, Gordes and Lourmarin, with comfort playing an equal part to defence, were built at this time, as were the rich Marseille town houses of the Maison Diamentée and the Hôtel Cabre. The facade of St-Pierre in Avignon shows the Renaissance finally triumphing over Provence's artistic backwardness.

The Wars of Religion

Though the Italian Wars temporarily disrupted social and productive advances, they were nothing compared with the **Wars of Religion** that put all France in a state of **civil war** for most of the second half of the sixteenth century. The clash between the new reforming ideas of Luther and Calvin and the old Roman Catholic order was particularly violent in Provence. Avignon, as papal domain, was inevitably a rigid centre of Catholicism. The neighbouring principality of Orange allowed Huguenots to practise freely and form their own organizations. Haute Provence and the Luberon became centres for the new religion due to the influx of Dauphinois and Piedmontais settlers.

Incidents began to build up in the 1540s, culminating in the massacre of Luberon Protestants and the destruction of Mérindol (see p.150). In Avignon heretics were displayed in the iron cages where they'd been slung to die; in Haute Provence churches were smashed by the reformers; while in Orange the Protestants pillaged the cathedral and took control of the city. The regent Catherine de Medici's **Edict of Tolerance** in 1562 only made matters worse. Marseille demanded and received an exemption; Aix promptly dispatched a Catholic contingent to massacre the Protestants of Tourves; Catherine's envoys prompted a massacre of Catholics at Barjols. The notorious Baron des Adrets, who had fought for the Catholics, now switched sides and carried out a series of terrifying attacks on Catholic towns and villages. The *parlement* chose to resign rather than ratify a new edict of tolerance in 1563, even though by this point Orange had been won back to the established Church, the garrison of Sisteron had been massacred for protecting the Protestants and the last armed group of reformers had fled north out of the province.

When Catherine de Medici and her son Charles XIV toured Provence in 1564, all seemed well. But within a few years fighting again broke out, with Sisteron once more under siege. In the mid-1570s trouble took a new turn with the rivalry between Henri III's governor and *sénéchal* adding to the hostile camps. This state of civil war was only terminated by another major outbreak of the **Plague** in **1580**.

With the Protestant **Henri de Navarre** (the future Henri IV) becoming heir to the throne in 1584, the *Guerres de Religion* hotted up even more. The pope excommunicated Henri; and the leaders of the French Catholics (the de Guises) formed the **European Catholic League**, seized Paris and drove out the king, Henri III. Provence found itself with two governors – the king's and the League's appointees; two capitals – Aix and Pertuis; and a split *parlement*. After Henri III's assassination, Catholic Aix called in the duke of Savoy whose troops trounced Henri de Navarre's supporters at Riez. At this point the main issue for the Provençaux was loyalty to the French Crown against invaders, rather than religion. Even the Aix *parlement* stopped short of giving Savoy the title to Provence, and after Marseille again withstood a siege, the duke gave up and went back home to Nice in 1592. For another year battles continued between the Leaguers and the Royalists, with Marseille refusing to recognize either authority. Finally Henri IV said his Mass; troops entered Marseille; and the war-damaged and impoverished Provence reverted back to **royal control**.

Louis XIII and Louis XIV

The **consolidation of the French state** initiated by Louis XIII's minister **Richelieu** saw the whittling away of Provençal institutions and ideas of independence, coupled with ever-increasing tax demands plus enforced "free gifts" to the king. The power and prestige of the États and *parlement* were reduced by force, clever negotiation or playing off the different cities' rival interests.

Political power switched from governors and *sénéchals*, who were part of the feudal structure, to *intendants*, servants of the state with powers over every aspect of provincial life, including the military. The États, having refused to provide the royal purse with funds in 1629, were not convoked again. These changes, along with the failure of the aristocratic rebellions during Louis XIV's minority (the Frondes), and the increasing number of titles bought by the bourgeoisie, left the *noblesse d'épée* (the real aristos) disgruntled but impotent. The clergy (the First Estate) also lost a measure of their former power.

It was a time of **plague**, **famine**, further outbreaks of **religious strife and war**. To deal with opposition the Château d'If became a state prison. The **war with Spain**, for which Toulon's fortifications were upgraded and forts added to Giens and the Îles d'Hyères, increased taxation, decimated trade and cost lives. Marseille attempted to hold on to its ancient independence by setting up a rebel council in 1658. The royal response was swift. Troops were sent in, rebels were condemned to the rack or the galleys, a permanent garrison was established and the foundations laid for the Fort St-Nicolas to keep an eye on "*ce peuple violent et libertin*".

While the various upheavals and ever-multiplying tax burden caused untold misery, progress in production (including the faïence industry), education and social provision (mostly the work of the burgeoning Pénitents orders outside the Church establishment) carried on apace. The town houses of Aix, Marseille and Avignon, the Hospice de la Charité in Marseille, the Baroque additions to churches and chapels, all show the wealth accumulating, gained, as ever, by maritime commerce. But the greatest Provençal sculptor of the period, **Pierre Puget**, never received royal patronage and Provençal was still the language of all classes in society, though French for the first time was imposed on certain disciplines at Aix University.

As the reign of **Louis XIV**, the **Sun King**, became more grandiose and more aggressive, Provence, like all of France outside Versailles and Paris, was eclipsed. The **war with Holland** saw Orange and the valley of Barçelonnette annexed; Avignon and the papal Comtat swung steadily into the French orbit; attempts were made again to capture Nice. But for the Provençaux, the people of Orange, Avignon and the Comtat had always been their fellow countrymen and women, while Nice was a foreign city they had never wished to claim. Wars that involved the English navy blockading the ports were as unwelcome to the local bourgeois as they were to those who had to fight.

As the *ancien régime* slowly dug its own grave the rest of the country stagnated. The pattern for Provence of wars, invasions and trade blockades became entrenched. To add to the gloom, another outbreak of the **Plague** killed half the population of Marseille in **1720**. The extravagance of Louis XV's court, where the Grassois painter Fragonard found his patrons, had few echoes in Provence. Aix had its grandiose town planning, Avignon its mansions, Grasse its perfume industry, but elsewhere there was complete stagnation.

The Revolution

Conditions were ripe for revolution in Provence. The region had suffered a disastrous silk harvest and a sharp fall in the price of wine in 1787, and the severe winter of 1788–89 killed off most of the olive trees. Unemployment and starvation were rife and the hurtling rise in the price of bread provoked serious rioting in the spring of 1789. There was no lack of followers for bourgeois *députés* exasperated by the incompetent administration and constant drain on national resources that the court represented.

So in **July 1789**, while the Bastille was stormed in Paris, Provençal peasants pillaged their local châteaux and urban workers rioted against the mayors, egged on by the middle classes. There was only one casualty, at Aups. The following year **Marseillaise revolutionaries** seized the forts of St-Jean and St-Nicolas, with again just one lashing of violence when the crowd lynched St-Jean's commander. **Toulon** was equally fervent in its support for the new order, and at **Aix** one counter-revolutionary lawyer and two aristocrats were strung up on lampposts. In the **papal lands**, where the crucial issue was reunion with France, Rome's representative was sent packing from Avignon and a revolutionary municipality installed.

Counter-revolutionaries regrouped in Carpentras and there were several bloody incidents, including the ice-house massacre. However, 1792 saw Marseille's staunchly Jacobin National Guard, the **Féderés**, demolish the counter-revolutionary forces in the Comtat and aristocratic Arles. Marseille's authorities declared that kingship was contrary to the principles of equality and national sovereignty. When the Legislative Assembly summoned all the Féderés to Paris to defend the capital and celebrate the third anniversary of the Bastille, five hundred Marseillais marched north singing Rouget de Lisle's **Hymn to the Army of the Rhine**. It was written for the troops at the front in the war declared that April with Germany and Austria. But for the Parisian *sans-culottes* it was a major hit, becoming the **Marseillaise**, France's national anthem – even more so after the attack on the Tuileries palace that was swiftly followed by the dethronement of the king. According to the Swedish ambassador of the time, "Marseille's Féderés were the moving force behind everything in August 1792."

Provence had by now incorporated the papal states and was divided into **four départements**. Peasants were once again on the pillage, and still starving, while royalists and republicans fought it out in the towns. In 1793 the Var military commander was ordered to take Nice, a hotbed of émigré intrigue and part of the great European coalition out to exterminate the French Revolution. Twenty thousand people fled the city but no resistance was encountered. The Alpes-Maritimes *département* came into existence.

In the summer of the same year, political divisions between the various factions of the Convention and the growing fear of a dictatorship by the Parisian *sans-culottes* provoked the **provincial Federalist revolt**. The populace was fed up with conscription to the wars on every frontier, and a hankering after their old Provençal autonomy reasserted itself. Revolutionary cities found themselves fighting against government forces – a situation speedily exploited by the real **counter-revolutionaries**. In Toulon the entire fleet and the city's fortifications were handed over to the English. (In the battle to regain the city, the government's victory was secured by the young Napoleon.) Reprisals, in addition to the almost daily executions of the Terror, cost thousands of lives.

Much of Provence, however, had remained Jacobin, and so fell victim to the **White Terror of 1795** that followed the execution of Robespierre. The prisons of Marseille, Aix, Arles and Tarascon overflowed with people picked up on the street with no charge. Cannons were fired into the cells at point-blank range and sulphur or lighted rags thrown through the bars. By the time the Revolution had given up all hopes of being revolutionary in terms of its 1789 manifesto, **anarchy reigned**. Provence was crawling with returned émigrés who had no trouble finding violent followers motivated by frustration, exhaustion and famine.

Napoleon and restoration

Provence's experience of **Napoleon's reign** differed little from that of the rest of France, despite the emperor's close connection with the region (childhood at Nice; military career at Antibes and Toulon; then the escape from Elba). Order was restored and power became even more centralized, with *préfets* enlarging on the role of Louis XIV's *intendants*. The **concordat with the pope** re-establishing Catholicism as the state religion was widely welcomed, particularly since the new ecclesiastical authorities were not all the old First Estate, *ancien régime* representatives. However, secular power reverted to the old seigneurs in many places – the new mayor of Marseille, for example, was a marquise.

It was the **Napoleonic wars** that lost the emperor his Provençal support. Marseille's port was again blockaded; conscription and taxes for military campaigns were as detested as ever; the Alpes-Maritimes *département* became a theatre of war and in 1814 was handed over (with Savoy) to Sardinia. Monaco followed suit the following year, though with the Grimaldi dynasty reinstalled in their palace.

The **restoration of the Bourbons** after Waterloo unleashed another White Terror. Provence was again bitterly divided between royalists and republicans. Despite this split there was no major resistance to the **1830 revolution** which put Louis-Philippe, the "Citizen King", on the throne. The new regime represented liberalism – well tinged with anti-clericalism and a dislike of democracy – and was welcomed by the Provençal bourgeoisie. Despite the ardent Catholicism of the *paysans*, and the large numbers of émigrés that had returned under the Bourbons' amnesties, the attempt by the duchess of Berry to bring back the "legitimate" royalty (which had some initial success in western France) failed totally here.

1848 and 1851

The first half of the nineteenth century saw the first major **industrialization** of France, and, overseas, the conquest of Algeria.

In Provence, Marseille was linked by rail with Paris and expanded its port to take steam ships; iron bridges over the Rhône and new roads were built; many towns demolished their ramparts to extend their main streets into the suburbs. By the 1840s the arsenal at Toulon was employing over three thousand workers.

This emerging proletariat was highly receptive to the visit by the socialist and feminist **Flora Tristan**, who was doing the rounds of France in 1844. A year later all the different trades in the arsenal went on strike. Throughout industrialized Provence – the Rhône Valley and the coast – workers overturned their traditional *compagnons* (guilds) to form more radical trade-union organizations. Things hardly changed, however, in inland Provence, as protectionist policies hampered the exchange of foodstuffs, and the new industries' demand for fuel eroded the forestry rights of the *paysans*. In 1847 the country (and most of Europe) was in severe economic crisis.

News of the **1848 revolution** arrived from Paris before the representatives of the new republic. Town halls, common lands and forests were instantly and peacefully reclaimed by the populace. In the elections that followed, very moderate republicans were returned, though they included three manual workers in Marseille, Toulon and Avignon. Two months later, however, the economic situation was deteriorating again, and newly won improvements in working hours and wages were being clawed back by the employers. A demonstration in Marseille turned nasty and the **barricades** went up.

Elsewhere, the most militant action was in Menton and Roquebrune, both under the rule of **Monaco**, where the people refused to pay the prince's high taxes on oil and fruit. Sardinian military assistance failed to quell the revolt and the two towns declared themselves independent republics. With his main source of income gone, the Grimaldi prince turned the focus of his state shrewdly towards tourism – already well established in Nice and Hyères – and opened the casino at Monte Carlo.

The 1848 revolution turned sour with the election of **Louis-Napoleon** as president in 1850. A law was introduced which in effect annulled the 1830 universal male suffrage by imposing a residency requirement. Laws against "secret societies" and "conspiracies" followed. Ordinary *paysans* discussing prices over a bottle of wine could be arrested; militants from Digne and Avignon were deported to Polynesia for belonging to a democratic party. Newly formed cooperatives were seen by the authorities as hotbeds of sedition. All this inevitably accelerated politicization of the *paysans*.

When Louis-Napoleon made himself emperor in the **coup d'état of 1851**, Provence, as many other regions of France, turned again to revolt. Initially there were insufficient forces in the small towns and villages to prevent the rebels taking control (which they did without any violence). In order to take the préfectures, villagers and townspeople, both male and female, organized themselves into disciplined "colonnes" which marched beneath the red flag. Digne was the only préfecture they held, though, and then for only two days. Reprisals were bloody – another White Terror in effect, with thousands of the rebels caught as they tried to flee into Savoy. Of all the insurgents in France shot, imprisoned or deported after this rebellion, one in five were from Provence.

The Second Empire

The **Second Empire** saw greater changes in everyday life than in any previous period. **Marseille** became the premier port of France, with trade enormously expanded by the colonization of North and West Africa, Vietnam and parts of China. The depopulation of inland Provence, which had been gradually increasing over the last century and a half, suddenly became a deluge of migration to the coast and Rhône Valley. While the railway was extended along the coast – encouraging the nascent Côte d'Azur tourism – communications inland were ignored.

At the end of the **war for Italian unification** in 1860, **Napoleon III** regained the Alpes-Maritimes as payment for his support of Italy against Austria. A plebiscite in Nice gave majority support for **reunion with France**. To the north, Tende and La Brigue voted almost unanimously for France but the result was ignored: the new king of Italy wished to keep his favourite game-hunting grounds. Menton and Roquebrune also voted for France. While making noises about rigged elections, Charles of Monaco agreed to sell the two towns – despite their independence – to France. The sum was considerably more than the fledgling gambling and tourism industry was as yet bringing in and saved the principality from bankruptcy. **Monaco's independence**, free from any foreign protector, was finally established.

One casualty of this dispersal of traditional Provence, combined with the spread of national primary education, was the Provençal language. This prompted the formation of the **Félibrige** in 1854, by a group of poets including Frédéric Mistral – a nostalgic, backward-looking and intellectual movement in defence of literary Provençal. There were other, more popularist, Provençal writers at the time, but they too were conservative, railing against gas lighting and any other modern innovation. The attempt to associate the language with some past golden age of ultra-Catholic primitivism only encouraged the association of progress with the French tongue – particularly for the Left.

By the end of the 1860s the **socialism** of the First International was gaining ground in the industrial cities, and in Marseille most of all. Opponents of the empire had the majority in the town hall, and in the plebiscite of 1870, in which the country as a whole gave Napoleon III their support, the Bouches-du-Rhône *département* was second only to Paris in the number of "nons". It was not surprising therefore that Marseille had its own commune (see p.177) when the Parisians took up arms against the right-wing republic established after the Prussians' defeat of France and the downfall of Napoleon III.

Honoré Daumier, the Marseillais caricaturist and fervent republican, was the great illustrator of both the 1851 and the 1871 events. In the middle of the century the **Marseille school of painting** developed under the influence of foreign travel and orientalism, attracting to the city such artists as Puvis de Chavannes and Félix Ziem. Provence's greatest native artist, **Cézanne**, though living in Paris from the 1860s to the 1880s, spent a few months of every year in his home town of Aix, or in Marseille and L'Estaque. He was sometimes accompanied by his childhood friend **Zola**, and by **Renoir** whom he introduced to this coast.

Third Republic: 1890–1914

Under the **Third Republic**, the division between inland Provence and the coast and Rhône Valley accentuated. Port activity at Marseille quadrupled with the opening of new trade routes along the Suez Canal and further colonial acquisitions in the Far East. Manufacturing began to play an equal role with commerce. The orchards of the Rhône Valley were planted on a massive scale, and light industries producing clothes, foodstuffs and paper developed in Aix and other cities to export to the North African colonies. Chemical works in Avignon produced the synthetics that spelt the rapid decline of the traditional industries of the small towns and villages of the interior – tanning, dyeing, silk and glass. Wine production, meanwhile, was devastated by phylloxera.

The one area of brilliance connected with the climate but not with commerce was art – painting in particular. Following on from Cézanne and Renoir, a younger generation of artists was discovering the Côte d'Azur. The Post-Impressionists and Fauves flocked to St-Tropez in the wake of the ever-hospitable Paul Signac. Matisse, Dufy, Seurat, Dérain, van Dongen, Bonnard, Braque, Friesz, Marquet, Manguin, Camion, Vlaminck and Vuillard were all intoxicated by the Mediterranean light, the climate and the ease of living. The escape from the rigours of Paris released a massive creative energy and resulted in works that, in addition to their radical innovations, have more *joie de vivre* than any other period in French art. Renoir retired to Cagnes for health reasons in 1907; for Matisse, Dufy and Bonnard the Côte d'Azur became their permanent home; and Van Gogh, always a man apart, had a spell in Arles.

Ignoring these bohemian characters, the **winter tourist season** on the coast was taking off. **Hyères** and **Cannes** had been "discovered" in the first half of the century (and Nice many years earlier). But increased ease of travel and the temporary restraint of simmering international tensions encouraged aristocratic mobility. The population of **Nice** trebled from 1861 to 1911; luxury trains ran from St Petersburg, Vienna and London; *belle époque* mansions and grand hotels rose along the Riviera seafronts; and gambling, particularly at Monte

Carlo, won the patronage of the Prince of Wales, the Emperor Franz Joseph and scores of Russian grand-dukes.

The native working class, meanwhile, were forming the first French Socialist Party, which had its opening congress in Marseille in 1879. Support came not just from the city but from towns and villages that had fought in 1851. In 1881 Marseille elected the first socialist *député*. By 1892 the municipal councils of Marseille, Toulon, La Ciotat and other industrial towns were in the hands of socialists. In Aix, however, the old legitimist royalists (those favouring the return of the Bourbons) still held sway, managing to block the erection of a monument to Zola in 1911.

World War I and the interwar years

The battlefields of **World War I** may have seemed far away in northern France and Belgium, but conscription brought the people of Provence into the war. The socialists divided between pacifists and patriots, but when, in 1919, France took part in the attack on the Soviet Union, soldiers, sailors and workers joined forces in Toulon and Marseille to support the mutinies on French warships in the Black Sea. The struggle to have the mutineers freed continued well into 1920, the year in which the **French Communist Party** (PCF) was born; the party's adherents in Provence were again the heirs to the 1851 rebellion.

The casualties of the war led to severe depopulation in the already dwindling villages of inland Provence, some of which were actually deserted. **Land use** also changed dramatically, from mixed agriculture to a monocrop of vines, in order to provide the army with its ration of one litre of wine per soldier per day. Quantity, thanks to the Provençal climate, rather than quality was the aim, leaving acres upon acres of totally unviable vineyards after demobilization. With the growth in tourism, it was easier to sell the land for construction rather than have it revert to its former use.

The **tourist industry** recovered fairly quickly from the war. The Front Populaire of 1936 introduced paid holidays, encouraging native visitors to the still unspoilt coast. International literati – Somerset Maugham, Katherine Mansfield, Scott and Zelda Fitzgerald, Colette, Anaïs Nin, Gertrude Stein – and a new wave of artists, Picasso and Cocteau amongst them, replaced the defunct grand-dukes, even if anachronistic titles still filled the palatial Riviera residences.

Marseille during the interwar years saw the evolution of characteristics that have yet to be obliterated. The activities of the fascist Action Française led to deaths during a left-wing counter-demonstration in 1925. Modern-style **corruption** snaked its way through the town hall and the rackets of gangsters on the Chicago model moved in on the vice industries. Elections were rigged and even revolvers used at the ballot boxes.

The increasing popularity of the Communist Party in the city was due to its anti-corruption platform. After the failure of the Front Populaire (which the great majority of Provençaux had voted for, electing several Communist *députés*), there were constant pitched battles between the Left and Right in Marseille. In 1939 a state administrator was imposed by Paris, with powers to obstruct the elected council.

World War II

France and Britain declared **war on Germany** together on September 3, 1939. The French Maginot line, however, swiftly collapsed, and by June 1940 the Germans controlled Paris and all of northern France. On June 22, Marshall Pétain signed the **armistice with Hitler**, which divided France between the Occupied Zone – the Atlantic coast and north of the Loire – and "unoccupied" Vichy France in the south. Menton and Sospel were occupied by the Italians, to whom the adjoining Roya Valley still belonged.

With the start of the British counteroffensive in 1942, **Vichy France** joined itself with the Allies and was immediately occupied by the Germans. The port of Toulon was overrun in November, with the French navy scuppering its fleet rather than letting it fall into German hands.

Resistance fighters and passive citizens suffered executions, deportations and the wholesale destruction of Le Panier quarter in Marseille (see p.176). The **Allied bombings** of 1944 caused high civilian casualties and considerable material damage, particularly to Avignon, Marseille and Toulon. The **liberation** of the two great port cities was aided by a general armed revolt by the people, but it was in the Italian sector – in Sospel and its neighbouring villages – that the fighting by the local populace was the most heroic.

Modern Provence

Before the Germans surrendered **Marseille** they made sure that the harbours were blown to bits. In the immediate **postwar years** the task of repairing the damage was compounded by a slump in international trade and passenger traffic. The nationalization of the Suez Canal was the next disaster to hit the city, spelling an end to its prime position on world trading routes. Company after company decamped to Paris, leaving a growing problem of unemployment.

Marseille's solution was to orient its **port** and industry towards the Atlantic and the inland route of the Rhône. The **oil industries** that had developed in the 1920s around the Étang de Berre and Fos were extended. The mouth of the Rhône and the Golfe de Fos became a massive tanker terminal. **Iron and steel works** filled the spaces behind the new Port de Marseille that stretched for 50km beyond the Vieux Port. In the process, the city's population boomed. The urgent demand for housing was met by badly designed, low-cost, high-rise estates proliferating north and east from the congested city centre.

The depopulation of **inland Provence** was never halted, but considerably slowed by the massive **irrigation schemes** and development of hydroelectric power which greatly increased the agricultural and industrial potential of regions impoverished earlier in the century. The isolated *mas* or farmhouses, positioned wherever there happened to be a spring, were left to ruin or linked up to the mains. Orchards, lavender fields and olive groves became larger, the competition for early fruit and vegetables fiercer, and the market for luxury foods greater. The rich **Rhône Valley** continued to export fruit, wine and vegetables, while the river was exploited for irrigation and power, both nuclear and hydroelectric, and made navigable for sizeable ships.

After Algeria won back its independence in 1962, hundreds of thousands of French settlers, the **pieds noirs**, returned to the mainland, bringing with them a virulent hatred of Arabic-speaking people. At the same time, the government encouraged immigration from its former colonies, North Africa in particular, with the promise of well-paid jobs, civil rights and social security, none of which was honoured. The resulting tensions, not just in Marseille but all along the coast, made perfect fodder for the **parties of the Right**. From being a bastion of socialism at the end of World War II, Provence gradually turned towards intolerance and reaction.

Municipal fiefdoms, corruption and vice

The activities of the local mafia, known as the **milieu**, with their invisible and inextricable ties to the town halls, have continued more or less unchecked since the 1920s. Not until the shocking assassination of Hyères' *député*, **Yann Piat**, in 1994 (see p.236) did the demand for a "clean hands" campaign really begin in earnest.

Drug trafficking became a major problem in Marseille in the early 1970s and is now prevalent all along the coast. Prostitution and protection rackets also flourish from Menton to Marseille, much of it controlled by either Eastern European crime rings, or the Cosonostra Italian mafia, which has been spreading its tentacles westwards, taking advantage of the large numbers of Italians running businesses along the coast, the casinos and cash sales of high-priced properties for money laundering, and the lack of specific anti-mafia laws in France.

As elsewhere in France, but particularly in Provence, **municipal fiefdoms** evolved – particularly with the huge budgets and planning powers that came with increasing decentralization – offering opportunities for patronage, nepotism and corruption, along with the financial muscle that, until very recently, ensured incumbents a more-or-less permanent position.

In **Marseille**, the town hall was controlled by **Gaston Defferre** for 33 years until his death in 1986. As well as being mayor, he was a socialist *député* and minister, and owned the city's two politically opposed regional newspapers. Though people had their suspicions about underworld links with the town hall, no one pointed the finger at Defferre.

In 1995, **Bernard Tapie**, the most popular politician in Marseille and millionaire owner of the town's football team, was unable to run for mayor because he'd just been sentenced to a year in prison for **match-rigging** his football team in the French League. A flamboyant businessman, *député* and European Member of Parliament for the Bouche-du-Rhône *département*, Tapie had already been debarred from all public office for four years due to **bankruptcy**. Despite – or perhaps because of – a self-admitted debt of over 100 million euros to Credit Lyonnais, and further investigations involving tax evasion, shady financial dealings and insulting the police, Tapie continues to remain a popular figure in the public eye, although he no longer has any official political power.

Nice's police and judiciary were accused by Graham Greene in 1982 of protecting organized crime. Greene claimed he slept with a gun under his pillow after his *J'Accuse* was published (and banned in France) in which he detailed the corruption. The late **Jacques Médecin**, who succeeded his father as mayor of Nice in 1966, controlled just about every facet of public life until his downfall in 1990 for political fraud and tax evasion – only when Médecin fled to Uruguay were his mafioso connections finally discussed in public. But Médecin had so successfully identified his name with all the city's glamour that after his departure most Niçois gladly supported his sister Géneviève Assemat-Médecin. Those who didn't, backed his daughter, Martine Cantinchi-Médecin, a Le Pen supporter. Finally extradited in 1994, Médecin served a very short prison term and was able to use his popularity to back the successful candidate in the 1995 municipal elections – one Jacques Peyrat, a close friend of Le Pen and former member of the *Front National*. Re-elected in 2001, Peyrat has made no secret of his desire to have the new public prosecutor, Eric de Montgolfier – who made his reputation fighting white-collar crime (notably Bernard Tapie) and political corruption – removed from his post, before his investigations into the Riviera underworld put yet another city magistrate into prison.

Toulon was another classic fiefdom, run for four decades by **Maurice Arreckx** and his clique of friends with their underworld connections, until he was put away when financial scandals finally came to light. His successor, and former director of finances, tried in vain to win back the voters but merely ran up more debts and lost to the *Front National* in 1995. Arreckx was sentenced to prison on two separate occasions (in 1997 and 2000), before dying of cancer in 2001. Previous to his death, investigators had found several Swiss bank accounts, under the names "Charlot [Charlie Chaplin]" and "Waterloo", where some of the money paid to Arreckx's campaign fund in return for a major construction contract was secreted.

In neighbouring **La-Seyne-sur-Mer** a planning officer who attempted to stop a corrupt planning deal was **murdered** in 1986. More recently, a British project for a World Sea Centre, that would have provided much-needed jobs after the closure of the shipyards, was disbanded after the British refused to pay protection money to the tune of £1 million.

François Léotard, the right-wing mayor of Fréjus, who held cabinet office (under Chirac in the late 1980s) and a seat in the Assemblée Nationale, was investigated for financial irregularities, but the case eventually ran out of time and the charges were dropped. **Cannes' mayor**, **Michel Mouillot**, was debarred from public office for five years and given a fifteen-month suspended sentence in 1989, then won his appeal and returned to the town hall only to be given an eighteen-month suspended sentence in 1996. **Pierre Rinaldi**, mayor of **Digne**, was investigated for fraud, **Jean-Pierre Lafond**, mayor of **La Ciotat**, for unwarranted interference, two successive mayors of **La Seyne** for corruption and abuse of patronage . . . and so the list goes on.

Ethnic tensions and the rise of the Front National

The corruption, waste and general financial incompetence of right-wing municipal power has been one element in the rise of **Jean-Marie Le Pen's neo-fascist Front National** (FN) party. Another has been the significance of military bases to the region's economy. While the right-wing national government has made cuts in defence spending, Le Pen has trumpeted his ardent support for France retaining its maximum military capability. However, the most important factor has been the combination of rampant racism, high unemployment and the rising crime rates in the region. Whichever way one looks at it, fear is the underlying current of the extreme right's success.

Although coastal Provence, and Marseille in particular, has always boasted a cosmopolitan mix, the experience of centuries has not bred tolerance. **North Africans** now suffer the discrimination meted out in the past to Jews, Armenians, Portuguese, Italians and other ethnic groups. Many locals are quick to complain of the high taxes they pay to support immigrants, while segregated low-income housing has not only helped to enforce the social boundaries, it has also created a severe gap in the level of education available, consequently serving to limit future opportunities and social integration for most foreigners. One of the ugliest ironies is in inland Provence, where many of the North African populations grew in response to the demand for seasonal labourers; thus, the vineyard owner who votes Le Pen is likely to employ Algerian, Moroccan or Tunisian workers when harvest season comes along.

Jean-Marie Le Pen's *Front National* party developed its major power base, after Paris, in **Marseille**, and in 1986 four FN *députés* were elected in the Bouches-du-Rhône *département*. They lost their seats when proportional representation was abandoned, but in 1989 the "respectable" parties of the right joined forces with the *Front National* in Grasse, Le Muy and elsewhere to oust Socialist and Communist mayors.

That the FN failed to win outright control of any councils then was due not to any great counterbalance to racism but rather to the similarity in policies of Gaullists such as Jacques Médecin of Nice, and because of the unassailable fortresses of municipal power.

In 1995, however, the *Front National* won **Toulon**, the ninth-largest city in France, plus **Orange** and **Marignane**. The main electoral promise was "Priority for the French", by which, of course, they meant the ethnically pure French. Despite the fact that giving priority to white citizens over non-white citizens is illegal, there were instances in Toulon of people of Algerian origin being overtaken in the housing queue. The town hall has also used municipal grants to promote their political preferences. So, for example, a book fair lost its subsidy when the organizers refused to include ten far-right authors, including a historian who denies the Holocaust took place. Other organizations, charities and cultural events were all pushed out of these towns, while the police force was quadrupled.

In December 1998 **internal feuding** split the party into two camps. **Bruno Mégret**, Le Pen's deputy, attempted to seize leadership of the party only to be expelled by Le Pen, along with several of Mégret's supporters including one of Le Pen's daughters. The ousted members immediately formed a new extreme-right breakaway party, the *Mouvement National Républicain* (MNR), headed by Mégret.

With the **municipal elections** of 2001, it looked as if the FN was splintering apart for good. Six years of misrule in Toulon convinced voters to back Hubert Falco of the *Démocratie Libérale* (DL) party, and Jacques Bompard of Orange was the only *Front National* mayor to be re-elected. The MNR made minor headway around Marseille, picking up Marignane and Vitrolles, though the victory in Vitrolles was later overturned in court due to "unfair campaigning techniques". Moreover, neither party managed to pick up any seats in the 2002 legislative elections for l'Assemblée Nationale.

It therefore came as a major shock when Le Pen returned in full force for the 2002 **presidential elections**, with first-round victories in five out of six *départements* in the PACA (Provence, Alpes, Côtes d'Azur) region, soundly defeating both Chirac and Jospin. A cursory glance at the results, even if one is familiar with the area's political leanings, is frightening. His highest support was registered in the Alpes-Maritimes (Nice, Cannes), where he took 26 percent of the vote, followed by the Vaucluse (25.8 percent) and the Var (23.5 percent); in the region's urban districts his most notable victories were Orange (33 percent), Carpentras (30 percent) and Marseille (22.4 percent). In most cases, the next-closest contender, Chirac, was at least ten percentage points behind, if not more. Le Pen's next target is the March 2004 PACA presidential elections, the equivalent of a regional governer, which could well result in the whole of Provence having an FN-led administration for the next few years.

At about the same time as the presidential elections, **ethnic tensions** of other kinds began to manifest themselves, notably among France's Arab and Jewish communities – both the largest of their kind in Europe. In April 2002, pro-Palestinian groups firebombed and burnt to the ground a number of French synagogues, including one in Marseille, and another in Montpellier. The series of attacks led to an outcry about "French anti-semitism" across Europe and the US, although since then no further incidents have taken place.

Mass tourism and the environment

A crucial factor in Provence's postwar history has been the development of **mass tourism**. Beginning with the St-Tropez boom in the 1960s, the number of visitors to the Côte d'Azur has steadily grown beyond manageable – in any sane sense – proportions. By the mid-1970s the coast had become a nearly uninterrupted wall of concrete, hosting eight million visitors a year. Agricultural land, save for a few profitable vineyards, was transformed into campsites, hotels and holiday housing. **Property speculation** and construction became the dominant economic activities, while the flaunting of planning laws and the ever-increasing threat to the **environment** – the area's prime asset – were ignored.

When **Brigitte Bardot** started to complain that her beloved **St-Tropez** was becoming a mire of human detritus, the media saw it as a sexy summer story. But when **ecologists** began warning that the main oxygenating seaweed in the Mediterranean was disappearing because of yacht anchors damaging the sea bed, new jetties and marinas modifying the currents, and dust from building sites clouding the water, no one was particularly interested. The loss of *Posidonia oceanica* is now affecting fish, and a toxic algae has appeared, spreading out from Monaco. According to some experts, nearly half of all current developments need to be demolished and a total embargo put on new developments, if the sea is to recover.

Short-term financial gain is still, of course, the overriding principle, so new marinas are still being built and new private villages and estates edge into supposedly protected areas such as the Esterel. A new resort, Antibes-les-Pins, was recently built alongside Juan-les-Pins. As for the pines themselves, fires are responsible for destroying great swathes of forest every year.

Since the late 1990s, Provence has been suffering from a further environmental menace – the **sanglochon**, a cross between a wild boar (*sanglier*) and a pig (*cochon*). These animals have been multiplying far beyond the constraints of their ever-shrinking natural habitat, and the boar population in the Var and elsewhere along the Riviera has rocketed from 3,000 to over 30,000 in the past decade – not including the 17,000 killed annually. Originally bred on special farms to provide hunters with prey, the hybrid species has two very undesirable characteristics: the first is an ability to reproduce two to three times faster than a regular wild boar; the second is their lack of timidity around people. The boars can wreak a fair amount of havoc, as well as cause considerable damage to property in built-up areas, with dustbins, vegetable gardens, orchards and golf courses being some of the more common casualties of their daily foraging. Locals shoot the animals freely in an attempt to keep numbers at bay, but so far have had little success in curbing the increasing population.

Urban expansion on the coast

If sun-worshipping set the region's tone for the first three postwar decades, the 1980s saw different forces at work. While the encouragement of summer tourism exacted its toll, a new type of visitor and resident was being encouraged: the expense-account delegate to **business conferences** and the well-paid employee of **multinational firms**. Towns like Nice and Cannes led the way in attracting the former, while the business park of **Sophia-Antipolis** north of Antibes showed how easy it was to persuade firms to relocate their information technology operations to the beautiful Côte d'Azur hinterland. The result is a further erosion of Provençal identity and greater pressure on the environment. The Dutch, American, Parisian and Lyonnais employees of the high-tech industries need more roads, more housing, more facilities, and Sophia-Antipolis is due to have not only its own new ring road but also a 25-kilometre métro line to Nice.

The business visitors, rather than countering the seasonal imbalance of tourism, have made consumption and congestion a year-round factor. A black market has even developed in game meat: venison and other game is shot with high-tech weaponry in areas such as the Clues de Haute Provence, and then sold to the promenade restaurants.

The money from business services and industry on the Riviera now outstrips the income from tourism, and whilst in the big cities the distinctive Marseillaise and Niçois identities have recognizably remained, elsewhere along the coast, and inland, continuities with the past have become ever harder to detect.

Inland Provence

Inland Provence has undergone a parallel transformation to the coast, with second homes in the sun becoming a requisite for the high-salaried French from the 1960s onwards.

Though some villages were certainly saved from extinction by the new property buyers, all suffered from the out-of-season closed shutters syndrome. With the growth of ski resorts, however, the population of the Alpine valleys started to increase, reversing a centuries-old trend. The damage to trees, soil and habitats caused by the ski resorts has in part been offset by the creation of the **Parc National du Mercantour**, an enclave that has saved several Alpine animal and plant species.

In central Provence the Durance Valley alongside the new Marseille–Grenoble *autoroute* has become the latest corridor for sunrise industries. Meanwhile, the *paysans* keeping goats and bees, a few vines and a vegetable plot are all of pensionable age. The cheeses and honey, the vegetables, olive oil and wine (unless it's A.O.C.) must compete with Spanish, Italian and Greek produce, from land that doesn't have the ludicrously high values of Provence. In order to exploit the consumption patterns of the 1990s the scale has to be larger than the traditional peasant plots, and there must be speedy access to the biggest markets.

Transport mania

Fast access to the Côte d'Azur has become the obsession of planners in Paris, the most recent move being the extension of the **TGV to Marseille**. However, whether or not the region's infrastructure can deal with the corresponding increase in tourist traffic is another matter. The Riviera has long suffered from the lack of a regional mass transportation system and the resulting chronic gridlock: planners predict that by 2005 traffic on the A8 will have slowed to a perpetual crawl between Monaco and Cannes.

A variety of alternatives has been proposed to ease the transport problems, ranging from a new commuter **train line** running between Grasse, Cannes, Nice and Monaco (RER Côte d'Azur), to the construction of an environmentally dubious *autoroute*, the **A8 bis**, which would shadow the A8 along the most congested stretch from Fréjus to Monaco. Unfortunately for residents and holiday-makers alike, the only immediate plans are to reopen rail services between Cannes and Grasse, tentatively scheduled for 2004, while the hotly contested Nice tramway – originally scheduled to open in 2006 – continues to be delayed by opponents at the final stages of planning.

Books

Most of the books listed below are in print and in paperback – those that are out of print (o/p) should be easy to track down in second-hand bookshops. Publishers are detailed with the British publisher first, separated by an oblique slash from the US publisher, where both exist. Where books are published in only one country, UK, US or France precedes the publisher's name; where the book is published by the same company in both the UK and US, the name of the company appears just once. Titles marked with the ★ symbol are particularly recommended.

History

Robin Briggs *Early Modern France, 1560–1715* (Oxford UP). Readable account of the period in which the French state started to assert control over the whole country. Strong perspectives on the provinces, including coverage of the Marseille rebellion of 1658.

James Bromwich *The Roman Remains of Southern France* (Routledge). The only comprehensive guide to the subject; detailed, well illustrated and approachable. In addition to accounts of well-known sites, it will lead you off the map to all sorts of discoveries.

Alfred Cobban *A History of Modern France* (3 vols: 1715–1799; 1799–1871; 1871–1962. Penguin/Viking Press). Definitive account of three centuries of French political, social and economic life, from Louis XIV to mid-de Gaulle.

Margaret Crosland *Sade's Wife* (Peter Owen/Dufour Editions). Expert on Provence's most notorious resident examines how Renée-Pélagie de Montreuil coped with being married to the Marquis de Sade.

FX Emmanuelli *Histoire de la Provence* (o/p). Huge, well-illustrated tome by a group of French academics, which covers the province in as much detail as anyone could conceivably want.

Colin Jones *The French Revolution: A Companion* (Addison Wesley Longman). Original quotes and documents, good pictures and an unusually clear explanation of events. Good background on Marseille's Fédéres and Mirabeau.

Emmanuel Le Roy Ladurie *Montaillou* (Penguin/Random House). Just outside the area but well worth reading, nevertheless, as the classic account of peasant life in a fourteenth-century Pyrenean village, reconstructed using the original court records of an anti-Cathar Inquisition.

★ **John Noone** *The Man Behind the Iron Mask* (Sutton/Palgrave Macmillan). Fascinating enquiry into the mythical or otherwise prisoner of Ste-Marguerite fort on the Îles de Lérins, immortalized by Alexander Dumas.

Jean Tulard *Napoléon: The Myth of the Saviour* (UK Weidenfeld & Nicolson). One of the classic French accounts of the rise and fall of the great man. Its interest is with the phenomenon rather than the personal life and characteristics of the man.

Simon Schama *Citizens* (Penguin/Vintage). A fascinating, accessible treatment of the history of the Revolution, with a fast-moving narrative and a reappraisal of the customary view of a stagnant, unchanging nobility in the years preceding the uprising.

 **Theodore Zeldin** *France, 1848–1945* (2 vols, Clarendon/Oxford UP). Two thematic and very accessible volumes on all matters French over the last century.

Society and politics

John Ardagh *France in the New Century* (Penguin). Long-time writer on France gets to grips with the country over the last twenty years. It attempts to be a comprehensive survey, but gets rather too drawn into party politics and statistics.

Roland Barthes *Mythologies* (Vintage/Noonday Press). Brilliant analyses of how the ideas, prejudices and contradictions of French thought and behaviour manifest themselves, in food, wine, travel guides and other cultural offerings.

Mary Blume *Côte d'Azur: Inventing the French Riviera* (o/p). This attempt to analyse the myth only reconfirms it, mainly because the people Blume has interviewed all have a stake in maintaining the image of the Côte as a cultured millionaires' dreamland. Great black and white photos.

Ann Tristan *Au Front* (France Gallimard). Compelling report by a Parisian journalist who infiltrated Le Pen's *Front National* in Marseille in 1987. Excellent on detail of the working-class milieu of Front sympathizers, but ultimately unconvincing in its attempt to explain the phenomenon.

Laurence Wylie *Village in the Vaucluse* (Harvard UP). Sociological study of Roussillon, full of interesting insights into Provençal village life.

Travel

MFK Fisher *Two Towns in Provence* (Vintage). Evocative memoirs of life in Aix-en-Provence and Marseille during the 1950s and 1960s.

John Flower and Charles Waite *Provence* (o/p). Waite's gorgeous photographs encompass landscapes, architectural details, markets and images obscure and familiar. Flower's text draws on over thirty years of residence and visits.

William Fotheringham *Put Me Back on My Bike: In Search of Tom Simpson* (Yellow Jersey Press). An in-depth study of Simpson's life as a cyclist, leading up to his tragic death on Mont Ventoux.

Peter Mayle *A Year in Provence* (Penguin/Vintage). A month-by-month account of the charms and frustrations of moving into an old French farmhouse in Provence; with entertaining accounts of everything from the local cuisine, tips for wooing fickle French contractors, handicapping goat races, and enduring winter's icy mistral.

Julian More *Tour de Provence* (Pavilion/Trafalgar Square). Easy-to-digest travelogue arranged by *département*, starting with More's home in northwestern Provence; good selection of colour photos.

Art and artists

Good introductions to the modern artists associated with Provence are published by Thames and Hudson (UK/US), Clematis and Phaidon (UK) and Abrams (US). Bracken Books (UK) publishes a series "Artists by Themselves" – small, attractively produced books with extracts of letters and diaries to accompany the pictures – which includes Matisse, Picasso, Cézanne, Van Gogh and Renoir. More substantial editions of artists' own writings include *Matisse on Art* (University of California Press), *My Life: Marc Chagall* (Peter Owen), and *Cézanne by Himself: Drawings, Paintings, Writings* (Little/Brown).

★ **Martin Bailey (ed)** *Van Gogh: Letters from Provence* (o/p). Attractively produced in full colour. Very dippable and very good value.

Françoise Gilot *Matisse & Picasso: A Friendship in Art* (UK Bloomsbury). A fascinating subject – two more different men in life and art would be hard to find.

D and M Johnson *The Age of Illusion* (UK Thames & Hudson). Links French art and politics in the interwar years, featuring Provençal works by Le Corbusier, Chagall and Picasso.

Jacques Henri Lartigue *Diary of a Century* (UK Penguin). Book of pictures by a great photographer from the day he was given a camera in 1901 through to the 1970s. Contains wonderful scenes of aristocratic leisure and Côte d'Azur beaches.

Nicholas Watkins *Matisse* (UK Phaidon). A brilliant and accessible analysis of Matisse's use of colour with beautiful reproductions.

Barbara Ehrlich *Renoir: His Life, Art and Letters* (Abrams). A thorough and interesting work.

Sarah Whitfield *Fauvism* (Thames & Hudson). Good introduction to a movement that encompassed Côte d'Azur and Riviera artists Matisse, Dufy and Van Dongen.

Provence and the Côte d'Azur in literature

The Côte d'Azur has inspired many twentieth-century English, American and French writers, indulging in the high life like Scott Fitzgerald, slumming it with the bohemians like Anaïs Nin, or trying to regain their health like Katherine Mansfield. The two best-known Provençal writers of the twentieth century, Jean Giono and Maurice Pagnol, wrote about peasant life in inland Provence; many of their works have been turned into films. Nineteenth-century Provence features in Alexander Dumas' rip-roaring tale of revenge, *The Count of Monte Cristo*, and in some of Aix-born Émile Zola's novels, while the horrors of eighteenth-century Provence are brought to life in Victor Hugo's *Les Misérables*.

Below is a selective recommendation of literary works in which the region plays a significant role, including poetry – spanning the ages from Petrarch troubadour songs to Bonnefoy and Mistral – and a play by Anouilh set in Marseille.

Jean Anouilh *Point of Departure*
Yves Bonnefoy *In the Shadow's Light*
Anthony Bonner (ed) *Songs of the Troubadours*
Colette *Collected Stories*
Alphonse Daudet *Letters from My Windmill; Tartarin de Tarascon; In the Land of Pain;* and *Tartarin on the Alps*
★ **Alexandre Dumas (Père)** *The Count of Monte Cristo*
Lawrence Durrell *The Avignon Quintet*
F. Scott Fitzgerald *Tender is the Night*
Sébastien Japrisot *One Deadly Summer*
★ **Jean Giono** *Joy of Man's Desiring; Blue Boy; The Man Who Planted Trees; The Horseman on the Roof; To the Slaughterhouse;* and *Two Riders of the Storm*
Graham Greene *Loser Takes All*
Victor Hugo *Les Misérables*
Katherine Mansfield *Collected Stories*
Frédéric Mistral *Mirèio*
Anaïs Nin *Diaries*
★ **Marcel Pagnol** *The Water of the Hills: Jean de Florette and Manon of the Springs; My Father's Glory and My Mother's Castle; Marius;* and *Fanny*
Francesco Petrarch *Canzoniere*
Françoise Sagan *Bonjour Tristesse*
★ **Patrick Süskind** *Perfume*
★ **Émile Zola** *Abbé Mouret's Transgression; Fortune of the Rougons;* and *The Conquest of Plassans*

Food and drink

Robert Carrier *Feasts of Provence* (UK Weidenfeld & Nicolson). Yummy cookery book.
Hubrecht Duijker *Touring in Wine Country: Provence* (Mitchell Beazley). Guide to the top vineyards and wine cellars of Provence.
Richard Olney *Lulu's Provençal Table* (Pavilion/Ten Speed Press). Classic Provençal recipes and interesting commentary from Lulu Peyraud, proprietor of the Domaine Tempier vineyard in Bandol. Great black and white photos.
Timothy Shaw *The World of Escoffier* (Vendome/St Martin). Biography of the famous chef who started his career on the Côte d'Azur.

Botany

W. Lippert *Fleurs de Haute Montagne* (France Miniguide Nathan Tout Terrain). Palm-sized colour guide to flowers, available from French bookshops in the trekking areas.

Language

Language

French

French can be a deceptively familiar language because of the number of words and structures it shares with English. Despite this, it's far from easy, though the bare essentials are not difficult to master and can make all the difference. Even just saying *"Bonjour, Madame/Monsieur"* and then gesticulating will usually get you a smile and helpful service. People working in tourist offices, campsites, hotels and so on, almost always speak English and tend to use it if you're struggling to speak French – be grateful, not insulted.

On the Côte d'Azur you can get by without knowing a word of French, with menus printed in at least four languages, and half the people you meet fellow foreigners. In Nice, Sisteron and the Roya Valley a knowledge of Italian would provide a common language with many of the natives. But if you can hold your own in French – however imperfectly – speak away and your audience will warm to you.

Provençal and accents

The one language you don't have to learn – unless you want to understand the meaning of the names of streets, restaurants or cafés – is **Provençal**. Itself a dialect of the *langue d'oc* (Occitan), it evolved into different dialects in Provence, so that the languages spoken in Nice, in the Alps, on the coast and in the Rhône Valley, though mutually comprehensible, were not precisely the same. In the mid-nineteenth century the *Félibrige* movement established a standard literary form in an attempt to revive the language. But by the time Frédéric Mistral won the Nobel Prize in 1904 for his poem *Mirèio,* Provençal had already been superseded by French in ordinary life.

Two hundred years ago everybody spoke Provençal whether they were counts, shipyard workers or peasants. Today you might, if you're lucky, hear it spoken by the older generation in some of the remoter villages. It just survives as a literary language: it can be studied at school and university and there are columns in Provençal in some newspapers. But unlike Breton or Occitan proper, it has never been the fuel of a separatist movement.

The French that people speak in Provence has, however, a very marked **accent**. It's much less nasal than northern French, words are not run together to quite the same extent, and there's a distinctive sound for the endings – *in*, *-en*, and for *vin*, and so on, that is more like *ung*.

Pronunciation

One easy rule to remember is that **consonants** at the ends of words are usually silent. *Pas plus tard* (not later) is thus pronounced "pa-plu-tarr". But when the following word begins with a vowel, you run the two together: *pas après* (not after) becomes "pazaprey".

Vowels are the hardest sounds to get right. Roughly:

a	as in h**a**t
e	as in g**e**t
é	between g**e**t and g**a**te
è	between g**e**t and g**u**t
eu	like the **u** in h**u**rt
i	as in mach**i**ne
o	as in h**o**t
o, au	as in **o**ver
ou	as in f**oo**d
u	as in a pursed-lip version of **u**se

More awkward are the **combinations** *in/im, en/em, an/am, on/om, un/um* at the ends of words, or followed by consonants other than n or m. Again, roughly:

in/im	like the **an** in **an**xious
an/am, en/em	like the **don** in **Don**caster when said with a nasal accent
on/om	like the **don** in **Don**caster said by someone with a heavy cold
un/um	like the **u** in **u**nderstand

Consonants are much as in English, except that: "*ch*" is always sh, "*c*" is s, "*h*" is silent, "*th*" is the same as t, "*ll*" is like the y in "yes", "*w*" is v, and "*r*" is growled (or rolled).

Learning materials

French Dictionary Phrasebook (Rough Guides). Mini dictionary-style phrasebook with both English–French and French–English sections, along with cultural tips for tricky situations and a menu reader.
Get By In French (BBC Publications). Phrasebook and cassette. A good stepping-stone before tackling a complete course.
Mini French Dictionary (Harrap/Larousse). French–English and English–French, plus a brief grammar and pronunciation guide.
Breakthrough French (Palgrave/McGraw Hill; book and two cassettes). An excellent teach-yourself course.
Pardon My French! Pocket French Slang Dictionary (UK Harrap). The key to understanding everyday French.
A Comprehensive French Grammar (Blackwell). Easy-to-follow reference grammar.
À Vous La France; France Extra; France-Parler (BBC Publications; EMC Paradigm). Comprising a book and two cassettes, these BBC radio courses run from beginner's to fairly advanced French.

French words and phrases

Basics

French nouns are divided into masculine and feminine. This causes difficulties with adjectives, whose endings have to change to suit the gender of the nouns they qualify. If you know some grammar, you will know what to do. If not, stick to the masculine form, which is the simplest – it's what we have done in this glossary.

today	**aujourd'hui**	later	**plus tard**
yesterday	**hier**	at one o'clock	**à une heure**
tomorrow	**demain**	at three o'clock	**à trois heures**
in the morning	**le matin**	at ten-thirty	**à dix heures et demie**
in the afternoon	**l'après-midi**	at midday	**à midi**
in the evening	**le soir**	man	**un homme**
now	**maintenant**	woman	**une femme**

here	**ici**
there	**là**
this one	**ceci**
that one	**cela**
open	**ouvert**
closed	**fermé**
big	**grand**
small	**petit**
more	**plus**
less	**moins**
a little	**un peu**
a lot	**beaucoup**
cheap	**bon marché**
expensive	**cher**
good	**bon**
bad	**mauvais**
hot	**chaud**
cold	**froid**
with	**avec**
without	**sans**

Talking to people

When addressing people you should always use *Monsieur* for a man, *Madame* for a woman, *Mademoiselle* for a girl. Plain *bonjour* by itself is not enough. This isn't as formal as it seems, and it has its uses when you've forgotten someone's name or want to attract someone's attention.

Excuse me	**Pardon**
Do you speak English?	**Vous parlez anglais?**
How do you say it in French?	**Comment ça se dit en français?**
What's your name?	**Comment vous appelez-vous?**
My name is . . .	**Je m'appelle . . .**
I'm English/ Irish/ Scottish Welsh/ American/ Australian/ Canadian/ a New Zealander	**Je suis anglais[e]/ irlandais[e]/ écossais[e]/ gallois[e]/ américain[e]/ australien[ne]/ canadien[ne]/ néo-zélandais[e]**
yes	**oui**
no	**non**
I understand	**Je comprends**
I don't understand	**Je ne comprends pas**
Can you speak slower?	**S'il vous plaît, parlez moins vite**
OK/agreed	**d'accord**
please	**s'il vous plaît**
thank you	**merci**
hello	**bonjour**
goodbye	**au revoir**
good morning/ afternoon	**bonjour**
good evening	**bonsoir**
good night	**bonne nuit**
How are you?	**Comment allez-vous?/ Ça va?**
Fine, thanks	**Très bien, merci**
I don't know	**Je ne sais pas**
Let's go	**Allons-y**
See you tomorrow	**À demain**
See you soon	**À bientôt**
Sorry	**Pardon, Madame/ Excusez-moi**
Leave me alone (aggressive)	**Fichez-moi la paix!**
Please help me	**Aidez-moi, s'il vous plaît**

Finding the way

bus	**autobus/bus/car**
bus station	**gare routière**
bus stop	**arrêt**
car	**voiture**
train/taxi/ferry	**train/taxi/ferry**
boat	**bateau**
plane	**avion**
train station	**gare (SNCF)**
platform	**quai**
What time does it leave?	**Il part à quelle heure?**
What time does it arrive?	**Il arrive à quelle heure?**
a ticket to . . .	**un billet pour . . .**
single ticket	**aller simple**
return ticket	**aller retour**
validate your ticket	**compostez votre billet**
valid for	**valable pour**
ticket office	**vente de billets**
how many kilometres?	**combien de kilomètres?**
how many hours?	**combien d'heures?**
hitchhiking	**autostop**
on foot	**à pied**
Where are you going?	**Vous allez où?**
I'm going to . . .	**Je vais à . . .**

I want to get off at . . .	**Je voudrais descendre à . . .**	on the corner of	**à l'angle de**
the road to . . .	**la route pour . . .**	next to	**à côté de**
near	**près/pas loin**	behind	**derrière**
far	**loin**	in front of	**devant**
left	**à gauche**	before	**avant**
right	**à droite**	after	**après**
straight on	**tout droit**	under	**sous**
on the other side of	**à l'autre côté de**	to cross	**traverser**
		bridge	**pont**

Questions and requests

The simplest way of asking a question is to start with *s'il vous plaît* (please), then name the thing you want in an interrogative tone of voice. For example:

Where is there a bakery?	**S'il vous plaît, la boulangerie?**	Which way is it to the Eiffel Tower?	**S'il vous plaît, la route pour la tour Eiffel?**

Similarly with requests:

We'd like a room for two.	**S'il vous plaît, une chambre pour deux.**	Can I have a kilo of oranges?	**S'il vous plaît, un kilo d'oranges?**

Question words

where?	**où?**	why?	**pourquoi?**
how?	**comment?**	at what time?	**à quelle heure?**
how many/how much?	**combien?**	what is/which is?	**quel est?**
when?	**quand?**		

Accommodation

a room for one/two people	**une chambre pour une/deux personnes**	sheets	**draps**
a double bed	**un lit double**	blankets	**couvertures**
a room with a shower	**une chambre avec douche**	quiet	**calme**
a room with a bath	**une chambre avec salle de bain**	noisy	**bruyant**
for one/two/three nights	**pour une/deux/trois nuits**	hot water	**eau chaude**
Can I see it?	**Je peux la voir?**	cold water	**eau froide**
a room on the courtyard	**une chambre sur la cour**	Is breakfast included?	**Est-ce que le petit déjeuner est compris?**
a room over the street	**une chambre sur la rue**	I would like breakfast	**Je voudrais prendre le petit déjeuner**
first floor	**premier étage**	I don't want breakfast	**Je ne veux pas de petit déjeuner**
second floor	**deuxième étage**	Can we camp here?	**On peut camper ici?**
with a view	**avec vue**	campsite	**un camping/terrain de camping**
key	**clef**	tent	**une tente**
to iron	**repasser**	tent space	**un emplacement**
do laundry	**faire la lessive**	youth hostel	**auberge de jeunesse**

Driving

service station	**garage**	to park the car	**garer la voiture**
service	**service**	car park	**un parking**

no parking	**défense de stationner/ stationnement interdit**
gas station	**station essence/ station service**
fuel	**essence**
(to) fill it up	**faire le plein**
oil	**huile**
air line	**ligne à air**
put air in the tyres	**gonfler les pneus**
battery	**batterie**
the battery is dead	**la batterie est morte**
plugs	**bougies**
to break down	**tomber en panne**
gas can	**bidon**
insurance	**assurance**
green card	**carte verte**
traffic lights	**feux**
red light	**feu rouge**
green light	**feu vert**

Health matters

doctor	**médecin**
I don't feel well	**Je ne me sens pas bien**
medicines	**médicaments**
prescription	**ordonnance**
I feel sick	**Je suis malade**
I have a headache	**J'ai mal à la tête**
stomachache	**mal à l'estomac**
period	**règles**
pain	**douleur**
it hurts	**ça fait mal**
chemist	**pharmacie**
hospital	**hôpital**

Other needs

bakery	**boulangerie**
food shop	**alimentation**
supermarket	**supermarché**
to eat	**manger**
to drink	**boire**
camping gas	**camping gaz**
tobacconist	**tabac**
stamps	**timbres**
bank	**banque**
money	**argent**
toilets	**toilettes**
police	**police**
telephone	**téléphone**
cinema	**cinéma**
theatre	**théâtre**
to reserve/book	**réserver**

Numbers

1	**un**
2	**deux**
3	**trois**
4	**quatre**
5	**cinq**
6	**six**
7	**sept**
8	**huit**
9	**neuf**
10	**dix**
11	**onze**
12	**douze**
13	**treize**
14	**quatorze**
15	**quinze**
16	**seize**
17	**dix-sept**
18	**dix-huit**
19	**dix-neuf**
20	**vingt**
21	**vingt-et-un**
22	**vingt-deux**
30	**trente**
40	**quarante**
50	**cinquante**
60	**soixante**
70	**soixante-dix**
75	**soixante-quinze**
80	**quatre-vingts**
90	**quatre-vingt-dix**
95	**quatre-vingt-quinze**
100	**cent**
101	**cent-et-un**
200	**deux cents**
300	**trois cents**
500	**cinq cents**
1000	**mille**
2000	**deux milles**
5000	**cinq milles**
1,000,000	**un million**

Days and dates

January	**janvier**	Monday	**lundi**
February	**février**	Tuesday	**mardi**
March	**mars**	Wednesday	**mercredi**
April	**avril**	Thursday	**jeudi**
May	**mai**	Friday	**vendredi**
June	**juin**	Saturday	**samedi**
July	**juillet**		
August	**août**	August 1	**le premier août**
September	**septembre**	March 2	**le deux mars**
October	**octobre**	July 14	**le quatorze juillet**
November	**novembre**	November 23	**le vingt-trois novembre**
December	**décembre**		
		1999	**dix-neuf-cent-quatre-vingt-dix-neuf**
Sunday	**dimanche**		

Food and drink terms

Basic terms

Pain	**Bread**	Cuillère	**Spoon**
Beurre	**Butter**	Cure-dent	**Toothpick**
Céréales	**Cereal**	Table	**Table**
Lait	**Milk**	L'addition	**Bill**
Huile	**Oil**	Offert/Gratuit	**Free**
Confiture	**Jam**	(Re)chauffé	**(Re)heated**
Poivre	**Pepper**	Cuit	**Cooked**
Sel	**Salt**	Cru	**Raw**
Sucre	**Sugar**	Emballé	**Wrapped**
Vinaigre	**Vinegar**	Sur place ou à emporter?	**Eat in or take away?**
Moutarde	**Mustard**		
Bouteille	**Bottle**	À emporter	**Takeaway**
Verre	**Glass**	Fumé	**Smoked**
Fourchette	**Fork**	Salé	**Salted/spicy**
Couteau	**Knife**	Sucré	**Sweet**

Snacks (*Casse-croûte*)

Un sandwich/ une baguette	**A sandwich**	nature/aux fines herbes	**plain/with herbs**
...au jambon/fromage	**...with ham/cheese**	au fromage	**with cheese**
...au jambon beurre/ ...fromage beurre	**...with ham & butter/ ...cheese & butter**	Croque-monsieur	**Grilled cheese and ham sandwich**
...au pâté (de campagne)	**...with pâté (country-style)**	Croque-madame	**Grilled cheese, ham or bacon and fried egg sandwich**
Oeufs ...	**Eggs...**		
au plat(s)	**Fried eggs**	Pan bagnat	**Bread roll with egg, olives, salad, tuna, anchovies and olive oil**
à la coque	**Boiled eggs**		
durs	**Hard-boiled eggs**		
brouillés	**Scrambled eggs**		
poché	**Poached eggs**	Tartine	**Buttered bread or open sandwich**
Omelette . . .	**Omelette . . .**		

Soups (*soupes*) and starters (*hors d'œuvres*)

Bisque	**Shellfish soup**
Baudroie	**Fish soup with vegetables, garlic and herbs**
Bouillabaisse	**Soup with five fish and other bits to dip**
Bouillon	**Broth or stock**
Bourride	**Thick fish soup with garlic, onions and tomatoes**
Consommé	**Clear soup**
Pistou	**Parmesan, basil and garlic paste or cream added to soup**
Potage	**Thick vegetable soup**
Rouille	**Red pepper, garlic and saffron mayonnaise served with fish soup**
Velouté	**Thick soup, usually fish or poultry**
Assiette anglaise	**Plate of cold meats**
Crudités	**Raw vegetables with dressings**
Hors d'œuvres variés	**Combination of the above plus smoked or marinated fish**

Pasta (pâtes), pancakes (crêpes) and flans (tartes)

Pâtes fraîches	**Fresh pasta**
Nouilles	**Noodles**
Raviolis	**Pasta parcels of meat or chard, a Provençal, not Italian invention**
Crêpe au sucre /aux œufs	**Pancake with sugar/ eggs**
Socca	**Thin chickpea flour pancake**
Panisse	**Thick chickpea flour pancake**
Pissaladière	**Tart of fried onions with anchovies and black olives**

Fish (*poisson*), seafood (*fruits de mer*) and shellfish (*crustaces* or *coquillages*)

Aiglefin	**Small haddock or fresh cod**
Anchois	**Anchovies**
Amande de mer	**Small sweet-tasting shellfish**
Anguilles	**Eels**
Araignée de mer	**Spider fish**
Baudroie	**Monkfish or anglerfish**
Barbue	**Brill**
Bigourneau	**Periwinkle**
Brème	**Bream**
Bulot	**Whelk**
Cabillaud	**Cod**
Calmar	**Squid**
Carrelet	**Plaice**
Chapon de mer	**Mediterranean fish (related to Scorpion fish)**
Claire	**Type of oyster**
Colin	**Hake**
Congre	**Conger eel**
Coques	**Cockles**
Coquilles St-Jacques	**Scallops**
Crabe	**Crab**
Crevettes grises	**Shrimp**
Crevettes roses	**Prawns**
Daurade	**Sea bream**
Écrevisse	**Freshwater crayfish**
Éperlan	**Smelt or whitebait**
Escargots	**Snails**
Favou(ille)	**Tiny crab**
Flétan	**Halibut**
Friture	**Assorted fried fish**
Gambas	**King prawns**
Girelle	**Type of crab**
Grenouilles (cuisses de)	**Frogs (legs)**
Grondin	**Red gurnard**
Hareng	**Herring**
Homard	**Lobster**
Huîtres	**Oysters**
Langouste	**Spiny lobster**

Langoustines	**Saltwater crayfish (scampi)**
Limande	**Lemon sole**
Lotte de mer	**Monkfish**
Loup de mer	**Sea bass**
Maquereau	**Mackerel**
Merlan	**Whiting**
Morue	**Salt cod**
Moules (marinière)	**Mussels (with shallots in white wine sauce)**
Oursin	**Sea urchin**
Pageot	**Sea bream**
Palourdes	**Clams**
Poissons de roche	**Fish from shoreline rocks**
Poulpe	**Octopus**
Poutine	**Small river fish**
Praires	**Small clams**
Raie	**Skate**
Rascasse	**Scorpion fish**
Rouget	**Red mullet**
Rouquier	**Mediterranean eel**
St-Pierre	**John Dory**
Saumon	**Salmon**
Sole	**Sole**
Telline	**Tiny clam**
Thon	**Tuna**
Truite	**Trout**
Turbot	**Turbot**
Violet	**Sea squirt**

. . . and fish terms

Aïoli	**Garlic mayonnaise/ or the dish when served with salt cod and vegetables**
Anchoïade	**Anchovy paste or sauce**
Arête	**Fish bone**
Assiette de pêcheur	**Assorted fish**
Béarnaise	**Sauce of egg yolks, white wine, shallots and vinegar**
Beignets	**Fritters**
Bonne femme	**With mushroom, parsley, potato and shallots**
Brandade	**Crushed cod with olive oil**
Colbert	**Fried in egg with breadcrumbs**
Croûtons	**Toasted bread, often rubbed with garlic, to dip or drop in fish soups**
Darne	**Fillet or steak**
En papillote	**Cooked in foil**
Estocaficada	**Stockfish stew with tomatoes, olives, peppers, garlic and onions**
La douzaine	**A dozen**
Frit	**Fried**
Friture	**Deep-fried small fish**
Fumé	**Smoked**
Fumet	**Fish stock**
Gelée	**Aspic**
Gigot de mer	**Baked fish pieces, usually monkfish**
Goujon	**Several types of small fish, also deep-fried pieces of larger fish coated in breadcrumbs**

Meat (*viande*) and poultry (*volaille*)

Agneau (de pré-salé)	**Lamb (grazed on salt marshes)**
Andouille, andouillette	**Tripe sausage**
Bœuf	**Beef**
Bifteck	**Steak**
Boudin blanc	**Sausage of white meats**
Boudin noir	**Black pudding**
Caille	**Quail**
Canard	**Duck**
Caneton	**Duckling**
Cervelle	**Brains**
Châteaubriand	**Porterhouse steak**
Cheval	**Horse meat**
Contrefilet	**Sirloin roast**
Coquelet	**Cockerel**
Dinde, dindon, dindonneau	**Turkey of different ages and genders**
Entrecôte	**Ribsteak**
Faux filet	**Sirloin steak**
Fricadelles	**Meatballs**
Foie	**Liver**
Foie gras	**Fattened (duck/ goose) liver**

Gésier	**Gizzard**
Magret de canard	**Duck breast**
Gibier	**Game**
Graisse	**Fat**
Jambon	**Ham**
Langue	**Tongue**
Lapin, lapereau	**Rabbit, young rabbit**
Lard, lardons	**Bacon, diced bacon**
Lièvre	**Hare**
Merguez	**Spicy, red sausage**
Mouton	**Mutton**
Museau de veau	**Calf's muzzle**
Oie	**Goose**
Os	**Bone**
Pintade	**Guinea fowl**
Porc, pieds de porc	**Pork, pig's trotters**
Poulet	**Chicken**
Poussin	**Baby chicken**
Ris	**Sweetbreads**
Rognons	**Kidneys**
Rognons blancs	**Testicles**
Sanglier	**Wild boar**
Saucisson	**Dried sausage**
Steack	**Steak**
Taureau/Toro	**Bull meat**
Tête de veau	**Calf's head (in jelly)**
Tournedos	**Thick slices of fillet**
Travers de porc	**Spare ribs**
Tripes	**Tripe**
Veau	**Veal**
Venaison	**Venison**

Meat and poultry dishes

Aïado	**Roast shoulder of lamb, stuffed with garlic and other ingredients**
Bœuf à la gardane	**Beef or bull meat stew with carrots, celery, onions, garlic and black olives, served with rice**
Canard à l'orange	**Roast duck with an orange-and-wine sauce**
Canard périgourdin	**Roast duck with prunes, pâté de foie gras and truffles**
Cassoulet	**A casserole of beans and meat**
Choucroute	**Pickled cabbage with peppercorns, sausages, bacon and salami**
Coq au vin	**Chicken cooked until it falls off the bone with wine, onions, and mushrooms**
Gigot (d'agneau)	**Leg (of lamb)**
Grillade	**Grilled meat**
Hâchis	**Chopped meat or mince hamburger**
Pieds et paquets	**Mutton or pork tripe and trotters**
Steak au poivre (vert/rouge)	**Steak in a black (green/red) peppercorn sauce**
Steak tartare	**Raw chopped beef, topped with a raw egg yolk**

Meat and poultry terms

Blanquette, civet, daube, estouffade, hochepôt, navarin and ragoût	**All are types of stew**
Aile	**Wing**
Blanc	**Breast or white meat**
Broche	**Spit-roasted**
Brochette	**Kebab**
Carré	**Best end of neck, chop or cutlet**
Civit	**Game stew**
Confit	**Meat preserve**
Côte	**Chop, cutlet or rib**
Cou	**Neck**
Cuisse	**Thigh or leg**
Épaule	**Shoulder**
Mariné	**Marinated**
Médaillon	**Round piece**
Pavé	**Thick slice**
En croûte	**In pastry**
Farci	**Stuffed**
Au feu de bois	**Cooked over wood fire**
Au four	**Baked**
Garni	**With vegetables**
Grillé	**Grilled**
Marmite	**Casserole**
Mijoté	**Stewed**
Rôti	**Roast**
Sauté	**Lightly cooked in butter**

For steaks:

Bleu	**Almost raw**
Saignant	**Rare**
À point	**Medium**
Bien cuit	**Well done**
Très bien cuit	**Very well cooked**

Garnishes and sauces:

Américaine	**White wine, Cognac and tomato**
Arlésienne	**With tomatoes, onions, aubergines, potatoes and rice**
Au porto	**In port**
Auvergnat	**With cabbage, sausage and bacon**
Beurre blanc	**Sauce of white wine and shallots, with butter**
Bonne femme	**With mushroom, bacon, potato and onions**
Bordelaise	**In a red wine, shallots and bone-marrow sauce**
Boulangère	**Baked with potatoes and onions**
Bourgeoise	**With carrots, onions, bacon, celery and braised lettuce**
Chasseur	**White wine, mushrooms and shallots**
Chatêlaine	**With artichoke hearts and chestnut purée**
Diable	**Strong mustard seasoning**
Forestière	**With bacon and mushroom**
Fricassée	**Rich, creamy sauce**
Galantine	**Cold dish of meat in aspic**
Mornay	**Cheese sauce**
Pays d'Auge	**Cream and cider**
Piquante	**Gherkins or capers, vinegar and shallots**
Provençale	**Tomatoes, garlic, olive oil and herbs**
Véronique	**Grapes, wine and cream**

Vegetables (*légumes*), herbs (*herbes*) and spices (*épices*), etc

Ail	**Garlic**
Anis	**Aniseed**
Artichaut	**Artichoke**
Asperges	**Asparagus**
Avocat	**Avocado**
Basilic	**Basil**
Betterave	**Beetroot**
Blette/bette	**Swiss chard**
Cannelle	**Cinnamon**
Câpre	**Caper**
Cardon	**Cardoon, a beet related to artichoke**
Carotte	**Carrot**
Céleri	**Celery**
Champignons:	**Mushrooms of cèpes, various kinds chanterelles, girolles, morilles**
Chou (rouge)	**(Red) cabbage**
Chou-fleur	**Cauliflower**
Ciboulettes	**Chives**
Concombre	**Cucumber**
Cornichon	**Gherkin**
Échalotes	**Shallots**
Endive	**Chicory**
Épinard	**Spinach**
Épis de maïs	**Corn on the cob**
Estragon	**Tarragon**
Fenouil	**Fennel**
Férigoule	**Thyme (in Provençal)**
Fèves	**Broad beans**
Flageolets	**White beans**
Fleur de courgette	**Courgette flower**
Genièvre	**Juniper**
Gingembre	**Ginger**
Haricots	**String (French)**
verts	**beans**
rouges	**kidney**
beurres	**butter**
blancs	**white**
Laitue	**Lettuce**
Laurier	**Bay leaf**
Lentilles	**Lentils**

Maïs	**Corn**
Marjoline	**Marjoram**
Menthe	**Mint**
Navet	**Turnip**
Oignon	**Onion**
Panais	**Parsnip**
Pélandron	**Type of string bean**
Persil	**Parsley**
Petits pois	**Peas**
Piment	**Pimento**
Pois chiches	**Chickpeas**
Pois mange-tout	**Snow peas**
Pignons	**Pine nuts**
Poireau	**Leek**
Poivron (vert, rouge)	**Sweet pepper (green, red)**
Pommes de terre	**Potatoes**
Radis	**Radishes**
Raifort	**Horseradish**
Riz	**Rice**
Romarin	**Rosemary**
Safran	**Saffron**
Sarrasin	**Buckwheat**
Sauge	**Sage**
Serpolet	**Wild thyme**
Thym	**Thyme**
Tomate	**Tomato**
Truffes	**Truffles**

Dishes and terms

Beignet	**Fritter**
Farci	**Stuffed**
Gratiné	**Browned with cheese or butter**
Jardinière	**With mixed diced vegetables**
À la parisienne	**Sautéed in butter (potatoes); with white wine sauce, and shallots**
À l'anglaise	**Boiled**
À la grecque	**Cooked in oil and lemon**
Râpé(e)s	**Grated or shredded**
Pistou	**Ground basil, olive oil, garlic and parmesan**
Primeurs	**Spring vegetables**
Salade verte	**Lettuce with vinaigrette**
Gratin dauphinois	**Potatoes baked in cream and garlic**
Mesclum	**Salad combining several different leaves**
Pommes château, fondantes	**Quartered potatoes sautéed in butter**
Pommes lyonnaise	**Fried onions and potatoes**
Ratatouille	**Mixture of aubergine, courgette, tomatoes and garlic**
Rémoulade	**Mustard mayonnaise, sometimes with anchovies and gherkins, also salad of grated celeriac with mayonnaise**
Parmentier	**With potatoes**
Sauté	**Lightly fried in butter**
À la vapeur	**Steamed**
Je suis végétarien(ne).	**I'm a vegetarian.**
Il y a des plats sans viande?	**Are there any non-meat dishes?**
Biologique	**Organic**
Raclette	**Toasted cheese served with potatoes, gherkins and onions**
Salad niçoise	**Salad of tomatoes, radishes, cucumber, hard-boiled eggs, anchovies, onion, artichokes, green peppers, beans, basil and garlic (rarely as comprehensive, even in Nice)**
Duxelles	**Fried mushrooms and shallots with cream**
Fines herbes	**Mixture of tarragon, parsley and chives**
Frisé(e)	**Curly**
Gousse d'ail	**Clove of garlic**
Herbes de Provence	**Mixture of bay leaf, thyme, rosemary and savory**
Petits farcis	**Stuffed tomatoes, aubergines, courgettes, peppers**
Tapenade	**Olive and caper paste**
Tomates à la provençale	**Tomatoes baked with breadcrumbs, garlic and parsley**

Fruits (*fruits*), nuts (*noix*) and honey (*miel*)

Abricot	**Apricot**	Marrons	**Chestnuts**
Amandes	**Almonds**	Melon	**Melon**
Ananas	**Pineapple**	Miel de lavande	**Lavender honey**
Banane	**Banana**	Mirabelles	**Small yellow plums**
Brugnon, nectarine	**Nectarine**	Myrtilles	**Bilberries**
Cacahouète	**Peanut**	Noisette	**Hazelnut**
Cassis	**Blackcurrants**	Noix	**Nuts**
Cerises	**Cherries**	Noix	**Walnut**
Châtaignes	**Chestnuts**	Noix de cajou	**Cashew nut**
Citron	**Lemon**	Orange	**Orange**
Citron vert	**Lime**	Pamplemousse	**Grapefruit**
Dattes	**Dates**	Pastèque	**Watermelon**
Figues	**Figs**	Pêche (blanche)	**(White) peach**
Fraises (de bois)	**Strawberries (wild)**	Pistache	**Pistachio**
Framboises	**Raspberries**	Poire	**Pear**
Fruit de la passion	**Passion fruit**	Pomme	**Apple**
Grenade	**Pomegranate**	Prune	**Plum**
Groseilles	**Redcurrants**	Pruneau	**Prune**
Mangue	**Mango**	Raisins	**Grapes**
		Reine-Claude	**Greengage**

. . . and terms

Agrumes	**Citrus fruits**	Flambé	**Set aflame in alcohol**
Beignet	**Fritter**	Fougasse	**Bread flavoured with orange flower water or almonds, can also be savoury**
Compôte	**Stewed fruit**		
Coulis	**Sauce of puréed fruit**		
Crème de marrons	**Chestnut purée**	Frappé	**Iced**

Desserts (*desserts or entremets*), pastries (*pâtisseries*) and confectionery (*confiserie*)

Bombe	**A moulded ice-cream dessert**	Fromage blanc	**Cream cheese**
Brioche	**Sweet, high-yeast breakfast roll**	Gaufre	**Waffle**
Calissons	**Almond sweets**	Glace	**Ice cream**
Charlotte	**Custard and fruit in lining of almond fingers**	Île flottante	**Soft meringues floating on œufs à la neige custard**
Chichis	**Doughnuts shaped in sticks**	Macarons	**Macaroons**
Clafoutis	**Heavy custard and fruit tart**	Madeleine	**Small sponge cake**
		Marrons	**Chestnut purée and cream on a Mont Blanc rum-soaked sponge cake**
Crème Chantilly	**Vanilla-flavoured and sweetened whipped cream**	Mousse au chocolat	**Chocolate mousse**
		Nougat	**Nougat**
		Palmiers	**Caramelized puff pastries**
Crème fraîche	**Sour cream**	Parfait	**Frozen mousse, sometimes ice cream**
Crème pâtissière	**Thick eggy pastry-filling**		
Crêpes suzettes	**Thin pancakes with orange juice and liqueur**	Petit Suisse	**A smooth mixture of cream and curds**

Petits fours	**Bite-sized cakes/pastries**	Tiramisu	**Layered pudding of mascarpone cheese, alcohol and coffee**
Poires Belle Hélène	**Pears and ice cream in chocolate sauce**		
Tarte Tropezienne	**Sponge cake filled with custard cream topped with nuts**	Truffes	**Truffles**
		Yaourt, yogourt	**Yoghurt**

Terms

Barquette	**Small, boat-shaped flan**	Crêpes	**Pancakes**
		En feuilletage	**In puff pastry**
Bavarois	**Refers to the mould, could be a mousse or custard**	Fondant	**Melting**
		Galettes	**Buckwheat pancakes**
		Gênoise	**Rich sponge cake**
Biscuit	**A kind of cake**	Pâte	**Pastry or dough**
Chausson	**Pastry turnover**	Sablé	**Shortbread biscuit**
Chocolat amer	**Unsweetened chocolate**	Savarin	**A filled, ring-shaped cake**
Coupe	**A serving of ice cream**	Tarte	**Tart**
		Tartelette	**Small tart**

Cheese (fromage)

The cheeses produced in Provence are all either *chèvre* (made from goats' milk) or *brebis* (made from sheeps' milk). The most renowned are the *chèvres*, which include Banon, Picodon, Lou Pevre, Pelardon and Poivre d'Ain.

Le plateau de fromages is the cheeseboard, and bread, but not butter, is served with it. Some useful phrases: *une petite tranche de celui-ci* (a small piece of this one); *je peux le gouter?* (may I taste it?).

And one final note: when in a restaurant or café always call the waiter or waitress Monsieur or Madame (Mademoiselle if a young woman). **Never** use garçon, no matter what you've been taught at school.

GLOSSARY

French terms

These are either terms you'll come across in the Guide, or come up against on signs, maps, etc while travelling around.

ABBAYE abbey
ARRONDISSEMENT district of a city
ASSEMBLÉE NATIONALE the French parliament
AJ (*Auberge de Jeunesse*) youth hostel
BASTIDE medieval military settlement, constructed on a grid plan
BEAUX-ARTS fine arts museum (and school)
BORIE dry-stone wall, or building made with same
CALANQUE steep-sided inlet on coast, similar to Norwegian fjord, but not glacially formed
CAR bus
CFDT Socialist trade union
CGT Communist trade union
CHAMBRE D'HÔTE room for rent in private house
CHASSE, CHASSE GARDÉE hunting grounds
CHÂTEAU mansion, country house or castle
CHÂTEAU FORT castle
CHEMIN path
CIJ (*Centre d'Informations Jeunesse*) youth information centre
CODENE French CND
COL mountain pass
CONSIGNE luggage store
CÔTE coast
COURS combination of main square and main street
COUVENT convent, monastery
DEFENSE DE . . . It is forbidden to . . .
DÉGUSTATION tasting (wine or food)
DÉPARTEMENT county – more or less
DL (*Démocratie Libérale*) free-market party led by Alain Madelin
DONJON castle keep
ÉGLISE church
EN PANNE out of order
ENTRÉE entrance
FAUBOURG suburb, often abbreviated to fbg in street names
FERME farm
FERMETURE closing period
FN (*Front National*) fascist party led by Jean-Marie Le Pen
FO Catholic trade union
FOUILLES archeological excavations
GARE station; **ROUTIÈRE** – bus station; **SNCF** – train station
GÎTE D'ÉTAPE basic hostel accommodation primarily for walkers
GOBELINS famous tapestry manufacturers, based in Paris; its most renowned period was in the reign of Louis XIV (seventeenth century)
GR (*grande randonée)* long-distance footpath
HALLES covered market
HLM public housing development
HÔTEL a hotel, but also an aristocratic town house or mansion
HÔTEL DE VILLE town hall
JOURS FÉRIÉS public holidays
MAIRIE town hall
MARCHÉ market
MNR (*Mouvement National Républicain*) extreme-right party led by Bruno Mégret
PCF Communist Party of France
PLACE square
PORTE gateway
PRESQU'ÎLE peninsula
PS Socialist party
PUY peak or summit
QUARTIER district of a town
RELAIS ROUTIERS truckstop café-restaurants
RC (*Rez-de-Chaussée)* ground floor
RN (*Route Nationale*) main road
RPR Gaullist party led by Jacques Chirac
SANTON ornamental figure used especially in Christmas cribs
SI (*Syndicat d'Initiative*) tourist information office; also known as OT, OTSI and maison du tourisme
SNCF French railways
SORTIE exit

TABAC bar or shop selling stamps, cigarettes, etc
TABLE D'HÔTE meal served in lodging at the family table
TOUR tower
TRANSHUMANCE Routes followed by shepherds for taking livestock to and from suitable grazing grounds
UDF (*Union pour la Démocratie Française*) centre-right party headed by François Bayrou
UMP Right-wing coalition consisting of the RPR, UDF and DL parties; formed in 2002
VAUBAN seventeenth-century military architect – his fortresses still stand all over France
VIEILLE VILLE old quarter of town
VIEUX PORT old port
VILLAGE PERCHÉ hilltop village
VOUSSOIR sculpted rings in arch over church door
ZONE BLEUE restricted parking zone
ZONE PIETONNÉ pedestrian precinct

Architectural terms

AMBULATORY covered passage around the outer edge of a choir of a church
APSE semicircular termination at the east end of a church
BAROQUE High Renaissance period of art and architecture, distinguished by extreme ornateness
CAROLINGIAN dynasty (and art, sculpture, etc) founded by Charlemagne, late eighth to early tenth century
CHEVET east end of church, consisting of apse and ambulatory, with or without radiating chapels
CLASSICAL architectural style incorporating Greek and Roman elements – pillars, domes, colonnades, etc – at its height in France in the seventeenth century and revived in the nineteenth century as **NEOCLASSICAL**
CLERESTORY upper storey of a church, incorporating the windows
FLAMBOYANT florid form of Gothic (see below)
FRESCO wall painting – durable through application to wet plaster
GALLO-ROMAN period of Roman occupation of Gaul (first to fourth century AD)
GOTHIC architectural style prevalent from the twelfth century to the sixteenth century, characterized by pointed arches and ribbed vaulting
MEROVINGIAN dynasty (and art, etc) ruling France and parts of Germany from the sixth to mid-eighth century
NARTHEX entrance hall of church
NAVE main body of a church
RENAISSANCE art-architectural style developed in fifteenth-century Italy and imported to France in the early sixteenth century by François I
RETABLE altarpiece
ROMANESQUE early medieval architecture distinguished by squat, rounded forms and naive sculpture
STUCCO plaster used to embellish ceilings, etc
TRANSEPT cross arms of a church
TYMPANUM sculpted panel above a church door
VOUSSOIR sculpted rings in arch over church door

Index

and small print

Index

Map entries are in **colour**

D

E

N

INDEX

A Rough Guide to Rough Guides

In the summer of 1981, Mark Ellingham, a recent graduate from Bristol University, was travelling round Greece and couldn't find a guidebook that really met his needs. On the one hand there were the student guides, insistent on saving every last cent, and on the other the heavyweight cultural tomes whose authors seemed to have spent more time in a research library than lounging away the afternoon at a taverna or on the beach.

In a bid to avoid getting a job, Mark and a small group of writers set about creating their own guidebook. It was a guide to Greece that aimed to combine a journalistic approach to description with a thoroughly practical approach to travellers' needs – a guide that would incorporate culture, history and contemporary insights with a critical edge, together with up-to-date, value-for-money listings. Back in London, Mark and the team finished their Rough Guide, as they called it, and talked Routledge into publishing the book.

That first *Rough Guide to Greece*, published in 1982, was a student scheme that became a publishing phenomenon. The immediate success of the book – with numerous reprints and a Thomas Cook prize shortlisting – spawned a series that rapidly covered dozens of destinations. Rough Guides had a ready market among low-budget backpackers, but soon also acquired a much broader and older readership that relished Rough Guides' wit and inquisitiveness as much as their enthusiastic, critical approach. Everyone wants value for money, but not at any price.

Rough Guides soon began supplementing the "rougher" information about hostels and low-budget listings with the kind of detail on restaurants and quality hotels that independent-minded visitors on any budget might expect, whether on business in New York or trekking in Thailand.

These days the guides – distributed worldwide by the Penguin group – offer recommendations from shoestring to luxury and cover more than 200 destinations around the globe, including almost every country in the Americas and Europe, more than half of Africa and most of Asia and Australasia. Our ever-growing team of authors and photographers is spread all over the world, particularly in Europe, the USA and Australia.

In 1994, we published the *Rough Guide to World Music* and *Rough Guide to Classical Music*; and a year later the *Rough Guide to the Internet*. All three books have become benchmark titles in their fields – which encouraged us to expand into other areas of publishing, mainly around popular culture. Rough Guides now publish:

- Travel guides to more than 200 worldwide destinations
- Dictionary phrasebooks to 22 major languages
- History guides ranging from Ireland to Islam
- Maps printed on rip-proof and waterproof Polyart™ paper
- Music guides running the gamut from Opera to Elvis
- Restaurant guides to London, New York and San Francisco
- Reference books on topics as diverse as the Weather and Shakespeare
- Sports guides from Formula 1 to Man Utd
- Pop culture books from *Lord of the Rings* to Cult TV
- World Music CDs in association with World Music Network.

Visit **www.roughguides.com** to see our latest publications.

Rough Guide Credits

Text editor: Mandy Tomlin
Managing Director: Kevin Fitzgerald
Series editor: Mark Ellingham
Editorial: Martin Dunford, Jonathan Buckley, Kate Berens, Ann-Marie Shaw, Helena Smith, Olivia Swift, Ruth Blackmore, Geoff Howard, Claire Saunders, Gavin Thomas, Alexander Mark Rogers, Polly Thomas, Joe Staines, Richard Lim, Duncan Clark, Peter Buckley, Lucy Ratcliffe, Clifton Wilkinson, Alison Murchie, Matthew Teller, Andrew Dickson, Fran Sandham, Sally Schafer, Matthew Milton, Karoline Densley (UK); Andrew Rosenberg, Yuki Takagaki, Richard Koss, Hunter Slaton (US)
Design & Layout: Link Hall, Helen Prior, Julia Bovis, Katie Pringle, Rachel Holmes, Andy Turner, Dan May, Tanya Hall, John McKay, Sophie Hewat (UK); Madhulita Mohapatra, Umesh Aggarwal, Sunil Sharma (India)
Cartography: Maxine Repath, Ed Wright, Katie Lloyd-Jones (UK); Manish Chandra, Rajesh Chhibber, Jai Prakesh Mishra (India)
Cover art direction: Louise Boulton
Picture research: Sharon Martins, Mark Thomas
Online: Kelly Martinez, Anja Mutic-Blessing, Jennifer Gold, Audra Epstein, Suzanne Welles, Cree Lawson (US); Manik Chauhan, Amarjyoti Dutta, Narender Kumar (India)
Finance: Gary Singh
Marketing & Publicity: Richard Trillo, Niki Smith, David Wearn, Chloë Roberts, Demelza Dallow, Claire Southern (UK); Geoff Colquitt, David Wechsler, Megan Kennedy (US)
Administration: Julie Sanderson
RG India: Punita Singh

Publishing Information

This fifth edition published October 2003 by
Rough Guides Ltd,
80 Strand, London WC2R 0RL.
4th Floor, 345 Hudson St,
New York, NY 10014, USA.
Distributed by the Penguin Group
Penguin Books Ltd,
80 Strand, London WC2R 0RL
Penguin Putnam, Inc.
375 Hudson Street, NY 10014, USA
Penguin Books Australia Ltd,
487 Maroondah Highway, PO Box 257,
Ringwood, Victoria 3134, Australia
Penguin Books Canada Ltd,
10 Alcorn Avenue, Toronto, Ontario,
Canada M4V 1E4
Penguin Books (NZ) Ltd,
182–190 Wairau Road, Auckland 10,
New Zealand
Typeset in Bembo and Helvetica to an original design by Henry Iles.

Printed and bound in China

512pp includes index

A catalogue record for this book is available from the British Library

ISBN 1-85828-892-4

4 6 8 9 7 5 3

Help us update

We've gone to a lot of effort to ensure that the fifth edition of **The Rough Guide to Provence** is accurate and up-to-date. However, things change – places get "discovered", opening hours are notoriously fickle, restaurants and rooms raise prices or lower standards. If you feel we've got it wrong or left something out, we'd like to know, and if you can remember the address, the price, the time, the phone number, so much the better.

We'll credit all contributions, and send a copy of the next edition (or any other Rough Guide if you prefer) for the best letters. Everyone who writes to us and isn't already a subscriber will receive a copy of our full-colour thrice-yearly newsletter. Please mark letters: "**Rough Guide Provence Update**" and send to: Rough Guides, 80 Strand, London WC2R 0RL, or Rough Guides, 4th Floor, 345 Hudson St, New York, NY 10014. Or send an email to **mail@roughguides.com**

Have your questions answered and tell

Acknowledgements

Chris Pitts would like to thank Francine Riou in Arles, Ian Holyman, Chris Kinsman, Miriam Bellecca, Géraldine Vigouroux, Dirk Jang with special thanks to Perrine, for her insight and infinite patience.

The forest fires of 2003

At the time of going to press, some areas of Provence and the Côte d'Azur were facing the worst forest fires seen for a generation. A dry spring followed by a long heatwave, coupled with high Mistral winds, had conspired to create tinderbox conditions, leading to blazes in much of the region, from Salon de Provence to the Riviera. As a result, some places listed in the Guide may have been affected. On the densely forested Massif des Maures, flames came closer to the coastal resorts than many could remember; 20,000 residents and holidaymakers were evacuated. People too frightened to return to their homes took to the beach for safety at Les Issambres, near Ste Maxime, while two holidaymakers died in the wooded country between Grimaud and La Garde Freinet. Campsites on the fringes of Fréjus were engulfed by fire, and 700 firefighters struggled to control a vast blaze at La Motte, near Draguignan. Following the discovery of Molotov cocktails the authorities introduced stop-and-search procedures, as it became clear that some of the fires had been started deliberately. But most probably started naturally or through carelessness, which sparked a wider debate among environmentalists about the wisdom of planting so many non-native pine trees – though picturesque, the pines dry out more thoroughly than native species and contain more fire-promoting resin.

Photo Credits

Cover Credits
Main front: Nice Robert Harding
Small front top picture: Nice Harbour Robert Harding
Small front lower picture: Mont Ventoux John Miller
Back top picture: Avignon John Miller
Back lower picture: Mardi Gras Robert Harding

Colour introduction
Lavendar Field © Roy Rainford / Robert Harding
Cotignac, Haut Var, Hardware Shop © J.Mann / TRIP
Avignon, Pont St Benezet & River Rhone © C.Martin / Robert Harding
Santons, Model Farmer © Ask Images / TRIP
Camargue-flamingoes © images-of-france
Aix-market-olives © images-of-france
Lavendar-shop © images-of-france
Marseilles fish market © Ray Roberts
Roman Amphitheatre, Arles © H.Rogers / TRIP
Matisse © Bridgeman Art Library/DACS
Brigitte Bardot relaxing between scenes © Bettmann/Corbis
Olive Trees © H.Rogers / TRIP

Things Not To Miss
Cote d'Azur, Calanque en Vau © Ask Images / TRIP
Nice, Place Felix, Street Cafes © T.Bognar / TRIP
The Yellow House by Vincent Van Gogh (1888) © Van Gogh Museum, Amsterdam (Vincent Van Gogh Foundation)
Cannes,Croisette,Winter © Neville Walker
Mont St Victoire by Paul Cezanne © Bridgeman Art Library
Abbaye de Senanque, Cloisters © H.Rogers / TRIP
Fondation Maeght © Neville Walker
Chateauneuf-du-pape © images-of-france
Marseilles, Notre Dame, Old Port © S.Grant/TRIP
Avignon, During the Festival © A.M.Bazalik / TRIP
Boullabaisse © Anthony Blake
Palais de Papes © B.Turner / TRIP
Nicois Village, Peille © Neville Walker
Camargue © Robert Harding
The Casino, Monte Carlo, Monaco © Neil Setchfield
Aix en Provence, Market Stalls © A.M.Bazalik / TRIP
Cassis, Boats, Cafes on Waterfront © Ask Images / TRIP
The River Verdon in the Grand Canyon of the Verdon © Tomlinson / Robert Harding
Parc National du Mercantour © Ask Images/TRIP
Cannes Beach, Pink Parasoles © Vanderharst / Robert Harding
Plage-de-pampelonne © images-of-france
Matisse Museum, Nice © Ellen Rooney / Robert Harding
Roman Amphitheatre, Orange © Roy Rainford / Robert Harding
Camargue, Ste Maries de la Mer, Gypsies Pilgrimage © A.Bloomfield / TRIP
Riviera corniche © images-of-france

Black and white photos
Avignon-tgv © images-of-france (p.60)
Cathedrale des Images, Val d'Enfer © Christopher Pitts (p.94)
Les Dentelles de Montmirail © Duncan Maxwell / Robert Harding (p.120)
Gargoyle in Le Crestet © Christopher Pitts (p.131)
Marseille Old Harbour, Cathedral, Major © A.Ghazzal / TRIP (p.164)
Cassis-route-des-Cretes © images-of-frances (p.213)
St.Tropez, Iles D'Hyeres © Don Wood / TRIP (p.230)
Cote d'Azur, St.Tropez, Vieux Port © Neil Setchfield (p.240)
Grand Canyon Du Verdon © Neville Walker (p.276)
Abbaye-du-Thoronet © images-of-trance (p.289)
Vieux Nice Rooftops © Neville Walker (p.314)
Cote d'Azur, Cannes, Hotel Carlton © H.P.Merten / Robert Harding (p.323)
Entrevaux, River, Medieval town © N & J.Wiseman / TRIP (p.396)
Alpine view near Valberg © Neville Walker (p.421)

Rough Guide Maps

Rough Guide Maps, printed on waterproof and rip-proof Polyart™ paper, offer an unbeatable combination of practicality, clarity of design and amazing value.

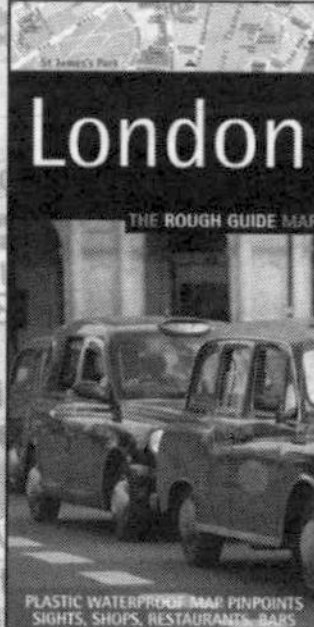

CITY MAPS

Amsterdam · Barcelona · Berlin · Boston · Brussels · Dublin
Florence & Siena · Frankfurt · London · Los Angeles
Miami · New York · Paris · Prague · Rome
San Francisco · Venice · Washington DC and more...

COUNTRY & REGIONAL MAPS

Andalucía · Argentina · Australia · Baja California · Cuba
Cyprus · Dominican Republic · Egypt · Greece
Guatemala & Belize · Ireland · Mexico · Morocco
New Zealand · South Africa · Sri Lanka · Tenerife · Thailand
Trinidad & Tobago Yucatán Peninsula · and more...

US$8.95 Can$13.50 £4.99

NOTES

NOTES

NOTES

NOTES

NOTES

NOTES

NOTES

NOTES

NOTES

NOTES

NORTH
SOUTH
TRAVEL

Es
London

by

SUSAN GROSSMAN

Susan Grossman is a travel writer, broadcaster and photographer, and is a former travel editor of the Telegraph Sunday Magazine. She has presented two series of the BBC's 'Food and Drink' programme, and has broadcast regularly on such radio programmes as 'Breakaway'.

AA

Produced by AA Publishing

Written by Susan Grossman
Peace and Quiet section
by Paul Sterry

Edited, designed and produced by AA Publishing. Maps © The Automobile Association 1994

Distributed in the United Kingdom by AA Publishing, Fanum House, Basingstoke, Hampshire, RG21 2EA.

The contents of this publication are believed correct at the time of printing. Nevertheless, the publishers cannot be held responsible for any errors or omissions, or for changes in details given in this guide or for the consequences of any reliance on the information provided by the same. Assessments of attractions, hotels, restaurants and so forth are based upon the author's own experience and, therefore, descriptions given in this guide necessarily contain an element of subjective opinion which may not reflect the publisher's opinion or dictate a reader's own experience on another occasion.
We have tried to ensure accuracy in this guide, but things do change and we would be grateful if readers would advise us of any inaccuracies they may encounter.

First published 1990
Revised Second edition 1993

A CIP catalogue record for this book is available from the British Library.

ISBN 0 7495 0840 X

Published by AA Publishing, which is a trading name of Automobile Association Developments Limited, whose registered office is Fanum House, Basingstoke, Hampshire, RG21 2EA.
Registered number 1878835.

Colour separation: Mullis Morgan, London

Printed by: Printers Trento, S.R.L., Italy

Cover picture: Guardsmen

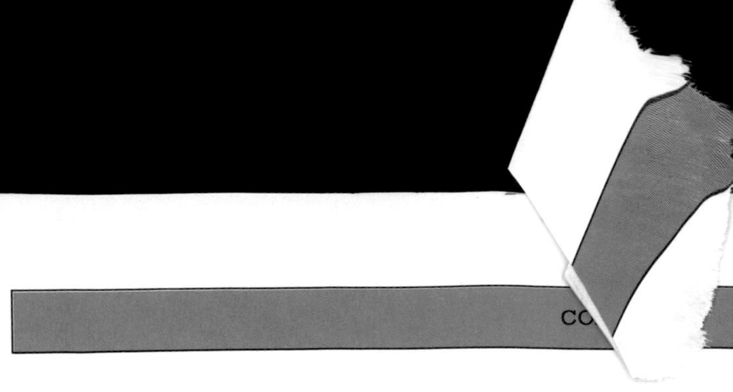

CO

This book employs a simple rating system to help choose which places to visit:

 'top ten'

◆◆◆ do not miss
◆◆ see if you can
◆ worth seeing if you have time

INTRODUCTION

Although London is changing rapidly, with new things to see and do appearing by the day, it is still a city with a profound and lively sense of history. This guide's aim is to provide the sort of information a Londoner would give to a friend visiting the capital. In it you will find everything from the newest museums to a personal selection of shops, hotels and restaurants. What you will not find is information on where to have an Elizabethan banquet; neither are there pages and pages of historical facts. This book does set out to show you a side of the British capital usually reserved for residents!

Present-day London

London had some 16 million visitors last year, over two times its population. For most, first impressions are not particularly inspiring, whether your approach is by train through the dreary south London suburbs from Gatwick, by coach from Heathrow in the west, or by tube into Piccadilly. Once in the city you may be shocked by the crowds, the traffic, the down-and-outs and the homeless teenagers asking for money at the foot of the escalators on the Underground. As for the litter, every year a pile of rubbish big enough to fill Trafalgar Square to five times the height of Nelson's Column is swept up.

Enough of the negatives. Get your bearings and you will discover a city with more green spaces than most, with enough culture to fill a filofax; culinary offerings that span the globe and an exciting future as whole areas of the capital are redeveloped.

London looks its best on a Sunday when the streets are relatively quiet (so long as plans for Sunday shop opening do not go ahead) and the office workers are at home eating roast beef and Yorkshire pudding after a pint in the pub. It looks its best in spring or early summer with the crocuses and daffodils carpeting the parks. And it looks pretty good at night, especially from Waterloo Bridge, with the main monuments lit up along the Embankment.

Open spaces are an essential part of London's character. They vary from parks so big as to be almost open countryside, to squares little bigger than suburban gardens. This is St James's Square

The Palace of Westminster (universally known as the Houses of Parliament) was rebuilt in the years after 1834, when its predecessor was burnt down. The Victoria Tower dominates this view, with 'Big Ben' looking small in the distance, an illusion which emphasises the huge size of the palace

Old London

Julius Caesar invaded Britain in 55BC, but it took another 100 years for his legions to land on the south coast and transform this site into a major town. It was Edward the Confessor who moved upstream from the City to establish Westminster, rebuilding the Abbey and the Royal Palace. The City retaliated by electing its own mayor; and it also established itself as the centre for trade, which it still is.

Monarchs came and went. The Black Death of 1348 did not stop the expansion and by the time Henry VIII came to power in 1509, London's population was 50,000. Henry, now famous for having had six wives, sparked off centuries of religious conflict when, in order to divorce his first wife and marry Anne Boleyn, he led the country in a break away from Papal authority. Under the rule of Henry and Anne's

daughter, Elizabeth I, London enjoyed a flourishing of literature and theatre: this was the age of Shakespeare and of the city's first theatre, the Globe, built in 1599. This was also a time of great debate between Parliament and monarch over the balance of political power. The 17th century brought civil war, when Parliament challenged Charles I's use of royal authority and his toleration of Catholicism. After the victory of Parliamentarian forces, led by Oliver Cromwell, the King was executed and a period of strict Puritan government ensued. The monarchy was restored in 1660, when Charles II ushered in a period of stability, earning the title of "Merry Monarch".
In 1665 yet another plague hit the capital and, a year later, a small fire in Pudding Lane triggered off flames that fed the Great Fire of London which destroyed four-fifths of the city.

Rebuilding was soon under way, and for the next few centuries London prospered. But many of the inhabitants lived in squalor, and crime was rife.

By the 19th century London had expanded enormously, but pockets of the capital were trapped in harsh poverty, vividly described in Charles Dickens' novels.

The first railway appeared during Queen Victoria's reign, as did the first Underground or 'tube' line, which first carried passengers in 1890. From then on suburbs began to spread alongside the railway tracks.

Government

London is the seat of British government, which is a constitutional monarchy. Its laws are made in Parliament, which has two 'Houses', both at Westminster: the House of Commons, where Members are returned by election; and the House of Lords, which can delay and amend

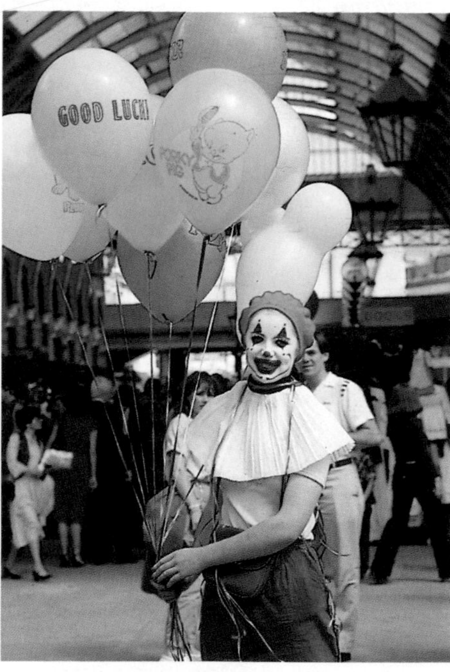

People! On an average day in London you can see bowler-hatted businessmen and penniless paupers, frantically rich yuppies and blue-bloods from the country, the genuinely eccentric and the desperately comic

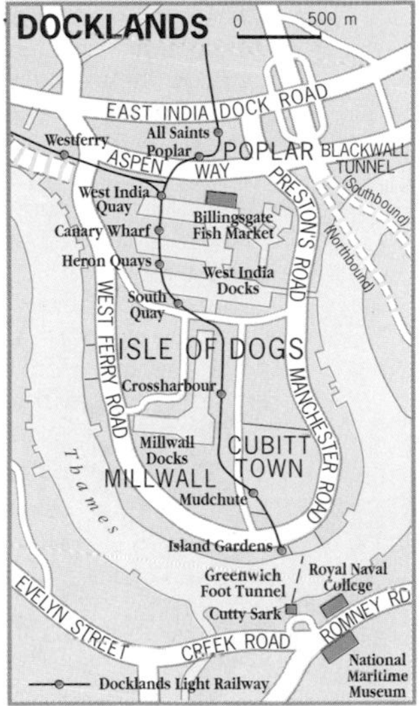

laws but can no longer veto them altogether. The House of Lords, denounced by some as unrepresentative and anachronistic, was once a powerful centre of patronage, and the creation of peers to add weight to one political party carried on well into this century. Britain has no written constitution – a subject of lively debate. Its form of government evolved through centuries of power struggles. In theory, the monarch can still veto the country's laws, and the Queen must still ratify all statutes. But this is now a formality which, like the approval of a new Prime Minister by 'kissing hands', has become one of the city's political rituals.

New London

They called it the largest building site in the world as the biggest building boom London had seen in 25 years got underway. But unless you base your visit in among the rapidly developing Docklands or in among the banks of the City, you would hardly know that some 20 million square ft (1,800,000 sq m) of new office space is being constructed.

Not all Londoners are happy about what's happening to their city, least of all Prince

Charles, who has complained that post-war architectural clutter has already obscured some of the famous 'views'. Rather late in the day, the Government finally agreed that views along the river and around the Palace of Westminster should be protected. The answer seems to lie in 'groundscrapers', a sort of tower block turned on its side, and they are mushrooming up.

To the east of the city centre, Docklands has already undergone an enormous change as the old warehouses of the West India Dock have been transformed into luxury office buildings and apartments. Of more interest to the visitor is the vast shopping centre at

Wapping's Tobacco Dock with its specialist shops, restaurants and pirate history ships. There is just one thing that might hinder Docklands' meteoric rise in status, and that is communications. Inadequate public transport and road links are, however, being improved. In the next few years a massive one-third of the part of London known as the City is being redeveloped in order to place it firmly on the 'global digital highway'. Many of the buildings will be offices, but entertainment and culture have not been forgotten. The Broadgate site of ultra-modern offices already has at its centre, a small open-air skating rink, while at Butler's Wharf, on the south bank of the Thames near

St Katharine's Dock. Originally built in the 1820s, the warehouses here stored wool and wine. They eventually closed in 1968, victims to new downriver ports. Today the expensive boats give a clue to the 'new money' that has transformed them

Nautical whimsy at Hays Galleria

Tower Bridge, there is a new Conran Foundation Design Museum, and 19th-century warehouses are being turned into shops. The thriving London Bridge City complex includes the impressive glass-domed Hays Galleria shopping centre overlooking the Thames, and by mid-1994 there will be a re-construction of Shakespeare's Globe Theatre on the Thames opposite St Paul's.

Buildings that went up in the 1960s elsewhere in London are being demolished or getting a facelift. The South Bank (Hayward Gallery, Queen Elizabeth Hall and Royal Festival Hall) and the ugly concrete high-level walkways linking them are getting a massive multi-million pound camouflage. A similarly large amount of money has been spent on turning the old Battersea Power Station into a mammoth shopping and leisure centre, but plans have faltered and its future is uncertain. Whether or not all these changes will enhance London's already rather haphazard appearance, only time will tell.

THE DIFFERENT AREAS

London is split into different areas, each with a distinctive character of its own, from the centre of commerce – the City – to the political world of Westminster. When you are trying to locate an address, the post code can provide useful information. Places in west, west central and southwest London have W, WC and SW respectively after their address, followed by a low number if they are central locations. Addresses with east (E) and east central (EC) after them are in the City, while northwest London (NW) includes areas like Hampstead. The higher the number, the further into the suburbs the location is. London is divided by the River Thames, and most of the action takes place north of it. Stay anywhere in the West End, Knightsbridge, Bayswater or Victoria and you will easily be able to reach the main shopping areas and places of interest.

Inner London

Bayswater

Part of Paddington, near Marble Arch and Hyde Park, and full of hotels. The busy Bayswater Road runs past Notting Hill (home of the famous carnival and Portobello Road antique market) and Holland Park to Shepherd's Bush in one direction and along to Marble Arch and Oxford Street in the other. The surrounding streets are quiet, and full of family homes and embassies. Knightsbridge is situated on the other side of Hyde Park.

Hyde Park Corner can be one of London's most unpleasant traffic bottlenecks, but these horses seem quite at home

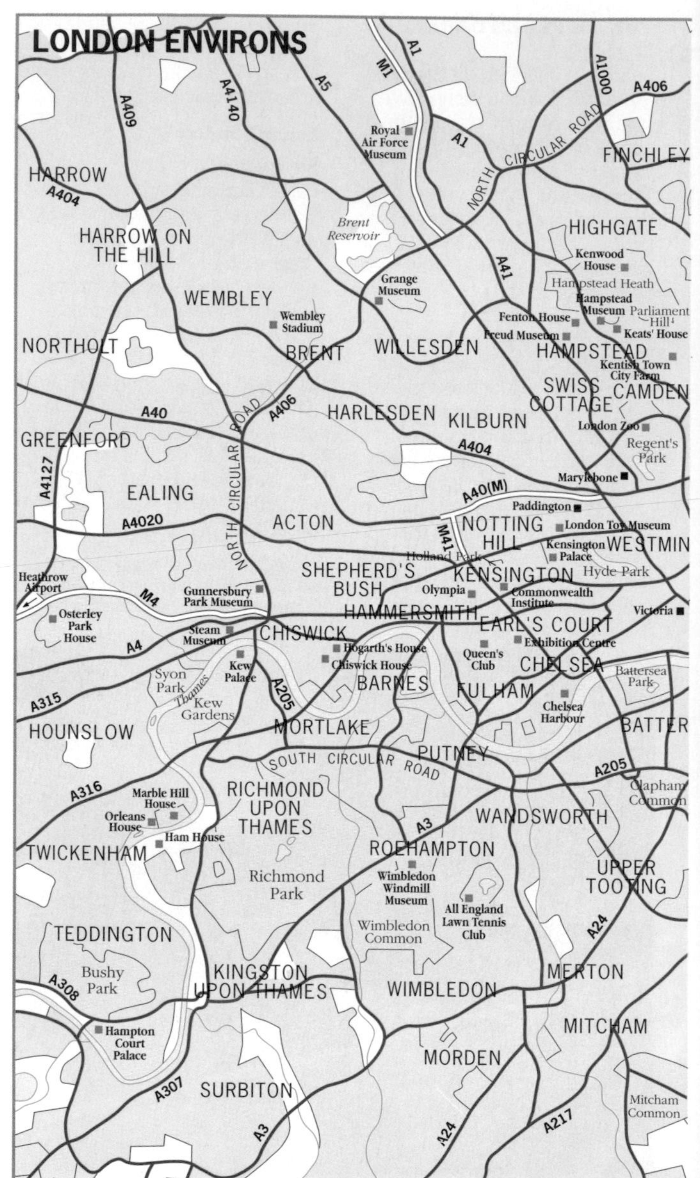
LONDON ENVIRONS
HARROW
HARROW ON THE HILL
WEMBLEY
NORTHOLT
GREENFORD
EALING
ACTON
BRENT
WILLESDEN
HARLESDEN
KILBURN
HAMPSTEAD
SWISS COTTAGE
CAMDEN
HIGHGATE
FINCHLEY
NOTTING HILL
KENSINGTON
SHEPHERD'S BUSH
HAMMERSMITH
CHISWICK
EARL'S COURT
CHELSEA
FULHAM
BARNES
MORTLAKE
PUTNEY
HOUNSLOW
RICHMOND UPON THAMES
WANDSWORTH
ROEHAMPTON
TWICKENHAM
UPPER TOOTING
TEDDINGTON
KINGSTON UPON THAMES
WIMBLEDON
MERTON
MITCHAM
MORDEN
SURBITON
Royal Air Force Museum
Brent Reservoir
Grange Museum
Wembley Stadium
Kenwood House
Hampstead Heath
Hampstead Museum
Parliament Hill
Fenton House
Freud Museum
Keats' House
Kentish Town City Farm
London Zoo
Regent's Park
Marylebone
Paddington
London Toy Museum
Kensington Palace
Holland Park
Hyde Park
Olympia
Commonwealth Institute
Victoria
Exhibition Centre
Queen's Club
Battersea Park
Chelsea Harbour
Heathrow Airport
Osterley Park House
Gunnersbury Park Museum
Steam Museum
Kew Palace
Hogarth's House
Chiswick House
Syon Park
Thames
Kew Gardens
Clapham Common
Marble Hill House
Orleans House
Ham House
Richmond Park
Wimbledon Windmill Museum
All England Lawn Tennis Club
Wimbledon Common
Bushy Park
Hampton Court Palace
Mitcham Common
NORTH CIRCULAR ROAD
SOUTH CIRCULAR ROAD
A1
M1
A5
A4140
A409
A1000
A406
A404
A41
A40
A4127
A4020
A40(M)
M41
M4
A4
A315
A205
A316
A3
A24
A308
A307
A217

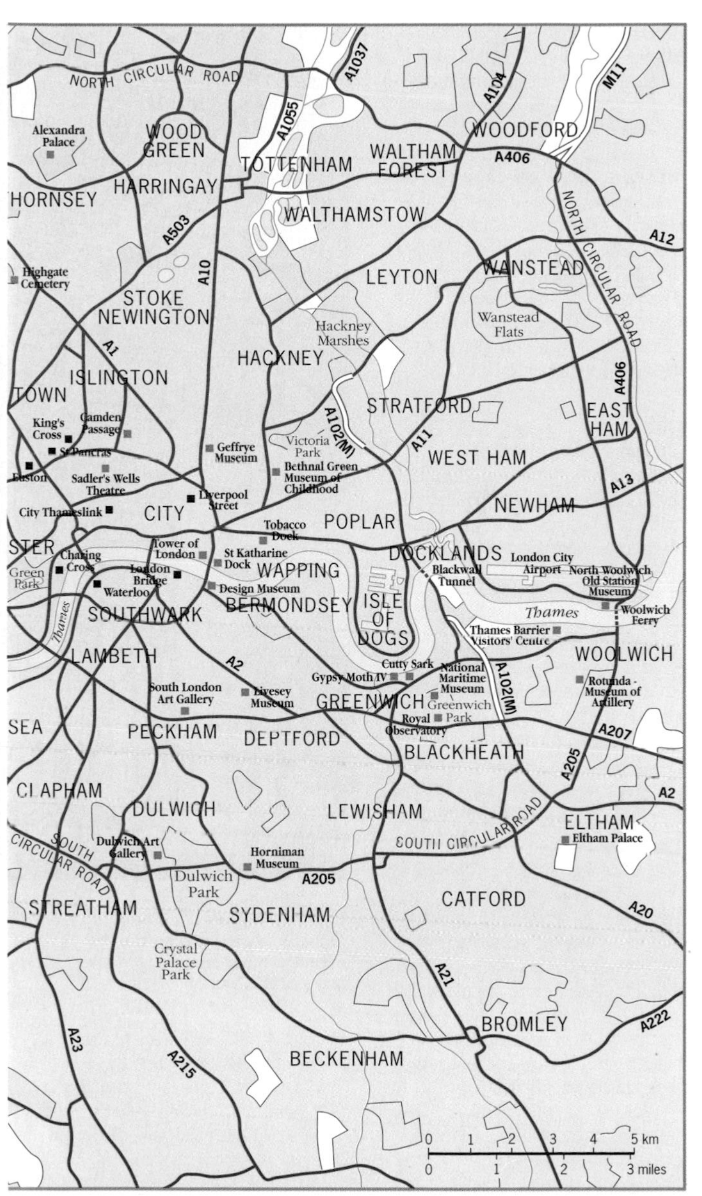
NORTH CIRCULAR ROAD
A1037
A104
M11
Alexandra Palace
WOOD GREEN
A1055
WOODFORD
TOTTENHAM
WALTHAM FOREST
A406
HARRINGAY
HORNSEY
WALTHAMSTOW
A503
NORTH CIRCULAR ROAD
A12
Highgate Cemetery
A10
LEYTON
WANSTEAD
STOKE NEWINGTON
Wanstead Flats
Hackney Marshes
A1
HACKNEY
ISLINGTON
A406
TOWN
STRATFORD
EAST HAM
King's Cross
Camden Passage
A102(M)
Victoria Park
A11
St Pancras
Geffrye Museum
WEST HAM
Euston
Sadler's Wells Theatre
Bethnal Green Museum of Childhood
A13
Liverpool Street
NEWHAM
City Thameslink
CITY
Tobacco Dock
POPLAR
Tower of London
St Katharine Dock
DOCKLANDS
London City Airport
Charing Cross
WAPPING
Blackwall Tunnel
North Woolwich Old Station Museum
Green Park
London Bridge
Waterloo
Design Museum
BERMONDSEY
ISLE OF DOGS
Thames
Woolwich Ferry
SOUTHWARK
Thames
Thames Barrier Visitors' Centre
LAMBETH
WOOLWICH
A2
Cutty Sark
Gypsy Moth IV
National Maritime Museum
A102(M)
South London Art Gallery
Livesey Museum
Rotunda - Museum of Artillery
GREENWICH
Greenwich Park
Royal Observatory
SEA
PECKHAM
DEPTFORD
A207
BLACKHEATH
A205
CLAPHAM
A2
DULWICH
LEWISHAM
SOUTH CIRCULAR ROAD
ELTHAM
Eltham Palace
SOUTH CIRCULAR ROAD
Dulwich Art Gallery
Horniman Museum
Dulwich Park
A205
CATFORD
STREATHAM
SYDENHAM
A20
Crystal Palace Park
A21
BROMLEY
A222
A23
A215
BECKENHAM
0 1 2 3 4 5 km
0 1 2 3 miles

Bloomsbury

Bloomsbury is behind New Oxford Street and Tottenham Court Road (with its hi-fi and furniture shops). It includes quiet squares, the British Museum, the University of London and University College Hospital. Famous residents in the 1920s and 30s were Virginia Woolf, E M Forster, Rupert Brooke, D H Lawrence and Bertrand Russell, all members of the intellectual circle of friends, the 'Bloomsbury Group'.

Chelsea

Chelsea has upmarket residential properties, many of them small terraced houses in quiet squares, with fashionable addresses like Cheyne Walk on the river. The new Chelsea Harbour development of restaurants, offices and expensive riverside flats overlooks the boats. The King's Road, the 'mecca' in the 1960s, is still one of London's fashion streets. Chelsea is a tube or bus ride from the West End's shops, a short way from Knightsbridge, and it runs into Kensington.

The City

The City is both the historic capital and the centre of commerce, with boundaries that have extended west into Holborn and east into Docklands. It is a hive of activity during the week as brokers do business on the foreign exchanges, nipping out to one of the many historic hostelries for lunch. At weekends it is relatively quiet, as the owners of the pinstripe suits and the occasional bowler hat desert the old Square Mile and head south of the river to the Stockbroker Belt. The younger 'yuppies' with their Porsches relax in a flat in Fulham, the Docklands or the Barbican. Meanwhile, the cockney heart

The nave of St Paul's. The monument on the left is the overwhelming memorial to the Duke of Wellington

(cockneys are Londoners born within the sound of Bow Bells) still throbs among the barrows in the East End markets, the historic centre still lives in the ancient Livery Halls, and wigged barristers still administer justice in the peace and inner sanctum of The Temple. The skyline is ever changing, though familiar landmarks like St Paul's Cathedral, the Bank of England and the Old Bailey are still distinguishable through the cranes. It is an area rich in things to see, including 39 city churches and the Museum of London. Close by though not strictly in the City, are the Tower of London, HMS *Belfast*, Tower Bridge, and the Hays Galleria shopping centre, in the London Bridge City Complex.

Covent Garden

A compact central area, next to Soho, immortalised in Shaw's *Pygmalion* where the young Eliza Doolittle sold flowers to the ladies and gents emerging from the Royal Opera House. The Opera House is still there, but the vegetable and flower market moved out in 1974. Today Covent Garden is a magnet for visitors, who throng the cobbled piazza to shop in the central market (idiosyncratic shops selling everything from doll's houses to flower perfumes) and watch the free live street entertainment. At weekends there are crafts and antiques sold from the original wrought-iron trading stands. During the week the open-air cafés, restaurants and wine bars, though few of high quality, are full of film and advertising executives from the surrounding offices. Attractions in the area include the London Transport Museum and several theatres, but there are only a few hotels.

Covent Garden is an essential destination for many shoppers and other visitors

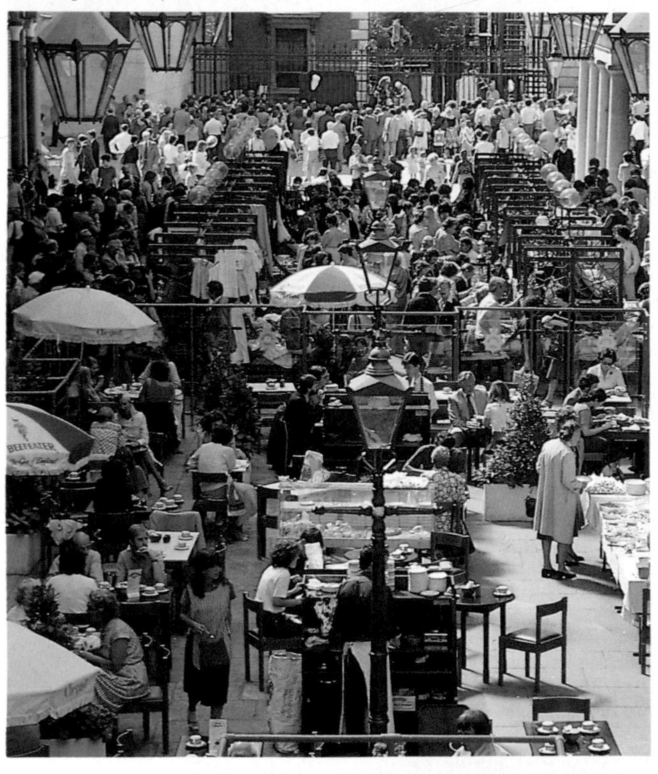

Docklands
Before World War II, London was the greatest port in the world, and 120,000 dockers handled cargoes of spices, furs, rubber and sugar. By the early 1960s the Docks were in irreversible decline and by 1982 everything had closed. Recently, some £2 billion has been invested in the area; Canary Wharf is set to become the new financial centre and hundreds of companies have already moved in, although it will be a while before the developers move out. The Docklands Light Railway, the London City Airport and some 12,000 new homes are already installed, as is the huge shopping centre at Tobacco Dock. The best way to see what is happening to Docklands is to travel on the Docklands Light Railway from Bank to Island Gardens on the Isle of Dogs. You can then take the old dockers' subway under the Thames across to Greenwich.

Fulham
Home of the 1980s yuppie brigade – who transformed the streets of this former working class suburbia – Fulham is a mix of seedy tenement houses and fashionable squares. Parts of Fulham are on the river. The Knightsbridge end is upmarket, with a good range of restaurants and shopping. Much of the rest is pretty nondescript. Fulham runs into neighbouring Chelsea.

Kensington
The High Street is now largely occupied by chain stores, but this Royal Borough still has its exclusive areas from the antique shops in Kensington Church Street to Kensington Palace and the surrounding gardens. Holland Park and the Commonwealth Institute are also in Kensington (see also South Kensington and Earl's Court, page 21).

Knightsbridge
A very central, exclusive location with some of the more expensive hotels and residences in quiet squares. Home of Harrods, Harvey Nichols, Bonham's auctioneers, quality fashion shops in Sloane Street and Knightsbridge, plus numerous galleries and antique shops. Opposite Hyde Park.

Mayfair and Park Lane
High rents render Mayfair, which includes the West End (see page 22), Bond Street and Park Lane, one of the most exclusive areas in London. Famous hotels line one side of Park Lane and overlook Hyde Park, and other well-known hotels like Claridges and the Connaught are nearby. Mayfair's village heart is Shepherd Market (home to high-class prostitutes). The area has famous squares like Berkeley and Grosvenor (home of the American Embassy), and includes Bond Street and the *haute couture* fashion houses, as well as Curzon Street's gaming clubs.
Attractions include the Museum of Mankind, near the Burlington Arcade, the Royal Academy, and, in Manchester Square, the Wallace Collection, with its 18th-century paintings and French furniture.

Piccadilly and St James's
Piccadilly is a busy thoroughfare connecting Hyde Park and Leicester Square. Green Park runs along one side of it. Within Piccadilly you will find the Ritz Hotel, the Burlington Arcade, the Royal Academy, Fortnum and Mason and airline offices. St James's, to the south, is a largely male-orientated area with tailors in Jermyn Street, and several gentlemen's clubs. There are theatres in the Haymarket.

Regent's Park
Nash's beautiful terraces dominate the architecture of Regent's Park, behind the busy Marylebone Road (Madame Tussaud's and the Planetarium) and Baker Street (Sherlock Holmes Museum). Attractions include Queen Mary's Rose Garden, the open-air theatre and the Zoo. The Regent's Canal leads to Camden Lock, with its weekend market, and Little Venice (Maida Vale).

Soho
Soho runs into Covent Garden. Once London's red-light district, Soho has cleaned up its act. Most of the sleazy nightclubs have shut and been replaced by designer restaurants and shops (although the famous Raymond Revuebar Theatre is still going strong). A handful of family-owned businesses still thrive in the area, including Continental delicatessens and patisseries. The Berwick Street market dates back to 1778 (Monday to Saturday 09.00 to 17.00). One of the few areas of London alive after midnight, with bars, brasseries and discos, Soho includes the cinemas in Leicester Square, the Trocadero Centre (shops and entertainment), the bookshops in Charing Cross Road and cinemas and theatres in Shaftesbury Avenue. Chinatown, south of Shaftesbury Avenue, is also part of Soho.

South Bank
The South Bank Arts Centre across Waterloo Bridge, overlooking the Thames, has for years been the most important landmark for visitors south of the river. It includes

'Little Venice' – the prettiest stretch of the Regent's Canal

the Royal Festival Hall, the National Theatre, the Queen Elizabeth Hall, the Hayward Gallery, the National Film Theatre and the Museum of the Moving Image (MOMI), all due for a £200 million facelift.

South Kensington and Earl's Court

This part of west London is a lively cosmopolitan area, useful to stay in if you are attending an exhibition at Earl's Court or Olympia and near to the main museums (Victoria and Albert, Science, Natural History and Geological) and public transport, but some way from theatres and the West End. It is full of reasonably priced small hotels and guesthouses, though you may find the neighbourhood a bit scruffy. Hotels in or around Kensington High Street are nearer the exclusive shops.

The Strand, Charing Cross

The Strand runs from Trafalgar Square, past Charing Cross Station to the Aldwych which adjoins Fleet Street. To the north is Covent Garden, to the south the river. The Strand's most famous landmark is the Savoy Hotel, and the street contains several theatres. At the Aldwych end are Bush House, the BBC's World Service headquarters, and Somerset House, which now houses the Courtauld Institute Galleries. If you listen to the bells at St Clement Danes Church (on weekdays at 09.00, 12.00, 15.00 or 18.00) you will hear the famous 'Oranges and Lemons' nursery rhyme. London's journalists have largely moved out of Fleet Street to Wapping and the Isle of Dogs, but the barristers are still at the Temple and in the four Inns of Court, a series of secluded cobbled courtyards (you can wander around the quadrangles) seemingly divorced from the hustle and bustle of the rest of London. The Royal Courts of Justice occupy an impressive cathedral-like building in the Strand.

Victoria

Numerous small hotels cater for new arrivals whose first view of London is the Station. Busy Victoria Street leads to the Palace of Westminster. Buckingham Palace is to the north, Knightsbridge to the west. It is fairly quiet at night.

West End

The West End is part of Mayfair and Soho, a large area that takes in the shops and department stores in Oxford Street and Regent Street and the theatres around Leicester Square and Covent Garden. North of Oxford Street, Harley Street and Wigmore Street are full of dentists' and doctors' consulting rooms.

Westminster

Seat of Royalty (Buckingham Palace) and Government, Westminster has the Houses of Parliament and Big Ben, Westminster Abbey, Westminster Cathedral, Whitehall and Horse Guards Parade leading up to Trafalgar Square. The area is near the river with good public transport to other parts of the capital. Other sights include the Tate Gallery. A relatively quiet area, especially in the evenings.

Outer London – North

Camden Town

A cosmopolitan residential area somewhat dominated by the crowds who descend at weekends to visit Camden Lock market (see page 80) or to take a boat trip on the Regent's Canal. A short ride by tube into central London. Good shopping for prints, pine furniture and

Buckingham Palace and the Queen Victoria Memorial

books (with many shops open on Sundays). Restaurants (brasseries and Greek) and wine bars. TV AM television studios, London Zoo, Regent's Park, Little Venice and Hampstead are nearby.

Hampstead

On the Northern Line tube into town. Village atmosphere with flats and houses occupied by writers, professionals and bohemians. Narrow pretty streets up behind the station, lots of pubs, restaurants and

boutiques and, at the top of the hill, the wide open spaces of Hampstead Heath. Join the Sunday afternoon kite flyers on Parliament Hill for fine views of the capital. In summer you can swim in the ponds, or watch an open-air concert, while picnicking in the grounds of Kenwood House.

Other Northern Suburbs

Swiss Cottage, down the road from Hampstead, has numerous cosmopolitan restaurants in the Finchley Road and good shopping. Lords, in **St John's Wood**, a short bus ride from Baker Street and near Regent's Park, will be familiar to cricket fans. Further north is **Highgate** (Karl Marx is buried here) and **Islington**, which has a good antique market on Wednesday and Saturday (Camden Passage) and the Sadler's Wells Theatre.

Outer London – South

It is more difficult to get into central London by public transport from most places south of the river.

Greenwich

Directly across the river from Docklands and the Isle of Dogs via the foot tunnel under the Thames, built in 1897 for dockers working in the West India Docks. Things to see include the *Cutty Sark*, National Maritime Museum and the Old Royal Observatory. River boats from Greenwich continue along the river to Westminster.

Richmond

Lies between Hampton Court (see What to See, page 25) and Hammersmith Bridge. The best way to get there is by boat (summer only) from Westminster Pier. Richmond also encompasses Mortlake, Twickenham, Ham, Barnes, Teddington and Kew (with its magnificent Royal Botanic Gardens). You can walk along the river or stroll through the 2,500 acres of Richmond Park.

Richmond Park is just like 'real' countryside except that the deer don't run away!

Other Southern Suburbs

Dulwich and **Blackheath** are affluent residential areas.

WHAT TO SEE

Museums, Exhibitions and Galleries

Among the most popular sights in London are the British Museum, the National Gallery, the Science Museum, Madame Tussaud's, the Tower of London (see page 42) and the Tate Gallery. Three of the major museums, the Science, Natural History and Victoria and Albert, are next to each other in South Kensington, although they are so large you may not find it possible to 'do' more than one or two at a time, and it may be best to stick to one section and 'do' it thoroughly.

Many museums are shut on some, but not necessarily all, public holidays. Most charge admission. Exceptions are indicated in the lists below and include the British Museum, the Tate Gallery, the Bank of England Museum and the National Gallery. Children and Senior Citizens usually pay less and under 5's nothing. Below is a selection out of the hundreds of museums around the capital.

Central London

◆

BANK OF ENGLAND MUSEUM

Bartholomew Lane, EC2

Opened at the end of 1988, this museum tells the story of the 300 years of history of the 'Old Lady of Threadneedle Street', with an exhibition that includes gold bars, banknotes and a video. Free.

Open: Monday to Friday 10.00 to 17.00; Sundays and Bank Holidays in summer 11.00–17.00

Tube: Bank

◆◆◆

BRITISH MUSEUM ✓

Great Russell Street, WC1

One of the biggest and best museums in the world with numerous treasures. Prehistoric Britain, Egyptian mummies, Islamic art, and Greek and Roman antiquities are just a few of the subjects covered. Do not miss the Magna Carta, the Sutton Hoo treasure or the Elgin Marbles. The ethnography collection is in the **Museum of Mankind** in Burlington Gardens. Shop, café and restaurant. Free.

Open: Monday to Saturday 10.00 to 17.00, Sunday 14.30 to 18.00

Tube: Russell Square, Holborn, Tottenham Court Road

◆◆

COURTAULD INSTITUTE GALLERIES

North Block, Somerset House, Strand, WC2

Some of the most exciting French paintings in London are here – with work by Monet, Bonnard, Degas, Seurat and Cézanne. There is also a fine collection of Old Masters. Bookshop and café.

Open: Monday to Saturday 10.00 to 18.00, Sunday 14.00 to 18.00

Tube: Aldwych, Temple, Covent Garden

◆

DESIGN MUSEUM

Butlers Wharf, 28 Shad Thames, SE1

Exhibitions of design and graphics in a modern white building converted from a 1950s warehouse. Magnificent river frontage overlooking Tower Bridge and the City. Run by the Conran Foundation and partly

INNER LONDON

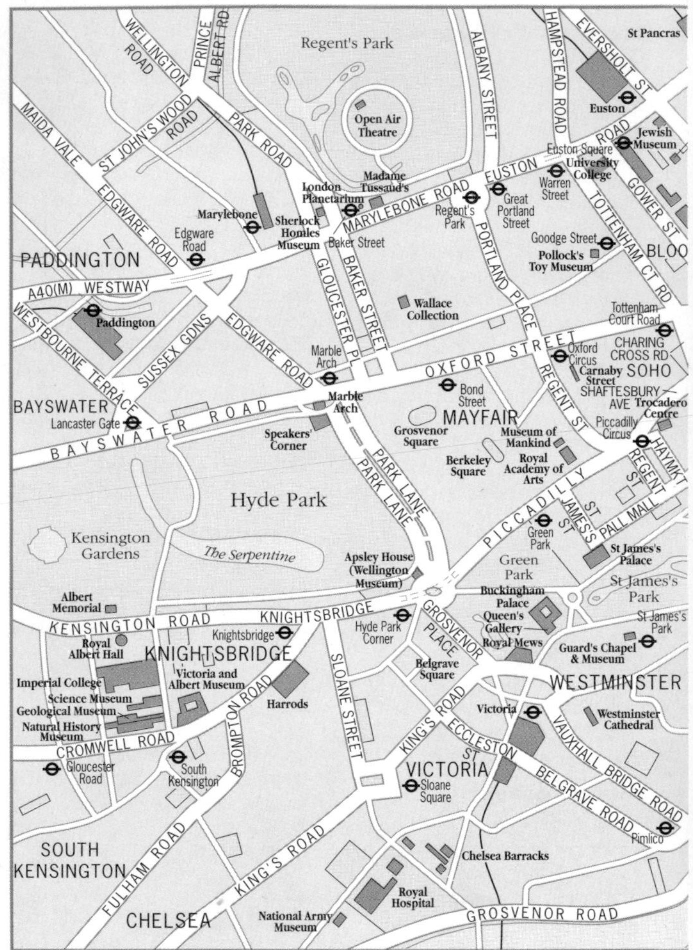

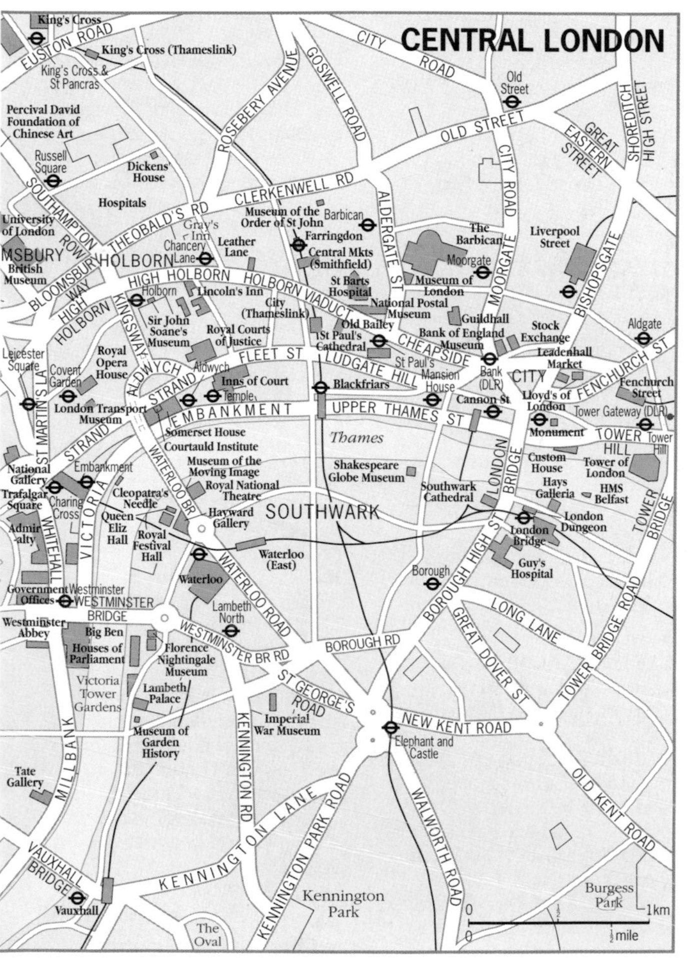
CENTRAL LONDON
King's Cross
EUSTON ROAD
King's Cross (Thameslink)
King's Cross & St Pancras
Percival David Foundation of Chinese Art
Russell Square
Dickens' House
Hospitals
SOUTHAMPTON ROW
University of London
MSBURY
British Museum
BLOOMSBURY WAY
HIGH HOLBORN
HOLBORN
THEOBALD'S RD
Gray's Inn
Chancery Lane
Leather Lane
CLERKENWELL RD
ROSEBERY AVENUE
GOSWELL ROAD
CITY ROAD
OLD STREET
Old Street
GREAT EASTERN STREET
SHOREDITCH HIGH STREET
Museum of the Order of St John
Barbican
Farringdon
Central Mkts (Smithfield)
ALDERSGATE ST
The Barbican
Moorgate
MOORGATE
Liverpool Street
BISHOPSGATE
Museum of London
St Barts Hospital
National Postal Museum
HOLBORN VIADUCT
Holborn
Lincoln's Inn
City (Thameslink)
KINGSWAY
Sir John Soane's Museum
Royal Courts of Justice
Old Bailey
St Paul's Cathedral
Guildhall
Bank of England Museum
Stock Exchange
Aldgate
Leicester Square
Covent Garden
Royal Opera House
ALDWYCH
Aldwych
FLEET ST
LUDGATE HILL
CHEAPSIDE
St Paul's
Mansion House
Bank (DLR)
CITY
Leadenhall Market
FENCHURCH ST
Fenchurch Street
ST MARTIN'S LA
London Transport Museum
STRAND
Inns of Court
Temple
Blackfriars
Cannon St
Lloyd's of London
Tower Gateway (DLR)
EMBANKMENT
UPPER THAMES ST
Monument
TOWER HILL
Tower Hill
Somerset House
Courtauld Institute
Thames
National Gallery
Embankment
WATERLOO BR
Museum of the Moving Image
Royal National Theatre
Shakespeare Globe Museum
LONDON BRIDGE
Custom House
Tower of London
Trafalgar Square
Charing Cross
VICTORIA
Cleopatra's Needle
Southwark Cathedral
Hays Galleria
HMS Belfast
Hayward Gallery
SOUTHWARK
London Dungeon
TOWER BRIDGE
Admiralty
WHITEHALL
Queen Eliz Hall
Royal Festival Hall
London Bridge
Waterloo (East)
BOROUGH HIGH ST
Guy's Hospital
Waterloo
Borough
Government Offices
Westminster
WESTMINSTER BRIDGE
Lambeth North
WATERLOO ROAD
LONG LANE
TOWER BRIDGE ROAD
Westminster Abbey
Big Ben
Houses of Parliament
WESTMINSTER BR RD
BOROUGH RD
GREAT DOVER ST
Florence Nightingale Museum
Victoria Tower Gardens
Lambeth Palace
ST GEORGE'S ROAD
Imperial War Museum
NEW KENT ROAD
Elephant and Castle
Museum of Garden History
KENNINGTON RD
MILLBANK
Tate Gallery
OLD KENT ROAD
KENNINGTON LANE
KENNINGTON PARK ROAD
WALWORTH ROAD
VAUXHALL BRIDGE
Vauxhall
Kennington Park
Burgess Park
The Oval
0
½
1km
0
½ mile

modelled on the Boilerhouse which they leased out in the basement of the Victoria and Albert Museum until 1986.
Open: Tuesday to Sunday 11.30 to 18.30; closed Mondays except Bank Holidays
Tube: Tower Hill or London Bridge (riverboat from Tower Pier)

◆
FLORENCE NIGHTINGALE MUSEUM
2 Lambeth Palace Road, SE1
A small museum dedicated to the life of the Lady of the Lamp, next to St Thomas's Hospital where she founded the first School of Nursing in 1860. Unique collection of memorabilia including the medicine chest and lamp she used during the Crimean War.
Open: Tuesday to Sunday 10.00 to 16.00; closed Mondays
Tube: Waterloo, Westminster

◆
GEOLOGICAL MUSEUM
(part of Natural History Museum) *Cromwell Road, SW7*
Gem stones, rocks and fossils plus an earthquake simulator and video of a volcano, part of 'The Story of the Earth'. Other exhibits include 'Britain before Man', 'Treasures of the Earth', 'Gem Stones' and 'Britain's Offshore Oil and Gas'. Combined ticket with Natural History Museum and linkway through. Films and activities for families.
Open: Monday to Saturday 10.00 to 18.00, Sunday 11.00 to 18.00. Free admission 16.30 to 18.00 (Monday to Friday), 17.00 to 17.50 (weekends and Bank Holidays)
Tube: South Kensington

◆
GUINNESS WORLD OF RECORDS
The Trocadero, Coventry Street, Piccadilly, W1
The first exhibition organised by Guinness. The displays illustrate feats from the *Guinness Book of Records*, one of the world's best-selling books. Fun for anyone interested in world records, this is a colourful exhibition of obscure feats and achievements from the tallest man to the fastest runner. Push-buttons and scale models.
Open: daily 10.00 to 22.00
Tube: Piccadilly Circus, Leicester Square

◆
HAYWARD GALLERY
South Bank Centre, Belvedere Road, SE1
Housed in a purpose-built, modern building, opened in 1968. On the South Bank (next to the National Theatre and the Festival Hall) the gallery has no permanent collection, but it is an important venue for major exhibitions concentrating on the work of 20th-century artists.
Open: daily 10.00 to 18.00 (Tuesday and Wednesday until 20.00), closed between exhibitions
Tube: Waterloo

◆◆
IMPERIAL WAR MUSEUM
Lambeth Road, SE1
Newly redesigned museum, with exhibits never previously displayed. Story of war from Flanders to the Gulf in a triple height exhibition hall with exhibits including aircraft, Polaris missiles and torpedoes.

Quiet recreation – inside the London Brass Rubbing Centre

The building which houses the museum, formerly the original 'Bedlam', Bethlehem Royal Hospital (a lunatic asylum), has been revamped and adapted to include such features as an enormous glazed atrium. Aircraft seem to fly around the room and visitors can roam among the displays. Interactive displays and various themes including the 'Blitz and Trench Experiences' and the 'Post War World'. Free after 16.30 daily.
Open: daily 10.00 to 18.00
Tube: Lambeth North, Elephant and Castle

◆

LONDON BRASS RUBBING CENTRE
St Martin-in-the-Fields Church, Trafalgar Square, WC2
Brass rub to medieval music. Some 70 replica church brasses to choose from – charge. (NB You can also rub brasses at Westminster Abbey – Monday to Saturday 09.00 to 17.00.)
Open: Monday to Saturday 10.00 to 18.00, Sunday 12.00 to 18.00
Tube: Charing Cross, Leicester Square

◆

LONDON DUNGEON
28–34 Tooley Street, SE1
Opposite Hays Galleria and near HMS *Belfast.* Gruesome, dimly lit exhibition of medieval history including the Plague, the Great Fire of London, Theatre of the Guillotine, astrology and witchcraft. Lots of torture and noises. Life-size reconstruction of Pudding Lane. No under 10's on their own.
Open: April to September daily 10.00 to 18.30 (17.30 winter)
Tube: London Bridge

◆◆

LONDON PLANETARIUM

Marylebone Road, NW1

Combined ticket with Madame Tussaud's. Spectacular views of the heavens with shows every 40 minutes. The Astronomers exhibition includes wax figures such as Einstein and Galileo and three-dimensional images of their discoveries. For times of shows tel: 071 486 1121.
Tube: Baker Street

◆◆

LONDON TRANSPORT MUSEUM

The Piazza, Covent Garden, WC2

All sorts of transport from trolley buses to trains housed in the old Flower Market building in the Covent Garden piazza. Lots of things to scramble over, and you can work signals on trains or 'drive' a bus or a tube train. Special events for children and families in the school holidays.
Open: daily, except Xmas, 10.00 to 18.00 (last entry 17.15). Exhibits currently being redisplayed – reopens Jan'94, tel: 071 379 6344 to check.
Tube: Covent Garden

◆◆

MADAME TUSSAUD'S

Marylebone Road, NW1

One of the most popular attractions in London, with life-like wax figures (continuously updated) of famous people including historical figures, film stars, sportsmen and pop stars. Plus the Chamber of Horrors, which includes reconstructions of some grisly and historic crimes. Combined ticket with the Planetarium (see separate entry) next door. Long queues.
Open: Monday to Friday 10.00 to 17.30, Saturday and Sunday 09.30 to 17.30
Tube: Baker Street

MUSEUM OF LONDON

150 London Wall, EC2

The Museum if you are interested in the history of London and Londoners. Open-plan galleries of well-displayed exhibits from pre-historic cave men to a lift from Selfridges department store. Also the Lord

Mayor's State Coach, reconstructed Victorian shops, a 1930s Ford motorcar, an air-raid shelter and a reconstruction of Newgate gaol. One of the highlights (but you may have to queue) is a short re-enactment of the Fire of London. Café. Free after 16.30. *Open:* Tuesday to Saturday 10.00 to 18.00, Sunday 12.00 to 18.00; closed Mondays, except Bank Holidays
Tube: Barbican, St Paul's, Moorgate

◆◆

MUSEUM OF THE MOVING IMAGE (MOMI)

South Bank Centre, SE1
The largest museum in the world devoted to cinema and television, tracing the history of film from the Chinese Shadow Plays of 2000 BC to the latest in optical technology. Watch yourself fly over London, appear in a TV chat show, or

The National Gallery's collections are superb

act in a cowboy film. Shop.
Open: daily 10.00 to 18.00
Tube: Waterloo, Embankment

◆◆◆
NATIONAL GALLERY ✓

Trafalgar Square, WC2
One of the world's finest collections of western European paintings from about 1250 to 1900. The information sheet *A Quick Visit to the National Gallery* highlights 16 masterpieces; and there are quiz sheets for children during the school holidays. The new Sainsbury Wing, with its extra gallery space, also has a shop and a restaurant. Free.
Open: Monday to Saturday 10.00 to 18.00, Sunday 14.00 to 18.00. Wednesdays in July and August open until 20.00
Tube: Charing Cross, Leicester Square

◆◆
NATIONAL PORTRAIT GALLERY
St Martin's Place, WC2
Around 9,000 portraits, arranged chronologically, of famous Britons from the Middle Ages to Princess Diana. Free (charge for some exhibitions).
Open: Monday to Friday 10.00 to 17.00, Saturday 10.00 to 18.00, Sunday 14.00 to 18.00
Tube: Charing Cross, Leicester Square

◆◆◆
NATURAL HISTORY MUSEUM ✓

Cromwell Road, South Kensington, SW7
Unstuffy museum with over 50

million specimens of animals (including insects), plants and fossils. Huge dinosaur skeletons, 'Creepy Crawly' exhibition, videos and an exciting interactive human biology hall. The Geological Museum is now amalgamated with the Natural History Museum, and the two have a combined entrance ticket.
Open: Monday to Saturday 10.00 to 18.00, (Sunday 11.00 to

The Natural History Museum – superb Victorian architecture

18.00). Free admission 16.30 to 18.00 (Monday to Friday), 17.00 to 17.50 (weekends)
Tube: South Kensington

◆
QUEEN'S GALLERY
Buckingham Palace, SW1
A rare chance to see works of art from the Royal Collection, in a former Palace chapel.
Open: (when an exhibition is being held) Tuesday to Saturday 10.00 to 17.00, Sunday 14.00 to 17.00
Tube: Victoria

◆
ROCK CIRCUS
London Pavilion, Piccadilly, W1
An audio animatronic spectacular on two floors with models of the immortals of rock and pop from Buddy Holly to Michael Jackson, plus instruments, authentic settings, spectacular lighting and sound effects. Revolving stage shows.
Open: daily 11.00 to 21.00 (from 12.00 Tuesday; until 22.00 Friday and Saturday), extended hours in summer
Tube: Piccadilly Circus

◆◆
ROYAL ACADEMY OF ARTS
Burlington House, Piccadilly, W1
The home of the Fine Art Society, founded in 1768. Changing exhibitions and famous annual Summer Exhibition (June to August) where you can buy the work of some 1,000 artists. Shop.
Open: daily 10.00 to 18.00
Tube: Piccadilly Circus, Green Park

◆◆◆
SCIENCE MUSEUM ✓
Exhibition Road, South Kensington, SW7
One of the most exciting museums for children. Original press-button Children's Gallery in the basement plus hi-tech 'Launch Pad' on the first floor. Measure your heartbeat or star in your own video. Also Space Gallery, medical history, gallery

of aeroplanes, films and scientific instruments.
Open: Monday to Saturday 10.00 to 18.00, Sunday 11.00 to 18.00
Tube: South Kensington

◆
SHERLOCK HOLMES MUSEUM
221b Baker Street
The famous address of super-sleuth sherlock Holmes his friend Dr Watson. The museum has maintained its Victorian atmosphere, and includes a range of exhibits from the published adventures of Mr Holmes. Shop.
Open: daily 10.00 to 18.00
Tube: Baker Street

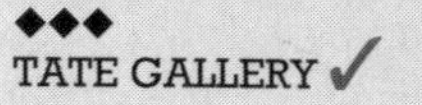

◆◆◆
TATE GALLERY ✓

Millbank, SW1
National collections of British art including 20th-century paintings and sculpture, Turners in the

Clore Gallery, modern prints and changing major exhibitions. Free except for exhibitions. Lunchtime restaurant (closed Sundays) and coffee shop.
Open: Monday to Saturday 10.00 to 17.50, Sunday 14.00 to 17.50
Tube: Pimlico

In 1871 the Cutty Sark beat the world record by sailing from China to England in 107 days. She is now moored at Greenwich

◆◆◆
VICTORIA AND ALBERT MUSEUM (V&A) ✓

South Kensington, SW7; entrances in Cromwell and Exhibition Roads
An outstanding museum of European and Oriental decorative and fine art and design, tracing the history of glass, furniture and jewellery, textiles and dress, from early Christian times to the present day. Exhibitions from around the world, with seven miles of galleries. Also here is a national collection of watercolours, sculpture and Constables, plus exhibitions. Gallery talks 14.30 daily. Restaurant. Donations.
Open: Monday to Saturday 10.00 to 17.50, Sunday 14.30 to 17.50
Tube: South Kensington

Forest Hill

◆
HORNIMAN MUSEUM AND GARDENS
London Road, Forest Hill, SE23
An Art Nouveau museum with a curious mix of exhibits, from stuffed birds to tribal masks. Also musical instruments and aquarium.There is a park with nature trail and good views of London. Changing exhibitions, lectures, and concerts. Café. Free.
Open: Monday to Saturday 10.30 to 17.30, Sunday 14.00 to 17.30
British Rail: Forest Hill (1½ miles east of Dulwich)

Greenwich

◆
CUTTY SARK AND GIPSY MOTH IV
Greenwich Pier, SE10
Two ships moored on the Thames at Greenwich. In 1869 the *Cutty*

The Freud Museum

Sark used to bring in tea from China and wool from Australia and was the fastest sailing clipper afloat. You can explore above and below decks, where an exhibition explains her history. The *Gipsy Moth IV* was the boat used by Francis Chichester on the first single-handed voyage around the world in 1966/67. *Open: Cutty Sark:* April to September 10.00 to 18.00, Sunday 12.00 to 18.00. Closes one hour earlier rest of year. *Gipsy Moth:* April to October only; Monday to Saturday 10.00 to 17.30, Sunday 12.00 to 17.30. *British Rail:* Cannon Street, Waterloo East, Charing Cross and London Bridge to Maze Hill or Greenwich; or boat from Westminster, Charing Cross or Tower Piers; or foot tunnel from Island Gardens (DLR).

◆

NATIONAL MARITIME MUSEUM

Romney Road, Greenwich, SE10
A wonderful museum, devoted to British seafaring, partly housed in England's first Palladian-style house, designed by Inigo Jones. Navigation room with instruments, contemporary ship models, paintings, barges and galleries devoted to Lord Nelson and Captain Cook.
Open: Monday to Saturday 10.00 to 18.00, Sunday 14.00 to 18.00. Closes 17.00 in winter
British Rail: see previous entry

Hampstead

FENTON HOUSE

Windmill Hill, Hampstead Grove, Hampstead, NW3
A William and Mary house built in 1693, with a collection of early musical instruments and porcelain and furniture.
Open: April to October, Saturday, Sunday and Bank Holidays, 11.00 to 18.00, Monday to Wednesday 13.00 to 19.00; also March weekends 14.00 to 18.00
Tube: Hampstead

FREUD MUSEUM

20 Maresfield Gardens, Hampstead, NW3
The imposing red-brick home of Sigmund Freud is now a small museum and research institute containing his furniture including the famous couch, books and collection of antiquities.
Open: Wednesday to Sunday 12.00 to 17.00; closed Mondays and Tuesdays
Tube: Finchley Road

KEATS' HOUSE

Keats Grove, Hampstead, NW3
The Regency house where Keats lived from 1818 to 1820 and where he wrote his finest poetry. Furniture of the period, his bedroom, plus cabinets of letters, manuscripts and relics relating to his friends and family, and the pretty garden in which he wrote *Ode to a Nightingale.* Keats' lover and nurse, Fanny Brawne, lived in the house next door. Voluntary donation.
Open: April to October, Monday to Friday 10.00 to 13.00, 14.00 to 18.00, Saturday 10.00 to 13.00, 14.00 to 17.00, Sunday 14.00 to 17.00. November to March, Monday to Friday 13.00 to 17.00, weekends as above
Tube: Hampstead

KENWOOD HOUSE

The Iveagh Bequest
Hampstead Lane, Hampstead, NW3
A beautiful Robert Adam mansion overlooking the Heath, with weekend open-air lakeside jazz and symphony concerts. Lord Iveagh gave the mansion and his collection of paintings to the nation in 1927. Magnificent English 18th-century paintings, a Rembrandt self-portrait and Vermeer's *Lady Playing the Guitar.* Free. Restaurant, café.
Open: April to September, 10.00 to 18.00. Closes two hours earlier from October to March
Tube: Walk across the Heath from Hampstead tube; or take the 210 bus from Archway or Golders Green

Hampton Court – Richmond on Thames

◆◆◆
HAMPTON COURT PALACE ✓

East Molesey, Surrey
Bought by Cardinal Wolsey in 1514, this 1,000-roomed palace is richly furnished with tapestries, and heavily panelled with gilded ceilings. It was enlarged by Henry VIII, who built the Great Hall, and again altered by Wren in 1689. Opulent state rooms, tapestries and famous paintings. Set in magnificent formal gardens.
Open: Monday 10.15 to 18.00, Tuesday to Sunday 09.30 to 18.00; closes 16.30 in winter. Gardens open dawn to half an hour before dusk
British Rail: Hampton Court (also river trips from Westminster Pier, Richmond and Kingston)

Twickenham

MARBLE HILL HOUSE

Richmond Road, Twickenham
Palladian villa built in the18th century as a summer residence for George II's mistress, Henrietta Howard, later the Countess of Suffolk. Gilded carvings and oil paintings. Landscaped gardens sweeping down to the Thames with concerts on Sunday evenings in July and August. Free.
Open: daily; April to September 10.00 to 18.00 (until 16.00 rest of year)
British Rail: Waterloo to St Margaret's; or river launches in summer from Westminster Pier to Richmond then by bus.

The entrance to Hampton Court Palace, flanked by heraldic 'King's Beasts'

Landmarks, Cathedrals and Monuments

HMS *BELFAST*

Morgan's Lane, off Tooley Street, SE1

Huge Royal Navy cruiser from World War II. Admire it from the river (good views in front of Hays Galleria), or clamber over the seven decks to see the gun turrets and galleys.

Open: daily, mid March to October 10.00 to 17.20; rest of year until 16.00

Tube: Tower Hill, Monument or London Bridge; Tower Gateway (Docklands Light Railway); or ferry from Tower Pier

BIG BEN

Clock Tower, Palace of Westminster, SW1

Probably named after Sir Benjamin Hall, who commissioned the enormous bell and completed work on the 316 ft (96m) tower in 1859. To climb the tower you must be in a group, be aged over 11 and have a letter of permission from your MP or embassy.

Tube: Westminster

BUCKINGHAM PALACE

The Mall, SW1

The Queen's residence; she is at home when the Royal Standard is flying. You can only go in during August and September, or if invited to a State banquet or a garden party. But you can watch the Changing of the Guard at 11.30 from early April to mid-August daily and in winter on alternate days, which is free.

Completed in 1882, the Law Courts are a superb example of Victorian Gothic architecture

Open: Palace daily August to 1 October 09.30–17.30.

Tube: Victoria, St James's Park, Green Park

HOUSES OF PARLIAMENT

St Margaret Street, SW1

The Palace of Westminster includes the House of Commons and the House of Lords. You can visit the Strangers' Gallery while the House is sitting; queue outside St Stephen's entrance. Call the Public Information Office (tel: 071 219 4272) for details. Free.

Tube: Westminster

LAW COURTS

Strand, WC2

The Royal Courts of Justice date

from 1874. Watch from the public galleries in 60 courts. Free.
Open to visitors: weekday sessions, 10.30 to 13.00 and 14.00 to 16.30
Tube: Temple, Aldwych

◆
LLOYD'S OF LONDON
1 Lime Street, EC3
International insurance market housed in an eye-catching, modern, rocket-like building designed by Richard Rogers. Exhibition depicting 300 years in the City and a viewing gallery of the Underwriting Room. Free.
Open: Monday to Friday 09.30 to 12.30, 14.00 to 16.00; closed weekends
Tube: Bank, Monument, Aldgate

◆
MONUMENT
Monument Street, EC3
Fluted hollow Doric column built by Sir Christopher Wren to commemorate the Great Fire of London. The view from the platform, just below the golden urn (311 steps up), is somewhat obscured by office blocks.
Open: April to September, Monday to Friday 09.00 to 18.00, Saturday and Sunday 14.00 to 18.00, October to March, Monday to Saturday 09.00 to 16.00, closed Sunday
Tube: Monument

◆
OLD BAILEY
Newgate Street, EC4
Central Criminal Court.
Open: Public Gallery Monday to Friday 10.30 to 13.00 and 14.00 to 16.00 when court is sitting; closed weekends
Tube: St Paul's

Construction of the huge Thames Barrier began in 1974

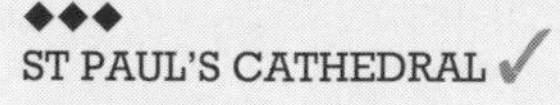

◆◆◆
ST PAUL'S CATHEDRAL ✓

Ludgate Hill, EC4
Largest and most famous church in the City, the fourth or fifth on the site, built by Sir Christopher Wren. Burial place of Nelson and the Duke of Wellington. Splendid interior views from the Whispering Gallery. The dome is more than 600 steps up, but once there the views are spectacular. Guided tours (except Sundays). Free, but donations requested. A charge is made for the crypt,

galleries and ambulatory.
Open: Monday to Saturday 07.15 to 18.00; Sunday: services only
Tube: St Paul's

◆

SOUTHWARK CATHEDRAL

London Bridge, SE1

Just across London Bridge from the City, a fine Gothic building with the Harvard Chapel dedicated to the founder of Harvard University. Burial place of Shakespeare's brother. Free.
Tube: London Bridge; or riverbus to London Bridge

10 DOWNING STREET

Off Whitehall, SW1

The official residence of the Prime Minister; the Chancellor of the Exchequer lives next door at No. 11. The buildings themselves have unpretentious Georgian façades. The world-famous street has a barrier at the end so you cannot get close.
Tube: Westminster, Charing Cross

THAMES BARRIER

Unity Way, Woolwich SE18

Between the Blackwall Tunnel and the Woolwich Ferry. The world's largest movable flood barrier stretching 1700 ft (520m) across the Thames to stop water pouring in on London. It consists of 10 impressive separate

movable steel gates which when raised stand as high as a five-storey building, as wide as the opening in Tower Bridge and weigh more than a Naval destroyer. Visitors' centre.
Open: Monday to Friday 10.00 to 17.00; Saturday, Sunday and Bank Holidays 10.30 to 17.30
British Rail: Charlton Station (then 15 mins walk); or river boat (1hr 15 mins from central London, 25 mins from Greenwich)

TOWER BRIDGE

Tower Bridge, SE1
Opened in 1894, it took eight years to build. Splendid views from the enclosed high-level walkway across the top of the towers (lift). Various exhibitions, plus Victorian engine rooms with the original steam pumps. The huge bascules are raised to let big ships through.
Open: daily; April to October 10.00 to 18.30, November to March 10.00 to 16.45
Tube: Tower Hill, London Bridge

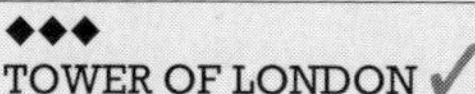

TOWER OF LONDON ✓

Tower Hill, EC3
William I's Tower, built on a vantage point on the river to defend the city from invaders. Its chequered past has included a prison (for the likes of Guy Fawkes and Sir Walter Ralegh), the Royal Mint and the Royal Observatory. Now the home of the Crown Jewels. The Keep is one of the earliest fortifications in western Europe. Galleries of armour and torture instruments. Yeoman Warders (popularly known as Beefeaters) wear Tudor uniform. The nightly 700-year-old Ceremony of the Keys can be watched only by written application to the Constable's Office, Queen's House, HM Tower of London, EC3N 4AB.
Open: March to October, Monday to Saturday 09.30 to 18.00, Sunday 10.00 to 18.00; November to February, Monday to Saturday only, 09.30 to 17.00
Tube: Tower Gateway, or Tower Hill (Docklands Light Railway)

◆◆◆

WESTMINSTER ABBEY ✓

Parliament Square, SW1
Famous kings and queens crowned and buried in the vaults, including Elizabeth I. Coronation Chair, Poet's Corner and the Stone of Scone. There is also a brass rubbing centre.
Open: Nave and cloisters (free), Sunday between services, weekdays 08.00 to 18.00 (19.45 Wednesdays). Royal Chapels (charge). Monday to Friday 09.00 to 16.45, Saturday 09.00 to 14.45 and 15.45 to 17.45. Also visit the Chapter House, Pyx Chamber, Abbey Museum and College Gardens
Tube: St James Park, Westminster

◆◆

WESTMINSTER CATHEDRAL

Ashley Place, SW1
Behind Victoria Street. The largest and most important Roman Catholic Church in England. Fine marble and mosaics. Free. You can take a lift to the top of the 273ft (83m) campanile (charge).
Open: bell tower, April to October 09.30 to 17.00, cathedral all year 07.00 to 20.00
Tube: Victoria

Tower Bridge is beautiful at any time of day

Parks, Gardens and Cemeteries

Few cities in the world can boast as many parks and open spaces, from the acres of Royal Parks, originally the hunting grounds of the Royal Palaces, to tiny grassed-over squares, a haven from the bustle of London.

Central London

◆

HOLLAND PARK

Behind Kensington High Street, a pleasant, almost suburban park, with many nannies pushing perambulators. Orangery with changing exhibitions, open-air theatre and summer concerts.
Tube: Holland Park, High Street Kensington

HYDE PARK

Once a hunting forest belonging to Henry VIII. Wide open spaces characterise Hyde Park, which is enclosed by Bayswater, Knightsbridge and Park Lane, and has the Serpentine Lake at its centre. It is the largest of the central London parks and is home to a surprisingly large range of birds. Hire a horse to ride down Rotten Row, take out a boat, swim if you can brave the British weather, or listen to the soapbox orators at Speaker's Corner.
Tube: Hyde Park Corner, Marble Arch

KENSINGTON GARDENS

Merges with Hyde Park at the bridge over the Serpentine. The formal gardens of Kensington Palace, opposite the Royal Albert Hall. Do not miss the statue of Peter Pan, the Round Pond, the Orangery, feeding the ducks or the Albert Memorial.
Tube: High Street Kensington, Queensway

REGENT'S PARK

The park with the most to offer: the Zoo, the open-air theatre

A detail from the Albert Memorial

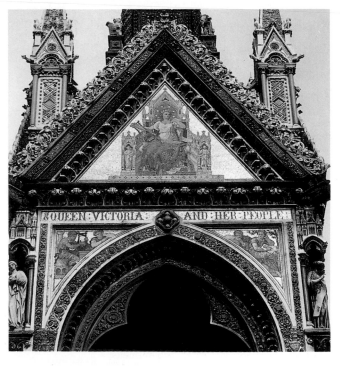

(Shakespeare), a boating lake and swings for children, rowing boats for adults, cafés and Queen Mary's splendid rose garden. Alongside the park runs the Outer Circle, which is lined with elegant, columned Nash terraces.
Tube: Baker Street (Regent's Park, Camden Town for Zoo)

◆
ST JAMES'S PARK
The oldest of the Royal Parks with a lake and good views of Buckingham Palace. Alongside the Mall it joins up with Green Park, which runs along Piccadilly. Once a favourite retreat of Charles II.
Tube: Green Park, St James's Park

Outer London

◆◆
GREENWICH PARK
Overlooking the Thames with the Old Royal Observatory, original home of Greenwich Mean Time, on the crest of the ridge, and the National Maritime Museum at the bottom. This is one of the most historic of the Royal Parks, laid out by Le Nôtre for Charles II in 1662. There is a hollow oak, reputedly danced around by Elizabeth I, the deer enclosure, a boating pool and a playground.
Tube: Docklands Light Railway from Bank to Island Gardens, then subway under the Thames; or British Rail from Charing Cross, Waterloo East, London Bridge and Cannon Street (weekdays only) to Maze Hill or Greenwich; or river boats from Westminster, Charing Cross and Tower Piers

◆
HAMPSTEAD HEATH
High open space in north London, with splendid views from Jack Straw's Castle pub and Parliament Hill, which is popular with kite flyers, Sunday afternoon walkers, dogs and joggers. Bank holiday fairground. Playground and bathing ponds. Wooded walk to Kenwood House (see separate entry) where there are lakeside concerts on summer weekend evenings.
Tube: Hampstead, Belsize Park

◆
HIGHGATE CEMETERY
Swain's Lane, N6
Last resting place of, among others, Karl Marx. Western side by guided tour only (weekends on the hour, and summer weekdays at 12.00, 14.00 and 16.00). Photos only with permit.
Open: Eastern side, April to October daily 10.00 to 17.00, rest of year until 16.00
Tube: Archway; or bus 210, C11, 143, 271

◆◆◆
KEW GARDENS (ROYAL BOTANIC GARDENS)
World-famous Royal Botanic Gardens, south of the river, with plant houses: alpines, palms, and a tropical conservatory. Splendid trees and flowering shrubs. You can have tea in the Orangery. Kew Palace is furnished in George III style.
Open: daily 09.30 to between 16.00 and 18.30 or 20.00 on Sundays depending on season
Tube: Kew Gardens; or British Rail to Kew Bridge; or buses 65, 27. Boats from Westminster Pier (summer)

Red deer stag – imposing resident of Richmond Park

RICHMOND PARK

In southwest London, 2,500 acres used as a hunting ground by Charles I, with deer, ancient oak trees and ponds. Horses for hire, riverside walks, cycle tracks and several magnificent residences.
Tube/British Rail: Richmond

SYON PARK GARDENS

In Brentford, Middlesex.
Around 55 acres of gardens that include a lake, rose garden, butterfly house, vintage cars, Great Conservatory and sculptures. The 16th-century house, which was remodelled by Robert Adam, is the London home of the Duke of Northumberland.
Open: House, April to September, Wednesday to Sunday and Bank Holidays 11.00 to 17.00, Sunday only in October; closed November to March. Gardens open daily year round 10.00 to 18.00 (17.00 winter); also Butterfly House 10.00 to 17.00, and the Heritage Motor Museum 10.00 to 17.30.
Tube: Gunnersbury; then bus 237 or 267 to Brent Lea Gate

PEACE AND QUIET

Wildlife and Countryside in and around London

by Paul Sterry

At first glance, the centre of London, like many other capitals, may not seem the most suitable place to observe wildlife: house sparrows, starlings and pigeons are often the only creatures to be seen. However, visit the right locations or travel as little as 30 miles (48km) from the centre and a fascinating array of plants and animals can be discovered. Even the central Royal Parks, such as St James's Park and Hyde Park, have squirrels and woodpigeons, and the presence of tame birds on their lakes lures wild birds into these rather unnatural settings. The same is true of London Zoo, set in Regent' s Park; sometimes it is difficult to tell the captive creatures from the wild ones. Examples of most habitats typical of southern England lie within a day's journey of the capital. The remains of once great hunting forests can be found at Windsor and Epping and freshwater habitats from lakes to rivers, abound many being associated with the course of the Thames, which bisects the city. Even specialised and wildlife-rich habitats such as heathland and chalk grassland lie close to the city and are well worth a visit.

The Royal Parks of Central London

In the heart of the capital, the Royal Parks provide a haven of comparative solitude. The vegetation of these parks is almost entirely dictated by man and the wildlife often exotic and introduced, but the presence of animals which are tolerant of humans often draws in more appealing wild species.

St James's Park is home to ubiquitous house sparrows which are bold enough to feed from people's hands, and flocks of feral pigeons come and go from nearby Trafalgar Square. A surprising resident of both this park and nearby Hyde Park is the woodpigeon. It is not persecuted here as it is in the rest of Britain and consequently has become extremely confiding.

Both St James's Park and Hyde Park contain lakes and ponds and, of these, the Serpentine is the most interesting. The lake winds its way along the northern side of Hyde Park and it contains numerous fish which are food for fish-eating birds. To explore the Serpentine, park on the northern shore just off The Ring, near Serpentine Bridge. Walk around the edge of the water and around the Long Water as well. Look for moorhens and coots among the tufted ducks, mallards and Canada geese. Grey herons are sometimes seen early in the morning and great crested grebes nest on the island near the Boat House. In spring, pairs of grebes perform elaborate displays on the water prior to mating and nest building.

Small patches of woodland in Hyde Park and adjoining Kensington Gardens sometimes harbour migrant birds such as spotted flycatchers, redstarts and willow warblers in spring, while jays are resident throughout the year. They will often come and investigate those visitors who seem a likely source of food, often with bold grey squirrels in hot pursuit. These charming animals were introduced from North America, but have adapted extremely well to British woodlands and urban environments. Grey squirrels are fascinating creatures to watch as they dextrously use their paws to eat, but be careful not to get too close because they can, and do, bite if provoked.

Richmond Park

Lying just south of the Thames in west London, Richmond Park is the most 'natural' and largest of the London Royal Parks and without doubt the one which holds the most wildlife interest. Famous for its deer, which are numerous and obligingly tame, the park is an enclave of attractive, rolling countryside set among the sprawling suburbs, and is popular with Londoners and visitors alike.

Richmond Park has ponds, open grassland with scattered trees and areas of more mature woodland. Rhododendron thickets provide a wonderful flowering display in June which attracts the admiration of both visitors and pollinating insects.

Insects are not confined to the flowers, however, and a careful search of the foliage may reveal the amazingly colourful rhododendron leafhopper, as well as oak bush crickets and speckled bush crickets.

Despite the houses and tower blocks which surround and almost overlook the park, the birdlife is surprisingly rich. Kestrels are frequently seen hovering over the grassland on the look-out for scurrying voles, and spotted flycatchers, great spotted woodpeckers, tits, nuthatches and treecreepers can be found in the wooded areas. The ponds sometimes attract interesting wildfowl and reed warblers have been known to attempt to nest around their margins.

As soon as you enter the park, you cannot fail to notice the deer. Sizeable herds of both red and fallow deer roam the grassland, and because they are forever confined within its boundaries, they are easily seen throughout the year. In the autumn, the red deer in particular are at their most spectacular: dominant stags with huge sets of antlers gather together their harems of hinds, and bellow warnings at other males. Visit the park on a cold October morning and you will be treated to the memorable sound of stags 'belling', their breath steaming in the damp air, and the sight of crashing antlers as rivals do battle.

For good views of the deer, park in designated spots at Robin Hood Gate and walk towards Pen Ponds. They are usually close to the road and are easiest to see on the north side where the grassland is more open. However, the lusher vegetation to the south provides a more appropriate setting. If you find a young deer in spring, leave it alone: otherwise the mother may desert.

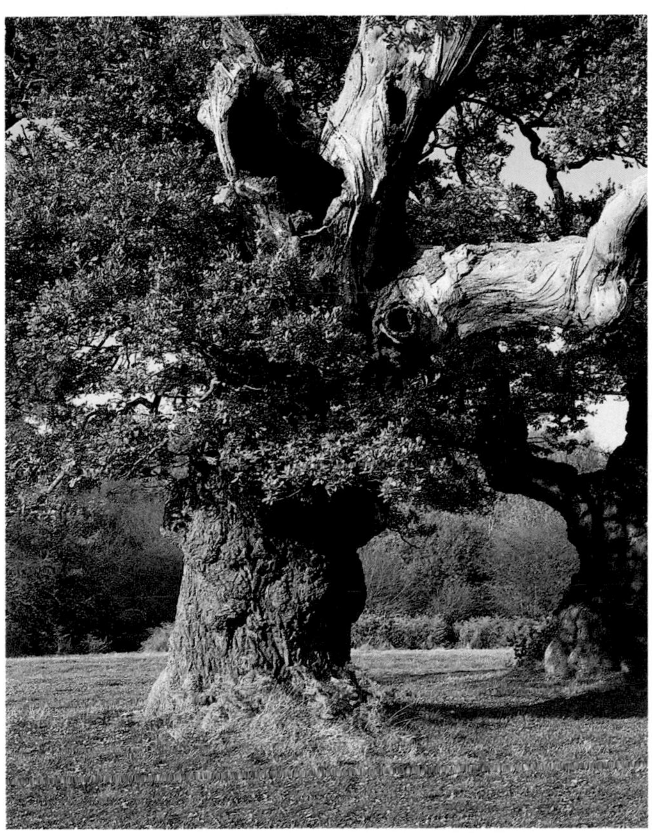

One of the ancient oaks in Windsor Great Park

Windsor Great Park and Virginia Water

Despite its popularity, Windsor Great Park, which lies to the west of London, is still a fine example of mature English parkland. The landscape is dotted with stately trees and, nestling within its woodlands, the tranquil surface of Virginia Water reflects its leafy surroundings like a mirror. Throughout the park, ancient oaks with gnarled and twisted trunks and withered looking branches play host to large numbers of insects, including several rare species of beetles not known elsewhere in the country. During July and August, purple hairstreak butterflies flit among the foliage, while at ground level, speckled woods and small tortoiseshells are common.

If you are lucky, you might see a purple hairstreak butterfly in Windsor Great Park

The birds also benefit from the variety and age of the trees. Diminutive lesser spotted woodpeckers feed unobtrusively throughout the park, while green and great spotted woodpeckers are conspicuous and noisy, making them easier to locate. Kestrels hunt over the open ground and, during the summer months, hobbies are occasionally seen as they scythe through the air in search of swallows and house martins.

The woodlands around Virginia Water are renowned for being one of the most reliable places in the counties around London to see hawfinches. Normally rather shy and elusive birds, hawfinches are frequently found in the vicinity of hornbeam trees close to the car park, and their massive, seed-cracking bills give them an unmistakable silhouette when perched high in a tree.

For a lovely circular walk, park either in the large car park beside the A30 or in the car park beside the A329 at Blacknest. From the shores of the lake Canada geese and ducks can be seen; this is the best place in England to see mandarin ducks. Carp, tench and other fish can be seen spawning from the bridges in the early summer. In October, when the leaves and seeds of most trees fall to the ground, and thereafter for the rest of the winter, chaffinches, bramblings and the occasional hawfinch can be seen feeding on the woodland floor.

During the winter months, this variety of birds is sometimes joined by small numbers of winter visitors such as scaup, goldeneye and smew. These are particularly easy to see as the water begins to freeze because the birds become concentrated as the area of open water reduces.

The Surrey Heaths

Lying to the southwest of London, the landscape of Surrey varies from mature woodland to chalk grassland. Above all, however, it is the open heathland for which the county is best known and, despite being so close to the capital, there are still areas, such as Chobham Common, which have escaped housing development. The heathers (from which the habitat gets its name) and the gorse are the glory of the heathlands and, from June to August, turn the landscape into seas of yellows and purples.

Although heathlands may look natural, their appearance is actually due to generations of tree clearance by man. The resulting nutrient-poor, acidic soils have an extremely specialised flora, with ling, bell heather, cross-leaved heath and gorse predominating, interspersed with tussocks of the characteristic purple moorgrass. In wetter areas, beautiful yellow spikes of bog asphodel grow among the carpet of *Sphagnum* moss, and carnivorous sundew plants digest insects caught on their sticky leaves.

Heathlands are renowned for their spiders, misty autumn mornings highlighting the tell-tale webs and strands of silk with dew. Insects also abound and colourful emperor moths are on the wing in March and April, while July and August are the months for grayling and silver-studded blue butterflies and numerous species of dragonfly and damselfly. Among the low vegetation, mottled grasshoppers hop to safety and bog bush crickets clamber among the cross-leaved heath.

The insect life supports a variety of birds, with stonechats and pipits being particularly conspicuous. Among the larger clumps of gorse, the more secretive Dartford warbler, long since extinct in its place of discovery in Kent, scolds intruders into its territory.

Emperor moths are big and spectacular and not uncommon on heathlands in spring

Although they prefer to skulk in the cover of vegetation, during March and April, males often perch aloft on the tops of gorse spikes, singing for all they are worth.

To visit Chobham Common, park in one of the car parks off the Chobham Road (B383) near Chertsey. Thursley Common is another fine example of southern heathland. Park on the west side of the common, which lies between Farnham and Haslemere, off the A287. Headley Heath has a car park to the west of the B2033 near Leatherhead.

Reservoirs

Vast quantities of water are consumed by Londoners. To quench this thirst, numerous reservoirs have been built around the outskirts of the city, these benefiting not only the human population but also large numbers of birds. These in turn lure birdwatchers, who find the variety of species and numbers of birds they offer as good as, if not better than, many rural areas. Most notable and easily accessible of the reservoirs is Staines, situated under the flight path of many of the jets which leave Heathrow. Although the noise may detract from some people's enjoyment, it certainly seems to do little to upset the birds, who carry on feeding regardless. From the central causeway which separates the two halves of the reservoir, huge numbers of ducks can be seen during the winter months, with unusual birds such as red-necked grebe and black-throated diver being recorded in most years. Black-throated divers are large water birds which swim low in the water. Although more usually associated with coastal waters, they regularly turn up inland on areas of water with lots of fish. Black-throated divers are superficially similar to cormorants but lack the hooked-tip to the bill of this species.

If the water is very low, green sandpipers might stop off to feed in muddy reservoir bottoms

From March to May, Staines Reservoir is a good spot to watch for passage migrants such as sand martins, swallows, swifts and black terns. Rarities such as white-winged black terns and whiskered terns appear occasionally and the list of unusual birds is not confined to water-loving species.

Every now and then, the water authorities have to drain one or other of the reservoirs in order to remove the build-up of silt.

This rich expanse of mud, teeming with small invertebrates, attracts waders such as dunlins and redshanks. To visit Staines Reservoir, park in one of the residential roads off Town Lane – this heads north from the A30 to the west of the reservoir – and walk to the causeway. Brent Reservoir is another good spot to visit. It lies near the junction of the North Circular Road and Edgware Road in West Hendon. Park off Church Lane.

The North Downs and Box Hill

Within easy reach of London, the North Downs, a long ridge of chalk running east to west through Surrey, provides fabulous views over rolling English countryside. The North Downs Way provides long-distance walks, but for those with less time to spare, the wildlife and scenery of Box Hill Country Park near Dorking is particularly rewarding. Although the park suffers a lot from public pressure, the range of plants and animals within its boundaries is immense. Centuries of woodland clearance and sheep grazing have combined to produce the close-cropped grassland so typical of chalky soils. On this land, known as 'downland', constant nibbling by sheep and rabbits has encouraged a rich diversity of flowering plants which would otherwise be crowded out by the grasses. During the summer months, yellow rattle, marjoram, thyme, sainfoin, kidney vetch and knapweeds provide a

Yellow rattle – a showy plant of downland in early summer

kaleidoscope of colour, and attract insects such as hoverflies, burnet moths, and butterflies including silver-spotted skipper, common blue and chalkhill blue.

In southern England, orchids are the real botanical speciality of chalk downland, with many colourful and extraordinary species being found around Box Hill. Purple spikes of fragrant orchids and the aptly named pyramidal orchid grow alongside the diminutive greenish-yellow plants of musk orchids, while where the scrub provides a degree of shade, common twayblades and man orchids can sometimes be found. Many of the downland invertebrates are also unique to the chalky soils, and snails are often abundant, the calcium providing building materials for their shells. Humbug-like shells of white-lipped and brown-lipped snails are conspicuous, while immense edible snails, introduced to Britain by the Romans, are best seen on damp days among the scrub.

On many slopes on the North downs, scrub and woodland still persist. Box Hill gains its name from the box tress which predominate in some areas, but elder and yew are also common. To find Box Hill Country Park car park, follow signs from the A24 just to the north of Dorking or from the A25 between Dorking and Reigate. Other superb areas of downland can be found at Ranmore Common. The car park is located on the minor road which runs from Dorking to East Horsley. The area is particularly well known for the wide range of butterflies that can be found during spring and summer.

The Thames Estuary

On its journey from London to the North Sea, the Thames fans out to form an extensive estuary bordered on the north by Essex and on the south by Kent. Although at times bleak and forbidding, and often industrialised, this habitat is the winter home to thousands of birds and a nursery ground for many commercially important species of fish. Access to the marshes is often difficult, but at Two-Tree Island near Southend in Essex and from Cliffe to High Halstow in Kent good views of the mudflats and their teeming birdlife can be had.

Much of coastal Kent and Essex is protected from floods and gales by sea walls, and to the naturalist both the landward and the seaward sides are of interest. Inland, the coastal marshes are grazed by cattle and are breeding grounds for redshank, snipe and yellow wagtail in the summer, while in the winter, short-eared owls and hen harriers hunt for small mammals. Hen harriers are graceful birds of prey that feed by quartering the ground. Both sexes have a conspicuous white rump. The plumage of the male is grey while that of the female is brown.

The vast areas of mud and silt which the Thames has deposited over the centuries become exposed at low tide and provide a rich feeding ground for birds. Shelduck dabble in the shallow water for small molluscs, while brent geese, visitors from Arctic Russia, alternate between feeding grounds in the creeks and the close-cropped fields behind the sea walls. Huge numbers of dunlin, knot, grey plover, redshank, curlew and godwit probe the mud for lugworms and molluscs, taking to the wing in tight flocks at the slightest disturbance.

Northward Hill is an RSPB reserve which protects part of the north Kent marshes as well as oak woodland. It lies northeast of Rochester and can be reached on Northwood Road from High Halstow village. Grey

Marshes such as this one in Kent are excellent for birds

herons and nightingales breed here and long-eared owls are seen in winter.

On the Isle of Sheppey is Elmley, another RSPB reserve. A signposted track heads east from the A249, 1 mile north of Kingsferry Bridge. There are grazing marshes and freshwater scrapes here which attract large numbers of waders and wildfowl, especially during the winter.

Epping Forest

Only a short distance from the centre of London, Epping Forest is an extensive area of ancient woodland with wide forest rides. Sadly, it no longer harbours the deer which once provided sport for kings, the disturbance caused by increased public pressure having driven them away. The decline in tree management has also had an adverse effect on the diversity of the forest's wildlife, especially its birds and mammals. Despite this, however, Epping Forest still has magnificent trees and is a wonderful escape from the city for both the casual stroller and those more interested in observing the plant and animal life of the woodland.

Epping Forest. It is difficult to believe that this great tract of ancient woodland is right on London's doorstep

During the winter months, flocks of redpolls, occasionally joined by small numbers of siskins, feed among the high branches of the trees. The flocks often form loose associations with blue tits, coal tits, long-tailed tits and goldcrests, whose high-pitched calls attract the attention of the observer. Since the trees lack leaves at this time of year, following the movements of the birds is comparatively easy. Winter is also the best season to observe the hawfinches of Epping Forest which, as elsewhere in Britain, are generally associated with hornbeam trees. Among European passerines, their massive bill is the only one powerful enough to crack the tree's hard seeds and the loud cracking sound can sometimes even help locate the birds. The buds burst into leaf in April and May just as many migrant birds are arriving from Africa.

Whitethroats, blackcaps and willow warblers are common songsters, and colourful redstarts flit amongst the dappled branches. As hole-nesting birds, redstarts benefit from the holes left in the tree trunks by fallen branches and ancient pollards but they often compete for nest sites with nuthatches and woodpeckers, who have similar preferences. Epping Forest lies northwest of Loughton. There are several car parks off the A11(T) as well as on minor roads through the forest. The Conservation Centre at High Beach provides information about the Forest and its long history of association with man. The area with the most wildlife interest is in Great Monk Wood. Woodland birds, butterflies and fungi are numerous.

The Thames

Although its role in the life of the city has dwindled over the centuries, the Thames is still a focal point and has much to offer the visitor. Beyond Docklands, the river opens out to form the vast Thames Estuary which is the haunt of thousands of wintering birds, while up-river towards Henley it gradually becomes more attractive as waterside vegetation and lush agricultural land appear along its banks. Once so polluted that no life survived in the waters that flowed through London, the Thames is now undergoing a slow process of being cleaned up and fish are beginning to recolonise. A variety of birds can also be seen along its course in central London, the most conspicuous being black-headed gulls, which are present for most of the year except the height of summer. Flocks of these noisy birds often include herring gulls or even common gulls, all of which commute between the Thames and London's many reservoirs and parkland lakes.

As the banks of the Thames become more rural, kingfishers occasionally fly by in a dazzling flash of blue and red and it is possible to see graceful mute swans more and more frequently.

These stately birds are considered Crown property and have benefited from the protection this has provided. In the spring, large nests of twigs and grasses are built among the riverside vegetation and are fiercely guarded by the male bird, which is known as a cob.
Along the course of the Thames from Wraysbury near Heathrow to Reading, there is a mosaic of hundreds of gravel pits.
To explore the network of gravel pits around Wraysbury, explore the minor road around Horton, Wraysbury, Datchet and Hythe End to the west of the M25. There are extensive gravel pit workings around Theale, which lies to the east of Reading. Explore the minor roads around Burghfield, Theale and Sheffield Bottom.
Where these gravel pits have not yet filled with water, they provide the ideal conditions for one of Britain's scarcest breeding waders. Little-ringed plovers lay their camouflaged eggs on the pebbly ground where they are almost impossible to spot. Adult birds, with their yellow eye-rings, are also inconspicuous as they quietly incubate the eggs until the young hatch.

Freshwater Habitats

Less than 25 miles (40km) north of central London, the valleys of the rivers Chess and Lea offer a rich variety of natural freshwater habitats which contrast markedly with the formal appearance of the ponds and lakes in the city's parks.
With both flowing rivers and still waters of marshes and lakes, the birdlife is fascinating throughout the year and from May to August colourful flowers catch the eye. The River Chess is an attractive, shallow river which between Rickmansworth and Chorley is bordered with rich waterside vegetation. Metallic-blue damselflies and mayflies dance around the bushes and family parties of mute swans regally paddle up and down, in places such as Chenies becoming quite tame. Patches of thick vegetation sometimes harbour breeding sedge warblers and overhanging branches serve as convenient perches for colourful kingfishers. During the winter months, small numbers of green sandpipers, easily recognised in flight by their white rumps, feed along the river margins. They also frequent the margins of gravel pits and man-made lakes such as Stocker's Lake near Rickmansworth.
Further east, the Lea Valley also holds interesting freshwater habitats. The RSPB's reserve at Rye House Marsh near Hoddesdon has a public birdwatching hide overlooking an interesting area of marsh. Both reed and sedge warblers sing from the cover of the reeds during May and June while common terns, which breed on man-made rafts in the reserve's pools, scream overhead.
During migration time, swallows, martins and black terns pass through the area and a wide selection of waders such as green and common sandpipers, redshank, ruff and little-ringed plovers put in brief appearances. During the winter

months, the reserve is frequented by good numbers of wildfowl, gulls and waders, such as snipe and jack snipe. Rye House Marsh lies to the east of Hoddesdon in Hertfordshire and there is a car park opposite Rye House railway station. The Old River Lea is another good wetland area and is especially rich in dragonflies. It can be reached by crossing footbridges from Waltham Abbey in Hertfordshire. There are numerous gravel pits to the north of nearby Cheshunt.

Water rail – retiring inhabitant of marshes and watersides

Kew Gardens

An entrance fee allows access to the world-famous Royal Botanic Gardens at Kew, which have been open to the public since 1841. To anyone interested in botany, the gardens are a paradise, containing plants from all over the world, and with over 30,000 species and varieties of plant on display, Kew provides an endless source of interest. Flowers are grown both outdoors and indoors within elaborate showpiece greenhouses, so there is plenty to see all year round. Spring, however, is especially colourful with blooms of every conceivable hue on show.

In contrast to the wonderful displays of flowers in the formal borders and those in the botanical study areas, part of the garden has been devoted to a more natural setting and was originally laid out by Capability Brown. Here the visitor can stroll through attractive, lakeside woodland, the ground carpeted with flowers early in the year, and be serenaded by woodland birds. Because they are not persecuted, many species have become remarkably confiding, and jays and woodpigeons in particular seem to have little fear of people.

Kew Gardens. As well as the various glasshouses, there are 300 acres of grounds to explore here

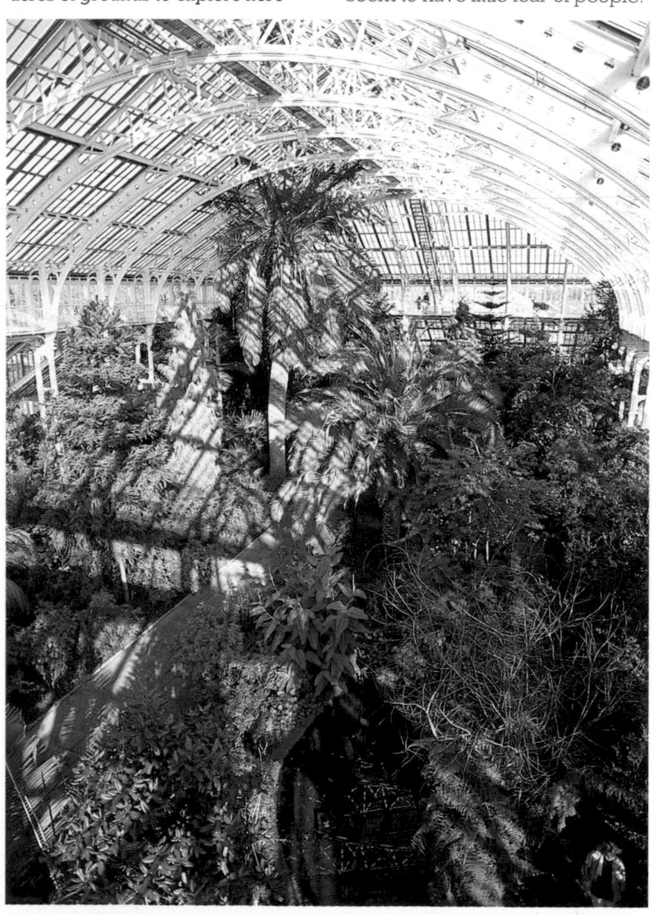

FOOD AND DRINK

Restaurants

Restaurants with the best food in the capital are generally pricey, especially in the evening. But there are exceptions and at lunchtime many offer the chance to try a fixed-price menu at a fraction of the evening price. A selection of outstanding restaurants is given here.

Alastair Little, 49 Frith Street, W1 (tel: 071 734 5183). A small, stylish, street-level, café-like restaurant, with bare black tables and a daily changing menu that roams Europe and further afield. Reasonably expensive (cash only). Closed Saturday lunchtimes and Sundays.

L'Arlequin, 123 Queenstown Road, Battersea, SW8 (tel: 071 622 0555). Small, south London restaurant (just over Chelsea Bridge) with dreary décor. Christian Delteil has little time for matching crockery or fussy garnishes but produces largely well-executed French dishes and desserts deserving of an Egon Ronay Restaurant of the Year award. Cheap set-lunch menu, otherwise very expensive. Popular with intellectuals. Closed weekends.

Bibendum, Michelin House (First Floor), 81 Fulham Road, SW3 (tel: 071 581 5817). First-floor, elegant, fashionable restaurant full of animated celebrities, with chef Simon Hopkinson rejecting *nouvelle cuisine* in favour of regional, usually classic French, though fish and chips or rice pudding may be on the changing menu at lunchtime. Open daily.

M. Bibendum oversees his restaurant

Chez Nico, 35 Great Portland Street, W1 (tel: 071 436 8846). Chef-proprietor Nico Ladenis recently exchanged his Victoria backwater (see Very Simply Nico) for this unlikely location near Oxford Circus (and the 'Simply' for 'Chez'). Simply one of the best restaurants in London, and Nico will not mind at all if you applaud. Expensive. Closed weekends.

The Four Seasons, Inn on the Park Hotel, Park Lane, W1 (tel: 071 499 0888). A dimly lit, florid, palm-filled, fussy room that somewhat detracts from the inventiveness of Bruno Loubet's classic cooking. Rather expensive, but Loubet is tipped as the chef of the 1990s.

Le Gavroche, 43 Upper Brook Street, W1 (tel: 071 408 0881). Owned by the famous Roux brothers. Serious French restaurant with an impressive menu taking in both simple dishes and elaborate creations. Very special and very expensive. Closed weekends.

Harvey's, 2 Bellvue Road, Wandsworth, SW17 (tel: 081 672 0114). Owned by the inspired young Marco Pierre White. He is already hailed as one of the best chefs in Britain, and his dishes are a colourful canvas of the finest ingredients, with a clarity of vision and taste few of his contemporaries can emulate. Reasonable lunch menu, and less expensive than most. Closed Sundays and Mondays.

The Oak Room, in Le Meridien London Hotel, 21 Piccadilly, W1 (tel: 071 734 8000). A rather grand, gilt and mirrored, baroque banqueting hall with an international feel and a rather loud pianist, offering *cuisine creative, traditionelle* or *gourmand* and changing specialities. Very expensive. Closed Saturday lunchtimes and Sundays.

One Ninety Queen's Gate, 190 Queen's Gate, SW7 (tel: 071 581 5666). Bastion of modern British cuisine in basement of restaurateurs' club. Rich seasonal menu, gargantuan portions, excellent wines. Closed Saturday lunchtimes and Sundays.

Le Soufflé, Inter-Continental London, Hamilton Place, W1 (tel: 071 409 3131). Arguably the best hotel food in London. A small, tastefully decorated dining room, where chef Peter

Exterior style reflects the interior qualities of La Tante Claire

Kromberg specialises in imaginative soufflés as well as outstanding French dishes. Closed weekend lunchtimes.

Sutherlands, 45 Lexington Street, W1 (tel: 071 434 3401). A stylish new wave Soho restaurant in a long narrow room. Superb breads, soups served at the table in copper pans. Immaculate presentation. Reasonably expensive. Closed Saturday lunchtimes and Sundays.

La Tante Claire, 68–69 Royal Hospital Road, SW3 (tel: 071

351 0227). Pierre Koffmann is at the helm of this small temple of gastronomy offering consistently high standards and good-value lunches, otherwise very expensive. Closed weekends.

The following is a mixed bag of restaurants (also see separate sections for **Vegetarian** and **Ethnic**) selected for their better than average food, ambience and value for money.

Expensive:
In Hotels. The legendary, oak-panelled restaurant in the **Connaught** in Carlos Place (tel: 071 499 7070) and the **Savoy's** Grill Room, The Strand (tel: 071 836 4343), much loved by businessmen, are both very expensive. The long-awaited, lavishly restored and refurbished **Dorchester** in Park Lane (tel: 071 629 8888) has a new Oriental restaurant to compliment the Grill and Terrace. The Chelsea Room in the **Hyatt Carlton Tower**, Cadogan Place (tel: 071 235 5411) near Harrods is a good choice for lunch (including wine); or try the club-like, wood-panelled Rib Room which specialises in roast meat and

shellfish. **Dukes Hotel** (tel: 071 491 4840), tucked away in St James's Place, offers traditional English and French food (from 18.00 onwards), immaculately presented in a small formal dining room. The Causerie at **Claridge's** in Brook Street, W1 (tel: 071 629 8860) is much loved by Royalty who come for the comfortable, elegant setting and the smörgåsbord lunch. The restaurant also offers early evening (from 17.30) buffets.

Tea at the Ritz – you will need to book if you want a table at this famous establishment

With Dancing. The **Savoy's** opulent River Restaurant (tel: 071 836 4343) overlooks the Thames and has a band most nights. There is also dancing (on Saturdays) in the sumptuous Louis XVI style French baroque dining room at the **Ritz** (tel: 071 493 8181) and big-band dancing

in the Ritz's Palm Court (where they serve afternoon teas) on Friday and Saturday nights.

Reasonable:
The Brackenbury, 129 Brackenbury Road, W6 (tel: 081 748 0107). Charming wine bar restaurant serving delicious, simple cuisine. Friendly service, interesting wine list. Closed Saturday lunchtimes and Sundays.
Caprice, Arlington House, Arlington Street, SW1 (tel: 071 629 2239). Chic, black and white brasserie with a large menu, in the heart of Mayfair, which attracts celebrities, especially for Sunday brunch. Open every day until midnight.
Chez Moi, 1 Addison Avenue, Holland Park, W11 (tel: 071 603 8267). Old-fashioned, French restaurant that has been in the food guides for over 20 years. Closed Saturday lunchtimes and Sundays.
Clarke's, 124 Kensington Church Street, W8 (tel: 071 221 9225). Sally Clarke, the chef-owner, offers a no-choice, changing menu and a short choice at lunch. She char grills in the open-plan kitchen and offers Californian, Italian or Japanese dishes. Closed weekends.
Kensington Place, 201-205 Kensington Church Street, W8 (tel: 071 727 3184). Noisy, hi-tech, street level, fashionable brasserie with an eclectic menu. Open daily.
Langan's Brasserie, Stratton Street, W1 (tel: 071 493 6437). Michael Caine's winning brasserie off Piccadilly, on two floors. Large, noisy and fashionable, with photographers outside ready to snap the inevitable celebrities. Closed Saturday lunchtimes, Sundays.
The Terrace Garden, Le Meridien London Hotel, Piccadilly, W1 (tel: 071 734 8000). Exotic fern and tree-filled split-level conservatory overlooking Piccadilly, relatively inexpensive snacks and meals served all day from 07.00 to 01.00.
Very Simply Nico, 48a Rochester Row, SW1 (tel: 071 630 8061). A cheaper, simpler version of Chez Nico, with Nico's sous chef in command. Closed Saturday lunchtimes and Sundays.
For Fish. The Pierre Martin chain of fish restaurants has been well established for over 15 years. Cannes-type atmosphere and dishes that include a vast cork platter of seafood, nestling on a crinkly bed of seaweed. Not overly expensive, the staff and everything down to the butter are all French. His restaurants include: **La Croisette**, 168 Ifield Road, SW10 (tel: 071 373 3694); **Le Suquet**, (the most popular with celebrities, ask for a table downstairs), 104 Draycott Avenue, SW3 (tel: 071 581 1785) and **Le Quai St Pierre**, 7 Stratford Road, W8 (tel: 071 937 6388).
For Oysters. There are oyster bars at **Wiltons**, 55 Jermyn Street, W1 (tel: 071 629 9955) or at **Green's**, 36 Duke Street, SW1 (tel: 071 930 4566), which also has a champagne bar.

Inexpensive:
There are relatively few good, cheap restaurants in London, but you can often eat cheaply in

Indian, Italian and Chinese restaurants (see separate **Ethnic** section).
Otherwise try:
Café in the Crypt, 5 St Martin's Place, WC2 (tel: 071 839 4342). Enormous brick-vaulted coffee bar/restaurant serving hot dishes, coffee and cakes and with a cheap set menu. Profits go towards the church. Open daily.
Chelsea Kitchen, 98 King's Road, SW3 (tel: 071 589 1330). Hearty basic cooking that has been giving sustenance to shoppers and students for over 30 years. No reservations. Open 08.00 to 23.45 (Sunday from noon).
The Chinoiserie, Hyatt Carlton Tower, Cadogan Place, SW1 (tel: 071 235 5411). Ground-floor, comfortable, though formal lounge, where snacks and light meals are served from 09.00 to 00.15. A harpist plays at teatime, a pianist during lunch and dinner.
Chinon, 25 Richmond Way, W14 (tel: 071 602 5968). Tiny French restaurant in a parade of shops in Shepherd's Bush. Excellent value no-choice set menu. Closed Saturday lunchtimes, Sundays and Mondays.
Pollo, 20 Old Compton Street, W1 (tel: 071 734 5917). Cheap and cheerful long-standing Soho Italian restaurant. Closed Sunday.
Stockport, 40 Panton Street, SW1 (tel: 071 839 5142). Hearty meals at rock-bottom prices; very studenty. The Stockpot at 6 Basil Street (tel: 071 589 8627), SW3 is similar.
Surinder's, 109 Westbourne Park Road, W2 (tel: 071 229 8968). Outstanding value. Small formal restaurant with pretty peach décor. Dinner Tuesday to Saturday; lunch Friday and Sunday only.

Vegetarian

Blah, Blah, Blah, 78 Goldhawk Road, W12 (tel: 081 746 1337). Tempting menus guaranteed to intrigue even non-vegetarians. Closed Sunday.
Food for Thought, 31 Neal Street, WC2 (tel: 071 836 0239). Monumental take-aways; some seating. Open daily.
Futures, 8 Botolph Alley, EC3 (tel: 071 623 4529) is a popular vegetarian take-away. Open 07.30 to 10.00 and 11.30 to 03.00.
Leith's, 92 Kensington Park Road, W11 (tel: 071 229 4481). Modern, expensive restaurant with excellent selection of vegetarian dishes using ingredients (often organic) from Prue Leith's own farm. Dinner only daily.
Neal's Yard Bakery, 6 Neal's Yard, WC2 (tel: 071 836 5199). Covent Garden hang-out for serious vegetarians (in among the wholefood shops). Cheap. Open 10.30 to 18.15 Monday to Friday, till 16.30 on Saturday.

Ethnic

Ethnic restaurants are generally cheap, provided their owners have not inflated their prices just because they have replaced paper tablecloths with linen, lager with wine, and added pot plants. You stand a good chance of getting a table without booking and of finding somewhere open early or late

Get American food at the Hard Rock Café

in the evening. Of the thousands of restaurants, a selection is listed below by nationality (with phone numbers where it is necessary to book).

American. The **Hard Rock Café**, 150 Old Park Lane, W1 (near Hyde Park Corner). Long queues. Very noisy and cheap. You cannot book. Open daily 11.30 to 00.30 (01.00 Friday and Saturday). **Joe Allen's** basement in Covent Garden's Exeter Street down an alley near the Aldwych (tel: 071 836 0651) is popular with actors after the show and is open until 00.45. **Henry J Bean's**, 195 King's Road in Chelsea SW3, (tel: 071 352 9255) is done out like a 1950s American bar; they serve whisky, cocktails, beer, burgers and other dishes. For a taste of the Deep South, head on down to **Old Orleans**, 29-31 Wellington Street, WC2 (tel: 071 497 2433). Cajun specialities like seafood gumbo, blackened fish and spicy ribs. Open daily 11.00 to 23.00.

Chinese. London's Chinatown centres around Soho's pedestrianised Gerrard Street. Many restaurants stay open late and although you may have to queue to get in you do not usually have to book a table. **Poons** at 27 Lisle Street, WC2 (tel: 071 437 4549) specialises in wind-dried food. **Chuen Cheng Ku** is vast, has been at 17 Wardour Street, W1 (tel: 071 437 1398) for over 20 years, and its reputation as the best *dim sum* palace is rivalled only by the even larger 600-seater **New World** in Gerrard Place (tel: 071 734 0677). **Fung Shing** at 15 Lisle Street (tel: 071 437 1539) is smarter than most while the largely Szechuan (spicy) **Dragon's Nest** at 58 Shaftsbury Avenue (tel: 071 437 3119) is somewhat more ambitious than its neighbours. If you are in a hurry, **Wong Kei**, on three floors, at 41 Wardour Street (tel: 071 437 8408) is quick, with brisk service. Insomniacs might like to know that **Yung's**, 23 Wardour Street (tel: 071 437 4986) and **China China**, a new fast-food restaurant at 3 Gerrard Street (tel: 071 439 7511) are both open until about 04.00.

Outside Chinatown, the best Chinese restaurants are usually more formal and more expensive. One of the first was **Ken Lo's Memories of China**, at 67–69 Ebury Street, SW1 (tel: 071 730 7734). **Ken Lo's Memories of China**, Harbour Yard, Chelsea Harbour, SW10 (tel: 071 352 4953), has views of boats and a reasonably priced *dim sum* brasserie open throughout the day. Ken Lo himself sometimes cooks Sunday brunch. There are three branches of the 'monosodium-free' fashionable **Zen** restaurants, all with modern European designer décor: **Zen Chelsea** in Chelsea Cloisters, Sloane Avenue, SW3 (tel: 071 589 1781) was the first, followed by **Zen W3** (with its cascading waterfall) at 83 Hampstead High Street, NW3 (tel: 071 794 7863) and **Zen Central**, in Mayfair at

Almost like an outpost of an old Empire: the Bombay Brasserie

20–22 Queen Street, W1 (tel: 071 629 8103). If you fancy a tasty bowl of noddles for elevenses, **New Yung Kee**, 51 Queensway, W2 (tel: 071 727 5753) is a basic Cantonese café open daily from 11.00. They also serve meals.

Greek/Cypriot. Few restaurants excel but one of the capital's finest is **Psistaria,**

82 Wilton Road, SW1 (tel: 071 821 7504). Mainly Cypriot-style grilled meats and fish served in an airy dining room (closed Sundays). There are several restaurants in Charlotte Street, W1, where you can throw plates and dance on the tables, while round the back of Bayswater, in Inverness Mews, there are two neighbouring 20-year-old branches of the taverna-like candelit **Kalamaras** (tel: 071 727 9122): No 66 (unlicensed) and 76 (Greek wine and ouzo), both offering genuine Greek food. These provide meals during the evenings only (closed on Sundays). The proprietor sometimes plays the bouzouki.

Indian. Among the best are the **Red Fort** in Soho's Dean Street (tel: 071 437 2115) and its new, popular with the media, sister **Jamdani** at 34 Charlotte Street, W1 (tel: 071 636 1178), where they specialise in unusual dishes. Equally sophisticated in a decadent colonial sort of way is the palm-strewn **Bombay Brasserie**, opposite Gloucester Road tube station, in Courtfield Close, Courtfield Road, SW7 (tel: 071 370 4040), with its evening and Sunday lunchtime piano music. Or try **Lal Qila**, 117 Tottenham Court Road, W1 (tel: 071 387 4570), where they specialise in North Indian food.

Italian. Leading the fashionable band of Italian restaurants is **Orso**, 27 Wellington Street, Covent Garden, WC2 (tel: 071 240 5269), a large, fashionable and relatively pricey 1930s-style restaurant (sister of Joe Allen's) with a daily changing menu. Open 12.00 to 24.00. **The River Café**, Thames Wharf, Rainville Road, W6 (tel: 071 381 8824), specialises in traditional farmhouse cooking (closed Saturday, lunch only on Sunday). **La Seppia** is a basement trattoria deep in the heart of Mayfair at 8a Mount Street, W1 (tel: 071 499 3385). Old-established fashionable favourites include the family run **San Martino**, 103 Walton Street, SW3 (tel: 071 589 3833), and **Santini**, 29 Ebury Street,

SW1, near Victoria (tel: 071 730 4094), which has an elegant younger sister, **L'Incontro** at 87 Pimlico Road, SW1 (tel: 071 730 6327).

Japanese. More reasonable than most are **Nanten Yakitori Bar**, 6 Blandford Street, W1 (tel: 071 935 6319), **Ginnan**, 5 Cathedral Place, EC4 in the City (tel: 071 236 4120), and **Ninjin**, 244 Great Portland Street, W1 (tel: 071 388 4657). All are part of the Ninjin group, who also have a Japanese restaurant in the Hilton International in Regent's Park and Kensington. Also worth trying is **Ikeda**, 30 Brook Street, W1 (tel: 071 629 2730), and the basement **Ikkyu**, 67 Tottenham Court Road, W1 (tel: 071 636 9280), with its excellent value set-meal lunches. Slightly more expensive, but with a cheaper set lunch, is **Miyama**, 38 Clarges Street, W1 (tel: 071 499 2443). Also see **Benihana**, Swiss Cottage, under Where to Eat with Children, page 104.

Jewish. **Bloom's**, 90 Whitechapel High Street, E1 (tel: 071 247 6001), serves chicken soup like mama makes. There is also a branch at 130 Golders Green Road, NW11 (tel: 081 455 1338).

Lebanese. **Al Hamra**, 31 Shepherd Market, W1 (tel: 071 493 1954), offers excellent Middle Eastern food. This fairly formal, busy restaurant (almost opposite the Curzon cinema), has an excellent selection of starters, huge baskets of salads and raw vegetables on every table. Less glamorous is **Maroush 1**, 21 Edgware Road, W2 (tel: 071 723 0773). The smarter **Maroush 11**, 38 Beauchamp Place, SW3 (tel: 071 581 5434), is near Harrods and is open until 04.30.

Spanish. London has few Spanish restaurants of note. **Navarro's Restaurant & Tapas Bar**, 67–69 Charlotte Street, W1 (tel: 071 637 7713) has a very pleasant and comfortable restaurant, with a bar down the street. If you want a genuine smoky *tapas* bar with a guitarist, try the **Meson Don Felipe**, 53 The Cut, SE1 (tel: 071 928 3237), which is near the Old Vic theatre.

Thai. Several of the better Thai restaurants are in Soho. They include **Bahn Thai**, 21A Frith Street, W1 (tel: 071 437 8504), **Sri Siam**, 14 Old Compton Street, W1 (tel: 071 434 3544), and **Chiang Mai**, 48 Frith Street, W1 (tel: 071 437 7444). The **Blue Elephant**, at the far end of the Fulham Road in Fulham Broadway, is a fern-filled jungle (tel: 071 385 6595). By comparison, **Tui**, 19 Exhibition Road, SW7 (tel: 071 584 8359), is rather plain.

Pubs

People have stopped counting the 10,000-plus pubs in London and lost track of how old some of them are. Needless to say, several of Dickens' and Shakespeare's watering holes are historic enough to be included in sightseeing as well as drinking itineraries.

Do not expect too much in the way of home comforts in a London pub, though you may get a game of skittles or darts. The food is unlikely to be anything out of the ordinary either. However, if you want to sample a pork pie, a ploughman's (cheese and bread), bangers (sausages) and mash (potatoes), or shepherd's pie, a pub is the place to do it at a reasonable cost.

New licensing laws mean you can eat or drink all day, though some pubs still shut for a few hours in the afternoon. Closing time is generally 23.00 (22.30 on Sundays) though a handful of pubs, several down the Old Kent Road (tube: Elephant and Castle), stay open until 02.00. If you want to take children the pub has to have a separate eating area. The following pubs are reasonably central or on the river:

Bloomsbury and Holborn

The Lamb, 94 Lamb's Conduit Street, WC1. Small, intimate and friendly pub near Holborn, good for a snack lunch. Small courtyard and original 'snob screens'.

The real test of any pub is the quality of its beer

At lunchtime most pubs fill to bursting point

Museum Tavern, 49 Great Russell Street, WC1. Old-fashioned Victorian pub open all day, once frequented by Karl Marx and Virginia Woolf.
Princess Louise, 208 High Holborn, WC1. Popular with Londoners. Rather grand Victorian pub, with lots of polished mahogany. The 'gents' toilet is quiet spectacular.

Chelsea

The Ferret and Firkin, Lots Road, SW10. Jolly pub with basic décor and a singalong piano or guitarist at night.
The Front Page, Old Church Street, SW3. Wealthy Chelsea residents' local. Good food.

Covent Garden

Lamb and Flag, 33 Rose Street, WC2. Low-ceilinged, 18th-century popular pub in an alley. Always packed.

Hampstead
The Holly Bush, Holly Mount, NW3. An 18th-century village pub tucked away in a cobbled courtyard (opposite the station).

Kensington
The Anglesea Arms, Selwood Terrace, South Kensington, SW7. Early Victorian pub owned by Lady Joseph (Sir Maxwell's widow). Comfortable and civilized, with a terrace and open fire.
Windsor Castle, 114 Campden Hill Road, W8. Just off the Bayswater Road in Holland Park, an old-fashioned pub with good food and an open terrace garden. Popular in the evenings and at weekends.

Victoria
The Albert, Victoria Street, SW1. Victorian pub frequented by Members of Parliament. Division bell upstairs, huge staircase lined with portraits of Prime Ministers.

The River (including the City and Docklands)
The Anchor, Bankside SE1, (near Southwark Bridge). Dates back to 1750, the third inn on the site, with lots of little rooms and a terrace overlooking the river. Samuel Pepys, the 17th-century diarist, watched the Great Fire of London from here. On the tourist route.
The Angel, 101 Bermondsey Wall East, SE16. A 19th-century pub with fantastic views of Tower Bridge from the back gallery overhanging the river.
Dickens Inn, St Katharine's Way, Docklands E1. Very popular pub especially at weekends. Overlooks the boats and quayside entertainers, and has an open terrace and exposed wooden beams.
The Dove, 19 Upper Mall, Hammersmith, W6. Cosy, 17th-century riverside pub with tables and chairs outside. Near Ravenscourt Park or Stamford Brook tube.
George Inn, 77 High Street, Southwark, SE1 (near London Bridge Station). The only remaining galleried coaching inn in London, famous during the 18th and 19th centuries and mentioned by Dickens in *Little Dorrit*. Now run by the National Trust. You can sit outside in the cobbled courtyard.
Horniman, Hays Galleria, SE1. Part of the new modern London Bridge City shopping development. On the Thames with views of HMS *Belfast* and Tower Bridge from the tables outside. Open all day.
Mayflower Inn, 117 Rotherhithe Street, SE16. On the Rotherhithe Walk through the Surrey Docks. The Pilgrim Fathers sailed from here and part of the pub dates back to the 16th century. Weekend barbecues.
Old Thameside, St Mary Wharf, Clink Street, SE1. New pub with a waterside setting between Tower and Blackfriars bridges, also champagne bar and riverside restaurant.
Prospect of Whitby, Wapping Wall, Docklands. Famous tavern with Tudor beams and flagstones. Live music nightly.
Samuel Pepys, High Timber Street, off 48 Upper Thames Street, EC4. Was a Victorian tea warehouse. Fine river views. There are two large bars and meals are served.

SHOPPING

Opening Hours

Most shops are open from 09.00 to 18.00, with late-night opening until 20.00 on Thursdays in the West End and Kensington High Street and on Wednesday in Knightsbridge, King's Road and Sloan Square. Some Bond Street shops are shut all day or half day on Saturdays. Many shops in 'tourist areas' like Covent Garden and Tobacco Dock are open until 20.00 nightly. Sunday opening laws are constantly under review, but you will find that some shops (not large stores) are open.

Sales

Prices get slashed at saletime. The winter sales start just before or after Christmas and run until early February. The summer sales begin in June or July and run through August. Look out for the last day of the sales in places like Harrods, where prices are reduced even further. The larger stores have special mid-season sales too.

VAT: See Money Matters section of Directory for relief from VAT for overseas visitors.

The Main Shopping Streets and Areas

There are enough shopping areas in London to fill a book on their own. Those below are the main areas.

The West End/Mayfair

Bond Street and South Molton Street

New Bond Street is synonymous with luxury. Once the home of Byron, Nelson and Beau Brummel, Bond Street begins at Oxford Street and runs south towards Piccadilly, becoming **Old Bond Street,** about two-thirds of the way down. Once the most exclusive street in London, it is now more of a mixed bag, though it still offers high quality goods from silver to haute couture. Two famous landmarks are Sotheby's the auctioneers (Phillips' is in nearby Blenheim Street), and Asprey's for exquisite gifts.

Fenwicks is good for accessories and women's fashion, while the rather more exclusive White House specialises in linens as well as hand-embroidered clothes for children. You can buy sheet music in Chappell's, shoe shops include Rayne's (suppliers to the Royal family), and you will find Cartier, Hermes, Chanel, Karl Lagerfeld, Ungaro and Ferragamo, and numerous antique shops, silversmiths and fine art galleries. Pedestrianised **South Molton Street** runs at an angle between Oxford Street and Brook Street which in turn leads into Bond Street. Here you will find several designer fashion outlets; Browns, Katherine Hamnett, Joseph Tricot, Kenzo and Bazaar among them, plus a few shoe shops. Café tables

Looking for that special something? Sotheby's might be the place for you

spill out onto the pavement in warm weather.

Burlington Arcade, Savile Row and Cork Street

Burlington Arcade, built in 1819, and one of the last bastions of Edwardian London, runs parallel with Old Bond Street, north of Piccadilly and next to the Royal Academy. It is a covered, glass-domed arcade, lined with quality shops selling everything from antique jewellery to cashmere jumpers and Irish linen. Several are 'by Royal Appointment', and supply the Queen or other Royals. Among the most tempting (running south from Burlington Gardens) are the Irish Linen Company, Christie (who specialise in bronze animals), Hummel (who do a good line in china dolls and tin soldiers) and Barrett and Co (whose window is full of almost priceless hand-painted miniature chess sets and Russian enamel jewellery). There is a branch of the herbalists Penhaligon's, several jewellers, and Zelli has an exquisite collection of fine porcelain.
If you are interested in art there are a number of galleries, several contemporary, in and around **Cork Street** opposite. Turn left at the end, just past Gidden's of London saddlers, and you are in New bond Street. Turn right if you want a hand-made suit from one of the exclusive tailors in the world-famous **Savile Row**.

Chelsea

The main shopping area of Chelsea is the **King's Road**, which was originally the path Charles II took to visit Nell Gwyn in Fulham. Livelier than most other fashion areas, there are boutiques of every description, some of them selling whatever is currently in vogue second hand.

Burlington Arcade

Covent Garden
A fashionable area that attracts young people and visitors. Shops are clustered round the covered central market building, with antiques and crafts sold from the original wrought-iron trading stands. The area is very expensive.

Kensington
A mixed area that includes **Kensington High Street** (department stores and boutiques), **Kensington Church Street** (antique shops), **Portobello Road** antique market, and the tiny newly fashionable **Brompton Cross**, round the corner from Harrods, with the Conran shop and Joseph's.

Knightsbridge
Knightsbridge is one of the most exclusive shopping areas. Harrods and Harvey Nichols at the top of **Sloane Street** are the two main stores, but you will also find the Scotch House and an Emporio Armani just before you reach **Beauchamp Place**. There are numerous designer boutiques selling fashion and jewellery, and a long line of some of the most stylish designer shops in London leads south down Sloane Street.

Oxford Street
Nearly a mile long, full of cheap fashion shops and chain stores, interspersed with good-value department stores: Marks & Spencer, Selfridges, C&A, House of Fraser, John Lewis, Debenhams and British Home Stores. Private cars are not allowed in part of Oxford Street, but even the widened pavements have not eased congestion. Illegal marketeers attract crowds that clog up the pavements (and their cheap perfumes will probably be water). Round the back of Selfridges, the pedestrianised **St Christopher's Place** offers quality fashion boutiques and a bit of peace and quiet.

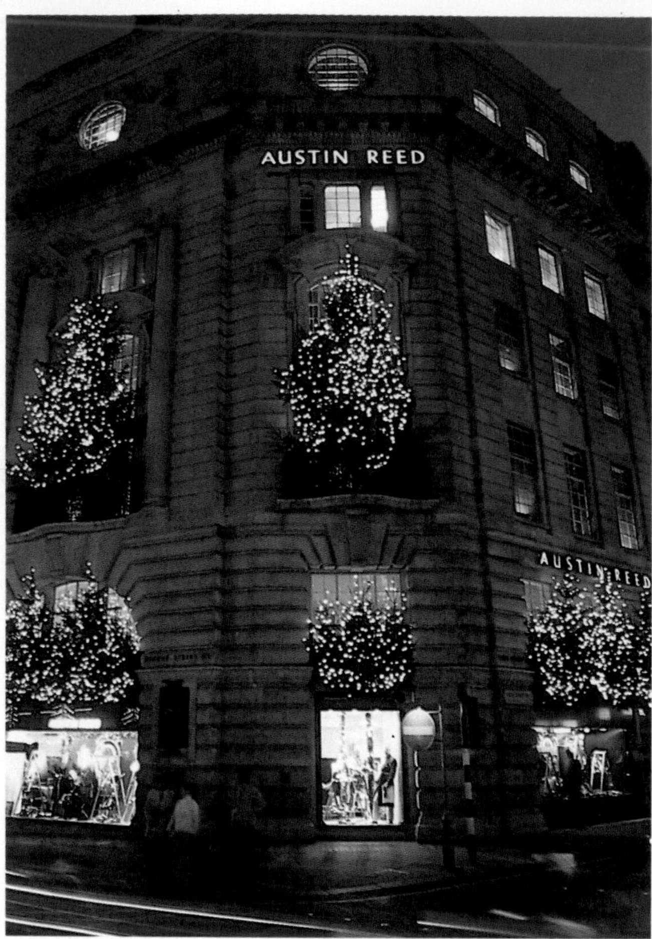

Austin Reed – famous for men's clothes

Piccadilly and St James's

Piccadilly is a busy thoroughfare with airline offices and car showrooms either side of the Ritz and the Royal Academy of Arts. It has old-fashioned shopping arcades (including Burlington Arcade) selling everything from luggage to crystal, Fortnum and Mason, with its exotic food hall, Simpson for clothes and Hatchards for books. Beyond Piccadilly are the indoor shopping complexes of the Trocadero and London Pavillion, while in the

Haymarket, Burberrys sell the famous trenchcoats.
Jermyn Street, south of Piccadilly in St James's, is unashamedly old fashioned and male orientated, offering hand-made shirts and shoes, Havana cigars, antiques, fine art and antique scientific instruments. There is also Floris, perfumiers to the Court of St James since George IV, and half-way along is Fortnum's Fountain Restaurant and a branch of Dunhill's.

Regent Street and Carnaby Street

Regent Street curves down from Oxford Circus to Piccadilly. Designed by John Nash, it houses some impressive buildings including the mock-Tudor façade of Liberty's department store. There are several airline offices, Dickins and Jones department store, a branch of Laura Ashley, Hamleys' toyshop and several shops selling china and crystal, plus the Queen's jewellers, Garrard. Shops specialising in classic British fashion include Jaeger, Austin Reed and Aquascutum. Round the back is the pedestrianised **Carnaby Street**. This used to be *the* street to be seen in during the 1960s, but now you should avoid it unless you like tourist junk.

Soho

Soho is changing fast but there are still long-established family firms, selling Continental food, coffee, cigars or cakes, though they may soon be pushed out by property developers and high rents as the area becomes even more desirable. The inevitable replacements are boutiques, bars and restaurants. **Gerrard Street** caters for its Chinese community and there is a lively fruit and vegetable market in **Berwick Street**.

Tobacco Dock

London's newest shopping centre in Docklands (opened in the spring of 1989) twice the size of Covent Garden, with over 100 shops (open until 20.00) and restaurants housed in a grade one listed Georgian building off The Highway. To get there take the East London Underground to Wapping, or Docklands Light Railway from Bank to Shadwell, then follow the signs.

Markets

London's market traders are a dying breed as the main wholesale markets get squeezed out of the capital by redevelopment. Covent Garden's fruit and vegetable traders are now in Nine Elms, Billingsgate fish market has moved to West India Dock, and the former Spitalfields' meat market area is set to be developed as an international banking centre.
At the turn of the century there were some 60,000 street sellers, called 'costermongers', hawking anything they could get their hands on. The markets of the East End were full of Romany fortune tellers, quack doctors and organ grinders. Food stalls sold pies and eels. You could get your shoes blacked or your knives sharpened. Illegal traders carted off half the food to be sold in poorer districts, talking in rhyming slang (*eg* 'apples and pears'; stairs) to fool the police. Today the street markets that

are left sell fruit, sometimes of dubious quality unless you know the stallholder, second-hand clothes, and rubbish that has 'fallen off the back of a lorry'. Antiques at largely inflated prices are sold off stalls in Portobello Road, but if you get up early enough there are bargains to be had at the New Caledonian Market on a Friday morning in Bermondsey. As for the old 'costermongers', they are still around in the East End, dressing up in their finest costumes as 'pearly Kings and Queens' for special occasions like the Lord Mayor's Show. The following markets are still going strong:

Antiques
Camden Passage, off Upper Street, Islington, N1 (tube: Angel). Individual stalls on Wednesday (06.45 to 16.00) and Saturday (08.00 to 17.00), also Thursday for prints and drawings (07.00 to 16.00), plus quality shops open all week in adjoining streets. **New Caledonian Market**, Bermondsey Square, SE1 (tube: London Bridge). Huge open-air market from 06.00 to 14.00 on Friday. Trade plus anyone else who gets there early enough. Lots of jewellery. **Portobello Road**, W11 (tube: Notting Hill Gate, Ladbroke Grove). The antique-stall holders turn up from 06.00 to 17.00 on Saturday. With 1,500 dealers competing for custom, prices can be cut throat. Shops are worth a visit.

Other Goods
Brick Lane, E1 (tube: Aldgate East). East End market. Sunday 08.00 to 13.00. Lots of rock-bottom rubbish.
Camden Lock, Camden Town, NW1 (tube: Chalk Farm, Camden Town). Several small markets, with crafts and jewellery sold under awnings in the crowded Lock area at weekends (09.00 to 18.00) when most of the local shops

(prints, furniture etc) are also open. Undergoing redevelopment. Fruit and vegetables are sold in Inverness Street daily, there is a small antique market in Camden High Street on Thursday and at weekends and more bric-à-brac in the **Chalk Farm** market down the road. **Covent Garden**, WC2 (tube: Covent Garden). Crafts and mostly British-made goods are sold on weekdays and weekends, with antiques on Sunday and Monday. Spills over into the more general Jubilee Market to the south of the piazza. 09.00 to 17.00.

A stall in Camden Passage

Petticoat Lane. Some stallholders have turned the business of attracting bored shoppers into an art form

Greenwich Market, Greenwich High Road, SE10 (British Rail: Greenwich). Weekend market (better on Sunday) selling antiques, crafts and second-hand clothes, 08.00 to 16.00.
Leather Lane, EC1 (tube: Chancery Lane). A bit of everything from cheap silk ties to cassettes, woolly jumpers to palm trees, 140 stalls. Monday to Friday 10.00 to 14.30.
Petticoat Lane, Middlesex Street, E1 (tube: Aldgate or Aldgate East). Do not look for Petticoat Lane itself because you will not find it. Sunday is the day for clothes. Try Goulston Street at the far end for designer clothes. Brick Lane specialises in electrical goods and furniture. 09.00 to 14.00, Sunday.

ACCOMMODATION

Nearly a quarter of all visitors to London stay with friends or relatives. For the rest the London Tourist Board produces two guides: *Where to Stay in London*, which covers hotels, b&b, guesthouses and apartments and *London Budget Hotels*. They also have a separate leaflet *Accommodation With Families*. The AA also publishes several guides to London.
The London Tourist Board can book accommodation if you call in at their office at Victoria Station or Heathrow on arrival, or you can write to them at 26 Grosvenor Gardens, London, SW1W 0DU, at least six weeks in advance of your visit. Alternatively, telephone 071 824 8844 (Access or Visa required). A deposit and communication charge is payable when making a reservation.

Apartments
There are numerous agencies dealing with short-let apartments (usually a minimum of one week). You can get a list from the London Tourist Board. Agencies include: Apartment Services (tel: 071 388 3558), Aston's (tel: 071 370 0737/1100) and Holiday Flats Services Ltd (tel: 071 373 4477).
London's universities and colleges make their halls of residence available to visitors at Easter and from July to September. To book telephone 071 636 2818.

Bed and Breakfast
The London Tourist Board lists b&b hotels (see Hotels) as well as agencies that will find you accommodation with a private family. Many of the private homes are in the suburbs and you have no guarantee that you will be included in family life. You may or may not get the option of an evening meal, or a packed lunch, and there may be a minimum stay. The b&b agencies for accommodation in private homes include:
Anglo World Travel (tel: 071 436 3601)
Capital Homes (tel: 081 440 7535)
Host & Guest Service (tel: 071 731 5340/736 5645)
London Homestead Services (tel: 081 949 4455)
Uptown Reservations (tel: 071 351 3445)
World Wide Bed and Breakfast Association (tel: 081 742 9123).

Hotels
London hotels are notoriously expensive although most also offer corporate rates and attractively priced weekend breaks. Some hotels offer free accommodation to children sharing your room and throw in all sorts of extras from rail travel to theatre tickets. Do not hesitate to ask either a travel agent or the hotel itself about bargain breaks; even the most exclusive establishments like the Ritz, the Savoy and the Hyatt Carlton Tower offer them. The following agencies will make hotel reservations for you:
British Hotel Reservation Centre (toll free) (tel: 0800 282888)
Concordia-Worldwide Hotel Reservations (tel: 071 730 3467)
Hotel Booking Service (tel: 071 437 5052)
The Leading Hotels of the World

(toll free) (tel: 0800 181123)
Room Centre (UK) (tel: 071 328 1790)
Small Luxury Hotels (toll free) (tel: 0800 282124).

Hotels are officially classified by a 'listed' or crown system from one to five. Those that display the crown have met certain criteria and have been inspected. Given here is a selection of London hotels in a variety of locations divided up according to price.

Very expensive:

The most exclusive hotels in the capital are in Piccadilly, Mayfair and Knightsbridge. The **Ritz** in Piccadilly (tel: 071 493 8181) opened in 1906 and soon became one of the most fashionable hotels in the world, frequented by Royalty and celebrities from Noël Coward to the Aga Khan. (The latter had a suite there for over 40 years.) If your finances do not run to staying there you can (if you book ahead) have tea in the Palm Court. The sumptuous **Dorchester** in Park Lane (tel: 071 629 8888) is also one of the world's ultimate luxury hotels. It has a traditionally English style and facilities include a spa and four restaurants. The rather less flamboyant **Athenaeum** (tel: 071 499 3464) near Hyde Park Corner, overlooks Green Park. The Savoy Group includes the Savoy, the Connaught, Claridge's and the Berkeley. The **Connaught** in Carlos Place, Mayfair (tel: 071 499 7070) was created as a London home for the landed gentry. The staff wear morning dress and it feels more like a country house than a hotel. **Claridge's** (tel: 071 629 8860) in Brook Street opened its doors in 1899. You may be welcomed by a Hungarian quartet. Royalty often drop in for lunch in the Causerie. The **Savoy** (tel: 071

The Connaught Hotel has a country house feel

836 4343) in the Strand recently celebrated its centenary and its standards are still exemplary. At the turn of the century it was so popular with Royalty that the special bell that heralded their arrival was abandoned. There are splendid river views from the highly acclaimed restaurant and an American Bar.

Italians will feel quite at home at the **Hyde Park Hotel** (tel: 071 235 2000) opposite Harvey Nichols in Knightsbridge, where the General Manager is from the Grand in Rome. It has wonderful views over the park from the rear.

If you like to work out or have a swim, the **Grosvenor House** (tel: 071 499 6363) in Park Lane has an attractive indoor pool, as does the **Berkeley** in Wilton Place, Belgravia (tel: 071 235 6000) where the sliding lid of the rooftop is removed in summer.

Le Meridien London in Piccadilly (tel: 071 734 8000) has a Champneys health club with a superb Roman-style pool complete with Grecian statues, and the **Hyatt Carlton Tower** in Cadogan Place off Sloane Street (tel: 071 235 5411) has a ninth and tenth floor gym and fitness club. The Peak, which also offers views over Knightsbridge. Overlooking Hyde Park, the **Hotel Inter-Continental London** (tel: 071 409 3131) and the **Four Seasons Inn on the Park** (tel: 071 499 0888) both cater well for businessmen. The Inter-Continental has a fitness centre and plunge pool. At the Inn on the Park the second-floor suites have conservatories. Both hotels have excellent restaurants.

Small Hotels

London's smaller hotels are often converted out of terraced houses, and furnished more like a home. Among the best are: **The Capital** in Basil Street near Harrods (tel: 071 589 5171); the pretty, chintzy **Halcyon** on the corner of Holland Park and Holland Park Avenue, with its fashionable Kingfisher garden restaurant (tel: 071 727 7288); the stylish **Blakes Hotel** owned by the celebrated Anouska Hempel in Roland Gardens, South Kensington (tel: 071 370 6701); and tiny **Dukes** in a cobbled alley behind St James's (tel: 071 491 4840) and the neighbouring **Stafford** (tel: 071 493 0111), both with excellent restaurants. **Brown's** (tel: 071 493 6020) started off small enough when it opened in 1837, but now occupies 12 elegant town houses in Albemarle and Dover Streets off Bond Street, while the **Chesterfield**, 35 Charles Street, Mayfair (tel: 071 491 2622), was once the home of the 4th Earl of Chesterfield.

Expensive enough:
The **Goring**, 15 Beeston Place (tel: 071 396 9000), near Buckingham Palace, has been going strong since 1910 and is still owned by the original family. **L'Hôtel** in Basil Street (tel: 071 589 6286), is essentially a b&b establishment but wonderfully central. For lovers of antiques the **Portobello Hotel** in Stanley Gardens (tel: 071 727 2777) is near the market of that name. For river views try the modern **Tower Thistle Hotel** in St Katharine's Way (tel: 071 481 2575), or the slightly more expensive **Royal Horseguards Thistle** in Whitehall Court (tel: 071 839 3400). There are six Hiltons in London, including the modern **London Regent's Park Hilton** (tel: 071 722 7722) in St John's Wood, which just about overlooks Lord's cricket ground and has a good Japanese restaurant and New York deli, and the **London Mews Hilton** (tel: 071 493 7222) in Stanhope Row, behind the **London Hilton on Park Lane** (tel: 071 493 8000).

Small Hotels

If you prefer a more personal atmosphere, the 28-roomed **Beaufort Hotel** (b&b and light snacks only) in peaceful Beaufort Gardens, near Harrods (tel: 071 584 5252), is a town house that gives guests

One of the bedrooms in Holland Park's Halcyon Hotel

their own front-door key. The Regency-style **Dorset Square Hotel** (tel: 071 723 7874) near Regent's Park is hot on chintzes and beautiful fabrics. The b&b only **Fenja**, 69 Cadogan Gardens near Sloane Square (tel: 071 589 7333), is a member of the Prestige group and is decorated with fine antiques and English Masters. You would not know that **11 Cadogan Gardens** (tel: 071 730 3426) was a hotel at all; four Victorian town houses (60 rooms) have been converted into an elegant hotel furnished with antiques and paintings. It offers 24-hour room service with light meals.

Reasonable:
One of London's best b&b hotels and a winner of awards is the **Claverley on Beaufort Gardens**, a few minutes from Harrods (tel: 071 589 8541). The **Pembridge Court**, a Victorian town house near Portobello Road, in Pembridge

Gardens (tel: 071 229 9977), has only 21 rooms and its own restaurant. Handy for Victoria Station is the b&b only **Elizabeth Hotel** in Eccleston Square (tel: 071 828 6812), as is the **Elbury Court** (tel: 071 730 8147), with accommodation in five adjoining houses. Similarly converted out of three terraced houses is **Hazlitt's** in Frith Street in Soho (tel: 071 434 1771). North of Oxford Street, **Durrants Hotel** (tel: 071 935 8131) in George Street near Baker Street is one of the oldest privately owned hotels in London. Reasonably priced for Knightsbridge is the recently renovated **Knightsbridge Green Hotel**, which is near Harrods (tel: 071 584 6274).

If you do not mind staying in North London, both the **Swiss Cottage Hotel** in Adamson Road (tel: 071 722 2281), and the **Sandringham** in Holford Road near Hampstead Heath (tel: 071 435 1569), offer b&b in a quiet location. The West End is a bus ride or a few stops away on the tube, and the areas themselves are worth exploring.

Quiet and unobtrusive: the Sandringham Hotel at Hampstead

ENTERTAINMENT

There is always an enormous choice of what to see in London, most of it in the West End or just across Waterloo Bridge in the rather ugly concrete South Bank Arts Centre. Opened in 1976, the latter is long overdue for a facelift. Alongside the National Theatre and Hayward Gallery is the Royal Festival Hall, built in 1951 for the Festival of Britain. The neighbouring Queen Elizabeth Hall and the Purcell Room were opened in 1967. The Barbican, in the City, is home to the Royal Shakespeare Company and London Symphony Orchestra, and is a major venue for art exhibitions and concerts. The Royal Opera and Royal Ballet perform at the Royal Opera House, and the English National Opera at the Coliseum.

Dress is fairly informal for concerts and the theatre, but most people dress up for the Royal Opera House. Theatres tend to be hot and stuffy, and although you can leave coats in cloakrooms, queues tend to be long, so a light coat you can fold up and put on your lap is the best idea. In the interval, bars sell drinks (you can order in advance) and light snacks.

Clubs/Discos/Live Music

It is not worth listing what is 'in', because it probably will not be by next week! Needless to say, most clubs are for members only. If you are staying at a top hotel the concierge may be able to get you into a nightclub like **Annabel's** for the evening. If you happen to have media friends in the capital you could be taken for a drink on a comfortable sofa or a meal at Groucho's in Soho. Trendy young Londoners belong to Fred's or Moscow's. But you have to know a member to get in. If you are from out of town and punk, funk, yuppie or anything else, the best you can do is to buy the weekly *Time Out* magazine and look up the clubs (that do not need membership) currently in vogue. The **Hippodrome**, Cranbourn Street, WC2 (tel: 071 437 4311) is where to go for a good dance. It is central, loud and expensive, with hi-tech décor and the best lasers in town. **Stringfellow's**, 16 Upper St Martin's Lane, WC2 (tel: 071 240 5534) is rather more intimate and sophisticated and you can also eat there. Notable live music venues include the **Brixton Academy**, 211 Stockwell Road, SW9 (tel: 071 326 1022); the **Marquee Club**, 105 Charing Cross Road, WC2 (tel: 071 437 6603); and the **Forum** (formerly the Town and Country Club), 9–17 Highgate Road, NW5 (tel: 071 284 2200). You can eat or drink, listen to live blues, jazz or soul and dance at the **Dover Street Restaurant and Wine Bar**, 8–9 Dover Street, W1 (tel: 071 629 9813), until 03.00 except Sunday.

Jazz

London has few central jazz venues but it does have some informal venues in pubs and restaurants. A selection is listed below.

The Bass Clef, 35 Coronet Street, off Hoxton Square, N1 (tel: 071 729 2476). Serious venue for young artists who

perform on a stage in a dim cellar. Cheap food.
The 100 Club, 100 Oxford Street, W1 (tel: 071 636 0933). A small smoky basement which offers jazz and blues nights with Caribbean food; also provides other forms of live music.
Ronnie Scott's, 47 Frith Street, W1 (tel: 071 439 0747). In the heart of Soho, this is London's most sophisticated jazz club, dimly lit and smoky, with regularly changing acts. You can eat here, but it is expensive. Booking essential for the most popular artists. Closed Sunday.
Restaurants with live jazz include:
Pizza Express, 10 Dean Street, W1 (tel: 071 437 9595). Jazz basement.
Pizza on the Park, 11–13 Knightsbridge, SW1 (tel: 071 235 5550/5273). Near Hyde Park Corner. Live music every night in separate basement jazz room.

Concerts/Classical Music

Concerts and classical music are performed at numerous venues. If you are in London during the summer, the **Henry Wood Promenade Concerts** (or Proms), held from the end of July to September in the red-brick Royal Albert Hall, are great fun, but queues for the standing area in the body of the hall can form early on in the day. The main classical music venues are:
The Barbican Hall, Silk Street, EC2 (tel: 071 638 8891/4141)
Purcell Room, South Bank, SE1 (tel: 071 928 3191)
Queen Elizabeth Hall, South Bank, SE1 (tel: 071 928 8800)

The Royal Opera House has been the setting for many memorable operatic evenings

Royal Albert Hall, Kensington Gore, SW7 (tel: 071 589 8212)
Royal Festival Hall, South Bank, SE1 (tel: 071 921 0600)
Wigmore Hall, 36 Wigmore Street, W1 (tel: 071 935 2141).
Free concerts take place in the foyers of the Barbican and the National Theatre on the South Bank, at weekends and early in the evening. Free lunchtime concerts of organ music, string quartets, piano recitals, brass

bands etc are held in churches, many of them in the City.

Dance

The Royal Ballet performs at the **Royal Opera House** in Covent Garden. In summer the English National Opera moves out of the **Coliseum** to make room for major ballet companies, while the London Contemporary Dance School as well as touring companies give performances at **The Place**. There are also major performances at **Sadler's Wells** in Islington and in the South Bank concert halls (see listings above). Addresses and phone numbers are:

London Coliseum, St Martin's Lane, WC2 (tel: 071 836 3161)
The Place, 17 Duke's Road, WC1 (tel: 071 387 0031)
Royal Opera House, Covent Garden, WC2 (tel: 071 240 1066)
Sadler's Wells, Rosebery Avenue, EC1 (tel: 071 278 8916).

Opera

The first opera at the **Royal Opera House**, in Covent Garden, was performed in 1817 and they have been playing to packed houses ever since. If you cannot afford a dress circle seat (very expensive) you can always sneak into the famous 'crush bar' during the interval to soak up the atmosphere. If you are lucky your visit may coincide with the odd summer night when a huge screen is erected and sound relayed into the Covent Garden piazza. Prices are a lot cheaper and the operas are sung in English at the English National Opera's home at the **Coliseum**. Operas are also occasionally performed at other venues including the concert halls on the South Bank. English National Opera, The London Coliseum, St Martin's Lane, WC2 (tel: 071 836 3161). Royal Opera House, Covent Garden, WC2 (tel: 071 240 1066).

Theatre
Most London theatres are in and around Soho and Covent Garden. The **National Theatre** and the **Old Vic** are across Waterloo Bridge on the South Bank, the **Barbican** is in the City. There are also numerous small repertory or 'fringe' theatres all over London (see below). Performances usually begin at 19.30 or 20.00 with matinées often on Wednesday and Saturday afternoons. Theatres are closed on Sundays. If your visit coincides with Christmas you will find that many theatres offer a traditional pantomime, while in the summer you can watch a Shakespearean play in the open-air setting of Regent's Park.
Fringe Theatre. London has an enormous network of fringe theatres extending into the suburbs. Performances are highly regarded, though companies are often ill-funded and perform on a shoe-string. Many take place in pub theatres, some at lunchtime. The most well-known venues include: The Almeida, Almeida Street, N1 (tel: 071 359 4404); Bush Theatre, Shepherds Bush Green, W12 (tel: 081 743 3388); ICA Theatre, The Mall, W1 (tel: 071 930 3647); King's Head, 115 Upper Street, N1 (tel: 071 226 1916); Riverside Studios, Crisp Road, W6 (tel: 081 748 3354). Be prepared for uncomfortable seats, and minimal scenery. There is no need to dress up. Admission charges are low and you usually have to become a member for a small charge which you can do at the door. For more information contact The Pub Theatre Network (tel: 071 835 1853) or see *Time Out*.

Tickets
To get tickets for shows and theatre you should use a reputable ticket agency (see **Directory**). The box offices of the individual theatres are usually open from 10.00 to 20.00 and you can book over the telephone by credit card or go along in person. You may also be lucky if you queue up for returns on the day. Seats for West End shows are not cheap. The National Theatre is more reasonable. For half-price tickets (to theatres and sometimes for the English National Opera) go in person on the day to the blue and red SWET ticket booth in Leicester Square. There is a small booking fee, and payment is by cash only. The booth is open

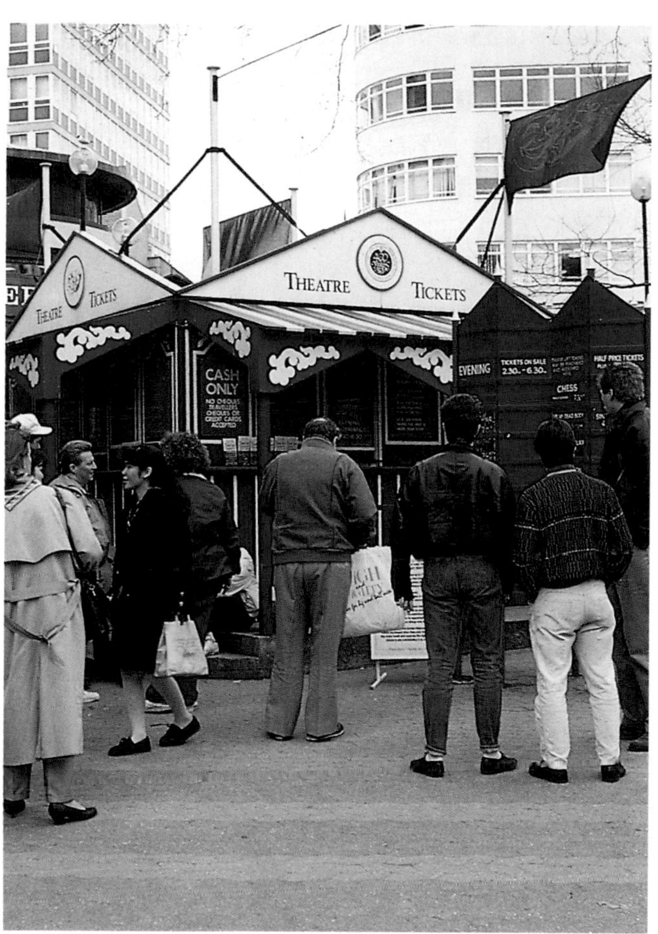

If you want bargain theatre tickets, the Leicester Square Ticket Booth is the place for you

from Monday to Saturday from noon until half an hour before the matinée performances and from 14.30 to 18.30 for evening performances. Up to four tickets per person only.

What's on

You can find out what is on from any of the quality daily or Sunday newspapers, or, with more lengthy (and fairly radical) reviews, in the weekly *Time Out* magazine.

Tourist Offices (see **Directory**) will also have information on entertainment in the capital.

WEATHER AND WHEN TO GO

Whenever you choose to travel to London, pack an umbrella and a light mackintosh. In the last few years, London's weather seems to have become totally unpredictable. There have been crocuses in bloom in February, the worst storms in memory in October, incessant rain in normally dry months, plus little summer to speak of. Traditionally the wettest month is November. July and August are also wet, but the average daily maximum temperatures reach 71 degrees Fahrenheit (22 degrees Centigrade). March and April are the driest months, despite what you may have heard about April showers. You may get snow in winter, but you cannot bank on it.

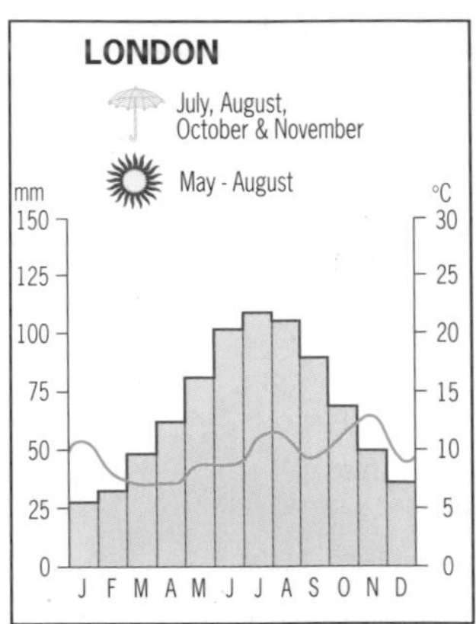

To listen to a recorded weather forecast for the London area phone 0898 500401.

Whatever the season, a military band might appear from nowhere to entertain the crowds

HOW TO BE A LOCAL

'Londoners' are hard to define. Cockneys refuse to extend the description to anyone not born within the sound of Bow Bells. North Londoners scoff at South Londoners' claims to be locals, and vice versa. In fact, most Londoners are not really Londoners in any strict sense. It is a diverse, cosmopolitan city – but there are plenty of ways to tell a 'local' from a tourist.

Londoners are always in a hurry. If you feel ignored, do not be offended; they do not talk to each other in public, let alone strangers.

Londoners do not go to the 'historic' pubs on the Thames unless they are next door to the office, and when a publican calls 'time gentlemen please', Londoners have already ordered their last drinks.

Londoners who want to eat their lunch in comparative peace go to the parks; those who are really in the know go to the Inns of Court or to the Temple, where the squares have never emerged into the 20th century.

In shops Londoners know better than to expect the assistant to offer much in the way of help and accept that purchases will be scrumpled up and shoved into a plastic bag. They remember to keep the receipt from Marks & Spencer if they think they might need a refund.

Londoners who can, avoid supermarkets and West End shops on a Saturday morning. They know that it is much easier to park (and the meters are free) on Saturday afternoon.

They never drive into town without plenty of change for meters and do not expect to get their windscreen washed when they fill up with petrol.

If they go to museums it is with the children in the holidays or on a Sunday afternoon, and they always eat before they go because they know the café will be full.

Londoners over 30 wait for new films to come round to their local cinema and rarely venture into the West End on a Saturday night except to see a play. They know better than to try to get into a decent film, play or restaurant without booking.

Many of the most exciting plays are staged outside the West End anyway, in alternative venues – such as rooms above pubs. Look for these and every other form of entertainment in the weekly magazine *Time Out*.

Londoners hate travelling by public transport. They resign themselves to long waits at bus stops followed by the sudden arrival of a convoy of buses all for the same route.

They know that the tubes will be horribly overcrowded during the rush hour (08.00–09.30 and 16.30–18.30) and they also know that delays are likely at any time. As for the railway network, well it brings many commuters close to tears on a regular basis and that is the only reliable thing about it.

Londoners claim to hate London, but regard anywhere outside the tube line as outer space. They like to describe the city as a series of villages, and enjoy having 'their own' shops and parks, off the beaten track.

If Londoners want to go for a walk in the City, they go on Sundays, when the whole of the 'square mile' is virtually deserted. If they want to buy trendy clothes they go to Camden Market and this is also where you can go to see the colourful and eccentric side of London.

Despite their generally grim outlook, Londoners love processions, festivals, marches, demonstrations and anything else that could be described as a 'bit of a do' (it really is true about the use of understatement, by the way).

Derby Day at Epsom. This is one of the great events in the British racing calendar

SPECIAL EVENTS

The London Tourist Board produces a leaflet on events. Some of those that take place on an annual basis are listed below. Exact dates vary from year to year.

January
Lord Mayor of Westminster's New Year's Day Parade.

Marching bands and dancers parade from Westminster Abbey to Berkeley Square, followed by a performance at the Royal Albert Hall.

February
Gun Salute on Accession Day (6th, day after if Sunday). 41-gun salute (noon) opposite the Dorchester Hotel in Hyde Park.
Cruft's Dog Show, Earl's Court.

March
The Oxford versus Cambridge University Boat Race, from Putney to Mortlake.

April
Easter Parade (sometimes in March, depending on when Easter falls) in Battersea Park on Easter Sunday, followed by the Horse Harness Parade in the Inner Circle of Regent's Park on Easter Monday.
Gun Salute on the Queen's Birthday (21st).

May
Chelsea flower Show in the Chelsea Royal Hospital Grounds. Some days open to members only. Apply in advance for tickets.
FA Cup Final, Wembley.

June
Beating the Retreat: Household Division, Horse Guards Parade, SW1. Military display of marching and drilling bands with massed bands and pipers.
Derby Day. Epsom's famous race for three-year-old colts and fillies.
Royal Academy Summer Exhibition, Royal Academy of Arts, Piccadilly (until mid-August).
Stella Artois Tennis

The Regatta always attracts leisurely crowds

Championships, Queen's Club, W14.
Beating the Retreat: Tri-Service Massed Bands, Horse Guards Parade, SW1.
Queen's Official Birthday (Saturday, mid June).
Trooping the Colour. Parade leaves Buckingham Palace at 10.40 and travels down The Mall to Horse Guards Parade. Return to Buckingham Palace with flypast by the RAF and appearance on the balcony at 13.00 with another gun salute at the Tower of London.
Royal Ascot, Ascot Racecourse, Berkshire. The Queen and the Royal family attend the famous races. Starts at 14.30 each day. Formal attire and a hat essential.
Wimbledon Lawn Tennis Championships, All England Club, Wimbledon, SW19. Late June to early July. Book well ahead for Centre Court tickets.
Henley Royal Regatta, Henley-on-Thames, Oxfordshire. Late

June to early July. International rowing regatta held since 1839.

July

Royal Tournament, Earl's Court, SW5. Spectacular by the Armed Forces in aid of service charities. Attended by the Royal Family.
Henry Wood Promenade concerts, the 'Proms' (informal jazz to symphonic), held at the Royal Albert Hall. Mid-July to mid-September. The last night is the most riotous.
Swan Upping. A traditional ceremony to 'mark' the swans and record their numbers. Takes place on the Thames from Sunbury to Whitchurch (3rd week of July).

August

London Riding Horse Parade, Rotten Row, Hyde Park. A competition to choose the best turned out horse and rider.
Notting Hill Carnival. Held over the Late Summer Holiday weekend in the streets of Notting Hill and Ladbroke Grove. A usually peaceful Caribbean-style procession and party with steel bands, dancing in the streets and lots of loud reggae until 21.00.

September

Horsemen's Sunday. Church service taken by a vicar on horseback at Church of St John and St Michael, Hyde Park Crescent, W2. Horses assemble at 11.30. Ends 13.00 then horses go on a procession through Hyde Park.

October

Pearly Harvest Festival Service, held at 15.00 at St Martin-in-the-Fields, WC2, attended by London's Pearly Kings and Queens (the traditional cockney costermongers).
Judges' Service. Opening of the legal year on the first weekday in October, with judges in full ceremonial robes. 11.00 at Westminster Abbey. View the procession from Westminster Abbey to the Houses of Parliament at 11.45.
Trafalgar Day Parade to celebrate Nelson's victory. Held in Trafalgar Square on the nearest Sunday to the 21st.

November

Guy Fawkes Night (5th). His attempt to blow up Parliament in 1605 is commemorated by bonfires and fireworks on high points in the capital's parks.
London to Brighton Veteran Car Run. Held on the first Sunday in November. Several hundred entrants and their pride and joys in gleaming condition leave Hyde Park Corner early in the morning and take the A23 to Brighton.
Lord Mayor's Show. Takes place on a Saturday in mid-November. The Lord Mayor rides in his gilded coach to the Law Courts for the declaration of office. Colourful floats and military bands start at around 11.00 from Gresham Street for Mansion House, passing St Paul's, Fleet Street and the Strand.
State opening of Parliament. Mid-November. The Royal Procession travels along The Mall, through Horse Guards Parade. Departs at 11.00.
Christmas Lights. Switched on in Oxford Street, Regent Street and Bond Street from mid-November until early January.

CHILDREN

There is no accounting for children's tastes. Some like museums, others hate them. The boredom factor may be alleviated by the quiz sheets provided by some of the major museums and galleries, and there are often special events, or films, either at weekends or during the holidays. If you have children who like 'doing things', both the Launch Pad at the Science Museum and the Human Biology Hall at the Natural History Museum will provide hours of educationally interactive fun for all ages. Children are charged half-price admission in museums and under 5's usually get in free. There are also numerous other possibilities, from cinemas and theatres that put on children's films and plays, to puppet shows and parks. Babysitters can be arranged via Childminders (tel: 071 935 9763) or Universal Aunts (tel: 071 738 8937).

One of the most useful sources of up-to-the-minute information is Capital Radio's *London for Kids* magazine (from good bookshops), or the children's section of *Time Out* magazine (available from newsagents).

For details of children's clubs, classes, sports and holiday entertainment, call Kidsline (tel: 071 222 8070), weekdays 09.00 to 16.00 during school holidays, 16.00 to 18.00 in term time.

The following should provide something of interest for most age groups (see pages 25–42 for further details).

Try it yourself – the Science Museum's Launch Pad

HMS *Belfast*, London Bridge
British Museum, Bloomsbury,
Buckingham Palace (and the Changing of the Guard every morning in summer and alternate mornings in winter at 11.30, also at Horse Guards in Whitehall)
Cutty Sark, Greenwich
Guinness World of Records, Piccadilly
Hampton Court Palace (and the maze), Hampton Court

Horniman Museum, Forest Hill
London Brass Rubbing Centre, Trafalgar Square
London Transport Museum, Covent Garden
Madame Tussaud's, Marylebone
Museum of the Moving Image, South Bank
Natural History Museum, South Kensington
Planetarium, Marylebone
Rock Circus, Piccadilly
Science Museum, South Kensington
Thames Barrier, Woolwich
Tower of London, City

Other places of interest for children include:

BETHNAL GREEN MUSEUM OF CHILDHOOD

Cambridge Heath Road, E2

A branch of the Victoria and Albert devoted to what man has made for children, with toys through the centuries, dolls and doll's houses, puppets, children's dress and nursery furniture. Saturday workshops

In the garden of the London Toy and Model Museum

in the art room at 11.00 and 14.00. Holiday activities. Free. *Open:* Monday to Thursday and Saturday 10.00 to 17.50, Sunday 14.30 to 17.50; closed Fridays *Tube:* Bethnal Green (next door)

◆

COMMONWEALTH INSTITUTE

Kensington High Street, W8
Centre for Commonwealth education and culture in Britain with changing exhibitions reflecting the people and issues of some 48 countries. Festivals, workshops and holiday activities. Free.
Open: Monday to Saturday 10.00 to 17.00, Sunday 14.00 to 17.00
Tube: High Street Kensington

◆

DICKENS' HOUSE

48 Doughty Street, near Gray's Inn Road, WC1
A museum since 1925. The house where Dickens lived with his family from 1837 to 1839, and where he wrote his first full-length novel, *The Pickwick Papers*, and later *Oliver Twist* and *Nicholas Nickelby*. Displays include manuscripts, furniture, letters and first editions.
Open: Monday to Saturday 10.00 to 17.00; closed Sunday and Bank Holidays
Tube: Russell Square, Chancery Lane

◆

GEFFRYE MUSEUM

136 Kingsland Road, E2

Collection of period furniture from 1600 to 1939, and 18th-century street. Playground in the garden. Workshops. Free.
Open: Tuesday to Saturday 10.00 to 17.00, Sundays and Bank Holidays 14.00 to 17.00
Tube: Liverpool Street then bus

◆

HAMLEYS

188–196 Regent Street, W1

Enormous toyshop with six floors devoted to everything you can possibly imagine from dolls and teddy bears to trains and computers. Soda bar.
Tube: Oxford Circus

◆

LONDON TOY AND MODEL MUSEUM

21-3 Craven Hill, W2

A charming small museum in two Victorian buildings in Bayswater with over 3,000 toys and models dating from the 18th century to the present day (but no touching). Trains, boats, planes and a steam train and playbus in the garden. Special events.
Open: Tuesday to Saturday 10.00 to 17.30, Sunday from 11.00
Tube: Lancaster Gate, Paddington, Queensway

◆◆◆

LONDON ZOO

Regent's Park, NW1

The Discover Centre offers an 'animal experience', where children can put on a helmet and see how a housefly views the world, or use a computer game to 'run like a leopard'. Also animal encounters, shows and chats to keepers. Summer Arklight laser shows with floats on the canal.
Open: daily 10.00 to 17.30 March to September; 10.00 to 16.00 or dusk October to February
Tube: Regent's Park, Camden Town

◆

POLLOCK'S TOY MUSEUM

1 Scala Street, W1 (annexe opposite and entrance in Whitfield Street)

Two tiny houses with pint-sized rooms and narrow staircases. Founded by the man who made Victorian toy theatres (which you can buy along with toys in the adjoining shop and also in the theatre shop in Covent Garden). Suitable for small adults and children.
Open: Monday to Saturday 10.00 to 17.00; closed Sundays
Tube: Goodge Street

◆

TOBACCO DOCK

The Highway, E1

Huge new shopping and restaurant complex converted out of a 19th-century warehouse in Docklands. Two replica sailing ships to explore. One is a Museum of Piracy through the Ages, the other, the *Sky Lark* schooner, a children's adventure ship themed to Robert Louis Stevenson's *Treasure Island*. Charge for ships.
Transport: Wapping or Shadwell Underground; or Docklands Light Railway to Shadwell from Tower Gateway or Bank. Then 5-minute (sign-posted) walk

Where to Eat
On the whole London restaurants do not take kindly to small children. Some even ban them altogether. You cannot take under 14's into a pub unless it has a separate dining area. Restaurants that do cater well for families include:
Benihana, 100 Avenue Road, Swiss Cottage, NW3 (tel: 071 586 9508). A Japanese/American restaurant on the ground floor of a modern red and cream building opposite the station. The first in Britain of a USA chain offering 'performing' Japanese chefs (juggling pepper pots) on tables for eight, each with its own Hibachi grill. On weekend lunchtimes they have a cheap menu for under 10's (all food grilled in front of them), plus crayons and a Punch and Judy show (Sundays) in the bar. Not so cheap for grown-ups.
Chicago Meat Packers, 96 Charing Cross Road, WC2 (tel: 071 379 3277). Very cheap children's menu until 20.00 every day. On Sundays (12.00 to 16.00) magicians work the tables. Crayons and cartoons in the bar area. Model railway.
Smollensky's Balloon, 1 Dover Street, W1 (tel: 071 491 1199). Opposite the Ritz. Noisy

Smollensky's Balloon is one of the places that welcomes children

basement, with weekend lunchtime fun (children's ½ hour show at 14.30) includes balloons, children's menus, a resident clown and a magician, plus videos, story time and Punch and Judy upstairs. Food is mostly steaks.

Entertainment

Barbican Centre, Silk Street, EC2 (tel: 071 638 4141). Changing exhibitions, workshops, concerts (free) and Saturday and holiday cinema club.
Tube: Moorgate, Barbican

Half Moon Theatre, 213 Mile End Road, E1 (tel: 071 790 4000). Saturday morning shows for young children.
Tube: Stepney Green

ICA Children's Cinema, Nash House, The Mall, SW1 (tel: 071 930 3647). Regular Saturday and holiday film shows.
Tube: Charing Cross, Piccadilly Circus

The Little Angel Marionette Theatre, 14 Dagmar Passage, off Cross Street, N1 (tel: 071 226 1787). Weekend and holiday puppet shows.
Tube: Highbury and Islington

National Film Theatre, South Bank, Waterloo, SE1 (tel: 071 921 0600). Weekend matinées of films. Also arts workshops at the National Theatre, Royal Festival Hall and Hayward Gallery (tel: 071 921 0848).
Tube: Waterloo

Polka Children's Theatre, 240 The Broadway, Wimbledon, SW19 (tel: 081 543 4888). Some way from central London but one of the best children's theatres in the capital with regular plays for all ages and also workshops. Puppets and playground. Closed Sundays and Mondays.
Tube: Wimbledon, South Wimbledon

Puppet Theatre Barge, Little Venice, Blomfield Road, W9 (tel: 071 249 6876). String puppet show on a moored Thames barge in Maida Vale.
Tube: Warwick Avenue

Unicorn Theatre for Children, 6 Great Newport Street, WC2 (tel: 071 836 3334). The only solely professional children's theatre in the West End. Plays for all ages. *Performances:* 13.30 Tuesday to Friday, 14.30 weekends and during school holidays.
Tube: Leicester Square

TIGHT BUDGET

Accommodation

- The Youth Hostels Association, 14 Southampton Street, WC2, near Covent Garden (tel: 071 836 1036) will help you find cheap accommodation.
- As an alternative, the London Tourist Board will direct you to bed and breakfast hotels.

Eating and Drinking

- Pubs with decent food are generally a lot cheaper than restaurants of whatever sort.
- Wine bars have reasonably priced food but the wine is expensive.
- The cheapest meals of all are to be found in cafés (sausage, bacon and egg, washed down by a cup of tea).
- You can get a cheapish meal at any number of restaurants serving pizzas.
- Indian and Chinese restaurants can also be cheap provided you steer clear of the new wave of 'designer' restaurants in and around Soho and Covent Garden.
- A cheap alternative to lunch is to buy a sandwich from any one of numerous sandwich bars.
- If you are prepared to start your evening off early, you can get half-price cocktails at bars that offer a Happy Hour.

Entertainment

- If you cannot afford a full-price ticket to a West End theatre, go to the SWET ticket booth in Leicester Square for half-price tickets on the day.
- Cheaper still are the tickets for pub or fringe theatres.
- National Theatre seats are cheaper than the West End.
- Free concerts are held in the National Theatre foyer, at the Barbican, in churches and in the piazza at Covent Garden.
- Several of London's museums are free, including the British Museum, though most expect some sort of donation (see **What to See** section).
- Some museums and galleries offer a reduction if you have got a student card.

St James's Park is free entertainment

Contents

DIRECTORY

Airports

Useful phone numbers:
Gatwick Flight Enquiries, tel: 0293 535353
Heathrow
Terminal 1, tel: 081 745 7724
Terminal 2, tel: 081 745 7115–7
Terminal 3, tel: 081 745 7412–4
Terminal 4, tel: 081 745 4540
London City Airport, tel: 071 474 5555
Luton, tel: 0582 405100
Stansted, tel: 0279 680500

• **Gatwick**. To the south. Regular British Rail trains (every 15 mins, or hourly before 06.20) leave from within the terminal and run into Victoria Station in 30–45 mins.

• **Heathrow**. To the west. You can get to and from central London by Underground, Airbus or taxi (very expensive). The **Airbus** runs from all four Terminals to Victoria or Euston, stopping at several points including major hotel areas *en route*. The journey takes between 50 and 85 mins, with services every 20 or 30 mins. Airbuses are equipped with wheelchair lifts and secure accommodation. At Victoria and Euston there are Carelink wheelchair-accessible bus services linking most of the central London main-line railway stations. You buy tickets (reasonably cheap) on the bus. Unless you are staying right in the centre of London this is the most relaxing bet, especially if you have heavy luggage, although it takes a bit longer than the tube.

The Piccadilly **Underground** line runs from Terminals 1, 2 and 3 with a separate stop for Terminal 4. Trains run every 4–7½ mins. Allow about 45 mins to Piccadilly Circus, where you can change tube lines. If you have got heavy luggage you will have to struggle up stairs and escalators.

A **Night Bus** service between Heathrow and Trafalgar Square (Route N97) operates nightly at about hourly intervals. Tickets bought onboard.

You can buy **Heathrow Transfer Tickets** in advance through overseas travel agents or in London hotels, Travel Information Centres and travel agents.

UNDERGROUND

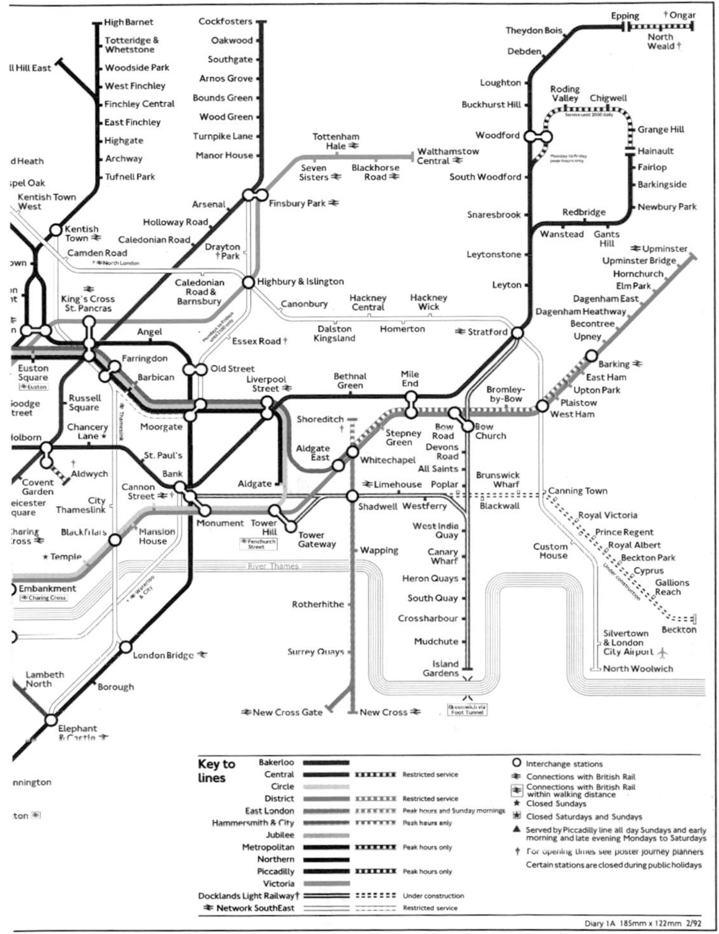
High Barnet
Totteridge & Whetstone
Woodside Park
West Finchley
Finchley Central
East Finchley
Highgate
Archway
Tufnell Park
Kentish Town West
Kentish Town
Camden Road
King's Cross St. Pancras
Cockfosters
Oakwood
Southgate
Arnos Grove
Bounds Green
Wood Green
Turnpike Lane
Manor House
Arsenal
Holloway Road
Caledonian Road
Drayton Park
Finsbury Park
Highbury & Islington
Caledonian Road & Barnsbury
Angel
Essex Road
Tottenham Hale
Seven Sisters
Blackhorse Road
Walthamstow Central
Canonbury
Hackney Central
Hackney Wick
Dalston Kingsland
Homerton
Stratford
Epping
Ongar
North Weald
Theydon Bois
Debden
Loughton
Buckhurst Hill
Roding Valley
Chigwell
Grange Hill
Hainault
Fairlop
Barkingside
Newbury Park
Woodford
South Woodford
Snaresbrook
Redbridge
Wanstead
Gants Hill
Leytonstone
Leyton
Upminster
Upminster Bridge
Hornchurch
Elm Park
Dagenham East
Dagenham Heathway
Becontree
Upney
Barking
East Ham
Upton Park
Plaistow
West Ham
Bromley-by-Bow
Bow Church
Bow Road
Mile End
Stepney Green
Bethnal Green
Liverpool Street
Old Street
Farringdon
Barbican
Moorgate
Euston Square
Russell Square
Chancery Lane
Holborn
Aldwych
Covent Garden
St. Paul's
Bank
Cannon Street
City Thameslink
Blackfriars
Mansion House
Temple
Embankment
Charing Cross
Monument
Tower Hill
Fenchurch Street
Tower Gateway
Aldgate
Aldgate East
Shoreditch
Whitechapel
Limehouse
Shadwell
Westferry
Devons Road
All Saints
Poplar
Brunswick Wharf
Blackwall
Canning Town
Royal Victoria
Prince Regent
Royal Albert
Beckton Park
Cyprus
Gallions Reach
Beckton
Custom House
Silvertown & London City Airport
North Woolwich
Wapping
West India Quay
Canary Wharf
Heron Quays
South Quay
Crossharbour
Mudchute
Island Gardens
Greenwich via Foot Tunnel
River Thames
Rotherhithe
Surrey Quays
New Cross Gate
New Cross
London Bridge
Borough
Lambeth North
Elephant & Castle
Key to lines
Bakerloo
Central
Restricted service
Circle
District
Restricted service
East London
Peak hours and Sunday mornings
Hammersmith & City
Peak hours only
Jubilee
Metropolitan
Peak hours only
Northern
Piccadilly
Peak hours only
Victoria
Docklands Light Railway†
Under construction
Network SouthEast
Restricted service
Interchange stations
Connections with British Rail
Connections with British Rail within walking distance
Closed Sundays
Closed Saturdays and Sundays
Served by Piccadilly line all day Sundays and early morning and late evening Mondays to Saturdays
For opening times see poster journey planners
Certain stations are closed during public holidays
Diary 1A 185mm x 122mm 2/92

• **London City Airport**. Poor public transport, but a fleet of taxis is likely to be on hand at the tiny airport in Dockland, 6 miles (9·5km) east of the Bank of England and the City. The Green Line 787 service runs from Victoria Station to the airport or trains run to Silvertown British Rail Station (less than a quarter of a mile from the airport) via West Ham or Stratford on the Underground. River Bus (tel: 071 512 0555) services to Charing Cross Pier, depart every 20 minutes Monday to Friday 07.00 to 19.40.

Car clamping is very effective – and very annoying

• **Luton**. British Rail have a combined rail and coach link between St Pancras and the airport via Luton Station. The journey takes about 45 mins. Trains from King's Cross Thameslink are more frequent.
• **Stansted**. Direct British Rail train services to Liverpool Street Station every 30 minutes. The journey takes 45 minutes. Trains also stop at Tottenham Hale Station where there is direct access to the Underground's Victoria Line.

Camping
Sites include:
Eastway Cycle Circuit, Temple Mills Lane, E15 (tel: 081 534 6085). 4 miles (6.5km) from the city centre. Open March to October.
Hackney Camping, Millfields Road, E5 (tel: 081 985 7656). 4 miles (6.5km) from the centre. Open mid-June to August.
Picketts Lock Centre, Picketts Lock Lane, N9 (tel: 081 345 6666). Open all year. 10 miles (16km) from the centre. Also caravans.

Chemists (see **Pharmacies**)

Crime
It is best not to travel alone on the Underground at night. Keep bags and wallets safe, especially in crowded places. Otherwise London is much the same as other capitals.

Driving
Londoners are not bad drivers. One-way streets and trying to park legally are the main problems. There are special 'bus and taxi only' lanes that operate during peak hours in

the West End and yellow 'boxes' in which you are not supposed to stop across junctions. Traffic in central London tends to snarl up during the 'rush hours' from 08.00 to 10.00 and from 17.00 to 19.00, with an additional jam after theatres close at around 22.30. Seat belts are compulsory.

Car breakdown. If you are not a member of a motoring organisation you can join on the spot. The AA is Britain's largest motoring organisation; for breakdown assistance, 'phone 0800 887766. This is a free call service.

Car de-clamping. Hyde Park Police Car Pound, NCP car-park, Park Lane, W1, is where to go if your car has been clamped in central London. After paying a fine you have to wait to get it released. Alternatively, the Car Clamp Recovery Club (tel: 071 235 9901) will, for a fee, do it for you.

Car hire. Agencies include:

AA Car Hire, tel: 071 262 2223
Avis Rent A Car, tel: 081 848 8733
Central Rent A Car, tel: 0800 282666 (toll free)
Century Self Drive, tel: 0442 216512
Guy Salmon Rentals, tel: 071 408 1255
Hertz Rent-A-Car, tel: 081 679 1799
Major Car Rentals, tel: 081 203 7666

Chauffeur-driven cars.
Berryhurst, tel: 071 582 0244
Brunswick Chauffeur Car Services, tel: 071 727 2611
Camelot Barthropp Chauffeur Driven Cars, tel: 071 235 0234
Hugh Damien Executive Chauffeur Drive, tel: 081 897 0555
Knightsbridge Chauffeurs, tel: 071 261 1422
Magnum Chauffeur Drive, tel: 081 994 9123

Parking. Car-parks (numerous National Car Park, NCP, parks) cost a little more than meters. Most meters in central London are blue and only take 20p and £1 coins. They all seem to gobble up coins. You are not allowed to 'feed' your meter when it has run out of time, but can use time already clocked up. Parking in some areas is free after lunchtime on Saturdays and all meters are free on Sundays. Traffic wardens are dressed in yellow and black; do not expect them to show you any mercy! You are not allowed to park in a resident's parking bay (unless you have got a permit), on a double yellow line (at any time) or on a single yellow line during working hours (usually including Saturday). Always check the little signs on lamp-posts to see exactly what the rules are. An illegally parked car may get clamped or towed away to a Police Pound and you have to pay a fine to get it back (see **Car de-clamping** above). If you cannot find your car, ask a policeman.

Petrol. Most petrol stations are self-service and some stay open 24 hours a day. Unlike their counterparts on the Continent you cannot expect your windscreen to be washed. If you need assistance you have to call the breakdown services (see **Car breakdown** above) or visit a garage with a mechanic. Most garages shut at weekends.

Electricity
240 volt, 50 cycle AC. Shavers operate on 240 or 110 volts. Plugs are three-prong.

Embassies and Consulates
Virtually every country is represented. Addresses are listed in the Yellow Pages phone book under 'embassies', or ask at the London Tourist Board.

Emergency Telephone Numbers
Dial 999 from any telephone, give the location, and state whether you want Fire, Police or Ambulance (which will take you to the nearest hospital).

Entertainment (see page 89). For what's on, see weekly events listings in *Time Out, City Limits* or in the quality Sunday papers.

Hospitals
There are **24-hour casualty departments** at: University College Hospital, Gower Street, WC1, (tel: 071 387 9300); Guy's Hospital, St Thomas Street, SE1 (tel: 071 955 5000); St Bartholomew's Hospital, West Smithfield, EC1 (tel: 071 601 8888)
Moorfields Eye Hospital is situated at City Road, EC1 (tel: 071 253 3411)
Private emergency treatment is available from Medical Express, 117A Harley Street, W1 (tel: 071 499 1991), Monday to Saturday only.

Lost Property
Go to the nearest police station to report any loss.
If you have left something on a bus or tube the London Transport Lost Property Office (tel: 071 486 2496) is at 200 Baker Street, NW1 (open 09.30 to 14.00 Monday to Friday). For losses on trains ring up the arrival/departure point of the train you were travelling on. If you have left something in a taxi try to remember its licence number (not number plate) and telephone 071 833 0996.

Familiar red buses in Oxford Street

Money Matters

Banks (see **Opening Times**). The terminals at Gatwick and Heathrow have 24-hour banks.

Currency. When banks are shut you can change money at major travel agencies like Thomas Cook, in the exchange offices at major department stores or in the numerous *bureaux de change* in high streets and at stations. Look for agencies that indicate that they follow the BTA Code of Conduct if you do not want to be cheated. There are exchange facilities at National Girobanks at some large post offices in central London.

VAT (Value Added Tax) is added to most goods and services at a standard rate of 17½ per cent. You can get relief from VAT on goods (*eg* shopping) but not services (*eg* restaurants) if you are a visitor from abroad. You may have to spend a minimum amount (usually over £100).

Opening Times

Banks. Monday to Friday 09.30 to 15.30 or 16.30. Also Saturday mornings (09.30 to 12.00) at some branches.

Business. Normal business hours are 09.00 or 10.00 to 17.30 or 18.00. Offices are shut at weekends.

Museums and Galleries. Most are shut Christmas Day, Boxing Day and New Year's Day, others on all public holidays and on Sunday mornings. Some museums and galleries are open shorter hours during the winter months.

Pubs. They are allowed to open from 11.00 to 23.00 Monday to Saturday and from 12.00 to 15.00 and again from 19.00 to 22.30 on Sundays and Bank Holidays. Not all pubs choose to stay open in the afternoon.

Shops. Most shops open at 09.00 or 09.30 and shut at 17.30. Shops open until 19.00 or

Chelsea Harbour, base for a waterborne commuter service

20.00 on Thursdays in the West End and on Wednesdays in Knightsbridge and Chelsea. They are open late daily in Covent Garden and Tobacco Dock. Some shops (the law is under review) open on Sundays.

Pharmacies
There are pharmacies all over London. Bliss, 5 Marble Arch, W1, Boots, 75 Queensway, W2 and 44 Piccadilly Circus, W1, are pharmacies which open late.

Places of Worship
Practically every religion is represented somewhere in London. See Places of Worship, in the Yellow Pages directory.

Public Holidays
New Year's Day, Good Friday, Easter Monday, May Day (first Monday in May), Spring Bank Holiday (last Monday in May), Late Summer Holiday (last Monday in August), Christmas Day, Boxing Day.

Pubic Transport
• **Buses**. From the upper deck of one of London's double-decker buses there is often a good view of the capital. Three million passengers a day use the buses. Bus stops show bus numbers and timetables, but make sure you ring the bell or put your hand out at a red 'request' stop. There are 41 miles (66km) of bus lanes in central London, so while the rest of the traffic stands still, buses (and taxis) keep moving. 'Pay-as-you-enter' night buses all stop at Trafalgar Square.
• **Coaches**. Victoria Coach Station is the main London terminal for longer distance express coaches. Information from National Express Coaches (tel: 071 730 0202). London Transport run coach tours in and around London and to places of interest nearby, with a courtesy pick up service from hotels. Most leave from Wilton Road Coach Station, near Victoria Station (tel: 071 227 3456). Green Line coaches connect central London with the suburbs. The main terminal at Eccleston Bridge near Victoria Station (tel: 081 668 7261).
• **Disabled**. London Regional Transport run a special unit to help disabled passengers, including braille maps for the visually impaired. There is a Dial-a-Ride minibus service and a Taxi-card scheme (tel: 071 483 2519) which enables disabled people to use taxis at reduced cost. Airbus services between Heathrow and central London have been converted to accept wheelchairs. At Victoria and Euston the Carelink wheelchair-accessible bus service links main-line stations. There are also Mobility Buses with wheelchair access on routes in and around London, and the Docklands Light Railway can accommodate wheelchairs. Details from London Regional Transport, 55 Broadway, SW1 (tel: 071 227 3312).
• **Docklands Light Railway (DLR)**. The Docklands Light Railway, built to cater for the redevelopment of the Docklands, opened in 1987. The toy-town-like, blue and red, driverless trains run on weekdays only (until 21.30), departing from Bank Underground station and Tower Gateway (take the

The tube stations are gradually being re-vamped

Underground to Tower Hill) via Shadwell through the Isle of Dogs to Island Gardens (walk to and from Greenwich through the Greenwich foot tunnel under the Thames). Trains also run between Island Gardens and Stratford, connecting with the Underground and British Rail. An extension east to Beckton in the Royal Docks is due to open shortly.

• Information.

British Rail Travel Centres (for personal visitors) are at: 14 Kingsgate Parade, Victoria Street, SW1; 407 Oxford Street, W1; and 87 King William Street, EC4. Telephone enquiries: 071 928 5100 (24-hour service).

Docklands Light Railway (tel: 071 222 1234).

London Transport 24-hour telephone information buses and Underground (tel: 071 222 1234). Recorded details (tel: 071 222 1200).

London Regional Transport, 55 Broadway, SW1H 0BD (tel: 071 222 1234).

London Transport (LT) Information centres can be found at the following stations: Piccadilly Circus, Oxford Circus, King's Cross, Euston, Victoria and at Heathrow Central at Terminals 1, 2 and 3, and in all the arrival halls. They also sell tickets for excursions.

• **Minicabs**. Minicabs cannot (at the time of writing) be hailed in the street. You have to telephone a central reservation number (see Yellow Pages). Drivers use their own private cars. Ask about the price before you set off. There are plans to license them like taxis

• **River Boats**. RiverBus (tel: 071 512 0555) run regular commuter services (weekday only) along the river using high-speed, 62–seat airline-style catamarans. They run from Chelsea Harbour to the City, and from Charing Cross to Greenwich or the London City Airport, at 20-minute intervals. Stops (piers) *en route* are; Festival (by the South Bank Centre), Swan Lane (by London Bridge), London Bridge City (by Hays Galleria) and West India Dock (the Docklands).

• **Taxis**. London taxicabs are black or maroon with a white licence plate at the back. You can hail them when the yellow taxi sign on the roof is alight. There are ranks outside main-line stations and major hotels. A taxi can be ordered by telephoning 071 286 0286, 071 253 5000 or 071 272 0272/3030. A tip of between 10 and 15 per cent is expected. Taxi drivers are a mine of information. The driver must use his meter (within the Metropolitan District). There is a minimum charge shown on the clock, and supplements for luggage, after 20.00 and at weekends.

• **Tickets**. The **Visitor Travelcard** is available to overseas visitors, for 1, 3, 4 or 7 days and must be bought abroad. It offers virtually unlimited travel on the tube and buses (as well as discount vouchers to top attractions) and saves money on the regular

Travelcard available once you get here. It can be bought from travel agents and London Transport sales agents abroad (you do not need a photo).

Heathrow Transfer Tickets (see **Airports**, page 107).

The regular **Travelcards** are available from any Underground station. They give freedom to travel on the buses or Underground for 1 or 7 days, or a month, within selected zones. You need a passport-sized photo for a 7-day or monthly card. Journeys for one-day cards have to start after 09.30 and are restricted between 16.30 and 18.30 (Monday to Friday) but you can travel any time at weekends. You can also get a bus pass (for a day, week or month) though they are not available for the central London zone.

Underground or tube tickets. Single or return tickets must be bought at the station before you begin your journey. They must be kept to show an inspector who might board the train, and be handed in at the other end. If you leave a station before you get to your destination you have to buy a new ticket.

On **buses** you pay the conductor if there is one or the driver (as you board) if there is not. Keep your ticket until you leave the bus in case an inspector gets on. London is divided up into six **zones** for fare purposes. Travel within central London is one zone. See maps at stations for details.

Children under 5 travel free. Under 14's get reduced rates (up to a third off the price), while 14 and 15-year-olds must carry a child-rate photocard (available from post offices and travel information centres with a photo and proof of age) for their reduction.

• **Trains**. British Rail trains terminate in central London at various stations. Each station serves a network of stations in certain directions, as indicated below.

Moorgate, King's Cross (Yorkshire, North East and East Coast to Scotland). Tel: 071 278 2477

Euston, St Pancras (Midlands, North Wales, North West and West Coast to Scotland). Tel: 071 387 7070

Paddington, Marylebone (West of England and South Wales). Tel: 071 262 6767

Blackfriars, Cannon Street, Charing Cross, Fenchurch Street, Holborn Viaduct, Liverpool Street, London Bridge, Victoria and Waterloo (East Anglia and Essex, South East and South). Tel: 071 928 5100

• **Underground**. The London Underground (or Tube) runs deep under the capital. Two and a half million people travel on it daily. There are 273 stations; those in central London are within a few minutes' walk of each other. You should not have to wait long for a train, but they can get uncomfortably crowded during the rush hour (roughly between 08.00 and 09.30 and 17.00 and 18.30).

The Underground is divided into lines: Bakerloo, Central, Circle, District, East London, Jubilee, Metropolitan, Northern (which has one of the longest continuous railway tunnels in the

Many London pubs now stay open all day long

world), Piccadilly and Victoria. Maps are easy to follow with each line having a different colour (see pages 108–9). The lines criss-cross making it easy to switch from one line to another although at some stations this can mean long walks down (well-lit) corridors or several rides on escalators.

Some stations have numerous platforms; Baker Street has ten. The destination will be marked on the front of the train and also on a board above the platform. Some lines branch into two so check the destination carefully. Most stations have automatic barriers which open when you insert a ticket. All the main-line stations have connections with the Underground.

It is not permitted to smoke

anywhere on the Underground. The Underground shuts at night with last trains leaving central London stations at midnight or soon after (an hour earlier on Sundays). First trains at 05.30 (07.00, Sundays).

Senior Citizens
Senior Citizens or OAPs get reduced entry into many museums and galleries. There are also reductions for women over 60 and men over 65 on public transport on production of a Senior Citizen Railcard (UK residents), or a Rail Europe Senior Card or a BritRail Pass (overseas visitors).

Sports
Sportsline (tel: 071 222 8000) provides information on what is on where. The *Time Out Guide to Sport, Health and Fitness in London*, from bookshops and newsagents, lists venues. For the major sporting events like Ascot, Wimbledon or Henley you will need to book tickets well in advance through a ticket agency such as First Call (tel: 071 240 7200).

Student and Youth Travel
London can seem like a pretty cruel city if you are a student. Essential reading is *Time Out's* free *Student Guide,* produced in conjunction with the NUS (National Union of Students), particularly if you are planning to stay for a while. Hang around the NUS in Malet Street, WC1, and you will soon meet fellow students.
An International Student Identity Card is essential is you want discounts in museums, galleries, theatres, cinemas and public transport. The main student organisations in London are: Student Travel Association, 74 and 86 Old Brompton Road, SW7 (tel: 071 937 9962 intercontinental, 071 937 9921 European).
University of London Union, Malet Street, WC1 (tel: 071 580 9551). See also **Tight Budget**.

Westminster Abbey is one of the great treasures of London

Telephones and Postal Services

Post Offices generally open 09.00 to 17.30 Monday to Friday; 09.00 to 12.00 on Saturdays. The post office behind Trafalgar Square in King William IV Street, WC2, is open from 08.00 to 20.00 Monday to Saturday. Stamps (only of certain values) are also available from machines outside some post offices, or as books of stamps in newsagents etc. The old red phone boxes have now almost all been replaced by open glass booths. You can use a phonecard in some of them (available from post offices or newsagents). If you are out of cash call the operator (dial 100) to reverse charges/call collect. For calls within London, you need only use the prefix 071 (inner London), or 081 (outer London),

if calling across the 071/081 boundary (check the number of the telephone you are calling on), otherwise simply dial the number. International numbers start with 010. Push-button phones take coins which you insert after you have lifted the receiver but before you dial. Useful numbers include:
Directory Enquiries (London) 142
Directory Enquiries (UK) 192
International Directory Enquiries 153
International Call Collect 155
Emergency 999

Ticket Agencies
Most agencies make a charge. They take credit card bookings over the phone. They include:
Edwards & Edwards, tel: 071 379 5822
First Call, tel: 071 240 7200
Keith Prowse, tel: 071 793 1000
Ticketmaster, tel: 071 379 3295
Wembley Box Office, tel: 081 900 1234

Time
British Summer Time (BST) begins in late March when the clocks are put forward one hour. In late October the clocks go back an hour to Greenwich Mean Time (GMT). The official date is announced in the daily newspapers and is always on a Saturday night. Just remember March forward and Fall back!

Tipping
Taxi drivers expect 10 to 15 per cent of the fare. Most restaurants include service in their bill, but even so some leave the total amount on credit card slips blank. Some ethnic restaurants do not include service. Doormen at hotels expect 50p plus for getting taxis etc. Porters at railway stations expect £1 (standard charge of £5 at Heathrow Airport).

Toilets
There are some sanitised booths in the centre of London, otherwise there are public toilets in main-line stations (both charge 10p) and most large stores. The parks all have toilets, and so do many squares.

Tourist Offices
For information on what to do and see, events, entertainment, maps and hotel bookings: The **British Travel Centre**, 12 Regent Street, SW1. Open weekdays 09.00 to 18.30 and 10.00 to 16.00 Saturdays and Sundays (until 17.00 on Saturdays in summer). Tel: 071 730 3400 from 09.00 to 18.30 Monday to Friday, 10.00 to 16.00 Saturday (extended in summer). Also American Express Travel Agency. The **London Tourist Board** operates Tourist Information Centres at: Victoria Station Forecourt, SW1. Open Easter to end October daily 08.00 to 19.00, and from November to Easter, Monday to Saturday 08.00 to 19.00, Sunday 08.00 to 16.00. Selfridges, Oxford Street, W1 (Basement). Open store hours. Heathrow Terminals 1, 2, 3, Underground Station Concourse. Open daily 08.00 to 18.00. Liverpool Street Underground Station. Open Monday 08.15 to 19.00; Tuesday to Saturday 08.15 to 18.00; Sunday 08.30 to 16.45. The **London Tourist Board** number is 071 730 3488. Monday to Saturday 09.00 to 18.00.

Part of Buckingham Palace's Changing of the Guard – a 'must' for many visitors

For travel outside London:
Northern Ireland Tourist Board, tel: 071 493 0601 (3201 for Eire)
Scottish Tourist Board, tel: 071 930 8661
Wales Tourist Board, tel: 071 409 0969
There are also regional tourist offices throughout Britain.

Tours of London

If you want a guided tour of the capital there are numerous possibilities.

• **By Boat**. The Regent's Canal runs from Camden Lock to the Zoo and Little Venice (Maida Vale): a quiet backwater with a towpath you can walk along.

Companies include:

Jason's Trip (tel: 071 286 3428). They use gaily painted narrow boats and trips last 1½ hours. Easter to early October. Refreshments and commentary on board. Also lunch and dinner cruises. Boats leave from Little Venice and Camden Lock.

Jenny Wren Cruises (tel: 071 485 4433). Leave from Camden Lock. They are based at 250 Camden High Street on the bridge over the canal. Sunday lunchtime cruises run all year.

London Waterbus Company (tel: 071 482 2550). Runs daily on the hour from Camden Lock to Little Venice from April to September (weekends only rest of year, every 90 minutes). The company also run day-long trips through East London to Limehouse and the Docklands.

The Thames. Covered cruise boats ply the river. Most boats have snack bars on board with informal commentaries (in English only). They depart from the following piers:

Richmond (tel: 081 892 0741) to Hampton Court and a circular cruise to Teddington Lock.

Westminster (tel: 071 930 4721/2062) down river to the Tower, the Thames Barrier and Greenwich (all year); up river to Kew, Richmond and Hampton Court (summer only). Also circular cruises and evening and lunch cruises.

Charing Cross (tel: 071 839 3572) to the Tower and Greenwich; also evening cruises.

Tower (tel: 071 488 0344) up river to Westminster and down river to Butler's Wharf and Greenwich (all year) with a ferry to see HMS *Belfast*.

Greenwich (tel: 081 858 3996) to Tower, Charing Cross, Westminster and down river to the Thames Barrier. Also lunch cruises every Sunday.

General riverboat information (tel: 071 730 4812).

• **By Bus**. London Transport run 1½ hour sightseeing tours by double-decker bus (open-topped in summer), with a commentary by a qualified guide. They start from Marble Arch, Victoria, Piccadilly and Baker Street, and French and German speaking guides are also available. There are sightseeing buses to the Zoo (between March and early September) from Oxford Circus and Baker Street stations.

• **By Coach**. Numerous companies offer coach tours of London as well as excursions to nearby places of interest.

• **On Foot**. Guided walks usually start at Underground stations. Some follow a theme – Cockney London, the Jewish East End and Jack the Ripper among them. Companies include: Citisights (tel: 081 806 4325). Led by archaeologists and historians working with the City of London Archaeological Trust at the Museum of London, City Walks (tel: 071 837 2841). Foreign language tours

available: Cockney London Walks (tel: 081 504 9159). Literary tours of Hampstead village: Exciting Walks (tel: 071 624 9981), Footloose in London (tel: 071 435 0259). Themed Walks: London Walks (tel: 081 441 8906). Hidden and unusual London: Streets of London (tel: 081 346 9255); Original Ghost Walks (tel: 071 247 5604). Tours by Tape (with a guidebook, in several languages) are available from the Tourist Information Centre bookshop at Victoria Station.

One of the most relaxing ways to see London is to take a boat trip. The view below is looking upstream from Tower Bridge. The Chelsea Pensioner (right) spends his time at the Royal Hospital. The hospital was founded in 1682 for veteran and invalid soldiers

INDEX

Page numbers in *italics* refer to illustrations

ACKNOWLEDGEMENTS

The Automobile Association would like to thank the following photographers, libraries and hotels for their assistance in the compilation of this book.

AA PHOTO LIBRARY 82 S & O Mathews, 34 R Surman.

SUSAN GROSSMAN 36 Freud Museum, 88 Sandringham Hotel, 104/5 Smollensky's Balloon.

HALCYON HOTEL 86/7.

NATURE PHOTOGRAPHERS LTD 46 Red deer stag (C B Carver) 49 Ancient oaks (F V Blackburn), 50 Purple hairstreak, 52 Green sandpiper, 53 Yellow rattle, 55 Grazing marsh, 56/7 Epping Forest, 59 Water rail (P R Sterry).

RITZ HOTEL 64.

SPECTRUM COLOUR LIBRARY Cover.

BARRY SMITH was commissioned to take all the remaining photographs, and these are now in the AA's Photo Library.

Author's Acknowledgement:
Susan Grossman thanks the London Tourist Board for their help in preparing this book.

The Automobile Association would also like to thank the **London Tourist Board** for their assistance in updating this revised edition.

For this revision: Copy editor and Verifier Jenny Fry